Indonesia

a Lonely Planet travel survival kit

Peter Turner
Brendan Delahunty
Paul Greenway
James Lyon
Chris McAsey
David Willett

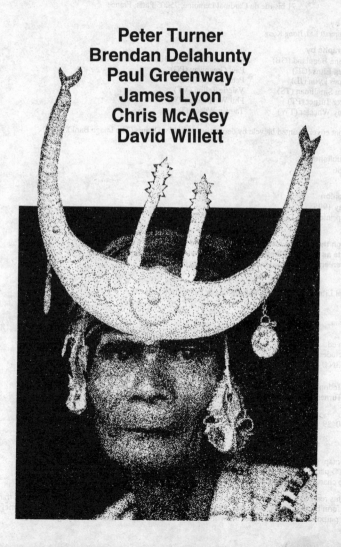

Indonesia

4th edition

Published by

Lonely Planet Publications

Head Office: PO Box 617, Hawthorn, Vic 3122, Australia
Branches: 155 Filbert St, Suite 251, Oakland, CA 94607, USA
               10 Barley Mow Passage, Chiswick, London W4 4PH, UK
               71 bis rue du Cardinal Lemoine, 75005 Paris, France

Printed by

Colorcraft Ltd, Hong Kong

Photographs by

Glenn Beanland (GB)	Brendan Delahunty (BD)
Greg Elms (GE)	Paul Greenway (PG)
James Lyon (JL)	Peter Morris (PM)
Tom Smallman (TS)	Valerie Tellini (VT)
Peter Turner (PT)	Phil Weymouth (PW)
Tony Wheeler (TW)	Tamsin Wilson (Tass)

Front cover: Painted bicycle by decorative wall, Lisl Dennis (The Image Bank).

First Published

1986

This Edition

May 1995
Reprinted with Update supplement June 1996

Although the authors and publisher have tried to make the information as
accurate as possible, they accept no responsibility for any loss, injury or
inconvenience sustained by any person using this book.

National Library of Australia Cataloguing in Publication Data

Indonesia.

4th ed.
Includes index.
ISBN 0 86442 263 6.

1. Indonesia – Guidebooks.
I. Turner, Peter. (Series : Lonely Planet travel survival kit).

915.980439

Brendan Delahunty

Brendan updated the Kalimantan and Sulawesi chapters. He is a would-be-poet with a passion for the glory days of Art-Deco. His brilliant career features forays into journalism, nursing, farming, AIDS outreach work and a brief stint of teaching Indonesian to young children in Australia. Frequent visits to Indonesia have taken him from Dili to Medan. Lonely Planet plucked Brendan from a moribund law course, sending him to study Kalimantan and Sulawesi instead.

Paul Greenway

Paul updated the Maluku and Irian Jaya chapters. He got his first tropical disease in 1985, and has had the 'travel bug' ever since. He has travelled to nearly 50 countries, and learnt to order 'one beer please' in just about every known language. During the rare times he is not travelling, or thinking, writing or reading about it, he lives in Darwin, listens to heavy rock, watches Australian Rules football and avoids marriage.

James Lyon

James updated the Bali chapter and the Lombok section of the Nusa Tenggara chapter. He is by nature a sceptic and by training a social scientist. He worked for five years as an editor at Lonely Planet's Melbourne office, imposing unreasonable demands on its authors, until he decided to 'jump the fence' and try for himself the life of a travel writer. He has travelled in Bali both by himself and also with his wife, Pauline, and their two young children. A keen gardener, he finds the flowers and landscapes of Bali a special delight. He also enjoys walking, which is another attraction of Bali and Lombok, and skiing, which isn't.

Chris McAsey

Chris updated the Nusa Tenggara chapter. After being weeded out of law school, Chris had varying levels of success as kitchenhand, professional footballer and clothing wholesaler. He left Australia in 1988 and travelled, worked and studied in Western and Eastern Europe, Japan and the USA. He returned to Australia in 1991 to complete a BA in professional writing and in 1993 published the imaginatively-titled *How to Live in Australia: A Guide for the Japanese*. This is his first Lonely Planet assignment.

Peter Turner

Peter updated the introductory chapters and the Java chapter. He was born in Australia and his long-held interest in South-East Asia has seen him make numerous trips to the region. He joined Lonely Planet as an editor and now works as a full-time travel writer. He is also the author of LP's guides to *Singapore*, *Jakarta*, *Java* and co-author of *Malaysia, Singapore & Brunei*.

David Willett

David updated the Sumatra chapter. He is a freelance journalist based on the mid-north coast of New South Wales, Australia. He grew up in Hampshire, England, and wound up in Australia in 1980 after stints working on newspapers in Iran and Bahrain. He spent two years working as a sub-editor on the *Melbourne Sun* before opting to live somewhere warmer. Between jobs, he has travelled extensively in Europe, the Middle East and Asia. He lives with his partner, Rowan, and their four-year-old son, Tom. David updated the Tunisia sections in LP's guides to *North Africa* and *Mediterranean Europe*.

From the Authors

Brendan Delahunty Special thanks to my patient coach Jeff le Chef, Catherine Logie of Makale for her insights into Torajan culture, Aprianus Dulimar and Pak Sudaryanto of Palangkaraya, Hanna, her sisters Gerry and Imo, Togian tourmaster Rudy Ruus, Jacqueline Hurlimann, and trans-Kalimantan adventurer Andrea Nitsche for her detailed advice.

Paul Greenway Paul would like to thank: Michelle de Kretser at LP for having faith in a new writer; Anne-Marie van Dam (Netherlands), Robert Hewat (Australia) in Wamena, Stefan & Claudia Kelbel (Germany), Peter & Anouk Pluymers (Belgium) in Ambon, and Menno & Nelleke Kuiper (Netherlands) for their help; and the wonderful people of Indonesia.

David Willet My thanks go first and foremost to my partner, Rowan, and our four-year-old son, Tom, for their patience and understanding during this project – and for their help in testing the hotels and restaurants of North Sumatra.

Covering some of the far-flung corners of Sumatra would have been infinitely more difficult without the enthusiastic assistance of local tourist officials. Mr Saharuna Amiruddin, from the Indonesian Tourist Promotions Board in Sydney, was especially helpful.

The list of those to thank at Lonely Planet is led by Tom Smallman, whose understanding of the Indonesian concept of *jam karet* (rubber time) was much appreciated.

James Lyon Thanks to Richard, Tini and Nancy at Lovina; Asri and Raka in Ubud; Hadji Radiah on Lombok; Yarnt and Simon in the Gili Islands; Debbie Cullen; and to the many other people who helped me and smiled at me. The tourist offices in Kuta, Ubud, Singaraja and Mataram were also very helpful. At home, thanks to Ansett airlines; the editors and artists; and to Pauline, my research assistant, administrator, wife and muse.

Chris McAsey Chris would like to thank Willy D Kadati and Edwin Lerrick (Kupang), Isabel Milner and Marjo Trinks, Kering Hammad (Waikabubak), Jack and Marion (Lamalera) and Bill Irwin.

Peter Turner Of the many people who helped in the preparation of the Java section, Peter would like to send a special thanks to Drew Coburn and Andreas Vecchiet in Jakarta, Jajang Nurjaman in Pangandaran, Alfin and Alan in Solo, Djohan in Malang, and the staff of the many helpful tourist offices in Java including Yuni Syafril of the Jakarta City Tourism office, Widijanti of the Central Java Diparda office in Semarang, Djoko Rahardjo in Kudus and Pak Sunardi in Malang. Above all, the research was made possible and enriched by my wife Lorraine and 2½-year-old daughter Ruby, who accompanied me through much of Java.

This Edition

Peter Turner, the coordinating author for this edition, updated the introductory chapters and the Java chapter. James Lyon updated the Bali and Lombok sections, Brendan

Delahunty did the Kalimantan and Sulawesi chapters, Paul Greenway did the Maluku and Irian Jaya chapters, Chris MacAsey updated the Nusa Tenggara chapter and David Willet the Sumatra chapter.

This Book

The monumental task of compiling the first edition was the collective work of Alan Samalgalski, who roamed the far reaches of the archipelago, Ginny Bruce, who covered Java, and Mary Covernton, who did Sumatra and Bali. For the second edition, Alan went to Sumatra and Sulawesi, Tony Wheeler explored Bali and Lombok as well as covering Sumatra, John Noble and Susan Forsyth island-hopped through Nusa Tenggara and Maluku, and Joe Cummings went to Java and Kalimantan. For the third edition, Robert Storey oversaw the project and researched Nusa Tenggara, Maluku and Sulawesi. Dan Spitzer updated Java and Kalimantan, Richard Nebesky went to Sumatra, and Bali was covered by Tony Wheeler along with James Lyon, who also explored Lombok.

From the Publisher

This 4th edition of *Indonesia* was edited and proofed at Lonely Planet's Melbourne office by Sharan Kaur, Kristin Odijk, Alison White, Tom Smallman, Greg Alford and Miriam Cannell. Kristin, Miriam, Susan Noonan, Megan Fraser and Frith Pike assisted with the proofreading and Ann Selby with the indexing. Sally Woodward coordinated the mapping and was assisted by Andrew Smith, Michelle Stamp, Glenn Beanland and Sandra Smythe. The cover was designed by Valerie Tellini. The illustrations were drawn by Tamsin Wilson, Joanne Ridgeway and Sally. Design and layout was done by Sally.

Louise Keppie and Valerie were responsible for the design and layout of the Arts & Crafts colour section.

Thanks

All those involved in producing this book greatly appreciate the contributions of those travellers who put so much effort into writing and telling us of their experiences. These people's names appear on page 1003.

Warning & Request

Things change – prices go up, schedules change, good places go bad and bad places go bankrupt – nothing stays the same. So if you find things better or worse, recently opened or long since closed, please write and tell us and help make the next edition better.

Your letters will be used to help update future editions and, where possible, important changes will also be included in an Update section in reprints.

We greatly appreciate all information that is sent to us by travellers. Back at Lonely Planet we employ a hard-working readers' letters team to sort through the many letters we receive. The best ones will be rewarded with a free copy of the next edition or another Lonely Planet guide if you prefer. We give away lots of books, but, unfortunately, not every letter/postcard receives one.

Contents

NUSA TENGGARA 617

Map Legend

BOUNDARIES

- International Boundary
- Provincial Boundary
- Marine Park Boundary

ROUTES

- Freeway
- Highway
- Major Road
- Unsealed Road or Track
- City Road
- City Street
- Railway
- Underground Railway
- Walking Track
- Walking Tour
- Ferry Route
- Cable Car or Chairlift

AREA FEATURES

- Park, Gardens
- National Park
- Built-Up Area
- Pedestrian Mall
- Market
- Cemetery
- Reef
- Beach or Desert
- Rocks

HYDROGRAPHIC FEATURES

- Coastline
- River, Creek
- Intermittent River or Creek
- Lake, Intermittent Lake
- Canal
- Swamp

SYMBOLS

CAPITAL — National Capital	Hospital, Police Station
Capital — Provincial Capital	Airport, Airfield
CITY — Major City	Swimming Pool, Gardens
City — City	Shopping Centre, Zoo
Town — Town	Petrol Station, Golf Course
Village — Village	A25 — One Way Street, Route Number
Hotel	Archaeological Site or Ruins
Restaurant	Stately Home, Monument
Pub, Bar	Meru, Tomb
Post Office, Telephone	Cave, Hut or Chalet
Tourist Information, Bank	Mountain or Hill, Lookout
Transport, Parking	Surf beach, Stupa
Museum, Youth Hostel	Pass, Spring
Caravan Park, Camping Ground	Ancient or City Wall
Church, Cathedral	Rapids, Waterfalls
Mosque, Synagogue	Cliff or Escarpment, Tunnel
Buddhist Temple, Hindu Temple	Railway Station

Note: not all symbols displayed above appear in this book

Introduction

Like a string of jewels in a coral sea, the 13,000-plus islands of the Indonesian archipelago stretch almost 5000 km from the Asian mainland into the Pacific Ocean. And like jewels the islands have long represented wealth. A thousand years ago the Chinese sailed as far as Timor to load up cargoes of sandalwood and beeswax; by the 16th century the spice islands of the Moluccas were luring European navigators in search of cloves, nutmeg and mace, once so rare and expensive that bloody wars were fought for control of their production and trade. The Dutch ruled for almost 350 years, drawing their fortunes from the islands whose rich volcanic soil could produce two crops of rice a year, as well as commercially valuable crops like coffee, sugar, tobacco and teak.

Endowed with a phenomenal array of natural resources and strange cultures, Indonesia became a magnet for every shade of entrepreneur from the West – a stamping ground for proselytising missionaries, unscrupulous traders, wayward adventurers, inspired artists. It has been overrun by Dutch and Japanese armies; surveyed, drilled, dug up and shipped off by foreign mining companies; littered with the 'transmigrants' of Java and Bali; poked and prodded by ethnologists, linguists and anthropologists turning fading cultures into PhD theses.

Now there is a new breed of visitor – the modern-day tourist. After the 1991 'Visit Indonesia Year', the government decided to promote the 'Visit Indonesia Decade' to encourage even larger numbers of visitors by the year 2000. Places like Bali, Lombok, Torajaland, and the Hindu-Buddhist monuments of Borobudur and Prambanan in Central Java attract huge numbers of visitors. On the other hand, much of the country remains barely touched by mass tourism, despite great improvements in communications and transport connections. Indonesia has thousands of islands with a myriad of different cultures, offering adventure that is hard to find in the modern world.

Indonesia possesses some of the most

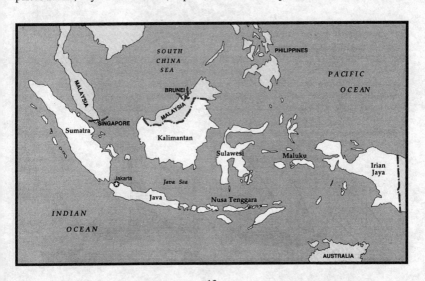

remarkable sights in South-East Asia and there are things about this country you will never forget: the flaming red and orange sunsets over the mouth of the Sungai (river) Kapuas in Kalimantan; standing on the summit of Keli Mutu in Flores and gazing at the coloured lakes that fill its volcanic craters; the lumbering leather-skinned dragons of Komodo Island; the funeral ceremonies of the Torajas in the highlands of Central Sulawesi; the Dani tribesmen of Irian Jaya wearing little else but feathers and penis gourds; the wooden *wayang golek* puppets manipulated into life by the puppet-masters of Yogyakarta; the brilliant coral reefs off Manado on the north coast of Sulawesi.

You can lie on your back on Kuta Beach in Bali and soak up the ultraviolet rays, paddle a canoe down the rivers of Kalimantan, surf at Nias off the coast of Sumatra, trek in the high country of Irian Jaya, catch giant butterflies in Sulawesi, eat your way through a kaleidoscope of fruit from one end of the archipelago to the other, stare down the craters of live volcanoes, learn the art of batik in Yogyakarta or kite-making from any Indonesian kid – almost anything you want, Indonesia has got!

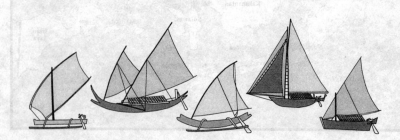

Facts about the Country

HISTORY
In the Beginning
It's generally held that the earliest inhabitants of the Indonesian archipelago came from India or Burma, while later migrants, known as 'Malays', came from southern China and Indochina. This second group is reckoned to have entered the Indonesian archipelago gradually over several thousand years.

Among its migrational phases, it's thought, was what's known as the Dongson Culture, which originated in Vietnam and southern China about 3000 years ago and spread to Indonesia, bringing with it techniques of irrigated rice growing, ritual buffalo sacrifice, bronze casting, the custom of erecting large monumental stones (megaliths) and some of the peculiar *ikat* weaving methods found in pockets of Indonesia today. Some of these practices have survived only in isolated islands or areas which were little touched by later arrivals and cultural currents – such as the Batak areas of Sumatra, Tanatoraja in Sulawesi, parts of Kalimantan and several islands of Nusa Tenggara.

From the 7th century BC there were well-developed and organised societies in the Indonesian archipelago. The inhabitants knew how to irrigate rice fields, domesticate animals, use copper and bronze, and had some knowledge of sea navigation. There were villages – often permanent ones – where life was linked to the production of rice, the staple crop.

These early Indonesians were animists, believing that all animate and inanimate objects have their own particular life force, *semangat* or soul. Certain people had more semangat than others – such as the tribal and village leaders, and the *shamans* or priests who had magical powers and could control the spirit world. The spirits of the dead had to be honoured because their semangat could still help the living; there was a belief in the afterlife, and weapons and utensils would be left in tombs for use in the next world. Supernatural forces were held responsible for natural events, and evil spirits had to be placated by offerings, rites and ceremonies. In a region where earthquakes, volcanic eruptions and torrential rainstorms are common events, a belief in malevolent spirits is hardly surprising.

Villages, at least in Java, developed into embryonic towns and, by the 1st century AD, small kingdoms (little more than collections of villages subservient to petty chieftains) evolved with their own ethnic and tribal religions. The climate of Java, with its hot, even temperature, plentiful rainfall and volcanic soil, was ideal for the wet-field method of rice cultivation, known as *sawah* cultivation. The well-organised society it required may explain why the people of Java and Bali developed a more sophisticated civilisation than those of the other islands. The dry-field or *ladang* method of rice cultivation is a much simpler form of agriculture and requires no elaborate social structure.

The social and religious duties of the rice-growing communities were gradually refined to form the basis of *adat* or customary law. This traditional law was to persist through waves of imported religious beliefs – Hinduism, Buddhism, Islam and Christianity – and still remains a force in Indonesia today.

Coming of Hinduism & Buddhism
One of the puzzles of Indonesian history is how the early kingdoms on Sumatra, Java, Kalimantan and Bali were penetrated by Hinduism and Buddhism. The oldest works of Hindu art in Indonesia, statues from the 3rd century AD, come from Sulawesi and Sumatra. The earliest Hindu inscriptions, in Sanskrit, have been found in West Java and eastern Kalimantan and date from the early 5th century AD.

Several theories regarding the influx of Hinduism and Buddhism have been proposed. Large-scale immigration from India is generally ruled out and there is no evidence for the theory that Indian princes, defeated in wars in India, fled to the islands of South-East Asia and established kingdoms on the Indian model. Certainly Indian traders brought Tamil, the language of southern India, but only Brahmins could have brought Sanskrit, the language of religion and philosophy. Some Brahmins may have followed the traders as missionaries – although Hinduism is not a proselytising religion. On the other hand, Buddhism *is* a proselytising religion and was carried far from its Indian homeland.

Another theory holds that the early Indonesians were attracted to the cultural life of India in much the same way as the Elizabethan English were to that of Italy. The Indonesian aristocracy may have played an active role in transferring Indian culture to Indonesia by inviting Brahmin priests to their courts. Possibly it was hoped that the new religions could provide occult powers

Borobodur relief

and a mythological sanction for the Indonesian rulers – as had happened in India. This theory fits in well with the mythological and mystical view of history which has persisted since the beginning of recorded Indonesian civilisation. In the Hindu period, the kings were seen as incarnations of Vishnu.

Even after the arrival of Islam the dynasties traced their lineage on one side back to Muhammed and from there to the prophets and Adam – but on the other side it was traced to the heroes of the *wayang*, the indigenous puppet theatre of Java, and to gods which orthodox Muslims considered pagan. One Sumatran dynasty even claimed descent from Alexander the Great, and as late as the second half of the 19th century, the rulers of Solo were boasting of a special alliance with Nyai Lara Kidul, the Goddess of the South Seas, and with Sunan Lawu, the ruler of the spirits on Gunung (Mt) Lawu.

Development of Early Sea Trade

Foreign traders were attracted by the Indonesian archipelago's unique local products. Foremost were spices, which were used as flavourings and also to preserve food (meat in particular). Sumatra was famous for gold, pepper and benzoin (an aromatic gum valued especially by the Chinese) but the real 'Spice Islands' were the tiny specks in the region now known as Maluku (the Moluccas): the islands of Ternate and Tidore off the coast of Halmahera, Ambon and Banda. These islands grew nutmeg and cloves, which could be used for spices and preservatives in the manufacture of perfumes, and for medicinal purposes.

By the 1st century AD, Indonesian trade was firmly established with other parts of Asia, including China and India. Indian trade, the more active of the two, linked India, China and Indonesia with Greece and Rome – Ptolemy mentions the islands of Indonesia in his writings as early as 165 AD.

Early Kingdoms

The Sumatran Hindu-Buddhist kingdom of Sriwijaya rose in the 7th century AD and, while its power has been romanticised, it

Top left: Woman at a funeral gathering, Ubud, Bali (VT)
Top right: Diamond miner, Cempaka, Kalimantan (BD)
Bottom: A young boy in traditional attire, Ubud, Bali (PM)

Fruit & vegetables for sale (BD & GB)

nevertheless maintained a substantial international trade – run by Tamils and Chinese. It was the first major Indonesian commercial seapower, able to control much of the trade in South-East Asia by virtue of its control of the Straits of Melaka between Sumatra and the Malay peninsula.

Merchants from Arabia, Persia and India brought goods to the coastal cities to exchange for both local products and goods from China and the Spice Islands. Silk, porcelain and Chinese rhubarb (peculiar for its medicinal properties) came from China in return for ivory, tortoise shell, rhinoceros horn, cloves, cardamom and pepper, as well as precious wood like ebony and camphor wood, perfumes, pearls, coral, camphor oil, amber and the dull reddish-white precious stone known as cornelian or chalcedony. Exports to Arabia included aloes for medicinal uses, camphor oil, sandalwood, ebony and sapanwood (from which a red dye is made), ivory, tin and spices. By the 13th century, woollen and cotton cloth, as well as iron and rice, were imported to Sumatra.

Meanwhile, the Buddhist Sailendra and the Hindu Mataram dynasties flourished on the plains of Central Java between the 8th and 10th centuries. While Sriwijaya's trade brought it wealth, these land-based states had far greater human labour at their disposal and left magnificent remains, particularly the vast Buddhist monument of Borobudur and the huge Hindu temple complex of Prambanan.

Thus two types of states evolved in Indonesia. The first, typified by Sriwijaya, were the mainly Sumatran coastal states – commercially oriented, their wealth derived from international trade and their cities highly cosmopolitan. In contrast, the inland kingdoms of Java, separated from the sea by volcanoes (like the kingdom of Mataram in the Solo River region), were agrarian cultures, bureaucratic and conservative, with a marked capacity to absorb and transform the Indian influences.

By the end of the 10th century, the centre of power had moved from Central to East Java where a series of kingdoms held sway

until the rise of the Majapahit kingdom. This is the period when Hinduism and Buddhism were syncretised and when Javanese culture began to come into its own, finally spreading its influence to Bali. By the 12th century, Sriwijaya's power had declined and the empire broke up into smaller kingdoms.

Hindu Majapahit Kingdom

One of the greatest of Indonesian states and the last important kingdom to remain predominantly Hindu until its extinction was Majapahit. Founded in East Java in 1293, the kingdom had a brief period of conquering glory but in the late 14th century the influence of Majapahit began to decline.

The power of the kingdom was largely due to the rigorous action of one of its early prime ministers, Gajah Mada. Gajah Mada was a royal guard who put down an anti-royalist revolt in the 1320s and then, during the reign of Hayam Wuruk, brought parts of Java and other areas under control. The kingdom has often been portrayed as an Indonesian version of Rome, with its own vast empire, but it is now thought that its power did not extend beyond Java, Bali and the island of

Gajah Mada, Majapahit's strongman prime minister, was a brilliant military commander who rose to prominence during Jayanegara's reign. Gajah Mada assumed virtual leadership from 1336, when Hayam Wuruk became king but was too young to rule. After Gajah Mada's death in 1364, the Majapahit kingdom declined.

Madura. If Gajah Mada did have some control over the other islands he did not govern them as the Romans governed Europe or the Dutch governed Indonesia. Instead, it's likely to have been trade which linked these regions, and at the Majapahit end, this trade was probably a royal monopoly.

Hayam Wuruk's reign is usually referred to as an Indonesian golden age, comparable with the Tang dynasty of China. One account, by the court poet Prapanca, credits the Majapahits with control over much of the coastal regions of Sumatra, Borneo, Sulawesi, Maluku, Sumbawa and Lombok, and also states that the island of Timor sent tribute. The kingdom is said to have maintained regular relations with China, Vietnam, Cambodia, Annam and Siam. However, by 1389 (25 years after the death of Gajah Mada), the kingdom was on the decline, and the coastal dependencies in northern Java were in revolt.

Penetration of Islam
Islam first took hold in north Sumatra, when traders from Gujarat (a western state in India) stopped en route to Maluku and China. Settlements of Arab traders were established in the latter part of the 7th century, and in 1292 Marco Polo noted that the inhabitants of the town of Perlak (present-day Aceh) on Sumatra's north tip had been converted to Islam.

The first Muslim inscriptions in Java date back to the 11th century and there may even have been Muslims in the Majapahit court at the zenith of its power in the mid-14th century. But it was not until the 15th and 16th centuries that Indonesian rulers turned to Islam and it became a state religion. It was then superimposed on the mixture of Hinduism and indigenous animist beliefs to produce the peculiar hybrid religion which predominates in much of Indonesia, especially Java, today.

By the time of Majapahit's final collapse at the beginning of the 16th century, many of its old satellite kingdoms had declared themselves independent Muslim states. Much of their wealth was based on their position as transhipment points for the growing spice trade with India and China. Islam spread across the archipelago from west to east and followed the trade routes. It appears to have been a peaceful transformation – unlike Arab and Turkish conversions made at the point of the sword.

While pockets of the Indonesian population are fundamentalist Muslims, such as the Acehnese in northern Sumatra, the success of Islam was due, on the whole, to its ability to adapt to local customs. The form of Islam followed in much of Indonesia today is not the austere form of the Middle East, but has more in common with Sufism. This is a mystical variant of Islam brought to India from Persia and possibly carried into Indonesia by wandering Sufi holy people and mystics.

Rise of Melaka & Makassar
By the 15th century, the centre of power in the archipelago had moved to the south-west of the Malay peninsula, where the trading kingdom of Melaka (also spelt Malacca) was reaching the height of its power. The rise of Melaka, and of trading cities along the north coast of Java, coincided with the spread of Islam through the archipelago – the Melaka kingdom accepted Islam in the 14th century. Though centred on the peninsula side of the Straits, the Melaka kingdom controlled both sides, based its power and wealth on trade and gathered the ports of northern Java within its commercial orbit. By the 16th century it was the principal port of the region, possibly one of the biggest in the world.

By the end of the 16th century, a sea power had risen in the Indonesian archipelago – the twin principalities of Makassar and Gowa in south-western Sulawesi. These regions had been settled by Malay traders who also sailed to Maluku and beyond. In 1607 when Torres sailed through the strait which now bears his name, he met Makassar Muslims in western New Guinea. Other Makassar fleets visited the northern Australian coast for several hundred years, introducing the Aborigines to metal tools, pottery and tobacco.

Arrival of the Portuguese

When the first Europeans arrived in the Indonesian archipelago they found a varying collection of principalities and kingdoms. These kingdoms were occasionally at war with each other, but were also linked by the substantial inter-island and international trade, over which successive powerful kingdoms – Sriwijaya, Majapahit and Melaka – had been able to exert control by virtue of their position or their sea power.

European influence from the 16th to 18th centuries was due to the penetration of individuals and organisations into the complex trading network of the archipelago. Marco Polo and a few early missionary-travellers aside, the first Europeans to visit Indonesia were the Portuguese. Vasco de Gama had led the first European ships round the Cape of Good Hope to Asia in 1498; by 1510 the Portuguese had captured Goa on the west coast of India and then pushed on to South-

East Asia. The principal aim of the first Portuguese to arrive in the Indonesian archipelago was the domination of the valuable spice trade in Maluku – the Molucca Islands. Under Alfonso d'Albuquerque they captured Melaka in 1511, and the following year arrived in Maluku.

Portuguese control of trade in Indonesia was based on their fortified bases, such as Melaka, and on their supremacy at sea due to the failure of their various foes to form a united front against them. This allowed them to exercise a precarious control of the strategic trading ports that stretched from Maluku to Melaka, Macau, Goa, Mozambique and Angola. From a European point of view, the Portuguese were the pioneers who opened up the trade routes from Europe to Asia and were the forerunners of European expansionism. From an Indonesian point of view, they were just another group of traders who found their way to the Spice Islands. The

Portuguese travellers in Banten, 1596

coming of the Portuguese to Indonesia did not represent a fundamental alteration of Indonesian society or trade – even the capture of Melaka did not change anything. The face and the colour of the rulers changed, but local traders took no notice of political boundaries and allegiances if they did not affect trade.

The initial Portuguese successes encouraged other European nations to send ships to the region – notably the English, the Dutch and the Spanish. The latter established themselves at Manila in 1571. By the time these new forces appeared on the horizon, the Portuguese had suffered a military defeat at Ternate in Maluku and were a spent force. It was the Dutch who would eventually lay the foundations of the Indonesian state we know today.

Coming of the Dutch

A badly led expedition of four Dutch ships, under the command of Cornelius de Houtman, arrived at Banten in West Java in 1596 after a 14-month voyage in which more than half of the 249 crew died. A Dutch account of Banten at the time gives a lively picture:

There came such a multitude of Javanese and other nations such as Turks, Chinese, Bengali, Arabs, Persians, Gujarati, and others that one could hardly move...that each nation took a spot on the ships where they displayed their goods the same as if they were in a market. Of which the Chinese brought of all sorts of silk woven and non-woven, spun and non-spun, with beautiful earthenware, with other strange things more. The Javanese brought chickens, eggs, ducks, and many kinds of fruits. Arabs, Moors, Turks, and other nations of people each brought everything one might imagine.

The Dutch got off to a poor start. They made a bad impression on the Javanese by killing a prince and some of his retainers, concluded a meaningless treaty of friendship with the ruler of Banten and lost one of their ships when attacked by the Javanese north of Surabaya. Nevertheless, they returned to Holland with goods that yielded a small profit for their backers. Other independent expeditions followed and met with varying success –

some ships were captured by the Spanish and Portuguese. The behaviour of the Dutch was uneven and so was their reception but Dutch trade expanded quickly. This was partly because regional Indonesian leaders took advantage of the higher prices which the Dutch and Portuguese competition generated.

Then in 1580, Spain, the traditional enemy of Holland, occupied Portugal and this prompted the Dutch government to take an interest in the Far East. The government amalgamated the competing merchant companies into the United East India Company, or the VOC (Vereenigde Oost-Indische Compagnie). The intention was to create a force to bring military pressure to bear on the Portuguese and the Spanish. Dutch trading ships were replaced by heavily armed fleets with instructions to attack Portuguese bases. By 1605 the Dutch had defeated the Portuguese at Tidore and Ambon and occupied the territory themselves – but it was another 36 years before they captured Melaka.

Foundation of a Dutch Empire

The founder of the Dutch empire in the Indies was Jan Pieterszoon Coen, an imaginative but ruthless man. Amongst his 'achievements' was the near-total extermination of the indigenous population of the Banda Islands in Maluku. Coen developed a grandiose plan to make his capital in Java the centre of the intra-Asian trade from Japan to Persia, and to develop the spice plantations using Burmese, Madagascan and Chinese labourers.

While the more grandiose plans were rejected he nevertheless acted vigorously in grabbing a monopoly on the spice trade as he had been instructed. An alliance with Ternate in 1607 gave the Dutch control over the source of cloves, and their occupation of Banda from 1609-21 also gave them control of the nutmeg trade. As the Dutch extended their power, they forced a reduction in spice production by destroying excess clove and nutmeg plantations, thus ruining the livelihoods of the local inhabitants but keeping European prices and profits high. After cap-

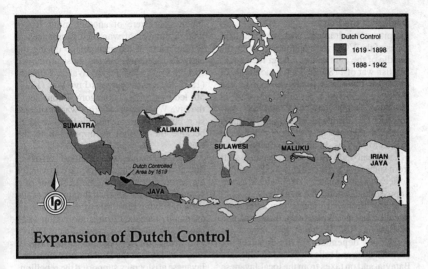

Expansion of Dutch Control

turing Melaka from the Portuguese in 1641, the Dutch became masters of the seas in the region. They not only held a monopoly of the clove and nutmeg trade, they also had a hold on the Indian cloth trade and on Japanese copper exports. By the middle of the century they had made their capital Batavia, on the island of Java, the centre of trade on a route from Japan to Persia via Ceylon and India. They defeated Makassar in 1667 and secured a monopoly of its trade, and eventually brought the Sumatran ports under their sway. The last of the Portuguese were expelled in 1660 and the English in 1667.

The first effect of Dutch power in the Indies was the disruption of the traditional pattern of trade by their attempts – with some success – to achieve a monopoly of the spice trade at its source. The VOC's policy at this stage was to keep to its trading posts and avoid expensive territorial conquests. An accord with the Susuhunan (literally 'he to whose feet people must look up') of Mataram, the dominant kingdom in Java, was established. It permitted only Dutch ships, or those with permission from the VOC, to trade with the Spice Islands and the regions beyond them.

Then, perhaps unintentionally, but in leaps and bounds, the Dutch developed from being one trading company to the masters of a colonial empire centred on their chief trading port at Batavia. Following a 'divide and rule' strategy, the Dutch exploited the conflicts between the Javanese kingdoms and, in 1678, were able to make the ruler of Mataram their vassal and dominate his successors.

They had already put Banten under their control by helping the ruler's ambitious son to overthrow his father. In 1755 the Dutch split the Mataram kingdom into two – Yogyakarta and Surakarta (Solo). These new states and the five smaller states on Java were only nominally sovereign; in reality they were dominated by the VOC. Fighting amongst the princes was halted, and peace was brought to East Java by the forced cessation of invasions and raids from Bali.

Thus Java was united – what the native kings had failed to do for centuries had been achieved towards the end of the 18th century by a foreign trading company with an army that totalled only 1000 Europeans and 2000 Asians.

Decline of the VOC

Despite some dramatic successes, the fortunes of the VOC were on the decline by the middle of the 18th century. After the Dutch-English war of 1780, the Dutch monopoly of the spice trade was finally broken by the Treaty of Paris which permitted free trade in the East. Dutch trade in China was outstripped by European rivals, and in India much of their trade was diverted by the British to Madras. In addition, the emphasis of European trade with the East began to shift from spices to Chinese silk, Japanese copper, coffee, tea and sugar – over which it was impossible to establish a monopoly.

Dutch trading interests gradually contracted more and more around their capital of Batavia. The Batavian government increasingly depended for its finances on customs dues and tolls on goods coming into Batavia, and on taxes from the local Javanese population. Increased smuggling and the illicit private trade carried on by company employees helped to reduce profits. The mounting expense of wars within Java and of administering the additional territory acquired after each new treaty also played a part in the decline.

The VOC turned to the Dutch government at home for support and the subsequent investigation of VOC affairs revealed corruption, bankruptcy and mismanagement. In 1800 the VOC was formally wound up, its territorial possessions became the property of the Netherlands government and the trading empire was gradually transformed into a colonial empire.

British Occupation

In 1811, during the Napoleonic Wars when France occupied Holland, the British occupied several Dutch East Indies posts, including Java. Control was restored to the Dutch in 1816 and a treaty was signed in 1824 under which the British exchanged their Indonesian settlements (such as Bengkulu in Sumatra) for Dutch holdings in India and the Malay peninsula. While the two European powers may have settled their differences to their own satisfaction, the Indonesians were of another mind. There were a number of wars or disturbances in various parts of the archipelago during the early 19th century, but the most prolonged struggles were the Paderi War in Sumatra (1821-38) and the famous Java War (1825-30) led by Prince Diponegoro. In one sense the Java War was yet another war of succession, but both wars are notable because Islam became the symbol of opposition to the Dutch.

In 1814, Diponegoro, the eldest son of the Sultan of Yogya, had been passed over for the succession to the throne in favour of a younger claimant who had the support of the British. Having bided his time, Diponegoro eventually vanished from court and in 1825 launched a guerrilla war against the Dutch. The courts of Yogya and Solo largely remained loyal to the Dutch but many of the Javanese aristocracy supported the rebellion.

Prince Diponegoro, of the Yogyakarta royal house, was the charismatic leader of a bloody guerrilla war against the Dutch from 1825 to 1830. Diponegoro was treacherously lured to discuss peace terms with the Dutch at Magellan, and then arrested. He was exiled to Sulawesi, where he died in 1856.

Diponegoro had received mystical signs that convinced him that he was the divinely appointed future king of Java. News spread among the people that he was the long-prophesied Ratu Adil, the prince who would free them from colonial oppression.

The rebellion finally ended in 1830 when the Dutch tricked Diponegoro into peace negotiations, arrested him and exiled him to Sulawesi. The five-year war had cost the lives of 8000 European and 7000 Indonesian soldiers of the Dutch army. At least 200,000 Javanese died, most from famine and disease, and the population of Yogyakarta was halved.

Dutch Exploitation of Indonesia

For 350 years, from the time the first Dutch ships arrived in 1596 to the declaration of independence in 1945, there was little stability in Indonesia. The first Dutch positions in the archipelago were precarious, like the first Portuguese positions. Throughout the 17th century the VOC, with its superior arms and Buginese and Ambonese mercenaries, fought everywhere in the islands. Despite Dutch domination of Java, many areas of the archipelago – including Aceh, Bali, Lombok and Borneo – remained independent.

Fighting continued to flare up in Sumatra and Java, and between 1846 and 1849 expeditions were sent to Bali in the first attempts to subjugate the island. Then there was the violent Banjarmasin War in south-eastern Borneo, during which the Dutch defeated the reigning sultan. The longest and most devastating war was the one in Aceh which had remained independent under British protection (the two had an active trade). In 1871 the Dutch negotiated a new treaty in which the British withdrew objections to a possible Dutch occupation of Aceh. The Dutch declared war on Aceh in 1873. The war lasted for 35 years until the last Aceh guerrilla leaders finally surrendered in 1908.

Even into the 20th century Dutch control outside Java was still incomplete. Large-scale Indonesian piracy continued right up until the middle of the 19th century and the

Dutch fought a war in Sulawesi against the Buginese. Dutch troops occupied south-western Sulawesi between 1900 and 1910, and Bali in 1906. The 'bird's head' of West Irian did not come under Dutch administration until 1919-20. Ironically, just when the Dutch finally got it all together they began to lose it. By the time Bali was occupied, the first Indonesian nationalist movements were getting under way.

The determined exploitation of Indonesian resources by the Dutch really only began in 1830. The cost of the Java and Paderi wars meant that, despite increased returns from the Dutch system of land tax, Dutch finances were severely strained. When the Dutch lost Belgium in 1830 the home country itself faced bankruptcy and any government investment in the Indies *had* to make quick returns. From here on Dutch economic policy in Indonesia falls into three overlapping periods: the period of the so-called 'Culture' System, the Liberal Period and the Ethical Period.

Throughout all three periods, the exploitation of Indonesia's wealth contributed to the industrialisation of the Netherlands. Large areas of Java became plantations whose products, cultivated by Javanese peasants and collected by Chinese intermediaries, were sold on the overseas markets by European merchants. Before WW II, Indonesia supplied most of the world's quinine and pepper, over a third of its rubber, a quarter of its coconut products and almost a fifth of its tea, sugar, coffee and oil. Indonesia made the Netherlands one of the major colonial powers.

Culture System A new governor-general, Johannes Van den Bosch, fresh from experiences of the slave labour of the West Indies, was appointed in 1830 to make the East Indies pay their way. He succeeded by introducing a new agricultural policy called the *cultuurstelsel* or Culture System. It was really a system of government-controlled agriculture or, as Indonesian historians refer to it, the *Tanam Paksa* (compulsory planting).

Forced labour was not new in Java – the

Dutch merely extended the existing system by forcing the peasants to produce particular crops, including coffee, which the Dutch introduced. Instead of land rent, usually assessed at about two-fifths of the value of the crop, the Culture System proposed that a portion of peasants' land and labour be placed at the government's disposal. On this land a designated crop, suitable for the European market, was to be grown.

In practice things did not work out that way and the system produced fearful hardship. The land required from each peasant was sometimes as much as a third or even a half of their total land. In some cases the new crops demanded more labour than the maximum allowed for, and the government did not bear the losses of a bad harvest. Often the Culture System was applied on top of the land tax rather than in place of it. When the cash crops failed the peasants had no money to buy the rice they would otherwise have planted on their land. In some regions the population starved because the Javanese regents (princes) and their Chinese agents forced the peasants to use almost all their rice land to grow other crops. In the 1840s there was severe famine in some areas because of the encroachment on rice lands.

The system was never applied to the whole population – by 1845 it involved only about 5% of the total cleared land, so its impact on the Javanese was very uneven. Amongst the crops grown was indigo (from which the deep blue dye is extracted), which required arduous cultivation, and sugar, which took twice the labour required of rice fields.

The Culture System was, however, a boon to the Dutch and to the Javanese aristocracy. The profits made Java a self-sufficient colony and saved the Netherlands from bankruptcy. That this gain was made by appropriating all available profits and making the peasants bear all the losses was irrelevant to the Dutch. They believed that the function of a colony was to benefit the coloniser and that the welfare of the indigenous people should not interfere with this.

Liberal Period In the 10 years after 1848, efforts were made to correct the worst abuses of the Culture System. The liberals in the Dutch parliament attempted to reform the system, while at the same time retaining the profits and alleviating the conditions of the peasants.

They were committed to reducing government interference in economic enterprises and were therefore opposed to the system of government-controlled agriculture in Indonesia. Their policies advocated opening up the country to private enterprise – in the belief that once the peasant was freed from compulsion, productivity would increase and everyone would be swept to prosperity by the forces of a free economy. But to make the archipelago safe for individual capitalists and to free the Indonesians from oppression were, in fact, two conflicting aims.

From the 1860s onwards, the government abolished monopolies on crops which were no longer profitable anyway. Things moved more slowly for other crops; in 1870 a law was passed by which control of sugar production would be relinquished over a 12-year period from 1878 onwards, while the monopoly of the most profitable crop, coffee, was retained right up until 1917.

The 1870 Agrarian Law and other new policies proved profitable for the Dutch but brought further hardships to the Indonesians. Sugar production doubled in 1870-85, new crops like tea and cinchona flourished, and a start was made with rubber, which eventually became a valuable export. At the same time, oil produced in south Sumatra and Kalimantan became a valuable export – a response to the new industrial demands of the European market.

The exploitation of Indonesian resources was no longer limited to Java but had filtered through to the outer islands. As Dutch commercial interests expanded, so did the need to protect them. More and more territory was taken under direct control of the Dutch government and most of the outer islands came under firm Dutch sovereignty.

Ethical Period At the turn of the century there were two increasingly vocal groups in the Dutch parliament – those who had a humanitarian interest in the welfare of the Indonesian people, and those who wanted to raise the purchasing power of the Indonesians in order to widen the market for consumer goods. The group who aimed at improving the welfare of the Indonesian people approached the task with a strong sense of a moral mission.

New policies were to be implemented, foremost among them irrigation, transmigration from heavily populated Java to lightly populated islands, and education. There were also plans for improved communications, credit facilities for Indonesians, agricultural advice, flood control, drainage, extension of health programmes, industrialisation and the protection of native industry. Other policies aimed for the decentralisation of authority with greater autonomy for the Indonesian government, as well as greater power to local government units within the archipelago.

There were four main criticisms of these new policies: as they were implemented they improved the lot of the Europeans in Indonesia, not the Indonesians themselves; those programmes which did benefit the Indonesians only reached a small percentage of the population; the programmes were carried out in a paternalistic, benevolent fashion which continued to regard the Indonesians as inferiors; and some of the policies were never implemented at all. Industrialisation was never implemented, because it was never seriously envisaged that Indonesia would compete with European industry, and because it was also feared that industrial development would result in the loss of a market for European goods.

Indonesian Nationalist Movements

Of all the policies of the Ethical Period, it was the education policies which had the least predictable and the most far-reaching effects. The diversification of economic activity and the increasing scope and range of government activity, banks and business houses, meant a growing need for Indonesians with some Western education to do the paperwork. As educational opportunities increased and some Indonesians attained higher levels of education, an educated elite developed which became increasingly aware and resentful of European rule.

The first Indonesian nationalist movements of the 20th century had their roots in educational organisations. Initially the nationalist organisations largely concerned the upper and middle-class Indonesians whose education and contact with Western culture had made them more conscious of their own cultural traditions and critical of the injustices of the colonial system. Then mass movements began to develop, drawing support from the peasants and the urban working class.

Islamic Association The first truly mass movement was Sarekat Islam (Islamic Association), which had its origins in a trading society formed in 1909 to protect Indonesians against Chinese dealers. It quickly became one of the most significant of the early nationalist movements. It was the first movement attempting to bridge the gap between the villagers and the new Western-educated elite.

Indonesian Communist Party Created in 1914, this small Marxist group, later known as the PKI (Perserikatan Kommunist Indonesia) built up influence in the Islamic Association until a showdown in 1921 forced the Communists out. The Communists organised strikes in urban businesses and in the sugar factories but Communist-led revolts in Java (1926) and Sumatra (1927) were both suppressed by the Dutch. The PKI was effectively destroyed for the rest of the colonial period, with its leaders imprisoned or self-exiled to avoid arrest.

Indonesian Nationalist Party The Partai Nasional Indonesia (PNI) was formed (under a different name) in 1927 and advocated an independent Indonesia as its ultimate objective. The party was chaired by and had arisen out of the Bandung Study Group which was formed by Achmed Soekarno, who later become the first president of independent Indonesia.

The PNI became the most powerful nationalist organisation. Its early success was partly a result of Soekarno's skill as an orator and his understanding of the common people from whom the party drew and built up its mass support. The Dutch quickly recognised the threat from the PNI, and Soekarno and three other PNI leaders were imprisoned in 1930. The party was outlawed and its membership split into factions.

Other nationalist groups arose. In 1932,

Muhammed Hatta and Sutan Sjahrir, who were to become important figures in the nationalist movement, returned from university in the Netherlands and established their own nationalist group. Soekarno was released and then re-arrested in 1933, and Hatta and Sjahrir were arrested in 1934. None of the three leaders were freed until the Japanese invasion of 1942.

As the 1930s progressed, the question of cooperation or non-cooperation with the Dutch in the face of growing European and Japanese fascism was raised. While some nationalist leaders attempted to formulate an anti-fascist solidarity pact with the Dutch in return for

Street Names & Indonesian Heroes

In every city, town and kampung in Indonesia, streets (as well as airports, parks and so on) are named after Indonesian heroes who, invariably, helped fight the Dutch during the colonial period, or after independence was declared by Indonesia in 1945. Some of the more well-known are:

Cockroaminoto, H O S (1883-1934) was from East Java, and helped establish the Islamic Federation, also known as the PSII.

Diponegoro, Pangeran (1785-1855) was a prince from Yogyakarta. He was a leader in the Java War of 1825-30 against the Dutch, during which he was captured, and later exiled to Ujung Pandang where he died.

Gajah Mada was prime minister and a brilliant military commander in the Javanese Majapahit kingdom in the 14th century. He helped defeat rebels who fought King Jayanegara (but Gajah Mada later arranged the king's murder because he took Gajah Mada's wife!).

Hasanuddin, Sultan (1631-70), born in South Sulawesi, helped with the resistance against the VOC.

Hatta, Mohammed (1902-80) was a Sumatran who was arrested in 1927 for promoting resistance against the Dutch. He was sent to the notorious prison, Boven Digul, and then Banda, but later released by the Japanese. On 17 August 1945, he declared Indonesian independence with Soekarno, and served as vice-president and/or prime minister from 1945-56.

Imam Bonjol (1772-1864) was an important Islamic leader, and a leader of the resistance against the Dutch in the Paderi war of 1803-37. He was captured by the Dutch, sent to Ambon and then Manado.

Kartini, Raden Ajeng (1879-1905) was a Javanese writer and activist, who became famous for her promotion of education and women's rights, especially through her letters which were discovered after her death during childbirth.

Monginsidi, Wolter (1925-49) was captured and shot at only 24 years of age by the Dutch during the resistance.

Indonesian independence, at no time – even after the Nazi occupation of the Netherlands – did the Dutch encourage the Indonesians to believe that their cooperation was needed, or that their independence aims would be recognised.

Japanese Invasion & Occupation

The first Japanese landings in Indonesia were in January 1942. The Dutch forces eventually surrendered, and to some extent the Japanese were hailed by the Indonesians as liberators. Sjahrir commented that:

...for the average Indonesian the war...was simply a struggle in which the Dutch colonial rulers finally

would be punished by Providence for the evil, the arrogance and the oppression they had brought to Indonesia.

An ancient prophesy was revived which predicted that Indonesia would be ruled by a white buffalo (interpreted as meaning the Dutch) and then by a yellow chicken (the Japanese) which would stay only for 'a year of corn' before independence was again achieved. The Japanese occupation lasted for 3½ years.

Japanese control was very much dependent on goodwill. Believing the anti-Dutch sentiments of the Indonesians to be stronger

---

Sisingamangaraja (1849-1907) was the last of a long line of Batak kings, first dating from the 16th century. His ancestors were spiritual leaders, and he became a leader of, and then was killed by, the resistance against the Dutch.

Subroto, Gatot (1907-62) fought for Indonesian independence in the 1940s, and helped quell communist rebels in 1948. He became Military Governor of Surakarta, then a General, and later a member of Soeharto's early cabinet.

Sudarso, Yos (1925-62) was a senior naval officer who died when his ship, the *Macan Tutul*, was sunk by the Dutch during the liberation of Irian Jaya.

Sudirman (1916-50) was a leader of the resistance against the Dutch during 1945-50. After independence, he was appointed General and Commander-in-Chief of the Indonesian Republic.

Supratman, W R (1903-38) composed the Indonesian national anthem *Indonesia Raya*, which was first performed by Supratman at the 2nd Indonesian Youth Congress in 1928.

Syahrir, Sutan (1909-66), also referred to as Sjahrir, was a leading nationalist leader in Java in the 1930s, but was opposed to Soekarno. Syahrir was arrested by the Dutch, exiled to Boven Digul, and later denounced the Japanese Occupation. He served as Prime Minister from 1945-47, and was instrumental in obtaining former Dutch territories for the new Indonesia.

Thamrin, Mohammed (1894-1941) was a nationalist leader and politician in the 1920s and 1930s. He was arrested by the Dutch in 1941, after cooperating with the Japanese, and died soon after.

Yamin, Mohammed (1903-62) a Sumatran writer, poet, lawyer and politician; he helped formed the Youth Pledge in 1928. He was arrested in 1946 by the Dutch, then became a cabinet minister, and later the instigator of 'Guided Democracy'.

Yani, Ahmad (1922-65) was responsible for suppressing Sumatran rebels in 1958. He was commander of the 'liberation' of Irian Jaya three years later, and became Army Chief of Staff in 1962. He was one of the generals killed in the ill-fated coup of September 1965. ■

than any anti-Japanese sentiments, the Japanese were prepared to work with the Indonesian nationalists. Soekarno and Hatta, the best known nationalists, worked above ground and collaborated with the Japanese. Sjahrir led one of the underground groups, among which were people who later became prominent in Indonesian politics.

The period of Japanese occupation was immensely important in the development of the nationalist movement and there is little doubt that it grew in strength. The Japanese sponsored mass organisations based on Islam and anti-Western sentiments. Soekarno and Hatta were allowed to travel about addressing gatherings of Indonesians, and Soekarno used these occasions to spread nationalist propaganda.

In 1943, the Japanese formed the Volunteer Army of Defenders of the Fatherland, a home defence corps which Indonesians joined in large numbers. Soekarno and Hatta were allowed to address the recruits and the corps soon became a hotbed of nationalism, later forming the backbone of the Indonesian forces fighting the Dutch after WW II.

Independence Struggle

In mid-1945, with the tide of war against them, the Japanese set up a committee of Indonesian nationalists entitled the 'Investigating Body for the Preparation of Indonesian Independence'. This committee represented an important point in the history of the nationalist movement because it outlined the geographical limits of a future independent Indonesia.

It also set out the philosophical basis which would underlie the government and social structure of the new state. This was based on a speech Soekarno made on 1 June 1945 to the committee announcing the *Pancasila* or 'Five Principles' on which an independent Indonesia would be based: Faith in God, Humanity, Nationalism, Representative Government and Social Justice. As Soekarno put it, it was a synthesis of Western democratic ideas, Islam, Marxism and indigenous village customs and traditions of government.

Three plans were drawn up for territorial boundaries and the vote came out strongly in favour of including all the territories of the Dutch East Indies, plus the territories of North Borneo, Brunei, Sarawak, Portuguese Timor, Malaysia, New Guinea and surrounding islands. Soekarno, according to a book by Hatta, argued for the inclusion of Malaysia in the belief that the interests of Indonesia would not be secure unless both sides of the Straits of Melaka were under its control. Despite majority feeling, the Japanese seemed to have influenced the Indonesians into accepting one of the other plans which claimed only the former territory of the Dutch East Indies.

On 6 August 1945, the USA dropped the atomic bomb on Hiroshima. On 9 August, the second atomic bomb was dropped on Nagasaki, and the next day Japan surrendered. Japan was no longer in a position to grant or guarantee Indonesian independence, but it still controlled the archipelago. The underground movements were now determined to rise against the Japanese and take over the administration. In the early morning of 16 August, a group of students – including Adam Malik, the future foreign minister of the Republic of Indonesia – kidnapped Soekarno, his wife and children, and Hatta, and held them outside Jakarta. The following day, outside his Jakarta home, Soekarno proclaimed the formation of an independent Indonesia. An Indonesian government consisting of 16 ministers was formed on 31 August, with Soekarno as president and Hatta as vice-president.

In September 1945, the first British and Australian troops landed in Jakarta, and from October onwards began arriving throughout the territories. They had three main tasks: to disarm the Japanese troops and send them back to Japan, to rescue Allied prisoners of war and, lastly, to hold the Indonesian nationalists down until the Dutch could return to the archipelago and reassert their 'lawful' sovereignty.

Most of the 'British' troops were in fact Indians – the soldiers of one colony being used to help restore colonialism in another –

and many deserted to the Indonesian side. Japanese troops tried to recapture towns held by the Indonesians, such as Bandung. Heavy fighting, which lasted for 10 days, broke out in Surabaya between Indonesians and the Indian troops led by British officers.

Against this background of turbulence, attempts were made to begin negotiations between the Dutch and the nationalists but the Dutch failed to recognise that their colonial empire was finished. Hatta said:

The Dutch are graciously permitting us entry into the basement while we have climbed all the way to the top floor and up to the attic. Indonesia today has achieved her own administration as a result of her own efforts. And what earthly reason is there for Indonesia to return to her former status as a colony of a foreign nation which did practically nothing to defend her from the Japanese? The Dutch should not remain under the delusion that they can thwart Indonesia's desire to remain independent.

The last British troops left at the end of November 1946, by which time 55,000 Dutch troops had landed in Java. In Bogor (Java) and in Balikpapan (Kalimantan), Indonesian republican officials were imprisoned. Bombing raids on Palembang and Medan in Sumatra prepared the way for the Dutch occupation of these cities. In southern Sulawesi, a Captain Westerling was accused of pacifying the region by murdering 40,000 Indonesians in a few weeks. Elsewhere, the Dutch were attempting to form puppet states among the more amenable ethnic groups.

The next three years saw a confusing struggle – half diplomatic and half military. Despite major military operations in 1947 and 1948, the nationalists continued to hold out, world opinion swayed heavily against the Dutch and it became obvious that only a concerted and costly campaign could defeat the nationalist forces. The Dutch were finally forced out by international pressure, particularly from the USA, which threatened the Dutch with economic sanctions. In December 1949, after negotiations in the Netherlands, the Dutch finally transferred sovereignty over the former Dutch East Indies to the new Indonesian republic.

Economic Depression & Disunity

The threat of external attacks from the Dutch had helped to keep the nationalists mostly united in the first five years or so after the proclamation of independence. With the Dutch gone, the divisions in Indonesian society began to reassert themselves. Soekarno had tried to hammer out the principles of Indonesian unity in his Pancasila speech of 1945 and while these, as he said, may have been 'the highest common factor and the lowest common multiple of Indonesian thought', the divisive elements in Indonesian society could not be swept away by a single speech. Regional differences in customs (adat), morals, tradition, religion, the impact of Christianity and Marxism, and fears of political domination by the Javanese all contributed to disunity.

In the early years of the republic there were a number of separatist movements which sprang out of the religious and ethnic diversity of the country. These included the militant Darul Islam (Islamic Domain) which proclaimed an Islamic State of Indonesia and waged guerrilla warfare in West Java against the new Indonesian republic from 1949 to 1962. There was also an attempt by former Ambonese members of the Royal Dutch Indies Army to establish an independent republic in Maluku, and there were revolts in Minahasa (the northern limb of Sulawesi) and in Sumatra.

Against this background lay divisions in the leadership elite, and the sorry state of the new republic's economy. When the Republic of Indonesia came into being, the economy was in tatters after almost 10 years of Japanese occupation and war with the Dutch. The population was increasing and the new government was unable to boost production of foodstuffs and clothing to keep pace with, let alone overtake, this increase in population. Most of the population was illiterate; there were few schools and few teachers. While there was a sufficiently large elite of Western-educated Indonesians to fill top levels of government, there were insufficient middle-level staff, technicians and people with basic skills such as typing and accountancy. Inflation was chronic, smuggling cost the central government badly needed foreign currency, and many of the plantations had been destroyed during the war.

Political parties proliferated and deals between parties for a share of cabinet seats resulted in a rapid turnover of coalition governments. There were 17 cabinets for the period 1945 to 1958. The frequently postponed elections were finally held in 1955 and the PNI – regarded as Soekarno's party – topped the poll. There were also dramatic increases in support for the Communist PKI but no party managed more than a quarter of the votes and short-lived coalitions continued.

Soekarno Takes Over – Guided Democracy

By 1956 President Soekarno was openly criticising parliamentary democracy. Its most serious weakness, he said, was that it was 'based upon inherent conflict' thus running counter to the Indonesian concept of harmony as the natural state of human relationships.

Soekarno sought a system based on the traditional village system of discussion and deliberation upon a problem in an attempt to find common ground and a consensus of opinion under the guidance of the village elders. He argued that the threefold division – nationalism *(nasionalisme)*, religion *(agaman)* and communism *(komunisme)* – would be blended into a cooperative government, or what he called a *Nas-A-Kom* government.

In February 1957, at a large meeting of politicians and others, Soekarno proposed a cabinet representing all the political parties of importance (including the PKI). This was his attempt to overcome the impasse in the political system, but it was not an attempt to abolish the parties. Soekarno then proclaimed 'guided democracy' and brought Indonesia's period of Western parliamentary democracy to a close. This was achieved with support from his own party, and with some support from regional and military leaders grown weary of the political merry-go-round in Jakarta.

Soekarno

Sumatra & Sulawesi Rebellions

As a direct result of Soekarno's actions, rebellions broke out in Sumatra and Sulawesi in 1958. Led by senior military and civilian leaders of the day, these rebellions were partly a reaction against Soekarno's usurpation of power and partly against the growing influence of the Communist Party which was winning increasing favour with Soekarno. The rebellions were also linked to the growing regional hostility to the mismanagement, inefficiency and corruption of the central government. This was intensified by Java's declining share in the export trade, while the foreign earnings of the other islands were used to import rice and consumer goods for Java's increasing population.

The central government, however, effectively smashed the rebellion by mid-1958, though guerrilla activity continued for three years. Rebel leaders were granted amnesty, but the two political parties which they had been connected with were banned and some of the early nationalist leaders were discredited. Sjahrir and others were arrested in 1962.

The defeat of the rebellion was a considerable victory for Soekarno, his supporters and the army, led by General Nasution, which had gained administrative authority throughout the country. The Communist Party had also benefited because it had been a target of criticism by the rebels. Soekarno was now able to exercise enormous personal influence and set about reorganising the political system in order to give himself *real* power.

In 1960 the elected parliament was dissolved and replaced by a parliament appointed by the president. It had no authority over the president and enacted laws subject to his agreement. A new body, the Supreme Advisory Council, with 45 members including a president who appointed the others, was established and became the chief policy-making body. An organisation called the National Front was set up in September 1960 to 'mobilise the revolutionary forces of the people'. The Front was presided over by the president and became a useful adjunct to the government in organising 'demonstrations' – such as sacking embassies during the period of 'Confrontation' with Malaysia.

Soekarno – Revolution & Nationalism

With his assumption of power, Soekarno set Indonesia on a course of stormy nationalism. During the early 1960s he created a strange language of capital letters: the world was divided between the NEFOS (New Emerging Forces) and the OLDEFOS (Old Established Forces), in which Westerners were the NEKOLIM (the Neo-Colonial Imperialists).

His speeches were those of a romantic revolutionary and they held his people spellbound. *Konfrontasi* become a term to juggle with. Malaysia would be confronted, as would its protector, the UK. The USA would be confronted, as would the whole Western world. The people sometimes called Soekarno *bapak* or father, but he was really *bung*, the daring older brother who carried

out the outrageous schemes they wished they could do themselves.

The Western world remembers Soekarno's flamboyance and his contradictions. No other Asian leader has so keenly offended the puritan values of the West; abstinence, monogamy and other virtues were conspicuously undervalued by Soekarno. His notorious liking for women and his real and/or alleged sexual exploits were certainly advantageous to him in Indonesia, where he was not expected to be the good family man, faithful to his wife in the best traditions (as opposed to actual practice) of Western politics.

He claimed to be a believer in God and also a Marxist – this peculiar blending of contradictory philosophies sprang from the time when he was trying to find common ground against the Dutch. Soekarno set himself up as a conciliator between the nationalist groups because he knew that unity was vital in order to achieve independence. He also made appeals to the emotions and mysticism of the Javanese because these were their characteristics.

Economic Deterioration

What Soekarno could not do was create a viable economic system that would lift Indonesia out of its poverty. Soekarno's corrosive vanity burnt money on a spate of status symbols meant to symbolise the new Indonesian identity. They included the Merdeka (Freedom) Monument, a mosque designed to be the biggest in the world, and a vast sports stadium built with Russian money. Unable to advance beyond revolution to the next stage of rebuilding, with its slow and unspectacular processes, Soekarno's monuments became substitutes for real development.

Richard Nixon, who became the US president in 1968, visited Indonesia in 1953 and presented this image of Indonesia under Soekarno:

In no other country we visited was the conspicuous luxury of the ruler in such striking contrast to the poverty and misery of his people. Jakarta was a collection of sweltering huts and hovels. An open sewer ran through the heart of the city, but Soekarno's palace was painted a spotless white and set in the middle of hundreds of acres of exotic gardens. One night we ate off gold plate to the light of a thousand torches while musicians played on the shore of a lake covered with white lotus blossoms and candles floating on small rafts.

A more aggressive stance on foreign affairs also became a characteristic of Soekarno's increased authority. Soekarno believed that Asia had been humiliated by the West and had still not evened the score. He sought recognition of a new state that was once a 'nation of coolies and a coolie amongst nations'. Indonesia was also surrounded, and from Soekarno's view, threatened by the remnants of Western imperialism: the British and their new client state of Malaysia; the hated Dutch who continued to occupy West Irian; and the Americans and their military bases in the Philippines.

From this point of view, Soekarno's efforts to take over West Irian and his Confrontation with Malaysia – however inadvisable – make some sense. Indonesia walked out of the United Nations in January 1965 after Malaysia had been admitted to the Security Council. Under Soekarno, Indonesia turned its attention towards attaining those territories it had claimed in August 1945. First on the agenda was West Irian, still under Dutch rule. An arms agreement with the Soviet Union in 1960 enabled the Indonesians to begin a diplomatic as well as military confrontation with the Dutch over West Irian. It was pressure from the USA on the Dutch that finally led to the Indonesian takeover in 1963.

The same year Indonesia embarked on Confrontation with the new nation of Malaysia, formed from a federation of the Malay peninsula and the states in northern Borneo which bordered on Indonesian Kalimantan. For Indonesia, the formation of Malaysia meant the consolidation of British military power on its own doorstep. Soekarno and Indonesian military leaders also suspected that the British and the Americans had aided the separatist rebels in the archipelago. It

took three years for the Confrontation to run its course. It tied up 50,000 British, Australian and New Zealand soldiers in military action along the Kalimantan-Malaysia border, but was never really a serious threat to the survival of Malaysia.

The critical effects of Confrontation were economic. The eight-year economic plan announced in 1963 was intended to increase revenue from taxes, stabilise consumer prices and strengthen the currency. The plan miscarried, in part due to half-heartedness and corruption on the part of military leaders and administrators but mainly because of the runaway inflation caused by the expenses of Confrontation. Foreign aid dried up because the USA withdrew its aid when Indonesia launched Confrontation.

Without finance the government had to look elsewhere for money. Government subsidies in several areas of the public sector were abolished, leading to massive increases in rail freight, and rail, bus and airfares. Similar increases occurred in electricity, tap water, post and telegraph charges. These rises flowed on to the market, with large increases in the price of basic consumer goods like rice, beef, fish, eggs, salt and soap. Salaries were increased in this period but not enough to keep up with the ever-mounting prices.

Soekarno, the Army & the Communists
Confrontation also alienated Western nations, and Indonesia came to depend more and more on support from the Soviet Union, then increasingly from Communist China. Meanwhile, tensions grew between the Indonesian Army and the PKI (Communist Party). Though Soekarno often talked as if he held absolute power, his position actually depended on maintaining a balance between the different political powers in Indonesia at the time, primarily between the army and the PKI. Soekarno is often described as the great *dalang*, or puppet master, who balanced the forces of the left and right just as competing forces are balanced in the Javanese shadow puppet shows.

The PKI was the third-largest communist

party in the world, outside the Soviet Union and China. By 1965 it claimed to have three million members, it controlled the biggest trade union organisation in Indonesia (the Central All-Indonesian Workers Organisation) and the largest peasant group (the Indonesian Peasant Front). It also had an influence in the major mass organisation (the National Front). The membership of affiliate organisations of the PKI was said to be 15 to 20 million. Except for the inner cabinet, it penetrated the government apparatus extensively.

It is possible that the successes of the party in the 1955 election suggested to Soekarno that the PKI could be the force that would end centuries of economic oppression of the Indonesian peasant – by feudal lords, the Dutch, the modern upper class, the army and the superstitions of the people – and to that end he gave the PKI his support.

Guided democracy under Soekarno was marked by an attempt to give the peasants better social conditions, but attempts to give tenant farmers a fairer share of their rice crops and to redistribute land led to more confusion. The PKI often pushed for reforms behind the government's back and encouraged peasants to seize land without waiting for decisions from land-reform committees. In 1964 these tactics led to violent clashes in Central and East Java and Bali, and the PKI got a reputation as a troublemaker.

The PKI was dissatisfied with what had been achieved domestically and wanted more control of policy making. It also wanted the workers and peasants armed and organised into self-defence units. The pressure increased in 1965 with growing tension between the PKI and the army. The crunch came with the proposal to arm the Communists. The story goes that after a meeting with Zhou Enlai (the then Premier of China) in Jakarta in April 1965, Soekarno secretly decided to accelerate the progress of the Communist Party. He created a 'fifth force' – an armed militia independent of the four branches of the armed forces (the army, navy, air force and police) – and arranged for 100,000 rifles to be brought in secretly from China.

Slaughter of the Communists

In the early hours of the morning of 1 October 1965, six of the Indonesian Army's top generals were murdered after military rebels raided their houses. They were the Army Commander and Army Minister, Lieutenant-General Ahmad Yani, who had all Indonesian troops under his control and who opposed the establishment of a fifth force, and five members of the Army Central High Command. Three of the generals – Yani, Harjono and Pandjaitan – were shot dead in their homes. Their bodies and the three other generals were taken to the rebel headquarters at the Halim air force base outside Jakarta, where those still alive were killed. The home of the Defence Minister, General Nasution, was also attacked but he managed to escape. His five-year-old daughter was killed, and his adjutant, Lieutenant Tendean (presumably mistaken for Nasution), was taken to Halim where he was shot with the generals.

Other rebel units occupied the national radio station and the telecommunications building on Merdeka Square, and took up positions around the Presidential Palace, yet there appears to have been little or no attempt to coordinate further revolt in the rest of Java, let alone in the rest of the archipelago. Within a few hours of the beginning of the coup, General Soeharto, head of the army's Strategic Reserve, was able to mobilise army forces to take counteraction. By the evening of 1 October, the coup had clearly failed, but it was not clear who had been involved or what its effects would be.

It has been argued that the coup was primarily an internal army affair, led by younger officers against the older leadership. The official Indonesian view is that it was an attempt by leaders of the PKI to seize power. There are some who think the Communists were entirely to blame for the coup and support the Indonesian Army's assertion that the PKI plotted the coup and used discontented army officers to carry it out. Another view is that military rebels and the PKI took the initiative separately and then became partners. And then there are those who believe that Soekarno himself was behind the coup – and yet another story that Soeharto was in the confidence of one of the conspirators. There is also a theory that Soeharto himself provoked the coup as a means of clearing out his rivals in the army as well as Soekarno, and seizing power himself – advocates of this theory point out that Soeharto was not on the rebels' execution list although he was more important than some of those who were killed.

If the Communists *were* behind the attempted coup then for what reason is anybody's guess. They had been fairly successful up until then, gaining mass support and influence in government, and had no apparent reason to risk it all on one badly organised escapade. It's been suggested that they may have reacted to Soekarno's apparently deteriorating health and, fearing a military coup once Soekarno was out of the way, decided to act. Yet there's no way that the Communists, if they were behind the coup, could have fought the army even if the 100,000 guns from China had arrived.

Whatever the PKI's real role in the coup, the effect on its fortunes was devastating. With the defeat of the coup, a wave of anti-Communism swept Indonesia; thousands upon thousands of Communists and their sympathisers were slaughtered and more imprisoned. The party and its affiliates were banned, and its leaders were killed, imprisoned or went into hiding. Aidit, Chairman of the Party, was eventually shot by government soldiers in November 1965.

Estimates of just how many people were killed vary widely. Adam Malik, the future Foreign Minister under Soeharto, said that a 'fair figure' was 160,000; and there are other estimates of 200,000 and 400,000. Army units were organised to kill villagers suspected of being PKI, and anti-Communist civilians were given arms to help with the job. Private grudges were settled and petty landlords seized the opportunity to rid themselves of peasants who, under local PKI leadership, had taken over fields in an attempt to enforce the government's ineffectual land reforms. Debtors also used the opportunity to rid themselves of their credi-

tors. On top of this, perhaps 250,000 people were arrested and sent to prison camps for allegedly being involved in some way with the coup.

Soekarno's Fall & Soeharto's Rise
General Soeharto took the lead in putting down the attempted coup with remarkable speed. He took over leadership of the armed forces, ended the Confrontation with Malaysia, and carried on a slow and remarkably patient, but not entirely peaceful, duel with Soekarno.

By mid-October 1965, Soeharto was in such a strong position that Soekarno appointed him Commander-in-Chief of the armed forces. Army units, under the command of Colonel Sarwo Edhie, began the massacre of the PKI and their supporters in Central Java. Soekarno was aghast at the killings and into the early part of the following year continued to make public statements in support of the Communists. He sacked General Nasution from his position as Defence Minister and Army Chief of Staff. The army responded by organising violent demonstrations made up largely of adolescents. One demonstration tried to storm the Presidential Palace and another ransacked the Foreign Ministry.

Soekarno still had dedicated supporters in all the armed forces and it seemed unlikely that he would topple, despite the street riots and the violence in the countryside. Soeharto obviously believed it was time to increase the pressure. On 11 March 1966, after troops loyal to Soeharto had surrounded the Presidential Palace, Soekarno signed the 11 March Order – a vague document which, while not actually handing over the full powers of government to Soeharto, officially allowed Soeharto to act on his own initiative rather than on directions from the president. While always deferring to the name of Soekarno and talking as if he was acting on Soekarno's behalf, Soeharto now set the wheels moving for his own outright assumption of power. The PKI was officially banned. Soeharto's troops occupied newspaper houses, radio, cable, telex and telephone offices, and the following day again block-aded the Presidential Palace. Pro-Soekarno officers, men in the armed forces and a number of cabinet ministers were arrested. A new six-man inner cabinet including Soeharto and two of his nominees, Adam Malik and Sultan Hamengkubuwono of Yogyakarta, was formed.

Soeharto then launched a campaign of intimidation to blunt any grassroots opposition to his steadily increasing power. Thousands of public servants were dismissed as PKI sympathisers, putting thousands more in fear of losing their jobs. Soeharto intensified his efforts to gain control of the People's Consultative Congress, the body whose function it was to elect the president. The arrest or murder after the abortive coup of 120 of its 609 members had already ensured a certain amount of docility but despite further pressure, Soekarno managed to hang onto the presidency into 1967. In March of that year, the Congress elected Soeharto acting president. On 27 March 1968, it 'elected' him president.

The New Order

Soeharto wanted the new regime to at least wear the clothes of democracy, and in 1971 general elections were held. Soeharto used the almost defunct Golkar party as the spearhead of the army's election campaign. Having appointed his election squad, the old parties were then crippled by being banned, by the disqualification of candidates and by disenfranchising voters. Predictably, Golkar swept to power with 236 of the 360 elective seats – the PNI was shattered and won just 20 seats. The new People's Consultative Congress also included 207 Soeharto appointments and 276 armed forces officers.

Soeharto then enforced the merger of other political parties. The four Muslim parties were merged into the Development Union Party, and the other parties into the Indonesian Democratic Party. Political activity between elections and below the district level – ie, in the villages – was prohibited. Since most people lived in the villages this meant there would be no political activity at all outside election campaigns. Effectively, it was the end of Indonesian democracy.

Under Soeharto, Indonesia turned away from its isolationist stance and rejoined the United Nations. It joined in the formation of the Association of South-East Asian Nations (ASEAN), reflecting an acceptance of its immediate neighbours in marked contrast to Soekarno's Confrontation with Malaysia. It made a determined effort to attract foreign investment. The largest proportion now comes from Japan, which is also Indonesia's biggest trading partner.

Unfortunately, Indonesia's invasion of East Timor in 1975 not only committed the country to a seemingly interminable war against the Fretilin guerrillas but also strained international relations. This again conjured up the shadow of Confrontation and the image of Indonesia as a potential aggressor. The Indonesians are also continually troubled by Irian Jaya's guerrillas, who have never accepted the Indonesian takeover of the province, consequently straining Indonesian relations with neighbouring Papua New Guinea.

Politically, Indonesia is much more stable but this is mainly because the government's authority rests squarely on a foundation of military power. Opposition has either been eliminated or is kept suppressed and muted. The government sees opposition from several sources including Muslim extremists, university students, Communists, racist groups (particularly anti-Chinese sentiment which could spill over into attacks on the Chinese who run many of the business enterprises) and various dissident groups.

Soeharto's main legacy has been stability – political and economic. Corruption is ever present, disparity of wealth seems to be increasing and real democracy is still a long way off, but the lot of the majority of Indonesians has improved substantially over the last 30 years.

The main political question now facing Indonesia is what will happen in the era after Soeharto, who has indicated that he will retire in 1998 at the end of his current five-year term. Talk of a more open, freer society is common in Jakarta these days, but progress to democratisation is painfully slow. Growing press liberalisation in the 1990s suffered a brutal set back in 1994 when three magazines were banned for criticising government minister Habibie, Soeharto's confidante in cabinet. While the political opposition, particularly the PDI (Partai Demokrasi Indonesia), grows in stature and popularity, and Soeharto has promoted even more civilian power in the government at the expense of the military, the military seems keen to reassert its dominance.

GEOGRAPHY

The Republic of Indonesia is the world's most expansive archipelago, stretching almost 5000 km from Sabang off the northern tip of Sumatra, to a little beyond Merauke in south-eastern Irian Jaya. It stretches north and south of the equator for a total of 1770 km, from the border with Sabah to the small island of Roti off the southern tip of Timor.

Officially, the archipelago contains 13,677 islands – from specks of rock to huge islands like Sumatra and Borneo – 6000 of which are inhabited. The five main islands are Sumatra, Java, Kalimantan (Indonesian Borneo), Sulawesi and Irian Jaya (the western part of New Guinea). Most of the country is water; the Indonesians refer to their homeland as *Tanah Air Kita*, literally 'Our Earth and Water'. While the total land and sea area of Indonesia is about 2½ times greater than the land area of Australia, Indonesia's total land area is only 1,900,000 sq km, or a little larger than Queensland.

Most of these islands are mountainous; in Irian Jaya there are peaks so high they're snowcapped all year round. North-central Kalimantan and much of central Sulawesi are also mountainous, but in most other parts of Indonesia volcanoes dominate the skyline. Running like a backbone down the western coast of Sumatra is a line of extinct and active volcanoes which continues through Java, Bali and Nusa Tenggara and then loops around through the Banda Islands of Maluku to north-eastern Sulawesi. Some of these have erupted, with devastating effects – the massive blow out of Krakatau in 1883 produced a tidal wave killing 30,000 people, and the 1963 eruption of Gunung Agung on Bali wasted large areas of the island. To many Balinese the eruption of this sacred mountain was a sign of the wrath of the gods, and in East Java the Tenggerese people still offer a propitiatory sacrifice to the smoking Bromo crater which dominates the local landscape. However, it is the ash from these volcanoes that has provided Indonesia with some of the finest, richest and most fertile stretches of land on the planet.

Unlike the large sunburnt neighbour to the south, Indonesia is a country of plentiful rainfall, particularly in west Sumatra, northwest Kalimantan, West Java and Irian Jaya. A few areas of Sulawesi and some of the islands closer to Australia – notably Sumba and Timor – are considerably drier but they're exceptions. The high rainfall and the tropical heat make for a very humid climate – but also for a very even one. The highlands of Java and Irian Jaya can get very cold indeed, but on the whole most of Indonesia is warm and humid year-round.

Because of this high rainfall and year-

round humidity, nearly two-thirds of Indonesia is covered in tropical rainforest – most of it on Sumatra, Kalimantan, Sulawesi and Irian Jaya. Most of the forests of Java disappeared centuries ago as land was cleared for agriculture. Today the rest of Indonesia's rainforest, which is second only to Brazil's in area, is disappearing at an alarming rate as local and foreign timber companies plunder the forests. Other contributing factors are the clearing of forest for agriculture, transmigration settlements and mining.

In 1983 Indonesia was the scene of probably the greatest forest fire ever recorded, when 30,000 sq km of rainforest were destroyed in the Great Fire of Kalimantan, which lasted nine months. The government blamed shifting 'slash-and-burn' cultivators for this, but outside experts say the fire was triggered by the waste wood and debris left by loggers, setting off peat and coal fires beneath the ground which burned for months. The fire was followed in 1991 and 1994 by more huge fires both in Sumatra and Kalimantan.

Along the east coast of Sumatra, the south coast of Kalimantan, Irian Jaya, and much of the northern coast of Java, there is swampy, low-lying land often covered in mangroves. In many areas the over-clearing of natural growth has led to a continual erosion as topsoil is washed down the rivers by heavy rains, simultaneously wreaking havoc with the Indonesian roads.

The tropical vegetation, the mountainous terrain and the break up of the country into numerous islands, have always made communication difficult between islands and between different parts of each island. But it is these factors which have had a marked effect on its history and culture, and also explain some of the peculiarities of the country and its people.

Firstly, Indonesia straddles the equator between the Indian Ocean to the west and the Pacific Ocean to the east. To the north are China and Japan, to the north-west India and beyond that Arabia. Because of this central position, the Indonesian islands – particularly Sumatra and Java – and the Malay peninsula have long formed a stopover and staging ground on the sea routes between India and China, a convenient midway point where merchants of the civilised world met and exchanged goods.

Secondly, the regular and even climate (there are some exceptions – in some of the islands east of Java and Bali the seasonal differences are pronounced, and even within Java some districts have a sufficiently marked dry season to suffer drought at times) means that a rhythm of life for many Indonesian farmers is based less on the annual fluctuations of the seasons than on the growth pattern of their crops. In areas with heavy rainfall and terraced rice-field cultivation, there is no set planting season or harvest season, but a continuous flow of activity where at any one time one hillside may demonstrate the whole cycle of rice cultivation, from ploughing to harvesting.

Java is the hub of Indonesia and its most heavily populated island. The capital of Indonesia, Jakarta, is located on the island's north-western coast. While the Javanese are the dominant group in Indonesian politics and in the military, their control over the other islands is a tenuous one for the reasons already mentioned. The diversity of the archipelago's inhabitants and the break-up of the country into numerous islands helps to fuel separatism; since the formation of the republic in 1949 the central administration in Jakarta has fought wars against separatists in West Java, Sumatra, Minahasa in northern Sulawesi, West Irian and Maluku.

Indonesia shares borders with Malaysia and Papua New Guinea. Relations with Malaysia were unhappy during the Soekarno era and the period of Confrontation but since then they have very much improved. Trouble with Papua New Guinea results from continuing problems with the OPM (Free West Papua) guerrillas who refuse to recognise Indonesian sovereignty over West Irian and take refuge in Papua New Guinea. East Timor remained a colony of Portugal up until independence but was invaded by Indonesia in 1975.

CLIMATE

Straddling the equator, Indonesia tends to have a fairly even climate all year round. There are no seasons comparable with the four that Westerners are familiar with, and you do not get the extremes of winter and summer as you do in Europe or some parts of Asia such as China and northern India.

Indonesians distinguish between a wet season and a dry season. In most parts of Indonesia the wet season falls between October and April, and the dry season between May and September. In some parts you don't really notice the difference – the hot season just seems to be slightly hotter and not quite so wet as the wet season; moreover the rain comes in sudden tropical downpours. In other parts – like Maluku – you really do notice the additional water; it rains almost non-stop and travelling during this period becomes more than difficult.

The Indonesians may tell you it gets cold in their country – you'll often see them running around in long-sleeved shirts and even winter coats in the stifling heat! In fact, it's invariably hot and generally humid during the day and warm during the night. Once you get up into the hills and mountains the temperature drops dramatically – in the evenings and during the night it can be amazingly cold! Camp out at night atop Gunung Rinjani in Lombok without a sleeping bag, and you'll be as stiff as those wood carvings they sell in Bali. Sleeping out at night on the deck of a small boat or ship can also be bitterly cold, no matter how oppressive the heat may be during the day. You don't exactly need Antarctic survival gear, but bring jeans and some warm clothes. There is a 'cold season' if you want to call it that, mainly July and August, but you're only likely to notice it in the 'deep south' (about 10° south of the equator) and again, mostly in the highlands.

At the other end of the thermometer, an hour's walk along Kuta Beach in the middle of the day will roast you a nice bright red – bring a hat, sunglasses and some sunscreen (UV) lotion.

See the Appendix at the back of the book for climate charts of Pulau Ambon, Bali, Balikpapan, Dili, Jakarta and Lake Toba.

Java

Across the island the temperature throughout the year averages 22 to 29˚C (78 to 85˚F) and humidity averages a high 75%, but the north coastal plains are usually hotter (up to 34˚C (94˚F) during the day in the dry season) and more oppressively humid than anywhere else. Generally the south coast is a bit cooler than the north coast, and the mountainous regions inland are very much cooler.

The wet season is from October to the end of April, so the best time to visit the island is during the dry season from May to September. The rain comes as a tropical downpour, falling most afternoons during the wet season and intermittently at other times of the year. The heaviest rains are usually around January-February. Regional variations occur – West Java is wetter than East Java, and the mountain regions receive a lot more rainfall. The highlands of West Java average over 4000 mm (160 inches) of rain a year while the north-east coastal tip of East Java has a rainfall of only 900 mm (35 inches).

Bali

Here it is much like Java; the dry season is between April and September. The coolest months of the year are generally May, June and July with the average temperature around 28˚C (82˚F). The rainy season is between October and March but the tropical showers alternate with clear skies and sunshine; the hottest months of the year are generally February and March, with the average temperature around 30˚C (86˚F).

Overall, the best time to visit the island is in the dry and cooler months between May and August, with cool evenings and fresh breezes coming in off the sea.

Sumatra

The climate of Sumatra resembles that of Java and is hot and extremely humid. The equator cuts this island into two roughly equal halves and, since the winds of northern

Sumatra differ from those of the rest of the archipelago, so does the timing of the seasons – though temperatures remain pretty constant year-round. North of the equator the heaviest rainfall is between October and April and the dry season is May to September. South of the equator the heaviest rainfall is in December to February, though it will have started raining in September. In Sumatra heavy rains can make bad roads impassable.

Nusa Tenggara

In the islands east of Bali the seasonal differences are more pronounced. The driest months are August and September, and the wettest months are November to February. However, the duration of the seasons varies from island to island. The seasons on Lombok are more like those on Bali, with a dry season from April to September and a wet season from October to March. Much the same applies to Sumbawa and Flores. The duration of the dry season increases the closer you get to Australia – the rusty landscapes of Sumba and Timor are a sharp contrast to well-vegetated Flores. At 11° south latitude, Timor is also the only island in Indonesia far enough from the equator to get typhoons (cyclones), but these are rare. Nearby northern Australia is not so lucky.

Sulawesi

The wettest months here tend to be from around November-December to March-April but in central and northern Sulawesi the rainfall seems to be a bit more evenly spread throughout the year. In the mountainous regions of central Sulawesi, even in the dry season it may rain by late afternoon – likewise in the northern peninsula. The south-eastern peninsula is the driest part of the island.

Temperatures drop quite considerably going from the lowlands to the mountains. Average temperatures along the coast range from around 26 to 30°C, but in the mountains the average temperature drops by 5°C.

Except in south-western Sulawesi and the Minahasa region of the north (or in odd places where foreign mining companies operate), the wet season turns the mostly unsurfaced roads into excruciatingly frustrating vehicle-bogging mud. It makes travel by road in some parts of the island either impossible or tedious at these times. There's some improvement being made to the roads so check out the current situation when you get there – be prepared to fly, skirt the coast in ships or even do some walking.

Kalimantan

It's permanently hot and damp; the wettest period is October to March, and the driest period is July to September. Although the sun predominates between April and September be prepared for heavy tropical downpours during this period.

Maluku

Maluku (the Moluccas) is the main exception to the climate rule in Indonesia. Whilst the wet season everywhere else is from October to April, in central Maluku the wet season is April through July, and may even carry on to the end of August. Travelling in Maluku during the wet is more difficult; the sea is rougher, inter-island connections are fewer, and heavy rainfall can interrupt travel plans. The best time to visit is September to March.

Maluku does have regional variations. Northern and central Maluku does not have an exclusive dry season and rainfall occurs throughout the year, and it is much drier in the south. Aru in far south-eastern Maluku has its wet season from September to April.

Irian Jaya

Irian Jaya is hot and humid in the northern coastal regions. In the highlands it's warm by day, but can get very cold by night – and the higher you go the colder it gets! August and September in the highlands will be gloomy and misty. In the northern part of Irian Jaya, May to October is the drier season and May is the hottest month. Southern Irian Jaya has a much more well-defined season than the northern part of the island, and Merauke has a more distinct dry season from April to October.

FLORA & FAUNA

Indonesia has one of the world's richest natural environments, harbouring an incredible diversity of plant and animal species. Lying across such a large area, Indonesia includes regions of separate natural history and unique ecosystems.

The British naturalist Alfred Wallace in his classic study *The Malay Archipelago* first classified the Indonesian islands into two zones – a western, Asian ecological zone and an eastern, Australian zone. The 'Wallace Line' dividing these two zones ran at the edge of the Sunda shelf between Kalimantan and Sulawesi and south through the straits between Bali and Lombok. West of this line, Indonesian flora & fauna shows great similarities to that of the rest of Asia, while to the east the islands gradually become drier and the flora & fauna more like Australia. Later scientists have further expanded on this classification to show distinct breaks between the ecologies of Sulawesi and Maluku, and further between Maluku and Irian Jaya.

Greater Sunda Islands
(Sumatra, Java, Kalimantan & Bali)

The western part of the country comprising Sumatra, Java, Kalimantan and Bali, lying on the Sunda shelf and known as the Greater Sunda Islands, was once linked to the Asian mainland. As a result some large Asian land animals, including elephants, tigers, rhinoceros and leopards, still survive, and the dense rainforests and abundant flora of Asia are in evidence.

Perhaps the most famous animal is the orang-utan ('man of the forest' in Indonesian), the long-haired red apes found only in Sumatra and Kalimantan. The Bukit Lawang Sanctuary in North Sumatra provides easy access to see orang-utans in their natural setting, as does the centre at the Tanjung Puting National Park in Kalimantan. Kalimantan is also home to the proboscis monkey, identified by its pendulous, almost comical nose. Various species of the graceful gibbon also exist throughout the Greater Sundas, as do other common varieties of primate.

The rafflesia is the world's largest flower and the largest of the species is Sumatra's *Rafflesia arnoldii*. For much of its life the rafflesia lies hidden in the base of jungle vines, until the hard bud bursts through the host plant and rapidly develops its huge cauldron flower. Pollinated by flies, it is a carrion plant, preying on insects.

Elephants are not numerous, but they still exist in the wild in Sumatra and can be seen at the Way Kambas Reserve in Sumatra's Lampung province. Kalimantan also has a few wild elephants in the north-east, but they are very rare and probably introduced.

The magnificent tiger once roamed freely throughout Asia and existed in large numbers on Sumatra, Java and Bali. A few places in Java and Bali claim to be the last refuge of the tiger on those islands, but tigers in Indonesia are now known only to exist in Sumatra. Leopards (the black leopard or panther is more common in South-East Asia) are also rare but exist in Sumatra and Java's Ujung Kulon National Park. This park is also home to the rare, almost extinct one-horned Javan rhinoceros. Rhinos have not fared well in Indonesia and the two-horned variety, found in Sumatra, is also on the endangered species list.

Of all Indonesia's flora, the most spectacular is the rafflesia, the world's largest flower growing up to one metre in diameter. This parasitic plant is found primarily in Sumatra, but smaller versions are found in Kalimantan and Java.

The rainforests are also disappearing at an

alarming rate. The mighty dipterocarp forests of Kalimantan are being logged ferociously, prized as they are for their durable tropical hardwoods, such as ironwood. Sumatran forests are also being logged and cleared as the jungle is pushed back for new settlements; however, both Sumatra and Kalimantan present some of the best opportunities in Indonesia to explore rainforest environments. The landscapes of crowded and heavily cultivated Java and Bali are dominated by wet-rice cultivation, but natural forest remains in national parks and in some remote mountain regions.

Irian Jaya & Aru Islands
Irian Jaya and the Aru Islands were once part of the Australian land mass and lie on the Sahul shelf. The collision between the Australian and Pacific plates resulted in a massive mountain range running along the middle of Irian Jaya, isolating a number of unique environments, but the fauna throughout is closely related to Australia. Irian Jaya is the only part of Indonesia to have kangaroos, marsupial mice, bandicoots and ring-tailed possums, all marsupials found in Australia. Aussie reptiles include crocodiles and frilled lizards. While the south is much drier, the mountain regions and the north are

covered with dense rain... includes Asiatic and endem... Jaya has over 600 species of bi... well known being the cassowary a... paradise species.

The isolated Aru Islands, though admini... tratively part of Maluku, share a common evolution and are more closely related to Irian Jaya.

Sulawesi, Nusa Tenggara & Maluku
Lying between the two shelves, the islands of Sulawesi, Nusa Tenggara (also known as the Lesser Sunda Islands) and Maluku have long been isolated from the continental land masses and have developed unique flora & fauna.

Endemic to Sulawesi is the anoa or dwarf buffalo, a wallowing animal which looks like a cross between a deer and a cow, standing only about 80 cm high. The babirusa ('deer pig') have great curving tusks that come out the side of the mouth and through the top of the snout. The bulbous beaked hornbills are some of Indonesia's most spectacular birds and are often considered sacred. They are found throughout most of the Greater Sundas as well as Sulawesi, but the enggang Sulawesi or Buton hornbill with its brightly coloured beak and neck is one of the most spectacular of the species.

Komodo Dragon *(Varanus komodoensisi)* – the world's largest lizard grows up to three metres long and weighs over 140 kg. It is only found on the islands of Komodo, Rinca and Padar near Flores in Nusa Tenggara. Known locally as the 'ora', the komodo uses its powerful tail to stun victims and its split yellow tongue is an olfactory organ, used to sniff out prey. These days the komodo's favourite meal is goat, kindly provided by tourist groups, but humans have also ended up on the komodo menu.

y, and teak

th Sulawesi,
& fauna. The
s are found, as
ms most of the
uku by. Maluku
eram Island has
species) and bird
life, p... raja or Amboina
king parrot (a la... nificently coloured
parrot).

The Wallace Line separates Lombok, the westernmost island of Nusa Tenggara, from Bali. From East Lombok eastwards, the flora & fauna of Nusa Tenggara reflect the more arid conditions of these islands. The large Asian mammals are nonexistent on Lombok, and in Nusa Tenggara mammal species in general are smaller and less diverse. Asian bird species diminish further east and Australian birds are found on the eastern islands. Nusa Tenggara has one astonishing and famous animal, the Komodo dragon, the world's largest lizard, found only on the island of Komodo and a few neighbouring islands. East Timor is noted for its stands of sandalwood, the scented wood used in woodcarving and the manufacture of the perfumed oil.

National Parks

Although environmentalists have blasted Indonesia's government for its logging and transmigration development schemes, it's only fair to mention that the past decade has seen a rapid increase in the number of national parks, nature reserves and historical sites. While it's true that loggers, farmers and hunters have even violated national parks, there has been a sincere effort to enforce the rules – no easy task in a country with so much sparsely inhabited jungle.

The Indonesian national park service, PHPA (Perlindungan Hutan dan Pelestarian Alam) maintains information offices at various points around the country, including posts in the national parks and in some reserves.

Sumatra Sumatra has some excellent national parks, Gunung Leuser being the most accessible and rewarding. Covering almost 10,000 sq km, this park contains the orang-utan sanctuary at Bukit Lawang on its eastern flank, and from there and Berastagi it is easy to arrange treks into the park.

The Bukit Barisan Selatan National Park in southern Sumatra is difficult to reach but contains varied flora from coastal to rainforest, and large mammal species, including tigers, elephants and tapirs. Way Kambas National Park in Lampung province is noted for its elephants, which are protected in the park but also exploited in an elephant training show. Lembah Anai Nature Reserve between Bukittinggi and Padang is known for its rafflesia.

Java The pick of Java's national parks is Ujung Kulon on the south-west tip of the island. Though not easy to reach, it has superb coastal scenery, lush rainforest and coral reefs and is home to the almost extinct Javan rhinoceros and leopards.

In complete contrast, Baluran National Park, on the dry north-eastern tip of Java, is one of the most easily visited parks in Indonesia with grasslands reminiscent of Africa or Australia. This drive-in park is noted for its buffaloes, banteng, deer and bird life.

Bromo-Tengger-Semeru National Park is justly famous for its spectacular volcanic craters and Mt Bromo is one of Java's main attractions. For mountain climbers, the park also contains Java's highest peak, Mt Semeru.

Pangandaran National Park, being on the doorstep of a popular beach resort, receives many visitors. Wildlife includes banteng, deer and Javan gibbon and this coastal headland park has good jungle walks. In the mountains south of Jakarta, Gunung Gede-Pangrango National Park is another for volcano climbing through submontane forest. One of Java's most spectacular walks is to the active crater lake of Kawah Ijen in the plateau reserve near Banyuwangi in East Java. East Java also has some fine coastal parks, Alas Purwo and Meru Betiri, but access is very difficult. Pulau Dua, off the north coast near Banten, is a major sanctuary for coastal sea birds.

Bali Bali Barat National Park takes up a significant chunk of the western part of the island. Most of the park is savanna with coastal mangroves and more tropical vegetation in the southern highlands. Over 200 species of plant inhabit the various environments, and animals include monkeys, deer, muncak, squirrel, wild pig, buffalo, iguana, python and green snake. The bird life is prolific, with many of Bali's 300 species represented.

Nusa Tenggara Gunung Rinjani, at 3726 metres, is the highest mountain in Indonesia outside Irian Jaya, and dominates the island of Lombok. It is a very popular three to five-day trek to the top and the huge crater contains a large green crescent-shaped lake, Segara Anak, six km across at its widest point. Some 40,000 hectares of Rinjani's slopes are protected forest.

Two-thirds of Pulau Moyo, off the coast just north of Sumbawa Besar, is a nature reserve with savanna and some forest. Good coral reefs are at the southern end of the island.

The mostly dry, savanna Komodo National Park encompasses much of Komodo and the Rinca islands, and is home to Indonesia's most famous beastie, the Komodo dragon. The islands also have coral reefs.

In Flores, the three-coloured lakes of Keli Mutu, one of Indonesia's most impressive sights, is a protected reserve managed by the PHPA.

Kalimantan Tanjung Puting is Kalimantan's national park, famous for its Camp Leakey orang-utan rehabilitation centre. Encompassing 3050 sq km of tropical rainforest, mangrove forest and wetlands, it is home to a vast variety of flora & fauna, including crocodiles, hornbills, wild pigs, bear cats, crab-eating macaques, orang-utan, proboscis monkeys, gibbons, pythons, dolphins, mudskippers (a kind of fish that can walk and

breathe on land!) and the dragon fish (a rare and valuable aquarium fish).

Kutai National Park in East Kalimantan is a strange mixture of national park and logging zone. The hardwood forests contain orang-utan, gibbons and leaf monkeys, but this park is difficult to reach and facilities are minimal. Tangkiling National Park is another nature reserve, 35 km north of Palangkaraya.

Sulawesi Lore Lindu in Central Sulawesi is a remote but untouched national park, rich in exotic plant and animal life. It is also home to several indigenous tribes, has ancient megalithic relics, great trekking as well as a couple of mountains for peak bagging.

Sulawesi's other major park is Dumoga-Bone National Park in North Sulawesi, a watershed area with intact forest, but it is less interesting than Lore Lindu. Sulawesi has some good reserves. Tangkoko Reserve, 30 km from Bitung, is home to black apes, anoas, babirusas and maleo birds (the maleo looks like a huge hen and lays eggs five times the size of a hen's). The reserve also includes the coastline and coral gardens offshore. The Morowali Reserve in Central Sulawesi is good for treks that can be organised out of Kolondale. Wildlife includes maleo birds.

Sulawesi's most famous natural attractions are its coral reefs, and the government is developing conservation zones in some areas. The easily accessible, fabulous reefs of Pulau Bunaken are famous, and the Togian Islands also have some fine reefs for snorkelling and diving.

Maluku Manusela National Park, forming a large chunk of Seram's centre, comprises remote mountain regions, and sandy beaches and coral off the north coast. Access is not easy and facilities are limited, but it is possible to organise treks within the park.

The coral reefs of the beautiful Banda Islands are protected and the islands have been declared a marine reserve.

Irian Jaya Wasur National Park near Merauke is the joint project between the World Wide Fund for Nature (WWF) and the traditional people. This large, remote park has wetlands, traditional villages, unique bird life and wildlife such as cuscus and even kangaroos.

Irian Jaya has some other reserves, and the Biak Utara Reserve protects the remaining forest of Biak Island, while much of nearby Superiori Island is a more unspoilt nature reserve with abundant bird life. The Baliem Valley is the main area for trekking in Irian Jaya.

GOVERNMENT

The ruling party is Golkar, which officially is not a political party but is designed to be an all-things-to-all-people 'group' representing wide interests inside and outside of government. One of the major interests that it represents is the army.

The opposition, what there is of it, is a two-party system resulting from the forced amalgamation of opposition parties in the 1970s to form the Partai Persatuan Pembangunan (PPP), representing Islamic groups, and Partai Demokrasi Indonesia (PDI), Soekarno's old party which became an amalgam of nationalists, Christians and 'the rest'.

Opposition parties must accept the national ideology of Pancasila. The government has the power to decide the opposition parties' policies, leaders and election candidates. The opposition is not allowed to destabilise the government by criticising it, the media is tightly controlled and Golkar, as the government party, has enormous resources to put into its election campaigns. Not surprisingly, the government wins elections by handsome majorities, typically capturing around 70% of the vote.

Elections are held every five years to elect 400 of the 500 members of the House of Representatives. The other 100 members are appointed by the armed forces. This is the

---

Pancasila

Since it was first expounded by Soekarno in 1945 the Pancasila (Five Principles) have remained the philosophical backbone of the Indonesian state. It was meant by Soekarno to provide a broad philosophical base on which a united Indonesian state could be formed. All over Indonesia you'll see the Indonesian coat of arms with its symbolic incorporation of the Pancasila, hung on the walls of government offices and the homes of village heads, on the covers of student textbooks or immortalised on great stone tablets. These principles are:

1. Faith in God – symbolised by the star. This is perhaps the most important and contentious principle. As interpreted by Soekarno and the Javanese syncretists who have ruled Indonesia since independence, this can mean any god – Allah, Vishnu, Buddha, Christ, etc. For many Muslims, it means belief in the only true God, Allah, but the government goes to great lengths to suppress both Islamic extremism and calls for an Islamic state in multi-ethnic and multireligious Indonesia.

2. Humanity – symbolised by the chain. This represents the unbroken unity of humankind, and Indonesia takes its place amongst this family of nations.

3. Nationalism – symbolised by the head of the buffalo. All ethnic groups in Indonesia must unite.

4. Representative government – symbolised by the banyan tree. As distinct from the Western brand of parliamentary democracy, Soekarno envisaged a form of Indonesian democracy based on the village system of deliberation (permusyawaratan) among representatives to achieve consensus (mufakat). The Western system of 'majority rules' is considered a means by which 51% oppress the other 49%.

5. Social justice – symbolised by the sprays of rice and cotton. A just and prosperous society gives adequate supplies of food and clothing for all – these are the basic requirements of social justice. ∎

real house of government, proposing and passing government legislation. It is divided into permanent committees which carry out the day-to-day business of government.

The highest political institution is the People's Consultative Congress (MPR), which is composed of all the members of the House of Representatives along with 500 appointees representing various groups and regions – the armed forces and Golkar are again well represented. In theory, the congress is the supreme ruling body but it seldom meets and the main function of this stacked house is to elect the president, ratify changes to the constitution and make sure the army has the numbers to force its will if need be. The congress also elects the vice-president and in 1993, General Try Sutrisno, the army's preferred candidate, was given the nod as the successor to the top job after Soeharto (but it's still a long way to 1998).

Executive power rests with the president, who is head of state and holds office for a period of five years. The president appoints cabinet ministers, and this inner sanctum is the core of government power in Indonesia. Of the current crop of 38 ministers, some of the more powerful and better known are: Minister of Defence & Security, Edi Sudradjat; Minister of Home Affairs, Yogie Suardi Memet; Minister of Foreign Affairs, Ali Alatas; and Minister of State for Research & Technology, Dr Habibie.

Regional Government

Though national policy, international wranglings and the multimillion dollar deals are the preserve of the central government, for most Indonesians Jakarta is far removed and real government is at the district or village level.

Politically, Indonesia is divided into 27 provinces, including the three special territories of Aceh, Jakarta and Yogyakarta. Java has five provinces: Jakarta, West Java, Central Java, Yogyakarta and East Java. Sumatra has eight: Aceh, North Sumatra, West Sumatra, Riau, Jambi, Bengkulu, South Sumatra and Lampung. Kalimantan has West, Central, South and East provinces.

Sulawesi has North, Central, South and South-Eastern provinces. Other provinces are: Bali, West Nusa Tenggara (Lombok and Sumbawa), East Nusa Tenggara (Sumba, West Timor, Flores, and the Solor and Alor archipelagos), East Timor, Maluku and Irian Jaya.

Each province has its own political legislature, headed by a governor, with extensive powers to administer the province. The 27 provinces are further broken down into 241 *kabupaten* (districts) headed by a *bupati* (district head) and 56 *kotamadya* (municipalities) headed by a *walikota* (mayor). The districts are further broken down into 3625 *kecamatan* (subdistricts), each headed by a *camat* (subdistrict head). Kecamatan are further broken down into *kelurahan* or village groupings.

Each level of government has its own bureaucracy, often with overlapping functions. For example, in one city you may find three or more separate tourist offices – a provincial government tourist office, a district tourist office, a city tourist office and regional representatives of the central government. Between them they may employ dozens if not hundreds of people, and still not be able to produce a decent map or intelligible brochure. Government is Indonesia's major employer, and its a major frustration if you have to deal with it.

But despite this extended hierarchy of government, often the most relevant level of government is at village level. In the *desa* or *kampung*, the day-to-day running of the village, neighbourhood disputes and local affairs are handled as they always have been. The village elects a *lurah* or *kepala desa* (village chief), though often the position of kepala desa is virtually hereditary, falling in the same family and passed from father to son, even extending back to some long since defunct Hindu principality when the kepala desa was *raja* (king). The kepala desa is the government representative at the most basic level, and the person to see if you wander into a village and need to spend the night or resolve a problem.

The village is the main social unit, providing welfare, support and guidance. If a fire destroys a house or a village needs a new well, then everyone pitches in. This grass-root system of mutual help and discussion is usually presided over by a traditional council of elders, but there are also village organisations or government representatives to carry out government policies and campaigns on economic development, population control, health, etc. One of the main community organisations is the *rukun tetangga*, which organises neighbourhood security (every village and kampung has a security post – *pos kamling*) and the registration of families and new arrivals.

Armed Forces

Though Soeharto prefers a civilian image, and the present cabinet contains few military men, political power ultimately lies with the army. Military personnel, both former and present, are widely represented in government and in business, and though the government rules with a degree of independence and not always to the military's liking, when push comes to shove the military dominates.

The military influence in Indonesian culture is instantly noticeable. Paramilitary uniforms abound, from government employees to parking lot attendants, and Indonesians love to march – school children drill even on their days off. Since the military-backed government came to power in 1965, the glorification of the military has increased but it existed long before Soeharto came to power.

The Indonesian military psyche developed during WW II when the Japanese organised village militia to defend Indonesia in the event of reoccupation. When the Dutch returned, independence was gained only after a bloody battle of village armies united under the banner of the new republic. Indonesian freedom fighters became heroes, and their leaders' names adorn Indonesian streets, their exploits are endlessly retold in schools, and their homes have become museums. Indonesia's history has become a military one, and even the most obscure leaders of ancient, easily crushed peasant rebellions have become national heroes. The military has been a part of the political process since independence, and it hardly regards itself as having usurped power that somehow 'rightfully' belongs to civilians.

Under Soekarno's guided democracy the military's powers and aspirations intensified. In 1958, General Nasution, Chief of Staff of the Army, expounded the doctrine of *dwifungsi* (dual function) to justify the army's expanded role in Soekarno's government after the establishment of martial law. This stated that the army not only played a security role and was responsible to the government, but it also had to play an independent social and political role as 'one of the many forces in society'.

At this time the army developed a national defence policy based on the army, since the navy and air force would never be strong enough to block an invasion, and only the army could continue, in the last resort, an indefinite guerrilla struggle. To be successful in such a war the army would have to be accepted and supported by the people, and so the army would need to establish contacts with the people at a local level so as to build up and sustain their goodwill. Thus developed the idea and the subsequent implementation of 'Territorial Management', a parallel administration down to village level where resident army personnel could supervise and prod the civil authorities.

With the 1965 coup the army became not just one of many, but the dominant force in society. Today the military still plays its dwifungsi role, with a civilianised government leading the country, but the military is the major behind-the-scenes player. However, as Indonesia slowly becomes more open politically, the government becomes more noticeably civilian and a nouveau riche and powerful middle class develops, the question being asked is: 'In these stable times, who needs the military?'. 'The people' is the military's answer, and it shows no signs of relinquishing its power. If anything, the military has indicated that it wants to play a stronger role in post-Soeharto Indonesia.

ECONOMY

Indonesia is part of the world's fastest developing economic region, and the Indonesian economy is bounding along with an annual growth rate of over 6%, a rate it has averaged for over 20 years. Jakarta is the centre for this economic boom and the signs of wealth are stamped all over the city – towering new office developments, freeways, multistorey shopping centres, thousands of imported luxury cars and horrendous traffic jams.

Away from the glossy business centre, Jakarta also has the worst slums in the country and most of the city is without sewerage and a decent water supply – and therein lies the dilemma of Indonesia's economy. The economy is booming, but with its huge population and the strain on resources,

President Soeharto

Soeharto was born in 1921 and spent his childhood amongst peasants in small villages in Central Java and in Solo, his father ensuring that he got a primary and middle school education. The time he spent from the age of 15 living in the house of a *dukun* (faith healer) appears to have imbued him with a sense of traditional Javanese mysticism which has lasted to this day. He joined the Royal Dutch Indies Army in 1940 and quickly became a sergeant. He served with the Japanese during the occupation and became an officer in the Japanese-sponsored Volunteer Army of Defenders of the Motherland. He led attacks against the Dutch during the independence struggle after WW II and rose rapidly through the ranks.

In 1962 he was promoted to Major-General by Soekarno and was put in charge of the forces which were set up to take West Irian from the Dutch. In 1961 he became commander of the army's Strategic Reserve (later to be known as KOSTRAD). This was an important posting because the reserve, set up by Nasution, was a well-equipped, highly mobile fighting force directly at the disposal of the top generals, thus avoiding any argument or even outright opposition from regional commanders.

Just why Soeharto took the role of overthrowing Soekarno is unclear – perhaps it was personal ambition, a reaction to the attempted coup, unease at the growing strength of the PKI, a reaction to the deterioration of the economy under Soekarno, or a mixture of all four. Certainly Soeharto cut through his opponents with exceptional determination.

Soeharto has shown himself to be remarkably resilient. His rule is certainly not unopposed but he has continually sought to reaffirm his authority and has successfully met any challenges. In recent years, the main threat to his position has come from the army, and Soeharto is keen to promote greater civilian power in government at the expense of the military. An interesting trend is that Soeharto has been sounding more and more Islamic, and made his first-ever pilgrimage to Mecca in 1991. Despite extolling secularism and suppressing Islamic fundamentalism throughout his career (as is the army line), he has been seen to court the Muslim lobby to counterfoil the military.

Exactly who will succeed Soeharto, and what tack Indonesia will take after him, are the burning political questions. One thing is certain – Soeharto, and his relatives, have become very rich since he came to power. For example, in 1991, the president's son, Tomboy Soeharto, was granted the lucrative clove monopoly. In Soeharto's 1989 autobiography, the president stated that his family's financial dealings were simply 'social work'. Being president of Indonesia is like riding a tiger – as the succession problem looms, unless Soeharto dies in the saddle, his real problem is to make sure he doesn't get eaten when he steps down. ■

Indonesia is still one of the poorest countries in South-East Asia. Furthermore, while the statistics show that life for the average Indonesian is getting better each year, the disparity between rich and poor grows even faster. Indonesia's middle-class, earning over US$30,000 per year, is estimated to be over 20 million people, but many workers – those lucky enough to have a job – earn less than US$2 per day and the average per capita income is still only US$650.

The mainstay and saviour of the Indonesian economy for many years has been oil and gas. During the 1970s and early 1980s, the majority of export earnings came from oil, but the mid-1980s slump in oil prices saw a concerted effort to increase non-oil exports, particularly manufacturing. Oil and gas exports still account for over US$10 billion annually, about one-third of all exports. Other major exports are timber and wood products (Indonesia is the world's biggest supplier of plywood), tin, coal, copper and bauxite, and substantial cash crops like rubber, coffee, copra and fishing. Helped by increased foreign investment, Indonesia has a rapidly developing light industrial base and is now a major producer of textiles and clothing, and is a growing exporter of footwear, chemicals, fertilisers, cement and glassware. The tourist dollar is also a growth industry, with Indonesia looking to increase the three-million plus visitors to five million within the next few years.

New Order Economy

During the Soeharto era, the Indonesian economy has largely been governed by an alliance between army leaders and Western-educated economists. Rigorous economic measures were taken in the first years of the regime designed to get Indonesia back on its feet after the economic mismanagement of the Soekarno years. Sufficiently large cuts were made in government expenditure to balance the budget; the plunge of the rupiah was halted; rice prices were kept temporarily in check by establishing a reserve which reduced speculation; inflation was dramatically reduced; and there was

some success in stabilising the price of other basic commodities.

Under Soeharto's rule the Planning Body for National Development (Bappenas) has implemented a series of five-year development plans, called Repelita, designed to rehabilitate and improve the economy.

Riding on the back of oil exports, Indonesian business grew up behind a protective wall of barriers. Import and export monopolies were granted to favoured clients, tariffs kept out imports, restrictions were placed on foreign ownership, and the government had monopoly control over key industries like banking, oil refining, airlines, telecommunications, etc. These measures were supposedly designed to protect the economy.

Instead, these rules gave birth to a bungling and corrupt bureaucracy. Protected industries like banks were so inefficient they could charge usurious interest rates. Keeping out foreign investment meant Indonesia had to instead seek foreign loans to develop its own industries, resulting in a build-up of debt. High import taxes and government-sanctioned import monopolies meant Indonesian companies found the cost of foreign-made components so high that they couldn't develop export industries. Export monopolies meant that coffee farmers, for example, could look forward to low prices while the exporter got rich.

From the late 1980s onwards there has been a change in attitudes and deregulation is the word. The banking industry was thrown open to foreign joint ventures, helping to spur investment. Import monopolies have been mostly eliminated, resulting in lower prices to consumers and export-oriented manufacturers. Rules on stock trading were liberalised in 1989, and 100% foreign ownership in now allowed in some industries. As a result, foreign money has started pouring in, much of it to Jakarta, Java and the island of Batam, a free-trade zone 20 km south of Singapore. The government still controls many enterprises, but privatisation is gaining speed.

All this has spurred economic growth in the past few years. The negative side of the coin is that privatisation and deregulation are a boon for middle-class investors with the capital to invest (especially if they have good government contacts), but the flow on to Indonesia's have-nots is painfully slow, if it reaches them at all. Indonesia's brave new economic world also has plenty of stories of corruption and incompetence. Banks have gone bust amid embezzlement and graft scandals, and while positive long-term investment is helping the country, non-productive speculation appealing to get-rich-quick merchants is also in evidence.

However, Indonesia's approach to freeing up the economy has been relatively cautious. Many tariffs remain and the government maintains some controls on foreign investment and borrowing. Despite a large foreign debt, high interest rates, an everpresent inflation rate of around 10% and the obvious problems confronting a developing country, Indonesia's long-term economic future is destined to be one of continuing improvement.

Poverty & Prospects for the Future

Government-sponsored programmes enabled Indonesia to become self-sufficient in rice production by 1982, and thus reduce its risky dependency on food imports. While this was a significant step forward, attempts to alleviate poverty have met with a mixed bag of successes and failures.

To help assure access to essential goods, both the Soekarno and the Soeharto governments operated a nationwide system of subsidies and price controls for necessities, including rice, wheat, sugar, cooking kerosene and gasoline. Increasing financial stringency in recent years has forced cutbacks on subsidies, plus the recognition that low prices hurt production. The free market is being given a freer hand, but the adjustments will be painful.

Health care has received high priority with considerable expansion in the number of health centres, and a noticeable drop in the infant mortality rate. Education also has a high priority and nearly all children have access to primary school education. However, many drop out early, there is a shortage of qualified teachers and, in rural areas, the quality of education doesn't ensure that the majority of children will leave school literate.

The establishment of new industries and increased employment opportunities has occurred mostly in the cities, but Indonesia's population is still overwhelmingly rural, with a large proportion working on small farms. The average Indonesian farm labourer gets by on very little. Unemployed rural residents tend to migrate to the cities in search of the elusive pot of gold, but with poor education and skills they often wind up as squatters in the slums of Jakarta and other cities.

The lack of protective legislation and free unions or other organisations to defend workers has seen Indonesia's labour record come increasingly under attack, particularly from the USA. The government is keen to show that it is making progress, but resistance is still confined to sporadic outbursts of violence by disenfranchised workers and villagers, often with tragic consequences.

As elsewhere in developing countries, the rich get richer and the poor get children. Although initially a burden, children are regarded as an economic asset because they provide a form of social security for the parents. Birth rates are highest among the poor. The unfortunate result is that the fastest growing segment of the population is the least educated and least likely to succeed economically.

Although Indonesia is better off than it was 20 years ago, the fruits of this economic growth are very unevenly distributed. Yet somehow even the poorest of Indonesians show a remarkable resilience and capacity to survive. They sell food, clothing, plastic shoes, sit on the side of the street all day flogging off a few combs or a couple of bunches of bananas or jump on crowded buses to hawk ice blocks, pineapple chunks, or single cigarettes. They sift through garbage, recycle the tobacco from cigarette ends, pedal *becaks* (three-wheeled bicycle-rickshaws), shine shoes, mind parked cars or scratch some of the money from the tourist industry as touts. And if they come home with nothing then their family or neighbours will help them to survive another day.

POPULATION

Indonesia's total population is around 185 million. Java alone has almost 110 million people.

Indonesia's population is growing at a rate of about 1.7% per year. If it continues at that rate it will have 220 million people by the turn of the century and almost 400 million by 2035. Overpopulation, however, is largely a Javanese and, to some extent, a Balinese problem. Java's population was estimated as six million in 1825, 9.5 million in 1850, 18 million in 1875, 28 million in

Rice Production

Although Indonesia produces a range of agricultural products, including exotic introductions from Latin America thanks to the early Spanish and Portuguese settlers, the staple produce remains rice.

With the exception of Bali and most of Java, plus a few much smaller patches across the archipelago, the soil is just as poor in Indonesia as it is elsewhere in the tropics. In sparsely populated areas of Sumatra, Kalimantan, Sulawesi and West Java, where the peasants moved from one place to another, a form of shifting cultivation or *ladang* developed. In ladang cultivation, the jungle is burned off to speed up the normal process of decomposition and enrich the soil in preparation for planting, but the soil quickly loses its fertility. When the top cover of forest is removed the intense heat and heavy rain soon leach the soil of its nutrients. As a result, settled agriculture is impossible without the continuous addition of soil nutrients.

On the other hand, the rich volcanic soils of most of Java, Bali and western Lombok have allowed wet rice, or *sawah*, cultivation in flooded rice fields. Rice cultivation in terraced sawah fields has been known for over 2000 years, the system being continually refined and developed, and is widely seen as a contributing factor to the development of the prolific civilisations on Java and later on Bali. The development of the fields, particularly in the highland areas where extensive terracing took place, required great organisation, either at a co-operative village level or through the suppression of a peasant work force.

The wonder of this method of agriculture is that sawah fields can keep producing two or even three crops a year, year after year, with little or no drop in soil fertility. The profundity of sawah fields cannot be attributed to soil fertility alone, however, for this astonishing ecosystem depends on the water to provide nutrients and the bacteria produced in the water also aids the extraction of nitrogen. Other nutrients are provided by the remains of the previous crop, the addition of extra organic material and the aeration of the soil through water movement in the field.

After each harvesting of rice, the stubble from the crop is ploughed back into the field, traditionally using bullocks. Small carpets of the best rice seed are planted and when ready, seedlings are prized apart and laboriously transplanted in even rows in an inundated field flooded to a few centimetres. The level of the water is crucial in the life cycle of the rice plant and the water is increased in depth as the plant grows and then slowly drained as harvest approaches, until the field is dry at harvest time. The field may also be drained during the growing period, to weed the field or to aerate the soil.

From 1968, the government has introduced schemes to improve productivity, such as the introduction of high-yield varieties of rice; however, the basic method of sawah farming has remained unchanged for generations. ■

1900, 36 million in 1925, 63 million in 1961 and 108 million in 1990.

Java and the island of Madura off Java's north coast have a total area of 130,000 sq km or about 1½ times the area of the UK. Java's population density is more than 800 people per sq km, more than twice that of either England or Holland (the two most densely populated countries in Europe) and more than twice that of Japan. Population in Indonesia is very unevenly distributed, as can be seen from the last census (1990) figures. The following table reflects the percentages of total area and population:

Island(s)	Area	Population
Java	6.89%	59.9%
Sumatra	24.67%	20.33%
Sulawesi	9.85%	6.98%
Bali & Nusa Tenggara	4.61%	5.67%
Kalimantan	28.11%	5.08%
Irian Jaya	21.99%	0.92%
Maluku	3.88%	1.03%

Population Control

Each year two million people are added to the Indonesian population, most of them in Java. However, Indonesia's birth control programme is making inroads into population growth.

After taking power, Soeharto reversed Soekarno's policies of continued population expansion to provide a work force to develop the outer islands. He set up a National Family Planning Co-ordinating Board which greatly expanded the network of private clinics providing free contraceptive services. Efforts were concentrated on Bali and Java at first and noticeable drops in the birth rate were reported. It was also reported that over 80% of the people who took part in the scheme were the wives of peasants, fisherpeople and labourers – the poorer end of the scale who normally have the most children. However, birth-control campaigns have been heeded more by better educated, urban families and have been less successful in highly traditional and strongly Muslim areas. In poorer, isolated rural areas large families are still common.

The campaign has been most successful in Java where many families are now firm believers in the slogan *Dua Anak Cukup* ('two children is enough'). As well as public awareness campaigns, coordinators are appointed at village level to advise on contraception, monitor birth rates and counsel, if not admonish, families that exceed two children.

Transmigration

As well as reducing the birth rate, attempts are also being made to take the pressure off heavily populated areas, particularly Java and Bali, by moving people out to less populated areas like Sumatra, Kalimantan, Irian Jaya and Maluku. These *transmigrasi* programmes started with Dutch efforts to relieve population pressure in Java in 1905. The Soeharto government's first Five Year Plan moved 182,000 people out of Java, Bali and Lombok – below target by only 8000. The second Five Year Plan aimed to move over a million people in the five years from 1974, but by 1976 the target figure had to be reduced by half. The third, fourth and fifth Five-Year Plans ambitiously aimed at shifting 500,000, 750,000 and 550,000 families respectively – more than seven million people.

So far, however, the transmigrasi programmes seem to have had little effect on the population burden of Java. The main problem is that insufficient numbers of people can physically be moved to offset the growth in population. Furthermore, transmigration settlements have developed a poor reputation – one of the underlying faults has been the tendency to attempt wet-rice cultivation in unsuitable areas. Settlers have frequently ended up as subsistence farmers no better off than they were back in Java, if not because of poor soil and water then because of inadequate support services and isolation from markets.

In addition, most government-sponsored transmigrants are not experienced farmers; two-thirds of transmigrants are landless peasants, the poorest of the countryside, and another 10% are homeless city dwellers. Up until 1973, the urban poor of Jakarta were often virtually press-ganged into moving out of Java – they turned out to be the least successful transmigrants, often returning to the towns they came from. The most successful transmigrants are often those who move 'spontaneously' – because they emigrate on their own initiative to the outer islands, and because they can choose where to live. Transmigration is a voluntary programme but as officials strain to meet new targets, there is increasing pressure on people to sign up.

Transmigration takes its toll on the natural environment through destruction of rainforest, loss of topsoil and degradation of water supplies. Tension, even conflict, with the indigenous people in some settled areas is not uncommon.

PEOPLE

The rugged, mountainous terrain and the fact that the country is made up of many islands has separated groups of people from each other and resulted in an extraordinary differentiation of language and culture across the archipelago. Indonesians are divided – according to one classification – into approximately 300 ethnic groups which speak some 365 languages and dialects.

Indonesia's national motto is *Bhinneka Tunggal Ika*, an old Javanese phrase meaning 'They are many; they are one', which usually gets translated as 'Unity in diversity'. The peoples of the archipelago were not 'Indonesian' until 1949, when a line was drawn on the map enclosing a group of islands which housed a remarkably varied collection of people.

Most Indonesians are of Malay stock, descended from peoples who originated in China and Indochina and spread into Indonesia over several thousand years. The other major grouping is the darker skinned, fuzzy-haired Melanesians who inhabit much of easternmost Indonesia.

Despite the Malay predominance, the culture and customs of the various islands are often quite different. There are different languages and dialects, different religions and differences in adat (the unwritten village law

which regulates the behaviour of everyone in every village in Indonesia). The Indonesian terrain is partly responsible for the incredible diversity; mountains and jungles cut off tribes and groups on certain islands from the outside world – like the Kubu tribe of south Sumatra, thought to be descendants of the original settlers from Sri Lanka. They were barely known to outsiders until guerrillas fighting against the Dutch came into contact with them. Other isolated groups have included the Papuan Dani people of the Balim Valley in Irian Jaya, and the Dayaks – the collective name given to the people who inhabit the interior of Borneo. There are also the Badui of West Java who withdrew to the highlands as the Islamic religion spread through the island, and have had little contact with outsiders. Other distinctive groups, like the Balinese and Javanese, have had considerable contact with the outside world but nevertheless have managed to maintain their traditional cultures intact.

Of all the ethnic minorities in Indonesia, few have had a larger impact on the country than the Chinese, or 'overseas Chinese' as they are commonly known. Although comprising less than 3% of the population, the Chinese are the major force in the economy, operating everything from small shops, hotels and restaurants to major banks and industries. The Chinese are by far the wealthiest ethnic group in the country and there is much anti-Chinese resentment in Indonesia that sometimes threatens to boil over into a pogrom along the lines of the slaughter following the 1965 coup attempt, when many of the victims were Chinese.

Despite the diversity of peoples, cultures, languages and religions and the inevitable conflicts that arise because of this diversity, Indonesia is surprisingly unified. When the republic was proclaimed, Indonesia was a group of hundreds of different societies, united through their subjection to Dutch colonialism, a tenuous reason upon which to build a nation. But Indonesia has done just that, through mass culture and prolonged campaigns, all conveyed through its national language, Bahasa Indonesia.

Dari Mana?

Dari Mana? Where do you come from?

You will be asked this question frequently, in Indonesian or English, along with many others like *Suduh kawin?* (Are you married?), and *Mau kemana?* (Where are you going?). Visitors can find these questions intrusive, irritating and even infuriating, but Indonesians regard them as polite conversation.

An Indonesian approaching a friend might ask, in their local language, 'What are you doing?', even if it's perfectly obvious. Similarly, someone obviously going to the market might be asked 'Where are you going?', simply as a form of greeting. Indonesians are a curious and very friendly people, and seemingly inane questions are used as small talk and to express positive feelings for others. Indonesians will ask foreign visitors such questions in English (it may be their only English!), and you should not get annoyed – a smile and a 'hello', or a greeting in Indonesian, is generally a polite and adequate response. If the questions continue, which is likely, you will need to take a different approach, as one new arrival in Indonesia found out...

She was introduced to a young man, who immediately began asking her all manner of personal questions – where did she come from? was she married? where was she staying? did she like Indonesia? what were her plans? Anxious to be friendly and polite, she tried to answer every question, while becoming increasingly dubious about his motives. But he never seemed to be satisfied with her responses, because as soon as she answered one question, he would ask her another, and he seemed to become more morose with each exchange. Finally, and with a note of utter despondency in his voice, the young man announced 'I have five children'.

The message is that you don't really have to answer every question, but you should ask some questions yourself, to show a polite interest in the other person. If the questioning becomes too nosey, try responding with an equally nosey question, and you might be surprised at the warmth of the response. When you've had enough chatter, you can answer the question 'Where are you going?', even if it wasn't asked. ■

Regional conflicts and loyalties remain, but the overwhelming majority of Indonesians now identify themselves proudly with their nation, flag and language.

EDUCATION

In Indonesia, education begins with six years of primary school (SD or Sekolah Dasar), then three years of junior high school (SMP or Sekolah Menengah Pertama) and three years of senior high school (SMA or Sekolah Menengah Atas), leading on to university. While school enrolments have risen to 90% for the seven to 12 year-old age group, less than half will make it to secondary school and less than half again will graduate. Schooling is not free in Indonesia, not even at the primary level, though government schools charge only about 1200 rp per month. Unfortunately, many families cannot afford even this, and send the children out to work rather than to school. The literacy rate is around 77%.

There are plenty of private schools, many operated by mosques and churches. Private schools generally have higher standards, and this is where the upper crust educate their children. Of course, private schools are more expensive.

Going to university is expensive and only a few can afford it. Higher education is concentrated in Java. Number one and biggest in Indonesia is UI (Universitas Indonesia) in Jakarta, a government-run university. Yogya is Indonesia's main educational centre, famous for its Universitas Gajah Mada. Bandung has the major high-tech school, ITB (Institut Teknologi Bandung). Lesser universities are located in the outlying provinces, such as Sulawesi's UNHAS (Universitas Hassanuddin) in Ujung Pandang.

ARTS

Indonesia has an astonishing array of cultures and all express themselves in different ways. The most readily identifiable arts are from Java and Bali. No travel documentary on Indonesia is complete without scenes of a *wayang kulit* (shadow puppet) performance or a Balinese dance, all performed to the haunting gongs and drums of the *gamelan* orchestra. Yet Java and Bali are only a small part of a vast archipelago, and Indonesia has an astonishing diversity of dance, music and especially crafts (see the Arts & Crafts section).

Theatre

Javanese *wayang* (puppet) plays have their origins in the Hindu epics, the *Ramayana* and the *Mahabharata*. There are different forms of wayang: wayang kulit are the leather shadow puppets, *wayang golek* are the wooden puppets. A detailed discussion about wayang theatre can be found in the Java chapter.

Dance

If you spend much time in Jakarta or Bali's · Kuta Beach, you could be forgiven if you thought that disco was Indonesia's traditional folk dance. But if you get out past the skyscrapers and tourist traps, you'll soon find that Indonesia has a rich heritage of traditional dance styles.

There are wayang dance dramas in Java. Yogyakarta has dance academies as well as its Ramayana Ballet, Java's most spectacular dance drama. Solo competes with Yogyakarta with its many academies of dance. Wonosobo (Central Java) has its Lengger dance, in which men dress as women. Jaipongan is a modern dance found in West Java with some erotic elements reminiscent of Brazil's lambada.

Central Kalimantan has the Manasai, a friendly dance in which tourists are welcome to participate. Kalimantan also has the Mandau dance, performed with knives and shields.

Some of the most colourful performances of all, including the Barong, Kecak, Topeng, Legong and Baris dances are found in Bali. For more information on these and other dances, see the Bali chapter.

Music

Indonesia produces a lot of indigenous pop music, most of which does not suit Western tastes. One thing you can be certain of is that Indonesians like their music *loud*.

Traditional *gamelan* orchestras are found primarily in Java and Bali. The orchestras are composed mainly of percussion instruments including drums, gongs and shake-drums *(angklung)*, along with flutes and xylophones. See the Java chapter for more detail.

Western rock music – both modern and vintage stuff from the 1960s – is also popular. Michael Jackson and the Rolling Stones have given concerts to packed audiences at the Senayan football stadium in south Jakarta.

One of Indonesia's rock idols is Iwan Fals and his band Kantata Takwa. Fals has a definite anti-Establishment and anti-government bent; his songs have gotten him arrested several times. However, he always seems to get released fairly quickly, probably because his father is a general in the Indonesian army.

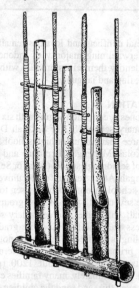

The angklung is a musical instrument made of differing lengths and thicknesses of bamboo suspended in a frame. When shaken, it produces xylophonic sounds.

CULTURE

Indonesia has a diverse mix of cultures rather than a single one, but the effects of mass education, mass media and a policy of government-orchestrated nationalism have created a sort of Indonesian national culture.

Traditional Lifestyle

'Keeping face' is important to Indonesians and they are generally extremely courteous – criticisms are not spoken directly and they will usually agree with what you say rather than offend. They will also prefer to say something rather than appear as if they don't know the answer. They mean well but when you ask how to get somewhere, you may often find yourself being sent off in the wrong direction!

Taboos

Indonesians will accept any lack of clothing on the part of poor people who cannot afford them; but for Westerners, thongs (flip-flops), bathing costumes, shorts or strapless tops are considered impolite except perhaps around places like Kuta. Elsewhere you have to look vaguely respectable.

Women are better off dressing modestly – revealing tops are just asking for trouble. Short pants are marginally acceptable if they are the baggy type which almost reach the knees.

While places of worship are open to all, permission should be requested to enter, particularly when ceremonies are in progress, and you should ensure that you're decently dressed. Always remove footware before entering a mosque, and it is customary to take shoes off before entering someone's house.

Avoiding Offence

Asians resent being touched on the head – the head is regarded as the seat of the soul and is therefore sacred. In traditional Javanese culture, a lesser person should not have their head above that of a senior person, so you may sometimes see Javanese duck their heads when greeting someone, or walk past with dropped shoulders as a mark of respect.

When handing over or receiving things remember to use the right hand – the left hand is used as a substitute for toilet paper. To show great respect to a high-ranking or elderly person, hand something to them using both hands. Talking to someone with your hands on your hips is impolite and is considered a sign of contempt, anger or aggressiveness – it's the same stance taken by characters in traditional dance and operas to signal these feelings to the audience. Handshaking is customary for both men and women on introduction and greeting.

The correct way to beckon to someone is with the hand extended and a downward waving motion of all the fingers (except the thumb). It looks almost like waving goodbye. The Western method of beckoning, with the index finger crooked upward, won't be understood and is considered rude.

An innate curiosity and interest in other people, combined with a desire to practise English, means that there's a set of stock questions that everybody asks you. It's hard to know how to react when you're sitting on a bus or boat and someone asks you 'Where are you going?'. The usual stock questions in Indonesia are: Where are you from? Where are you going? What is your name? How long have you been in Indonesia? Are you married? What is your religion?

The question to be careful of is the one on religion; Indonesians presume that Westerners are Christian. If you are an atheist you'll be better off not telling them; in Indonesia the logic is that Communists are atheists, and therefore if you are an atheist you must be a Communist.

The question about marriage should be treated carefully too. Indonesians find it absurd that anyone would not want to be married, and being divorced is a great shame. Your social relations will go more smoothly if you say you are 'already married' or 'not yet married'. If you are over age 30, it's better to be 'married' or else people will assume there must be some defect in your personality. If you really can't handle being 'married', you could say your spouse is dead, which is considered less of a tragedy than being divorced.

In the tourist areas, the relaxed morals of Westerners are tolerated, but elsewhere unmarried couples sharing a hotel room may cause embarrassment if not moral outrage. Say you are married.

Sport

Pencak silat, a form of martial arts, is most popular in West Java and West Sumatra. This form of fighting uses not only hands, but also some weapons including sticks and knives.

These days, badminton is the most popular sport. Indonesian Susi Susanti is reputed to be the best female badminton player in the world. Alan Budikusuma is a world-famous Indonesian male badminton player.

Soccer is the second most popular sport, often shown on national TV. Tennis is catching on too, and Indonesia has produced one world-famous female tennis player, Yayu Basuki from Yogya.

RELIGION

The early Indonesians were animists and practised ancestor and spirit worship. The social and religious duties of the early agricultural communities that developed in the archipelago were gradually refined to form a code of behaviour which became the basis of adat, or customary law. When Hindu-Buddhism spread into the archipelago it was overlaid on this already well-developed spiritual culture.

Although Islam was to become the predominant religion of the archipelago, it was really only a nominal victory. What we see in ostensibly Islamic Indonesia today is actually Islam rooted in Hindu-Buddhism, adat and animism. Old beliefs carry on and in Java, for example, there are literally hundreds of holy places where spiritual energy is said to be concentrated; amongst them are the Sendang Semanggi spring near Yogya, the Gua Sirandil sea-cave near Cilacap, and the misty uplands of the Dieng Plateau – all places where, with patient meditation and

self-denial, the spiritual force may be absorbed. Today a holy stone on Gunung Bromo in East Java still receives regular offerings from some Tenggerese villagers as it did when animism was the predominant religion.

As for Christianity, despite the lengthy colonial era, the missionaries have only been successful in converting pockets of the Indonesian population – the Bataks of Sumatra, the Minahasans and Toraja of Sulawesi, some of the Dayaks of Kalimantan, the Florinese, Ambonese and some of the West Irianese. Christian beliefs are also usually bound up with traditional religious beliefs and customs.

There are still a few pockets where animism survives virtually intact, such as in west Sumba and some parts of Irian Jaya.

Hinduism

Outside India, Hindus predominate only in Nepal and Bali. It is one of the oldest extant religions, its roots extending back beyond 1000 BC, in the civilisation which grew up along the Indus River Valley in what is now modern-day Pakistan.

The Hindus believe that underlying a person's body, personality, mind and memories there is something else – it never dies, it is never exhausted, it is without limit of awareness and bliss. What confuses Westerners is the vast pantheon of gods found in Hinduism – you can look upon these different gods as representations of the many attributes of an omnipresent god. The symbols and images of Hinduism are meant to introduce the worshipper to what they *represent* – the images should not be mistaken with idolatry, and the multiplicity of them with polytheism. The three main physical representations of the one omnipresent god are Brahma the creator, Vishnu the preserver and Shiva the destroyer.

Central to Hinduism is the belief that we will all go through a series of rebirths or reincarnations. Eventual freedom from this cycle depends on your karma – bad actions during your present life result in bad karma and this results in a lower reincarnation.

Conversely, if your deeds and actions have been good you will be reincarnated on a higher level and you'll be a step closer to eventual freedom from rebirth. Hinduism specifies four main castes: the highest is the Brahmin priest caste; next is the Kshatriyas, who are soldiers and governors; the Vaisyas are tradespeople and farmers; and lowest are the Sudras, who are menial workers and craftspeople. You cannot change your caste – you're born into it and are stuck with it for the rest of that lifetime.

Centuries ago Hinduism pervaded Java and spread to Bali. Today, Hinduism in Bali bears only a vague resemblance to the form practised on the Indian sub-continent. In Indonesia, Hinduism survives in a much more tangible form in the remains of great temples like Prambanan near Yogyakarta and those on the Dieng Plateau, and in stories and legends still told in dance and in the wayang puppet performances of both Bali and Java.

Ganesh

These stories are drawn from a number of ancient Hindu texts including the *Bhagavad Gita*, a poem credited to the philosopher-soldier Krishna in which he explains the duties of a warrior to Prince Arjuna. The *Bhagavad Gita* is contained in the *Maha-bharata*, which tells of a great battle said to have taken place in northern India. The *Ramayana* is another story; it tells of Prince Rama's expedition to rescue his wife, Sita, who had been carried away by the demon-prince Rawana. In this epic Rama is aided by the monkey-god Hanuman and by an army of monkeys. Rama is regarded as the person-ification of the ideal human and as an incarnation of the god Vishnu. Vishnu has visited the earth a number of times; the seventh time as Rama and the eighth time as Krishna.

The gods are also depicted in statues and reliefs in the ancient Hindu temples of Java. Often they can be identified by the 'vehicle' upon which they ride; Vishnu's vehicle is Garuda, the half-man half-eagle after whom Indonesia's international airline is named. Of all the Hindu gods, Shiva the destroyer is probably the most powerful and

the most worshipped, but out of destruction comes creation and so the creative role of Shiva is frequently represented as the lingam – a phallic symbol. Shiva's consort is Parvati, by whom he had two children, one of whom is Ganesh the elephant-headed god. Coming back from a long trip, Shiva discov-ered Parvati in her room with a young man and, not pausing to think that their son might have grown up during his absence, lopped his head off! He was then forced by Parvati to bring his son back to life but could only do so by giving him the head of the first living thing he saw – which hap-pened to be an elephant. Ganesh's vehicle is the rat.

Buddhism

Buddhism was founded in India around the 6th century BC by Siddhartha Gautama. He was a prince brought up in luxury, but in his 20s he despaired of ever finding fulfilment on the physical level since the body was inescapably involved with disease, decrepi-tude and death. At around the age of 30, he made his break from the material world and plunged off in search of 'enlightenment'. After various unsuccessful stratagems, one evening he sat beneath a banyan tree in deep meditation and achieved enlightenment.

Buddha founded an order of monks and for the next 45 years preached his ideas until his death around 480 BC. To his followers he was known as Sakyamuni. Gautama Buddha is not the only Buddha; but rather the fourth, and neither is he expected to be the last one.

Buddha taught that all life is suffering and that happiness can only be achieved by overcoming this suffering through following the 'eight-fold path' to *nirvana*, a condition beyond the limits of the mind, where one is no longer oppressed by earthly desires. Strictly speaking, Buddhism is more of a philosophy and a code of morality than a religion, because it is not centred on a god. Buddhism appears to retain some of the Hindu concepts, such as the idea of reincarnation and karma.

Hinduism & Buddhism in Indonesia

It remains one of the puzzles of Indonesian history how the ancient kingdoms of the archipelago were penetrated by Hinduism and Buddhism. The evidence of Hindu-Buddhist influence is clear enough in different parts of Indonesia, where there are Sanskrit inscriptions dating back to the 5th century AD, and many Hindu and Buddhist shrines and statues have been found in the archipelago. Disentangling the two is difficult, because there is usually a blending of Hindu and Buddhist teachings with older religious beliefs. It's been suggested, for instance, that the wayang puppet shows of Java have their roots in primitive Javanese ancestor worship, though the wayang stories that have been passed on are closely linked with later Hindu mythology or with Islam.

The elements of Indian religion and culture which had the greatest influence in Indonesia were those to do with courts and government: the Indian concept of the god-king, the use of Sanskrit as the language of religion and courtly literature and the introduction of Indian mythology. Even the events and people recorded in epics like the *Ramayana* and the *Mahabharata* have all been shifted out of India to Java. Various

Hindu and Buddhist monuments were built in Java, of which the Buddhist stupa of Borobudur and the Hindu temple complex at Prambanan are the most impressive. The Sumatran-based Sriwijaya kingdom, which arose in the 7th century, was the centre of Buddhism in Indonesia.

Bali's establishment as a Hindu enclave dates from the time when the Javanese Hindu kingdom of Majapahit, in the face of Islam, virtually evacuated Java to the neighbouring island – taking with them their art, literature and music as well as their religion and rituals. It's a mistake, however, to think that this was purely an exotic seed planted on virgin soil. The Balinese probably already had strong religious beliefs and an active cultural life and the new influences were simply overlaid on the existing practices – hence the peculiar Balinese variant of Hinduism.

The Balinese worship the Hindu trinity of Brahma the creator, Shiva the destroyer and Vishnu the preserver, but they also have a supreme god, Sanghyang Widhi. In Bali, unlike in India, the threesome is always alluded to, never seen – a vacant shrine or an empty throne says it all. Secondary Hindu gods, such as Ganesh, may occasionally appear, but there are many other purely Balinese gods, spirits and entities. Other aspects of Balinese Hinduism separate it from Indian Hinduism – like the widow-witch Rangda. She bears a close resemblance to Durga, the terrible side of Shiva's wife Parvati, but the Balinese Barong dance (in which she appears) certainly isn't part of Indian Hinduism.

Islam

Islam is the most recent and widespread of the Asian religions. The founder of Islam was the Arab prophet Muhammed but he merely transmitted the word of God to his people. To call the religion 'Muhammed-anism' is wrong, since it implies that the religion centres around Muhammed and not around God. The proper name of the religion is Islam, derived from the word *salam* which means primarily 'peace', but in a secondary sense 'surrender'. The full connotation is something like 'the peace which comes by surrendering to God'. A person who follows Islam is a Muslim.

The prophet was born around 570 AD and came to be called Muhammed, which means 'highly praised'. His descent is traditionally traced back to Abraham. There have been other true prophets before Muhammed – among them Moses, Abraham and Jesus – but Muhammed is regarded as the culmination of them, as there will be no more prophets.

Muhammed taught that there is one all-powerful, all-pervading God, Allah. 'There is no God but Allah' is the fundamental tenet of the Islamic religion. The initial reaction to Muhammed's message was one of hostility; the uncompromising monotheism conflicted with the pantheism and idolatry of the Arabs. Apart from that, Muhammed's moral teachings conflicted with what he believed was a corrupt and decadent social order, and in a society afflicted with class divisions Muhammed preached a universal humanity in which all people are equal in the eyes of God. Muhammed and his followers were forced to flee from Mecca to Medina in 622 AD, and there Muhammed built up a political base and an army which eventually defeated Mecca, although Muhammed died two years later in 632 AD.

Muhammed's teachings are collected in the Koran (or Qur'an), the holy book of Islam, compiled after Muhammed's death. Much of the Koran is devoted to codes of behaviour, and much emphasis is placed on God's mercy to humankind. Muhammed's teachings are heavily influenced by two other religions, Judaism and Christianity, and there are some extraordinary similarities including belief in hell and heaven, belief in a judgement day, and a creation theory almost identical to the Garden of Eden and myths like Noah's Ark and Aaron's Rod.

Islam hangs on four pegs: God, creation, humankind and the day of judgement. Everything in Islam centres on the fact of God or Allah but the distinctive feature of Islam is the appreciation of the value of the individual. In Hinduism and Buddhism, the individual is just a fleeting expression with no permanence or value but the Islamic religion teaches that individuality, as expressed in the human soul, is eternal, because once created the soul lives forever. For the Muslim, life on earth is just a forerunner to an eternal future in heaven or hell as appropriate.

Islam is a faith that demands unconditional surrender to the wisdom of Allah. It involves total commitment to a way of life, philosophy and law. Theoretically it is a democratic faith in which devotion is the responsibility of the individual, unrestricted by hierarchy and petty social prerequisites, and concerned with encouraging initiative and independence in the believer. Nor, in theory, is it bound to a particular locale – the faithful can worship in a rice field at home, in a mosque or on a mountain. It is also a fatalistic faith in that everything is rationalised as the will of Allah.

It is a moralistic religion and has its own set of rituals and laws, such as worshipping five times a day, recitation of the Koran, almsgiving, and fasting annually during the month of Ramadan. Making the pilgrimage to Mecca is the foremost ambition of every devout Muslim – those who have done this, called *haji* if they are men or *haja* if women, are deeply respected. Other Muslim customs include scrupulous attention to cleanliness, including ritualistic washing of hands and face. The pig is considered unclean and is not kept or eaten by strict Muslims.

Islam also called on its followers to spread the word – by the sword, if necessary. In succeeding centuries Islam was to expand over three continents. By the time a century had passed the Arab Muslims had built a huge empire which stretched all the way from Persia to Spain. The Arabs, who first propagated the faith, developed a reputation as ruthless opponents but reasonable masters, so people often found it advisable to surrender to them.

At an early stage Islam suffered a fundamental split that remains to this day. The third caliph, successor to Muhammed, was murdered and followed by Ali, the prophet's son-in-law, in 656 AD. Ali was assassinated in 661 by the governor of Syria, who set himself up as caliph in preference to the descendants of Ali. Most Muslims today are Sunnites, followers of the succession from the caliph, while the others are Shias or Shi'ites, who follow the descendants of Ali.

Islam only travelled west for a hundred years before being pushed back at Poitiers in France in 732, but it continued east for centuries. It regenerated the Persian Empire which was then declining from its protracted struggles with Byzantium. In 711, the same year in which the Arabs landed in Spain, they sent dhows up the Indus River into India. This was more a raid than a full-scale invasion but in the 11th century all of north India fell into Muslim hands. From India the faith was carried into South-East Asia by Arab and Indian traders.

Islam in Indonesia

Indonesia first came in contact with Islam through Muslim traders, primarily from India, who introduced a less orthodox form of Islam than that of Arabia. The state of Perlak in Aceh adopted Islam near the end of the 13th century, then the ruler of Melaka accepted the faith in the early part of the 15th century. Melaka became the centre of South-East Asian trade, and a centre of Islamic study, and trading ships carried the new religion to Java, from where it spread to the spice islands of eastern Indonesia via Makassar (now Ujung Pandang) in Sulawesi. Islam caught on in Java in the 16th and 17th centuries, and at about the same time, Aceh developed as a major Islamic power and the religion took root in west and south Sumatra, in Kalimantan and Sulawesi.

By the 15th and 16th centuries, centres for the teaching of Islam along the northern coast of Java may have played an important role in disseminating the new religion, along with previously established centres of Hinduism, which adopted elements of Islam. Javanese tradition holds that the first propagators of Islam in Java were nine holy men, the *wali songo*, who possessed a deep knowledge of Islamic teaching as well as exceptional supernatural powers. Another theory holds that Islam was adopted by the rulers of the coastal trading ports, who broke with the dominant Hindu kingdoms of the interior that claimed suzerainty over the north. The common people followed suit in much the same way as Europeans adopted the religions of their kings.

Whatever the reasons for the spread of Islam, today it is the professed religion of 90% of Indonesians and its traditions and rituals affect all aspects of their daily life. Like Hinduism and Buddhism before it, Islam also had to come to terms with older existing traditions and customs.

Indonesian Islam is rather different from the austere form found in the Middle East; customs in Indonesia often differ from those of other Muslim countries. Respect for the dead throughout most of Indonesia is not expressed by wearing veils but in donning traditional dress. Muslim women in Indonesia are allowed more freedom and shown more respect than their counterparts in other Muslim countries. They do not have to wear facial veils, nor are they segregated or considered to be second-class citizens. Muslim men in Indonesia are only allowed to marry two women and even then must have the consent of their first wife – Muslims in other parts of the world can have as many as four wives. Throughout Indonesia it is the women who initiate divorce proceedings. The Minangkabau society of Sumatra, for example, is a strongly Muslim group but their adat laws allow matriarchal rule, which conflicts strongly with the assumption of male supremacy inherent in Islam.

Like other Muslims, Indonesian Muslims practise circumcision. The laws of Islam require that all boys be circumcised and in Indonesia this is usually done somewhere between the ages of six and 11.

One of the most important Islamic festivals is Ramadan, a month of fasting prescribed by Islamic law, which falls in the ninth month of the Muslim calendar. It's often preceded by a cleansing ceremony, Padusan, to prepare for the coming fast.

Traditionally, during Ramadan people get up at 4 am to eat and then fast until sunset. During Ramadan many Muslims visit family graves and royal cemeteries, recite extracts from the Koran, sprinkle the graves with holy water and strew them with flowers. Special prayers are said at mosques and at home. The first day of the 10th month of the Muslim calendar is the end of Ramadan. Mass prayers are held in the early morning and these are followed by two days of feasting. Extracts from the Koran are read and religious processions take place; gifts are exchanged and pardon is asked for past wrongdoings during this time of mutual forgiveness.

Islam not only influences routine daily living but also Indonesian politics. It was with the Diponegoro revolt in the 19th century that Islam first became a rallying point in Indonesia. In the early part of the 20th century Sarekat Islam became the first mass political party. Its philosophy was derived from Islam and its support was derived from the Muslim population. In post-independence Indonesia it was an Islamic organisation, the Darul Islam, which launched a separatist movement in West Java. Despite the Islamic background of the country and the predominance of Muslims in the government, the Indonesian government has not followed the trend towards a more fundamentalist Islamic state.

LANGUAGE

The 300-plus languages spoken throughout Indonesia, except those of North Halmahera and most of Irian Jaya, belong to the Malay-Polynesian group. Within this group are many different regional languages and dialects. Sulawesi has at least six distinct language groups and the tiny island of Alor in Nusa Tenggara no fewer than seven. The languages of the Kalimantan interior form their own distinct sub-family. Sumatra is no less diverse, and languages range from Acehnese in the north, to Batak around Lake Toba, and in southern Sumatra the main language is Bahasa Melayu (Malay Language) from which Bahasa Indonesia is derived.

Java has three main languages: Sundanese, spoken in West Java; Javanese, spoken in Central and East Java; and Madurese,

The Mosque

A mosque is an enclosure for prayer. The word *mesjid* means 'to prostrate oneself in prayer'. Mosques can be differentiated according to function: the *jami mesjid* is used for the Friday prayer meetings; the *musalla* is one that is used for prayer meetings but not for those on Friday; the 'memorial mosque' is for the commemoration of victorious events in Islamic history; and a *mashad* is found in a tomb compound. There are also prayer houses which are used by only one person at a time, not for collective worship – you'll often find that larger hotels and airport terminals in Indonesia have a room set aside for this purpose.

The oldest mosques in Indonesia – in Cirebon, Demak and Palembang, for example – have roofs with two, three or five storeys. It is thought that these multistoreyed roofs were based on Hindu *meru* (shrines) that you'll still see in Bali. Today's mosques are often built with a high dome over an enclosed prayer hall. Inside there are five main features. The *mihrab* is a niche in a wall marking the direction to Mecca. The *mimbar* is a raised pulpit, often canopied, with a staircase. There is also a stand to hold the Koran, a screen to provide privacy for important persons praying, and a fountain, pool or water jug for ablutions. Outside the building there is often a *menara* – a minaret, or tower, from which the *muezzin* summons the community to prayer.

Apart from these few items the interior of the mosque is empty. There are no seats and no decorations – if there is any ornamentation at all it will be quotations of verses from the Koran. The congregation sits on the floor.

Friday afternoons are officially decreed as the time for believers to worship and all government offices and many businesses are closed as a result. All over Indonesia you'll hear the call to prayer from the mosques, but the muezzin of Indonesia are now a dying breed – the wailing will usually be performed by a cassette tape. ■

spoken on the island of Madura (off the north coast of Java) and parts of East Java. The Balinese have their own language.

Bahasa Indonesia

Today, the national language of Indonesia is Bahasa Indonesia, which is almost identical to Malay. Most Indonesians speak Bahasa Indonesia as well as their own regional language.

A few essentials are listed here. For a more comprehensive overview, try Lonely Planet's *Indonesian phrasebook* or the *CD/Audio Pack*. They're set out with a view to helping you communicate easily, rather than just listing endless phrases.

An English/Indonesian and Indonesian/English dictionary is also very useful. They're sold quite cheaply in Indonesia, and you can also get bilingual dictionaries in French, German, Dutch and Japanese.

Pronunciation

a	like the 'a' in 'father'
e	like the 'e' in 'bet' when unstressed. When stressed it is more like the 'a' in 'may'.
i	like the 'ee' sound in 'meet'
o	like the 'oa' in 'boat'
u	like the 'u' in 'flute'
ai	like the 'i' in 'line'
au	like a drawn out 'ow' as in 'cow'
ua	at the start of a word, like a 'w' – such as *uang* (money), pronounced 'wong'

The pronunciation of consonants is very straightforward. Most sound like English consonants except:

c	like the 'ch' in 'chair'
g	like the 'g' in 'garden'
ng	like the 'ng' in 'singer'
ngg	like the 'ng' in 'anger'
j	like the 'j' in 'join'
r	like Spanish trilled r
h	like English 'h', but a bit stronger. Almost silent at the end of a word.
k	like the English 'k', except at the end of the word, when you stop just short of actually saying the 'k'

ny	is a single sound like the beginning of 'new'

Greeting & Civilities

Good morning. (until 11 am)	*Selamat pagi.*
Good day. (11 am to 3 pm)	*Selamat siang.*
Good afternoon. (3 to 7 pm)	*Selamat sore.*
Good night.	*Selamat malam.*
Welcome.	*Selamat datang.*
Goodbye. (said by the person who is leaving to the person who is staying)	*Selamat tinggal.*
Goodbye. (said by the person who is staying to the person who is going)	*Selamat jalan.*
Thank you.	*Terima kasih.*
Thank you very much.	*Terima kasih banyak.*
You're welcome.	*Kembali.*
Please. (asking for help)	*Tolong.*
Please open the door.	*Tolong buka pinta.*
Please. (giving permission)	*Silakan.*
Please come in.	*Silakan masuk.*
Sorry.	*Ma'af.*
Excuse me.	*Permisi.*
How are you?	*Apa kabar?*
I'm fine.	*Kabar baik.*
What is your name?	*Siapa nama anda?*
My name is...	*Nama saya...*

Questions

How much?	*Berapa?*
How much is the price?	*Berapa harga?*
How much money?	*Berapa uang?*
How many kilometres?	*Berapa kilometer?*
Where is...?	*Di mana ada?*
Which way?	*Ke mana?*

ticket	*karcis, tiket*
bus	*bis*
train	*kereta api*
ship	*kapal*
aeroplane	*kapal terbang*
motorcycle	*sepeda motor*
station	*stasiun*
here	*di sini*
stop (verb)	*berhenti*
straight on	*terus*
right	*kanan*
left	*kiri*
slow	*pelan-pelan*

Useful Words

matches	*korek api*
mosquito coil	*obat nyamuk*
mosquito net	*kelambu*
postage stamp	*perangko*
soap	*sabun*
towel	*handuk*
telephone card	*kartu telepon*
telephone number	*nombor telepon*
toilet	*kamar kecil WC* (pronounced 'way say')
toilet paper	*kertas WC*
air-conditioning	*ac* (pronounced as 'ah-say')

Accommodation

price list	*daftar harga*
hotel	*hotel*
bed	*ranjang/tempat tidur*
room	*kamar*
quiet room	*kamar tenang*
bathroom	*kamar mandi*
with private bath	*kamar mandi didalam*
with shared bath	*kamar mandi diluar*
I want to pay now.	*Saya mau bayar sekarang.*

Numbers

1	*satu*	6	*enam*
2	*dua*	7	*tujuh*
3	*tiga*	8	*delapan*
4	*empat*	9	*sembilan*
5	*lima*	10	*sepuluh*

After the numbers one to 10, the 'teens' are *belas*, the 'tens' are *puluh*, the 'hundreds' are *ratus* and the 'thousands' *ribu*. Thus:

11	*sebelas*
12	*duabelas*
13	*tigabelas*
20	*duapuluh*
21	*duapuluh satu*
25	*duapuluh lima*
30	*tigapuluh*
90	*sembilanpuluh*
99	*sembilanpuluh sembilan*
100	*seratus*
200	*duaratus*
250	*duaratus limapuluh*
254	*duaratus limapuluh empat*
888	*delapanratus delapanpuluh delapan*
1000	*seribu*
1050	*seribu limapuluh*

A half is *setengah*, which is pronounced 'stengah', so half a kilo is 'stengah kilo'. 'Approximately' is *kira-kira*.

Time

rubber time	*jam karet*
When?	*Kapan?*
tomorrow/yesterday	*besok/kemarin*
hour	*jam*
week	*minggu*
month	*bulan*
year	*tahun*
7 o'clock	*jam tujuh*
5 o'clock	*jam lima*
five hours	*lima jam*
What is the time?	*Jam berapa?*
How many hours?	*Berapa jam?*

Days of the Week

Monday	*Hari Senin*
Tuesday	*Hari Selasa*
Wednesday	*Hari Rabu*
Thursday	*Hari Kamis*
Friday	*Hari Jumat*
Saturday	*Hari Sabtu*
Sunday	*Hari Minggu*

Emergency

I'm sick.	*Saya sakit.*	Thief!	*Pencuri!*
Call the police.	*Panggil polisi.*	Fire!	*Kebakaran!*
Help!	*Tolong!*	hospital	*rumah sakit*

Arts & Crafts

Indonesia's arts & crafts reflect the regional histories, religions and influences of the archipelago's mind-boggling array of ethnic groups. Indonesian arts & crafts can be classified into three major groupings, which roughly parallel the three cultural streams within Indonesia – a loose generalisation but a useful one.

The first is that of 'outer' Indonesia, the islands of Sumatra, Kalimantan, Sulawesi, Nusa Tenggara, Maluku and Irian Jaya, which have strong animist traditions. Carvings, weavings, pottery etc have developed from a tribal art in which art objects are part of worship, for example, the ancestor statues from Nias in Sumatra, or are representational art adorning everyday objects, imbuing them with the power of the spirits.

The second stream is that of 'inner' Indonesia, the islands of Java and Bali that have come under the greatest influence from Hindu-Buddhist tradition. The techniques and styles that built Borobudur and the Indian epics such as the *Mahabharata* that form the basis for wayang theatre are still a major influence on arts & crafts.

The third influence is that of Islam, which not so much introduced its own art tradition but modified existing traditions. Its more rigid style and its ban on human and animal representation restricted art, yet because of it the existing artistic traditions became more stylised and refined.

These days the religious influence or magic associated with many art objects is disappearing. For example, the *sahan*, the Batak medicine holder of buffalo horn with a wooden carved stopper, or the *tunggal*, the medicine man's wand, line Lake Toba craft shops. These copies of the increasingly rare real thing have no significance to the maker apart from its sale value.

Front page: Kenyah Dyak basket (GB)

Top: Modern Batak sahan, carved buffalo horn medicine holder from Lake Toba, North Sumatra (GB)

Bottom: Stone axe from Baliem Valley, Irian Jaya (GB)

But while one can lament at the passing of traditional meaning and methods, it would be wrong to assume that the tourist trade is destroying traditional crafts. The sophistication and innovation of the craft 'industry' is growing. For example, Batak carvers now produce large sahan that are much bigger and more intricately carved than the original. Whilst they lack spiritual meaning, they are fine pieces of craftwork and show increasing sophistication. The designs have changed to suit the market – small, simple sahan just don't sell and, anyway, the spiritual meaning of an original sahan has no relevance for most buyers.

Of course, many of the trinkets turned out for the tourist trade are of poor quality and there is an increasing cross-fertilisation of craft styles. The 'primitif' Asmat or Kalimantan statues so in vogue in Balinese art shops may well have been carved just up the road in Peliatan. On the other hand, Javanese woodcarvers are turning out magnificent traditional panels and innovative furniture commissioned by large hotels, and Balinese jewellers influenced by Western designs are producing new work of stunning quality.

Top Left: Angklung *from West Java, a bamboo musical instrument which is shaken to produce notes (GB)*

Top Right: Gerantang *or* tingklik *bamboo xylophone from Bali (GB)*

Bottom: Pottery from Lombok (GB)

Asmat fertility statue from Irian Jaya (GB)

Woodcarving

Woodcarving is the most enduring and widespread medium for artistic expression in Indonesia. Each culture has its own style, and the diversity and sophistication of Indonesia's woodcarvers is remarkable.

In Indonesia a house not only protects its inhabitants from the elements but repels unwanted spirits. Woodcarvings that adorn houses are usually more than just ornament, for example, the horned *singa* (lion) heads that protect Batak houses, the water buffalo representations on Toraja houses signifying prosperity or the serpents and magical dog carvings on Dayak houses in Kalimantan.

Woodcarvings and statues are an important expression of the spirits in the outer islands. Statues of the ancestors are an integral part of spiritual life on Nias and Sumba. The Toraja's famed funerals are important events for the artist also and a realistic statue is carved of the dead and the coffin is adorned with animal heads. In Ngaju and Dusun villages in Kalimantan, giant carved ancestor totems or *temadu* depict the dead.

Perhaps the most famous and mythologised of Indonesia's woodcarvers are the Asmat of south-west Irian Jaya. Shields, canoes, spears, drums and everyday objects are carved but the most distinctive and easily recognisable Asmat woodcarvings are the ancestor poles *(mbis)*. These poles show the dead one above the other, and the open carved 'wing' at the top of the pole is a phallic symbol expressing fertility and power. The poles are also an expression of revenge and were traditionally carved to accompany a feast following a headhunting raid.

Woodcarving also has a decorative as well as spiritual function and everyday objects from the outer islands are often intricately carved. Some of the most readily seen objects are the baby carriers and ironwood stools from Kalimantan, lacquered bowls from South Sumatra, carved bamboo containers from Sulawesi and even doors from Timor and horse effigies from Sumba.

Right: Bamboo containers etched with Batak calendar from Lake Toba, North Sumatra (GB)

Bottom: Frontispiece of Toba Batak house, with singa head to protect the house and ward off unwanted spirits (PT)

*Top: Asmat carved
wooden bowl,
Irian Jaya (GB)*

*Middle Left: Modern
Balinese wood carving
from Celuk, Bali (TS)*

*Middle Right: Asmat
shields (GB)*

*Bottom: Batak coconut
container used to carry
spices, with carved totem
stopper showing rider and
animals (GB)*

Top: Carved buffalo horn tobacco holder from Lombok (GB)

Middle: Wooden surveying tool (plumb line) from Lombok (GB)

Bottom Left: Mancala, carved board game from Java. This popular board game is found throughout Asia and Africa (GB)

Bottom Right: Carving a serpent frieze in teak, Karduluk, Madura (PT)

The islands of Bali and Java also have strong woodcarving traditions. Balinese woodcarving is the most ornamental and intricate in Indonesia. Carved statues, temple doors and relief panel are decorated with swirls of the gods and demons of Balinese cosmology. While religion still plays an important part in traditional Balinese woodcarving, nowhere in Indonesia has Western art and souvenir demand made so much impact. Western influence saw a revolution in woodcarving akin to that in Balinese painting, and many years ago Balinese woodcarvers began producing simpler, elongated statues of purely ornamental design with a natural rather than a brightly painted finish. Nowadays Bali also turns out art copies from all over the archipelago, producing their own interpretations of Asmat totems or Kalimantan fertility statues, as well as unique modern statues.

The centre for woodcarving on Java is Jepara on the north coast of Central Java. The intricate style is obviously of the same tradition as the Balinese, but Muslim and other influences has seen human representation replaced by heavily carved and stylised leaves, flowers and birds. Furniture is the main business in Jepara, and cupboards, sideboards, beds, chairs etc are all heavily carved. Other centres on Java are Kudus, which produces mostly intricate panels seen in traditional houses, and Madura.

The most favoured wood in Indonesia is teak *(jati)*, though this is an increasingly expensive commodity. Teak is widely used in Java and sometimes Bali. and is one of the best woods because it is easily carved and less susceptible to warping, splitting, insects and rot. Sandalwood, which is grown in East Timor, is also occasionally seen in Balinese carvings. Mahogany is also used, though not common, while ebony imported from Sulawesi and Kalimantan is used on Bali. This very heavy wood is also very expensive. Jackfruit is a common wood and cheap, though it tends to warp and split. Above all, local carvers use woods at hand so, for example, heavy ironwood and meranti are used in Kalimantan woodcarving and *belalu*, a quick growing light wood, is used on Bali.

Left: Serving ladles (GB)

Right: Topeng masks from Yogyakarta, Central Java (PT)

Carved Masks

Masks are also a specialised form of woodcarving. Though they exist throughout the archipelago and may be in funerary rites and the like, the most readily identifiable form of mask is the *topeng* used in the wayang topeng dances of Java and Bali. The introduction of wayang topeng is attributed to Sunan Kalijaga, an Islamic saint of the 16th century, but dances are of the Hindu-Buddhist tradition. Dancers perform tales from the Indian epics such as the *Mahabharata* or distinctly local tales and the masks are used to represent the characters. Masks vary from the stylised but plain masks of Central and West Java to the heavily carved masks of East Java. Balinese topeng masks are less stylised and more naturalistic – the Balinese save their love of colour and detail for the masks of the *barong* dance, which is more strongly pre-Hindu in influence.

Top Left: Topeng masks from Java are more stylised, as seen in this intricately carved topeng kartolo mask from Lumajang, East Java (PT)

Top Right: Balinese topeng mask depicting a more kasar (unrefined) character. The teeth are made from gleaming mother-of-pearl shells (GB)

Middle: Balinese wayang topeng masks. These white masks with refined features depict royal characters (GB)

Bottom Left: Balinese Rangda witch mask, from the Barong dance (GB)

Bottom Right: Barong mask. The Barong is a mythical lion/dragon creature that battles with and defeats Ranga, the queen of witches, in a dance that is often performed to purge evil spirits (TW)

Intricate tulis *batik from Cirebon, West Java (PT)*

Textiles

Indonesian textiles come in a dazzling variety of fabrics, materials, techniques, colours and motifs. Basically there are three major textile groupings.

The first is *ikat*, a form of tie-dyeing patterns onto the threads before weaving them together; this technique is associated with the proto-Malay people of the archipelago such as the various ethnic groups of Nusa Tenggara (see the Nusa Tenggara chapter for more on ikat). The second is *songket*, where gold or silver threads are woven into silk cloth. This is strongest where Islam has made the most impact, eg in places like Aceh in Sumatra and amongst the Malays of coastal Kalimantan. The third group is *batik*, the alternate waxing and dyeing technique most clearly associated with those parts of central Java where the great Javanese kingdoms were established. It was also taken up in Bali, Madura and in Jambi in Sumatra, all of which have been subject to considerable Javanese influence.

Ikat

The Indonesian word ikat, which means to tie or bind, is used as the name for intricately patterned cloth whose threads are tie-dyed by a very painstaking and skilful process *before* they are woven together.

Ikat cloth is made in many scattered regions of the archipelago, from Sumatra to Maluku, but it's in Nusa Tenggara that this ancient art form thrives most strongly. Ikat garments are still in daily use in many areas, and there's an incredible diversity of colours and patterns. The spectacular ikat of Sumba and the intricate patterned work of Flores are the best known, but Timor and Lombok and small islands like Roti, Sawu, Ndao and Lembata all have their own varied and high-quality traditions, as do Sulawesi, Kalimantan and Sumatra. On Bali the rare double ikat method, in which both warp and waft threads are pre-dyed is used in the weavings of Gringseng.

Lion figures, shown in this detail from a Sumbanese blanket (GB)

Making Ikat Ikat cloth is nearly always made of cotton, still often hand spun, though factory-made threads have come into use. Dyes are traditionally handmade from local plants and minerals, and these give ikat its characteristic earthy brown, red, yellow and orange tones as well as the blue of indigo.

Ikat comes in a variety of shapes and sizes including *selendang* (shawls); sarongs; two-metre long tubes which can be used as a cloak or rolled down to the waist to resemble a sarong; *selimut* (blankets); and four-metre long pieces (known as *kapita* in Flores) used as winding cloths for burial of the dead.

Some aspects of ikat production are changing with the use of manufactured dyes and thread. A description of the traditional method follows.

All the work belongs to the women – they produce the dyes and they plant, harvest, spin, dye and weave the cotton. Spinning is done with a spindle or sometimes a simple spinning wheel. The thread is strengthened by immersion in stiffening baths of grated cassava, fine stamped rice, or a meal made of roasted maize, and then threaded onto a winder. The product is usually thicker and rougher than machine-spun cotton.

Traditional dyes are made from natural sources. The most complex processes are those concerned with the bright rust colour, known on Sumba as *kombu*, which is produced from the bark and roots of the kombu tree. Blue dyes come from the indigo plant, and purple or brown can be produced by dyeing the cloth deep blue and then overdyeing it with kombu.

Each time the threads are dipped in dye, the sections that are not due to receive colour are bound together ('ikatted') beforehand with dye-resistant fibre. A separate tying-and-dying process is carried out for each colour that will appear in the finished cloth – and the sequence of dying has to consider the effect of over-dying. This tying-and-dying stage is what makes ikat and it requires great skill, since the dyer has to work out – *before* the threads are woven into cloth – exactly which parts of the thread are to receive each colour in order to give the usually complicated pattern of the final cloth. After dying, the cloth is woven on a simple hand loom.

There is a defined schedule of work for the traditional production of ikat. On Sumba the thread is spun between July and October, and the patterns bound between September and December. After the rain ends in April, the blue and kombu dyeing is carried out. In August the weaving starts – more than a year after work on the thread began.

Origins & Meaning of Ikat The ikat technique probably came to Indonesia over 2000 years ago with the migrants bringing the Dongson culture from southern China and Vietnam. It has survived in more isolated areas that were bypassed by later cultural influences.

Ikat styles vary according to the village and sex of the wearer, and some types of cloth are reserved for special purposes. In parts of Nusa

The skull tree motif is featured extensively in Sumbanese weavings. Sumbanese head-hunters would display the heads of their enemies on trees (GB)

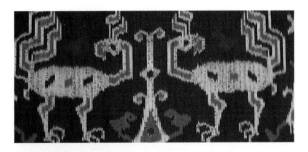

Sumba weaving with animal motifs (GB)

Tenggara high-quality ikat is part of the 'dowry' that a bride's family must give to the bridegroom's family. On Sumba, less than 90 years ago only members of the highest clans could make and wear ikat textiles. Certain motifs were traditionally reserved for noble families (as on Sumba and Roti) or members of a particular tribe or clan (Sawu or among the Atoni of Timor).

In the 20th century, traditional motifs have become mixed up with some of European origin, and ikat's function in indicating its wearer's role or rank has declined.

Motifs & Patterns An incredible range of designs is found on ikat. Some experts believe that motifs found on Sumba such as face-on people, animals and birds, stem from an artistic tradition even older than Dongson. The main Dongson influence was in geometric motifs like diamond and key shapes (which often go together), meanders and spirals.

A particularly strong influence was cloths known as *patola* from Gujarat in India. In the 16th and 17th centuries these became highly-prized in Indonesia and one characteristic motif was copied by local ikat weavers. It's still a favourite today – a hexagon framing a sort of four-pronged star. On the best patola and geometric ikat, repeated small patterns combine to form larger patterns, and the longer you look at it the more patterns you see – rather like a mandala.

Judging Ikat Not so easy! Books on the subject aren't much use when you're confronted with a market trader telling you that yes, this cloth is definitely hand spun and yes, of course the dyes are natural. Taking a look at the process is informative: you can see women weaving in many places, and at the right time of year you may see dye-making, thread-spinning or tie-dying. Cloths made in villages will nearly always be hand spun and hand-woven. Here are some tips on distinguishing the traditional product:

Thread Hand spun cotton has a less perfect 'twist' to it than factory cloth.

Weave Handwoven cloth, whether made from hand spun or factory thread, feels rougher and, when new, stiffer than machine-woven cloth. It will probably have imperfections (perhaps minor) in the weave.

Dyes Until you've seen enough ikat to get a feel for whether colours are natural or chemical, you often have to rely on your instincts as to whether they are 'earthy' enough. Some cloths contain both natural and artificial dyes.

Dyeing Method The patterns on cloths which have been individually tie-dyed by the authentic method will rarely be perfectly defined, but they're unlikely to have the detached specks of colour that often appear on mass-dyed cloth.

Age No matter what anybody tells you, there are very few antique cloths around. Most of what you'll be offered for sale will be new or newly second-hand. There are several processes to make cloth *look* old.

Songket

Songket is silk cloth with gold or silver threads woven into it, though these days imitation silver or gold is often used. Songket is most commonly found in West Sumatra, but can be seen in parts of Kalimantan and Bali.

Gold thread is also used in embroidery typically in the more Islamic areas of Indonesia.

Top: The use of gold thread in weavings, known as songket, *have long been prized in Indonesia. Real gold thread is traditionally used but look-alike thread is common (GB)*

Bottom: Gold embroidery is used in this Minangkabau wedding scarf from Bukittinggi, West Sumatra (GB)

Batik

The technique of applying wax or some other type of dye-resistant substance (like rice-paste) to cloth to produce a design is found in many parts of the world. The Javanese were making batik cloth at least as early as the 12th century but its origins are hard to trace. Some think the skills were brought to Java from India, others that the Javanese developed the technique themselves. The word 'batik' is an old Javanese word meaning 'to dot'.

The development of batik in Indonesia is usually associated with the flowering of the creative arts around the royal courts – it's likely that the use of certain motifs was the preserve of the aristocracy. The rise of Islam in Java probably contributed to the stylisation of batik patterns and the absence of representations of living things from most designs. More recently batik has grown from an art mainly associated with the royal courts into an important industry with a number of noted production centres.

Left: Hand-worked or tulis batik involves drawing designs in wax with the use of a copper pen (canting) (PT)

In the older method of making batik the wax is applied hot to the smooth cloth with the *canting*, a pen-like instrument with a small reservoir of liquid wax. The design is first traced out onto the prepared cloth and the patterns drawn in wax on the white cloth, or on a cloth previously dyed to the lightest colour required in the finished product. The wax-covered areas resist colour change when immersed in a dye bath. The waxing and dyeing are continued with increasingly dark shades until the final colours are achieved. Wax is added to protect previously dyed areas or scraped off to expose new areas to the dye. Finally, all the wax is scraped off and the cloth boiled to remove all traces of the wax. The wax mixture usually includes beeswax, paraffin, resins and fats mixed in varying proportions. This type of batik is called *batik tulis* or 'written batik', because the patterns are drawn onto the cloth in freehand style.

Below: In cap batik, copper stamps (cap) are made with the desired design, dipped in wax and then pressed on to the fabric (PT)

From the mid-19th century production was speeded up by applying the wax with a metal stamp called a *cap*. The cap technique can usually be identified by the repetition of identical patterns, whereas in the freer composition using the canting even repeated geometric motifs vary slightly. Some batik combines the cap technique with canting work for the fine details. It's worth noting that batik cap is true batik; don't confuse it with screen-printed cloth which completely bypasses the waxing process and is often passed off as batik.

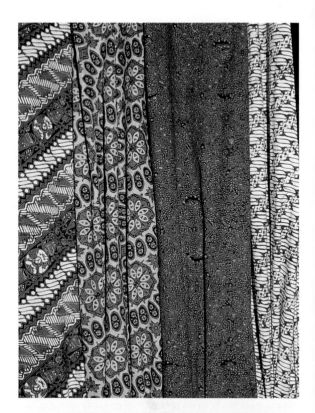

Top: Batik featuring
traditional colours and
designs from Yogyakarta
and Solo (PT)

Bottom: Batik
silk from Cirebon,
West Java (PT)

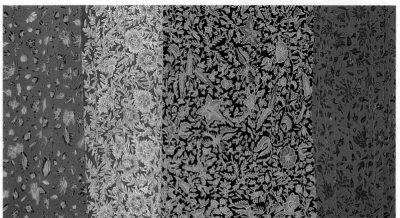

Java is the home of Indonesian batik, and each district produces its own style. The court cities of Yogyakarta and Solo in Central Java are major batik centres. Traditional court designs are dominated by brown, yellow and indigo blue. These days both cities produce a wide range of modern as well as traditional batiks. Solo is a major textile centre and many of the large batik houses are based there.

Batiks from the north coast of Java have always been more colourful and innovative in design. As the trading region of Java, the north coast came in contact with many influences and these are reflected in its batik. Pekalongan is the other major batik centre on the north coast, and traditional floral designs are brightly coloured and show a Chinese influence. Floral and bird motifs are popular traditional designs. Many modern designs are now employed and some of Indonesia's most interesting batik comes from Pekalongan. Cirebon also produces very fine traditional tulis work that is colourful.

Top Left: Pekalongan batik, noted for its intricate design, use of bright colours and floral motifs (GB)

Top Right: Floral motif on traditional Pekalongan batik (GB)

Bottom: Modern cap batik sarongs, produced mainly in Solo (PW)

The wavy bladed kris *is said to have spiritual power and will rattle in its scabbard to warn the owner of impending danger. The hilt is often carved with* raksasa *(demon) figures to ward off evil spirits and the blade is beaten, rolled and etched, and may include inlaid jewels. (Tass)*

Metalwork

The Bronze age in Indonesia began with the metalworking introduced from the Dongson culture in present-day Vietnam. Bronze work peaked with the Hindu-Buddhist empires of Java and brasswork is now more common, but in the eastern islands the ancient hourglass-shaped bronze drums are still produced.

Brassware was mostly of Indian and Islamic influence and fine brass vessels and ornaments are produced in Indonesia. Some of the best workmanship is that of the Minangkabau in Sumatra, but brassware is also produced in Java, South Kalimantan and Sulawesi.

Minangkabau betel container from West Sumatra (left), and etched brass bowl from Madura. (GB)

The most important ironwork objects are knives. As well as the famous kris, the *parang* of Kalimantan are sacred weapons used in everything from hacking through the jungle to head-hunting. Scabbards for ceremonial parang are intricately decorated with beads, shells and feathers.

Kris

Some think the Javanese kris – from the word *iris*, to cut – is derived from the bronze daggers produced by the Dongson culture around the 1st century AD. Bas-reliefs of a kris appear in the 14th-century Panataran temple-complex in East Java, and the carrying of the kris as a custom in Java was noted in 15th-century Chinese records. The kris is still an integral part of men's formal dress on ceremonial and festive occasions. A dalang will wear his kris while giving a wayang performance, and the kris is still part of the uniform of the guards at the palace in Yogyakarta.

The kris is no ordinary knife. It is said to be endowed with supernatural powers; adat law requires that every father furnish his son with a kris upon his reaching manhood, preferably an heirloom kris enabling his son to draw on the powers of his ancestors stored in the sacred weapon. Distinctive features and the number of curves in the blade, and the damascene, are read to indicate good or bad fortune for its owner. Damascening is a technique whereby another metal is hammered onto the blade of the kris to produce a design. The number of curves in the blade also has symbolic meaning: five curves symbolise the five Pandava brothers of the *Mahabharata* epic; three stand for fire, ardour or passion. Although the blade is the most important part of the kris, the hilt and scabbard are also beautifully decorated.

Before the arrival of Islam, Hindu-inspired images were often used to decorate the wooden hilts – the mythological Garuda was a popular figure. After the spread of Islam such motifs were discouraged, but were often preserved in stylised forms. In any case, the origins and symbolism of the kris lay too deep in Javanese mysticism to be eradicated by the laws of Islam.

Though the kris is mostly associated with Java and Bali, it is also found in Sumatra, Kalimantan and Sulawesi. Kris from the outer islands are larger and less ornate than those on Java and Bali.

Jewellery

Gold and silver work have long been practised in Indonesia. Some of the best gold jewellery comes from Aceh in the very north of Sumatra where fine filigree work is produced, and chunky bracelets and earrings are produced in the Batak lands. Gold jewellery can be found all over Indonesia, and while some interesting traditional work can be found throughout the islands, the ubiquitous *toko mas* (gold shop) found in every Indonesian city is mostly an investment house selling gold jewellery by weight, while design and workmanship take a back seat.

The best known jewellery is the silver jewellery of Bali, and Kota Gede in Yogyakarta. Balinese work is nearly always hand constructed and rarely involves casting techniques. Balinese jewellery is very innovative, employing traditional designs but more often than not adapting designs or copying from other jewellery presented by Western buyers. The range is stunning and Bali is a major producer of export fashion jewellery. The traditional centre for Balinese jewellery is Cleek.

The ancient city of Kota Gede within the city boundaries of Yogyakarta is another major silver centre famous for its fine filigree work. Silverware tends to be more traditional but is also starting to branch out and adapt new designs. As well as jewellery, Kota Gede produces a wide range of silver tableware.

Top Left: Modern Balinese bracelet (Tass)

Top Right: Silver earring from Timor, used by the Tetum people as a wedding ornament. (GB)

Bottom Left: Balinese silver jewellery (GB)

Bottom Right: Necklace with painted wooden carved flowers (GB)

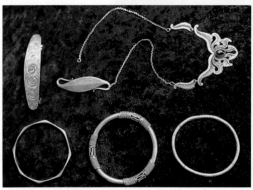

Top: Silver coffee set from Kota Gede, Yogyakarta (PT)

Bottom Left: Kota Gede silverwork is noted for its fine filigree work, shown here on a large peacock ornament (PT)

Bottom Right: Silversmith handbeating designs onto a silver bowl, Kota Gede, Yogyakarta (PT)

Antique Chinese ceramics, common throughout the archipelago (GB)

Pottery

Indonesia's position on the trade routes saw the import of large amounts of ceramics from China. Indonesia is a fertile hunting ground for antique Chinese ceramics, which date back as far as the Han dynasty. The best examples of truly indigenous ceramics are the terracottas from the Majapahit Empire of East Java.

Indonesian pottery is usually unglazed and hand worked, though the wheel is also used. It may be painted but is often left natural. Potters around Mojokerto, close to the original Majapahit capital, still produce terracottas but the best known pottery centre on Java is just outside Yogyakarta at Kasongan, where intricate, large figurines and pots are produced.

In the Singkiwang area of West Kalimantan, the descendants of Chinese potters produce a unique style of utilitarian pottery.

Lombok pottery is very fashionable and has an earthy 'primitive' look with subtle colourings. Balinese ceramics show a stronger Western influence and are more inclined to use glazing.

Top Left: Dragon figurine from Kasongan, Central Java (PT)

Top Right: Detail on bowl from Lombok (GB)

Bottom Left: Lombok pots (JL)

Bottom Right: Potter, Kasongan, Central Java (PT)

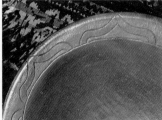

Balinese temple festival scene, showing barong dance, by A A Rai (RvD)

Painting

Painting is widespread in Indonesia as an accompaniment to other art forms, for example, woodcarvings, masks and pottery are often painted, as are religious items such as calendars or religious designs painted on houses, eg the tree of life paintings in Dayak longhouses. An individual painting on canvas that is an art form in itself is a modern Western concept.

Temple and other painting exists on Java but after the conversion to Islam, Bali became the centre for painting in Indonesia. The traditional wayang narratives were moral tales or told of the exploits of the gods. They were mostly wall paintings or decorative hangings for temples and palaces.

Top: Batik painting from Yogyakarta (TW)

Bottom: Temple painting at Tirta Empul, Tampaksiring, Bali (TW)

Balinese painting was turned around in the 1930s by Western artists such as Walter Spies and Rudolf Bonnet who came to live and work on Bali. They encouraged painting as an art form and Balinese artists started to depict scenes from everyday life rather than religious narratives. Balinese paintings were still packed with detail but rice harvesting and market scenes replaced the cartoon-like narratives of the Hindu epics like the *Ramayana*. Further transformations occurred with the naive 'young artists' style that developed in the 1950s, and Balinese painting continues to evolve with many noted modern artists producing innovative work.

Of course, Indonesia has many exponents of Western-style painting using the same media as artists all over the world but expressing Indonesian themes and incorporating traditional Indonesian styles. The Javanese painter Raden Saleh is credited with being one of the first modern Indonesian artists in the 19th century. Present-day artists cover all painting styles. Of particular note are the batik painters that sprung up in Yogyakarta in the 1960s. Using batik techniques they depicted traditional and modern themes and inspired a whole craft tourist industry. Like much of the painting on Bali, batik painting can be very imitative and of poor quality, but some is original.

Top: Rural scene by I Dab Alit, Ubud (GB)

Bottom Left: Modern Balinese painting moved away from depicting traditional myths to showing everyday life. In this painting by I Made Nyana, surfing and the tourist industry are portrayed (TW)

Bottom Right: Painter in Ubud (TW)

Top: Painter in Ubud (PW)

Bottom: Young Artist
painting by I Nyoman
Dana (TW)

Bone and cowrie shell necklace, fibre purse and dog teeth choker from Irian Jaya (GB)

Basketwork & Beadwork

Some of the finest basketwork in Indonesia comes from Lombok. The spiral woven rattan work is very fine and large baskets are woven using this method, or smaller receptacles topped with wooden carvings are also popular.

In Java, Tasikmalaya is a major cane-weaving centre, often adapting baskets and vessels to modern uses, with the introduction of zips and plastic lining. The Minangkabau, centred around Bukittinggi, also produce interesting palm leaf bags and purses, while the lontar palm is used extensively in weaving in Timor, Roti and other outer eastern islands.

The Dayak of Kalimantan produce some superb woven baskets and string bags and they also produce some fine beadwork which can be seen on their baby carriers.

Some of the most colourful and attractive beadwork is produced by the Toraja of Sulawesi, and beadwork can be found throughout Nusa Tenggara from Lombok to Timor.

Small, highly prized cowrie shells are used like beads and are found on Dayak and Lombok artefacts, though the best application of these shells is in the Sumbanese tapestries intricately beaded with shells.

Top & Middle: Lombok is noted for its fine basketwork and cane ware (GB)

Bottom Left: Beaded basket, Lombok (GB)

Bottom Right: Modern Indonesian leatherwork uses traditional materials, such as cane weaving and ikat, to great effect, as shown in these bags from Yogyakarta (GB)

Of the many forms of wayang, the three-dimensional wayang golek puppets are most popular in West Java. Shown here is a puppet of a Javanese nobleman. (GB)

Puppets

The most famous puppets of Indonesia are the carved leather *wayang kulit* puppets. The intricate lace figures are cut from buffalo hide with a sharp, chisel-like stylus and then painted. They are produced on Bali and Java, particularly Central Java. The leaf-shaped *kayon* representing the 'tree' or 'mountain of life' is used to end scenes in the wayang and is also made of leather.

Wayang golek are the three-dimensional wooden puppets found in Central Java but are most popular amongst the Sundanese of West Java. The *wayang klitik* puppets are a rarer flat wooden puppet of East Java.

Wayang klitik puppets are carved and painted two-dimensional wooden puppets, most popular in East Java (GB)

Sumba weaving with animals and star motifs

Facts for the Visitor

VISAS

For many nationalities, a visa is not necessary for entry and a stay of up to 60 days. This includes, but is not limited to, the following: Argentina, Australia, Austria, Belgium, Brazil, Canada, Chile, Denmark, Finland, France, Germany, Greece, Iceland, Ireland, Italy, Japan, Liechtenstein, Luxembourg, Malaysia, Malta, Mexico, Morocco, the Netherlands, New Zealand, Norway, the Philippines, Singapore, South Korea, Spain, Sweden, Switzerland, Thailand, the UK, the USA, Venezuela and Yugoslavia.

If you're from one of these countries, a 60-day tourist pass (which is a stamp in your passport) is issued on arrival, as long as you enter and exit through recognised entry ports. Officially (but not always in practice), you must have a ticket out of the country when you arrive. Officially (and almost certainly), you cannot extend your visa beyond 60 days. If you're really intending to explore Indonesia in some depth, then 60 days is inadequate and you will have to exit the country and re-enter.

Make sure to check your passport expiry date. Indonesia requires that your passport has six months life left in it on your date of arrival.

Social & Work Visas

Visas for social or study purposes can be arranged if you have a sponsor, such as an educational institution, in Indonesia. These are normally one-month visas that are extended every month for up to six months or more. If you are contemplating a three or four-month trip to Indonesia and see this as an alternative to a tourist pass, it is rarely worth the trouble of first hassling with an overseas embassy and then with the local immigration office every month. By the time you pay visa fees and possibly bribes, it can be almost as cheap as leaving the country and returning after 60 days. Perhaps the Indonesian government will one day realise that the 60-day restriction is losing them valuable tourist dollars and issue longer tourist passes.

Work visas are an almighty hassle to get and should be arranged by your employer. The Indonesian Embassy in Singapore is the busiest and most troublesome for issuing working visas – foreign companies usually hire agents who know the ropes.

Recognised Entry/Exit Points

Entry and exit to Indonesia on a tourist pass is restricted to the following airports or seaports (remembering that the approved gateways do change):

Bali
    Ngurah Rai Airport, Denpasar
    Benoa & Padangbai Seaports
Irian Jaya
    Frans Kaisiepo Airport, Biak
Java
    Soekarno-Hatta Airport & Tanjung Priok Seaport, Jakarta
    Juanda Airport & Tanjung Perak Seaport, Surabaya
    Tanjung Emas Seaport, Semarang
Kalimantan
    Sepinggan Airport, Balikpapan
    Soepadio Airport, Pontianak
Maluku
    Pattimura Airport & Yos Sudarso Seaport, Ambon
Nusa Tenggara
    El Tari Airport, Kupang, Timor
Riau Archipelago
    Tanjung Pinang Seaport, Bintan Island
    Simpang Tiga Airport, Pekanbaru
    Batu Besar Airport, Sekupang Seaport & Batu Ampar Seaport, Batam Island
Sulawesi
    Sam Ratulangi Airport & Bitung Seaport, Manado
Sumatra
    Polonia Airport & Belawan Seaport, Medan

If you plan to arrive through an unrecognised 'gateway', eg to Jayapura from Papua New Guinea, then you have to get an Indonesian visa before arriving. A visa is also required to *leave* Indonesia through a non-designated port, even if you entered through a designated one. Travellers have left through a non-designated port without a visa – details on the situation in some of these places are given in the relevant town sections of this book.

Visas are only valid for one month, not 60 days as for visa-free entry, and can only be extended for two weeks. Indonesia embassies are usually not keen on issuing visas.

Visa Extensions

Tourist passes are not extendable beyond 60 days. You may get a few extra days in special circumstances, like missed flight connections or illness, but don't count on it. Whatever you do, do not simply show up at the airport with an expired visa or tourist pass and expect to be able to board your flight. You may be sent back to the local immigration office to clear up the matter or you might be asked to 'pay a fine'. If you overstay and immigration takes a disliking to you, they could stamp your passport so you can't re-enter Indonesia.

If you arrived in Indonesia on a one-month tourist visa, it is usually extendable only for two weeks. An extension costs around 50,000 rp, and is obtained through any immigration office.

Onward Ticket

The best answer to the 'ticket out' requirement is to buy a return ticket to Indonesia, or include Indonesia as a leg on a through ticket. The main problem is for people with open-ended travel plans, for whom an onward ticket may not be an attractive option. One straightforward option is to buy a Medan-Penang ticket with Malaysian Airline System (MAS), which is reasonably cheap and able to be refunded if you don't use it. If coming from South-East Asia, Singapore-Jakarta return tickets are also quite cheap.

However, the ticket out requirement is (unofficially) less strictly enforced these days, and evidence of sufficient funds is usually acceptable in lieu. US$1000 seems to be the magic number. If you fly in to

Kupang from Darwin, or take the ferry to Batam from Singapore, it's unlikely that any great fuss will be made. In Kupang, they may ask to see a wad of travellers' cheques, but Batam is a breeze. Expect to flash your cash if arriving in Medan on the ferry from Penang. In the more 'normal' entry points, like Bali or Jakarta, they may still ask to see a ticket but most Bali visitors are on short-stay package trips, so you're unlikely to be troubled.

You may be very unlucky and be forced by Indonesian immigration to buy a ticket out on arrival, but the main problem can occur with airlines flying into Indonesia, which may insist that you have an onward ticket before allowing you to board the plane.

EMBASSIES
Indonesian Embassies Abroad

Australia
> Embassy, 8 Darwin Ave, Yarralumla, ACT 2600 (☎ (06) 2733222)
> Consulate-General, 236-238 Marcubra Rd, Sydney, NSW 2035 (☎ (02) 3449933)
> Consulate, 18 Harry Chan Ave, Darwin, NT (☎ (089) 410048)
> Consulate, 72 Queens Rd, Melbourne, Vic (☎ (03) 5252755)
> Consulate, Judd St, South Perth, WA 6151, (☎ (09) 3671178)

Belgium
> Avenue de Turvueren 294, 1150 Brussels, Belgium (☎ (02) 7715060)

Brunei
> KG Sungai Hanching Baru, Simpang 528, Lot 4494, Jalan Muara, Bandar Seri Begawan (☎ 330180)

Canada
> 287 Maclaren St, Ottawa, Ontario K2P OL9 (☎ (613) 236 7403-5)
> Consulates in Vancouver and Toronto

Denmark
> Orehoj Alle 12900, Hellerup, Copenhagen (☎ 624422)

France
> 47-49 Rue Cortambert 75116, Paris (☎ (1) 45030760)
> Consulate in Marseille

Germany
> 2 Bernakasteler Strasse, 5300 Bonn 2 (☎ (228) 382990)
> Consular offices in Berlin, Bremen, Dusseldorf, Hamburg, Hannover, Kiel, Munich and Stuttgart

India
    50-A Chanakyapuri, New Delhi (☎ 602348)
Italy
    53 Via Campania, Rome 00187 (☎ 4825951)
Japan
    9-2 Higashi Gotanda 5 Chome, Shinagawa-ku, Tokyo (☎ (03) 34414201)
Luxembourg
    Ave Guillaume 62, L-1650 Luxembourg (☎ 455858)
Malaysia
    Embassy, 233 Jalan Tun Razak, Kuala Lumpur (☎ (03) 9842011)
    Consulates: 467 Jalan Burma, Penang (☎ 04-374686); 5A Pisang Rd, Kuching, Sarawak (☎ 082-241734); Jalan Karamunsing, Kota Kinabalu, Sabah (☎ 088-219578); Jalan Apas, Tawau, Sabah (☎ 089-765930)
Netherlands
    8 Tobias Asserlaan, 2517 KC Den Haag (☎ (070) 3108100)
New Zealand
    70 Glen Rd, Kelburn, Wellington (☎ (04) 4758669)
Norway
    Inkonitogata 8, Oslo 2 (☎ (2) 441121)
Papua New Guinea
    1+2/140, Kiroki St, Sir John Guise Drive, Waigani, Port Moresby (☎ 253116, 253118, 253544)
Philippines
    185/187 Salcedo St, Legaspi Village, Makati, Manila (☎ (2) 855061 to 67)
    Consular office in Davao
Singapore
    7 Chatsworth Rd (☎ 7377422)
Spain
    13 Caile del Cinca, Madrid (☎ 4130294)
Sweden
    Strandvagen 47/V, 11456 Stockholm (☎ (08) 6635470)
Switzerland
    51 Elfenauweg, 3006 Bern (☎ 440983)
Thailand
    Embassy, 600-602 Petchburi Rd, Bangkok (☎ 252 3135 to 40)
UK
    Embassy, 38 Grosvenor Square, London W1X 9AD (☎ (0171) 4997661)
USA
    Embassy, 2020 Massachussetts Ave NW, Washington DC 20036 (☎ (202) 7755200)
    Consulates in Chicago, Honolulu, Houston, Los Angeles, New York and San Francisco

Foreign Embassies in Indonesia

Countries with diplomatic relations with Indonesia will generally have their consular offices in Jakarta, the capital. Australia, Denmark, Finland, France, Germany, Italy, Japan, the Netherlands, Norway, Sweden, Switzerland and the USA have representatives in Bali – see the Bali chapter for details. Some of the more useful foreign embassies in Jakarta include:

Australia
    Jalan Rasuna Said, Kav 15-16 (☎ 5227111)
Austria
    Jalan Diponegoro 44 (☎ 338090)
Belgium
    Wisma BCA, Jalan Jenderal Sudirman, Kav 22-23 (☎ 5710510)
Brunei
    Wisma BCA, Jalan Jenderal Sudirman (☎ 5712180)
Canada
    5th Floor, Wisma Metropolitan I, Jalan Jenderal Sudirman, Kav 29 (☎ 5250709)
Denmark
    Bina Mulia Building, 4th Floor, Jalan Rasuna Said, Kav 10 (☎ 5204350)
Finland
    Bina Mulya Building, 10th Floor, Jalan Rasuna Said, Kav 10 (☎ 5207408)
France
    Jalan Thamrin 20 (☎ 3142807)
Germany
    Jalan Raden Saleh 54-56 (☎ 3849547)
India
    Jalan Rasuna Said 51, Kuningan (☎ 5204152)
Italy
    Jalan Diponegoro 45 (☎ 337445)
Japan
    Jalan Thamrin 24 (☎ 324308)
Malaysia
    Jalan Rasuna Said Kav X/6/1-3 (☎ 5224947)
Myanmar (Burma)
    Jalan H Augus Salim 109 (☎ 3140440)
Netherlands
    Jalan Rasuna Said, Kav S-3, Kuningan (☎ 511515)
New Zealand
    Jalan Diponegoro 41 (☎ 330680)
Norway
    Bina Mulia Building, 4th Floor, Jalan Rasuna Said, Kav 10 (☎ 5251990)
Pakistan
    Jalan Teuku Umar 50 (☎ 3144009)
Papua New Guinea
    6th Floor, Panin Bank Centre, Jalan Jenderal Sudirman 1 (☎ 7251218)
Philippines
    Jalan Imam Bonjol 6-8 (☎ 3100345)

Poland
    Jalan Diponegoro 65 (☎ 3140509)
Russia
    Jalan Thamrin 13 (☎ 327007)
Singapore
    Jalan Rasuna Said, Block X, Kav 2 No 4
    (☎ 5201489)
South Korea
    Jalan Jenderal Gatot Subroto 57 (☎ 5201915)
Spain
    Jalan Agus Salim 61 (☎ 331414)
Sri Lanka
    Jalan Diponegoro 70 (☎ 3161886)
Sweden
    Bina Mulia Building, Jalan Rasuna Said, Kav 10
    (☎ 5201551)
Switzerland
    Jalan Rasuna Said, B-1, Kav X-3 (☎ 516061)
Taiwan
    Chinese Chamber of Commerce to Jakarta, Jalan
    Banyumas 4, (☎ 351212)
Thailand
    Jalan Imam Bonjol 74 (☎ 3904055)
UK
    Jalan Thamrin 75 (☎ 330904)
USA
    Jalan Merdeka Selatan 5 (☎ 360360)
Vietnam
    Jalan Teuku Umar 25 (☎ 3100357)

DOCUMENTS

A passport is essential and, if yours is within
a few months of expiration, you should get a
new one now – many countries will not issue
a visa if your passport has less than six
months of validity remaining. Also, be sure
it has plenty of space for visas and entry and
exit stamps.

Losing your passport is very bad news –
getting a new one means a trip to your
embassy or consulate and usually a long wait
while they send faxes or telexes (at your
expense) to confirm that you exist. If you're
going to be spending a long time in Indonesia, many embassies will allow you to
register your passport, which makes replacement easier. Registered or not, it helps if you
have a separate record of passport number,
issue date, and a photocopy of your old passport or birth certificate. While you're
compiling that info add the serial numbers of
your travellers' cheques, details of health
insurance and US$200 or so as emergency
cash – and keep all that material totally sep-

arate from your passport, cheques and other
cash.

If you plan to be driving abroad get an
International Driving Permit from your local
automobile association. They are valid for
one year only.

A Hostelling International (HI) card is of
very limited use in Indonesia, but there are a
few hostels which will recognise it and give
a slight discount.

If you plan to pick up some cash by
working, photocopies of university diplomas,
transcripts and letters of recommendation
could prove helpful. If you're travelling with
your spouse, a photocopy of your marriage
licence just might come in handy should you
become involved with the law, hospitals or
other bureaucratic authorities. Useful
(though not essential) is an International
Health Certificate – see the Health section
later in this chapter for more details.

The International Student Identity Card
(ISIC) can perform all sorts of miracles, such
as getting you a discount on some international and domestic flights, as well as
discounts at a few museums. Small wonder
there is a worldwide trade in fake cards, but
the authorities have tightened up on the
abuse of student cards in several ways. You
may be required to provide additional proof
of student status – such as 'student' in your
passport, or a letter from your university or
college stating that you are a student. In
additional, there are now maximum age
limits (usually 26) for some concessions, and
the fake-card dealers have been clamped
down on. Nevertheless, fake cards are still
widely available and useable, but some are
of quite poor quality.

Remember that a student is a very respectable thing to be, and if your passport has a
blank space for occupation you are much
better off having 'student' printed there than
something nasty like 'journalist' or 'photographer'.

CUSTOMS

Customs allow you to bring in a maximum
of two litres of alcoholic beverages, 200
cigarettes or 50 cigars or 100 grams of

tobacco, and a 'reasonable' amount of perfume per adult. Bringing narcotics, arms and ammunition, cordless telephones, TV sets, radio receivers, pornography, fresh fruit, printed matter in Chinese characters and Chinese medicines into the country is prohibited. The rules state that 'film, pre-recorded video tape, video laser disc, records, computer software must be screened by the Censor Board', presumably to control pornography. You are permitted to bring in one radio or cassette recorder as long as you take it out on departure. Officially, your personal goods are not supposed to have a value exceeding US$250, but in effect customs officials rarely worry about how much gear tourists bring into the country – at least if you have a Western face. Personal effects are not a problem.

MONEY

Try and bring as much money as possible, preferably in relatively safe travellers' cheques issued by a major bank. Also bring at least a few hundred US dollars in cash – there are a few odd towns where banks do not accept travellers' cheques.

US dollars are the most widely accepted foreign currency. If you intend travelling extensively around Indonesia then bring US dollars – either in cash or travellers' cheques from a major US company such as American Express (the most widely accepted), Citicorp or Bank of America – or you'll be sorry. In big cities like Jakarta and in major tourist areas such as Bali, it's also easy to change Australian dollars and major European currencies such as Deutschmarks, Netherlands guilders, pounds sterling, French or Swiss francs. Slightly more obscure currencies such as Canadian dollars can be difficult to change outside of the main tourist areas. If you bring other than US dollars, be prepared to put in more legwork – first to find a bank that will accept them and secondly to find one that gives a good rate.

Rates vary from bank to bank, and from town to town, so it pays to shop around. The rate for US dollars rarely varies by more than 5% but other currencies can vary by up to

15%. Banks sometimes give a slightly better rate for travellers' cheques but overall you usually get a slightly better rate on cash. Banks may charge a transaction fee (ask first), and a 500 rp 'stamp duty' (tax) is payable if changing more than 100,000 rp, but some banks absorb this fee.

Many banks handle foreign exchange, but some of the most common ones are Bank Central Asia, Bank Rakyat Indonesia, Bank Dagang Negara, Bank Expor Impor and Bank Negara Indonesia. Bank Niaga is one that likes to charge fees, Lippobank and Bank Bali are efficient but rates are not always good. Overall, Bank Central Asia is one of the best. They usually give good rates, accept most currencies and brands of travellers' cheques without fuss, and give cash advances on credit cards, but are only found in large regional cities outside Java, Sumatra and Bali. Try Bank Expor Impor in the eastern islands.

The best rates of exchange are found in Jakarta and Bali. Touristy places have lots of moneychangers as well as the banks, but their exchange rates are usually lower than the banks, except in Bali where moneychangers offer some of the best rates in Indonesia.

If you are travelling away from the major cities and tourist areas, change enough money to tide you over until you reach another major centre. For really remote places, carry stacks of rupiah because there won't be anywhere to change foreign cash or cheques. Places where you can change cash and travellers' cheques are noted in the relevant sections.

There are other problems to consider; it's often difficult to change big notes – breaking even a 10,000 rp note in a warung can be a major hassle and out in the villages it's damn near impossible.

Currency

The unit of currency in Indonesia is the rupiah (rp). Coins of 25, 50, 100 and 500 rp are in circulation, both the old silver-coloured coins and the new bronze-coloured coins. The five and 10 rp coins have vanished, as has the new 1000 rp coin, and the 25 rp coin is going the same way. Notes come in 100, 500, 1000, 5000, 10,000, 20,000 and 50,000 rp denominations.

There is no restriction on the import or export of foreign currencies in cash, travellers' cheques or any other form, but you're not allowed to take in or take out more than 50,000 rp.

Exchange Rates

Australia	A$1	=	1675 rp
France	FF1	=	423 rp
Germany	DM1	=	1465 rp
Japan	Y100	=	2235 rp
Malaysia	M$1	=	866 rp
Netherlands	G1	=	1308 rp
Singapore	S$1	=	1530 rp
Switzerland	SFr1	=	1744 rp
United Kingdom	UK£1	=	3526 rp
USA	US$1	=	2216 rp

The rupiah has a floating rate, and in recent years it has tended to fall by about 4% a year against the US dollar.

Credit Cards

If you have a credit card, don't leave home without it. If you are travelling on a low budget, credit cards are of limited use for day-to-day travel expenses in Indonesia as only expensive hotels, restaurants and shops accept them, but they are very useful for major purchases like airline tickets though smaller offices in the back blocks may not accept credit cards.

Another major advantage is that you can draw cash over the counter at selected banks. Credit cards can be a convenient way to carry your money. You don't have money tied up in travellers' cheques in a currency that is diving, you don't pay commission charges and the interbank exchange rates are often better than those offered by local banks for cash or travellers' cheques. The disadvantages are that interest is charged unless your account is always in the black, and not all banks will give cash advances on a credit card. You can always find a bank that will accept Visa or MasterCard in the major

centrés on Java and Bali, and in the big regional cities like Medan or Ujung Pandang, but it can be difficult outside major cities and impossible in remote areas. Carry cash or travellers' cheques as a back up. An American Express card is less widely accepted; cash can be obtained at Amex agents, usually PT Pacto, in the major cities.

Indonesian banks don't usually charge transaction fees for cash advances on credit cards, but always ask first. Also check with your home bank to make sure they don't charge transaction fees.

Giro

Dutch travellers with a Dutch post office account can conveniently obtain cash from Indonesian post offices. These girobetaalkaarten are useful in the many Indonesian towns where there is no bank.

Costs

How much it will cost to travel in Indonesia is largely up to the individual and depends on what degree of comfort you desire or what degree of discomfort you're prepared to put up with. It also depends on how much travelling you do. But most importantly in Indonesia it's where you go that makes or breaks the budget – some parts of the country cost *much* more to travel through than others.

If you follow the well-beaten tourist track through Bali, Java and Sumatra, you'll find Indonesia is one of the cheapest places in South-East Asia (exceptions like Jakarta apart) in which to travel. Travellers' centres like Bali, Yogyakarta and Lake Toba are excellent value for food and accommodation, while Nusa Tenggara is marginally more expensive than Bali but cheap by most standards.

On the other hand, in the outer provinces, like Kalimantan, Maluku or Irian Jaya, cheap hotels are not as easy to find and you'll pay a lot more. Food prices don't vary as much as room prices, though food quality deteriorates in eastern Indonesia.

Transport expenses also increase once you get into the outer provinces. On Bali, Java, Sumatra and Nusa Tenggara there's very little need to take to the air, while in the interior of Irian Jaya you have no choice but to fly. In the outer islands like Maluku, you really can't rely on ships – there may be only one ship every week or two between any two islands. If you're not prepared to fly you'll spend a good deal of your 60-day tourist pass just waiting around in port towns.

If you confine yourself to Sumatra, Java, Bali and Nusa Tenggara, rock-bottom budget travel works out to around US$10 per day, not including what you spent to reach Indonesia in the first place. Hotels and especially transport costs are a lot higher if you're heading towards Maluku and Irian Jaya. Count on more like US$50 a day if you need such luxuries as air-conditioning and tour guides, or want to buy woodcarvings, batik paintings and other souvenirs. You should keep in mind that in places like Kuta, where living expenses are low, there are more things to buy: massages, admission charges to discos, copious quantities of alcohol to consume, and tours and dance performances in abundance. Before you go out of your way to set new records for austerity, you should remember that travelling is not meant to be some sort of endurance test. If you want to find out how long you can stay away and how little money you can spend doing it, go ahead, but being in a permanent state of discomfort is not going to earn you any credit in heaven.

Tipping

Tipping is not a normal practice in Indonesia so please don't try to make it one. Jakarta taxi drivers, however, expect (demand?) a tip – the fare is usually rounded up to the next 500 rp. Hotel porters expect a few hundred rupiah per bag.

Bargaining

Many everyday purchases in Indonesia require bargaining. This applies particularly to handcrafts, clothes and artwork but can also apply to almost anything you buy in a shop. Restaurant meals, transport and, often, accommodation are generally fixed in price – restaurants usually have their menus and

Market scene

prices posted up on the wall and hotels usually have a price list. Sometimes when supply exceeds demand hotels may be willing to bend their prices rather than see you go next door. Though transport prices are fixed, bemos throughout Indonesia have a well-earned reputation for charging Westerners whatever they're willing to pay – or even more than they're willing to pay!

Your first step should be to establish a starting price. It's usually easiest to ask them their price rather than make an initial offer, unless you know very clearly what you're willing to pay. As a rule of thumb your starting price could be anything from a third to two-thirds of the asking price – assuming that the asking price is not completely crazy. Then with offer and counter-offer you move closer to an acceptable price. Don't show too much interest when bargaining, and if you can't get an acceptable price walk away. You will often be called back and offered a lower price.

A few rules apply to good bargaining. First of all it's not a question of life or death, where every rupiah you chisel away makes a difference. Don't pass up something you really want that's expensive or unobtainable at home because the seller won't come down a few hundred rupiah more – it is nothing compared with the hundreds of dollars you spent on the airfare! Secondly, when your offer is accepted you have to buy it – don't then decide you don't want it after all. Thirdly, while bargaining may seem to have a competitive element in it, it's a mean victory knocking a poor becak driver down from 500 to 400 rp for a ride.

Bargaining is sometimes fun – and often not. A lot depends on whether you and the vendor are smiling or yelling at each other. Sometimes it seems as if people don't want your money if they can't overcharge you. Sometimes they will ask ludicrous prices and will get very upset if you offer a ridiculously low price back, even if you mean it as a joke. This also works in the other direction; there is a nauseating category of Westerner on the Asian trail who will launch into lengthy bitch sessions about being overcharged five cents for an orange.

Ask Indonesian friends or hotel staff for information about correct prices. If you don't know what the right price for transport is you might try asking another passenger what the regular price *(harga biasa)* is. Then you offer the correct fare. There's not much point doing this when you're buying something in a shop or at a market – onlookers naturally side with their own people.

Don't get hassled by bargaining and don't go around feeling that you're being ripped off all the time – too many people do. It is too easy to become obsessed with getting the 'local' price. Even locals don't always get the local price – Indonesian visitors to Bali will be overcharged on the bemos just like Westerners. In Indonesia, if you are rich it is expected that you pay more, and *all* Westerners are rich when compared to the grinding poverty of most Indonesians. Above all, keep things in perspective. The 500 rp you may overpay for a becak ride wouldn't buy a newspaper at home, but it is a meal for a poor becak driver.

WHEN TO GO
The dry season from May to October is the best time to visit much of Indonesia, but there are also distinct tourist seasons when prices rise, and accommodation and transport, particularly air travel, can be fully booked in some places.

Bali is Australia's favourite Asian getaway and everyone is duty-bound to make the pilgrimage eventually. The Christmas holiday period until the end of January brings a wave of migratory Australians, as do the shorter school breaks during the year. An even bigger tourist wave during the European summer holidays bring crowds of Germans, Dutch, French etc, in July and August to Bali, Java, Sumatra and Sulawesi, the big European destinations. The main Indonesian holiday periods are the end of Ramadan, when some resorts are packed to overflowing and prices skyrocket, Christmas and the end of the school year from mid-June to mid-July when graduating high school students take off by the bus load to tourist attractions, mainly in Java and Bali.

So that leaves May/June and September/October as the pick of the months to visit Indonesia, though even during the peak tourist months you can always find a place away from the crowds and travel in the wet season is not usually a major problem.

WHAT TO BRING
Bring as little as possible. It is better to buy something you've left behind than to have to throw things away because you've got too much to carry. Except in the very remote areas, you can buy almost anything you can get at home.

Before deciding what to bring, decide what you're going to carry it in. For budget travellers the backpack is still the best single piece of luggage. Travel-packs, which can be used as either a backpack or a carry bag, are a good all-round option. They zip right to the bottom, allowing you easy access to your gear, and can usually be locked, providing difficult access for others. If you will be doing a lot of hiking and carrying all your gear with you on the trail, then take a properly designed hiking pack. Adding some thief-deterrent by sewing on a few tabs so you can shut your pack with a padlock is a good idea. A small day pack is also very useful. Whatever you bring, try and make it small; in some parts of Indonesia bemos are packed to the hilt with passengers and there's next to no space left over to stow baggage.

Temperatures are uniformly tropical year-round in Indonesia so short-sleeved shirts and T-shirts are the order of the day. Bring at least one long-sleeved shirt for the cool evenings. A few places in Indonesia get bloody cold at night, eg the Baliem Valley in Irian Jaya, Kintamani in Bali and the Dieng Plateau in Java. You don't need Antarctic survival gear, but long jeans, shoes and possibly a jacket are necessary. Clothing is quite cheap in Indonesia and you can always buy more, though it can be hard to find clothes and shoes in sizes to fit Western frames.

Modesty prevails. If you must wear shorts, they should be the loose-fitting type which come down almost to the knees, but shorts are considered very low class in Indonesia and only for the beach. Higher dress standards apply particularly whenever you're visiting a government office; have something suitable for more formal occasions.

Dark-coloured clothes hide the dirt better. Artificial fibres like rayon and nylon are too hot and sticky in this climate; drip-dry cotton or silk are best. You need clothes which will dry fairly quickly in the humidity – thicker jeans are a problem in this regard. You'll need some heavy clothing if you travel by motorcycle.

A hat and sunglasses are essential, and don't forget sunscreen (UV) lotion. A water bottle is a good idea but you can easily buy water in plastic throwaway bottles.

A sarong is an all-purpose Indonesian marvel. Besides wearing it, a sarong can serve as an impromptu blanket during cold evenings; or lie on it on a white-sand beach; wrap it round your head to counter the pounding sun; use it as a top sheet or, alternatively, as a barrier between yourself and an unhealthy-looking mattress in an unhealthy-looking hotel; pin it up over the window of your hotel room to block the outside lights that burn fiercely all night long; and even use it as a towel – if it still seems clean enough.

A sleeping bag is really only useful if you intend doing a lot of high-altitude camping.

Toiletries like soap, shampoo, conditioner, toothpaste and toilet paper are all readily available in Indonesia. Dental floss and shaving cream are hard to find, however, and tampons can be found with some difficulty.

Stock up on some passport or visa photos – these are readily obtained at photographic shops in Indonesia but you can never find these shops when you need them. A couple of places in Indonesia require permits to visit (like the interior of Irian Jaya) and photos are needed.

The following is a checklist of things you might consider packing, but don't feel obligated to bring everything on this list:

Passport, money, address book, namecards, visa & passport photos, Swiss army knife, electric immersion coil (for making hot water), cup, padlock, camera & accessories, sunglasses, alarm clock, leakproof water bottle, flashlight with batteries, comb, compass, daypack, long pants, short pants, long shirt, T-shirt, nylon jacket, sweater, raincover for backpack, rainsuit or poncho, razor, razor blades, shaving cream, sewing kit, spoon, sunhat, sunscreen, toilet paper, tampons, toothbrush, toothpaste, dental floss, deodorant, shampoo, underwear, socks, thongs, nail clipper, tweezers, mosquito repellent, vitamins, Panadol (Tylenol), laxative, Lomotil, birth control (including condoms) and any special medications you use.

A final thought: airlines do lose bags from time to time – you've got a much better chance of not losing your bag if it is tagged with your name and address *inside* as well as outside. Other tags can always fall off or be removed.

TOURIST OFFICES
Local Tourist Offices
Unlike many other Asian countries, Indonesia has neither an excellent tourist information service pumping out useful brochures, nor well-equipped offices with all the facts at their fingertips.

The Indonesian national tourist organisation, the Directorate General of Tourism (which has its base in Jakarta) maintains tourist offices called Kanwil Pariwisata in each province, but these are not the places to go for information. Each province has a tourist office called DIPARDA, usually located in the capital or major cities. In addition many kabupaten (districts) have their own tourist departments and city governments may have their own tourist offices. The sign on the building is usually written only in Indonesian. Look for *dinas pariwisata* (tourist office).

The usefulness of the tourist offices varies greatly from place to place. This happens in Java, where the city tourist offices in Jakarta, Yogya and Solo attract lots of tourists and provide excellent maps and information about the city and its immediate vicinity, while offices in the less-visited areas may have nothing at all – they'll always try to help, but it's pretty hopeless if they don't speak English and you don't speak Indonesian. For more details of local offices read the information sections listed under the main cities. Literature is sometimes not displayed so ask to see what they've got. Sometimes their stocks are severely limited and they can't give anything away. Useful publications are the *Tourist Map of Indonesia* and the *Calendar of Events* for the whole country.

Representatives Abroad

There are a number of Indonesian Tourist Promotion Offices (ITPO) abroad where you can get some brochures and information about Indonesia. The ITPO headquarters is at the Directorate General of Tourism (☎ 3101146), Jalan Kramat Raya 81, PO Box 409, Jakarta. There are also offices in Frankfurt, Los Angeles, Singapore, Sydney and Tokyo. Overseas, Garuda Airlines offices are also worth trying for information.

Australia
   Level 10, 5 Elizabeth St, Sydney, NSW 2000 (☎ (02) 233 3630)
Germany
   Wiessenhuttenstrasse 17 D.6000, Frankfurt am Main 1 (☎ (069) 233677)
Japan
   2nd Floor, Sankaido Building, 1-9-13 Akasaka, Minatoku, Tokyo 107 (☎ (03) 3585-3588)
Singapore
   10 Collyer Quay, Ocean Building, Singapore 0104 (☎ 5342837)
USA
   3457 Wilshire Blvd, Los Angeles, CA 90010 (☎ (213) 3872078)

USEFUL ORGANISATIONS

When it comes to useful organisations, many travellers think first of their nation's embassy. In fact, embassies often prove to be a disappointment. If you lose your passport your embassy can issue a new one, and if you die they'll probably pass the message on to your next of kin eventually, but if you've got malaria or all your money gets stolen, it's likely you'll be left twisting in the wind. Still, you've nothing to lose by giving them a call – there are a few embassy staff who actually take their job seriously.

Tim Sar (☎ 5501111) in Jakarta is the search and rescue organisation. In other cities, Tim Sar is listed on the first page of the telephone book, often just with the heading 'SAR'.

The Summer Institute of Linguistics (or Bible Translators) is an international missionary organisation with branches in 56 countries. Whether or not you are interested in their religious activities, they do linguistics courses and operate medical clinics around Indonesia. They also dispense vaccinations and medical advice, and can keep you informed of the latest epidemics ravaging the country. You can ring them in Jakarta (☎ (21) 330710) or write to PO Box 373 KBY, JKSMG, Jakarta 12001. Their head office is in Huntington Beach, California, USA.

BUSINESS HOURS & HOLIDAYS

Government offices are variable (sometimes very variable) but are generally open Monday to Thursday from 8 am to 2 pm, Friday until 11 am, and Saturday until 1 pm. Go early in the morning if you want to get anything done. Most post offices have similar opening hours, but central post offices in the large cities often have extended hours and open on Sunday for basic postal services. The main Telkom offices are open 24 hours for phone calls, while private telephone agencies are usually open until midnight. Some of the better tourist offices are open beyond normal government office hours and sometimes on Sunday.

Private business offices have staggered

hours: Monday to Friday from 8 am to 4 pm or 9 am to 5 pm, with a lunch break in the middle of the day. Offices are also open on Saturday morning until about noon.

Banks are open Monday to Friday, usually from 8 am to 2 pm, and on Saturday usually until 11 am. Bank branches in hotels stay open longer, and moneychangers in places like Kuta Beach stay open until the evening.

Shops tend to open around 8 am and stay open until around 9 pm. Sunday is a public holiday but some shops and many airline offices open for at least part of the day. In the big cities, shopping complexes, supermarkets and department stores stay open from 9 am to 9 pm every day and often on Sunday.

Public Holidays

Indonesia has many faiths and many festivals celebrated on different days throughout the country. Islam as the major religion provides many of the holidays. The most important time for Muslims is Ramadan (Bulan Puasa), the traditional Muslim month of daily fasting from sunrise to sunset. It falls in the ninth month of the Muslim calendar. It's a good time to avoid fervent Muslim areas of Indonesia – you get woken up in your losmen at 3 am in the morning to have a meal before the fasting period begins. Many restaurants shut down during the day, leaving you searching the backstreets for a restaurant that's open. Lebaran (Idul Fitri) marks the end of Ramadan, and is a noisy two-day public holiday when half the country seems to be on the move and hotels fill up and prices sky rocket.

National Holidays

All government offices and large businesses will be closed though many small businesses such as restaurants and shops will be open. For those festivals that do not follow the Western calendar and change each year, the likely month they will fall is given.

Day	Event	
1 January	New Year's Day	
February	Isra Mi'raj Nabi Mohammed	– celebrates the ascension of the Prophet
March-April	Good Friday	
	Lebaran (Idul Fitri)	– marks the end of Ramadan and is a noisy celebration at the end of a month of gastronomic austerity lasting for two days.
	Nyepi – Balinese New Year	– marks the end of the Hindu saka calendar. This one is not much fun – everything in Bali closes and everyone stays at home.
April-May	Waisak Day	– marks the Buddha's birth, enlightenment and death
	Idul Adha	– a Muslim festival commemorating Abraham's willingness to sacrifice his son, Isaac, it's celebrated with prayers and feasts. In many places, goats are slaughtered and the meat offered to the poor.
	Islamic New Year	
24 May	Ascension of Christ	
August	Maulud Nabi Muhammed	– the birthday of the Prophet Muhammed (Hari Natal)
17 August	Independence Day	– Soekarno proclaimed Indonesian independence (Hari Proklamasi Kemerdekaan) on 17 August 1945 in Jakarta. Throughout the country parades are held and special events organised, particularly in Jakarta.
25 December	Christmas Day	

CULTURAL EVENTS

With such a diversity of people in the archipelago there are many local holidays, festivals and cultural events. On Sumba, for example, mock battles and jousting matches harking back to the era of internecine warfare are held in February and March. The Balinese have the Galungan Festival, during which time all the gods, including the supreme deity Sanghyang Widi, come down to earth to join in. In Tanatoraja, in central Sulawesi, the end of the harvest season is the time for funeral and house-warming ceremonies. In Java, Bersih Desa takes place at the time of the rice harvest – houses and gardens are cleaned, village roads and paths repaired. This festival was once enacted to remove evil spirits from the village but it's now used to express gratitude to Dewi Sri, the rice goddess. Because most Indonesians are Muslims, many holidays and festivals are associated with the Islamic religion. Muslim festivals are affected by the lunar calendar

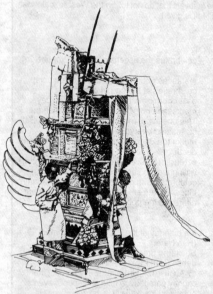

Cremation tower carrying the remains of a priest

and dates move back 10 or 11 days each year, so it's not easy to list what month they will fall in.

A regional *Calendar of Events* is generally available from the appropriate regional tourist office. It lists national holidays, festivals particular to that region and many of the music, dance and theatre performances held throughout the year. There's also an *Indonesia Calendar of Events* booklet which covers holidays and festivals throughout the archipelago. You should be able to pick up a copy from any of the overseas Indonesian Tourist Promotion Offices, or overseas Garuda Airlines offices.

POST & TELECOMMUNICATIONS
Post

Postal Rates International airmail rates for letters (up to 20g) are 1000 rp to Australia and the Pacific, 1400 rp to Europe and 1600 rp to the USA and Canada. Postcards cost a flat 600 rp. Parcels up to a maximum weight of 10 kg can be sent by sea mail, though rates are high. If you want to send more than 10 kg, break it up into several parcels.

Sending Mail Letters and small packets bound for overseas or domestic delivery may be registered for an extra fee at any post office branch. There are also two forms of express service available for mail within Indonesia: blue *kilat* envelopes are for regular airmail; yellow *kilat khusus* are for airmail express. These envelopes, plus aerogrammes, can be bought at all post offices.

Overseas parcels can be posted, insured and registered *(tercatat)*, from a main post office but staff may want to have a look at the contents first so there's not much point in sealing it up before you get there. If you're going to Singapore you'll find it considerably cheaper to post overseas packages and parcels from there than from Indonesia.

Most post offices are open government hours, ie Monday to Thursday from 8 am to 2 pm, Friday until 11 am, and Saturday until 1 pm. In the larger cities, the main post offices are open extended hours, including Sunday, for basic postal services (go during normal hours for poste restante). Warpostels and warparpostals are private postal agencies that are open extended hours and provide an efficient service for slightly higher rates. Outside big post offices in Java, parcel-wrapping services and stationery are available from street vendors.

Receiving Mail The postal service in Indonesia is generally pretty good and the poste restantes at Indonesian *kantor pos* – at least in major travellers' centres like Jakarta, Yogya, Bali, Medan and Lake Toba – are efficiently run. Expected mail always seems to arrive. Have your letters addressed to you with your surname in capitals and underlined, the poste restante, Kantor Pos, and city in question. 'Lost' letters may have been misfiled under Christian names so always check under both your names.

Telephone

Telkom, the government-run telecommunications company, has offices (kantor Telkom) in most cities and towns. They are usually open 24 hours, and often offer fax service as well as telephone and telegraph. These are the cheapest places to make phone calls, and the place to make collect calls. Private telecommunications agencies, usually called wartel, warpostal or warparpostel, may be marginally more expensive but are often more convenient. They are usually open from around 7 am until midnight, but sometimes 24 hours. As a rule, wartels don't offer a collect-call service, or in the rare cases that they do, a first-minute charge may apply.

Public pay phones can be found in some post offices, at the airports and in public phone booths in the major cities and towns. They are blue in colour and take 50 rp and 100 rp coins. When the phone begins to beep, feed in more coins or you'll be cut off. With private pay phones, normally you must dial the number first and drop the coin into the slot *after* the other party has answered – otherwise, you will be able to hear them but they won't be able to hear you!

Telephone cards (*kartu telepon*) can be used at the phones that accept them (*telepon*

kartu). A local call requires one unit, which works out to 82.50 rp. Telephone cards are sold in the following denominations: 20 units (1650 rp); 60 units (4950 rp); 80 units (6600 rp); 100 units (8250 rp); 280 units (23,100 rp); 400 units (33,000 rp); and 680 units (56,100 rp).

Domestic calls are charged according to a system of zones. For example, if you're ringing from Biak in Irian Jaya, Zones I, II and III include the local area around Biak plus Nabire and Manok; Zone IV is the rest of Irian Jaya plus Ambon and Ternate; and Zone V is Java, Sumatra, Sulawesi, Nusa Tenggara and Kalimantan. The rates per minute are: Zone I, 900 rp; Zone II, 1000 rp; Zone III, 1200 rp; Zone IV, 1500 rp; and Zone V, 2000 rp. There is a 50% discount on calls placed between 9 pm and 6 am.

There are two types of calls: normal *(biasa)* and immediate *(segera)*. The latter is a type of express call that gets you through faster than a normal call. Express calls cost twice as much as normal calls.

International direct dialling (IDD) is available to many countries – dial ☎ 001, then the country code, area code (minus the initial zero if it has one) and then the number you want to reach. Public phones rarely support this facility and you'll have to go to a Telkom office or wartel. The country code for dialling Indonesia is 62.

As with domestic calls, international calls are charged according to zones.

IDD Rates Rates for IDD telephone calls are:

Zone I:	Singapore, Malaysia and Brunei; 2600 rp per minute
Zone II:	Hong Kong, Thailand and the Philippines; 3900 rp per minute
Zone III:	Australia, New Zealand, Japan, South Korea, India and the USA; 4550 rp per minute
Zone IV:	Canada and the UK; 5200 rp per minute
Zone V:	Western Europe (minus the UK), Alaska, South America and Africa; 6180 rp per minute

For most countries, there is a 25% discount for IDD calls placed between midnight and

7 am. For a few countries, this discount is in effect from 9 pm until 6 am. Check with the phone company to see which night-time discount, if any, applies to the country you wish to call.

With operator assistance, you can reverse charges. Another way to reverse charges is to use Home Country Direct Dialling, available from special telephones in some Telkom offices, airports, luxury hotels etc. These phones can be used for placing collect calls only to specified countries. Just press the button for your country (Australia, the USA etc) and an operator from that country will come on the line.

Home Country Direct calls can also be made from phones where exchanges support the service by dialling ☎ 00 801 and then the country code. It usually isn't available from public telephones and is not available to all countries.

Some useful numbers include:

Directory assistance, local:	☎ 108
Directory assistance, long-distance:	☎ 106
Operator assistance, domestic:	☎ 100
Operator assistance, international:	☎ 101

Fax, Telex & Telegraph

You can send messages by fax, telex and telegraph from the government-run telecommunications office in most cities and many mid-sized towns, or from wartels. Faxes cost 4400 to 6600 rp per page for ASEAN countries, 7700 rp to Australia, New Zealand, Japan, South Korea, India and the USA; 8800 rp per page to Canada and 10,450 rp per page to the rest of Europe, Africa and South America.

TIME

There are three time zones in Indonesia. Sumatra, Java, and West and Central Kalimantan are on Western Indonesian Time, which is seven hours ahead of GMT, and one hour ahead of Singapore. Bali, Nusa Tenggara, South and East Kalimantan, and Sulawesi are on Central Indonesian Time, which is eight hours ahead of GMT. Irian

Jaya and Maluku are on East Indonesian Time, which is nine hours ahead of GMT. In a country straddling the equator, there is of course no daylight-saving time.

Allowing for variations due to daylight-saving, when it is noon in Jakarta it is 1 pm in Ujung Pandang, 2 pm in Jayapura, 5 am in London, 3 pm in Melbourne or Sydney, 12 midnight in New York and 9 pm the previous day in San Francisco or Los Angeles. Because of a detour in the time zones, Singapore is one hour ahead of Sumatra and Java.

Strung out along the equator, Indonesian days and nights are approximately equal in length, and sunrises and sunsets occur very rapidly with almost no twilight. Sunrise is around 5.30 to 6 am and sunset is around 5.30 to 6 pm, varying slightly depending on distance from the equator.

ELECTRICITY

Electricity is almost always 220 V, 50 cycles AC, but a few rare places are still wired for 110 V – so check first before you plug in a foreign electrical appliance. Sockets are designed to accommodate two round prongs of the European variety. Recessed sockets are designed to take earth (ground) facilities, but wiring in many hotels and most appliances aren't earthed, so take care. Electricity is usually pretty reliable in cities, but occasional blackouts occur in rural areas. It's wise to keep a flashlight or candles handy for such occasions. Safe adaptors for foreign plugs are hard to find, so bring your own.

In some small towns, or even in parts of larger towns, electricity is still a fairly futuristic thing – you find the odd isolated hotel where lighting is provided with oil lamps. Even where there is electricity you're likely to find the lighting can be very dim. Electricity is expensive (for most Indonesians), so cheaper hotels have light bulbs of such low wattage that you can almost see the electricity crawling laboriously around the filaments. If you can't get by with just 25 watts then it might be worth carrying a more powerful light bulb with you.

Street lighting can also be a problem –

sometimes there's very little, sometimes none at all. Walking down dark, pot-holed streets in some Indonesian cities is like walking through a minefield. Falling into a sewage canal is a real drag, so be sure you bring a flashlight.

LAUNDRY

Virtually every hotel – from the smallest to the largest – has a laundry service, and in most places this is very inexpensive. About the only thing you need be concerned about is the weather – clothes are dried on the line, so a hot, sunny day is essential. Give staff your laundry in the morning – they like to wash clothes before 9 am so it has sufficient time to dry before sunset.

WEIGHTS & MEASURES

Indonesia has fully adopted the international metric system.

BOOKS

Indonesia is not a straightforward country. Its history, economics, politics and culture – and their bizarre interactions – are wide open to interpretation, and different writers come up with astoundingly different interpretations of events. If you want to read about Java or Bali you'll be suffocated beneath the literature – but trying to find out anything about the outer islands is like putting together bits and pieces of a jigsaw.

People & Society

Indonesians: Portraits from an Archipelago by Ian Charles Stewart is a photographic essay on Indonesian life and culture which took the Australian photographer/author three years to compile. It's a very large, expensive book but the photographs are excellent.

Robin Hanbury-Tenison's *A Pattern of Peoples* was based on his trip to Indonesia in 1973, visiting minority groups like the Danis of Irian Jaya and the Torajas of Sulawesi. It comments on the effects that tourism and other developments have had on what were, until recently, isolated peoples.

A compilation of some of the intriguing

religious, social and mystical customs of the diverse peoples of Indonesia is Lee Khoon Choy's *Indonesia: Between Myth & Reality*. It's a journalistic travelogue, derived from the author's short spells in the country as a journalist and politician and his stay as Singapore's Ambassador to Indonesia from 1970 to 1975.

The best account of the top echelons of the Indonesian government and military is Australian journalist David Jenkin's *Soeharto and his Generals: Indonesian Military Politics 1975-1983* (Monograph Series No 64, Cornell Modern Indonesia Project, South East Asia Program, Cornell University, 1984). Jenkins interviewed many of Indonesia's leading generals, including those both in and out of power. The final product is an intriguing and illuminating work.

Twilight in Jakarta by the Indonesian journalist Mochtar Lubis, is an outspoken condemnation of political corruption and one of the most vivid documentations of life in the capital at the beginning of the 1960s, particularly of Jakarta's lower depths – the prostitutes, becak drivers and rural immigrants. Lubis is well known for his forthright views and he was twice imprisoned during the Soekarno regime for his political convictions.

For a good general introduction to Indonesian culture, customs, language and food, designed for the expat or the traveller, *Culture Shock: Indonesia* by Cathie Draine and Barbara Hall is part of the well-known series.

Another excellent general guide to living in Indonesia is *Introducing Indonesia: A guide to Expatriate Living* by the American Women's Association of Indonesia.

Fiction

Pramoedya Ananta Toer, a Javanese author, has written four novels about life in colonial Indonesia. The first two – *This Earth of Mankind* and *Child of All Nations* – are available in Penguin paperback. Both novels were bestsellers in Indonesia but the Soeharto government banned them in 1981, claiming that, while they might be skilful accounts of the colonial era, they were also subtle Marxist parodies of President Soeharto's Indonesia. The author has spent more than 17 years in prison ever since he started writing: the Dutch jailed him during the independence struggle; he was briefly detained by the Army in the 1960s, as an anti-Soekarno move, and his history of the Chinese in Indonesia was banned; and in 1965 he was jailed by Soeharto's New Order government and exiled to Buru Island for 14 years.

Pramoedya now lives in Jakarta under house arrest. *The Fugitive* by Pramoedya is set in East Java in WW II. Pramoedya wrote the book while at Bucket Durra Prison, a forced labour camp, where he was imprisoned from 1947 to 1949 for his active role in the Indonesian revolution that followed the end of WW II. *House of Glass* by the same author is the final volume of a quartet of novels set in the Indonesia of Dutch colonialism.

Christopher Koch's *The Year of Living Dangerously* is an evocative reconstruction of life in Jakarta during the final chaotic months of the Soekarno period and a sympathetic portrayal of the Indonesians and their culture and society. The movie by Australian director Peter Weir packs a feel for the place that few other movies could ever hope to achieve.

Much of Joseph Conrad's *Victory* is set in Surabaya, in a hotel very reminiscent of the Hotel Majapahit (see under Surabaya in the Java chapter later in this book). Though not particularly evocative of Indonesia, it gives a wonderful account of the sea traders of the time.

History

A good general history that pieces together some of the jigsaw is *A History of Modern Indonesia* by M C Ricklefs, Professor of History at Monash University in Melbourne, Australia. It takes you through from 1300, and while it mainly concerns itself with Java and the Dutch conquest it also ties in what was happening in the outer islands.

Indonesia – an Alternative History by aca-

demics Malcolm Caldwell and Ernst Utrecht, is an interesting book. Utrecht was once a member of Indonesia's Supreme Advisory Council which Soekarno set up to advise him on government policy. In a blow-by-blow account of Dutch economic policy in Indonesia, they argue that it is the Dutch who are responsible for Indonesia's economic problems. They also criticise the Western attitude which sees Indonesia only as a cornerstone of defence against Communism and as a lucrative place of investment.

Australian journalist Bruce Grant's *Indonesia* gives background info about the country and takes you through the tumultuous Soekarno years. The book was first published in 1964, with later reprints taking in the events just after the attempted coup of 1965. His biography of the leader and translations of some of Soekarno's speeches make for some fascinating reading.

An interesting and very readable account of the Soeharto years is *Soeharto's Indonesia* by Australian journalist Hamish McDonald, who worked as a free-lance correspondent in Jakarta from 1975 to 1978.

One of the more evocative books on contemporary Indonesia is *The Indonesian Tragedy* by Australian journalist Brian May. Much of the book, as May himself says, 'is a tale of Western-aided despotism' that Indonesia has suffered under Soeharto's rule. It also gives a rather more sympathetic account of Soekarno than has generally been afforded.

Travel

If you think travel through the outer islands of Indonesia is time-consuming now, then just read Helen & Frank Schreider's *Drums of Tonkin* (published 1965) – they overcame the lack of transport by island hopping all the way from Java to Timor in a tiny amphibious jeep, defying landslides, oncoming monsoons, hostile (or just over-enthused?) indigenous inhabitants and the strange propensity Jakarta soldiers once had to shoot at vehicles making illegal turns.

Whilst the Schreiders took only their pet dog with them, zoologist-TV personality

David Attenborough left the UK with practically nothing and returned from the archipelago with an orang-utan, a couple of pythons, civets, parrots and assorted other birds and reptiles. The whole saga of the enterprise, eventually to be dignified by the title 'expedition', is recounted in his book *Zoo Quest for a Dragon*, published in 1957.

Gavin Young's *In Search of Conrad* is an interesting account of this British author's retracing of Conrad's journeys by boat around Sumatra, Java, Kalimantan, Bali and Sulawesi.

The Tropical Traveller by John Hatt (Pan Books, London) is a good practical introduction to travel in the tropics.

If you intend trekking, camping out or heading off to the great outdoors beyond everything, or are just interested in doing something different, get Christina Dodwell's *An Explorer's Handbook – Travel, Survival & Bush Cookery* (Hodder & Stoughton, London).

Other Lonely Planet guidebooks covering Indonesia are *South-East Asia* and *Bali & Lombok*.

Language

Bookshops in Indonesia stock plenty of cheap Bahasa Indonesia/English text books and dictionaries, but most are of poor quality.

A good introduction to Bahasa Indonesia is Lonely Planet's *Indonesia Phrasebook* by Paul Wood or the *Indonesian CD/Audio Pack*. They are structured to provide a good working knowledge of basic Indonesian with emphasis on the day-to-day vocabulary needed to travel around the country. John Barker's *Practical Indonesian* is another phrasebook emphasising travel vocabulary.

For something a little more advanced, *How to Master the Indonesian Language* by AM Almeister is widely available in Indonesia and cheap. This slim volume provides a good introduction to the language and introduces Indonesian grammar, but is a little old fashioned and not structured to get you up and using the language straight away.

For serious students, *Bahasa Indonesia: Langkah Baru – a New Approach*, Book I,

by Yohanni Johns is a standard text used in schools and universities around the world. Though not really designed for self study, if you master this one you will have a substantial vocabulary and a solid grounding in Indonesian grammar. It can be bought in Indonesia and overseas.

Cheap pocket dictionaries abound in Indonesian bookstores but are riddled with errors and omissions. The only really decent dictionaries are *An Indonesian-English Dictionary* and its companion volume *An English-Indonesian Dictionary* by John Echols and Hassan Shadily. Nothing else matches these comprehensive, scholarly dictionaries but they are expensive (especially outside Indonesia) and far too weighty to lug around. *Kamus Lengkap* by S Wojowasito and Tito Wasito is a complete Indonesian-English/English-Indonesian dictionary in one volume. Despite a number of odd and inaccurate translations, it is about the best comprehensive dictionary in a manageable (though still large) size for travelling. It is cheap in Indonesia.

One of the better pocket dictionaries is the small *MIP Concise Indonesian Dictionary*, but it is not available in Indonesia.

Bookshops

Books in English, usually only cheap novels, can be found in bookshops in the main cities, airport shops and in some of the large hotels. Good bookshops are hard to find, impossible in the outer islands and smaller cities. Bring your own as they're expensive and the supply and range are extremely limited. Jakarta has the best bookshops in the country. Well-touristed places like Ubud and Yogya have second-hand bookshops, and these are the best bet for books in other languages such as Dutch, French, German etc.

MAPS

The best series of maps and the most widely available, both within and outside Indonesia, is the Nelles maps. They cover all the major areas of Indonesia. Periplus also produce useful maps that include plans of the major cities.

Maps produced in Indonesia can be surprisingly poor. City maps, when you can get them, are usually good, but regional maps are often inaccurate and dated. P T Pembina publishes a useful map of all Indonesia and reasonable individual maps of Java, Sumatra, Kalimantan and Sulawesi.

The Directorate General of Tourism publishes a useful give-away information booklet, the *Indonesia Tourist Map*, which includes maps of Java, Bali, Sumatra and Sulawesi, and a good overall map of Indonesia. Maps of major Javanese, Sumatran and Balinese cities are easy enough to come by – ask at the tourist offices or try bookshops, airports and major hotels, particularly in Jakarta, Denpasar and Kuta.

In the outer islands the odd good map may pop up but quite often you'll be lucky to come across anything at all, or else only fairly simple maps. Hotels often have a good, detailed map of the town or city hanging on the wall of their foyer. The local police station should have a good map and will often allow foreigners to photocopy it.

Virtually every town and city has a *Kantor Pekerjaan Umum*, usually just known as *Kantor PU*. This office is responsible for mapping the city in question, and sometimes they have copies for sale. If not, they will probably allow you to make photocopies of their master map.

MEDIA

The news media is expected to – and does – practise self-censorship. 'Politeness' is the key word, and in typically indirect Javanese style, stories of corruption, wastage of funds and government ineptitude are frequently run, but care is always taken not to point the finger too closely. Most importantly, criticism of Soeharto and his immediate family is not tolerated.

Through the early '90s the press enjoyed greater liberalisation and became increasingly bold. New magazines like *Detik* and *Editor* exposed scandals and corruption and ran articles critical of the government. Government tolerance was seen as a step towards a more open and mature society, until June 1994, when the government banned *Detik*, *Editor* and the long-running and highly respected *Tempo* magazine. The move prompted widespread criticism and demonstrations in Jakarta, and the openness policy has remained clouded.

Newspapers & Magazines

Whenever you buy newspapers and magazines in Indonesia, take a close look at the date. It is not uncommon for vendors to try to sell old news from two or three weeks ago.

Domestic The English-language press is limited mostly to the *Jakarta Post*, published daily (except Sunday) and available around the country, though difficult to get outside Jakarta and the major tourist areas. While subject to the same 'self-censorship' as other Indonesian publications, it manages to tell you quite a lot about Indonesia – and the rest of the world – in a roundabout way.

The other English-language newspaper is the *Indonesian Observer* but its coverage and independence are a long way behind that of the *Jakarta Post*.

Of course, Indonesian-language newspapers are on sale throughout the country. Two of the leading newspapers are the Jakarta daily *Sinar Harapan* and the Catholic newspaper *Kompas. Suara Karya* is the mouthpiece of Golkar, the government political party.

Foreign For information on what's happening in Indonesia today (including Indonesian politics, history and culture) take out a subscription to *Inside Indonesia*, published in Australia at PO Box 190, Northcote, Vic 3070, Australia. Excellent articles cover everything from power plays within the army, to the environment, and it discusses issues not raised in the Indonesian media and rarely covered overseas.

The *International Herald-Tribune, Asian Wall Street Journal* and major Asian dailies are sold in Indonesia. Western magazines like *Time, Newsweek, The Economist* and the excellent Hong Kong-published *Far Eastern Economic Review* are available in Indonesia.

Radio & TV

Radio Republik Indonesia (RRI) is the national radio station, which broadcasts 24 hours in Indonesian from every provincial capital. Indonesia also has plenty of privately run stations.

Thanks to satellite broadcasting, TV can be received everywhere in Indonesia. You'll see plenty of satellite dish antennas around the country, aimed almost straight up, as broadcast satellites are put in geostationary orbit – they travel around the equator at the same speed the earth rotates at. You'll also see plenty of Indonesians in geostationary orbit around the TV set in any hotel – they are among the world's foremost TV addicts.

Televisi Republik Indonesia (TVRI) is the government-owned Indonesian-language TV station, which is broadcast in every province. It broadcasts on two channels, but the second channel is not available in more remote areas.

Private stations are Rajawali Citra Televisi Indonesia (RCTI) with many shows in English, SCTV (Surya Citra Televisi), Televisi Pendidikan Indonesia (TPI), a government-owned educational station and AN-TV (Andalas Telvisi).

Satellite dishes also pick up uncensored overseas stations transmitting in the region, which has worried some government sources and Islamic groups complaining about moral corruption. Other neighbouring governments such as Singapore have simply banned satellite receivers and are pursuing cable TV, a much more controllable medium.

Overseas TV can be seen at the large tourist hotels, and while many smaller hotels have satellite dishes, they are not usually interested in tuning them in to programmes in a foreign language they cannot understand. CNN, BBC, Television Australia and Malaysian TV can all be received, though the most popular in the foreign stakes seems to be French TV. Apart from soccer games, French TV occasionally shows kissing and even bare flesh.

FILM & PHOTOGRAPHY

Indonesia is an incredibly photogenic country and you can easily whip through large quantities of film. Colour print film is preferred to anything else, so slide film and black & white film are not as readily available. Nevertheless, in Jakarta, Bali and the major cities you can usually find most types of film, even Polaroid film, movie film and video tape. Fuji is by far the most widely available brand, for prints and slides, while Kodachrome is rarely seen and has to be sent overseas for developing. Film is cheap.

Developing and printing is quite good and much cheaper than in the West. You can get Ektachrome and Fujichrome slide film developed in two or three days and colour print film can be done same day through photographic shops in major Indonesian towns all across the archipelago. Many of these have machines which churn out prints in 45 minutes, and the quality is usually very good.

In the small towns and particularly in the outer islands or where few tourists go, many types of film aren't available at all. Turnover of stock is often slow, so it's best to check the expiry date of the film. Film manufacturers warn that films should be developed as quickly as possible once exposed – although in practice they seem to last for months without deterioration even in Asia's summer heat.

Camera batteries and other accessories are readily available from photographic shops in major cities.

Technical Problems

Shoot early or late as from 10 am to 1 or 2 pm the sun is uncomfortably hot and high overhead, and you're likely to get a bluish washed-out look to your pictures. A polarising filter helps reduce glare and darkens an otherwise washed-out sunlit sky. A lens hood will reduce your problems with reflections and direct sunlight on the lens. Beware of the sharp differences between sun and shade – if you can't get reasonably balanced overall light you may have to opt for exposing only one area or the other correctly. Or use a fill-in flash.

Those lush, green rice fields come up best

if backlit by the sun. For those sunset shots at Kuta, Kalibukbuk or Pontianak set your exposure on the sky without the sun making an appearance – then shoot at the sun. Photography from fast-moving trains and buses doesn't work well unless you use a fast shutter speed. Dust can be a problem – hazy days will make it difficult to get sharp shots.

People Photos

You get a fantastic run for your money in Indonesia – not only are there 180 million or so portraits to choose from but the variation in ethnic types is phenomenal.

Few people expect payment for their photos, the Baliem Valley in Irian Jaya being an odd exception. What Indonesians *will* go for is a copy of the photo – if you hang around Indonesia long enough you'll wind up with a pocketful of bits of paper with addresses of people to send their photos to.

There are three basic approaches to photographing people: one is to be polite, ask permission and pose the shot; another is the no-holds-barred and upset everyone approach; and the other is surreptitious, standing half a km away with a metre-long telescopic lens. Some Indonesians will shy away from having their photo taken and duck for cover; some are shy but only too pleased to be photographed; some are proud and ham it up for the camera; and others won't get out of the way of the bloody lens when you want them too!

Whatever you do, photograph with discretion and manners. Hardly surprisingly, many people don't like having a camera lens shoved down their throats – it's always polite to ask first and if they say no then don't. A gesture, a smile and a nod are all that is usually necessary. In some places you may come up against religious barriers to taking photographs – such as trying to photograph Muslim women in the more devoutly Islamic parts of the archipelago. The taboo might also apply to the minority groups. Don't take photographs at public bathing places – intruding with your camera is no different to sneaking up to someone's bathroom window and pointing your camera through. Remem-

ber, wherever you are in Indonesia, the people are *not* exotic birds of paradise and the village priest is *not* a photographic model. And finally, don't be surprised if Indonesian people turn the tables on you – they have become fond of sneaking up on Westerners and shooting a few exotic photos to show their friends!

Prohibited Subjects

Be careful of what you photograph in Indonesia – they're touchy about places of military importance and this can include airports, bridges, railway terminals and stations, seaports and any military installations or bases. Ask if in doubt.

HEALTH

Being a tropical country with a low level of sanitation and a high level of ignorance, Indonesia is a fairly easy place to get ill. The climate provides a good breeding ground for malarial mosquitoes, but the biggest hazards come from contaminated food and water. You should not worry excessively about all this. With some basic precautions and adequate information few travellers experience more than upset stomachs.

In most cases you can buy virtually any medicine across the counter in Indonesia without a prescription. If you need some special medication, take it with you. However, you shouldn't have any trouble finding common Western medicines in Indonesia, at least in big cities like Jakarta and Denpasar where there are lots of well-stocked pharmacies *(apotik)*. In rural areas, pharmacies are scarce, but grocery stores will gladly sell you all sorts of dangerous drugs, which are often long beyond their expiry dates. Many of the big tourist hotels also have drugstores.

In each apotik there is an English-language copy of the IIMS (Indonesian Index of Medical Specialities), a guide to pharmaceutical preparations available to doctors in Indonesia. It's updated three times a year and it lists drugs by brand name, generic name, manufacturer's name and therapeutic action. Drugs may not be of the same strength as in

Vital Signs
A normal body temperature is 98.6°F or 37°C; more than 2°C higher is a high fever. A normal adult pulse rate is 60 to 80 beats a minute (80 to 100 for children, 100 to 140 for babies). You should know how to take a temperature and a pulse rate. As a general rule the pulse increases by about 20 beats a minute for each °C rise in fever.

Respiration (breathing) rate is also an indicator of illness. Count the number of breaths per minute: between 12 and 20 is normal for adults and older children (up to 30 for younger children, 40 for babies). People with a high fever or serious respiratory illness (like pneumonia) breathe more quickly than normal. More than 40 shallow breaths a minute usually means pneumonia.

Many health problems can be avoided by taking care of yourself and dressing appropriately for the climate. Minimise insect bites by covering bare skin when insects are around or by using insect repellents. ■

other countries or may have deteriorated due to age or poor storage conditions.

As for medical treatment, Catholic or missionary hospitals or clinics are often pretty good, and in remote areas may be your only hope other than prayer beads and chanting. Missionary hospitals frequently have English-speaking staff. Back in the developed world, you can often locate a competent doctor (*dokter*) or a dentist (*dokter gigi*) and hospitals (*rumah sakit*) by asking at hotels or offices of foreign companies in places where large expatriate communities work. In the towns and cities there seems to be a fair supply of doctors and dentists to choose from. In the outback of places like Irian Jaya there are the clinics set up by the missionaries. There are also public hospitals in the cities and towns.

Hospitals are open during the day, but private clinics operate mostly in the evening from 6 pm. It's first come, first served, so go early and be prepared to wait. Medical costs are generally very cheap, but drugs are expensive.

Jakarta has the best medical facilities in the country. In south Jakarta, most expatriates use Pondok Indah (☎ 7500157), Jalan Metro Duta Kav UE, a perfectly modern hospital that rivals the best hospitals in the West, although it charges modern prices. Better known hospitals in central Jakarta (near Jalan Jaksa) are the Rumah Sakit Cipto Mangunkusumo (☎ 330808), Jalan Diponegoro 71, a government public hospital (reasonably priced but very crowded); and

St Carolus Hospital (☎ 4214426), Jalan Salemba Raya 41, a private Catholic hospital charging mid-range prices.

Also popular is Medical Scheme (☎ 515367, 5201034) in the Setiabudi Building, Jalan H Rasuna Said, Kuningan. It's a private practice but they deal with all emergencies, and vaccinations are given to non-members for a small fee. Doctors speak English and Dutch.

For serious illnesses, Singapore has the best medical facilities in South-East Asia and is only a short flight away. Alternatively, Darwin is close for eastern Indonesia.

Travel Health Guides
There are a number of books on travel health:

Staying Healthy in Asia, Africa & Latin America, Moon Publications. Probably the best all-round guide to carry, as it's compact but very detailed and well organised.
Travellers' Health, Dr Richard Dawood, Oxford University Press. Comprehensive, easy to read, authoritative and also highly recommended, although it's rather large to lug around.
Where There is No Doctor, David Werner, Hesperian Foundation. A very detailed guide intended for someone, like a Peace Corps worker, going to work in an undeveloped country, rather than for the average traveller.

Predeparture Preparations
Health Insurance A travel insurance policy to cover theft, loss and medical problems is a wise idea. There are a wide variety of policies and your travel agent will have recommendations. Some policies offer lower

and higher medical expenses options, and a mid-range one is usually recommended for Asia where high medical costs are not so high. Check the small print:

- Some policies specifically exclude 'dangerous activities' which can include scuba diving, even trekking and motorcycling (no doubt because of the legendary accident rate of tourists in Bali). A motorcycle licence acquired in Bali may not be valid under your policy. If such activities are on your agenda you don't want that sort of policy.
- You may prefer a policy which pays doctors or hospitals direct rather than you having to pay on the spot and claim later. If you have to claim later make sure you keep all documentation. Some policies ask you to call back (reverse charges) to a centre in your home country where an immediate assessment of your problem is made.
- Check if the policy covers ambulances or an emergency flight home. If you have to stretch out you will need two seats and somebody has to pay for them!

Medical Kit A small, straightforward medical kit is a wise thing to carry. A possible kit list includes:

- Aspirin or Panadol – for pain or fever.
- Antihistamine (such as Benadryl) – useful as a decongestant for colds, allergies, to ease the itch from insect bites or stings or to help prevent motion sickness. Antihistamines may cause sedation and interact with alcohol so be careful.
- Antibiotics – useful if you're travelling well off the beaten track, but they must be prescribed and you should carry the prescription with you. Some individuals are allergic to commonly prescribed antibiotics such as penicillin or sulfa drugs. It would be sensible to always carry this information when travelling.
- Kaolin preparation (Pepto-Bismol), Imodium or Lomotil – for stomach upsets.
- Rehydration mixture – for treatment of severe diarrhoea. This is particularly important if travelling with children, but is recommended for everyone.
- Antiseptic such as Betadine, which comes as impregnated swabs or ointment, and an antibiotic powder or similar 'dry' spray – for cuts and grazes.
- Calamine lotion – to ease irritation from bites or stings.
- Bandages and Band-aids – for minor injuries.
- Scissors, tweezers and a thermometer (note that mercury thermometers are prohibited by airlines).

- Insect repellent, sunscreen, suntan lotion, chapstick and water purification tablets.
- A couple of syringes, in case you need injections. Indonesian medical workers are not always scrupulous about using new equipment. Ask your doctor for a note explaining why they have been prescribed.

Health Preparations Make sure you're healthy before you start travelling. If you are embarking on a long trip make sure your teeth are OK; there are lots of places where a visit to the dentist would be the last thing you'd want to do. If you wear glasses take a spare pair and your prescription. Losing your glasses can be a real problem, although in many places you can get new spectacles made up quickly, cheaply and competently.

If you require a particular medication take an adequate supply, as it may not be available locally. Take the prescription or, better still, part of the packaging showing the generic rather than the brand name (which may not be locally available), as it will make getting replacements easier. It's a wise idea to have a legible prescription with you to show you legally use the medication – it's surprising how often over-the-counter drugs from one place are illegal without a prescription or even banned in another.

Immunisations Indonesia requires no vaccinations to enter the country, apart from yellow fever if you are arriving from a yellow fever infected area within six days. While not compulsory, other vaccinations are highly recommended. Record vaccinations on an International Health Certificate, which is available from your physician or government health department. While you may not ever be required to show it, a record of your vaccinations is useful for future travels, getting boosters etc.

Plan ahead for getting your vaccinations: some require an initial shot followed by a booster, while some vaccinations should not be given together. It is recommended you seek medical advice at least six weeks prior to travel.

Most travellers from Western countries

will have been immunised against various diseases during childhood but your doctor may still recommend booster shots against measles or polio, diseases still prevalent in many developing countries. The period of protection offered by vaccinations differs widely and some are contra-indicated if you are pregnant.

Recommended vaccinations for Indonesia include:

Tetanus & Diptheria Boosters are necessary every 10 years.

Typhoid Available either as an injection or oral capsules. You may get some side effects such as pain at the injection site, fever, headache and a general unwell feeling. A new single-dose injectable vaccine, which appears to have few side effects, is now available but is more expensive. Side effects are unusual with the oral form but occasionally an individual will have stomach cramps.

Hepatitis A The most common travel-acquired illness which can be prevented by vaccination. A new vaccine, Havrix, provides long-term immunity (possibly more than 10 years) after an initial course of two injections and a booster at one year. The second injection should be administered at least three weeks prior to departure.

The other alternative is the less-effective gammaglobulin, which is not a vaccination but a ready-made antibody which has proven very successful in reducing the chances of hepatitis infection. Because it may interfere with the development of immunity, it should not be given until at least 10 days after administration of the last vaccine needed; it should also be given as close as possible to departure because its effectiveness tapers off gradually between three and six months.

Basic Rules

Food & Water Much of the water that comes out of the tap in Indonesia is little better than sewage water. Depending on how dirty it is and how sensitive you are, it might not even be safe to brush your teeth with tap water; use bottled or boiled water instead.

Bottled water is widely available in Indonesia. It's expensive at hotels and restaurants, but is reasonably priced in grocery stores or supermarkets. You can boil your own water if you carry an electric immersion coil and a large metal cup (plastic will melt), both of which are available in department stores and

supermarkets in Indonesia. For emergency use, water purification tablets will help. Water is more effectively sterilised by iodine than by chlorine tablets, because iodine kills giardia and amoebic cysts. However, iodine is not safe for prolonged use, and also tastes horrible. Bringing water to a boil is sufficient to kill most bacteria, but 20 minutes of boiling is required to kill amoebic cysts. Fortunately, amoebic cysts are relatively rare and you should not be overly concerned about these.

It's a good idea to carry a water bottle with you. You are dehydrating if you find you are urinating infrequently or if your urine turns a deep yellow or orange; you may also find yourself getting headaches. Dehydration is a real problem if you go hiking in Indonesia.

Fruit juices, soft drinks, tea and coffee will not quench your thirst – when it's really hot, you need water – *clean* water.

When it comes to food, use your best judgement. Have a good look at that restaurant or warung – if it looks dirty, think twice. Street food generally runs a higher risk, but may be better than restaurants if it is cooked on the spot before your eyes. To be absolutely safe, everything should be thoroughly cooked – you can get dysentery from salads and unpeeled fruit. Fish, meat and dairy products are generally OK provided they are fresh – if they spoil, you could become violently ill. Fish can also be a problem if they lived in contaminated water, and shellfish is a much higher risk. Fish from the 'black rivers' of Indonesia are the fastest ticket to the hepatitis clinic.

Other Precautions Sunglasses will protect your eyes from the scorching Indonesian sun. Amber and grey are said to be the two most effective colours for filtering out harmful ultraviolet rays.

Sunburn is also a problem. Bring sunscreen (UV) lotion and something to cover your head. You can also buy sunscreen in better Indonesian pharmacies – two popular brands are Pabanox and Parasol.

If you're sweating profusely, you're going to lose a lot of salt and that can lead to fatigue and muscle cramps. If necessary you can make it up by putting extra salt in your food (a teaspoon a day is plenty), but don't increase your salt intake unless you also increase your water intake.

Take good care of all cuts and scratches. In this climate they take longer to heal and can easily get infected. Treat any cut with care; wash it out with sterilised water, preferably with an antiseptic (Betadine), keep it dry and keep an eye on it – they can turn into tropical ulcers! It would be worth bringing an antibiotic cream with you, or you can buy one in Indonesia ('NB' ointment). Cuts on your feet and ankles are particularly troublesome – a new pair of sandals can quickly give you a nasty abrasion which can be difficult to heal. For the same reason, try not to scratch mosquito bites.

The climate may be tropical, but you *can* catch a cold in Indonesia. One of the easiest ways is leaving a fan on at night when you go to sleep, and air conditioners are even worse. You can also freeze your hide by sleeping out on the decks of ships at night, or going up to mountainous areas without warm clothes.

Medical Problems & Treatment

Diarrhoea Diarrhoea is often due simply to a change of diet. A lot depends on what you're used to eating and whether or not you've got an iron gut. If you do get diarrhoea, the first thing to do is wait – it rarely lasts more than a few days.

Diarrhoea will cause you to dehydrate, which will make you feel much worse. The solution is not simply to drink water, since it will run right through you. You'll get much better results by mixing your water with oral rehydration salts, which are available at pharmacies. The most common brand is Oralit, but the generic term is *bubuk glukosa elektrolit* (glucose electrolyte powder). Dissolve the powder in *cool* water (never hot!) and drink, but don't use it if the powder is wet. The quantity of water is specified on the packet. Oralit is also useful for treating heat exhaustion caused by excessive sweating.

If the diarrhoea persists then the usual treatment is Lomotil or Imodium tablets. The maximum dose for Lomotil is two tablets three times a day. Both Lomotil and Imodium are prescription drugs in the West, but are available over the counter in most Asian countries, though apparently not in Indonesia. Fortunately, Indonesia has its own local brands – a good one to look for is Entrostop. Anti-diarrhoeal drugs don't cure anything, but slow down the digestive system so that the cramps go away and you don't have to go to the toilet all the time. Excessive use of these drugs is not advised, as they can cause dependency and other side effects. Furthermore, the diarrhoea serves one useful purpose – it helps the body expel unwanted bacteria.

Activated charcoal, while not actually considered a drug, can provide much relief from diarrhoea and is a time-honoured treatment. A local brand available in Indonesia is Norit, also known generically as 'carbo-tablet'.

Fruit juice, tea and coffee can aggravate diarrhoea – again, water with oral rehydration salts is the best drink. It will help tremendously if you eat a light, fibre-free diet. Yoghurt or boiled eggs with salt are basic staples for diarrhoea patients. Later you may be able to tolerate plain white rice, and rice porridge with chicken *(bubur ayam)* is also very good for this condition. Keep away from vegetables, fruits and greasy foods for a while. If the diarrhoea persists for a week or more, it's probably not simple travellers' diarrhoea – it could be dysentery and it might be wise to see a doctor.

Dysentery This serious illness is reasonably common in Indonesia and is caused by contaminated food or water, and is characterised by severe diarrhoea, often with blood or mucus in the stool. There are two kinds of dysentery. Bacillary dysentery is characterised by a high fever and rapid onset; headache, vomiting and stomach pains are also symptoms. It generally does not last longer than a week, but it is highly contagious.

Amoebic dysentery is often more gradual in the onset of symptoms, with cramping abdominal pain and vomiting less likely;

fever may not be present. It is not a self-limiting disease: it will persist until treated and can recur and cause long-term health problems.

A stool test is necessary to diagnose which kind of dysentery you have, so you should seek medical help urgently. In case of an emergency the drugs norfloxacin or ciprofloxacin can be used as presumptive treatment for bacillary dysentery, and metronidazole (Flagyl) for amoebic dysentery.

For bacillary dysentery, norfloxacin 400mg twice daily for seven days or ciprofloxacin 500mg twice daily for seven days are the recommended dosages. If you're unable to find either of these drugs then a useful alternative is co-trimoxazole 160/800mg (Bactrim, Septrin, Resprim) twice daily for seven days. This is a sulfa drug and must not be used in people with a known sulfa allergy.

Giardiasis The parasite causing this intestinal disorder is present in contaminated water. The symptoms are stomach cramps, nausea, a bloated stomach, watery, foul-smelling diarrhoea and frequent gas. Giardiasis can appear several weeks after you have been exposed to the parasite. The symptoms may disappear for a few days and then return; this can go on for several weeks. Tinidazole, known as Fasigyn, or metronidazole (Flagyl) are the recommended drugs for treatment. Either can be used in a single treatment dose. Antibiotics are of no use.

Cholera Cholera vaccination is not recommended. However, outbreaks of cholera are generally widely reported, so you can avoid such problem areas. The disease is characterised by a sudden onset of acute diarrhoea with 'rice water' stools, vomiting, muscular cramps and extreme weakness. You need medical help – but treat for dehydration, which can be extreme, and if there is an appreciable delay in getting to hospital then begin taking tetracycline. See under Dysentery earlier in this section for dosages and warnings.

Typhoid Typhoid fever is another gut infection that travels the faecal-oral route – ie, contaminated water and food are responsible. Vaccination against typhoid is not totally effective and it is one of the most dangerous infections, so medical help must be sought.

In its early stages typhoid resembles many other illnesses: sufferers may feel like they have a bad cold or flu on the way, as early symptoms are a headache, a sore throat and a fever which rises a little each day until it is around 40°C or more. The victim's pulse is often slow relative to the degree of fever present and gets slower as the fever rises – unlike a normal fever where the pulse increases. There may also be vomiting, diarrhoea or constipation.

In the second week the high fever and slow pulse continue and a few pink spots may appear on the body; trembling, delirium, weakness, weight loss and dehydration are other symptoms. If there are no further complications, the fever and other symptoms will slowly go during the third week. However, you must get medical help before this because pneumonia (acute infection of the lungs) or peritonitis (burst appendix) are common complications, and because typhoid is very infectious.

The fever should be treated by keeping the victim cool and dehydration should also be watched for.

The drug of choice is ciprofloxacin at a dose of one gram daily for 14 days. It is quite expensive and may not be available. The alternative, chloramphenicol, has been the mainstay of treatment for many years. In many countries it is still the recommended antibiotic but there are fewer side affects with ampicillin. The adult dosage is two 250 mg capsules, four times a day. Children aged between eight and 12 years should have half the adult dose; younger children should have one-third the adult dose.

People who are allergic to penicillin should not be given ampicillin.

Malaria This serious disease is spread by mosquito bites. If you are travelling in endemic areas it is extremely important to take malarial prophylactics. Jakarta is the only place in Indonesia that has been classified as definitely malaria free. Bali and Java officially fall within the malarial zone but if you are travelling only to the main cities and tourist areas the risk is very minimal. Irian Jaya on the other hand is definitely a high-risk area, as are some of the more remote parts of the other islands.

Symptoms include headaches, fever, chills and sweating which may subside and recur. Without treatment malaria can develop more serious, potentially fatal effects.

Antimalarial drugs do not prevent you from being infected but kill the parasites during a stage in their development.

There are a number of different types of malaria. The one of most concern is falciparum malaria. This is responsible for the very serious cerebral malaria. Falciparum is the predominant form in many malaria prone areas of the world, including South-East Asia. Contrary to popular belief cerebral malaria is not a new strain.

The problem in recent years has been the emergence of increasing resistance to commonly used antimalarials like chloroquine, maloprim and proguanil. Newer drugs such as mefloquine (Lariam) and doxycycline (Vibramycin, Doryx) are often recommended for chloroquine and multidrug resistant areas. Expert advice should be sought, as there are many factors to consider when deciding on the type of antimalarial medication, including the area to be visited, the risk of exposure to malaria-carrying mosquitoes, your current medical condition, and your age and pregnancy status. It is also important to discuss the side effects of the medication, so you can work out some level of risk versus benefit ratio. It is also very important to be sure of the correct dosage of the medication prescribed to you. Some people inadvertently have taken weekly medication on a daily basis, with disastrous effects. While discussing dosages for prevention of malaria, it is often advisable to include the dosages required for treatment, especially if you are travelling to remote areas in high risk areas like Irian Jaya.

The main messages are:

1. Primary prevention must always be in the form of mosquito avoidance measures. The mosquitoes that transmit malaria bite from dusk to dawn and during this period travellers are advised to:

- wear light coloured clothing
- wear long pants and long sleeved shirts
- use mosquito repellents containing the compound DEET on exposed areas
- avoid highly scented perfumes or aftershave
- use a mosquito net – it's worth taking your own

2. While no antimalarial is 100% effective, taking the most appropriate drug significantly reduces the risk of contracting the disease.
3. No-one should ever die from malaria. It can be diagnosed by a simple blood test. Symptoms range from fever, chills and sweating, headache and abdominal pains to a vague feeling of ill health, so seek examination immediately if there is any suggestion of malaria.

Contrary to popular belief, once a traveller contracts malaria he/she does not have it for life. One of the parasites may lie dormant in the liver but this can also be eradicated using a specific medication. Malaria is curable, as long as the traveller seeks medical help when symptoms occur.

Dengue Fever There is no prophylactic available for this mosquito-spread disease; the main preventative measure is to avoid mosquito bites. A sudden onset of fever, headaches and severe joint and muscle pains are the first signs before a rash starts on the trunk of the body and spreads to the limbs and face. After a further few days, the fever will subside and recovery will begin. Serious complications are not common.

Eye Infections Trachoma is a common eye infection; it's easily spread by contaminated towels which are handed out by restaurants and even airlines. The best advice about wiping your face is to use disposable tissue paper. If you think you have trachoma, you need to see a doctor – the disease can damage your vision if untreated. Trachoma is normally treated with antibiotic eye ointments for about four to six weeks.

Hepatitis Hepatitis A is a potential problem for travellers to Indonesia. Fortunately long-term protection is available through the new vaccine Havrix. The alternative to Havrix is the short-lasting antibody gammaglobulin.

The disease is spread by contaminated food or water. The symptoms are fever, chills, headache, fatigue, feelings of weakness and aches and pains, followed by loss of appetite, nausea, vomiting, abdominal pain, dark urine, light coloured faeces, jaundiced skin and the whites of the eyes may turn yellow. In some cases you may feel unwell, tired, have no appetite, experience aches and pains and be jaundiced. You should seek medical advice, but in general there is not much you can do apart from rest, drink lots of fluids, eat lightly and avoid fatty foods. People who have had hepatitis must forego alcohol for six months after the illness, as hepatitis attacks the liver and it needs that amount of time to recover.

Hepatitis B, which used to be called serum hepatitis, is spread through contact with infected blood, blood products or bodily fluids, for example through sexual contact, unsterilised needles and blood transfusions. Other risk situations include having a shave or tattoo in a local shop, or having your ears pierced. The symptoms of type B are much the same as type A except that they are more severe and may lead to irreparable liver damage or even liver cancer. Although there is no treatment for hepatitis B, an effective prophylactic vaccine is readily available in most countries. The immunisation schedule requires two injections at least a month apart followed by a third dose five months after the second. Persons who should receive a hepatitis B vaccination include anyone who anticipates contact with blood or other bodily secretions, either as a health care worker or through sexual contact with the local population, particularly those who intend to stay in the country for a long period of time.

Hepatitis Non-A Non-B is a blanket term formerly used for several different strains of hepatitis, which have now been separately identified. Hepatitis C is similar to B but is less common. Hepatitis D (the 'delta particle') is also similar to B and always occurs in concert with it; its occurrence is currently limited to IV drug users. Hepatitis E, however, is similar to A and is spread in the same manner, by water or food contamination.

Tests are available for these strands, but are very expensive. Travellers shouldn't be too paranoid about this apparent proliferation of hepatitis strains; they are fairly rare (so far) and following the same precautions as for A and B should be all that's necessary to avoid them.

Sexually Transmitted Diseases Sexual contact with an infected sexual partner spreads these diseases. While abstinence is the only 100% preventative, using condoms is also effective. Gonorrhoea and syphilis are the most common of these diseases; sores, blisters or rashes around the genitals, discharges or pain when urinating are common symptoms.

Symptoms may be less marked or not observed at all in women. Syphilis symptoms eventually disappear completely but the disease continues and can cause severe problems in later years. The treatment of gonorrhoea and syphilis is by antibiotics. There are numerous other sexually transmitted diseases, for most of which effective treatment is available. However, there is no cure for herpes and there is also currently no cure for AIDS.

HIV/AIDS HIV, the Human Immunodeficiency Virus, may develop into AIDS, Acquired Immune Deficiency Syndrome. Any exposure to blood, blood products or bodily fluids may put the individual at risk. Official HIV figures in Indonesia are pathetically low, though it is widely believed that the real figures are much higher and set to increase significantly unless the promotion of safe sex and hospital practices are improved. The primary risk for most travellers is contact with workers in the sex industry, and in Indonesia the spread of HIV is primarily through heterosexual activity. Apart from abstinence, the most effective prevention is always to practise safe sex using condoms. It is impossible to detect the HIV-positive status of an otherwise healthy-looking person without a blood test.

HIV/AIDS can also be spread through infected blood transfusions; most developing countries cannot afford to screen blood for transfusions. It can also be spread by dirty needles – vaccinations, acupuncture, tattooing and ear or nose piercing can potentially be as dangerous as intravenous drug use if the equipment is not clean. If you do need an injection, ask to see the syringe unwrapped in front of you, or better still, take a needle and syringe pack with you overseas – it is a cheap insurance package against infection with HIV.

Fear of HIV infection should never preclude treatment for serious medical conditions. Although there may be a risk of infection, it is very small indeed.

Rabies Rabies is rare in Indonesia but can be caused by a bite or scratch by an infected animal. Dogs are noted carriers as are monkeys and cats. Any bite, scratch or even lick from a warm-blooded, furry animal should be cleaned immediately and thoroughly. Scrub with soap and running water, and then clean with an alcohol solution. If there is any possibility that the animal is infected medical help should be sought immediately. Even if the animal is not rabid, all bites should be treated seriously as they can become infected or can result in tetanus. A rabies vaccination is now available and should be considered if you are in a high-risk category – eg, if you intend to explore caves (bat bites could be dangerous) or work with animals.

Fungal Infections Hot weather fungal infections are most likely to occur on the scalp, between the toes or fingers (athlete's foot), in the groin (jock itch or crotch rot) and on the body (ringworm). You get ringworm (which is a fungal infection, not a worm) from infected animals or by walking on damp areas, like shower floors.

To prevent fungal infections wear loose, comfortable clothes, avoid artificial fibres, wash frequently and dry carefully. If you do get an infection, wash the infected area daily with a disinfectant or medicated soap and water, and rinse and dry well. Apply an antifungal powder like the widely available Tinaderm. Try to expose the infected area to air or sunlight as much as possible and wash all towels and underwear in hot water as well as changing them often.

Worms These parasites are most common in rural, tropical areas and a stool test when you return home is not a bad idea. They can be present on unwashed vegetables or in undercooked meat and you can pick them up through your skin by walking in bare feet. Infestations may not show up for some time, and although they are generally not serious, if left untreated they can cause severe health problems. A stool test is necessary to pinpoint the problem and medication is often available over the counter.

Snakes Indonesia has several poisonous snakes (*ular* is the Indonesian word for snake), the most famous being the cobra (*ular sendok*). There are many other poisonous species. *All* sea snakes are poisonous and are readily identified by their flat tails. Although not poisonous, giant-sized pythons lurk in the jungle. They do not generally consume humans, but have been known to do so. They do frequently eat pigs, and are thus an enemy of non-Muslim farmers.

To minimise your chances of being bitten always wear boots, socks and long trousers when walking through undergrowth where snakes may be present. Don't put your hands into holes and crevices, and be careful when collecting firewood.

Snake bites do not cause instantaneous death and antivenenes are usually available. Keep the victim calm and still, wrap the bitten limb tightly, as you would for a sprained ankle, and then attach a splint to immobilise it. Then seek medical help, if possible with the dead snake for identification. Don't attempt to catch the snake if there is even a remote possibility of being bitten again. Tourniquets and sucking out the poison are now comprehensively discredited.

Jellyfish Heeding local advice is the best way of avoiding contact with these sea creatures with their stinging tentacles. The box jellyfish found in inshore waters in some parts of Indonesia is potentially fatal, but stings from most jellyfish are simply rather painful. Dousing in vinegar will deactivate any stingers which have not 'fired'. Calamine lotion, antihistamines and analgesics may reduce the reaction and relieve the pain.

Women's Health

Gynaecological Problems Poor diet, lowered resistance due to the use of antibiotics for stomach upsets and even contraceptive pills can lead to vaginal infections when travelling in hot climates. Keeping the genital area clean, and wearing skirts or loose-fitting trousers and cotton underwear will help to prevent infections.

Yeast infections, characterised by a rash, itch and discharge, can be treated with a vinegar or even lemon-juice douche or with yoghurt. Nystatin suppositories are the usual medical prescription. Trichomonas is a more serious infection; symptoms are a discharge and a burning sensation when urinating. Sexual partners must also be treated, and if a vinegar-water douche is not effective medical attention should be sought. Metronidazole (Flagyl) is the prescribed drug.

Pregnancy Most miscarriages occur during the first three months of pregnancy, so this is the most risky time to travel as far as your own health is concerned. Miscarriage is not uncommon, and can occasionally lead to severe bleeding. The last three months should also be spent within reasonable distance of good medical care. A baby born as early as 24 weeks stands a chance of survival, but only in a good modern hospital.

Pregnant women should avoid all unnecessary medication, but vaccinations and malarial prophylactics should still be taken where possible. Additional care should be taken to prevent illness and particular attention should be paid to diet and nutrition. Alcohol and nicotine, for example, should be avoided.

Women travellers often find that their periods become irregular or even cease while they're on the road. Remember that a missed period in these circumstances doesn't necessarily indicate pregnancy. There are health posts or Family Planning clinics in many small and large urban centres, where you can seek advice and have a urine test to determine whether you are pregnant or not.

WOMEN TRAVELLERS

Indonesia is a Muslim society and very much male oriented. Nevertheless, lots of Western women travel in Indonesia either alone or in pairs – most seem to enjoy the country and its people, most seem to get through the place without any problems, or else suffer only a few minor hassles with the men. Your genetic make-up plays a part – blonde-haired, blue-eyed women seem to have more hassles than dark women. Some cities are worse than others – a lot of women have complained about Yogyakarta. There are some things you can do to avoid being harassed; dressing modestly helps a lot.

Indonesians, both men and women, are generally not comfortable being alone – even on a simple errand they are happier having a friend along. Travelling alone is considered an oddity – women travelling alone, even more of an oddity. Nevertheless, for a woman travelling alone or with a female companion, Indonesia can be easier going than some other Asian countries.

You might spare a thought for Indonesian women, who are given the privilege of doing backbreaking labour and raising children, but never trusted in positions of authority. The whole concept of feminism, equality between the sexes etc, would seem absurd to most Indonesians.

DANGERS & ANNOYANCES

Theft

While violent crime is very rare in Indonesia, theft can be a problem. If you are mindful of your valuables and take precautions, the chances of being ripped off are small. Most thefts are the result of carelessness or naivety.

A money belt worn under your clothes is the safest way to carry your passport, cash and travellers' cheques, particularly when travelling on the crowded buses and trains. Keep a separate stash of money (say US$200) hidden in your luggage, with a record of the travellers' cheque serial numbers and your passport number; you'll need the money if you have got a long trip to the replacement office. If you get stuck, try ringing your embassy or consulate.

Pickpockets are common and crowded bus and train stations are favourite haunts, as are major tourist areas. The thieves are very skilful and often work in gangs – if you find yourself being hassled and jostled, check your wallet, watch and bag. 'Pencuri' is the Indonesian word for thief.

Don't leave valuables unattended, and in crowded places, hold your handbag or day pack closely. At the same time, don't be too worried if your luggage is put on the roof of a bus or in the hold of a boat. It is often safer there than next to you where a stray hand can delve inside unnoticed or it can be slashed. It is good insurance to have luggage that can be locked, such as a travel pack. It is worth sewing on tabs to hiking packs to make them lockable.

Always lock your hotel room door and windows at night and whenever you go out, even if momentarily. If you leave small things like sunglasses and books lying around outside your room, expect them to disappear. It's also a depressing reality that sometimes it's your fellow travellers who rip you off. Don't leave valuables lying around in dorms. Bring your own locks for dorm lockers and for those hotel rooms that are locked with a padlock.

Drugs

In most of Indonesia, recreational plants and chemicals are utterly unheard of. Being caught with drugs will result in jail or, if you are lucky, a large bribe. Most marijuana in Indonesia is grown in the north Sumatran province of Aceh, and some of this filters down to the tourist resorts such as Lake Toba.

Hotel owners are required by law to turn offenders in. Bali used to be the place to float sky high, but the scene has all but disappeared. You'll still get plenty of offers, but nine times out of ten those 'buddha sticks' are banana leaves, and remember that there are still Westerners soaking up the sunshine in Bali's prison.

Crocodiles

The situation here is much like in northern Australia. Crocodiles *(buaya)* mostly inhabit low swampy jungle areas and slow-moving rivers near the sea coast. They wisely avoid contact with humans since they are liable to be turned into fashionable handbags. They *can* be dangerous, but unless you go stomping around the swamps of Irian Jaya, you probably won't see one. Still, if you intend to jump into any rivers for a refreshing swim, it would be wise to first make local enquiries.

Noise

If you're deaf, there's no problem. If you're not deaf, you might be after a few months in Indonesia. The major sources of noise are radios and TVs – Indonesians always set the volume knob to maximum. You can easily escape the racket at remote beaches and other rural settings by walking away, but there isn't much you can do on a bus with a reverberating stereo system. In hotels, the lobby often contains a booming TV set, but if you choose your room carefully, you might be able to avoid the full impact. If you complain about the noise, it's likely the TV or radio will be turned down, but then turned back up again five minutes later.

Another major source of noise is the mosques, which start broadcasting the calls to prayer at 4 am, repeating the procedure four more times during the day. Again, choose your hotel room carefully.

'Hello Mister' Fatigue

This is the universal greeting given to foreigners regardless of whether the person being addressed is male or female. The less advanced English students know only 'Mister', which they will enthusiastically *scream* in your ear every five seconds – 'Mister Mister Mister!' Most have no idea what it means, but they have been told by their school teachers that this is the proper way to greet foreigners. After two months of listening to this, some foreigners go over the edge. Try to remember that they think it's polite. It's mainly a problem in the outer islands, not in Java, Bali and the main tourist areas, where foreigners are ubiquitous and English-speaking abilities are higher.

Other Hassles

You tend to get stared at in Indonesia, particularly in places where few foreigners go. But on the whole the Indonesians stand back and look, rather than gather round you. Those who do come right up to you are usually kids, though some teenagers also do this. Getting stared at is nothing new; almost 500 years ago when the first Portuguese arrived in Melaka the *Malay Annals* recorded that:

...the people of Melaka...came crowding to see what the Franks (Portuguese) looked like; and they were all astonished and said, 'These are white Bengalis!' Around each Frank there would be a crowd of Malays, some of them twisting his beard, some of them fingering his head, some taking off his hat, some grasping his hand.

The insatiable curiosity of Indonesians manifests itself in some peculiar ways. Many Indonesians take their holidays in Bali not for the beach, but just so they can stare at foreigners. Sometimes you get people who start following you on the street just to look at you – such people are called *buntut* (tails). If you read a book or write something down, it's not unusual for people to poke their nose right into your book or writing pad, or take it from your hands so that they can have a better look.

The other habit which is altogether ordinary to Indonesians is touching. The

Indonesians are an extraordinarily physical people; they'll balance themselves on your knee as they get into a bemo, or reach out and touch your arm while making a point in conversation, or simply touch you every time they mean to speak to you or when they want to lead you in a new direction if they're showing you around a house or museum. All this is considered friendly – some Indonesians just have to be friendly regardless of the time or situation, even if it means waking you from your peaceful slumber!

While casual touching among members of the same sex is regarded as OK, body contact between people of different sexes is not. Walking down the street holding hands with a member of the opposite sex will provoke stares, pointing, loud comments and shouting. Public displays of affection (like kissing) may incur the wrath of moral vigilantes.

Sometimes you'll come across young guys who hang around bus stations, outside cinemas and ferry docks with not much else to do except stir foreigners. They'll crack jokes, laugh, and sometimes make obscene gestures. Don't give them their entertainment by chucking a fit – just ignore their puerile antics.

On the whole you'll find the Indonesians (including the army and the police, despite the nasty reputation they have with the locals) *extraordinarily* hospitable and very easy to get on with.

Travelling with Children

Travelling anywhere with children requires energy and organisation. The Indonesians are generally very friendly and receptive to children. Of course some areas of Indonesia are hard going, probably too hard for most people to want to tackle with the additional burden of small children. Other areas, such as Bali, are easy.

A real problem exists with little children who have blond hair and blue eyes. Many Indonesians just can't resist pinching them on the cheek and, while no harm is meant, most children don't like it and will start crying.

For more information on travelling in Asia with children see LP's *Travel with Children*.

WORK

It is possible for foreigners to work in Indonesia, provided you are willing to make some long-term commitments. Although Indonesia is still a Third-World country, in some situations you can be paid well. Given the low cost of living, you could eventually save quite a bundle if you don't live extravagantly.

People with valuable technical skills, like engineers, computer programmers and the like may be able to find jobs with foreign multinational corporations, primarily in Jakarta, though most expats are managerial. By far the best way to arrange this is through a company overseas. By fronting up in Jakarta and finding work, you may miss out on the benefits that most expats get as standard – accommodation, car and driver etc.

There are a few jobs available for Westerners as bartenders in five-star hotels. The pay is good, but note that these jobs are for men only. For most travellers, both male and female, the easiest way to pick up decent work is to teach English. There are good opportunities for doing this in large cities like Jakarta, Surabaya, Bandung and Yogya, and somewhat fewer opportunities in tourist centres like Bali. The best paying jobs by far are in Jakarta. Salaries start at 30,000 rp per hour, and can go as high as 50,000 rp per hour if you teach at banks, five-star hotels and other large companies. It's not quite as good as it sounds though. Most banks and big companies will not offer you full-time work – you'll have to do some commuting between jobs in Jakarta's insane traffic if you want to work 20 hours a week, which is about as much as most teachers can stand. Also, it takes connections to get the really plumb jobs.

To get good-paying work, there are a few qualifiers. First of all, you have to look 'decent' – forget the thongs, T-shirts and short pants. To teach at a bank, men will probably need a white shirt and tie, while women will be expected to wear a dress. Scraggly beards and punk haircuts will not impress your potential employers. Academic credentials and letters of reference will help,

but are not essential. Finally, companies prefer someone who has been around awhile, not a traveller who just fell off the plane at Denpasar with a guitar and a surfboard. But if you're persistent, you can usually find something.

You'll also have to consider your visa. The words 'employment prohibited' are stamped on your two-month tourist pass and most other visas. It is possible to get a working visa, but that involves more bureaucracy. Although enforcement of the regulations has not been rigid, you are vulnerable to getting fined and booted out of the country if the authorities take a dim view of your activities. Sometimes your employer will help you to deal with the immigration authorities, but usually you're on your own. Some foreigners have paid bribes to get work visas, but we aren't recommending that you do this. If you do get a work visa, you may have to pay taxes. All this is worth keeping in mind.

ACTIVITIES

Surfing

Indonesia has long had a reputation as a surfing Mecca, and intrepid surfers have been roaming the archipelago for decades in their search for the ideal break. Bali is the main destination – the living's good and the surf easy to reach, but the waves can be crowded. Surfing on Bali is well established with plenty of surf shops and information in Kuta. Surf tours are available to best spots on Bali and boat-based trips go to more remote breaks on nearby islands especially Grajagan on Java and Desert Point on Lombok.

Kuta & Legian have the only beach breaks suitable for beginners; all the others are reef breaks for experienced surfers. The following work best with an easterly wind, in the dry season from about April to October: Kuta & Legian, Kuta Reef, Ulu Watu, Padang Padang, Bingin, Balangan, Canggu, Medewi and Nusa Lembongan.

During the wet season, roughly October/November to March/April, good surf can be found on the east side of the island at Nusa Dua, Sanur, Ketewel and Lebih.

Nyang Nyang and Green Ball on the extreme south coast, round the end of the Bukit peninsula, can be surfed any time of the year providing there is a northerly wind, or no wind at all.

On Lombok, there is good surf at Bangko Bangko (the break is called Desert Point) and Ekas, and numerous 'secret' reef breaks along the south coast, off Kuta and Silong Blanak. For full details on surfing and what to bring with you (apart from your board) see *Bali & Lombok – a travel survival kit*.

Apart from Bali, Nias off the west coast of Sumatra has long had a reputation as Indonesia's second surfing Mecca, though the smaller islands further south are now receiving attention. On the south-east tip of Java, Grajagan has received such legendary status that there are even boat tours operated from Bali. The entire south coast of Java is pounded by surf, much of it on shallow reef, but a few less-popular surfing destinations can be found right across to Ujung Kulon National Park in the west.

Out in Nusa Tenggara, Huu on Sumbawa is the number one surfing destination, but despite its isolation even that is getting crowded. More obscure destinations in Nusa Tenggara include Nemberala on Roti, south-east of Timor, and surfers are even hunting waves on Sumba.

Windsurfing

Obviously, Bali is the place where windsurfing is most common, followed by Lombok. It's caught on in Manado in North Sulawesi too. Indonesians windsurf the Sungai (river) Kapuas at Pontianak in West Kalimantan, and there's a place at Pantai Waiara near Maumere on Flores that rents windsurfing equipment.

Scuba Diving

With so many islands and so much coral, Indonesia presents all sorts of possibilities for diving.

For much of Indonesia, diving may not be as good during the wet season, from about October to April, as storms tend to reduce

visibility. Bring your scuba certification – most of the main qualifications are recognised, including those of PADI, NAUI, BSAC, FAUI and SSI.

Bali has the best established dive operators in Indonesia, found in the major resorts and hotels. Baruna Water Sports, (☎ 753820; fax 752779), Jalan Bypass Ngurah Rai 300B, Kuta, is one of Bali's most reliable operators. Sanur also has a good selection of dive shops.

Some of Bali's best known dive sites include: Nusa Dua, Sanur, Padangbai, Candidasa, Tulamben (the big attraction is the wreck of the USS *Liberty*), Amed, Lovina Beach and Pulau Menjangan (in the Bali Barat National Park), and perhaps Bali's best diving is on Nusa Penida. Dive operators in Bali's southern tourist area can arrange trips to the main dive sites around the island for US$45 to US$80 per person for two dives with a group of four.

Diving is not as well developed on Lombok, though new diving areas are being explored, such as Gili Petangan off the east coast. Most dive operators are found on Sengigi. Further afield in Nusa Tenggara, Waira near Maumere has dive operators though much of the nearby reefs suffered damage in the earthquake of 1992. Kupang and more remote Roti also have diving possibilities.

Further afield there are the brilliant coral reefs around Bunaken Island off Manado in northern Sulawesi, and Sulawesi has many other good dive spots, including the Togian islands.

In Maluku, the Bandas are popular and Ambon also has diving sites and well established dive operators. Increasingly popular islands are Northern Halmahera and Morotai, and around Biak and the Cenderawasih Bay in Irian Jaya, with so many WW II wrecks.

Java is not a great diving destination as the waters tend to be less than clear and Java doesn't have the well-developed reefs of some of the other islands. A number of dive operators can be found in Jakarta, and in the hotels on the west coast around Carita. Pulau Seribu, just of the coast north of Jakarta has diving opportunities, as does the waters of West Java, around Krakatau and Ujung Kulon National Park.

On Sumatra, the best diving opportunities are around Pulau We and Pulau Banyak.

Snorkelling

If diving is beyond your budget then try snorkelling. Many of the dive sites can also be explored with a snorkel, and there are beautiful coral reefs on almost every coastline in Indonesia. Whilst you can usually buy or rent the gear when you need it, packing your own snorkel, mask and fins is a good idea.

Trekking

For information about trekking see the Walking section in the Getting Around chapter later in this book.

White-Water Rafting

Although the art of floating down raging rivers is not very well developed in Indonesia, there is great potential. A few commercial operators now cater to this peculiar Western custom. The Sungai Hamputung in Kalimantan offers a fairly easy float down a river with an impressive jungle canopy above. The canyon of the Sungai Sadan in Torajaland, Sulawesi, is becoming popular. There are a number of other rivers in Central Sulawesi which are also attracting Western tour groups. Inquire with local travel agents if interested.

White-water enthusiasts get quite a thrill out of being the first to raft a particular river, and in this regard Indonesia offers quite a few opportunities. There are a number of unrafted rivers in Irian Jaya, but tackling these will require expedition-style preparations – roads are nonexistent, crocodiles will probably find Western food delightful and there may be unexpected surprises like waterfalls. But if you survive all this, it will certainly be the adventure of a lifetime.

HIGHLIGHTS

Indonesia has beaches, volcanoes, ancient cultures, magnificent wilderness, vibrant cities, archaeological ruins – the problem is which to visit in a limited time. The following is a rundown on the most popular destinations throughout Indonesia. Indonesian highlights for each region are shown under the relevant chapters.

Planning an Itinerary

It is impossible to see all of Indonesia in the 60 days allowed by a tourist pass, if not a lifetime. Most visitors to Indonesia have one month or less to travel the vast archipelago, and it pays to choose only one, two or a maximum of three regions to explore.

The most visited islands tend to be Bali, Java and Sumatra, and it is possible to see the main highlights of these three islands in one month, but that doesn't leave much time for relaxation. Sulawesi is a growing tourist destination, and can be comfortably combined with a trip to another region. More visitors are heading out through Nusa Tenggara, but Maluku, Irian Jaya and Kalimantan are still unexplored territory for the vast majority of visitors to Indonesia. The outer islands are not so inaccessible these days, though travel costs are higher because flying becomes essential unless you have huge amounts of time.

If you are prepared to fly extensively you can easily visit a funeral in Torajaland, lie on the beach in Bali, hear gamelan at the kraton in Yogya, see the orang-utans in Sumatra and climb up to the coloured lakes of Keli Mutu in Flores – all in one month (we met one Dutchman who did just that, and much more!). For this sort of trip you need stamina and a great deal of luck, especially if travelling to the outer islands where transport is limited and subject to cancellation, and bookings often go astray.

Always allow yourself some extra time. Travel can sometimes be hard and you may need extra time to recuperate, or you may find yourself sidetracked to some wonderful place that you never knew existed. Remember that schedules in Indonesia are flexible, and you may be forced to bend yours.

ACCOMMODATION

One thing you'll have to learn to deal with is the *mandi*. The word mandi simply means to bath or to wash. A mandi is a large water tank beside which you'll find a plastic saucepan. The popularity of the mandi is mainly due to a frequent lack of running water in Indonesia – sometimes the tank is refilled by a hose attached to a hand-pump.

Climbing into the mandi is very bad form indeed – it's your water supply and it's also the supply for every other guest that comes after you, so the idea is to keep the water clean. What you're supposed to do is scoop water out of the mandi and pour it over yourself. Most of the better tourist hotels have showers and hot water, and even bathtubs.

Another thing which may require adjustments to your way of thinking are Indonesian toilets. These are basically holes in the ground, footrests on either side, over which you squat and aim. In some tourist areas, Asian toilets are fading away as more places install Western-style toilets. The lack of running water makes flushing toilets a problem, so what you do is reach for that plastic saucepan again, scoop water from the mandi and flush it that way.

As for toilet paper, you'll seldom find it supplied in public places, though you can easily buy your own. In fact, Indonesians seldom use the stuff. This is partly to save money, but mainly because Indonesian plumbing systems don't handle toilet paper too well and easily become clogged up. The Indonesian method is to use the left hand and copious quantities of water – again, keep that saucepan handy. Some Westerners easily adapt to this method, but many do not. If you need to use toilet paper, see if there is a wastebasket next to the toilet. If there is, then that's where the paper should go, not down the toilet. If you plug up the hotel's plumbing with toilet paper, the management is going to get really angry.

Kamar kecil is Bahasa Indonesia for toilet, but they usually understand 'way-say' (WC). *Wanita* means women and *pria* means men.

Camping

Camping grounds are relatively rare, but there are plenty of opportunities for back-country camping. It is important that you camp away from civilisation, unless you want Indonesian spectators all night.

You can probably get by without a sleeping bag below 1000 metres, but at higher elevations you'll certainly need one. Rain is a possibility even in the dry season, especially as you gain altitude, so bring some sort of tent or rainfly. You'll also want to guard against insects and other things that crawl and slither in the night, so a tent or mosquito net would be appropriate.

Hostels

Indonesia doesn't have much in the way of hostels, mainly because there are so many low-cost hotels. One exception is Jakarta, where accommodation is relatively dear, so there are a number of places offering cheap dormitory accommodation. There are a handful of hostels in a few other places, like Surabaya and Kupang, but it's entirely possible to travel through Indonesia on a tight budget without ever staying in a hostel.

The main thing to be cautious about in hostels is security. Few places provide lockers, and it's not just the Indonesians you must worry about – foreigners have been known to subsidise their vacation by helping themselves to other people's valuables. While it's not a huge problem, it is something to be aware of.

If you want to avoid nocturnal visits by rats, don't put food in your room, or at least have it sealed in ratproof jars or containers. Rats have a keen sense of smell, and they can and will chew through a backpack to get at food.

Bedbugs are occasionally a problem in this climate. Examine the underside of the mattress carefully before retiring. If you find it crawling with bugs, either change rooms or have the management spray copious quantities of poison which, hopefully, will eliminate the bugs rather than you.

Hotels

Hotels in Indonesia come in different grades of price and comfort. At the bottom end of the scale is the *(penginapan)*. A slightly more up-market penginapan is called a *losmen*. *Wisma* and *pondok* are slightly more up-market again, but still cheap.

The Indonesian government has embarked on a campaign to get all penginapan, losmen, wisma and pondok to change their names to 'hotel'. Not all the hotel owners are happy about this, since the old naming system gave potential guests some idea of the price.

By way of compensation, there is now an official rating system: a hotel can be either a flower *(melati)* or *yasmin* hotel, which is relatively low standard, or a star *(bintang)* hotel, which is more luxurious. A hotel at the bottom of the barrel would be one melati whereas a five-star hotel *(lima bintang)* occupies the top end. Most star hotels post signs indicating star rating as set by the government. All hotels are required to pay a 10% tax to the government, and this may be passed on to the customer, but most cheap hotels either avoid the tax or absorb it into their room rates. Upper-crust places charge a whopping 21% tax and service charge.

The real budget hotels are spartan places with shared bath, costing as little as 2500 rp per person. Mid-range hotel rooms often come with private bath and typically cost from 15,000 rp for a single. The five-star hotels can match the best in the West, with prices piercing the US$100 level. But in Indonesia, what you pay depends more on where you are; the cost of accommodation varies considerably across the archipelago. If you follow the well-beaten tourist track through Bali to Java and Sumatra, you'll find Indonesia one of the cheapest places in South-East Asia (exceptions like Jakarta apart). Travellers' centres like Bali, Yogyakarta and Lake Toba are superb value for food and accommodation. Nusa Tenggara is marginally more expensive than Bali, but cheap by any standards. On the other hand, once you get to some of the outer provinces, like Kalimantan, Maluku, or Irian Jaya, you could be paying five times as much as you'd pay in Yogyakarta for equivalent accommodation.

If you get into a town and the cheap places mentioned in this book are full, or you have no information on cheap places to stay, then ask taxi drivers, becak drivers or even the police what's available. Other travellers who have come from where you're heading are also good sources of information.

You may have to bargain for your room price just as you do for other purchases. Rather than argue, the most polite way to do this is to simply ask for a discount. Ask to see the printed price list *(daftar harga)* when you front up at a hotel. For many cheap and mid-range hotels, the price is often fixed to this rate. Seeing the price list will also give you an idea of the range of rooms – many hotels have a huge range of rooms from cheap to expensive, but you may only be offered the most expensive. If there is no price list, assume you can bargain, but the existence of a price list doesn't necessarily mean you can't bargain. Some hotels, especially in resort areas, have more than one price list, and if a hotel is overpriced or empty they will often give a discount.

Ironically, it's high-class places where you can bargain most. They seem to put their prices up every year regardless of occupancy rates or good sense, and accordingly the discounts also grow every year. As a rule, never pay the published rate at a top-end hotel. Always ask for a discount, which are readily available and range from 10 to 50%. Top-end hotels often quote prices in US dollars, and some mid-range hotels also engage in this dubious practice. The exchange rate they use for converting to rupiah is often higher than the rate you can obtain from a bank.

On the whole it's cheaper if two people travel together and split the cost of the room – the price for a two-person room is nearly always well below the cost of two singles. You rarely get dormitory accommodation in Indonesia, although there are a few hotels catering to Western budget travellers, notably in Jakarta, that provide dorm beds.

Even the cheapest hotels tend to be reasonably clean, if spartan, though some stand out as long overdue for demolition. Some places can be abominably noisy, with the inevitable TV booming in the passageway outside your room or punching up through the floorboards until after midnight. Other hotels are just several layers of hot little sweat boxes and slimy bathrooms. The tendency in the last few years has been to tear down the old firetraps and replace them with more wholesome accommodation, but of course prices have risen to reflect the improved conditions. The best way to survive some of the more dismal places is to go to Indonesia with a level of saintly tolerance, a good pair of earplugs, or enough money to afford some upper-market accommodation now and then and avoid the worst places.

How good a time you have in Indonesia often depends on where you're staying – ie, the friendliness and location of your hotel. If you want to enjoy yourself or learn something about the country then there's no point incarcerating yourself in the large tourist hotels. If you want to meet the local people and/or other travellers then you've got to stay in the cheap places. So pick your hotel carefully; while some places may not have such comfy beds the people you meet more than make up for it.

Staying in Villages

In many places in Indonesia you'll often be welcome to stay in the villages. Ask for the village head – the *kepala desa*. They're generally very hospitable and friendly, offering you not only a roof over your head but also meals. Obviously you don't get a room of your own, just a bed. What you pay for this depends on the bargain you reach with the kepala desa. Sometimes he may offer it to you for nothing but more often some payment will be expected: about 5000 rp a night as rule of thumb. If you intend to stay with a kepala desa it's a good idea to have one or two gifts to offer – cigarettes, postcards and photographs are popular.

Staying with the Police

In places where there's no accommodation available you can often stay in the local police station. Indonesian police and military are actually quite friendly to foreigners – how they treat the locals is another matter.

Rental

Given the wide assortment of cheap hotels, it almost doesn't pay to bother with renting a house or apartment. Trying to find a house for short-term rental – one or two months – is difficult and depends on personal contacts or luck. Real estate agents are virtually nonexistent in Indonesia. Ask your Indonesian friends, at your hotel, restaurants etc. Something may turn up, but it can take time. Negotiating a proper price may also take some time, and it's wise to obtain the help of an Indonesian friend.

However, if you're working in Indonesia for a long time, you will want to get your own place. Rents vary wildly depending on where you want to live. Jakarta's rates are very high, and rent is required in advance, even for three-year leases. Prices are lower elsewhere. More than a few foreigners have taken up semipermanent residence in Bali, either renting houses on long-term lease or leasing the land and building their own homes with an Indonesian partner.

FOOD

You'll generally eat well in most parts of Indonesia. There are some gastronomic voids in the more poverty-stricken areas, but the variety is stunning in cities like Jakarta and touristy regions like Bali. There are occasional surprises too, like midyear in Tanatoraja (Sulawesi), when harvest and funeral ceremonies are at their height and you can try pig and buffalo meat barbecued in bamboo tubes, washed down with copious quantities of white and red alcoholic *tuak* tapped from a palm tree. Of course, food like this is not available from your average pushcart.

Jalan Malioboro in Yogyakarta is the longest restaurant in the world – lined in the evening with innumerable food stalls serving up genuine Yogya food, which you eat while sitting on mats laid out on the footpath –

though the innumerable stalls strung along Pantai Losari in Ujung Pandang also vie for the title. Pontianak and Samarinda in Kalimantan have the biggest river prawns you've probably ever seen in your life; Jayapura has the best selection of barbecued fish *(ikan bakar)*.

Many general books on Asian food include a section on Indonesian cuisine, including *South-East Asia Food* by Rosemary Brissenden. *Indonesian Food & Cookery* by Sri Owen is a straightforward cookery book without the glossy photos, but it gives an excellent rundown on Indonesian food and ingredients and authentic Indonesian recipes.

Restaurants

At the bottom of the barrel in terms of price are the *warungs*. These are the poor person's restaurants, and they can be seen everywhere in Indonesia. They're usually just a rough table and bench seats, surrounded by sheets or canvas strung up to act as walls. In Yogya on Jalan Malioboro, they're basically food trolleys and you sit on mats laid out on the footpath. Often the food is as drab as the warung looks, but occasionally you find something outstanding. One thing you can be sure about is that warungs are cheap. A night market *(pasar malam)* is often a congregation point for warungs.

One step up from the warungs, sometimes in name only, is the *rumah makan* – literally the 'house to eat', often only distinguished from the warung by its fixed position and the addition of solid walls – but many such places call themselves warungs so it's a hazy distinction.

A *restoran* is a restaurant – once again often nothing more than the name distinguishes it from a rumah makan. But in many cases a restoran will be an up-market place, often Chinese-run and with a Chinese menu. Chinese food is nearly always more expensive than Indonesian food, but there is usually a more varied menu.

Kuta Beach and Jakarta are the two main places in Indonesia where Western food has grabbed hold. In Kuta you would be forgiven

if you thought there was no such thing as Balinese cooking – while the food you get around Kuta is good, traditional Balinese food has just about dropped out of the picture, and Indonesian food is succumbing to the onslaught of hamburgers, steaks, yoghurt, fish & chips, banana muesli and – for homesick Aussies – vegemite on toast, mate!

Jakarta has the most cosmopolitan range of culinary delights in Indonesia, from European and Mexican to Indian, Chinese, Thai, Korean and Japanese. Parts of Indonesia where there are large expatriate communities working for foreign firms, Balikpapan for example, are also sources of foreign food.

Western fast food has come to roost in the main cities, complete with air-conditioning, laminex tables and a statue of the ever-smiling Colonel or Ronald the clown. If you made as much money as they do, you'd smile too. Indonesia also has a growing contingent of Pizza Hut, Wendy's and other outlets.

In spite of the wide variety of food, many travellers lose weight, and some say a trip through Indonesia is the best crash diet they know of. This has more to do with illness than lack of tasty food, so take care – in some places, 'hygiene' is just a slogan. As a general guide, the cleanliness of a warung or restaurant is a good indicator as to how sanitary its kitchen is likely to be. A bad meal at the local Rumah Makan Dysentery can spoil your trip – be wary of uncooked vegetables and fruits, rubbery seafood and 'boiled' drinking water straight from the tap.

Snacks

Indonesians are keen snackers and everywhere you'll find lots of street stall snacks, such as peanuts in palm sugar, shredded coconut cookies or fried bananas. Potatoes and other starchy roots are eaten as a snack – either steamed, with salt and grated coconut added, or thinly sliced and fried.

Main Dishes

Food in Indonesia, particularly meat dishes, is generally Chinese-influenced, although there are a number of purely Indonesian dishes. Pork is not widely used since it is regarded by Muslims as unclean, but it sometimes appears in Chinese dishes and is eaten in Christian areas. Javanese cooking uses fresh spices and a mixture of ingredients, the chilli mellowed by the use of sugar in many dishes. Sumatran cooking, on the other hand, blends fresh and dry spices to flavour the main ingredient. The types of fresh spices that Indonesians use are known to most Westerners only as dried ground powders. There is also some Dutch influence in the use of vegetables from temperate zones in some recipes.

Rice is the basis of the meal, with an assortment of side dishes, some hot (with chilli) and spicy, and some just spicy. Many dishes are much like soup, the water being used to moisten the large quantity of rice eaten.

Indonesian Food

Some of the dishes you're likely to encounter in Indonesia are listed here:

abon – spiced and shredded dried meat often sprinkled over nasi rames or nasi rawon
acar – pickle; cucumber or other vegetables in a mixture of vinegar, salt, sugar and water
apam – delicious pancake filled with nuts and sprinkled with sugar
ayam – chicken; *ayam goreng* is fried chicken

babi – pork. Since most Indonesians are Muslim, pork is generally only to be found in market stalls and restaurants run by Chinese, and in areas where there are non-Muslim populations such as in Bali, Irian Jaya and Tanatoraja.
bakmi – rice-flour noodles, either fried *(bakmi goreng)* or in soup
bakso or *ba'so* – meatball soup
bawang – onion
bubur ayam – Indonesian porridge with chicken. The porridge is generally sweetened and made from rice, black sticky rice or mung beans.
bubur kacang – mung bean porridge cooked in coconut milk
buncis – beans

cap cai – usually pronounced 'chop chai'. This is a mix of fried vegetables, although it sometimes comes with meat as well.
cassava – Known as tapioca to Westerners, this is a long, thin, dark brown root which looks something like a shrivelled turnip.
cumi cumi – squid

daging babi – pork
daging sapi – beef
daging kambing – goat or mutton
dragonflies – a popular Balinese snack, caught with sticky sticks and then roasted!

emping – powdered and dried *melinjo* nuts, fried as a snack to accompany a main meal
es krim – ice cream. In Indonesia you can get Western brands like Flipper's and Peters, and also locally manufactured varieties.

fu yung hai – a sort of sweet & sour omelette

gado gado – another very popular Indonesian dish of steamed bean sprouts, various vegetables and a spicy peanut sauce
garam – salt
gula – sugar
gula gula – lollies (sweets, candy)

continued overleaf

gulai/gule – thick curried-meat broth with coconut milk

ikan – fish. Understandably there's a wide variety to choose from in Indonesia: *ikan laut* is saltwater fish, *ikan danau* is freshwater fish. *Ikan asam manis* is sweet and sour fish and *ikan bakar* is barbecued fish. If you're buying fresh fish (you can often buy these at a market and get your hotel to cook them up), the gills should be a deep red colour, not brown, and the flesh should be firm to touch.
ikan belut – eels. Another Balinese delicacy; kids catch them in the rice paddies at night.

jahe – ginger

kacang – peanuts or beans
kacang hijau – mung bean sprouts. These can be made into a sweet filling for cakes and buns.
kare – curry; as in *kare udang* (prawn curry)
kecap asin – salty soy sauce
kecap manis – sweet soy sauce
keju – cheese
kentang – potatoes; usually the size found in the West and used in various ways, including dishes of Dutch origin and as a salad ingredient
kepiting – crab; features in quite a few dishes, mostly of Chinese origin
kodok – frog; plentiful in Bali and caught in the rice paddies at night
kroket – mashed potato cake with minced meat filling
krupuk – is made of shrimp and cassava flour or of fish flakes and rice dough, cut in slices and fried to a crisp
krupuk melinjo (emping) – is made of the seeds of the melinjo fruit *(gnetum-gnemon)*, pounded flat, dried and fried to make a crisp chip and served as a snack with a main course
kueh – cake

lemper – sticky rice with a small amount of meat inside, wrapped up and boiled in a banana leaf; a common snack found throughout the country
lombok – chilli. There are various types: *lombok merah* (large, red); *lombok hijau* (large, green); and *lombok rawit* (rather small but deadliest of them all, often packaged with *tahu* etc).
lontong – rice steamed in a banana leaf
lumpia – spring rolls; small pancake filled with shrimp and bean sprouts and fried

madu – honey
martabak – found on food trolleys all over the archipelago. A martabak is basically a pancake but there are two varieties. The one that seems to be everywhere is the sickeningly sweet version guaranteed to set your dentist's bank account soaring when you get back home. But (at least in Java) you can also get a delicious savoury martabak stuffed with meat, egg and vegetables. Some people think the sweet version isn't all that bad.
mentega – butter
mentimun – cucumber
merica – lada
mie goreng – fried wheat-flour noodles, served sometimes with vegetables, sometimes with meat
mie kuah – noodle soup
mentega – butter

nasi campur – steamed rice topped with a little bit of everything – some vegetables, some meat, a bit of fish, a krupuk or two – a good, usually tasty and filling meal
nasi goreng – This is the most common of Indonesian dishes; almost like hamburgers are to Americans, meat pies to Australians, fish & chips to the British – popular at any time of day, including breakfast time. Nasi goreng simply means fried (goreng) rice (nasi) – a basic nasi goreng may be little more than fried rice with a few scraps of vegetable to give it some flavour, but sometimes it includes some meat. *Nasi goreng istimewa* (special) usually means nasi goreng with a fried egg on top. The dish can range from dull and dreary to very good.

nasi gudeg – unripe jackfruit cooked in santan and served up with rice, pieces of chicken and spices

nasi padang – Padang food, from the Padang region of Sumatra, is popular all over Indonesia. It's usually served cold and consists of the inevitable rice, with a whole variety of side dishes, including beef, fish, fried chicken, curried chicken, boiled cabbage, sometimes fish and prawns. The dishes are laid out before you and your final bill is calculated by the number of empty dishes when you've finished eating. Nasi padang is traditionally eaten with the fingers and it's also traditionally very hot (pedas not panas) – sometimes hot enough to burn your fingers, let alone your tongue! It's sometimes wonderful, and sometimes very dull. It's also one of the more expensive ways to eat in Indonesia and you generally end up spending a couple of thousand rupiah on a meal, although it can be well worth it.

nasi pecel – similar to gado gado, with boiled papaya leaves, tapioca, bean sprouts, string beans, fried soybean cake, fresh cucumber, coconut shavings and peanut sauce

nasi putih – white (putih) rice – usually steamed; glutinous rice is mostly used in snacks and cakes

nasi rames – rice with a combination of egg, vegetables, fish or meat

nasi rawon – rice with spicy hot beef soup, fried onions and spicy sauce

nasi uduk – rice boiled in coconut milk or cream

opor ayam – chicken cooked in coconut milk

pete – a huge broad bean, quite spicy, which is often served in the pod

pisang goreng – fried banana fritters; a popular street-side snack

rijsttafel – Dutch for 'rice table'; Indonesian food with a Dutch interpretation, it consists of lots of individual dishes with rice. Rather like a glorified nasi campur or a hot nasi padang. Bring a big appetite.

roti – bread. The stuff you get in Indonesia is nearly always snow white and sweet.

sago – a starchy, low protein food extracted from a variety of palm tree. Sago is the staple diet of the Maluku islands.

sambal – a hot, spicy chilli sauce served as an accompaniment with most meals

sate – One of the best known of Indonesian dishes, sate (satay) are small pieces of various types of meat on a skewer served with a spicy peanut sauce. Street sate-sellers carry their charcoal grills around with them and cook the sate on the spot.

saus tomat – tomato sauce; ketchup

sayur – vegetables

sayur-sayuran – vegetable soup with coconut milk

sembal pedis – hot sauce

sop – clear soup with mixed vegetables and meat or chicken

soto – meat and vegetable broth, often a main meal eaten with rice and a side dish of sambal

tahu – tofu, or soybean curd; soft bean cake made from soybean milk. It varies from white and yellow to thin and orange-skinned. It's found as a snack in the food stalls and is sometimes sold with a couple of hot chillies or with a filling of vegetables

tempe – made of whole soybeans fermented into cake, wrapped in plastic or a banana leaf; rich in vegetable protein, iron and vitamin B. Tempe goreng is pieces of tempe (tempeh) fried with palm sugar and chillies.

telur – egg

ubi – sweet potato; spindle-shaped to spherical with a pulpy yellow or brown skin and white to orange flesh

udang – prawns or shrimps

udang karang – lobster ■

Salad is usually served, along with *sambal* (a spicy side dish) and *acar* (pickles). Many dishes are cooked in *santan*, the liquid obtained when grated coconut is squeezed. *Bumbu* is a combination of pounded ingredients used to flavour a dish. Indonesians use every part of a plant, including the leaves of cassavas, papayas, mangoes and beans.

A few basic words and phrases will help make ordering a meal easier.

makan	to eat
minum	to drink
makanan	food
nasi bungkos	take-away food
minuman	drink
makan pagi	breakfast
makan siang	lunch
makan malam	dinner
enak	delicious
daftar makanan	the menu
bon	the bill
manis	sweet
asam manis	sweet and sour
dingin	cold
panas	hot (temperature)

Fruit

It's almost worth making a trip to Indonesia just to sample the tropical fruit – apples and bananas curl and die before the onslaught of nangkas, rambutans, mangosteens, salaks and sirsaks.

apel – apple. Most are imported from the Australia, New Zealand and the USA, and are expensive. Local apples grown in mountain areas, such as Malang in Java, are much cheaper and fresher.

apokat – avocado. They are plentiful and cheap; try an avocado and ice-cream combo.

belimbing – The 'starfruit' is a cool, crispy, watery tasting fruit – if you cut a slice you'll immediately see where the name comes from.

durian – the most infamous tropical fruit, the durian is a large green fruit with a hard, spiky exterior. Inside are pockets of creamy white fruit. Stories are told of a horrific stench emanating from an opened durian – hotels and airlines often ban them because of their foul odour. Some don't smell so bad – unpleasant yes, but certainly not like holding your nose over an overflowing sewer. The durian season is in the later part of the year.

jambu air – water apple or wax jambu. These glossy white or pink bell-shaped fruit come from a popular street and garden tree found throughout Indonesia. Children can often be seen selling the fruit skewered on a sliver of bamboo. The jambu air is crisp and refreshing eaten chilled, but fairly tasteless. The single seed should not be eaten.

jambu batu – guava. Also known as jambu klutuk, the guava comes from Central America and was bought to Asia by the Spanish. The fruit comes in many colours, shapes and sizes, the most common are light green and pear-shaped, turning yellow when fully ripe. The pinkish flesh is full of seeds. Ripe guava have a strong smell that some find overpowering. In Asia, the unripe fruit are also popular sliced and dipped in thick soy sauce with sliced chilli, and mango can also be served this way.

jeruk – the all-purpose term for citrus fruit. There are several kinds available. The main ones include the huge *jeruk muntis* or *jerunga*, known in the West as the pomelo. It's larger than a grapefruit but has a very thick skin, tastes sweeter, more like an orange and has segments that break apart very easily. Regular oranges are known as *jeruk manis* – sweet jeruk. The small tangerine-like oranges which are often quite green are *jeruk baras*. Lemons are *jeruk nipis*.

kelapa – coconut; as plentiful as you would expect! *Kelapa muda* means young coconut and you'll often get them straight from the tree. Drink the milk and then scoop out the flesh.

mangga – mango. The mango season is the second half of the year.

manggis – mangosteen. One of the most famous of tropical fruits, this is a small purple-brown fruit. The outer covering cracks open to reveal pure-white segments with an indescribably fine flavour. Queen Victoria once offered a reward to anyone able to transport a mangosteen back to England while still edible. From November to February is the mangosteen season. Beware of stains from the fruit's casing, which can be permanent.

pedas	spicy hot
goreng	fried
bakar	barbecued
rebus	boiled
pisau	knife
garpu	fork
sendok	spoon
Saya mau makan.	I want to eat.

Self-Catering

In any medium to large-sized city, you'll find well-stocked supermarkets. It's here that you'll find a wide variety of both local and imported foods. The other alternative is to explore the outdoor markets where you find fresh fruits, vegetables, eggs, chickens (both living and having recently passed away), freshly ground coffee and just about anything else. There are no price tags in the market and bargaining is often necessary.

An easy guide to the identification of weird-looking food is *A Jakarta Market* by Kaarin Wall, published by the American Women's Association – it should be possible for you to pick up a copy in Jakarta. It's got pictures and descriptions of vegetables, roots

Coconuts

Durians

Starfruits

Jackfruit

nangka – also known as jackfruit this is an enormous yellow-green fruit that can weigh over 20 kg. Inside are individual segments of yellow fruit, each containing a roughly egg-shaped seed. The segments are held together by strong white fibres. The fruit is moist and fairly sweet, with a slightly rubbery texture. It is used mostly in cooking. As each nangka ripens on a tree it may be individually protected in a bag. The skin of a nangka is green when young, yellow when ripe. The *cempadak* is a close relative of the nangka, but smaller, sweeter and more strongly flavoured.

nanas – pineapple

papaya – or paw paw are not unusual in the West. It's actually a native of South America and was brought to the Philippines by the Spanish, and from there spread to other parts of South-East Asia.

pisang – banana. The range in Indonesia is astonishing – from midgets to specimens well over a foot long. A bunch of bananas, by the way, is *satu sisir pisang*.

rambutan – a bright red fruit covered in soft, hairy spines – the name means hairy. Break it open to reveal a delicious white fruit closely related to the lychee. From November to February is the rambutan season.

salak – found chiefly in Indonesia, the salak is immediately recognisable by its perfect brown 'snakeskin' covering. Peel it off to reveal segments that, in texture, are like a cross between an apple and a walnut, but in taste are quite unique. Each segment contains a large, brown oval-shaped seed. Bali salaks are much nicer than any others.

sawo – brown-skinned, looks like a potato and has honey-flavoured flesh

sirsak – the sirsak is known in the West as soursop or zurzak. Originally a native of tropical America, the Indonesian variety is one of the best. The warty green skin covers a thirst-quenching, soft, white, pulpy interior with a slightly lemonish, tart taste. You can peel it off or slice it into segments. Sirsaks are ripe when the skin has begun to lose its fresh green colouring and become darker and spotty. It should then feel slightly squishy rather than firm. ■

and herbs, dry goods, fish, fresh fruit and other foods you'll find in the markets in Jakarta, which are also relevant to the rest of Indonesia.

Betel Nut

Not exactly a food, betel nut (*sirih* in Bahasa Indonesia) is popular, especially in the villages. It's what causes that red stain on what's left of their teeth and gums. The betel nut *pinang* is chewed in combination with sirih leaf, *kapor sirih* (powdered lime) and a brown substance called *gambir*.

DRINKS

Indonesians have enthusiastically embraced Western soft drink culture. In a country where delicious, fresh fruit juices are sold you can still rot your teeth on Coca Cola, 7-Up, Sprite and Fanta. Prices are typically around 750 rp and up for a bottle, and from 1200 rp for a can.

There is a saying that while the British built roads in their colonies, the Dutch built breweries. Many of these still exist and, while beer is comparatively expensive (normally 3000 rp, often more), it's also good. The three popular brands are Bintang, San Miguel and Anker. Bintang is the most popular. Some other popular Indonesian drinks, both alcoholic and non-alcoholic, include:

air – water. You may get a glass of it with a restaurant meal. It should have been boiled (and may not have cooled down since), but often it won't be boiled at all. Ask for *air putih* (literally white water) or drink tea. Hygienic bottled water is available everywhere.
air jeruk – citrus fruit juice. *Jeruk manis* is orange juice and *jeruk nipis* is lemon juice.
air minum – drinking water
arak – a stage on from brem (distilled rice wine). It's usually home-produced, although even the locally bottled brands look home-produced. It makes quite a good drink mixed with 7-Up or Sprite. Taken in copious quantities it has a similar effect to being hit on the head with an elephant.
Aqua – the most common brand of mineral water. It is highly recommended if you're dubious about drinking other water, although it's not cheap, at around 1000 rp for a 1½ litre bottle.

brem – rice wine; either home produced or there's the commercially bottled 'Bali Brem'. A bit of an acquired taste, but not bad after a few bottles!
es juice – although you should be a little careful about ice and water the delicious fruit drinks are irresistible. Just take one or two varieties of tropical fruit, add crushed ice and pass it through a blender. You can make mind-blowing combinations of orange, banana, pineapple, mango, jackfruit, soursop or whatever else is available.
es buah – more a dessert than a drink; a curious combination of crushed ice, condensed milk, shaved coconut, syrup, jelly and fruit. Sickening say some, wonderful say others.
Green Sands – a pleasant soft drink, made not from sand, but from malt, apple and lime juice.
kopi – coffee. Excellent coffee is grown in Indonesia. The best comes from Sulawesi, though Java and Sumatra also produce some mean brews. It is made, Turkish style, by pouring boiling water on finely ground coffee beans spooned into a glass. Served sweet and black with the coffee granules floating on top, it is a real kick start in the mornings. Travellers' restaurants have adopted the odd habit of serving kopi without sugar. *Kopi susu* is white coffee, usually made with sweetened, condensed milk.
stroop – cordial
susu – milk; fresh milk is found in supermarkets in large cities, although life-long milk in cartons is more common. Cans of condensed Indomilk are also sold in Indonesia and are very sweet. Another common one is Bear Brand canned milk from every Third World country's favourite multinational, Nestlé. Fresh milk (*susu segar*) is served in warungs in Yogya and Solo.
teh – tea; Some people are not enthusiastic about Indonesian tea but if you don't need strong, bend-the-teaspoon-style tea you'll probably find it's quite OK. *Teh tawar* or *teh pahit* is tea without sugar and *teh manis* is tea with sugar.
tuak – an alcoholic drink fermented from the sap tapped from a type of palm tree.

TOBACCO

If you're an anti-smoking activist, you'll have your work cut out for you in Indonesia. Most Indonesian men (rarely women) smoke like chimneys. Some say Indonesian chain smokers only need one match a day – they light the first cigarette in the morning, and then continue to light the next cigarette with the one currently being smoked, ad infinitum.

If you have the habit yourself, you might be pleased by the local selection of tobacco products. Indonesia is justly famous for its unique 'kretek' cigarettes, produced by blending cloves with tobacco. The fragrant odour is quite unlike any you've ever smelled before. Imported cigarettes like Dunhill, Lucky Strike and Marlboro are available but more expensive.

ENTERTAINMENT

Cinemas

Indonesians are great movie fans and cinemas can be found in all but the smallest village. In large cities like Jakarta, Surabaya, Denpasar etc, the latest Western films can be seen, usually with English dialogue and Indonesian subtitles. As one gets into the backwaters, the films tend to be of vintage age – old hits from the 1960s are still being shown! Besides Western movies, there are plenty of violent kung fu epics from Hong Kong and weird science-fiction films from Japan.

Cinemas usually only operate in the evening, starting from 5 pm, but a few places open on Sunday around 1 pm.

Discos

Young Indonesians have taken to disco dancing like ants to honey. Obviously, discos are easiest to find in large cities like Jakarta and resort areas like Kuta Beach in Bali. Some discos are independent, but many are located in five-star hotels. Prices vary, but in general there's a small cover charge and expensive drinks.

Spectator Sports

Most of Indonesia's live spectator sports are male-oriented and associated with gambling. You'll certainly have plenty of chance to see cockfighting, especially in Bali and Kalimantan.

THINGS TO BUY

Souvenir vendors positively swarm around touristy places like Kuta Beach and Yogyakarta. Off the beaten track, shopping is more relaxed. If you're an art collector, you'll find plenty of chances to stock up on unusual items. Wood carvings are on sale everywhere. Batik and ikat (see the Arts & Crafts colour section) attract a steady stream of foreign art enthusiasts. Good pottery is available, mostly in Java.

If you have little or no interest in art, there are still plenty of more practical, everyday items that make good buys. Sarinah Department Store in Jakarta, and other various up-market shops, have export-quality clothing in large sizes for dirt cheap prices. You can even find jackets, ski caps and other winter clothing.

If you can figure out a way to get it home, rattan and bamboo furniture is a very cheap and practical item to buy in Indonesia.

Many foreigners get addicted to Indonesian coffee, which is superb. Kapal Api is a popular brand name for packaged coffee, but the best coffee is the stone-ground stuff you buy in markets. If you're going to keep it a long time, it's best to buy whole coffee beans and grind it yourself when you're ready to drink it. Cheap coffee grinders can also be bought in Indonesia.

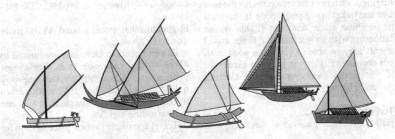

Getting There & Away

AIR

The principal gateways for entry to Indonesia are Jakarta and Bali. Jakarta is serviced by more airlines, but with its huge tourist trade Bali gets almost as much traffic.

There are also international flights from neighbouring countries to various cities in the outer islands and a couple of possible land and sea entry routes. Singapore has some of the cheapest flights to Indonesia, and is a major travel hub in the region. It may be cheaper to fly to Singapore, from where you can enter Indonesia by air or ship. The same applies to Penang in Malaysia, from where you can take a short flight or ferry to Medan in Sumatra.

For bargain fares, it is usually better to go to a travel agent than to an airline, as the latter can only sell fares by the book. Budget tickets may come with lots of restrictions. Check for how long the ticket is valid, the minimum period of stay, stopover options, cancellation fees and any amendment fees if you change your date of travel. Plenty of discount tickets are valid for six or 12 months, allowing multiple stopovers with open dates. Make sure you get details in writing of the flights you've requested (before you pay for the ticket). 'Round-the-world' tickets may also be worth looking into.

Fares quoted below are an approximate guide only. Fares vary depending on the season (high, shoulder or low) and special deals are often available. Fares can vary from week to week, and it pays to shop around by ringing a variety of travel agents for the best fare and ticket to suit your needs. If you want to combine some domestic flights within Indonesia with an international flight, travel agents may be able to get you a good deal, but domestic flights can be more expensive if purchased overseas (see the Getting Around chapter).

To/From Australia

Bali is the major gateway to Australia, with almost all flights to/from Indonesia routed via Denpasar. Direct flights connect Denpasar with Sydney, Melbourne, Brisbane, Perth, Darwin and Port Hedland. Garuda, Qantas and Ansett Australia are the main carriers and compete on most of these runs, but the Port Hedland-Denpasar flight on Saturdays is operated only by Merpati. From Denpasar you can connect to other Indonesian cities.

Other direct flights to Indonesia are limited. They include Darwin-Kupang (Merpati), Perth-Jakarta (Garuda and Sempati), and Sydney-Jakarta (Qantas and UTA). The most interesting of these is the flight from Darwin to Kupang (on the island of Timor) on Wednesdays and Saturdays. From Kupang, regular flights go to Bali (which is slightly cheaper than flying Darwin-Bali direct) or you can island-hop through the Nusa Tenggara archipelago. Natrabu (☎ (089) 813695), 12 Westlane Arcade off Smith St Mall, is one of the biggest Merpati agents in Darwin.

Sample fares in Australian dollars, ranging between the low season (February to December) and the high season (December and January), are:

From	To	One Way	Return
Melbourne, Sydney, Brisbane	Denpasar	650-750	800-1100
Darwin, Perth	Denpasar	450-550	700-900
Port Hedland	Denpasar	390-457	616-722
Darwin	Kupang	198-248	330-407

Flights to Jakarta cost around A$100 more than to Denpasar.

Return tickets to Denpasar are limited to 45 or 90-day excursion fares. For longer periods, you'll have to buy two one-way tickets, or Garuda has six-month return tickets to Jakarta (via Denpasar, if you can fathom airline logic).

Travel agents are the best place to shop for

cheap tickets, but because Bali is such a popular destination flight discounting is not large and most agents prefer to sell Bali packages. Merpati has no competition on its Port Hedland-Denpasar and Darwin-Kupang flights, so discounts are virtually non-existent on these runs.

Travel agents to try include the big networks like STA Travel or Flight Centres International, with offices in the main cities, or check the travel pages of the main newspapers. It is also worth ringing the airlines direct. The highest demand for flights is during school holidays and especially the Christmas break – book well in advance.

Of course Bali is one of Australia's favourite 'OS' holiday destinations and package tours can offer good, cheap deals. Packages including return airfare with five to 10-days accommodation in a three or four-star hotel can cost little more than the price of an airfare alone. If you are thinking of taking one of these packages and then extending your stay – forget it. They are strictly for the period on offer.

To/From New Zealand

Garuda and Air New Zealand have direct flights between Auckland and Denpasar. Air New Zealand's fares are generally a little lower than Garuda's. The return economy airfare from Auckland to Denpasar or Jakarta is about NZ$1300 to NZ$1500, depending on the season.

Check the latest fare developments and discounts with the airlines, or shop around a few travel agents for possible deals. As in Australia, STA Travel and Flight Centres International are popular travel agents.

To/From the UK

Ticket discounting is a long-established business in the UK and it's wide open – the various agencies advertise their fares and there's nothing under the counter about it at all. To find out what is available and where to get it, pick up a copy of the giveaway newspapers *TNT, Southern Cross,* or *Trailfinder* or the weekly 'what's on' guide *Time*

Out. Discounted tickets are available all over the UK, and they're not just a London exclusive. The magazine *Business Traveller* also covers fare possibilities.

A couple of excellent places to look are Trailfinders and STA Travel. Trailfinders is at 194 Kensington High St, London W8 (☎ 0171-938 3939) and at 46 Earls Court Rd (☎ 0171-938 3366). It also has offices in Manchester (☎ 061-839 6969) and Glasgow (☎ 041-353 2224). STA Travel is at 74 Old Brompton Rd, London W7 (☎ 0171-581 1022) and at Clifton House, 117 Euston Rd (☎ 388 2261).

Garuda is one of the main discounters to Indonesia, with flights from around £500 return to Jakarta in the low season, slightly more to Denpasar. High season prices are about 30% more. Travel agents also put together cheap tickets via Singapore, or you can do it yourself. Flights from London to Singapore start at around £225 one-way, £400 return. From Singapore you can reach Indonesia by boat or a one-way ticket to Jakarta will cost around £50, but Denpasar flights will cost more than triple that.

It's also easy to find cheap fares to Australia with a stopover in Indonesia, starting at about £350 one-way in the low season or £600 in the high season. Round-the-World (RTW) tickets including Indonesia, Australia, New Zealand and the USA start at around £850.

To/From Europe

The Netherlands, Brussels and Antwerp are good places for buying discount air tickets. In Antwerp, WATS has been recommended. In Zurich try SOF Travel and Sindbad. In Geneva try Stohl Travel. In the Netherlands, NBBS is a reputable agency.

As well as Garuda and other Asian airlines, KLM and Lufthansa have a number of flights to Indonesia. Usually it is cheaper to fly to Jakarta than Denpasar, eg Lufthansa's regular discount fares from Germany are around 1600 DM to Jakarta and 1900 DM to Denpasar, but package deals and specials to Bali can make fares about the same to either destination. The cheapest way to reach Indonesia is often via Singapore, with the East European airlines offering some of the cheapest flights. Aeroflot's flight into Jakarta once a week is especially cheap.

Garuda has flight connections between Jakarta and several European cities: Paris, Amsterdam, Zurich, Frankfurt and Rome.

To/From the USA

There are some very good open tickets which remain valid for six months or one year (opt for the latter), but don't lock you into any fixed dates of departure. For example, there are cheap tickets between the US west coast and Singapore with stopovers in Japan, Korea, Taiwan, Hong Kong and Bangkok for

---

Air Travel Glossary

Apex Apex ('advance purchase excursion') is a discounted ticket which must be paid for in advance. There are penalties if you wish to change it.

Baggage Allowance This will be written on your ticket: usually one 20-kg item to go in the hold, plus one item of hand luggage.

Bucket Shop An unbonded travel agency specialising in discounted airline tickets.

Bumped Just because you have a confirmed seat doesn't mean you're going to get on the plane – see Overbooking.

Cancellation Penalties If you have to cancel or change an Apex ticket there are often heavy penalties involved – insurance can sometimes be taken out against these penalties. Some airlines impose penalties on regular tickets as well, particularly against 'no show' passengers (see No Shows).

Check In Airlines ask you to check in a certain time ahead of the flight departure (usually two hours on international flights). If you fail to check in on time and the flight is overbooked, the airline can cancel your booking and give your seat to somebody else.

Confirmation Having a ticket written out with the flight and date you want doesn't mean you have a seat until the agent has checked with the airline that your status is 'OK' or confirmed. Meanwhile, you could just be 'on request'. It's also wise to reconfirm onward or return bookings directly with the airline 72 hours before departure (see Reconfirmation).

Discounted Tickets There are two types of discounted fares: officially discounted (see Promotional Fares) and unofficially discounted. The lowest prices often impose drawbacks like flying with unpopular airlines, inconvenient schedules, or unpleasant routes and connections. A discounted ticket can save you other things than money – you may be able to pay Apex prices without the associated Apex advance booking and other requirements. Discounted tickets only exist where there is fierce competition.

Full Fares Airlines traditionally offer 1st-class (coded F), business-class (coded J) and economy-class (coded Y) tickets. These days there are so many promotional and discounted fares available from the regular economy class that few passengers pay full economy fare.

Lost Tickets If you lose your airline ticket, an airline will usually treat it like a travellers' cheque and, after enquiries, issue you with another one. Legally, however, an airline is entitled to treat it like cash and if you lose it then it's gone forever. Take good care of your tickets.

No Shows No shows are passengers who fail to show up for their flight, sometimes due to unexpected delays or disasters, sometimes due to simply forgetting, sometimes because they made more than one booking and didn't bother to cancel the one they didn't want. Full fare passengers who fail to turn up are sometimes entitled to travel on a later flight. The rest of us are penalised (see Cancellation Penalties).

On Request An unconfirmed booking for a flight (see Confirmation).

very little extra money – the departure dates can be changed and you have one year to complete the journey. However, be careful during the peak season (summer and Chinese New Year) because seats will be hard to come by unless reserved months in advance.

San Francisco is the bucket shop capital of the USA, though some good deals can be found in Los Angeles, New York and other cities. Bucket shops can be found through the Yellow Pages or the major daily newspapers. Those listed in both Roman and Oriental scripts are invariably discounters. The *New York Times*, the *LA Times*, the *Chicago Tribune* and the *San Francisco Examiner* all produce weekly travel sections in which

Open Jaws A return ticket where you fly out to one place but return from another. If available, this can save you backtracking to your arrival point.

Overbooking Airlines hate to fly empty seats, and since every flight has some passengers who fail to show up (see No Shows), airlines often book more passengers than they have seats. Usually the excess passengers balance those who fail to show up but occasionally somebody gets bumped. If this happens, guess who it is most likely to be? The passengers who check in late.

Promotional Fares Officially discounted fares like Apex fares which are available from travel agents or direct from the airline.

Reconfirmation At least 72 hours prior to departure time of an onward or return flight you must contact the airline and 'reconfirm' that you intend to be on the flight. If you don't do this the airline can delete your name from the passenger list and you could lose your seat. You don't have to reconfirm the first flight on your itinerary or if your stopover is less than 72 hours. It doesn't hurt to reconfirm more than once.

Restrictions Discounted tickets often have various restrictions on them – advance purchase is the most usual one (see Apex). Others are restrictions on the minimum and maximum period you must be away, such as a minimum of 14 days or a maximum of one year. See Cancellation Penalties.

Standby A discounted ticket where you only fly if there is a seat free at the last moment. Standby fares are usually only available on domestic routes.

Tickets Out An entry requirement for many countries is that you have an onward or return ticket – in other words, a ticket out of the country. If you're not sure what you intend to do next, the easiest solution is to buy the cheapest onward ticket to a neighbouring country or a ticket from a reliable airline which can later be refunded if you do not use it.

Transferred Tickets Airline tickets cannot be transferred from one person to another. Travellers sometimes try to sell the return half of their ticket, but officials can ask you to prove that you are the person named on the ticket. This is unlikely to happen on domestic flights, but on international flights, tickets may be compared with passports. Also, if you're flying on a transferred ticket and something goes wrong with the flight (hijack, crash), there will be no record of your presence on board.

Travel Agencies Travel agencies vary widely and you should ensure you use one that suits your needs. Some simply handle tours while full-service agencies handle everything from tours and tickets to car rental and hotel bookings. A good one will do all these things and can save you a lot of money, but if all you want is a ticket at the lowest possible price, then you really need an agency specialising in discounted tickets. A discounted ticket agency, however, may not be useful for other things, like hotel bookings.

Travel Periods Some officially discounted fares, Apex fares in particular, vary with the time of year. There is often a low (off-peak) season and a high (peak) season. Sometimes there's an intermediate or shoulder season as well. At peak times, when everyone wants to fly, not only will the officially discounted fares be higher but so will unofficially discounted fares, or there may simply be no discounted tickets available. Usually the fare depends on your outward flight – if you depart in the high season and return in the low season, you pay the high-season fare. ■

you'll find any number of travel agents' ads. The magazine *Travel Unlimited* (PO Box 1058, Allston, Mass 02134) publishes details of courier and cheap airfares to destinations all over the world from the USA.

It's not advisable to send money (even cheques) through the post unless the agent is very well established – some travellers have reported being ripped off by fly-by-night mail order ticket agents.

Council Travel is the largest student travel organisation and, although you don't have to be a student to use them, they do have specially discounted student tickets. Council Travel has an extensive network in all major US cities and is listed in the telephone book. There are also Student Travel Network offices which are associated with Student Travel Australia.

One of the cheapest and most reliable travel agents on the west coast is Overseas Tours (☎ (800) 3238777 in California, (800) 2275988 elsewhere), 475 El Camino Real, Room 206, Millbrae, CA 94030. Another good agent is Gateway Travel (☎ (214) 9602000, (800) 4411183), 4201 Spring Valley Rd, Suite 104, Dallas, TX 75244, who seem to be reliable for mail order tickets.

From the US west coast, fares to Singapore, Bangkok or Hong Kong cost around US$700/1000 one-way/return, while Bali flights cost from US$650/1100 in the low season (outside summer and Christmas).

Alternatively, Garuda has a Los Angeles-Honolulu-Biak-Denpasar route which is an extremely interesting back-door route into Indonesia. Biak is a no-visa entry point so that's no problem, and from there you can explore Irian Jaya, or continue on to Bali. The return fare from Los Angeles to Bali is about US$1100 or US$600 one way in the low season.

To/From Canada

Getting discount tickets in Canada is much the same as in the USA – go to the travel agents and shop around until you find a good deal. Again, you'll probably have to fly into Hong Kong or Singapore and carry on from there to Indonesia.

CUTS is Canada's national student bureau and has offices in a number of Canadian cities including Vancouver, Edmonton, Toronto and Ottawa – you don't necessarily have to be a student. There are a number of good agents in Vancouver for cheap tickets, CP-Air are particularly good for fares to Hong Kong.

The *Toronto Globe & Mail* and the *Vancouver Sun* carry travel agents' ads. The magazine *Great Expeditions* (PO Box 8000-411, Abbotsford BC V2S 6H1) is useful.

To/From Singapore

There are direct flights from Singapore to Jakarta, Denpasar and several cities in Sumatra, such as Medan, Pekanbaru, Padang and Palembang. Merpati has flights to Pontianak in Kalimantan for around S$260, and to Balikpapan. Silk Air flies from Singapore to Manado (in Sulawesi) direct.

Of most interest to travellers are the numerous Singapore-Jakarta tickets which are discounted to as low as US$70. Sempati is regularly one of the cheapest, but Gulf Air and Air India are also cheap.

Singapore is also a good place to buy a cheap air ticket if you're leaving South-East Asia for the West. Cheap air tickets from Singapore are available at Airmaster and Airpower travel agents. Also try STA Travel.

To/From Malaysia

The most popular flight is from Penang to Medan in Sumatra with Sempati Air or Malaysian Air Service (MAS) for around US$60. Sempati flies from Kuala Lumpur to Medan for around US$80 and to Padang, while Pelangi Air flies from KL to Padang via Pekanbaru for US$107.

There are also twice-weekly flights between Kuching in Sarawak and Pontianak in Kalimantan for around US$70. Similarly at the eastern end of Borneo there is also a connection between Tawau in Sabah and Tarakan in Kalimantan.

To/From Philippines

Bourac's has a twice weekly flight from Manado in Sulawesi to Davao in the Philippines, as well as regular Manila-Jakarta flights.

To/From Papua New Guinea

From Papua New Guinea there is a twice-weekly flight between Vanimo and Jayapura in Irian Jaya for 50 PNG kina or roughly US$50. For more details see the Irian Jaya chapter.

LAND

The only open land crossing is at Entikong, between Kalimantan and Sarawak (eastern Malaysia). This border post on the Pontianak-Kuching highway is now an official international entry point. Visas are not required and a 60-day tourist pass is issued on the spot. See the Kalimantan chapter for more details.

SEA
To/From Malaysia

Most sea connections are between Malaysia and Sumatra. The comfortable, high-speed ferry from Penang (Malaysia) to Medan (Sumatra) is one of the most popular ways to reach Indonesia. Ferries also connect Medan with Port Kelang and Lumut in Malaysia, and Dumai (Sumatra) with Melaka and Port Kelang. See Sumatra Getting There & Away for full details.

A new passenger ship operates from Pasir Gudang, about 30 km from Johor Bahru, to Surabaya. SS Holidays (☎ 07-511577), Level 3, 12-13, Kompleks Pusat Bandar, Pasir Gudang has a ship to Surabaya at 5 pm on Saturdays which takes 60 hours. Fares range from RM200 in an eight-berth economy cabin to RM280 in a two-berth cabin. See under Surabaya for more details.

To/From Singapore

An increasingly popular way to reach Indonesia is via Sumatra's Riau Archipelago (see the Sumatra chapter for full details). The main stepping stones are the islands of Batam and Bintan, both only a short high-speed ferry ride from Singapore.

Batam is the bigger travel hub and from

this island speedboats run through to Pekanbaru on the Sumatran mainland.

From Bintan, Pelni ships run to Jakarta. The problem with the Pelni ships has always been the difficulty of finding out the constantly changing Pelni schedule before arriving in Indonesia, but now there is also another regular twice-weekly service from Bintan to Jakarta. This is an interesting way to reach Jakarta, though only marginally cheaper than flying.

To/From Australia

For those with plenty of time up their sleeves, the *Golden Star*, a modified 35-metre Indonesian sailing vessel, departs monthly from Hudson Creek, in Darwin, to Benoa Harbour (in South Bali). The journey takes from 10 to 13 days, and accommodation is in basic two, four or eight berths. The one-way fare is A$270/320/340 in an eight/four/two berth. In Australia, contact All Points Travel (☎ 089-410066; fax 089-411602), Unit 7, Anthony Plaza, Smith St Mall, PO Box 2561, Darwin NT 0801. The agent in Bali is Tall Ship Cruises (☎ & fax 287431), Jalan Danau, Posio 20A, Sanur, Bali.

Other

With a bit of effort it's still possible to get yacht rides around South-East Asia. Very often, yacht owners are travellers too and need another crew member or two and often all it costs you is the contribution to the food kitty. As for where to look – well, anywhere that yachts pass through or in towns with Western-style yacht clubs. We've had letters from people who have managed to get rides from Singapore, Penang, Phuket (in Thailand) and Benoa (in Bali). Other popular yachting places include the main ports in Papua New Guinea and Hong Kong.

It is possible to get a lift as a passenger or crew member from Darwin, especially at the time of the Darwin-Ambon yacht race in July, but make sure you go to a recognised entry port if you don't have a visa. The Darwin Yacht Club, at Fannie Bay, Darwin has a noticeboard for crews.

TOURS

Tours tend to be oriented towards Bali. Most are accommodation and airfare only packages, which are very popular and can be good value for short stays. Choose your accommodation so that you are not too isolated and forced to rely on expensive hotel services. Other more expensive tours include sightseeing, all transfers, meals, etc.

Tours to other parts of Indonesia range from adventure/trekking tours of Irian Jaya and Kalimantan to temple tours of Java. There are so many tours that it's impossible to list them all here, but the European market probably has the biggest selection, especially Dutch tour companies that have very competitively priced tours ranging from big luxury groups to small, interesting off-the-beaten-track tours. Prices range according to the standard of accommodation. Some try so hard to maximise luxury and minimise hassles that participants are hermetically isolated from Indonesia and Indonesians. Smaller groups that provide some independence generally provide a more worthwhile experience.

Some of the more deluxe tours also include luxurious boat trips to neighbouring islands. One note of caution – the more upmarket tours may be comfortable and fun, but some of the staged ceremonies you'll be shown are basically little more than theatre. We ran into one tour group on the island of Lembata while they were attending a 'traditional ceremony' imported from Hawaii, complete with female dancers in grass skirts and flower necklaces, moving to the beat of bongo drums. Nice, but not exactly authentic Indonesian culture.

Of course you can make your own way to Indonesia and take day tours to surrounding attractions. The major tourist centres such as Kuta in Bali and Yogyakarta on Java, offer some of the best value tours in Indonesia.

LEAVING INDONESIA

Jakarta is no discount centre compared to Singapore or Bangkok, but it is the best place to buy international tickets in Indonesia. Of most interest to travellers are the short hop tickets such as Jakarta-Singapore and Kupang-Dili. Small agents specialising in services for travellers may advertise international tickets, but you will usually get much better discounts at one of the bigger flight specialists. At travel agencies, you usually save at least 3% if you pay cash rather than use a credit card.

International student-card holders should ask about discounts (up to 25%) if buying international tickets in Indonesia. These discounts are generally only available on overpriced published fares anyway, and not for already discounted tickets.

Indonesian airports are dull affairs. Jakarta's Soekarno-Hatta airport is spacious, modern and surprisingly efficient but only has a few overpriced food and shopping outlets. Bali's smaller Ngurah Rai airport is slightly more interesting. Shopping is also overpriced but more varied, and the airport can be exciting if you like crowds. In peak tourist seasons when a few jumbos land, it is standing room only and the queues can be long. Standard duty free items are on sale at both airports, but local cigarettes are much cheaper than the duty free variety, and there are no great bargains for alcohol either.

Departure Tax

Airport tax on international flights varies with the airport: 21,000 rp from Jakarta, 20,000 rp from Denpasar and 15,000 rp from most other airports. On domestic flights, airport tax is usually between 5500 and 8800 rp, depending on the airport, but this is normally included in the ticket price.

Getting Around

AIR

Indonesia has a variety of airlines, a bizarre collection of aircraft and an extensive network of flights that make some pretty remote corners of the country easily accessible. The main airlines are Garuda, Merpati, Sempati, Bouraq and Mandala and there are several smaller ones. Tickets bought through the airline offices will cost the same regardless of the airline, but some travel agents in Jakarta, and a few other big cities (mostly on Java), sell discounted domestic tickets. Discounts are often small (5 to 10%), but can be substantial for return tickets (up to 40%).

On top of the basic fares, a 10% tax is charged, as well as domestic departure tax, which varies from around 5500 to 8800 rp, depending on the airport. These taxes are normally paid when you buy the ticket, and will be written on the ticket. Baggage allowance is usually 20 kg, or only 10 kg on the smaller planes. Sometimes a fee is charged for excess baggage.

Most airlines offer student discounts of up to 25%. You need a valid International Student Identity Card (ISIC) to take advantage of this, as well as a letter from the school or institution. For domestic flights, there is no age limit for claiming the student discount, but for international flights the age limit is 26.

Airlines accept credit cards but don't expect to be able to use them in small offices in the outer islands.

Each airline publishes a nationwide timetable – definitely worth picking up if you're going to do a lot of flying, but not always easy to get. Minor changes to schedules are frequent, so always check with local airline offices about what's available.

Book as far in advance as possible during Indonesian holiday periods and the peak tourist season around August. During these times, on the more popular routes, flights can be fully booked two or three weeks in advance. Indonesian airlines are generally reliable, even efficient these days, but it is essential to *reconfirm*. Overbooking is common and if you don't reconfirm at least a few days before departure you may well get bumped. Expect problems in the outer islands where flights are limited, communications poor and booking procedures haphazard. Here you should reconfirm and reconfirm again.

Travel agents overseas can usually include discounted domestic flights with an international ticket if you enter Indonesia with Garuda. Otherwise domestic tickets bought overseas are quoted in US dollars and cost around 50% more than if bought in Indonesia in rupiah.

Visit Indonesia Decade Pass

Garuda issues this internal airpass starting at US$300 for three sectors, with each additional sector costing US$100. A sector can comprise a number of connecting flights, so, in theory at least, it is possible to fly from one end of the country to the other for only US$100. You must buy the airpass overseas or within 14 days of arrival in Indonesia, and it is valid for 60 days. A few other restrictions apply – inquire at a Garuda office. If your travel was restricted to Java and Sumatra, you might not save any money with these passes but you can make big savings if you fly to Irian Jaya, Maluku or Sulawesi. The pass is currently available for use on Merpati as well as Garuda flights.

Local Air Services

Garuda The major national airline is Garuda, named after the mythical man-bird vehicle of the Hindu god Vishnu. Garuda operates most of Indonesia's international flights and has a useful domestic network between the major cities only. Garuda operates wide-bodied jets on the domestic runs and has an efficient booking network. Its airpass can be very good value.

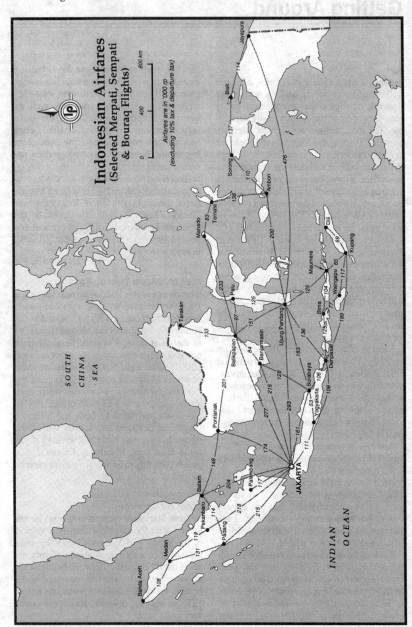

Indonesian Airfares
(Selected Merpati, Sempati
& Bouraq Flights)

Airfares are in '000 rp
(excluding 10% tax & departure tax)

0   400   800 km

Merpati Merpati was taken over by Garuda in 1989, but it has been announced that the marriage will be annulled. In effect both airlines have operated independently and run their own network of offices since the merger, so the change will make little difference. One major advantage has been that Merpati flights can be tacked on to a Garuda ticket (including the Visit Indonesia Decade Pass) but this may change.

Merpati runs a mind-boggling collection of aircraft – everything from modern jets to single-engine eggbeaters. It has the most extensive domestic network, and part of its charter is to cover obscure locations that would otherwise be without an air service. Merpati also flies a few back-door international routes, including Darwin-Kupang, Denpasar-Port Hedland and Pontianak-Kuching.

Merpati has a not-undeserved reputation for poor service, bungled bookings and cancelled flights. However, it is important to remember that Merpati operates two networks – its commercial flights and its 'Perintis' (Pioneer) flights in the rural backblocks of Indonesia. On the commercial flights, large aircraft run between the major cities, where many of the offices now have computerised booking systems. These flights are competitive in standards with the other airlines. On Perintis flights, small aircraft land on grass strips in obscure towns that may not even have telephones. Seats are hard to get, flights get cancelled, and the radio booking system is haphazard. Expect hassles on these flights, which cover many of the flights in Irian Jaya, Maluku and Nusa Tenggara (including some popular tourist runs in Flores), as well as a few rural services in Kalimantan, Sulawesi and Java.

Sempati Sempati is Indonesia's fastest growing airline with a fleet of modern jets and impeccable government contacts. It serves most of the major cities throughout Indonesia, and its growing international network includes flights to Singapore, Kuala Lumpur, Malacca, Penang, Perth and Taipei. Sempati has a good reputation for reliability and service, and it has some nice touches like in-flight lotteries and compensation for late flights (both in the form of discount vouchers on Sempati flights).

Bouraq The network of this privately run airline is nowhere near as extensive as Merpati's or Garuda's, but it has some useful flights in Kalimantan, Sulawesi, Maluku and Nusa Tenggara, including connections between Java and Bali. Bouraq also has some interesting international flights: Tarakan-Tawau (Malaysia) and Manado-Davao (Philippines).

Mandala Mandala is the smallest of the all-Indonesia airlines and apart from a few new jets runs a largely clapped out collection of rattle traps. They serve a couple of main routes connecting Jakarta with Ambon, Biak, Medan, Padang, Surabaya and Ujung Pandang, as well as Yogya-Denpasar-Kupang.

Other There are some intriguing possibilities for flying in Indonesia. The mission aircraft which operate in places like Kalimantan, Central Sulawesi and Irian Jaya fly to some really remote parts of the interior of these islands and will take *paying* passengers if they have room. You're most likely to use the flights around Irian Jaya – see the Irian Jaya chapter for details.

Various aircraft and helicopters are used by the foreign mining and oil companies – if you meet the right people in the right place, if they like the look of your face, and if they're not yet sick of every self-proclaimed Marco Polo looking for a free ride, you never know where you could end up.

Other airlines include SMAC, Deraya and DAS (Dirgantara Air Service), which operate back routes in Sumatra and Kalimantan.

BUS

At any time of the day, thousands of buses in all shapes and sizes are moving thousands of people throughout Indonesia. Buses are the mainstay of Indonesian transport.

Classes

Bus services vary throughout the islands, but are usually dependent on the roads. Java, for example, has all types of buses including luxury air-con coaches that ply the well-paved highways. Luxury buses can also be found on the Trans-Sumatran Highway and the good roads on Bali, Lombok and Sumbawa. The 'Wallace Line' for the evolution of buses lies between Sumbawa and Flores, for luxury buses just don't exist on Flores and the islands further east. Only small, overcrowded rattlers ply the narrow, pot-holed roads on Flores that would soon wreck an expensive bus. In Indonesia the further off the beaten track you get, the more beaten-up the track becomes and the less choice you have in buses.

The bottom line in buses are the ordinary, everyday *ekonomi* buses that run set routes between towns. They stop at bus stations in every town en route, but will also stop for anyone, anywhere in the search for more paying customers – there is no such thing as 'full'. These buses are the lifeline for many communities, delivering the post, and passengers may include goats, pigs and chickens on the rural runs. They can be hot, slow and incredibly crowded but they are also ridiculously cheap and provide a never-ending parade of Indonesian life. They are often beat up rattle traps with limited leg room, but if you get a seat and the road is good, they can be quite tolerable for short distances, especially on the main highways.

The next class up are the express or *patas* buses. They can be much the same as the ekonomi buses, but stop only at selected bus stations en route and don't pick up from the side of the road. Air-con patas buses are more luxurious, and seating is often guaranteed. Usually there is no need to book and you can just catch one at bus stations in the big cities.

The luxury air-con buses come in a variety of price categories, depending on if they have reclining seats, on-board toilets, TV, karaoke, snacks, etc. These buses should be booked in advance. Ticket agents often have pictures of the buses and seating plans, so check to see what you are getting when you choose your seat. Through Sumatra, Java and Bali, many of the luxury buses are night buses *(bis malam)*, travelling the highways when the traffic is lighter.

Bring as little luggage as possible – there is rarely any room to store anything on buses. A large pack with a frame will be a positive abomination to find a space for – so if you can travel with a small bag, do so.

Reservations

For short routes on good roads you'll probably find frequent vehicles departing all through the day. For longer routes you'll have to get down to the station early in the morning to get a vehicle; on bad roads there'll be fewer vehicles, so buying a ticket beforehand can be a good idea. In many places the bus companies will have an office from which you can buy a ticket and reserve a seat; there may be shops which act as agents (or own the buses) from which you can buy tickets in advance. Often, hotels will act as agents or will buy a ticket for you and arrange to have the bus pick you up at the hotel – sometimes they will charge a few hundred rupiah for this service but it's easily worth it.

Costs

Ekonomi buses are ridiculously cheap and you can travel over 100 km for less than 2000 rp. Prices vary from region to region and with the condition of the road. The daytime buses that depart early in the morning – carrying chickens, pigs and goats – are usually the cheapest. You'll rarely have to pay more than 6000 rp for a full-day journey.

By way of comparison, the most luxurious overnight buses from Jakarta to Bali cost around 55,000 rp, including the ferry crossing. A non-air-con express bus will do the same run for around 28,000 rp.

MINIBUS (BEMO)

Public minibuses are used both as local transport around cities and towns and on short intercity runs, but their speciality is delivering people out into the hills and villages.

They service the furthest reaches of the transport network.

The great minibus ancestor is the *bemo*, a small pick-up truck with a row of seats down each side but they are more like regular minibuses these days. The word 'bemo' (a contraction of *becak* – three-wheeler bicycle-rickshaw, and *motor)* is rarely used now but is still applied on Bali and universally understood. In other regions, minibuses go by a mind-boggling array of names such as *opelet*, *mikrolet*, *angkot* or *angkudes*. Just to make things confusing they are called *taksi* in many parts of Irian Jaya and East Java. Often they will be called simply by their brand name such as Suzuki or Toyota, but the most popular make by far is the Mitsubishi Colt, and *colt* is widely used.

Most minibuses operate a standard route, picking up and dropping off people and goods anywhere along the way. They can be very cramped with even less room for luggage than the buses, and if there is a choice, the buses are usually more comfortable.

Within cities, there is usually a standard fare no matter how long or short the distance. On longer routes between cities, you may have to bargain a bit. Minibus drivers often try to overcharge foreigners – more in some places than in others. It's best to ask somebody, such as your hotel staff, about the *harga biasa* (normal price) before you get on. Otherwise see what the other passengers are paying and offer the correct fare.

Beware of getting on an empty minibus; you may end up chartering it! One annoying problem you come across in Indonesia is wandering into the minibus station to search out a minibus going where you want to go, and being told by driver after driver how much it will cost you to charter it! On the other hand, sometimes chartering a bemo is worth considering – for a few people it can work out cheaper than hiring a motorcycle by the day and much cheaper than hiring a car. Regular bemos carry around 12 people, so multiplying the usual fare by 12 should give you a rough idea of what to pay.

As with all public transport in Indonesia,

the drivers wait until their vehicles are crammed to capacity before they contemplate moving, or they may go *'keliling'*, driving endlessly around town looking for a full complement of passengers. Often there are people, produce, chickens, stacks of sarongs, laden baskets, even bicycles hanging out the windows and doors and at times it seems you're in danger of being crushed to death or at least asphyxiated. There's no such thing as air-con on any of these vehicles. Many Indonesians don't travel well; many people have amazingly weak stomachs and chuck up last night's gado-gado the first time the vehicle crosses a ripple in the road.

Door-to-Door Minibus

Express minibuses also operate between cities, mostly on Java, but tourist minibuses also run between the main tourist centres in Sumatra and on Bali. These minibuses are often luxurious seven or eight seaters with air-con and lots of leg room. Often called *travel*, they will pick you up from your hotel and drop you at your destination at the other end. Cheaper non-air-con minibuses also operate, and sometimes you will have to go to a depot to catch them.

TRUCK

One of the great ironies of Indonesia is that farm animals ride in buses and people ride in the backs of farm trucks! Trucks come in many different varieties. The luxurious ones operate with rows of bench seats in the tray at the back to sit on. More likely, you will have to sit on the floor or stand. It's imperative to try and get a seat in front of the rear axle, otherwise every time the truck hits a pothole you get to find out what it's like to be a ping-pong ball. Trucks are most common in Nusa Tenggara, but you'll also find them in other places where the road is so rough as to be impassable to other vehicles. Trucks can even been found in parts of developed Java.

TRAIN

Train travel in Indonesia is restricted solely to Java and Sumatra – for full details see those chapters. Briefly, there is a pretty good railway service running from one end of Java to the other – in the east it connects with the ferry to Bali, and in the west with the ferry to Sumatra. There are a few lines tacked down in Sumatra, but most of that island is reserved for buses. There are no railways on any of the other islands.

Trains vary – there are slow, miserable, cheap ones; fast, comfortable, expensive ones; and in-between ones. Some major towns like Jakarta and Surabaya have several railway stations so check where you'll be going to and where you have to leave from. Reservations should be made well in advance (up to one week) for the luxury trains.

CAR & MOTORBIKE
Road Rules
Basically, there aren't any. People in Indonesia drive on the left (usually!) of the road, as in Australia, Japan, the UK and most of South-East Asia. Opportunities for driving yourself are fairly limited in Indonesia unless you bring your own vehicle with you, except in Bali and Java – see the Bali and Java chapters for more details. In other places where tourists congregate, you can usually hire a jeep or minibus with driver included.

Punctures are usually repaired at roadside stands known as *tambal ban*. Whatever you do, try not to have an accident – if you do, as a foreigner, it's *your* fault.

Petrol
Petrol is reasonably cheap in Indonesia – it's currently around 700 rp a litre. There are petrol stations around the larger towns, but out in the villages it can be hard to find. Small wayside shops sell small amounts of petrol – look for signs that read *press ban*, or crates of bottles with a sign saying *bensin*. Some of the stuff off the roadside stands is said to be of dubious quality, so it's probably best to refill whenever you see a petrol station (*pompa bensin*).

Motorbike
Hiring or bringing your own motorbike could be one of the most interesting ways to travel through Indonesia. They've long been a favourite means of getting around Bali but they're also suited to many other parts of the country – particularly where there are poor, unsurfaced roads on which large vehicles get bogged. In fact, you'll avoid a bone-shattering ride on some of these roads if you can hire a trail bike! Outside Java and Bali, traffic is generally not heavy until you hit the cities and towns. Ferries and ships between the islands are more regular these days and will transport motorcycles.

The main disadvantage of motorcycles are danger and distance. Other disadvantages are that you don't meet people the way you do on public transport, you don't see life as it's lived, you just rush round keeping your eye on the road. Furthermore, motorcycles are an unpleasant intrusion in many places – noisy, distracting, annoying and unwanted. But by the same token, the major plus is the enormous flexibility a motorcycle gives you, allowing you to get to places that people without their own transport have to walk to, and it saves having to wait endlessly for transport. And if you see something you like you can stop and continue 10 minutes or 10 hours later.

There is no denying the dangers of bike riding in Indonesia – combined with all the normal hazards of motorcycle riding are narrow roads, unexpected potholes, crazy drivers, buses and trucks which (through size alone) reckon they own the road, children who dart onto the road, bullocks that lumber in, dogs and chickens that run around in circles, and unlit traffic at night. Take it slowly and cautiously around curves to avoid hitting oncoming traffic – this includes very large and heavy buses, buffaloes, herds of stray goats, and children. Rocks, boulders and landslides on poor stretches of roads are another hazard. Watch out for animals that are tethered to one side of the road and then wander over to the other side, stretching their ropes across the road at neck height of a motorcyclist.

Roadworks are another hazard – you round a corner and come slap up against a grader, rocks piled into the middle of the road or 55-gallon drums of tar. They rarely, if ever, put up warning signs that there are roadworks in progress. Up in the mountains there are perilous and unprotected drops down sheer cliff faces to the valleys below – this limits your opportunities for swerving round these obstacles!

At home, most people would never dream of hopping on a motorcycle in shorts and thongs and without a crash helmet – but in Bali they take one rudimentary test, stick their bikes in first gear and their brains in reverse and charge off. Indonesia is no place to learn how to ride a motorcycle.

If you're willing to throw caution to the wind, motorcycles can be hired in Java, and more easily in Bali. Those for hire in Bali are almost all between 90 and 125 cc, with 100 cc as the usual size. You really don't need anything bigger – the distances are short and the roads are rarely suitable for going very fast. Anyway, what's the hurry? In any case, for long-distance travel, a small bike is better if it breaks down or runs out of gas and you have to push – particularly if it breaks down on some of those hilly islands like Flores or Sumbawa where it's a long way between service stations! If you have to load and unload the thing on and off boats, it's much easier with a small bike.

Rental charges vary with the bike and the period of hire. The longer the hire period, the lower the rate: the bigger or newer the bike, the higher the rate. Typically, in Bali you can expect to pay at least 9000 to 12,000 rp per day. It's virtually impossible to hire a bike in Bali and take it to another island.

You need to have a licence, but in Bali getting that is as easy as opening a cornflakes packet. See the Bali chapter for details of how to rent a motorcycle there and how to get a licence.

Car

A car offers much the same advantages and disadvantages as a motorcycle. Another major disadvantage is price – at least five times that of a motorcycle.

The price for hiring a car varies according to both location and vehicle. Indonesia has regular car-rental agencies in big cities like Jakarta, where a car without a driver costs over 100,000 rp per day, or around 150,000 rp with a driver. Bali is one of the cheapest places to rent a car. A Suzuki jeep costs around 35,000 to 40,000 rp a day including insurance and unlimited km; or a *kijang* (Indonesia's popular family car that is a cross between a sedan and an off-road vehicle) costs from around 55,000 rp per day. In most cases, the price includes unlimited mileage but you supply the petrol.

In Jakarta there are a number of car-rental agencies: Hertz, Mandarin Oriental Hotel (☎ 321397, ext 1268); Avis, Jalan P Diponegoro 25 (☎ 334495); Indo Rent, Jalan Hayam Wuruk 6 (☎ 355326). National Car Rental has offices in a number of cities: Jakarta (☎ 333423), Bandung (☎ 433025), Yogyakarta (☎ 87078), Medan (☎ 327641), Surabaya (☎ 60527) and Denpasar (☎ 71906). There are plenty of other places that rent vehicles and, if you're in a city that has a government tourist information centre, it's not a bad idea to inquire there first.

Driving yourself is not much fun in many parts of Indonesia. It requires enormous amounts of concentration, and the legal implications of accidents can be a nightmare, that is if you survive an angry mob should someone be hurt. It is more common, and often cheaper, to rent a car or minibus with driver.

Renting a minibus can be a particularly good deal for a group. The Mitsubishi Colt L300 is a favourite model – they are comfortable, sturdy, go-almost-anywhere vehicles and can take up to six people and luggage in comfort.

Travel agents in the travellers' centres are good places to try for minibus rental. Go to the cheap tour operators – agents in the big hotels will charge big prices. Through the agents you have a better chance of finding a good, experienced driver that speaks some English and knows what tourists want.

Failing that ask at a tourist information centre or your hotel. There is always someone with a vehicle that is looking for work. Bali is a good place for renting on this basis on Java, Yogyakarta is the best, and on Lombok try around Sengigi. It is less common (and often more expensive) in other parts of Indonesia, but always possible.

Car or minibus rental starts at around 60,000 rp per day, including driver but excluding petrol. Bargaining is usually required. It is harder, but certainly possible, to find a driver for longer trips lasting a few days or even weeks. Negotiate a deal covering food and accommodation – either you provide a hotel room each night and pay a food allowance, or negotiate an allowance that covers both – figure on about 10,000 to 15,000 rp per day. It pays to see what your driver is like on a day trip before heading off on a lengthy expedition.

BICYCLE
Bicycles can be rented in the main centres of Java, Bali and also Lombok, but they're not used very much by Indonesians or by travellers. A few odd places like Solo are exceptions, with plenty of bicycles in common use.

The main advantage of cycling is the quality of the experience. You can cover many more km by bemo, bus or motorcycle but you really don't see more. Bicycles also tend to bridge the time gap between the rush of the West and the calm of rural Asia – without the noise of a motorcycle engine you can hear the wind rustling in the rice paddies, or the sound of a gamelan practising as you pass a village in Bali.

The main problems with seeing Indonesia by bicycle are the traffic in Java and the hills and enormous distances everywhere, which make it rather impractical or tough going to ride all over Indonesia. Seeing Bali by pushbike has become much more popular in recent years. More people are giving it a try and more places are renting bikes. At all the main sights in Java there are bicycle parking areas (usually 100 rp) where an attendant keeps an eye on your bicycle.

For serious bicycle touring, bring your own. Good quality bicycles and components can be found in the major cities, particularly on Java and Bali, but are difficult to find elsewhere.

HITCHING
Hitching is not part of the culture in Indonesia but if you put out your thumb someone may give you a lift. Confusion may arise as to whether payment is required or not. On the back roads where no public transport exists, hitching may be the only alternative to walking and passing motorists or trucks are often willing to help.

Bear in mind, however, that hitching is never entirely safe in any country in the world, and we do not recommend it. Travellers who decide to hitch should understand that they are taking a small but potentially serious risk. People who do choose to hitch will be safer if they travel in pairs and let someone know they are planning to go.

WALKING
Indonesia is too large to seriously consider walking across the country, but there are numerous trekking possibilities.

If you hike at high-altitude locations like Gunung Rinjani in Lombok or Puncak Trikora in Irian Jaya, you must be prepared for unstable mountain weather. Sudden rainstorms are common in all high altitudes, and Indonesia is no longer tropical once you get above 3000 metres. The rain will not only make you wet, but freezing cold. Forget umbrellas – a good rain poncho is essential. Bring warm clothing, but dress in layers so you can peel off each item of clothing as the day warms up. Proper footwear is essential. A compass could be a real life-saver if you're caught in the fog.

Be sure to bring sunscreen (UV) lotion – it's even more essential at high altitudes than in the lowlands.

It should go without saying that you must bring sufficient food and water. Don't underestimate your need for water – figure on about two litres per day, more in extreme heat.

If you haven't done much long-distance

walking or jogging recently, work up to it gradually rather than trying to 'get in shape' all at once. Do a few practice runs at home before disappearing into the Indonesian jungles.

Guides

A big decision is whether or not you need a guide. If you do need one, be prepared to haggle over the price. Guides in Indonesia sometimes ask for ridiculous amounts of money. Unless hired through a travel agency, a guide will typically cost around 10,000 rp per day. A travel agency may ask 10 times this amount, or more. Take some time to talk to your guide to make sure he (Indonesian guides are always male) really understands the route and won't simply help you get lost.

The Indonesian government has a policy of licensing guides. Licensed guides are not necessarily better than unlicensed ones, but usually are. If a guide is licensed, he is almost certainly a local, not a transient just passing through looking to pick up some quick cash from tourists. In any event, if your guide claims to be licensed, you should ask to see the licence and copy down his name and number. That way, if you encounter some really big problems (eg the guide abandons you on a mountainside, or rips off your camera and disappears) you can report him. On the other hand, if your guide turns out to be exceptionally good, you can then recommend him to other travellers you meet.

BOAT

Along with the roads, the shipping connections between the various islands of the archipelago have also improved greatly over the last few years, particularly in Nusa Tenggara. There are regular ferries connecting Sumatra and Java, Bali and Java, and almost all the islands of Nusa Tenggara – see the relevant chapters in this book for details. These ferries run either daily or several times a week so there's no longer any need to spend days in sleepy little port towns, reading big thick books, waiting for the elusive piece of driftwood to take you to the next island. Some of these ferries can transport large vehicles, and all of them will take motorcycles.

Pelni Ships

Indonesia has an extensive inter-island passenger ship network run by the national shipping line Pelni (P T Pelayaran Nasional Indonesia). They have modern, all air-con ships which operate regular fortnightly or monthly routes around the islands and are surprisingly comfortable. The ships usually stop for four hours in each port, so there's time for a quick look around.

Boats follow set routes but schedules change every few months – copies of the latest schedule are available from Pelni offices.

Classes Travel on Pelni ships is comprised of four cabin classes, followed by Kelas Ekonomi, which is the modern version of the old deck class. There you are packed in a large room with a space to sleep but, even in ekonomi, it's air-con and can get pretty cool at night, so bring warm clothes or a sleeping bag.

Class I is luxury plus with only two beds per cabin and a price approaching air travel. Class II is a notch down in style, with four to a cabin and no TV, but still very comfortable. Class III has six beds and Class IV has eight beds to a cabin. Classes I and II have a dining room while in ekonomi you queue up to collect a meal on a tray and then sit down wherever you can to eat it.

Ekonomi is fine for short trips but Class IV is the best value for longer hauls. Some ships, however, only offer Classes I and II in addition to ekonomi. As a rough cost approximation, Class IV is 50% more than ekonomi, Class III 100%, Class II 200% and Class I 400%.

Reservations You can book tickets up to 10-days ahead and it's best to book at least a few days in advance. Pelni is not a tourist operation, so don't expect any special service although there is usually somebody hidden away in the ticket offices who can help foreigners.

Important seaports to know include Belawan (port of Medan, Sumatra), Makasar (port of Ujung Pandang, Sulawesi), Tanjung

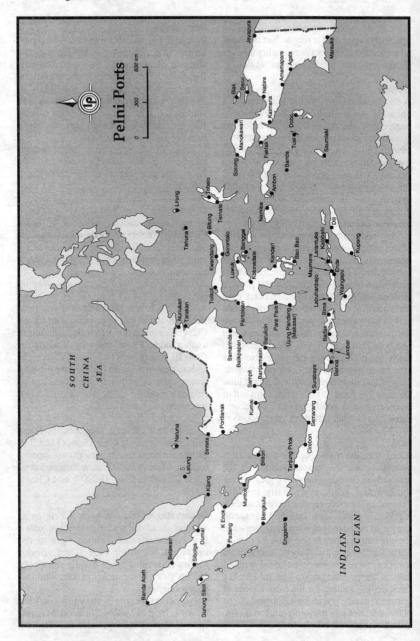

Pelni Ports

Priok (port of Jakarta), Bima (Sumbawa), Bitung (port of Manado, Sulawesi), Dili (east Timor), Ende (Flores), Kijang (Riau Islands), Kupang (west Timor), Kwandang (near Gorontalo, Sulawesi), Lembar (Lombok), Pantoloan (port of Palu, Sulawesi), Sibolga (north-west Sumatra), Ternate (north Maluku) and Waingapu (Sumba).

As well as their luxury liners, Pelni has Perinitis ('Pioneer') routes that ply many of the other ports not covered by the passenger liners. They can get you to just about any of the remote outer islands, as well as the major ports. The ships are often beaten up old crates that also carry cargo. They offer deck class only, but you may be able to negotiate a cabin with one of the crew.

Other Ships

Apart from Pelni ships, getting a boat is generally a case of hanging around a port until something comes by. Check with the

Pelni Routes

The following are the routes of the main Pelni passenger ships. Pelni is in the process of expanding its fleet, and as more ships are delivered the following routes may be adjusted slightly.

KM *Lawit*
Tanjung Priok, Pontianak, Semarang, Kumai, Semarang, Pontianak, Tanjung Priok, Panjang, Enggano, Padang, Gunung Sitoli, Sibolga, Padang, Enggano, Panjang, Tanjung Priok

KM *Kerinci*
Tanjung Priok, Surabaya, Makasar, Bau Bau, Ambon, Bitung, Ternate, Ambon, Bau Bau, Makasar, Surabaya, Tanjung Priok

KM *Rinjani*
Tanjung Priok, Surabaya, Makasar, Bau Bau, Ambon, Banda, Tual, Fak Fak, Banda, Ambon, Bau Bau, Makasar, Tanjung Priok, Muntok, Kijang, Dumai, Kijang, Muntok, Tanjung Priok

KM *Kambuna*
Tanjung Priok, Surabaya, Makasar, Balikpapan, Toli Toli, Bitung, Toli Toli, Pantoloan, Balikpapan, Makasar, Surabaya, Tanjung Priok, Belawan, Tanjung Priok

KM *Tidar*
Surabaya, Pare Pare, Pantoloan, Nunukan, Tarakan, Balikpapan, Pare Pare, Surabaya, Makasar, Balikpapan, Tarakan, Pantoloan, Makasar, Surabaya, Balikpapan, Surabaya

KM *Umsini*
Tanjung Priok, Surabaya, Makasar, Balikpapan, Pantoloan, Kwandang, Bitung, Kwandang, Pantoloan, Balikpapan, Makasar, Surabaya, Tanjung Priok, Muntok, Kijang, Dumai, Kijang, Muntok, Tanjung Priok

KM *Kelimutu*
Makasar, Jampea, Maumere, Dili, Kalabahi, Kupang, Ende, Waingapu, Bima, Lembar, Banyuwangi, Kalianget, Masalembo, Batu Licin, Masalembo, Kalianget, Banyuwangi, Benoa, Lembar, Bima, Waingapu, Ende, Kupang, Kalabahi, Dili, Maumere, Jampea, Makasar

KM *Ciremei*
Makasar, Tanjung Priok, Makasar, Bau Bau, Banggai, Bitung, Temate, Sorong, Manokwari, Biak, Jayapura, Biak, Manokwari, Sorong, Ternate, Bitung, Banggai, Bau Bau, Makasar

KM *Dobonsolo*
Sorong, Manokwari, Biak, Jayapura, Biak, Manokwari, Sorong, Ambon, Dili, Kupang, Benoa, Surabaya, Tanjung Priok, Surabaya, Benoa, Kupang, Dili, Ambon, Sorong

KM *Sirimau*
Makasar, Lembar, Kangean, Surabaya, Sampit, Cirebon, Pontianak, Tanjung Priok, Pontianak, Cirebon, Sampit, Surabaya, Kangean, Lembar, Makasar

KM *Tatamailau*
Tual, Dobo, Timika, Agats, Merauke, Tual, Kaimana, Fak Fak, Sorong, Manokwari, Nabire, Serui, Jayapura, Serui, Nabire, Manokwari, Sorong, Fak Fak, Kaimana, Tual

KM *Awu*
Makasar, Labuanbajo, Bima, Badas, Banyuwangi, Benoa, Badas, Bima, Labuanbajo, Makasar, Bau Bau, Kendari, Kolonedale, Luwuk, Gorontalo, Bitung, Lirung, Tahuna, Bitung, Gorontalo, Luwuk, Kolonedale, Kendari, Bau Bau, Makasar

KM *Leuser*
Samarinda, Pare Pare, Batu Licin, Surabaya, Kumai, Pontianak, Kumai, Surabaya, Batu Licin, Pare Pare, Samarinda, Toli Toli, Tarakan, Nunukan, Toli Toli, Samarinda

KM *Binaiya*
Tanjung Priok, Biliton, Sintete, Natuna, Tarempa, Letung, Kijang, Enok, Tanjung Priok

KM *Bukitraya*
Makasar, Batu Licin, Surabaya, Sampit, Semarang, Pontianak, Tanjung Priok, Pontianak, Semarang, Sampit, Surabaya, Batu Licin, Makasar ■

shipping offices, Pelni, the harbour master's office, and anyone else you can think of. Tickets can be bought at shipping offices, although for some ships and in some ports (big ones like Jakarta and Surabaya aside) it may be possible and cheaper to negotiate your fare on-board rather than buy tickets from the office in advance.

Unscheduled cargo and passenger ships – even those run by Pelni – are tough going. Most of them are filthy, with overflowing toilets, poor food, and the decks covered in an intricately lumpy carpet of people and their belongings, often fencing off their own little patch of deck with their cases, bunches of bananas and the occasional chicken. If you're travelling deck class then unroll your sleeping bag and make yourself comfortable – a good idea is to take some newspapers with you and lay them out on the floor to cover up the dirt and chicken crap. Deck class in the rainy season can be very cold and wet. The crew have their own cabins and they often rent these out – it's one way they make some extra money. Bring some food and water of your own. Here are some readers' comments and recommendations regarding boat travel in Indonesia:

Unless it's really wet I reckon deck class is as good as cabin but get as high in the ship as possible. Privacy and security are major considerations. If you want fresh air in your cabin you get a lot of Indonesian faces too. If you keep your ultra-valuables on you, an official will give you somewhere to stick your pack. Cabins get very hot, windows often don't help. Rats and cockroaches do not abound on the higher decks...

If you're travelling in a cabin take 1st class – very little more than 2nd class, but you get reasonable food, a private cabin and your own private collection of cockroaches and mice!

Definitely a once-only experience...

Another possibility worth investigating is getting a passage on one of those magnificent Bugis schooners you see lined up at the Pasar Ikan in Jakarta. They sail between Java, Kalimantan and Sulawesi, often going as far as Nusa Tenggara.

Small Boat

There's a whole range of floating tubs you can use to hop between islands, across rivers, down rivers and over lakes. Just about any sort of vessel can be rented in Indonesia. Fishing boats or other small boats can be chartered to take you to small offshore islands. Some of these boats are *not* reliable and engine trouble is an occasional problem. Check out the boat before you rent it – it would be nice if it had a two-way radio and a lifeboat, just in case.

The *longbot* (longboat) is a long, narrow boat powered by a couple of outboard motors, with bench seats on either side of the hull for passengers to sit on. You find these mainly on the rivers of Kalimantan where they're a common means of transport.

Outrigger canoes powered by an outboard motor are a standard form of transport for some short inter-island hops – like the trip out from Manado in northern Sulawesi to the coral reefs surrounding nearby Pulau Bunaken. On Lombok these elegant, brilliantly painted fishing boats, looking rather like exotic dragonflies, are used for the short hop from Bangsal Harbour to the offshore islands of Gili Air and Gili Trawangan. There are standard fares for standard routes, and you can charter these boats.

Speedboats are not all that common, although they are used on some routes on the rivers of Kalimantan, or for some short inter-island hops in some parts of Indonesia. They are, of course, considerably faster than longbots or river ferries, but considerably more expensive.

River ferries are commonly found in Kalimantan, where the rivers *are* the roads. They're large, bulky vessels that carry people and goods up and down the water network.

LOCAL TRANSPORT
To/From the Airport

There are generally taxis waiting outside the airports – even if the taxi has no meter (*argo*) there will usually be a fixed fare into town; tickets for the journey can be bought from the taxi desk in the airport terminal. From the

Old men outside the Vihara Dharma Bhakti Temple, Glodok, Jakarta, Java (GB)

Top left: A man cleaning the hull of a Schooner, Sunda Kelapa, Jakarta (GB)
Top right: A local woman at Sunda Kelapa, Kota, Jakarta (GB)
Middle: A Fishing boat, Thousand Islands (GB)
Bottom: Schooners moored at Sunda Kelapa, Jakarta (GB)

town to the airport, go on the meter or bargain a fare with the driver. In other towns, local buses or bemos may pass within walking distance of the airport; they are considerably cheaper than taking a taxi. In some of the smaller outer islands, like those of Nusa Tenggara, where some of the airports are quite far from the town and have no regular road transport between them, the airlines have taxis or bemos to take passengers to the airport. The cost of these airline taxis is not included in the ticket so you have to pay extra, but often it's the only reliable way of getting to your flight.

Bus

Large buses aren't used much as a means of local transport except in Java, perhaps because most Indonesian towns aren't that big; smaller vehicles suffice.

There's quite an extensive system of buses in Jakarta and these are universally cheap, but be *very* careful about pickpockets. These guys usually work in gangs and can empty your pockets faster than you can say 'gado-gado'.

Taxi

Metered taxis are readily available in major cities, especially in Java and Bali. Elsewhere, you may have to bargain the fare in advance. If a taxi has a meter, make sure it is used. Most drivers will use them without fuss, and Indonesian taxi drivers usually provide a good service. Jakarta undoubtedly has the worst taxi drivers in the country.

Metered taxis charge about 900 rp for the first km, and 450 rp for each additional km.

Bemo

Bemos are the usual form of transport around Indonesian towns and cities – most run on standard routes with standard fares.

Becak

These are three-wheeler bicycle-rickshaws. Unlike the version found in India where the driver sits in front of you, or the Filipino version with the driver at the side, in Indonesia the driver sits at the rear, nosing your

life ever forwards into the traffic. Many drivers rent their machines, but those who own them add personal touches: brightly painted pictures, tinkling bells or whirring metal discs strung across the undercarriage. In Yogyakarta one guy peddled furiously around the streets at night with a tiny flashing light-bulb on the point of his coolie hat! Whilst becaks are now banned from the main streets of large Javanese cities (they are banned from Jakarta altogether), in just about any town of any size in Java as well as in some other parts of Indonesia (like Ujung Pandang in Sulawesi), they're the most basic form of transport – for people and anything else that has to be shifted.

Bargain your fare *before* you get into the becak! And make sure, if there are two of you, that it covers both people – otherwise you'll be in for an argument when you get to your destination. Indonesian becak drivers are hard bargainers – they have to be to survive! But they will usually settle on a reasonable fare – say 300 to 500 rp per km. Fares vary from city to city and increase with more passengers, luggage, hills, and at night. Hiring a becak by time or for a round-trip often makes good sense if you're planning to cover a lot of ground in one day, particularly in large places like Yogyakarta or Solo.

Bajaj

These are noisy, smoke-belching three-wheeled vehicles with a driver at the front, a small motorbike engine below and seats for two passengers behind. They're a common form of local transport in Jakarta, but you don't see them very often elsewhere.

Dokar

Dokars are the jingling, horse-drawn carts found all over Indonesia. The two-wheeled carts are usually brightly coloured with decorative motifs and fitted with bells which chime when they're in motion. The small horses or ponies that pull them are often equipped with long tassels attached to their gear. A typical dokar has bench seating on either side, which can comfortably fit three people, four if they're all slim; their owners

Dokar

generally pack in as many people as possible plus bags of rice and other paraphernalia. It's a picturesque way of getting around if you don't get upset by the ill-treatment of animals – although generally the ponies are looked after pretty well since they mean the difference between starvation and survival. The price depends on the colour of your skin – the bidding starts at around 1000 rp. After negotiations, count on paying about 300 rp per person per km.

In Java you also see the *andong* or *delman* which is a larger horse-drawn wagon designed to carry six people. In some parts of Indonesia like Gorontalo and Manado in northern Sulawesi you also see the *bendi* which is like a small dokar, designed to carry two people.

Other
There are various other ways of getting around.

Ojek are motorcycle riders that take pillion passengers for a bargainable price. They are found at bus stations and markets, or just hanging around at crossroads. They will take you around town and go where no other public transport exists. They can tackle roads impassable to any other vehicle. They can also be rented by the hour (starting at around 3000 rp) for sightseeing.

In many of the hill resorts in Java you can hire horses. Likewise, just about anywhere in Indonesia where horses are raised it's

often possible to hire one – this is possibly the ideal solution to getting over some of that rough terrain and actually enjoying those abominable roads! In Jakarta, bicycles with little seats at the rear are used as a taxi service – see them near the Pasar Ikan.

TOURS
A wide range of tours can be booked from travel agents within Indonesia. Most of these take in places where tourists are numerous, such as Jakarta, Yogyakarta, Bali, Lombok, Komodo and Lake Toba.

You can be absolutely certain that taking a tour will work out to be more expensive than going by yourself, but some are good value. For example, you can take a day tour to Borobudur and the Dieng Plateau from Yogyakarta and be picked up and dropped off at your hotel for only 25,000 rp. Yogya and Bali tend to have the cheapest tours and the best range, but cheap tours are available in all the main travellers' centres.

Tours are normally much less expensive if you book through a hotel rather than through a travel agent. For example, in Waikabubak (Sumba), hotels can arrange a jeep with tour guide/driver for 80,000 rp per day for three people, and this is probably the best way of visiting villages in the area. In Labuhanbajo (west Flores), boat and snorkelling tour abound; they are numerous and cheap.

There are, of course, expensive all-inclusive tours available from travel agencies in Jakarta, Bali and elsewhere. Some of the major national operators are Vayatour, Pacto and Natour, with offices throughout the country. You can find many other agents by looking in the yellow pages of the telephone directory. Most travel agents have some economy tours, but they prefer to sell packages with accommodation at a luxurious hotel like the Hilton or Sheraton, banquet-style meals and prices beginning at around 200,000 rp per day.

Java

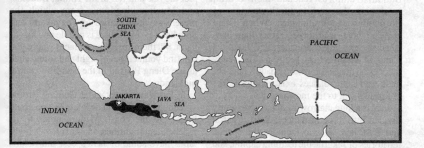

Java is the political, geographic and economic centre of Indonesia. With an area of 132,000 sq km, Java is a little over half the size of the island of Great Britain but its population is almost double Britain's at 110 million. With such vast human resources, Java is the powerhouse and dictator of Indonesia.

Java presents vivid contrasts of wealth and squalor, majestic open country and crowded filthy cities, quiet rural scenes and bustling modern traffic. The main cities can be overwhelming, but rural Java is still an island of astonishing beauty. A string of high volcanic mountains runs through the centre of the island, providing a smoking backdrop to the fertile green fields and terraces. The rich volcanic soils that have long been the secret to Java's abundance extend north to the flat coastal plain and the murky Java Sea, while

Highlights

The favourite travellers' centre is the cultural centre of Yogyakarta, centred around the sultan's *kraton* (palace). Yogya has excellent, cheap facilities and makes an ideal base for trips to awe-inspiring Borobudur, Indonesia's most famous landmark, and the equally impressive temple complex at Prambanan. Nearby, Solo is another quieter court city and repository of Javanese culture, as is Cirebon on the north coast.

Java's big cities, such as Jakarta, Bogor, Bandung and Surabaya, are intense, crowded and disorienting. To appreciate contemporary Indonesia or the Dutch heritage, a visit to Java's cities is essential, but for many travellers they are mostly transit points with only a few 'must sees'.

Away from the main highway and major cities, Java's vast urban sprawl gives way to some superb natural attractions. A string of volcanoes runs through the island, and Mt Bromo is one of the most spectacular in Indonesia. Krakatau, Indonesia's most famous volcano, can be visited from the west coast of Java. Other volcanic mountains such as Ijen, Papandayan, Merapi and Gede have superb scenery and good trekking yet see few tourists. Java also has the highest concentration of national parks in the country – Ujung Kulon has unique wildlife and wilderness in crowded Java.

Java's beaches don't match the superb beaches of Sulawesi and Maluku or those of nearby Bali, but Pangandaran is deservedly Java's No 1 beach resort. The living is cheap, relaxed and the adjoining national park is good for walks.

The typical route through Java is a variation on: Jakarta to Bogor and/or Bandung, then on to Pangandaran, Yogya, Solo, Surabaya and Mt Bromo before heading to Bali. This route can be done comfortably in about three or four weeks, less if the big cities are bypassed. For a whirlwind trip, some just fly into Yogya, with a quick trip out to Borobudur and Prambanan. ■

the south coast fronts the crashing waves of the Indian Ocean.

It was on plentiful Java that the Hindu-Buddhist empires reached their zenith, producing the architectural wonders of Borobudur and Prambanan. When Islam came to Java, it absorbed rather than banished the existing influences, and Java is a blend of cultures and religion. The ready Indonesian images of *wayang* shadow puppets, batik and court dances exist alongside the muezzin's call to the mosque.

Java is a long, narrow island, conveniently divided into three provinces: West, Central and East Java. It also includes the special territories of Jakarta, the teeming capital, and Yogyakarta, a centre for Javanese culture and one of Indonesia's premier tourist destinations.

West Java, home to the Sundanese people, has places of interest such as Bandung in the Sundanese heartland, the court city of Cirebon, the beach at Pangandaran, famous Krakatau and the wilds of the Ujung Kulon National Park.

In Central Java, temples and royal cities plot the rise and fall of the Hindu, Buddhist and Muslim kingdoms, from which the present-day court cities of Yogyakarta and Solo have evolved. Java is people and lots of them, but there are isolated places where you can find yourself out of sight and sound such as the Dieng Plateau in the beautiful central highlands.

In East Java, spectacular Gunung Bromo volcano is as wild and desolate as you could hope. Off the coast, Madura holds to its independent traditions, and East Java's highlands have some of Java's best hill resorts and hiking opportunities.

HISTORY

The history of human habitation in Java extends back over half a million years when 'Java Man' lived along the banks of Bengawan Solo River in Central Java. Waves of

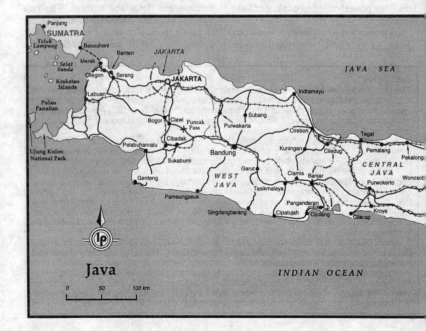

migrants followed, coming down through South-East Asia to inhabit the island. The Javanese are an Austronesian people, closely related to the people of Malaysia and the Philippines.

Early Javanese Kingdoms

The island's exceptional fertility allowed the development of an intensive *sawah* (wet-rice) agriculture, which in turn required close cooperation between villages for the maintenance of the irrigation systems. From this first need for local government small kingdoms eventually developed, but the first major principality appears to have been that of King Sanjaya's. Around the beginning of the 8th century he founded the kingdom of Mataram, which controlled much of central Java. Mataram's religion centred on the Hindu god Shiva, and the kingdom produced some of the earliest of Java's Hindu temples on the Dieng Plateau.

Sanjaya's Hindu kingdom was followed by a Buddhist interlude under the Sailendra dynasty; it was during this time that Mahayana Buddhism was established in Java and work began (probably around 780 AD) on Borobudur. Hinduism continued to exist alongside Buddhism and the massive Hindu Prambanan complex was built and consecrated around 856 AD. Hinduism and Buddhism often fused into one religion in Java.

Mataram eventually fell, possibly as a result of conflict with the Sumatra-based Sriwijaya kingdom which invaded Java in the 11th century. Sriwijaya, however, also suffered attacks from the Chola kingdom of southern India and Javanese power revived under King Airlangga, a semi-legendary figure who brought much of Java under his control and formed the first royal link between Java and Bali. Airlangga divided his kingdom between his two sons, resulting in the formation of the Kediri and Janggala kingdoms.

Early in the 13th century, the commoner Ken Angrok usurped the throne of Singosari

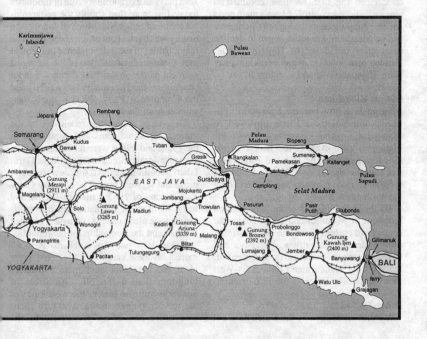

(a part of the Janggala kingdom), defeated Kediri and then brought the rest of Janggala under his control. His new kingdom of Singosari expanded its power during the 13th century up until its last king, Kertanegara, was murdered in a rebellion in 1292.

Majapahit Kingdom

Kertanegara's son-in-law and successor, Wijaya, established the Majapahit kingdom, the greatest kingdom of the Hindu-Javanese period. Under Hayam Wuruk, who ruled from 1350 to 1389, the Majapahit kingdom claimed sovereignty over the entire Indonesian archipelago, although its territorial sovereignty was probably restricted to Java, Madura and Bali. Hayam Wuruk's strongman prime minister, Gajah Mada, was responsible for many of Majapahit's territorial conquests.

While previous Javanese kingdoms based their power on the control of the rich Javanese agricultural areas, the Majapahits established the first Javanese commercial empire by taking control of Java's main ports and the shipping lanes throughout Indonesia.

The Majapahit kingdom began to decline soon after the death of Hayam Wuruk. Various principalities began breaking away from Majapahit rule and adopting Islam.

Islamic Kingdoms

Islam in Java now became a powerful religious and political force opposed to Majapahit, making converts amongst the Majapahit elite even at the height of the kingdom's power. The 15th and 16th centuries saw the rise of new Islamic kingdoms such as Demak, Cirebon and Banten along the north coast.

By the end of the 16th century the Muslim kingdom of Mataram had taken control of central and eastern Java. The last remaining independent principalities, Surabaya and Cirebon, were eventually subjugated, leaving only Mataram and Banten (in West Java) to face the Dutch in the 17th century.

Dutch Period

The conquest of Java by the Dutch need not be recounted here, but by the end of the 18th century practically all of the island was under Dutch control. (See the History section in the Facts about the Country chapter for more details.)

During the Dutch period there were strong Muslim powers in Java, most notably Mataram. The Javanese were great warriors who continually opposed the Dutch but they were never a united force because of internal conflict or battles with the Sundanese or the Madurese. The last remnants of the Mataram kingdom survived as the principalities of Surakarta (Solo) and Yogyakarta until the foundation of the Indonesian republic. Javanese kings claimed to rule with divine authority and the Dutch helped to preserve the vestiges of a traditional Javanese aristocracy by confirming them as regents, district officers or sub-district officers in the European administration.

Java Today

Java plays an extraordinary role in Indonesia today. It is more than simply the geographical centre of Indonesia. Much of Indonesian history was hacked out on Javanese soil. The major battles of the independence movement took place on Java and two of the strongest political parties in the first decade of independence – the Nationalist Party (PNI) and the Communist Party (PKI) – drew their support from the Javanese.

To a large extent the rebellions of the Sumatrans, Minahasans and Ambonese in the 1950s and 1960s were rebellions against Javanese domination. Furthermore the Darul Islam rebellion against the new republic broke out in West Java. The abortive Communist coup of 1965 started in Jakarta and some of its most dramatic and disastrous events took place in Java. Java has provided the lead and the leadership for the republic.

It has been said that Soeharto is much more a Javanese king than an 'elected' president, and Indonesia much more a Javanese kingdom than a republic. Admirers of Soeharto compare him to the wise kings of the wayang puppet shows, who turn chaos into order and bring prosperity to the kingdom. Critics respond that he rules much more like a Javanese king or sultan, with systems of palace-centred patronage, favouritism and officially sponsored corruption. The ultimate base for Soeharto's authority is always the military, which is overwhelmingly Javanese at the top level.

A strong consciousness of ancient religious and mystical thought carries over into modern-day Java, from the peasant farmer to the high-ranking government official. Soekarno identified with Bima, the strong-willed prince of the wayang. Soeharto is said to identify strongly with the clown-god Semar, who in the traditional wayang plays often steps in to save the situation when more refined characters have failed.

Java also dominates economic life in Indonesia. Java has the bulk of Indonesia's industry and is the recipient of most of the new foreign investment pouring into the country. The island is the most developed part of Indonesia by far, but its big test for the future is to manage economic growth and make inroads into the everpresent problems of overpopulation and poverty.

PEOPLE & CULTURE

Java has three main groups of people, each speaking their own language: the Javanese of Central and East Java, the Sundanese of West Java and the Madurese from Madura island off the north-east coast. The divisions are blurred – the Madurese, for example, have settled in large numbers in East Java and further afield, and Indonesians from all over the archipelago have come to seek work in the cities. Smaller pockets of pre-Islamic peoples also remain, like the Badui in the mountains of West Java and the Hindu Tenggerese centred on Gunung Bromo in East Java, while polyglot Jakarta identifies its own tradition in the Betawi, the name for the original inhabitants of the city.

Today the Javanese are Muslim. Though most are *santri* (or devout) Muslim, and Java is slowly becoming more orthodox, Javanese culture owes much to pre-Islamic animism and Hinduism. India has had probably the most profound and enduring influence on religion in Java, yet the Indian poet Rabindranath Tagore, when visiting the country, said: 'I see India everywhere, but I do not recognise it.'

The Javanese cosmos is composed of different levels of belief, stemming from older and more accommodating mysticism, the Hindu court culture and a very real belief in ghosts and numerous benevolent and malevolent spirits. Underneath the unifying code of Islam, magic power is concentrated in amulets and heirlooms (especially the Javanese dagger known as the *kris*), in parts of the human body like the nails and the hair, and in sacred musical instruments. The traditional medicine man, or *dukun*, is still consulted when illness strikes.

The *halus* (refined) Javanese is part of the Hindu court tradition, which still exists in the heartland of Central Java. In contrast to Islam, the court tradition is an hierarchical world view, based on privilege and often guided by the gods or the spirits of nature. Refinement and politeness are highly regarded, and loud displays of emotion and flamboyant behaviour is *kasar* (coarse and rough, bad manners).

Indirectness is a Javanese trait, and stems from an unwillingness to make anyone else feel uncomfortable or ashamed. It is impolite to point out mistakes, embarrassments, sensitive or negative areas, or to directly criticise authority. Even the Javanese language reinforces this deference to authority. Like Balinese, Javanese has 'high' and 'low' forms; different words are used when speaking to superiors, elders, equals or inferiors. This underlines differences in status, rank, relative age, and the degree of acquaintance between the two people talking.

The Javanese of East Java speak Javanese and have inherited many of the same traditions as the Javanese from Central Java, but since the fall of the great Hindu Majapahit empire, East Java has been more of a backwater, more removed from the Islamic tradition. Pockets of Hinduism still survive in East Java. The most well-known group is the Tengger people of the Bromo area. The Tengger are regarded as the survivors of

Majapahit, the commoners that were left behind after the Majapahit elite fled to Bali.

While the southern and central part of East Java shows a greater Hindu influence, the north coast is the stronghold of Islam, and much of the population is Madurese. From the hot dry island to the north, the Madurese are a blunt, strong and proud people that migrated to the north-east coast and then further into East Java. Surabaya is the melting pot of all East Java, and as the gateway to Madura, shows strong influence from the more devoutly Islamic Madurese. Javanese as spoken in Surabaya is considered very kasar, without the intricacies and deferences of Central Java.

The Sundanese of West Java are likewise less concerned with the flourishes and hierarchies of Central Java. Their culture and traditions have much in common with the Javanese. Sundanese is also a hierarchical language of high and low forms, but Islam has taken stronger root in Sunda and the people are earthier, more direct and more egalitarian. Yet even in this more Islamic atmosphere, the older traditions remain. The Badui in the western highlands are distinguished by their history of resistance to Islam.

ARTS

Javanese culture is a product of pre-Hindu, Hindu and Islamic influences. The rise of the 16th-century Islamic states brought a rich new cultural heritage, but the Hindu heritage also managed to continue its influence.

Wayang

Javanese wayang theatre has been a major means of preserving the Hindu-Buddhist heritage in Java. The most well-known form is the *wayang kulit*, the shadow-puppet theatre using puppets made of leather (*kulit* means leather).

Wayang Kulit In the shadow-puppet theatre perforated leather figures are manipulated behind an illuminated cotton screen. The stories are usually based on the Hindu epics, the *Ramayana* and the *Mahabharata*,

although other purely Javanese stories are also performed. In a traditional performance a whole night might be devoted to just one drama (*lakon*) from a legend. A single puppeteer (the *dalang*) animates the puppets and narrates and chants through the entire night to the accompaniment of the *gamelan* orchestra.

Many wayang kulit figures and even whole stories have a specific mystical function; certain stories are performed for the purpose of protecting a rice crop (these incorporate the rice goddess Dewi Sri), the welfare of a village or even individuals.

Shadow-puppet theatre is not unique to Java; it can also be found in Turkey, India, China and parts of South-East Asia, and wayang kulit owes much to Indian tradition.

By the 11th century wayang performances with leather puppets flourished in Java and by the end of the 18th century wayang kulit had developed most of the details of puppet design and performance techniques we see today. The standardisation of the puppet designs is traditionally attributed to King Raden Patah of Demak, a 16th-century Islamic kingdom.

The puppets are made of leather, with water-buffalo leather from a young animal being the most favoured material. The outline of the puppet is cut using a thin knife and the fine details carved out using small chisels and a hammer. When the carving is finished the movable arms are attached and the puppet is painted. Lines are drawn in and accentuated with black ink, which is also used to increase the contrast of the carved holes. The *cempurit*, the stick of horn used to hold the puppet upright, is then attached.

The leaf-shaped *kayon* represents the 'tree' or 'mountain of life' and is used to end scenes or to symbolise wind, mountains, obstacles, clouds or the sea. Made of the same flexible hide as the other puppets, the kayon might be waved softly behind the cloth screen while a puppet figure is held horizontally – a surprisingly effective way of indicating flight through the cloudy sky. Symbolic decorations on the kayon include the face in the centre of the tree which symbolises the danger and risk that all people must confront in life.

The characters in wayang are brought to life by the dalang. To call the dalang a puppeteer belittles the extraordinary range of talents a dalang must possess. Sitting cross-legged on a mat before the white screen, the dalang might manipulate dozens of figures in the course of a performance.

The dalang recounts events spanning centuries and continents, improvising from the basic plot a complex network of court intrigues, great loves, wars, philosophy, magic, mysticism and comedy. The dalang must be a linguist capable of speaking both the language of the audience and the ancient *kawi* language spoken by the aristocratic characters of the play. The dalang must also be a mimic capable of producing a different voice for each of the characters, and have great physical stamina to sustain a performance lasting from evening until the early hours of the morning.

The dalang must be a musician, able to direct the village's gamelan orchestra which accompanies the performance, be versed in history and have a deep understanding of philosophy and religion. The dalang must be a poet capable of creating a warm or terrifying atmosphere, but must also be a comedian able to introduce some comic relief into the performances. Understandably, the dalang has always been regarded as a very special type of person.

The dalang directs the gamelan orchestra using a system of cues, often communicating the name of the composition to be played using riddles or puns. The player of the *kendang* (drum) liaises between the dalang and the other gamelan players by setting the proper tempo and changes of tempo for each piece, and in executing the important signals for ending pieces. The dalang may communicate with the orchestra using signals tapped out with the wooden *cempala* (a mallet) held in the left hand. Or there may be other types of cues – for example, one of the clowns in the performance may announce that a singing contest is to be held, then

Wayang kulit puppet

announce the song he intends singing and the gamelan will play that song.

The mass of the audience sits in front of the screen to watch the shadow figures, but some also sit behind the screen with the dalang, to watch the expert at work.

Wayang Golek These three-dimensional wooden puppets have movable heads and arms and are manipulated in the same way as shadow puppets – but without using a shadow screen. Although *wayang golek* is found in Central Java it is most popular amongst the Sundanese of West Java. Sometimes a wayang golek puppet is used right at the end of a wayang kulit play to symbolise the transition back from the world of two dimensions to the world of three.

Wayang golek uses the same stories as the

wayang kulit, including the *Mahabharata* and the *Ramayana*, as well as stories about the mythical Javanese king, Panji, and other legendary kings. It also has its own set of stories, for which there is some direct Islamic inspiration. These include the elaborate romances inspired by legends about the Prophet Mohammed's uncle, Amir Hamzah.

Wayang Klitik In East Java the wayang kulit is replaced by the *wayang klitik* or *keruchil*, a flat wooden puppet carved in low relief; this type of wayang is performed without a shadow screen. The wayang klitik is associated with the Damar Wulan stories which are of particular historical relevance to East Java. The stories relate the adventures of a handsome prince and his rise to become ruler of the Majapahit kingdom.

Wayang Orang Known as *wayang wong* in Javanese, the *wayang orang* is a dance drama in which real people dance the part of the wayang characters.

Wayang Topeng The *wayang topeng* is similar to wayang orang but uses masks. The two forms of dance drama were cultivated at varying times in the courts of Central Java. Wayang topeng is the older of the two and dates back as far the Majapahit kingdom. In more recent times wayang wong was performed only as the official court dance drama, while wayang topeng was also performed outside the walls of the palace. The stylisation of human features seen in the shadow puppets is also seen in the wayang topeng masks; elongation and refinement are the key notes of the noble (halus) characters, while grotesque exaggeration denotes the vulgar (kasar) characters.

Mahabharata & Ramayana

Ancient India, like ancient Greece, produced two great epics. The *Ramayana* describes the adventures of a prince who is banished from his country and wanders for many years in the wilderness. The *Mahabharata* is based on the legends of a great war. The first story is a little reminiscent of the *Odyssey*, which relates the adventures of Ulysses as he struggles to return home from Troy; the second has much in common with the *Iliad*.

When Hinduism came to Java so did the *Ramayana* and the *Mahabharata*. The Javanese shifted the locale to Java; Javanese children were given the names of the heroes and by tradition the kings of Java were descendants of the epic heroes.

Mahabharata The great war portrayed in the *Mahabharata* is believed to have been fought in northern India around the 13th or 14th century BC. The war became a centre of legends, songs and poems and at some point the vast mass of stories accumulated over the centuries were gathered together into a narrative called the 'Epic of the Bharata Nation (India)' – the *Mahabharata*. Over the following centuries more was added to it until it was seven times the size of the Iliad and the Odyssey combined!

The central theme of the *Mahabharata* is the power struggle between the Kurava brothers and their cousins, the Pandava brothers. Important events along the way include: the appearance of Krishna, an incarnation of Lord Vishnu, who becomes the adviser of the Pandava; the marriage of Prince Arjuna of the Pandavas to the Princess Drupadi; the Kuravas' attempt to kill the Pandavas; and the division of the kingdom into two in an attempt to end the rivalry between the cousins. Finally, after 13 years in exile and hiding, the Pandavas realise there is no alternative but war, the great war of the *Mahabharata*, which is a series of bloody clashes between the cousins.

It is at this time that the Pandava warrior, Arjuna, becomes despondent at the thought of fighting his own flesh and blood, so Krishna, his charioteer and adviser, explains to him the duties and obligations of the warrior in a song known as the 'Bhagavad Gita'. Krishna explains that the soul is indestructible and that whoever dies shall be reborn and so there is no cause to be sad; it is the soldier's duty to fight and he will be accused of cowardice if he runs away.

In the course of the battles many of the great heroes from both sides are slain one by one; many others also lose their lives but in the end the Pandavas are victorious over the Kuravas.

Ramayana The *Ramayana*, the story of Prince Rama, is thought to have been written after the *Mahabharata*. Long before Prince Rama was born the gods had determined that his life would be that of a hero – but like all heroic lives it would be full of grave tests. Rama is an incarnation of the god Vishnu, and it will be his destiny to kill the ogre king

Rawana (also known as Dasamuka and Dasakhantha).

Due to scheming in the palace, Rama, his wife the beautiful Sita (or Shinta in Javanese) and his brother Laksamana are all exiled to the forest, where Sita is abducted by the ogre king. Rawana takes the form of a golden deer, luring Rama and Laksamana into the forest as they try to hunt the deer. Rawana then carries off Sita to his island kingdom of Lanka.

Rama begins his search for Sita, and is joined by the monkey god Hanuman and the monkey king Sugriwa. Eventually a full-

---

The Mahabharata & Ramayana Characters

Bima Bima is the second-eldest of the Pandavas. He is physically big, burly, aggressive and not afraid to act on what he believes; he can be rough, even using the language of the man of the street to address the gods. He is able to fly and is the most powerful warrior on the battlefield, but he also has infinite kindness and a firm adherence to principle, which makes him a heroic figure who can't really be criticised for his faults.

Arjuna Arjuna is a Pandava and is the handsome and refined ladies' man, a representative of the noble class, whose eyes look at the ground because it's *kasar* to stare into people's faces. He can also be fickle and selfish, and that is his weakness. He has one single quality which outweighs his failings: he is *halus*, never speaking ill to offend others, polite and humble, patient, careful, the direct opposite of *kasar*. Arjuna's charioteer is Krishna, the incarnation of the god, Vishnu, a spiritual adviser, but also a cunning and ruthless politician.

Semar A purely Javanese addition to the story is Arjuna's servant, the dwarf clown Semar. An incarnation of a god, Semar is a great source of wisdom and advice to Arjuna – but his body is squat with an enormous posterior, bulging belly, and he sometimes has an uncontrollable disposition for farting. Semar has three sons: Gareng, with his misshapen arms, crossed eyes, limp and speech impediment; Petruk, with his hilarious long nose, enormous smiling mouth, and a general lack of proportion both in physical stature and thinking; and Bagong, the youngest of the three, who speaks as though he has a mouthful of marbles. Though they are comic figures, they play the important role of interpreting the actions and speech of the heroic figures in the wayang kulit plays. Despite their bumbling natures and gross appearance they are the mouthpieces of truth and wisdom.

Kurava Characters On the Kurava side is Duryudana, a handsome and powerful leader, but too easily influenced by the prevailing circumstances around him and thus often prey to the evil designs of his uncle and adviser, Sangkuni. Karna is the good man on the wrong side, whose loyalty is divided between the Kuravas and the Pandavas. He is actually a Pandava but was brought up a Kurava; adhering to the code of the warrior he stands by his king as a good Javanese should and, as a result, he dies at the hands of Arjuna.

Ramayana Characters The characters of the *Ramayana* are a little more clear-cut. Like Arjuna, Rama is the epitome of the ideal man – a gentle husband, a noble prince, a kindly king, a brave leader. His wife Sita is the ideal wife who remains totally devoted to her husband. But elements of the *Mahabharata* can also be found in the *Ramayana*: Rawana's warrior brother knows that the king is evil but is bound by the ethics of the Ksatria warrior and remains loyal to his brother to the end, consequently dying a horrible death by dismemberment. ∎

scale assault is launched on the evil king and Sita is rescued.

Performances & Characters The *Mahabharata* and the *Ramayana* are the basis of the most important wayang stories, and also appear in Balinese dances and theatre. While they often come across like ripping yarns, both are essentially moral tales, which for centuries have played a large part in establishing traditional Javanese values. In the *Mahabharata*, the Kuravas are essentially the forces of greed, evil and destruction, while the Pandavas represent refinement, enlightenment and civilised behaviour.

The division between good and evil is never absolute; the good heroes have bad traits and vice versa. Take, for example, Yudistra, the eldest of the Pandava brothers. His moral integrity is high, but his great fault is his extravagant generosity. Although the forces of good usually triumph over evil, more often than not the victory is an ambivalent one: both sides suffer grievous loss and though a king may win a righteous war he may lose all his sons in the process. In the *Mahabharata*, when the great battle is over and the Pandavas are victorious, one of their enemies sneaks into the encampment and kills all the Pandava women and children.

Wayang Kulit Performances It's fairly easy to tell the kasar figures from the halus figures. The halus figures tend to be smaller in size and more elegant in proportion; their legs are slender and close together, and their heads are tilted downwards presenting an image of humility and self-effacement. The kasar characters are often enormous, muscular and hairy, with their heads upturned. Eye shape (bulging eyes indicate a person is kasar) and the colour of the figures, particularly on the faces, are of great importance. Red often indicates aggressiveness, greed, impatience, anger or simply a very forthright personality. Black, and often blue, indicates calmness, spiritual awareness and maturity. Gold and yellow are reserved for kings and the highest nobles. White can symbolise purity or virtue, high moral purpose and the

like. Hair styles, ornamentation and clothing are all important in identifying a particular puppet.

A traditional wayang kulit performance transmits the desirable values and characteristics of the heroes of the *Ramayana* and *Mahabharata* – inner control, dedication and self-sacrifice – and stresses the importance of refined behaviour over the violent and crude. One's passions, desires, lust and anger must be disciplined; in the 'Bhagavad Gita' Krishna tells Arjuna that these cause people to do evil, even against their own will. All is clouded by desire, says Krishna, as a fire by smoke, as a mirror by dirt. The performance portrays the forces upon which all life depends, the meaning and purpose of life, the inconsistencies, weakness and greatness of its epic heroes and, by implication, human society as a whole.

Although the wayang theatre still teaches the traditional Javanese values it's difficult to determine its current direction. Some argue that its ritual function seems to be disappearing and that it's becoming more and more purely a form of entertainment, with much of the mystical aura and traditional philosophy being lost. In the past the skills of the dalang were handed down from father to son, but for years now there have been schools in Java – some more traditional than others – which also teach the techniques. Even puppet design is changing, and on TV, characters from the wayang cackle, sing and shriek about such matters as paying taxes on time, birth control and agricultural development.

Gamelan

The musical instruments of Indonesia can be grouped into four main strata: those from pre-Hindu days; those from the Hindu period from the first centuries AD until about the 15th century; the Islamic period from about the 13th century AD; and the last from the 16th century, which is associated with Christian and European influences.

The oldest known instruments in Indonesia are the bronze 'kettle drums' belonging to the Dongson culture which developed in

Gamelan Instruments

Bonang The bonang consists of a double row of bronze kettles (like small kenongs) resting on a horizontal frame; there are three kinds, although the lowest in pitch is no longer used in gamelan orchestras. The bonang is played with two long sticks bound with red cord at the striking end. Although in modern Javanese gamelan the bonang has two rows of bronze kettles, originally it had only one row, as it still does in Bali.

Celempung This is a plucked, stringed instrument, looking somewhat like a zither. It has 26 strings arranged in 13 pairs. The strings are stretched over a coffin-shaped resonator which stands on four legs; the strings are plucked with the thumb nails. The sitar is a smaller version of the celempung, with fewer strings and a higher pitch; the body is box-shaped and without legs.

Gambang The gambang is the only gamelan instrument with bars made not of bronze, but of hardwood, and laid over a wooden frame. They are struck with two sticks made of supple buffalo horn, each ending with a small, round, padded disc. Unlike the gender keys the gambang keys do not need to be damped.

Gender This is similar to a slentem in structure, but there are more bronze keys and the keys and bamboo chambers are smaller. The gender is played with two disc-shaped hammers, smaller than those used for the slentem. The hand acts as a damper, so that each hand must simultaneously hit a note and damp the preceding one.

Gong Ageng The *gong ageng* or *gong gede* is suspended on a wooden frame. There is at least one such gong, sometimes more, in a gamelan orchestra. The gong is made of bronze and is about 90 cm in diameter. It performs the crucial task of marking the end of the largest phrase of a melody.

Kempul This is a small hanging gong, and marks a smaller musical phrase than the big gong.

Kendang These drums are all double-ended and beaten by hand (with the exception of the giant drum, the *bedug*, which is beaten with a stick). The drum is an important leading instrument; it is made from the hollowed tree-trunk sections of the jackfruit (nangka) tree with cow or goat skin stretched across the two ends. There are various types of drums but the middle-sized *kendang batangan* or *kendang ciblon* is chiefly used to accompany dance and wayang performances; the drum patterns indicate specific dance movements or movements of the wayang puppets.

Kenong The kenong is a small gong laid horizontally on crossed cord and sitting inside a wooden frame.

Ketuk The ketuk is a small kenong tuned to a certain pitch, which marks subdivisions of phrases; it is played by the kenong player. The sound of the ketuk is short and dead compared with the clearer, resonant tone of the kenong.

Rebab The rebab is a two-stringed bowed instrument of Arabic origin. It has a wooden body covered with fine, stretched skin. The moveable bridge is made of wood. The bow is made of wood and coarse horsehair tied loosely, not stretched tight like the bows of Western instruments. The rebab player sits cross-legged on the floor behind the instrument.

Saron This is the basic instrument-type of the gamelan, a xylophone with bronze bars which are struck with a wooden mallet. There are three types of saron: high, medium and low-pitched. The high one is called *saron panerus* or *saron peking* and is played with a mallet made of buffalo horn rather than wood.

Slentem The slentem carries the basic melody in the soft ensemble, as the saron does in the loud ensemble. It consists of thin bronze bars suspended over bamboo resonating chambers; it is struck with a padded disc on the end of a stick.

Suling The suling, or flute, is the only wind instrument in the gamelan orchestra. It is made of bamboo and played vertically. ■

Saron

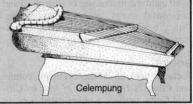

Celempung

what is now northern Vietnam and spread into the Indonesian archipelago – they are not really drums as they have bronze rather than membrane heads. These instruments have been found in Sumatra, Java, Bali, Kalimantan and other parts of South-East Asia; amongst the most curious examples are those of the island of Alor in Nusa Tenggara.

Other instruments, particularly those made of bamboo (like flutes and reed pipes), are also thought to be very old. By the time of the Hindu period there was a wealth of metallic as well as wooden and bamboo instruments played in Java, and these are depicted on the stone reliefs of Borobudur and Prambanan, and other shrines. On Borobudur there are reliefs of drums (waisted, hourglass, pot and barrel-shaped), two-stringed lutes, harps, flutes, mouth organs, reed pipes, a keyed metallophone *(saron)*, xylophone, cymbals and others. Some of these instruments are direct imports from India, whilst others resemble the instruments now used in the Javanese gamelan orchestra.

One interesting and ancient instrument is the *calung*, a Sundanese instrument which is also found in a few places in Java and in southern Thailand. The basic version consists of a set of bamboo tubes, one end of each tube closed off by the natural node of the bamboo, and the other end pared down for part of its length like a goose-quill pen. The instrument is played with one or two sickle-shaped wooden hammers *(panakol)* padded with cotton or rubber. The calung is still commonly found in Java.

The oldest instruments still in use include drums, gongs, various wind instruments and plucked strings. The large Javanese gamelan, whose total complement comprises from 60 to 80 instruments, has sets of suspended and horizontal gongs, gong chimes, drums, flutes, bowed and plucked string instruments, metallophones and xylophones.

BOOKS

A classic book on Javanese religion, culture and values is *The Religion of Java* by Clifford Gertz, perhaps a rather dated book (it was based on research done in the 1950s), but nevertheless fascinating reading. Also worth reading is *Indonesia: Between Myth & Reality* by Lee Khoon Choy. Choy was the Singaporean ambassador to Indonesia from 1970 to 1975 and has written a readable journalistic account of the customs, traditions and spirituality of Indonesia. The chapters on Kebatinan (Javanese spiritualism) and Java's isolated minorities (the Badui and the Tenggerese) are particularly interesting.

The *Oxford in Asia* paperback series (Oxford University Press) has a number of excellent books including *Javanese Wayang Kulit – An Introduction* by Edward C van Ness and Shita Prawirohardjo, *Javanese Gamelan* by Jennifer Lindsay and *Borobudur* by Jacques Dumarcay.

An excellent way to become familiar with the *Ramayana* and *Mahabharata* epics is to read the English adaptations written by William Buck. Buck's inspired versions read like fantasy novels and will give you a greater appreciation of these Indian epics. They make good train and bus reading.

GETTING THERE & AWAY
Air

Jakarta is Indonesia's busiest entrance point for overseas airlines and, though not in the same class as Singapore, it is the best place in Indonesia to shop around for cheap international air tickets. One of the most popular short-hop international connections is the Jakarta-Singapore run for around US$70.

Jakarta is also the hub of the domestic airline network. Garuda, Merpati and Sempati are the main airlines serving the outer islands from Java, though Bouraq and Mandala also have useful services.

Sea

There are, of course, shipping services from other Indonesian islands, but about the only regular international connection to Java is from Pasir Gudang (just outside Johor Bahru in Malaysia) to Surabaya.

The more usual route to reach Java by sea is to take a ferry from Singapore to Tanjung

Pinang on Bintan Island in the Riau Archipelago, and then take a ship to Jakarta. Pelni operates boats between Bintan and Jakarta's Tanjung Priok harbour, and the *Bintan Permata* also sails twice a week.

To/From Bali Ferries run round-the-clock between Banyuwangi/Ketapang harbour on Java and Gilimanuk on Bali. Coming from Bali you can take a local bus to Gilimanuk, then catch one of the frequent ferries to Ketapang, from where numerous buses and trains go to the rest of Java. An easier alternative are the through buses from Denpasar to any major city on Java, and these include the ferry journey. From Denpasar you can get a bus straight to Probolinggo (7½ hours) for Gunung Bromo, Surabaya (nine hours) or head through to Yogyakarta (16 hours) or even Jakarta. A few buses also run between Javan cities and Lovina/Singaraja and Pandangbai on Bali.

To/From Sumatra Ferries shuttle 24 hours a day between Merak in Java and the southern Sumatran port of Bakauheni.

Regular buses go to Merak from Jakarta's Kalideres bus station. In Bakauheni buses take you north to Bandarlampung's Rajabasa bus station, from where other buses can take you all over Sumatra. The easy option are the long-distance buses that run from Jakarta (and other cities in Java) straight through to the main Sumatran destinations such as Padang, Bukittinggi, Sibolga, Prapat, Medan and even Aceh. Most of these leave from Jakarta's Pulo Gadung bus station.

The long bus journeys in Sumatra can take their toll, and as most points of interest are in North Sumatra, many travellers prefer to take a Pelni boat or fly between Jakarta and Padang.

GETTING AROUND

Most travellers going through Java follow the well-worn route from Jakarta to Bogor, Bandung, Pangandaran, Yogyakarta, Solo, Surabaya, Gunung Bromo and on to Bali, with short diversions from points along that route.

Air

There's no real need to fly around Java unless you're in a real hurry or have money to burn, as there's so much transport at ground level. If you do take to the air you'll get some spectacular views of Java's many mountains and volcanoes – try to get a window seat!

Bus

Buses are the main form of transport on Java, and so many operate that you can often just front up to the bus terminal and catch one straight away, especially the big public buses which constantly shuttle between the cities and towns.

Buses are convenient, and quick and comfortable if you pay extra. Java has a huge variety of services from ordinary, public buses that can be very crowded and slow because they pick up and drop off anywhere en route, to super-luxury coaches running directly between the main cities, sometimes at night to avoid the worst of the traffic.

Tickets for express and luxury buses can be bought in advance at bus terminals, or more conveniently at bus agents in the city centres. Many tourist hotels also arrange tickets.

One drawback to bus travel is that the bus terminal can be a long way from the centre of town, especially in the big cities like Jakarta, Surabaya and Bandung. In these cities, the train is often a better alternative because railway stations are conveniently central.

Small minibuses also cover the shorter routes and back runs. They may be called *bemo*, *oplet*, *mikrolet*, *angkot*, etc – there is a mind-boggling array of names with many regional variations in Java – but colt (after Mitsubishi Colt) is the most common term. Like the public buses they pick up and drop off anywhere on request and can get very crowded.

On buses and colts where the fare isn't ticketed or fixed, it's wise to check the fare with other passengers – colt drivers are the worst culprits for jacking up fares for foreigners. Beware of the practice of taking your money and not giving you your change until later.

Java also has an excellent system of door-to-door minibuses, which can pick you up at your hotel (though sometimes you have to go to a depot) and will drop you off wherever you want to go in the destination city. These minibuses (usually called *travel*) run all over Java, and are usually roomy, deluxe air-con minibuses.

Train

Java has a pretty good rail service running from one end of the island to the other. In the east (at Ketapang/Banyuwangi) it connects with the ferry to Bali and in the west (at Merak) it connects with the ferry to Sumatra. The two main lines run between Jakarta and Surabaya – the longer central route goes via Yogyakarta and Solo or the shorter northern route goes via Semarang.

Choose your trains carefully for comfort and speed. Fares and journey times for the same journey and in the same class will vary widely from train to train. Trains range from very cheap squalid cattle trains and reasonably cheap faster trains to very expensive expresses. The schedules change and although departures may be punctual, arrivals will be late for most services and very late for others, particularly the cheap trains.

Ekonomi trains are no frills with bare wooden seats (if you can get one), hawkers, beggars and all manner of produce. They can be very crowded and horrendously slow. Ekonomi trains on the back runs are to be avoided at all costs, but some of the limited-express ekonomi trains on the main routes, eg Surabaya-Solo, provide a reasonably efficient service and are fine for shorter hops. Ekonomi trains cannot be booked; just front up before departure time and buy a ticket.

The best trains to catch are the expresses that offer *bisnis* and *eksekutif* carriages. In bisnis class you get a guaranteed, comfortable seat with plenty of room and fans (but not air-con). Eksekutif is similar but with air-con, reclining seats and video (maybe). Both classes usually include snacks or dinner in the train ticket price. These trains can be booked the day before departure, but outside peak travel times you can usually get a seat on the day of departure.

Top of the range are the luxury trains that run between Jakarta and Surabaya, such as the *Bima* via Yogyakarta and the *Mutiara Utara* via Semarang. These trains also have sleeping carriages and are the next best thing to flying, and almost as expensive. They should be booked as far in advance as possible, usually one week ahead.

When choosing a train, try to get one that begins in the city you are departing from. Seats are more difficult to get on a train coming through from somewhere else, and in ekonomi you may be a standing-room-only sardine. Try also to get a train that ends in the city of your destination. Even if you are only going part way on a train's journey, the fare is almost the same for the full journey, eg Yogyakarta-Jakarta costs the same as Surabaya-Jakarta on the *Bima*.

Another factor to bear in mind when choosing your trains is that some cities, such as Jakarta and Surabaya, have several stations, some far more convenient than others. Both these cities have convenient central stations, compared to the bus terminals out in the sticks, making the train a good alternative to the buses.

As well as having central stations, train travel can be less tiring and the better trains can be more comfortable (if slower) than the buses, particularly on long hauls. One drawback is that there are far fewer train departures and while you can get a bus almost any time, you may be in for a long wait at the railway station.

Buying tickets is usually straightforward, but ticket windows can be crowded and trying to get information can be a frustrating experience. Some cities, such as Yogya and Bandung, have helpful tourist information booths at the station, or the station master *(kepala stasiun)* can help. Stations display timetables on boards, and at main stations you can often get a printed timetable *(jadwal)* for that station, but all-Java timetables are almost impossible to get.

Train tickets can also be bought through travel agencies in main cities. They charge for this service, but it can be worth the money to save a lot of time and hassle at the station.

Sector by sector the main train routes through Java are as shown below. Scheduled times are given – expect overruns.

Jakarta-Yogyakarta All trains between Jakarta and Yogyakarta pass through Cirebon on the north coast, and some continue on through Solo and Madiun to Surabaya.

From Jakarta to Yogyakarta takes from nine to 12 hours with fares from 5000 rp in ekonomi on the *Kerata Api Ekspres* up to 94,000 rp for a sleeper on the *Bima*.

The express *Bima* costs from 26,000 rp in bisnis class to 94,000 rp for a sleeper. It departs Jakarta (Kota) at 4 pm, arriving in Yogya at 12.30 am before continuing on to Surabaya, arriving at 5.15 am. In the other direction it leaves Surabaya at 4 pm, goes through Yogya at 9 pm and arrives in Jakarta at 5.30 am the next day.

The *Fajar Utama Yogya* and *Senja Utama Yogya* services are also good, but don't provide sleepers. Between them, departures leave Jakarta (Gambir) at 5.55 and 7 am, 7.15 and 7.35 pm. Trains leave Yogya in the other direction at 7 and 9 am, 6 and 8 pm. Both cost from 21,000 rp in bisnis class to 44,000 rp in eksekutif A (top class), and the journey time is around nine hours.

Other express services include the slower *Jayabaya* (18,000 rp bisnis, 10½ hours), which runs between Jakarta and Surabaya and stops in Yogya. The *Senja Utama Solo* leaves Gambir at 6.25 pm for Solo (12 hours), and passes though Yogya.

At the other end of the comfort scale are the crowded ekonomi class-only trains departing Jakarta's Pasar Senen station: the *Gaya Baru Malam Selatan* and *Matamaja* (both 7500 rp, 10 hours), or the *Kerata Api Ekspres* (5000 rp, 12 hours). In comparison, the cheapest bus is 11,000 rp from Jakarta to Yogyakarta and takes 12 hours, but given inevitable delays on ekonomi trains, the bus may be quicker.

Jakarta-Surabaya The quickest trains between Jakarta and Surabaya are the night trains that take the shorter northern route via Semarang. Trains that take the longer south-ern route via Yogya include the luxury *Bima* (13½ hours), the bisnis-class only *Jayabaya* (26,000 rp, 15 hours), and the ekonomi *Gaya Baru Malam Selatan* (10,000 rp, 16 hours).

The deluxe *Mutiara Utara* takes the northern route from Jakarta (Kota) to Surabaya (Pasar Turi), departing Jakarta at 4.30 pm, Surabaya at 5 pm. The 12-hour trip ranges from 26,000 rp in bisnis to 94,000 rp for a sleeper.

The cheapest services taking the north coast route are the ekonomi class-only *Gaya Baru Malam Utara* (10,000 rp, 14 hours), which goes from Jakarta (Kota) to Surabaya's Pasar Turi at 5 pm, and the *Parcel* (10,000 rp, 14 hours) from Jakarta (Pasar Senen) at 5.45 pm. Overruns can turn this into a 20-hour journey on the ekonomi trains.

Yogyakarta-Surabaya There are more than half a dozen trains a day between Yogya and Surabaya. The trip takes from 5½ to 7½ hours and costs from 3300 rp in ekonomi. The deluxe *Bima* between Jakarta and Surabaya operates through Yogyakarta. The *Argopuro* (3700 rp, seven hours) is one of the best ekonomi services leaving Yogya at 7.30 am, Surabaya at 1 pm. Solo is on the main route from Yogyakarta to Surabaya.

Car

Self-drive cars can be hired in Jakarta but rates are very high through the international companies like Avis and National, typically around US$100 per day. Local companies are slightly cheaper. To hire a car you must have a valid local or international driving licence, and the age limit is usually 19, sometimes higher. Surabaya and Yogya have cheaper car hire.

While it is possible to drive yourself in Java, you need the patience of a saint and the concentration powers of a chess grand master. The main Jakarta-Bandung-Yogya-Solo-Surabaya route is no fun. Apart from a few toll roads, and the odd quiet stretch with stunning scenery, driving along this highway is a procession of towns and villages, with constant traffic – buses, trucks, cars, motorbikes, food carts, bicycles, pedestrians and chickens – all competing for the narrow stretch of tarmac.

The usual alternative is to rent a car or minibus with driver, which can be a lot cheaper than hiring a self-drive car. The big car-rental agencies prefer to rent cars with drivers. Much cheaper are the private operators that cost as little as 70,000 rp (US$35) per day with driver. Cars can be hired through travel agents and hotels, who have regular drivers or may know of a driver looking for work. Check out the driver for experience and language ability, and get licence and identity-card details. (See the Getting Around chapter for more information.) Good places for hiring cars on this basis are the main cities and tourist destinations such as Yogya, Jakarta, Surabaya, Bogor, Bandung, Pangandaran and Malang.

For shorter trips around town you can rent taxis or minibuses quite easily through car-rental companies, some travel agencies and hotels in main cities. Rates vary but it's likely to be around 10,000 rp an hour for a minimum of two hours, or a flat rate for a set route. It is cheaper through the private operators, but heavy bargaining is usually required.

Boat

There are plenty of ferries and boats from Java to the outer islands but there is also a boat trip across the inland sea between Cilacap and Kalipucang on the south coast which is really worth doing. If you're travelling between Central Java and Pangandaran in West Java the boat is an excellent alternative to taking the bus and/or train all the way.

There are daily boat services to Pulau Seribu in the Bay of Jakarta, but trips to the small islands off the coast usually involve chartering a fishing boat – an outrigger vessel with sails or a motorised boat – and are dependent on the weather. There are regular daily ferries between Java and Madura, Bali and Sumatra.

Local Transport

Taxis are to be found around hotels and at airport, train and bus terminals. Most are metered and drivers will use them – insist if they don't, or catch another. The metered rate is around 900 rp for the first km and 450 rp for each subsequent km. Private cars and minivans also operate where taxis don't exist, or in opposition to taxis. Bargaining is the definitely the rule with private operators, and taxis are a better alternative for the uninitiated.

Indonesia has all sorts of weird and wonderful means of transport, and most can be found in Java. Bargaining is required for all these forms of transport. The *bajaj* (pronounced 'ba-jai') is a farting, noisy three-wheeler, a Jakarta speciality. Java has more becaks (trishaws) than just about anywhere in the world. The horse-drawn *andong* can be found through Java, or in Jakarta bicycles with passenger seats on the back can take you around the streets. If you really want to get off the beaten track, or simply get home from the market, the *ojek* rider will give you a lift on his motorbike and go where no buses do or dare.

Jakarta

Jakarta is all Indonesia rolled into one huge urban sprawl of nearly nine million people. Indonesians come from all over the archipelago to seek fame and fortune, or just to eke out a living. Bataks and Minangkabau from Sumatra, Ambonese from Maluku, Dani from Irian Jaya, Minahasans from Sulawesi, Balinese, Madurese and Timorese are all united by Bahasa Indonesia and a desire to make it in the capital. For it is in Jakarta that the latest styles and thoughts are formed, the important political decisions made. Jakarta is the main centre for the economy, the place to find work, do deals and court government officials.

Over the last decade or so, Jakarta has undergone a huge transformation. Once, its miserable poverty and crumbling infrastructure made it one of the hell holes of Asian travel. Now the city's face is being changed by the constant construction of more sky-

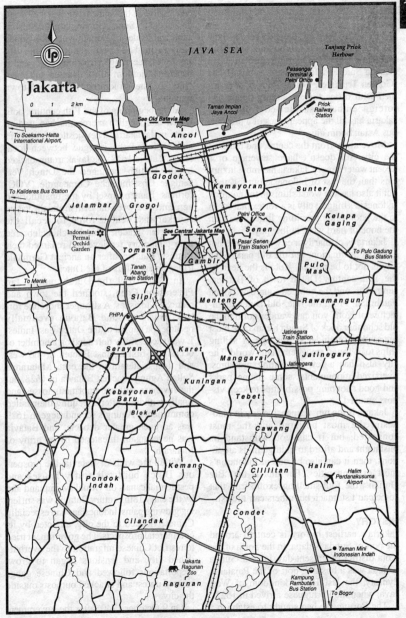

Jakarta

JAVA SEA

0 1 2 km

Tanjung Priok
Harbour

Passenger
Terminal &
Pelni Office

Priok
Railway
Station

See Old Batavia Map

Taman Impian
Jaya Ancol

To Soekarno-Hatta
International Airport,

Ancol

Glodok

Kemayoran

Sunter

To Kalideres Bus Station

Jelambar

Grogol

Pelni Office

Kelapa
Gagling

Indonesian
Permai
Orchid
Garden

Tomang

See Central Jakarta Map

Senen

Pasar Senen
Train Station

To Pulo Gadung
Bus Station

Tanah Abang
Train Station

Gambir

Pulo
Mas

To Merak

Silpi

Menteng

Rawamangun

PHPA

Jatinegara
Train Station

Serayan

Karet

Manggarai

Jatinegara
Jatinegara

Kuningan

Tebet

Kebayoran
Baru

Blok M

Cawang

Kemang

Cililitan

Halim

Halim
Perdanakusuma
Airport

Pondok
Indah

Cilandak

Condet

Taman Mini
Indonesian Indah

Jakarta
Ragunan
Zoo

Kampung
Rambutan
Bus Station

Ragunan

To Bogor

scrapers, flyovers, hotels and shopping malls.

The showpiece of the prosperous new Jakarta is the central business district bounded by Jalan Thamrin/Sudirman, Jalan Rasuna Said and Jalan Gatot Subroto. The 'Golden Triangle', as it is known, is crammed with office towers, luxury hotels and foreign embassies. Viewed from here, Jakarta has all the appearances of a prosperous Asian boom city.

Move away from the centre, and much of the city still doesn't have sewerage or a decent water supply. Jakarta has more luxury cars than the rest of Indonesia put together, but it also has the worst slums in the country. Indonesia's biggest city is a vortex that sucks in the poor, often providing little more than the hope of hard work at low pay.

Jakarta is primarily a city of business not a tourist destination, but the old part of the city is not to be missed. Kota is the heart of the 17th-century Dutch town of Batavia, centred around the cobbled square of Taman Fatahillah. From the fine, old Dutch architecture of Kota, you can wander north to the old schooner dock of Sunda Kelapa, the most impressive reminder of the age of sailing ships to be found anywhere in the world. The city also has a few interesting museums, oversized monuments, some theme parks and good shopping possibilities to keep visitors amused.

Jakarta is the most expensive city in Indonesia, the most polluted and the most congested, but if can you withstand its onslaught and afford to indulge in its attractions, then it can also be one of Indonesia's most exciting cities. For this is the 'Big Durian', the foul-smelling exotic fruit that some can't stomach but others can't resist.

HISTORY

Jakarta's earliest history is centred around the port of Sunda Kelapa, in the north of the Kota district of present-day Jakarta. Sunda Kelapa was a bustling port of the Pajajaran dynasty, the last Hindu kingdom of West Java, when the Portuguese arrived in 1522.

The Portuguese had sought to establish a concession in the spice trade but they were driven out by Sunan Gunungjati, the Muslim saint and leader of Demak who took Sunda Kelapa in 1527. He renamed the city Jayakarta, meaning 'victorious city', and it became a fiefdom of the Banten sultanate. None of the structures of this old town remain.

At the beginning of the 17th century, both Dutch and English merchants had trading posts in Jayakarta. They jostled for power and exploited the intrigue between local rulers. Late in 1618, the Jayakartans, backed by the British, besieged the Dutch Vereenigde Oost-Indische Compagnie (VOC) fortress. Banten, upset by the unauthorised agreement between the British and the vassal Jayakartans, sent a force to recall the Jayakartan leader. The Dutch celebrated their temporary reprieve and renamed their fortress 'Batavia' after an ancient Germanic tribe, the ancestors of the Dutch.

In May 1619 the Dutch, under Jan Pieterszoon Coen, stormed the town and reduced it to ashes. A stronger shoreline fortress was built and Batavia eventually became the capital of the Dutch East Indies. It was successfully defended on a number of occasions, first against Banten in the west and then Mataram in the east. Mataram's Sultan Agung attacked Batavia in 1628, but the Javanese suffered enormous losses and finally withdrew after executing their failed commanders. Agung's second siege in 1629 was an even greater debacle, and Batavia was never again threatened by an army of Mataram.

Within the walls of Batavia, the prosperous Dutch built tall stuffy houses and pestilential canals on virtual swampland and by the early 18th century Batavia was suffering growing pains. Indonesians and especially Chinese flocked to the city, attracted by its commercial prospects. The government tried to restrict Chinese migration to the overburdened city, and tensions began to grow. Deportations followed and Chinese gangs created unrest and attacked outposts outside the city.

On 9 October 1740, after the government

ordered a search of Chinese premises for weapons, the good citizens of Batavia went berserk and massacred 5000 Chinese within the city. A year later Chinese inhabitants were moved to Glodok, outside the city walls. Other Batavians, discouraged by the severe epidemics between 1735 and 1780, moved when they could and the city began to spread far south of the port. The Koningsplein, now Merdeka Square, was finished in 1818 and Merdeka Palace in 1879; Kebayoran Baru was the last residential area to be laid out by the Dutch after WW II.

Dutch colonial rule came to an end when the Japanese occupied Java and the name 'Jakarta' was restored to the city. The republican government of the revolution retreated to Yogyakarta when the Dutch returned after the war, but in 1950, after Indonesian independence was finally secured, Jakarta was made the capital of the new republic.

In 1945 Jakarta had a population of 900,000; since then there has been a continual influx of migrants from depressed rural areas and newcomers continue to crowd into the urban slums. Today the population is over nearly nine, or 17 million including the surrounding districts that form a greater Jakarta.

Soekarno's image of Jakarta was of a city of grand structures that would glorify the republic and make Jakarta a world centre. The 14-storey Jakarta Hotel broke the skyline, the six-lane Jalan Thamrin was constructed and a massive sports stadium was erected for the 1962 Asian Games. Work on Jakarta's massive mosque was begun, and the National Monument took root.

With Soekarno's architectural ambitions cut short in 1965, the job of sorting out the city was left to Lieutenant General Ali Sadikin, governor of Jakarta from 1966 to 1977. Although he is credited with rehabilitating the roads and bridges, building several hospitals and a large number of new schools, he also began the campaign of ruthlessly cleaning up the city by clearing out slum dwellers, banning becaks and street pedlars. He also started the control of migration to the city, to stem hopeless overcrowding and poverty.

New arrivals from the countryside, without Jakarta residence permits, still constantly face the possibility of expulsion from the city. But the lure of the big lights continues, and a even roadside *parkir* directing traffic and parking cars can still earn a good living compared to an existence of village unemployment.

ORIENTATION

Jakarta sprawls over 25 km from the docks to the suburbs of South Jakarta, covering 661 sq km in all. The centre of the city fans out from around Merdeka Square, which contains the central landmark of Soekarno's towering gold-tipped National Monument. Merdeka Square itself is just a barren, deserted field, a product of grand urban planning gone wrong. Jakarta's main problem is that it doesn't really have a centre that can be explored on foot, but a number of centres, all separated by vast traffic jams and heat.

For most visitors, Jakarta revolves around the modern part of the city to the south of the monument. Jalan Thamrin, running from the south-west corner of Merdeka Square down to the Welcome Monument roundabout, is the main thoroughfare, containing many of the big hotels and a couple of major shopping centres – the Sarinah department store and the Plaza Indonesia.

Just east of Jalan Thamrin and south of the National Monument is Jalan Jaksa, the likeable oasis of backpackers' hotels and restaurants.

North of the National Monument, the old city of Jakarta has Jakarta's main tourist attractions. It includes the Chinatown area of Glodok, the old Dutch area of Kota, and the schooner harbour of Sunda Kelapa. The modern harbour, Tanjung Priok, is several km along the coast to the east past the Taman Impian Jaya Ancol recreation park.

The main railway station, Gambir, is just to the east of the National Monument. The intercity bus stations – Kalideres in the west, Kampung Rambutan in the south and Pulo Gadung in the east – are on the outskirts of Jakarta.

Jalan Thamrin heading south becomes

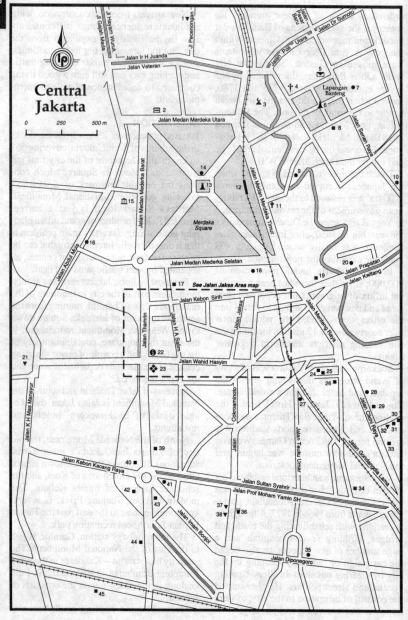

Central Jakarta

0   250   500 m

See Jalan Jaksa Area map

PLACES TO STAY

8	Borobudur Inter-Continental Hotel
17	Sabang Metropolitan Hotel
19	Aryaduta Hyatt Hotel
24	Sofyan Hotel Betawi
25	Gondia Guest House
26	Hotel Menteng I
29	Sofyan Hotel Cikini
30	Yannie International Guest House
31	Karya II Hotel
33	Hotel Menteng II
34	Hotel Marcopolo
39	President Hotel
40	Grand Hyatt Jakarta Hotel
42	Hotel Indonesia
43	Mandarin Oriental Jakarta Hotel
44	Kartika Plaza Hotel
45	Shangri-La Hotel

PLACES TO EAT

1	Seafood Night Market
21	Pasar Tanah Abang
32	Oasis Bar & Restaurant
37	Tamnak Thai Restaurant
38	Gandy Steakhouse

OTHER

2	Presidential Palace
3	Istiqlal Mosque
4	Catholic Cathedral
5	Post Office
6	Free Irian Monument
7	Mahkamah Agung & Ministry of Finance Building
9	Gedung Pancasila
10	Bharata Theatre
11	Emanuel Church
12	Gambir Railway Station
13	National Monument (Monas)
14	Entrance to Monas
15	National Museum
16	Tanamur Disco
18	US Embassy
20	4848 Taxis
22	Jakarta Theatre Building & Visitor Centre
23	Sarinah Department Store
27	Immigration Office
28	Taman Ismael Marzuki (TIM)
35	Adam Malik Museum
36	Casa Pub
41	British Embassy

Jalan Jenderal Sudirman, home to more hotels, large banks and office blocks. Further south are the affluent suburban areas of Kebayoran Baru, Pondok Indah and Kemang, with their own centres and busy shopping districts such as Blok M in Kebayoran.

INFORMATION
Tourist Offices
The Jakarta Tourist Information Office (☎ 332067, 364093) is opposite the Sarinah department store in the Jakarta Theatre building on Jalan Thamrin. They can answer most queries and have a good giveaway map of Jakarta, and a number of excellent leaflets and publications including the *Jakarta Official Guide*. The office is open every day except Sundays and holidays from 9 am to 4.30 pm. There is also a branch office (☎ 5507088) at the airport.

The headquarters of the Indonesia Tourist Promotion Organisation is the Directorate-General of Tourism (☎ 3103117), at Jalan Kramat Raya 81. This is not the best place to have your travel queries answered but they have some useful publications including the

Calendar of Events, the *Indonesia Tourist Map*, and you might be able to squeeze a copy of the useful *Indonesia Travel Planner* out of them. The office is open government office hours only.

Money
Jakarta is crawling with banks and money-changers. Jakarta banks offer some of the best exchange rates in Indonesia, but it pays to shop around. Banks offer better rates than moneychangers. Many foreign-exchange banks are found on and around Jalan Thamrin and most are open from 8 am to 4 pm Monday to Friday, and from 8 to 11 am Saturday.

Handy banks to Jalan Jaksa are the Lippobank and Bank Duta on Jalan Kebon Sirih. The Lippobank gives cash advances on credit cards and good (though not necessarily the best) rates for cash and travellers' cheques. Bank Duta on the other side of the street also has good rates.

In the Sarinah department-store building, on Jalan Wahid Hasyim, the branch of the BDN bank usually has good exchange rates.

The moneychanger inside Sarinah is open until 9 pm and changes foreign cash at below bank rates. The Plaza Indonesia has a selection of banks and in the Sogo supermarket in the basement, Bank Dagang Nasional Indonesia has a foreign-exchange booth, open every day from 10 am to 9 pm for after-hours transactions. It changes US$ cash at reasonable rates, travellers' cheques and other currencies at poorer rates. Many of the big hotels also have bank branches that offer good exchange rates.

The American Express Bank (☎ 5501152) headquarters in Jakarta is at Jalan Rasuna Said Block X-1. Pacto Ltd is the American Express agent throughout Indonesia and handles postal services and Amex cheque and card transactions at their Hotel Borobudur Inter-Continental branch (☎ 3865952).

Post & Telecommunications

The main post office and efficient poste restante is behind Jalan Pos Utara, off to the north-east of the National Monument (Monas). It's a good half-hour walk from the centre of town, or you can take a No 12 bus from Jalan Thamrin. Post restante is open from 8 am to 4 pm Monday to Friday, from 8 am to 1 pm Saturday. For basic postal services, a few windows open from 6 am to 10 pm Monday to Saturday (closed from 11 am to noon Friday) and from 9 am to 4 pm Sunday.

For international and intercity phone calls, the efficient Telkom centre is next to the tourist office in the Jakarta Theatre building. It's open 24 hours and has Home Country Direct phones and a fax service.

Convenient for those staying around Jalan Jaksa is the privately run RTQ Warparpostel (☎ 326221, fax 3904503), Jalan Jaksa 25, opposite Nick's Hostel. This place offers international and domestic postal, telephone and fax services. You can receive faxes here for 1500 rp per page. Business centres in the major hotels also have more expensive postal and fax services.

Immigration Office

There is a central immigration office (☎ 349811) at Jalan Teuku Umar 1 in Menteng.

Travel Agencies

For international flights, the travel agencies on Jalan Jaksa are convenient places to start looking: try Seabreeze Travel (☎ 3902996), at No 38, and Balimaesti near Angie's Cafe. Travel International (☎ 3905188) in the President Hotel on Jalan Thamrin is also a good place for cheap tickets, as is Vayatour (☎ 3100720) next door. Other agents worth checking are Natrabu (☎ 331728), Jalan Agus Salim 29A (near Jalan Jaksa) and Pacto Ltd (☎ 3810837) in the Hotel Borobudur Inter-Continental.

Indo Shangrila Travel (☎ 6256080), Jalan Gajah Mada 219G, is the STA Travel agent and often has good deals.

Bookshops

Singapore's Times Bookshop chain has a branch in the Plaza Indonesia on Jalan Thamrin. It has the best stock of English language books, and a good range of travel books. On the other side of the roundabout, the bookshop in the Hotel Indonesia is expensive but has a very good range of books on Indonesia.

The big Indonesian book chains are good for maps, dictionaries and travel books and have a few English-language books. Gramedia has shops at Jalan Gajah Mada 109 and Jalan Melawai IV/13 in Blok M, while Gunung Agung has a huge shop at Jalan Kwitang 6, just east of Jalan Jaksa. Sarinah department store also has a good book and map section.

Media

The daily English-language *Jakarta Post* (1000 rp from street vendors) gives a useful run down of what's on, temporary exhibitions and cinema programmes.

Film & Photography

Jalan Agus Salim, between Jalan Jaksa and Jalan Thamrin, has photographic shops for film, developing and equipment, but 'tourist prices' may apply and bargaining might be necessary. Otherwise, Jakarta has plenty of places for film developing. Fuji is the most common brand of film.

Dangers & Annoyances

Jakarta's buses tend to be hopelessly crowded, particularly during rush hours. Its pickpockets are notoriously adept and they're great bag slashers too. So take care. Indeed, if you are carrying a camera or anything else of value, you would be wise to spring for a taxi.

Libraries & Organisations

The Ganesha Society (☎ 360551) at the National Museum is an organisation of volunteer museum workers that holds weekly lectures or films about Indonesia at the Erasmus Huis (☎ 512321) on Jalan Rasuna Said, beside the Dutch Embassy in South Jakarta.

The Indonesian/American Cultural Center (Perhimpunan Persahabatan Indonesia Amerika) (☎ 8583241), Jalan Pramuka Kav 30, has exhibits, films and lectures related to Indonesia each week. The Australian Cultural Centre (Pusat Kebudayaan Australia), at the embassy on Jalan Rasuna Said, has a good library, open from 10.30 am to 3.30 pm Monday to Friday. The British Council (☎ 5223311) also has a good library in the Widjojo Centre, Jalan Jenderal Sudirman 56. The French Cultural Centre (☎ 3908585), Jalan Salemba Raya 25, has a French library and screens French films. The Goethe Institut (☎ 8581139) is at Jalan Mataram Raya 23.

National Parks/Nature Reserves

The national parks body, the PHPA, is in the Forestry Department (Departemen Kehutanan) building, Jalan Gatot Subroto. Take bus No 210 or 213 from Jalan Jenderal Sudirman. Entry permits to national parks and/or reserves can be acquired directly from local offices located on-site throughout Indonesia.

OLD BATAVIA (KOTA)

The old town of Batavia, known as Kota today, at one time contained Coen's massive shoreline fortress, the Kasteel, and was surrounded by a sturdy defensive wall and a moat. In the early 19th century Governor-General Daendels did a good job of demolishing much of the unhealthy city but there is still a Dutch flavour to this old part of the town. A few of Batavia's old buildings remain in active use, although others were restored during the 1970s and have become museums.

The centre of old Batavia is the cobblestone square known as **Taman Fatahillah**. A block west of the square is the **Kali Besar**, the great canal along Sungai Ciliwung. This was once the high-class residential area of Batavia and on the west bank overlooking the canal are the last of the big private homes dating from the early 18th century. The **Toko Merah** or Red Shop, now occupied by the Dharma Niaga company, was formerly the home of Governor-General van Imhoff. At

Old Batavia (Kota)

the north end of the Kali Besar is a small 17th-century Dutch drawbridge, the last in the city, called the **Chicken Market Bridge**.

Jakarta History Museum

On the south side of Taman Fatahillah Square, the museum is housed in the old town hall of Batavia, which is probably one of the most solid reminders of Dutch rule to be found anywhere in Indonesia. This large bell-towered hall, built in 1627 and added to between 1707 and 1710, served the administration of the city. It was also used by the city law courts and its dungeons were the main prison compound of Batavia. In 1830 the Javanese hero Prince Diponegoro was imprisoned here for a time on his way into exile in Manado.

Today it contains lots of heavy, carved furniture and other memorabilia from the Dutch period. Amongst the more interesting exhibits is a series of gloomy portraits of all the Dutch governors-general, and early pictures of Batavia.

In the courtyard at the back of the building is a strange memorial stone to one Pieter Erbervelt, who was put to death in 1722 for allegedly conspiring to massacre the Dutch inhabitants of Batavia.

The museum is open every day but Monday: from 9 am to 4 pm Tuesday to Friday, from 9 am to 1 pm Saturday and from 9 am to 4 pm Sunday. Entry costs 150 rp.

Wayang Museum

Also on Taman Fatahillah, this museum has one of the best collections of wayang puppets in Java and includes puppets not only from Indonesia but also China, Malaysia, India and Cambodia.

Formerly the Museum of Old Batavia, the building itself was constructed in 1912 on the site of the Dutch Church of Batavia which was demolished by Daendels in 1808. In the downstairs courtyard there are memorials to the Dutch governors-general once buried here. These include Jan Pieterszoon Coen, founder of Batavia, who died of cholera in 1629 during the siege by Mataram,

and Anthony van Diemen, former governor-general and discoverer of Australia.

Closed on Monday, the museum is open Tuesday to Thursday and Sunday from 9 am to 3 pm, on Friday until 11 am, and Sunday until 1 pm. Entry costs 150 rp.

The best time to visit is Sunday morning. Wayang golek or wayang kulit performances are put on every Sunday from 10 am to 2 pm.

Balai Seni Rupa (Fine Arts Museum)

Built between 1866 and 1870, the Palace of Justice building is now a museum housing a collection of contemporary Indonesian paintings, with works by Indonesia's most prominent painters including Raden Saleh, Affandi and Ida Bagus Made. Part of the building is also a ceramics museum with Chinese ceramics and Majapahit terracottas.

Closed on Monday, the museum is open Tuesday to Thursday from 9 am to 4 pm, Friday from 9 to 11 am, Saturday 9 am to 1 pm and Sunday from 9 am to 2 pm. Entry costs 150 rp.

Cannon Si Jagur

This huge bronze cannon in Taman Fatahillah is adorned with a Latin inscription, *Ex me ipsa renata sum*, which means 'Out of myself I was reborn'. The cannon tapers at one end into a large clenched fist, with the thumb protruding between the index and middle fingers. This suggestive fist is a sexual symbol in Indonesia and childless women would offer flowers and sit astride the cannon in the hope of gaining children. Si Jagur is a Portuguese cannon brought to Batavia as a trophy of war after the fall of Melaka in 1641.

Gereja Sion

On Jalan Pangeran Jayakarta, near Kota railway station, this church dates from 1695 and is the oldest remaining church in Jakarta. Also known as Gereja Portugis or Portuguese Church, it was built just outside the old city walls for the so-called 'black Portuguese' – the Eurasians and natives captured from Portuguese trading ports in India and Malaya and brought to Batavia as slaves.

Most of these people were Catholics but they were given their freedom on the condition that they joined the Dutch Reformed Church, and the converts became known as the Mardijkers or 'Liberated Ones'.

The exterior of the church is very plain, but inside there are copper chandeliers, the original organ and a Baroque pulpit. Although in the year 1790 alone, more than 2000 people were buried in the graveyard here, very few tombs remain. One of the most interesting is the ornate bronze tombstone of Governor-General Zwaardecroon, who died in 1728 and, as was his wish, was buried among the 'ordinary' folk.

Sunda Kelapa

Just a 10-minute walk north of Taman Fatahillah, the old port of Sunda Kelapa has more sailing ships, the magnificent Macassar schooners called *pinisi*, than you ever thought existed. This is one of the finest sights in Jakarta. These brightly painted ships are still an important means of transporting goods to and from the outer islands. Most of them come from Kalimantan, spending up to a week in port unloading timber and then reloading cement and other supplies for the return journey.

Old men will take you in row boats around the schooners for about 2000 rp. You can spend a good half-hour or so rowing around the schooners, but try to avoid decapitation by mooring ropes or gangplanks and occasionally having rubbish thrown on you from the ships.

Entry to the dock is just around from the Museum Bahari and costs 200 rp. There is a small tourist cafe with expensive drinks at the dock.

Museum Bahari (Maritime Museum)

Near the entrance to Sunda Kelapa, an old VOC warehouse built in 1645 has been turned into a maritime museum. It exhibits craft from around Indonesia, and has an interesting collection of old photographs recreating the voyage to Jakarta from Europe via Aden, Ceylon and Singapore. The build-

ing itself is worth a visit and the sentry posts outside are part of the old city wall.

The museum is open every day but Monday from 9 am to 3.30 pm Tuesday to Thursday, from 9 am to 3 pm Friday and Sunday, and from 9 am to noon on Saturday. Admission is 150 rp (100 rp on Sundays).

Just before the entrance to the museum is the **old watchtower** back near the bridge. It was built in 1839 to sight and direct traffic to the port. Although there are good views over the harbour from the top, the watchtower is usually locked.

Further along the same street from the museum is the early-morning fish market, **Pasar Ikan**. Around dawn when the day's catch is sold it is an intense, colourful scene of busy crowds. Later in the day it sells household items and a growing collection of souvenirs.

Glodok

After the Chinese massacre of 1740, the Dutch decided there would be no repetition and prohibited all Chinese from residing within the town walls, or even from being there after sundown. In 1741 a tract of land just to the south-west of Batavia was allocated as Chinese quarters. The area became Glodok, Jakarta's Chinatown, and the city's flourishing commercial centre.

Glodok is bounded to the east by Jalan Gajah Mada, a wide road lined with offices, restaurants and modern shopping plazas. But if you walk in from Jalan Pancoran, beside the Glodok Plaza, old Glodok still consists of winding lanes, narrow crooked houses with balconies, slanting red-tiled roofs and tiny obscure shops. In between there are numerous eating places, markets and street hawkers. It can be a fascinating area to wander around. Just south of Jalan Pancoran, you'll find the Chinese **Dharma Jaya Temple**, one of the most interesting in Jakarta. Built in 1650, it was the chief temple for the Chinese of Batavia and was once known for its casino and Chinese wayang kulit.

If you're walking from Glodok back along Jalan Gajah Mada, it's worth pausing to have a glance at two old Jakarta buildings along this street. The **Candra Naya**, at No 188, was once the home of the Chinese 'captain' employed by the Dutch to manage the affairs of Batavia's Chinese community. Since 1946 the building has housed the offices of a social work society but you may be able to have a short wander inside. Further south at No 111, the **Arsip Nasional** (National Archives) building dates from 1760 and was formerly the country house of Governor-General Reinier de Klerk.

NATIONAL MUSEUM

On the west side of Merdeka Square, the National Museum, built in 1862, is the best museum in Indonesia and one of the best in South-East Asia. Its collection includes a huge ethnic map of Indonesia and an equally big relief map on which you can pick out all those volcanoes you have climbed.

The museum has an enormous collection of cultural objects of the various ethnic groups – costumes, musical instruments, model houses and so on – and numerous fine bronzes from the Hindu-Javanese period, as well as many interesting stone pieces salvaged from Central Javanese and other temples. There's also a superb display of Chinese ceramics dating back to the Han dynasty (300 BC to 220 AD) which was almost entirely amassed in Indonesia.

One of the best places to start a tour of the museum is the Treasure Room upstairs from the entrance. The gold exhibits are interesting, but the real attraction is the air-con if you have walked to the museum.

Just outside the museum is a bronze elephant which was presented by the King of Thailand in 1871; thus the museum building is popularly known as the Gedung Gajah or Elephant House.

The museum is open from 8.30 am to 2.30 pm Tuesday to Thursday and Sunday, to 11 am on Friday and to 1.30 pm on Saturday. It's closed on Monday. Entry costs 200 rp, and a 1000 rp camera fee applies. It's well worth a visit, for here you will find some reminder of almost anywhere you have been

in Indonesia. The Ganesha Society offer excellent guided tours in English (free) on Tuesday, Wednesday and Thursday at 9.30 am, and the last Sunday of the month at 10.30 am. Tours are also conducted in French (9.30 am Wednesday), German (10 am Thursday) and Japanese (10 am Tuesday).

OTHER MUSEUMS

Jakarta has a number of other museums apart from the excellent National Museum and those in old Batavia. North-west of the National Museum is the **Taman Prasasti Museum**, or Park of Inscription, on Jalan Tanah Abang. This was once the Kebon Jahe Cemetery and some important figures of the colonial era are buried here, including Olivia Raffles (wife of British Governor-General Sir Stamford Raffles) who died in 1814. The cemetery is open from 9 am to 3 pm Monday to Thursday, to 1 pm on Friday, and until 2 pm on Saturday. It's closed on Sunday and holidays.

The **Textile Museum** is in a Dutch colonial house on Jalan Satsuit Tubun 4, near the Tanah Abang district bus station. It has a large collection of batik and woven cloth from all over Indonesia, as well as looms and batik-making tools, and it's well worth a visit. This museum is open from 9 am to 4 pm Tuesday to Thursday, from 9 am to 11.30 am on Friday, from 9 am to 1 pm on Saturday and until 3 pm on Sunday. Admission is 150 rp.

In Menteng, the **Adam Malik Museum**, Jalan Diponegoro 29, was the home of the former vice-president and foreign minister. Now a museum crammed with his private collection of Indonesian wood carvings, sculpture and textiles, a huge display of Chinese ceramics, and even Russian icons from when he was ambassador to Moscow. You can wander around the house, a Dutch villa in the old-money suburb of Menteng not far from Jalan Thamrin, and poke into the man's bedroom and even his bathroom, remaining much as he left it in 1984. The museum is open from 9 am to 3 pm every day except Monday. Entry is 1000 rp.

NATIONAL MONUMENT (MONAS)

This 132-metre-high column towering over Merdeka Square is both Jakarta's principal landmark and the most famous architectural extravagance of Soekarno. Commenced in 1961, the monument was not completed until 1975, when it was officially opened by Soeharto. This phallic symbol topped by a glittering flame symbolises the nation's independence and strength (and, some would argue, Soekarno's virility). The National Monument is constructed 'entirely' of Italian marbles', according to a tourist brochure, and the flame is gilded with 35 kg of gold leaf.

In the base of the National Monument, the **National History Museum** tells the history of Indonesia's independence struggle in 48 dramatic dioramas. The numerous uprisings against the Dutch are overstated but interesting, Soekarno is barely mentioned and the events surrounding the 1965 Untung coup are a whitewash.

The highlight of a visit is to take the lift to the top, for dramatic, though rarely clear, views of Jakarta. Avoid Sundays and holidays when the queues for the lift are long.

The National Monument is open weekdays from 8.30 am to 5 pm, and until 7 pm on weekends and holidays. Admission is 500 rp to the museum in the base, or 2000 rp for both the museum and a ride to the top of the monument.

OTHER SOEKARNO MONUMENTS

Inspired tastelessness – in the Russian 'heroes of socialism' style – best describes the plentiful supply of statues Soekarno left to Jakarta. Many have acquired descriptive nicknames. At the end of Jalan Jenderal Sudirman in Kebayoran, the Semangat Pemuda (Spirit of Youth) statue is a suitably muscular young man holding a flaming dish above his head. He is more commonly known as the 'Pizza Man'.

On Jalan Thamrin, the **Selamat Datang (Welcome) Monument** – 'Hansel & Gretel' – was built by Soekarno as a symbol of Indonesian friendliness for the 1962 Asian Games held in Jakarta. Now that the airport

has moved, most visitors' first view is from behind, so it is really the Selamat Jalan (Goodbye), rather than Selamat Datang, Monument.

The propaganda element reaches its peak in the **Free Irian Monument** at Banteng Square near the Borobudur Hotel. Here another muscle-bound gent breaks the chains around his wrists. An almost identical statue can be found a few thousand km away in Dili where, surprise, surprise, the statue is the Free East Timor Monument.

The **Farmer's Monument**, near south of Gambir station on the Jalan Menteng Raya roundabout, is another heart-rending bronze showing a mother offering rice to her returning-hero son after the battle for independence.

On the northern side of Merdeka Square, not far from the National Monument, is a more classical statue of freedom fighter, Prince Diponegoro, astride his horse.

LAPANGAN BANTENG

Just east of Merdeka Square in front of the Hotel Borobudur Inter-Continental, Lapangan Banteng Square (formerly the Weltevreden) was laid out by the Dutch in the 19th century and the area has some of Jakarta's best colonial architecture.

The **Catholic cathedral** with its twin spires was built in 1901 to replace an earlier church. Facing the cathedral is Jakarta's principal place of Muslim worship. The modernistic **Istiqlal mosque**, a Soekarno construction, is reputedly the largest in South-East Asia.

To the east of Lapangan Benteng is the **Mahkamah Agung**, the Supreme Court built in 1848 and next door is the **Ministry of Finance** building, formerly the Witte Huis (White House). This grand government complex was built by Daendels in 1809 as the administration centre for the Dutch government.

To the south-west, on Jalan Merdeka Timur, is the **Gedung Pancasila**, an imposing neoclassical building built in 1830 as the Dutch army commander's residence. It later became the meeting hall of the Volksraad (People's Council), but is best known as the place where Soekarno made his famous Pancasila speech in 1945, laying the foundation for Indonesia's constitution. Just east along Jalan Pejambon from Gedung Pancasila is the **Emanuel Church**, another classic, pillared building dating from 1893.

TAMAN MINI INDONESIA INDAH

In the south-east of the city, near Kampung Rambutan, Taman Mini is another of those 'whole country in one park' collections popular in Asia. The idea for the park was conceived by Madame Tien Soeharto, and in 1971 the families inhabiting the land were cleared out to make way for the project (then estimated to cost the awesome total of US$26 million) and the park was duly opened in 1975.

This 100-hectare park has 27 full-scale traditional houses from the 27 provinces of Indonesia with displays of regional handicrafts and clothing, and a large 'lagoon' where you can row around the islands of the archipelago or take a cable car across for a bird's eye view. There are also museums, theatres, restaurants, an orchid garden and a bird park with a huge walk-in aviary. There's even a mini Borobudur. The park is quite good value and Indonesians will tell you that if you see this there's no need to go anywhere else in the country!

Other attractions include 'Indonesia Indah', a three-dimensional screen show of the Indonesian panorama which takes place at the Keong Mas (Golden Snail) Theatre. In 30 minutes the film packs a lot in a special effects travelogue. Admission is 2000 rp and showings are from noon to 4 pm Monday to Friday, and from 10 am to 5 pm Sunday. On Saturdays an imported film plays.

You can walk or drive your own car around Taman Mini. Or you can go by horse and cart, take the mini-train service that shuttles around the park, or the cable car that goes from one end to the other. The park is open from 8 am to 5 pm daily, the houses and Museum Indonesia from 9 am to 4 pm. Admission is 2000 rp (children 1000 rp). On Sunday mornings there are free cultural performances in most regional houses from 10

am to 2 pm. For other cultural events here, check the Taman Mini monthly programme available from the tourist information office.

Taman Mini is about 18 km from the centre so you need to allow about 1½ hours to get out there and at least three hours to look round. Take any bus to Kampung Rambutan bus station and from there a T55 metro-mini to the park entrance. A taxi will cost around 12,000 rp from central Jakarta.

TAMAN IMPIAN JAYA ANCOL

Along the bay-front between Kota and Tanjung Priok, the people's 'Dreamland' is built on land reclaimed in 1962. This huge landscaped recreation park, providing non-stop entertainment, has hotels, nightclubs, theatres and a variety of sporting facilities.

Taman Impian Jaya Ancol's prime attractions include the **Pasar Seni** (Art Market) (see Things to Buy later), its many sidewalk cafes and a gallery where there are often interesting exhibitions of modern Indonesian art and photography. Pasar Seni has live music on Friday and Saturday nights. Near the Pasar Seni there's an **oceanarium** *(gelanggang samudra)* and an amazing **swimming pool complex**, including a wave pool and slide pool *(gelanggang renang)*. The **Ancol Beach**, so close to the city, is not the greatest place for a swim but you can take a boat from the marina here for day trips to some of Jakarta's Pulau Seribu islands.

The big drawcard at Ancol is **Dunia Fantasi** ('Fantasy Land'), a fun park that must have raised eyebrows at the Disney legal department. Resemblances to Disneyland start at the 'main street' entrance, and the Puppet Castle is a straight 'it's a small world' replica. But the Indonesian influence prevails – Western World is the old west complete with a 'rumah jahil' for miscreants and a Sate Corner snack bar. Dunia Fantasi is actually very well done and great for kids, with a host of fun rides. It is open daily, on Monday to Saturday from 2 to 9 pm, Sundays and holidays from 10 am to 9 pm. Standard entry is 6000 rp, or including all rides it is 13,000 rp during the week, 14,000 rp on Saturday, and 16,000 rp on Sunday and holidays.

Basic admission to Ancol is 800 rp during the week and 1000 rp on Saturday, Sunday and holidays (half price for children). The Pasar Seni is open from 9 am to 10 pm daily, and the swimming pool complex from 7 am to 9 pm daily. The oceanarium costs 6000 rp during the week, 8000 rp on weekends. The pool costs 2500 rp on weekdays, 3000 rp on weekends and the slides are extra. Apart from initial entry, discounts for children are virtually nonexistent at Ancol attractions.

The park can be very crowded on weekends, but on weekdays it's fairly quiet and a great place to escape from the hassles of the city. For more information, call ☎ 681511 in Jakarta.

TAMAN ISMAIL MARZUKI

On Jalan Cikini Raya, not far from Jalan Jaksa, the Taman Ismail Marzuki (TIM) (☎ 322606) is Jakarta's cultural showcase. There is a performance almost every night and here you might see anything from Balinese dancing to poetry readings, gamelan concerts to overseas jazz groups, an Indonesian Communist Party (PKI) film to a New Zealand film festival! The TIM monthly programme is available from the tourist office, the TIM office and major hotels, and events are also listed in the *Jakarta Post*.

Jakarta's **planetarium** (☎ 337530) is also here, but shows are generally given in Indonesian. Phone for information about shows in English. The whole complex is open from morning until midnight and there are good outdoor cafes, so it can be a useful place. The No 34 bus from Jalan Thamrin stops nearby.

RAGUNAN ZOO

Jakarta's Ragunan Zoo is about 10 km south of the city centre in the Pasar Minggu area. It's large and spacious but the animal enclosures are shabby and the landscaping consists of half-successful attempts to replace jungle with grass. The zoo has komodo dragons, orang-utans and other Indonesian wildlife. It's open daily from 9 am to 6 pm. Admission is 1000 rp, half-price for children.

OTHER ATTRACTIONS

Jakarta has several gardens specialising in cultivating orchids and the **Taman Anggrek Indonesia Permai**, just north of Taman Mini, is the best place to see them. Entry is 1000 rp.

Indonesia's independence was proclaimed at **Gedung Perintis Kemerdekaan**, Jalan Proklamasi 56 in Menteng, on the site of the former home of Soekarno. A monument to President Soekarno and Vice President Hatta marks the spot.

The **Pasar Burung**, on Jalan Pramuka in Jatinegara, is Jakarta's market for captive birds from all over Indonesia.

At Lubang Buaya (meaning 'crocodile hole'), a few km east from Taman Mini, the **Pancasila Cakti** is a memorial to the six generals and the army officer killed here by the communists in 1965.

The **swimming pools** at Ancol are great, but many of the closer hotels open their pools to the public for a fee – the Hotel Indonesia has a large pool costing 7500 rp for non-guests.

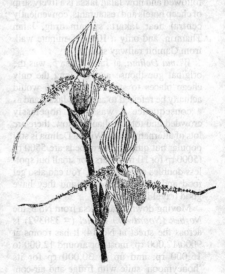

Orchid

JAVA

FESTIVALS

The Jakarta Anniversary on 22 June celebrates the establishment of the city by Gunungjati back in 1527 with fireworks, a 'Miss & Mr Jakarta' competition and the Jakarta Fair. The latter is an annual commercial and country fair event, with displays from all over the country and lots of music. It's held at the Jakarta Fair Grounds, northeast of the centre in Kemayoran, from late June until mid-July.

Indonesia's independence day is 17 August and the parades in Jakarta are the biggest in the country.

PLACES TO STAY

Places to Stay – bottom end

Jalan Jaksa Area Once upon a time, so the story goes, a backpacker arrived at Jakarta's Gambir railway station and wandered off looking for a hotel, without success. He chanced down Jalan Jaksa and a family took pity on him and gave him a bed for the night. The word spread and soon other backpackers started arriving at the house, so the family decided to open a hostel. Other guesthouses followed and now Jalan Jaksa is a lively strip of cheap hotels and restaurants, conveniently central near Jakarta's main drag, Jalan Thamrin, and only a 10 to 15-minute walk from Gambir railway station.

Wisma Delima, at Jalan Jaksa 5, was the original guesthouse and for long the only cheap places to stay. In fact No 5 would actually be referred to as 'Jalan Jaksa' and as a consequence it was often hopelessly crowded and totally chaotic. Now, there are lots of alternatives and Wisma Delima is still popular but quieter. Dorm beds are 5500 rp (5000 rp for HI members), or small but spotless doubles are 12,000 rp. You can also get food and cold drinks here, and they have good travel information.

Moving down Jalan Jaksa from No 5, the *Norbek (Noordwijk) Hostel* (☎ 330392) is across the street at No 14. It has rooms at 9000/12,000 rp, most for around 12,000 to 15,000 rp, and up to 30,000 rp for its 'honeymoon' suite with fridge and air-con. It's a dark rabbit warren, but many of the rooms are air-conditioned. It is one of those places which likes to have lists of rules posted on every vertical surface.

Nick's Corner Hostel (☎ 336754), at No 16, advertises itself as the 'cleanest' in town, and it's hard to disagree. It's a mini version of the Hyatt – all mock granite and fresh paint – and a dorm bed costs 7500 rp in immaculate, if somewhat cramped, eight and 12-bed air-con dorms. Good doubles are 30,000 rp and 35,000 rp or 45,000 rp and 65,000 rp with bathroom. Breakfast is included.

Continue down the street to the *Djody Hostel* at Jalan Jaksa 27. This is another old standby with dorm beds for 7500 rp, and double rooms from 22,000 to 30,000 rp, but it is getting overpriced. A few doors further up is the related *Djody Hotel* (☎ 33 2368), at No 35, where rooms without bath cost 15,000 rp and 20,000 rp. Rooms with bath and air-con cost 45,000 rp and 60,000 rp.

The *International Tator Hostel* (☎ 32 5124/3940), Jalan Jaksa 37, is a small place and a notch above most of the others in quality. Rooms start at 17,500 rp with bath up to 35,000 rp with air-con but renovations and extensions are planned.

More places can be found in the small streets running off Jalan Jaksa. Gang 1 is a small alley connecting Jalan Jaksa to Jalan Kebon Sirih Timur (running east off Jalan Jaksa). A short distance down are two small, quiet places. The *Kresna Homestay* (☎ 325403), at No 175, and the *Bloem Steen Homestay* next door at No 173. They're a bit cramped, but popular and good value for Jakarta. At the Kresna rooms are 12,000/18,000 rp without/with bath; the Bloem Steen has singles/doubles for 9000/12,000 rp or larger rooms for 15,000 rp.

At Kebon Sirih Barat Dalam 35, running west off Jalan Jaksa, *Borneo Hostel* (☎ 320095) packs them in and has a lively cafe, despite the mediocre food. The dorm beds at 5000 rp are about the cheapest around. The rooms for 15,000 to 20,000 rp are well kept but no bargain. Still, it's popular, well run and friendly. Avoid the annexe next door, which is under different

A: Welcome Monument, from the Hyatt Hotel, Jakarta (GB)
B: National Museum, Jakarta (GB)
C: Free Irian Monument, Lapangan Banteng, Jakarta (GB)
D: Arjuna statue, Jakarta (GB)
E: National Monument (Monas), Merdeka Square, Jakarta (GB)

Top: Karimunjawa, Central Java (PT)
Bottom: Fishermen hauling in the nets, Ambuten, Madura, East Java (PT)

management – it's boring and the rooms are badly in need of maintenance.

There are more places dotted along this lane, such as the similarly priced *Bintang Kejora* (☎ 323878), at No 52, which has a small cafe and very clean rooms for 15,000/ 20,000 rp. Further down, there's the *Hostel Rita* with rooms from 9000 rp, *Pondok Wisata Kebon Sirih*, at No 16, with doubles for 12,000 rp, and the *Pondok Wisata Jaya Hostel*, at No 10, but these are less popular with travellers.

If you walk along Jalan Wahid Hasyim, at the southern end of Jalan Jaksa, and keep going across Jalan Thamrin, you'll come to the *Wisma Ise Guesthouse* (☎ 33 3463) at No 168. It has single/double rooms for 9900/ 15,400 rp and some rooms with bath for 25,000 or with air-con for 35,000 rp. The basic rooms are fairly spartan, but it's a clean and friendly place, and there's a pleasant balcony bar at the back where you can look out over Jakarta.

Kuningan Apart from Wisma Delima, Jakarta has other youth hostels popular with local school groups and university students, but they tend to be a long way from the centre. The best and most convenient is the *Graha Wisata Mahasiswa* (☎ 516922), Jalan Rasuna Said, in Kuningan about four km south of Jalan Thamrin. Good dormitory accommodation costs 7500 rp (2500 rp for students) in six-bed dorms. Twin-bed, air-con rooms are about the best deal in Jakarta and cost 15,000 rp per person (7500 rp for students). The hostel has a cafeteria and sports facilities. To get there take bus No P11 or 407 from Gambir railway station.

Places to Stay – middle
Jalan Jaksa Area Each year new hotels are being built and old ones renovated in the Jalan Jaksa area, pushing it slowly more up-market. These middle-bracket hotels all charge 21% tax and service on top of the rates, but discounts of around 20% are readily available if you ask.

The *Hotel Karya* (☎ 320484), Jalan Jaksa 32-34, is undergoing big renovations but in the interim their older rooms cost US$35 and US$55. They are worn but comfortable enough with hot water, TV and telephone.

Jalan Wahid Hasyim has better hotels that are popular with local business people. They all have coffee shops and air-con rooms with hot water, minibar and TV. The new *Arcadia Hotel* (☎ 2300050), at No 114, has a lobby with impressive modern decor and a pleasant coffee shop/bar. The rooms for US$69 and US$78 are very comfortable but quite small.

The best hotel on Jalan Wahid Hasyim is the *Cemara Hotel* (☎ 324417), on the corner with Jalan Cemara. The rooms and service are very good, and it is competitively priced with rooms for US$60 and US$70.

The larger *Sabang Metropolitan Hotel* (☎ 373933), Jalan H A Salim 11, is looking a little old but rooms have all the facilities, it has a swimming pool and it's in a good location. Rooms cost from US$60 to US$90.

Cikini The Cikini area, east of Jalan Thamrin and close to the TIM cultural centre, has a selection of mid-range hotels and some good guesthouses.

The *Gondia Guest House* (☎ 3909221), Jalan Gondia Kecil 22, is in a quiet side street off Jalan R P Soeroso. Comfortable air-con rooms around small garden areas cost 86,000 rp, including breakfast. It has a pleasant, homey atmosphere. Bookings are advisable.

The big *Hotel Marcopolo* (☎ 325409), at Jalan Teuku Cik Ditiro 19, is better value than most in this range. Air-con rooms with fridge, TV and hot water cost 129,000 rp, single or double. The hotel has a good swimming pool and a reasonably priced restaurant with excellent buffet breakfasts for only 4000 rp.

Another good and very popular guesthouse near the TIM cultural centre is the *Yannie International Guest House* (☎ 3140012), Jalan Raden Saleh Raya 35. Spotless, bright rooms with air-con and hot water cost US$32/35, including a US-style breakfast. It is exceptional value for Jakarta and consequently often full. If so, try the *Karya II Hotel* (☎ 325078) next door at No 37. Comfortable air-con rooms range from 55,000 to

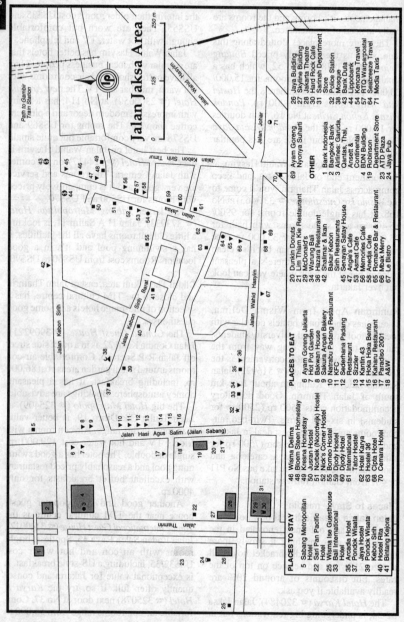

Jalan Jaksa Area

0   125   250 m

Path to Gambir Train Station

PLACES TO STAY

5   Sabang Metropolitan Hotel
22 Sari Pan Pacific Hotel
25 Wisma Ise Guesthouse
33 Bali International Hotel
35 Arcadia Hotel
37 Pondok Wisata
38 Jaya Hostel
39 Pondok Wisata
40 Kebon Hotel
41 Bintang Kejora
46 Wisma Delima
48 Bloem Steen Homestay
49 Kresna Homestay
50 Jusenny
51 Nordek (Noordwijk) Hostel
52 Nick's Corner Hostel
55 Borneo Hostel
59 Djody Hostel
60 Djody Hotel
61 International Tator Hostel
62 Hotel Karya
63 Hostel 36
68 Cipta Hotel
70 Cemara Hotel

PLACES TO EAT

6   Ayam Goreng Jakarta
7   Fat Fat Garden
8   Bakmi Gajah Mada
9   Sakura Anpan Bakery
10 Natrabu Padang Restaurant
12 Sederhana Padang Restaurant
13 Sizzler
14 Kantin 43
15 Hoka Hoka Bento
16 Kaharu Restaurant
17 Paradiso 2001
18 A&W
20 Dunkin Donuts
21 Lim Thiam Kie Restaurant
29 McDonald's
34 Warung Bali
36 Bakwa House
42 Shalimar & Ikan Bakar Kebon Sirih Restaurants
45 Senayan Satay House
47 Angie's Cafe
53 Asmat Cafe
56 Memories Cafe
58 Anedja Cafe
65 Romance Bar & Restaurant
66 Mbak Merry
67 Le Bistro
69 Ayam Goreng Nyonya Suhari

OTHER

1   Bank Indonesia
2   Bangkok Bank
3   Airlines: Garuda, Qantas, Thai, Ansett & Continental
4   BDN Building
19 Robinson Department Store
23 ATD Plaza
24 Jaya Pub
26 Jaya Building
27 Skyline Building
28 Jakarta Theatre
30 Hard Rock Cafe
31 Sarinah Department Store
32 Police Station
38 Mosque
43 Bank Duta
44 Lippobank
54 Kencana Travel
57 RTO Warparpostal
64 Seabreeze Travel
71 Media Taxis

88,000 rp. Downstairs rooms are dark – the best value are the upstairs rooms with hot water, TV and phone for 66,000 rp.

At the top of this range are the three-star Sofyan hotels: the new *Sofyan Hotel Betawi* (☎ 3905011), Jalan Cut Mutiah 9, just east of Jalan Jaksa, and the *Sofyan Hotel Cikini* (☎ 3140695), Jalan Cikini Raya 79. The Betawi has well-furnished, classy rooms from US$59/85, but the singles are very small. The Cikini is slightly better value with rooms from US$57/69.

Places to Stay – top end

Most, but not all, hotels readily offer discounts for walk-in customers, usually around 20% if you ask, but this may increase if it looks like you will walk out the door.

If you're arriving by air, hotel-booking counters at Jakarta's Soekarno-Hatta international airport have a big list of hotels with the current discount rates. Travel agents in Jakarta and elsewhere also offer some of the best discounts.

Following is a list of the top hotels in Jakarta:

Hotel Atlet Century Park, Jalan Pintu Satu Senayan (☎ 5712041; fax 5712191); rooms US$95/105 to US$130/140, suites US$200 to US$500

Aryaduta Hyatt Hotel, Jalan Prapatan 44-48 (☎ 3861234; fax 380990); rooms US$180 to US$210, suites US$230 to US$1350

Borobudur Inter-Continental Jakarta, Jalan Lapangan Banteng Selatan (☎ 3804444; fax 3805555); rooms US$190 to US$200, suites US$310 to US$750

Grand Hyatt Jakarta, Jalan Thamrin (☎ 3901234; fax 3906426); rooms US$265 and US$295, suites US$530 to US$5000

Hilton Hotel, Jalan Gatot Subroto (☎ 5703600; fax 5733089); rooms US$180/200 to US$220/235, suites US$310 to US$2000

Hotel Indonesia, Jalan Thamrin (☎ 3140008; fax 3141508); rooms US$130/140 to US$150/160, suites US$300 to US$800

Kartika Plaza Hotel, Jalan Thamrin 10 (☎ 3141008; fax 3905301); rooms US$95/105 to US$125/135, suites US$200

Le Meridien Jakarta, Jalan Jenderal Sudirman Kav 18-20 (☎ 5711414; fax 5711633); rooms US$180 to US$275, suites US$300 to US$1500

Mandarin Oriental Jakarta, Jalan Thamrin (☎ 3141307; fax 3148680); rooms US$180 to US$235, suites US$480 to US$1500

President Hotel, Jalan Thamrin 59 (☎ 2301122; fax 3143631); rooms US$132/155 to US$215, suites US$400 and US$480

Sahid Jaya Hotel, Jalan Jenderal Sudirman 86 (☎ 5704444; fax 5733168); rooms US$170, suites US$190 to US$3000

Sari Pan Pacific Hotel, Jalan Thamrin (☎ 323707; fax 323650); rooms US$155/170 to US$185/200, suites US$225 to US$1000

Shangri-La Hotel, Jalan Jenderal Sudirman Kav 1 (☎ 5707440; fax 5703531); rooms US$220/250 to US$270/300, suites US$380 to US$1800

The main centre for luxury hotels is the Welcome Statue roundabout on Jalan Thamrin. The Hotel Indonesia, Grand Hyatt, Mandarin and President are all on the roundabout and nearby on Jalan Thamrin are the Kartika Plaza and the Sari Pacific.

The Hotel Indonesia was the first of Indonesia's international hotels and in the 1960s was the refuge for foreigners surrounded by the turmoil of Soekarno's 'year of living dangerously'. It certainly has history and some nice 1960s touches, but it is looking a little tired, however the regularly offered big discounts make it a good buy.

Also on the Welcome Statue roundabout, the Grand Hyatt Jakarta is widely considered to be the capital's best and is favoured by many visiting dignitaries and VIPs. Diagonally across from the Hyatt, the Mandarin Oriental has no grounds, but it is an excellent business hotel and the well-furnished rooms have good extras. The nearby President Hotel is a smaller and more old-fashioned looking hotel. Just south from the welcome statue, the Kartika Plaza is also an older hotel without the gloss of its neighbours, but it has large rooms, a pool and good discounts.

More hotels can be found heading south down Jalan Thamrin, which runs into Jalan Jenderal Sudirman. Just off Jalan Thamrin, one of the newest and most opulent hotels is the Shangri-La, with its impressive lobby of granite, glass and gold. The Sahid Jaya Hotel on Jalan Jenderal Sudirman is a rambling hotel, while further south, Le Meridien is up there with the best. The Hilton Hotel is at the bottom corner of the 'Golden Triangle' business district. It has large grounds and a good range of facilities. Near the Hilton, the Hotel Atlet Century Park is a cheaper three-star hotel but it has good facilities and well-appointed rooms.

To the north-east of the centre near the National Monument, the Borobudur Intercontinental Hotel is one of the older generation of luxury hotels but still one of the best. Nearby the Aryaduta Hotel is a good business-class hotel with all the trimmings.

PLACES TO EAT

Jakarta has the best selection of restaurants of any major Indonesian city, although a meal in a better-class restaurant is expensive. Plenty of street hawkers and night markets cater for cheaper meals.

Jalan Jaksa Area

Jalan Jaksa's cafes are convivial meeting places dishing out the standard travellers' menu. They are certainly cheap and the breakfasts are very good value. Food is quasi-European or bland Indonesian. The cheapest eats on Jalan Jaksa are in the warungs at the north end, and in the side alleys towards Jalan H A Salim, but some look remarkably dirty.

Topping the popularity polls on Jalan Jaksa is the *Asmat Cafe*, at No 16-18, next to Nick's Corner Hotel. The food is only average, but people come here for the lively atmosphere, video movies in the evening and the disco at the back.

Angie's Cafe, at No 15, is another popular cafe, good for cheap Western breakfasts and fruit salads. Indonesian dishes are particularly bland here. *Memories Cafe* on the same stretch is similar. Many of the hostels, such as the Borneo Hostel, also have their own cafes.

Romance Bar & Restaurant, Jalan Jaksa 40, is the fanciest restaurant in the street with air-con and a small bar. The menu is a varied hotchpotch including Mexican, pasta and pizza for around 5000 rp, and, while not outstanding, it is reasonably priced and a pleasant place to dine.

Jalan Kebon Sirih, at the top end of Jalan Jaksa, has some interesting possibilities. At Jalan Kebon Sirih 31A on the corner of Jalan Jaksa, *Senayan Satay House* is air-con and more expensive but the food is good and the sate superb. Heading west towards Jalan H A Salim, on the other side of the street at No 40, the *Ikan Bakar Kebon Sirih*, specialises in that popular Sulawesi dish, ikan bakar (Macassar-style roast fish).

Jalan H A Salim (Jalan Sabang)

The next street west of Jalan Jaksa has a string of cheap to mid-range restaurants. Though Jalan Sabang was renamed Jalan Haji Agus (H A) Salim years ago, everyone still knows it by its former name.

Throughout Java, Jalan Sabang is famed as the sate capital of Indonesia. Dozens of sate hawkers set up on the street in the evening and the pungent smoke from their charcoal braziers fills the air. Most business is take away, but benches are scattered along the street if you want to sit down and eat it there.

Restaurants line both sides of Jalan Sabang, and the most famous is *Natrabu* at No 29A. This would have to be the classiest Padang restaurant in Indonesia, and if you only try Padang food once then do so here. You can have a filling meal for 10,000 rp.

For standard Chinese fare, the *Lim Thiam Kie*, at No 49, has air-con, but the pretensions to being a fancy restaurant stop there. Most dishes are in the 5000 to 10,000 rp range. Down a little alley close to the A&W is the *Paradiso 2001*, an interesting little Chinese vegetarian restaurant. The restaurant is nothing fancy but the food is tasty, healthy and cheap and they do good fruit juices.

Jalan Thamrin

In the Jakarta Theatre building, the *Green Pub* features Mexican food with a meal averaging about 20,000 rp and a happy hour from 3 to 6 pm with half-price drinks. In the evening, the place is jammed, as Indonesians turn out to enjoy a local live band perform in Mexicano cowboy garb! Also in the Jakarta

Theatre building, there's a *California Fried Chicken* joint as well as a *Pizza Hut*.

Across the road, the Sarinah department store has a very good, but very expensive, food-stall area in the basement next to the supermarket. Try the excellent *soto betawi* – a thick coconut-based offal soup, a Jakarta speciality. Sarinah is also home to Indonesia's first *McDonald's* and the *Hard Rock Cafe*, which is one of the best places for US-style grills and imported steaks. The *Jaya Pub* at the back of the Jaya building, Jalan Thamrin 12, is another music venue that also puts on good grills.

Further down Jalan Thamrin at the Welcome Statue roundabout, Plaza Indonesia under the Grand Hyatt Jakarta Hotel is the fanciest shopping mall in Jakarta. The *Happy Times Food Court* on the top floor is a salubrious, Singapore-style hawker's centre with a range of international food stalls. Excellent Indonesian, Chinese, Thai, Singaporean and Japanese dishes as well as pizza, French pastries and Western fast food can be enjoyed for around 5000 rp. Plaza Indonesia also has an abundance of fast-food emporia.

Almost every shopping centre has a supermarket. The Sogo supermarket in the basement of the Plaza Indonesia is one of the best in the city centre and features Japanese groceries. You can also find one in the basement of Sarinah department store or across the road in the Jakarta Theatre building.

Elsewhere

Street Food Jakarta has plenty of street food, served from push carts called *kaki lima* ('five feet') or slightly more permanent warungs with canvas overhangs. As Indonesia's melting pot, Jakarta's street food has specialities from all over the archipelago – delicious *srabi* pancakes from Solo, sate from Madura or Sulawesi-style *ikan bakar*. Those new to Indonesia should exercise caution with street food and gradually introduce themselves to the local microbes.

Jakarta's markets always have plenty of street-side warungs. Pasar Tanah Abang, west along Jalan Wahid Hasyim from Jalan

Thamrin, has a collection of cheap and popular night warungs. South of the Welcome roundabout, a string of stalls can be found along Jalan Kendal – walk south past the bars on Jalan Blora, and turn left (where the transvestites hang out) along Jalan Kendal, which runs parallel to the railway line.

One of the fanciest and best warung areas is on Jalan Pecanongan, about one km north of the National Monument. These night warungs start setting up large marquees around 5 pm and serve excellent Chinese seafood at moderate prices.

Restaurants Along Jalan Gajah Mada towards Glodok are numerous restaurants, bakeries, and fast-food and ice-cream parlours. *Bakmi Gajah Mada* is a busy noodle-house chain with stores all over Jakarta. The original restaurant at Jalan Gajah Mada 92, just south of Arsip Nasional, has been pumping out noodles since the 1950s and is still a very popular, efficient place for cheap eats. The air-con Gajah Mada Plaza shopping centre nearby has fast food.

Right in the middle of historic Kota on Taman Fatahillah, *Cafe Batavia* is very 'in'. Housed in a tastefully renovated Dutch building, the restaurant is not cheap but not outrageously expensive for good Chinese and international cuisine.

The historic *Oasis Bar & Restaurant* (☎ 327818), on Jalan Raden Saleh 47 in Cikini, is housed in a large, old Dutch villa and has the feel of an extravagant 1930s Hollywood film set, with prices to match. More than a dozen waitresses serve up a traditional rijsttafel, while you are serenaded by a group of Batak singers from Sumatra. Reservations are recommended. It's closed on Sundays.

For southern Indian cuisine served in banana leaves, *Mutu Curry* is adjacent to the Tanamur Disco on Jalan Tanah Abang Timur.

About one km east of Jalan Thamrin on Jalan Cokroaminoto is the well-to-do Menteng shopping centre, where a number of more up-market dining possibilities can be found. You can have Thai, Japanese, noodles, seafood or steak (try the *Gandy Steakhouse* or *Black Angus*). *Tamnak Thai*, Jalan Cokroaminoto 78, is recommended for good, moderately priced Thai food and Chinese seafood.

The wealthy southern suburbs are the favourite residential district for Jakarta's elite and expatriate community. While the city centre is a much more convenient place to dine, South Jakarta has some excellent restaurants. An expat favourite is the *Orient Express*, Wijaya Grand Centre, Block H37-39, Jalan Baramwangsa Raya in Kebayoran Baru. It serves a bit of everything: Indian, seafood, pizza, Mexican. The food is consistently good and the prices moderate.

ENTERTAINMENT

Check the entertainment pages of the *Jakarta Post* for films, concerts and special events. Films, lectures and discussions of Indonesian culture are often sponsored by foreign embassies and the Ganesha Society, a volunteer organisation devoted to affording an appreciation of the nation's rich cultural heritage.

Cultural Performances

The already-mentioned *Taman Ismael Mazurki (TIM)* cultural centre in Menteng is the one of the best places to see traditional and modern performing arts and cultural events.

The *Bharata Theatre*, on Jalan Kalilio in Pasar Senen, has wayang orang performances from 8.15 pm to midnight every evening, except Monday and Thursday when there are *ketoprak* (popular comedy) performances.

Wayang kulit/golek puppet shows are held outdoors in the *Jakarta Fair* area every second Saturday of the month during the Jakarta Fair in late June and July. These all-night performances start around 9 pm. The Jakarta fair features plenty of other cultural events.

Nightlife

Jakarta is the most sophisticated, broadminded and corrupt city in Indonesia and has nightlife to match. Hundreds of bars, discos, karaoke lounges and night clubs range from the sleazy to the refined. Local bands are found in profusion, doing everything from Beatles and Rolling Stones impersonations to jazz and the latest hits. European and Black American bands are definitely in vogue and provide the pick of the music. Bands start around 10 or 11 pm, and continue on until 2 or 3 am, sometimes later on the weekends. During the week many places close at 1 am.

Many don't have cover charges, though sometimes a first-drink cover charge applies, especially in the discos. A beer or a mixed drink costs from 6000 rp in the cheaper bars, double that in exclusive hotel bars.

Live Music The *Hard Rock Cafe*, on Jalan Thamrin, has the usual blend of rock memorabilia, music and food. It is always lively and has decent bands or occasional top-line imports. The music starts around 11 pm, when dinner finishes, and keeps going until around 3 am. The dance floor is dominated by a huge stained-glass portrait of the King, though this Elvis looks vaguely Indonesian.

The *Jaya Pub*, next to the car park behind the Jaya building, Jalan Thamrin 12, is a Jakarta institution that has live pub music most evenings.

Oreilly's, in the Grand Hyatt Jakarta Hotel, is a salubrious place for a business drink, but it also gets some very good bands on Friday and Saturday nights, when the ties come off, the crowds pack in and the place starts jumping.

The historic, restored *Cafe Batavia*, at Taman Fahillah, is another up-market venue and a popular spot to be seen. The music is mostly jazz and soul from imported bands.

Discos Many discos are found at the big hotels, and dress requirements – no jeans, sneakers, T-shirts – usually apply.

Jakarta's most infamous disco is *Tanamur* at Jalan Tanah Abang Timur 14. This long-running institution is jammed nightly with gyrating revellers of every race, creed and sexual proclivity, and innumerable ladies of the night. It is unbelievably crowded after midnight on Friday and Saturday nights. Wear what you like here.

THINGS TO BUY

Good buys in Jakarta include batik and antiques but Jakarta has bits and pieces from almost everywhere in Indonesia. If this is your first stop, it's a good place to get an overall view of Indonesian crafts and, if it's your last stop, then it's always a last chance to find something that you missed elsewhere in the country.

A good place to start is Sarinah on Jalan Thamrin. The 3rd floor of this large department store is devoted to batik and handicrafts from all over the country. The batik floor is divided into different concessions sponsored by the big batik manufacturers like Batik Keris and Batik Danar Hadi. Handicrafts are souvenirs rather than true collectibles, but the quality is high and the prices reasonable.

In the same vein, but possibly even bigger, is Pasar Raya Big & Beautiful in Blok M.

The Pasar Seni, at Ancol recreation park, is an excellent place to look for regional handicrafts and to see many of them actually being made. Whether it's woodcarvings, paintings, puppets, leather, batik or silver, you'll find it here.

In Menteng, Jalan Surabaya is Jakarta's famous fleamarket. Here you'll find woodcarvings, furniture, brassware, jewellery, batik, oddities like old typewriters and many (often instant) antiques. It is always fun to browse, but bargain like crazy – prices may be up to five times the worth of the goods.

Jalan Kebon Sirih Timur, the street east of Jalan Jaksa, has a number of shops for antiques and curios. The quality is high, but so are the prices.

Jakarta has plenty of shopping centres and markets to explore. Clothes and shoes are cheap, but it can take some hunting to find Western sizes and styles. Pasar Baru pedestrian mall, just across the canal from the post office, is a good place to shop for cheap clothes and shoes.

Pasar Senen, west of Gambir railway station, is another lively shopping area with a large, active market.

Jakarta has plenty of malls. The most exclusive and expensive is the Plaza Indonesia on Jalan Thamrin. It's a great place to browse at designer labels, but the prices are very high. Other big, dazzling malls include the Pondok Indah Mall in the southern suburbs and the Citraland Mall in West Jakarta on the way to the airport.

Blok M is one of the biggest and best shopping areas in Jakarta. Here you'll find the huge Block M Mall above the large bus terminal. This is a more down-to-earth mall with scores of small, reasonably priced shops offering clothes, shoes, music tapes, household goods, etc. More up-market shopping can be found at the multistorey Blok M Plaza just across the way, and Pasaraya Big & Beautiful department store is also right next to the mall. Jalan Palatehan 1, just to the north of the Blok M bus terminal has some interesting antique and craft shops.

GETTING THERE & AWAY

Jakarta is the main international gateway to Indonesia and for details on arriving there from overseas see the introductory Getting There & Away section at the start of this chapter. Travel agencies worth trying for discounted air fares on international flights out of Jakarta are listed under Information, at the start of the Jakarta section.

Jakarta is also a major centre for domestic travel, with extensive bus, rail, air and sea connections.

Air

International and domestic flights both operate from the Soekarno-Hatta international airport. Airport tax is 21,000 rp on international departures, 8800 rp on domestic flights. The domestic tax is usually included in the ticket. Flights depart from Jakarta to all the main cities in Java and to places all over the archipelago. The main domestic airlines have offices open normal business hours, and usually Sunday mornings as well.

Garuda, BDN Building, Jalan Thamrin 5 (☎ 2300925); Garuda flies to the major cities throughout Indonesia; Garuda also has offices at the Borobudur Hotel (☎ 2310339), Hotel Indonesia (☎ 2300568), Wisma Dharmala Sakti

(☎ 5706155) and Jakarta International Trade Centre (☎ 2600244)

Merpati, Jalan Angkasa 2, Kemayoran (☎ 4247404); this office is inconveniently located, but travel agents sell tickets; Merpati is the main domestic carrier with flights throughout the archipelago

Sempati, Hotel Borobudur Inter-Continental (☎ 3805555); most travel agents can book Sempati; Sempati often has the cheapest flights to Singapore, discounted to around US$70, and also flies to most of the main cities in Indonesia; Sempati also has offices in many of the major hotels including the Hotel Indonesia (☎ 320008), Sari Pan Pacific (☎ 323707), Le Meridien (☎ 5711414), Sahid Jaya (☎ 5704444), etc

Bouraq, Jalan Angkasa 1, Kemayoran (☎ 6295150); Bouraq has direct flights from Jakarta to Bandung, Semarang, Pangkal Pinang, Pontianak, Balikpapan and Banjarmasin with connections further afield in the eastern islands

Mandala, Jalan Veteran I No 34 (☎ 368107)

Bus

Jakarta has three major bus stations, all a long way from the centre. In some cases it can take longer getting to the bus station than the bus journey itself, making the trains a better alternative for arriving at or leaving Jakarta. This is especially true for buses to/from Kampung Rambutan bus station. The bus stations are:

Kalideres Buses to the west of Jakarta go from the Kalideres station, about 15 km north-west of Merdeka Square. Frequent normal/air-con buses run to Merak (2500/4000 rp, three hours), Labuan (2700 rp, 3½ hours), Serang (1800 rp, 1½ hours) and Rankasbitung (2000 rp, 3½ hours). A couple of midday buses go through to Sumatra from Kalideres, but most Sumatra buses leave from Pulo Gadung.

Kampung Rambutan The big, new Kampung Rambutan terminal, handles buses to areas south and south-west of Jakarta. It was designed to carry much of Jakarta's inter-city bus traffic, but it really only handles buses to West Java including: Bogor (1000/1500 rp, 40 minutes), Bandung (3200/6500 rp, 4½ hours), Tasikmalaya (4700/8100 rp, 7½ hours) and Banjar (5100/8600 rp, nine hours). Buses also go to Sumatra,

Cirebon, Yogya, Surabaya and other long-distance destinations, but Pulo Gadung still has most of the long-distance services. Kampung Rambutan is about 18 km to the south of the city centre and takes at least an hour by city bus. For Bogor or Bandung, take the train.

Pulo Gadung Pulo Gadung is 12 km to the east of the city centre and has buses to Cirebon, Central and East Java, Sumatra and Bali. Most of the air-con, deluxe buses operate from here. Tickets can be bought in advance through agents in town. Many can be found on Jalan Ankasa in the Pasar Baru area, bus companies operating to Sumatra are found along Jalan K H Mansyur, or Jalan Jaksa agents sell bus tickets. Jalan Jaksa agents not only sell tickets, but can include travel to the bus stations or to the bus-company depots, usually located in South Jakarta. Ticket prices tend to be considerably higher, but doing this can save a lot of hassle. Advance bookings are a good idea for peak-travel periods, but so many buses operate to the main destinations that if you just front up at the terminal you won't have to wait long to find one.

This wild bus station is the busiest in Indonesia with buses, crowds, hawkers and beggars everywhere.

The terminal is divided into two sections: one for buses to Sumatra and the other for all buses to the east.

Most buses to Sumatra leave between 11 am and 6 pm and you can catch a bus right through to Aceh if you are crazy enough. Destinations and fares for normal/air-con buses include: Palembang (12,500/21,000 rp), Bengkulu (15,000/26,000 rp), Padang (24,000/41,000 rp) and Bukittinggi (25,000/42,000 rp). Deluxe buses with reclining seats and toilets will cost about 50% more than the air-con buses – well worth it for those long hauls through Sumatra. For Bukittinggi, two good companies are ALS (☎ 8503446) with a bus at 4 pm and ANS (☎ 352411) with a bus at 11.30 am. Both charge 60,000 rp for the 30-hour plus journey.

To the east, frequent buses go to Central

and East Java and on to Bali. Destinations include: Cirebon (4700/7900 rp, four hours), Yogya (11,000/18,000 rp, 12 hours), Surabaya (13,500/23,000 rp), Malang (15,000/25,000 rp) and Denpasar (28,000/45,000 rp). Most buses to Yogya leave between 8 am and midnight. Some of the better deluxe bus companies are Raya, Harta Sanjaya and Muncul; tickets cost around 25,000 rp. The best buses to Denpasar cost around 55,000 rp and take 24 hours.

Train

Jakarta has four major railway stations.

Gambir, on the east side of Merdeka Square, is conveniently central for Jalan Jaksa. It handles most of the trains to the south and east, including Bogor, Bandung, Cirebon, Yogya and Surabaya. If you're travelling light, it is possible to walk the one km from Gambir to Jalan Jaksa. Taxi drivers at Gambir aren't very interested in the short fare, and meters will be 'broken'. They will ask the earth, so it is better to hail a taxi on the street or take one that is dropping off a passenger. Bajaj will also require some hard bargaining to around 1500 rp to Jalan Jaksa.

Kota, in the old part of the city, is on the same line as Gambir, and some Gambir trains also leave from or arrive at Kota. Some only depart from Kota, such as the deluxe night express trains to Surabaya – the *Bima* (via Yogya) and the *Mutiara Utara* (via Semarang). If departing from Kota, allow adequate time to wind your way through the rush-hour traffic snarls. From Jalan Thamrin, bus Nos 70, P1 and P11 go to Kota. A taxi will cost around 4000 to 5000 rp from the centre.

Pasar Senen, further east of Gambir, has a few ekonomi services to Surabaya via Semarang, as well as Yogya.

Tanah Abang station, directly to the west of Jalan Thamrin, has trains to Merak, for Sumatra, and a few other ekonomi services. Departures to Merak (1500 rp, four hours) are at 7 am and 2.35 pm, but the buses are much quicker.

To Bogor The train to Bogor runs every 20 minutes or so from Kota, stopping at Gambir on the way through. The trains are slow and crowded, and should be avoided during rush hours, but otherwise provide a reasonable service and are much more convenient than the buses. The fare is 700 rp from Kota, and 650 rp from Gambir for the 1½-hour trip. The best trains are the express *Pakuan* (2000 rp, one hour) offering bisnis-class carriages at 7.30 and 10.30 am, 2.15 and 4.40 pm.

To Bandung The train to catch is the efficient *Parahyangan*, an express service between Jakarta and Bandung, which goes through some picturesque countryside. It departs roughly every hour between 6 am and 8.30 pm from Gambir, and takes three hours. Fares are 12,000 rp in bisnis, 16,000 to 23,000 rp in air-con eksekutif class.

To Cirebon Most trains along the north coast leave from Gambir. Many ekonomi and express trains, including those to Yogya, go through Cirebon. One of the best services is the *Cirebon Express* departing Kota and also stopping at Gambir station at 6.45, 9.45 and 4.30 pm. It costs 9000 rp bisnis, 14,000 to 20,000 rp in eksekutif and takes 3½ hours. It may run an hour over schedule, but it is still quicker and more convenient than the buses. Other services continue on to Semarang via Cirebon.

To Yogyakarta & Surabaya Jakarta to Yogyakarta takes nine to 10 hours and most departures are from Gambir station. Fares vary from 5000 rp in ekonomi up to 94,000 rp for a sleeper. The *Fajar Utama Yogya* and *Senja Utama Yogya* are good bisnis-class services.

Trains between Jakarta and Surabaya either take the shorter northern route via Semarang or the longer southern route via Yogyakarta. The trip takes 10 to 17 hours although, in practice, the slower 3rd-class trains can take even longer. Fares start at 10,000 rp in ekonomi, 26,000 rp in bisnis.

See the introductory Getting There & Away section to this chapter for full details on these routes. Bookings (with the exception of ekonomi trains) can be made at the stations or some travel agents for a small charge.

Taxi

There are also intercity taxis and minibuses to Bandung that will pick you up and drop you off at your hotel. Fares start at 12,000 rp per person; they're fast and convenient but taxis will only depart when they have five passengers. Media Taxis (☎ 3140343) are at Jalan Johar 15, near Jalan Jaksa. The 4848 Taxis (☎ 364488) are at Jalan Prapatan 34, just beyond the Aryaduta Hyatt Hotel. Door-to-door minibus services are also available to Bandung, Yogya and other destinations and can be booked through travel agents.

Boat

Pelni has lots of services out of Jakarta, departing from and arriving at the Tanjung Priok Harbour. Of main interest are the connections to Tanjung Pinang on Pulau Bintan, from where you can catch a ferry to Singapore, the service to Padang in Sumatra, saving the long bus journey, and direct connections to Kalimantan and Sulawesi.

Pelni ships link Jakarta to Tanjung Pinang (from 37,000 rp economy class), Padang (from 37,000 rp economy class), Ujung Pandang (from 55,000 rp economy class), Belawan (from 56,000 rp economy class) and Pontianak (36,000 rp economy class).

The Pelni ticketing office (☎ 421 1921) is at Jalan Angkasa No 18, to the north-east of the centre. Pelni agents charge a small premium but are much more convenient – try Panintama Tour & Travel (☎ 390 2076), in the Sarinah department-store building on Jalan Thamrin, near the Jalan Jaksa area.

As well as the Pelni boats, the more luxurious MV *Bintan Permata* leaves Jakarta every Wednesday and Saturday at 4 pm for Tanjung Pinang, arriving at 2 pm the following day. It costs 91,500 rp in economy or 111,500 rp in 1st class. Bookings can be made through travel agents or PT Admiral Lines, 21 Jalan Raya Pelabuhan.

The best place to get information on non-Pelni cargo boats is the old harbour, Sunda Kelapa. The staff at the harbour master's office *(kantor syahbander)* are the people to see first. Most of them speak excellent English and they're very helpful. It's also worth going around all the ships at the dock.

GETTING AROUND
To/From the Airport

Jakarta's Soekarno-Hatta international airport is 35 km west of the city centre. A toll road links the airport to the city and a journey between the two takes 45 minutes to an hour, although it can take longer in the rush hour.

The Damri airport bus departs every 30 minutes between 3 am and 10 pm to Gambir station (near Jalan Jaksa), and continues on to Blok M, Kemayoran and Rawamangun. It costs 3000 rp per person.

Alternatively, a metered taxi to Jalan Thamrin costs about 24,000 rp, including the airport surcharge (2300 rp, payable from but not to the airport) and toll-road charges (4000 rp between the airport and Bandara and then another 2000 rp into the city centre). Catch metered taxis from taxi ranks outside the terminal, and avoid offers of 'transport' from unregistered taxis unless you want to pay double.

To/From Tanjung Priok Harbour

The Pelni ships all arrive at (and depart from) Pelabuhan or Dock No 1. It's half a km from the dock to the Tanjung Priok bus station. The best bus to get is the P14 bus from Jalan Kebon Sirih, at the north end of Jalan Jaksa, to Tanjung Priok. The harbour is 13 km from the centre of the city so allow an hour, at least, to get there, particularly on public transport. A taxi should cost around 8000 rp.

Bus

In Jakarta everything is at a distance. It's hot and humid and hardly anybody walks – you will need to use some form of transport to get from one place to another. Jakarta has probably the most comprehensive city bus network of any major Indonesian city.

Around town there are lots of big regular city buses charging a fixed 250 rp fare. The big express 'Patas' buses charge 550 rp and the air-con Patas buses cost 1300 rp; these are usually less crowded and by far the best option. These services are supplemented by orange toy-sized buses and, in a few areas, by pale-blue mikrolet buses which cost between 300 rp and 500 rp.

The visitor information centre in the Sarinah department store on Jalan Thamrin can provide information on the city buses. Some of the more useful Patas buses include:

P11, P10 (air-con)
  Kampung Rambutan to Kota via Jalan Thamrin
P1
  Blok M to Kota via Jalan Thamrin
P14
  Tanjung Priok to Tanah Abang via Jalan Kebon Sirih
P7A
  Pulo Gadung to Kalideres via Jalan Juanda

Taxi

Taxis in Jakarta are metered and cost 900 rp for the first km and 450 rp for each subsequent km. Make sure the meter is used. Many taxi drivers provide a good service, but Jakarta has enough rogues to give its taxis a bad reputation. Tipping is expected, if not demanded, but not obligatory. If good service is provided, it is customary to round the fare up to the next 500 rp. Carry plenty of small notes. Jakarta taxi drivers *never* have change under 1000 rp.

Jakarta has a large fleet of taxis and it's usually not too difficult to find one. Bluebird cabs (pale blue) (☎ 3143000, 7999000) have the best reputation and well-maintained cars.

Typical taxi fares from Jalan Jaksa/ Thamrin are: Kota (4000 rp), Ancol (5000 rp), Pulo Gadung (6000 rp), Kalideres (9000 rp), Kampung Rambutan or Taman Mini (12,000 rp).

Bajaj & Other

Bajaj (pronounced ba-jai) are nothing less than Indian auto-rickshaws: orange three-wheelers that carry two passengers (three at a squeeze if you're all dwarf-size) and sputter around powered by noisy two-stroke engines. Short trips – Jalan Jaksa to the post office, for example – will cost about 1500 rp.

They're good value, especially during rush hours, but hard bargaining is required. Always agree on the price beforehand. Bajaj are not allowed along main streets such as Jalan Thamrin, so make sure they won't simply drop you off at the border.

Jakarta has other weird and wonderful means of getting around. 'Morris' bemos are old English Morris vans than operate around Glodok and other parts of Jakarta. In the backstreets of Kota, pushbikes with a padded 'kiddy carrier' on the back will take you for a ride! The *helicak*, cousin to the bajaj, is a green motorcycle contraption with a passenger car mounted on the front. They are found only in the back streets of Menteng. Jakarta also has ojeks, motorbikes that take pillion passengers, but weaving in and out of Jakarta's traffic on the back of an ojek is decidedly risky. Becaks have disappeared from the city, and only a few tourist becaks remain at Ancol.

Car

If you feel up to driving yourself around, Jakarta has branches of three major rent-a-car operators. National Car Rental (☎ 3143423) is in the Kartika Plaza Hotel, Jalan Thamrin 10. Avis Rental Car (☎ 3904745) is at Jalan Diponegoro 25 and they also have a desk at the Hotel Sari Pacific (☎ 3203707, ext 1281) on Jalan Thamrin. Hertz Car Rental (☎ 371208) is at the Mandarin Hotel on Jalan Thamrin.

Organised Tours

Numerous travel agents offer daily tours of Jakarta but they tend to be expensive. Information on many of them is available from the tourist office and major hotels. They include Vayatour (☎ 3800202), Nitour (☎ 346347) and Setia Tours (☎ 6390008). All tour buses pick up from the major hotels, and tour prices and sights are very similar. A four-hour morning city tour, for example, costs US$20, and includes the National Museum, National Monument, Sunda Kelapa and Kota.

There are also a variety of tours to nearby towns in West Java which basically go to

Bogor, the Puncak Pass and Tangkuban Prahu volcano near Bandung. A six-hour tour to the Bogor botanical gardens and zoological museum costs US$35; to the Puncak Pass costs US$40.

AROUND JAKARTA
Pulau Seribu (Thousand Islands)

Scattered across the Java Sea to the north of Jakarta are the tropical islands of Pulau Seribu or Thousand Islands, although they are actually only 105 in number. The area is a marine national park, though 37 of the islands are permitted to be exploited.

Jakarta's 'offshore' islands start only a few km out, in the Bay of Jakarta. The waters closest to Jakarta are murky – the islands are better the further you go from Jakarta. **Pulau Bidadari** is the closest resort island and popular for day trips with Jakarta residents. It is one of the least interesting resorts, but from Bidadari you can visit other nearby islands like **Pulau Kahyangan**, **Pulau Kelor** (which has the ruins of an old Dutch fort), or **Pulau Onrust** where the remains of an old shipyard from the 18th century can be explored.

Further north, **Pulau Ayer** is another popular day-trip destination. It has a comfortable resort with a small stretch of good beach, though the waters are still cloudy. **Pulau Laki**, another resort island, is also close to the coast, being about 40 km west of Jakarta.

The entire island group has a population of 15,000, with the district centre on **Pulau Panggang**, about 15 km north of Jakarta, but most people live on just one island, **Pulau Kelapa**, further north. These poor fishing communities have yet to share in the wealth generated by the resorts. Near Kelapa, **Pulau Panjang** has the only airstrip in the islands. Around this group of islands are two more resorts on **Pulau Kotok**, which has a good reef for snorkelling and diving, and the Matahari resort on **Pulau Macan Besar**, which is surrounded by a retaining wall. **Pulau Bira** has, believe it or not, a golf course.

The best resorts lie around four km north of Kelapa, all close to each other. **Pulau Putri** is notable for its aquariums. **Pulau Sepa** is a small sandy island surrounded by wide stretches of pristine sand. Nearby **Pulau Pelangi** also has some good stretches of beach. **Pulau Papa Theo** is a divers' island with a dive camp. **Pulau Antuk Timur** and **Pulau Antuk Barat** are separated by a small channel and both house the fanciest resort on the islands with the best facilities.

Places to Stay All the resorts have individual bungalows with attached bathrooms, and provide water-sport facilities including diving. While comfortable, none are international-standard resorts despite the high prices. Most of the resorts offer packages that include buffet-only meals and transport. Weekends are up to 50% more expensive than those quoted below.

Pulau Bididari Resort, Marina Ancol, Taman Impian Jaya Ancol (☎ 680048); simple cottages accommodating two to four people cost from 51,000 to 68,500 rp

Pulau Ayer Resort, PT Sarotama Prima Perkasa, Jalan Ir H Juanda III/6 (☎ 3842031); spacious, very comfortable cottages range from US$92 to US$231

Pulau Laki Resort, PT Fadent Gema Scorpio, Jalan HOS Cokroaminoto 116 (☎ 3144885); cottages from US$70, up to US$162 for three-bedroom cottages

Kotok Island Resort, 3rd Floor, Duta Merlin Shopping Arcade, Jalan Gajah Mada 3-5 (☎ 362948); packages start at US$73 per person

Matahari Resort, PT Jakarta International Hotels Management, Suite 103, Hotel Borobudur Intercontinental, Jalan Lapangan Banteng Selatan (☎ 3800521); bungalow rooms cost US$60 to US$80 per person, including all meals

Pulau Putri Resort, PT Buana Bintang Samudra, Jalan Sultan Agung 21 (☎ 8281093); cottages start at US$60 and go up to US$110 for excellent, Balinese-style, cottages; including meals, the package rate is US$70 per person

Pulau Sepa Resort, PT Pulau Sepa Permai, Jalan Kali Besar Barat 29 (☎ 6928828); air-con bungalows from US$78 to US$110 are comfortable though fairly basic for the price

Pulau Pelangi Resort, PT Pulau Seribu Paradise, Jalan Wahid Hasyim 69 (☎ 335535); older bungalows cost US$85 to US$110, or full-board packages are US$80 per person

Pulau Seribu Marine Resort, PT Pantara Wisata Jaya, Jalan Jen Sudirman Kav 3-4 (☎ 5723161); located on Antuk Timur and Antuk Barat islands, this is the most up-market resort; full-board packages cost US$113/86/77 for single/double/triple occupancy

Getting There & Away The resorts have daily boats from Jakarta's Ancol Marina for guests and day trippers, usually leaving around 8 or 9 am and returning around 3 pm. Boats to Laki leave from Tanjung Kait, 40 km to the west of Jakarta. The resorts provide speedboats, and even the furthest islands take only a little over two hours. The KM *Betok* is a ferry operating from Ancol to the villages on Tidung (3500 rp) and Kelapa (4000 rp), but from these islands it is necessary to charter boats to other islands. If you want to rent a speed boat from Ancol expect to pay around 750,000 rp for a day.

West Java

The province of West Java has a population of 35.4 million, an area of 46,229 sq km and Bandung as its capital. It is historically known as Sunda, the home of the Sundanese people and their culture.

Away from Jakarta and the flat, hot coastline to the north, West Java is predominantly mountainous and agricultural, with lush green valleys and high volcanic peaks surrounding the capital, Bandung, at the core of the region. West Java is also strongly Islamic, yet in the remote Kendeng mountains there is still a small isolated community known as the Badui, believed to be descendants of the ancient Sundanese who fled from Islam more than 400 years ago. The name Sunda is of Sanskrit origin and means 'pure' or 'white'.

For travellers, West Java has tended to be a place to whiz through between Jakarta and destinations east, but, apart from its historic and cultural centres, West Java has a good beach resort at Pangandaran and a fine backwater trip along the coastal lagoons to Central Java. Other major attractions, though remote and isolated, are the famous Krakatau off the west coast and the unique Ujung Kulon National Park in the south-west of the province.

HISTORY

Early in its history, Sunda was primarily dependent on overseas trade. It was not only an important spice centre in its own right but also a transhipment point for trade with Asia. West Java was the first contact point in Indonesia for the Dutch and earlier it was one of the first regions to come into contact with Indian traders and their culture.

Ancient stone inscriptions record an early Hindu influence during the reign of King Purnawarman of Taruma and one of his rock edicts can be seen near Bogor. In the 7th century Taruma was destroyed by the powerful Sumatran-based Buddhist kingdom of Sriwijaya. Much later, Hinduism reasserted itself alongside Buddhism when the Pajajarans ruled the region. They're chiefly remembered for constructing the first trading settlement on the site of Old Batavia when it was called Sunda Kelapa, and for establishing trading relations with the Portuguese.

The first half of the 16th century saw the military expansion of the Muslim state of Demak and in 1524 Muslim power first made itself felt in West Java. In that year Demak's leader, Sunan Gunungjati, took the port of Banten and then Sunda Kelapa. Some time after 1552 he became the first of the kings of Cirebon, which today is the least visited and thus the most surprising of Java's surviving sultanates. Banten, on the other hand, was the maritime capital of the only Muslim state to remain independent of the great Javanese power, Mataram, but today it is little more than a small fishing village.

After the fall of Melaka in 1511 Chinese, Arabs and Indians poured into Banten and it became a major trading centre for Muslim merchants who made use of the Sunda Straits (Selat Sunda) to avoid the Portuguese. Gunungjati's successor, Hasanuddin, spread Banten's authority to the pepper-producing district of Lampung in south Sumatra. His

JAVA

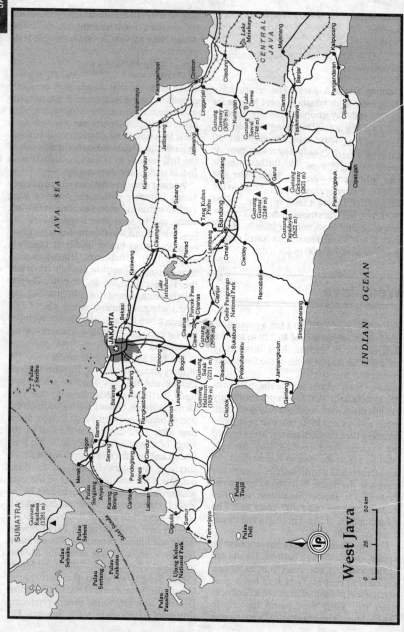

West Java

son, Maulana Yusuf, finally conquered the inland Hindu kingdom of Pajajaran in 1579 and so carved out a huge slice of Sunda as Banten's own domain.

Towards the end of the century Banten felt the first impact of a new force – the Europeans. In 1596 the Dutch made their first appearance at Banten, in 1600 the English established an East India Company trading post and two years later the Dutch formed a counterpart company, the Vereenigde Oost-Indische Compagnie (VOC). Banten naturally became a centre of fierce Anglo-Dutch competition and the Dutch soon moved out and seized Jakarta instead, henceforth to be their capital as Batavia.

The VOC's most formidable opponent was the Mataram empire which was extending its power over parts of West Java but Banten, so close to their own headquarters, remained a troublesome rival. It not only harboured foreign competitors but a powerful ruling house. Hostilities reached their peak with the accession of Banten's greatest ruler, Sultan Agung, in 1651. With the help of European captains Agung established an impressive trading network. He defied both Mataram and the VOC on more than one occasion before civil war within the ruling house led to Dutch intervention and his defeat and capture in 1683.

By the end of the 17th century Dutch power had taken a great step forward in the west, and throughout the colonial era West Java remained under more direct control than the rest of the country. It was closer to Batavia but, more importantly, much of the land was ceded to the Dutch by Mataram in return for military aid, while in Central and East Java the kingdoms became Dutch protectorates.

SUNDANESE ARTS
Music
The most characteristic Sundanese instrument is the *kecapi*, accompanied by the *suling*. The kecapi is a type of lute (it looks like a dulcimer) which is plucked; the suling is a soft-toned bamboo flute which fades in

and out of the long vibrating notes of the kecapi. Another traditional instrument is the *angklung* – a device of bamboo pieces of differing lengths and diameter loosely suspended in a bamboo frame, which is shaken to produce hollow echoing sounds. Originally the angklung was tuned to a five-note scale but it's now being revived using Western octaves and can be played by a single performer or a large orchestra. In Cirebon there's a variation on Bandung-style kecapi-suling music, called *tarling* because it makes use of gui*tar* and su*ling*.

Another traditional Sundanese music form is *gamelan degung*. This dynamic gamelan style is played by a small ensemble similar to the Central Javanese gamelan with the addition of the *degung*, which is a set of small suspended gongs, and the suling. It is less soporific and more rhythmic than Central Javanese gamelan music, yet not as hectic as the Balinese forms.

Nowadays, West Java is famous for the more modern music and dance form called Jaipongan, which is found mostly in Bandung and Jakarta. Jaipongan features dynamic drumming coupled with erotic and sometimes humorous dance movements that include elements of *pencak silat* (Indonesian martial arts) and even New York-style break dancing. Jaipongan dance/music is a rather recent derivation of a more traditional Sundanese form called Ketuktilu, in which a group of professional female dancers (sometimes prostitutes) dance for male spectators. The newer form involves males and females dancing alone and together, although in lengthy performances Jaipongan songs are usually interspersed with the older Ketuktilu style.

Other Sundanese dance forms include Longser, Joker and Ogel. Longser and Joker are couples' dances which involve the passing of a sash between the couples. Ogel is an extremely difficult form that features very slow dance movements. Traditional Ogel is in danger of dying out, because few younger performers are patient enough to endure the many years of training required to master the subtle movements.

Wayang Golek

Although the wayang golek puppet play can be seen elsewhere in Java, it is traditionally associated with West Java and the Sundanese prefer it to the shadow play. First used in north-coast towns for Muslim propaganda, this type of puppet play was Islamic and a popular, robust parody of the stylised aristo-cratic wayang kulit play. In the early 19th century a Sundanese prince of Sumedang had a set of wooden puppets made to corre-spond exactly to the wayang kulit puppets of the Javanese courts. With these he was able to perform the Hindu epics with the tradi-tional splendour of his rivals, but at the same time preserve his regional identity by using puppets long associated with anti-Javanese art. In West Java the stories are still usually based on the *Mahabharata* and *Ramayana* legends and the puppets are larger and more vivid than those found in Central Java.

JAKARTA TO MERAK

Most visitors just head straight through from Jakarta to Merak on their way to (or from) Sumatra, but along this route, you can also branch off and head for the west coast.

The Jakarta to Merak road runs through a flat coastal area with plenty of industrial development. It's one of the busiest in Java, with a great deal of traffic of all types. Getting out of Jakarta from Kalideres can be slow but once on the toll road it is a quick journey.

Serang

Serang, 90 km west of Jakarta, is a crossroad town and the only reason to stop here is if you are visiting Banten. Serang has some very basic hotels, but if you take an early-morning bus from Jakarta and a late-afternoon bus back (or on to the west coast) you're going to have all the time in the world to fit in a trip to explore Banten's ruins.

Getting There & Away Buses run to/from Jakarta (Kalideres) (1800 rp; two hours) and Merak (600 rp; one hour). Patas buses between Jakarta and Merak bypass Serang, which is south of the highway. From Serang minibuses run to Banten for 500 rp. Buses also go to Labuan (1200 rp); for Anyer and the coast road, first take a bus to Cilegon (300 rp).

Banten

Due north of Serang, on the coast, are the few fragments of the great maritime capital of the Banten sultanate where the Dutch and English first landed on Java to secure trade and struggle for economic supremacy.

Banten reached its peak during the reign of Sultan Agung (1651-83) but he unwisely declared war on the Dutch in Batavia in 1680. Before he could make a move, internal conflict within the royal house led to Dutch intervention on behalf of the ambitious crown prince. Agung fled Banten but finally surrendered in 1683 and his defeat marked the real beginning of Dutch territorial expan-sion in Java. Not only was Banten's independence at an end but their English East India Company rivals were driven out, which effectively destroyed British interests in Java.

The Dutch maintained trading interests in Banten for a time but they did a good job of demolishing the place in the 19th century. Then the coastline silted up and Banten became a ghost town. Banten today is just a small dusty fishing village.

The chief landmark of a prosperous era is the 16th-century **Mesjid Agung** mosque, which dominates the village. This is the main sight in Banten, and is a good example of early Islamic architecture, though the mosque's great white lighthouse of a minaret was reputedly designed by a Chinese Muslim.

Next to the mosque is an **archaeological museum** (open from 9 am to 4 pm, closed Mondays) with a modest collection of mostly clay artefacts found in the area and weapons including a few of the long, iron, chained spikes which the 'Debus players' are famous for. Banten has long been a centre for practitioners of the Debus tradition, which is supposed to have come from India. These Islamic ascetics engage in masochistic activ-ities such as plunging sharp weapons into their bodies (without drawing blood!), and are able to control pain and fear by the strength of their faith. It's said that in Banten this was originally part of the training of the invincible special soldiers to the court.

Directly across from the mosque is the large grass-covered site of Hasanuddin's fortified palace, the **Surosowan**, which was wrecked in the bloody civil war during the reign of Sultan Agung and rebuilt, only to be razed to the ground by the Dutch in 1832.

Other points of interest around the mosque include the massive ruins of **Fort Speelwijk** to the north-west, which now overlook an expanse of sand-silt marsh, although at one time it stood on the sea's edge. The fort was built by the Dutch in 1682 and finally abandoned by Governor-General Daendels at the beginning of the 19th century. Opposite the entrance to the fort is a **Chinese temple**, dating from the 18th century, which is still in use. Back along the road to Serang are the huge crumbling walls and archways of the **Kaibon** palace and near it is the **tomb of Maulana Yusuf**, who died in 1580.

Getting There & Away The usual way to reach Banten is to take a bus to Serang, 10 km south of Banten, and then a minibus (500 rp; half an hour), which will drop you right by the mosque. A slightly quicker alternative is to take any bus between Jakarta and Merak and get down at the mosque in Kramatwatu village on the main highway, from where an ojek (2000 rp) will take you the five km to Banten.

Pulau Dua Bird Sanctuary

Off the coast at Banten, Pulau Dua is one of Indonesia's major bird sanctuaries. The island has a large resident population – mainly herons, storks and cormorants – but peak time is between March and July when great numbers of migratory birds flock here for the breeding season. At low tide the island may be accessible by land now that the mudflats between it and the mainland have silted up; otherwise it's a half-hour boat ride from the Karanghantu harbour in Banten. A PHPA guard is stationed on the island and there's a watchtower and guesthouse but if

you are planning to stay bring both food and water. For more information you can contact the PHPA office in Jakarta. Tours are arranged from Carita.

MERAK

Right on the north-western tip of Java, 140 km from Jakarta, Merak is the terminal for ferries shuttling to and from Bakauheni on the southern end of Sumatra. Merak is just an arrival and departure point, and most people pass straight through this small, noisy village.

Pantai Florida is a reasonable beach five km north of Merak, but the west coast beaches to the south have more appeal and plenty of facilities.

Places to Stay

If you do have a reason to stay, the *Hotel Anda* (☎ 71041) on Jalan Florida (Pulorida) has reasonably clean rooms with fan and mandi for 9000 rp and 12,000 rp, or air-con rooms cost 25,000 rp. The *Hotel Robinson* next door is similarly priced but not as good. These standard losmen are just across the railway line opposite the bus station.

For those determined to pay more, the modern *Merak Beach Hotel* (☎ 71015) is two km out of town on the road to Jakarta. Comfortable but small air-con units are sandwiched between the bad beach and the noisy highway. Singles/doubles are an overpriced 107,000/142,000 rp.

Getting There & Away

The bus and railway stations in Merak are right at the ferry dock.

Bus Frequent normal/air-con buses run between Merak and Jakarta (2500/4000 rp, three hours). Most terminate at Jakarta's Kalideres bus station, but buses also run to/from Pulo Gadung and Kampung Rambutan terminals for 3500 rp. From Merak other buses include: Bogor (4000 rp), Bandung (5500/11,000 rp), Cirebon (7500 rp), Yogya (15,000/28,000 rp), Solo, Wonosobo and Banjar.

Local minibuses or larger, more comfort-

JAVA

able buses leave from out the front of the bus terminal and go to Serang (600 rp) and Ciregon (400 rp). Buses to Labuan via Anyer and Carita leave from the Ciregon terminal, or from Merak it is quicker to get down on the western side of Ciregon at the Simpang Tiga turn-off to Anyer and catch a bus from there.

Train Misnamed *cepat* (fast) trains depart Jakarta's Tanah Abang station for Merak at 7 am and 2.35 pm, and from Merak they depart at 6 am and 2 pm. They cost 1500 rp (ekonomi class only) and take a long four hours.

Boat Ferries to Bakauheni in Sumatra depart about every 40 minutes around the clock. Ferries cost 2400/1900/1300 rp in 1st/2nd/3rd class and take two hours. Bicycles cost 2100 rp, motorbikes 3500 rp and cars 24,200 rp. The Merak to Bakauheni crossing is one of the busiest waterways in Indonesia and traffic jams can occur during the holiday seasons.

WEST COAST BEACHES

At Cilegon, south-east of Merak, the road branches south to Anyer and runs close to the sea all the way to Labuan. The road passes Cilegon's massive steel works and chemical, cement and other industrial plants until it reaches Anyer market. From there the road runs south to Labuan along a flat, green coastal strip bordered by a rocky, reef-lined coast that is punctuated by stretches of white-sand beach.

This picturesque coast has masses of coconut palms and banana trees, and because of its easy access by toll road from Jakarta, it is a popular weekend beach strip. Though not world beaters, the beaches are good and make a fine escape from Jakarta's heat and crowds. The main place of interest is Carita, where you can arrange tours to Krakatau and Ujung Kulon National Park.

The area is sparsely populated with small fishing settlements and coconut ports. This is perhaps simply because the land isn't suitable for intensive rice agriculture but it's also

said that survivors of the Krakatau eruption, and succeeding generations, believed it to be a place of ill omen and never returned.

Anyer

Anyer, 12 km south-west of Cilegon, is an up-market beach resort popular with Jakarta residents. Anyer was once the biggest Dutch port in Selat Sunda before being totally destroyed by tidal waves generated by Krakatau. The Anyer lighthouse was built by the Dutch at the instigation of Queen Wilhelmina in 1885 after the disaster.

From here you can hire a boat to make the 1½ hour trip to explore the deserted island of **Sangiang**, which has coral reefs.

Karang Bolong

There's another good beach here, 11 km south of Anyer and 30 km north of Labuan, where a huge stand of rock forms a natural archway from the land to the sea.

Carita

This is a popular base for visits to the Krakatau islands and the Ujung Kulon National Park. The wide, sandy beach has good swimming, and there are plenty of opportunities to go wandering along the beach or inland. About two km from Carita across the rice paddies you can see the village of **Sindanglaut** ('End of the Sea') where the giant tsunami of 1883 ended.

The **Hutan Wisata Carita** is a forest reserve with walks through the hills and jungle. The **Curug Gendang** waterfall is a three-hour return hike through the reserve.

Organised Tours The Black Rhino (☎ 81072) and the privately run Tourist Information Service (☎ 81330), opposite the Desiana cottages, have almost identical tours to Krakatau (40,000 to 65,000 rp per person), Ujung Kulon (US$150 per person for four days/three nights), Badui villages (US$125), Pulau Dua (US$125) and even Jakarta (US$90 for a one-day tour to Sunda Kelapa, Jakarta Museum and Sarina). They can also arrange boat hire to nearby coral reefs and islands. The Carita Beach Resort (☎ 202222 ext 8364) also rents out speed boats and arranges quite expensive diving tours and trips to Krakatau.

Places to Stay

Because of the easy access from Jakarta, the resorts along this stretch of coast are over-priced, but standards are generally high. Dozens of hotels and villas (many private but some for rent) are spaced out along the 30-km stretch from Anyer to Carita. Prices drop the further south you head from Anyer, and the only cheap accommodation is found in Carita.

On weekends the hotels fill up and prices are 20 to 30% more than the weekday rates quoted here, and 21% tax and service is added. During the week, big discounts are available.

Anyer Most hotels in Anyer have swimming pools, restaurants and rooms with air-con, parabola (satellite) TV and hot-water showers. They are spaced out over a five km stretch and start just south of the Anyer market, but the better places are past the Anyer lighthouse. The first one south of the lighthouse is *Mambruk Quality Resort* (☎ 601602) with large gardens, a swimming pool, tennis courts and diving facilities. It is the best in Anyer and excellent rooms with all the trimmings range from US$80 up to the big cottages for US$165. They have man-ufactured a small beach, but the coast is still rocky here and unsuitable for swimming.

A little further south, *Marina Village* (☎ 601288) is similar but not as good. It has a boat marina and a dive shop. Speed boats can be hired for a mere US$500 per day.

Keep heading south until you reach *Ancotte* (☎ 601556), right on a fine stretch of sandy beach, the best in Anyer. This hotel is moderately priced and very popular with expats. It has a pool and good rooms from US$50, or large, attractive cottages, many with kitchens, for US$85 to US$120.

Karang Bolong Coming in to Karang Bolong from Anyer, *Anyer Beach Hometel* (☎ 629224) is on the beach and has a pool.

Rooms range from US$75 up to three-bedroom cottages for US$200. Some need maintenance but this is still one of the best places in Karang Bolang.

Lalita Cottages (☎ 7806514) is on the beach right next to the recreational park. Large two-bedroom cottages with kitchen are quite simple but very comfortable and reasonably priced at 125,000 rp, before dis-count.

The friendly *Matahari Park Resort* (☎ 42167) has well-appointed air-con rooms facing the beach start at 100,000 rp but big discounts are usually available.

Carita Heading north from Labuan, the usual access point, at the five km mark is the four-star *Carita Beach Resort* (☎ 202222). It is the most luxurious on the coast with rooms starting at US$75, but the beach fronts a rocky reef that is unsuitable for swimming.

Further north past Carita village, is a sweeping bay with one of the best beaches on the coast and good swimming. This is the area for budget and mid-range accommoda-tion. Bargaining is usually required.

Past the eight km mark is the *Carita Krakatau Beach Hotel*. It used to be a budget favourite but is undergoing massive renova-tions that will turn it into a big-league hotel. Opposite is the *Hotel Wira Carita* (☎ 200016) which has a swimming pool. Simple rooms with mandi cost 40,000 rp or 65,000 rp with air-con; cottages are 140,000 rp.

Around the nine km mark is the *Carita Beach Bungalow* (☎ 81126). Three-bedroom bungalows with kitchens are way overpriced at US$100, but they rent large rooms in the bungalows to travellers for 30,000 rp and the restaurant on the beach is good. A little further on, *Desiana Cottages* (☎ 201010) has clean rooms with mandi for 37,500 rp or overpriced cottages from 150,000 rp.

Just past the Hutan Wisata Carita, across from the beach park, is the popular *Black Rhino* (☎ 81072), the only really cheap place in Carita. Rooms with shared mandi are quite basic but cost only 5000 rp and 7000 rp. This friendly place also organises tours to Krakatau, Ujung Kulon, etc.

Next door is the good *Sunset View* (☎ 81075) where clean rooms with mandi cost 15,000 rp, after bargaining.

Places to Eat

The coast doesn't have a lot of restaurants and dining is usually done at the hotels, which can work out to be quite expensive at the higher priced establishments. In Anyer and Karang Bolang, unless you have your own transport you virtually have to eat at your hotel because everything is so spread out.

In Carita, *Rumah Makan Nyenil*, opposite the Carita Krakatau Beach Hotel, is a pleasant budget restaurant with a wide range of Indonesian dishes and traveller-oriented fare. The restaurant at the Carita Beach Bungalow is right on the beach and also worth trying. The small warung next to the Black Rhino has very limited food but is cheap and a convivial place to eat. Further north, the *Cafe de Paris* is an oddity – it has air-con and European food, and they accept credit cards.

Getting There & Away

To get to Carita from Jakarta, take a bus to Labuan and then a colt or angkot to Carita (500 rp). Overcharging is common.

Most visitors to Anyer go by car from Jakarta – 2½ to three hours via the toll road and the turn-off at Cilegon. By bus from Jakarta, take a Merak bus (2500 rp) and get off at Cilegon from where infrequent buses run to Labuan via Anyer and Karang Bolong. Minibuses are much more frequent and run to Anyer market from where you can catch other minibuses further south. It usually takes three minibuses to get to Carita and Labuan from Cilegon.

LABUAN

The dreary little port of Labuan is merely a jumping-off point for Carita or the Ujung Kulon National Park.

Ujung Kulon Permits

For permits and reservations for accommodation at Ujung Kulon National Park, the Labuan PHPA office is about one km from the centre of town on the road to Carita. This very helpful and informative office has maps of the reserve and the staff can also help arrange boat transport to the Ujung Kulon peninsula. The office is open normal government office hours.

Places to Stay & Eat

The very basic *Hotel Citra Ayu* costs a ridiculous 20,000 rp, or the *Hotel Caringin* has better rooms with mandi for 15,000 rp. The *Rawa Yana Hotel* is the best hotel in town and has rooms with bath from 25,000 rp, but Carita is only a few km up the road and has much better accommodation.

Getting There & Away

Frequent buses depart Kalideres station in Jakarta for Labuan (2700 rp; 3½ hours) via Serang and Pandeglang. Overcharging is common. Angkots for Carita (500 rp; half an hour) leave from the market, 100 metres from the Labuan bus station, as do minibuses to Sumur (4000 rp; 4½ hours). Other buses to/from Labuan include: Bogor (3000 rp; four hours), Bandung (5000 rp; seven hours), Rangkasbitung (1200 rp; 1½ hours), Serang (1200 rp; 1½ hours), Merak (1700 rp; two hours) and destinations further afield such as Garut, Banjar and Kuningan. Frequent buses go from Labuan to Jakarta, Bogor, Rangkasbitung and Serang, but other departures are less frequent and usually leave in the morning only.

KRAKATAU

The legendary Krakatau lies only 50 km from the West Java coast. Today only a small part of the original volcano remains but when Krakatau blew itself apart in 1883, in one of the world's greatest and most catastrophic eruptions, the effects were recorded far beyond Selat Sunda and it achieved instant and lasting infamy.

For centuries Krakatau had been a familiar nautical landmark for much of the world's maritime traffic which was funnelled through the narrow Selat Sunda straits. The volcano had been dormant since 1680 and was widely regarded as extinct, but from

May through to early August in 1883 passing ships reported moderate activity. By 26 August Krakatau was raging and the explosions became more and more violent.

At 10 am on 27 August 1883 Krakatau erupted with the biggest bang ever recorded on earth. On the island of Rodriguez, more than 4600 km to the south-west, a police chief reported hearing the booming of 'heavy guns from eastward'; in Alice Springs, 3500 km to the south-east, residents also reported hearing strange explosions from the north-west.

With its cataclysmic explosions, Krakatau sent up a record column of ash 80 km high and threw into the air nearly 20 cubic km of rock. Ash fell on Singapore 840 km to the north and on ships as far as 6000 km away; darkness covered the Selat Sunda straits from 10 am on the 27th until dawn the next day. Far more destructive were the great ocean waves triggered by the collapse of Krakatau's cones into its empty belly. A giant tsunami more than 40 metres high swept over the nearby shores of Java and Sumatra, and the sea wave's passage was recorded far from Krakatau, reaching Aden in 12 hours over a distance 'travelled by a good steamer in 12 days'. Measurable wave effects were even said to have reached the English Channel. Coastal Java and Sumatra were devastated: 165 villages were destroyed and more than 36,000 people were killed.

The following day a telegram sent to Singapore from Batavia (160 km east of Krakatau) reported odd details such as 'fish dizzy and caught with glee by natives'! Three months later the dust thrown into the atmosphere caused such vivid sunsets in the USA that fire engines were being called out to quench the apparent fires, and for three years it continued to circle the earth, creating strange and spectacular sunsets.

The astonishing return of life to the devastated islands has been the subject of scientific study ever since. Not a single plant was found on Krakatau a few months after the event; 100 years later – although the only fauna are snakes, insects, rats, bats and birds – it seems almost as though the vegetation was never disturbed.

Krakatau basically blew itself to smithereens but, roughly where the 1883 eruption began, Anak Krakatau (the 'Child of Krakatau') has been vigorously growing ever since its first appearance in 1928. It has a restless and uncertain temperament, sending out showers of glowing rocks and belching smoke and ashes, but boats can land

The Formation of Krakatau
Thousands of years ago Krakatau built up a cone-shaped mountain which which eventually formed a huge caldera over six km across and mostly beneath water level. The peaks of the rim projected as four small islands – Sertung on the north-west, Lang and the Polish Hat on the north-east, and Rakata ('Crab' in old Javanese) on the southeast. Later volcanic activity threw up two cones, Perbunan and Danan, which merged with the Rakata cone to form a single island – Krakatau – that extended almost completely across the caldera. When an eruption in 1883 ended, Lang and the Polish Hat had disappeared and only a stump of the original Krakatau with the caldera of Rakata remained above sea level. ∎

Krakatau
0   1.5   3 km
······ Islands before 1883 eruption

on the east side and it is possible to climb right up the cinder cones to the caldera. It is a hard scramble up the loose slopes to the rim of the crater with fine views of the fuming caldera and the surrounding sea and islands. Be careful – in 1993, Krakatau belched a load of molten rock on one unfortunate tourist who ventured too close. Krakatau is still a menacing volcano, and in its more active phases Krakatau's intermittent rumblings can be heard on quiet nights from the west coast beaches.

Getting There & Away

The islands of Krakatau are about 50 km from the nearest point on Java. During the rainy season (November to March) there are strong currents and rough seas, but even during the dry season strong south-east winds can whip up the swells and make a crossing inadvisable. When weather conditions are fine it's a long one-day trip, four or five hours there and four or five hours back, but having visited Krakatau we'd say it's definitely worth the effort – *if* you can hire a safe boat.

By far the easiest way to reach Krakatau is to take a tour from Carita. The tour operators (see under Carita) charge 40,000 rp per person (minimum of 10) for a day trip to Anak Krakatau, with two hours on the island. During the peak July/August tourist season a boat goes every day or two. In the quieter periods, it can take longer to fill a tour and prices may be higher. The large hotels also arrange expensive tours.

It is cheaper to charter a boat yourself from Labuan or Carita, but make sure you get a seaworthy vessel. The PHPA office in Labuan can be helpful in arranging a larger boat, or you can haggle with the fishermen on the beach and get a much smaller boat. If you do decide to take one of the fishing boats, be sure to take along a food reserve, some water and warm clothes in case you go adrift. In 1986, two foreigners and their Indonesian crew drifted for nearly three weeks before washing up near Bengkulu, Sumatra. A few years ago, Lonely Planet almost lost one of its writers, Joe Cummings,

who spent the night adrift on such a boat in high swells along with 10 other travellers.

UJUNG KULON NATIONAL PARK

Ujung Kulon National Park is on the remote south-western tip of Java, covering about 760 sq km of land area including the large Pulau Panaitan. Because of its isolation and being difficult to access, Ujung Kulon has remained an outpost of primeval forest and untouched wilderness in heavily developed Java. The park presents some fine opportunities for hiking and wildlife spotting, and has some good beaches with intact coral reefs. Despite its remoteness and the relatively high cost of visiting the park, it is one of the most popular national parks in Java.

Ujung Kulon is best known as the last refuge on Java for the once plentiful one-horned rhinoceros, now numbering only around 60. The shy Javan rhino, however, is an extremely rare sight and you are far more likely to come across less-exotic animals such as banteng (wild cattle), wild pigs, otters, squirrels, leaf monkeys and gibbons. Panthers also live in the forest, and crocodiles in the river estuaries, but these too are a rare sight. Green turtles nest in some of the bays and Ujung Kulon also has a wide variety of birdlife. On Peucang Island, rusa deer, long-tailed macaques and big monitor lizards are common, and there is good snorkelling around coral reefs.

The main park area is on the peninsula but the park also includes the nearby island of Panaitan and the smaller offshore islands of Peucang and Handeuleum. Much of the peninsula is dense lowland rainforest and a mixture of scrub, grassy plains, swamps, pandanus palms and long stretches of sandy beach on the west and south coasts. Walking trails follow the coast around much of the peninsula and loop round Gunung Payung on the western tip.

Information

Secure your permit and book accommodation at the very helpful PHPA office in Labuan. Pick up a copy of the excellent *Visitor's Guidebook to the Trails of Ujung*

Kulon National Park. Entry to the park costs 4500 rp.

The best time for visiting Ujung Kulon is the dry season (April to October) when the sea is generally calm and the reserve is not so boggy. Malaria has been reported in Ujung Kulon, and anti-malarials are advisable and appropriate measures to prevent mosquito bites should be taken.

Guides must be hired for hiking in the park. The PHPA in Tamanjaya will arrange this for around 10,000 rp per day, plus food. Gili Peucang has a restaurant but otherwise bring your own food, for yourselves and your guide, which the guide can cook. Bring lightweight food, such as packaged noodles, and drinking water if you will be doing a lot of trekking. Limited supplies are available in Tamanjaya, but it is best to stock up in Labuan.

Exploring the Park

Access to the park is either by boat, usually from Labuan or Tamanjaya, or you can walk into the park from Tamanjaya. From Tamanjaya it is a three-day hike across to the west coast and on to Gili Peucang.

The other popular way to enter the park is to take a boat to Handeuleum or Peucang islands. From Handeuleum boats or canoes can be hired for the short crossing to the mainland. From Cigenter, on the mainland opposite Handeuleum Island, a hiking trail leads six to eight hours along the coast to the Jamang rangers' hut, where it is possible to overnight. From Jamang it is a full day's hike to Cidaon, on the mainland directly opposite Gili Peucang.

Cidaon links up with the trail to Tamanjaya, or another coastal trail leads to the westernmost tip of mainland Java.

From Tamanjaya it is also possible to walk south across the Gunung Honje Range to Cegog village, where homestay accommodation is available, and then along the south coast to Kalejatan or Karang Ranjang and back to Tamanjaya. This is certainly the cheapest way to explore Ujung Kulon, though the main attractions of the park lie to the west.

Remote Pulau Panaitan also has some fine beaches, hiking and surfing.

Places to Stay

The PHPA guesthouse at Tamanjaya has rooms for 20,000 rp and 30,000 rp, or you can stay at homestay accommodation in the village for around 10,000 rp per night.

The pleasant guesthouse at Gili Handeuleum has doubles/triples for US$15/20, but accommodation is limited. If it is full you can sleep at the rangers' post. Gili Peucang has double rooms in the old guesthouse for US$25, including breakfast, or quite luxurious accommodation with air-con, hot water and refrigerators in the new guesthouses for US$60 and US$80 a double. Peucang also has a restaurant. Advance booking is essential for accommodation at both islands, particularly for weekends. Bookings can be made at the Labuan PHPA office (☎ 81217) or more easily through PT Wanawisata Alamhayati (☎ Jakarta 5710392), a private company which runs the accommodation in conjunction with the PHPA.

Within the park you can camp, or PHPA posts in the park can also accommodate hikers. A tent is handy for the hikes, though not essential for small groups.

Rhinoceros: Standing 1½ metres tall and weighing over 1500 kg, the Javan one-horned rhino once roamed from India through to Java, but now exists only at Ujung Kulon National Park. Sightings are very rare but numbers of this endangered species have increased to around 60.

Getting There & Away

The easiest way to get to the park is by boat from Labuan. The KV *Wanawisata* leaves Labuan on Mondays and Fridays for Tamanjaya, Gili Handeuleum and Gili Peucang, returning on Thursdays and Sundays, but check with the Labuan PHPA or PT Wanawisata Alamhayati in Jakarta. The cost to Gili Peucang is US$30 per person one way and it takes about six hours. Otherwise, to charter a boat which can carry 15 to 20 people to Gili Peucang or Pulau Panaitan will cost around 350,000 rp one-way. You can hire a smaller local fishing boat for about half that, but you'll have to bargain hard. As with boat rides to Krakatau, it can be a rough and dangerous crossing, so make sure you hire a seaworthy boat.

A cheaper alternative is to take a colt from Labuan south to Sumur (4000 rp, 3½ hours) and then an ojek (5000 rp) to Tamanjaya. In Tamanjaya, local boats (maximum 10 people) to Gili Handeuleum can be hired for around 65,000 rp one way. It is also possible to hire boats in Sumur.

BADUI VILLAGES

When Islam swept through Java, the temples were sacked and the outward manifestations of Hinduism all but disappeared. Yet throughout the mountains of Java, small isolated pockets of the old religions remain. The most mysterious of all these groups are the Badui. They have preserved their traditions through a strict policy of isolation, shunning visitors and attempts by the government to make them part of the modern world.

Badui religion is a blend of animism and Hinduism and the Badui priests are regarded as powerful mystics. This is particularly true of the Badui Dalam ('Inner Badui') or 'White Badui' as they are known because of their white dress. The three inner villages of Cibeo, Cikartawana and Cikeusik are off-limits to outsiders and are surrounded by Badui Luar ('Outer Badui') villages that have contact with the outside world and act as intermediaries for the Badui Dalam.

Permits are required to visit the Badui villages, access is difficult and a guide is usually necessary. Permits must be obtained from the tourist office (Dinas Parawisata), Jalan Pahlawan 13, in Rangkasbitung, 64 km east of Labuan. Cibolger, at the border of Badui territory, is the official entry point. In Cibolger it is possible to stay with the village head.

Getting There & Away

Rangkasbitung is easily reached by bus from Labuan (1200 rp; 1½ hours), Jakarta (2000 rp; three hours), Bogor (2000 rp; 108 km) and Serang (700 rp; 44 km). The Rangkasbitung bus terminal is over two km from town (200 rp by angkot).

Most visitors to Cibolger tend to be small tour groups that make the trip by minibus; public transport is infrequent and difficult. Tours from Carita cost US$125, including transport and guide.

BOGOR

Bogor, 60 km south of Jakarta, is most famous for its botanical gardens. In the days before independence, however, this was the most important Dutch hill station, midway between the mountains and the heat-ridden plains. Governor-General van Imhoff is credited with its discovery in 1745. He built a large country estate which he named Buitenzorg ('Without a Care'), but it was not until 1811 that it was first used as a country residence by Sir Stamford Raffles, during the British interregnum, and not until many years later that Bogor became the semi-official capital.

Raffles judged it as 'a romantic little village', but Bogor has grown and, other than the botanical gardens, its beauty has faded somewhat. Nevertheless, Bogor has become an important centre for scientific research, including botany, agronomy and forestry. Although the town itself has almost become a suburb of Jakarta, it makes a good base for nearby mountain walks. Many people visit the gardens from Jakarta or stop off on their way to Bandung and points further east, but Bogor could also be used as a Jakarta base since it is only about an hour away.

Though Bogor stands at a height of only

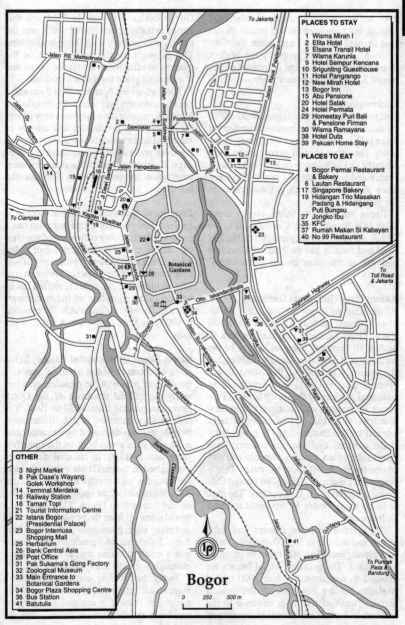

PLACES TO STAY
1 Wisma Mirah I
2 Efita Hotel
5 Elsana Transit Hotel
7 Wisma Karunia
9 Hotel Sempur Kencana
10 Srigunting Guesthouse
11 Hotel Pangrango
12 New Mirah Hotel
13 Bogor Inn
15 Abu Pensione
20 Hotel Salak
24 Hotel Permata
29 Homestay Puri Bali
   & Pensione Firman
30 Wisma Ramayana
38 Hotel Duta
39 Pakuan Home Stay

PLACES TO EAT
4 Bogor Permai Restaurant
   & Bakery
6 Lautan Restaurant
17 Singapore Bakery
19 Hidangan Trio Masakan
   Padang & Hidangang
   Puti Bungsu
27 Jongko Ibu
35 KFC
37 Rumah Makan Si Kabayan
40 No 99 Restaurant

OTHER
3 Night Market
8 Pak Dase's Wayang
   Golek Workshop
14 Terminal Merdeka
16 Railway Station
18 Taman Topi
21 Tourist Information Centre
22 Istana Bogor
   (Presidential Palace)
23 Bogor Internusa
   Shopping Mall
25 Herbarium
26 Bank Central Asia
28 Post Office
31 Pak Sukarna's Gong Factory
32 Zoological Museum
33 Main Entrance to
   Botanical Gardens
34 Bogor Plaza Shopping Centre
36 Bus Station
41 Batutulis

Bogor

0   250   500 m

290 metres it's appreciably cooler than Jakarta, but visitors in the wet season should bear in mind the town's nickname: the 'City of Rain'. Bogor has probably the highest annual rainfall in Java and is credited with a record 322 thunderstorms a year.

Information

The tourist information centre (☎ 321075), on the west side of the botanical gardens at Jalan Ir H Juanda 10, has a rough map of the town. The office is open from 8 am to 2 pm Monday to Thursday, from 8 am to 11 am on Friday and from 8 am to 1 pm on Saturday. They also have a branch at the entrance to the gardens.

Bogor has plenty of banks, mostly along Jalan Ir H Juanda. Bank Central Asia at No 28 has a foreign currency counter on the 2nd floor and usually has the best rates, no fees and will accept most brands of travellers' cheques.

Kebun Raya (Botanical Gardens)

At the heart of Bogor are the huge, world-class botanical gardens, known as the Kebun Raya (Great Garden), covering an area of around 80 hectares. They are said to be the inspiration of Governor-General Raffles, but the spacious grounds of the Istana Bogor (Presidential Palace) were converted to botanical gardens by the Dutch botanist Professor Reinwardt, with assistants from Kew Gardens (London, UK), and officially opened by the Dutch in 1817. It was from these gardens that various colonial cash crops such as tea, cassava, tobacco and cinchona were developed during the so-called Forced Cultivation Period in the 19th century. The park is still a major centre for botanical research in Indonesia.

The gardens contain streams and lotus ponds and more than 15,000 species of trees and plants, including 400 types of magnificent palms. The gardens' orchid houses are reputed to contain more than 3000 orchid varieties but are not open to the general public. North of the main entrance to the gardens is a small monument in memory of Olivia Raffles who died in 1814 and was buried in Batavia, and further north, near the palace, is a cemetery with Dutch headstones. The cafeteria on the eastern side of the gardens has fine view across the lawns and is a pleasant place for a snack or drink.

The gardens are open between 8 am and 5 pm and, although they tend to be crowded on Sundays, on other days they are a very peaceful escape from the hassles and crowds of Jakarta. The entrance fee is 1500 rp during the week and 1000 rp on Sundays and holidays. The southern gate is the main entrance; other gates are only open on Sundays and holidays.

Zoological Museum Near the botanical gardens' main entrance, this museum has a motley but interesting collection of zoological oddities, including the skeleton of a blue whale and a stuffed Javan rhinoceros. If you ever heard about the island of Flores having a rat problem, one glance at the stuffed Flores version in the showcase of Indonesian rats will explain why. Admission to the museum is 400 rp and it's open from 8 am to 4 pm daily.

Istana Bogor (Presidential Palace) In the north-west corner of the botanical gardens, the summer palace of the president was formerly the official residence of the Dutch governors-general from 1870 to 1942. The present huge mansion is not 'Buitenzorg' though; this was destroyed by an earthquake and a new palace was built on the site a few years later in 1856. In colonial days, deer were raised in the parklands to provide meat for banquets, and through the gates you can still see herds of white-spotted deer roaming on the immaculate lawns. The Dutch elite would come up from the pesthole of Batavia and many huge, glamorous parties were held there. Following independence, the palace was a much-favoured retreat for Soekarno, although Soeharto has ignored it.

Today the building contains Soekarno's huge art collection of 219 paintings and 156 sculptures (which is reputed to lay great emphasis on the female figure), but the palace is only open to the public by prior arrangement. The tourist information centre can arrange tours for groups or you can write directly to the Head of Protocol at the Istana Negara, Jalan Veteran, Jakarta. You need to give at least five days notice. If a tour is going the tourist information centre will try to include interested individuals. Abu Pensione (see Places to Stay) also makes regular bookings for tours.

Other Attractions
The **Batutulis** is an inscribed stone dedicated to Sri Baduga Maharaja by his son King Surawisesa in 1533. Sri Baduga Maharaja (1482-1521) was a Pajajaran king accredited with great mystical power. The stone is housed in a small shrine visited by pilgrims – almost any old rock stuck in the ground in Java is bound to attract worshippers. Remove your shoes and pay a small donation before entering. Batutulis is 2½ km south of the gardens, on Jalan Batutulis and almost opposite the former home of Soekarno. Soekarno chose this spot for his home supposedly because of the stone's mystical power, but his request to be buried here was ignored by Soeharto who wanted

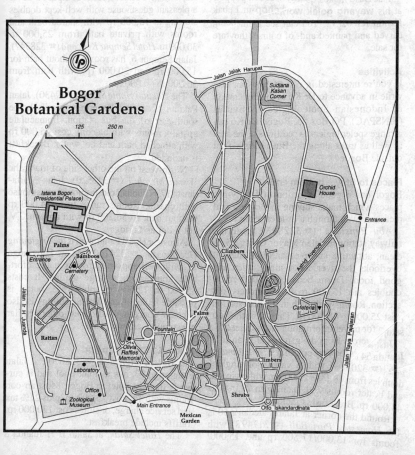

the former president's grave as far away from the capital as possible.

One of the few remaining gongsmiths in West Java is Pak Sukarna, and you can visit his **gong factory** at Jalan Pancasan 17. Gongs and other gamelan instruments are smelted over a charcoal fire in the small workshop out the back. A few gongs and wayang golek puppets are on sale in the front showroom. The gong factory is a short walk south from the garden gates down Jalan Empang and west across the river. Look for the 'Pabrik Gong' ('Gong Factory') sign.

Pak Dase makes quality wooden puppets at his **wayang golek workshop** in Lebak Kantin RT 02/VI. You can see them being carved and painted and, of course, they are for sale.

Activities

If you're interested in caving, you can also write in advance to Dr Ko at the Federation of Indonesian Speleological Activities (FINSPAC), PO Box 55, Bogor. Dr Ko can arrange speleological expeditions in the area as well as treks along the Buena Vista Trail outside Bogor.

Places to Stay – bottom end

Bogor has a good selection of family-run places which make staying in Bogor a real pleasure, even though a little expensive.

Abu Pensione (☎ 322893), near the railway station at Jalan Mayor Oking 15, is clean, attractive and pleasantly situated. It overlooks the river, has a nice garden and good food. Dorm beds cost 5000 rp or doubles are 15,000 rp in the rickety old section. Rooms with bath in the new section cost 25,000 to 45,000 rp. They have the best setup for travel information and services.

Just across from the gardens at Jalan Ir H Juanda 54 is the very colonial *Wisma Ramayana* (☎ 320364) with a variety of singles/doubles from 18,000/19,000 rp without bath, and better rooms with bath from 29,000 to 44,000 rp. Breakfast is included.

Round the corner at Jalan Paledang 50 is the *Homestay Puri Bali* (☎ 317498) with rooms for 13,000/17,500 rp and 15,000/

20,000 rp. All rooms have a bath and there is an attractive garden restaurant. Next door at No 48, *Pensione Firman* (☎ 323426) is a budget favourite and the cheapest around with dorm beds at 6000 rp, and rooms for 10,000/13,000 rp or 15,000/20,000 rp with bath, all including breakfast. It is undergoing some renovation.

Places to Stay – middle

Two more places, across the river and north of the botanical gardens, are a little out of the way but quiet and reasonably priced. *Wisma Karunia* (☎ 323411), Jalan Sempur 33-35, is a pleasant guesthouse with well-kept doubles starting at 15,000 rp with shared bath and rooms with private bath from 25,000 to 30,000 rp. *Hotel Sempur Kencana* (☎ 328347), Jalan Sempur 6, has rooms without bath for 15,000 rp and 20,000 rp, with bath from 30,000 to 40,000 rp.

The *Pakuan Home Stay* (☎ 319430), Jalan Pakuan 12, is in a large, new family home south-east of the bus station. Immaculate upstairs rooms with balcony cost 45,000 rp with attached bath and hot water. Breakfast is included.

North-west on the other side of town, the *Wisma Mirah I* (☎ 323520), Jalan Martadinata 17, is another old-fashioned guesthouse with charm. Rooms range from 24,000 rp without bath to 56,200 rp with air-con, TV, hot water and fridge.

Also near Hotel Pangrango is the *Srigunting Guesthouse* (☎ 324160), Jalan Pangrango 21, with well-appointed rooms in a comfortable house with a large garden. It costs 65,000 to 72,500 rp, plus 15%, but it is possible to negotiate. The Srigunting is also a chain concern, with three other similar guesthouses around town.

Places to Stay – top end

The *Hotel Pangrango* (☎ 328670), at Jalan Pangrango 23, has a small pool and is currently the best hotel in Bogor. Most air-con rooms with TV cost 75,000 rp, plus 21% tax and service charge, or suites cost 120,000 rp. Tariffs include breakfast.

The *Hotel Salak*, at Jalan Ir H Juanda 8

opposite the palace, is a big colonial hotel that is undergoing a massive facelift. When it is finally completed it will probably have little colonial atmosphere left, but will be Bogor's biggest hotel.

Places to Eat

Cheap food stalls appear at night along Jalan Dewi Sartika and during the day you'll find plenty of food stalls and good fruit at Pasar Bogor, the market close to the garden gates. In the late afternoon along Jalan Raja Permas next to the railway station, street vendors cook up delicious snacks such as deep-fried tahu and pisang goreng. Also near the railway station, Taman Topi is a recreational park with fun rides for the kids, and the spotless rumah makan here, such as *Tatos Cafe*, have better-than-average Indonesian food and ice juices.

The *Pujasera* is an air-con hawkers' centre on the top floor of the Bogor Plaza shopping centre opposite the entrance to the botanical gardens. One of the better little eateries here is the *Es Teler KK*, serving inexpensive lunches and good fruit juices.

Another good restaurant for Sundanese food is the *Jongko Ibu* opposite the post office at Jalan Ir H Juanda 36. Prices are moderate and you can dine buffet-style and try a number of dishes. *Rumah Makan Si Kabayan* (☎ 311849), Jalan Bina Marga I No 2, is one of Bogor's most pleasant Sundanese restaurants. You dine on mats in individual bamboo huts arranged around an attractive garden. You'll need to order a number of dishes to get your fill, but this restaurant is reasonably priced.

The *Bogor Permai Restaurant & Bakery*, Jalan Jenderal Sudirman 23A, is a large, semi-modern restaurant and bakery complex offering Chinese and Western fare, including steaks. The nearby *Lautan Restaurant* at No 15 is a large, no-frills eating house serving Chinese cuisine at moderate prices.

Bogor also has a *KFC* south of the gardens near the bus station, and a *Pizza Hut* in the Bogor Internusa shopping mall on Jalan Raya Pajajaran. The Bogor Internusa also has a supermarket, as does the Bogor Plaza.

Getting There & Away

Bus Buses from Jakarta (1000/1500 rp aircon) depart every 10 minutes or so from the Kampung Rambutan bus station, and can do the trip in a little over half an hour via the Jagorawi Highway toll road. The only problem is that it takes at least double that time to travel between Kampung Rambutan and central Jakarta.

Buses depart frequently from Bogor to Bandung (2800/4700 rp; three hours). On weekends, buses are not allowed to go via the scenic Puncak Pass (it gets very crowded) and have to travel via Sukabumi (3100/5200 rp; four hours). Other bus destinations from Bogor include Pelabuhanratu (2000 rp), Rangkasbitung (2000 rp), Labuan (3000 rp) and Merak (4000 rp).

Air-con, door-to-door minibuses go to Bandung for 11,000 rp, with connections to destinations further afield. The main travel agents are Erny (☎ 322563), Mitra (☎ 321486) and Suci (☎ 325360). Ring for pick-up, or the guesthouses such as Abu Pensione can arrange it.

Angkots to villages around Bogor, including Ciampea (No 5), depart from the Terminal Merdeka near the railway station.

Train The easiest way to reach central Jakarta is to take the trains, which run about every 20 minutes until 8.20 pm and take 1½ hours. They cost 650 rp to Gambir station or 700 rp to Kota. The ekonomi trains are reasonably efficient but best avoided during peak hours when they can be horribly crowded with commuters. More comfortable *Pakuan* ekspres trains (2000 rp bisnis class; one hour) leave Bogor at 6.20, 9.20 am and 3.25 pm, with extra services on Sundays and holidays.

Slow ekonomi trains operate between Bogor and Sukabumi; they depart Bogor at 7.30 am, 1.10 and 5.25 pm, and take about two hours. There is no through railway service to Bandung.

Getting Around

Efficient angkots shuttle around town, particularly between the bus and railway stations. The three wheelers cost 250 rp and the four wheelers 300 rp. Most are green, while the blue angkots run to outlying districts and most terminate at Terminal Merdeka, west of the railway station. Angkots leave from the street behind the bus station, Jalan Bangka. Also from the bus station, angkot No 3 does an anti-clockwise loop of the botanical gardens on its way to Jalan Muslihat, near the railway station.

Becaks are banned from the main road encircling the gardens – in any case, getting them to go where you want to go is not always easy! Metered taxis are nonexistent, but you can haggle with the minivan drivers that hang out near the entrance to the botanical gardens. Abu Pensione rents bicycles.

AROUND BOGOR
Purnawarman Stone (Batutulis)
From the village of Ciampea, which is about 12 km north-west of Bogor, you can take a colt to the village of Batutulis, where sits a huge black boulder on which King Purnawarman inscribed his name and made an imprint of his footstep around 450 AD. The inscription on the stone is still remarkably clear after more than 1500 years.

Other Attractions
Several travellers have recommended hiking in the Lokapurna area in the **Mt Halimun Reserve** near Bogor. To get there, take a colt to Cibadak, then another to Pasar Jumbat. From Pasar Jumbat it's a five-km walk to Lokapurna, about 1½ hours. Most people spend the night in Lokapurna (ask at the kepala desa's house) so they can get in a full day's hiking the next day. From Lokapurna, you can hike either to the local hot springs (*air panas*), to the volcano crater of Kawa Ratu or, if you're feeling fit, all the way to Pelabuhanratu on the south coast.

SUKABUMI & SELABINTANA
Sukabumi is a thriving commercial town of 110,000 people at the foot of Pangrango and Gede volcanoes. The main reason visitors are likely to come here is to visit Selabintana,

a small hill resort seven km to the north of town.

Selabintana is much less developed but much less crowded than the Puncak Pass resort area to the north of Gunung Gede. It is possible to walk up the hillside to **Sawer Waterfall** and on to **Gunung Gede**, but there is no PHPA post in Selabintana. Selabintana has a golf course, swimming pools and a selection of mid-range hotels. Otherwise Selabintana is simply a quiet place to relax and soak up the mountain air.

Places to Stay
Angkots to Selabintana run straight up to the foot of Gunung Gede and terminate at the old-fashioned, slightly faded *Hotel Selabintana* (☎ 221501), Jalan Selabintana Km 7. It has a golf course, tennis and volleyball courts, three swimming pools and three restaurants. Small, dark rooms opposite the golf course cost 40,000 rp, rooms in the hotel section are good value at 50,000 rp, or bungalows are 75,000 to 150,000 rp for those with three bedrooms.

Hotel Selabintana is *the* place to stay, and there is not a lot to do if you stay elsewhere. Nevertheless Selabintana has plenty of other hotels, such as *Pondok Asri Selabintana*, with modern, well-appointed flatettes from 70,000 rp, or the *Hotel Pangrango* has large, musty rooms for 20,000 rp up to 45,000 rp.

The main village, around the six-km mark, has cheaper hotels including the *Pondok Mandari* and *Melinda Hotel*. Cheapest of all is the *Hotel Intan* at 22,000 rp for good, clean rooms with bath.

PELABUHANRATU
Pelabuhanratu, 90 km south of Bogor, is a seaside resort popular with Jakarta residents. Located on a large horseshoe bay, this small fishing town has black-sand beaches and lush scenery, with rice paddies coming almost to the water's edge. Though quiet during the week, it can be crowded at weekends and holidays, and accommodation is quite expensive.

Swimming is possible when the sea is quiet, but like most of Java's south coast, the crashing surf can be treacherous. Drownings do occur in spite of the warning signs.

If you want to enter the realms of legend, Pelabuhanratu ('Harbour of the Queen') actually witnessed the creation of Nyai Loro Kidul, the malevolent Goddess who takes fishers and swimmers off to her watery kingdom. Don't wear green on the beach or in the water (it's her colour), and in the Samudra Hotel a room is set aside for offerings to the Queen of the South Seas.

Orientation

Pelabuhanratu is essentially a two-street town – Jalan Siliwangi, which leads into town and to the harbour, and Jalan Kidang Kencana, which runs around the harbour and out to the western beaches. The bus station is near the intersection of these two streets. The beach road continues on to Cisolok, 15 km to the west, and a number of places to stay are scattered along this road.

Things to See & Do

Pelabuhanratu town has little of interest, but the harbour is dotted with brightly painted prahu and the fish market is lively in the mornings.

The beaches to the west hold the main interest and **Cimaja**, eight km west of Pelabuhanratu, has a pebble beach and good surf. At the 13-km mark, **Pantai Karang Hawu** is a towering cliff with caves, rocks and pools which were created by a large lava flow that pushed over the beach. According to legend, it was from the rocks of Karang Hawu that Nyai Loro Kidul leapt into the mighty ocean to regain her lost beauty and never returned. Stairs lead up to a small *kramat* (shrine) at the top.

Further west, about two km past Cisolok, are the **Cipanas hot springs** where boiling water sprays into the river, and you can soak downstream where the hot and cold waters mingle. It is a very scenic area, and you can walk a few km upstream through the lush forest to a waterfall.

Further afield **Cikotok**, about 30 km to the north-west, is the site of Java's most important gold and silver mines. About 80 km

south-east, **Genteng** is a turtle-spawning area and also has good surfing at Ombak Tujuh.

Places to Stay

Pelabuhanratu has plenty of mid-range accommodation, but only a few vaguely cheap options. The beach, and the best places to stay, start one km west from the town.

Two cheap losmen can be found in town on Jalan Siliwangi, a few hundred metres before the harbour. *Penginapan Laut Kidul*, at No 148, has simple but clean rooms with bath for 12,500 rp. *Wisma Karang Nara*, at No 82, is a notch up in quality and price at 15,000 rp for a room.

The *Pondok Dewata* (☎ 41022) is the first place in town on the beach. Air-con Balinese-style cottages are comfortable but expensive at US$25 to US$45, plus 20% tax and service. Rates are up to 100% more in holiday periods.

Next along on a headland, *Buana Ayu* (☎ 41111) has some rooms for 45,000 rp, though most cost 60,000 rp. The comfortable rooms and the good seafood restaurant have fine sea views. Further around the headland, the *Bayu Amrta* (☎ 41031), run by the same proprietor, has rooms for 25,000 to 40,000 rp.

In Citepus village, three km from Pelabuhanratu, *Losmen Asry* is a friendly budget place and the owner speaks excellent English. Rooms with bath start at 15,000 rp.

About five km west of town, the best hotel on the coast, the *Samudra Beach Hotel* (☎ 41023), is a modern high-rise with several restaurants and a good swimming pool. Singles/doubles cost US$65/75 for slightly faded rooms; those for US$75/90 are better. All rooms face the sea. There's an additional 21% for tax and service, but substantial discounts are available.

Eight km out, Cimaja, the surfing beach, has a couple of very basic, overpriced penginapan with rooms for 15,000 rp. The *Mustika Rata* is much better and has rooms from 15,000 to 25,000 rp plus 20% tax and service, more on weekends and holidays.

A few km further towards Cisolok, the *Pantai Mutiara* (☎ 41330) is one of the best hotels. It has a swimming pool, and rooms from 30,000 to 135,000 rp, plus 15.5%.

Getting There & Away

The road from Bogor cuts south over the pass between Gunung Salak and Pangrango through valleys and hillsides of rubber, coconut, cocoa and tea plantations and terraced rice fields. Local buses run throughout the day from Bogor (2000 rp; three hours) via Cibadak or Sukabumi (1500 rp; 2½ hours). From Sukabumi buses connect with Bandung. Buses from Sukabumi continue on to Cisolok from Pelabuhanratu or minibuses run between Pelabuhanratu and Cisolok for 500 rp, less for shorter journeys.

From Labuan you can take various buses through the towns of Saketi and Malingping (seven hours) – it's a little-travelled and very scenic route.

BOGOR TO BANDUNG
Puncak Pass

If you take the bus from Bogor to Bandung you cross over this beautiful 1500-metre-high pass on a narrow, winding mountain road which passes through small resort towns and tea plantations. At high altitudes it's cool and often misty but in the early mornings the views across the valleys can be superb. It is a popular escape from the heat and crowds of Jakarta.

The resort strip, with its hotels and villas, starts about 10 km out of Bogor at Ciawi, continues up through Cibogo, Cipayung and Cisarua to the Puncak Pass and then over the other side to Cipanas. From Jakarta's Kampung Rambutan station any Bandung bus can drop you off at any of the resort towns on the highway (but not on Sundays when they aren't allowed to use this highway). From Bogor frequent buses and colts (which do run on Sundays) also ply the highway. While somewhat overdeveloped, the area has fine scenery, a refreshing climate and some good walks, especially from Cisarua on the Bogor side of the pass or Cibodas on the other side. Avoid weekends when the crowds and traffic jams are horrendous.

Cisarua

Ten km from Bogor on the slopes of the Puncak, there are good walks to picnic spots and waterfalls around Cisarua, which has good budget accommodation. **Curug Cilember** is a waterfall about 30 minutes, walk from Cisarua.

Just east of Cisarua is the turn-off to **Taman Safari Indonesia**, a wildlife park. As well as indigenous and African 'safari' animals in the drive-through game park, there is a bird park, white-tiger pavilion, children's rides, a programme of animal shows and for 1000 rp you can get your photo taken with an orang-utan or panther. This spacious park with its well-cared for animals is streets ahead of any of Indonesia's zoos. Any Bogor-Bandung bus can drop you at the turn-off, from where minibuses go to the park (500 rp, 2½ km). Entry is 5000 rp for adults, 4000 rp for children; cars are 5000 rp or a minibus is 10,000 rp. A park bus also does tours of the safari park. Park facilities include a swimming pool, restaurants and accommodation.

In the foot hills just before the Puncak summit, you can stop at the huge **Gunung Mas Tea Estate** for a free tour of the tea factory, a couple of km from the highway. Almost at the top of the pass, the Rindu Alam Restaurant has fine views of the surrounding tea estates if it is not shrouded in mist. From there you can walk down through the tea plantations to **Telaga Warna**, a small 'lake of many colours' just below the top of the pass which reflects different colours with changing daylight (if you're lucky).

Places to Stay The *Kopo Hostel* (☎ 4296), Jalan Raya Puncak 557 in Cisarua, has the only budget accommodation in the Puncak area. It's excellent value: the four or six-bed dorms cost 6000 rp per person or comfortable rooms cost from 22,000 to 34,000 rp, including breakfast. Rates are slightly higher on weekends and holidays; HI cardholders can get a small discount. The hostel has quiet garden grounds, a small restaurant, maps of walks and information on places of interest in the area.

Apart from the Kopo, scores of mid-range hotels and villas are spread out along the highway from Ciawi to Cipanas. Many of the villas are private – quite a few are owned by large corporations and foreign embassies – but some are for rent and worth looking into for longer stays.

The top hotel, in terms of facilities and elevation, is the *Puncak Pass Hotel* (☎ 512503), right near the pass itself. Mostly modern bungalows are scattered over the hillside below the old colonial central building. Rates range from US$47 a room up to US$175 for two-bedroom bungalows, 20% less during the week.

Getting There & Away From Bogor take a bus or colt to Cisarua (700 rp; 45 minutes) or a bus from Jakarta (1500 rp; 1½ hours). The Kopo Hostel is on the highway, next to the Cisarua petrol station ('Pompa Bensin Cisarua').

Cibodas
At Cibodas, over the Puncak Pass, is a beautiful high-altitude extension of the Bogor botanical gardens, the **Kebun Raya Cibodas**, surrounded by thick tropical jungle on the slopes of the twin volcanoes of Gunung Gede and Gunung Pangrango. The 80-hectare gardens were originally planted in 1860. Entry to the gardens is 1500 rp. Beside the entrance to the gardens is the entrance to the Gede Pangrango National Park.

Cibodas has limited facilities and is more difficult to reach than the resort strip along the Puncak Highway. Consequently it gets much fewer visitors, but it has fine scenery and excellent walks.

Places to Stay The modern *Pondok Pemuda Cibodas* (☎ 512807) near the Cibodas PHPA office has large dorms costing 4600 rp per person. It caters mostly to groups, but outside of weekends and holidays you'll probably have the place to yourself. There's cheap food at the warungs near the gardens and in the village, 500 metres down the hill.

A truly tranquil place to lodge is within the gardens themselves at the colonial *Cibodas Botanical Gardens Guesthouse* (☎ 512233). You certainly can't beat the surrounding ambience, and large old rooms cost 30,000 to 45,000 rp. Food is also served, at 12,500 rp for three meals. Bookings are essential and you can make reservations at the Bogor Botanical Gardens as well as the Cibodas gardens.

Getting There & Away The turn-off to Cibodas is on Bogor-Bandung highway, a few km west of Cipanas. The gardens are then five km off the main road. Angkots run from Cipanas (500 rp; ½ hour), or coming from the west you can catch them at the turn-off (300 rp).

Gede Pangrango National Park
The Cibodas gardens are also the main entrance to the Gede Pangrango National Park, the highlight of which is the climb to the 2958-metre peak of volcanically active Gunung Gede. From the top of Gede on a clear day you can see Jakarta, Cirebon and even Pelabuhanratu on the south coast – well, Raffles reported that he could.

Permits for the climb cost 4500 rp from the PHPA office just outside the garden entrance. The office has an information centre and pamphlets on the park.

From Cibodas, the trail passes Telaga Biru (15 minutes), a blue/green lake, and Cibeureum Falls (one hour) and another waterfall (another hour) where the water drops deep into a steaming gorge, fed by a hot water stream. Many visitors to the park only go to this waterfall. The 10-km hike right to the top of Gunung Gede takes at least 10 hours there and back, so you should start as early as possible and take warm clothes (night temperatures can drop to 5°C). Most climbers bring sleeping bags and camping equipment to camp out on the mountain, allowing them to be at the summit for dawn when the views are spectacular. There is also a steeper trail to the top of Gunung Pangrango (3019 metres) which requires an extra one to two hours.

Dense fog is common on the mountain so

take extra care when on the steeper trails. The best time to make the hike is from May to October. An alternative approach is to climb Gede Selabintana to the south.

Cipanas

Cipanas, five km beyond the Cibodas turn-off, has hot springs noted for their curative properties. The **Istana Cipanas** is another seldom-used summer presidential palace favoured by Soekarno. Built in 1750, it is an elegant country house in beautiful gardens but, like the Bogor palace, it is not normally open to the public. Apart from that, Cipanas is another resort town with plenty of hotels and a few restaurants. The *Hotel Flamboyant* (☎ 512586), Jalan Raya Pasekon 69, is one of the cheaper hotels with rooms for 30,000 rp.

BANDUNG

With its population of over two million, Bandung is the capital of West Java and Indonesia's third largest city. At 750 metres above sea level it has a cool and comfortable climate, and it attracts people from all over Indonesia, and from abroad, seeking work and higher education. The majority of the population are the native Sundanese of West Java, who not only have a reputation as extroverted, easy-going people compared with the extremely refined Javanese, but also as zealous guardians of their own ancient culture. In contrast, the city itself is relatively new.

Bandung was originally established in the late 19th century as a Dutch garrison town of some 90,000 Sundanese, Chinese and Europeans. It rapidly acquired importance as a commercial and educational centre, renowned in particular for its Institute of Technology.

Bandung's most notable entry in the history books was as host of the Asia-Africa conference in 1955, which placed Bandung in the world spotlight. On the industrial front, Bandung has maintained some of its European-created production centres, and its major industries include textiles, telecommunications, tea and food processing. Bandung's multi-million dollar aircraft factory has been promoted by the Minister for Research & Technology, Professor Habibie, despite widespread scepticism about its viability.

Although in the past Bandung was described as the 'Paris of Java', due to its many fine parks and gardens, much of the city's former glamour has faded. Today it is a mishmash of dilapidated colonial architecture and modern buildings, though the northern suburbs still have graceful residential areas. Art Deco architecture is in abundance, one of the best examples being the Savoy Homann Hotel.

Bandung is an excellent place to visit if you're interested in Sundanese culture; otherwise, its main attractions lie in the beautiful countryside around the city. To the north and south there's a wild tangle of high volcanic peaks, including the famous Tangkuban Prahu, and several huge tea plantations. There are some fine walks in the area – one of the best is the river walk from the village of Maribaya to Dago Hill on the outskirts of Bandung.

Orientation

Bandung sprawls out over the northern foothills of a huge plateau surrounded by high mountain ridges. The main part of the city lies south of the railway line, and is centred around Jalan Asia Afrika and the city square (*alun-alun*). Along Jalan Asia Afrika are the tourist office, the post office and most of the banks, airline offices, restaurants and top-range hotels. Jalan Braga, on the north side, was the ritzy shopping area in Dutch times and has a few useful shops and cafes.

The budget-hotel area in Bandung lies on either side of the railway station. Across the railway tracks to the north is the residential area studded with tree-lined streets and parks, and bordered on the northernmost edge by the hills of Dago.

Information

Tourist Offices The Bandung visitor information centre (☎ 4206644), at the alun alun on Jalan Asia Afrika, is the place to go for detailed information. The office staff are very helpful and can give you all the latest information about cultural events in and around Bandung. It's open from 9 am to 5 pm, Monday to Saturday. The knowledgeable Makmun Rustina and other staff can organise day trips to Papandayan volcano near Garut and Situ Patenggang.

The West Java Regional Tourist Office (Diparda Jawa Barat) is way out on the north side of the city at Jalan Cipaganti 151. More convenient is their office at the south side of the railway station, open from 7 am to 7 pm every day.

Money Bandung has plenty of banks and moneychangers. The Golden Megah Corp Moneychanger, Jalan Otista 180, usually has the best rates in town and no fees. It is open from 8.30 am to 4.30 pm Monday to Friday, from 8.30 am to 4 pm Saturday.

Post & Telecommunications The main post office, at the corner of Jalan Banceuy and Jalan Asia Afrika, is open 24 hours a day. Poste restante is just a tin of jumbled letters out the back. For international telephone calls, the wartel on Jalan Asia Afrika opposite the Savoy Homann Hotel is central and has a fax service.

Medical Services For medical attention, the Adventist Hospital (☎ 82091), at Jalan Cihampelas 161, is a missionary hospital with English-speaking staff.

Gedung Merdeka (Freedom Building)
If you're interested in learning more about the Afro-Asian conference, visit the Museum Konperensi (Conference Museum) in the Gedung Merdeka on Jalan Asia Afrika. There you'll see photographs and exhibits of the meeting between Soekarno, Chou En-Lai, Ho Chi Minh, Nasser and other Third-World leaders of the 1950s. The building itself dates from 1879 and was originally the 'Concordia Societeit', a meeting hall of Dutch associations and the centre for high society. The museum is open from 8 am to 1 pm, Monday to Thursday, from 8 to 11 am Friday and from 8 am to noon Saturday.

Museum Geologi (Geological Museum)
North across the railway tracks, at Jalan Diponegoro 57, the museum and the office of the Geological Survey of Indonesia are housed in the massive old headquarters of the Dutch Geological Service. There are some interesting exhibits such as relief maps, volcano models and an array of fossils, including one of the skull of a *Pithecanthropus erectus*, the famous pre-historic Java man. You can also buy topographical and geological maps of all places in Indonesia from the museum's publications department. It's open daily from 9 am to 2 pm Monday to Thursday, from 9 to 11 pm Friday and from 9 am to 1 pm Saturday. Entrance is free. From the railway station you can take a colt bound for 'Terminal Gang Tilil' and get off at the Gedung Sate, about 200 metres from the museum.

Other Museums
The **Museum Negeri Propinsi Jawa Barat** (West Java Cultural Museum), to the south-west of the city at Jalan Oto Iskandardinata 638, has an interesting display of Sundanese artefacts. It is open every day except Monday from 8 am to noon.

The **Museum Mandala Wangsit** (Army Museum), at Jalan Lembong 38, is devoted to the history and exploits of the West Java Siliwangi division (based in Bandung). It is open from 8 am to noon every day.

The **Museum Pos dan Giro** (Post & Giro National Stamp Museum) is in the north-east corner of the Gedung Sate (Regional Government) complex on Jalan Diponegoro. Apart from thousands of stamps from around the world, the museum has everything from post boxes to pushcarts used since colonial times to ensure that the mail must go through. It is open from 8 am to 2 pm every day.

Bandung Institute of Technology (ITB)
North of town on Jalan Ganeca is the Bandung Institute of Technology, constructed at the beginning of the century. The university has large grounds and gardens and the main campus complex is notable for its

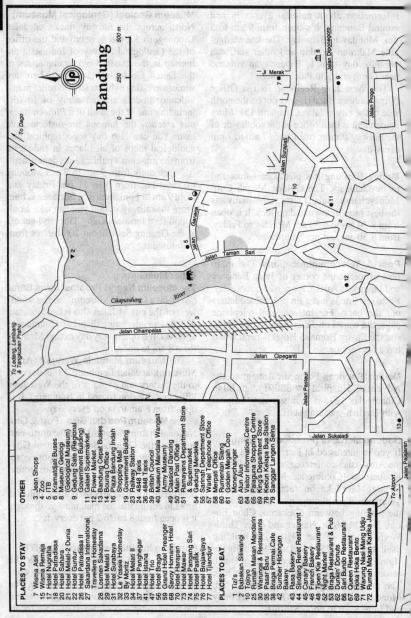

Bandung

0 250 500 m

PLACES TO STAY

7   Wisma Asri
15   Wisma Remaja
17   Hotel Nugraha
18   Hotel Patradissa
20   Hotel Sahara
21   Hotel Melati-2 Dunia
22   Hotel Guntur
23   Hotel Patradissa II
27   Sakardana International
     Travellers Homestay
28   Hotel Trio Sukarna
29   Hotel Melati I
31   Hotel Surabaya
32   Le Yossie Homestay
33   By Moritz
34   Hotel Melati II
37   Hotel Panghegar
41   Hotel Istana
47   Hotel Trio
56   Hotel Braga
59   Grand Hotel Preanger
68   Savoy Homann Hotel
73   Hotel Harapan
73   Hotel Mawar
74   Hotel Pangang Sari
75   Hotel Pasifik
76   Hotel Brajawijaya
77   Hotel Tjiandjur

PLACES TO EAT

1   Tizi's
12   Babakan Siliwangi
24   Soyoyo
25   Rumah Makan Mandarin
30   Warungs & Restaurants
35   Pasar Baru
38   Braga Permai Cafe
42   Sumber Hidangan
     Bakery
43   Rasa Bakery
44   Sindang Reret Restaurant
45   Canary Bakery
46   French Bakery
48   Njonja Rumah Restaurant
53   Braga Restaurant & Pub
62   Dunkin' Donuts
66   Sari Bundo Restaurant
67   Queen Restaurant
69   Hoka Hoka Bento
71   Warung Nasi Mang Udju
72   Rumah Makan Karfika Jaya

OTHER

3   Jean Shops
4   Zoo
5   ITB
6   Kramatdjati Buses
8   Museum Geologi
     (Geological Museum)
9   Gedung Sate (Regional
     Government Building)
11   Balesi Supermarket
13   Pasar Ujungberung
14   Bandung Cepat Buses
16   Bouraq Office
19   Plaza Bandung Indah
     Shopping Mall
19   Government Building
23   Railway Station
24   4848 Taxis
36   4848 Taxis
39   British Council
40   Museum Mandala Wangsit
     (Army Museum)
49   Ramayana Department Store
50   Main Post Office
51   Ramayana Department Store
     & Supermarket
54   Gedung Merdeka
55   Sarinah Department Store
57   Wartel Telephone Office
58   Merpati Office
60   Rumentan Siang
61   Golden Megah Corp
     Moneychanger
63   Layoyo
64   Visitor Information Centre
65   Palaguna Shopping Centre
69   King's Department Store
78   Kebun Kelapa Bus Station
79   Sangar Langen Selna

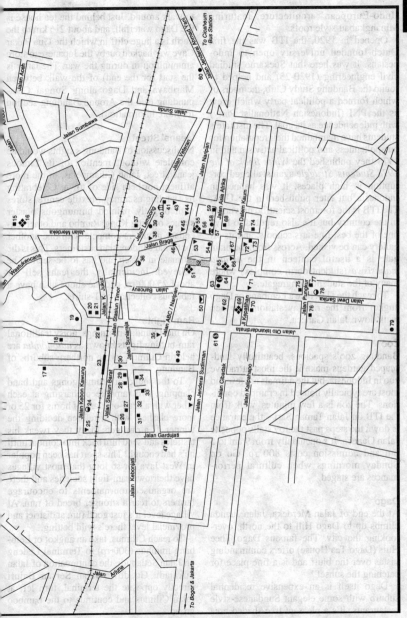

'Indo-European' architecture, featuring Minangkabau-style roofs.

Opened in 1920, the ITB was the first Dutch-founded university open to Indonesians. It was here that Soekarno studied civil engineering (1920-25) and helped to found the Bandung Study Club, members of which formed a political party which grew as the PNI (Indonesian Nationalist Party) with independence as its goal. The institute's students have maintained their reputation for outspokenness and political activism and in 1978 they published the *White Book of the 1978 Students' Struggle* against alleged corruption in high places. It was banned in Indonesia but later published in the USA. The ITB is the foremost scientific university in the country but it's also reputed to have one of the best fine-arts schools, and its art gallery can be visited. Across from the main gate is a useful canteen in the *asrama mahasiswa* (student dorm complex) where many of the students congregate.

To reach the ITB, take a Lembang or Dago angkot from the railway station and then walk down Jalan Ganeca.

Zoo

Bandung zoo's spacious, beautifully landscaped gardens make it the most attractive zoo in Indonesia, but the animals are few and most are typically housed in cramped conditions. The zoo is a few minutes' walk from the ITB on Jalan Taman Sari – the entrance is down the steps past the toy stalls opposite Jalan Ganeca. It's open daily from 9 am to 5 pm and admission costs 800 rp. Go on Sunday mornings when cultural performances are staged.

Dago

At the end of Jalan Merdeka, Jalan Juanda climbs up to Dago Hill to the north, overlooking the city. The famous Dago Thee Huis (Dago Tea House) offers commanding vistas over the bluff and is a fine place for catching the sunset.

Dago itself is an expensive residential suburb with some elegant Sundanese-style restaurants. It's a pleasant tree-shaded area

to walk around. Just behind the tea house is the Dago waterfall, and about 2½ km to the north is a huge cliff in which the Gua Pakar Cave was hacked out by the Japanese to store ammunition in during the war. The latter is the start (or the end) of the walk between Maribaya and Dago along Sungai Cikapundung (see the Around Bandung section for more information).

'Jeans' Street

No discussion of Bandung's sights would be complete without mention of its famous jeans street, Jalan Cihampelas, in the more affluent northern side of town. Celebrating its standing as a major textile centre, stores with brightly painted humungous plaster statues of King Kong, Rambo and other legendary monsters compete with one another for teenage Indonesian customers. This is the ultimate in kitsch and has to be seen to be believed. Incidentally, the jeans sell for about 25,000 rp, and the shops also have a fabulous collection of T-shirts.

Ram Fights

On most Sunday mornings, noisy traditional ram-butting fights known as *adu domba* are held in Cilimus, in the northern suburbs of Bandung.

To the sound of drums, gongs and hand clapping, two rams keep charging at each other with a head-on clash of horns for 25 or more clashes, with a referee deciding the winner. If a ram gets dizzy they tweak his testicles and send him back into combat until he's had enough! This sport has been popular in West Java for so long that most villages have their own ram-fight societies and there are organised tournaments to encourage farmers to rear a stronger breed of ram. At village level it's just good fun; at district and provincial level there's wild betting.

To reach Cilimus, take an angkot or Lembang minibus (300 rp) to Terminal Ledeng on Jalan Setiabudi, the continuation of Jalan Sukajadi. Go down Jalan Sersan Bajuri directly opposite the terminal, turn left at Jalan Cilimus and continue to the bamboo grove.

Places to Stay – bottom end

Bandung's hotels are fairly expensive but Jalan Kebonjati, near the railway station and the city centre, has some good options. The new, German-run *By Moritz* (☎ 437264), Kompleks Luxor Permai 18, Jalan Kebonjati, is an excellent, well-managed travellers' hotel. Dorm beds cost 5000 rp and immaculate singles/doubles are 10,500/ 15,000 rp. Breakfast is included.

Le Yossie Homestay (☎ 4205453), 53 Jalan Kebonjati, is another new place and good value, though not as well run as the By Moritz. A dorm bed costs 4000 rp per person; and singles/doubles/triples are available for 8500/12,000/15,000 rp. The rooms are light, free tea and coffee are provided and there is a downstairs cafe.

Other guesthouse options are the two Sakadarnas. At Jalan Kebonjati 34, the *Sakardana International Travellers Homestay* is a good information source and has a good restaurant. It used to be the place to stay though it's looking a little tired. It's clean with dorm beds at 4000 rp or basic doubles at 10,000 rp. The original *Losmen Sakardana* (☎ 439897) is down a little alley beside the Hotel Melati I at No 50/7B. Basic but well-kept rooms are 7000/11,000 rp.

Jalan Kebonjati also has a few hotels. The *Hotel Surabaya* (☎ 444133), at No 71, is a rambling old hotel with plenty of colonial ambience (check out the old photographs in the lobby) but is rather run down. Cheaper, spartan rooms without bath are 10,000/ 17,500 rp or 15,000/20,000 rp with bath; more expensive rooms in the 'renovated' section range up to 45,000 rp, but are only marginally better.

A few hotels, mostly mid-range, are near the Kebun Kelapa bus station. The pick of these is the well-run *Hotel Tjiandjur* (☎ 446384), 60 Jalan Pungkur, with rooms for 15,000 rp or 20,000/25,000 rp with bath.

Other places include *Wisma Remaja* in a government youth centre at Jalan Merdeka 64, next to the big Plaza Bandung Indah shopping mall. A bed costs 7500 rp per person in twin or triple rooms. It is good value, but can be crowded. It's a 20-minute walk from the railway station or you can take a Dago minibus and ask for the youth centre, Gelanggang Generasi Muda Bandung.

Places to Stay – middle

North of the railway station leading off Jalan Kebon Kawung, the *Hotel Nugraha* (☎ 436146), at Jalan H Mesri 11, is an attractive Balinese-style hotel. Pleasant rooms around an indoor garden are 30,000 rp without bath or 40,000 rp with bath and TV, but they need maintenance.

A block away, the popular *Hotel Patradissa* (☎ 4206680), at Jalan H Moch Iskat 8, has clean, modern rooms with bath. Small singles are 15,000 rp, larger singles 20,000 rp, while doubles range from 25,000 rp up to 50,000 rp. *Hotel Patradissa II* (☎ 4202645), Jalan Pasirkaliki 12, just around the corner from Jalan Kebonjati, is a new offshoot that offers spotless rooms with attached bathroom and hot water showers for 25,000 rp, including breakfast. A good deal.

At Jalan Oto Iskandardinata 20, the *Hotel Guntur* (☎ 443763) is a good hotel with a pleasant garden. Doubles with bath, hot water and TV are 37,000 rp and 40,000 rp.

Wisma Asri (☎ 707131), Jalan Merak 5, is a delightful, older-style guesthouse out near the Gedung Sate. Very comfortable rooms without bath cost 35,000 to 38,000 rp and deluxe rooms with air-con, fridge, TV and hot water are around 55,000 rp, all plus 16%.

Places to Stay – top end

All of the following have swimming pools and add an additional 21% tax and service charge. Bookings are advisable for weekends.

The *Savoy Homann Hotel* (☎ 432244) is conveniently central at Jalan Asia Afrika 112. Once 'the' hotel of Bandung, it is still a stylish old Art Deco building with spacious rooms off a small courtyard garden. Singles/doubles with bathroom cost US$90/100 or 'superior' rooms are US$105. The hotel has a garden restaurant and superb Art Deco dining room facing the street.

Built in 1928, the *Grand Hotel Preanger* (☎ 431631), at Jalan Asia Afrika 181, competes with the Savoy Homann for colonial style. It doesn't quite match the Savoy Homann on that score but it is Bandung's best hotel. Rooms in the new tower cost US$110/140 or the superb rooms in the old wing are US$170.

The *Hotel Panghegar* (☎ 447751) at Jalan Merdeka 2 is a popular business hotel and has all the modern facilities. Rooms cost from US$75/80.

The *Sheraton Inn* (☎ 2500303) at Jalan Juanda 390 is a typical Sheraton with all the modern amenities, such as a swimming pool, gym and satellite TV. Standard rooms run at US$90.

Places to Eat

Bandung has some excellent food venues. In the railway station area, the restaurant at *Sakardana International Travellers Home-stay*, at Jalan Kebonjati 34, is popular, even among travellers who aren't staying there. Directly in front of the railway station, in the area where the bemos stop between the station and Jalan Kebonjati, is a selection of good night-time warungs and restaurants.

A lively area for night-time cheap eats is on Jalan Gardujati, just around the corner from Jalan Kebonjati, opposite the Hotel Trio. You'll find a whole string of good street-side warungs and a selection of Chinese restaurants.

Restaurants in the centre of town can be fairly expensive, but for excellent warung food head for the night warungs on Jalan Cikapundung Barat, across from the alun alun near the Ramayana department store. There are stalls for all kinds of food, from soto and sate to gado-gado and seafood, and probably the number-one *martabak manis* in Java. Nearby on the ground floor in the Ramayana department store is a good, squeaky clean food-stall area open in the daytime and evening.

Bandung also has a number of excellent Chinese restaurants. The *Rumah Makan Mandarin*, on Jalan Kebon Kawung, is a no-frills place with excellent dishes served in steaming cast-iron pans. Seafood is a spe-

ciality and the restaurant is popular with Bandung's Chinese community.

Jalan Braga has a string of fancy coffee shops and bakeries where you can indulge yourself in a sort of east-west food fantasy. The centrepiece of this quasi-European avenue is the *Braga Permai* sidewalk cafe at No 74. Most meals are in the 6000 to 12,000 rp range, with simpler dishes like nasi goreng, sandwiches, plus a variety of cakes and superb ice cream. At No 17 is the *Braga Restaurant & Pub*, a shiny place with reasonable Indian, Indonesian and light Western meals. On the corner of Jalan Braga and Jalan ABC/Naripan is the *Canary Bakery*, with hamburgers and Western fare; the upstairs balcony is pleasant, if a little noisy. A little further along are the *Sumber Hidangan Bakery* and the *French Bakery*, good places for a snack or light meal – try croissants, Danish pastries or chicken curry puffs.

Apart from the Westernised places along Jalan Braga, the shopping malls also have plenty of fast food. Plaza Bandung Indah on Jalan Merdeka also has a host of Western-style eateries, including a *McDonald's*.

For modestly priced Padang food, eat at *Sari Bundo Restaurant*, Jalan Dalem Kaum 75. All the big hotels have restaurants – for a minor splurge with style try the rijsttafel in the *Savoy Homann Hotel* restaurant. The up-market *Tizi's* on Jalan Juanda is well known for its steaks and German breads.

Sundanese Restaurants Bandung is a good place to try traditional Sundanese food. The *Warung Nasi Mang Udju*, on Jalan Dewi Sartika just south of the square, is a simple place, but the food is excellent and you can eat well for about 3500 rp.

For a real treat, take a taxi to the Dago area in the north of the city to the lovely *Peni-neungan Endah*, Jalan Tubagus Ismail Raya 60. Here, each party has its own individual tearoom in which to try Sundanese food, surrounded by Japanese-style gardens bounded by tranquil brooks. From the waters which surround your teahouse, sizeable goldfish are freshly netted to serve as the Sundanese delicacy *ikan mas*. Delicious!

Tojoyo, Jalan Juanda 64, is housed in a 1920s Dutch villa and has a pleasant porch area and a wide range of Sundanese dishes. It is moderately priced, despite the expensive cars parked out front.

The *Sindang Reret Restaurant*, Jalan Naripan 9, just around the corner from Jalan Braga, is central and has good, but slightly expensive Sundanese food. It is noted more for its Saturday-night cultural performances.

Entertainment

Bandung is an excellent place to see Sundanese performing arts. Many performance are irregular – the visitor's information office can tell you when events are on, and also knows of special programmes.

Wayang golek puppet performances are held every other Saturday night at *Rumentang Siang*, Jalan Baranangsiang 1, near Pasar Kosambi on Jalan Ahmad Yani. They cost 2000 rp and are presented between 9 pm and 4 am. You can also catch a scaled-down exhibition with a meal every Saturday night from 7 to 11 pm at the *Sindang Reret Restaurant*, Jalan Naripan 9.

Sundanese dance is held every Wednesday and Saturday at 7.30 pm at the *Hotel Panghegar*, for the price of the hotel's expensive dinners. Some of the other large hotels, including the *Grand Hotel Preanger* on Jalan Asia Afrika, also have programmes of Sundanese music and dancing.

Sanggar Langen Selna, Jalan Oto Iskandar-dinata 541A, is a Jaipongan dance club that features Ketuktilu and Jaipongan every evening from 9 pm to 2 am. A cover charge applies and if you join the performers for a dance, 1000 rp is added to your bill for each song. The club is about one km south of the Kebon Kelapa bus station. While owing much to traditional dance, Jaipongan is a modern social dance and hostesses dance primarily to entertain male clients – something like traditional bar girls.

Every Sunday at the zoo, from 9 am to noon, traditional performances such as pencak silat or wayang golek are held. The

Museum Negeri Propinsi Jawa Barat (West Java Cultural Museum) also has occasional performances.

The *ASTI-Bandung* (or Kokar-Konservatori Karawitan), also in the southern part of the city at Jalan Buah Batu 212, is a school for traditional Sundanese arts – music, dancing and pencak silat (the art of self defence). Check with the tourist office for events, or it is open to interested visitors every morning, except Sunday. You can get there by Buah Batu angkot from Kebun Kelapa bus station.

Pak Ujo's *Saung Angklung* ('Bamboo Workshop') (☎ 71714), on Jalan Padasuka, has angklung performances some afternoons at 3.30 pm, but it's expensive at 7500 rp and tailored to Western tastes. To get there, take a Damri city bus towards Cicaheum and ask for 'Saung Angklung' or 'Pak Ujo'. Some drivers may only know the stop called 'Padasuka' – ask directions from there.

Things to Buy

In the centre of town, down a small alley behind Jalan Pangarang 22, near the Hotel Mawar, Pak Ruhiyat at No 78/17B produces wayang golek puppets and masks and you can see them being carved.

The Cupu Manik puppet factory is on Gang Haji Umar, off Jalan Kebon Kawung just north of the railway station. Traditional Sundanese musical instruments can be bought at Pak Ujo's Saung Angklung (Bamboo Workshop) or the Toko Musik at Gang Suniaraja 3, off Jalan ABC.

Jalan Cibaduyut, in south-west Bandung, is to shoes as Jalan Cihampelas is to jeans, but without the gaudy statues. Dozens of shops sell high-quality shoes and bags at competitive prices.

Jalan Braga used to be the exclusive shopping street of Bandung, though it is fairly quiet these days. Jakarta's Sarinah department store has a small branch here with a broad selection of crafts. The Leather Palace, Jalan Braga 113, is known for its custom-made coats, bags and shoes.

These days the shopping malls dominate the town – Plaza Bandung Indah is Bandung's biggest and brightest mall. For everyday goods, the liveliest shopping district is on Jalan Dalem Kaum and nearby streets, just west of the alun alun. Supermarkets can be found in the Ramayana department stores on Jalan Cikapundung Barat and Jalan Dalem Kaum, and in the Plaza Bandung Indah.

Pasar Baru is Bandung's big, somewhat grotty central market, with fruit, vegetables and all manner of goods. Bandung's title of the 'City of Flowers' comes true at the flower market on Jalan Wastukencana, on the way to the zoo. Pasar Jatayu, one km west of the railway station on Jalan Arjuna, is a flea market where you may be able to find some collectibles if you sift through the junk.

Getting There & Away

Air Garuda, Bouraq and Merpati fly from Bandung to Jakarta for 48,000 rp. You can also fly to Yogyakarta with Bouraq for 71,000 rp.

The Merpati/Garuda office (☎ 441226) is at Jalan Asia Afrika 73, opposite the Savoy Homann Hotel. The Bouraq office (☎ 437896) is at Jalan Cihampelas 27. Sempati (☎ 430477) is in the Hotel Panghegar, Jalan Merdeka 2.

Bus Kebun Kelapa bus station, on Jalan Dewi Sartika, about 10 minutes' walk south of the city square, has buses to the west to places like Bogor (2600 rp; 3½ hours), Sukabumi (1900 rp; three hours) and Jakarta. Buses to Bogor are not allowed to take the scenic Puncak Pass route on weekends when the trip is slower and costs more. To Jakarta's Kampung Rambutan terminal the fare is 3200 rp (air-con 7200 rp) and by the Jagorawi Highway it only takes about four hours. Door-to-door minibuses to Bogor via Puncak (11,000 rp; four hours) are operated by Suci (☎ 305892) and Erny Travel (☎ 639860).

Buses to the east leave from the Cicaheum bus station, on the eastern outskirts of the city. Normal/air-con buses go to Cirebon (2200/3600 rp; 3½ hours), Garut (1100 rp; two hours), Tasikmalaya (2000/3000 rp; four hours), Banjar (3000/4500 rp; five hours)

and Yogya (8000/13,500 rp; 12 hours). Most departures to Yogya leave around 3 to 7 pm.

For luxury buses, conveniently located companies include Bandung Cepat, Jalan Doktor Cipto 5, with departures at 7 pm to Yogya, and Kramatdjati (☎ 2502317) on Jalan Juanda near the ITB. Kramatdjati has buses to Jakarta (8000 rp), Yogya (16,000 rp), Solo (16,000 rp), Semarang (16,000 rp), Malang (34,000 rp), Surabaya (30,000 rp) and Denpasar (45,000 rp). Ring for departure times.

For Pangandaran, by public bus you must change in Tasikmalaya or Banjar then take another bus. Alternatively, Sari Bhakti have air-con buses from Bandung's Cicaheum bus station to Pangandaran at 6 am, noon and 6 pm for 7500 rp. Budiman has non air-con, express buses at 6 and 9 am, and 3 and 6 pm for 5500 rp. Easiest of all are the door-to-door minibuses operated by Sari Harum (☎ 708110), Jalan Ahmad Yani 279. They leave for Pangandaran at 6 am and 2 pm and cost 9000 rp for the non air-con service or 11,000 rp for the much better air-con minibuses. Ring for pick up, or hotels make bookings but charge extra.

Apart from the regular buses, 4848 Taxis has door-to-door services between Jakarta and Bandung for 11,000 rp per person or 65,000 rp per taxi. They leave from the 4848 Taxis office (☎ 434848), Jalan Suniaraja Timur 14, east of the railway station. From this office there is also an eight-seater, air-con minibus to Yogya (19,000 rp; nine hours) at 8 pm. From another 4848 Taxis office (☎ 420 8448), on Jalan Kebon Kawung north of the railway line, minibuses go to Pangandaran (7900 rp) at 7 am and 2 pm, Cirebon (5500 rp), Garut (3500 rp) and other destinations. These are cramped 14-seater minibuses without air-con.

Train The efficient *Parahyangan* service is the best way to travel between Jakarta and Bandung. From Gambir station in Jakarta trains depart at 5.05, 5.30 and 7.30 am, and then every hour until 6.30 pm. Trains depart Bandung every hour from 4 am to 5 pm. Fares are 12,000 rp in bisnis class, 23,000 rp in eksekutif and it's a comfortable, hassle-free train for the three-hour trip. Though the train avoids the hills around the Puncak, it cuts east of the huge dam and lake at Jatiluhur, and the views are quite spectacular at times along this route.

To Yogya, the *Badra Surya* (5000 rp ekonomi; eight hours) departs at 5.30 am. The *Cepat Yogya* (4500 rp ekonomi, 9½ hours) departs at 8.30 am, the more comfortable *Pajajaran* (14,000 rp bisnis; 7¾ hours) departs at 7.30 am or the *Kahuripan* (7000 rp ekonomi; 7½ hours) departs at 10.30 pm. Expect delays, especially for the ekonomi trains. The luxurious *Mutiara Selatan* is a night express train that leaves Bandung at 5.30 pm and arrives in Yogya at 12.54 am. It costs 21,000 rp bisnis or 36,000 rp eksekutif, but bookings should be made up to a week in advance. All but the *Cepat Yogya* continue on to Solo.

Getting Around

To/From the Airport Bandung's Husein Sastranegara airport is four km north-west of town, about half an hour away and 5000 rp by taxi.

Bus Bandung has a fairly good, if crowded, Damri city bus service which charges a fixed 250 rp. The most useful service is the Cicaheum-Kebon Kelapa bus, which operates between 7 am and about 9 pm. It runs between Cicaheum and Kebon Kelapa bus terminals via Jalan Asia Afrika and Jalan Jenderal A Yani.

Angkot, Becak & Taxi Downtown bemos (angkots) run set routes all over town between numerous terminals. Stasiun Hall terminal is on the southern side of the railway station and from here angkots go to Dago, Ledeng and other terminals. When returning catch any angkot showing 'St Hall'. Abdul Muis ('Abd Muis'), at the Kebon Kelapa bus station, is the other central terminal, with angkots to Dago, Ledeng, Cicaheum bus station and other terminals. Angkot fares range from 200 to 500 rp depending on the length of journey – most trips cost around 300 rp.

From the terminal outside the railway station, colts also run to Lembang and Subang (for Tangkuban Prahu and Ciater).

As in other cities the becaks are being relegated to the back streets and are no longer seen in great numbers. From the railway station to the alun alun will cost around 1000 to 1500 rp depending on bargaining skills.

Taxis are numerous and metered.

NORTH OF BANDUNG

Lembang

On the road to Tangkuban Prahu, 16 km north of Bandung, Lembang was once a hill resort though most visitors now keep heading further up into the hills.

Places to Stay The *Grand Hotel Lembang* (☎ 286671), Jalan Raya Lembang 272, harks back to the days when Lembang was a fashionable resort for Bandung's Dutch community. It is old-fashioned and comfortable with beautiful gardens, a swimming pool and tennis courts, as well as a pleasant bar and a restaurant. Standard rooms in the new wing cost 90,000 rp, although there are some economy rooms with shared bath in the old wing for 34,000 rp, or 47,000 rp with bath.

Maribaya Hot Springs

Maribaya, five km east of Lembang, has a thermal spa, landscaped gardens and a thundering waterfall. It's another tourist spot, crowded on Sundays, but worth visiting. You can extend your Tangkuban Prahu trip by walking from the bottom end of the gardens down through a brilliant, deep and wooded river gorge all the way to Dago. There's a good track and if you allow about two to three hours for the walk (six km) you can be at a Dago vantage point for sunset. From there it's only a short trip by colt back into Bandung.

Tangkuban Prahu

The 'overturned prahu' volcano crater stands 30 km north of Bandung. Years ago the centre of Tangkuban Prahu collapsed under the weight of built-up ash and, instead of the usual conical volcano shape, it has a flat elongated summit with a huge caldera more than seven km across.

There is, of course, a legend to explain this phenomenon.

An estranged young prince returned home and unwittingly fell in love with his own mother. When the queen discovered the terrible truth of her lover's identity she challenged him to build a dam and a huge boat during a single night before she would agree to marry him. Seeing that the young man was about to complete this impossible task, she called on the gods to bring the sun up early and as the cocks began to crow the boat builder turned his nearly completed boat over in a fit of anger.

Tangkuban Prahu still simmers and bubbles, sending up noxious sulphurous fumes. Its last serious eruption was in 1969.

Tangkuban Prahu is easily accessible by car, so it's very much a tourist attraction. Up at the crater there are car parks and warungs. A helpful information centre is at the top and a parade of peddlers hustling postcards, souvenirs and other junk are further down. While the scene is still more commercial than most other Javanese volcanoes, you can escape this bedlam of activity, and Tangkuban Prahu is an impressive sight.

The main crater is divided into two parts.

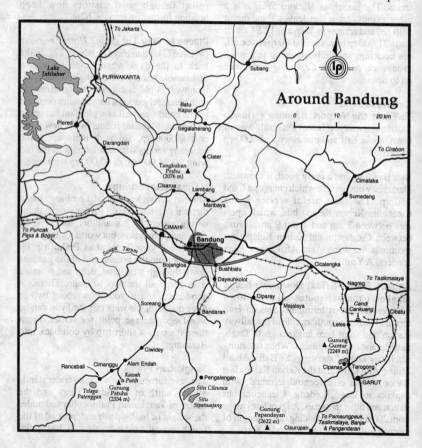

Around Bandung

Ignoring the obnoxious guides, walk away from the car park around the rim of the first part for almost 20 minutes before the second is fully visible. From the top you can also head off across country towards Ciater.

Getting There & Away At 1830 metres, Tangkuban Prahu can be quite cool and around noon the mist starts to roll in through the trees so try to go early. From Bandung's minibus station in front of the railway station, take a Subang colt (1200 rp) via Lembang to the park entrance. Entry is 1250 rp per person. Minibuses go to the top for 1000 rp per person – go in the morning when there is a better chance of sharing with other passengers or you'll have to charter. Traffic is heavy throughout the day on Sundays. Or you can walk. It's four km along the road or it's possible to take the more interesting shortcut through the jungle. There's no need for a guide; start up the road and take the first turning on the right. The path leads through the jungle to the Kawah Domas crater, an active open area of bubbling hot geysers, and another steep path with steps cut up to the main crater.

An alternative is to get dropped off at Bukit Jayagiri, just outside Lembang, and from there you can walk up through the forest to the crater (about eight km).

Drivers in Bandung can be bargained down to around 40,000 rp for a visit to Tangkuban Prahu, including petrol but excluding entry (4300 rp for a sedan or minibus).

Ciater Hot Springs
Eight km north-east of Tangkuban Prahu, Ciater is a pretty little place in the middle of huge tea and clove estates. The area has good walks and a tea factory on the south side of Ciater can be visited.

At the end of the road through the village, Ciater's main attraction is the **Sari Ater Hot Spring Resort**. Although quite commercialised, the pools are probably the best of all the hot springs around Bandung and if you've been climbing around the volcano on a cool, rainy day there's no better way to get

warm. There is a 1500 rp admission into the resort area and it costs extra to use the pool. You can walk to Ciater – about 12 km across country – from the main crater of Tangkuban Prahu, or flag down a colt (300 rp) at the entrance point.

From Ciater is it possible to visit the less-commercialised **Batu Kapur Hot Springs**, 10 km west from the main road on the way north to Subang. From Ciater take a colt to the Jalan Cagak junction (400 rp), then another to Segalaherang (250 rp), from where ojek (1000 rp) will take you to the hot springs.

Places to Stay The big *Sari Ater Hot Springs Resort* (☎ 200319) has a variety of rustic, bamboo bungalows spread out in spacious grounds. It has all the facilities of a big hotel, but the rooms are losing their shine. Most cost from US$43 to US$100, plus 15.5% and around 20% more on weekends.

Ciater has plenty of small penginapan with rooms starting at around 15,000 rp – the ones on the main road are cheaper. *Hotel Permata Sari* (☎ 203891) is close to the hot springs and has rooms for 20,000 rp without bath, 35,000 rp with bath and cottages with kitchens for 50,000 rp and 80,000 rp.

Lake Jatiluhur & Dam
This artificial lake *(waduk* in Indonesian), 70 km north-west of Bandung in the hills near Purwakarta, is a popular resort for swimming, boating and water-skiing. The tourist blurb certainly raves about the giant Jatiluhur Dam which stretches 1200 metres across, is 100 metres high, and has created a lake some 80 hectares in surface area. It's part of a hydro-electric generating system supplying Jakarta and West Java and also providing irrigation water for a large area of the province. Jatiluhur is also the site of the country's ITT earth satellite station, opened in 1969. The village was built by the French for their staff when they were building the dam. Purwakarta is the access point either from Jakarta (125 km by rail or road) or from Bandung (by road).

SOUTH OF BANDUNG

The mountains south of Bandung also have popular weekend retreats, though the area is less developed compared with the resorts north of the city. The picturesque road south of Bandung through Bojongloa leads to **Ciwidey**, a small town noted for its metal-working, especially knives, and for its stylish Sundanese restaurants.

The road winds through the hills to the turn-off to **Kawah Putih**, a volcanic crater with a beautiful turquoise lake. The turn-off is six km before Rancabali, and then it is eight km to the small crater lake just below Gunung Patuha (2334 metres). Though only a small crater, Kawah Putih is exceptionally beautiful and eerily quiet when the mists roll in and mingle with the steam of the warm lake and the bubbling sulphur deposits.

Back on the road a few km further south are the hot springs at **Cimanggu**, with landscaped gardens and large swimming pools filled by hot water piped from the springs on Gunung Patuha. A little further is the Walini Hot Springs, which also has a hot water pool.

Rancabali, 42 km from Bandung, is a tea-estate town surrounded by the rolling green hills of the tea plantations. Just two km south of the town is **Telaga Patenggang**, a pretty lake lined with boats available for a leisurely row. You can take a stroll around the lake and in the nearby forest area, and warungs and tea rooms cater to the Sunday crowds.

Also south of Bandung, **Situ Cileunca** is an artificial lake damned for a hydro-electric scheme.

Places to Stay

Accommodation is limited, and empty during the week. In Ciwidey, *Penginapan Sederhana* on the main road opposite the market has dismal rooms for 6000 rp. The *Sindang Reret Hotel* (☎ 237602) and *Motel Sukarasa Endah* (☎ 610601) are both on the highway north of town and have large Sundanese restaurants built over fish ponds. The Sindang Reret is slightly better and has comfortable rooms with hot water showers from 38,500 to 71,500 rp.

At Alam Endah ('Beautiful Nature'), about five km south of Ciwidey, you can stay at the *Pondok Endah Sari* on the main road. Basic rooms are expensive at 15,000 rp. *Pondok Taman Unyil Lestari*, half a km from the main road, has rooms and thatched cottages for 25,000 to 40,000 rp, plus 10%. The rooms are ordinary for the price, but compensated by fine views, a nice garden and a good restaurant.

Getting There & Away

Frequent buses run between Bandung's Kebon Kelapa station and Ciwidey (700 rp, 1½ hours). From Ciwidey local angkots run to Telaga Patenggang (800 rp). Kawah Putih is not serviced by regular public transport, but you'll find plenty of ojeks in Alam Endah.

BANDUNG TO PANGANDARAN

Heading south-east from Bandung, the road passes through a scenic and fertile stretch of hilly countryside and volcanic peaks. This is the Bandung-Yogya road as far as Banjar; the Bandung to Yogya railway line passes through Tasikmalaya and Banjar, but not Garut. The district is part of the Parahyangan highlands around Bandung.

Garut

Sixty-three km south-east of Bandung, Garut is a highland town and a centre for vegetable, orange, tea and tobacco growing. The town is ringed by impressive volcanic peaks that have provided the valley's fertility. Garut itself is just another town, but the surrounding area has a number of attractions.

On the outskirts of town, six km to the north-west, are the hot springs at **Cipanas**, a small resort at the foot of Gunung Guntur and an ideal base to explore the area. From Cipanas, the **Curug Citiis** waterfall is a one-hour walk away up the mountain and it is possible to walk all the way to the peak of Gunung Guntur.

Ngamplang, five km on the south-eastern outskirts of Garut, has a nine-hole golf course and adu domba (ram fights) are held here on the 1st and 3rd Sundays of the month.

Garut is famed for its *dodol* – a confectionery made of coconut milk, palm sugar and sticky rice. At the bus station hawkers selling tubes of sweet dodol besiege the passing buses and it's sold at many shops around town. The 'Picnic' brand is the best quality, and it is possible to visit the Picnic factory on Jalan Pasundan.

Places to Stay Garut has plenty of hotels and guesthouses, but Cipanas is the nicest place to stay.

In the centre of Garut, *Wisma PKPN* (☎ 21508), Jalan Ciledug 79, has clean rooms with attached mandi for 11,000 rp, but some bargaining may be required. *Penginapan Kota Baru* is a passable, cheap hotel on Jalan Merdeka near the bus station. The pleasant *Sarimbit Guest House* (☎ 21033), Jalan Oto Iskandardinata 236, is on the outskirts of town in Taragong, on the way to Cipanas. Rooms with attached bathroom are 10,000/15,000 rp and 15,000/20,000 rp, plus 10% tax. Meals are available and they can arrange tours.

Cipanas has over a dozen hotels strung along Jalan Raya Cipanas, the resort's single road. All have rooms with large baths with water piped in from the hot springs – pamper yourself after a hard day's trekking. The *Penginapan Cipta Rasa* (☎ 21351) is the best bet for a cheap hotel with good rooms for 10,000 rp or five-bed rooms for 50,000 rp. Rates double on weekends. Other reasonable, cheaper hotels are the *Pondok Kurnia Artha*, *Hotel Tirta Merta* and *Hotel Banyu Arta*.

As well as hot baths, the following hotels have swimming pools heated by the springs. Tax and service are added to the rates. *Cipanas Indah* (☎ 81736) is a reasonable mid-range hotel favoured by tour groups. Rooms start at 30,500 rp and good VIP rooms are 44,000 rp (around 5000 rp more on weekends). The *Sumber Alam* (☎ 21027) is the most attractive hotel with rooms built over the water. Rooms range from 27,000 to 150,000 rp (50% more on weekends).

Getting There & Away Buses and angkots

leave from Garut's Terminal Guntur, in the north of town. Garut is easily reached by bus from Bandung (1100 rp, two hours) and Tasikmalaya (1000 rp, two hours). For Pangandaran take another bus from Tasikmalaya. Buses also go to Jakarta (4000 rp or 7500 rp express).

Regular angkots run around town (300 rp), including Cipanas and Ngamplang, and to the nearby villages.

Around Garut
Near Leles, about 10 km north of Garut, is **Candi Cangkuang**, one of the few stone Hindu temples found in West Java. Dating from the 8th century, some of its stones were found to have been carved into tombstones for a nearby Islamic cemetery. The small, restored temple lies on the edge of Situ Cangkuang, a small lake, and has become something of a tourist trap. From Garut take a No 10 angkot to Leles on the highway and then an andong for the four km to Candi Cangkuang. Boats across the lake to the temple want 6000 rp.

Twenty-eight km to the south-west, **Gunung Papandayan** (2662 metres) is one of the most active volcanoes in West Java. Papandayan has only existed since 1772 when a large piece of the mountain exploded sideways in a catastrophe that killed more than 3000 people. It last erupted in 1925. The bubbling yellow crater (Kawah Papandayan) just below the peak is an impressive sight and clearly visible from Garut valley on fine mornings. To get there, take Cikajang minibus and get down at the turn-off on the outskirts of Cisurupan where you can catch a waiting ojek (2500 rp; 13 km). From the car-park area it is an easy half-hour walk to the crater. For fine views, go very early in the morning before the clouds roll in. Gunung Papandayan summit is a two-hour walk beyond the crater, and there are fields of Javan edelweiss near the top. Entry is 1000 rp per person at the PHPA hut. If you want to camp or trek, they can arrange a camping permit, guide and entry for 10,000 rp.

To the east, **Gunung Telagabodas** (2201 metres) has a bubbling bright-green crater lake alive with sulphur. To get to Tela-gabodas, take an angkot to Wanaraja (400 rp), then an ojek (2000 rp) and walk to the crater. Other craters to the west of Garut that can be visited are **Kawah Kamojang**, 23 km away, the site of a geothermal plant, and **Kawah Darajat**, 26 km away.

Pameungpeuk & Around
The picturesque, twisting road south from Garut leads through vegetable plots, tea plantations and pine forests to Pameungpeuk on the south coast. This area has some reasonable beaches, though swimming is usually out of the question. Very few travellers visit the area. Pameungpeuk itself is a fair-sized town – big enough to have a small tourist office, PHPA office and a handful of penginapan.

Pantai Sayang Heulang has an attractive white-coral beach fronting a reef that can be explored on foot at low tide, but swimming is out of the question. The village consists of three penginapan and a few warung and is two km west of Pameungpeuk via the main road, then a further two km down a rough road to the beach.

Further west, **Pantai Santolo** is the best beach, on a sheltered bay where swimming is possible when the sea is calm. Prahus can take you across the river to a small forest reserve on the headland. *Penginapan Citra Agung* is on the main road directly opposite the turn-off and has good rooms with mandi for 10,000 rp.

Isolated **Leuweung Sancang**, 35 km east of Pameungpeuk, is a nature reserve noted for its Banteng, gibbon and jungle trekking. For permits and information check with the PHPA in Pameungpeuk.

Getting There & Away From Garut, regular minibuses go to Pameungpeuk (1500 rp, three hours) and some continue on to Cikelet. To reach Sayang Heulang or Santolo you either have to walk from the main road or catch an ojek from Pameungpeuk.

Tasikmalaya
Sixty km east of Garut, Tasikmalaya is the centre for the district of the same name. It is noted for rattan crafts: palm leaf and bamboo are used to make floormats, baskets, trays, straw hats and paper umbrellas. Tasikmalaya (usually called simply Tasik) also has a small batik industry, and is also noted for its *bordel* lacework and *kelom geulis* (wooden sandals). For travellers, it is merely a transit town on the way to Pangandaran but the surrounding area has a few points of interest.

Places to Stay An inexpensive place to stay is the central *Hotel Kencana*, Jalan Yudanegara 17, close to the mosque with adequate rooms for 9000 rp and 15,000 rp, more on weekends and holidays. Jalan Yudanegara has plenty of other hotels including the *Wisma Galunggung* in an old Dutch house. The best for the price is the *Abadi Hotel* (☎ 33789), Jalan Empang 58. Spotlessly clean rooms with bath cost 15,000 rp, including breakfast.

Getting There & Away From Tasikmalaya buses operate to Bandung (2000/3000 rp; four hours), Garut (1000 rp; 1½ hours), Jakarta (4700/8100 rp; six hours), Banjar, Pangandaran, Cipatujah, Cirebon, etc. Tasikmalaya is also on the main rail line.

Around Tasikmalaya
For cheap rattan crafts, visit the village of **Rajapolah**, 12 km north of Tasikmalaya on the road to Bandung, where many of the weavers work.

Cipanas Galunggung, 20 km to the north-west, is a hot spring at the foot of Gunung Galunggung, a volcano which exploded dramatically in 1982. From the hot springs recreation park, a trail leads to a small waterfall and then on to Galunggung crater, three km away. A road to the crater, suitable only for 4WD vehicles, is an easier walk but less interesting. From Tasikmalaya's main bus station take an angkot to Bantar (300 rp) on the highway and then an ojek (3000 rp) can take you the 14 km along a very bad road.

Situ Lengkong, 40 km north of Tasikmalaya and a half km from the village of

Panjalu, is a serene lake formed when the Hindu ruler of Panjalu damned the valley. A forested island in the middle is home to thousands of flying foxes and contains a shrine dedicated to the rulers of Panjalu. Boats can be hired for around 5000 rp to take you around the island. Panjalu village has a small museum containing the heirlooms of the kings of Panjalu. Siti Lengkong can be reached by bus from Tasikmalaya (1000 rp; one hour) or Terminal Kawali in Ciamis (600 rp, 45 minutes).

Halfway between Tasikmalaya and Garut is **Kampung Naga**, a traditional village and museum piece of Sundanese architecture and village life. The old ways are very much preserved in Kampung Naga – the many tour groups that visit wouldn't come otherwise. Despite the fact that it can be crowded some mornings when the big bus loads arrive, there's no denying the beauty of the place. Kampung Naga with its thatched-roof houses is nestled next to a river and surrounded by steep hills terraced with rice paddies – a photographer's dream. Kampung Naga is 26 km from Garut. From Neglasari on the main highway more than 300 steps lead down into the valley.

Banjar

Banjar, 42 km east of Tasikmalaya, is the junction point where the Pangandaran road branches from the Bandung to Yogya road and rail route. Banjar has some basic hotels if you get stuck en route to Pangandaran – but try not to.

Getting There & Away The railway station is only five minutes' walk from the bus station. Banjar bus station has a bad reputation – watch your gear, and be wary being overcharged on the fare to Pangandaran. From Banjar buses go to Jakarta (5100/8600 rp air-con; 7½ hours), Pangandaran (2000 rp; one hour), Bandung (2900 rp), and Purwokerto (2000 rp). Buses also go from the Banjarsari bus station, half an hour south of Banjar, to Jakarta (9000 rp; seven hours) at 7.30 pm.

Ekspres trains from Banjar to Bandung

(4500 rp; four hours) leave at 5.15 am, 2.55 and 3.15 pm. For Yogya the 12.10 pm train costs 2700 rp ekonomi and takes six hours, more like eight with overruns.

PANGANDARAN

The fishing village of Pangandaran is Java's most popular beach resort. It lies on the narrow isthmus of a peninsula with broad sandy beaches that sweep back along the mainland, and at the end of the bulbous peninsula is the Pangandaran National Park.

On weekends Pangandaran is popular with Bandung residents, and during holidays – Christmas and the end of Ramadan in particular – the beaches have a temporary population of literally thousands. At any other time this is still just an overgrown fishing village where brightly painted prahu fish the waters and whole families work together to pull in the nets. It is an idyllic place to take a break from travelling; the people are exceptionally friendly, accommodation is cheap and the seafood excellent. If lazing around the beaches and trekking through the jungle of the national park begins to pall, you can head off east or west to other quieter beaches and attractions nearby.

As if all this isn't enough, at Pangandaran it's possible to enjoy the unique experience of seeing the sun set and the moon rise over the ocean simultaneously at full moon, and every evening at dusk a mass of fruit bats fly west across the setting sun.

Orientation & Information

Pangandaran extends for about three km from the bus station and market to the national park boundary in the south. The town is flanked by the west and east beaches, and dissected by the main street, Jalan Kidang Pananjung. The west beach is a wide sweep of sand and the main resort strip. The east beach is a quieter, fishing beach, and not much sand remains since a retaining wall was built.

A 1000 rp admission charge is levied at the gates on entering Pangandaran, and it costs

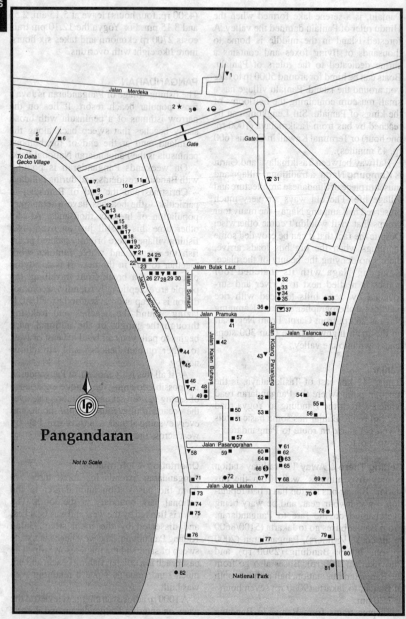

PLACES TO STAY			
	53	Samudra Hotel	58 Rumah Makan Nanjung
5 Yuli Beach Resort	54	Sunrise Beach Hotel	61 Chez Mama Cilicap
6 Bouganville	55	Panorama Hotel	67 Sympathy Cafe
7 Hotel Citra	56	Adem Ayem Hotel	68 Inti Laut
8 Surya Beach Hotel	57	Sari Harum Losmen &	69 Lonely Planet
9 Hideaway		Restaurant	Restaurant
10 Mini 3	59	Pondok Pelangi	
11 Bamboo House	60	Rawamangun Lodge	OTHER
12 Adam's Homestay	62	Setia Famili	
13 Duta Beach Hotel	64	Pondok Pelangi	2 Police Station
15 Putri Duyung Hotel	65	Losmen Mini	3 Market
16 Uni Beach Hotel & Uni	71	Mangkubumi Beach	4 Bus Station
Restaurant		Hotel	31 Telkom Office
17 Inti Laut Hotel & Res-	73	Mangkubumi Indah	32 Cinema
taurant		Hotel	33 Agung Travel
18 Sandaan Hotel	74	Nyiur Indah Hotel &	35 Luta Travel
19 Dahlia Indah Hotel		Restaurant	36 Villa Electric (Minibus
20 Bulak Laut Bungalows	75	Penginapan Saputra	Agent)
22 Bulak Laut Bungalows	76	Pangandaran Beach	37 Post Office
23 Bayu Indah Hotel		Hotel	38 Fish Market
24 Pantai Sari Hotel	77	Pondok Moris	44 Pasar Seni (Souvenir
26 Lambada Hotel	79	Wismawan Beach Hotel	Market)
27 Paradise Hotel			45 Disco
29 Holiday Inn	PLACES TO EAT		49 Bicycle Hire
30 Mutiara Selatan			63 Visitor Information
39 Hotel Bumi Pananjung	1	Hillman's Fish Farm	Centre
40 Pantai Indah Timur		Restaurant	(Guide Service)
Hotel	14	Putri Duyung	66 Bank Rakyat Indonesia
41 Losmen Pusaka	21	Skandinavian	70 Bookshop
42 Wisma Galuh		Restaurant	72 Toha Guide Service
46 Bumi Nusantara Hotel	25	Relax Coffee Shop	78 Fish Market
48 Dewi Laut	28	Bunga Laut Restaurant	(Wholesale)
50 Susan's Guest House	34	Warung Gypsy	80 Souvenir Stalls
51 Losmen Mini Dua	43	Number One	81 PHPA Office
52 Pantai Indah Barat		Restaurant	82 PHPA Office
Hotel	47	Warungs	

another 1000 rp for each visit to the national park.

Tourist Offices Pangandaran has plenty of travel agents and private 'tourist information centres'. They sell bus tickets and arrange good, cheap tours. Most provide a good service, though you may prefer guides registered with the Indonesian Guide Association.

Money The Bank Rakyat Indonesia on Jalan Kidang Pananjung changes most currencies and major brands of travellers' cheques at poor rates. It is open from 7 am to noon Monday to Thursday, and from 7 to 11 am Friday and Saturday. For after-hours' transactions, moneychangers change cash at even poorer rates.

Post & Telecommunications The post office and Telkom office (open 24 hours) are both on Jalan Kidang Pananjung.

Things to See & Do
Cloaked in jungle, **Pangandaran National Park** is teeming with *banteng* (wild cattle), *kijang* (barking deer), hornbill and monkeys, including Javan gibbon, and small bays within the park enclose tree-fringed beaches.

Like most south coast **beaches**, Pangandaran has black-sand beaches and the surf can be treacherous. The northern end of the west beach is dangerous, but the southern end is sheltered by the headland and provides safe swimming. The national park has some sheltered white-sand beaches with rocky reefs for snorkelling at high tide.

Organised Tours

Pangandaran has a host of tour operators that are constantly thinking up new tours and hyperbole to describe them. Tours to the national park are most popular.

Other tours are to Green Canyon (30,000 rp per person), and 'countryside' or 'home industry' tours (15,000 to 25,000 rp), which take you to plantations and local industries to see the making of tofu, krupuk, sugar, etc as well as a wayang golek maker. Then there are cycling, boating, walking, snorkelling tours to just about anywhere within a 50 km radius of Pangandaran. Tours are usually well run, informative and good value.

Places to Stay

Pangandaran has over 100 places to stay. At Christmas and Lebaran (the end of Ramadan) holidays, Pangandaran is packed and prices sky rocket. It can also get busy during school holidays and in the peak European holiday season around July/August, but for much of the year most hotels are empty and Pangandaran is quiet. It's worth asking for a discount in the quiet periods, especially for longer stays.

Places to Stay – bottom end

Most of Pangandaran's cheapest hotels are around the main street at the southern end of town.

Losmen Mini is on the main road, Jalan Kidang Pananjung. It is clean, convenient, popular and singles/doubles with mandi cost 7500/10,000 rp, including a good breakfast.

On Jalan Kalen Buhaya is a second Mini, *Losmen Mini Dua*. This long-popular place is clean but a little cramped and getting overpriced at 7500 rp for a simple room or 15,000 rp for better rooms with attached mandi, including breakfast.

On the eastern beach, the best value is the *Panorama Hotel* (☎ 379098), which straddles the bottom end and mid-range. Pleasant verandah rooms facing the sea cost 15,000/20,000 rp with attached bathroom and breakfast, or rooms behind are 10,000/15,000 rp with shared facilities.

Right near the national park, *Pondok*

Moris (☎ 379490) is in a small, quiet alleyway and has rooms for 10,000/15,000 rp per night. This well-run homestay organises tours.

While the southern end of town has much more of a village atmosphere, the northern end around Jalan Bulak Laut is more popular with travellers. Most places tend to be midrange, but Bulak Laut has some good budget buys.

It is hard to beat the *Holiday Inn* (☎ 379285), Jalan Bulak Laut 50, for value. Good bamboo rooms with individual porches and attached mandi cost 5000/7000 rp, or cheaper rooms upstairs cost 6000 rp. Next door at No 49, *Mutiara Selatan* (☎ 379416) is also good value. Rooms with porch and attached bathroom cost 10,000 rp including breakfast.

Closer to the beach, the popular *Pantai Sari Hotel* (☎ 379175) has downstairs rooms with fan for 10,000/15,000 rp, less for longer stays, but it pays to check a few out as the quality varies considerably. The best value are the very good upstairs rooms with air-con for 20,000 rp – the cheapest air-con rooms in Pangandaran. All rooms have attached bathroom.

Bamboo House (☎ 379419) is to the north and away from the beach, but this small, family-run place is well worth considering. Attractive singles/doubles with mandi are very good for the price – 7500/10,000 rp including breakfast; or there are bungalows for 15,000 rp.

Along the beach road to the west, four km from Pangandaran, *Delta Gecko Village* in Cikembulan is the place to get right away from it all. This travellers' hangout has rooms from 7500 rp, a vegetarian restaurant, bicycles for rent, art shop, etc.

Places to Stay – middle & top end

The west beach strip along Jalan Pamugaran near Jalan Bulak Laut is Pangandaran's Riviera, with a host of good value mid-range hotels popular with Europeans.

An oldie but a goodie is *Bulak Laut Bungalows* (☎ 379171), on the corner of Jalan Pamugaran and Bulak Laut and at the annexe a few doors further north. Attractive bungalows, most with their own sitting rooms, cost 25,000 rp and 30,000 rp, including breakfast. Discounts are available for longer stays, making them exceptional value.

Further north, *Sandaan Hotel* (☎ 379165) has plain fan rooms with shower costing 20,000/30,000 rp for singles/doubles, or more luxurious air-con rooms for 45,000/60,000 rp, including breakfast. The main attractions are the small swimming pool and the good restaurant.

The delightful *Adam's Homestay* (☎ 379164) has eclectic architecture, a book shop and good cappuccinos. This excellent German-run establishment has large rooms for 40,000 rp or luxurious bungalows at the back for 80,000 rp.

Surya Beach Hotel (☎ 379428) is a big resort hotel with a swimming pool, expensive restaurant and rooms for 80,000 rp or luxury suites for 150,000 rp. A few pokey economy rooms and rundown bungalows in the old section are also available.

Yuli Beach Resort (☎ 379375) is a long hike from the nearest restaurant, but it is quiet, has a pool and the boutique bungalows with sunken lounge areas offer some of the best accommodation in Pangandaran. Bungalows cost 60,000 rp, but the rate reduces by 5000 rp per night, down to 40,000 rp for stays of five days or more. Tax and service charges apply.

More mid-range hotels can be found towards the southern end of the west beach.

Pondok Pelangi, around the corner on Jalan Pasanggrahan, has old but comfortable bungalows in an attractive garden, each with a mandi, living room and small terrace. A bungalow with kitchen facilities and two or three bedrooms costs 60,000 to 80,000 rp. They're good for families.

One of Pangandaran's most pleasant hotels is the *Sunrise Beach Hotel* (☎ 379220), at Jalan Kidang Pananjung 175, on the east beach. It has a swimming pool, good restaurant and attractive, sizeable rooms from 42,500 to 57,500 rp for a double with fan, 70,000 to 85,500 rp for a room with air-con.

Across the street from the Sunrise, the *Pantai Indah Barat* (☎ 379006), along with its plush cousin on the east beach *Pantai Indah Timur* (☎ 379327), offer top-of-the-range accommodation; both are usually empty. The Timur has a huge pool and tennis courts, while the Barat has a more modest pool, tennis courts and a restaurant. Attractive air-con rooms with TV, refrigerator and hot water start at 75,000 rp for a standard double at the Barat and 90,000 rp at the Timur.

Places to Eat

Pangandaran has plenty of restaurants catering to Western tastes, with Western-style breakfasts, seafood (shrimps, lobster and fish), pancakes and a variety of fruit juices and fruit salads. Of course, Indonesian dishes are widely available too, as is Chinese seafood. Seafood is usually very good, other meals are of variable quality.

Popular places for cheap eats are the small, warmly lit warungs on Jalan Kidang Pananjung. The basic *Sympathy Cafe* is on the grotty side but is usually packed out because its prices are so reasonable; it serves excellent fruit salads, gado-gado and a variety of grilled fish. Over the road, the *Inti Laut* restaurant serves grilled fish and Indonesian fare. On weekends and holidays it turns over more fish than the average fishing boat, but it is often closed in the quiet periods.

Chez Mama Cilacap, at Jalan Kidang Pananjung 187, is one of Pangandaran's best restaurants, despite surly service, with an extensive menu, moderate prices, fresh fish and icy fruit juices.

On the west beach at the southern end, the no frills *Rumah Makan Nanjung* has a pleasant open-air dining area and good cheap seafood. They really know how to barbecue fish, and the sauces are excellent, or you could try the 'Fried Frog Balls' for 5000 rp. Further south, the restaurant at the *Nyiur Indah Hotel* is a little more expensive but one of Pangandaran's best Chinese seafood restaurants. Next to the Bumi Nusantara is a warung area with cheap Indonesian dishes and exposed to sea breezes.

The Bulak Laut area has plenty of eateries. On Jalan Bulak Laut, the *Pantai Sari Hotel* has a good restaurant with Indonesian dishes, reasonable Western fare and excellent fish. The German-run *Relax Coffee Shop* is one of Pangandaran's fanciest restaurants. The food is overpriced, though it is worth shelling out for a weighty slice of their delicious volkenbrot bread. On the other side of the street, the *Holiday Inn* has the usual travellers' menu. The fare is average, but very cheap and the breakfasts are good. A few doors along, the *Bunga Laut Restaurant* is shamefully underpatronised because it serves only Indonesian food. Sundanese dishes are a speciality – photographs of the dishes accompany the menu, so there is no excuse for eating spaghetti all the time.

The big hotels have restaurants for more-expensive dining. The *Sunrise Beach Hotel* has good food and service and is recommended for a splurge. *Hillman's Fish Farm Restaurant*, north of the bus station, is one of Pangandaran's classier establishments and good for seafood.

In addition to the restaurants, the new fish market just back from the east beach sells fresh fish and a number of seafood warungs have sprung up here. The market is to the north of the Pantai Indah Timur Hotel near the post office (not the fish market to the south, which is the wholesale market). The main market near the bus station is the place to stock up on fruit.

Women also do the rounds of the hotels with buckets of prawns, lobster, fish, squid or whatever else is in season and will return in the evenings with a complete meal cooked up for you.

Getting There & Away

Pangandaran lies halfway between Bandung and Yogya. Coming from Yogya by bus or rail, Banjar is the transit point, though the most popular way to reach Pangandaran is via the pleasant backwater trip from Cilicap to Kalipucang. From Bandung, plenty of direct buses go to Pangandaran, or it's possible to change for connections in Tasikmalaya.

Pangandaran's on-again-off-again airport is being built 20 km to the west.

Bus Local buses run from Pangandaran to Tasikmalaya (2600 rp; three hours), Ciamis (2400 rp; 2½ hours), Banjar (2000 rp; 1½ hours) and Kalipucang (500 rp; 40 minutes). Buses also run along the west coast as far as Cijulang (700 rp; 40 minutes).

The Sari Bakti and Budiman companies between them have buses to/from Bandung (5500/7500 rp air-con; six hours) at 6 and 9 am, 12.30, 3 and 6 pm. The most comfortable alternative is the Sari Harum Losmen's door-to-door minibus service for 9500 rp or the much better air-con service for 11,000 rp. The 4848 Taxis company also has cramped minibuses for 7900 rp.

Agents in Pangandaran sell bus tickets to Jakarta via Bogor, but this usually involves a change in Bandung or Banjar. Typical fares are 17,500 rp or 22,500 rp air-con for the 11-hour journey. Coming from Jakarta, take a bus from the Kampung Rambutan terminal to Tasikmalaya or Banjar and then another to Pangandaran, though the best alternative is to take the train to Bandung and then the minibus. Jalan Jaksa agents in Jakarta also sell through-tickets to Pangandaran.

The best way to reach Central Java is via the Kalipucang-Cilacap ferry (see Boat below) with bus connections at either end. If for some reason the boat doesn't appeal, take a bus to Banjar then a train to Yogya or another bus to Purwokerto for onward buses to Yogya or Wonosobo.

Car Pangandaran is a good place to rent cars for day trips or for extended touring. Try the travel agents such as Luta.

Boat One of the highlights of a trip to Pangandaran is the interesting backwater trip between Cilacap and Kalipucang. From Pangandaran it starts with a 17-km bus trip to Kalipucang (500 rp; 45 minutes). From Kalipucang the ferry travels across the wide expanse of Segara Anakan and along the waterway sheltered by the island of Nusa Kambangan. It's a fascinating, peaceful trip, hopping from village to village in a rickety 25-metre wooden boat. As well as carrying a regular contingent of tourists, it's very much a popular local service.

Ferries (1100 rp; four hours) leave Kalipucang at 6, 7 and 8 am, noon and 1 pm, but catch one of the early morning ferries to reach Yogya or Wonosobo in one day. Coming the other way, boats depart from Cilacap until 1 pm. From the Cilacap harbour it is about one km to the main road (no more than 500 rp by becak) from where bemos go to the Cilacap bus station (300 rp). From Cilacap direct buses go to Yogya or Wonosobo for the Dieng Plateau.

The trip is made very easy by the door-to-door services between Pangandaran and Yogya. Bus-ferry-bus services (12,500 rp, eight hours) are operated by Luta and Agung Travel in Pangandaran. Tickets costs about 5000 rp more from Yogya! Connections to Wonosobo are also advertised, but these only go if there is enough demand.

Getting Around

Pangandaran's brightly painted becaks cost a fixed 1000 rp around town regardless of the length of the journey. Bicycles are also an ideal way to get around and can be rented for as little as 3000 rp per day. Big rental shops are next to the Pasar Seni (Souvenir Market) and in front of the Dewi Laut on Jalan Kalen Buhaya. Motorbikes will cost around 9000 rp per day and are ideal for exploring the area around Pangandaran.

AROUND PANGANDARAN

The scenic coast road west from Pangandaran to Cipatujah skirts along the surf-pounded beaches and runs through small villages and padi fields. **Cikembulan**, four km from Pangandaran, has accommodation (see under Pangandaran) and local industries that can be visited, including the krupuk factory on the main road just west of the bridge, and a wayang golek workshop.

Karang Tirta, 16 km from Pangandaran and two km from the highway, is a lagoon set back from the beach with *bagang*, night fishing platforms. **Batu Hiu** (Shark Rock), 23 km from Pangandaran and one km from the highway, has a recreational park atop the cliffs with views along the coast.

Batu Karas, 42 km from Pangandaran and 10 km off the highway, is a relaxed fishing village with a surfing beach. Accommodation, favoured by Australian surfers, can be found one km beyond the fishing village at the headland beach. *Teratai Cottage* is the best value. Good rooms are 10,000 rp, or bungalows with a small sitting room are 20,000 rp. All have attached mandis and the swimming pool is a winner. Next door, *Alana's Bungalows* has bamboo decor and rooms for 10,000 to 20,000 rp, all with mandi. Batu Karas can be reached from Pangandaran by taking a bus to Cijulang (700 rp) and then an ojek for 1000 rp.

Pangandaran's number-one tour is to **Green Canyon**. Many tour operators in Pangandaran run trips here for around 30,000 rp, and usually include 'countryside' excursions on the way. To get there yourself, hire a boat from the various jetties on the highway near the turn-off to Batu Karas. A boat should cost around 15,000 rp and can

take six people. They travel up the emerald-green river through the forest to a waterfall and a steep rock canyon. The boats stop at the canyon for swimming. Count on two hours for this excellent trip.

The coast road ends at the village of **Cipatujah**, which has a wide but uninspiring beach with dangerous swimming, and a couple of cheap hotels. Five km before Cipatujah is a small PHPA post that monitors the green turtles that lay their eggs at **Sindangkerta** beach. The post welcomes interested visitors.

To the east of Pangandaran, **Karang Nini** is a recreational park perched high on the cliffs. Trails lead down the cliff face to the beach and crashing surf below. Apart from the occasional pair of young lovers, Karang Nini is deserted during the week. The park is run by the PHPA and it is possible to stay in their guesthouse, *Pondok Perhutanan*.

Getting There & Away

Buses run to Cijulang from Pangandaran, but to get to Cipatujah requires catching a host of local buses and *ankutan pedesaans* (village bemos). Cipatujah is well serviced by buses from Tasikmalaya and some continue to Ciparanti. From Cipatujah there are even buses to Jakarta. The best way to see this stretch of coast is to hire a motorbike in Pangandaran.

For Karang Nini, take any Kalipucang-bound bus to the Karang Nini turn-off (400 rp), nine km east of Pangandaran on the highway. It is then a three-km walk to the park, or 500 rp by ojek (if you can find one).

CIREBON

Few people make the trip out to Cirebon, but it's an interesting seaport and the seat of an ancient Islamic kingdom with a number of attractions for visitors. Located on the north coast, near the border with Central Java, the city's history has been influenced by both the Javanese and Sundanese with a bit of Chinese culture thrown in for good measure. A multi-ethnic city, many of the people speak a local dialect blending Sundanese and Javanese.

Cirebon was one of the independent sultanates founded by Sunan Gunungjati of Demak in the early 16th century. Later the powerful kingdoms of Banten and Mataram fought over Cirebon, which declared allegiance to Sultan Agung of Mataram but was finally ceded to the Dutch in 1677. By a further treaty of 1705 Cirebon became a Dutch protectorate, jointly administered by three sultans whose courts at that time rivalled those of Central Java in opulence and splendour. During the Dutch Culture System (see the History section in the Facts about the Country chapter for details), a flourishing trade in colonial crops attracted many Chinese entrepreneurs, and the Chinese influence can still be seen in the batik designs for which Cirebon is famous. Two of Cirebon's kratons (palaces) are open to visitors and, although a bit run-down compared with the palaces of Yogya and Solo, they still deserve more recognition.

Cirebon has long been a major centre for batik, and is also famous for its tari topeng, a type of masked dance, and tarling music, blending guitar, suling (bamboo flute) and voice. Cirebon is also important as the major port and fishing harbour between Jakarta and Semarang, with the added bonus that it has excellent seafood.

Remember that the north coast, particularly in the dry season, can be a sweltering contrast to the cooler heights inland. Other than that, Cirebon is a well-kept city small enough not to be overwhelming and makes a worthwhile stopover.

Information

Tourist Office The tourist office is inconveniently located five km out of town on the by-pass road, near Gua Sunyaragi. It has a few brochures in Indonesian – not worth the trip.

Money Bank Central Asia, Jalan Karanggetas 24, changes travellers' cheques and foreign cash at good rates. Bank Bumi Daya, Jalan Siliwangi 137, and Bank Niaga, Jalan Siliwangi 110, are also convenient.

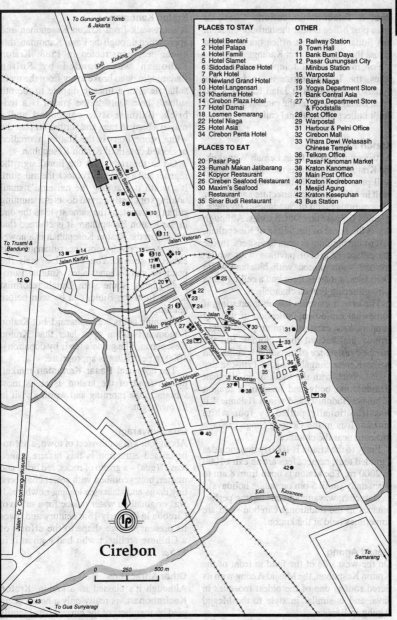

PLACES TO STAY

1 Hotel Bentani
2 Hotel Palapa
4 Hotel Famili
5 Hotel Slamet
6 Sidodadi Palace Hotel
7 Park Hotel
9 Newland Grand Hotel
10 Hotel Langensari
13 Kharisma Hotel
14 Cirebon Plaza Hotel
17 Hotel Damai
18 Losmen Semarang
22 Hotel Niaga
25 Hotel Asia
34 Cirebon Penta Hotel

PLACES TO EAT

20 Pasar Pagi
24 Rumah Makan Jatibarang
26 Kopyor Restaurant
27 Cirebon Seafood Restaurant
30 Maxim's Seafood Restaurant
35 Sinar Budi Restaurant

OTHER

3 Railway Station
8 Town Hall
11 Bank Bumi Daya
12 Pasar Gunungsari City Minibus Station
15 Warpostal
16 Bank Niaga
19 Yogya Department Store
21 Bank Central Asia
27 Yogya Department Store & Foodstalls
28 Post Office
29 Warpostal
31 Harbour & Pelni Office
32 Cirebon Mall
33 Vihara Dewi Welasasih Chinese Temple
36 Telkom Office
37 Pasar Kanoman Market
38 Kraton Kanoman
39 Main Post Office
40 Kraton Kecirebonan
41 Mesjid Agung
42 Kraton Kesepuhan
43 Bus Station

Cirebon

0   250   500 m

To Gunungjati's Tomb & Jakarta

To Trusmi & Bandung

To Gua Sunyaragi

To Semarang

Post & Telecommunications Cirebon's main post office is near the harbour on Jalan Yos Sudarso or a post office branch is just across the canal on Jalan Karanggetas.

For international telephone calls and faxes, the Telkom office is on Jalan Yos Sudarso. Warpostals at Jalan Kartini 7 and Jalan Bahagia 40 offer the same services, but don't collect international calls.

Kraton Kesepuhan

At the south end of Jalan Lemah Wungkuk, the Kraton Kesepuhan is the oldest and most well preserved of Cirebon's kratons. It was built in 1527 and its architecture and interior are a curious blend of Sundanese, Javanese, Islamic, Chinese and Dutch styles. Although this is the home of the Sultan of Kesepuhan, part of the building is open to visitors. Inside the palace is a cool pavilion with white-washed walls dotted with blue-and-white Delft tiles, a marble floor and a ceiling hung with glittering French chandeliers.

The kraton museum has an interesting, if somewhat run-down, collection of wayang puppets, kris, cannon, furniture, Portuguese armour and ancient royal clothes. But the *pièce de résistance* of the sultan's collection is the Kereta Singabarong, a 17th-century gilded coach with the trunk of an elephant (Hindu), the body and head of a dragon (Chinese-Buddhist) and wings (Islamic)! It was traditionally pulled by four white buffalo. It is in the Gedong Singa carriage museum near the entrance.

Entry to the kraton is 1000 rp and includes a guided tour; camera fees are an extra 1000 to 2000 rp. The kraton is open from 8 am to 4 pm daily (until 5 pm on public holidays).

Gamelan, wayang and tari topeng performances in the traditional Cirebon style are sometimes held at the kraton.

Mesjid Agung

On the west side of the field in front of the Kraton Kespuhan, the Mesjid Agung with its tiered roof is one of the oldest mosques in Java, and is similar in style to the Mesjid Agung in Banten.

Kraton Kanoman

A short walk from Kraton Kesepuhan and approached through the Pasar Kanoman, this kraton was constructed in 1588. Kraton Kanoman was founded by Sultan Badaruddin, who broke away from the main sultanate after a lineage dispute to the 6th sultan's heir. Outside the kraton is a red-brick, Balinese-style compound and a massive banyan tree, and further on past the white, stone lions is the kraton, a smaller, neglected cousin of Kraton Kesepuhan.

Go to the right past the lions, sign the register and a guide will unlock the museum. It's worth it – among the museum's small holdings of mostly carved doors is a stunning sultan's chariot, in the same style as the one in the Kraton Kesepuhan. It is claimed that the one in the Kraton Kesepuhan is a newer copy – the rivalry for the sultanate stills exists it seems. You can also visit the pendopo and its inner alter. Antique European plates, some with Dutch reformist scenes from the Bible, can be seen before entering.

Opening hours are haphazard, but Kraton Kanoman is often open later than Kraton Kesepuhan. The guide's fee is by donation – 1000 rp per visitor is appropriate.

The colourful **Pasar Kanoman** market, just in front of the kraton, is at its most vibrant in the morning and worth a visit in its own right.

Gua Sunyaragi

About four km south-west of town, a not-to-be-missed attraction is this bizarre ruined 'cave' (gua) – a grotto of rocks, red brick and plaster, honeycombed with secret chambers, tiny doors and staircases leading nowhere. It was originally a water palace for a sultan of Cirebon in the early 18th century and owes its present strange shape to the efforts of a Chinese architect who had a go at it in 1852.

Other Attractions

Although it's classed as a kraton, **Kraton Kecirebonan**, is really only a house occupied by members of the current royal family and is not open to the public. Built in 1839, it is worth a quick look for its exterior architecture, a blend of Dutch and Indonesian styles.

Places to Stay – bottom end

Inexpensive hotels can be found opposite the railway station. Very basic rooms can be had in the *Penginapan Budi Asih* and *Penginapan Lesana* for around 6000 rp, but a little further along, the *Hotel Palapa* (☎ 202380), Jalan Station 8, is better. While still rather dreary it is OK for the price: singles for 6000 rp or 10,000/12,500 rp for doubles/triples with mandi, including breakfast. On the corner of the same street, at Jalan Siliwangi 66, the brighter *Hotel Famili* (☎ 207935) has better singles/doubles for 6000/10,000 rp or 16,000 rp doubles with mandi.

Other cheap but uninspiring hotels in the centre of town on Jalan Siliwangi are the *Hotel Damai* (☎ 203045), at No 130, with singles for 7000 rp or doubles with mandi for 10,000 to 15,000 rp. *Losmen Semarang*, next door at No 132, has rooms for 7500/14,000 rp.

The best bet is the *Hotel Asia* (☎ 202183), at Jalan Kalibaru Selatan 15, alongside the tree-lined canal near the Pasar Pagi. This fine, old Dutch-Indonesian inn has a terraced courtyard where you can sit and have breakfast. It's about a 15-minute walk or 1000 rp by becak from the railway station. This very well-kept and friendly hotel has rooms with shared mandi for 13,900 rp and 16,000 rp, including breakfast. More expensive rooms with private mandi and fan cost 26,500 to 30,800 rp.

Places to Stay – middle

The *Newland Grand Hotel* (☎ 208623) at Jalan Siliwangi 98, is a pleasantly old-fashioned place with a big front verandah. Worn but large rooms with separate sitting areas have air-con, hot water and TV costing 38,000 rp for internal rooms, 48,000 rp for those with a view of the town square and 58,000 rp for suites with office areas.

Cheaper hotels on Jalan Siliwangi are *Hotel Slamet* (☎ 203296), at No 95, which has reasonable fan rooms with attached bathroom from 20,000 rp, air-con rooms from 36,000 rp.

The *Sidodadi Palace Hotel* (☎ 202305), Jalan Siliwangi 74, is a pleasant motel-style place built around a quiet courtyard. Very comfortable rooms range from 48,000 to 86,000 rp (plus 22% tax and service) and have air-con, hot water and parabola TV.

Hotel Niaga (☎ 206718), Jalan Kalibaru Selatan 47, is rather dull but has clean, carpeted rooms with air-con, TV, telephone and hot water for 35,000/50,000 rp, plus 10% tax.

Places to Stay – top end

Cirebon's better hotels charge 21% tax and service, but include breakfast. Always ask for a discount.

The *Kharisma Hotel* (☎ 2795), Jalan R A Kartini 48, straddles the middle and top-end ranges. Very ordinary singles/doubles in the old section cost 63,000/73,500 to 84,00/94,500 rp, but rooms in the new section for 115,500/126,000 rp are quite luxurious. The hotel has a pool, restaurants and bars.

The central *Cirebon Penta Hotel* (☎ 203328), Jalan Syarif Addurakhman 159, is small but classy. Excellent, new rooms cost US$50/60, including tax and service – much less after discount. The hotel has a rooftop garden and a health centre. It is above the KFC restaurant, opposite the Cirebon Mall.

Further south, the large *Park Hotel* (☎ 205411, fax 205407), Jalan Siliwangi 107, is Cirebon's best. It has a pool, tennis court, health centre, business centre, restaurants and bar. Rooms cost US$50/60 to US$70/80 depending on the view. Buffet breakfast is included and discounts of up to 30% apply.

Places to Eat

Apart from Cirebon's fine seafood, a local speciality to try is *nasi lengko*, a delicious rice dish with bean sprouts, tahu, tempe, fried onion, cucumber and peanut sauce. One good place for nasi lengko as well as other local and standard Indonesian dishes is *Rumah Makan Jatibarang*, on the corner of Jalan Karanggetas and Jalan Kalibaru Selatan.

The central market, or Pasar Pagi, has a great array of fruits and plenty of food stalls and basic warungs which stay open till evening. You also find plenty of good warungs along Jalan Kalibaru Selatan between the Asia and Niaga hotels. Delicious, cheap prawns in oyster sauce can be had at the *Moel Seafood* warung, or the *Seafood 31* rumah makan is also good. Ayam goreng and good sate can also be enjoyed along this stretch. The Yogya department store on Jalan Karanggetas (not the older Yogya store on Jalan Siliwangi) has a food-stall area on the ground floor, with plenty of the usual Indonesian favourites in squeaky clean surroundings.

Jalan Bahagia has a number of restaurants, and is also good for seafood. *Cirebon Seafood*, at No 9, has a varied menu, but check the prices first. One of the best seafood restaurants is the cavernous *Maxim's* at No 45, which specialises in Chinese, shrimp and crab dishes – most seafood dishes are in the 5000 to 10,000 rp range.

Western fast food hasn't really hit Cirebon, but the big, new Cirebon Mall has home-grown chicken-and-fries restaurants or *KFC* is right opposite under the Cirebon Penta Hotel. The Hero supermarket in the Cirebon Mall is the best in Cirebon for packaged goodies.

Getting There & Away
The road and rail route to Cirebon from Jakarta follows the flat north coast or from Bandung the road runs through scenic hilly country.

Air Cirebon's airport is to the south-west past the bus station. Merpati has a limited service from Jakarta for 83,600 rp.

Bus The Cirebon bus station is four km south-west of the centre of town.

Regular local buses run between Cirebon

and Jakarta (4700 rp; five hours; 256 km), Bandung (2300 rp; 3½ hours; 130 km), Semarang (4000 rp; six hours; 245 km), Pekalongan (2400 rp; 3½ hours; 137 km) and Yogya (6000 rp; nine hours; 365 km) as well as Bogor, Solo, Merak, Surabaya and other destinations. Less-frequent, air-con services also operate from the bus station on the major routes.

For express minibuses from Cirebon, the ACC Kopyor 4848 office (☎ 204343) is conveniently located in town at Jalan Karanggetas 7, next door to the Kopyor Restaurant. They have air-con minibuses to Jakarta (15,000 rp, four hours), Bandung (9000; 3½ hours), Semarang (5500 rp; five hours), and Yogya (12,500 rp; eight hours). Ring to arrange pick-up from your hotel.

Train Cirebon is on both the main northern Jakarta-Semarang-Surabaya railway line and the southern Jakarta-Yogya-Surabaya line, so there are frequent day and evening trains. The following are some of the better services, but often run over schedule and ekonomi trains can be very crowded. Bisnis trains also have air-con eksekutif carriages for around double the bisnis price.

To Jakarta's Gambir station, the *Cirebon Express* (9000 rp bisnis; 3½ hours) departs Cirebon at 5.40 am, 12.50 and 3.30 pm. It often runs up to an hour over schedule, but is still quicker and more convenient than the buses.

To Semarang, via Tegal and Pekalongan, the *Fajar Utama Semarang* (14,000 rp bisnis; 4½ hours) departs at 11.05 am. The *Cepat Semarang* (3500 rp ekonomi; five hours) departs at 1 pm.

To Yogyakarta, the *Fajar Utama Yogya* (18,000 rp bisnis; five hours) departs at 9.35 am. The *Senja Ekonomi Yogyakarta* (7500 rp ekonomi; seven hours) departs at 12.12 am.

Boat The Pelni office is at the harbour past the harbour entrance. The KM *Tatamailau* stops in Cirebon on its zig-zagging course between Pontianak and Banjarmasin in Kalimantan.

Getting Around

Cirebon's city minibus (angkutan kota) service operates from the Pasar Gunungsari a couple of blocks west of Jalan Siliwangi. They're labelled G7, GG, etc and charge a fixed 300 rp fare around town – some even offer 'full music'!

Cirebon has hordes of becaks ringing through the streets. A becak from the railway station to Pasar Pagi costs around 1000 rp. Taxis congregate around the bus and railway stations, but are unwilling to use their meters from these destinations and are hard to find elsewhere.

AROUND CIREBON
Sunan Gunungjati Tomb

In the royal cemetery, five km north of Cirebon, is the tomb of Sunan Gunungjati, who died in 1570. The most revered of Cirebon's kings, Gunungjati was also one of the nine walis who spread Islam throughout Java and his tomb is still one of the holiest places in the country. The inner tombs are only open once a month on Kliwon Thursday of the Javanese calendar, and at Idul Fitri and Maulud Nabi Mohammed. Pilgrims sit in contemplation and pray outside the doors on other days, and along from Sunan Gunungjati's tomb is the tomb of his first, Chinese wife and this tomb attracts Chinese worshippers.

Trusmi

Some of Cirebon's finest batik is made in the village of Trusmi, five km west of town. Take a G4 or GP angkot from Gunungsari station to Plered, on the Bandung road. Walk past the market from the main road, and then down a country lane of whitewashed cottages (or take a becak for 400 rp). At the end of the lane, Ibu Masina's is the best known studio where you can see batik tulis being made. Her showroom has a wide range of colours and designs. Also worth visiting is the workshop of Ibu Ega Sugeng – before you enter the lane to Ibu Masina's, follow Jalan Trusmi around to the right and continue 200 metres to No 218.

Surrounding villages, each specialising in their own crafts, include **Tegalwangi**, where rattan workshops line the Bandung road, one km on from Plered.

Linggarjati & Sangkan Hurip

Linggarjati's place in the history books was assured when, in 1946, representatives of the Republican government and the returning Dutch occupying forces met to negotiate a British-sponsored cooperation agreement. Terms were thrashed out in a colonial hotel at the foot of Gunung Cirema, once a retreat from the heat for Cirebon's Dutch residents. Soekarno briefly attended, but the Linggarjati Agreement was soon swept aside as the war for independence escalated. The hotel is now the **Gedung Naksa**, a museum recreating the events.

Linggarjati is not one of Java's premier hill resorts, but it has a few mid-range hotels and can still make a pleasant sojourn from the heat of the northern plains. It is possible to climb **Gunung Cirema** (3078 metres), which erupted dramatically last century, but a guide is necessary to negotiate the 10-hour walk through the forested slopes to the crater.

Sangkan Hurip, three km away, is a fairly nondescript hot-springs resort with a large hot-water swimming pool, hot baths and a dozen or so hotels in all price ranges.

Getting There & Away Linggarjati and Sangkan Hurip are 23 km south of Cirebon, lying two km to the west of the Kuningan road and one km to the east respectively. From Cirebon take a Kuningan bus to Cilimus (700 rp), and then a colt (250 rp) to either resort. Andongs also go to Sangkan Hurip.

Indramayu

Some say the 'very best' Cirebon batik comes from the small workshops of Pamuan village near Indramayu, 30 km north along the coast. The patterns of the batik are more involved and some of the batik tulis is still coloured with traditional vegetable dyes. You can get there by taking a colt to Indramayu, and from the colt station it's about a 1½-km walk, or a becak ride, to the village of Pamuan.

Central Java

Central Java has a population of about 29 million, an area of 34,503 sq km and Semarang as its capital. It's at the heart of Java and is the most 'Indonesian' part of Indonesia. This was the centre of Java's first great Indianised civilisation and much of the island's early culture. Later, the rise of Islam created powerful sultanates centred around the *kratons* or courts of Yogyakarta and Surakarta (Solo).

Although the north coast was the early Muslims' first foothold on Java, further inland the new faith was gradually infused with strong Hindu-Buddhist influences and even older indigenous beliefs. The old Javanese traditions and arts, cultivated by the royal courts, are at their most vigorous here. The years of Dutch rule made little impact and even though the Indonesian revolution stripped the sultans of their political powers, the influence of kraton culture still lingers in the minds of many Javanese.

Within the province, the 'special territory' of Yogyakarta forms an enclave shaped like

Central Java

a triangle with its base on the south coast and its apex at the volcano, Gunung Merapi. Although the capital of Central Java is Semarang, the cities of Yogya and Solo are the emotional and cultural centres, having both been capitals of Javanese kingdoms and, frequently, rival cities. Most of Central Java's main attractions are in, or close to, these two cities and include the magnificent Borobudur and Prambanan temples. There are also earlier temples in Central Java, particularly the ancient shrines of Dieng, and the province also has some fine hill resorts like Kaliurang.

Despite its population pressure, Central Java is a relaxed, easy-going state. The enclave of Yogyakarta in particular remains one of Indonesia's most important tourist destinations.

HISTORY

Central Java has been a great religious centre for both Hindus and Buddhists. Under the Sailendra and Old Mataram kings, the Hindu-Javanese culture flourished between the 8th and 10th centuries AD and it was during this time that Java's most magnificent religious monuments were built. The province has also been the major centre for the political intrigues and cultural activities of the Islamic states of old Java, and it was here too that some of the most significant historical events took place.

The renaissance of Central Java's political ascendancy began in the late 16th century with the disintegration of the Hindu Majapahit empire. Strong maritime Muslim states arose in the north but in the south the most powerful of the later Javanese dynasties had started to develop. According to the legend, the founder of this second Mataram empire sought the support of Nyai Loro Kidul, the 'Goddess of the South Seas', who was to become the special protector of the House of Mataram and is still very much a part of court and local traditions.

From its capital at Kota Gede, near Yogya, the Mataram empire eventually dominated Central and East Java and Madura. It reached its peak under Sultan Agung, one of the classic warrior figures of Java's history. Agung also sent missions further afield to Palembang, Banjarmasin and Macassar. The only permanent defeats of his career were his failure to take Dutch Batavia and the sultanate of Banten in the west. Sultan Agung's tomb at Imogiri near Yogyakarta is still revered as a holy place.

Following Agung's death in 1646 the empire rapidly began to disintegrate and ultimately fell to growing Dutch power. Amangkurat I followed Sultan Agung and devoted his reign to destroying all those he suspected of opposing him. In 1647 he moved to a new palace at Plered, not far from the old court. His tyrannical policies alienated his subjects and revolts soon broke out on all sides, which eventually led to the start of Dutch intervention in Javanese affairs. Rebellion broke out in 1675 and Plered fell to a predatory raid by Prince Trunojoyo of Madura, who then withdrew to Kediri, taking the Mataram treasury with him.

After Amangkurat's death in 1677, his son and successor made an alliance with the Dutch and began his reign from a new capital at Kartosuro, near present-day Solo. In 1678, Dutch and Javanese troops destroyed Trunojoyo's stronghold at Kediri, and the Mataram treasury was plundered by the victors, although some of it was later restored.

In the 18th century, intrigues and animosities at the Mataram court erupted into what became known as the First and Second Javanese Wars of Succession. Later, the repercussions of the Batavian Chinese massacre in 1740 spilled into Central Java and the fighting lasted almost 17 years. Pakubuwono II unwisely joined those Chinese who escaped slaughter in their siege of Dutch headquarters along the north coast, but was forced to retreat. Madurese intervention on behalf of the Dutch added to the confusion and in 1742 the court of Mataram was once again conquered by Madurese troops. The struggle was finally resolved by the treaty of 1743, by which Pakubuwono II was restored to his battered court but at the cost of enormous concessions to the Dutch.

Kartosuro was now abandoned and in 1745 Pakubuwono II established a new court at Surakarta which is still occupied by his descendants. The new court, however, was no more stable than the old and in 1746 the Third Javanese War of Succession began and continued until 1757. The Dutch, rapidly losing patience, finally adopted a policy of divide and rule – a tactic which was also adopted by the British when they took control during the five-year interregnum from 1811. By 1757 the former Mataram empire had been split into three rival, self-governing principalities – the realm of Surakarta was partitioned and the Sultanate of Yogyakarta was formed in 1755 and, finally, a smaller domain called Mangku-negara was created within Surakarta.

The founder of Yogya, Hamengkubuwono I (1755-92), was the most able Mataram ruler since Sultan Agung. During his reign the sultanate was the predominant military power in Central Java. Yet, within 40 years of his death, his successor had brought about the destruction of Javanese independence and the beginning of the truly colonial period of Central Javanese history. The deterioration of Hamengkubuwono II's relations both with his rivals in Surakarta and with the Dutch was followed by equal hostility towards the British. In 1812 European troops, supported by the sultan's ambitious brother and Mangkunegara, plundered the court of Yogya, and Hamengkubuwono was exiled to Penang. He was replaced as sultan by his son and his brother was appointed Prince Paku Alam of a small enclave within the sultanate.

At this time Java was in a state of flux due to corruption at court, continual European interference and increased hardship among the Javanese villagers. Into this turbulent picture stepped one of the most famous figures of Indonesian history, Prince Dipo-negoro, to launch the Java War of 1825-30. At the end of the war the Dutch held Yogya responsible and all of its outer districts were annexed. Just to maintain the principle of equality, the outer districts of Surakarta were annexed. Pakubuwono IV was so disturbed

by this apparent injustice that he set out for the Indian Ocean to confer with the 'Goddess of the South Seas' but the Dutch, fearing yet more rebellion, brought him back and exiled him to Ambon.

The Java War was the last stand of the Javanese aristocracy. For the rest of the colonial period the courts became ritual establishments and Dutch residents exercised control. With no real room or will for political manoeuvre, the courts turned their energies to traditional court ceremonies and patronage of literature and the arts. Their cultural prestige among the masses was high and this, combined with their political impotence, possibly explains why the royal elite were not major targets for the nationalist movement which arose in the 20th century. In fact Yogyakarta for a time became the capital of the Republican government and the progressive sultan at that time was so popular that he later served in several government posts. The sultanate has also remained administratively autonomous from Central Java as a 'special territory' with the status of a province.

CILACAP

Cilacap, just over the border from West Java, is a medium-sized city in a growing industrial area and has the only natural harbour with deep-water berthing facilities on Java's south coast. Apart from its fort, Cilacap has no real tourist attractions and the main reason to come here is to make the backwater trip to Kalipucang for Pangandaran.

Things to See
Benteng Pendem is an impressive fort complex at the entrance to the old harbour. Though sometimes erroneously referred to as the 'Portuguese fort', it is in fact a Dutch fort built between 1861 and 1879. With intact barracks, gun rooms and massive ramparts, it is the best preserved fort on Java, and relatively little stone has been carted off for use in local construction. Bring a torch to explore some of the tunnels and rooms, and wear sandals – one tunnel leads to the sea and lies in shallow water.

The fort overlooks a long stretch of dirty sand, **Pantai Teluk Penyu**, which, rather sadly, is a very popular local beach with souvenir stalls selling a dazzling array of shells.

Places to Stay & Eat
Losmen Tiga, in the centre of town at Jalan Mayor Sutoyo 61, is clean and friendly with spartan singles/doubles with shared mandi for 5225/6000 rp. Around the corner at Jalan Anggrek 16, *Losmen Anggrek* is also good with slightly larger rooms for 6600/9600 rp, or 10,600 to 19,000 rp with mandi.

Jalan Sudirman has some basic cheap hotels: the *Akhmad* at No 9 or the *Bahagia* at No 51. The *Cilacap Inn* (☎ 21543) at No 1 is definitely number one on this street. This good mid-range hotel has air-con rooms with hot water, TV and minibar for 35,000 to 80,000 rp, including breakfast.

At the top end is the *Hotel Wijaya Kusuma* (☎ 22871), Jalan Jenderal A Yani 12A, on Cilacap's main downtown street. All rooms have air-con, hot water and colour TV; rates start at 90,000 rp.

The *Restaurant Perapatan/Sien Hieng* at Jalan Jenderal A Yani 62, just around the corner from Losmen Tiga, has a large Chinese menu. Along Jalan Mayor Sutoyo, just east of Losmen Tiga, are a number of good warungs.

Getting There & Away
Air Merpati has a limited service from Jakarta to Cilacap for 126,500 rp. Cilacap's airport is 14 km north of the city.

Bus Buses to/from Cilacap include Yogya (3700 rp; five hours; 232 km), Purwokerto (1700 rp; 1½ hours) and Wonosobo (2700 rp; four hours; 150 km) for Dieng. The last bus to Yogya leaves around 3 pm. Alternatively, from Yogya take a train to Kroya and then a colt or bus for the one-hour ride to Cilacap.

Cilacap is also well served on the door-to-door private minibus network. Rahayu (☎ 21301), Jalan L E Martadinata 122, and the SAA agent, Toko Jaji (☎ 21490), Jalan Jenderal A Yani 72 both have non-air-con minibuses to Yogya (7000 rp; four hours). Erny Travel (☎ 22926), Jalan Mayjen Sutojo 54, has air-con minibuses to Bogor and Jakarta.

Boat Boats to Kalipucang (1100 rp; four hours) leave from the jetty a few km northwest of town, inland on the river estuary. To get there take a bemo (300 rp) to the jetty turnoff, and then a becak for the one km or so to the jetty. A becak from the bus station or the centre of town all the way to jetty should cost about 1500 rp. The jetty is near the big Pertamina installations – no photography! The last ferry leaves at 1 pm, so if coming from Yogya or Dieng you'll have to start early unless you want to spend the night in Cilacap. See under Pangandaran in the West Java section for full details of this fascinating trip.

PURWOKERTO
This medium-sized city is primarily a transport hub and you may find yourself here coming between Wonosobo or Cilacap, or on the way to Baturaden. Purwokerto is an unhurried, remarkably clean city with some architectural reminders of Dutch colonialism.

For a cheap hotel, the clean, well-run *Hotel Sampurna*, Jalan Gerilya 47, is near the bus station and has good rooms to suit most budgets or try the *Hotel Baru*, Jalan Pasarwage 27, in the centre of town near the market. *Hotel Borobudur*, Jalan Yosodarmo 32, is the best hotel in town.

Getting There & Away
Purwokerto's bus terminal is about two km south of town. Buses run to all major centres including Cilacap (1700 rp), Wonosobo (2000 rp), Banjar (2000 rp) and Yogya (3000 rp). Jaya Indah (☎ 61607), Jalan Mayjen Sutoyo 63, have door-to-door minibuses to Yogya (8500 rp) and other destinations. Purwokerto is also a major rail hub and the station is close to the centre of town.

Infrequent direct buses go to Baturaden, or catch a red angkot No B1 to Langentirto (250 rp) and then a minibus to Baturaden (500 rp).

JAVA

BATURADEN

Baturaden, 14 km north of Purwokerto, is one of Java's most attractive mountain resorts on the slopes of Gunung Slamet. Savour the mountain air on quiet weekdays and go for walks to waterfalls and through the pine-forested slopes. The recreation park also has a swimming pool, boat rides, etc.

Gunung Slamet, the second-highest peak in Java at 3432 metres, is a Fujiesque volcanic cone that dominates the landscape of western Central Java. Trails lead from Baturaden to the peak, but this is a very tough route. The usual ascent is from the north side, from the village of Serang. From Purwokerto take a bus to Belik (1500 rp) and then a pick-up to Moga (500 rp) to report to the police and obtain a permit. The climb involves a night on the mountain, and a guide and all-weather gear are essential.

Places to Stay

Wisma Kartika Asri has fine views and is in a good position right outside the gates to the recreation park. Comfortable rooms with mandi cost 15,000 rp; less with bargaining on weekdays. Near the bus station, the *Penginapan Kusuma Sari* is similarly priced. The rock-bottom *Losmen Harapan* is one of the cheapest around with rooms from 6000 rp.

Top of the range is the big, modern *Hotel Rosenda* (☎ 32570); the older *Rosenda Cottages* are simpler, homier and better value with doubles for 70,000 rp.

GUA JATIJAJAR

This huge limestone cave is a popular local tourist attraction, about 130 km west of Yogya. From the parking area, make your way through the souvenir sellers to the recreation park and up to the cave, which is spattered with graffiti. A concrete path wends its way over natural springs and through the halls of the cave, which are decorated with life-size statues relating the story of legendary lovers Raden Kamandaka and Dewi Ratna Ciptarasa. It is all very tacky, which is unfortunate because this is an otherwise impressive natural cave.

More difficult to explore, but larger and

unspoilt, **Gua Petruk** is seven km south of Gua Jatijajar. It has impressive stalactite and stalagmite formations. A guide (3000 rp) has to be hired from the PHPA post at the caves.

Black-sand beaches are to the south: **Pantai Indah Ayah** (aka Pantai Logending), five km beyond Gua Petruk, and **Pantai Karang Bolong**, where the people make a living collecting the nests of sea swallows from the steep cliff faces above the surf. The nests are collected every three months and sold to Chinese restaurants at home and abroad.

Getting There & Away

Gua Jatijajar is 21 km south-west of Gombong, which is on the main road and rail line between Yogya and Bandung. Gombong has hotels and is reached by bus from Cilacap (1500 rp; 1½ hours), Yogya (4000 rp; 3½ hours) and other centres such as Purwokerto and Semarang. Regular microbuses run from Gombong to Gua Jatijajar (500 rp).

WONOSOBO

Wonosobo is the main gateway to the Dieng Plateau. At 900 metres, in the hills of the central mountain range, Wonosobo has a good climate and is a fairly typical country town with a busy market. For most of the year it's not a particularly interesting place, but on national holidays it comes alive as people from the surrounding villages gather for festivities held in the main square. You might see the kuda kepang dance from nearby Temanggung, or the local lengger dance in which men dress as women and wear masks.

Information

The tourist office at Jalan Pemuda 2 is helpful and has maps of Wonosobo and the Dieng Plateau.

Places to Stay – bottom end

Pondok Duta Homestay (☎ 21674), Jalan Rumah Sakit 3, is the best budget option with comfortable, clean rooms with attached bathroom for 8000/10,000 rp including

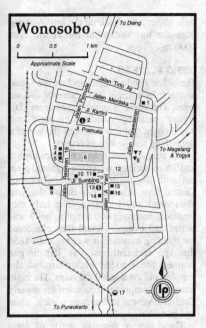

Wonosobo

1	Hotel Arjuna
2	Tourist Office
3	Hotel Nirwana
4	Losmen Widuri
5	Losmen Rahayu
6	Market
7	Dieng Restaurant
8	Asia Restaurant
9	Pondok Duta Homestay
10	Hotel Famili
11	Hotel Jawa Tengah
12	Plaza
13	Bank BNI
14	Hotel Perama
15	Hotel Sri Kencono
16	Hotel Petra
17	Bus Terminal

breakfast. It is well set up for travellers and provides good travel information.

Wonosobo also has plenty of cheap, uninspiring losmen. The *Hotel Jawa Tengah* (☎ 21802), Jalan A Yani 45, is one of the best of these. Small, clean rooms with three beds cost 7000 rp, larger rooms are 8000 rp or 12,500 rp with bath. It is set back from the street down a small alleyway. *Hotel Petra* (☎ 21152), Jalan A Yani 97, is also good value, with small singles at 4000 rp and 5000 rp and larger rooms with attached mandi from 10,000 rp.

A row of cheap losmen can be found on Jalan Resimen 18 near the market. Nearby at Jalan Sumbing 6, the similarly priced *Hotel Famili* is clean and comfortable.

Places to Stay – middle
Wonosobo doesn't have any top class hotels and those in the mid-range are fairly expensive for the standards on offer. *Hotel Perama* (☎ 21788), Jalan A Yani 96, is reasonable

value. Comfortable rooms with hot water showers cost 20,000 rp and 29,000 rp. A few spartan rooms with cold water are available for 12,500 rp.

The very popular *Hotel Nirwana* (☎ 21066) at Jalan Resimen 18 No 34 is clean, secure, quiet and friendly. Comfortable rooms cost 35,000 rp with hot shower and Western toilet, or 50,000 rp for larger rooms with a sitting area. The rates are inflated, but a substantial breakfast is included.

The *Hotel Arjuna* (☎ 21389), Jalan Sindoro 7A, is further out but it is quiet and pleasant. Rooms around courtyard areas start at 10,000 rp or 15,000 rp with bath. Those with bath, TV and hot water are good value at 30,000 rp or 35,000 rp with a sitting room. Breakfast is included.

Hotel Sri Kencono (☎ 21522), Jalan A Yani 72, is the best hotel in town. Spotless rooms with hot water showers and parabola TV cost 40,000 rp plus tax. Breakfast is included.

Places to Eat
The popular *Dieng Restaurant*, Jalan Kawedanan No 29, has good Indonesian, Chinese and European food served buffet-style. Most dishes cost around 1500 rp per portion. The Dieng closes at 9 pm. The owner, Mr Agus Tjugianto, is a good source of information on Dieng and sometimes arranges Dieng tours. The photograph albums are worth a look.

The *Asia*, two doors down, is one of Wonosobo's best restaurants and serves Chinese food.

The market area along Jalan Resimen 18 also has a host of warung for cheap eats.

Getting There & Away

To/From Yogya From Yogya take a bus or colt to Magelang (800 rp; one hour) and from there another bus to Wonosobo (1200 rp; two hours). Door-to-door minibuses also do the Yogya-Wonosobo run. Rahayu Travel (☎ 21217), Jalan A Yani 111, has minibuses to Yogya at 6, 8 am, noon, 2 and 4 pm for 4500 rp per person. Hotels can arrange pickup.

To/From Semarang A few buses run daily to Semarang (2200 rp; four hours) via Secang and Ambarawa. If you miss these, take a bus to Ambarawa (1500 rp; three hours) and then another to Semarang. Alternatively take the frequent colts that go to Secang, on the main Semarang-Yogya bus route.

To/From Cilacap From Wonosobo take a bus to Purwokerto (1800 rp; three hours) and then another to Cilacap (1600 rp; two hours). Leave early in the morning if you want to catch the ferry to Kalipucang and on to Pangandaran.

Direct minibuses from Pangandaran, via the Segara Anakan ferry, go to Wonosobo (12,500 rp; nine hours) but only if there are enough passengers. Otherwise you will be dropped at Purworejo and will have to negotiate a tedious series of buses, via Magelang, to get to Wonosobo.

To/From Dieng Frequent buses to Dieng (1200 rp; 1½ hours) leave from the colt station at the Wonosobo market in the centre of town. They leave throughout the day and continue on to Batur.

Getting Around

Buses coming into Wonosobo turn down Jalan A Yani to the bus station, and can drop you off in the centre – otherwise you'll have to walk about a km back up the hill. Andong from the bus station to the centre cost 1000 rp.

DIENG PLATEAU

The oldest Hindu temples in Java are found on this lofty plateau, 2000 metres above sea level. The name 'Dieng' comes from 'Di-Hyang', meaning 'Abode of the gods', and it is thought that this was once the site of a flourishing temple-city of priests.

The temples, mostly built between the 8th and 9th centuries, covered the highland plain but with the mysterious depopulation of Central Java, this site, like Borobudur, was abandoned and forgotten. The holy city reputedly had over 400 temples, but it was buried and overgrown and then plundered for building material. It was not until 1856 that the archaeologist Van Kinsbergen drained the flooded valley around the temples and catalogued the ruins. The eight remaining temples are characteristic of early Central Javanese architecture – stark, squat and box-like.

These simple temples, while of great archaeological importance, are not stunning. Rather Dieng's beautiful landscape is the main reason to make the long journey to this isolated region. Steep mountain sides terraced with vegetable plots enclose the huge volcanically active plateau, a marshy caldera of a collapsed volcano. Any number of walks to cool mineral lakes, steaming craters or other quiet, lonely places can be made around Dieng – to the highest village in Central Java if you're feeling energetic.

To really appreciate Dieng, it is best to stay in Dieng village. Alternatively, Wonosobo has better facilities and can be used as a base. Yogya companies also run tours to Dieng. The temples and the main 'natural' sights can be seen in one day on foot – be in Dieng in the morning before the afternoon mists roll in. It is a pleasant three or four-hour loop south from Dieng village to Telaga Warna, Candi Bima, Kawah Sikidang, and then back to Candi Gatutkaca, the Arjuna Complex and the village. Many other lakes and craters around Dieng are scattered over a large area, but they are difficult to reach.

Information

In Dieng village a kiosk sells tickets to Dieng for 2000 rp. The tourist office almost next door is helpful and knowledgeable.

Temples

The five main temples that form the **Arjuna Complex** are clustered together on the central plain. They are Shiva temples but like the other Dieng temples have been named after the heroes of the wayang stories of the

Mahabharata epic – Arjuna, Puntadewa, Srikandi, Sembadra and Semar. Raised walkways link the temples (as most of this land is waterlogged), but you can see the remains of ancient underground tunnels which once drained the marshy flatlands.

Just to the south of the Arjuna Complex is **Candi Gatutkaca** and the small site **museum** containing statues and sculpture from the temples. The museum is often locked but can be opened upon request. Further south, **Candi Bima** is unique in Java, with its *kudu*, strange sculpted heads like so many spectators looking out of windows.

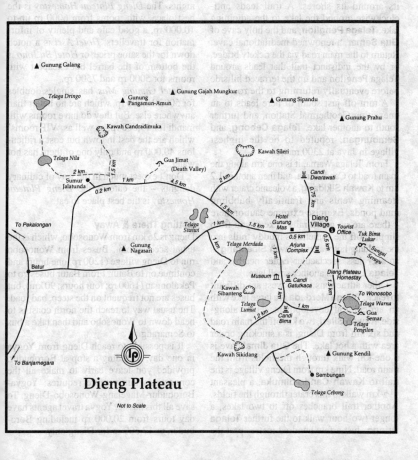

Dieng Plateau

Not to Scale

The restored **Candi Dwarawati** is on the northern outskirts of the village. Near the entrance to Dieng at the river, **Tuk Bima Lukar** is an ancient bathing spring where water spouts from the stone wall. It was once holy and has a fountain of youth legend attached.

Other Attractions

The road south from the Dieng Plateau Homestay passes a mushroom factory and a flower garden before the turnoff to beautiful **Telaga Warna** ('Coloured Lake'), which has turquoise hues from bubbling sulphur deposits around its shores. A trail leads anticlockwise around the lake to the adjoining lake, **Telaga Pengilon**, and the holy cave of **Gua Semar**, a renowned meditational cave. Return to the main road via the rickety bridge, or by the indistinct trail that leads around Telaga Pengilon and up the terraced hillside before eventually returning to the road.

A turn-off just south of here leads to an unexciting Geothermal Station, and further south to another lake, **Telaga Cebong**, and **Sembungan**, reputed to be the highest village in Java at 2300 metres.

From Telaga Warna, it is one km along the main road to Candi Bima, and then another 1.2 km to **Kawah Sikidang**, a volcanic crater with steaming vents and frantically bubbling mud ponds. Exercise extreme caution here – there are no guard rails to keep you from slipping off the sometimes muddy trails into the scalding hot waters. **Kawah Sibentang** is another less spectacular crater nearby and **Telaga Lumut** is another small lake.

Other attractions to the west are difficult to reach. **Telaga Merdada** is a large lake with an agricultural development centre alongside. **Kawah Sileri**, two km off the main road and six km from Dieng, is a smoking crater area with a hot lake. The **Gua Jimat** cave is a one-km walk through the fields from the main road. Nine km from Dieng village is the trail to **Kawah Candradimuka**, a pleasant 1½-km walk to this crater through the fields. Another trail branches off to two lakes, a longer two-hour walk to the further **Telaga Dringo**. Just a few hundred metres past the

turnoff to Kawah Candradimuka is **Sumur Jalatunda**. This 'well' (as 'sumur' translates) is in fact a deep hole some 100 metres across whose vertical walls plunge down to bright green waters.

For breathtaking views of the valley, the viewpoint on the slopes of **Gunung Sondoro** is five km from Dieng just off the main road towards Wonosobo.

Places to Stay & Eat

Dieng has a handful of spartan hotels. They provide little in the way of amenities, except for blankets, which are essential for the cold nights. The *Dieng Plateau Homestay* is the best place, with rooms from 6000 rp up to 10,000 rp, a good cafe and plenty of information for travellers. *Hotel Asri* is a notch down for the same price, or *Hotel Bu Jono* is the bottom of the barrel but cheapest with rooms for 5000 rp and 7500 rp.

Hotel Gunung Mas has singles/doubles for 5000/10,000 rp, which are no better than anywhere else. But they do have rooms with mandi for 15,000 rp, as well as 'VIP rooms' which are the best in town but cost a ridiculous 40,000 rp and only one of them has hot water.

Don't expect much in the way of culinary delights – the cafe at the *Dieng Plateau Homestay* is the best place to eat.

Getting There & Away

Dieng is 26 km from Wonosobo, which is the usual access point. Buses from Wonosobo run to Dieng village (1200 rp; one hour) and continue on to Batur. From Batur buses go to Pekalongan (1600 rp; four hours; 90 km), but buses are not frequent on the steep, bad road. The usual way to reach the north coast is to head down to Wonosobo and then take a bus to Semarang.

It is possible to reach Dieng from Yogya in one day, including a stop at Borobudur, provided you leave early to make all the connections this venture requires: Yogya-Borobudur-Magelang-Wonosobo-Dieng. To save all this hassle, Yogya travel agents have day tours from 20,000 rp including Borobudur, or 17,500 rp for Dieng only.

MAGELANG

Magelang was formerly a Dutch military garrison and it was here that the Javanese hero, Prince Diponegoro, was tricked into captivity in 1829. In the house where he was captured is a museum of Diponegoro memorabilia.

Magelang is 42 km north of Yogya, on the main road to Semarang. Shortly before the town is Gunung Tidar, which legend credits as the 'Nail of Java', a mountain planted there by the gods to stop Java from shaking.

BOROBUDUR

From the plain of Kedu, 42 km north-west of Yogya, a small hill rises up out of a pattern of palm trees and fields of rice and sugar cane. It's topped by one of the greatest Buddhist relics of South-East Asia – up there with Cambodia's Angkor Wat and Burma's Bagan.

Rulers of the Sailendra dynasty built the colossal pyramid of Borobudur sometime between 750 and 850 AD. Little else is known about Borobudur's early history but the Sailendras must have recruited a huge workforce, for some 60,000 cubic metres of stone had to be hewn, transported and carved

Borobudur

during its construction. According to tradition, the main architect was Gunadharma. The name Borobudur is possibly derived from the Sanskrit words 'Vihara Buddha Uhr', which means the 'Buddhist monastery on the hill'.

With the decline of Buddhism and the shift of power to East Java, Borobudur was abandoned soon after completion, and for centuries lay forgotten, buried under layers of volcanic ash. It was only in 1815, when Raffles governed Java, that the site was

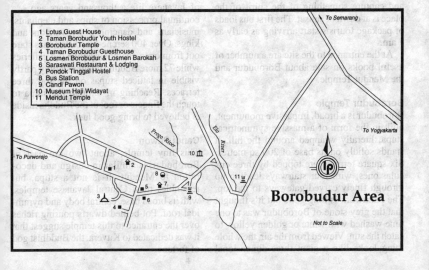

1 Lotus Guest House
2 Taman Borobudur Youth Hostel
3 Borobudur Temple
4 Taman Borobudur Guesthouse
5 Losmen Borobudur & Losmen Barokah
6 Saraswati Restaurant & Lodging
7 Pondok Tinggal Hostel
8 Bus Station
9 Candi Pawon
10 Museum Haji Widayat
11 Mendut Temple

Borobudur Area

Not to Scale

cleared and the sheer magnitude of the builders' imagination and technical skill was revealed. Early in the 20th century the Dutch began to tackle the restoration of Borobudur but over the years the supporting hill had become waterlogged and the whole immense stone mass started to subside. A mammoth US$21 million restoration project was undertaken between 1973 and 1984.

Although easily forgotten, standing as they do in the shadow of the great Borobudur, two smaller structures – Mendut and Pawon temples – form a significant part of the complex.

Orientation & Information

The small village of Borobudur consists of warungs, souvenir stalls and a few hotels that face the monument. The bus station is less than 10 minutes' walk from the monument.

The temple site is open from 6 am to 5.30 pm and admission is 4000 rp for foreign tourists, 1000 rp for domestic tourists. The higher price includes a guide (in most major foreign languages), camera fees and entry to the museum. Borobudur is Indonesia's single most popular tourist attraction, and it can be crowded and noisy, especially on weekends. The finest time to see Borobudur and capture something of the spirit of the place is at dawn or sunset. The first bus loads of package tourists start arriving as early as 7 am.

At the entrance to the site are a number of useful books on sale about Borobudur and the Mendut Temple.

Borobudur Temple

Borobudur is a broad, impassive monument, built in the form of a massive symmetrical stupa, literally wrapped around the hill. It stands solidly on its base of 200 sq metres. Six square terraces are topped by three circular ones, with four stairways leading up through finely carved gateways to the top. The paintwork is long gone but it's thought that the grey stone of Borobudur was at one time washed with white or golden yellow to catch the sun. Viewed from the air, the whole thing looks like a giant three-dimensional tantric mandala. It has been suggested, in fact, that the Buddhist community that once supported Borobudur were early Vajrayana or Tantric Buddhists who used it as a walkthrough mandala.

The entire monument was conceived as a Buddhist vision of the cosmos in stone, starting in the everyday world and spiralling up to nirvana – eternal nothingness, the Buddhist heaven. At the base of the monument is a series of reliefs representing a world dominated by passion and desire, where the good are rewarded by reincarnation as some higher form of life and the evil are punished by a lowlier reincarnation. These carvings and their carnal scenes are covered by stone to hide them from view, but they are partly visible on the south side.

Starting at the main eastern gateway, go clockwise (as one should around all Buddhist monuments) around the galleries of the stupa. Although Borobudur is impressive for its sheer bulk, it is the close-up sculptural detail which is quite astounding. The pilgrim's walk is about five km long. It takes you along narrow corridors past nearly 1500 richly decorated relief panels in which the sculptors have carved a virtual textbook of Buddhist doctrines as well as many aspects of Javanese life a thousand years ago – a continual procession of ships and elephants, musicians and dancing girls, warriors and kings. Over 400 serene-faced Buddhas stare out from open chambers above the galleries while 72 more Buddha images sit only partly visible in latticed stupas on the top three terraces. Reaching in through the stupa to touch the fingers or foot of the Buddha inside is believed to bring good luck.

Candi Pawon

This tiny temple, about two km east of Borobudur, is similar in design and decoration to Mendut. It is not a stupa, but resembles most Central Javanese temples, with its broad base, central body and pyramidal roof. Pot-bellied dwarfs pouring riches over the entrance to this temple suggest that it was dedicated to Kuvera, the Buddhist god of fortune.

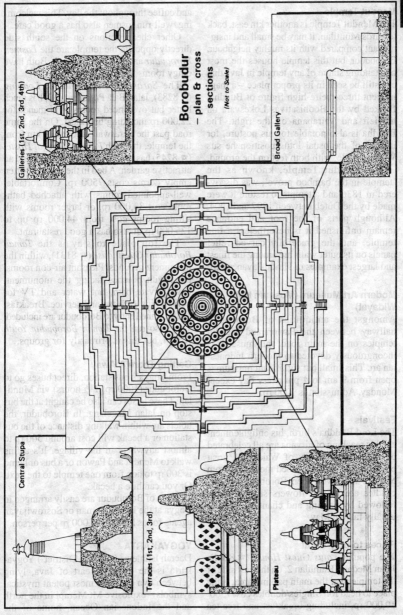

Borobudur
– plan & cross
sections
(Not to Scale)

Galleries (1st, 2nd, 3rd, 4th)

Broad Gallery

Central Stupa

Terraces (1st, 2nd, 3rd)

Plateau

Mendut Temple

The Mendut Temple is another km east, back towards Muntilan. It may be small and insignificant compared with its mighty neighbour, Borobudur, but this temple houses the most outstanding statue of any temple in Java that can still be seen in its proper place – a magnificent three-metre-high figure of Buddha, flanked by the Bodhisattvas Lokesvara on the left and Vairapana on the right. The Buddha is also notable for his posture, for instead of the usual lotus position he sits Western-style, with both feet on the ground.

The Mendut Temple, known as the 'temple in the bamboo grove', was discovered in 1836 and attempts to restore it were made by the Dutch between 1897 and 1904. Although parts of the roof and entrance remain unfinished it is nevertheless a fine temple, and the gracefully carved relief panels on its outer walls are among the finest and largest examples of Hindu-Javanese art.

Modern Art Museum (Museum Haji Widayat)

Amongst the antiquities of Borobudur, halfway between the Pawon and Mendut temples on the main road, this museum is incongruously devoted to modern Indonesian art. This small but significant museum is open from 9 am to 4 pm every day except Monday. Admission is 1000 rp.

Festivals

The Lord Buddha's birth, his enlightenment and his reaching of nirvana are all celebrated on the full-moon day of Waicak. A great procession of saffron-robed monks go from Mendut to Pawon then Borobudur, where candles are lit and flowers strewn about, followed by praying and chanting. Waicak usually falls in May.

Places to Stay & Eat

The popular *Lotus Guest House* (☎ 8281), Jalan Medang Kamulan 2, on the east side of the temple near the main parking area, is the place to head for. Singles/doubles cost 7500/ 10,000 rp, including breakfast and free tea

and coffee throughout the day. This welcoming, well-run losmen also has a good cafe.

Other cheap options on the south side directly opposite the temple are the *Losmen Borobudur* and *Losmen Barokah*. Both have dingy rooms for 7500 rp.

The *Saraswati Restaurant & Lodging* (☎ 8283), Jalan Bala Putradewa 10, has much better but overpriced rooms with mandi for 22,000 rp including breakfast. On the same road past the Saraswati, about one km from the temple, the flash *Pondok Tinggal Hostel* (☎ 8245) has bamboo-style rooms around an attractive garden. A bed in the spotless, often empty dorms costs 7500 rp. Comfortable, well-appointed rooms with attached bathroom cost 33,000 rp, or larger rooms with sitting rooms cost from 44,000 rp up to 125,000 rp. It also has a good restaurant.

The top place to stay is the *Taman Borobudur Guesthouse* (☎ 8131), within the monument grounds. Pleasant air-con rooms, most with porches facing the monument, have private bath, hot water and TV for US$35 plus 18% tax and service. Breakfast and unlimited entry to Borobudur are included. They also run the *Taman Borobudur Youth Hostel*, but this is primarily for groups.

Getting There & Away

From Yogya's bus station, direct buses go to Borobudur (1000 rp; 1½ hours) via Muntilan. These buses can also be caught at the bus stop on Jalan Magelang. In Borobudur, the hotels are within walking distance of the bus station or a becak will cost around 500 rp to almost anywhere in the village. It's a fine walk to Mendut and Pawon or a bus or bemo is 300 rp to hop from one temple to the next. Or you can hire a becak.

Tours of Borubudur are easily arranged in Yogya at the Prawirotaman or Sosrowijayan agents for as little as 15,000 rp per person.

YOGYAKARTA

Daerah Istimewa ('Special District') Yogyakarta is the cultural heart of Java, lying between two of Java's most potent mystical symbols – explosive Mt Merapi in the north and the Indonesian Ocean, home of the

'Queen of the South Seas', in the south. Yogyakarta, or Yogya (pronounced 'Jogja') for short, is the most active centre for Javanese arts, and spoken Javanese is at its most *halus* (refined) here. It is also an intellectual centre, crammed with prestigious universities and academies, and Yogya's influence and importance far outweigh its size. Yogya has always strived to maintain its independence, clinging proudly to its traditions, and is still headed by its sultan. The sultan's walled palace or kraton remains the hub of traditional life.

The district of Yogyakarta has a population of just over three million and an area of 3186 sq km, while the population of the city itself is around 500,000. No longer the city of bicycles, Yogya has noisy and chaotic traffic like any Javanese city, but just a short stroll behind the main streets are the kampungs where life is still unhurried. Despite its veneer of modernity and Westernisation, Yogya clings strongly to its traditional values and philosophies.

The city provides easy access for an insight into Javanese culture. Batik, silver, pottery, wayang kulit and other craft industries are easily visited, traditional Javanese performing arts can readily be seen, and the contemporary arts are also flourishing. Yogya is also a good base to explore numerous nearby attractions, including Indonesia's most important and awe-inspiring archaeological sites, Borobudur and Prambanan.

Yogya is Java's No 1 tourist centre and Indonesia's most popular city for visitors. It's easy to see why – apart from its many attractions, Yogya is friendly and easygoing, with an excellent range of economical hotels and restaurants.

History

Yogyakarta owes its foundation to Prince Mangkubumi who, in 1755, after a land dispute with his brother, the Susuhunan of Surakarta, returned to the former seat of Mataram and built the kraton of Yogyakarta. He took the title of 'sultan' and adopted the name of Hamengkubuwono, meaning literally 'the universe on the lap of the king', which all his successors have used. He created the most powerful Javanese state since the 17th century but his son was less competent and during the period of British rule the Yogya kraton was sacked, Hamengkubuwono II was exiled and the smaller Paku Alam principality created within the sultanate.

For the Javanese, Yogya has always been a symbol of resistance to colonial rule. The heart of Prince Diponegoro's Java War (1825-30) was in the Yogya area. More recently, Yogya was again the centre of revolutionary forces and became the capital of the Republic from 1946 until independence was achieved in 1949. As the Dutch took control of other Javanese cities, part of the kraton was turned over to the new Gajah Mada University which opened in 1946. Thus, as one of the sultan's advisers observed, in Yogya 'the Revolution could not possibly smash the palace doors, because they were already wide open'.

When the Dutch occupied Yogya in 1948, the patriotic sultan locked himself in the kraton, which became the major link between the city and the guerillas who retreated to the countryside. The Dutch did not dare move against the sultan for fear of arousing the anger of millions of Javanese who looked upon him almost as a god. The sultan let rebels, including Soeharto, use the palace as their headquarters and as a result of this support and the influence of the sultan, come independence Yogya was granted the status of a special territory. Yogya is now a self-governing district answerable directly to Jakarta and not to the governor of Central Java.

Under Soeharto's government, the immensely popular Sultan Hamengkubuwono IX was Indonesia's vice-president until he stepped down in March 1978. The sultan passed away in October 1988 and in March 1989 Prince Bangkubumi, the eldest of 16 sons, was installed as Sultan Hamengkubuwono X. The coronation involved great pomp and ceremony and included a procession of dwarfs and albinos. The new sultan is a member of the National Assembly and, like his father, is intent on preserving the traditions of Yogya.

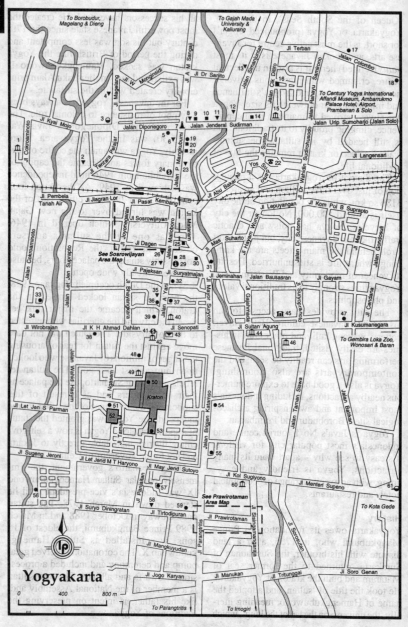

To Borobudur,
Magelang & Dieng

To Gajah Mada
University &
Kaliurang

See Sosrowijayan
Area Map

See Prawirotaman
Area Map

Kraton

To Century Yogya International,
Affandi Museum, Ambarrukmo
Palace Hotel, Airport,
Prambanan & Solo

To Gembira Loka Zoo,
Wonosari & Baran

To Kota Gede

To Parangtritis   To Imogiri

Yogyakarta

0   400   800 m

PLACES TO STAY		OTHER		40	Benteng Vredeburg
				41	Bank BNI
9	Phoenix Heritage Hotel	1	Museum Sasana	42	Sono-Budoyo Museum
10	Hotel Santika		Wiratama	43	Main Post Office
14	Java Palace Hotel		(Monumen	44	Museum Biologi
16	Indraloka Home Stay		Diponegoro)	45	Pakualaman Kraton
20	Arjuna Plaza Hotel	3	Pingit Bus Stop for	46	Sasmitaluka Jenderal
21	New Batik Palace Hotel		Borobudur		Sudirman
25	Hotel Puri	5	Minibus Agents	47	Batik Research Centre
28	Mutiara Hotel	7	Tugu Monument	48	Mesjid Besar
30	Melia Purosani Hotel	15	Army Museum	49	Museum Kareta Kraton
		17	ISI Dance Faculty	50	Kraton Entrance
PLACES TO EAT		18	RRI Auditorium	51	Pasar Ngasem Bird
		19	Garuda Airways		Market
2	Pesta Perak	22	Telkom Office	52	Taman Sari (Water
4	Valentino's	24	Bank BCA		Castle)
6	Restaurant Rama	29	Tourist Information	53	Sasono Hinggil
8	Pizza Hut		Office	54	Purawisata
11	Rumah Makan Tio Ciu	31	Papillon Disco		(Amusement Park)
12	Colt Station to	32	Terang Bulan Batik	55	Dalem Pujokusuman
	Kaliurang &		Shop		Theatre
	Prambanan	33	Amri Yahya's Gallery	56	Agastya Art Institute
13	Pujayo	34	ISI (Fine Arts Faculty)	57	Swasthigita Wayang
23	Tip Top	36	Mirota Batik		Kulit Workshop
26	Oshin Restaurant	37	Pasar Beringharjo	59	Tulus Warsito's Batik
27	Colombo Restaurant		Market		Gallery
35	Cherry Cafe	38	Nitour	60	Museum Perjuangan
58	Baleanda Restaurant	39	Gedung Negara	61	Bus Station Umbulharjo
			(Governor's Building)		

Orientation

It is easy to find your way around Yogya. Jalan Malioboro, named after the Duke of Marlborough, is the main road and runs straight down from the railway station to the kraton at the far end. The tourist office and many souvenir shops and stalls are along this street and most of the cheap-accommodation places are just off it, in the enclave near the railway line.

The old, walled kraton is the centre of the intriguing area of old Yogya where you will also find the Taman Sari, bird market and numerous batik galleries. A second mid-range hotel enclave is south of the Kraton area around Jalan Prawirotaman.

Information

Tourist Office The Tourist Information Office (☎ 66000), Jalan Malioboro 16, is open from 8 am to 8 pm Monday to Saturday. They have useful maps of the city, produce a number of publications (including a calendar of events) and can answer most queries.

The railway station and the airport also have tourist office counters.

Money Yogya has plenty of banks and moneychangers for changing cash. Banks usually give better exchange rates.

The BNI bank, Jalan Trikora 1 opposite the post office, is efficient and has good rates for most currencies. The BCA bank, just north of the railway station on Jalan Mangkubumi, gives good rates for major currencies and accepts most brands of travellers' checks. It gives cash advances on credit cards but charges 5000 rp. The money-change counter upstairs is open 8 am to 1 pm Monday to Friday and 8 to 11 am Saturday.

PT Baruman Abad, in the Hotel Garuda shopping arcade behind Lippobank, is one moneychanger that gives excellent rates. Opposite the railway station, PT Haji La Tunrung, Pasar Kembang 17, has passable rates and is open until 9.30 pm every day.

Post & Telecommunications The main

post office is on Jalan Senopati at the bottom of Jalan Malioboro and is open from 8 am to 8 pm Monday to Thursday, 8 to 11 am and 2 to 8 pm on Friday and 8 am to 5 pm on Saturday.

For international calls, convenient wartels are those behind the post office at Jalan Trikora 2 and opposite the railway station at Jalan Pasar Kembang 29. The Telkom office, one km east of Jalan Malioboro on Jalan Yos Sudarso, is open 24 hours and has Home Country Direct phones.

Bookshops The best bookshop in Yogyakarta, with a good selection of books in English and books on Indonesia, is the Prawirotaman International Bookshop.

Dangers & Annoyances Yogya has its fair share of pickpockets and thieves. Be particularly wary when catching buses to Borobudur and Prambanan.

Kraton

In the heart of the old city the huge palace of the sultans of Yogya is effectively the centre of a small walled-city within a city. Over 25,000 people live within the greater kraton compound, which contains its own market, shops, batik and silver cottage industries, schools and mosques.

The innermost group of buildings, where the current sultan still lives, were built between 1755 and 1756, although extensions were made over almost 40 years during the long reign of Hamengkubuwono I. European-style touches to the interior were added much later by the sultans of the 1920s, but structurally this is one of the finest examples of Javanese palace architecture, providing a series of luxurious halls, and spacious courtyards and pavilions. The sense of tradition holds strong in Yogya, and the palace is attended by very dignified and elderly retainers who still wear traditional Javanese dress.

The centre of the kraton is the reception hall known as the Bangsal Kencana, or Golden Pavilion, with its intricately decorated roof and great columns of carved teak. A large part of the kraton is used as a museum

and holds an extensive collection including gifts from European monarchs and gilt copies of the sacred *pusaka* (the heirlooms of the royal family), gamelan instruments, royal carriages and a huge bottle-shaped wooden alarm gong. One of the most interesting rooms contains the royal family tree, old photographs of grand mass weddings and portraits of the former sultans of Yogya.

An entire museum within the kraton is dedicated to Sultan Hamengkubuwono IX, with photographs and personal effects of the great man. Other points of interest within the kraton palace include the small European bandstand with stained-glass images of musical instruments. In another part of the kraton there are 'male' and 'female' entrances indicated by giant-sized 'he' and 'she' dragons, although they look pretty much alike. Outside the kraton, in the centre of the northern square, are two sacred *waringin* or banyan trees where, in the days of feudal Java, white-robed petitioners would patiently sit, hoping to catch the eye of the king.

The kraton is open from 8 am to 1 pm daily, except Friday when it closes at noon. It is closed on national and kraton holidays. Admission is 1500 rp, which includes an excellent guided tour. Booklets about the palace and excellent postcards of the old sultans are on sale inside. In the inner pavilion from 10.30 am to noon you can see gamelan on Mondays, Tuesdays and Thursdays, wayang on Wednesdays and Saturdays or classical dancing on Sundays.

Water Castle (Taman Sari)

Just west of the kraton is the Taman Sari or Fragrant Garden. Better known in Yogya as the Water Castle, this was once a splendid pleasure park of palaces, pools and waterways for the sultan and his entourage. The architect of this elaborate retreat, built between 1758 and 1765, was Portuguese and from Batavia, and the story goes that the sultan had him executed to keep his hidden pleasure rooms secret. They were damaged first by Diponegoro's Java War, and an earthquake in 1865 helped finish the job. Today most of the Water Castle has tumbled down amidst dusty alleys, small houses and batik galleries, but it's an interesting place of eerie ruins with underground passages and a large subterranean mosque.

The bathing pools have been restored, not terribly well perhaps, but it is possible to imagine life in the harem. Once surrounded by gardens, the sultan and ladies of the harem relaxed here, and from the tower overlooking the pools the sultan was able to dally with his wives and witness the goings-on below.

The main entrance on Jalan Taman leads first to the restored bathing pools, which are open from 7 am to 5 pm daily and cost 500 rp entry. Alternatively, wander through from the bird market to the old ruins and the underground mosque before proceeding to the bathing pools. Guides will attach themselves to you, and offer a free guided tour that will inevitably end at a batik gallery – either shake them off, establish a price for a guided tour first up, or be prepared to put up with the hard sell at the end.

Bird Market (Pasar Ngasem)

At the edge of Taman Sari, the Pasar Ngasem is a colourful bird market crowded with hundreds of budgies, orioles, roosters and singing turtle-doves in ornamental cages. Lizards and other small animals are also on sale, as are big trays of bird feed consisting of swarming maggots and ants. From the back of the bird market, an alleyway leads up to the broken walls of Taman Sari for fine views across Yogya.

Other Palaces

The smaller **Pakualaman Kraton**, on Jalan Sultan Agung, is also open to visitors and has a small museum, a *pendopo* which can hold a full gamelan orchestra (performances are held every fifth Sunday) and a curious colonial house with fine cast-iron work. The kraton is open Tuesday, Thursday and Sunday from 9.30 am to 1.30 pm.

The **Ambarrukmo Palace**, in the grounds of the Ambarrukmo Palace Hotel, was built in the 1890s as a country house for Hamengkubuwono VII and is another good example of Javanese palace architecture.

Museums

On the north side of the main square in front of the kraton, the **Sono-Budoyo Museum** is the pick of Yogya's museums. Though not particularly well-maintained or labelled, it has a first-rate collection of Javanese arts, including wayang kulit puppets, topeng masks, kris and batik, and an outside courtyard which is packed with Hindu statuary. Artefacts from further afield are also on display, including some superb Balinese carvings. It's open from 8 am to 1.30 pm Tuesday to Thursday, to 11.15 am on Friday and to noon on weekends. Entrance is 250 rp. Wayang kulit performances are held here every evening from 8 to 10 pm.

Between the kraton entrance and the Sono-Budoyo Museum in the palace square, the **Museum Kereta Kraton** holds some opulent chariots of the sultans. It's open from 8 am to 4 pm daily and admission is 250 rp.

Dating from 1765, **Benteng Vredeburg** is the old Dutch fort opposite the post office at the southern continuation of Jalan Malioboro. The restored fort now houses a museum with dioramas showing the history of the independence movement. The fort architecture is worth a look, but the dioramas are mostly for Indonesian patriots. Opening hours are 8.30 am to 1.30 pm Tuesday to Thursday, to 11 am on Friday and to noon on weekends. Admission is 200 rp.

Up until his death in 1990, Affandi, Indonesia's internationally best known artist, lived and worked in an unusual tree-house studio about six km from the centre of town overlooking the river on Jalan Solo. The **Affandi Museum** in the grounds exhibits his impressionist works, as well as paintings by his daughter Kartika and other artists. Affandi is buried in the back yard. It's open from 9 am to 3 pm and entry costs 500 rp.

The **Sasmitaluka Jenderal Sudirman** on Jalan B Harun is the memorial home of General Sudirman, the Commander of the Revolutionary forces. Wasted by tuberculosis, Sudirman reputedly often led his forces from a litter. He died shortly after the siege of Yogya in 1948. The house is open every morning except Monday.

The **Museum Sasana Wiratama**, also known as the Monumen Diponegoro, honours the Indonesian hero, Prince Diponegoro, leader of the bloody but futile rebellion of 1825-30 against the Dutch. A motley collection of the prince's belongings and other exhibits are kept in a small museum built at the site of his former Yogya residence. There's still a hole in the wall which Diponegoro is supposed to have shattered with his bare fists so that he and his supporters could escape. The museum is open from 8 am to 1 pm daily.

The **Museum Biologi** at Jalan Sultan Agung 22 has a collection of stuffed animals and plants from the whole archipelago. It is closed on Sundays. The **Museum Perjuangan**, in the southern part of the city on Jalan Kol Sugiyono, has a small and rather poor collection of photographs documenting the Indonesian Revolution. The large **Army Museum** (Museum Dharma Wiratama), on the corner of Jalan Jenderal Sudirman and Jalan Cik Ditiro, displays more documents, home-made weapons, uniforms and medical equipment from the revolution years. Records also trace Soeharto's rise in the ranks of Yogya's Diponegoro Division. It is open 8 am to 1 pm Monday to Thursday and 8 am to noon Saturday and Sunday.

Kota Gede

Kota Gede has been famous since the 1930s as the centre of Yogya's silver industry, but this quiet old town, now a suburb of Yogya, was the first capital of the Mataram kingdom founded by Panembahan Senopati in 1582. Senopati is buried in the small mossy graveyard of an old mosque near the town's central market. The sacred tomb is open only on Sunday, Monday and Thursday from around 9 am to noon, and on Friday from around 1 to 3 pm. Visitors should wear conservative dress. On other days there is little to see here but a murky mandi and a few goldfish.

The main street leading into town from the north (Jalan Kemasan) is lined with busy silver workshops where you're free to wander round and watch the silversmiths at work. Most of the shops have similar stock, including hand-beaten bowls, boxes, fine filigree and modern jewellery. See Shopping & Handicrafts for information on Kota Gede's silversmiths.

Kota Gede is about five km south-east of Jalan Malioboro – take bus No 4 or No 8. You can also take a becak, but andong (about 1000 rp) is cheaper, more agreeable and more human. Cycling is also pleasant on the back road and it is pretty flat all the way.

Other Attractions

In the evenings, if you are bored, you can always head along to the **Purawisata** on Brigjen Katamso. This amusement park is noted more for its dance performances, but there are also rides, fun fair games and a Pasar Seni (Art Market) with a basic collection of souvenirs.

Yogya's **Gembira Loka Zoo** is a spacious but sad affair – dusty and hot in the dry season, muddy in the wet and the rag-bag collection of animals are a miserable-looking bunch.

Organised Tours

Yogya is the best place in Java to arrange tours. Tour agents can be found on Jalan Prawirotoman, Jalan Sosrowijayan, Jalan Dagen and Jalan Pasar Kembang – there are so many offering similar tours at very competitive prices that it is difficult to recommend one in particular. The big national travel agents are also represented in Yogya – Pacto, Nitour, Natrabu, etc – but prices are much higher.

Typical day tours and per person rates through the budget operators are: Borobudur (15,000 rp), Dieng (20,000 rp), Prambanan (15,000 rp), Parangtretes and Kota Gede (20,000 rp), Mt Merapi (20,000 rp) and Gedung Songo (27,000 rp). Longer tours, such as to Mt Bromo (80,000 rp; two days/one night) and Bali, are also offered. Tours are often dependent on getting enough people to fill a minibus (usually four at minimum), and prices will vary depending if air-con and snacks are provided. Check if the price includes entry to the attractions such as Borobudur.

If you want to put together your own tour,

tour operators also arrange cars with driver at some of the best rates in Java.

Festivals
The three special Garebeg festivals held each year are Java's most colourful and grand processions. Palace guards and retainers in traditional court dress and large floats of flower-bedecked *gunungans* (mountains) of rice all make their way to the mosque west of the kraton to the sound of prayer and the inevitable music of gamelan. These are ceremonies not to be missed if you're anywhere in the area at the time.

Places to Stay – bottom end
Accommodation in Yogya is remarkably good value and there is a superb choice. It's certainly the best city in Java for places to stay and places to eat. The central Sosro area has the really cheap places and the best location, while the Prawirotaman area, a couple of km south of the kraton, has mostly mid-range places and a few cheap options.

Sosrowijayan Area Most of the cheap hotels are in the Sosrowijayan area, immediately south of the railway line between Jalan Pasar Kembang and Jalan Sosrowijayan. Running between these two streets are the narrow alleyways of Gang Sosrowijayan I & II with most of the cheap accommodation and popular eating places. More good places to stay are in other small gangs in this area. Despite mass tourism, the gangs are quiet and still have a kampung feel to them. The area is central and Jalan Malioboro is a short stroll away.

Gang Sosrowijayan I has some very low-cost places. At the north end, the first place is *Losmen Sastrowihadi*, about as basic as you can get with singles/doubles for 4000/5000 rp. *Losmen Beta* is similar in price and standards but is more geared to travellers. A bit further along this gang is *Sari Homestay* with immaculate rooms built around a courtyard. Rooms with bath for 7000/10,000 rp are good value. Just around the corner, *Losmen Lucy* is in a newer, more salubrious establishment and good rooms are 7500/

10,000 rp. *Lima Losmen*, in the alley east of Gang I, is a dive but they don't come any cheaper at 3000 rp.

On Gang Sosrowijayan II is the clean, good-value *Hotel Bagus*. It's built around a central courtyard and clean rooms with fan cost 4500/6000 rp. Further south, the *Gandhi Losmen*, in its own garden, is a popular place with basic rooms for 6000 rp.

There are a host of small losmen around Gang II and the small alleys off it, most of them in a similar rock-bottom price range. *Hotel Selekta* is popular and friendly. It's roomier and lighter than most, and good value at 5000 rp or 7500 rp with bath. Further along the same alley, *Utar Pension* and *Isty Losmen* have rooms from 5000 rp. Both are good but a little dark and less popular. The *Supriyanto Inn* is good value with bright rooms at 4000/5000 rp.

Between Gang I and Gang II, the friendly *Dewi Homestay* is a brighter place with a garden and is deservedly popular. Rooms start at 6000 rp, and rooms with mandi are 10,000 rp.

On Jalan Sosrowijayan, between Gang I and Malioboro, is the security-conscious *Aziatic*, an old Dutch-style hotel. It is clean and cool. Large but run-down doubles are 10,000 rp and you can sit and chat in the wide central hallway/cafe. Across the road from the Aziatic, the large *Hotel Indonesia* has nice courtyard areas and good-sized rooms at 6000 rp; rooms with bath cost 7500 rp, 9000 rp and 12,000 rp.

At the western end of the street, 100 metres down an alley, is the popular and well-run *Ella Homestay*. It's good value with rooms from 5000/7000 rp up to 7000/9000 rp with bath, including breakfast.

Jalan Pasar Kembang also has plenty of cheap losmen, but the cheapest places are seedy and it is mostly a street for mid-range hotels.

Jalan Prawirotaman This area does have some cheaper places like the neat, clean and helpful *Vagabond Youth Hostel* (☎ 71207) at Jalan Prawirotaman MG III/589. Dormitory beds cost 5000 rp, singles cost from 5500 to

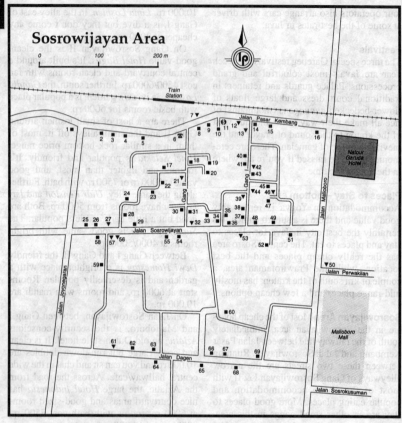

Sosrowijayan Area

13,000 rp and doubles from 10,000 to 15,000 rp. Student and HI card holders can get a small discount.

The quiet *Didi's Hostel*, down an alleyway opposite the Duta Guest House, is part of the Duta chain. The small, clean rooms with outside bath are a little expensive at 8500/11,000 rp but you can use the pool at the Duta.

If you spend a little extra, Jalan Prawirotaman has some good-value places that straddle the bottom end and mid-range. Breakfast is included in the tariff. The new *Indraprastha Homestay* (☎ 74087) has bright

rooms with shower and toilet for 10,000/15,000 rp. It is one of the best buys.

The next street south, Jalan Prawirotaman II, is quieter and cheaper. *Guest House Makuta* has a pleasant garden and clean rooms with attached bathroom for 8000/11,000 rp, 11,000/15,000 rp or 13,000/20,000 rp with hot water. The *Muria Guest House* (☎ 87211) at MGIII/600 is reasonable at 12,500 rp for doubles with attached bathroom. Others include the more spartan *Post Card Guest House*, run by the bigger Metro, with rooms from 10,000 rp, and the *Merapi* with rooms for 10,000/15,000 rp.

PLACES TO STAY		34	Dewi Homestay	69	Wisma Perdada
		35	Losmen Happy Inn		
1	Hotel Kota	36	Losmen Rama	**PLACES TO EAT**	
2	Berlian Palace	37	Hotel Rama		
3	Nusantara	38	Hotel Jogja	7	Mama's Warung
4	Losmen Tugu	40	Losmen Sastrowihadi	12	Borobudur Bar &
5	Hotel Mendut	41	Losmen Beta		Restaurant
8	Batik Palace Hotel	43	Sari Homestay	13	Cheap Warungs
9	Hotel Asia-Afrika	45	Losmen Lucy	21	Anna's Restaurant
10	Hotel Ratna	47	Lima Losmen	27	Bladok Restaurant
14	Kencana Hotel	48	Hotel Kartika	32	Es Puter Tanjung
15	Trim Guest House	49	Hotel Aziatic	39	New Superman's
16	Hotel Trim	51	Marina Palace Hotel		Restaurant
17	Losmen Setia	52	Hotel Indonesia	42	Superman's Restaurant
18	Hotel Bagus	54	Bakti Kasih	44	Eko Restaurant
19	Supriyanto Inn	55	Wisma Gambira	46	Bruin Cafe
20	Losmen Setia Kawan	58	Oryza Hotel	50	Legian Restaurant
22	Isty Losmen	59	Ella Homestay	53	Ris Restaurant
23	Utar Pension	60	Batik Palace Cottages	56	Caterina Restaurant
24	Hotel Selekta	62	Puntodewo Guest	57	Apapaya
25	Hotel Sala Baru		House	61	Manna Restaurant
26	Hotel Karunia	63	Wisma Nendra		
28	Losmen Wisma Wijaya	64	Kombokarno Hotel	**OTHER**	
29	Losmen Morris	65	Peti Mas		
30	Jaya Losmen	66	Blue Safir Hotel	6	Wartel Telephone Office
31	Gandhi Losmen	67	Lilik Guest House	11	PT Haji La Tunrung
33	Losmen Atiep	68	Sri Wibowo Hotel		Moneychanger

Places to Stay – middle

Sosrowijayan Area Jalan Pasar Kembang, opposite the railway, has a number of mid-range hotels. The *Asia-Afrika* (☎ 66219), 21 Jalan Pasar Kembang, has a pool and an attractive garden cafe. Prices start at 16,000/22,000 rp for very ordinary singles/doubles with mandi up to 50,000/57,000 rp for good air-con rooms with hot water showers.

A notch up in quality, the *Hotel Mendut* (☎ 3114) at No 49 also has a swimming pool and air-con rooms starting at 45,000 rp plus 20% tax and service. At No 62, *Berlian Palace* (☎ 60312) is a new hotel typical of the area. It looks flash, and the rooms are comfortable enough, but it is cheaply built and destined to quickly drop in standards and price. Air-con rooms with hot water cost 55,000 to 75,000 rp. *Hotel Trim* (☎ 4113), Jalan Pasar Kembang 2, is another newer hotel, reasonably priced at 35,000/45,000 rp for a room with shower and hot water, or with air-con from 45,000/50,000 rp.

Part of a chain, the *Batik Palace Hotel* (☎ 63824), Jalan Pasar Kembang 29, has a nice garden and rooms starting at US$20/25.

The sister *New Batik Palace Hotel* (☎ 62229), nearby at Jalan Mangkubumi 46 (see the main Yogya map), is better and has a swimming pool and rooms from US$27/33. Better still, *Batik Palace Cottages* (☎ 61828) has spacious grounds and a large pool. It is in the quiet back alleys, just north of Jalan Dagen and only a short stroll from Jalan Malioboro. Air-con rooms cost US$22/27 or bungalows start at US$27/33. All these three charge 10% tax.

Jalan Sosrowijayan, one street south of Pasar Kembang, also has some good mid-range hotels. At No 78, the very friendly *Hotel Karunia* (☎ 65057) is a cheaper alternative with a good rooftop restaurant. Fan rooms cost 10,000/12,000 rp, rooms with mandi cost 16,000/18,000 rp or air-con rooms are 30,000 rp – a pretty good deal. At No 49, *Oryza Hotel* (☎ 2495) is a renovated villa with some style. Pleasant rooms with shared mandi cost 17,500 rp and rooms with private bath cost 20,000 to 37,500 rp.

Jalan Dagen, one street further south from Jalan Sosrowijayan, is another slightly over-priced mid-range enclave – ask for a discount.

The clean, well-kept *Peti Mas* (☎ 2896), Jalan Dagen 39, is a European favourite. It has a pool and an attractive garden restaurant, but the rooms are not stunning for the price: doubles with bathroom and fan cost 30,000/33,000 to 40,000/44,000 rp, with aircon from 53,000/58,000 to 79,000/84,000 rp, including breakfast. Nearby at No 23, the *Sri Wibowo* (☎ 63084) has rooms with shared mandis from 19,500 rp, singles/doubles with mandis run 30,500/40,500 rp, and air-con rooms start at 42,500 rp. The *Wisma Perdada* at No 6, *Blue Safir* at No 34-36 and *Kombokarno Hotel* at No 49 have a similar range of rooms and prices. Cheaper hotels are the *Wisma Nendra* and the *Puntodewo Guest House*, with rooms for around 20,000 rp.

Other *Indraloka Home Stay* (☎ 64341), Jalan Cik Ditiro 14, is north of the centre near the Gajah Mada University and so is popular with overseas students and longer term visitors. Singles/doubles with air-con and hot water in this old colonial house cost US$18/21 plus 20% tax and service. Tours are organised, and a network of family homestay accommodation is run from here – ring for details on homestays in Yogya and elsewhere in Java. The *Gadjah Mada Guest House* (☎ 95225), further north, is similar in price and also popular with students.

Jalan Prawirotaman This street, a couple of km south of the city centre, is a more upmarket enclave than Sosrowijayan. Many of the hotels are converted old houses that are spacious, quiet and have central garden areas. Swimming pools are the norm.

The *Airlangga Guest House* (☎ 63344) at No 6-8 has fan rooms for 35,000/40,000 rp and air-con rooms for 40,000/50,000 rp, plus 20% tax and service. This high-density hotel is somewhat cramped but the rooms are some of the best on offer in Prawirotaman (but avoid those directly above the noisy nightclub).

Further down the street, the smaller *Prambanan Guest House* (☎ 76167) at No 14 is a new place with a pool, attractive garden and very comfortable rooms for 30,000/

40,000 rp with fan and hot water or 50,000/60,000 rp for larger rooms with air-con.

At No 26, the big *Duta Guest House* (☎ 72064) is favoured by European tour groups. This is one of the more luxurious places and the garden is very inviting, but it is often crowded and service can be lacking. Rooms range from 25,500/32,000 rp with fan up to 72,000/81,000 rp for the air-con rooms around the pool. The quality varies enormously, so check out a few first.

A lot of the guesthouses in the old villas are pleasant enough but the rooms can be dingy. The *Sumaryo Guest House* (☎ 73507) at No 22 is one of the better ones and has a pool. Rooms range from 15,000 to 45,000 rp. Others with pool in the same price range are the *Wisma Indah* (☎ 76021) at No 16 and the *Sriwijaya* (☎ 71870) at No 7.

The *Kirana Guest House* (☎ 76600) doesn't have a pool but is furnished with antiques and has plenty of colonial style. Even so, it is a little faded and expensive at 33,000/40,000 to 44,000/52,000 rp.

Around the corner from Jalan Prawirotaman, at Jalan Sisingamangaraja 74, the new *Ayodya Hotel* (☎ 72475) has a large pool and is the best hotel in the area. Immaculate air-con rooms with hot water and TV cost US$31/34 or bigger rooms with mini-bar are US$39/42.

The next street south is Jalan Prawirotaman II, where the Pasar Pagi (morning market) is located. This street is quieter than Jalan Prawirotaman I, and the hotels are not as flash. The *Metro* (☎ 5004) at No 71, often filled with Europeans, is the most popular and has a garden area and pool (in the annexe across the street). Rates start at 9000/15,000 rp for lousy rooms with shared bathroom to 40,500/46,000 rp for reasonable rooms with air-con and hot water showers. *Agung Guest House* (☎ 5512) at No 68 is also popular. The *Delta Homestay* (☎ 55135) at No 597A, another in the Duta chain, has a pool and good rooms for 10,500/15,000 rp or 21,000/25,000 rp with bathroom.

Places to Stay – top end
Yogya has a glut of luxury hotels and dis-

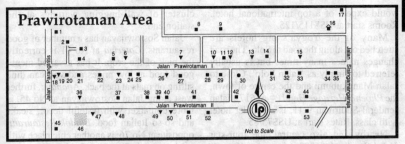

Prawirotaman Area

Not to Scale

PLACES TO STAY		
1	Hotel Sri Timur	
2	Indraprastha Homestay	
3	Puri Pertiwi	
4	Borobudur Guest House	
5	Sriwijaya Guest House	
8	Didi's Hostel	
9	Wisma Harto	
11	Gunarto Guest House	
14	Perwita Sari Guest House	
16	Vagabond Youth Hostel	
17	Ayodya Hotel	
20	Wisma Gajah	
21	Airlangga Guest House	
22	Putra Jaya Guest House	
24	Prambanan Guest House	
25	Wisma Indah	
27	Sumaryo Guest House	
28	Duta Guest House	
29	Rose Guest House	

31	Wisma Pari Kesit	
32	Prayogo Guest House	
33	Galunggung Guest House	
34	Kirana Guest House	
35	Sartika Homestay	
37	Delta Homestay	
38	Merapi Guesthouse	
39	Muria Guest House	
40	Gayatri Guest House	
41	Metro Guest House	
42	Agung Guest House	
43	Kroto Homestay	
44	Palupi Guest House	
45	Sunarko Guest House	
51	Metro Guest House	
52	Makuta Guest House	
53	Post Card Guest House	

PLACES TO EAT

6	Hanoman's Forest Restaurant	
7	Griya Bujana Restaurant	

10	Putri Restaurant	
12	Simco Restaurant	
13	French Grill Restaurant	
15	Galunggung Restaurant & Pub	
18	Tante Lies (Warung Java Timur)	
19	Melati Garden	
23	Palm House Restaurant	
26	La Beng Beng Restaurant	
36	Lotus Garden	
47	Bamboo House Restaurant	
48	Nini Restaurant	
49	Ramayana Restaurant	
50	Cafe Lotus	

OTHER

30	Prawirotaman International Bookshop	
46	Morning Market (Pasar Pagi)	

counts of 20 to 40% are readily available for the asking. If arriving by air, the hotel booking desk at the airport has tariffs substantially below the published rates listed here. Most of the big hotels are on the Solo/airport road or on Jalan Malioboro. All the following have swimming pools and add 21% tax and service.

The big *Natour Garuda Hotel* (☎ 2113) at Jalan Malioboro 60 was once a grand colonial edifice, Yogya's premier hotel in Dutch times. Numerous renovations over the years has seen it lose much of its colonial grace, but it is still one of Yogya's best and the position is hard to beat. Singles/doubles are US$90/105 and suites start at US$185.

Further down Jalan Malioboro at No 18, the *Mutiara Hotel* (☎ 63814) is also very central, right next to the Tourist Information Centre. It is a definite notch below Yogya's best hotels but reasonably priced at 94,500/105,000 rp. The old part of the hotel a few doors along has good mid-range rooms for half the price.

Just to the east of Malioboro is the huge, new *Melia Purosani Hotel* (☎ 89521), Jalan Suryotomo 31. So far, this is Yogya's only five-star hotel with all the facilities you

JAVA

would expect of a top international hotel. Rooms start at US$115/125.

Many of the Yogya's big hotels are stretched out along the road to Solo. The road changes names many times but is usually referred to simply as 'Jalan Solo'. Close to Jalan Mangkubumi and the centre of town, the *Phoenix Heritage Hotel* (☎ 66617), Jalan Jenderal Sudirman 9-11, is a smaller hotel with class. Rates start at US$75/85.

Nearby and also central, the four-star *Hotel Santika* (☎ 63036) is one of Yogya's best hotels. Rooms start at US$95/105.

On Jalan Solo about five km from the centre, the *Ambarrukmo Palace Hotel* (☎ 88488), Jalan Adisucipto, is a 1960s Soekarno-inspired construction and contains the old Ambarrukmo Palace in its grounds. For long the most prestigious hotel in Yogya, it now has a lot of good competition and is looking a little tired. Singles/doubles begin at US$95/105.

Places to Eat

Sosrowijayan Area The area is overrun with cheap eating houses featuring Western breakfasts and snacks, as well as Indonesian dishes, and no travellers' menu is complete without fruit salads and banana pancakes. The food is distinguished by big helpings and low prices.

A whole host of good warungs line Jalan Pasar Kembang, beside the railway line, but *Mama's* is definitely number one in the evenings. On Jalan Pasar Kembang at No 17, *Borobudur Bar & Restaurant* has average fare at high prices, but they have unlimited cold beer and bands later in the evening.

Gang Sosrowijayan I is a favourite hunting ground for cheap eats. The original *Superman's* has been serving up hippy fodder for decades, though its offshoot *New Superman's*, a bit further down Gang I, is better and more popular. Cheap no-frills eateries on Gang I include *N & N* and *Anna's*. *Eko Restaurant* serves steaks, which are not as good or as famous as they would have you believe, but are certainly cheap. For the cheapest eats on Gang I, head to the little

cluster of wall-hugging warungs at the station end.

Jalan Sosrowijayan has a number of good restaurants. *Caterina* at No 41 is currently the pick of the crop. It has a varied menu, good food at low prices and you can dine sitting on mats at the back. *Apapaya*, further west along Jalan Sosrowijayan at No 45, is more upmarket with tasteful decor, steaks and so-so Italian food. *Bladok Restaurant*, opposite at No 76, is another chic place with predominantly European food.

Jalan Malioboro After 9 pm, the souvenir vendors pack up and a *lesahan* area comes alive along the north end of Malioboro, staying open till early morning. Food stalls serve Yogya's specialities, such as *nasi gudeg* (rice with jackfruit in coconut milk) and *ayam goreng* (fried chicken). Here young Indonesians sit around strumming guitars and playing chess into the wee hours. Dine cross-legged on mats and take in the nightlife.

Hidden away upstairs on the corner of Jalan Malioboro and Jalan Perwakilan (see the Sosro Area map), the *Legian Restaurant* has Indonesian, Chinese, French and Italian food served by Balinese waiters in a roof-garden setting. It's very classy and they do a great claypot *gudeg ayam* (chicken with jackfruit), but the Western dishes are uninspiring and expensive.

That big new intrusion on Jalan Malioboro – Malioboro Mall – is not complete without fast food, and *McDonald's* takes pride of place at the front of this monument to Western consumerism. The top floor of the mall also has a squeaky clean food stall area with food of questionable quality, but the juice stall is good.

An excellent little eatery is *Cherry Cafe*, upstairs at Jalan Jenderal A Yani 57, the southern extension of Jalan Malioboro. This spotless cafe is a great place to sit overlooking Malioboro after a hard shopping session. They serve tasty Western, Chinese and Indonesian dishes at moderate prices – the *opor ayam* (chicken in coconut milk) is particularly good. The cafe is hard to find – take the narrow flight of stairs next to the Tatiana Batik shop opposite the market.

At Jalan Mangkubumi No 28, the *Tip Top* has been serving up excellent ice cream and cakes since Bill Dalton was a boy. The aircon *Restaurant Rama* at No 99 is one of Yogya's best Chinese restaurants.

Jalan Prawirotaman Several medium-priced restaurants along this street seem to specialise in slow service and mediocre food for tourists. Fortunately, there are some exceptions. The primary budget recommendation is *Tante Lies*, also known as *Warung Java Timur* at the Jalan Parangtritis intersection. They serve excellent sate, nasi pecel, soto ayam and other Central and East Javanese dishes at very reasonable prices.

Hanoman's Forest Restaurant features moderately priced Indonesian and Western cuisine, but the main attraction is the classical Javanese dance, wayang golek or wayang kulit shows each night. A cover charge of 2000 rp applies for each performance.

The *Griya Bujana* is very clean and the food is reasonable. For savoury soy chicken and some good fish dishes, dine at the *Palm House*.

On Jalan Tirtodipuran, the continuation of Prawirotaman, *Baleanda Restaurant* at No 3 (see the main Yogya map) is in a beautiful garden setting with an art gallery at back. The expensive food is no better than anywhere else, but this has to be one of Yogya's most attractive restaurants.

Other Good eats can be found to the north of the city out towards Gajah Mada University. *Pujayo*, Jalan Simanjuntak 73, out towards the university, is Yogya's best food stall restaurant. A dozen food vendors split over two floors serve a mind-boggling array of dishes and drinks at low prices in ultra hygienic surrounds – and karaoke is thrown in as well (6 to 8 pm is the time for songless dining).

The *Pesta Perak*, Jalan Tentara Rakyat Mataram 8, about one km west of Jalan Malioboro, has a delightful garden ambience and sometimes puts on gamelan music.

Excellent lunch and dinner buffets for 10,000 rp feature a whole range of Javanese dishes. Not surprisingly it is a very popular tourist restaurant.

The famous Yogya fried chicken leaves the colonel's recipe for dead. Yogya chicken is boiled in the water of young coconuts and then deep fried – absolute heaven when done well. One of the most famous purveyors was Mbok Berek out on Jalan Solo just before Prambanan, and in her wake a host of eateries have appeared nearby with similar names. *Nyonya Suharti*, Jalan Adiscupto 208 just past the Ambarrukmo Palace, has restaurants all over Java and is popular with tour groups.

Entertainment

Yogya is by far the easiest place to see traditional Javanese performing arts, and you can see performances of one sort or another every day of the week. Performances of dance, wayang or gamelan are held every morning at the kraton (see above) and are a good introduction to Javanese arts. Check with the tourist office for any special events.

Most famous of all is the spectacular *Ramayana* ballet held at nearby Prambanan during full moon in the dry season. See under Prambanan for details.

Wayang Kulit Leather puppet performances can be seen at several places around Yogya on virtually every night of the week. Most of the centres offer shortened versions for tourists but at Sasono Hinggil, in the alun alun selatan of the kraton, marathon all-night performances are held every second Saturday from 9 pm to 5 am.

Abbreviated wayang kulit performances are held every day, except Saturday, at the Agastya Art Institute, Jalan Gedong Kiwo MD III/237, where dalang are trained. The two-hour show begins at 3 pm.

The Sono-Budoyo Museum, near the kraton, also has two-hour performances every day from 8 pm for 3000 rp.

One-hour, tourist-oriented shows are held at the Yogyakarta Craft Centre on Jalan Adisucipto near the Ambarrukmo Hotel, about seven km from the city centre. Shows are at 8 pm every day. The Arjuna Plaza Hotel, Jalan Mangkubumi 48, also has two-hour wayang kulit shows on Tuesday at 7 pm.

Wayang Golek Wooden puppet plays are also performed frequently. The Nitour performance, from 11 am to 1 pm every day except Sunday, has a useful handout explaining the history of the wayang and the *Ramayana* story. Performances are held at Jalan Ahmad Dahlan 71.

On Saturday there are wayang golek performances at the Agastya Art Institute from 3 to 5 pm, and at the Arjuna Plaza Hotel from 7 to 9 pm. You can also see wayang practice sessions at Agastya daily between 3 and 5 pm.

Wayang Orang 'People wayang' (wayang wong in Javanese) performances are usually based on the *Ramayana*, or at least billed as 'Ramayana ballet' because of the famed performances at Prambanan.

Those at the Purawisata theater in the amusement park on Jalan Katamso are excellent; they are performed nightly from 8 to 10 pm.

Another fine troupe performs at Dalem Pujokusuman at Jalan Katamso 45 on Monday, Wednesday and Friday evenings from 8 to 10 pm for 6000 rp. The Ambarrukmo Palace Hotel has *Ramayana* ballet performances most nights at the hotel's Borobudur Restaurant on the 7th floor, and sometimes at the palace pavilion in the garden. The schedule changes, so check with the hotel (☎ 88984). Arjuna Plaza Hotel has *Ramayana* performances from 8 to 10 pm every Thursday night.

Schools ISI (Indonesia Institute of Arts) Dance Faculty on Jalan Colombo in north Yogya is open to visitors from 8 am to 2 pm, Monday to Saturday. Bagong Kussudiarja, one of Indonesia's leading dance choreographers, has a school at Jalan Singosaren 9 (off Jalan Wates) where modern and classical dance practice sessions are held. Kussudiarja's main studio is at Padepokan, five km from

Yogya, where he runs courses for foreign students.

Other *Ketoprak* (traditional folk drama) performances are held at the RRI auditorium, Jalan Gejayan, from 8 pm to midnight on the first Saturday of every month.

Some of the big hotels, such as the Ambarrukmo Palace and the Garuda, have gamelan music in their lobbies during the day. Other hotels and restaurants have gamelan or wayang performances. On Jalan Prawirotoman, Hanoman's Forest Restaurant has different wayang performances every night of the week.

Things to Buy

Yogya is a noted batik centre, but other craft industries in and around Yogya include silver, leather, pottery and wayang puppets. Even if you don't intend to buy, galleries and workshops are open free of charge for visitors to observe traditional Javanese crafts.

For serious shoppers, Yogya has a great array of crafts and antiques, primarily from Java, but bits and pieces from all over the archipelago can be found. By way of comparison, Yogya's prices are reasonable without being really cheap.

Jalan Malioboro is one great long colourful bazaar of souvenir shops and stalls and is a good place to start shopping. The street stalls offer a wide selection of cheap cotton clothes, leatherwork, batik bags, topeng masks and wayang golek puppets. They are the cheapest place to buy souvenirs, depending on your bargaining skills. Look in some of the fixed priced shops on Jalan Malioboro to get an idea of prices. Mirota Batik, Jalan A Yani 9, is a good place to start. It specialises in batik but also has a wide selection of handicrafts at reasonable prices. Malioboro's labyrinthine and newly renovated market, Pasar Beringharjo, is always worth a browse, especially for cheap batik and textiles.

The other major area to shop is Jalan Tirtodipuran, the continuation of Jalan Prawirotoman. Here you'll find a string of batik factories, galleries and art shops. This is an interesting, more upmarket shopping stretch, with furniture, antiques and a variety of crafts and curios from Java and further afield.

On Jalan Adisucipto, opposite the Ambarrukmo Palace, the government-promoted, fixed price Yogyakarta Craft Centre, has a sad collection of overpriced souvenirs. Other shops can be found nearby, and the hotel itself has a few expensive art shops. The Purawisata amusement park also has souvenirs and crafts, but these are less interesting shopping areas.

Batik Batik in the markets is cheaper than in the stores, but you need to be careful about quality and be prepared to bargain. A good place to start looking is the Terang Bulan shop, Jalan A Yani 108 (just before the market as you head south on Jalan Malioboro), which will give you an idea of what you should be paying. Other shops in town include Ramayana Batik, Jalan Ahmad Dahlan 21, specialising in Yogya-style batik, and the more expensive Batik Keris, a branch of the big Solo batik house on Jalan A Yani 71. Many other reasonably priced shops are on Jalan Malioboro/ A Yani.

Most of the batik workshops and several large showrooms are along Jalan Tirtodipuran to the south of the kraton. Many, such as Batik Indah, Jalan Tirtodipuran 6A, give free guided tours of the batik process.

Batik Painting Some artists who pioneered and grew famous from batik painting still produce some batik works. Kuswadji, in the north square next to the Museum Kereta Kraton, has classical batik art on display, and 'new wave' abstract pieces. Tulus Warsito has a gallery with a contemporary orientation at Jalan Tirtodipuran 19A. Top of the scale is Amri Yahya's very expensive gallery at Jalan Gampingan 67, near Yogya's ISI (Fine Arts Faculty), though he mostly produces abstract oil paintings these days.

Prices are high at the better known galleries, ridiculously cheap at the mass-production galleries, most of which are found around Taman Sari (Water Castle).

Styles go through cycles – from the psyche-delic mushroom era, to endless birds, butterflies and soaring moons over rice paddies. Now in vogue are more palatable traditional scenes from the wayang, *Ramayana*, etc, as well as abstract paintings. Most are very similar, so shop around for something unique and always bargain hard.

Yogya is crawling with batik salesmen, who'll strike up a conversation on Malioboro or follow you around Taman Sari, pretending to be guides or simply instant friends. Inevitably you'll end up at a gallery where they'll rake in a commission if you buy.

Batik Courses If you want to have a go at batik yourself there are lots of batik courses and classes in Yogya.

Hadjir Digdodarmojo has been teaching batik for years and has three and five-day courses. His studio is on the left of the main entrance to the Water Castle at Taman Kp 3/177. Tulus Warsito at Jalan Tirtodipuran 19A is one of Yogya's top batik artists and also conducts classes. The most thorough course with the best facilities is likely to be at the Batik & Handicraft Research Centre, Jalan Kusumanegara 2, which offers comprehensive one-month courses.

Antiques, Curios & Furniture While a few antiques can be found, they are best left to collectors who know their stuff. Yogya art shops spend an inordinate amount of time defacing wayang golek puppets and topeng masks in the name of antiquity, and many other items get similar treatment.

Along Jalan Tirtodipuran you can buy artefacts from all over Java and Indonesia. Shops to try include Dieng at No 30, Delly at No 22B and their offshoot Hanoman at No 57. Griya Kristaya Nugraha at No 65 has a good collection of old chests and furniture, or Borneo Boutique at No 49 specialises in textiles, particularly ikat from Nusa Tenggara.

Silver Silverwork can be found all over town, but the best area to shop is in the silver village of Kota Gede. Fine filigree work is a

Yogya speciality but many styles and designs are available. Kota Gede has some very attractive jewellery, boxes, bowls, cutlery and miniatures.

You can get a guided tour of the process, with no obligation to buy, at the large factories such as Tom's Silver, Jalan Ngeski Gondo 60, HS at Jalan Tegal Gendu 22, and MD, Jalan Pesegah KG 8/44, down a small alley off the street. Tom's has an extensive selection and some superb large pieces, but prices are very high. HS is marginally cheaper, as is MD, but always ask for a substantial discount off the marked prices. Kota Gede has dozens of smaller silver shops on Jalan Kemesan and Jalan Mondorakan where you can get some good buys if you bargain.

Other Crafts Yogya's leatherwork can be excellent value for money, and the quality is usually high, but always check stitching, etc. Shops and street stalls on Jalan Malioboro are the best places to shop for leatherwork.

Good quality wayang puppets are made at the Mulyo Suhardjo workshop on Jalan Taman Sari and also sold at the Sono-Budoyo museum shop. Swasthigita, Ngadinegaran MJ 7/50, just north of Jalan Tirtodipuran, is another wayang kulit puppet manufacturer.

Kasongan, the potters' village a few km south-west of Yogya, produces an astonishing array of pottery, mostly large figurines and pots.

Along Jalan Malioboro, *stempel* vendors create personalised stamps hand-carved on leather. Expect to pay 5000 rp or less for a reasonably sized stamp with name, address and a simple design.

Getting There & Away
Air Garuda (☎ 4400), Jalan Mangkubumi 56, has direct flights to Jakarta (128,100 rp) and Denpasar (120,400 rp) with onward domestic and international connections.

The Merpati office (☎ 4272) is in the Java Palace Hotel at Jalan Jenderal Sudirman 63. Merpati flies directly to Surabaya (64,300 rp), from where connections go to Ujung Pandang (266,100 rp), Banjarmasin

(190,200 rp), Kupang (339,800 rp), Maumere (318,900 rp), Mataram (167,100 rp), Denpasar and other regional centres.

Bouraq (☎ 65840), Jalan Mataram 60, has direct flights to Bandung (83,200 rp) and Banjarmasin (189,900 rp). Other flights to Balikpapan, Samarinda, Tarakan and Palu are routed through Banjarmasin.

Sempati (☎ 61475), in the Hotel Garuda at Jalan Malioboro 60, has direct flights to Jakarta and Surabaya, with a host of connections including Pekanbaru (350,800 rp), Padang (365,100 rp) and Balikpapan (433,300 rp).

Bus Yogya's Umbulharjo bus station is four km south-east of the city centre. From the terminal, buses run all over Java and to Bali. Ordinary/air-con buses include: Solo (1200/2000 rp; two hours), Magelang (900/1500 rp; 1½ hours), Semarang (1800/3200 rp; 3½ hours), Wonogiri (1500 rp; 2½ hours), Purwokerto (3000/5000 rp; 4½ hours), Cilacap (3700 rp; five hours), Bandung (8700/14,700 rp; 10 hours), Jakarta (11,000/18,700 rp; 12 hours) via Purwokerto and Bogor, Surabaya (5500/9300 rp; eight hours), Probolinggo (7300/14,500 rp; nine hours) and Denpasar (13,000/22,000 rp; 16 hours).

For the long hauls you are better off taking the big luxury buses. Agents can be found at the bus station or along Jalan Mangkubumi but it's less hassle to simply check fares and departures with the ticket agents along Jalan Sosrowijayan, near the Hotel Aziatic, or on Jalan Prawirotaman. These agents can also arrange pickup from your hotel. Typical fares are: Denpasar (35,000 rp), Surabaya and Malang (16,000 rp), Bandung (22,000 rp), Bogor (23,000 rp) and Jakarta (23,000 rp right up to 40,000 rp for super luxury). Direct minibuses to Pangandaran (17,500 rp air-con) and Mt Bromo (25,000 rp non-air-con) are also arranged.

From the main bus station, buses also operate regularly to all the towns in the immediate area: Borobudur (1000 rp; 1½ hours), Parangtritis (1000 rp; one hour) and Kaliurang (500 rp; one hour). For Prambanan (250 rp), take the yellow Pemuda bus.

For Imogiri (350 rp; 40 minutes) take a colt or the Abadi bus No 5 to Panggang and tell the conductor to let you off at the *makam* (graves). Buses to Imogiri and Parangtretes can also be caught on Jalan Sisingamanga- raja at the end of Jalan Prawirotaman. You can catch the Borobudur bus going north along Jalan Magelang at the Pingit bus stop.

Apart from the main bus station, colts operate to the outlying towns from various sub-terminals. The most useful is the Terban sub-terminal to the north of the centre on Jalan Simanjuntak. From here colts go to Kaliurang (800 rp), and Solo (1500 rp) passing the airport en route.

Buses, and colts in particular, to the tourist attractions around Yogya are renowned for overcharging. Know the correct fare before boarding, and tender the right money.

Minibus Door-to-door minibuses run to all major cities from Yogya. Many companies are found on Jalan Diponegoro, or the Sosrowijayan and Prawirotaman agents also sell tickets. Most will pick up from hotels in Yogya, but not for the short runs like Solo (they will drop off at your Solo hotel, however).

On Jalan Diponegoro, SAA (☎ 63238) at 9A has minibuses to Solo (4000 rp air-con, two hours), Jakarta (30,000 rp; 12 hours), Malang and Surabaya (15,000 rp; seven hours), Cilacap (7000 rp; five hours), Semarang (5000 rp; three hours), as well as Purwokerto and Pekalongan.

Rahayu (☎ 61322) is another big agent at No 15 with frequent minibuses to Solo (3000 rp non-air con), Wonosobo (4500 rp non-air-con), Bandung (17,000 rp air-con, nine hours) and other destinations.

Erny Travel (☎ 87970) at No 47A have good air-con minibuses to Bogor (30,000 rp) and Jakarta.

Train Yogya's railway station is conveniently central. See the introductory Getting Around Java section for details of Jakarta-Yogya and Surabaya-Yogya travel.

Solo is on the main Yogya-Surabaya rail route, only about 1½ hours out of Yogya.

Four daily trains operate on the Bandung- Banjar-Yogya route. Trains to Bandung range from the ekonomi-only *Cepat* (4,500 rp; 12 hours), to the *Senja Utama* and *Ekspres* bisnis trains (15,000 rp; nine hours) and the luxury *Mutiara Selatan* night express (21,000 rp bisnis; 7½ hours).

Getting Around
To/From the Airport Taxis from Yogya's airport, 10 km to the east, operate on a coupon system and cost 5500 rp to Sosro- wijayan or 6000 rp to Prawirotaman.

If you stroll out to the main road, only 200 metres from the terminal, you can get a Solo colt to Yogya's Terban colt terminal (about 1½ km from Sosrowijayan) or a Solo bus to the bus terminal (about one km from Prawirotaman) for 250 rp.

Bus Yogya's city buses *(bis kota)*, operate on 17 set routes around the city for a flat 250 rp fare. They work mostly straight routes – going out and then coming back the same way – and all start and end at the bus station.

Bus No 2 is one of the more useful ser- vices. It runs from the bus station then turns down Jalan Sisingamangaraja, past Jalan Prawirotaman, then loops around, coming back up Jalan Parangtritis and on to Jalan Mataram a block from Jalan Malioboro, before continuing to the university, and return.

For Kota Gede, bus No 4 runs down Jalan Malioboro and on to Jalan Ngeksigondo – get off at Tom's Silver and walk one km south to the centre of the village. Bus No 8 from the bus terminal runs through the centre of Kota Gede.

Becak & Andong Yogya is over-endowed with becaks and it is impossible to go any- where in the main tourist areas without being greeted by choruses of 'becak'. They cost around 500 rp a km, but the minimum fare for tourists is usually 1000 rp, and the asking rate is a lot more. The trip from Jalan Prawirotaman to Jalan Malioboro should cost 1500 rp. Unless you are a patient and expert bargainer, metered taxis are usually cheaper. Avoid becak drivers who offer cheap hourly rates unless you want to do the rounds of all the batik galleries that offer commission. There are also horse-drawn andong around town, costing about the same, or cheaper, than the becaks.

Taxi Taxis in Yogya are metered, efficient, courteous and, unlike their counterparts in Jakarta, willing to give change. They cost 800 rp for the first km, then 400 rp for each subsequent km.

Car & Motorbike Travel agents on Sosrowijayan and Prawirotaman rent out cars from as little as 60,000 rp per day, including driver but excluding petrol. A good minibus will cost a little more. For day trips, agents like to rent on an all-inclusive basis – from 80,000 rp including driver and petrol for trips around the city, more for long distances. Work out exactly what is included in the price before you hire a car, and be prepared to bargain.

Bali Car Rental (☎ 87548) in front of the Adisucipto airport is a registered car rental agency for self-drive hire.

Motorcycles can be hired for around 10,000 rp a day. An international licence is required by law, but nobody seems to bother.

Bicycle Yogya traffic is becoming increasingly heavy but a bicycle is still a viable way to explore the city. Pushbikes can be rented from hotels and agents around Jalan Sosrowijayan and Jalan Prawirotaman for around 3000 rp a day.

AROUND YOGYAKARTA
Imogiri
Perched on a hilltop 20 km south of Yogya, Imogiri was built by Sultan Agung in 1645 to serve as his own mausoleum. Imogiri has since been the burial ground for almost all his successors and for prominent members of the royal family, and it is still a holy place. The cemetery contains three major courtyards – in the central courtyard are the tombs of Sultan Agung and succeeding Mataram

kings, to the left are the tombs of the Susuhunans of Solo and to the right those of the sultans of Yogya. The tomb of Hamengkubuwono IX, the father of the present sultan, is one of the most visited graves.

The point of major interest for pilgrims is the tomb of Sultan Agung. The tomb is only open from 10 am to 1 pm on Monday and from 1.30 to 4 pm on Friday and Sunday, and there is no objection to visitors joining the pilgrims then.

It's an impressive complex, reached by an equally impressive flight of 345 steps. From the top of the stairway, a walkway circles the whole complex and leads to the real summit of the hill. Here you have a superb view over Yogya to Gunung Merapi.

Colts and buses from Yogya (350 rp) stop at the parking lot from where it is about 500 metres to the base of the hill and the start of the steps. Like most pilgrimage sites, there will be various, insistent demands for 'donations'. The only compulsory entry charge (500 rp) is payable when you sign the visitors' book, inside the main compound at the top of the stairs.

To enter the tombs you must don full Javanese court dress, which can be hired for another 1000 rp.

Kasongan
This is Yogya's pottery centre. Dozens of workshops produce pots and some superb figurines, including two-metre-high dragons and pony-sized horses. Kasongan pottery is sold painted or unpainted – very little glazing work is done.

Getting There & Away Catch a Bantulbound bus and get down on the main road at the entrance to the village, 6½ km from Yogya. It is then about a one-km walk to the centre of the village and most of the pottery workshops.

Parangtritis
Twenty-seven km south of Yogya, Parangtritis has rough surf and a long sweep of shifting, black sand dunes backed by high, jagged cliffs. It's a place of superstition and,

Around Yogyakarta

INDIAN OCEAN

0   15   30 km

like so many places along the south coast, a centre for the worship of Nyai Loro Kidul, the 'Queen of the South Seas'. Legend has it that Senopati, the 16th-century Mataram ruler, took her as his wife and thus established the strong tie between the goddess and the royal house of Mataram. Their sacred rendezvous spot is at **Parangkusumo**, one km west down the beach, where the sultans of Yogya still send offerings every year at Labuhan to appease this consort of kings. Just beyond Parangkusumo are hot springs at **Parang Wedang**.

The currents and undertows at Parangtritis

are reputed to be dangerous, though swimming is sometimes possible. Just don't wear green – Nyai Loro Kidul's favourite colour. You can swim safely in freshwater pools (*pemandian*) at the base of the hill near the village, where spring water spills out through high bamboo pipes from the hilltop. The beach promenade of straggling warungs and souvenir stalls is nothing to rave about, but this is a quiet, simple place if you want a break from Yogya. Most visitors day trip. Avoid weekends and holidays when the beach is swamped by mobs from Yogya.

Trails along the hills above the sea to the

east of Parangtritis, lead to caves used for meditation. A couple of km from town is **Gua Langse**, reached by narrow trails, rickety bamboo ladders and ropes down the cliff face to the cave opening. Branches of the cave extend deep into the hillside where would-be mystics sit in contemplation, sometimes for days on end.

Places to Stay The centre of the village is the plaza, marked by the Diponegoro monument. Leading down to the beach, the main street/promenade has plenty of cheap hotels and rumah makan, all of the same basic standard.

One of the best is the *Agung Garden*, which has good information on the area and a reasonable restaurant. Singles/doubles with shower cost 7500/10,000 rp, including breakfast. Other reasonable places are the *Wisma Lukita*, which has rooms with mandi for 8000 rp, or the *Budi Inn* and the *Losmen Widodo*.

The best hotel by far is the *Queen of the South* (☎ 67196), perched on the clifftops high above town. It has excellent views, a fine pendopo-style restaurant and a swimming pool. Clientele includes the sultan of Solo, who comes for the meditation. Rooms are comfortable but expensive at US$60 and US$67, plus 21%; however, discounts are available.

Getting There & Away From Yogya's main bus terminal it costs 1000 rp by bus (including 'entry' to Parangtritis) for the one-hour journey but only 700 rp back to Yogya. The Parangtritis bus can also be caught on Jalan Sisingamangaraja, at the end of Jalan Prawirotaman. The last bus back from Parangtritis leaves at around 5.30 pm. You can also reach Parangtritis via Imogiri, but this is a much longer route.

Other Beaches
Yogya has several other uninspiring beaches besides Parangtritis. The only ones of any minor interest are the isolated beaches to the south-east. **Baron**, 60 km from Yogya, has safe swimming inside a sheltered cove.

Kukup is a white-sand beach one km east of Baron.

Krakal, eight km east of Baron, has a fine, usually deserted, white-sand beach, but the shallow reef rules out swimming. If you really want to get away from it all, the *Krakal Beach Hotel* has a restaurant, simple rooms for 8500 to 11,000 rp and cottages with mandi for 20,000 rp.

To reach these beaches, take a bus from Yogya to Wonosari (1000 rp), then an infrequent minibus to the beaches (400 rp), but you may have to charter or take an ojek.

Kaliurang & Mt Merapi

Kaliurang, 25 km north of Yogya, is the nearest hill resort to the city . It stands at 900 metres on the slopes of Mt Merapi (the 'Fire Mountain'), one of Java's most destructive volcanoes. Pick a clear, cloudless day during the week when it's quiet and this is a great place to escape from the heat of the plains. There are good forest walks, waterfalls, two chilly swimming pools and superb views of the smoking, fire-spewing mountain.

Merapi (2911 metres) can be climbed from Kaliurang but this is one of the most difficult climbs in Java. Day trippers and the less adventurous can explore the forest park (Hutan Wisata Kaliurang) on the slopes of the mountain. For views of Merapi in action, it's a one-hour walk from the park entrance to the observatory at Pos Plawangan (1260 metres), the vulcanology post that monitors Merapi. Another good walk is to Mt Turgo, a small mountain to the west, which has great views of Merapi and right across to the Indonesian Ocean on a fine day.

Climbing Merapi It's a safer and easier climb from Selo, to the north of Merapi (see Around Solo), but many people do climb from Kaliurang. There are times when the summit is off limits because of dangerous sulphurous fumes. In late 1994, mud slides and fires caused dozens of deaths of local people – before approaching the mountain, check on local conditions.

The trail up the mountain begins at the main, east entrance to the forest park, next to the car park where colts from Yogya terminate. From here the trail leads one hour around the mountain to Kinahrejo, and then it is a gruelling five or six hours up to the summit. Moreover, climbers usually start around midnight to reach the summit during the few early morning hours when the volcano is free of clouds and mist.

Should you decide to go for the top, the owner of the Vogel hostel, Christian Awuy, holds an excellent briefing every evening at 7 pm except Saturday (when ascents should be avoided, as too many locals climb, sending dangerous small rocks falling onto those beneath them).

Places to Stay & Eat *Vogels Hostel* (☎ 95208), Jalan Astamulya 76, has deservedly been the travellers' favourite for years. As well as being the local tourist information office, Christian Awuy also has one of the best travel libraries in Indonesia with books on Indonesia and further afield. There is a variety of rooms to suit most tastes and budgets starting at 3500 rp in the dorm or doubles range from 6000 rp up to bungalows at the back with bath for 22,000 rp. HI card holders get a small discount. The old part of the hostel, the former residence of a Yogya prince, has a good, very cheap restaurant.

Kaliurang has over 100 other places to stay. Kaliurang is a down-market resort with no star-classified hotels, but some of the guesthouses are pleasant, older style places. The *Wisma Tamu Gadjah Mada* (☎ 95225) has good views and Indo-European architecture. Run-down rooms cost 10,000 rp or large family rooms cost 40,000 to 60,000 rp, hot water included. *Wisma Wijaya Kusuma* is similar. The *Satriafi* is newer and one of the best in town with standard rooms for 17,500 rp or more luxurious VIP rooms with hot water for 35,000 rp.

Vogel Hostel has a varied menu, or the *Restaurant Joyo* is a bright, clean place with good Chinese and Indonesian food.

Getting There & Away From Yogya's Terban sub-terminal take a colt for 800 rp

(overcharging is common) or a crowded bus from the main bus terminal for 500 rp.

PRAMBANAN

On the road to Solo, 17 km east of Yogya, the temples at Prambanan village are the cream of what remains of Java's period of Hindu cultural development. Not only do these temples form the largest Hindu temple complex in Java, but the wealth of sculptural detail on the great Shiva Temple makes it easily the most outstanding example of Hindu art.

All the temples in the Prambanan area were built between the 8th and 10th centuries AD, when Java was ruled by the Buddhist Sailendras in the south and the Hindu Sanjayas of Old Mataram in the north. Possibly by the second half of the 9th century these two dynasties were united by the marriage of Rakai Pikatan of Hindu Mataram and the Buddhist Sailendra Princess Pramodhavardhani. This may explain why a number of temples, including the Prambanan Temple and the smaller Plaosan group, reveal Shivaite and Buddhist elements in architecture and sculpture. On the other hand, you find this mixture to some degree in India and Nepal, too, so it's hardly a novel idea.

Following this two-century burst of creativity, the Prambanan Plain was abandoned when the Hindu-Javanese kings moved to East Java. In the middle of the 16th century there is said to have been a great earthquake which toppled many of the temples and, in the centuries that followed, their destruction was accelerated by greedy treasure hunters and local people searching for building material. Most of the restoration work of this century has gone into the preservation of Prambanan. Of the outlying temple sites, some are just decayed fragments. Perhaps half a dozen are of real interest.

Orientation & Information

The Prambanan temples *(candi)* can be visited using either Yogya or Solo as a base. The Shiva Mahadeva Temple, the largest of the temples, is locally called Candi Loro

Jonggrang, or 'Slender Virgin', and sometimes the entire complex is referred to by this name. Prambanan village is tiny and has little in the way of accommodation facilities. On its northern boundary is the temple complex and the outdoor theatre where the *Ramayana* ballet is performed on full-moon nights. The temple enclosure is open daily from 6 am to 6 pm. Entry costs 4000 rp and, as at Borobudur, this includes camera fees and a guided tour (if you are prepared to wait to join a large enough group) in most major languages. An audio-visual show on Prambanan plays every 30 minutes for another 2000 rp.

At the temple complex there is little in the way of free brochures or maps – you can buy a copy of *Guide to Prambanan Temple*, which is detailed and covers most of the temple sites on Prambanan Plain.

Most of the outlying temples are spread out within a five-km radius of Prambanan village. You'll need at least half a day to see them on foot, or you can hire a horsecart by the hour in Prambanan. As with any of Java's major tourist attractions, the best time to visit Prambanan is early morning or late in the day when it's quiet, though you can never expect

to get Prambanan to yourself. Very few people visit the other sites and the walk can be as much of a pleasure as the temples themselves.

Prambanan Temple Complex

The huge Prambanan Complex was constructed in about the middle of the 9th century – around 50 years later than Borobudur – but remarkably little is known about its early history. It's thought that it was built by Rakai Pikatan to commemorate the return of a Hindu dynasty to sole power in Java. Some have even suggested it was intended as a counterpart to Borobudur, but more likely it was a counterpart to Candi Sewu, a Buddhist complex three km away.

Prambanan was in ruins for years and although efforts were made in 1885 to clear the site, it was not until 1937 that reconstruction was first attempted. Of the original group the outer compound contains the remains of 244 temples. Eight minor and eight main temples stand in the highest central courtyard, and most have been restored.

Shiva Mahadeva The temple dedicated to Shiva is not only the largest of the temples,

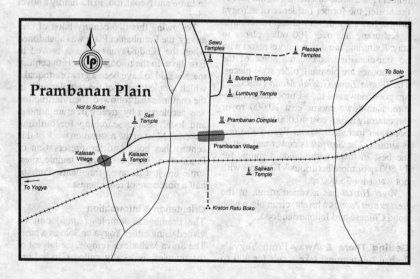

it is also artistically and architecturally the most perfect. The main spire soars 47 metres high and the temple is lavishly carved. The 'medallions' which decorate its base have the characteristic 'Prambanan motif' – small lions in niches flanked by 'trees of heaven' (or *kalpaturas*) and a menagerie of stylised half-human and half-bird heavenly beings *(kinnaras)*. The vibrant scenes carved onto the inner wall of the gallery encircling the temple are from the *Ramayana* – they tell how Lord Rama's wife, Sita, is abducted and how Hanuman the monkey god and Sugriwa his white monkey general eventually find and release her. To follow the story, ascend the main eastern stairway and go around the temple clockwise. The reliefs break off at the point where the monkey army builds a bridge to the island of Lanka; the end of the tale is found on the smaller Brahma Temple.

In the main chamber at the top of the eastern stairway, the four-armed statue of Shiva the Destroyer is notable for the fact that this mightiest of Hindu gods stands on a huge lotus pedestal, a symbol of Buddhism. In the southern cell is the pot-bellied and bearded Agastya, an incarnation of Shiva as divine teacher; in the western cell is a superb image of the elephant-headed Ganesha, Shiva's son. In the northern cell, Durga, Shiva's consort, can be seen killing the demon buffalo. Some people believe that the Durga image is actually an image of Loro Jonggrang, the 'Slender Virgin' who, legend has it, was turned to stone by a giant she refused to marry. She is still the object of pilgrimage for many who believe in her and the name of the cursed princess is often used for the temple group.

Brahma & Vishnu Temples These two smaller temples flank the large Shiva Mahadeva Temple. The Brahma Temple to the south, carved with the final scenes of the *Ramayana*, has a four-headed statue of Brahma, the god of creation. Reliefs on the Vishnu Temple to the north tell the story of Lord Krishna, a hero of the *Mahabharata* epic. Inside is a four-armed image of Vishnu the Preserver.

Nandi Temple This small shrine, facing the Shiva Mahadeva Temple, houses one of Prambanan's finest sculptures – a huge, powerful figure of the bull, Nandi, the vehicle of Shiva.

The shrines to the north and south of Nandi may once have contained Brahma's vehicle, the swan, and Vishnu's sun-bird, the Garuda.

Northern Group

Of the northern group of temples, the Sewu and Plaosan temples are the most interesting and they are within three km of Prambanan. They can be reached on foot by the sign-posted path leading north from the main Prambanan complex.

Sewu Temples The 'Thousand Temples', dating from around 850 AD, originally consisted of a large central Buddhist temple surrounded by four rings of 240 smaller 'guard' temples. Outside the compound stood four sanctuaries at the points of the compass, of which the Bubrah Temple is the southern one.

All but a few of the minor temples are in various stages of collapse, a great jumble of stone blocks littering the field. Only the shell of the main temple remains but this is interesting for the unusual finely carved niches around the inner gallery, with shapes resembling those found in the Middle East. Once these would have held bronze statues but plundering of the temple went on for many years – some of the statues were melted down and others disappeared into museums and private possession.

Plaosan Temples One or two km east of Sewu, you walk across rice paddies and sugar cane fields to this temple group. Believed to have been built at about the same time as the Prambanan temple group by Rakai Pikatan and his Buddhist queen, the Plaosan temples combine both Hindu and Buddhist religious symbols and carvings. Of the original three main temples, once linked by a multitude of small shrines and solid stupas, one has been reconstructed and is notable for its unusual three-part design. It is a two-storey, six-room structure with an imitation storey above and a tiered roof of stupas rising to a single larger one in the centre. Inside the temple are impressive stone Bodhisattvas on either side of an empty lotus pedestal within the various cells and intricately carved *kala* (dragon) heads above the many windows. The Buddhas that once sat on the lotus pedestals are now in the National Museum in Jakarta.

Southern Group

Sajiwan Temple Not far from the village of Sajiwan, about 1½ km south-east of Prambanan, are the ruins of this Buddhist temple. Around the base are carvings from the Jataka (episodes from the Buddha's various lives).

Kraton Ratu Boko A steep rocky path (opposite the 'Yogya 18 km' signpost) leads up to the main site, two km south of Prambanan village on a small plateau in the Gunung Kidul hills. Ratu Boko, the 'Palace of the Eternal Lord', is believed to have been a huge Hindu palace complex dating from the 9th century. Although little remains apart from a large gateway and a series of bathing places, it is worth the walk. The view from this site across the Prambanan plains is magnificent. On a smaller plateau a few hundred metres further south is a large platform of waterspouts and staircases and, below, a group of pools which are still used by the local villagers.

Western Group

There are three temples in this group between Yogya and Prambanan, two of them close to Kalasan village on the main Yogya road. Kalasan and Prambanan villages are three km apart, so it is probably easiest to take a colt or bus to cover this stretch.

Kalasan Temple Standing 50 metres off the main road near Kalasan village, this temple is one of the oldest Buddhist temples on the Prambanan Plain. A Sanskrit inscription of 778 AD refers to a temple dedicated to the

female Bodhisattva, Tara, though the existing structure appears to have been built around the original one some years later. It has been partially restored during this century and has some fine detailed carvings on its southern side, where a huge, ornate kala head glowers over the doorway. At one time it was completely covered in coloured shining stucco, and traces of the hard, stone-like 'diamond plaster' that provided a base for paintwork can still be seen. The bat-infested inner chamber of Kalasan once sheltered a huge bronze image of Buddha or Tara.

Sari Temple About 200 metres north of Kalasan Temple, in the middle of coconut and banana groves, the Sari Temple has the three-part design of the larger Plaosan Temple but is probably slightly older. Some students believe that its 2nd floor may have served as a dormitory for the Buddhist priests who took care of the Kalasan Temple. The sculptured reliefs around the exterior are similar to those of Kalasan but in much better condition.

Sambisari Temple A country lane runs to this isolated temple, about 2½ km north of the '10.2 km Yogya' post on the main road. Sambisari is a Shiva temple and possibly the latest temple at Prambanan to be put up by the Mataram rulers. It was only discovered by a farmer in 1966. Excavated from under ancient layers of protective volcanic ash and dust, it lies almost six metres below the surface of the surrounding fields and is remarkable for its perfectly preserved state. It has some fine decorations and in the niches you can see the stone images of Durga, Ganesh and Agastya.

Places to Stay Very few visitors stay at Prambanan, but there are a few basic hotels such as *Muharti Penginapan*, on the main highway near the entrance, with nondescript rooms for 10,000 rp. Other include *Sari's Hotel* and the quieter *Wisma Ramayana* on the east side of the complex.

Entertainment The *Ramayana Ballet* held at the outdoor theatre in Prambanan, is Java's most spectacular dance-drama. The ballet is performed over four successive nights, twice each month of the dry season, from May to October, leading up to the full moon. With the magnificent flood-lit Shiva Mahadeva Temple as a backdrop, more than 100 dancers and gamelan musicians take part in a spectacle of monkey armies, giants on stilts, clashing battles and acrobatics.

Performances last from 7 to 9 pm. Tickets are sold through the Tourist Information Office and travel agents in Yogya at the same price you'll pay at the theatre box office, but they usually have packages that include transport direct from your hotel. There are no bad seats in the amphitheatre – all have a good view and are not too far from the stage, but the cheapest seats are side on to the action.

If you miss the full moon ballet, the 'Ramayana Ballet Full Story' is a two-hour performance in a less spectacular setting indoors at Prambanan's Trimurti covered theatre at 7.30 pm every Tuesday, Wednesday and Thursday throughout the year. Tickets range from 7500 to 15,000 rp.

Ramayana ballet dancer

Getting There & Away
From Yogya, take the yellow Pemuda bus (250 rp; ½ hour) from the main bus station, or a Solo colt from the Terban sub-terminal. From Solo, buses take 1½ hours and cost 1000 rp.

By bicycle, you can visit all the temples. The secret is to avoid as much of the Solo road as possible. Past the Ambarrukmo Palace Hotel in Yogya, turn left down Jalan Babarsari, go past the Sahid Garden Hotel, then follow the road anti-clockwise around the school to the Mataram Canal. You can follow the canal for about six km, most of the way to Prambanan.

SOLO (SURAKARTA)
On the Yogya to Surabaya road, 65 km north-west of Yogya, the old royal city of Surakarta lies on the west bank of one of Java's most important rivers – the Bengawan Solo. More popularly known as Solo, its founding in 1745 has a mystical past. Following the sacking of the Mataram court at Kartasura in 1742 the susuhunan (king), Pakubuwono II, decided to look for a more auspicious site. The transfer of the capital had something to do with voices from the cosmic world – according to legend the king was told to go to the village of Solo because 'it is the place decreed by Allah and it will become a great and prosperous city'.

By the end of the 18th century Solo had already reached the peak of its political importance and the realm of Mataram had crumbled, split by internal conflict into three rival courts, of which Yogya was one. From then on the ruler of Surakarta and the subsidiary prince of Mangkunegara remained loyal to the Dutch, even at the time of Diponegoro's Java War. During the revolution they fumbled opportunities to play a positive role and with the tide of democracy in the 1940s, the kratons of Solo became mere symbols of ancient Javanese feudalism and aristocracy.

Solo is an excellent source of high quality batik and other textiles. Solo also competes with Yogya as a centre for Javanese culture, attracting many students and scholars to its academies of music and dance.

Solo has two kratons, one even larger and more venerable than Yogya's. It's quite possible to make a day-trip to Solo from Yogya but the place is worth far more than a day, particularly if you visit attractions such as Sukuh Temple outside the city.

Orientation

The oldest part of the city is centred around the Kraton Surakarta to the east where the Pasar Klewer, the main batik market, is also located. Kraton Mangkunegara is the centre of Solo. Away from these tranquil palaces Solo can be as busy as any other Javanese city, but it is less congested than its younger sister city, Yogya, and not overwhelmed by tourists. It is perhaps the least Westernised of Java's cities and there are corners with narrow walled streets and a strong village atmosphere.

Jalan Slamet Riyadi, the broad tree-lined avenue running east-west through the centre of Solo, is the main thoroughfare. Here the city's double-decker buses run their course. You will also find the tourist office at one end and most of the banks at the east end, near Kraton Surakarta. Solo's Balapan railway station is in the northern part of the city, about two km from the centre, and the main bus station is just a few hundred metres north again. Most hotels and restaurants are in the area between Jalan Slamet Riyadi and the railway station.

Information

Tourist Office The Solo Tourist Office (☎ 41435), Jalan Slamet Riyadi 275, has useful pamphlets, a map of Solo and information on cultural events in town and places to visit in the area. The office is open from 8 am to 5 pm. The tourist office also has a helpful stand at the bus station.

Post & Telecommunications The efficient main post office on Jalan Jenderal Sudirman is open from 8 am to 4 pm Monday to Friday, and 8 am to 1 pm on Saturday for poste restante, but is open until 8 pm every day for basic postal services. The telephone office for international calls is near the post office on Jalan Mayor Kusmanto, or there is a small wartel on Jalan Slamet Riyadi.

Other You can use the swimming pool at the Kusuma Sahid Prince Hotel for 3500 rp a day.

Kraton Surakarta

In 1745, Pakubuwono II moved from Kartasura to Kraton Surakarta (also known as the Kraton Kasunanan) in a day-long procession which transplanted everything belonging to the king, including the royal banyan trees and the sacred Nyai Setomo cannon (the twin of Si Jagur in old Jakarta), which now sits in the northern palace pavilion. Ornate European-style decorations were later added by Pakubuwono X, the wealthiest of Surakarta's rulers, from 1893 to 1939.

Entry to the kraton is through the north entrance, fronting the alun alun. Here the Pagelaran is the main audience hall where the susuhunan held court in front of his people. Crossing over the street behind the Pagelaran, is the kraton proper, though the main gateway is not open to the public and entry is from around the east side at the museum/art gallery. Much of the kraton was destroyed by fire in 1985, attributed by the Solonese to the susuhunan's lack of observance of tradition. Many of the inner buildings, including the pendopo (audience hall), were destroyed and have been rebuilt. One that has survived is the distinctive tower known as Panggung Songgo Buwono, built in 1782 and looking like a cross between a Dutch clock tower and a lighthouse. It's upper storey is a meditation sanctum where the susuhunan is said to commune with Nyai Loro Kidul, 'Queen of the South Seas'.

A heavy carved doorway leads through from the museum across the inner courtyard of shady trees to the pendopo, but most of the kraton is off-limits and is in fact the *dalem* or residence of the susuhunan. The main sight for visitors is the Sasono Sewoko museum/art gallery; exhibits include fine silver and bronze Hindu-Javanese figures,

Javanese weapons, antiques and other royal heirlooms.

Admission is 1000 rp, which includes entry to the kraton complex and museum and a guide. Entry is only from the north side opposite the alun alun, and the kraton is open from 8 am to 1.30 pm every day except Friday. Dancing practice, usually classes for children, can be seen on Sundays from 10 am to noon.

Kraton Mangkunegara

In the centre of the city, Kraton Mangkunegara, dating back to 1757, is the palace of the second ruling house of Solo. It was founded after a bitter struggle against the susuhunan of Surakarta, launched by Raden Mas Said, a member of the Surakarta aristocracy, and an ancestor of Madam Tien Soeharto, wife of the president. Though much smaller in scale and design, this kraton is much better maintained and obviously wealthier than the more important Kraton Surakarta. Members of the royal family still live at the back of the palace.

The centre of the palace compound is the pendopo pavilion, bordered on its northern side by the dalem, which now forms the palace museum. The pavilion has been added to over the centuries and is one of the largest in the country. Its high rounded ceiling was painted in 1937 and is intricately decorated with a central flame surrounded by figures of the Javanese zodiac, each in its own mystical colour. In Javanese philosophy yellow signifies a preventative against sleepiness, blue against disease, black against hunger, green against desire, white against lust, rose against fear, red against evil and purple against wicked thoughts. The pavilion contains one of the kraton's oldest sets of gamelan known as 'Kyai Kanyut Mesem', which translates as 'Drifting in Smiles'.

The museum here is a real delight. Most of the exhibits are from the personal collection of Mangkunegara VII. Amongst the items are gold-plated dresses for the royal Srimpi and Bedoyo dances, jewellery and a few oddities including huge Buddhist rings and a gold genital cover for a queen. There's also a magnificent collection of masks from various areas in Indonesia, a series of royal portraits and a library collection of classical literary works by the Mangkunegara princes.

The palace is open every day from 8.30 am to 2 pm, except Sundays when it closes at 1 pm. Admission is 1500 rp. At the pavilion, you can see dance practice sessions on Wednesday morning from 10 am until noon. The palace shop sells wayang puppets and other craft items.

Radya Pustaka Museum

This small museum, next to the tourist office on Jalan Slamet Riyadi, has good displays of gamelan instruments, jewelled kris, wayang puppets from Thailand and Indonesia, a small collection of wayang beber scrolls and another hairy muppet figurehead from a royal barge. It's open from 8 am to noon every day, except Friday when it closes at 11 am, and Monday when it remains closed. Entrance is 500 rp.

Markets

The **Pasar Klewer** is the ever-busy, crowded textile market near the main kraton. This is the place to look for batik.

Solo's antique market, **Pasar Triwindu**, is always worth a browse. It sells all sorts of bric-a-brac (not all of it old), though half the market is also devoted to car and motorbike parts.

The **Pasar Gede** is the city's largest every day market selling all manner of produce, while the **Pasar Depok** is Solo's bird market, at the north-west end of Jalan R M Said.

Other Attractions

On the west side of the alun alun, the **Mesjid Agung** (Grand Mosque) is the largest and most sacred mosque in Solo, featuring classical Javanese architecture.

Sriwedari is Solo's amusement park with fair rides, side-show stalls and other somewhat dated diversions. Unlike other cities in Java with similar amusement parks, Sriwedari can still draw a crowd on a Saturday night. The main reason to come is for the

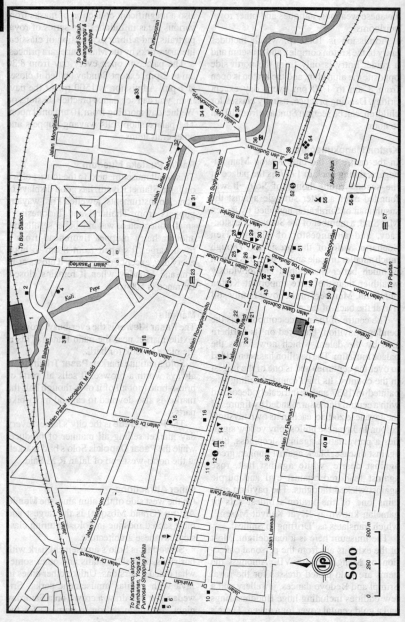

Solo

To Candi Sukuh,
Tawangmangu &
Surabaya

Jl Purwosari

Jalan Urip Sumoharjo

Jalan Sultan Sahir

Jalan Monginsidi

To Bus Station

Jalan Sugiyopranoto

Jalan Imam Bonjol

Jl Jen Sudirman

Jalan Pasagei

Kali Pepe

Jalan Teuku Umar

Jalan Yos Sudarso

Alun-Alun

Jl A Dahlan

Jalan Secoyudan

Jalan Balapan

Jalan Gajah Mada

Jalan Ronggowanito

Jalan Slamet Riyadi

Jalan Gatot Subroto

To Pacitan

To Kraton

Jalan Pisar Nongko/H. M. Said

Jalan Honggowongso

Jalan
Station

Jalan Dr Supomo

Jalan Dr Rajiman

Jalan Bayang Kara

Jalan Lawean

Jalan Tursari

Jalan Yosodipuro

Jalan Dr Muwardi

To Kartasuro, airport
Prambanan, Yogya &
Purwosari Shopping Plaza

Wahidin

0   250   500 m

PLACES TO STAY		PLACES TO EAT		13	Radya Pustaka Museum
2	Hotel Jayakarta	8	Swensen's & KFC	15	Toko Bedoyo Srimpi
3	Hotel Agung	9	Adem Ayam Restaurant	22	Garuda (Lippobank
5	Riyadi Palace Hotel	14	Pujosari & Oriental		Building)
6	Hotel Putri Ayu	17	Cipta Rasa Restaurant	23	Kraton Mangkunegara
7	Solo Inn	19	Tio Ciu 99	24	Pasar Triwindu
10	Ramayana Guest	25	Warung Baru	33	SMKI School
	House	26	Jalan Teuku Umar	35	Pasar Gede
16	Hotel Dana		Night Market	36	Telkom Office
18	Sahid Sala Hotel	27	American Donut Bakery	37	Main Post Office
20	Hotel Cakra	30	Superman's Restaurant	38	Adpura Kencana
21	Wisata Indah	32	Pringgondani		Monument
28	Solo Homestay	43	New Holland Bakery	41	Singosaren Plaza
29	Hotel Central	46	Kasuma Sari Restau-	42	Taxi Stand
31	Kusuma Sahid Prince		rant	44	Wartel Telephone Office
	Hotel			50	Vihara Rahayu
34	Hotel Trio	**OTHER**			Chinese Temple
39	Bamboo Homestay			52	Bank BCA
40	Happy Homestay	1	Balapan Railway	53	Gamelan Factory
45	Hotel Kota		Station	54	Matahari Department
47	Relax Homestay	4	RRI Radio Station		Store
48	Paradise Guest House	11	Sriwedari Amusement	55	Mesjid Agung
49	Westerners		Park	56	Pasar Klewer
51	Mama Homestay	12	Tourist Office	57	Kraton Surakarta

nightly wayang orang performances, and other regular cultural performances.

The **Dullah Museum** on Jalan Dr Cipto 15 is the museum and studio of a well-known Indonesian artist, popular during the Soekarno era for paintings depicting the struggle for independence. His works and collection of antiques, ceramics and crafts are on display from 8 am to noon every day except Monday.

Meditation

Solo has a number of contemporary mystical groups, of different philosophies and religions, which come under the broad umbrella of Kebatinan (Mysticism), one of the recognised religious streams in Indonesia. A few schools in Solo have followings of Westerners and most gatherings are generally held informally at private homes.

Pak Suwondo, on Gang 1 Jalan Kratonan, teaches the traditional theory and practice of Javanese meditation and has a reputation as a patient teacher. Or Ananda Suyono is a Javanese 'New Age' eclectic, who lives at Jalan Ronggowarsito 60. The guesthouses can steer you towards a school, and many

meditators stay at the Joyokusuman guesthouse.

Organised Tours

Warung Baru and some of the homestays, such as Bamboo Homestay, run bike tours of Solo and of sites outside the city limits. These tours are reasonably priced and have earned the praise of numerous travellers. For 8000 rp one full-day tour takes you through beautiful countryside to see batik weaving, gamelan making, and tofu, arak and rice-cracker processing.

Various travel agents around town also run more conventional tours. City tours will cost around 20,000 rp, Sukuh-Tawangmangu costs 25,000 rp, Prambanan-Kota Gede-Parangtritis costs 40,000 rp, and there are also Dieng-Borobudur tours for 60,000 rp and others, including Bromo tours. Ratna (☎ 37634), Jalan Yos Sudarso 3, at the intersection of Jalan Slamet Riyadi, is one conveniently located tour operator.

Places to Stay – bottom end

The best value is found in the travellers' homestays which are springing up everywhere. They are friendly, family-run places with good travel information and most offer tours, make bus bookings, have bicycles, and provide breakfast, free tea and drinking water.

The *Westerners* (☎ 33106) at Kemlayan Kidul 11, the first alley north of Jalan Secoyudan off Jalan Yos Sudarso, is spotlessly clean, well run and secure. Solo's original homestay, it is still one of the most popular, though it can be cramped. The five-bed dormitory costs 4000 rp per night, small singles/doubles cost 6000/7000 rp and better doubles range from 7500 rp up to 11,000 rp. Breakfast is available for 1750 rp.

In the same alley at No 1/3, the new *Paradise Guest House* (☎ 52960) is a classy little place with a pendopo-style lobby/sitting area and dazzlingly white rooms for 8000 to 15,000 rp. Look for the sign offering 'Westerner's' accommodation, an attempt to lure the competition's trade.

A couple of *gang* north is *Relax Homestay*, 28 Gang Empu Sedah, one of the best homestays. The rooms are built around a large courtyard and this place has a bar and cafe. Good-sized rooms cost 6000/7000 rp or more luxurious rooms are 7000/8000 rp and 10,000 rp.

Another good homestay is *Mama Homestay* (☎ 52248), Kauman Gang III, also off Jalan Yos Sudarso, costing 6000/8000 rp including breakfast. Batik courses are available here. *Solo Homestay*, in an alley near Warung Baru, is reputedly the best place for batik courses, and many of the guests stay here just for the courses. It's friendly, if a little dingy, and rooms cost 5000/6000 rp.

The other guesthouses are not so central, but also offer good accommodation. *Bamboo Homestay* (☎ 35856), Jalan Setyaki 1 Kebonan behind the Sriwedari amusement park, lives up to its name. The walls and all the furniture are made of bamboo, and this is one of the most attractive homestays. There's a pleasant sitting area, and rooms including breakfast cost 5000/8000 rp or 6000/9000 rp with fan. Rooms with attached bath cost 17,500 rp. In the same area is *Happy Homestay* (☎ 57149), Gang Karagan 12, off Jalan

Honggowongso (look for the sign). This friendly, family concern has very small but comfortable singles for 4000 rp or larger doubles for 8000 rp.

Solo has dozens of hotels, but they tend to be anonymous places.

In a more central location, the long-running *Hotel Kota* (☎ 32841), Jalan Slamet Riyadi 125, is a double-storey place built around a large open courtyard. Rooms cost from 7000/10,000 to 12,500/20,000 rp for singles/doubles with mandi. At Jalan Ahmad Dahlan 32 is the open and airy *Hotel Central* (☎ 42814). With its very fine art deco woodwork, a thorough restoration would turn this hotel into a real showpiece. Meanwhile the rooms, all without bath, are 6000 rp and 7500 rp for doubles.

Places to Stay – middle

Many of the hotels in this bracket are strung out along or just off Jalan Slamet Riyadi, west of the town centre. Solo's mid-range hotels are expensive for what you get, but the well-maintained *Hotel Putri Ayu* (☎ 36154), Jalan Slamet Riyadi 331, is good value. Quiet rooms around a courtyard garden cost 25,000 rp with mandi, fan and TV, or air-con rooms with bath are 38,000 rp, including breakfast.

The *Ramayana Guest House* (☎ 32814), 22 Jalan Dr Wahidin, is an attractive house with a guest wing set around a garden. It has reasonable doubles with bath for 25,300 rp and from 42,500 rp with air-con, including breakfast, though it's the garden and stylish dining/lobby area decorated with artefacts that make this place special.

Conveniently located across the street from the tourist office and museum is the colonial *Hotel Dana* (☎ 33891), Jalan Slamet Riyadi 286. The peaceful grounds surround an impressive tiled-floor lobby in the main building, and rooms behind have private sitting areas. Rates are 25,000 rp without bath, or air-con rooms are 50,000 to 70,000 rp, including breakfast. The rooms are overpriced, so ask for a discount.

The *Solo Inn* (☎ 46075), Jalan Slamet Riyadi 366, is at the top of this range. Slightly faded but well-appointed rooms with fridge, hot water, TV, etc cost 80,000/90,000 rp, after discount.

Places to Stay – top end

The *Kusuma Sahid Prince Hotel* (☎ 46356), Jalan Sugiyopranoto 22, has been designed around a former Solonese palace. It's a grand place set in beautiful grounds with a swimming pool. Other facilities include a coffee shop serving Indonesian and Western meals, a bar, shopping arcade, Javanese herb shop and massage service. In the lobby, guests are serenaded by a gamelan. Older singles/doubles cost 180,000/205,000 rp or excellent bungalow suites start at 292,000 rp and range up to US$450 for the 'royal' suites. Discounts are available for the asking.

The *Said Sala Hotel* (☎ 45889), Jalan Gajah Mada 82, is undergoing massive renovations and extensions and when it re-opens will be Solo's other four-star hotel with pool, restaurants, bars, etc.

Out of the centre, but well worth considering, is the *Riyadi Palace Hotel* (☎ 33300), Jalan Slamet Riyadi 335. This new three-star hotel has immaculate rooms with all conveniences from 92,500 to 186,500 rp, including breakfast.

Places to Eat

For the cheapest food listen for the weird and distinctive sounds which are the trademarks of the roaming street hawkers. The bread seller sings (or screeches) a high-pitched 'tee'; 'ding ding ding' is the *bakso* seller; 'tic toc' is *mie*; a wooden buffalo bell advertises sate; a shrieking kettle-on-the-boil sound is the *kue putu*. Kue putu are coconut cakes, which are pushed into small bamboo tubes to cook over a steam box and then served hot, sprinkled with coconut and sugar.

Nasi gudeg is popular but the speciality of Solo is *nasi liwet*, rice with chicken and coconut milk. Another local speciality to try at night is *srabi*, the small rice puddings served up on a crispy pancake with banana, chocolate or jackfruit on top – best eaten piping hot. *Lesahan* dining (on mats) is very much a part of eating in Solo.

Jalan Ahmad Dahlan is the centre for budget travellers' eateries. Without question, the most popular is *Warung Baru* at No 23 run by the ebullient Suntari Haryono. Try the famous black bread, along with substantial breakfasts and Indonesian and Western fare at most reasonable prices. The warung is the meeting place for travellers to dine, and also runs bike tours of Solo and environs.

Across the street, *Superman's* turns out good Indonesian dishes but is definitely second in the popularity stakes. Further down at No 58, *Monggo Pinarak* is an excellent, cheap cafe. The varied menu includes good curries cooked by the well-travelled Bangladeshi owner.

Some of the cheapest and best food is to be found in Solo's numerous warungs. Everyone has their favourites and you can get a feed any time of the night at numerous dusk to dawn warungs, the only real nightlife in Solo despite its title of the 'city that never sleeps'.

Some years ago Solo's night market warungs were given more permanent housing next to the museum and tourist office in the Sriwedari Park area. Now a dozen or so *rumah makan* offer a good selection of Solonese and other Indonesian dishes. The biggest and best are the *Pujosari*, a 24-hour lesahan place that sometimes has bands on Saturday evenings, and the more restaurant-like *Oriental*. The ayam kampung (village chicken) at Pujosari is delicious, and the Oriental has a wide range of good Chinese dishes, including seafood. The only drawback at both these ever-busy eateries is that service can be slow.

On fine evenings, straw mats are laid out on the pavement on Jalan Yos Sudarso or just around the corner on Jalan Slamet Riyadi and the sate is superb. Or try the warungs on Jalan Teuku Umar for an inexpensive taste of local specialities, including nasi liwet. Wash your meal down with *susu segar* or fresh milk – hot or cold milk with optional egg and honey.

On Jalan Gatot Subroto, look out for the *Bu Mari* warung, which has miniature chairs around a low table on the sidewalk. It has great nasi gudeg and chicken curry with rice and sambal, open until the wee hours of the morning.

Decent Chinese restaurants along Jalan Slamet Riyadi include the Cipta Rasa at 245, and the popular Tio Ciu 99. The unpretentious Cipta Rasa has cheap, filling fare, though for a little extra the Tio Ciu 99 is a better bet for good Chinese food.

Also on Jalan Slamet Riyadi at No 342, the Adem Ayam is split into two restaurants, one serving Chinese food and the other Javanese. The gudeg is their best dish.

For those willing to spend more in a restaurant for excellent Solonese specialities served in a pleasant ambience, try the Pringgondani, north of the river at Jalan Sultan Sahrir 79. Here you can dine seated on casual yet comfortable furniture, or local-style on a bamboo floor. The savoury ayam bakar (roast chicken) is not to be missed.

Apart from the travellers' places on Jalan Ahmad Dahlan, Western food is not widely available in Solo. One exception is the Kusama Sari, on the corner of Jalan Slamet Riyadi and Jalan Yos Sudarso, which has seductive air-con, good hot platter grills and ice creams. It is also one of those rarities in Indonesia – a non-smoking restaurant (well, almost). Another branch is next to the BCA bank. Bakeries along Jalan Slamet Riyadi include the American Donut and the New Holland. The latter has a bewildering array of baked goods and delicious savoury martabak rolls, as well as a restaurant upstairs.

Entertainment

Surakarta is an excellent place to see traditional Javanese performing arts.

Wayang orang performances of the Ramayana can be seen at the Sriwedari Amusement Park, Jalan Slamet Riyadi, from 8 to 11 pm Monday to Saturday. The Sriwedari theatre boasts one of the most famous wayang orang troupes in Java. Performances are held in the theatre at the back of the park behind the tourist office. Seats are cheap – 750 rp for the cheapest, 1000 rp for quite good ones. There is no need to book –

the only time the theatre is even half full is on a Saturday night. On the first Saturday night of the month, wayang kulit is also held at Sriwedari, at the open pavilion near the tourist office.

Various cultural performances are held at the broadcasting station of Radio Republik Indonesia (RRI), Jalan Abdul Rahman Saleh 51. The RRI performances are popular and often excellent. The station has all-night wayang kulit shows on the third Saturday of every month from 9 pm to around 5 am; on the second Tuesday evening of the month there is wayang orang from 8 pm to midnight; ketoprak performances are held on the fourth Tuesday of the month from 8 pm to midnight.

At the STSI (Sekolah Tinggi Seni Indonesia), the arts academy, you can see dancing practice from around 7.30 am to noon from Monday to Saturday. STSI is at the Kentingan campus in Jebres, in the north-east of the city. SMKI, the high school for the performing arts on Jalan Kepatihan Wetan, also has dance practice every morning expect Sunday from around 8 am.

Both kratons also have traditional Javanese dance practice. The Wednesday performances from 10 am to noon at the Kraton Mangkunegara are usually more rewarding than the Sunday morning performances at the Kraton Surakarta.

The tourist office has details of other cultural events around Solo. Wayang kulit shows are occasionally performed by the famous dalang, Ki Anom Suroto, at Jalan Notodiningran 100, in the area behind the Hotel Cakra. You can count on all-night performances there every Tuesday Kliwon in the Javanese calendar, occurring every five weeks. Anom also occasionally performs at the Sriwedari Amusement Park. Ki Mantep Sudarsono is one of Indonesia's most famous dalang and performs all around Java and overseas. He sometimes has performances in his village, 27 km from Solo, near Karangpandan.

Things to Buy

Solo is one of Indonesia's main textile

centres, producing not only its own unique, traditional batik but every kind of fabric for domestic use and export. Many people find it better for batik than Yogya, though Solo doesn't have Yogya's range for other crafts and curios.

Batik Pasar Klewer, a three-storey 'hanging market' near the susuhunan's palace, has hundreds of stalls selling fabrics. This is a good place to buy batik, mainly cap but you can also find tulis batik and *lurik* homespun. Bargaining is obligatory, and it pays to know your batik and prices before venturing into the market.

The big manufacturers have showrooms with a range of often very sophisticated work. You can see the batik process at the Batik Keris factory in Lawiyan, west of the city, or at their shop at Jalan Yos Sudarso 62. Another big Solonese manufacturer is Batik Danarhadi, with shops at Jalan Dr Rajiman 164 and Jalan Slamet Riyadi 217. They have a good range of batik fabrics and ready-made clothes. Batik Semar, Jalan R M Said 148, is good for modern cotton and beautiful silk batiks. In the mornings (weekdays only) you can see the batik being made.

Smaller batik industries include Batik St Senari, Jalan Slamet Riyadi 298; Batik Srimpi, Jalan Dr Supomo 25; and Batik Arjuna, Jalan Dr Rajiman 401.

You can take batik courses in Solo. Solo Homestay (see Places to Stay) has a good reputation and is the most popular place to do batik.

Curios Pasar Triwindu on Jalan Diponegoro is Solo's flea market. All kinds of bric-a-brac plus a few genuine antiques are sold here – old buttons and buckles, china dogs and fine porcelain, puppets, batik tulis pens, lamps, bottles, bell jars and furniture – but if you're looking for bargains you have to sift carefully through the rubbish and be prepared to bargain hard. Many of the 'antik' are newly aged. Some of the dealers have larger collections at their homes, so it is worth asking if they have other pieces.

Toko Bedoyo Srimpi, Jalan Ronggo-

warsito 116, is the place for wayang orang dancers' costumes and theatrical supplies, such as gold gilt headdresses and painted arm-bands. They also sell masks and wayang kulit puppets.

Jalan Dr Rajiman (Secoyudan) is the goldsmiths' street. Krises and other souvenirs can be purchased from street vendors at the east-side alun alun to the north of the Kraton Surakarta, and at Sriwedari.

Getting There & Away

Air The Adi Sumarmo airport is 10 km northwest of the city centre; 10,000 rp by taxi or take a bus to Kartosuro (200 rp) and then another to the airport. Garuda and Sempati have direct flights to Jakarta (129,800 rp) and Surabaya (59,400 rp) with connections further afield, while Merpati flies to Surabaya.

The Garuda office (☎ 44955) is in the Lippobank building, Jalan Slamet Riyadi 136. Sempati (☎ 46240) is in the Solo Inn, Jalan Slamet Riyadi 366.

Bus The main Tirtonadi bus station is just north of the railway station, three km from the centre of town, 1000 rp by becak.

Frequent buses go to Prambanan (1000 rp; 1½ hours), Yogya (1200 rp; two hours), Semarang (1900/3000 rp air-con, 2½ hours), Salatiga (900 rp; 1½ hours), Madiun (2000 rp), Bandung (8000/15,000 rp) via Semarang or Yogya, and Jakarta (11,000/18,000 rp to 30,000 rp).

Going east, buses include those to Tawangmangu (700 rp; one hour), Pacitan (2200 rp; four hours), Blitar (4700 rp; six hours), Surabaya (5000/9000 rp air-con, six hours), Malang (6500/13,000 rp; eight hours) and Probolinggo (6000/13,000 rp; eight hours). Luxury buses also do these runs and agents can be found at the bus station and in the main tourist area around Jalan Yos Sudarso/ Slamet Riyadi; or many of the homestays and Warung Baru also sell tickets.

Near the main bus station, the Gilingan bus station has express minibuses to nearly as many destinations as the buses. Deluxe door-to-door minibuses cost 4000 rp to

Yogya or 13,000 rp to Surabaya or Malang. Homestays or agents next to Losmen Kota or Warung Baru sell tickets, or go straight to Gilingan. Ranta (☎ 37634), Jalan Yos Sudarso 3, has a minibus service to Bromo for a hefty 25,000 rp non-air-con or 35,000 rp air-con.

Train Solo is on the main Jakarta-Yogya-Surabaya train route so there are frequent day trains, as well as night trains. The most comfortable way to get to Jakarta is to take the fast *Bima Express*, which departs Solo at 8 pm, arriving at Jakarta Kota at 5.30 am; fares range from 36,000 rp for a seat in bisnis to 94,000 rp for a sleeping berth.

Trains from Solo to Surabaya take around five hours, with fares ranging from 3500 rp on the ekonomi *Argopuro* to 77,000 rp in a 1st-class sleeper on the *Bima Express*.

Up to eight trains run between Bandung and Solo: the *Kereta Api Ekspres* (7000 rp ekonomi, 14,000 rp bisnis, nine hours) is a reasonable cheap service or the *Mutiara* is a luxury service. Ekonomi services also run to Cirebon via Purwokerto, and some of the luxury trains to Jakarta also take this route. Yogya is only about 1½ hours away by train.

Getting Around

A becak from the railway station or bus station into the town centre is around 1000 rp. The orange minibus No 06 costs 250 rp to Jalan Slamet Riyadi.

The city double-decker bus runs between Kartasura in the west and Palur in the east, directly along Jalan Slamet Riyadi, and costs a flat fare of 200 rp. Bicycles can be hired from the homestays.

Solo has metered taxis (☎ 45678 for bookings). The main taxi stand is at the corner of the Singosaren Plaza shopping centre. A taxi to the airport will cost around 9000 rp.

AROUND SOLO
Sangiran

Fifteen km north of Solo, Sangiran is an important archaeological excavation site, where some of the best examples of fossil skulls of prehistoric 'Java Man' (*Pithecanthropus erectus*) were unearthed by a Dutch

professor in 1936. While of great archaeological significance, the only thing to see is a small museum with a few skulls (one of *homo erectus*), various pig and hippopotamus teeth and fossil exhibits including mammoth bones and tusks. Souvenir stalls outside sell bones, 'mammoth tusks' carved from stone, and other dubious fossil junk. Guides will also offer to take you to the area where fossils have been found – it's a hot walk to see a few shells, if you are lucky.

The museum is open daily, except Sunday, from 9 am to 4 pm. Admission is 500 rp. From the Solo bus station, take a Purwodadi bus to Kalijambe (400 rp). Ask for Sangiran and you will be dropped at the turnoff, 15 km from Solo. It is then four km to the museum (1000 rp by ojek).

Candi Sukuh

One of Java's most mysterious and striking temples, the Candi Sukuh stands 900 metres high on the slopes of Gunung Lawu, 36 km east of Solo. In form it is a large truncated pyramid of rough-hewn stone with a curious Inca look and, while the sculpture is carved in the 'wayang style' found particularly in East Java, the figures are crude, squat and distorted. The temple is hardly as wildly erotic as it is sometimes made out to be but there are fairly explicit and humorous representations of a stone penis or two and the elements of a fertility cult are quite plain.

Built in the 15th century during the declining years of the Majapahit, Sukuh seems to have nothing whatsoever to do with other Javanese Hindu and Buddhist temples, and the origins of its builders and strange sculptural style remain a mystery. It is the most recent Hindu-Buddhist temple in the region, yet it seems to mark a reappearance of the pre-Hindu animism and magic that existed 1500 years before. It's a quiet, isolated place with a strange and potent atmosphere.

At the gateway before the temple is a large stone lingga and yoni. Flowers are still often scattered over it and there's a story that the symbol was used mainly by villagers to determine whether a wife had been faithful or a wife-to-be was still a virgin. The woman

Java Man

Charles Darwin's *Evolution of the Species* inspired a new generation of naturalists in the 19th century, and his theories sparked acrimonious debate across the world. Ernst Haeckel's *The History of Natural Creation* published in 1874 expounded further on Darwin's theory of evolution and attributed the evolution of primitive humans from a common ape-man ancestor, the famous 'missing link'.

One student of the new theories, Dutch physician Eugene Dubois, set sail for Sumatra in 1887 where he worked as an army doctor. In 1889, he left his position and went to Java after hearing of the uncovering of a skull at Wajak, near Tulung Agung in East Java. Dubois worked at the dig, uncovering other human fossils closely related to modern man. Later in 1891, at Trinil in East Java's Ngawi district, Dubois unearthed an older skull and other remains that he later classified as *Pithecanthropus erectus*, a low-browed, prominent-jawed early human ancestor, dating from the Middle Pleistocene era. His published findings of 'Java Man' caused a storm in Europe and were amongst the earliest findings in support of Darwin's theories.

Since Dubois' findings, many older examples of *Homo erectus* have been uncovered on Java. The most important and most numerous findings have been at Sangiran where in the 1930s Ralph von Koenigswald found fossils dating back to around one million BC. Meanwhile, in 1936 at Perning near Mojokerto the skull of a child was discovered and some, possibly sensationalist, estimates have dated it as 1.9 million years old. Most findings have been along the Bengawan Solo River in Central and East Java, though Pacitan on East Java's south coast is also an important archaeological area.

Discoveries in Kenya now date the oldest hominid human ancestors, *Australopithecine*, to 4.5 million years old. Ancient man migrated from Africa to Asia and came to Java via the land bridges that existed between the Asian mainland and the now insular Indonesian lands. It is thought that Java Man eventually became extinct, and the present inhabitants are descendents of a much later migration. ∎

Pithecanthropus skull found at Sangiran, exhibiting the low brow and prominent jaw of early humans.

had to wear a sarong and stride across the lingga – if the sarong tore, her infidelity was proven. Other interesting cult objects stand further in amongst the trees, including a tall-standing monument depicting Bima, the *Mahabharata* warrior hero, with Narada, the messenger of the gods, in a stylised womb followed by Bima dropping through at his birth. In the top courtyard three enormous flat-backed turtles stand like sacrificial altars.

From the site the views are superb, to the west and north across terrace fields and mountains.

Getting There & Away From Solo, take a Tawangmangu bus to Karangpandan (500 rp), then a Kemuning minibus to the turnoff to Candi Sukuh (500 rp). On market days (Wage and Pahing in the Javanese calendar), a 9 am bus from Karangpandan stops right beside the temple but otherwise, it's a couple of km uphill walk to the site. The trip takes about 1½ hours in total. There is a 300 rp admission charge to the site, and the ubiquitous visitors' book makes an appearance.

Candi Ceto

Further up the slopes of Gunung Lawu, Candi Ceto dates from the same era as Candi Sukuh. Combining elements of Shivaism and fertility worship, it is a larger temple than Sukuh, spread over terraces leading up the misty hillside. It is a spartan complex, with little carving, and the closely fitted stonework, some of it new, gives the temple a medieval atmosphere. Along with Sukuh, it

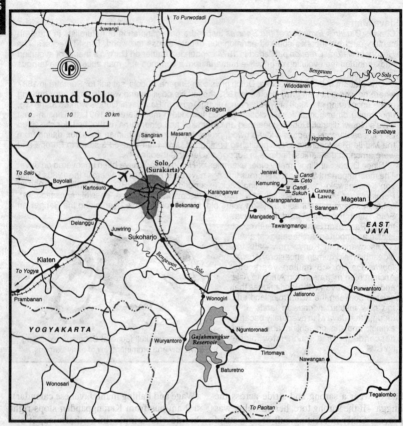

Around Solo

0   10   20 km

To Purwodadi

Juwangi

Bengawan   Solo

Widodaren

Sragen

Sangiran   Masaran

To Surabaya

Ngrambe

Solo
(Surakarta)

Jenawi   Candi
Ceto

To Selo   Boyolali   Kemuning   Candi   Gunung
Kartosuro   Karanganyar   Sukuh   Lawu

Magetan

Karangpandan

Bekonang   Sarangan

Delanggu   Mangadeg

Juwiring   Tawangmangu   EAST
Sukoharjo   JAVA

Klaten   Bengawan   Solo

To Yoga
Prambanan   Wonogiri   Jatisrono   Purwantoro

YOGYAKARTA   Nguntoronadi

Wuryantoro   Gajahmungkur   Tirtomaya
Reservoir   Nawangan

Baturetno

Wonosari

Tegalombo

To Pacitan

is reputed to be the most recent Hindu temple in Java, built when the wave of Islamic conversion was already sweeping the island.

Because of the difficulty in reaching Ceto, few visitors make it here – one of the attractions. Ceto is nine km by road past the Sukuh turnoff. Take a bus as far as Kemuning, then an ojek (3000 rp) or walk the six km through the hills covered in tea plantations, clove trees and vegetable plots.

Tawangmangu

Trekkers can make an interesting 2½-hour walk from Candi Sukuh along a well-worn cobbled path to Tawangmangu, a hill resort on the other side of Gunung Lawu. Or you can get there by bus from Solo via Karangpandan, which is just as fine a trip along a switchback road through magnificent tightly terraced hills. At Tawangmangu is **Grojogan Sewu**, a 100-metre high waterfall and favourite playground for monkeys. It's reached by a long flight of steps down a hillside from the village and you can swim in the very chilly pool at the bottom.

The cave of **Gua Maria** is a three-km walk from the road. Tawangmangu is packed on Sundays.

Places to Stay & Eat In Tawangmangu, the *Pak Amat Losmen* is right by the bus station. Rooms with their own enclosed verandahs are good value at 7500 rp, though the attached mandis could do with a good scrub. The losmen has a decent restaurant.

Prices and quality increase as you head up the hill. The *Pondok Garuda* (☎ 97239) has good rooms to suite most budgets, ranging from 7500 rp ekonomi rooms or from 20,000 to big 50,000 rp bungalows with hot water, TV and breakfast thrown in.

Further up the hill, the friendly *Pondok Indah* (☎ 97024) has spacious old rooms with sitting rooms for 35,000 rp, or new, motel-style rooms from 60,000 rp.

The best place in town is the *Komajaya Komaratih Hotel* (☎ 97125), near the turn-off to the waterfall. It is favoured by tour groups and rooms in the old wing cost 42,000 rp and 53,000 rp, or new rooms accommodating up to four people cost from 95,000 rp.

For good Indonesian dishes, eat at *Sapto Argo* on Jalan Raya Lawu. Continue down Jalan Raya Lawu and you may dine in the tranquil ambience of *Lesahan Pondok Indah* while seated cross-legged on bamboo mats overlooking the rice paddies.

Getting There & Away Buses go to Solo (700 rp) and Sarangan (1000 rp). Mitsubishi minibuses (300 rp) loop through town from the bus station up the main road, across to the waterfall and around back to the bus station.

Sarangan

An interesting alternative to backtracking to Solo is to take a colt to Sarangan, 14 km from Tawangmangu on the mountain road to Madiun. This picturesque hill town lies on the slopes of Gunung Lawu with hotels clustered at the edge of Telaga Pasir, a crater lake. At 1287 metres the climate is refreshing and this is one of the most pleasant hill resorts in Java, with the lake providing opportunities for boating and water-skiing, and walking opportunities include the four-hour ascent of Gunung Lawu (3265 metres). Sarangan is just over the provincial border in East Java, though most visitors come via Solo.

Places to Stay This is an upmarket resort without really being luxurious. There is little in the way of budget accommodation. The only cheap places are found away from the lake to the east of town in Ngerong, near the smaller Telaga Wahyu. On the main road, *Losmen Indrawati* (☎ 98057) is basic but OK for 12,000 rp.

The mid-range and expensive hotels are all around Telaga Pasir. *Hotel Sarangan* (☎ 98022) has fine views and colonial atmosphere and is very popular with Dutch tourists.

Selo

On the northern slopes of volatile Gunung Merapi, 50 km from Solo, it is roughly a four-hour trek from Selo to the summit of the volcano (2911 metres) – and this is a safer and easier climb than the one from Kaliurang to the south. (For more information, see the Around Yogya section.) However, you shouldn't try to hike around the side of the peak from Selo to see the crater, as this is a very dangerous climb. From the Kaliurang side you can hike to both crater and summit if you're in good shape. In Selo, you can stay at the *Agung Merapi*, which has rooms from 6000 rp. Guides can be hired in Selo.

Getting There & Away From Solo, take the Masa bus to Selo (700 rp) or a Semarang bus to Boyolali and from there a colt to Selo. From Yogya take a Magelan bus to Blabak and then a colt to Selo. In Yogya, the Kartika Travel Agency at Jalan Sosrowijayan 10 arranges guided treks to the summit of Gunung Merapi, including transport, food, accommodation in Selo and a guide.

NORTH COAST

For many centuries Java's north coast was the centre for trade with merchants from Arabia, India and China. Through trade the north coast came in contact with different cultures and ideas, and became the birthplace of Islam in Java. During the 15th and 16th centuries, Islam was adopted by the rulers of the trading principalities, in opposition to the Hindu kingdoms of inland Central Java.

Islam in Indonesia has immortalised the wali songo, or nine saints, to whom the establishment of Islam in Java is credited. With the exception of Sunan Gunungjati in Cirebon, the tombs of the saints all lie between Semarang and Surabaya and are important pilgrimage points for devout Muslims. A number of these places lie on the road to Surabaya and can also be visited using Semarang as a base.

While the coast attracts many pilgrims, few tourists venture north. The flat, hot coastal plain bordered by low hills doesn't have fine beaches or the spectacular scenery of the central mountains. The massive monuments of ancient Java are missing, and apart from some impressive mosques, the reminders of the north coast's trading heyday are not obvious. Yet while the north coast doesn't have any 'must see' tourist attractions and is conspicuously absent from tour group itineraries, it has an interesting mix of cultural influences, a lazy Middle Eastern atmosphere and makes an interesting diversion for the more adventurous with time to spare.

PEKALONGAN

On the north coast between Semarang and Cirebon, Pekalongan is known as Kota Batik (Batik City) and its batiks are some of the most sought after in Indonesia. Positioned on the trading routes between China, India and Arabia, the city absorbed many influences and these are reflected in its style of batik. Pekalongan batik is less formal, more colourful and innovative in design compared to the traditional styles of Yogyakarta and Solo.

Pekalongan is a must for batik freaks, but otherwise it is not a tourist destination. The town has a neglected, old-fashioned atmosphere and a mixed population. While the main street, Jalan Gajah Mada/Hayam Wuruk can bustle, Pekalongan is a relatively quiet town, especially during the afternoon siesta.

Javanese Mosques

When Islam came to Java it absorbed existing traditions, and many Javanese mosques used Hindu architectural details. The three-tiered *meru* roof topped by a *mustaka* is found in many Javanese mosques and is the same as those on Balinese Hindu temples. In Bali, three-tiers represent the Hindu trinity of gods while 11 roofed temples are devoted to Sanghyang Widi, the supreme Balinese deity. Similarly, some early mosques on Java, such as the Al-Manar Mosque in Kudus, have Hindu *candi bentar* (split gateways), designed to keep out evil spirits. ■

Mustaka (crowning ornament)

Javanese mosque with *meru* roof

Balinese temple with *meru* roof.

Information

The tourist office in the town hall (Balai Kota) has maps of Pekalongan and will try to answer most queries.

The main post office (Kantor Pos dan Giro) is opposite the Bali Kota, and for international telephone calls, the Telkom office is next door at Jalan Merak 2. There is also a Warpostal at the railway station.

Things to See

Pekalongan's small **Batik Museum**, two km south of the railway station on Jalan Majapahit, exhibits examples of different batik styles, with explanations in Indonesian. It's open from 9 am to 1 pm and closed on Sundays. Of more interest is the **bird market** nearby on Jalan Kurinci.

The most interesting area of town is around the **Pasar Banjarsari**, a lively market and good place for batik shopping. Nearby Jalan Blimbing is the old **Chinese quarter** and along this street is a Chinese temple and old terraced houses. To the east, Jalan Patiunus and the streets leading off it, is the **Arab quarter**, and this is also a good area for batik (see Things to Buy).

Facing the alun alun with its massive banyan trees is the **Mesjid Al Jami**. The lighthouse-styled minaret and Arabic architecture enclosing an older Javanese-style mosque is especially impressive when lit at night.

Places to Stay

Pekalongan has decent budget accommodation directly opposite the railway station on Jalan Gajah Mada. The best is the friendly and very clean *Hotel Gajah Mada* (☎ 41185) at No 11 with doubles for 7000 rp, or 10,000 rp with mandi. A few doors along, the *Losmen Damai* is slightly cheaper with rooms from 6000 rp.

In the centre of town, Pekalongan's best budget-to-moderate bet is the *Hotel Hayam Wuruk* (☎ 41823) at Jalan Hayam Wuruk 152-158. A variety of good rooms cost from 18,000/24,000 rp for singles/doubles with fan and mandi, and with air-con from 23,000/29,000 to 35,000/41,000 rp for those

with hot water and TV. Breakfast is included. The *Hotel Istana* (☎ 61581), near the railway station at Jalan Gajah Mada 23, is a good mid-range hotel with fan rooms from 24,000/30,000 rp and air-con rooms from 42,000 to 96,000 rp.

The *Nirwana Hotel* (☎ 41691), Jalan Dr Wahidin 11, is the best hotel in town. It has a large pool, coffee shop and restaurant. Air-con rooms cost from 49,000/50,000 to 82,000/88,000 rp, including breakfast.

Places to Eat

Coming into town from the railway station, one of the first restaurants you will see signposted on Jalan Gajah Mada (there is no number) is *A Karim* in the Pasar THR. It may look like a hole-in-the-wall, but the Madurese sate is superb. The *Purimas Bakery* on Jalan Hayam Wuruk has cakes, pastries, cold drinks and a sit-down area to enjoy them. A smaller branch is on Jalan Gajah Mada near A Karim.

On Jalan Merdeka, the *Mie Rasa* is spotless little place with noodle dishes and excellent icy fruit juices. At the *Remaja*, Jalan Dr Cipto 20, good and reasonably cheap Chinese food is available. Seafood is a speciality. The *Es Teler 77* at No 66 has a selection of Indonesian dishes, cold ice juices and a cool, shady garden.

Things to Buy

Batik, of course. Pekalongan batik is constantly evolving and new designs are more suited to Western and modern Indonesian tastes. Traditional batik is still popular, however, and for formal occasions Indonesians are often required to don batik.

Street peddlers casually wave batik from the doorways of hotels and restaurants – mostly cheap clothes and poor quality sarongs. Shops around town, many on Jalan Hayam Wuruk, sell ready-made clothes, lengths of cloth and sarongs in cotton and silk.

The Pasar Banjarsari is a great place to browse for cheap, everyday batik, and some better pieces can be found. In the same area, Tobal, Jalan Teratai 24, is a large rag trade business that produces clothes for the export market and you can view the process. Jacky, nearby at Jalan Surabaya 5A, has a showroom down an alley with a large range of clothes and lengths of good-quality cloth.

Most of the traditional batik is produced in the villages around Pekalongan. In the batik village of Kedungwuni, nine km south of town, Oey Soe Tjoen's workshop is one of the most famous. Intricate and colourful batik tulis are still produced, and these are regarded as among the highest quality you will find. You can see them being made every day of the week except Friday.

Getting There & Away
Pekalongan is on the main Jakarta-Semarang-Surabaya road and rail route. There is also a road linking Pekalongan and the Dieng Plateau.

Bus Pekalongan's bus station is about four km south-east of the centre of town, 300 rp by colt or 1500 rp by becak. Buses from Cirebon can drop you off in town on their way through.

Frequent buses go to Semarang (1800 rp; 2½ hours) and Cirebon (2400 rp; 3½ hours) and air-con buses also operate on these routes. Most buses to Wonosobo (2100 rp; 3½ hours) go in the morning or the most direct route to Dieng is to take a bus to Batur (1600 rp; four hours) and then a colt to Dieng, but buses are not frequent and this is a bone-rattling journey along a bad road.

The agents for door-to-door minibuses are clustered together on Jalan Alun Alun, just north of the square. Fares and journey times include: Jakarta (25,000 rp air-con, eight hours), Yogyakarta (8000 to 10,000 rp air-con, five hours) and Semarang (6000 rp non-air con, two hours). Hotels can ring for pickup.

Train As Pekalongan is midway for most train routes, the buses are a better bet. The *Senja Utama* (18,000 rp bisnis), *Fajar Utama* (14,000 rp bisnis) and *Cepat* (4500 rp ekonomi) run from Semarang to Jakarta and stop in Pekalongan and Cirebon. To

Semarang, the *Cepat* (2700 rp ekonomi) leaves in the afternoon.

Getting Around
Pekalongan has plenty of becaks, costing around 500 rp per km. Most journeys around town are 500 rp, or for 1000 rp you can go halfway across town. Orange bemos run all over town for a standard 300 rp. For Keduwangi, take a bemo down Jalan Mansyur.

SEMARANG
The north coast port of Semarang, the capital city of Central Java province, is a strong contrast to the royal cities of Solo and Yogyakarta. Under the Dutch it became a busy trading and administrative centre, and great numbers of Chinese traders joined the Muslim entrepreneurs of the north coast. Even in the depressed 1950s, great wealth flowed through the city, with sugar and other agricultural produce going out, and industrial raw materials and finished goods coming in.

Today, Semarang is the only port open to large ships on the central coast. Deep-water berthing facilities were built so that ocean-going vessels no longer had to anchor out in the mouth of Sungai Kali Baru.

1 Terboyo Bus Terminal
2 Airport
3 Puri Maerakaca
4 Gedung Batu
5 Green Guesthouse
6 Hotel Candi Baru
7 Patra Jasa Hotel
8 Jamu Jago

JAVA SEA

To Demak

See Central Semarang map

Jalan Siliwangi

To Cirebon

Jalan Majapahit

Dr Wahidin

To Solo

0   2   4 km

Semarang

More a commercial centre than a city for tourists, Semarang's main points of interest are the old city and the famous Chinese Gedung Batu Temple. This little-visited city can also be a good starting point for trips along the north coast or south to the central mountains. It can be a pleasant place to stop in for a night or two, for it seems less crowded and more relaxed than its large size and population (just over 1.3 million) would indicate.

Orientation

Semarang is split into two parts. 'Old' Semarang is on the coastal plain, sandwiched between the two Banjir canals, while the new town has spread out to the wealthy residential areas in the southern hills of Candi. An important hub in the old town is the Pasar Johar on the roundabout at the top of Jalan Pemuda.

Jalan Pemuda, Semarang's premier boulevard in Dutch times, is still a major artery and shopping street, though nowadays the Simpang Lima ('Five Ways') square has more life.

Information

Tourist Offices The Central Java tourist office (Dinas Pariwisata or DIPARDA), at Jalan Pemuda 171, has lots of maps and brochures on the province, including a regional *Calendar of Events* and an excellent map of Semarang. They are available if you ask for them. The city tourist office is in the old amusement park, Tegal Wareng, at Jalan Sriwijaya 29.

Both tourist offices are open from 7 am to 2 pm from Monday to Thursday, to 11 am on Friday and to 12.30 pm on Saturday.

Other The big banks can be found along Jalan Pemuda. The BCA bank, Jalan Pemuda 90-92, has good rates for cash and travellers' cheques and will give cash advances on Visa and MasterCard.

Semarang's main post office is on Jalan Pemuda near the river. The Telkom Office for international calls is at Jalan Suprapto 7, and it has a Home Country Direct phone.

The best hospital and first choice of the sizeable Semarang expat community is R S Saint Elizabeth (☎ 315345) on Jalan Kawi in the Candi district.

Old City

Semarang's decrepit old city has just enough relics of bygone days to make it an interesting place to wander around. On Jalan Let Jenderal Suprapto, the **Gereja Blenduk** is a Dutch church built in 1753 and still functioning. It has a huge dome and inside is a baroque organ. This area was the main port area in Dutch times, and towards the river from the church are numerous old Dutch warehouses, many still housing shipping companies.

Heading south of the Gereja Blenduk, you plunge into the narrow streets of Semarang's old **Chinatown**. The highlight here is the brightly painted **Tay Kak Sie Temple**, one of the finest examples of a Chinese temple in Indonesia. This temple complex dates from 1772 and is on Gang Lombok, the small alley running along the river off Jalan Pekojan. Also in Chinatown, the **Pasar Cina**, also called Pasar Gang Baru, is a fascinating market to wander around. It's a morning market, at its best before 7 am.

Back towards the centre of the city, **Pasar Johar** is Semarang's most intriguing market. You can find a little bit of almost everything from food to hardware to clothing and it's worth an hour or so of wandering around. Facing the market is Semarang's **Grand Mosque**.

Gedung Batu (Sam Po Kong Temple)

This well-known Chinese temple stands five km south-west of the centre of town. It was built in honour of Admiral Cheng Ho, the famous Muslim eunuch of the Ming dynasty who led a Chinese fleet on seven expeditions to Java and other parts of South-East and West Asia in the early 15th century. Cheng Ho has since become a saint known as Sam Po Kong and is particularly revered in Melaka, Malaysia. He first arrived in Java in 1405, and is attibuted with having helped spread Islam. This temple is also revered by Muslims.

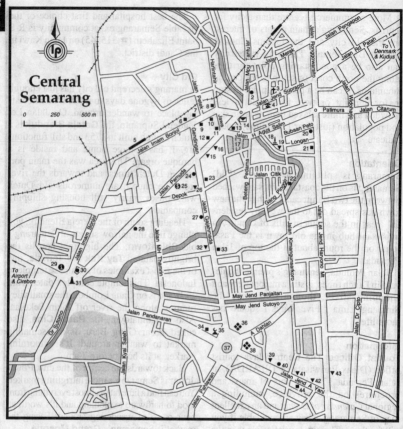

Central Semarang

0   250   500 m

To Denmark & Kudus

To Airport & Cirebon

Jalan Pandanaran

May Jend Panjaitan

May Jend Sutoyo

A Dahlan

Jalan Jend A. Yani

The main hall of the temple complex is built around an inner chamber in the form of a huge cave flanked by two great dragons. Hence the temple's popular name, *gedung batu*, meaning 'stone building'. Inside the cave is the idol of Sam Po Kong.

To get to Gedung Batu, take Damri bus No 2 from Jalan Pemuda to Karang Ayu, and then a Daihatsu from there to the temple. It takes about half an hour from central Semarang.

Puri Maerakaca

Often referred to as 'Taman Mini Jawa Tengah', this large theme park is Semarang's version of Jakarta's Taman Mini, with traditional houses representing all of Central Java's kabupaten (regencies). While mostly of interest to domestic tourists, it is well done and worth a look if you will be exploring Central Java in depth. Most houses have a small display of crafts and a map showing points of interest in the regency.

Puri Maerakaca is open from 7 am to 8 pm every day, and entry is 1000 rp. It is way out near the airport, and not accessible by public transport. Go in the late afternoon or on Sundays, as many of the exhibits are closed during the heat of the day.

PLACES TO STAY

6	Losmen Arjuna
7	Losmen Rahayu
8	Hotel Oewa Asia
9	Hotel Surya
10	Losmen Singapore
11	Natour Dibya Puri
12	Hotel Blambangan
13	Metro Hotel
21	Losmen Jaya
22	Hotel Nendra Yakti
23	Queen Hotel
33	Telomoyo
34	Hotel Graha Santika
44	Hotel Santika

PLACES TO EAT

15	Toko Oen
16	Sari Medan
19	Loenpia Semarang
26	Depot Naga
32	Rumah Makan Tio Cio
39	Bu Nani
41	Mbok Berek
42	Timlo Solo
43	Istana, Matsuri & Istana Baruna Restaurants

OTHER

1	Tawang Station
2	Pelni Office
3	Gereja Blenduk
4	Telkom Office
5	Poncol Station
14	Main Post Office
17	Pasar Johar
18	Tay Kak Sie Temple
20	Minibus Agents
24	Merpati
25	BCA Bank
27	Bouraq & Mandala
28	Ngesti Pandowo Theatre
29	Central Java Tourist Office
30	Lawang Sewu
31	Tugu Muda Monument
35	Mesjid Baiturrakhman
36	Citraland Mall
37	Simpang Lima
38	Plaza Simpang Lima
40	RRI

Jamu

Semarang is known for its two large *jamu* (herbal medicine) manufacturers – **Jamu Jago**, Jalan Raya Kaligawe Km 4 near the bus station, and **Jamu Nyonya Meneer**, Jalan Setia Budi 273, about six km from town on the Ambarawa road. Jamu Jago are well known for their adverts that use a squad of dwarfs! Both have museums open Monday to Friday from 10 am to 3.30 pm, and tours of the factories are available upon request.

Other Attractions

The **Tugu Muda**, at the southern end of Jalan Pemuda, is a candle-shaped monument commemorating Semarang's five-day battle against the Japanese in October 1945. Nearby is an impressive European-style building, known to the Javanese as **Lawang Sewu** ('1000 doors'). It was formerly Dutch offices, later headquarters of the Japanese forces and is now Indonesian army offices.

Simpang Lima square is where you'll find Semarang's cinema complexes and big shopping malls. Crowds congregate in the evenings and browse aimlessly at goods they can't afford to buy.

The **Semarang Harbour** is worth a look to see the pinisi and other traditional ocean-going vessels. The **Ronggowarsito Museum** is the provincial museum with antiquities from all over the state. It is on Jalan Abdulrachman, about one km from the airport.

Places to Stay – bottom end

You don't get a lot for your money in Semarang. The cheaper hotels are often dives and many are full with long-term residents. When you can get a room, conditions are not the best. The main budget hotel area is close to the centre on or just off Jalan Imam Bonjol. It's about 15 minutes' walk from the Tawang railway station (800 rp by becak).

The best cheap hotel (but often full) is the friendly *Losmen Arjuna* (☎ 544186) at No 51, Jalan Imam Bonjol, a colonial relic with some style. Cool and fairly comfortable rooms with high ceilings and mandi cost 12,500 rp. The *Losmen Singapore* (☎ 543757) at No 12 is a bit seedy but the no-frills rooms with shared mandis are clean and reasonable value at 9000 rp.

The popular *Hotel Oewa Asia* (☎ 542547), Jalan Kol Sugiono 12, spans the lower-to-middle bracket. This old colonial hotel is antiquated but comfortable and reasonably well maintained. Simple, clean rooms with fan and mandi cost 15,000 rp and 17,500 rp including breakfast. Air-con rooms cost

25,000 to 40,000 rp. It's in a good central location, near Pasar Johar and the post office.

Right in the action at Jalan Pemuda 23A, the well-run *Hotel Blambangan* (☎ 541649) has clean doubles/triples with mandi for 18,000/24,000 rp.

Over at Jalan M T Haryono 85-87, but still central, the *Losmen Jaya* (☎ 543604) is a good budget option with rooms for 9000 rp or doubles/triples with mandi for 14,500/ 17,500 rp, including breakfast.

For a little more, the *Hotel Nendra Yakti* (☎ 542538) at Gang Pinggir 68 is the best in this range. It is in an interesting area and good rooms with fan and mandi cost 18,000 to 20,000 rp or air-con rooms are 35,000 rp and 40,000 rp.

Places to Stay – middle
In the centre of town, the *Natour Dibya Puri* (☎ 547821) at Jalan Pemuda 11 is a rambling old hotel with loads of colonial atmosphere, but badly in need of renovation. Large air-con rooms have terraces overlooking the garden, hot water, TV and fridge for 48,000 to 80,000 rp, but nothing seems to work and they are grubby for the price. The best value are the bare but big fan rooms without bathroom for 25,000 rp – you can savour the colonial ambience but don't have to pay for non-existent facilities.

Also central, Jalan Gajah Mada has two good hotels. The *Telomoyo* (☎ 545436) at No 138 has a few fan rooms for 21,000 rp, but most are good, air-con rooms with balconies for 57,500 to 74,000 rp. The motel-style *Queen Hotel* (☎ 547063) at No 44-52 is well run and fully air-con. Spotless rooms with a private bathroom cost from 40,000 to 80,000 rp, including breakfast and afternoon tea.

The best value in Semarang is found in the tranquil residential districts in the hills to the south of the city. Two excellent options are in Candi Baru, a popular expat suburb about three km south-west of Simpang Lima. Candi Baru can be reached by bus, but be prepared do some walking, or catch taxis.

Green Guesthouse (☎ 312642), Jalan Kesambi 7, is a fine old hotel with terraced areas overlooking the city. Air-con rooms cost 25,000 to 50,000 rp – for 35,000 rp you have can a large bungalow with TV, fridge and hot water. *Hotel Candi Baru* (☎ 315272) is a magnificent, rambling old villa with even better views of the city. Air-con rooms here range from 38,000 to 77,000 rp, plus 21%. The On-On Pub at the hotel is the hash hangout and well patronised by expats, especially on Friday nights.

Places to Stay – top end
Once the top hotel in Semarang, the three-star *Metro Hotel* (☎ 547371) at Jalan H Agus Salim 2 is right in the middle of town. Standard singles/doubles for US$48/55 are comfortable but don't have windows, or the better rooms cost US$58/65 to US$68/75. Add 21% tax and service, but discounts usually apply.

The top luxury hotel in Semarang is the *Hotel Graha Santika* (☎ 318850), Jalan Pandanaran 116-120. Among the amenities are a pool, restaurant, gym and satellite TV. Rooms cost US$88/97 and US$103/114, plus 21%.

The other major hotel is the *Patra Jasa Hotel* (☎ 314441) at Jalan Sisingamangaraja in Candi, offering fine view of Semarang, a pool, bowling alleys and tennis. Rooms cost US$90/100 to US$115/130.

Places to Eat
The *Toko Oen*, Jalan Pemuda 52, is not to be missed. It's a large, old-fashioned tea room where white tableclothes, basket chairs and ancient waiters in white jackets are all part of the genteel colonial atmosphere. It has an Indonesian, Chinese and European menu, good food and a great selection of ice creams.

At night you'll find dozens of warungs around Pasar Johar (or Pasar Ya'ik as it is known in the evenings), Semarang's best speciality market. The southern side of Simpang Lima also has plenty of warungs. Of course, Simpang Lima's malls are the place for fast food, including a *McDonald's* in the Citraland Mall.

Semarang is renowned for its lumpia (Chinese spring rolls). They can be found all over town, but one of the most famous and original purveyors is the small *Loenpia Semarang*, near the Tay Kak Sie Temple at Gang Lombok No 11. Other cheap, hole-in-the-wall places are on the same stretch – a good place to have a meal after touring Chinatown.

Jalan Gajah Mada is another hunting ground for Chinese restaurants. Try *Rumah Makan Tio Cio*, opposite the Telemoyo Hotel, a popular place with reasonably priced seafood. At Jalan Gajah Madah 37A, *Depot Naga* is a scrupulously clean, open-sided cafe, with a wide selection of dishes, including excellent grilled fish and sate.

The *Timlo Solo*, Jalan A Yani 182, has good, inexpensive Javanese food. Try the lontong timlo or nasi timlo. A few doors away, *Mbok Berek* has Yogya-style fried chicken. Also on Jalan A Yani, near the RRI, *Bu Nani* at No 136 has good seafood.

Entertainment

Every evening there are wayang orang performances at the long-established *Ngesti Pandowo Theatre* at Jalan Pemuda 116. Performances start at 8 pm. *RRI* on Jalan A Yani puts on wayang kulit shows on the first Saturday of the month.

Getting There & Away

Air Merpati (☎ 20178), Jalan Gajah Mada 11, has direct flights between Semarang and Bandung (92,400 rp), Jakarta (114,400 rp, nine flights per day), Pangkalanbun (161,700 rp) and Surabaya (69,300 rp).

Sempati (☎ 414086) is in the Hotel Graha Santika and has direct flights to Jakarta and Surabaya.

Bouraq (☎ 515921) at Jalan Gajah Mada 61 D has a direct flight to Banjarmasin (170,500 rp).

Mandala (☎ 543021) at Jalan Gajah Mada 61 C has direct flights to Jakarta.

Bus Semarang's Terboyo bus terminal is

four km east of town, just off the road to Kudus. Destinations for non-air-con/air-con buses include: Yogya (2000/3400 rp; 3½ hours), Solo (1900/3000 rp; 2½ hours), Magelang (1400/2200 rp), Wonosobo (2200/3600 rp; four hours), Pekalongan (1800/3000 rp; 2½ hours), Cirebon (4000/6500 rp; six hours), Kudus (1000/1600 rp; one hour) and Surabaya (5200/8800 rp; nine hours).

Most ticket-agent offices for night and luxury buses can be found on Jalan Haryono near the Losmen Jaya. They have departures for all major long-haul destinations, including Jakarta for around 20,000 rp and Denpasar for 31,000 rp. To Jakarta, it's a long nine-hour haul and buses arrive at ungodly hours at the remote Pulo Gadung station.

Agents for express minibuses are found all over town. Or on Jalan Haryono, try the Rahayu agent at No 9 (☎ 543935), or the Nusantara Indah agent at No 9B (☎ 548648). Non air-con/air-con minibuses go to Solo (4000/5000 rp) and Yogya (4500/5000 rp) every hour from 7 am to 6 pm. Other non-air-con services include Kudus (2500 rp) and Wonosobo (8000 rp), or air-con buses include Cirebon (15,000 rp), Surabaya (20,000 rp) and Jakarta (30,000 rp).

Train Semarang is on the main Jakarta-Cirebon-Surabaya train route and there are frequent services operating to and from these cities. Tawang is the main railway station in Semarang.

Trains between Jakarta and Semarang include the *Cepat* (5000 rp ekonomi, 11 hours), *Senja Utama* (18,000 rp bisnis, eight hours) and *Fajar Utama* (14,000 rp bisnis, eight hours). They all stop in Pekalongan and Cirebon and usually run over schedule. The luxury *Mutiara Utara* passes through Semarang between Surabaya and Jakarta and costs 31,000 rp bisnis to either destination.

To Solo, the *Pandaran* (1300 rp ekonomi, four hours) leaves from Poncol station, but the bus is a much better option.

Boat The Pelni office (☎ 20488) is at Jalan Tantular 25, near the Tawang railway station. It's open from 8 am to 4 pm Monday to

Friday and to 1 pm on Saturday. Pelni's *Lawit* and *Bukitraya* run between Semarang and the Kalimantan ports of Pontianak, Kumai and Sampit. There are also occasional cargo boats from Semarang to Banjarmasin which take passengers – inquire in the harbour area.

Getting Around
To/From the Airport Ahmad Yani Airport is six km to the west of town. A taxi into town costs 6000 rp, less going to the airport. Damri bus No 2 goes to the airport.

Local Transport Semarang has becaks, taxis and a big Damri city bus service, supplemented by orange Daihatsu minivans. City buses charge a fixed 200 rp fare and terminate at the Terboyo bus station. Bus Nos 1 and 5 run south along Jalan Pemuda to Candi. Daihatsus cost 250 to 350 rp and operate all around town.

A becak from Tawang railway station or the bus station to the Oewa Asia Hotel will cost about 800 rp. You shouldn't pay more than 1000 rp for most becak rides in town. Becaks aren't allowed along Jalan Pemuda.

Semarang has a limited number of metered taxis, and they can be hard to find on the street. They tend to congregate around the big hotels or in front of the post office. Private minibuses for hire can be found at the post office and bus station, but bargain furiously.

AROUND SEMARANG
Ambarawa
At the junction where the Bandungan road branches from the Yogya to Semarang road, this small market town is the site of the **Ambarawa Railway Station Museum** (Museum Kereta Api Ambarawa). At the old Ambarawa depot, steam locomotives built between 1891 and 1928 are on show, including a 1902 cog locomotive still in working order. Most of the engines were made in Germany and assembled in Holland. The museum is open from 7 am to 4.30 pm every day.

Though the line has closed, groups can charter a train for the 18-km round trip from Ambarawa to Bedono on the old cog railway. The train can take up to 100 passengers for a total cost of 500,000 rp. Book in Ambarawa or through the Central Java Exploitation Office (Exploitasi Jawa Tengah) (☎ 524500), PJKA, Jalan Thamrin 3, Semarang.

Getting There & Around Ambarawa can be reached by public bus from Semarang (600 rp; one hour; 40 km), and Yogya (1400 rp; 2½ hours; 90 km) via Magelang. From Solo, you have to change buses at Salatiga.

You can get around Ambarawa by dokar; they quote around 500 rp from the bus station to Pasar Projo or the Railway Museum.

Bandungan
Bandungan at 980 metres is a pleasant enough hill resort to savour the mountain air, but the main attraction is nearby Gedung Songo. On Bandungan's main street, just before the road turns off to Gedung Songo, is an excellent roadside market with locally grown fruit and vegetables. In the same area are several cheap eating places. At around 7 am, a flower market gathers here briefly before dispersing to outlying towns and villages.

Places to Stay Bandungan has dozens of losmen and more expensive hotels. The *Losmen Riana I* has simple rooms with small mandi for 7000 rp. The *Pura Mandira Karya* (☎ 91454) is a notch up in quality and has rooms from 9000 to 15,000 rp. Some have hot water – very welcome in the mornings. The *Kusuma Madya Inn* (☎ 91136) has rooms with mandi costing from 12,000 rp, though most are from 22,000 to 45,000 rp. The hotel has friendly staff and comfortable rooms. Blankets and hot water in the mornings are provided.

The *Hotel Rawa Pening I* (☎ 91134), about one km out of town towards Gedung Songo, is a lovely old colonial-style wood bungalow with a front terrace, fine gardens, tennis courts and a restaurant. This is also *the* place to stay for fantastic views but, as you might imagine, it is often full at weekends. Rooms in the old building range from 22,500 o 27,500 rp and other rooms and cottages ost 30,000 to 77,500 rp. The nearby *Rawa Pening II* is at the more expensive end of the scale and has a pool and tennis courts.

At the top end is the new *Hotel Nugraha Wisata* (☎ 91501) which has a swimming pool and rooms for 45,000 to 70,000 rp or suites ranging up to 160,000 rp (50% more on weekends).

Getting There & Away Buses run directly from Semarang to Bandungan (500 rp) or coming from the south, get down in Ambarawa and then take a colt to Bandungan.

Gedung Songo Temples

These nine small Hindu temples are scattered along the tops of the foothills around Gunung Ungaran. Like those in Dieng, the Gedung Songo are small and simple temples, among the oldest Hindu temples in Java. The architecture may not be overwhelming, but the setting is simply superb. This 1000-metre perch gives one of the most spectacular views in Java – south across the shimmering Danau Rawa Pening to Gunung Merbabu and behind it smouldering Gunung Merapi, and west to Gunung Sumbing and Gunung Sundoro.

Gedung Songo means 'nine buildings' in Javanese. Built in the 8th and 9th century AD and devoted to Shiva and Vishnu, the temples are in good condition after major restorations in the 1980s, but many of the carvings have been lost. A well-trodden path ventures up the hill past three groupings – the temples at the third grouping are the most impressive. Halfway, the trail leads down to a ravine and gushing hot sulphur springs, and then up again to the final temple and its expansive views. The three-km loop can be walked in an hour, but allow longer to savour the atmosphere. Horses can also be hired.

The site is open from 6.15 am to 5.15 pm every day. Get there early in the morning for the best views.

Getting There & Away

The temples are about six km from Bandungan. From Bandungan's bustling marketplace, catch a colt for the three km to the turnoff to the temples. From the turnoff, take an ojek for the final three km to Gedung Songo (1000 rp, or only 500 rp for the return, downhill journey).

Demak

Twenty-five km east of Semarang on the road to Surabaya, Demak was once the capital of the first Islamic state on Java and the most important state during the early 16th century. At the time this was a good seaport but silting of the coast has now left Demak several km inland.

The **Mesjid Agung** (Grand Mosque) dominates the village of Demak and is one of Indonesia's most important places of pilgrimage for Muslims. It's so holy that seven pilgrimages to it are said to be the equivalent of a pilgrimage to Mecca. It is the earliest mosque known on Java, founded jointly by the wali songo in 1478, and it combines Javanese-Hindu and Islamic elements in its architecture. Constructed entirely of wood, it has four main pillars, called the *soko guru*, in the central hall. The pillars are said to have been made by four of the saints – one of them, erected by Sunan Kalijaga, is made of chips of wood glued together.

The mausoleum of Sunan Kalijaga is at **Kadilangu**, two km south of Demak.

KUDUS

Fifty-five km north-east of Semarang, Kudus was founded by the Muslim saint, Sunan Kudus. Like Demak, it is an Islamic holy city and an important place of pilgrimage. Its name comes from the Arabic *al-Quds*, which means 'holy', and it is the only place in Java that has permanently acquired an Arabic name.

Kudus is strongly Muslim, yet, strangely, some old Hindu customs prevail and there is still a tradition that cows may not be slaughtered within the town. Kudus is also a prosperous town and a major centre of Java's kretek (clove cigarette) industry.

Old Town

West of the river on the road to Jepara,

Kauman, the oldest part of town, can be an interesting place to wander around. Its streets are narrow and winding, stark white and almost Middle-Eastern in atmosphere, crowded with boys in sarong and topi and women in full orthodox Muslim dress. Some of the buildings are colourful traditional houses with ornately carved wooden fronts.

In the centre of the old town, the **Al-Manar** (or Al-Aqsa) **Mosque** was constructed in 1549 by Sunan Kudus. The mosque is named after the mosque of Jerusalem and, like so many of Java's early mosques, it displays elements of Islamic and Hindu-Javanese design such as the old Javanese carved split doorways. In fact it was probably built on the site of a Hindu-Javanese temple and is particularly famous for its tall red-brick minaret, or *menara*, which may have originally been the watchtower of that temple.

In the courtyards behind the mosque is the imposing **Tomb of Sunan Kudus**, which is now a shrine. His mausoleum of finely carved stone is hung with a curtain of lace. The narrow doorway, draped with heavy gold-embroidered curtains, leads through to an inner chamber and the grave. During Buka Luwur held once a year on 10 Muharram of the Islamic calendar, the curtains around the tomb are changed and thousands of pilgrims flock to Kudus for the event.

Kretek Production

Kretek, the sweet clove-flavoured cigarettes were invented by a Kudus man, Nitisemito and now Kudus has nearly 50 businesses accounting for roughly a quarter of Indonesia's annual production of kretek. Kudus is kretek city and it is possible to visit a number of factories.

The main companies are Djambu Bol, Nojorono, Sukun and the Chinese-owned

---

Kretek Cigarettes

One of those distinctive 'aromas' of Indonesia is the sweet spicy smell, almost like incense, of clove flavoured cigarettes. The *kretek* cigarette has only been around since the start of the century, but today the kretek addiction is nationwide and accounts for 90% of the cigarette market, while sales of *rokok putih* (ordinary non-clove cigarettes) are languishing. So high is the consumption of cloves for smoking that Indonesia, traditionally a supplier of cloves in world markets, has become a substantial net importer from centres like Zanzibar and Madagascar.

The invention of the kretek has been attributed to a Kudus man, Nitisemito, who claimed they relieved his asthma. He mixed tobacco with crushed cloves rolled in corn leaves, and these *rokok klobot* were the prototype for his Bal Tiga brand which he began selling in 1906. Nitisemito was a tireless promoter of his product – on the radio, by air (dropping advertising leaflets) and by touring van which took a musical troupe across Java in an attempt to sell the new cigarettes.

Kudus in Java became the centre for the kretek industry and at one stage the town had over 200 factories, though today less than 50 cottage industries and a few large factories remain. Rationalisation in the industry has seen kretek production dominated by the big producers such as Bentoel in Malang, Gudang Garam in Kediri, and Djarum in Kudus. Nitisemito became a victim of the industry he started and died bankrupt in 1953.

Although filtered kreteks are produced by modern machinery, non-filtered kreteks are still rolled by hand on simple wooden rolling machines. The manual process is protected by law. Women work in pairs with one rolling the cigarettes and the other snipping ends. They work an eight to 10-hour day, and typical rates are: 850 rp per 1000 cigarettes; 1350 rp per 1000 after the first batch of 4000 cigarettes. The best rollers can turn out about 7000 cigarettes in a day.

As to the claim that kreteks are good for smokers' cough, cloves are a natural anaesthetic and so do have a numbing effect on the throat. Any other claims to aiding health stop there, because the tar and nicotine levels in the raw, slowly cured tobaccos used in kreteks are so high that some countries have banned or restricted their import. The Srintil tobacco from Muntilan is said to be the best.

Filtered kreteks now dominate the market and popular brands include Bentoel, Gudang Garam and Sukun. The Bentoel company has even produced a 'light' range of kreteks, Sampoerna, though tar levels are still quite high. For the kretek purist, the conical, crackling, non-filtered kretek has no substitute – the Dji Sam Soe brand is regarded as the Rolls Royce of kreteks. ∎

Also worth a visit is the **Kretek Museum**. Although all explanations are in Indonesian, a number of interesting photographs and implements used in kretek production are on show.

Other Attractions

Next to the Kretek Museum, the **Rumah Adat** is a traditional wooden Kudus house exhibiting the fabulous carving work for which Kudus is famous. It is said that the Kudus style originated from Ling Sing, a 15th-century Chinese immigrant and Islamic teacher. While nearby Jepara is now the famous wood-carving centre, a few work-shops in Kudus still make intricately carved panels and doorways, primarily works commissioned by architects for public buildings, hotels or Jakarta mansions.

In front of the Plasa Kudus, the **Tugu Identitas**, styled after the menara, can be climbed for views over the town.

Places to Stay

The central *Losmen Slamet*, Jalan Jenderal Sudirman 63, is a rambling old place with spartan rooms from 7000 rp. It's just OK – some rooms are better than others. The motel-style *Air Mancur* (☎ 22514) at Jalan Pemuda 70 is much better but expensive, with decent doubles with mandi for 17,500 rp and 23,000 rp, or air-con rooms for 35,000 rp and 38,000 rp.

The *Hotel Notasari Permai* (☎ 21245), Jalan Kepodang 12, is a good mid-range hotel with a swimming pool, quiet courtyard and restaurant and the staff are friendly. Comfortable rooms with mandi start at 23,000 rp including breakfast; air-con rooms start at 40,000 rp, but don't get palmed off with a windowless room.

The *Kudus Asri Jaya Hotel* (☎ 22449) is the best hotel in town. The only drawback is that it is a long way from the centre, a few hundred metres north of the bus station. Rooms with mandi start at 12,500 rp but most are air-con rooms ranging from 65,000 rp to the 125,000 rp suites. It has a pool, bar and restaurant.

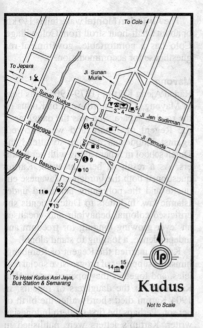

Kudus

Not to Scale

1 Al-Manar Mosque
2 Garuda Restaurant
3 Telkom
4 Post Office
5 Losmen Slamet
6 BCA Bank
7 Air Mancur Hotel
8 Hotel Notasari Permai
9 Tourist Office
10 Djarum Kretek Factory
11 Plaza Kudus
12 Tugu Identitas Tower
13 Rumah Makan Hijau
14 Kretek Museum
15 Rumah Adat

Djarum company which started in 1952 and is now the biggest producer in Kudus. Djarum's modern factory on Jalan A Yani is central, but they usually require a week's notice to tour the factory. Sukun, outside the town, still produce some *rokok klobot*, the original kreteks rolled in corn leaves. For a tour, contact the tourist office who can recommend a factory to visit.

JAVA

Places to Eat

Local specialities to try include *soto Kudus* (chicken soup) and *jenang Kudus*, which is a sweet made of glutinous rice, brown sugar and coconut.

The *Rumah Makan Hijau*, near the Plasa Kudus shopping centre at Jalan A Yani 1, is cheap and good for Indonesian food and super-cool fruit juices. It's closed on Fridays.

The *Hotel Notasari* restaurant is reasonably priced for the big helpings you get. The *Garuda* at Jalan Jenderal Sudirman 1 has Indonesian, Chinese and Western food.

Getting There & Away

Kudus is on the main Semarang to Surabaya road. The bus station is about four km south of town. City bemos run from behind the station to the centre, or you can take an ojek or becak, but they want 2500 rp.

From Kudus you can get buses to Semarang (1000 rp; one hour; 54 km), Surabaya (4400 rp; 286 km), Solo (2600 rp; 3½ hours; 156 km), Jepara (600 rp; 45 minutes; 35 km), Rembang (1000 rp), Lasem (1200 rp) and Mantingan (600 rp).

Colts go to Colo for 600 rp (1000 rp in holiday periods!). Kembang Express (☎ 22153) at Jalan A Yani 90 has express buses to Surabaya (12,500 rp) at 9.30 am and 10-seater, air-con minibuses to Yogya for 5500 rp.

AROUND KUDUS
Colo

This small hill resort lies 18 km north of Kudus at an altitude of 700 metres on the slopes of Gunung Muria.

Colo is most famous for its **Tomb of Sunan Muria** (or Raden Umar Said), one of the wali songo, who was buried here in 1469. The mosque surrounding the tomb is perched high on a ridge overlooking the plains to the south. It was built around the middle of the 19th century though it has had many later additions. Pilgrims regularly come to pray at the tomb, and during Buka Luwur, held in Colo on 16 Muharram of the Islamic calendar, up to 10,000 pilgrims line the road to the top.

The **Air Terjun Montel** waterfall is 1½ km or about a half-hour stroll from Colo village. Colo has a comfortable, government-run guesthouse for accommodation.

Mayong

Raden Ajeng Kartini (1879-1904) was born in Mayong, 12 km north-west of Kudus on the road to Jepara. She was the daughter of the Regent of Jepara and was allowed, against Indonesian custom, to attend the Dutch school in Jepara along with her brothers. As a result of her education, Kartini questioned both the burden of Javanese etiquette and the polygamy permitted under Islamic law. In letters to Dutch friends she criticised colonial behaviour and vocalised an 'ever growing longing for freedom and independence, a longing to stand alone'.

Kartini married the Regent of Rembang, himself a supporter of progressive social policies, and together they opened a school in Rembang for the daughters of regents. In 1904 Kartini died shortly after the birth of her son. Perhaps the first modern Indonesian writer, Kartini's letters were published in 1911 in the original Dutch, entitled *Through Darkness to Light*; the English edition is available in paperback.

At Mayong there is a monument to Kartini, which marks the spot where her placenta was buried according to Javanese custom. Jepara and Rembang are other important places where ceremonies are held on 21 April to celebrate Kartini Day.

JEPARA

Jepara, only 35 km north-west of Kudus, is famed as the centre for the best woodcarvers in Java. The road into Jepara passes workshops stacked high with furniture, so you get a fair idea of places to visit as you arrive.

Jepara is a small, peaceful country town but it has a colourful history. An important port in the 16th century, it had both English and Dutch factories by the early 1600s and was involved in a violent dispute between the VOC and Sultan Agung of Mataram. After some of the Dutch reputedly compared

Agung to a dog and relieved themselves on Jepara's mosque, hostilities finally erupted in 1618 when the Gujarati who governed Jepara for Agung attacked the VOC trading post. The Dutch retaliated by burning Javanese ships and much of the town. In 1619 Jan Pieterszoon Coen paused on his way to the conquest of Batavia to burn Jepara yet again and with it the English East India Company's post. The VOC headquarters for the central north coast was then established at Jepara.

Apart from furniture, Jepara's attractions are limited, but it has enough to keep visitors occupied during a short stay.

Things to See
Kartini's father was regent of Jepara and she grew up in the regent's house, Pendopo Kabupaten Jepara, now government offices on the east side of the alun alun. The small **Museum R A Kartini**, next to the tourist office on the north side of the alun alun, has photos and furniture from the family home. It is open from 7 am to 5 pm every day.

Heading north from the museum, cross the river and veer left up the hill to the old Dutch fort, the **Benteng VOC**. Over the last 50 years the stonework has been pillaged for building material and not much remains, but the site has good views across the town and out to the Java Sea, and the nearby cemetery has some Dutch graves.

Jepara has some surprisingly decent, white-sand beaches. **Tirta Samudra**, eight km north-east from town, is the most popular beach, but can be littered and is best avoided on weekends.

Places to Stay
The best budget choice is the *Menno Jaya Hotel* (☎ 91143), in the centre of town at Jalan Diponegoro 40B, which has basic singles/doubles without mandi for 8000/12,500 rp. The owner, Mr Teopilus Hadiprasetya, is an excellent host. He speaks good English and will proudly show you his photo albums and the 'thank you' letter from Prince Charles and Lady Di for a carved plaque he sent them as a wedding present.

Other places include the *Losmen Asia* at Jalan Kartini 32, which has rooms from 8000 rp or the more expensive *Hotel Terminal* right by the bus station, but it can be a bit noisy.

The *Kalingga Star* (☎ 91054), Jalan Dr Soetomo 16, is a reasonable mid-range hotel with economy rooms for 12,000 rp or air-con rooms from 30,000 rp. The *Ratu Shima* (☎ 91406), Jalan Dr Soetomo 13-15, is a better choice and the best hotel in town. Fan rooms range from 8,500 to 22,500 rp or air-con rooms are 30,000 to 47,500 rp. The rooms are spotless and it's a good deal.

Places to Eat
Depot Milo, Jalan Dr Soetomo 16-19, is a pleasant little restaurant next to the Kalingga Star with bamboo decor and Indonesian/Chinese dishes. Just across the river from the alun alun, the *Pondok Rasa*, Jalan Pahlawan 2, is Jepara's premier restaurant with Indonesian dishes at very reasonable prices. It has a pleasant garden and a lesahan eating area, as well as tables and chairs. The *Ratu Shima Hotel* also has a decent restaurant.

Things to Buy
Intricately carved wooden cupboards, divans, chests, chairs, tables, relief panels and the like are carved from teak *(jati)* or sometimes mahogany. Jepara's consumption of teak is so high that demand is outstripping supply in Java. Furniture shops and factories are all around Jepara, but the main centre is the village of Tahunan, four km south of Jepara on the road to Kudus.

Brightly coloured ikat weavings using motifs from Sumba are sold in Bali but they come from the village of Torso, 14 km south of Jepara, just off the main road. Other designs are produced and the men do the weaving, allowing broader looms to be used.

Pecangaan, 18 km south of Jepara, produces rings, bracelets and other jewellery from *monel*, a stainless steel alloy.

Getting There & Away
From Jepara's conveniently central terminal, frequent buses run from Jepara to Kudus (600 rp; 45 minutes) and Semarang (1200 rp;

1½ hours). Buses also go to Surabaya at 6 am, but Kudus has more connections. Night buses run to Jakarta and cost around 15,000 rp or Muji Jaya has more luxurious buses.

AROUND JEPARA
Mantingan

The mosque and tomb of Ratu Kali Nyamat are in this village, four km south of Jepara. Kali Nyamat was the great warrior-queen of Jepara who twice laid siege to Portugal's Melaka stronghold in the latter part of the 16th century. The campaigns against Melaka were not successful but she scared the Portuguese witless.

The mosque dating from 1549 was restored some years ago, and the tomb lies around the side. It is noted for its Hindu-style embellishments and medallions.

Mantingan is easily reached from Jepara. Angkudes from the bus terminal can drop you outside the mosque for 250 rp.

KARIMUNJAWA

These 27 islands, lying around 90 km north-west of Jepara, have been declared a marine national park. Though they are being promoted as a tropical paradise, facilities are limited, the islands are difficult to reach and few visitors make it to this forgotten part of Java.

The main island of **Pulau Karimunjawa** has homestay accommodation, but apart from peace and quiet the island's attractions are few – you can swim in the calm, clear waters but the island is mostly ringed by mangroves and has no decent beaches. Nearby islands do have magnificent beaches and coral reefs but can only be reached by chartered boat.

Pulau Tengah to the north is a small island ringed by a reef and beautiful, sandy beaches. The small resort here has the best accommodation on the islands. Other nearby deserted islands with good beaches are **Pulau Burung** and **Pulau Geleang** to the west.

Getting There & Away

A new, well-equipped ferry leaves from Pantai Kartini in Jepara (1000 rp by becak

from the town centre) and costs 10,000 rp or 15,000 rp in air-con 1st class for the 4½-hour journey. It leaves Jepara at 9 am on Mondays and Fridays, and returns from Karimunjawa at 8 am on Tuesdays and Saturdays, but schedules are unreliable. Smaller fishing boats (5000 rp; seven hours) battle the Java Sea swells and leave most mornings from Jepara's main harbour by the river, but they don't carry life jackets or rafts. Crossings in the wet season are rugged.

East Java

The province of East Java, or Jawa Timur, officially includes the island of Madura off the north-west coast. Including Madura it has a total population of 29.2 million and an area of 47,922 sq km. The majority of its population are Javanese, but many Madurese farmers and fishermen live in East Java. They are familiar faces, particularly around Surabaya, the capital of the province. In the Bromo area is a small population of Hindu Tenggerese.

Geographically, much of the province is flatter than the rest of Java. In the north-west is lowland with deltas along the rivers Brantas and Bengawan Solo, and km upon km of rice-growing plain. But the rest of East Java is mountainous and hilly, containing the huge Bromo-Tengger massif and Java's highest mountain (Gunung Semeru). This region offers a raw, natural beauty and magnificent scenery.

Major attractions for the visitor include the magnificent Gunung Bromo, still one of Java's most active volcanoes. Then there's a host of other mountains, pleasant walks and fine hill towns, like Malang. In the north-east corner of the province there is also the important Baluran National Park, the most accessible of Java's wildlife reserves. Finally, although East Java is closely related culturally to Central Java, the Madurese are best known for their rugged sport called *kerapan sapi*, the famous bull races which take place on the island during August and September.

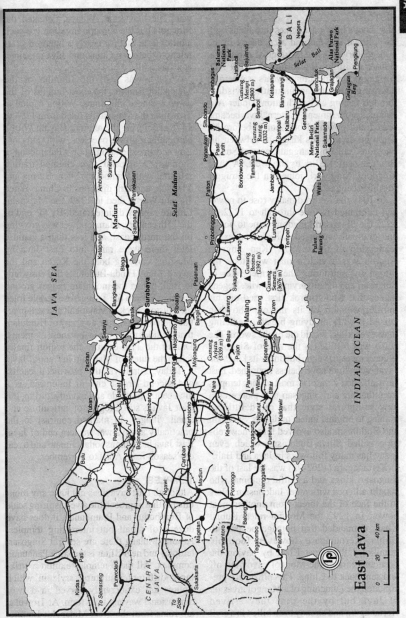

East Java

0   20   40 km

HISTORY

East Java's hazy past comes into focus with its political and cultural ascendancy in the 10th century AD, and the reign of Airlangga. Before claiming the throne in 1019 AD, Airlangga had spent many years as a hermit, devoting time to accumulating wisdom through fasting and meditation. Under Airlangga's government, eastern Java became united and powerful but shortly before his death he divided his kingdom between his two sons, creating Janggala, east of Sungai Brantas, and Kediri to the west. A third kingdom, Singosari, joined in the struggle for the ascendancy.

In 1049 the Kediri dynasty rose to power and continued its rule through to 1222. In 1222 the Singosari kingdom came to power and gradually superseded Kediri under the leadership of the usurper, Ken Angrok. Angrok was a violent man who took the throne by murdering the former ruler of Singosari and then marrying his wife. Legend relates that Ken Angrok first tried out his murder weapon on its maker, who then cursed it with his dying breath, predicting that seven kings would die by the sword. The curse was fulfilled – the rule of Singosari lasted a mere 70 years, but under its kings the Javanese culture nevertheless flourished. East Java inherited some of its most striking temples from that era and Singosari also pioneered a new sculptural style that owed little or nothing to original Indian traditions. Shivaism and Buddhism also evolved into a new religion called Shiva-Buddhism, which even today has many followers in Java and Bali.

Kertanagara (1262-92) was the last of the Singosari kings and a skilful diplomat who sought alliance with other Indonesian rulers in the face of the threat from another great power. In 1292 the Mongol ruler, Kublai Khan, demanded that homage be paid to China. Kertanagara, however, foolishly humiliated the Great Khan by having the nose and ears of the Mongol envoy cut off and sent back to China. This effrontery precipitated the launching of a Mongol invasion of Java but by the time they arrived Kertanagara had already been killed in a civil war. The new king, Wijaya, defeated the Mongols but the barbaric invasion left such a bitter taste that for nearly a hundred years relations between China and Java remained at a standstill.

Wijaya was also the founder of the Majapahit Empire, the most famous of the early Javanese kingdoms. With a capital at Trowulan the Majapahits ruled from 1294 to 1478 and during the reign of Hayam Wuruk carried their power overseas, with raids into Bali and an expedition against Palembang in Sumatra. Majapahit also claimed trading relations with Cambodia, Siam, Burma and Vietnam, and sent missions to China. When Hayam Wuruk died in 1389, the Majapahit Empire rapidly disintegrated. By the end of the 15th century, Islamic power was growing on the north coast, and less than a century later there were raids into East Java by Muslims carrying both the Koran and the sword. Many Hindu-Buddhists fled eastwards to Bali, but in the mountain ranges around Gunung Bromo the Tenggerese people trace their history back to Majapahit and still practise their own religion, a variety of Hinduism that includes many proto-Javanese elements. During the 17th century the region finally fell to the rulers of Mataram in Central Java.

Today, Surabaya, the provincial capital and second-largest city in Indonesia, is a vital centre for trade and manufacturing, but East Java is still a region of agriculture and small villages. In marked contrast to the practically always-wet western end of Java, East Java has a monsoonal climate and a real dry season from April to November.

TEMPLES

Although East Java does not have any monuments that approach the awe-inspiring scale of Borobudur and Prambanan, it does have dozens of small but interesting temples. Around Malang there are several Singosari temples and near Blitar is the large Panataran complex. All these temples exhibit a strikingly different sculptural style in which figures are exuberantly carved in a two-dimensional wayang kulit form. At Trowulan are ruins from the great Majapahit Empire.

Stone statues, Borobudur, Central Java (PM)

Top left: Candi Jalatunda, near Tretes, East Java (PT)
Top right: Pura Balekambang (a modern Hindu temple), Balekambang, East Java (PT)
Bottom: Hindu temple, Gedung Songo, Central Java (PT)

Overall, the innovative East Javan temple style is an obvious prototype for later Balinese sculpture/architecture.

The decorative imagination of the East Javanese sculptors also found expression in richly ornamented items cast in bronze and more costly metals. A great variety of ritual objects, weapons, and other utensils have been preserved, and many can be seen in Jakarta's National Museum.

MALANG

Malang is one of Java's finest and most attractive hill towns. Situated on the banks of Sungai Brantas, it was established by the Dutch around the end of the 18th century when coffee was first grown as a colonial cash crop in this area. In more recent years, local farmers have grown tobacco and apples; cigarette factories and the army have set themselves up here. It's a cool, clean place with a well-planned square, and the central area of town is studded with parks, tree-lined streets and old Dutch architecture.

The main attractions lie outside the city, but apart from being a good base for many points of interest in East Java, it is also worth a day or two's visit for its own sake. Unlike many Javanese towns, which are planned on a grid pattern, this one sweeps and winds along the river bank, with surprising views and quiet backwaters to explore. The living is good and the atmosphere easy-going.

Orientation

Life in Malang revolves around the town square and the busy streets of Agus Salim and Pasar Besar near the central market. Here are the main shopping plazas, restaurants, cinemas and many of Malang's hotels. The square in particular is a very popular area in the evenings, when families and students promenade and buskers perform. North-west of the square along Jalan Basuki Rachmat you'll find banks, the telephone office and restaurants.

Information

Tourist Office The East Java Government tourist bureau (DIPARDA) has a good information centre at Jalan Semeru 2. It is open from 8 am to 7 pm Monday to Saturday and until 1 pm on Sunday. The city tourist office at Jalan Tugu 1 is open from 8 am until 1.30 pm Monday to Thursday, until 10.30 am Friday and 12.30 pm Saturday.

Post & Telecommunications The main post office is opposite the alun alun on Jalan Kauman Merdeka.

The Telkom office on Jalan Basuki Rachmat is open 24 hours and has Home Country Direct phones. The Toko Oen restaurant and the Kartika Prince Hotel also have Home Country Direct phones. You'll find a Telkom wartel on Jalan Agus Salim, near the Hotel Santosa.

Money Malang has plenty of banks and moneychangers. Compare the BNI and BCA banks on Jalan Basuki Rachmat for the best rates.

Other The best bookshops are Sari Agung, next to the Sarinah department store, and Gramedia, on the other side of the street. The Sarinah department store has a small selection of crafts and souvenirs.

Things to See & Do

The major attractions are outside town, but Malang has a few diversions to stave off boredom.

Malang is noted for its colonial architecture, though in fact several other Javanese cities are better endowed with Dutch buildings. The **Balai Kota** (Town Hall) on Tugu Circle is a sprawling Dutch administrative building, and nearby are some former old mansions such as the **Splendid Inn** and the **Wisma IKIP** next door on Jalan Majapahit. For reliving colonial dreams, nothing beats the **Toko Oen restaurant**. Another good example of Art Deco colonial architecture is the **Hotel Pelangi** and its tiled restaurant with scenes of old Holland. Near the Toko Oen, the **Gereja Kathedral Kuno** is the old Dutch reform church. **Jalan Besar Ijen** is Malang's millionaire's row. Most of the

Malang

0   250   500 m

large houses date from the colonial era, but many have been substantially renovated, losing architectural detail in the process.

On the north-west outskirts of town, **Candi Badut** is a small Shivaite temple dating from the 8th century. West of town on Jalan Besar Ijen, the modern **Army Museum** is devoted to Malang's Brawijaya Division.

Malang has some good markets. The huge central market, the **Pasar Besar**, is always worth a browse. The flower market, **Pasar Bunga**, has a pleasant aspect down by the river, and it is the place to stroll in the morning. At the same time, you can also take in the nearby **Pasar Senggol**, once Malang's thriving night market, now a bird market. **Pasar Kebalen**, near the Chinese temple, is the most active market in the evenings until around 9 pm most nights.

Taman Rekreasi Senaputra is Malang's cultural and recreational park. Every Sunday morning, *kuda lumping* 'horse trance' dances (*jaran kepang* in Javanese) are held here. The dancers ride plaited cane horses until they fall into a trance, allowing them to eat glass and perform other masochistic acts without harm.

PLACES TO STAY		PLACES TO EAT		12	Tugu Transport Travel Agent
2	Regent's Park Hotel	7	Rumah Makan Minang Jaya	13	City Tourist Office
3	Hotel Palem			15	Balai Kota (Town Hall)
4	Hotel Helios	21	Minang Agung	19	Wisma IKIP
5	Kartika Prince Hotel	26	Toko Oen Restaurant	20	Pasar Senggol & Pasar Bunga
11	Hotel Menara	33	Rumah Makan Agung		
14	Hotel Aloha	34	Gloria Restaurant	22	BNI Bank
16	Splendid Inn	38	Depot Pangsit Mie	23	Cinema Complex
17	Tugu Park Hotel			25	Telkom Office
18	Montana Hotel	**OTHER**		28	Gereja Kathedral Kuno
24	Bamboe Denn			29	Sarinah Dept Store
27	Hotel Riche	1	Cathedral	30	Mosque
31	Hotel Pelangi	6	Army Museum	32	Main Post Office
36	Hotel Santosa	8	Tourist Office(DIPARDA)	35	Mitra & Gajah Mada Plaza
39	Hotel Tosari				
40	Losmen Semarang	9	BCA Bank	37	Malang Plaza
41	Hotel Margosuko	10	Taman Rekreasi Senaputra	42	Pasar Besar & Matahari Dept Store
				43	Chinese Temple

Organised Tours

A number of operators have tours to the Singosari temples, Batu and Bromo (via Tosari from around 50,000 rp per person). The Hotel Helios and the private Tourist Information Service (☎ 64052) at the Toko Oen are two well-known operators and speak Dutch as well as English. They can also arrange car hire with driver.

Places to Stay – bottom end

The most popular hotel and the best value in town is the *Hotel Helios* (☎ 62741), Jalan Pattimura 37. Doubles cost 10,000 to 15,000 rp with shared mandi and newer rooms with private bath cost 20,000 rp or 27,500 rp for three people. It's clean, comfortable and all rooms have balconies overlooking the garden. Good travel information, bus bookings and tours are provided.

For dormitory accommodation, the *Bamboe Denn* (☎ 66256), Jalan Arjuna 2, is a small branch-hostel of the famous Surabaya institution. A bed in the eight-bed dorm costs 2500 rp, or the one, often-full, private room is 10,000 rp. While it can be a little cramped, the staff are friendly, it has good travel information and it is certainly cheap.

If both the above are full, and they can be in the peak July/August tourist season, other budget options are poor. Near the Hotel

Helios, the *Hotel Palem* (☎ 25129), Jalan Thamrin 15, has passable rooms with mandi for 17,500 to 25,500 rp. The cheaper rooms on the top floor are the best value.

In the lively central area, the rambling *Hotel Riche* (☎ 24560) is well placed near the Toko Oen at Jalan Basuki Rachmat 1, but the rooms are dingy and cost 15,000 rp or 20,000 rp with mandi.

Other central hotels are the uninspiring *Hotel Santosa* (☎ 23889), in the thick of things at Jalan Agus Salim 24, with rooms from 17,000 rp; or, a better option is the *Hotel Tosari* (☎ 26945), Jalan Achmad Dahlan 31, with bare but very clean rooms with mandi for 20,000 rp. Opposite the Tosari, *Losmen Semarang*, Jalan Achmad Dahlan 30, is a rundown old hotel but has some style. Rooms cost from 12,500 rp.

Places to Stay – middle

The most fashionable area to stay is in the area around Jalan Tugu. This is the old Dutch administrative district with impressive public buildings and old villas. For the colonial feel, the *Splendid Inn* (☎ 66860), Jalan Mojopahit 2-4, is an expat favourite just off the Jalan Tugu circle. This fine old Dutch villa has slightly worn but very comfortable rooms with immense bathrooms, hot water, TV and air-con for 42,000 to 52,000 rp. It also has a good restaurant and bar, which is the meeting place for the hash-house harriers.

Nearby at Jalan Kahuripan 8, the *Montana Hotel* (☎ 62751) is at the top of this range but overpriced. Older, standard rooms for 70,000 rp with fan or 85,000 rp with air-con are tatty for the price. The deluxe rooms in the new section are much better and cost 110,000 rp and 135,000 rp, plus 21%.

The friendly, well-run *Hotel Menara* (☎ 62871), Jalan Pajajaran 5, has comfortable rooms with mandi from 25,000 to 31,000 rp, or quite luxurious rooms with air-con, hot water and TV for 43,000 rp and 53,000 rp. The tariff includes breakfast, and there is a good sitting area for meals.

Right on the town square, the *Hotel Pelangi* (☎ 65156), Jalan Kauman Merdeka 3, is a large, pleasant old Dutch hotel with spacious rooms. Simple economy rooms for 15,000 to 25,000 rp are good value, or fan rooms with bath, hot water and TV cost 55,000 and 66,000 rp. Air-con rooms range from 80,000 to 100,000 rp. Rates include buffet breakfast in the delightful hotel restaurant.

The well-run *Hotel Margosuko* (☎ 25270, Jalan Achmad Dahlan 40-42, is also central. Good rooms with mandi and hot water cost 25,000/30,000 rp or VIP rooms are 50,000 rp. The hotel has a small coffee shop and good service, but can be noisy.

Places to Stay – top end
The best hotel in town is the *Tugu Park Hotel* (☎ 63891) at Jalan Tugu 3. This beautifully designed hotel has a pool, business centre, a good restaurant and a tea house facing the Tugu square. Rooms cost US$78 and excellent suites are US$98 and US$130.

The *Kartika Prince* (☎ 61900) is a modern glass-and-marble hotel with good facilities, including a pool, restaurants and bars. Very good rooms cost US$62 to US$92 or suites cost US$120 and US$230.

The *Regent's Park Hotel* (☎ 63388) is a little worn and a notch below the other top-end hotels, but it still provides good three-star accommodation and has a pool.

Rooms range from US$70 to US$90, and suites start at US$135.

All these hotels charge 21% tax and service, but will usually give a similarly sized discount.

Places to Eat
The *Toko Oen*, opposite the Sarinah shopping complex, is an anachronism from colonial days, with tea tables and comfortable basket chairs. Relax and read a newspaper while being served by waiters in white sarongs and black *peci* hats. They have Chinese and Western dishes plus good Indonesian food and delicious home-made ice cream. This is one of the most relaxing places for a meal and a good place for breakfast. It's open from 8.30 am to 9 pm every day except Monday.

For a drink or a snack, the *Melati Restaurant* in the Hotel Pelangi is even more architecturally impressive than the Toko Oen. This cavernous colonial relic has towering pressed metal ceilings, and painted tiles around the walls feature picture postcard scenes from old Holland. While guaranteed to make any Dutchman homesick, the Indonesian and Western food is only average.

The similarly named *Melati Pavilion Restaurant* in the Tugu Park Hotel restaurant serves good Indonesian, Chinese and continental cuisine at upscale prices. Dutch dishes are featured, and of course there is rijsttafel. The Tugu rijsttafel for 9500 rp has a selection of East Javanese dishes.

For cheap and varied eats, head for Jalan Agus Salim. The Chinese *Gloria Restaurant* at No 23, specialises in pangsit mie, a bowl of delicious noodles, meat and vegetables served with a side bowl of soup for you to mix. Closer to the alun alun, *Rumah Makan Agung* has excellent savoury murtabak and chicken biryani as well as Indonesian dishes.

The big shopping centres have a variety of places to eat. The best is the *Food Centre*, sandwiched between the Mitra department store and the Gajah Mada Plaza. The busy food stalls here offer a great selection of dishes, including local specialities such as nasi rawon (beef soup served with rice). Street vendors on Jalan Agus Salim also have tasty sweets and dumplings.

The shopping centres on Jalan Agus Salim, as well as the Matahari on Jalan Pasar Besar, have well-stocked supermarkets. For Western fast food, *KFC* and *Swensens* are in the Variety department store building next to the Malang Plaza. *McDonald's* is next to Sarinah on Jalan Basuki Rachmat, or, further north, the cinema complex next to the BNI bank has *KFC* and *Pizza Express*, and *Fran's Bakery* has delicious cakes and pastries.

The *Rumah Makan Minang Jaya* at Jalan Basuki Rachmat 111 has good Padang food at reasonable prices.

Getting There & Away

Malang can be approached from a number of directions. The back route between Yogya and Banyuwangi takes you through some beautiful countryside. For an interesting trip, you could take a train from Solo to Jombang, then colts south to Blimbing, Kandangan, Batu and finally Malang.

Air Malang's military airport has been opened to commercial flights, but as yet the only services are irregular Merpati flights to Jakarta (181,500 rp).

Bus There are three bus terminals in Malang.

Arjosari, five km north of town, is the main bus station with regular buses to northern route destinations such as Surabaya (1500 rp; two hours), Probolinggo (1700 rp; 2½ hours), Jember (3600 rp; 4½ hours), Banyuwangi (5000 rp; seven hours via Probolinggo and Jember) and Denpasar (6500 rp; 10 hours). Air-con express buses also cover these routes, and travel to Yogya and Solo. Mikrolets run from Arjosari to nearby villages such as Singosari (500 rp) and Tumpang (600 rp).

Terminal Gadang is five km south of the town centre and has buses along the southern routes to destination such as Blitar (1500 rp; two hours), Tulung Agung (2100 rp; three hours) and Turen (500 rp; one hour).

Terminal Landungsari, five km north-

west of the city, has buses to the west to destinations such as Kediri (2100 rp; three hours), Madiun and Jombang. Frequent mikrolet run to Batu (500 rp; half an hour).

Malang has plenty of bus companies offering luxury express services for the long hauls. Buses to Bandung (30,000 to 34,000 rp), Bogor and Jakarta (35,000 to 55,000 rp) leave around 1 pm. Numerous buses to Solo and Yogya cost from 10,000 rp and leave around 7 pm; or, for Bali, companies such as Bali Cepat have morning buses to Denpasar at 6.30 am for around 20,000 rp, and these continue on to Padangbai and Mataram in Lombok. They leave from the company offices and usually pick up at the Arjosari terminal.

It is easiest to buy tickets from the agents found all over town. There are plenty of agents on Jalan Basuki Rachmat, south of the tourist office, or the tourist office itself is helpful. Tugu Transport (☎ 68363), Jalan Kertanegara 5, is handy for the Tugu area or try the travel agent at the Toko Oen.

Minibus Plenty of door-to-door minibus companies operate from Malang, and hotels and travel agents can book them. The Yobel company has minibuses to Banyuwangi (12,500 rp), Kediri (5000 rp), Solo (14,000 rp) and Yogya (15,000 rp). Timbul Jaya goes to Solo and Yogya via Blitar (5000 rp), and Arjosari also have a number of minibuses to Solo and Yogya. ABC go to Madiun and Magetan (6000 rp).

Simpatik and Bali Indah have minibuses to Denpasar (20,000 rp). Nusantara goes to Probolinggo (7000 rp). Wiedes and Mandala go to Surabaya (6000 rp), and are well worth considering as they will drop off at hotels in Surabaya, thus saving the long haul from Surabaya's bus terminal.

Train Ekonomi trains run from Surabaya to Blitar via Malang, or the *Pattas* express train on this route provides a good service and costs 2300 rp to Surabaya or Blitar. Most other services tend to go via Surabaya. Trains from points west such as Solo and Yogya are ekonomi only and very slow. Buses are a much better choice on these routes.

Getting Around

Mikrolet run all over town from the main bus terminals and to other mikrolet terminals. The most useful services are those running between the bus stations and passing through the centre of town. These are marked A-G (Arjosari to Gadung and return), A-L (Arjosari-Landungsari), G-L (Gadang-Landungsari) etc. A trip anywhere around town costs 350 rp.

Becaks and metered taxis are also available, but not from the bus stations.

AROUND MALANG
Singosari Temples

The Singosari Temples lie in a ring around Malang and are mostly funerary temples dedicated to the kings of the Singosari dynasty (1222 to 1292 AD), the precursors of the Majapahit kingdom.

Candi Singosari Right in Singosari village, 12 km north of Malang, this temple stands 500 metres off the main Malang to Surabaya road. One of the last monuments erected to the Singosari dynasty, it was built in 1304 AD in honour of King Kertanagara, the fifth and last Singosari king who died in 1292 in a palace uprising. The main structure of the temple was completed but, for some reason, the sculptors never finished their task. Only the top part has any ornamentation and the kala heads have been left strangely stark, with smooth bulging cheeks and pop eyes. Of the statues that once inhabited the temple's chambers, only Agastya, the Shivaite teacher who walked across the water to Java, remains. Statues of Durga and Ganesha were carted off to the Netherlands, but have since been returned and are now in the Jakarta Museum.

About 200 metres beyond the temple are two enormous figures of *dwarapala* (guardians against evil spirits) wearing clusters of skulls and twisted serpents. These may have been part of the original gates to the palace of the Singosari kingdom.

To reach Singosari, take a green mikrolet (500 rp) from Malang's Arjosari Terminal and get off at the Singosari market on the highway, then walk or take a becak.

Candi Sumberawan This small, plain Buddhist stupa is five km north-west of Singosari. Dating from a later period than the Singosari temples, it was built to commemorate the visit of Hayam Wuruk, the great Majapahit king, who visited the area in 1359. Sumberawan lies in the foothills of Gunung Arjuna, about five km north-west of Singosari.

Take a colt from the Singosari market on the highway to Desa Sumberawan (350 rp), and then from where the colts terminate, walk half a km down the stony road to the canal, turn right and then follow the canal through the picturesque rice paddies for one km to the temple. This delightful walk is the highlight of the visit.

Candi Jago Along a small road near the market in Tumpang (18 km from Malang), Candi Jago (or Jajaghu) was built in 1268 AD and is thought to be a memorial to the 4th Singosari king, Vishnuvardhana. The temple is in fairly poor condition but it still has some interesting decorative carving – in the two-dimensional wayang kulit style typical of East Java – which tells tales from the *Jataka* and the *Mahabharata*. The caretaker describes it as a Buddhist temple, but scattered around the garden are Javanese-Hindu statues, including a six-armed death-dealing goddess and a lingga, the symbol of Shiva's virility and male potency.

To reach Candi Jago take a white mikrolet from the Malang's Arjosari Terminal to Tumpang (600 rp). If coming from Singosari, go to Blimbing where the road to Tumpang branches off the highway, and then catch a mikrolet. In Tumpang, the temple is only a short stroll from the main road.

Candi Kidal The Kidal temple, a small gem and a fine example of East Javanese art, is seven km south of Candi Jago. Built around 1260 AD as the burial shrine of King

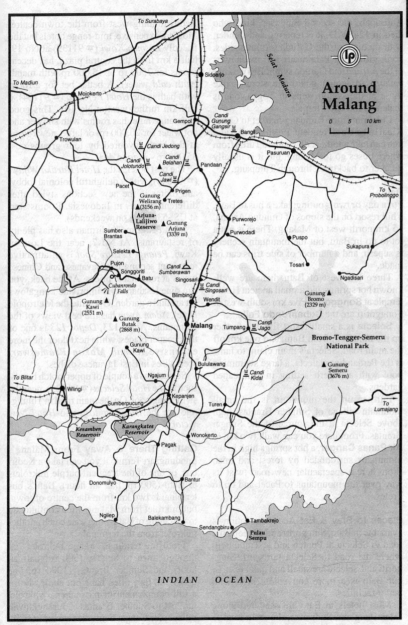

To Surabaya

To Madiun

To Madiun

Mojokerto

Sidoarjo

Selat Madura

Around Malang

0   5   10 km

Trowulan

Gempol

Candi
Gunung
Gangsir

Bangil

Pasuruan

Candi Jedong

Candi
Belahan

Pandaan

To
Probolinggo

Candi
Jolotundo

Candi
Jawi

Pacet

Prigen

Gunung Welirang
(3156 m)

Tretes

Purworejo

Arjuna-
Lalijiwo
Reserve

Gunung
Arjuna
(3339 m)

Purwodadi

Puspo

Sumber
Brantas

Sukapura

Selekta

Candi
Sumberawan

Tosari

Ngadisari

Pujon

Songgoriti

Batu

Singosari

Candi
Singosari

Gunung
Bromo
(2329 m)

Cubanrondo
Falls

Blimbing

Wendit

Gunung
Kawi
(2551 m)

Gunung
Butak
(2868 m)

Malang

Tumpang

Candi
Jago

Bromo-Tengger-Semeru
National Park

Gunung
Kawi

Bululawang

Gunung
Semeru
(3676 m)

To Blitar

Ngajum

Candi
Kidal

Wlingi

Kepanjen

Turen

To
Lumajang

Sumberpucung

Karangkates
Reservoir

Wonokerto

Kesamben
Reservoir

Pagak

Bantur

Donomulyo

Ngilep

Balekambang

Tambakrejo

Sendangbiru

Pulau
Sempu

INDIAN   OCEAN

Anusapati, the second Singosari king who died in 1248 AD, it is tapering and slender, with pictures of the Garuda on three sides, bold, glowering kala heads and medallions of the *haruna* and Garuda symbols. Two *kala makara* (dragons) guard the steps – like those at the kraton steps in Yogya, one is male and the other female.

Colts run from Tumpang market to Candi Kidal but are not frequent. From Candi Kidal you can take another colt south to Turen from where buses go to Malang, but it is usually quicker to backtrack through Tumpang.

Batu

For a day or two's outing, take a bus to Batu, a hill resort on the slopes of Gunung Arjuna, 15 km north-west of Malang. There is not a lot to do in Batu, but the mountain scenery is superb, and a number of side trips can be made.

Three km west of Batu there are well-known hot springs and a small ancient Hindu temple at **Songgoriti**. Five km south-west of Songgoriti are the **Cubanrondo Falls**.

Selecta is a small resort five km further up the mountain from Batu, and one km off the main road. Selecta's main claim to fame is the Pemandian Selecta, a large swimming pool with a superb setting in landscaped gardens.

Further up the mountain is the small mountain village of Sumber Brantas, high above Selecta at the source of the Sungai Brantas. From here you can walk two km to **Air Panas Cangar**, a hot springs high in the mountains surrounded by forest and mist. From here a spectacular new road twist its way over the mountains to Pacet and on to Tretes.

Places to Stay & Eat Accommodation is available in Batu, Singgoriti and all along the road to Selecta at Punten and at Tulungrejo where the road to Selecta turns off. Singgoriti and Selecta are small and quiet resorts, but Batu is a more convenient base with better facilities.

Most hotels in Batu are scattered along Jalan Panglima Sudirman, the main road to

Kediri running west from the town centre. Most are expensive, mid-range hotels but the friendly *Losmen Kawi* (☎ 91139) at No 19, half a km from the central plaza, has decent rooms for 7500 rp or 15,000 rp with mandi (with *cold* water). A better bet for a room with bath is the *Hotel Perdana* (☎ 91104), a half km further west at No 101. This good mid-range hotel has rooms with shower and hot water for 20,000 rp, or large, new rooms at the back favoured by tour groups cost 35,000 rp – a good deal.

The best hotel is the *Hotel Kartika Wijaya* (☎ 92600), with a delightful colonial lobby, and rooms in the new sections styled after different regions in Indonesia. Rooms start at US$53 (more on weekends).

Jalan Panglima Sudirman also has plenty of restaurants. At No 7, near the Losmen Kawi, *Pelangi Leisure Spot* is an attractive restaurant serving East Javanese and Chinese meals at reasonable prices. At the back, you can dine lesahan-style in private bungalows set around a garden. Opposite the Metropole Hotel, *Adem Ayem* has the best views of the mountains. At no 123, *Depot 123* is one of the cheaper places, while next door the more expensive *Rumah Makan Prameswari* specialises in East Javanese dishes.

Selecta has a couple of upper-notch hotels, such as the *Hotel Selecta* (☎ 91025), near the swimming pool. On the main road in Tulungrejo are the *Hotel Santosa* and *Hotel New Victory*.

Getting There & Away From Malang's Landungsari Terminal you can take a Kediri bus, or one of the frequent purple mikrolets to Batu (500 rp; half an hour). Batu's bus terminal is two km from the centre of town, but mikrolet from Malang often continue on to the centre of Batu, otherwise catch another mikrolet from the terminal.

From the terminal, orange mikrolet run through town to Selecta (500 rp; half an hour) and Sumber Brantas (1000 rp; one hour), but they often hang out endlessly for a full complement of passengers. Mikrolet turn off to Sumber Brantas at Jurangkuwali village; for Cangar continue two km straight ahead. Cangar can be reached by car but public transport won't tackle the twisting, dipping road.

Gunung Kawi

On Gunung Kawi, west of Malang and 18 km north-west of Kepanjen, is the tomb of a Muslim sage, Mbah Jugo, who died in 1871. Also buried in the tomb is Raden Imam Sujono, of Yogya's royal Hamengkubuwono family and grandson of Dipenogoro. From the parking area, a long path leads up the slope past shops, souvenir stalls and beggars. Before the tombs at the top are a Chinese temple and the house of Mbah Jugo, which attracts non-Muslim, Chinese worshippers. Legend has it that the saint will answer the prayers of fortune-seeking pilgrims, and did so for one Chinese couple that went on to form one of Indonesia's biggest kretek companies.

Malam Jumat Legi in the Javanese calendar is the most propitious time, but pilgrims visit Gunung Kawi throughout the year, especially at night.

This strange cross-religious mountain resort can be experienced on a day trip, or Gunung Kawi has plenty of basic penginapan and restaurants if you want to stay the night. Gunung Kawi can be reached by taking a Blitar bus to Kromengan and then a colt to Gunung Kawi.

South Coast Beaches

The coast south of Malang has some good beaches, but facilities are limited. **Sendangbiru** is a picturesque fishing village separated by a narrow channel from **Pulau Sempu**, an island nature reserve with a lake in the middle ringed by jungle.

A few km before Sendangbiru, a rough track to the left leads three km to **Tambakrejo**, a small fishing village with a sweeping sandy bay, which despite the surf is generally safe for swimming.

Balekambang is best known for its picturesque Hindu temple on the small island of Pulau Ismoyo, connected by a footbridge to the beach. This is Java's answer to Bali's Tanah Lot and was built by Balinese artisans in 1985 for the local Hindu communities.

Accommodation is limited to the *Pesanggrahan Balekambang*, which has a few rough rooms for 15,000 rp per night. Balekambang is one of the most popular beaches and is crowded on weekends.

Nyilep further west is a rocky beach and also very popular. It has a pesanggrahan for basic accommodation.

Getting There & Away Minibuses from Malang's Gadang Terminal go to Sendangbiru (2000 rp; two hours; 69 km), past the turn off to Tambakrejo; otherwise take a bus to Turen and then another to Sendangbiru.

For Balekambang, first take a minibus to Bantur (1000 rp), and then another along the rough road to Balekambang (500 rp), or take an ojek (2000 rp). Nyilep is also reached via Bantur, from where you will usually have to take a bus to Donomulyo first, and then another to Nyilep.

Purwodadi

A few km north of Lawang, the **Kebun Raya Purwodadi** are big dry-climate botanical gardens, open daily from 7 am to 4 pm. The entrance is right on the main highway, and if you want more information and maps of the gardens, visit the garden offices to the south of the entrance. The Air Terjun Jobanbau is a high waterfall next to the gardens.

BLITAR

Blitar is the usual base from which to visit Panataran. It's quite a pleasant country town to stay in overnight, and is also of interest as the site of President Soekarno's grave.

Information

The BNI bank, Jalan Kenanga 9, changes cash at reasonable rates, but not travellers' cheques.

The post office is next to the railway station. For international telephone calls, Telkom is at Jalan A Yani 10 (the continuation of Jalan Merdeka), about one km east of the Hotel Lestari.

Makam Bung Karno

At Sentul, about two km north of the town centre on the road to Panataran, an elaborate monument now covers the spot where former President Soekarno was buried in 1970. Soekarno is looked on by many as the 'father of his country', although he was only reinstated as a national hero in 1978 by the present regime.

Soekarno was given a state funeral but, despite family requests that he be buried at his home in Bogor, the hero of Indonesian independence was buried as far as possible from Jakarta in an unmarked grave next to his mother in Blitar. His father's grave was also moved from Jakarta to Blitar. It was only in 1978 that the lavish million-dollar monument was built over the grave and opened to visitors.

A becak from the town centre will cost about 1500 rp or take a Panataran angkudes (yellow minibus) for 300 rp and get off at the rows of souvenir stalls. Entry, amazingly, is free.

Other Attractions

The house that Soekarno lived in as a boy functions as the **Museum Soekarno**. Photos and memorabilia line the front sitting room, and you can see the great man's bedroom. The house, still owned by relatives of Soekarno, though they now live in Jakarta, is at Jalan Sultan Agung 59, about 1½ km from the centre of town.

The **Museum Blitar**, on the north side of the alun alun, houses some fine examples of Hindu statuary removed from Panataran.

Blitar's large **Pasar Legi**, next to the bus station, is also worth a browse. In the north-east corner a few stalls sell krises, woodcarvings and bronze walking sticks.

Places to Stay & Eat

Blitar is a small compact town and the bus station is very central. Right next to the bus station, the *Hotel Santosa*, Jalan Manur 2, is convenient but no great shakes. Rooms cost 7000 rp or 15,000 rp with mandi.

The best hotel in town, and most popular place to stay, is the *Hotel Sri Lestari* (☎ 81766) at Jalan Merdeka 173, a few hundred metres from the bus station. This good mid-range hotel has budget rooms for 7000 rp at the back, but the rooms sleeping three or four people in the impressive old colonial building are nicer and cost 8000 to 12,000 rp with shared mandi. A variety of better rooms with bathroom are available in the new wings for 24,000 to 90,000 rp; the cheapest air-con rooms start at 40,000 rp. The hotel also has a good, if slightly expensive, restaurant.

The *Hotel Sri Rejeki* (☎ 81770), Jalan TGP 13, is cheaper and also worth considering. It is another mid-range hotel with rooms to suit most budgets.

Blitar has some good Chinese restaurants on Jalan Merdeka. The no-frills *Rumah Makan Jaya* is at No 128, the larger *Rumah Makan Sarinah* is at No 170 and the fancier *Ramayana* is at No 65, east of the alun alun.

Getting There & Away

Buses from Blitar include: Malang (1500 rp; two hours; 80 km), Ponorogo (2200 rp; 4½ hours), Kediri (1100 rp; 1½ hours), Trenggalek (1300 rp; 2½ hours), Madiun (2700 rp), Solo (4700 rp; six hours) and Surabaya (2800 rp). Colts also run from the bus station to Malang for 1500 rp.

Rosalia Indah (☎ 82149), Jalan Mayang 45 opposite the bus station, and Timbul Jaya (☎ 82583), next door at No 47, have express air-con minibuses to Solo (12,500 rp; five hours) and Yogya (13,000 rp; 6½ hours) at 9 am and 9 pm.

Angkudes run from the bus station to Panataran for 600 rp and stop right outside the temple. They also pass Makam Bung Karno (300 rp). The Hotel Lestari can arrange a car for a visit to Makam Bung Karno and Panataran for 20,000 rp, or you can hire an ojek.

Several trains a day run from Blitar to Malang (1200 rp ekonomi; three hours). The best one to catch is the 12.30 pm *Pattas* express train (2300 rp; two hours).

AROUND BLITAR
Panataran

The Hindu temples at Panataran are the largest remaining Majapahit sanctuaries and perhaps the finest examples of East Javanese architecture and sculpture. Construction began around 1200 AD during the Singosari dynasty but the temple complex took some 250 years to complete. Most of the important surviving structures date from the great years of the Majapahit during the 1300s and are similar to many temples in Bali.

Around the base of the first level platform, which would once have been a meeting place, the comic-strip carvings tell the story of a test between the fat meat-eating Bubukshah and the thin vegetarian Gagang Aking.

Farther on is the small Dated Temple, so called because of the date 1291 (1369 AD) carved over the entrance. On the next level are colossal serpents snaking endlessly around the Naga Temple which once housed valuable sacred objects.

At the rear stands the Mother Temple – or at least part of it, for the top of the temple has been reconstructed alongside its three-tiered base. Followed anticlockwise, panels around the base depict stories from the *Ramayana*. The more realistic people of the Krishna stories on the second tier of the base show an interesting transition from almost two-dimensional representation to three-dimensional figures.

Behind is a small royal mandi with a frieze of lizards, bulls and dragons around its walls.

The temple complex is open from 7 am to 5 pm, and entry is by donation.

Getting There & Away Panataran is 16 km from Blitar, and three km north of the village of Nglegok. It is possible to see the Panataran temples comfortably in a day from Malang – and possibly from Surabaya.

PACITAN

On the south coast near the provincial border, the village of Pacitan is three km from a large bay ringed by rocky cliffs. Pacitan's beach, **Pantai Ria Teleng**, is one of the best in East Java, with fine views of the coastline and the hills surrounding Pacitan Bay. Swimming is possible when the seas are calm – the safest area is towards the fishing boats at the end of the bay. Apart from a few day trippers the beach is quiet, and you can wander further along the beach to find a deserted spot.

Information

The Bank Rakyat Indonesia will change US$ cash and travellers' cheques, as well as other currencies (cash only), but the rates are poor.

There is a wartel next to the Hotel Remaja, or the Telkom office is further west on Jalan A Yani before the Hotel Remaja.

Places to Stay & Eat

The best place to stay is four km out of town at Pantai Ria Teleng. *Happy Bay Beach Bungalows* (☎ 81474), run by an Australian and his Indonesian wife, has attractive singles/doubles with bathroom for 12,500/17,000 rp or private bungalows for 24,000 rp. Happy Bay is right opposite the beach, has a good restaurant, and you can rent bicycles (3000 rp) or arrange a boat trip.

Budget hotels in Pacitan are along Jalan A Yani, the main street. The cheapest is the *Losmen Remaja* (☎ 81088) at No 67, about one km west of the town centre. Rooms without mandi are only 3500 rp or 5000 to 8000 rp with bath, and VIP air-con rooms are 17,000 rp. The rooms are good for the money, but it's not the friendliest place in town.

In the town centre opposite the alun alun, the welcoming *Hotel Pacitan* (☎ 81244), Jalan A Yani 37, is the pick of the hotels in town. Pleasant rooms with fan and mandi are 12,500 rp and 17,500 rp, or air-con rooms are 30,000 rp and 40,000 rp. Ask to see a selection of rooms – the internal rooms are dark but no cheaper.

For food, the *Depot Makan Bu Jabar*, Jalan H Samanhudi 3, a block behind the police station on Jalan Yani, has excellent gado-gado, nasi campur, fish and fruit juices. The best restaurant in town is the *Rumah Makan Srikandi*, Jalan A Yani 67A, near the Hotel Remaja. It is spotlessly clean, has cheap Indonesian dishes and fruit drinks, and you can dine looking across the rice paddies.

Getting There & Away

Pacitan can be approached by bus from Solo (2200 rp; four hours), or along the scenic road to Ponorogo (1500 rp; 3½ hours), just south of Madiun. From Ponorogo, buses run to Surabaya, via Madiun and Nganjuk (for buses to Kediri), and direct buses to Blitar (2200 rp; 4½ hours) leave Ponorogo until 1 pm; if you arrive too late, take a bus first to Trenggalek (1000 rp; two hours) and then another to Blitar (1300 rp; 2½ hours). From Blitar to Malang take a colt or bus (1500 rp; two hours).

For Yogya, take a Solo bus to Baturetno (1000 rp; 1½ hours; 56 km) and then another to Yogya.

Pacitan's bus terminal is half a km from the centre of town on the road to Solo and the beach. When coming from Solo, buses can drop you off at the turn off to the beach. Happy Bay is a half-km walk or becak ride away.

AROUND PACITAN

Other beaches accessible from Pacitan are Watu Karung (22 km) and Latiroco Lorok (41 km).

Just beyond Punung village, 30 km north-west of Pacitan, the **Gua Tabuhan** (Musical Cave) is a huge limestone cavern said to have been a refuge for the 19th-century guerilla leader Prince Diponegoro. Here you can listen to an excellent 'orchestral' performance, played by striking rocks against stalactites, each in perfect pitch and echoing pure gamelan melodies. You have to hire a guide and a lamp (for about 1000 rp) and the concert lasts about 10 minutes; it's 15,000 rp for seven tunes. Bargaining is obligatory! This is also agate country and there are lots of people at the cave selling very reasonably priced polished stones and rings.

To get to the cave, take a Solo bus to the turn off (800 rp), four km beyond Punung, and then an ojek (1000 rp) for the last four km to the cave.

MADIUN

On the Solo to Surabaya road, Madiun is a major travel hub in the western part of East Java. This unhurried city has some interesting colonial architecture and decaying steam locomotives in the rail yard for train buffs, but the real attractions lie outside the city.

AROUND MADIUN

In Ngawi, 33 km north-west of Madiun, the **Benteng Pendem** is an impressive Dutch fort (formerly the Benteng Van Den Bosch) built between 1839 and 1845.

In 1891 at **Trinil**, a Dutchman, Eugene Dubois, unearthed a skull of *Pithecanthropus Erectus*, commonly known as Java Man. Dubois' discovery and his 'ape man' revelations in support of Darwin's theory of evolution caused a furore in Europe. A museum displaying fossils found in the area has been built at the site. The turn off from the main highway to Trinil is 11 km west of Ngawi and then it's a further three km.

Ponorogo, 30 km south of Madiun, is famed as the home of the *reyog* dance, in which gaily costumed performers enact the battle between a court official of Ponorogo and the *singa barong*, the ruler of the forest. Combining elements of the horse trance dance, the barong and possibly the Chinese lion dance, the reyog is performed in Ponorogo's alun alun on 1 Suro (New Year) of the Javanese calendar, falling around May.

SURABAYA

The capital of East Java, the industrial city of Surabaya is second only to Jakarta in size and economic importance, and has a population of over four million. For centuries it has been one of Java's most important trading ports, and it is also the main base for the Indonesian navy. Surabaya is a city on the move, yet signs of poverty are always in sight and the narrow streets in the old part of the city, crowded with warehouses and jostling becaks, contrast strongly with the modern buildings and shopping centres of the showpiece central city.

For most visitors, Surabaya is merely a commercial centre or a transit point on the way to or from Bali or Sulawesi. Surabaya has an interesting old city and if you thrive on big cities, then teeming Surabaya is certainly lively, but otherwise its tourist attractions are few.

Orientation
The centre of this sprawling city is the area around Jalan Pemuda, which runs west from Gubeng railway station past the tourist office, the Plaza Surabaya and a number of big hotels and banks. Jalan Pemuda runs into Jalan Tunjungan/Basuki Rahmat, another main commercial street where you'll find the Tunjungan Plaza. Most of the hotels are in this area.

The old city is centred around the Jembatan Merah bus station and Kota railway station to the north. Further north is Tanjung Perak Harbour. Surabaya's zoo is five km south of the city centre, and the main bus station, Bungurasih, is just outside the city limits, 10 km to the south of the centre.

Information
Tourist Office The tourist office is at Jalan Pemuda 118, and the head office of the East Java Regional Tourist Office is at Jalan Darmokali 35 near the zoo. Both are closed on Sunday. You can book tickets for the Pandaan ballet performance (see under Around Surabaya later in this chapter), get a few maps, some information on places to visit in the province and a regional calendar of events. The Bamboe Denn has better information.

Money Many Indonesian banks barely make a profit but that doesn't stop them erecting gigantic edifices right across the country, and Surabaya has more than its fair share of extravagant bank real estate. Jalan Pemuda has plenty – Bank Duta and Bank BNI usually have good rates and accept credit cards. Jalan Tunjungan also has a string of banks.

Post & Telecommunications Surabaya's main post office and poste restante, on Jalan Kebon Rojo, is four km north of the city centre.

For telephone calls, a good Telkom wartel is in the ground floor of the Tunjungan Plaza and the Plaza Surabaya has a small wartel on the 2nd floor.

Other As Indonesia's second city, Surabaya has a number of foreign consular representatives, such as the USA, the Netherlands and France, but in general they handle only limited functions.

There is a French Cultural Centre (☎ 68639) at the French Consulate, Jalan Darmokali 10-12, and a Goethe Institute (☎ 43735) at Jalan Taman Ade Irma Suryani Nasution 15.

For a swim (3000 rp), there is an excellent public pool just behind the Radisson Hotel.

For supermarkets, bookshops and everyday shopping needs, Surabaya's huge malls – Plaza Surabaya, Tunjungan Plaza and Surabaya Mall – are well stocked.

Dangers & Annoyances In most large Javanese cities it is hard to cross the street, but it is almost impossible on Surabaya's big, four-lane roads which have constant traffic and few traffic lights or pedestrian bridges. The only way to cross the street is to wait for the traffic to subside (it never stops), head out onto the road and motion with one hand for the traffic to stop. Cross yourself in prayer with the other hand.

Old City
This is the most interesting part of Surabaya, albeit the grottiest. When the central business district was cleaned up all the garbage must have been moved here.

It was at the **Jembatan Merah** (Red Bridge) that Brigadier Mallaby, chief of the British forces, was killed in the lead-up to the bloody battle of Surabaya for Indonesian independence. Some rundown but good examples of **Dutch architecture** can be seen here. Jalan Jembatan Merah, running south of the bus station along the canal, is a grungy replica of Amsterdam. The area further south around the post office and Pelni office also has some fine old buildings, though the most impressive is the Persero government office building just west of Jalan Jembatan Merah along Jalan Cendrawasih. This superb

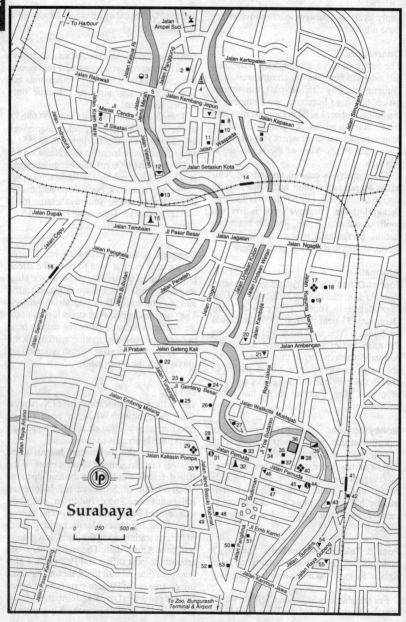

Surabaya

0   250   500 m

PLACES TO STAY		PLACES TO EAT			
8	Hotel Rejeki	7	Kiet Wan Kie	12	Post Office
9	Hotel Ganefo	20	Soto Ambengan	13	Pelni Office
10	Hotel Irian	21	Cafe Venezia	14	Kota Railway Station
11	Hotel Semut	30	Galael Supermarket,	15	Tugu Pahlawan
23	Hotel Paviljoen		KFC & Swensen's	16	Pasar Turi Railway
25	Hotel Majapahit	34	Zangrandi Ice Cream		Station
27	Bamboe Denn		Palace	17	Surabaya Mall
28	Natour Simpang	45	Turin	18	THR
35	Garden Hotel	46	Granada Modern	19	Taman Remaja
37	Garden Palace Hotel		Bakery	22	Garuda Office
38	Radisson Plaza Suite	54	Gandy Steakhouse	24	Genteng Market
	Hotel	55	Kuningan Seafood	26	Andhika Plaza
42	Said Surabaya Hotel			29	Tunjungan Plaza
43	Hotel Gubeng	**OTHER**		31	Bank Duta
47	Hotel Remaja			32	Joko Dolog
48	Ramayana Hotel	1	Mesjid Ampel	33	Governor's Residence
50	Elmi Hotel	2	Pasar Pabean	36	World Trade Centre
51	Tanjung Hotel	3	Jembatan Merah Bus	39	Public Swimming Pool
52	Hyatt Regency		Station	40	Plaza Surabaya
	Surabaya	4	Kong Co Kong Tik Cun	41	Gubeng Railway
			Ong		Station
		5	Jembatan Merah	44	Tourist Office
		6	Persero Building	49	Minibus Agents
				53	Bouraq Office

building is fashioned in the Indo-European style.

To the east of the Jembatan Merah is Surabaya's Chinatown, where hundreds of small businesses and warehouses ply their trade. Becaks and hand pulled carts are still the best way to transport goods in the crowded, narrow streets. **Pasar Pabean** on Jl Pabean is a sprawling, dark market where you can buy everything from Madurese chickens to Chinese crockery.

Further east, on Jalan Dukuh near the canal, **Kong Co Kong Tik Cun Ong** temple is primarily Buddhist but has a variety of Confucian and Taoist altars. On the full moon, wayang performances are held at the temple at 10 am and in the evenings.

The highlight of a visit to the old city is the **Mesjid Ampel** in the heart of the Arab Quarter. From the Chinese temple, proceed north along Jalan Nyamplungan and then take the second left down Jalan Sasak. A crowd of becaks marks the way to the mosque. Through the stone entrance is Jalan Ampel Suci, a narrow, covered bazaar lined with shops selling perfumes, sarongs, pecis and other religious paraphernalia. Follow the

pilgrims past the beggars to the mosque. This is the most sacred mosque in Surabaya, for it is here that Sunan Ampel, one of the wali songo who brought Islam to Java, was buried in 1481. Pilgrims chant and offer rose petal offerings at the grave around the back.

From the old city you can then head north to the **Kalimas Harbour**, where brightly painted pinisi schooners from Sulawesi and Kalimantan unload their wares.

Surabaya Zoo

On Jalan Diponegoro, near the Joyoboyo bus station, the Surabaya Zoo (kebun binatang) specialises in nocturnal animals, exotic birds and fish. The animals look just as bored as they do in any other zoo, but the park is quite well laid-out, with large open enclosures, a great collection of pelicans and lively otters, and a some rather dazed-looking Komodo dragons.

The zoo is open from 7 am to 5 pm. Entry costs 1000 rp and another 200 rp for the aquarium or the nocturama. This park is popular with Surabayans and outside there are warungs and a permanent gaggle of vendors selling drinks, and peanuts for the monkeys.

MPU Tantular Museum

Across the road from the zoo, this small historical and archaeological museum is housed in a superb example of Dutch architecture. It is open from 8 am to 2 pm Monday to Saturday.

Other Attractions

On Jalan Pemuda, across from the governor's residence, is the statue of **Joko Dolog** which dates from 1289 and commemorates King Kertanagara of Singosari. It's known as the 'fat boy'.

The **Taman Remaja** (Youth Park), has occasional performances of wayang orang, ketoprak and *srimulat* (East Javanese comedy), while next door the Taman Hiburan Rakyat or People's Amusement Park (THR) is Surabaya's amusement centre after dark. The nearby Surabaya Mall shopping centre is usually much livelier, though on Thursday evenings the transvestites come out and dangdut music is performed at the Taman Remaja.

Places to Stay – bottom end

If you're staying in this busy port town – and many people do at least overnight here between Yogya and Bali – there's really only one very cheap place. The *Bamboe Denn* (☎ 40333), Jalan Ketabang Kali 6A, a 20-minute walk from Gubeng railway station, is a Surabaya institution and has been the No 1 travellers' centre in Surabaya for over 20 years. Beds in the large dorm are 4000 rp and a few, tiny singles/doubles are 5000/7500 rp. It can be full in the peak tourist season, but they will always rustle up a mattress on the floor. You may well get roped into a little English conversation with Indonesian students at the language school, which also runs from this youth hostel. The Denn master is the famous Bruno, who provides excellent travel information on Surabaya and other parts of Indonesia.

Apart from the Bamboe Denn, Surabaya doesn't have a great choice of cheap accommodation. Across the river from the Bamboe Denn on Jalan Genteng Besar, the *Hotel PavilJoen* (☎ 43449) is in an old colonial house at No 94. Old rooms without bath are decrepit but reasonable value at 14,000 rp. Renovated rooms with mandi are of mid-range standard and a good deal at 27,500 rp or 35,000 rp with air-con, including breakfast. The hotel has style and the friendly owners speak Dutch as well as English.

The *Hotel Gubeng* at Jalan Sumatra 18 is close to the Gubeng station and OK if you can't be bothered going any further. Basic rooms cost 18,000 rp or 24,000 rp with bath.

Well north of the town centre, near the Kota railway station and Jembatan Merah bus station, *Hotel Ganefo* (☎ 311169) is at Jalan Kapasan 169-171. This spacious old hotel has real character with gigantic ceilings, stained glass, wood panelling and old furniture. Well-kept but very simple rooms with shared mandi cost 18,000 rp. Larger rooms cost 25,000 rp and 36,000 rp with bath and air-con. In the same area, another hotel with some colonial style is the *Hotel Irian* (☎ 20953), Jalan Samudra 16, which has doubles for 16,500 rp or rooms with bath for 30,000/35,000 rp.

Places to Stay – middle

Conveniently located, and a good middle-range deal in expensive Surabaya, is *Hotel Remaja* (☎ 41359) on quiet little Jalan Embong Kenongo 12, not far from Jalan Pemuda. Immaculate singles/doubles with air-con, TV and hot water cost 57,000/60,000 rp and 69,000/72,000 rp, including breakfast.

Nearby, the *Tanjung Hotel* (☎ 44031), Jalan Panglima Sudirman 43-45, is a larger hotel with a variety of rooms. Rooms without bath are overpriced at 43,500/53,500 rp, or better air-con rooms with satellite TV, hot-water showers and telephone cost 66,500/77,500 to 91,000/102,00 rp, including breakfast.

The *Hotel Semut* (☎ 24578), in the old part of town at Jalan Samudra 9-15, offers reasonable value. Dating from the Art Deco era, it has good-sized rooms facing large verandas around a central quadrangle. Air-con rooms with shower or bath and TV cost 46,000 rp and 62,000 rp, including breakfast.

Behind a rather ugly later facade, the central *Hotel Majapahit* (☎ 43351), Jalan Tunjungan 65, is a superb colonial hotel with a fine garden. Built in 1910, it was originally named the Oranje Hotel and it bears a striking resemblance to Schomberg's hotel described in Joseph Conrad's *Victory*. Though fallen from grace, it is currently undergoing major renovations and when completed in 1996 it may well emerge as one of Surabaya's finest hotel.

Places to Stay – top end

All hotels in this category have a 21% service charge and government tax on top of the room charge, but discounts range from 20% up to 50% for the most expensive hotels.

Surabaya has a number of three-star hotels. The *Natour Simpang* (☎ 42151) is very central at Jalan Pemuda 1-3 and has a pool, though the rooms are quite average for the price, starting at US$90/110. The similar *Said Surabaya Hotel* (☎ 522711) is near the Gubeng railway station at Jalan Sumatra 1. Rooms cost from US$78/83. The *Elmi Hotel* (☎ 471571), Jalan Panglima Sudirman 42-44, is good value in this range and has a restaurant, bar, disco, fitness centre and a rooftop swimming pool. Well-appointed rooms cost from 127,500/149,000 rp.

The *Garden Palace Hotel* (☎ 479250) at Jalan Yos Sudarso 11 is a good four-star hotel. Luxurious rooms start at 196,000 rp. There are three restaurants and a pub with live jazz music. The *Garden Hotel* (☎ 470001), Jalan Pemuda 21, is its cheaper sister with slightly rundown rooms for US$80/90 or better deluxe rooms for US$140.

Surabaya's best hotel is the five-star *Hyatt Regency Surabaya* (☎ 511234) at Jalan Basuki Rahmat 124-128. It has a pool, business centre, a host of restaurants and bars and all the other facilities of a top hotel, but it is a little sterile. Very plush rooms start at US$220 and suites start at US$375.

The Hyatt is getting a lot of competition from the new *Radisson Plaza Suite Hotel* (☎ 516833), Jalan Pemuda 31-37. Though not quite as flash as the Hyatt, it is in an excellent position right next to the Plaza Surabaya and opposite the World Trade Centre. It has a swimming pool, tennis courts, fitness centre etc. It has a variety of rooms and suites ranging from US$170 to US$550.

Places to Eat

Food in Surabaya can be expensive. Restaurants are scarce in the city centre, and the greatest concentration of eating places is found in the shopping malls.

On the ground floor of the Plaza Surabaya, the *Food Plaza* has a range of restaurants with Korean, Cantonese and Indonesian food, and there is also a *Pizza Hut*, *McDonald's* and a French patisserie elsewhere on the ground floor. The 2nd floor has an outdoor food stall near the rooftop children's play area but the best deal is the *Food Bazaar* on the 4th floor with a large variety of moderately priced stalls.

The Tunjungan Plaza is similarly well stocked with restaurants and fast-food outlets, starting with a *McDonald's* and *KFC* on the ground floor. On the 4th level *Mon Cheri* is a classy ice cream parlour with a view, while the *New Singapore* has Chinese dishes and steamboats or the cheaper *Es Teler 77* has Indonesian dishes. The 5th floor has a host of more expensive restaurants, including the *Tirtomoyo* for East Javanese dishes, *Winda Grill & Steak* and *Pizza Hut*.

The *Granada Modern Bakery* on the corner of Jalan Pemuda and Jalan Panglima Sudirman is a good place for buns and cakes.

Surabaya has almost as many ice cream parlours as banks. At Jalan Yos Sudarso 15, the *Zangrandi Ice Cream Palace* is an old establishment parlour favoured by wealthy Surabayans. Relax in arm chairs at low tables and somehow ignore the traffic noise. Another good place for ice cream is the *Turin* on Jalan Embong Kenongo.

For cheap eats, the Genteng Market on Jalan Genteng Besar, just across the river from the Bamboe Denn, has good night warungs – sate ular (snake sate) is sometimes available. Another cluster of warungs is found further along Jalan Genteng Besar in front of the Hotel Paviljoen. There is a good hawkers' centre open at night near the flower market on Jalan Kayoon and on Jalan Pandegiling.

Kiet Wan Kie, Jalan Kembang Jepun 51, is a air-conditioned retreat from the Surabaya heat with dark but pleasant decor. This good Chinese restaurant has a varied menu.

For soto famed throughout the island, enjoy Pak Sadi's lemon grass, coriander Madurese chicken soup at *Soto Ambengan*, Jalan Ambengan No 3A. Further down the street at No 16, *Cafe Venezia* is a very classy establishment in an old villa with a delightful garden. Considering the setting, the prices are reasonable. Steaks cost around 7500 to 9000 rp, hamburgers are 4000 rp and Japanese and Korean dishes are also available.

There is plenty of money in Surabaya and plenty of upmarket restaurants to spend it in. The big hotels have a wide selection of restaurants – the *Radisson* has an Italian restaurant and a reasonable Indian restaurant.

Entertainment

Surabayans are big on discos. Popular places include the *Top Ten* and *Fire* in Tunjungan Plaza, *Studio East*, Andhika Plaza, Jalan Simpang Dukuh 38-40 and *Atum*, Jalan Bunguran 45.

Surabaya's brothels are (in)famous, and the most well-known of all is Dolly, a red light district named after its madam founder. Bangurejo is another large red-light area, but less safe than Dolly.

Getting There & Away

Air Surabaya is an important hub for domestic flights. Merpati has direct flights to Jakarta (183,700 rp), Denpasar (92,400 rp), Bandung (147,400 rp), Yogyakarta (64,900 rp), Solo (59,400 rp), Banjarmasin (147,400 rp), Balikpapan (218,900 rp) and Ujung Pandang (207,900 rp), with numerous other connections. Merpati (☎ 516040) has its office at the Plaza Surabaya.

Garuda has limited direct flights to Denpasar, Jakarta and Ujung Pandang. Garuda (☎ 515590) has offices at Jalan Tunjungan 29, the Hyatt Regency and the Bank Duta Building on Jalan Pemuda.

Sempati flies directly to Jakarta, Denpasar, Yogyakarta, Mataram, Banjarmasin, Balikpapan and Ujung Pandang, and they fly twice a week direct to Kuala Lumpur in Malaysia. Sempati has an office in the Tunjungan Plaza (☎ 526680) and in the Hyatt Regency.

Bouraq (☎ 42383), Jalan Panglima Sudirman 70, operates direct flights from Surabaya to Jakarta, Denpasar, Banjarmasin, Balikpapan and Ujung Pandang.

Mandala (☎ 578973), Jalan Raya Diponegoro 73, has flights to Jakarta, Ujung Pandang and Manado.

Bus Most buses operate from Surabaya's main Bungurasih bus station, 10 km south of the city's centre. Crowded Damri buses run between the bus station and the centre – the P1 service (400 rp) from the bus station can drop you at the Jalan Tunjungan/Jalan Pemuda intersection. A metered taxi costs around 7000 rp. Buses along the north coast to Semarang depart from the Jembatan Merah station.

Normal/air-con buses from Bungurasih include: Pandaan (1000 rp; one hour), Malang (1600/2400 rp; two hours), Blitar (2900/2200 rp; four hours), Mojokerto (750 rp; one hour), Probolinggo (1700/3000 rp; 2½ hours), Banyuwangi (4800/8400 rp; seven hours), Tuban (1900/3200 rp; three hours), Bondowoso (3750/6800 rp; 4½ hours), Jember (3200/5600 rp), Solo (4600/9200 rp; 6½ hours), Yogya (6000/9000 rp; eight hours) and Semarang (7100/12,200 rp; nine hours). Buses also operate from this terminal to Madura.

Luxury buses from Bungurasih also do the long hauls to Solo, Yogya, Bandung, Bogor and further afield. For Bali, night buses to Denpasar (21,000 rp; nine hours) depart between 4 and 8 pm. Night buses to Jakarta (35,000 to 50,000 rp; 16 hours) depart between 2 and 8 pm. Bookings can be made at Bungurasih or more conveniently at travel agents in the centre of town. The most convenient bus agents are those on Jalan Basuki

Rahmat (see under Minibus below). Intercity buses are not allowed to enter the city so you will have to go to Bungurasih to catch your bus.

From Jembatan Merah buses go to north coast destinations such as Gresik (400 rp), Tuban (1900 rp), Kudus (4500 rp) and Semarang (5500 rp). Only normal buses operate from this station; air-con express services to Semarang operate from Bungurasih.

Minibus Door-to-door *travel* minibuses are a good alternative to the buses, because they pick up at hotels, saving a long haul to the bus station. They are not always quicker, however, because it can take a long time to pick up a full load of passengers in sprawling Surabaya.

Minibuses run from Surabaya to all the major towns in East Java and to the rest of Java and Bali. Destinations and sample fares include: Malang (6000 rp), Banyuwangi (12,500 rp), Denpasar (25,000 rp), Solo (13,000 rp), Yogya (14,000 rp) and Semarang (15,000 rp). Hotels can make bookings and arrange pickup, or a selection of agents can be found on Jalan Basuki Rahmat including: Surya Jaya (☎ 42463) at No 72, Tunggal (☎ 523069) at No 70 and Tirta Jaya (☎ 523393) at No 66.

Train Trains from Jakarta, taking the northern route via Semarang, arrive at the Pasar Turi station. Trains taking the southern route via Yogya, and trains from Banyuwangi and Malang, arrive at Gubeng and most carry on to Kota. The Gubeng station is much more convenient for central places than Kota or Pasar Turi.

The trip from Jakarta takes 12 to 17 hours, although in practice the slower ekonomi trains can take even longer. Fares vary from 10,000 rp in ekonomi class, to 26,000 rp in bisnis and from 44,000 rp in eksekutif. The best services are with the deluxe *Bima Express* via Yogya or the slightly quicker *Mutiara Utara* via Semarang. The cheapest are the ekonomi services like the *Gaya Baru Malam Utara* (14 hours) or the *Parcel* (14

hours) on the northern route or the *Gaya Baru Malam Selatan* (17 hours) on the southern route.

Trains to or from Solo (4½ to six hours) and Yogyakarta (5½ to seven hours) cost from 3700 rp in ekonomi, from 14,000 rp in bisnis. The train is faster and cheaper than the buses. The 8.25 am *Purbaya* and the faster 1 pm *Argopura* are good ekonomi services.

Apart from services to the main cities, there are six trains per day to Malang (two hours), including an express service at 6.20 pm. Most of these trains continue on to Blitar. Two per day go to Banyuwangi (3500 rp ekonomi/7000 rp bisnis; seven hours) at 8 am and 10 pm.

Boat Surabaya is an important port and a major travel hub for ships to the outer islands.

Pelni Popular Pelni connections are those to Sulawesi, with at least four Pelni boats doing the Surabaya-Ujung Pandang run, and to Kalimantan with boats to Kumai, Batu Licin and Sampit. See the Getting Around chapter earlier in this book for Pelni route details.

Ekonomi fares include: Ujung Pandang 35,000 rp, Jakarta 24,000 rp, Banjarmasin 30,000 rp, Balikpapan 45,000 rp, Waingapu 62,000 rp and Kupang 76,000 rp. Boats depart from Tanjung Perak harbour – bus P1 or C will get you there.

The Pelni ticket office (☎ 293347) at Jalan Pahlawan 112 is open from 9 am to 1.30 pm Monday to Friday, and from 8 am to 1 pm Saturday. The front ticket counter can be chaotic but tourists often get preferential treatment.

Other Ferries to Kamal on Madura (350 rp; half an hour) leave every half hour from the Perak Terminal at the end of Jalan Kalimas Baru, reached by P1 (400 rp) or C bus (200 rp).

Kalla Lines (☎ 21024), Jalan Perak Timur 158, also have a ship once a week to Pasir Gudang, just outside Johor Bahru in Malaysia. The cost is around US$80 per person for the cheapest eight-berth cabins, and the journey takes 60 hours.

PT Wisata Bahari Mas Permai (☎ 291633), Jalan Tanjung Priok 6, does 'East Java Pinisi Traditional Cruises' to Bali, Lombok, Sumbawa, Komodo, Flores and further afield.

Getting Around

To/From the Airport Taxis from the Juanda airport (15 km) operate on a coupon system and cost 9000 rp to the city centre. To the airport on the meter is slightly cheaper. The Damri airport bus drops off at hotels in the city and costs 2000 rp, but departures are not frequent.

Bus Surabaya has an extensive Damri city bus network with normal buses (costing 200 rp anywhere around town) and *patas* express buses (400 rp per journey). They can be very crowded, especially the normal buses, and are a hassle if you have a lot of luggage.

One of the most useful services is the patas P1 bus which runs from Bungurasih bus terminal past the zoo and into the city along Jalan Basuki Rahmat. It then turns down Jalan Embong Malang and continues on the Pasar Turi railway station, Pelni office and Tanjung Perak harbour. In the reverse direction, it runs to the zoo and Bungurasih Terminal and can be caught on Jalan Tunjungan or at the bus stop in front of the Natour Simpang Hotel on Jalan Pemuda. The normal C buses also cover the same route.

Surabaya also has plenty of bemos labelled A, B, C etc, and all charge a standard 250 rp.

Taxi Surabaya has air-con metered taxis charging 900 rp for the first km and 450 rp for every subsequent km. Typical fares from central Surabaya are: Pelni office 3000 rp, harbour 4500 rp, Bamboe Denn to Gubeng station 2000 rp and airport 8000 rp. Surabaya also has yellow pickups that are non-metered taxis – they should be slightly cheaper than taxis, but you will have to bargain hard.

Becak Becaks aren't allowed on the main streets of Surabaya, but in neighbourhoods where they are, expect to pay about 500 rp per km.

AROUND SURABAYA

Gresik

On the road to Semarang, 25 km from Semarang, this port was once a major centre for international trade and a major centre of Islam in the 15th century. Close by, at Giri, is the tomb of the first Sunan Giri, who is regarded as one of the greatest of the nine wali songo. He was the founder of a line of spiritual lords of Giri which lasted until it was overwhelmed by Mataram in 1680. According to some traditions, Sunan Giri played a leading role in the conquest of Majapahit and ruled Java for 40 days after its fall – to rid the country of pre-Islamic influences. Gresik also has a colourful pinisi harbour.

Pandaan

Pandaan is 40 km south of Surabaya on the road to Tretes. At the **Candra Wilwatika Amphitheatre** ballet performances takes place every second and fourth week of the month from June to November. The varied programme usually consists of dances based on indigenous tales and East Java's history. Bookings can be made at the tourist office in Surabaya and seats cost 500 rp on the concrete benches, or VIP seats are 1500 rp. To reach the amphitheatre take a bus from Surabaya, and then a Tretes-bound colt. The theatre is one km from Pandaan, right on the main road to Tretes.

Also on the main road to Tretes, a few km from Pandaan before Pringen, **Candi Jawi** is an early 14th-century Hindu temple. Basically a Shivaite structure built to honour King Kertanegara, a Buddhist stupa was later added on top.

Tretes

This hill town, standing at 800 metres on the slopes of Arjuna and Welirang, is renowned for its cool climate and fine views. Tretes also has an intriguing reputation as a redlight district. If you have to kill time in Surabaya, it can be a pleasant enough place to escape to but there's not a great deal to do. The **Kakek Bodo** ('stupid grandfather'), **Putuh Truno** and **Alap-alap** waterfalls are nearby and there are a number of interesting walks around the town, including the trek to the Lalijiwo Plateau and Gunung Arjuna.

Places to Stay & Eat Accommodation in Tretes is overpriced, and haggling seems to bring only minor reductions. Most of Tretes' cheap hotels, and many of the more expensive hotels, are little more than brothels. Unattached males looking for a room to sleep are considered an oddity. The best place to stay is towards the top of the hill, and hotels lower down around Prigen are generally cheaper. Cottages can be rented for longer stays.

On the main road towards near the Natour Bath Hotel, *Mess Garuda* has large rooms with attached mandi for 15,000 rp. It is a reasonable, cheap wisma. The *Wisma Semeru Indah* (☎ 81701), Jalan Semeru 7, is below the main shopping area and has fine views from the garden. The large rooms with mandi are quiet but very ordinary for 30,000 rp.

If you are going to get ripped off, you might as well go the whole hog and stay at the three-star *Natour Bath Tretes Hotel* (☎ 67157) in a commanding position towards the top of the hill. This is the 'old money' hotel with some style and a good range of facilities. Large, slightly rundown rooms cost US$60 and US$70, or the smaller, renovated rooms cost US$80. The other luxury hotel is the new *Hotel Surya* (☎ 81991), a concrete-and-glass upstart with better facilities and good rooms from US$95.

For cheap eats, *Depot Abadi*, Jalan Raya 27, opposite the Mess Garuda, has standard fare. A line of mid-range restaurants can be found along the road from the Natour Bath Hotel, including the *Mandarin* for Chinese food and the *Istana Ayam Goreng* for chicken.

Getting There & Away From Surabaya take a bus to Pandaan (1000 rp) and then a minibus to Tretes (500 rp).

Gunung Arjuna-Lalijiwo Reserve

This reserve includes the dormant volcano Arjuna (3339 metres), the semi-active Gunung Welirang (3156 metres) and the Lalijiwo Plateau on the north slopes of Arjuna. From Tretes, there is a track used by people collecting sulphur which leads to the summit of Arjuna. It's a stiff four-hour climb from Tretes to the plateau and another two hours to the saddle between the mountains. To the summit and back would be a long day's climb. Arjuna has meadows and, on the higher slopes, forests where deer and wild pigs are common. On the Lalijiwo Plateau, there's a shelter used by the sulphur gatherers but you would have to take camping gear, food and drinking water.

Gunung Penanggungan

The remains of no less than 81 temples are scattered over the slopes of Gunung Penanggungan (1650 metres), a sacred Hindu mountain said to be the peak of holy Mt Mahameru which broke off and landed at its present site when the holy mountain was being transported from India to Indonesia.

This was an important pilgrimage site for Hindus. Pilgrims made their way to the top of the mountain and stopped to bath in the holy springs adorned with Hindu statuary. The two main bathing places are Belahan and Jolotundo, the best examples of remaining Hindu art. Both are difficult to reach.

Between Pandaan and Gembol, a rough read leads west and then a turn off leads south to Genengan village, four km away. From here an even rougher stone road leads two km up through the fields and villages to **Candi Belahan**. The bathing pool is presided over by Vishnu's consorts Sri and Lakshmi, who once flanked the magnificent statue of Airlangga-as-Vishnu, which now lies in the Trowulan Museum. From Laskmi's cupped breasts (and with aid of plastic tubing!), water spouts into the pool still used as a bathing spot by the villagers. From Belahan the road continues further up the hill, and the peak of Gunung Penanggungan lies six km away.

Candi Jolotundo is the bathing place on the western side of the mountain. Dating from the 10th century, it is set into the hillside

JAVA

like Belahan but many of its carved reliefs have been removed. It lies about six km south of Ngoro on the Gempol-Mojokerto road. Ojek hang around the turn off and can take you to the temple along another bad road.

MADURA

Madura is a large and rugged island, about 160 km long by 35 km wide, and separated from Surabaya on the East Java coast by a narrow channel. It is famous for its bull races, the kerapan sapi, but also has a few historical sites, some decent beaches and an interesting, traditional culture. The sarong and peci is still normal dress here, mall fever has not found its way to Madura, and very few tourists go beyond a day trip to the bull races.

The people of Madura are familiar faces in East Java, particularly in Surabaya where many have gone to look for work. Since independence, Madura has been governed as part of the province of East Java but the island has had a long tradition of involvement with its larger neighbour and with the Dutch. The Dutch were not interested in the island itself, which was initially of little economic importance, but rather in the crucial role the Madurese played in Javanese dynastic politics.

Madurese men claim that the name Madura is derived from *madu* (honey) and *dara* (girl), and Madura's 'sweet' girls are famed throughout Java for their sexual prowess. Madura is, however, a very traditional and devoutly Islamic society. The Madurese are rugged *kasar* (unrefined) people (according to the Javanese), and are said to be adept at wielding knives when disputes arise. While the Madurese can be disconcertingly blunt at times, and in remote areas you may attract a crowd of curious onlookers, the Madurese can also be extremely hospitable.

The southern side of the island, facing Java, is shallow beach and cultivated lowland, while the northern coast alternates between rocky cliffs and beaches of great rolling sand dunes, the best of which is at Lombang. At the extreme east is tidal marsh

and vast tracts of salt around Kalianget. The interior of this flat and arid island is riddled with limestone slopes and is either rocky or sandy, so agriculture is limited. There are goat farms, tobacco estates, some orchards and extensive stands of coconut palms but the main industries of this dry, sun-burnt land are cattle, salt and fishing.

History

In 1624 the island was conquered by Sultan Agung of Mataram and its government united under one Madurese princely line, the Cakraningrats. Until the middle of the 18th century the Cakraningrat family fiercely opposed Central Javanese rule and harassed Mataram, often conquering large parts of the kingdom. Prince Raden Trunojoyo even managed to carry off the royal treasury of Mataram in 1677, which was restored only after the Dutch intervened and stormed Trunojoyo's stronghold at Kediri. In 1705 the Dutch secured control of the eastern half of Madura following the conflict of the First Javanese War of Succession between Amangkurat III and his uncle, Pangeran Puger. Dutch recognition of Puger was largely influenced by Cakraningrat II, the lord of West Madura. He probably supported Puger's claims simply because he hoped a new war in Central Java would give the Madurese a chance to interfere but, while Amangkurat was arrested and exiled to Ceylon, Puger took the title of Pakubuwono I and concluded a treaty with the Dutch which, along with large concessions in Java, granted them East Madura.

The Cakraningrats fared little better by agreeing to help the Dutch put down the rebellion in Central Java that broke out after the Chinese massacre in 1740. Although Cakraningrat IV attempted to contest the issue, a treaty was eventually signed in 1743 in which Pakubuwono II ceded full sovereignty of Madura to the Dutch. Cakraningrat fled to Banjarmasin and took refuge on an English ship but was robbed, betrayed by the sultan and finally captured by the Dutch and exiled to the Cape of Good Hope (South Africa).

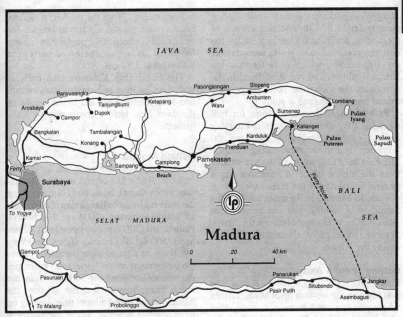

Under the Dutch, Madura continued as four states, each with its own *bupati*, or regent. Madura was initially important as a major source of colonial troops but in the second half of the 19th century it acquired greater economic value as the main supplier of salt to Dutch-governed areas of the archipelago, where salt was a profitable monopoly of the colonial government.

Kerapan Sapi (Bull Races)

As the Madurese tell it, the tradition of bull races began long ago when plough teams raced each other across the arid fields; this pastime was encouraged by an early king of Sumenep, Panembahan Sumolo. Today, when stud bull breeding is big business in Madura, the kerapan sapi are as much an incentive for the Madurese to breed good stock as simply a popular form of entertainment and sport. Only bulls of a certain standard can be entered for important races and the Madurese keep their young bulls in

superb condition, dosing them with an assortment of medicinal herbs, honey, beer and raw eggs.

Traditional races are put on in bull-racing stadiums all over Madura. Practice trials are held throughout the year, but the main season starts in late August and September when contests are held at district and regency level. The cream of bulls fight it out for the big prize in October at the grand final in Pamekasan, the island's capital.

This is, of course, the biggest and most colourful festival. As many as 100 bulls, wearing fancy halters and yokes of gilt, ribbons and flowers, are paraded through town and around the open field of the stadium to a loud fanfare of drums, flutes and gongs. For each race two pairs of bulls, stripped of their finery, are matched against each other with their 'jockeys' perched behind on wooden sleds. Gamelan is played to excite the bulls and then, after being given a generous tot of arak, they're released and charge flat out down the track – just as often plunging right into the seething crowds of spectators! The race is over in a flash – the best time recorded so far is nine seconds over the 100 metres, which is faster than the human world track record. After the elimination heats the victorious bulls are proudly trotted home to be used at stud.

Pamekasan is the main centre for bull races but they can also be seen in the other regency centres, Bangkalan, Sampang and Sumenep, and in the surrounding villages. The *East Java Calendar of Events*, available from the tourist office in Surabaya, has a general schedule for the main races, but if you are in Madura in the main season on a Saturday or Sunday, you can be sure that races will be held somewhere on the island. Surabaya travel agents also arrange day trips during the season.

Getting There & Away
From Surabaya, ferries sail to Kamal, the port town on the western tip of Madura, from where you can catch buses or colts to other towns on the island. It's a half-hour trip by ferry and they cost just 350 rp, operating about every half hour until midnight. Buses go directly from Surabaya's main bus station via the ferry right through to Sumenep, but if you're already based in the centre of town it's easier to take P1 express city bus (400 rp) or C bus (250 rp) to the ferry terminus at Tanjung Perak, take the ferry across to Kamal, and then take local buses around the island.

Another possibility, if you're coming from Bali, say, is to take the DLU (☎ 0338-41142) passenger ferry from Jangkar harbour (near Asembagus) to Kalianget on the eastern tip of Madura. The fare is 3400 rp, and the journey takes 4½ hours, but if the winds are up this rough journey can take a lot longer. Motorbikes and bicycles (not cars) can be taken on the ferry, which departs daily from Jangkar at 1.30 pm, except Wednesday and Sunday. To get to Jangkar, catch any bus heading along the main highway between Situbondo and Banyu-wangi and get down at the Pasar Kambong

in Asembagus. From the market, countless becaks make the 4½-km trip to Jangkar for an incredibly cheap 500 rp, or take an andong for 400 rp. To Jangkar, the ferry departs from Kalianget at 7.30 am.

The Pelni ship *Kelimutu* also calls at Kalianget on its way between Banyuwangi and Maselembo, an island in the middle of the Java Sea, before continuing to Kalimantan.

Getting Around
On arrival, negotiate what can be a wild melee to find a bus or colt to your destination. From Kamal, buses and colts run along the main highway to Bangkalan (600 rp; half an hour), Sampang (2000 rp; 1½ hours), Pamekasan (2000 rp; two hours) and Sumenep (3500 rp; 3½ hours). Buses run every 1½ hours or so, and from Surabaya's Bungurasih station seven 'eksekutif' buses per day run to Sumenep for 5000 rp. Colts are much more frequent and run all over the island but can spend a lot of time picking up passengers. Colts run along the northern route to Arosbaya (600 rp), Sapulu (1500 rp), Tanjungbumi (2000 rp), Pasongsongan (3000 rp) and Ambunten.

To see something of the island, it's interesting to take a colt from Pamekasan inland through tobacco country to Waru (1000 rp), and another to Pasongsongan (600 rp) from where you can head back to Sumenep (800 rp), via Ambunten and Slopeng.

Madura's roads are almost all paved and in excellent condition with relatively little traffic. As the island is mostly flat, Madura is a good cycling destination, though it does get very hot.

Bangkalan
This is the next town north of Kamal along the coast and because it is so close to Surabaya, many visitors only day trip for the bull races. The **Museum Cakraningrat** is also a small museum of Madurese history and culture, open from 8 am to 2 pm Monday to Saturday, except Friday when it closes at 11 am.

Places to Stay & Eat Central at the alun-alun on Jalan Veteran, the *Wisma Pemda* has all of two rooms with shared mandi, a six-bed room for 16,000 rp and a room with nine beds for 25,000 rp. Nearby are several small restaurants – the *Citra Rasa* is decent. For good Chinese food, try the *Mirasa Restaurant* at Jalan Trunojoyo 75A, near the police station.

The *Hotel Ningrat* (☎ 95388) at Jalan Kahaji Muhammed Cholil 113, on the main road south of town, is one of Madura's best hotels. It is very clean and comfortable, but expensive for what you get. Small singles are 8000 rp, simple singles/doubles with mandi are 20,000/30,000 rp. The much more attractive air-con rooms are decorated in traditional Madurese style and cost 45,000/60,000 rp.

Sampang

Sampang, 61 km from Bangkalan, is the centre of the regency of the same name and also stages bull races.

Camplong (nine km east of the town) is a popular beach on the south coast and safe for swimming. The Pertamina storage tanks nearby do nothing for its visual appeal; however, it is a breezy oasis from the hot interior of Madura. Impressive flotillas of twin-outrigger dugout canoes are used for fishing along the coast and the prahus carry huge, triangular striped sails.

Places to Stay At Camplong, the *Pondok Wisata Pantai Camplong* (☎ 21569) provides some of the best accommodation in Madura. Attractive cottages on the beach cost 25,000 to 45,000 rp.

Pamekasan

On the southern side of the island, 100 km east of Kamal, the capital of Madura is a quiet and pleasant enough town, although during October each year it comes alive with the festivities of the Kerapan Sapi Grand Final. Bull races are held in and around Pamekasan every Sunday from the end of July until the big day in early October. To see tulis batik being made, visit Batik Kristal,

Jalan Jokotole 29, across the road from the BCA bank.

About 35 km east of Pamekasan before Bluto, **Karduluk** is a wood carving centre that produces mostly cupboards.

Information The BCA bank, just east of the alun alun on Jalan Jokotole, changes money and travellers' cheques at good rates and gives cash advances on credit cards.

Places to Stay & Eat In the centre of town opposite the alun alun, the *Hotel Garuda* (☎ 81589) at Jalan Mesigit 1 has doubles with shared mandi at 4000 rp and big, old rooms with mandi for 9000 rp up to 20,000 rp with air-con. It's good value but noisy and not well-run.

The best hotel in town is the *Hotel Trunojoyo* (☎ 81181), Jalan Trunojoyo 48. It is clean, quiet and good value. Rooms cost 5500 rp or 12,500 rp with mandi, and from 17,500 to 33,000 rp with air-con, including breakfast.

Losmen Bahagia, further up Jalan Trunojoyo, is basic and less than immaculate, but cheap, and the family who run it are friendly. Singles/doubles cost 5000/8000 rp.

The Garuda and Trunojoyo hotels both have attached restaurants.

Sumenep

At the eastern end of the island, Sumenep is Madura's most interesting town. It is centred around the kraton, mosque and market, and is considered to be the most *halus* (refined) area of Madura. This small, quiet, easy-going town makes a fine base to explore the island.

Sumenep's decaying villas with white-washed walls, high ceilings and cool porches give the town a Mediterranean air, which is mixed with the Arabic influence typical of Java's north coast. Sumenep is also a champion bull breeding centre, and on most Saturday mornings practice bull races can be seen at the Giling stadium.

Information The post office is on the road to Kalianget and the Telkom office is further

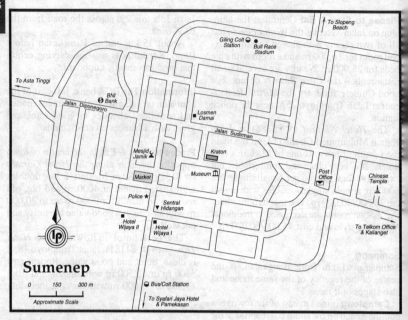

Sumenep

0   150   300 m

Approximate Scale

Map labels:
- To Sloneng Beach
- Giling Colt Station
- Bull Race Stadium
- To Asta Tinggi
- BNI Bank
- Jalan Diponegoro
- Losmen Damai
- Jalan Sudirman
- Mesjid Jamik
- Kraton
- Market
- Museum
- Post Office
- Chinese Temple
- Police
- Sentral Hidangan
- Hotel Wijaya II
- Hotel Wijaya I
- To Telkom Office & Kalianget
- Bus/Colt Station
- To Syafari Jaya Hotel & Pamekasan

out past the Chinese temple. Cash only can be changed at poor rates at the BNI bank – change money in Pamekasan.

Things to See The **kraton** and its **taman sari** (pleasure garden) are worth visiting. It was built in the 18th century by Panembahan Sumolo, son of Queen Raden Ayu Tirtonegoro and her spouse, Bendoro Saud, who was a commoner but a descendant of Muslim scholars. The architect is thought to have been the grandson of one of the first Chinese to settle in Sumenep after the Chinese massacre in Batavia. The kraton is occupied by the present bupati of Sumenep, but part of the building is a small museum with an interesting collection of royal possessions, including Madurese furniture, stone sculptures and *binggels*, the heavy silver anklets worn by Madurese women. Opposite the kraton, the royal carriage house museum contains the throne of Queen Tirtonegoro and a Chinese-style bed reputedly 300 years

old. Entry is 200 rp to the museum, and from here you will be taken on a guided tour of the kraton.

Sumenep's 18th century **Mesjid Jamik** (Mosque) is notable for its three-tiered Meru-style roof, Chinese porcelain tiles and ceramics. Sumenep also has a **Chinese temple.**

The tombs of the royal family are at the **Asta Tinggi cemetery**, which looks out over the town from a peaceful hilltop two km away. The main royal tombs are interesting and decorated with carved and painted panels, two depicting dragons said to represent the colonial invasion of Sumenep. One of the small pavilions in the outer courtyard still bears the mark of an assassin's sword from an unsuccessful attempt to murder Bendoro Saud.

Places to Stay & Eat The best place to head for is the *Hotel Wijaya I* (☎ 21433), Jalan Trunojoyo 45-47. Good clean rooms cost

7000 rp and 8000 rp without mandi, 10,000 and 12,000 rp with mandi, and air-con rooms cost 22,000 to 60,000 rp. The sister *Hotel Wijaya II* (☎ 21532) is also clean and well-run. It is quieter, though many of the rooms are dark. Doubles with common mandi start at 6000 rp and range up to the excellent value air-con rooms with mandi, fridge and TV for 25,000 rp. The *Syafari Jaya* (☎ 21989), on the southern outskirts of town at Jalan Trunojoyo 90, is a big hotel where rooms range from 6500 to 15,500 rp with air-con. It is also good value but dull and a long way from town. The other option is the basic *Losmen Damai* on Jalan Sudirman where rooms cost 5500 to 11,000 rp.

A good place to eat is the *Sentral Hidangan*, Jalan Trunojoyo 49. Dine inside or out in this pleasant food stall centre which has a variety of good dishes, ice juices and cold beer. Decent restaurants to try around town include the *Mawar* at Jalan Diponegoro 105 and *Rumah Makan 17 Agustus* at Jalan Sudirman 34, serving both budget Chinese and Indonesian. There are good day and night markets in the area around the mosque.

Things to Buy Sumenep is a centre for batik on Madura, though Madurese batik isn't as fine as that in Java. Try the market or you can visit home workshops around town.

The main business in town is antiques, but unfortunately the best antiques have been carted off by the truck load to Bali and Jakarta.

Getting There & Away The main bus station, about half a km south of the Hotel Wijaya I, has buses to Surabaya via Pamekasan and Kamal. Seven eksekutif buses leave between 5.30 am and midnight for Surabaya's Bungurasih terminal. The Giling bus stand for colts to the north is right near the bull-race stadium, 1½ km from the market or around 500 rp by becak. From Giling, colts go to Lombang (1500 rp), Slopeng (700 rp), Ambunten (800 rp) and other north coast destinations.

Around Sumenep

From Sumenep, the road to **Kalianget**, 10 km to the south-east, passes many fine villas with frontages of thick, white Roman-style columns under overhanging red-tiled roofs. Kalianget is a centre for salt production, and from here you can take boats to the other islands of Sumenep district. You can go snorkelling at Talango Island just offshore, and the larger islands include Sapudi, Rass and Kangean, well to the east. The ferry from Kalianget to Jangkar runs every day except Wednesday and Sunday when it goes to Kangean.

Lombang beach, 30 km north-east of Sumenep, is one of the best beaches on the island with a sweeping stretch of sand.

North Coast

Fishing villages and their brightly painted prahus dot the north coast. The coast is lined with sandy beaches where you can swim to escape the heat. Madura's beaches are pleasant enough but not the reason to visit the island.

Near Arosbaya, 27 km north of Kamal, the tombs of the Cakraningrat royalty are at the **Air Mata** cemetery, which is superbly situated on the edge of a small ravine overlooking a river valley. The ornately carved gunungan headstone on the grave of Ratu Ibu, consort of Cakraningrat I, is the most impressive and is on the highest terrace. The turn off to Air Mata is shortly before Arosbaya and from the coast road it's a four-km walk inland. *Air mata* means 'tears'.

The village of **Tanjungbumi** is on the north-west coast of Madura, about 60 km from Kamal. Although primarily a fishing village, it's also a centre for the manufacture of traditional Madurese batik and Madurese prahus. On the outskirts is Pantai Siring Kemuning beach.

Pasongsongan, a fishing village on the beach, has a good homestay which is geared to travellers.

Further east, **Ambunten** is the largest village on the north coast and has a bustling market. Just over the bridge, you can walk along the picturesque river lined with prahus and through the fishing village to the beach.

Just outside Ambunten to the east, **Slopeng** has a wide beach with rolling sand dunes, coconut groves and usually calm waters. Men fish the shallower water with large cantilevered hand nets which are rarely seen elsewhere in Java. In Slopeng, Pak Supakra continues the tradition of topeng mask-making handed down by his father, Madura's most noted topeng craftsmen. From Slopeng it is only 20 km to Sumenep, a half-hour colt ride away.

Places to Stay In Pasongsongan, Pak Taufik takes in travellers at his friendly homestay, *Coconut Rest House*, for 5000 rp per night. This is the place to relax and enjoy the beach, and Pak Taufik is only too happy to explain Madurese customs and culture.

Slopeng has a fairly expensive *pesanggrahan* (government rest house), but the beach is better visited on a day trip from Sumenep.

TROWULAN

Trowulan was once the capital of the largest Hindu empire in Indonesian history. Founded by a Singosari prince, Wijaya, in 1294 it reached the height of its power under Hayam Wuruk (1350-89), who was guided by his powerful prime minister, Gajah Mada. During his time Majapahit claimed control over, or at least received tribute from, most of today's Indonesia and even parts of the Malay peninsula. The capital was a grand affair, the kraton forming a miniature city within the city and surrounded by great fortified walls and watchtowers.

Its wealth was based both on the fertile rice-growing plains of Java and on control of the spice trade. The religion was a hybrid of Hinduism with Shiva, Vishnu and Brahma being worshipped, although, as in the earlier Javanese kingdoms, Buddhism was also prominent. It seems Muslims too were tolerated and Koranic burial inscriptions, found on the site, suggest that there were Javanese Muslims within the royal court even in the 14th century when this Hindu-Buddhist state

was at the height of its glory. The empire came to a sudden end in 1478 when the city fell to the north coast power of Demak and the Majapahit elite fled to Bali, thus opening up Java for conquest by the Muslims.

The remains of Majapahit are scattered over a large area around the small village of Trowulan, 12 km from Mojokerto. The Majapahit temples were mainly built from red clay bricks and did not stand the test of time. Many have been rebuilt and are fairly simple compared to some of Java's other ruins, but you can get an idea of what was once a great city. It's possible to walk around the sites in one day if you start early, but unless you have a strong interest in Majapahit history, this is a very hot way to see a few relatively simple archaeological remains. You really need a car, or hire a becak.

Trowulan Museum

One km from the main Surabaya-Solo highway, the museum houses superb examples of Majapahit sculpture and pottery from throughout East Java. Pride of place is the splendid statue of Kediri's King Airlangga-as-Vishnu astride a huge Garuda, taken from Belahan. It should be your first port of call for an understanding of Trowulan and Majapahit history, and it includes descriptions of the other ancient ruins in East Java. The museum is open from 7 am to 4 pm; closed Monday and public holidays. Admission is 150 rp.

Ruins

Some of the most interesting sites include the **Kolam Segaran** (a vast Majapahit swimming pool); the gateway of **Bajang Ratu** with its strikingly sculptured kala heads; the **Tikus Temple** (Queen's Bath) and the **Siti Inggil Temple** with the impressive tomb of Wijaya (people still come to meditate here and in the early evening it has quite a strange spiritual atmosphere). The **Pendopo Agung** is an open-air pavilion built by the Indonesian Army. Two km south of the pavilion, the **Troloyo Cemetery** is the site of the oldest Muslim graves found on Java, the earliest being from 1376 AD.

Getting There & Away

Trowulan can be visited from Surabaya, which is 60 km to the east. Trowulan has a few restaurants on the highway but no accommodation. If you want to stay nearby, Mojokerto has plenty of cheap hotels.

From the Bungurasih bus station in Surabaya it's a one-hour trip to Trowulan. Take a Jombang bus, which can drop you at the turn off to the museum, or a Mojokerto bus which will stop at the bus station on the outskirts of town, then another bus or colt to Trowulan. A becak can be hired to get you around the sites.

When leaving Trowulan, flag a bus down on the road from Surabaya to Solo. Heading east to Probolinggo or south to Malang, take a bus or colt to Gempol and then another. For Malang, an interesting alternative is to travel by colt via Jombang and the hill town of Batu.

PROBOLINGGO

Probolinggo, on the Surabaya-Banyuwangi coastal road, is a transit centre for people visiting Gunung Bromo. It grows the finest mangos in Java, and its well-stocked fruit stalls are a delight, but otherwise Probolinggo is nothing special.

The main post office and most of the banks, including Bank Central Asia, and government buildings are on Jalan Suroyo.

Places to Stay & Eat

Hotels and some cheap restaurants can be found along the main street, Jalan P Sudirman. The *Hotel Bromo Permai II* (☎ 22256) at No 237 is the most popular travellers' hotel and has comfortable, clean rooms for 7500 rp, 9000 to 15,600 rp with bath, or air-con rooms cost 18,000 rp and 25,000 rp. It's a sister hotel of the Bromo Permai I up at the Gunung Bromo crater. It is close to the centre of town at the eastern end.

Hotel Ratna (21597) further west at No 16 is one of the best in town. Good economy rooms cost 7000 and 8000 rp, or rooms with bath range from 20,000 to 40,000 rp with air-con.

The *Hotel Tampiarto Plaza* (☎ 21280),

Jalan Suroyo No 16, is the best hotel in town, but only just. It has a swimming pool and comfortable rooms for 10,000 to 98,000 rp, but the Ratna is better value.

Most of the hotels have restaurants and Probolinggo has some good Chinese restaurants. The *Restaurant Malang*, Jalan P Sudirman 104, has a wide range of items on the menu and the food is good. You'll find plenty of small restaurants and 'depots' at the night market around Pasar Gotong Royong.

Getting There & Away

Bus Probolinggo's Terminal Bayuangga is about five km out of town on the road to Bromo. Yellow angkutan run to/from the main street and the railway station for 300 rp. The bus station is overrun with 'tourist office' bus agents offering dubious information and some charge outrageous prices for buses. It pays to shop around, or just simply bargain for a good fare. Some of the luxury night buses to Bali and Yogya may cost a little more than the fares quoted here, but not much more.

Normal/patas buses include: Surabaya (1700/3000 rp; two hours), Malang (1700/3000 rp; 2½ hours), Yogya (7300/14,500 rp; eight hours), Bondowoso (2700/3000 rp; three hours), Banyuwangi (3400/6000 rp; five hours) via Situbondo, and Denpasar (7500/13,000 to 15,000 rp; eight hours). Coming from Bali, evening buses depart around 7.30 to 8.30 pm and arrive in Probolinggo about 4 am.

Travel minibuses also operate to Yogya for around 17,500 rp air-con or 12,000 rp non-air-con, slightly less to Solo, and to Malang for 7000 rp.

To/From Gunung Bromo Minibuses from Probolinggo go to Ngadisari (1500 rp; 1½ hours) and Cemoro Lawang (2500 rp; two hours) from in front of the bus station. They sometimes cruise over to the railway station in search of passengers, otherwise take a yellow G bemo (300 rp) from the train to the bus station.

Minibuses to Cemoro Lawang run every one to two hours from morning until around midnight. Buses also run as far as Ngadisari, but it is better to take the minibus if you are heading straight to Cemoro Lawang. Otherwise you may find yourself at the mercy of the Ngadisari jeep mafia – a jeep from Ngadisari to Cemoro Lawang should cost 1000 rp per person if there is a full load of passengers.

Jeeps also take passengers directly from Probolinggo to Cemoro Lawang in one hour and cost 3500 rp per person for a minimum of four people.

Train The railway station is about six km from the bus station. Probolinggo is on the Surabaya-Banyuwangi line. The *Blambangan* and *Argopuro* are ekonomi trains and take about two hours to Surabaya (2700 rp), or the *Mutiara* costs 6000 rp in bisnis. The *Argopuro* continues on to Yogya for a long, slow trip. To Banyuwangi takes about five hours and costs 2700 rp in ekonomi, but the buses are quicker and better.

GUNUNG BROMO & BROMO-TENGGER-SEMERU NATIONAL PARK

Gunung Bromo is an active volcano lying at the center of the Tengger Massif, a spectacular volcanic landscape and one of the most impressive sights in Indonesia. The massive Tengger crater stretches 10 km across and its steep walls plunge down to a vast, flat sea of lava sand. From the crater floor emerges the smoking peak of Gunung Bromo (2392 metres), the spiritual centre of the highlands. This desolate landscape has a strange end-of-the-world feeling, particularly at sunrise, the favoured time to climb to the rim of Bromo's crater.

Bromo is the best known peak, and often the whole area is simply referred to as 'Mt Bromo', but it is only one of three mountains that have emerged within the caldera of the ancient Tengger volcano, and Bromo is flanked by the peaks of Batok (2440 metres) and Kursi (2581 metres). Further south the whole supernatural moonscape is overseen by Gunung Semeru (3676 metres), the highest mountain in Java and the most active volcano in these highlands. The whole

area has been incorporated as the **Bromo-Tengger-Semeru National Park**.

Legend has it that the great Tengger crater was dug out with just half a coconut shell by an ogre smitten with love for a princess. When the king saw that the ogre might fulfil the task he had set, which was to be completed in a single night, he ordered his servants to pound rice and the cocks started to crow, thinking dawn had broken. The coconut that the ogre flung away became Gunung Batok, and the trench became the Sand Sea – and the ogre died of exhaustion.

The Bromo area is also home to the Hindu Tengger people who cultivate market vegetables on the steep mountain slopes and are found only on the high ranges of the Tengger-Semeru massif. When the Majapahit Empire collapsed and its aristocracy fled to Bali to escape the tide of Islam on Java, the Tengger highlands provided a haven for Hindus left behind. Hinduism has in fact made a resurgence in the area, and a Hindu temple has been built near the base of Gunung Bromo and the area has growing cultural ties with Bali.

Each year, Bromo is the site for the Kasada (Kasodo) festival, with a colourful procession of Tenggerese who come to throw offerings into the crater at sunrise to pacify the god of the volcano.

Access is usually via Probolinggo, but Bromo can be approached from a number of routes. The ideal time to visit Bromo is during the dry season, April to November. In the wet season the dawn and the clouds are likely to arrive simultaneously so an early rise may not be worth the effort – you might as well stroll across later when it's warmer. At any time of year it's cold on these mountains and night temperatures can get down to around 2 to 5°C.

Probolinggo Approach

This is the easiest and by far the most popular route. From Probolinggo, it's 28 km to Sukapura, then another 14 km to Ngadisari, and then another three km to Cemoro Lawang. Minibuses run all the way to Cemoro Lawang from Probolinggo. At

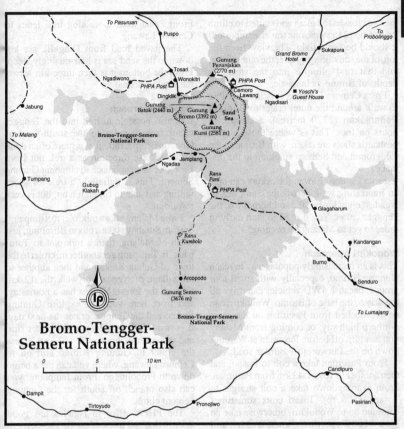

Bromo-Tengger-Semeru National Park

To Pasuruan • Puspo

To Probolinggo

• Sukapura

Grand Bromo Hotel ■

Gunung Penanjakan (2770 m)

Ngadiwono • Tosari

PHPA Post □ Wonokitri

Cemoro Lawang

PHPA Post ■

• Yoschi's Guest House

Dingklik

• Ngadisari

Jabung •

Gunung Batok (2440 m)

Gunung Bromo (2392 m)

Sand Sea

To Malang

Bromo-Tengger-Semeru National Park

Gunung Kursi (2581 m)

• Jemplang

Ngadas

Ranu Pani

PHPA Post □

Tumpang •

Gubug Klakah •

• Glagaharum

Ranu Kumbolo

• Kandangan

Arcopodo

• Bumo

Gunung Semeru (3676 m)

• Senduro

Bromo-Tengger-Semeru National Park

To Lumajang

0   5   10 km

• Candipuro

Dampit •

Tirtoyudo •

• Pronojiwo

• Pasirian

Ngadisari, you have to pay your 2100 rp at the entrance post; don't believe any stories that only hired jeeps can take you on to Cemoro Lawang. The road is steep but regularly negotiated by minibuses and cars.

As with mountain scaling anywhere in Asia, it is all important to be at the top of Gunung Bromo for the impressive sunrise, but don't despair if you can't make it for the dawn. Because of the rising hot air from the Tengger crater, visibility is good throughout the day in the dry season even though the slopes below Cemoro Lawang may be covered in mist.

From Cemoro Lawang, it's another three km down the crater wall and across the Sand Sea to Bromo, about a one-hour walk. Sunrise is at about 5 am, so if you're staying in Ngadisari you'll have to leave around 3 am, from Cemoro Lawang at 4 am. There's no real need for a guide or horses, although if you want to ride across to Bromo it costs 10,000 rp from Cemoro Lawang. It's cold and windy in the early morning so take warm gear, and a flashlight is handy. Once you're on the sand sea *(lautan pasir)*, white-painted rocks mark the trail straight across to the Hindu temple and Bromo. By the time you've crossed the plain and started to climb up Bromo (246 steps, one traveller reported) it should be fairly light. The view from the top, of the sun sailing up over the outer crater, and that first glimpse into the steaming depths of Bromo, is fantastic.

From Cemoro Lawang, it is also possible to walk around the outer crater to **Gunung Penanjakan** (2770 metres), a steep two hours on foot. This is where those picture postcards shots are taken, with Bromo in the foreground and Semeru smoking in the distance.

From Cemoro Lawang, trekkers can take an interesting walk across the Sand Sea to Ngadas (eight km) on the southern rim of the Tengger crater. You'd need to start early in order to get to Malang by evening.

Wonokitri Approach

This is an increasingly popular way to reach Gunung Bromo, especially with small tour groups, because 4WD vehicles can drive all the way to the base of Bromo. Wonokitri can be approached from Pasuruan on the main northern highway, or coming from Malang you can turn off before Pasuruan at Warungdowo on the Purworejo-Pasuruan road.

From Pasuruan take a colt to Puspo, and then another to Tosari, 42 km from Pasuruan. From Warungdowo take a colt straight to Tosari (1500 rp). Tosari colts sometimes continue on to Wonokitri, otherwise take an ojek (1000 rp; three km). Tosari and Wonokitri have accommodation (see under Places to Stay later in this section).

At Wonokitri check in at the PHPA office on the southern outskirts of town and pay your 2100 rp park entry fee. In Wonokitri you can hire a jeep to Bromo for 50,000 rp return or 60,000 rp, including a side trip to Gunung Penanjakan. An ojek will cost 15,000 rp for a return trip to Bromo or 10,000 rp to Penanjakan.

From Wonokitri, it is five km along a good road to Dingklik. The views from Dingklik, right on the edge of the outer crater, are superb. From Dingklik the road forks – down to Bromo or four km up along the paved road to Gunung Penanjakan for even better views.

From Penanjakan a walking trail leads to Cemoro Lawang.

The paved road from Dingklik six km down to the sand sea is hair-raisingly steep. From the bottom it is then three km across the sand to Bromo.

Ngadas Approach

It is also possible to trek into the Tengger crater from Ngadas to the south-west of Gunung Bromo, though it is more often done in the reverse direction as a trek out from Bromo or as an approach to climbing Gunung Semeru. This is definitely a trek for those willing and able to rough it a bit, but is very rewarding.

From Malang take a mikrolet to Tumpang, or from Surabaya take a bus to Blimbing, just north of Malang, then a mikrolet to Tumpang. In Tumpang get another mikrolet to the town of Gubug Klakah and then another to the village of Ngadas, or walk the 12 km through the forest. Ngadas has a homestay, and from here you can explore Gunung Bromo and the Tengger crater the next day. It is two km to Jemplang at the crater rim, and then a three-hour walk (12 km) across the crater to Gunung Bromo and on to Cemoro Lawang, where you can get a bemo down to Probolinggo. From Jemplang, you can also branch off south for the Gunung Semeru climb.

The PHPA office in Ngadas has good information and maps of the Bromo-Semeru area.

Lumajang Approach

This route to Bromo is rarely used by travellers but is an alternative from the south-east. From Lumajang take a mikrolet to Senduro (18 km), then another to Burno (seven km). From Burno it is then 18 km to Ranu Pani, from where you can walk to Bromo (14 km) or to Semeru.

Climbing Gunung Semeru

Part of the huge Tengger massif, Gunung Semeru is the highest mountain in Java at 3676 metres. Also known as Mahameru, the Great Mountain, it has been looked on by

A	B
C	D
E	F

A: Kampung children near Jalan Jaksa (GB)
B: A kampung near Jalan Jaksa (GB)
C: Art for sale, Ancol (GB)
D: An artist at work, Ancol (GB)
E: Street vendors, Blok M (GB)
F: Street vendors (GB)

White tiger, Taman Safari, Cisarua, West Java (PT)

Hindus since time immemorial as the most sacred mountain of all and father of Gunung Agung on Bali. It is a rugged three-day trek to the summit, and you must be well equipped and prepared for camping overnight. Nights on the mountain are freezing and inexperienced climbers have died of exposure. The best time to make the climb is May to October.

Hikers usually come through Ngadas, from where jeeps run to Ranu Pani (2500 rp per person), the start of the trek. It is also possible to cross the Tengger Sand Sea from Gunung Bromo (12 km) to Jemplang, two km from Ngadas at the Tengger crater rim. From Jemplang, the road skirts around the crater rim before heading south to Ranu Pani (six km; 1½ hours on foot).

Ranu Pani is a lake with a small village nearby. Accommodation is available in the village homestay and the warung serves basic meals. Ranu Pani is the usual overnight rest spot, and the Ranu Pani PHPA post is a few hundred metres past the lake. Register here and obtain advice on the climb, and they can help arrange guides.

Volcanoes

Indonesia is a virtual chain of volcanic islands. Some have caused extraordinary destruction, yet they are often the lifeblood of the local people who cling to the volcanoes because they produce such fertile soil and their height produces rain. The word for volcano in Bahasa Indonesia is 'gunung api', which literally means, appropriately, 'fire mountain'. Most can be climbed relatively easily and, naturally, offer uniquely spectacular views, particularly at sunrise, and, sometimes craters and temples can be seen. Many are still active, smoking and rumbling constantly.

The most famous is probably Krakatau between Sumatra and Java. In August 1883, it exploded killing more than 36,000 people and destroying most of the island. The noise was reported several thousand km away in Indonesia and Australia. Its ash was spread as far, and tidal waves were felt as far as England.

The highest mountain in Indonesia, outside of Irian Jaya, Gunung Kerinci (3800 metres) is along the western coast of Sumatra. Around the beautiful area of Padang and Bukittinggi (which means 'high mountain') are the active Merapi (2891 metres; last erupted in 1994), and Singgalang, volcanoes. Stunning Lake Toba is a crater lake 800 metres above sea level, but the area is inactive: the last eruption was maybe 75,000 years ago.

In Java, Gunung Bromo is quite magnificent and still active. Nearly 2400 metres high, it is well cultivated and the site of an annual festival by the local Tenggerese people who throw offerings into the crater to pacify the gods. Gunung Semeru, 3676 metres high, is regarded by all Hindus as the 'father mountain'; further east are the joint Gunung Merapi (2800 metres) and Gunung Raung (3332 metres), where coffee is planted. There are several other volcanic peaks over 3000 metres in Java.

In 1963, Gunung Agung, in Bali, erupted with immense destruction, which was interpreted by the Balinese as a sign of anger from the gods. Revered as the 'mother mountain', about 1000 metres up the 3142-metre slope of Agung is Pura Besakih, regarded as Bali's most important temple. Nearby, Gunung Batur (1717 metres) erupted in 1917, killing thousands and destroying untold number of homes and temples. It erupted again in 1963 and 1974.

Near Banda, in Maluku, jutting out of the sea spectacularly, is the unimaginatively named Gunung Api. It remains a constant threat to the nearby islands and villages perched around the volcano. The first eruption caused massive destruction in 1778 but less damage (because of warnings) during eruptions in 1901 and 1988. In northern Maluku, villages hug the ever-smoking Gunung Api Gamalama (1721 metres), on Ternate Island, which erupted in 1980, 1983, and in October 1994.

The 2820-metre high Gunung Tambora on the island of Sumbawa, Nusa Tenggara, erupted in 1815, killing at least 10,000; many more – up to two-thirds of the island's population – died from resulting starvation or disease. On Flores, one of the great sights in Indonesia is the three-coloured lakes at the top of the omnipotent Keli Mutu (1600 metres) volcano. Sulawesi has several more in the south, not far from Ujung Pandang, and more active ones in the far northern parts and islands around Manado.

Paul Greenway

The next day from the PHPA post it is a couple of km to the shelter at the end of the road. Jeeps and motorbikes can make it this far. From here the trail climbs to the beautiful Ranu Kumbolo crater lake (2400 metres), 10 km or about three hours away. The lake is the last place to replenish water supplies. Just past the lake is another shelter and the trail from here climbs to Kalimati (three hours) at the foot of the mountain. From Kalimati it is a steep one-hour climb to Arcopodo, where there is a campsite for the second night on the mountain.

The next day from Arcopodo the fun begins. It is short steep climb to the start of the volcanic sands, the result of Semeru's eruption, and then a struggling three-hour climb through loose scree to the peak. On a clear day, there are breathtaking views of Java's north and south coasts, as well as Bali. To see the sunrise it is necessary to start at 2 am for the summit. It is possible to make it back to Ranu Pani on the same day.

Places to Stay & Eat

Cemoro Lawang This is the best place to stay as it is right at the lip of the Tengger crater with fine views. Cemoro Lawang is a small village and all the hotels are within easy walking distance of each other.

The cheap and very popular *Cafe Lava Hostel* has comfortable single/doubles with shared mandi for 5000/7000 rp, or a bed in the 14-bed dormitory costs 3000 rp. It is very good value and staff provide good information.

One hundred metres past the Cafe Lava, at the lip of the crater and the start of the walk to Gunung Bromo, the *Hotel Bromo Permai I* (☎ 23459) is the best hotel. It has a restaurant in the moderate price range, a bar and evening entertainment. Rooms with shared mandi cost 10,000 to 15,000 rp and doubles with attached bathroom and hot water range from 33,500 rp up to 77,000 rp for the luxury suites.

The *Cemara Indah Hotel* (☎ 23457) is on the road that branches off to Gunung Penanjakan. It is also on the lip of the crater and has even better views. The hotel has an excel-

lent, airy restaurant, though the cheap rooms for 6000/10,000 rp are quite spartan. The 14-bed dormitory costs 3000 rp, or very comfortable rooms with bathroom and hot water cost 35,000 rp and 45,000 rp.

Ngadisari Ngadisari is a less convenient place to stay than Cemoro Lawang, but one good reason to stay here is *Yoschi's Guest House* (☎ 23387), two km below Ngadisari village. This attractive, friendly inn has a garden and fine views across the valley. Singles cost 5000 rp, or doubles range from 7000 to 15,000 rp with attached mandi. Cottages with hot water showers cost 18,000 to 25,000 rp, or 50,000 rp for four or more people. It also serves food, and offers tours and transport to Bromo.

Right nearby, the *Bromo Home Stay* (☎ 23484) has older rooms for 10,000 rp or spotless, comfortable rooms with bath for 15,000 rp. It also has a large restaurant, but lacks atmosphere.

Sukapura The plush *Grand Bromo Hotel* (☎ 711802) is a few km up the mountain from Sukapura village and a full nine km from the crater. If you want luxury accommodation and have a car this may be your place, otherwise it is too far from the crater to be convenient. Rooms cost US$45 and US$60, or cottages start at US$125. The hostel section next door has large but barren rooms with three beds for 25,000 rp.

Tosari & Wonokitri The *Bromo Cottages* (☎ Surabaya 336888) in Tosari are well-appointed cottages perched on the hillside with fine mountain views. Singles/doubles cost an inflated US$65/70, plus 21%, and expensive meals are available.

Wonokitri village has three penginapan with simple accommodation. The going rate is 30,000 rp per night, which includes all meals, but this is very expensive for what you get. It is best to negotiate for a room only and then eat at the couple of basic warung in town.

Getting There & Away

Most visitors come through Probolinggo (see under Probolinggo earlier in this chapter for transport details). Hotels in Cemoro Lawang and Ngadisari can make bookings for onward bus tickets from Probolinggo for a slight premium. A direct minibus service usually operates to/from Solo and Yogya right through to Cemoro Lawang in the tourist season, and hotels can arrange tickets.

For Ngadas, frequent mikrolet go to Tumpang from Malang (600 rp). From Tumpang irregular minibuses go to Ngadas from where jeeps go to Ranu Pani for 2500 rp per person. Jeeps can be chartered in Tumpang or Ngadas for high rates. From Tumpang you can even charter a jeep to Bromo for 100,000 rp but this is a long journey there and back.

Bromo tours are easily arranged in Malang, and you can also arrange jeep hire in hotels and travel agents there. Bromo tours are also widely available in Solo and Yogya.

PASIR PUTIH

Roughly halfway between Probolinggo and Banyuwangi, on the north coast road, this is East Java's most popular seaside resort and is mobbed on weekends by sun'n'sand worshippers from Surabaya. It has picturesque outrigger boats and safe swimming, but its name *(pasir putih* means 'white sand') is a misnomer – the sand is more grey-black than white. This quite ordinary beach would make a pleasant enough stopover if the accommodation wasn't so bad.

Places to Stay

Pasir Putih's hotels, sandwiched between the beach and the noisy main road, are appallingly overpriced. The *Hotel Bhayangkara* (☎ 91083) is the cheapest. There's nothing wrong with this place that a bucket of disinfectant, a good scrub and a 50% discount wouldn't fix. Dirty, stuffy rooms start at 6500 rp or dirty, larger rooms with mandi cost 15,500 to 25,000 rp, more for air-con.

The *Pasir Putih Inn* (☎ 91522) is only slightly better and has singles/doubles with mandi from 10,500/14,500 rp up to 48,000

rp with air-con. The *Mutiara Beach Hotel* is similar and has rooms from 15,000 rp.

The *Hotel Sido Muncul* (☎ 91352) is the best hotel – at least it is clean. Rooms with fan and mandi facing the road cost 21,000 rp, and air-con rooms cost 32,000 to 52,000 rp for those facing the beach.

BONDOWOSO

Bondowoso, 34 km south of Situbondo, is one of the cleanest towns in Java, in itself an attraction, but otherwise it is merely a transit point for nearby attractions such as Ijen. *Hotel Anugerah*, Jalan Sutoyo 12, is a very good cheap hotel, or the *Palm Hotel*, Jalan A Yani 32, is the best in town and also exceptional value.

On Saturday and Sunday in **Tapen**, 15 km from Bondowoso towards Situbondo, traditional Madurese horn-locking bullfights *(aduan sapi)* are held.

Getting There & Away

Buses from Bondowoso include: Situbondo (800 rp; one hour), Jember (600 rp; 45 minutes), Probolinggo (1600 rp; two hours) and Surabaya (3300/6000 rp patas; 4½ hours). For Tapen (500 rp) take any Situbondo bound bus.

JEMBER

Jember is the thriving service centre for the surrounding coffee, cacao, rubber, cotton and tobacco plantations. It has all the amenities of a large city, but is relatively uncongested and competes with Bondowoso for the tidy town award. The *Hotel Widodo*, Jalan Letjen Suprapto 74, about one km south of the town centre, is a good cheap hotel and on the ball with travel information.

From Jember groups can arrange a plantation tour, though Kalibaru is the usual centre for plantation visits. PT Perkubunan XXVI (Persero) (☎ 21061), Jalan Gadjah Mada 249, is the state-owned company that controls most of the plantations and has day or overnight tours with accommodation on the plantations.

Getting There & Away

The main bus terminal, Tawung Alun, is six km west of town. Normal/patas buses include: Probolinggo (1600/3000 rp; three hours), Surabaya (3100/6000 rp; five hours), Malang (3600/6500 rp; five hours), Bondowoso (600 rp; 45 minutes), Banyuwangi (1900 rp; three hours) and Kalibaru (850 rp; one hour). Buses from Bondowoso usually terminate at the sub-terminal, five km north of town, and there are also sub-terminals to the east (for Banyuwangi) and south (for Watu Ulo). Damri city buses (200 rp) and yellow Lin bemos (250 rp) run from the terminals to the centre of town.

Jember is also on the Surabaya-Banyuwangi line and the station is close to the centre of town.

WATU ULO & PAPUMA

Watu Ulo is a popular weekend resort, but like most of the beaches on the Java's south coast, it has grey sands and crashing surf with dangerous swimming. The real surprise lies just west around the headland from Watu Ulo. Papuma is a small beach with white sand, turquoise waters and sheltered swimming. Further around from Papuma, the rugged coastline with spectacular rocky outcrops is again pounded by the surf, but deserted patches of white sand can be found for sunbathing. Nearby caves and the **Wana Wisata Londolapesan** forest area can also be explored.

Watu Ulo has one hotel, *Hotel Vishnu*, which has basic rooms with mandi for 15,000 rp, but a new hotel is planned for Papuma.

Getting There & Away

In Jember, take a city bemo (250 rp) to the Ajung sub-terminal and then a colt to Ambulu (600 rp; 25 km). From Ambulu yellow bemos go to Watu Ulo (300 rp; 12 km). Papuma is then a half-hour walk along the paved road over the steep headland.

KALIBARU

The picturesque road from Jember to Banyuwangi winds around the foothills of Gunung Raung up to the small hill town of Kalibaru. Kalibaru has a refreshingly cool climate and makes a pleasant stop on the way between Jember and Banyuwangi. The village itself is unremarkable – the attraction here is the chance to visit nearby plantations around **Glenmore**, 10 km east. Java's finest coffee, both *arabica* and *robusta* varieties, is produced in the Ijen plateau area, as well as cacao, cloves and rubber. In Kalibaru town, to the north of the railway station, are smaller, easily visited plots of coffee and cloves.

Places to Stay & Eat

The only cheap hotel is the *Losmen Darmo*, on the main road at the eastern end of town, but it is a brothel first and a hotel second. If you are desperate, dirty rooms with mandi cost 6000 rp.

Undoubtedly, the best hotel is the delightful *Margo Utomo* (☎ 97123), an old Dutch inn that has maintained its colonial feel. It has new, colonial-style cottages with private balconies built around a pretty garden. Cottages cost US$19/25, including breakfast, and all-you-can-eat meals cost 5000 rp for lunch or 7500 rp for dinner. Plantation tours are available for 20,000 rp per person as well as a host of fairly expensive tours to Ijen, Alas Purwo, Sukamade etc.

The *Raung View Hotel* (☎ 14) looks very flash and is comfortable but the rooms for 36,000 rp are quite simple. *Kalibaru Cottages* (☎ 97333) has a swimming pool and all conveniences for US$45/58.

Getting There & Away

Any bus between Jember (1200 rp; one hour) and Banyuwangi (1300 rp; two hours) can drop you near the hotels. The railway station is right near the Margo Utomo and a scenic ekonomi service runs from Kalibaru to Banyuwangi (550 rp; 2½ hours).

MERU BETIRI NATIONAL PARK

Covering 580 sq km, the Meru Betiri National Park is on the south coast and lies between Jember and Banyuwangi districts.

It receives few visitors because access is difficult.

The major attraction is the protected **Sukamade** ('Turtle Beach'), a three-km sand strip where four species of turtle come ashore to lay their eggs. Green turtles are common, but the giant leatherbacks have also been reported.

In the mountain forests there are wild pigs, muncaks, squirrels, civets, jungle cats and some leopards; the silvered-leaf monkey and long-tailed macaque are common. Meru Betiri is also said to be the last home of the Javan tiger but chances are it is already extinct.

The reserve contains pockets of rainforest and the area is unusually wet for much of the year. The best time to visit is the dry season, from April to October; at other time access can be very difficult because of the condition of the road.

The area has some fine coastal scenery, both in the park and along the coast on the approach to the park. **Lampon**, just south of Pesanggaran, is a passable beach popular on weekends. **Pancer**, on a sweeping bay, has a fine beach with good swimming and a small island, **Pulau Merah**, at one end. The Hindu community here has a temple and make offerings at the island. The now-rebuilt Pancer was obliterated by the 1994 tsunami with appalling loss of life. At **Rajegwesi**, at the entrance to the park, is a large bay with a beach, though further into the park one of the prettiest spots on the coast is **Teluk Ijo** (Green Bay). The walk between Sukamade and Green Bay makes a good day trip.

Places to Stay

About four km from the beach, *Mess Sukamade* is part of the large plantation that was in the area long before the establishment of the national park. It has about 30 beds and costs 17,000 rp plus meals per person. Visitors can tour the plantations, which include coffee, cacao, coconut and rubber. The PHPA visitor centre at Rajegwesi also has accommodation for around the same price, with food available by arrangement.

Outside the park, the nearest hotels are in Jajag if you get stuck. The *Hotel Widodo*, Jalan Sudirman 124, is very basic and costs 7000 rp with mandi. *Hotel Baru Indah*, right near the bus station, has excellent rooms with mandi from 7000 to 20,000 rp, but the nocturnal liaisons can be very noisy. The flash, new *Hotel Surya* (☎ 94126) has a swimming pool and rooms for 17,500 to 35,000 rp.

Getting There & Away

This is one of the most isolated parts of Java, and it is a long bumpy trip, even by 4WD which is how most visitors travel to the park. By public transport take a bus first to Jajag (south of the highway) from Jember (1500 rp; two hours) or Banyuwangi (800 rp; one hour). Then take a minibus to Pesanggaran (800 rp; 22 km), or the Minto Putrajaya bus runs direct from Banyuwangi (1500 rp; two hours). From Pesanggaran the road gets progressively worse and the pot holes larger. A *taksi* (the confusing name for a public minibus in these parts) leaves Sukamade for Pesanggaran (2000 rp; 2½ hour; 41 km) at 6 am, returning mid-morning. On busy days (ie, weekends) it may do two trips, returning to Sukamade around 1 pm. Otherwise infrequent trucks to Sukamade cost the same. You may be forced to charter a truck or ojek.

An even rougher road to Sukamade runs from Glenmore, but only 4WD vehicles can make the trip and it is quicker to go via Jajag.

ALAS PURWO NATIONAL PARK

Also known as Blambangan, this national park occupies the whole of the remote Blambangan peninsula at the south-eastern tip of Java. This is perhaps the last area in Indonesia where the fast-dwindling species of Indonesian wild dog (*ajak*, a subspecies of the Indian dhole) still exists in any numbers. The reserve is also noted for its turtle-nesting beaches which, sadly, are often raided by Balinese turtle hunters for grey and green turtles. There are jungle fowl, leaf monkeys, muncaks, rusa deer, leopards and wild pigs.

Entry to the park is via Kendalrejo where you register at the PHPA office and proceed to Rowobendo (10 km) and then Trianggulasi (two km), a village within the park that has accommodation. Using Trianggulasi as a base it is a three-km walk north-east to the viewing tower at Sadengan where wildlife to spot includes banteng, ajak, rusa (deer) and merak (peacocks). From Rowobendo it is an eight-km trek to Ngagelan, a turtle spawning beach. Goa Padepokan cave is inland from the camping ground at Pancur, three km south of Trianggulasi.

Continuing 12 km along the coast from Pancur, a walking track leads around Grajagan Bay and along some fine beaches to **Plengkung**. The small surfing camp on the beach at Plengkung has reached legendary proportions among surfers who are willing to pay for the boat tours to Grajagan (as Plengkung is known among surfers) that operate out of Bali. The beach is superb, but it is the left-hand reef break that has made Grajagan world famous among surfers. Accommodation is in simple bamboo huts, and controlled access is limited to organised tours – try travel agents in Kuta Beach, or Wanawisata, Jalan Jaksagung, in Banyuwangi. Some surfers experienced the terrifying ride of their lives when the 1994 tsunami hit the camp in the middle of the night, carrying huts and surfers 60 metres back into the jungle.

Places to Stay
Accommodation in the park is very limited, but the park receives few visitors and the PHPA can help if rooms are full. The *Penginapan Trianggulasi* in Trianggulasi has accommodation in basic rooms for 4500 rp. The surf camp at Plengkung is for tours only, but you may be able to rent a hut if they are not full. There is also a camping ground at Pancur.

Getting There & Away
From Banyuwangi's Karang Ente terminal, the Purwo Indah company has five taksi (public minibuses) to Kalipahit (1300 rp; 1½ hours) via Tegaldelimo until mid-afternoon. From Kalipahit occasional trucks battle the bad road to Trianggulasi. Alternatively, take an ojek from Kalipahit to

Kendalrejo PHPA (1000 rp) and the rangers can provide transport to Trianggulasi for a small donation.

If coming from Jember, take a bus to Jajag then another to Benculuk (300 rp), from where buses go to Tegaldelimo and Kalipahit or to the town of Grajagan on the northern end of Grajagan Bay. From Grajagan, you can rent a fishing boat or a speedboat to Plengkung. Tours come this way, but this is a very expensive way to reach the park.

BANYUWANGI
Although there are no particular attractions to drag you here, schedules or just the urge to be somewhere different might take you to Banyuwangi, the ferry departure point for Bali. The ferry terminus, main bus station and train terminal are all at Ketapang, eight km north of town, so everyone goes straight though to Gunung Bromo, Yogya or elsewhere. While Bali is teeming with tourists, Banyuwangi, just a stone's throw away, is a quiet, neglected backwater.

The main reason to stay here is to overnight on the way to Kawah Ijen, or the national parks to the south. If you are desperate for something to do, the **Museum Daerah Blambangan**, opposite the alun alun on Jalan Sritanjung, has a small collection of artefacts. In Desa Temenggungan, the kampung just behind the museum, Banyuwangi-style batik, *gajah oleng*, is produced. Ask around to see it being made. The town's market, **Pasar Banyuwangi**, with its crowded, narrow alleyways, is also worth a look.

Information
The Banyuwangi Tourist Office, Jalan Diponegoro 2, is at the cultural centre/sports field. A helpful branch at the LCM Ferry Building in Ketapang is open every day from 8 am to 7 pm.

The post office is opposite the tourist office. Change money at the BCA bank on Jalan Banterang.

For information on the national parks and accommodation bookings, the PHPA office (☎ 41119) is at Jalan A Yani 108, about two km south of the town centre.

Places to Stay

The *Hotel Baru* (☎ 21369), Jalan Pattimura 82-84, is the budget travellers' choice. It's clean, quiet, friendly and has a good restaurant. Most rooms have private balconies, and doubles with mandi and fan cost 6800 to 9000 rp, or with air-con from 15,500 to 28,300 rp, including breakfast.

Nearby *Hotel Slamet*, next to the old railway station at Ka'am Wahid Hasyim 96, is another friendly place with a restaurant. Singles/doubles start at 8000/9000 rp and range up to 25,000 rp with air-con. Some of the rooms are dark, so it pays to check a few out.

For something better, the popular *Hotel Pinang Sari* (☎ 23266) at Jalan Basuki Rachmat 116 is a few hundred meters north of the Blambangan bemo terminal. It has a very attractive garden and a restaurant. All rooms with bath and balcony cost 12,000 to 18,000 rp, or with air-con from 30,000 to 48,000 rp.

The *Hotel Ikhtiar Surya* (☎ 21063), Jalan Gajah Mada 9, is the best in town with large grounds and a huge variety of rooms, all with bath, ranging from 12,500 rp up to the 82,500 rp VIP rooms. It is very quiet but a long 1½ km hike to the centre of town.

The motel-style *Manyar Garden Hotel* (☎ 24741) is about one km south of the ferry terminal on the road to Banyuwangi. It is arguably the best hotel in the area, but is dull and overpriced. Rooms range from 20,000 to 110,000 rp.

Places to Eat

For snacks, Jalan Pattimura has night food stalls; delicious *air jahe* (ginger tea) and *dadak jagung* (egg and sweetcorn patties), *ketan* (sticky rice topped with coconut) and fried banana.

The *Rumah Makan Surya* around the corner at Jalan W Hasyim 94 has moderately priced Chinese food and serves a good ayam goreng. *Depot Asia*, Jalan Dr Sutomo 12, also has good, if slightly expensive, Chinese food and boasts air-con. For the best Madurese-style sate in town, in the evenings go to *Pak Amat* on Jalan Basuki Rachmat.

Getting There & Away

Bus Banyuwangi has two bus stations. Terminal Ketapang is right in front of the Bali ferry terminal eight km north of town. Buses from here go to northern destinations such as: Baluran (1200 rp; one hour), Pasir Putih (2200; 2½ hours), Probolinggo (3300/6000 rp patas; three hours) for Gunung Bromo, Surabaya (5000/9000 rp patas; five hours) and Malang (4900 rp). Buses also go right through to Yogya and Jakarta.

Terminal Brawijaya (more commonly referred to as Karang Ente) is four km south of town and has buses to the south. Buses include: Kalipahit (1300 rp; 1½ hours),

Pesanggrahan (1500 rp; two hours), Kalibaru (1300 rp; two hours) and Jember (1900 rp; three hours).

Train The railway station is just a few hundred metres north of the ferry terminal and bus station. Bisnis trains leave at 8 am and 9 pm for Probolinggo (6000 rp; five hours) and Surabaya (7000 rp; seven hours). Economy trains include the *Blambangan* to Probolinggo (2100 rp; six hours) at 1 pm and *Kalibaru* to Kalibaru (550 rp; 2½ hours) at 2.30 pm. The *Argopuro* provides an excruciating trip to Yogya (7000 rp; 15 hours) at 5 am. Schedules are subject to change and expect overruns on journey times. Trains can be very crowded at peak travel times such as Sunday.

Ferry to Bali Ferries from Ketapang depart every 40 minutes round the clock for Gilimanuk on Bali. The ferry costs 650 rp for passengers, 1800 rp for motorbikes and 7400 rp for cars. Through buses between Bali and Java include the fare in the bus ticket.

Pelni Ship Pelni's *Kelimutu* stops in Banyuwangi, coming from Lembar on Lombok before continuing on to Kalianget on Madura. In the opposite direction it comes from Kalianget and continues on to Bali's Benoa harbour.

Getting Around

Banyuwangi has a squadron of bemos running between the bus stations and terminating at the Blambangan colt terminal; they're marked Lin 1, 2, 3 etc and charge a fixed 300 rp fare around town. Lin 6 will get you from Ketapang to Blambangan, then take Lin 2 to the Hotel Baru area. Lin 3 goes from Blambangan to Sasak Perot, where you get colts on to the Ijen Plateau.

IJEN PLATEAU

The Ijen Plateau, part of a reserve area which stretches north-east to Baluran, was at one time a huge active crater complex 134 sq km in area. Today Ijen is dormant, not dead, and the landscape is dominated by the volcanic cones of Ijen (2400 metres) and Merapi (2800 metres) on the north-eastern edge of the plateau and Raung (3332 metres) on the south-west corner. Coffee plantations cover much of the western part of the plateau, where there are a few settlements. The plateau area has a number of difficult-to-reach natural attractions, but most visitors come for the hike to spectacular Kawah Ijen.

Kawah Ijen Hike

Kawah Ijen (Ijen Crater) is surrounded by sheer walls rising up from a magnificent turquoise sulphur lake. From the crater lip it is possible to climb down to the smoking sulphur deposits, and at the south-western end the crater walls plunge down to a 'safety-valve' dam which was built to regulate the flow of water into the Banyu Pahit, the 'Bitter River'. There are few people in this totally unspoilt area. Sulphur is extracted from the lake and a vulcanology post just below the crater monitors sulphur collection and is staffed year-round.

The best time to make the hike is in the dry season between April and October. Sulphur collectors hike up in the morning and return around 1 pm when the clouds roll in. Trekkers are advised to do the same, but the clouds often disappear in the late afternoon.

The starting point for the trek to the crater is the PHPA post at Paltuding, which can be reached from Banyuwangi or from Bondowoso. The steep well-worn path up to the vulcanology post takes about an hour. Just past the vulcanology post the road forks – to the left is the easy walk to the dam, but the more interesting walk is the right fork another half hour to the top of the crater and its stunning views. From the crater a steep, gravelly path leads down to the sulphur deposits and the steaming lake. The walk down takes about 20 minutes, double the time for the walk up. The path is slippery in parts and the sulphur fumes towards the bottom can be overwhelming – take care.

Back at the lip of the crater, turn left for the steep half hour climb to the peak and magnificent views of the lake and the surrounding mountains.

You can also keep walking anti-clockwise around the crater for equally superb views. On the other side of the lake opposite the sulphur deposits, the trail disappears into crumbling volcanic rock and deep ravines.

Places to Stay & Eat

Most people visit Kawah Ijen on a day trip but it is possible to stay and explore the plateau area. Sempol, 13 km from the Pos Paltuding on the Bondowoso side, has three simple homestays with rooms from around 10,000 rp and meals can be arranged. Sempol has little else in the way of facilities.

You can always stay at the PHPA posts for a small donation.

To the south of Sempol, *Guest House Jampit* provides the best accommodation in the area. It is an old Dutch house in the government-run Persero plantation. Persero (see under Jember earlier in this chapter) run Ijen tours with overnight stays in Jampit, or tours can be arranged through Bondowoso hotels.

Getting There & Away

The starting point for the main trek to Kawah Ijen is at the PHPA post of Pos Paltuding, which can be reached from either Banyuwangi or Bondowoso.

From Banyuwangi This is the most popular route. It is shorter and cheaper than coming from Bondowoso, though it is a much longer trek. Start at 5.30 am to reach the crater in time for good views.

From Banyuwangi's Blambangan bemo terminal, take a Lin bemo to Sasak Perot (300 rp) on the eastern outskirts of town, and then a Licin-bound colt which can drop you off in Jambu (500 rp) at the turnoff to Kawah Ijen. From here ojek can take you along the paved road for the nine km to Sodong for 3000 rp (they will ask for more). Sodong is nothing more than a bamboo shed where the sulphur collectors bring their loads to be taken by truck to Banyuwangi. You may be lucky enough to get a ride on the trucks to or

from Sodong but don't count on it. The expensive alternative to all this is to hire a car – the tourist office, Hotel Baru and other hotels can arrange one for 75,000 rp for the return journey.

From Sodong the road becomes very steep and is not negotiable by vehicle. The eight-km walk to Pos Paltuding goes through some brilliant, dense forest and takes three to four hours. On the way you will pass another PHPA post, Pos Totogan.

From Bondowoso If you are prepared to charter transport, then the route from Bondowoso is the easiest way to reach Kawah Ijen. From Wonosari, eight km from Bondowoso towards Situbondo, an asphalt road runs via Sukosari all the way to Pos Paltuding. It is potholed in parts but the 64-km trip from Bondowoso to Pos Paltuding can be easily made in about 2½ hours by car.

Colts run from Bondowoso to Sukosari, but there is no regular public transport for the remaining 40 km to Pos Paltuding. Expect to have to charter a pickup or truck in Sukosari to Pos Paltuding for 45,000 rp return. If you make it to Sempol by public transport, you can then hire an ojek to Pos Paltuding (5000 rp; 13 km).

KALIKLATAK

Kaliklatak, 20 km north of Banyuwangi, is another 'agro-tourism' venture where you tour large coffee, cocoa, rubber, coconut and clove plantations. Accommodation is available at the *Wisata Irdjen Guesthouse* (☎ 41061 in Kaliklatak, 41896 in Banyuwangi), but is expensive. Note that tours and accommodation must be booked in advance.

BALURAN NATIONAL PARK

On the north-east corner of Java, Baluran National Park covers an area of 250 sq km. The parklands surround the solitary hump of Gunung Baluran (1247 metres) and contain extensive dry savanna grassland threaded by stony-bedded streams and coastal mangrove. It is surprisingly reminiscent of Australia or the African grasslands, and is billed as Indonesia's 'African safari park'. It is also very easy to reach, lying on the main Banyu-wangi-Surabaya highway, and easy car access makes it one of Java's most visited parks.

The main attractions are the herds of feral water buffalo, banteng (wild cattle), rusa deer, muncaks (barking deer), monkeys, and the wild pigs, leopards and civets that live in the upland forest. Birds include the green junglefowl, peacocks, bee-eaters, kingfishers and owls.

PHPA staff can arrange a jeep to the more remote parts of the savanna for a price. At Bekol, where the main guesthouse is located, you can see deer and water buffalo at the waterhole, usually in the early morning or late afternoon, so you should stay here for the night. Bekol also has a tower for wildlife spotting. From Bekol you can walk or drive the three km to Bama on the coast. Bama also has accommodation, a waterhole and viewing tower, and a half decent beach where you can snorkel. Trails lead around the coast and through the savanna.

The main service area for Baluran is the village of Wonorejo, on the main coast road between Surabaya and Banyuwangi, where food supplies can be bought – the PHPA office and visitor centre is just inside the park entrance. Baluran is open daily from 7 am to 5 pm and, if you're not staying overnight, baggage can be left safely at the PHPA office.

Baluran can be visited at any time of the year but the best time is the dry season, between May and November, because this is when the animals come to the park waterholes.

Places to Stay

At Bekol, 12 km into the park, the *Pesang-grahan* has seven rooms and costs 4000 rp per person; there's a mandi and kitchen but you must take your own provisions. *Wisma Tamu* next door has three very comfortable rooms with attached mandi for 8000 rp per person. The canteen at Bekol sells drinks and some provisions, but meals are cooked only for groups if advance notice is given. You might be able to arrange something with the PHPA staff, but you should bring your own food.

Bama Guesthouse is three km east of Bekol on the beach and provides rooms for 5000 rp per person, and there are also cooking facilities here if you bring your own food. Bookings for both can be made in advance at the PHPA office in Banyuwangi. Most visitors tend to day trip so accommodation is not usually full, but it pays to book especially in the main June/July holiday period when school groups visit the park.

Getting There & Away

Surabaya to Banyuwangi buses, taking the coast road via Probolinggo, can drop you right at the park entrance and when leaving the park buses are easily flagged down. From Banyuwangi (or Ketapang ferry, if you're coming from Bali) it's only a half-hour journey on the Wonorejo bus, which costs 750 rp. Ask the driver to let you off at the park and at the entrance ask a PHPA ranger to arrange an ojek (2000 rp) or car (10,000 rp) to take you the 12 km to Bekol. The park entry fee is 2000 rp. Coming from the west, Baluran is 3½ hours from Probolinggo/Gunung Bromo.

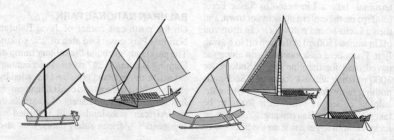

Bali

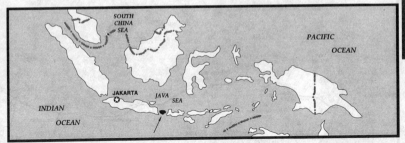

For many Westerners, Bali doesn't extend beyond the tourist leaflet: idyllic tropical beaches, lush green forests and rice fields tripping down hillsides like giant steps. This vision of paradise has been turned into a commodity for the hundreds of thousands of tourists who flood into Bali every year. But Bali has much more than this – you can still discover the extraordinary richness of Balinese culture, which remains unique and authentic despite the tourist invasion, and it's not hard to find out-of-the-way places where tourists are a rarity.

HISTORY

There is no trace of the Stone Age in Bali, although the island was certainly populated before the Bronze Age commenced there about 300 BC. Nor is much known of Bali during the period when Indian traders

---

Highlights

Bali can be all things to all people: relax in decadence on a luxury beach resort, visit traditional villages, indulge in Western delights after less developed parts of Indonesia, shop till you drop or experience Balinese dance, music and rich art traditions. You can easily spend months doing all these things, or Bali is compact and developed enough to do it all in one day.

Bali is by far the most touristed part of Indonesia, and the visitor's dream of idyllic Bali is often shattered by the commercial reality. Either indulge yourself and treat Bali as a well-equipped, scenic and cheap resort, or be prepared to put in some work to seek the richness of Balinese culture, which may take some hunting, but is often right in front of you, hidden under the tourist glitz.

Bali is wonderfully scenic, with brilliant green sculptured rice terraces, lush jungle gorges and deep blue sea. Some highlights of a trip round the island are the descent from Bedugul to the north coast, the spectacular volcanic crater and lake of Gunung Batur, and the panorama from the southern slopes of Gunung Agung.

For Balinese culture, head for the hills. Ubud has always been the cultural centre of Bali, and the tag still fits despite mass tourism. From here, it is possible to get out and explore the surrounding villages and their rich traditions.

Balinese culture often takes a back seat to the lure of Bali's famed beach resorts. Kuta has a host of good hotels, restaurants and bars, great shopping and a fine stretch of sand, but the maddening, chaotic hustle for the tourist dollar is an unfortunate aspect of Bali. Sanur is in the same mould but much quieter, more up-market and family oriented, while Nusa Dua is more up-market again. Candidasa and Lovina don't have Bali's best stretches of sand but they are more relaxed and relatively low key. ■

BALI

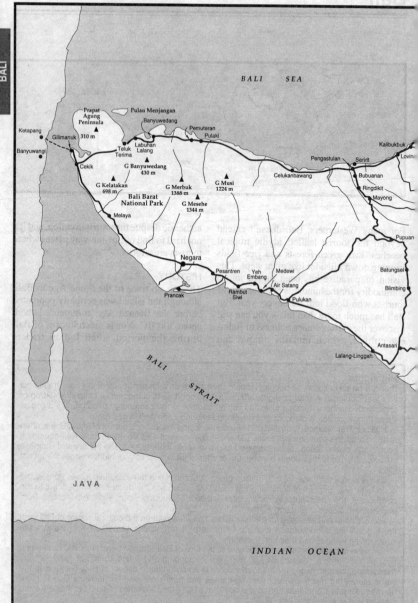

BALI

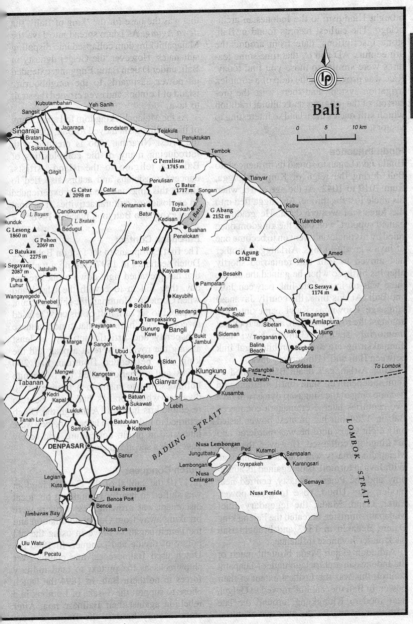

Bali

0   5   10 km

Kubutambahan   Yeh Sanih
Sangsit
Singaraja   Jagaraga   Bondalem   Tejakula
Bratan   Penuktukan
Sukasade
Gitgit   Tembok
                          G Penulisan
L Buyan   1745 m
unduk   G Catur   Penulisan   Tianyar
        2098 m   Catur   G Batur   Songan   Kubu
Candikuning   1717 m
G Lesong   Kintamani   Toya   G Abang   Tulamben
1860 m   Batur   Bunkah   2152 m
G Pohon   Bedugul   Kedisan   Buahan
2069 m   Penelokan
G Batukau   Jati   Amed
2275 m   Taro   G Agung   Culik
Segayang   Pacung   Kayuanbua   3142 m
2087 m   Jatuluih   Besakih   G Seraya
Pura   Pujung   Pampatan   1174 m
Luhur   Sebatu   Kayubihi
Wangayegede   Penebel   Rendang   Muncan   Tirtagangga
                    Tampaksiring   Selat   Amlapura
        Marga   Gunung   Bangli   Sibetan   Asak   Ujung
              Sangeh   Kawi   Iseh Sideman
                    Payangan   Bukit   Tenganan
                    Ubud   Pejeng   Jambul   Balina
        Mengwi   Bedulu   Sidan   Beach   Bugbug
Tabanan   Kangetan   Mas   Klungkung   Padangbai   Candidasa
Kedri   Batuan   Gianyar   Goa Lawah   To Lombok
Kapal   Lukluk   Celuk Sukawati   Lebih
Tanah Lot   Batubulan   Kusamba
        Sempidi   Ketewel
                          BADUNG STRAIT
DENPASAR
                    Nusa Lembongan   Ped   Kutampi   Sampalan
        Sanur   Jungutbatu   Karangsari
                    Lembongan   Toyapakeh
Legian   Nusa
Kuta   Pulau Serangan   Ceningan   Semaya
        Benoa Port   Nusa Penida
Jimbaran Bay   Benoa   LOMBOK STRAIT
        Nusa Dua
Ulu Watu
Pecatu

brought Hinduism to the Indonesian archipelago. The earliest records found in Bali, stone inscriptions, date from around the 9th century AD and by that time some features were similar to those you find today. Rice was grown with the help of a complex irrigation system, and there were the precursors of the religious and cultural tradition which still makes the island so interesting to visitors.

Hindu Influence

Hindu Java began to spread its influence into Bali during the reign of King Airlangga, from 1019 to 1042. At the age of 16, when his uncle lost the throne, Airlangga fled into the forests of western Java. He gradually gained support, won back the kingdom once ruled by his uncle and went on to become one of Java's greatest kings. Airlangga's mother had moved to Bali and remarried shortly after his birth, so when he gained the throne there was an immediate link between Java and Bali. At this time, the courtly Javanese language known as Kawi came into use amongst the royalty of Bali, and the rock-cut memorials seen at Gunung Kawi near Tampaksiring are a clear architectural link between Bali and 11th-century Java.

After Airlangga's death Bali retained its semi-independent state until Kertanagara became king of the Singasari dynasty in Java two centuries later. Kertanagara conquered Bali in 1284 but his greatest power lasted only eight years until he was murdered and his kingdom collapsed. However, the great Majapahit dynasty was founded by his son. With Java in turmoil, Bali regained its autonomy and the Pejeng dynasty, centred near modern-day Ubud, rose to great power. Later, Gajah Mada, the legendary chief Majapahit minister, defeated the Pejeng king Dalem Bedaulu in 1343 and brought Bali back under Javanese influence.

Although Gajah Mada brought much of the Indonesian archipelago under Majapahit control, this was the furthest extent of their power. In Bali the 'capital' moved to Gelgel, near modern Klungkung, around the late 14th century and for the next two centuries

this was the base for the 'king of Bali', the *dewa Agung*. As Islam spread into Java the Majapahit kingdom collapsed into disputing sultanates. However, the Gelgel dynasty in Bali, under Dalem Batur Enggong, extended its power eastwards to the neighbouring island of Lombok and even crossed the strait to Java.

As the Majapahit kingdom fell apart many of its intelligentsia moved to Bali, including the priest Nirartha, who is credited with introducing many of the complexities of Balinese religion to the island. Artists, dancers, musicians and actors also fled to Bali at this time and the island experienced an explosion of cultural activities. The final great exodus to Bali took place in 1478.

European Contact

The first Europeans to set foot on Bali were Dutch seafarers in 1597. Setting a tradition that has prevailed right down to the present day, they fell in love with the island and when Cornelius Houtman, the ship's captain, prepared to set sail, half of his crew refused to come with him. At that time Balinese prosperity and artistic activity, at least among the royalty, were at a peak and the king who befriended Houtman had 200 wives and a chariot pulled by two white buffaloes, not to mention a retinue of 50 dwarves whose bodies had been bent to resemble kris handles! Although the Dutch returned to Indonesia in later years they were interested in profit, not culture, and barely gave Bali a second glance.

Dutch Conquest

In 1710 the capital of the Gelgel kingdom was shifted to nearby Klungkung but local discontent was growing, lesser rulers were breaking away from Gelgel domination and the Dutch began to move in using the old policy of divide and conquer. In 1846 the Dutch used Balinese salvage claims over shipwrecks as the pretext to land military forces in northern Bali. In 1894 the Dutch chose to support the Sasaks of Lombok in a rebellion against their Balinese raja. After some bloody battles, the Balinese were

BALI

defeated on Lombok, and with the north of Bali firmly under Dutch control, south Bali was not likely to retain its independence for long. Once again it was disputes over salvage of wrecked ships that gave the Dutch the excuse they needed to move in. A Chinese ship was wrecked off Sanur in 1904 and ransacked by the Balinese. The Dutch demanded that the raja of Badung pay 3000 silver dollars in damages. This was refused, and in 1906 Dutch warships appeared at Sanur and Dutch forces landed and, despite Balinese opposition, marched the five km to the outskirts of Denpasar.

On 20 September 1906 the Dutch mounted a naval bombardment on Denpasar and then commenced their final assault. The three princes of Badung (south Bali) realised that they were outnumbered and outgunned and that defeat was inevitable. Surrender and exile, however, was the worst imaginable outcome so they decided to take the honourable path of a suicidal *puputan* – a fight to the death. First the palaces were burnt. Then, dressed in their finest jewellery and waving golden krises, the raja led the royalty and priests out to face the modern weapons of the Dutch.

The Dutch begged the Balinese to surrender rather than make their hopeless stand but their pleas went unheard and wave after wave of the Balinese nobility marched forward to their death. In all, nearly 4000 Balinese died in defence of the two Denpasar palaces. Later, the Dutch marched east towards Tabanan, taking the raja of Tabanan prisoner, but he committed suicide rather than face the disgrace of exile.

The kingdoms of Karangasem and Gianyar had already capitulated to the Dutch and were allowed to retain some of their powers, but other kingdoms were defeated and their rulers exiled. Finally, the raja of Klungkung followed the lead of Badung and once more the Dutch faced a puputan. With this last obstacle disposed of, all of Bali was now under Dutch control and part of the Dutch East Indies. Fortunately, the Dutch government was not totally onerous and the common people noticed little difference between rule by the Dutch and rule by the rajas. Some far-sighted Dutch officials encouraged Balinese artistic aspirations which, together with a new found international interest, sparked off an artistic revival. Dutch rule over Bali was short-lived, however, as Indonesia fell to the Japanese in WW II.

Independence

On 17 August 1945, just after the end of WW II, the Indonesian leader Soekarno proclaimed the nation's independence, but it took four years to convince the Dutch that they were not going to get their great colony back. In a virtual repeat of the puputan nearly half a century earlier, a Balinese resistance group was wiped out in the battle of Marga on 20 November 1946, and it was not until 1949 that the Dutch finally recognised Indonesia's independence. The Denpasar airport, Ngurah Rai, was named after the leader of the Balinese forces at Marga.

The huge eruption of Gunung Agung in 1963 killed thousands, devastated vast areas of the island and forced many Balinese to accept transmigration to other parts of Indonesia. Only two years later, in the wake of the attempted Communist coup, Bali became the scene of some of the bloodiest anti-Communist killings in Indonesia, perhaps inflamed by some mystical desire to purge the land of evil, but equally because the radical agenda of land reform and abolition of the caste system was a threat to traditional Balinese values. The brutality of the killings was in shocking contrast to the stereotype of the 'gentle' Balinese.

The tourist boom, which started in the 1970s, has brought many changes, and has helped pay for improvements in roads, telecommunications, education and health. Though tourism sometimes seems to threaten the survival of the remarkable culture which makes Bali so interesting, the offerings of food, flowers and incense, which are reverently placed outside every home and business every morning, even in tourist ghettos like Kuta, testify to the amazing resilience of Balinese culture.

BALI

GEOGRAPHY
Bali is a tiny, extremely fertile and dramatically mountainous island just 8° south of the equator. It is only 140 km by 80 km, with an area of 5620 sq km. Bali's central mountain chain includes several peaks over 2000 metres and many active volcanoes, including the 'mother' mountain Gunung Agung (3142 metres). Bali's volcanic nature has contributed to its exceptional fertility and the high mountains provide the dependable rainfall which irrigates the island's complex and beautiful rice terraces.

South of the central range is a wide, gently sloping area where most of Bali's abundant crops of rice are grown. The northern coastal strip is narrower, rising more rapidly into the foothills. Here the main export crops of coffee and copra are produced, along with some rice, vegetables and cattle. Bali also has arid areas; the lightly populated western mountain region, the eastern and northeastern slopes of Gunung Agung, the Bukit Peninsula in the south and the island of Nusa Penida get little rain and have only limited agriculture.

PEOPLE
Something like 2.7 million people are crammed onto this tiny island. The Balinese have a traditional caste system which resembles the Indian Hindu system, although there are no untouchables. Nor is there an intricate division of labour based on caste, except for the Brahmana priesthood. Over 90% of the population belong to the common Sutra caste, which now includes many wealthy Balinese. The main significance of caste is in religious roles and rituals, and in the language, but its importance in other aspects of life is declining.

Balinese Society
Balinese society is an intensely communal one; the organisation of villages, the cultivation of farmlands and even the creative arts are communal efforts – a person belongs to their family, clan, caste and the village as a whole. Religion permeates all aspects of life and ceremonies and rituals mark each stage in the life cycle. The first ceremony takes place before birth, at the third month of pregnancy, when a series of offerings is made at home and at the village river or spring to ensure the wellbeing of the baby. When the child reaches puberty its teeth are filed to produce an aesthetically pleasing straight line – even teeth symbolise an even temperement while crooked fangs are characteristic of witches and demons.

Balinese women are not cloistered away, although the roles of the sexes are fairly well delineated, with certain tasks handled by women and others reserved for men. For instance, the running of the household is very much the women's task, while caring for animals is mostly a male preserve.

Balinese society is held together by a sense of collective responsibility. If a woman enters a temple during menstruation, for instance, it is a kind of irreverence, an insult to the gods, and their displeasure falls not just on the transgressor, but on the community as a whole. This collective responsibility produces considerable pressure on the individual to conform to traditional values and customs, called *adat*.

Households
Despite the strong communal nature of Balinese society, traditional houses are surrounded by a high wall and the compound is usually entered through a gateway backed by a small wall known as the *aling aling*. It serves a practical and a spiritual purpose – both preventing passers-by from seeing in and stopping evil spirits from entering. Evil spirits cannot easily turn corners so the aling aling stops them from scooting straight in through the gate. Inside there will be a family temple in one corner, a garden and a separate small building *(bale)* for each household function: cooking, sleeping, washing and the toilet.

Village Organisation
Each village is subdivided into *banjars*, which all adults join when they marry. It is the banjar which organises village festivals, marriage ceremonies and even cremations.

Throughout the island you'll see the open-sided meeting places known as *bale banjar* – they're nearly as common a sight as temples. Gamelan orchestras are organised at the banjar level and a glance in a bale banjar at any time might reveal a gamelan practice, a meeting going on, food for a feast being prepared, even a group of men simply getting their roosters together to raise their anger in preparation for the next round of cockfights.

One of the important elements of village government is the *subak*. Each individual rice field is known as a *sawah* and each farmer who owns even one sawah must be a member of the local *subak*. The rice fields must have a steady supply of water and it is the job of the subak to ensure that the water supply gets to everybody. It's said that the head of the local subak will often be the farmer whose rice fields are at the bottom of the hill, for he will make quite certain that the water gets all the way down to his fields, passing through everybody else's on the way!

ARTS & CRAFTS

The Balinese have no words for 'art' and 'artist' because traditionally, art has never been regarded as something to be treasured for its own sake. Prior to the tourist invasion art was just something you did – you painted or carved as a part of everyday life and what you produced went into temples or palaces or was used for festivals. Although res-pected, the painter or carver was not considered a member of some special elite; there was no cult of the artist as there is in the West, the artists' work was not signed and there were no galleries or craft shops.

It's a different story today, with thousands of galleries and craft shops in every possible crevice a tourist might trip into. Although much of Balinese art is churned out quickly for people who want a cheap souvenir, buried beneath the reproductions of reproductions there's still quite a lot of beautiful work to be found – if you dig deep enough.

Even the simplest activities are carried out with care, precision and artistic flair. Just glance at those little offering trays thrown down on the ground for the demons every morning – each one a throwaway work of art. Look at the temple offerings, the artistically stacked pyramids of fruit or other beautifully decorated foods. Look for the *lamaks*, long woven palm-leaf strips used as decorations, the stylised female figures known as *cili* and the intricately carved coconut-shell wall-hangings. At funerals you'll be amazed at the care and energy that goes into constructing huge funeral towers and exotic sarcophagi, all of which go up in flames.

There are, however, some traditional objects which are not only made to last, but are imbued with great spiritual significance. An example is the sacred kris, a knife which is thought to contain great spiritual force and thus require great care in manufacture and use. The *wayang kulit* shadow-puppet

Cockfights

Cockfights are a regular part of temple ceremonies – they're a convenient combination of excitement, sport, gambling and a blood sacrifice all rolled into one. Men keep fighting cocks as prized pets: carefully groomed and cared for, they are lovingly prepared for their brief moment of glory or defeat. On quiet afternoons the men will often meet in the banjars to compare their roosters, spar them against one another and line up the odds for the next big bout.

You'll often see the roosters by the roadside in their bell-shaped cane baskets – they're placed there to be entertained by passing activity. When the festivals take place the cocks are matched one against another, a lethally sharp metal spur tied to one leg and then, after being pushed against each other a few times to stir up the blood, they're released and the feathers fly. It's usually over in a flash – a slash of the spur and one rooster is down and dying. Occasionally a cowardly rooster turns and flees but in that case both roosters are put in a covered basket where they can avoid fighting. After the bout, the successful betters collect their pay-offs and the winning owner takes home the dead rooster for his cooking pot. ∎

BALI

figures cut from buffalo hide are also magical items since the plays enact the eternal battle between good and evil. The Balinese weave a variety of complex fabrics for ceremonial and other important uses, including *songket* cloth (silk cloth with gold or silver threads woven into it).

Architecture & Sculpture

Of all the Balinese arts it's said that architecture and stone sculpture have been the least affected by Western influence and the tourist boom, because they don't make convenient souvenirs. Traditionally, stone and wooden sculpture was used only for architectural decoration, particularly on temples, so architecture and sculpture are inextricably bound together.

Architecture A basic element of Balinese architecture is the *bale*, a rectangular, open-sided pavilion with a steeply pitched hip roof of palm thatch. A family compound will have a number of *bale* for eating, sleeping and working. The focus of a community is the *bale banjar*, a large pavilion for meeting, debate, gamelan practice etc. Large, modern buildings like restaurants and the lobby areas of new hotels are often modelled on the *bale* – they are airy, spacious and handsomely proportioned.

Like the other arts, architecture has traditionally served the religious life of Bali. Balinese houses, though often attractive places, have never been lavished with the architectural attention that is given to temples. Even Balinese palaces are modest compared with the more important temples. Temples are designed to set rules and formulas, with sculpture serving as an adjunct, a finishing touch to these design guidelines.

Sculpture In small or less important temples, the sculpture may be limited or even nonexistent, while in other temples – particularly some of the exuberantly detailed temples of north Bali – the sculpture may be almost overwhelming in its detail and intricacy. A temple gateway, for example, might be carved over every square cm, with a dimin-

ishing series of demon faces above it as protection. Even then it's not finished without a couple of stone statues to act as guardians.

Door guardians, of legendary figures like Arjuna or other protectors, flank the steps to the gateway. Above the main entrance to a temple, a kala's monstrous face often peers out, sometimes a number of times – its hands reach out beside its head to catch any evil spirits which try to sneak in. The ancient swastika symbol indicates good fortune and prosperity. Carved panels on the walls may show scenes of local significance or everyday life. The front of a *pura dalem* (temple of the dead) will often feature images of the *rangda* (witch) and sculptured panels may show the horrors that await evildoers in the afterlife.

Painting

The art form probably most influenced both by Western ideas and demand is painting. Traditional painting was very limited in style and subject matter, and was used primarily for temple decoration. The arrival of Western artists after WW I expanded painting beyond these limitations, introduced new subject matters and brought new materials for artists to work with. The best place to see examples of the various Balinese painting styles is in Ubud at the Puri Lukisan Museum and the Museum Neka.

Traditional Painting Balinese painting was strictly limited to three basic kinds: *langse*, *iders-iders* and calendars. Langse are large rectangular hangings used as decoration or curtains in palaces or temples. Iders-iders are scroll paintings hung along the eaves of temples. The calendars were usually astrological, showing auspicious days of each month.

Most of the paintings were narratives with mythological themes, illustrating stories from Hindu epics and literature – rather like a cartoon strip with a series of panels each telling a segment of the story. These paintings were always executed in the wayang style, the flat two-dimensional style imitative of the wayang kulit shows, the figures invariably shown in three-quarters view. Even the colours artists could use were strictly limited to a set list of shades (red, blue, brown, yellow and a light ochre for flesh).

In these narratives the same characters appeared in several different scenes, each depicting an episode from the story. The individual scenes were usually bordered by mountains, flames or ornamental walls. The deities, princes and heroes were identified by their opulent clothing, jewellery, elaborate headdresses and their graceful postures and gestures; and the devils and giants by their bulging eyes, canine teeth, bulbous noses and bulky bodies. Klungkung is still a centre for the traditional wayang style of painting and the painted ceiling of the Hall of Justice in Klungkung is a fine example.

Foreign Influences Under the influence of Walter Spies and Rudolf Bonnet, who settled in Bali in the 1930s, Balinese artists started painting single scenes instead of narrative tales, and using scenes from everyday life rather than romantic legends as their themes. More importantly, they started painting pictures purely as pictures – not as something to cover a space in a palace or temple. The idea of a painting being something you could do by itself (and for which there might be a market!) was wholly new.

In one way, however, the style remained unchanged – Balinese paintings are packed full; every spare millimetre is filled in. A forest scene will have leaves and flowers filling every corner, and a whole zoo of birds and other creatures. Other themes include idyllic rural scenes, energetic festivals or engagingly stylised animals and fish.

This new artistic enthusiasm was interrupted by WW II and by the political turmoil of the 1950s and 1960s. As the 1930s style degenerated into stale copying, a new style emerged in Ubud, with particular encouragement from the Dutch painter Aries Smit. His 'young artists', as they were known (they weren't necessarily young), picked up where those of the 1930s had left off,

painting Balinese rural scenes in brilliant technicolour.

Woodcarving

Like painting, woodcarving is no longer done simply for decoration or other symbolic purposes in temples and palaces, but is now created for its own sake. As with painting, it was influences from outside which inspired new subjects and styles, and some of the same Western artists who provided the stimulus.

Especially around Ubud, carvers started producing highly stylised and elongated figures, leaving the wood in its natural state rather than painting it, as was the traditional practice. Others carved delightful animal figures, some totally realistic and others wonderful caricatures, while other artists carved whole tree trunks into ghostly, intertwined 'totem poles' or curiously exaggerated and distorted figures.

MUSIC, DANCE & DRAMA

Music, dance and drama are all closely related in Bali. In fact, drama and dance are synonymous, though some 'dances' are more drama and less dance, and others more dance and less drama. Most dancers are not specialists, but ordinary people who dance in the evening or in their spare time. They learn the dances by long hours of practice, usually carefully following the movements of an expert.

There's little of the soaring leaps of classical ballet or the smooth flowing movements often found in Western dance. Balinese dance tends to be precise, jerky, shifting and jumpy, like the accompanying gamelan music, which has abrupt shifts of tempo, and dramatic changes between silence and crashing noise. There's virtually no contact in Balinese dancing – each dancer moves independently but every movement of wrist, hand and finger is important. Even facial expressions are carefully choreographed to convey the character of the dance.

Balinese dance is not a static art form – old dances fade out and new dances, or new versions of old dances, become popular.

BALI

The Oleg Tambulilingan, for example, was developed in the 1950s as a solo female dance, but later a male part was added and the dance now mimics the flirtations of two *tambulilingan* or bumblebees.

The Balinese like a blend of seriousness and slapstick and their dances show this. Basically, the dances are straightforward ripping yarns, where you cheer on the goodies and cringe back when the baddies appear. Some dances have a comic element, with clowns who counterbalance the staid, noble characters. The clowns often have to put across the story to the audience, since the noble characters may use the classical Javanese Kawi language while the clowns (usually servants of the noble characters) converse in everyday Balinese.

Dances are a regular part of almost every temple festival and Bali has no shortage of these. There are also dances virtually every night at all the tourist centres; admission to a first-class performance in Ubud costs around 5000 rp for foreigners. Some performances are offered as entertainment at a restaurant or hotel, often with a mixture of dances – a little Topeng, a taste of Legong

and some Baris to round it off. This is not a good way to see Balinese dance, and it's worth looking around for a better performance. The authenticity, quality and level of drama varies widely, but excellent dances can be seen, where the audience includes many appreciative Balinese. Some of the more common dances are:

The Gamelan

As in Sumatra and Java, Balinese music is based around the gamelan orchestra – for more details see the Java chapter. The whole gamelan orchestra is known as a *gong* – an old fashioned *gong gede* or a more modern *gong kebyar*. There are even more ancient forms of the gamelan such as the *gong selunding*, still occasionally played in Bali Aga villages like Tenganan.

Though the instruments used are much the same, Balinese gamelan is very different from the form you'll hear in Java. The Yogyakarta style, for example, is the most reserved, formal and probably the gentlest and most 'refined' of gamelans. Balinese gamelan often sounds like everyone going for it full pelt. Perhaps a more telling point

---

Balinese Dances

Kecak Probably the best known of the many Balinese dances, the Kecak is also unusual because it doesn't have a gamelan accompaniment. Instead, the background is provided by a chanting 'choir' of men who provide the 'chak-a-chak-a-chak' noise which distinguishes the dance. Originally this chanting group was known as the Kecak and they were part of a Sanghyang trance dance. Then in the 1930s the modern Kecak developed in Bona, a village near Gianyar, where the dance is still held regularly.

The Kecak tells the tale of the *Ramayana* (see the Java chapter for a rundown of the story) and the quest of Prince Rama to rescue his wife Sita after she had been kidnapped by Rawana, the King of Lanka. Rama is accompanied to Lanka by Sugriwa, the king of the monkeys, with his monkey army. Throughout the Kecak dance the circle of men, all bare-chested and wearing checked cloth around their waists, provide a nonstop accompaniment, rising to a crescendo as they play the monkey army and fight it out with Rawana and his cronies. The chanting is accompanied by the movements of the 'monkey army' whose members sway back and forth, raise their hands in unison, flutter their fingers and lean left and right, all with an eerily exciting coordination.

Barong & Rangda Like the Kecak, the Barong & Rangda or kris dance is a battle between good and evil. Barongs can take various forms but in this dance it takes the form of the Barong Keket, the most holy of the Barongs. The Barong Keket is a strange creature – half shaggy dog, half lion – and is played by two men in much the same way as a circus clown-horse. Its opponent is the rangda, or witch.

The barong personifies good and protects the village from the rangda, but is also a mischievious and fun-loving creature. It flounces into the temple courtyard, snaps its jaws at the gamelan, dances around and enjoys the acclaim of its supporters – a group of men with krises. Then the rangda makes her appearance, her long tongue lolling, her pendulous breasts wobbling, human entrails draped around her neck, fangs protruding from her mouth and sabre-like fingernails clawing the air.

Now the barong is no longer the clown, but the protector. The two duel with their magical powers and the barong's supporters draw their krises and rush in to attack the witch. The rangda puts them in a trance and the men try to stab themselves, but the barong also has great magical powers and casts a spell which stops the krises from harming the men. This is the most dramatic part of the dance – as the gamelan rings crazily the men rush back and forth, waving their krises around, all but foaming at the mouth, sometimes even rolling on the ground in a desperate attempt to stab themselves. Finally, the rangda retires defeated – good has won again. Good must always triumph over evil on Bali, and no matter how many times the spectators have seen the performance or how well they know the outcome, the battle itself remains all-important.

The end of the dance still leaves a large group of entranced Barong supporters to be brought back to the real world. This is usually done by sprinkling them with holy water, sanctified by dipping the Barong's beard in it.

Legong This is the most graceful of Balinese dances and, to sophisticated Balinese connoisseurs of dancing, the one of most interest. A Legong, as a Legong dancer is always known, is a girl, often as young as eight or nine years and rarely older than her early teens. Such importance is attached to the dance that even in old age a classic dancer will be remembered as a 'great Legong' even though her brief period of fame may have been 50 years ago.

There are various forms of the Legong but the Legong Kraton, or Legong of the palace, is the one most usually performed. Peliatan's famous dance troupe, which visitors to Ubud often get a chance to see, is particularly noted for its Legong. A performance involves just three dancers – the two Legongs and their 'attendant' known as the *condong*. The Legongs are identically dressed in tightly bound gold brocade. So tightly are they encased that it's something of a mystery how they manage to move with such agility and speed. Their faces are elaborately made up, their eyebrows plucked and repainted and their hair decorated with frangipanis.

Legong dancer

It's a very stylised and symbolic dance – if you didn't know the story it would be impossible to tell what was going on. The dance relates how a king takes a maiden, Rangkesari, captive. When Rangkesari's brother comes to release her he begs the king to let her free rather than go to war. The king refuses and on his way to the battle meets a bird bringing ill omens. He ignores the bird and continues on to meet Rangkesari's brother, who kills him. The dance, however, only relates the lead-up to the battle and ends with the bird's appearance. When the king leaves the stage he is going to the battle that will end in his death.

The dance starts with the condong dancing an introduction. The condong departs as the Legongs come on. The Legongs dance solo, in close identical formation, and even in mirror image when they dance a nose-to-nose love scene. They relate the king's sad departure from his queen, Rangkesari's request that he release her and the king's departure for the battle. Finally, the condong reappears with tiny golden wings as the bird of ill fortune and the dance comes to an end.

BALI

Baris The warrior dance known as the Baris is a male equivalent of the Legong in which femininity and grace give way to the energetic, warlike martial spirit. The solo Baris dancer has to convey the thoughts and emotions of a warrior preparing for action and then meeting an enemy in battle. The dancer must show his changing moods not only through his dancing, but also through facial expression. Chivalry, pride, anger, prowess and, finally, regret, all have to be there. It's said that the Baris is one of the most complex of the Balinese dances, requiring a dancer of great energy, skill and ability.

Ramayana The *Ramayana* is a familiar tale in Bali but the dance is a relatively recent addition to the Balinese repertoire. It tells much the same story of Rama and Sita as told in the Kecak but without the monkey ensemble and with a normal gamelan orchestra accompaniment. It's also embellished with many improvisations and comic additions. Rawana may be played as a classic bad guy, the monkey god Hanuman can be a comic clown, and camera-wielding tourists amongst the spectators may come in for some imitative ribbing.

Kebyar This is a male solo dance like the Baris, but with greater emphasis on the performer's individual abilities. Development of the modern Kebyar is credited in large part to the famous prewar dancer Mario. There are various forms of the dance, including the seated Kebyar Duduk where the 'dance' is done from the seated position and movements of the hands, arms and torso plus, of course, facial expressions, are all important. In the Kebyar Trompong the dancer actually joins the gamelan and plays an instrument called the *trompong* while still dancing.

Janger Both Covarrubias and Powell, in their between-the-wars books on Bali, comment on this strange new, almost un-Balinese, dance which appeared in the 1920s and 1930s. Today it is part of the standard repertoire and no longer looks so unusual. It has similarities to several other dances including the Sanghyang, where the relaxed chanting of the women is contrasted with the violent chak-a-chak-a-chak of the men. In the Janger dance, formations of 12 young women and 12 young men perform a sitting dance where the gentle swaying and chanting of the women is contrasted with the violently choreographed movements and loud shouts of the men.

Topeng The word Topeng means 'pressed against the face', as with a mask. In this mask dance, the dancers have to imitate the character their mask indicates they are playing. The Topeng Tua, for example, is a classic solo dance where the mask is that of an old man and requires the performer to dance like a creaky old gentleman. In other dances there may be a small troupe who dance various characters and types. A full collection of Topeng masks may number 30 or 40.

Another mask dance is the Jauk, but this is strictly a solo performance. The dancer plays an evil demon, his mask an eerie face with bulging eyes, fixed smile and long, wavering fingernails. Mask dances require great expertise because the character's thoughts and meanings cannot be conveyed through the dancer's facial expressions, so the character of the unpleasant, frenetic, fast-moving demon has to be conveyed entirely through the dance.

Pendet This is an everyday dance of the temples, a small procedure gone through before making temple offerings which doesn't require arduous training and practice. You may often see the Pendet being danced by women bringing offerings to a temple for a festival, but it is also sometimes danced as an introduction and a closing for other dance performances.

Sanghyang Dances The Sanghyang trance dances originally developed as a means of driving out evil spirits from a village. The Sanghyang is a divine spirit which temporarily inhabits an entranced dancer.

The Sanghyang Dedari is performed by two girls who dance a dream-like version of the Legong. The dancers are said to be untrained in the intricate pattern of the dance and, furthermore, they dance in perfect harmony but with their eyes firmly shut. A female choir and a male Kecak choir provide a background chant but when the chant stops the dancers slump to the ground in a faint. Two women bring them round and at the finish a priest blesses them with holy water and brings them out of the trance. The modern Kecak dance developed from the Sanghyang.

In the Sanghyang Jaran a boy in a trance dances round and through a fire of coconut husks riding a coconut-palm hobby horse – it's labelled the 'fire dance' for the benefit of tourists. Once again the priest must be on hand to break the trance at the close of the dance. ■

is that Javanese gamelan music is rarely heard except at special performances, whereas in Bali you seem to hear gamelans playing all the time everywhere you go.

RELIGION

The Balinese are nominally Hindus but Balinese Hinduism is half a world away from that of India. When the Majapahits evacuated to Bali they took with them their religion and its rituals as well as their art, literature, music and culture. The Balinese already had strong religious beliefs and an active cultural life, and the new influences were simply overlaid on existing practices – hence the peculiar Balinese interpretation of Hinduism.

The Balinese worship the same gods as the Hindus of India – the trinity of Brahma, Shiva and Vishnu – but they also have a supreme god, Sanghyang Widhi. Unlike in India, the trinity is never seen – a vacant shrine or empty throne tells all. Nor is Sanghyang Widi often worshipped, though villagers may pray to him when they have settled new land and are about to build a new village. Other Hindu gods such as Ganesh, Shiva's elephant-headed son, may occasionally appear, but a great many purely Balinese gods, spirits and entities have far more relevance in everyday life.

The Balinese believe that spirits are everywhere, an indication that animism is the basis of much of their religion. Good spirits dwell in the mountains and bring prosperity to the people, while giants and demons lurk beneath the sea and bad spirits haunt the woods and desolate beaches. The people live between these two opposites and their rituals strive to maintain this middle ground. Offerings are carefully put out every morning to pay homage to the good spirits and nonchalantly placed on the ground to placate the bad ones. You can't get away from religion in Bali – there are temples in every village, shrines in every field and offerings made at every corner. Although it enforces a high degree of conformity it is not a fatalistic religion – there are rules and rituals to placate

or drive out the bad spirits, and ensure the favour of the gods and the good spirits.

Temples

The word for temple in Bali is *pura*, which is a Sanskrit word literally meaning a space surrounded by a wall. As in so much of Balinese religion the temples, although nominally Hindu, owe much to the pre-Majapahit era. Their alignment towards the mountains *(kaja)*, the sea *(kelod)* or the sunrise *(kangin)* is in deference to spirits which are more animist than Hindu.

There are an amazing number of temples, with almost every village having at least three. The most important is the *pura puseh* or 'temple of origin', which is dedicated to the village founders and is located at the kaja end of the village. In the middle of the village is the *pura desa* for the spirits which protect the village community in its day-to-day life. At the kelod end of the village is the *pura dalem* or temple of the dead. The graveyard is also located here and the temple will often include representations of Durga, the terrible incarnation of Shiva's wife. Apart from these three basic temple types, others include the temples dedicated to the spirits of irrigated agriculture.

Families worship their ancestors in family temples, clans in clan temples and the whole village in the pura puseh. Certain special temples in Bali are of such importance that they are deemed to be owned by the whole island rather than by individual villages. These 'world sanctuaries' include Pura Besakih on the slopes of Gunung Agung.

The simple shrines or thrones you see, for example in rice fields or next to sacred old trees, are not real temples as they are not walled. You'll find these shrines in all sorts of places, often overlooking crossroads, intersections or dangerous curves in the road, to protect road users.

Temple Design Balinese temples usually consist of a series of courtyards entered from the sea side. In a large temple the outer gateway will generally be a *candi bentar*, modelled on the old Hindu temples of Java.

These gateways resemble a tower cut in halves and moved apart, hence the name 'split gate'. The first courtyard is used for less important ceremonies, and will have a number of bale for preparing food and holding meetings. There will also be a *kulkul* (alarm drum) tower in this outer courtyard and perhaps a banyan or frangipani tree.

The innermost and holiest courtyard (small temples may have just two courts) is entered by another candi-like gateway. A passage through the middle of it symbolises the holy mountain through which you must pass to enter the inner court. This gateway will be flanked by statues of guardian figures or by small protective shrines.

In the inner court there will usually be two rows of shrines, the most important on the mountain side and the lesser on the sunrise side. These shrines vary in number and design from temple to temple, although there are detailed rules to cover all of them. In the major temples the shrines will include multi-roofed thatched pagodas known as *meru*. The number of roofs are, apart from some rare exceptions, always odd and the holiest meru will have 11 roofs. The inner court may also contain simple little thrones for local and less important gods to use.

Behaviour There are a couple of rules for visiting temples. Except on rare occasions anyone can enter, anytime, but you are expected to be politely dressed. You should always wear a temple scarf – a sash tied loosely around your waist. Many of the larger, more touristed temples rent them to visitors for a few hundred rupiah. You can buy one yourself quite cheaply, and it's a nice thing to have when visiting temples where sashes are not available for rent. You might save on the cost of renting a sash, but you should regard this as part of a donation.

Priests should be shown respect, particularly at festivals. They're the most important people and should, therefore, be on the highest plane. Don't put yourself higher than them by climbing up on a wall to take photographs. There will usually be a sign outside temple entrances asking you to be well dressed, to wear a temple scarf, be respectful and also requesting that women not enter the temple during their periods.

Nearly every temple (or other site of interest to tourists) will levy an entry charge or ask for a donation from foreigners – any non-Balinese is a foreigner. Usually this is around 500 rp – occasionally less, occasionally more. If there is no fixed charge and a donation is requested, 500 rp is a suitable amount, though the donation book may indicate that people have paid thousands – zeros are sometimes added.

Temple Festivals For much of the year Balinese temples are deserted, but on holy days the deities and ancestral spirits descend from heaven to visit their devotees and the temples come alive with days of frenetic activity and nights of drama and dance. Temple festivals come at least once every Balinese year – 210 days. Because most villages have at least three temples, you're assured of at least five or six annual festivals in every village. The full moon periods around the end of September to beginning of October or early to mid-April are often times of important festivals. One such festival is the Galungan, which takes place throughout the island. During this 10-day period all the gods, including the supreme deity, Sanghyang Widi, come down to earth for the festivities.

Temple festivals are as much a social occasion as a religious one. Cockfights (where two cocks fight with sharp barbs attached to their legs) are a regular part of temple ceremonies: a combination of excitement, sport and illicit gambling. They also provide a blood sacrifice to dissuade evil spirits from interfering with the religious ceremonies that follow. While the men slaughter their prized pets, the women bring beautifully arranged offerings of foods, fruit and flowers artistically piled in huge pyramids, which they carry on their heads to the temple. Outside, warungs offer food for sale, stalls are set up to sell toys, trinkets and batik and there are sideshows with card games, gambling, buskers, mystic healers, music and dancing, while the gamelan orchestra plays on in the outer courtyard.

Inside, the *pemangkus* (temple priests) suggest to the gods that they should come down and enjoy the goings on. The small thrones in the temple shrines are symbolic seats for the gods to occupy during festivals, although sometimes small images called *pratimas* are placed in the thrones to represent them. At some festivals the images and thrones of the deities are taken out of the temple and ceremonially carried down to the sea (or to a suitable expanse of water) for a ceremonial bath. Inside the temple the proceedings take on a more formal, mystical tone as the pemangkus continue to chant their songs of praise before shrines clouded by smoking incense. The women dance the stately pendet, in itself an offering to the gods through the beauty of their motions.

As dawn approaches, the entertainment and ceremonies wind down and the women dance a final pendet, a farewell to the deities. The pemangkus politely suggest to the gods that it's time they made their way back to heaven, and the people make their own weary way back to their homes.

Funerals

A Balinese funeral is an amazing, colourful, noisy and exciting event – a stark contrast to the solemn ceremony practised in the West. Basically it is a happy occasion, as it represents the destruction of the body and the release of the soul so that it can be united with the supreme god.

The body is carried to the cremation ground in a high multi-tiered tower made of bamboo, paper, string, tinsel, silk, cloth, mirrors, flowers and anything else bright and colourful. Carried on the shoulders of a group of men, the tower represents the cosmos and the base, in the shape of a turtle entwined by two snakes, symbolises the foundation of the world. On the base is an open platform where the body is placed – in the space between heaven and earth. The size of the group carrying the body and the number of tiers on the tower varies according to the caste of the deceased.

On the way to the cremation ground the tower is shaken and run around in circles to disorientate the spirit of the deceased so that it cannot find its way home. A gamelan sprints along behind, providing a suitably exciting musical accompaniment and almost trampling the camera-toting tourists. (Tourists are accepted in the procession because they add to the noise and confusion, further disorienting the spirits.) At the cremation ground the body is transferred to a funeral sarcophagus and the whole lot – funeral tower, sarcophagus and body – goes up in flames. Finally, the colourful procession heads to the sea (or a nearby river if the sea is too far away) to scatter the ashes.

LANGUAGE

Balinese language, as distinct from Indonesian, the national language, reflects caste distinctions. Traditionally there are five forms of the language, with the usage governed by the social relationship between the two people having a conversation. Modern usage is described in terms of three forms: Low Balinese (Ia) is used between intimates, between equals and when talking to inferiors; Polite or Middle Balinese (Ipun) is used when speaking about superiors, or when addressing superiors or strangers, mainly when one wishes to be very polite but doesn't want to emphasise caste differences; and High Balinese (Ida) is used when talking to superiors, particularly in the context of religious ceremonies.

FOREIGN CONSULATES IN BALI

The Australian Consulate, in the Renon district of Denpasar, will also help citizens of other Commonwealth countries while they're in Bali, including those from Canada, New Zealand, Papua New Guinea and the UK. Japan also has a full consulate in Denpasar, but all the others listed below are consular agents and may offer only a limited range of services.

Australia
    Jalan Prof Mochammad Yamin 51, Renon, Denpasar; PO Box 243 (☎ 235092/3; fax 231990)
France
    Jalan Raya Sesetan 46D, Banjar Pesanggaran, Denpasar; (☎ & fax 233555)
Germany
    Jalan Pantai Karang 17, Sanur; PO Box 3100 Denpasar (☎ 288535; fax 288826)
Italy
    Jalan Cemara, Banjar Semawang, Sanur Kauh; PO Box 158 Denpasar (☎ 288996; fax 287642)
Japan
    Jalan Mochammad Yamin 9, Renon, Denpasar (☎ 234808; fax 231308)

Netherlands
  Jalan Iman Bonjol 599, Kuta; PO Box 337
  (☎ 751517; fax 752777)
Norway & Denmark
  Jalan Jaya Giri VIII/10, Renon, Denpasar; PO
  Box 188 Denpasar (☎ 235098; fax 234834)
Sweden & Finland
  Segara Village Hotel, Jalan Segara Ayu, Sanur
  (☎ 288407/8)
Switzerland
  Swiss Restaurant, Jalan Pura Bagus Taruna,
  Legian (☎ 751735; fax 754457)
USA
  Jalan Segara Ayu 5, Sanur (☎ 288478; fax
  287760)

BOOKS

There are many publications about Bali. The
classic work is *Island of Bali* (Oxford paperback) by Mexican artist Miguel Covarrubias.
First published in 1937, it is still available as
an Oxford in Asia paperback. Despite many
changes, much of Bali is still as Covarrubias
describes it, and few people have come to
grips with the island as well as Covarrubias.

Colin McPhee's *A House in Bali* is a
lyrical account of a musician's lengthy stay
in Bali to study gamelan music. *The Last
Paradise* by Hickman Powell and *A Tale
from Bali* by Vicki Baum also date from that
heady period in the 1930s when so many
Westerners 'discovered' Bali. All three are
available as Oxford paperbacks. K'Tut
Tantri's *Revolt in Paradise* (available in an
Indonesian paperback) again starts in the
1930s but this Western woman who took a
Balinese name remained in Indonesia
through the war and during part of the subsequent struggle for independence from the
Dutch.

Our Hotel in Bali by Louis G Koke
(January Books, Wellingtom, NZ) tells of the
original Kuta Beach Hotel which was established by Americans Robert and Louis Koke
during the 1930s and run by them until WW
II spread to the Pacific. From the same publisher comes Hugh Mabbett's *The Balinese*,
an interesting collection of anecdotes, obser-
vations and impressions, and *In Praise of
Kuta*, a sympathetic account of that much
maligned beach resort.

For a rundown on Balinese arts and

culture look for the huge and expensive *The
Art & Culture of Bali* by Urs Ramseyer
(Oxford University Press). From the same
publisher comes *Dance & Drama In Bali* by
Beryl de Zoete and Walter Spies. Originally
published back in 1938, this book draws
from Walter Spies' deep appreciation and
understanding of Bali's arts and culture. An
economical and handy introduction to Balinese painting is *Different Styles of Painting in
Bali* published by the Neka Gallery in Ubud
– it covers the various schools of painting
and also has short biographies of well-
known artists, including many of the foreign
artists who have worked in Bali. *Balinese
Paintings* by A A M Djelantik (Oxford University Press) is a concise and handy overview
of the field.

Periplus Editions publish a range of titles
on Balinese food, fruit, flowers, textiles etc,
which will appeal to those with specific
interests. Bookshops in Kuta, Sanur and
Ubud have a wide range of English-language
books, particularly on Indonesia. Big hotels,
some supermarkets and various tourist shops
and galleries have more limited selections,
and there are numerous places selling
second-hand books.

GETTING THERE & AWAY

Bali has direct international flights from a
number of countries, and more which
connect via other Indonesian airports. Frequent domestic flights go to Java in the west,
the island of Lombok in the east and to many
other islands of Indonesia. Regular ferries go
to/from Java and Lombok, which carry vehicles as well as passengers, and there are also
fast boat services between Bali and Lombok.

Air

Bali's Denpasar airport is actually a few km
to the south, just beyond Kuta Beach. Officially the airport is named Ngurah Rai, after
a hero of the struggle for independence from
the Dutch.

The airport has a hotel-booking counter,
which covers only the more expensive
places. There's also a tourist information
counter with some useful brochures and

helpful staff, a left-luggage room and a couple of moneychanging desks.

On departure there's an expensive duty-free shop and some souvenir shops at the airport – they only accept foreign currency. The departure lounge cafeteria takes rupiah, but it's much more expensive than the shop outside. You can change excess rupiah back into hard currency at the bank counter by the check-in desks, but keep 20,000 rp for departure tax on international flights. The 7700 rp domestic departure tax is usually included in the ticket price.

International The number of direct international flights to Bali has increased in recent years. See the introductory Getting There & Away chapter for more details.

If you're flying out of Bali, reconfirm your bookings at least 72 hours before departure. Most travel agents in the main tourist areas can do this, but make sure you get the piece of computer printout that shows you are actually confirmed on the flight. There are Garuda offices in Denpasar, Kuta and Sanur, and most of the other airlines have offices in the Hotel Bali Beach in Sanur.

Domestic Garuda, Merpati, Sempati and Bouraq have flights between Denpasar and other Indonesian airports. Merpati is combined with Garuda, and there are offices in Kuta, Sanur and Denpasar. The Bouraq office is in Denpasar and Sempati is in Sanur at the Bali Beach Hotel. Denpasar is a major travel hub with direct flights to Bima, Dili, Jakarta, Kupang, Mataram, Maumere, Surabaya, Ujung Pandang and Waingapu. With connections you can fly to almost anywhere in Indonesia from Denpasar.

Sea
To/From Java The ferry that shuttles back and forth across the narrow strait between Gilimanuk (Bali) and Ketapang (Java) takes only 15 minutes to cross one way. Costs are 550 rp for an adult, 450 rp for a child. You can take a car across for about 7400 rp (the cost depends on the size of the car), a motorbike for 1800 rp and a bicycle for 950 rp. On the Java side the ferry terminus is at Ketapang, on the outskirts of Banyuwangi. The main bus terminal is right next to the ferry terminal for buses to most other parts of Java, and the train terminal is just a few hundred metres north.

You can also get direct buses to Denpasar from the main cities on Java, which include the ferry trip and sometimes a meal at a rest stop along the way. Generally you have to book a day or more in advance and air-con and non-air-con buses are available. Check the arrival times to avoid reaching your destination at an absurdly early, pre-dawn hour.

Direct buses from Denpasar depart from Ubung terminal to Surabaya (from 18,000 rp) or beyond. The straight-through buses will drop you in Probolinggo if you want to climb Gunung Bromo. Ubung terminal is the cheapest place to buy tickets but you can also buy them from agents at Kuta Beach and elsewhere – they can usually arrange transport to Ubung for about 5000 rp extra.

Direct bus services also go between Java and Singaraja, on Bali's north coast; Singaraja to Surabaya costs around 20,000 rp. If the times aren't convenient, get a local bus to Gilimanuk and take the ferry from there. From the main tourist centres in Java, such as Yogyakarta, a few buses also go to Lovina/Singaraja and on to Padangbai.

There are also bus and ferry services connecting with trains at Ketapang in Java; tickets are available from the railways office in Denpasar or from agents in Kuta. Combined tickets include the bus to Gilimanuk, the ferry crossing to Java, another bus for the ½ km to the railway station and the train from there. The through buses generally provide a better, more convenient service than the trains.

To/From Lombok There are ferries every two hours between Padangbai (Bali) and Lembar (Lombok) at 6, 8, and 10 am, noon, 2, 4, 6 and 8 pm, though they may leave later or earlier than these scheduled departure times. Departures from Lembar to Padangbai are scheduled at the same times. Ekonomi costs around 4800 rp (children 2500 rp), 1st class

BALI

8700 rp (children 4700 rp). You can take a bicycle (800 rp) or motorbike (5300 rp).

Tourist shuttle buses (see the following Getting Around section) make direct connections between the main tourist centres on Bali and Lombok. From Kuta or Sanur on Bali to Mataram or Senggigi on Lombok costs 20,000 rp, including the ferry.

The *Mabua Express* is a luxury jet-powered catamaran, providing a fast boat service between Lembar Harbour on Lombok and Benoa Port on Bali. It leaves from Benoa Port at 8.30 am and 2.30 pm, and leaves from Lembar at 11.30 am and 5 pm, and takes about two hours. It costs US$17.50 for 'Emerald Class' and US$25 for 'Diamond Class'; the latter includes transfer from the port of arrival, and drinks and a snack on the boat. For details, telephone their office in Bali (☎ 0361 72370, 72521) or Lombok (☎ 0364 25895, 37224).

Another fast boat service operates between Padangbai and western Lombok (20,000 rp), but is not always reliable and it may not operate throughout the year. It's supposed to take two hours, but sometimes takes much longer. Phone for the latest information (☎ 0361 34428 in Padangbai, 0364 93045 ext 339 on Lombok).

To/From Nusa Tenggara The national shipping line, Pelni, has passenger ships doing regular loops through the islands of Indonesia, typically calling at Benoa once a fortnight. The exact dates and routes can change, so inquire well in advance. The Pelni office in Bali is at Jalan Pelabuhan, Benoa (☎ 238962; fax 228962). The KM *Kelimutu* and KM *Tatamailau* stop in Benoa on their way out through Nusa Tenggara.

GETTING AROUND

Bali is a small island with good roads and regular, inexpensive public transport. Traffic is heavy from Denpasar south to Kuta and Sanur, east about as far as Klungkung and west as far as Tabanan. Over the rest of the island, the roads are remarkably uncrowded. If you rent your own vehicle it's easy to find your way around – roads are well signposted

and maps are readily available. Off the main routes, most roads are surfaced, but often very potholed.

To/From the Airport

The Ngurah Rai Airport is just south of Kuta Beach. Outside is a taxi counter where you pay for your taxi in advance. Fares from the airport are:

Destination	Fare
Kuta Beach (to Jalan Bakung Sari)	4500 rp
Kuta-Legian (to Jalan Padma)	6500 rp
Legian (beyond Jalan Padma)	9000 rp
Denpasar	9000 rp
Sanur	12,000 rp
Nusa Dua	12,000 rp
Oberoi Hotel (beyond Legian)	10,000 rp
Ubud	34,000 rp

The impecunious should walk across the airport car park and continue a couple of hundred metres to the airport road where there's a public bemo to Denpasar's Tegal terminal via Kuta. You could walk all the way to Kuta – it's only a few km, on the Tuban road or along the beach.

Bemo

Denpasar is the transport hub of Bali and has bus/bemo terminals for the various destinations – see the Denpasar section later in this chapter for details. Unfortunately, travel in southern Bali often requires you to travel via one or more of the Denpasar terminals, and this can make for an inconvenient and time-consuming trip.

The fare between main towns is usually posted at the terminals and you should get the right price as the operators will be competing for your business. On the longer routes the vehicle may be a full sized bus. On shorter routes the vehicle may be a minibus or a small truck with bench seats which stops anywhere along its route. Bali bemos are notorious for overcharging, with visitors often being charged the *harga turis* (tourist price) – ask a Balinese the correct fare before embarking on a journey. Otherwise try to see what the other passengers pay, or make your best estimate of the correct fare, and offer the exact amount when you get off.

You can charter a whole vehicle for a trip, which may be more convenient, and between a few people not much more expensive than the standard fare. You can also charter bemos by the day, from around 40,000 rp depending on the distance; the price includes the driver and petrol. In tourist areas you can only charter vehicles with yellow plates; regular bemos are only licenced to work fixed routes. In non-tourist areas this doesn't seem to be enforced, and bemo charter is cheaper but you have to pay for petrol and buy food for the driver.

Beware of pickpockets on bemos – they often have an accomplice to distract you, or use a package to hide the activity.

Tourist Shuttle Bus

As well as the public buses and bemos, there are a growing number of shuttle bus services between various tourist centres such as Kuta, Sanur, Candidasa, Kintamani and Lovina – look for the advertisements outside tour and travel agencies. There are also connections to the ports of Gilimanuk, Padangbai and Benoa, and you can book direct-tickets to destinations on Java, Lombok and Sumbawa. They are more expensive than the bemos, but much quicker and more convenient. Usually you have to book the day before. The Perama company seems to have the most comprehensive service, but there are others. Make sure that the bus is going direct to your destination and not by some roundabout route. If they promise to deliver you to a specific hotel, have it written on your ticket.

Taxi

Taxis are becoming more common in Denpasar and some tourist areas. They're blue and yellow with meters and air-con. The fare is 800 rp for the first km, then 500 rp a km. They're a lot less hassle than haggling with bemo jockeys and charter minibus drivers. You can always find them at the airport, but taxis can be unpopular in areas where charter operators are trying to hustle tourist business

at rip-off rates. Taxis probably won't stop on Jalan Legian or near Bemo Corner in Kuta. Don't get in a taxi if the driver says the meter isn't working – it may fix itself immediately, but if not, get another taxi.

Car Rental

Car rental is becoming very common. The usual vehicle is a small Suzuki jeep (Jimny), but for more than two adults, a Kijang minibus will be more comfortable. Typical costs for a Suzuki are around 35,000 to 40,000 rp a day including insurance and unlimited km; a Kijang costs from around 55,000 rp per day. It's substantially cheaper by the week. You can also find regular cars, but they cost more and are not as well suited to steep, rough, winding roads. Just look around for 'car for rent' signs. You need to have an international driving permit to legally drive a car.

Motorbike Rental

Motorbikes are a popular way to get around Bali, but can be dangerous. Most rental motorbikes are between 90 and 125 cc, with 100 cc the usual size. Rental charges vary with the bike, the period of hire and demand. The longer the hire period the lower the rate; the bigger or newer the bike the higher the rate. Typically you can expect to pay from around 9000 to 12,000 rp a day. This incudes a flimsy helmet which is compulsory, and provides protection against sunburn but not much else.

There are a few places around Kuta which specialise in bike hire, but it's often just a travel agent, restaurant, losmen or shop with a sign saying 'motorbike for rent'. Kuta is the main bike-hire place but you'll have no trouble finding a motorbike to rent in Ubud, Sanur, Candidasa or Lovina. Check the bike over before riding off – some are very poorly maintained.

There's a scattering of petrol stations around Bali but they often seem to be out of petrol, out of electricity or out on a holiday. In that case look for the little roadside fuel shops where you fill up with a plastic jug and a funnel. They often have a hand-painted sign saying 'Premium'.

Motorbike Licence If you've got an international driving permit endorsed for motorbikes, you've got no problems. If not, you'll have to get a local licence, which is easy to get but time-consuming. Your bike owner will take you to Denpasar, stopping to be photographed on the way. You're fingerprinted, given a written test (20 multiple-choice questions; the owner will make sure you know the answers) and then comes the hard part. After a friendly send off from the police examiner, you ride a short slalom and do a figure eight round some cones, and if you don't put your feet down, fall off or bump into anything you'll pass. Eventually everyone passes and is judged fit to be unleashed on Bali's roads. It costs 50,000 rp and the whole process takes about four hours. Driving without a licence can get you a 2,000,000 rp fine.

Motorbike Registration & Insurance Apart from your licence you must also carry the bike's registration paper with you – make sure the bike's owner gives it to you before you ride off. Insurance is compulsory, but provides only limited cover and is usually quite expensive. Read the small print on your own travel insurance policy as you may find you're not covered for motorbike accidents unless you have a home motorbike licence, not just a Balinese one.

Bicycle
In the main tourist areas it is quite easy to rent a pushbike by the hour or the day, and it's a good way to get around locally. Mostly they're 10-speed mountain bikes, and asking prices start around 8000 rp per day for one in reasonable condition. You should be able to bargain the price down to about 4000 rp per day for a few days or longer. Check the bike carefully – many are in bad condition and few are perfect.

Touring the island by bicycle is quite popular and a great way to see Bali. If you want to try it, it's probably best to bring your own bike with you; airlines will generally carry a bike as part of your 20 kg baggage allowance. Otherwise be prepared to spend some time looking for a good machine to rent, and/or some effort making it suitable for long-distance touring. Good brakes, seat, tyres and a lock are essential; bells, lights and luggage racks are desirable. You can use short bemo trips to scale the central mountains (the bike goes on the roof, and costs the same as a passenger) you can accomplish a beautiful, 200-km circle trip of Bali, level or downhill almost the whole way. Once you're out of the congested southern region traffic is relatively light and the bumpy roads are no great problem if you invest in a good, padded seat.

Bicycles are used extensively by the Balinese and even the smallest village has some semblance of a bike shop. Some shops will allow you to borrow tools to work on your own bike. The best shops for extensive repairs are in Denpasar.

A 200-km Bicycle Tour This route is designed to take in the greatest number of points of interest with the minimum use of motorised transport and the maximum amount of level or downhill roads. For convenience the tour is divided into six days of actual riding in a clockwise direction, which takes advantage of evening stops where there are convenient losmen.

Day 1 – Kuta to Bedugul (57 km) The first 37 km is level cycling, but from the village of Luwus it's uphill so you can catch a bemo – on a good bicycle even this section is quite manageable. Estimated riding time is seven hours.

Day 2 – Bedugul to Singaraja (30 km) Estimated riding time is three hours, a steep climb then downhill most of the way. You can detour to the Lovina beaches.

Day 3 – Singaraja to Penelokan (60 km) The 24 km from the coast up to Penulisan is very steep, so a bemo is recommended. The first 10 km and the final 10 km are fine. Detour down to Lake Batur and Toya Bunkah to climb Gunung Batur.

Day 4 – Penelokan to Klungkung via Rendang (31 km) You can detour to Besakih by bemo, but the direct ride is only about four hours. An alternative would be via Tampaksiring to Ubud.

Day 5 – Klungkung to Denpasar (40 km) Estimated riding time is six hours. This road has heavy traffic.

Day 6 – Denpasar to Kuta If you go via Sanur and Benoa this is a 24-km ride and estimated riding time is five hours. Again there are some stretches of heavy traffic on this run.

Organised Tours

There are countless tours organised from the main tourist areas, and they can be booked through the many travel agencies or through your hotel. Day and half-day tours are offered to all of the tourist attractions on Bali, though they vary widely in price and quality. Some are nothing more than shop crawls, carting you from one warehouse to another with a brief pause at a temple or an over-priced restaurant. Check the itinerary carefully and compare a few offerings.

A good tour will let you see a variety of hard-to-reach places in a short time. A good day trip might take in silver workshops at Celuk, a hand-weaving factory in Gianyar, the Kerta Ghosa at Klungkung, the 'mother temple' of Besakih, the 'bat cave' of Goa Lawah and a traditional salt-making operation, with some superb rice-field scenery along the way. An excursion to Bona village to see the Kecak dance, the Sanghyang Dedari and the Sanghyang Jaran (fire) dance could make a memorable evening tour. Prices start at around 20,000 rp for a full day trip.

There are also specialist operators, with scuba diving, white-water rafting, pony trekking, cycling, sailing and surfing tours.

Tours to Other Islands Tours also go to Mt Bromo in East Java and as far as Yogyakarta, including all accommodation, transport and entry charges. Others take in the main sights on Lombok, and tours to Komodo or Sulawesi are also available. Generally these seem expensive for what they offer. For example: US$125 for a two-day, one-night trip to climb Mt Bromo; US$500 for a three-day, two-night trip to Flores, Komodo and Rinca. It would be much better value to organise your own transport to the area you're interested in, and arrange any sightseeing trips locally.

Denpasar

The capital of Bali, with a population of around 300,000, Denpasar has been the focus of a lot of the growth and wealth in Bali over the last 15 or 20 years. It has an interesting museum, an arts centre and lots of shops. Denpasar means 'next to the market', and the main market (called Pasar Badung) is said to be the biggest and busiest in Bali. The city, sometimes referred to as Badung, is the capital of the Badung district which incorporates most of the tourist areas of southern Bali and the Bukit peninsula. Denpasar still has some tree-lined streets and pleasant gardens, but the traffic, noise and pollution make it a difficult place to enjoy.

Many of Denpasar's residents are descended from immigrant groups such as Bugis mercenaries and Chinese, Arab and Indian traders. More recent immigrants have been attracted by the wealth in Denpasar, including Javanese civil servants, tradespeople and workers, and Balinese from all over the island. They give the city a cosmopolitan air, and it is increasingly a Java-oriented modern Indonesian city rather than a parochial Balinese capital. As the city grows it is engulfing the surrounding villages, but their banjars and village life continue amid the urbanisation. The recent immigrants tend to occupy detached houses outside the family compounds, and may eventually supplant the traditional communal way of life.

If you're one of those who feel that Bali is overcrowded with tourists, you'll find that tourists are vastly outnumbered in Denpasar – it mightn't be a tropical paradise, but it's as much a part of 'the real Bali' as the rice fields and temples.

Orientation & Information

The main street of Denpasar, Jalan Gajah Mada, is called Jalan Gunung Agung where it enters the west side of town. It then changes to Jalan Wahidin, then Gajah Mada in the middle of town, then Jalan Surapati,

BALI

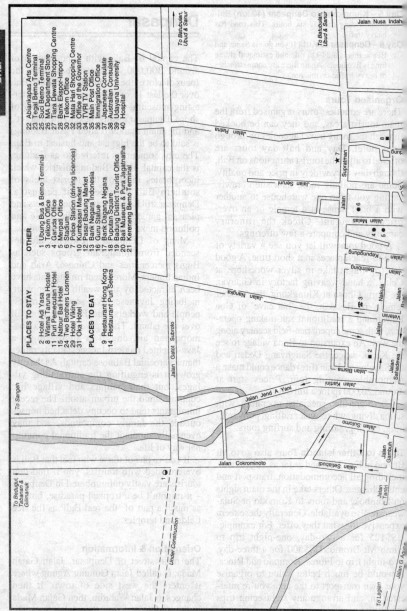

PLACES TO STAY

2 Hotel Adi Yasa
8 Wisma Taruna Hostel
11 Puri Pemecutan Hotel
15 Natour Bali Hotel
24 Two Brothers Losmen
26 Hotel Viking
31 Oka Hotel

PLACES TO EAT

9 Restaurant Hong Kong
14 Restaurant Puri Selera

OTHER

1 Ubung Bus & Bemo Terminal
3 Telkom Office
4 Garuda Office
5 Merpati Office
6 Stadium
7 Kereneng Station (driving licences)
10 Kumbasari Market
12 Pasar Badung Market
13 Bank Negara Indonesia
16 Guru Statue
17 Bank Dagang Negara
18 Puputan Square
19 Badung District Tourist Office
20 Bali Museum & Pura Jagatnatha
21 Kereneng Bemo Terminal
22 Abiankapas Arts Centre
23 Tegal Bemo Terminal
25 Suci Bemo Terminal
27 MA Department Store
28 Tiara Dewata Shopping Centre
29 Bank Ekspor-Impor
30 Telkom Office
32 Mata Hari Shopping Centre
34 Office of the Governor
35 TVRI TV Station
36 Main Post Office
37 Immigration Office
38 Japanese Consulate
38 Australian Consulate
39 Udayana University
40 Hospital

To Batubulan, Ubud & Sanur

Jalan Nusa Indah

Jalan Ratna

Jalan Supratman

Jalan Senur

Jalan Melati

Jalan Kapundung

Jalan Belimbing

Jalan Nangka

Jalan Veteran

Jalan Nakula

Jalan Sahadewa

Jalan Bisma

Jalan Kartini

Jalan Jend A Yani

Jalan Sulomo

Jalan Gumbuh

Jalan Cokrominoto

Jalan Seladodi

Jalan Tantri

Jalan G Agung

Jalan Gatot Subroto

To Sangeh

To Beduqul, Tabanan & Gilimanuk

To Legian

Under Construction

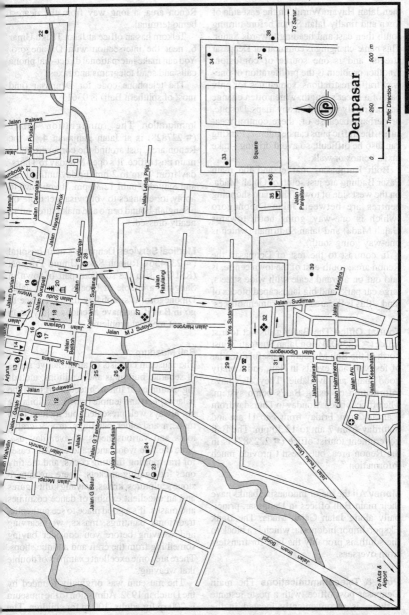

Denpasar

To Sanur

To Kuta &
Airport

Square

Traffic Direction

0   250   500 m

BALI

then Jalan Hayam Wuruk on the east side of town and finally Jalan Sanur before turning south then east and heading towards Sanur. This name-changing is common for Denpasar streets, and is one source of confusion. Another problem is the proliferation of one-way traffic restrictions, sometimes for only part of a street's length, which often change and are rarely marked on any maps. Despite, or perhaps because of, these control measures, the traffic jams can be intense. Parking can also be difficult, so avoid driving – take taxis, bemos or walk.

Both Kumbasari market and the main Pasar Badung are just south of Gajah Mada, on the west side of town. The main shopping centres are between Jalan Diponegoro (which is one-way, going north towards Gajah Mada) and Jalan Sudirman (which is one-way going south).

In contrast to the rest of Denpasar, the Renon area, south-east of the town centre, is laid out on a grand scale with wide streets, large car parks and big landscaped blocks of land – this is the area of government offices.

Tourist Office The Badung district tourist office (☎ 223602) is on Jalan Surapati 7, just north of the Bali Museum. A useful calendar of festivals and events in Bali, and a pretty good map, are available. They also have information on using Bali's bemo system. The office is open Monday to Thursday from 7 am to 2 pm, Friday from 7 to 11 am and Saturday from 7 am to 12.30 pm. The Bali government tourist office (☎ 222387) is in the Renon area, but doesn't provide much information.

Money All the major Indonesian banks have their main Bali offices in Denpasar, principally along Jalan Gajah Mada. The Bank Ekspor-Impor Indonesia, which is a block to the south, is probably the best for transfers from overseas.

Post & Telecommunications The main Denpasar post office, with a poste-restante service, is inconveniently located in the Renon area, a long way from the nearest bemo terminal.

Telkom has an office at Jalan Teuku Umar 6, near the intersection with Diponegoro. You can make international direct-dial phone calls and send telegrams and faxes.

The telephone code for Denpasar (and most of southern Bali) is 0361.

Immigration The immigration office (☎ 227828) is at Jalan Panjaitan 4, in the Renon area, just around the corner from the main post office. It's open Monday to Thursday from 7 am to 2 pm, Friday until 11 am and Saturday until 12.30 pm. If you have to apply for changes to your visa, get there on a Sanglah-bound bemo and make sure you're neatly dressed.

Medical Services Denpasar's main hospital (☎ 235456), Rumah Sakit Umum Propinsi (RSUP), is in the southern part of town in Sanglah, a couple of blocks west of Jalan Diponegoro. It's probably the best place to go in Bali if you have a serious injury or an urgent medical problem.

Bali Museum
The museum consists of an attractive series of separate buildings and pavilions, including examples of the architecture of both the palace (*puri*) and temple (*pura*). Exhibits are not always well presented, but include both modern and older paintings, arts & crafts, tools and various items of everyday use. Note the fine wood and cane-carrying cases for transporting fighting cocks, and the tiny ones for fighting crickets. There are superb stone sculptures, krises, wayang kulit figures and an excellent exhibit of dance costumes and masks. It's a good place to see authentic, traditional paintings, masks, woodcarving and weaving before you consider buying something from the craft and antique shops. There are some excellent examples of double ikat weaving.

The museum was originally founded by the Dutch in 1932. Admission to the museum is 200 rp for adults, 100 rp for children. The museum is open daily (except Monday) from 8 am to 5 pm and closes 1½ hours earlier on Friday.

Pura Jagatnatha

Adjacent to the museum is the state temple Pura Jagatnatha. This relatively new temple is dedicated to the supreme god, Sanghyang Widi and his shrine, the *padmasana*, is made of white coral. The padmasana (throne, symbolic of heaven) tops the cosmic turtle and the *naga* (mythological serpent) which symbolise the foundation of the world.

Arts Centres

The Abiankapas arts centre, quite a large complex on Jalan Nusa Indah, has an exhibit of modern painting and woodcarving together with a dancing stage, craft shop, restaurant and other facilities. Dances are held regularly and temporary exhibits are held along with the permanent one. It's open from 8 am to 5 pm Tuesday to Sunday; costs are 250 rp entry and 200 rp car parking.

Further out of town is the Conservatory of Performing Arts (SMKI), a training institution for high-school age students where, in the mornings, you can watch dance practices and hear a variety of gamelan orchestras. Sekolah Tinggi Seni Indonesia (STSI, formerly ASTI), is near the arts centre and runs more advanced courses. Here you may also see dance practices. Both groups hold public performances at the Abiankapas centre, particularly during the summer arts festival in June and July.

Places to Stay

Most people who stay in Denpasar are Indonesian visitors, mostly business travellers. There are also domestic tourists, especially in July-August and around Christmas, and hotels can fill up. There are plenty of places to stay, however, and you won't be bothered by a surfeit of foreign tourists.

Places to Stay – bottom end

Adi Yasa (☎ 222679) at Jalan Nakula 23B was once one of the most popular travellers' hotels in Bali. The rooms are arranged around a garden, and it's a pleasant, well-kept and friendly place, and quite a few people still stay here, even if it's no longer a travellers' mecca. Rooms are 8000/10,000 rp with shared mandi, 10,000/12,000 rp with private bathroom, breakfast included. Make sure you lock your room carefully here.

Two Brothers, near the Tegal bemo terminal, is another old-style losmen, and there are several other cheap places around. *Bali Yuai Mansion* (☎ 228850) at Jalan Satelit 22 in Sanglah, has been recommended by some readers. Rooms are from 10,000/15,000 rp and the owner is very helpful. It's about 500 metres south of the hospital; call first for directions, or staff may pick you up from Tegal bemo terminal.

Recently opened is the Bali International Youth Hostel, with 120 beds in two and four-bed Bali-style rooms, some with air-con. The address is Jalan Mertesari, Desar Sidakarya, Denpasar; it's south of Denpasar and west of Sanur, and it's signposted from the Airport-Sanur Bypass road.

Places to Stay – middle

There are a number of mid-range places on or near Jalan Diponegoro, the main road on the south side of town. The *Hotel Viking* (☎ 223992) at No 120 has a wide variety of accommodation, from economy rooms at 15,000 rp for singles up to air-con rooms at 50,000 rp.

Further south on the eastern side of Diponegoro is the *Hotel Rai*, a mid-range to expensive place catering mainly to business travellers. Other hotels in the southern part of Diponegoro include the *Dirgapura* (☎ 226924), the *Artha*, and the *Oka*.

The *Puri Pemecutan Hotel* (☎ 223491) is in the rebuilt palace at the junction of Jalan Hasanudin and Jalan Imam Bonjol (the road to Kuta), handy to the Tegal bemo terminal. Singles/doubles with air-con, phone, TV and private bathroom cost 40,000/50,000 rp, 12,000 rp for an extra bed.

Places to Stay – top end

There are no real luxury hotels in Denpasar, but the once-popular Hotel Denpasar at

BALI

Diponegoro 103 is being rebuilt, and will be be the first new top-end hotel in quite a while. The former Bali Hotel is now the Government-owned *Natour Bali* (☎ 225681/5) at Jalan Veteran 3, and is a notch down from luxury standard. A pleasantly old-fashioned place dating from the Dutch days, it still has some nice Art-Deco details (look at the light fittings in the dining room) but incongruous Balinese decorations are being added, like

The Best Hotel on Bali

The 'best' hotel is obviously a matter of opinion, but if the best means the most expensive, then the best place to stay in Bali is the Presidential Suite at The Grand Bali Beach Hotel in Sanur, at US$3000 per night (plus 17½% tax and service, which adds another US$525). If the best is the most luxurious, then it's impossible to differentiate at the top end – they all have large, luxurious air-con rooms and neither an extra metre of marble nor an extra channel on the in-house video system will make them any more comfortable.

How do the top hotels differentiate among themselves? To judge by their brochures, the most important things are the swimming pool and the view. On the first score we can be reasonably objective – the best swimming pool in Bali is at the Sheraton Lagoon Resort at Nusa Dua. It's so large they call it a lagoon, and it's complete with sandy beaches, islands, waterfalls, bridges, and bars. For a few extra dollars you can get a room with a balcony overhanging the lagoon, so you can drop in anytime.

As for the best view in Bali – do you look towards the mountains or the sea? The best mountain view may well be from a five-dollar flea-pit in Penelokan, while the best ocean view is a matter of how much water you can look at – looking south from the Bali Cliffs Hotel you will see nothing else. But if you want a view that is uniquely Balinese it must be of sculptured rice terraces stepping down a steep hillside in fifty shades of green, and for that you can do no better than looking at the Ayung river gorge from a room at Kupu Kupu Barong, a few km west of Ubud.

If you think the best hotel is the one with the richest history and the strongest links with a place and its past, then Ubud has two top contenders. The Hotel Tjampuan was originally the home of the artist Walter Spies, and his house guests included Noel Coward, Charlie Chaplin, Margaret Mead and a constellation of the celebrated artists, writers and musicians of the era. The hotel now has little resemblance to the guesthouse of the 1930s, but the site on the lush ravine of the Campuan river is still special, as are the many paintings which are a legacy of the revolution in Balinese art which commenced on this very spot.

Another hotel (of sorts) with a history, is actually a part of Ubud's royal family palace, the Puri Saren Agung – though it's not as old as it looks. The late Tjokorde Sukawati was one of Spies' patrons, and he saw the potential of 'cultural tourism' before the term was coined. After a fire in the 1950s, the palace was rebuilt with a number of *bale* for guests, in classic Balinese style but with modern Western facilities. The rooms are almost casually decorated with the sort of antiques and artworks you would expect in the home of a Balinese prince and patron of the arts. There's no swimming pool and no air-con, and the rooms are appropriately dusty, but the ambience is so thick you can chew on it.

You could judge a hotel by how it feels and how it makes you feel – as a sort of walk-in work of art which should leave an impression long after check-out time. By this standard, any one of the three Aman hotels is a masterpiece. They all have sensational views, superb decor, sublime architecture and swimming pools so perfect it seems a shame to swim in them. The Amankila, for example combines its spectacular view over the Badung Strait with three swimming pools, which step down towards the sea in matching shades of blue. While every other top-end hotel in Nusa Dua has a huge and imposing lobby with a formidable front desk, the Amanusa has a simple, open sided pavilion with two low tables and a view of half of Bali. Many hotels put on Balinese dances as a special attraction, but the Amandari, near Ubud, sponsors a local Legong troupe, and they practise in a pavilion a few metres from the front desk. Instead of in-house video movies the Aman resorts offer a sound system in every room. Instead of a disco, they have a library. Instead of a big building with hundreds of rooms, they have a few dozen free-standing suites.

Are they expensive enough to be the best? With US$100 price differences between almost identical suites, you can pay as much as you think is necessary, starting at US$300. Do they offer five-star luxury? They do not have a star rating at all, apparently because they refuse to provide a TV in their rooms – that's class. ■

the carved panels next to the leadlight windows in the lobby. Standard singles/doubles start at about US$60/65 including breakfast and air-con; 'superior rooms' cost an extra US$5 and a suite is US$90. Some of the rooms are actually on the other side of Jalan Veteran, so you'll have to walk across the road to use the dining room, bar and swimming pool.

Places to Eat
The eating places in Denpasar cater for local people, recent immigrants and Indonesian visitors, rather than for Western tourists, so they offer a good selection of authentic food from Indonesia's various cuisines. A number of restaurants along and near Jalan Gajah Mada are operated by and for the Chinese community, and many of them serve very good Chinese food.

The *Restaurant Atoom Baru*, at Gajah Mada 98, is a typical Asian (as opposed to Western) Chinese restaurant. It's interesting menu has lots of seafood, and dishes such as beef balls soup and pig's bladder with mushrooms. Other main courses are from 3000 to 7000 rp. Across the road is the *Restaurant Hong Kong*, with Chinese and Indonesian food and cafeteria-style self-service or table service. It's a bit classier, with tablecloths, and a bit pricier. The *Ha Ha Restaurant*, 20 metres to the west, has good food at reasonable prices.

Around the corner in the Kumbasari market, *Restaurant Hawaii* has oriental and European set menus, and there are food stalls available, especially in the evening. Further down Gajah Mada is the relatively expensive *Restaurant Puri Selera*, which does excellent Chinese food. There are also several Padang food restaurants along Gajah Mada.

You'll find excellent and cheap food at the market stalls by the Suci bemo terminal and at the other markets, especially in the evenings. South of there, Jalan Diponegoro has more eating possibilities, like the *Melati Indah*, next to the MA department store, and the *Minang Indah*, further south, with good Padang food. A number of rumah makans down Jalan Teuku Umar, like *Kak Man*, serve real Balinese food, as well as the standard Indonesian fare. *Ayam Bakar Taliwag*, in the same street, does Lombok-style food – very *pedas* (hot, spicy). To try street-stall type food in a very clean, hygienic setting, try the food hall at *Tiara Dewata Shopping Centre*.

The *Natour Bali Hotel*, on Jalan Veteran, still has some features in the Dutch East Indies colonial style, and you can get a rijsttafel in the old-fashioned dining room for 10,000 rp.

Entertainment
There are regular Kecak performances at the Abiankapas arts centre, and a Barong & Rangda dance every morning at the SMKI or STSI schools. Wayang kulit performances can be seen a couple of times a week at the Puri Pemecutan Hotel.

There are a number of cinemas (bioskop) in Denpasar, though they are losing ground to TV and videos. US movies are popular, particularly 'action movies', along with kung fu titles from Hong Kong, the occasional Indian epic and some Indonesian productions. Movies are usually in the original language, subtitled in Bahasa Indonesia. The Thamrin Wisita Cineplex, on Jalan Thamrin, has a number of cinemas so you'll have a choice.

Things to Buy
There are many shops selling crafts from Bali and from other Indonesian islands. You'll find some craft shops on Jalan Gajah Mada, and some more round the corner on Jalan Thamrin. Shops often close around 12.30 pm and reopen around 5 or 6 pm.

The main market, the three-storeyed building of the Pasar Badung, is near the east bank of the river. Fruit and vegetables are on the ground floor; household goods, foods, spices etc are on the 2nd floor; and clothing, sarongs, baskets, ceremonial accessories and other handcrafts on the top floor. It's very busy in the morning and evening, and would be a great place to browse and bargain if it were not for the women who attach themselves to you as unsolicited guides-cum-commission takers; even so, it's pretty interesting, colourful and pungent. Jalan Sulawesi, near the market, has many shops with batik, ikat and other fabrics. Gold jewellery is also a speciality in this area, known as Kampung Arab· for the many people of Middle Eastern or Indian descent. Kumbasari is another market/shopping centre on the opposite side of the river from Pasar Badung, with handcrafts, fabrics and gold work.

Other places that have been recommended include Bali Nusa at Jalan Diponegoro 98 and also Jalan Sumbawa 24 for batik; Emi at Jalan Hasanudin 53 for woodcarving; and Arts of Asia, just west of Jalan Thamrin, for antiques.

The Western-style shopping centres in Denpasar are quite a recent innovation. As the number of affluent citizens in Denpasar has increased, so has the number and quality of retail outlets, and the variety of goods on offer. Visitors go to the large, fixed-price shopping centres, not so much for Balinese handcrafts, but for clothing, shoes, toys and electronic goods.

The MA department store on Jalan Diponegoro was one of the first, but has been eclipsed by the bigger, newer places and now feels like a general store in a large country town. The Tiara Dewata shopping centre on Jalan MJ Sutoyo has a much better range. It incorporates a miniature fun fair with amusements which will entertain very young children, and includes a video arcade and swimming pool (500 rp) for older kids. Mata Hari, on Jalan Dewi Sartika between Surdiman and Diponegoro, is one of the newest and biggest department stores with a big range of clothes, cosmetics, leather goods, sportswear, toys and baby things. Genuine name brands like Calvin Klein, Reebok and Elizabeth Arden are competitively priced.

Getting There & Away

Denpasar is the focus of road transport in Bali, with terminals for buses and bemos to all corners of the island. There are also direct buses to destinations in Java, and agents for

boat, bus and train tickets, and the Garuda, Merpati, Bouraq and Sempati airline offices.

Air It's not necessary to come into Denpasar to arrange booking, ticketing or reconfirmation of flights. Most of the travel agencies in Kuta, Sanur, Ubud or other tourist areas can provide these services.

The Garuda office (☎ 225245) at Jalan Melati 61 is open Monday to Friday from 7.30 am to noon and 1 to 4.45 pm, and Saturday from 9 am to 1 pm. Merpati (☎ 235358) is just down the road at Jalan Melati 51, and is open from 7.30 am to 9 pm every day. Merpati has flights to Lombok and the other islands of Nusa Tenggara. Bouraq (☎ 223564) at Jalan Sudirman 19A has similar fares to Merpati and flies to destinations in Java and Nusa Tenggara. Sempati Air (☎ 288823, 288824), a good choice for domestic flights, is on Jalan Hang Tuah, the Denpasar-Sanur road.

Bus & Bemo Denpasar has five terminals for bemos and buses, so in many cases you'll have to transfer from one terminal to another if you're making a trip through Denpasar. If, for example, you were travelling from Kuta to Ubud you'd get a bemo from Kuta to the Tegal bemo terminal in Denpasar (500 rp), transfer to Batubulan (700 rp), then take a bemo from there to Ubud (1000 rp).

The cute little three-wheeled mini-bemos are only used within the congested city itself – 500 rp between the terminals, less for shorter trips in the city. More conventional looking four-wheeled minibuses do the routes between towns, while full-sized buses are also used on many of the longer, more heavily travelled routes. Buses tend to be cheaper than smaller vehicles on the same route, but they are less frequent and do not usually stop at intermediate points. Anyone who uses the bemos will know how difficult it is to get a precise figure for the 'harga biasa' on any bemo trip. The following should be accurate to within a couple of hundred rupiah, but try to confirm them with a local source before you get on.

BALI

Tegal – south of the city centre on the road to Kuta, this is the terminal for the southern peninsula.

Destination	Fare
Airport	800 rp
Batubulan terminal	700 rp
Kereneng terminal	500 rp
Kuta	500 rp
Legian	600 rp
Nusa Dua	1000 rp
Sanur (blue bemo)	600 rp
Suci terminal	300 rp
Ubung	500 rp
Ulu Watu	1500 rp

Ubung – north of the city centre on the Gilimanuk road, this is the terminal for the north and west of Bali.

Destination	Fare
Batubulan terminal	500 rp
Bedugul	1800 rp
Gilimanuk	4500 rp
Kediri	1000 rp
Kereneng terminal	500 rp
Mengwi	900 rp
Negara	3500 rp
Singaraja	2000 rp
Tegal terminal	500 rp

Ubung is also the main terminal for buses to Surabaya, Yogyakarta and other destinations in Java.

Destination	Time	Fare
Jakarta	30 hours	56,000 rp (air-con)
Surabaya	10-12 hours	18,000 rp
Yogyakarta	16 hours	25,000 rp
		36,000 rp (air con)

Kereneng – east of the city centre, off the Ubud road, this is mainly an urban transfer terminal, but it does have direct bemos to Sanur (500 rp).

Destination	Fare
Batubulan terminal	600 rp
Suci terminal	500 rp
Tegal terminal	500 rp
Ubung terminal	500 rp

Batubulan – about six km north east of the city centre, this is the terminal for the east and central area of Bali.

Destination	Fare
Amlapura	3000 rp
Bangli	1200 rp
Candidasa	2200 rp
Gianyar	1000 rp
Kintamani	2000 rp
Klungkung	1200 rp
Padangbai	2000 rp
Tampaksiring	1200 rp
Tegal terminal	700 rp
Ubud	1000 rp

Suci – south of the city centre, this terminal is mainly just the bemo stop for Benoa (500 rp).

Getting Around

Squadrons of three-wheeled mini-bemos *(tiga rodas)* shuttle around the city centre – all the bigger minibus bemos have to go round the central area between the various Denpasar bus/bemo terminals and also to various points in town. The Jalan Thamrin end of Jalan Gajah Mada, for example, is a stop for the transfer bemos. You'll find transfer bemos lined up for various destinations at, or just outside, each of the terminals; the set fares between terminals are around 500 rp. They are marked with a letter on the back that indicates which route they take; you can get a list of these routes from the tourist office. You can also charter bemos (from 4000 rp) or little three-wheelers (cheaper) from the various terminals for short trips. Agree about all prices before getting on board because there are no meters.

Taxis Blue and yellow taxis are also available, for 800 rp plus around 500 rp per km, but there are far fewer of them than the bemos. They should have meters – if the driver says it's not working, get another taxi.

Dokars Despite the traffic, *dokars* (horse-drawn carts) are still very popular around Denpasar. They should cost the same as a bemo, but they always charge tourists more

BALI

because of the novelty value; agree on prices before departing. Note that dokars are not permitted on Jalan Gajah Mada and may also be barred from some other streets with heavy vehicle traffic.

South Bali

The southern part of Bali, south of the capital Denpasar, is the tourist end of the island. The overwhelming mass of visitors to Bali is concentrated down here. Nearly all the package tour hotels are found in this area and many tourists only get out on day trips; some never get out at all.

KUTA

Kuta is Bali's biggest tourist beach area. Counting the areas of Tuban, Kuta, Legian and Seminyak, the *kelurahan* (local government area) of Kuta extends for nearly eight km along the beach and foreshore. Most visitors come to Kuta sooner or later, because it's close to the airport, has the biggest range of cheap tour and travel agents, and the biggest concentration of shops and services. Some people will find Kuta overdeveloped and seedy, but if you have a taste for a busy beach scene, shopping and nightlife, you can have a great time here. Just don't expect a quiet, unspoilt, tropical hideaway. It's not pretty, but it's not dull either, and the amazing growth is evidence that a lot of people find something to like in Kuta.

It's still the best beach in Bali, especially since the activities of the hawkers have been restricted, and watching the spectacular sunset is almost an evening ritual. Kuta has the only surf on the island which breaks over sand instead of coral, and beginning surfers can wipe out without being cut to pieces on the reefs. Lots of cheap accommodation is available, as well as good-value mid-range places and luxury hotels. There's a huge choice of places to eat, and a growing number of shops with everything from genuine antiques to fake fashion items. The tourists themselves have become a tourist attraction, and visitors come from Java to ogle the topless bathers, and from the other resorts to tut-tut at the tackiness of it all.

History

Mads Lange, a Danish copra trader and adventurer, established a successful trading enterprise near modern Kuta, and had some success in mediating between local rajas and the Dutch, who were encroaching from the north. His business soured in the 1850s, and he died suddenly. His grave, and a monument erected later, are near Kuta's night market.

The original Kuta Beach Hotel was started by a Californian couple in the 1930s, but closed with the Japanese occupation of Bali in 1942. It was rebuilt in 1991, and is now run by the government's hotel chain as the Natour Kuta Beach. In the late 1960s, Kuta became known as a stop on the hippie trail between Australia and Europe, and an untouched secret surf spot. Accommodation opened and, by the early 1970s, Kuta had a delightfully laid-back atmosphere. Enterprising Indonesians seized opportunities to profit from the tourist trade, often in partnership with foreigners who wanted a pretext for staying longer. When Kuta expanded, Legian further north became the quiet alternative, but now you can't tell where one ends and the other begins. Legian has now merged with Seminyak, the next village north. To the south, new developments are filling in the area between Kuta and the airport.

All this development has taken its toll, and the area presents a chaotic mixture of shops, bars, restaurants and hotels on a confusing maze of streets and alleys, often congested with heavy traffic, thick with fumes and painfully noisy. Now Kuta is trying to move up-market, and shopping is the big growth area. Nearly all the clothing sold in Kuta is locally made, and a growing Balinese garment industry is exporting worldwide. Lots of expatriate businesspeople rent houses or bungalows round Seminyak; many are married to Balinese and are permanent residents.

Modern Kuta is an international scene, but

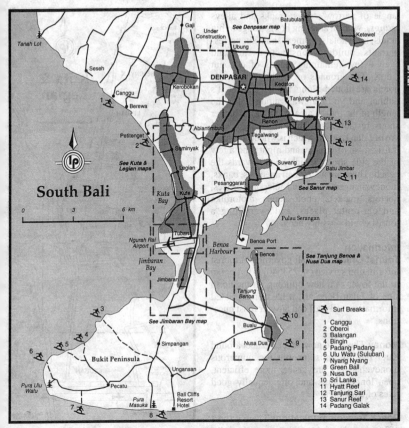

South Bali

0   3   6 km

	Surf Breaks
1	Canggu
2	Oberoi
3	Balangan
4	Bingin
5	Padang Padang
6	Ulu Watu (Suluban)
7	Nyang Nyang
8	Green Ball
9	Nusa Dua
10	Sri Lanka
11	Hyatt Reef
12	Tanjung Sari
13	Sanur Reef
14	Padang Galak

a traditional Balinese community remains. The religious practices are observed, and the banjars are still active in governing the local community. Temples are impressive and well-kept, processions and festivals are elaborate and the offerings are made every day. The observance of nyepi, the day of stillness when no work is done, has left many tourists perplexed at the closure of their favourite bar or restaurant.

Orientation

Kuta can be disorienting – it's flat, with few landmarks or signs other than a riot of adver-

tising; the streets and alleys are crooked and often walled on one or both sides so it feels like a maze. The main road is Jalan Legian, which runs roughly parallel to the beach from Seminyak in the north, through Legian, to Kuta. The south end of Jalan Legian is 'Bemo Corner', its junction with Jalan Pantai Kuta (Kuta Beach Rd). This one-way street runs west from Bemo Corner then north along the beach to Jalan Melasti, which goes back to Jalan Legian. From Melasti down to Bemo Corner, Jalan Legian is one-way, going south).

Between Jalan Legian and the beach is a

tangle of narrow streets, tracks and alleys *(gangs)*, with an amazing hodgepodge of big hotels, little hotels, losmen, small shops, restaurants, building construction sites and even a few remaining stands of coconut palms. The grounds of the big, expensive hotels are dotted along the beach, but it's public, and you can walk along it for the length of the tourist area. Most of the bigger shops, restaurants and bars are along several km of Jalan Legian (which is wheel-to-wheel traffic most of the day and night) and a few of the side streets which head towards the beach. There are also travel agencies, banks, moneychangers, post and telepone offices, doctors, markets, photo shops, motorbike and car-rental places, and everything a tourist could possibly need.

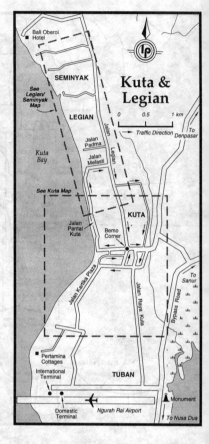

Information

Tourist Office The Bali government tourist information service (☎ 753540) is in Legian in the foyer of a new building on the north side of Jalan Benesari; it has some printed information and staff can answer most questions.

Money There are now several banks around Kuta but for most people the numerous moneychangers are faster, more efficient, open longer hours and offer equally good rates of exchange.

Post & Telecommunications There's a post office near the night market, on a small dirt road off Jalan Raya Kuta, the airport road. It's small, efficient and has a sort-it-yourself poste-restante service. There's also a postal agency on Jalan Legian, about half a km along from Bemo Corner; another on Jalan Melasti in Legian, and another in Seminyak on the main road.

There are several wartels on Jalan Legian and on Jalan Bakung Sari in Kuta (see the Kuta map). Opening hours are generally from 7 am to 9 pm. In most of them you can dial international calls yourself and send faxes, and payment is in cash. There are some card phones available in Kuta and outside the airport's international terminal.

There's a Home Country Direct phone in the Natour Kuta Beach Hotel. Private phone offices are more expensive than Telkom ones.

The whole Kuta-Legian area is in the 0361 telephone zone. Phone numbers were changed in October 1993; the new numbers have six digits starting with 75. If you have an old five-digit number, just add 7 to the front of it.

Dangers & Annoyances Theft is not an enormous problem, but visitors do lose things from unlocked hotel rooms or from

BALI

the beach. Always lock your room, even at night. Valuable items should be checked with reception or, if not needed, left in a security box. There are also some pickpockets and snatch theives, so hang on to your bag and keep your money belt under your shirt.

Some years ago Kuta had a number of muggings but the problem was handled with quite amazing efficiency and in a very traditional fashion. The local banjars organised vigilante patrols and anybody they came across who wasn't a tourist or a local Balinese had to have a damn good reason for being there. Thefts in the dark gangs stopped dead and there has been no repeat performance.

Water Safety The surf can be tricky, with a strong current on some tides, especially in Legian. There are drownings every year, many of them visitors from other Asian countries who are not good swimmers. The number of deaths has diminished greatly since the formation of the efficient Kuta Lifesaving Club, modelled on the Australian system. Patrolled areas are indicated by red-and-yellow flags on the beach.

Hawkers & Hasslers The activities of hawkers, touts and would-be guides are a major annoyance in Kuta. Beach selling is restricted to the upper part of the beach; closer to the water, you can lie on the sand in peace – you'll soon find out where the invisible line is. The best way to deal with unwanted sales pitches is to ignore them completely – even saying 'no' seems to encourage them.

Places to Stay

Kuta and Legian have hundreds of places to stay with more still being built. Even cheap losmen have bathrooms these days, and the squat toilet is a rarity. Don't be unduly influenced by Kuta hotel names – places with 'beach' in their name may not be anywhere near the beach and a featureless three--storeyed hotel block may rejoice in the name 'cottage'.

Places to Stay – bottom end

Outside busy seasons you can find a good basic losmen for around 10,000 rp a double, with private bathroom, a table fan, a light breakfast and a pleasant relaxed atmosphere. As you move up the price scale you get bigger rooms, a ceiling fan, better furnishings and a generally less spartan appearance. Bottom end places usually quote their prices in rupiah, up to about 30,000 rp per night for a double (US$15); above that is middle range. The following selections are grouped by location, from the south of Kuta to the areas north of Legian. The location key number on the Kuta or Legian-Seminyak map is indicated after the name.

South of Kuta There are mostly mid-range to expensive places down Jalan Kartika Plaza, but some cheapies are appearing on the back streets. Closer to central Kuta, the streets south of Jalan Pantai Kuta have some of the area's longest running low-budget places.

Bamboo Inn (☎ 751935) (Kuta No 97) – this traditional little losmen in central Kuta is some distance from the beach but close to the restaurants and bars. It's in a gang south of Jalan Bakung Sari, but far enough away to be quiet. Good rooms cost from 12,000/17,000 rp including breakfast.

Jesen's Inn II (☎ 752647) & *Zet Inn* (☎ 753135) (Kuta No 97) – are pleasant little places near the Bamboo Inn, at around 17,500/20,000 rp.

Anom Dewi Youth Hostel (☎ 752292) (Kuta No 77) – close to Bemo Corner, is a cheap but well-run youth hostel-associated losmen with standard rooms at 10,000 and 12,000 rp, superior rooms at 12,000/15,000 rp, and a 3000 rp high season supplement.

Jalan Pantai Kuta A number of cheap places are on this street between Bemo Corner and the beach. Rooms away from the road aren't too noisy.

Budi Beach Inn (☎ 751610) (Kuta No 66) – an old-style losmen with a garden and rooms from 10,000/15,000 rp up to 20,000/25,000 rp.

Kodja Beach Inn (☎ 752430) (Kuta No 64) – some rooms are set well away from the road; fan-cooled rooms are 10,000/12,500 rp, rooms with air-con and hot water are up to 45,000 rp.

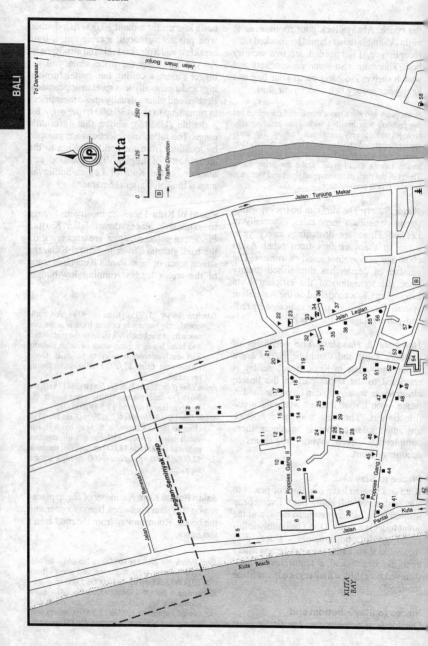

Kuta

To Denpasar
Jalan Imam Bonjol

0   125   250 m

Banjar
Traffic Direction

B

Jalan Tunjung Mekar

Jalan Legian

See Legian-Seminyak map

Jalan Benesari

Poppies Gang I

Poppies Gang II

Jalan Pantai Kuta

Kuta Beach

KUTA BAY

BALI

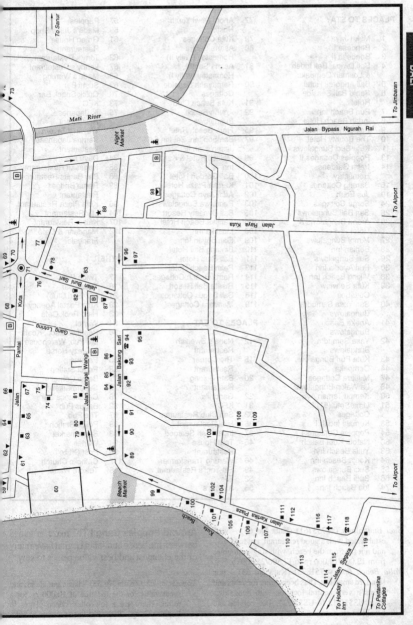

To Sanur

Mati River

Jalan Bypass Ngurah Rai

To Jimbaran

Night Market

B

98

B

88

Jalan Raya Kuta

To Airport

77

69 70

71

78

83

Jalan Buni Sari

96 97

76

Kuta

69

B

82

87

B

Gang Lotring

Pantai

B

86

94

95

Jalan Bakung Sari

93

Jalan Tegal Wangi

84 85

92

Jalan

75

74

81

91

66

67

65

79 80

90

64

63

108 109

62

61

103

60

Beach Market

89

102

104

To Airport

Kuta Beach

99

Jalan Kartika Plaza

100

101

105

106

107

111

112

116 117

118

110

119

113

115

114

Jalan Segara

To Holiday Inn

To Pertamina Cottages

PLACES TO STAY

1	Meka Jaya	77	Anom Dewi Youth Hostel	57	Poppies
2	Bendesa I	79	Kuta Cottages	59	Made's Juice Shop
3	Bendesa II	80	Asana Santhi Homestay (Willy II)	61	Green House Restaurant
4	Bali Dwipa, Bali Indah & Losmen Cempaka	81	Asana Santhi Homestay (Willy I)	62	Tony's Restaurant
5	Bali Anggrek Hotel	90	Ramayana Seaside Cottages	67	Lenny's Restaurant
6	Sahid Bali Seaside Hotel	91	Kuta Beach Club	68	Made's Warung
7	Puri Beach Inn	92	Agung Beach Bungalows	69	Sushi Bar
8	Indah Beach Hotel	95	Flora Beach Hotel	70	Quick Snack Bar
9	Bali Sandy Cottages	97	Bamboo Inn, Zet Inn & Jesen's Inn II	73	KFC
10	The Bounty Hotel	99	Melasti Hotel & Karthi Inn	75	Iki Japanese Restaurant
11	Kuta Suci Bungalows	100	Bali Garden Hotel	76	Wayan's Tavern
13	Poppies Cottages II	101	Kartika Plaza Hotel	83	Serrina Japanese Restaurant
14	Palm Gardens Homestay	102	Adhi Jaya Cottages	84	Dayu I
16	Barong Cottages	103	Pendawa Bungalows	85	Nagasari Restaurant
19	Jus Edith	105	Bali Dynasty Resort	86	Bali Bagus Restaurant
24	Sorga Cottages	106	Santika Beach Hotel	89	Rama Bridge Restaurant
25	Sari Bali Bungalows	108	Mustika Inn	96	Kuta Plaza Restaurant
26	Arena Bungalows & Hotel	109	Flamboyan Inn	104	Lily Restaurant
27	Mimpi Bungalows	110	Bintang Bali Hotel	107	Kaiser Restaurant
28	Berlian Inn	111	Bali Rani Hotel	112	Mandarin & Café Français
29	Suji Bungalows	113	Palm Beach Hotel		
30	Puri Ayodia Inn	114	Rama Beach Cottages		
38	Viking Beach Inn	115	Risata Bali Resort		**OTHER**
39	Kuta Seaview Cottages	116	Bali Bagus Cottages	17	Twice Pub
40	Sari Yasa Samudra Bungalows	119	Mandara Cottages	18	Tubes Bar
41	Aneka Beach Bungalows			21	SC (Sari Club)
42	Yasa Samudra Bungalows		**PLACES TO EAT**	23	Kuta Postal Agency
43	Kuta Puri Bungalows			33	Hard Rock Cafe
44	Cempeka	12	Nana's Swedish Restaurant	34	Wartel
47	Mutiara Cottages	15	The Corner Restaurant	36	Peanuts Disco, Koala Blu Pub, Warehouse & Crazy Horse
48	La Walon Bungalows	20	Batu Bulong Restaurant	56	Perama
50	Kempu Taman Ayu	22	Gandhi's	58	Petrol Station
51	Lima Satu (51) Cottages	31	KFC	71	Bemo Corner
53	Komala Indah I	32	Sari Club Restaurant	72	Supermarket
54	Poppies Cottages I	35	Mini Restaurant	78	Casablanca Bar
60	Natour Kuta Beach	37	Indah Sari Seafood	82	Bagus Pub
63	Yulia Beach Inn	45	Tree House Restaurant	87	The Pub
64	Kodja Beach Inn	46	Warung Transformer	88	Police Station
65	Suci Bungalows	49	Fat Yogi's Restaurant	93	Supermarket
66	Budi Beach Inn	52	TJs	94	Wartel
74	Ida Beach Inn	55	Aleang's	98	Post Office
				117	Catholic Church
				118	Telkom Wartel

Suci Bungalows (☎ 753761) (Kuta No 65) – well established with a good restaurant, not too noisy and not far from the beach, with singles/doubles from 12,000/15,000 rp to 17,500/25,000 rp.

Yulia Beach Inn (☎ 751893) (Kuta No 63) – this standard small hotel has been going for years and offers a very central location with bungalows from US$10/12 to US$22/25. Tax, service and breakfast are extra.

Around Poppies Gang I The maze of gangs between the beach and Jalan Legian have many of the cheapest and best-value places to stay.

Komala Indah I (Kuta No 53) – basic but clean, and great value for the location at 10,000 rp for a room. There are a few other cheap places in Poppies Gang – *Rita's* has been recommended.

Kempu Taman Ayu (Kuta No 50) – in a back lane off Poppies Gang, just round the corner from TJ's restaurant, this long running and friendly little place has fairly standard cheap rooms from 9000 to 12,000 rp.

Berlian Inn (Kuta No 28) – just off Poppies Gang, with good rooms from 16,000/20,000 rp including breakfast, this place is good value in a good location.

Arena Bungalows & Hotel (Kuta No 26) – a new place, with a pool, a bit of style and rooms from 15,000/25,000 rp upwards.

Sorga Cottages (☎ 751897) (Kuta No 24) – there's a pool, the location is quiet and the rooms are from 17,500 to 25,000 rp with fan or from 25,000 to 35,000 rp with air-con. The open meals area upstairs is a pleasant bonus.

Bali Sandy Cottages (Kuta No 9) – still manages to be in a coconut plantation close to the beach and Poppies Gang II; small, nice and inexpensive at 15,000/20,000 rp.

Puri Ayodia Inn (Kuta No 30) – this small and very standard losmen is in a quiet but convenient location and has rooms for just 10,000 rp.

Jus Edith (Kuta No 19) – a basic place, but quiet and central, with rooms from 7000/10,000 rp to 12,000/15,000 rp.

Around Poppies Gang II There are lots of cheap places on and around Poppies Gang II. It's about the best place to look for cheap accommodation.

Palm Gardens Homestay (☎ 752198) (Kuta No 14) – a neat and clean place, good value from 15,000 to 20,000 rp, including breakfast, and the location is convenient but reasonably quiet.

Arthawan Losmen – on Poppies Gang II about 30 metres west of Tubes bar, with clean rooms from 8000 rp, including breakfast.

Bali Dwipa, Bali Indah & Losmen Cempaka (Kuta No 4) – on the gang going north of Poppies Gang II. They don't have a lot of character or comfort, but they're well located and cheap at around 12,000 rp a double, including breakfast.

Bendesa No 2 & No 3, Meka Jaya No 1 & Beneyasa Beach Inn (Kuta No 1, 2 & 3) – are on the same gang, and also have cheap rooms from 12,000/15,000 rp, including breakfast and tax.

Kuta Suci Bungalows (Kuta No 11) – on a cul de sac off Poppies Gang II, this is a plain two-storey place with rooms from 12,500/15,000 rp.

Legian Cheap accommodation in Legian tends to be north of Jalan Padma. There's no road along the beach up here, so there are places fronting the beach which you reach on side streets from Jalan Legian. If you really want a beachfront place, walk along the beach and look from that angle.

Sayang Beach Lodging (Legian No 83) (☎ 751249) – tucked away on a windy lane south of Jalan Melasti, but handy to the beach and not too far from the action. It has a pool, and a variety of rooms from the basic variety at 7000/10,000 rp to larger air-con ones at 30,000/40,000 rp.

Legian Mas Beach Inn (Legian No 79) – a basic place in a quiet location, it has clean rooms from 10,000/12,000 rp.

Legian Beach Bungalows (Legian No 60) – in the centre of Legian on busy Jalan Padma, with singles from US$10 to US$15 and doubles from US$12 to US$18. It's friendly and the rooms are OK, back from the street in a nice garden.

Puspasari Hotel (Legian No 56) (☎ 751088) – also well located on Jalan Padma, this place is a bit cramped but has a pool and special low-season prices from 15,000/24,000 rp for its standard single/double rooms, including tax and breakfast.

Puri Damai Cottages (Legian No 57) (☎ 751965) – also on Jalan Padma, this budget place has singles/doubles from 15,000/20,000 rp.

North Legian & Seminyak The development up here is quite spread out, and there's not much public transport so getting around can be difficult. But there are places within an easy walk of both the beach and the facilities on Jalan Legian.

Sinar Indah (Legian No 45) – on Jalan Padma Utara, the rough lane between Jalan Padma, in central Legian, and Jalan Purana Bagus Taruna, in north Legian, this standard-style losmen has singles/doubles from 12,000/15,000 rp (without breakfast), plus bigger rooms with kitchen facilities.

Sinar Beach Cottages (Legian No 42) – east of Jalan Padma Utara at the north end of Legian, this pleasant little place has a thriving garden and rooms at 15,000 rp.

Sari Yasai Beach Inn (Legian No 31 – on Jalan Pura Bagus Taruna, this is a small losmen with rooms at 7000/12,000 rp.

LG Beach Club Hotel (☎ 751060) (Legian No 15) – well located behind the beachfront restaurant, this is budget accommodation near Legian beach at 25,000 rp for a room. There are other places to stay behind the beachfront bar/restaurants around here.

Mesari Beach Inn (☎ 751401) (Legian No 5) – one of the few budget places up in Seminyak, off Jalan Dhyana Pura behind the stables, with single/double rooms for 12,000/15,000 rp, and bungalows at around 140,000 rp per week.

Surya Dharma Cottage (☎ 753028) (Legian No 9) – at Jalan Dhyana Pura 9A, this is another cheapie by Seminyak standards at 40,000/50,000 rp plus 15% tax and service.

Places to Stay – middle

There are a great many mid-range hotels, which at Kuta means something like US$15 to US$60. Prices quoted in US dollars on a printed sheet are the 'publish rates' for the package tour market – this rate is always negotiable, up to 50% off in low season, especially when a lot of rooms are empty. All but the cheapest places add 15 to 17.5% for tax and service. Many of the newer package-tour hotels are utterly featureless and dull. The best of the mid-range hotels are former budget places which have proved popular and improved their facilities. Most of the following have air-con and swimming pools unless otherwise noted. Again, they are listed by location, going from south to north.

South of Kuta New places are going up around Jalan Segara, at the south end of Jalan Kartika Plaza. It's quiet and near the beach, but otherwise the area is not very interesting. The north end of Jalan Kartika Plaza is closer to central Kuta, and the beach market is an attraction.

Risata Bali Resort (☎ 753340) (Kuta No 115) – on Jalan Segara at the south end of Jalan Kartika Plaza, a new place with nice rooms, pool and garden. Prices start at US$60/65 but they give big discounts at quiet times.

Palm Beach Hotel (☎ 751661) (Kuta No 113) – off Jalan Segara and close to the beach, this is a motel-style place with rooms stacked three-storeys high, from US$50/55.

Adhi Jaya Cottages (☎ 753607) (Kuta No 102) – near the north end of Jalan Kartika Plaza, this place is nothing special to look at, but it has a pool and fan-cooled rooms from US$15/20, air-con suites up to US$42.

Karthi Inn (☎ 754810) (Kuta No 99) – at the north end of Jalan Kartika Plaza, and surrounded on three side by the more expensive Melasti Hotel, Karthi has a pool and offers all the mod cons in the rooms packed around it. Standard rooms are US$35/40, but with the 40% low-season discount it's only US$21/24.

Around Jalan Bakung Sari This area is close to the beach, has all the facilities you'll need and it's only a few hundred metres to Bemo Corner. There is some redevelopment at the beach end of these streets.

Ramayana Seaside Cottages (☎ 751864) (Kuta No 90) – on Jalan Bakung Sari, this long-established place has lots of rooms fitted in a limited space, with the cheapest ones around US$35/45.

Kuta Cottages (☎ 751101) (Kuta No 79) – close to the beach, on Jalan Tegal Wangi, this old hotel has been relocated, but is still central and reasonably priced from US$15/20 for fan-cooled rooms up to US$35/50 with air-con.

Asana Santhi (Willy I) Homestay (☎ 751281) (Kuta No 81) – this attractive small hotel is surprisingly quiet and relaxed for its location. The well-kept rooms have interesting furnishings and art, and there's a good central swimming pool. Air-con rooms are US$30 to US$35. *Willy II Homestay*, a little further west, is not as attractive but cheaper at US$20/25.

Ida Beach Inn (☎ 751205) (Kuta map No 74) – in a secluded location south of Jalan Pantai Kuta, there are a lot of rooms on a small site but the place has some style and a nice garden. Air-con rooms are US$20/25, or US$15/20 with fan.

Bali Summer Hotel (☎ 753947) (Kuta No 52) – one of several places along busy Jalan Pantai Kuta, where it goes west to the beach. The rooms are back from the street in a three-storey block, with air-con but not much character, from US$30/35.

Central Kuta The back lanes between Jalan Legian and the beachfront road have a mixture of cheap to mid-range places, which are handy both to the beach and to shops and restaurants. They don't have much traffic so it's a relatively quiet area.

La Walon Bungalows (☎ 752463) (Kuta No 48) – on Poppies Gang I, handy for the beach and the Kuta 'scene', La Walon is an established budget hotel which has acquired a pool and some air-con units, but it still has pleasant little rooms with verandahs, open-air bathrooms and ceiling fans for US$19/25.

Mutiara Cottages (☎ 752091) (Kuta No 47) – conveniently located on Poppies Gang I, the Mutiara is excellent value with a pool, spacious lush garden and plain, slightly tatty, fan-cooled rooms at US$12/15, including breakfast.

Poppies Cottages I (☎ 751059) (Kuta No 54) – still setting the standard for what a good Bali hotel should be, Poppies has an exotically lush garden with beautiful cottages. It's in the centre of things on Poppies Gang I and has a lovely swimming pool. At US$58/63 for singles/doubles it's right at the top of the mid-range category. Make a reservation as it's very popular.

Mimpi Bungalows (Kuta No 27) – on a back lane north of Poppies Gang I, this small hotel is good value in a pleasant location with a nice little pool. Rooms cost US$17 to US$35.

Kuta Seaview Cottages (☎ 751961) (Kuta No 39) – on Jalan Pantai Kuta at the end of Poppies Gang I, it's opposite the beach but separated from it by the busy beach road. Most of the rooms are in a three-storey block, definitely not cottages, and don't have any view of the sea. The site is a bit cramped, but it's still a good, central location, with rooms from US$40/45 for singles/doubles.

Poppies Cottages II (Kuta No 13) – the original Poppies (despite the name), is not as fancy nor as central as newer Poppies I, and there are only four cottages, but they are nice and spacious, at US$23/28. Guests can use the pool at Poppies I.

Legian There are plenty of mid-range places around Jalan Benesari in Legian, some near the beach, others on the lanes behind.

Kuta Bungalows (Legian No 90) – well located on Jalan Benesari, the bungalows are a bit stark but OK, at US$35/40.

Bruna Beach Hotel (☎ 751565) (Legian No 77) – this simple place has a good central location on the beach road. The rooms are nothing special but they're cheap with prices from US$15/18 up to US$30/35 with air-con.

Ocean Blue Club (Legian No 78) – pitched at the young Aussie package tourists, this is the only place that quotes prices in Australian dollars; A$60/120 for singles/doubles (about US$40/80).

Legian Beach Hotel (☎ 751711) (Legian No 66) – PO Box 308, Denpasar – on the beach at Jalan Melasti in the heart of Legian this large, popular hotel has a wide variety of rooms, most of them in three-storeyed blocks, with singles/doubles from US$50/60 to US$80/90.

Garden View Cottages (☎ 751559) (Legian No 52) – well located, just north of Jalan Padma in Legian, the rooms have hot water, phone and fridge, but look a little like concrete boxes at US$34/38.

Bali Sani Hotel (☎ 752314) (Legian No 46) – on Jalan Padma Utara (the lane going north of Jalan Padma), this smaller hotel is a short walk from the beach and has attractively designed rooms, some of them with a touch of eccentricity. Rooms are US$50/55 for singles/doubles.

Maharta Beach Inn (☎ 751654) (Legian No 40) – on a lane off Jalan Padma Utara, this is a pretty place with cottages around a pool in a lush garden which extends to the beach; US$60 for singles or doubles.

Bali Niksoma Inn (☎ 751946) (Legian No 38) – right on the beach towards the northern end of Legian this smaller hotel has two-storeyed units in relatively spacious grounds with rooms from US$21/25 to US$65/80.

Baleka Beach Inn (Legian No 32) – at the north end of Legian on Jalan Pura Bagus Taruna, this place asks from US$15/20 to US$30/35, but it's worth discussing the price.

Seminyak This area starts around Jalan Pura Bagus Taruna (also called Rum Jungle Road). Some of the best restaurants and most popular nightspots are up here, and some good mid-range accommodation. It's a bit remote so phone first, and they may pick you up. There are also houses and bungalows to rent by the week or month.

Legian Garden Cottages (☎ 751876) (Legian No 16) – on Legian Cottages Road (also called Double Six Street and Jalan Legian Kaja), off Jalan Legian but close to the beach, this attractive place is well-located with pool, gardens and standard rooms from US$38/45.

Prince of Legian Cottages – halfway along the same road, have serviced bungalows with kitchen facilities and room for at least four people, for 60,000 rp per night, but would really suit a longer stay.

Sing Ken Ken (☎ 752980) (Legian No 17) – also on Legian Cottages Road, this new, nice-looking place charges US$35/40 in the high season, but only US$20 at other times.

Ramah Village (☎ 753793) – for longer stayers, this place has 15 comfortable bungalows, sleeping up to six people, from US$450 to US$1050 per week. It's on Gang Keraton, off Jalan Legian near the Alas Arum supermarket.

Bali Holiday Resort (☎ 753547) (Legian No 6) – in a beachfront location south off Jalan Dhyana Pura, and close to popular restaurants and nightclubs, this place is good value with rooms from US$55/60.

Dhyana Pura Hotel (☎ 751422) (Legian No 3) – on Jalan Dhyana Pura in Seminyak, with a beach frontage, this is a YMCA-affiliated hotel run by Bali's Protestant Christian Church. Air-con rooms and bungalows are set in an attractive garden and have all the usual facilities at very reasonable prices – from US$35/45, including tax and breakfast. There's no proselytising, but occasionally large groups of visitors dominate the place.

Bali Agung Village (☎ 754267; fax 754269) (Legian No 1) – this small new place is off Jalan Dhyana Pura, on the northern edge of the tourist area next to the rice fields (at least for a little while). It's in nice Balinese style, and is quite good value at US$55/60.

Nusa di Nusa (☎ 751414) (Legian No 4) – right on the beach, but some distance from the Jalan Legian restaurant and shops, it's still in a trendy area. Very pleasant rooms start at US$30/35 for singles/doubles, but check the room first – some readers say it's not as well kept as it should be.

Places to Stay – top end

Kuta has quite a few places in the top-end category, and more luxury hotels are going up. There will be at least 17.5% tax and service charge on top of the quoted prices. They nearly all have beach frontage, so they're easy to locate on a map. Going from south (the airport end) to north, some of the more popular or interesting top-end places include:

Pertamina Cottages (☎ 751161) PO Box 3121, Denpasar – on the beach at Tuban, the airport end of Kuta, this large deluxe hotel has rooms from US$120. It's one of the first luxury hotels in Kuta and has lovely beachfront gardens and an excellent Japanese restaurant.

Holiday Inn Bali Hai (☎ 753035) – this place has excellent Balinese architecture, despite being part of an international chain, and a beautiful pool and gardens. Rooms cost from US$120, bungalows from US$180.

Bintang Bali Hotel (☎ 753810) (Kuta No 110) – this hotel is new, big (400 rooms) and has a range of sports facilities (gym, pool, tennis), disco and karaoke. Rooms start at US$95/105.

Santika Beach Hotel (☎ 751267) (Kuta No 106), PO Box 1008 Tuban – on Jalan Kartika Plaza, with swimming pools, tennis courts, all the usual facilities and a variety of rooms from US$80.

Bali Dynasty Resort (☎ 7524003) (Kuta No 105), PO Box 20047 Kuta – a large new place on Jalan Kartika Plaza, with rooms from US$95.

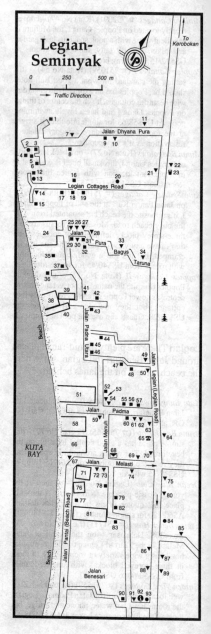

BALI

PLACES TO STAY		56	Puspasari Hotel	59	Padma Club Restaurant
1	Bali Agung Village	57	Puri Damai Cottages	61	Rama Garden
3	Dhyana Pura Hotel	58	Bali Mandira Cottages		Restaurant
4	Nusa di Nusa Hotel	60	Legian Beach	62	Norman Garden
5	Mesari Beach Inn		Bungalows		Restaurant
6	Bali Holiday Resort	66	Legian Beach Hotel	63	MS Restaurant
8	Tjendana Paradise	71	Bali Intan Cottages	64	Ned's Place
	Hotel	76	Kul Kul Resort	67	Karang Mas Restaurant
9	Surya Dharma	77	Bruna Beach Hotel	69	Gosha Restaurant
	Cottages	78	Ocean Blue Club	70	Do Drop Inn
12	Sheraton Hotel	79	Legian Mas Beach Inn	72	Restaurant Puri Bali
15	LG Beach Club Hotel	81	Kuta Jaya Cottage		Indah
16	Legian Garden	82	Puri Tanah Lot	73	Legian Garden
	Cottages	83	Sayang Beach Lodging		Restaurant
17	Sing Ken Ken	90	Kuta Bungalows	74	Orchid Garden
18	Bali Subak				Restaurant
19	Suri Bunga Bungalows	**PLACES TO EAT**		75	Manhattan Restaurant
24	Kuta Palace Hotel				& Bar
29	Orchid Garden	7	Pino Lotus Restaurant	80	Made's Restaurant
	Cottages	10	Jimbaro Cafe	85	Il Pirata
31	Sari Yasai Beach Inn	11	Benny's Cafe II	86	The Bounty
32	Baleka Beach Inn	14	Puri Naga	87	Depot Viva
35	Mabisa Beach Inn	22	Goa 2001 Pub	88	Za's Bakery &
36	Puri Tantra Beach		Restaurant		Restaurant
	Bungalows	25	Topi Koki Restaurant	89	Mama's German
37	Mabisa Hotel	26	Swiss Restaurant		Restaurant
38	Bali Niksoma Inn	27	Twice Cafe	91	Midnight Oil Restaurant
39	Bali Coconut Hotel	28	Rum Jungle Road Bar		
40	Maharta Beach Inn		& Restaurant	**OTHER**	
42	Sinar Beach Cottages	30	Sawasdee Thai		
43	Adika Sari Bungalows		Restaurant	2	Chez Gado Gado
44	Surya Dewata Beach	33	Bamboo Palace	13	66 Club
	Cottages		Restaurant	20	Strand Bar
45	Sinar Indah	34	Benny's Café	21	Luna Cafe
46	Bali Sani Hotel	41	Poco Loco Mexican	23	Jaya Pub
47	Sri Ratu Cottages		Restaurant	65	Wartel
48	Three Brothers	49	Restaurant Glory	68	Postal Agent
51	Bali Padma Hotel	50	Warung Kopi	84	Peanuts II
52	Garden View Cottages	53	Legian Snacks	92	Government Tourist
55	Legian Village Hotel	54	Joni Sunken Bar &		Information
			Restaurant	93	Krishna Bookshop

Kartika Plaza Hotel (☎ 751067) (Kuta No 101), PO Box 3084, Denpasar – right on the beach, just south of central Kuta, this large hotel has rooms from US$100/110.

Natour Kuta Beach (☎ 751361) (Kuta No 60), PO Box 3393, Denpasar – this hotel is a successor to the original Kuta Beach Hotel, which was close by. Unfortunately, there's no sense of history at all, but there are nice views and the location is very central, at the beach end of Jalan Pantai Kuta. Singles/doubles are from US$65/75 to US$300.

The Bounty Hotel (☎ 753030) (Kuta No 10) – away from the beach, but still central and a nice looking place, this hotel has a young clientele. The published rates start at US$80 (including tax and service), but it gives big off-season discounts.

Kul Kul Resort (☎ 752520) (Legian No 76), PO Box

3097, Denpasar – just south of Jalan Melasti in Legian, this big and popular hotel has two and three-storeyed blocks plus bungalows in relatively spacious grounds. Rooms cost from US$83.

Bali Intan Cottages (☎ 51770; fax 751891) (Legian No 71) – on Jalan Melasti, close to the beach in Legian, this very standard large hotel has rooms in two-storeyed blocks plus cottages with rooms from US$80/85 to US$90/95.

Bali Padma Hotel (☎ 752111) (Legian No 51), PO Box 1107 TBB, Legian – a big 400-room hotel by the beach on Jalan Padma in the middle of Legian, with some of the lushest gardens in Bali. Rooms are in two or three-storeyed blocks or in six-room units and cost from US$100/110 to US$120/130 for singles/doubles, with a US$20 high-season supplement; suites are from US$165 to US$1500.

Kuta Palace Hotel (☎ 751433) (Legian No 24), PO Box 3244, Denpasar – at the northern end of Legian, this big hotel is right on the beach at the end of Jalan Pura Bagus Taruna, and has pleasant swimming pools and gardens. Rooms cost from US$85/100 to US$95/110.

Bali Imperial Hotel (☎ 754545; fax 751545) – at the beach end of Jalan Dhyana Pura in Seminyak, it's not central but it offers a shuttle service to Kuta. The architecture is very imposing, and the prices are substantial, with rooms from US$140, villas from US$400 and the Imperial Villa for US$1600.

Bali Oberoi Hotel (☎ 751061) PO Box 3351, Denpasar – right on the beach at Seminyak, at the end of its own road way up beyond Legian, the Bali Oberoi is isolated and decidedly deluxe with beautiful individual bungalows (US$175 to US$240) and even some villa rooms with their own private swimming pools (from around US$400).

Persona Bali (☎ 753914; fax 753915) – just north of the Oberoi, this is a new, nice-looking beachfront place with friendly staff and all the usual mod cons; rooms cost from US$70 to US$110.

Puri Ratih Bali (☎ 751146; fax 751549) – Petitenget, the area north of Seminyak, this place has a swimming pool, gym, tennis court and two-bed bungalows from US$80 to US$250.

Places to Eat

There are countless places to eat around Kuta and Legian, from tiny hawker's carts to fancy restaurants, cheap warungs to bars and pubs, steakhouses to juice bars. Indonesian food is available, but mostly the cuisine is international and multicultural. The restaurant business is very competitive, and they're quick to pick up on new trends – Japanese dishes (perhaps not authentic, but very tasty) are appearing on many menus, and Thai dishes are starting to become popular.

If you want to eat cheaply, try the places which cater to local workers. Food carts appear in the afternoon near Legian beach, and there are warungs at the night market near the post office, and also at the beach market at the end of Bakung Sari.

For middle-budget eating, most tourist restaurants serve the standard Indonesian dishes (nasi goreng, nasi campur etc), depending on the restaurant, but hamburgers, jaffles, spaghetti and salads are common offerings for a light meal (between 2000 rp and 4500 rp at most places), while a pizza, seafood or steak dish will cost between 6000 rp and 10,000 rp. The quality varies from average to excellent, and seems to depend as much on when you go and what you order as on the establishment and the price. The very big, barn-like places, often seafood specialists, can be inconsistent.

There are French, German, Italian, Japanese, Korean, Mexican, Swiss and Swedish restaurants – the more expensive places really specialise, but the cheaper ones have a variety of dishes regardless of their name. Wine is expensive, but some places serve Australian wine by the glass for around 4000 rp. Beer goes well with most meals, and is a fair index of prices – in cheap places a large beer is around 3000 rp; in expensive places it costs from 4000 rp upwards.

South of Kuta The *Café Français* on Jalan Kartika Plaza is a good patisserie for a croissant (1300 rp), coffee and fruit juice breakfast. *Bali Seafood*, opposite the Bintang Bali Hotel, is a big place where you can select your main course while it's still swimming. The Cantonese restaurant at the Dynasty Hotel has a good reputation.

Around Kuta The beach market, at the north end of Jalan Kartika Plaza, has some cheap food stalls. Going east on Bakung Sari there are several reliable restaurants, including *Dayu I* and *Nagasari*, and a supermarket which has many Western supermarket-style goods.

Jalan Buni Sari has some more long-term survivors, including the *Bali Indah, Wayan's Tavern* and *Dayu II*. Further along this short street are some popular pubs, including *The Pub* itself, the original Kuta pub. You'll also find *Restaurant d'Este*, which has great Italian food.

Along Jalan Pantai Kuta, between Bemo Corner and the beach, is popular *Made's Warung*, a simple open-front place which is good for people watching – the food is very good though a touch expensive. The *Suci Restaurant*, on the south side, is good value with delicious fruit drinks.

Poppies Gang, the tiny lane between Jalan Legian and the beach, is named for *Poppies Restaurant* (☎ 751059), one of the oldest and most popular in Kuta – make a reservation. The prices are quite high, from 7000 to 10,000 rp for main courses, but the food is well prepared and presented, and the garden setting and the atmosphere are delightful. A few steps west of Poppies is *TJ's* (☎ 751093), a deservedly popular Mexican restaurant, also with a good atmosphere and main courses cost from 8000 to 12,000 rp. Further down Poppies Gang, towards the beach, there are several popular places for light meals – try *Warung Transformer* or the pleasant *Tree House Restaurant*, a good place for an excellent and economical breakfast.

Along Jalan Legian There are lots of possibilities along Jalan Legian, though a table near the road can be very noisy. Right on Bemo Corner is the *Quick Snack Bar*, a good place for a snack or breakfast and the yoghurt is particularly delicious. A little further up is a *Sushi Bar*, with excellent sushi for 1200 to 3000 rp, and sashimi from 7000 to 10,000 rp. Continue north and you reach the *Twice Bar & Bakery*, which might be good for a breakfast but is noisy and a little overpriced for dinner. The *Mini Restaurant* is a huge place despite the name, but busy serving good straightforward food at low prices. The *Sari Club Restaurant* is similar in style, price and quality. There's a new *KFC* on a side alley here, and a new *McDonalds* just up the road.

Around the corner, Poppies Gang II has a lot of cheap eateries, like the popular *Batu Bulong*, *Nana's Swedish Restaurant*, *Twice Pub* and *The Corner Restaurant*.

Continue north to *Mama's German Restaurant* (see the Legian map), which has pretty authentic German food for 7000 to 8000 rp for main courses. The *Depot Viva* is an open-roofed place with surprisingly good Indonesian and Chinese food despite its bare and basic appearance. The prices are pleasantly basic too, which accounts for its steady popularity. Across the road is *Za's Bakery & Restaurant*, a good spot for breakfast, which

also has a menu featuring everything from pasta dishes to curries.

A little further along Jalan Legian is *Il Pirata*, noted both for its very good pizzas for 5000 to 7000 rp, and for its late opening hours. Continuing north to the heart of Legian, you'll come to the ever popular *Do Drop Inn*, the well-regarded *Warung Kopi* and the long standing *Restaurant Glory*.

Around Legian The streets west of Jalan Legian have numerous restaurants and bars. On Jalan Melasti is the big *Orchid Garden Restaurant*, the *Legian Garden Restaurant*, and the *Restaurant Puri Bali Indah*, which serves excellent Chinese food. Jalan Padma has a number of tourist restaurants, and *Legian Snacks*, just north of Padma, serves lighter meals. At the *Joni Sunken Bar & Restaurant*, on Padma, you can eat and drink while semi-immersed in a swimming pool – if your hotel doesn't cater to this indulgence, here's your chance to try it.

Further north, things get more expensive but the standards are higher. Some of the most interesting places are on Jalan Pura Bagus Taruna (also known as Rum Jungle Road). Right by the Kuta Palace Hotel entrance is the *Topi Koki Restaurant*, which serves pretty good French food in a lovely setting, and is about the most expensive place around – a full meal for two with drinks will cost over 50,000 rp. A little further back from the beach is the *Swiss Restaurant*, which is adjacent to the Swiss consul so should have some credibility. Other restaurants along this street include the *Sawasdee Thai Restaurant*, *Yudi Pizza* and, nearer to Jalan Legian, the distinctive and very popular *Bamboo Palace Restaurant*, and the smaller, but also popular, *Benny's Café*, with delicious pastries and coffee for a splurge breakfast.

Seminyak Good, though not cheap, places to eat up here include the *Ibiza* Italian restaurant and the *Goa 2001*, both on Jalan Legian. On Jalan Dhyana Pura you'll find *Benny's Café II* and *Jimbaro Cafe*, which are mid-range places. On a beach track past the

Oberoi, near the Petitenget temple, *La Lucciato* is an Italian place with food that people rave about, and prices which are expensive but not excessive – main courses around 9000 rp.

Entertainment

Nightspots are scattered around Kuta, Legian and Seminyak, many along Jalan Legian. The wild, drunken excesses of Kuta are mostly a scene for young Australians on cheap package holidays. The scene centres around a short side alley off Jalan Legian, with *Peanuts Disco* at the far end, and bars like *Crazy Horse*, the *Warehouse* and *Koala Blu Club* on either side. Peanuts gets going around 11 pm, and charges 6000 rp admission, which includes one drink. The bars start earlier and entry is free. The whole Peanuts complex is due to be closed and redeveloped as a shopping centre (a sign of the times!), and the owners have established *Peanuts II*, up in Legian, to continue the reputation (or notoriety) of the original. Other nearby drinking places include the *Sari Club* (or 'SC' for short), just up the road, *Norm's Life Be In It* bar, further up, and *Tubes Bar*, around the corner in Poppies Gang II, which is a surfer's hangout. The glossy *Hard Rock Cafe*, just north of the Peanuts alley, is a new landmark in Kuta.

Up in Legian you'll find a few more Aussie drinking places on Jalan Padma. There are also a few bars/pubs in the south of Kuta, like *Un's Pub* near Bemo corner and, on Jalan Buni Sari in order of noisiness, *The Pub*, one of Kuta's original bars, the *Pub Bagus* and *Casablanca*.

There is somewhat classier nightlife further north in Seminyak – the sophisticates start with drinks and/or dinner at the *Goa 2001 Pub Restaurant*. They then move on (but not before 10 pm) to the *Jaya Pub* for relaxed music and conversation, or do some café society at *Luna Cafe*, across the road. Later on, but *never* before 1.00 am, the action shifts to the beachside *66 Club* (pronounced 'double six'), or the chic *Chez Gado Gado*, at the beach end of Jalan Dyana Pura; if you don't like one, you can stroll along the beach

to the other. After some hours of this, you could do breakfast at *Benny's Café*, if you haven't found a better option.

Large-screen video (or laser disk) movies, are featured at some of the restaurants/pubs, including the *Batu Bulong*, the *Twice Bar* and the *Bounty*. They're pretty loud and easy to find, but only go if you want to see the movie – they're impossible to ignore and the service slows down as the staff get involved in the interesting bits.

Things to Buy

Parts of Kuta are now almost door-to-door shops and over the years these have become steadily more sophisticated. For arts & crafts from Bali and all over Indonesia, there are many art and 'antique' shops on the main streets. Countless boutiques for men and women display budget Balinese versions of the latest styles from all over the world. Many shops sell silver and jewellery, but the quality is often suspect – well-established places like Jonathon's and Mirah are probably best. There are also many simple stalls selling an endless range of T-shirts and beachwear, many of them crowded together in 'art markets' like the one at the beach end of Jalan Bakung Sari. For everyday purchases, like food, toiletries and stationery, there are supermarkets on Jalan Legian, Jalan Bakung Sari and Jalan Raya Kuta. The

biggest is the Galael Supermarket on the road to Denpasar. The big duty-free shop is nearby, though it seems expensive. The department store at Plaza Bali, on the airport road, has a good selection of clothing and leather at reasonable prices.

Music shops sell a huge variety of cassette tapes, from about 8000 rp. CDs are also available, at around 26,000 rp, but the range is not as good. Mahogany, in Legian, has an excellent selection, including gamelan music on tape and CD.

Getting There & Away

Air Kuta has lots of travel agencies but if you're looking for onward tickets, Bali is no place for air-travel bargains. For reconfirmations, it's better to contact the airline directly. There's a small Garuda office (☎ 751179) in the Natour Kuta Beach Hotel. The Air New Zealand office is at the Kartika Plaza Hotel (☎ 751067). Most other airlines have offices at the Grand Bali Beach Hotel in Sanur – their numbers are listed in the Sanur entry later in this section.

Bus Lots of agents in Kuta sell bus tickets to Java, although they're cheaper from the bus companies at the Ubung bus terminal, from where the buses depart. The agents can arrange transport to Ubung for an extra 5000 rp or so.

There are regular tourist shuttle buses to other places in Bali. Services include Ubud for 7500 rp, Padangbai and Candidasa for 10,000 rp and Lovina for 12,500 rp. Perama (☎ 751551), on Jalan Legian, is the best known operator, but other shuttle bus companies have similar fares. Perama also operates bus-ferry-bus services to Lombok.

Bemo For a public bemo to virtually any destination in Bali you'll have to go to one (or more) of the Denpasar terminals first. Kuta bemos go to/from the Tegal terminal in Denpasar (500 rp). Most 'S' bemos go only to the terminal area in Kuta, just beyond Bemo Corner, but the S1 does a loop round the beach road. In practice you will probably have to go to the terminal near Bemo Corner

to get a bemo out of town (see under Public Bemo in the following Getting Around section).

Car & Motorbike Rental Groups of motorbikes for rent are assembled at various points along Jalan Legian. There are lots of car-rental places, large and small, and it's cheaper here than in Sanur, Ubud or other tourist centres. The moneychanger just up from Bemo Corner (☎ 751738) advertises the cheapest rates around, and you don't even have to haggle – a Suzuki hardtop jeep with air-con is 33,000 rp per day including insurance, with a 10% discount if you take it for a week. A larger Kijang is 55,000 rp per day. There are lots of other car-rental places – try to bargain them down to these levels.

Getting Around

Kuta is a pain to get around because it's so spread out, and the guys with charter minibuses try to preclude any cheaper transport alternatives.

To/From the Airport There are set taxi fares from the airport to Kuta, Legian, Seminyak and as far as the Oberoi Hotel. From Kuta to the airport you should be able to charter a minibus for about the same fares (haggle like crazy), or get a metered taxi. Perama buses to the airport cost 5000 rp. Theoretically, you could get to the airport from Kuta by regular public bemo for just a few hundred rp, but you'd have to walk to the S1 bemo route (near the corner of Jalan Bakung Sari and Jalan Raya Kuta would be a good place to try) and it's also a fair walk from the closest stop on the bemo route to the airport terminal.

Taxi & Charter There are plenty of taxis around Kuta Beach. They're blue and yellow, with meters and are air-con. They charge 800 rp flag fall and 500 rp per km. They seem reluctant to stop for passengers on Jalan Legian or round Bemo Corner, where the transport touts hustle for business.

Minibuses available for charter are easy to find – listen for the offers of 'transport' which follow any pedestrian. Vehicles which can legally be chartered by tourists have yellow licence plates. They don't have meters so you have to negotiate the fare before you get on board. You should be able to get from the middle of Kuta to the middle of Legian for around 3000 rp. A full day charter should run to about 45,000 or 50,000 rp, and shorter periods should cost proportionally less, but you'll have to bargain hard. The 'first price' for transport can be truly outrageous.

Public Bemo In theory, S1 bemos do a loop through Kuta and Legian on their route from Tegal terminal in Denpasar to Kuta, the airport and back to Tegal. In practice, it's almost impossible for tourists to use the system for local transport within Kuta, at the public price. They only do a limited route – from Bemo Corner, west then north on Jalan Pantai Kuta, south on Jalan Legian back to Bemo Corner, then continuing their route to the airport or Denpasar. They don't seem to go down Jalan Legian very often during the day, and even less in the evening. For many short trips you're almost certainly going to have to charter transport.

Bicycle There are lots of places to rent bikes, for around 5000 rp per day. Lock your bike when you leave it, and beware of thieves who might snatch things from the basket or luggage rack.

BEREWA

This beach is a few km up the coast from the north end of the Kuta strip, but to reach it you have to take the small roads west of Kerobokan – there's no coast road north of Petitenget. Signs point to *Bolare Beach Hotel* (☎ 0361 262358), which has a great beachfront location, pool, restaurant etc for US$50/55. *Legong Keraton Beach Cottages* (☎ 0361 238049; fax 238050) is just next door and not quite as fancy, but still very nice, from US$45. The top-end option at Berewa is the *Dewata Beach Hotel* (☎ 0361 237663; fax 234990), a member of the Best Western chain.

CANGGU

A well known surf spot with right and left hand breaks, Canggu has a nice beach, though sometimes there is polluted water at the river mouth. There's a warung, and you can stay at the *Canggu Beach Club* for 20,000/25,000 rp; less if you stay longer. To get there, go west at Kerobokan and follow signs to Pererenan. There's no public transport.

SANUR

Sanur is a quieter, more up-market alternative to Kuta for those coming to Bali for sea, sand and sun. It does have some cheaper places to stay, and there are some good restaurants, so you don't have to swallow the high prices at hotel restaurants.

An early home for visiting Western artists, Sanur is still an artistic centre, famed for its gamelan orchestras and the courtly Arja opera, and wayang kulit are also popular.

The beach is pleasant, and sheltered by a reef, but shallow at low tide. At high tide the swimming is fine, and there is an array of water sports on offer – windsurfing, snorkelling, water-skiing, parasailing, paddle boards etc – all for a price, and a classic but fickle surf break.

Orientation

Sanur stretches for about three km along an east-facing coastline, with the landscaped grounds and restaurants of expensive hotels fronting right onto the beach. The conspicuous, 1960s style Hotel Bali Beach (now officially the Natour Grand Bali Beach Hotel, but still commonly called by the original name) is at the northern end of the strip. West of the beachfront hotels, the main drag is called Jalan Danau Toba in the north, but changes to Jalan Danau Tamblingan (formerly Jalan Tanjung Sari) in the middle.

Information

Sanur has travel agencies, moneychangers, film processing, supermarkets and other facilities, mostly along Jalan Danau Tamblingan.

Post & Telecommunications Sanur's post office is on the southern side of Jalan Danau Buyan (the part of Jalan Segara west of the Bypass road). If you're an American Express customer you can have your mail sent to their office, c/o PT Pacto Ltd, PO Box 52, Sanur (☎ 288449), which is in the Hotel Bali Beach.

There's a Telkom wartel at the top end of Jalan Danau Toba, on the corner of Jalan Segara, and a private wartel near the south end of Jalan Tamblingan. A Home Country Direct phone is next to the Malaysian Airlines office in the Hotel Bali Beach.

Museum Le Mayeur

Sanur was one of the places in Bali favoured by Western artists during their prewar discovery of the island. The home of the Belgian artist Le Mayeur, who lived here from 1932 to 1958, is now squeezed between the Hotel Bali Beach and the Diwangkara Beach Hotel. It displays paintings and drawings by Le Mayeur, but, unfortunately, many of them are yellowed, dirty and badly lit. They are nevertheless interesting, impressionist-style paintings from his travels in Africa, India, Italy, France and the South Pacific. The more recent works, from the 1950s, are in much better condition, with the vibrant colours of Bali and the scenes of daily life which later became popular with Balinese artists. All the works have titles, descriptions, dates, etc in both Indonesian and English. The museum is also an interesting example of architecture in its own right. Notice the beautifully carved window shutters which recount the story of Rama and Sita from the *Ramayana*.

Admission is 200 rp (children 100 rp) and it's open from 8 am to 2 pm Sunday, Tuesday, Wednesday and Thursday until 11 am Friday and until noon on Saturday. It's closed on Monday.

Places to Stay

Principally, Sanur is a medium to high-price package-tour resort, although there are a few cheapies and a handful of mid-range places. The prices quoted in the following sections

don't include the 17.5% additional charge for tax and service.

Places to Stay – bottom end

The cheapest places are away from the beach, and at the northern end of town. On Jalan Danau Bayan, west of the main road, there are three lower-priced places side by side. The *Hotel Sanur-Indah*, closest to Denpasar, is the most basic and the cheapest at about 15,000 rp for a room. The *Hotel Taman Sari* and the *Hotel Rani* (☎ 288578) have singles/doubles for around 12,500/17,000 rp, up to 45,000 rp with air-con and hot water.

There are three basic homestays at the northern end of Jalan Danau Toba, the *Yulia*, the *Luisa* and the *Coca*, where clean, simple rooms with private mandi go for around 20,000 rp per night. They're inconspicuously located behind shops at Nos 38, 40 and 42. Further south, on a side street west of the main road, the *Bali Wirasana* (☎ 288632) is cheap at 20,000/40,000 rp; it doesn't have a pool but guests can use the one at Swastika Bungalows.

Places to Stay – middle

At the northern end of Sanur Beach the *Ananda Hotel* (☎ 288327) is behind the restaurant of the same name, right by the beach. It's neat and clean; rooms with fan and cold water cost 25,000/30,000 rp for singles/doubles.

The *Watering Hole Homestay*, (☎ 288289) on Jalan Hang Tuah (the Sanur to Denpasar road), opposite the Hotel Bali Beach entrance, has clean, pleasant rooms from 25,000 rp for a single. It's a friendly, well-run place, and has recently been remodelled; the food is good and there's a bar. On Hang Tuah, on the other side of the Bypass road, the *Hotel Bali Continental* (☎ 288250) is mainly for Indonesian guests, with singles and doubles with air-con, TV and hot water from 50,000 rp.

The *Kalpataharu Homestay & Restaurant* (☎ 288457), on the west side of Jalan Danau Toba, is a pleasant place with a garden and swimming pool. It's clean, and not bad value at US$25/30 for budget rooms, US$30/35 rp for better rooms with air-con.

A little further south, on a side road which runs towards the beach between some government buildings, is the *Werdha Pura*. It's a government-run 'beach cottage prototype', the service is OK, and it's cheap enough at 25,000/50,000 rp for singles/doubles and 60,000 rp for family rooms.

The more expensive mid-range places tend to quote their prices in US dollars and add on about 15% for tax and service. Starting again from the northern end of town, the *Sanur Village Club* (one of the Bali Sanur Bungalows group), on Jalan Hang Tuah, costs US$40/45 with air-con but is not in a good location. *Alit's Beach Bungalows* are also on Hang Tuah, a bit closer to the beach, and cost US$37/40 with air-con and hot water.

On Jalan Segara, the *Tourist Beach Inn* (☎ 288418) is new, clean and well located, but expensive at US$45/50. On Jalan Pantai Sindhu, a block further south and right on the beach, is the *Baruna Beach Inn* (☎ 288546), with a great location and only nine rooms from US$30/45, including breakfast, tax and air-con. Rooms cost a few dollars extra in the high season. On the south side of Jalan Pantai Sindhu, a bit further from the beach, the *Queen Bali Hotel* (☎ 288054) has standard rooms at US$25/30 and bungalows at US$30/35; extra beds are US$7.50. The price includes tax, breakfast, air-con and hot water.

Next to the night market, and running through to the Bypass road, *Abian Srama* has a little swimming pool and over 50 rooms on a small site, but some of them are pretty cheap at US$12/16, while better air-con rooms are US$25/30. It caters mostly to Indonesian guests.

Going down the main drag, you'll find the small *Respati Beach Village* (☎ 288046) which asks US$45 to US$55 for ordinary motel-style double rooms, but should give a discount in the off season. Next door is the *Gazebo Beach Hotel*, a popular beachfront place with a lush garden and singles/doubles from US$35/40 to US$47/55 (US$15 extra in high season).

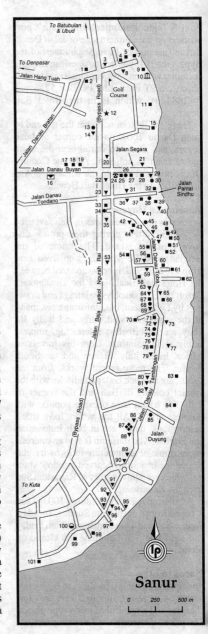

Sanur

0   250   500 m

PLACES TO STAY

1 Bali Sanur
  Bungalows Sanur
  VillageClub
2 Hotel Bali Continental
4 Watering Hole
  Homestay &
  Restaurant
5 Alit's Beach
  Bungalows &
  Restaurant
7 Ananda Hotel &
  Restaurant
9 Diwangkara Beach
  Hotel
11 Natour Grand Bali
  Beach
15 Natour Grand Bali
  Beach - Cottage
  Section
17 Hotel Sanur-Indah
18 Hotel Taman Sari
19 Hotel Rani
25 Puri Kelapa Cottages
27 Tourist Beach Inn
28 Segara Village Hotel
32 Baruna Beach Inn
33 Abian Srama
37 Queen Bali Hotel
39 Natour Sindhu Beach
43 Homestays Yulia,
  Luisa & Coca
48 La Taverna Bali Hotel
49 Respati Beach Village
50 Gazebo Beach Hotel
51 Bali Sanur
  Bungalows Irama
52 Tandjung Sari Hotel
54 Bumi Ayu Bungalows
55 Made Homestay &
  Pub
56 Kalpatharu Homestay
  & Restaurant
58 Prima Cottages
60 Besakih Beach Hotel
61 Santrian Beach
  Cottages
62 Werdha Pura
66 Laghawa Beach Inn
67 Swastika Bungalows
70 Bali Wirasana Hotel
71 Hotel Ramayana
78 Hotel Satai
83 Bali Sanur
  Bungalows
  Peneeda View
84 Bali Hyatt Hotel
97 Santrian Beach
  Resort
98 Semawang Beach Inn
99 Hotel Sanur Beach
101 Surya Beach Hotel

PLACES TO EAT

3 Si Pino Restaurant
8 Bali 16 Pizza
14 Kentucky Fried
  Chicken &
  Swensens Ice
  Cream
20 Lenny's Restaurant
21 Rana's Coffee Shop
22 The Corner
  Restaurant
23 Merry Bar &
  Restaurant
29 Warungs
31 Borneo Restaurant
35 Aga Restaurant
36 Queen Bali
  Restaurant
40 Mango Bar &
  Restaurant
41 Bali Moon
  Restaurant
42 Lotus Pond
  Restaurant
44 Swastika I Restaurant
46 Sindhu Corner
  Restaurant
47 Kuri Putih Restaurant
53 Sita Restaurant
57 Ratu's Pizza
59 Arena Restaurant
63 Bayu Garden
  Restaurant
64 Warung Aditya
65 Laghawa Grill

69 Swastika II
  Restaurant
72 Jineng Restaurant
73 Nam Ban Kan
  Japanese
  Restaurant
76 Penjor Restaurant
77 New Seoul Korean
  Restaurant
79 Karya Seafood &
  Taiwanese
  Restaurant
80 Kulkul Restaurant
81 Melanie Restaurant
82 Restaurant Telaga
  Naga
86 Paon Restaurant
88 Legong Restaurant
89 Oka's Bar Restaurant
90 Cafe Jepun
91 Kesumasari
92 Norman's Bar
93 Donald's Cafe &
  Bakery
94 Alita Garden
  Restaurant
95 Trattoria da Marco
96 Pualam Restaurant

OTHER

6 Boats to Nusa
  Lembongan
10 Museum Le Mayeur
12 Police Station
13 Supermarket
16 Post Office
24 Telkom Wartel
26 US Consular Agency
30 Sanur Beach Market
34 Night Market
38 Rumours Nightclub
45 Subec Disco
68 Temptation
74 Handcraft Market
75 Number One Club
85 Supermarket
87 Double U Shopping
  Centre
100 Bemo Stop

A small side track west of Jalan Danau Tamblingan leads to a T-junction, north of which you'll find *Bumi Ayu Bungalows* (☎ 289101), which are nice but pricey at US$45/50 for a place this far from the beach, going south on the same back lane brings you to *Prima Cottages* (☎ 289153), a clean place with a pool and a friendly atmosphere, and about half the price.

Continuing along Jalan Danau Tamblingan, you'll find the *Laghawa Beach Inn* (☎ 288494, 287919) on the beach side of the road, with air-con singles/doubles for US$35/40; fan-cooled rooms are US$10 less and all prices include continental breakfast. An extra bed costs US$7. The inn has an attractive garden setting, restaurant and bar, and looks like quite good value for Sanur. On the other side of the road, *Swastika Bunga-lows* (☎ 288693; fax 287526) has pretty gardens, two swimming pools, and comfortable rooms for US$27.50/35, or US$37.50/45 with air-con. A few metres further south is the *Hotel Ramayana* (☎ 288429) with air-con rooms at US$23 for singles or doubles, excluding tax and breakfast. South again is the *Hotel Satai* (☎ 287314), a two-storey place with rooms facing inwards to the pool – nothing special, but clean and comfortable, and only US$23/ 25 including breakfast.

At the southern end of town, on a small road between the big hotels, the *Semawang Beach Inn* (☎ 288619) is close to the beach and offers good facilities and breakfast for US$22 to US$30 for air-con singles or doubles.

Places to Stay – top end

The Hotel Bali Beach was Bali's first 'big' hotel. Dating from the Soekarno era of the mid-60s, it was built as a Miami Beach-style rectangular block facing the beach and is still one of the biggest hotels on Bali. Damaged by fire in 1992, it has been substantially remodelled with a Bali-style lobby, and renamed *The Grand Bali Beach* (☎ 288511; fax 287917), PO Box 3275, Denpasar. Managed by the government Natour group, it has all the usual facilities from bars, restaurants and a nightclub to swimming pools and tennis courts, as well as the adjacent golf course and the bowling alley. Air-con rooms in the main block cost from US$115/135 to US$150/170, and there are suites from US$190 to US$400, some with kitchenettes. Adjoining the hotel to the south is the cottage section, with a more Balinese style, from US$110/130.

Immediately north of the Bali Beach and adjacent to the Museum Le Mayeur is the partially secluded *Diwangkara Beach Hotel* (☎ 288577; fax 288894), PO Box 3120, Denpasar. Air-con rooms with breakfast cost from US$45 to US$55 a double. On Jalan Segara, the new *Puri Kelapa Cottages* is a smaller place, away from the beach, and not great value at US$50/60. At the beach end of Jalan Segara, the *Segara Village Hotel* (☎ 288407/8; fax 287242) has motel-style rooms and two-storeyed cottages from US$66 to US$200. The hotel is in a pleasant landscaped area with swimming pools and a children's playground, and it's one of the few places with an organised programme of kids' activities; only US$5 for a 9 am to 2 pm session. Unfortunately, they charge US$20 for an extra bed, which makes it pretty expensive if you have a couple of kids, but it's a nice place with a good atmosphere.

The *Natour Sindhu Beach* (☎ 288351/2; fax 289268), right on the beach, has 50 air-con rooms from US$55/66 to US$77/88, but seems to specialise in conferences and package groups. The *La Taverna Bali Hotel* (☎ 288497), PO Box 40, Denpasar, also right on the beach, is an attractive place with air-con rooms from US$80/90 and suites from US$160 (US$15 extra in the high season).

The main street has several places to stay in the Bali Sanur Bungalows (BSB) group (☎ 288421; fax 288426). Heading south you come first to the *Irama* then to the *Respati*, both priced from US$50 a double. Further south you come to the *Peneeda View* bunga-lows, which are more expensive at US$60/70. Breakfast, tax and service are extra. The *Besakih Beach Hotel* is no longer a member of the BSB group, but it's a nice beachfront place with rooms from US$60/70.

In between the Irama and the Besakih is the *Tandjung Sari Hotel* (☎ 288441; fax 287930), one of the original Balinese beach bungalow accommodation, which started as an extension of a family home in 1962. Individual bungalows are in traditional style and beautifully decorated with crafts and antiques. There's a swimming pool and the restaurant has an excellent reputation, but it's an expensive place, with the bungalows starting at US$200.

The *Santrian Beach Cottages* (☎ 288181; fax 288185), PO Box 3055 Denpasar, have private cottages set in a lush garden with a pool and a beach frontage. It's a very attractive place, well located and quite good value at US$60/65 to US$70/75.

Going south on Jalan Danau Tamblingan, the next top-end place is the *Bali Hyatt* (☎ 288271/7), PO Box 392, Denpasar, one of the biggest hotels in Sanur with 36 acres of grounds between the main road and the beach. It's an interesting contrast with the Hotel Bali Beach built 10 years earlier; with its sloping balconies overflowing with tropical vegetation, the Hyatt blends in remarkably well. Air-con rooms start at around US$160.

The *Santrian Beach Resort* (☎ 288184; fax 288185), on the beachfront, has air-con double rooms from around US$70, plus two swimming pools and tennis courts. The newer *Sativa Sanur Cottages* (☎ 287881), also near the beach, are attractively arranged around a swimming pool and gardens, with air-con rooms from US$62/72 to US$85/95; US$15 extra in high season.

Further south is the huge *Hotel Sanur Beach*, (☎ 288011; fax 287566), with hundreds of air-con rooms from US$110/120 to US$175/200, and suites and bungalows from US$350 to US$900. The *Surya Beach Hotel* (☎ 288833; fax 287303) is the southernmost place in the Sanur strip, so it's pretty tranquil with a frontage to an uncrowded beach – rooms and suites cost from US$90 to US$350.

Places to Eat

All the top-end hotels have their own restaurants, snack bars, coffee bars and just plain bars – generally with top-end prices too! The tourist restaurants are mostly along the main street so it's easy to compare a few as many have similar menus and prices. For cheaper and more authentic Indonesian food, try the rumah makans on the Bypass road, the warungs at the night market, and the food carts and stalls at the northern end of the beach, close to where boats leave for Nusa Lembongan.

The *Jineng Restaurant* serves Balinese feasts, and quite a few hotels offer Balinese buffet dinners with Balinese dancing, from about US$15 up to US$75 per head, though you couldn't vouch for the authenticity of either the food or the dancing at some of these functions.

Trattoria da Marco, down at the southern end of the beach road, boasts the best Italian food on Bali, and has the honorary Italian consul to guarantee it. *Ratu's Pizza* is recommended for pizza, as is the *Pualam Restaurant*, at the south end of the main street. The large and conspicuous tourist restaurants on the main street are useful landmarks (that's why they're on the map), but the service can be slow and the food is often disappointing.

For Asian food, there's the *New Seoul Korean Restaurant* halfway down Jalan Danau Tamblingan on the beach side, and the *Nam Ban Kan* Japanese restaurant a bit further north. *Karya* serves Taiwanese food and seafood. *Telaga Naga*, opposite the Bali Hyatt which owns it, is about the most expensive place to eat in Sanur, but it offers excellent Szechuan-style Chinese food.

For breakfast, *Donald's Cafe & Bakery* and the *Merry Restaurant* both have excellent coffee, pastries and fruit drinks. The *Borneo Restaurant* is one of several places which advertise 'the coldest beer in town', but it is also recommended for breakfast. The restaurants at the *Sanur Beach Market* are quite OK. The *Swastika I* and *Swastika II* restaurants get mixed reports, but they're not expensive, and some people say they're great, so they might be worth a try. Agung and Sue's *Watering Hole*, opposite the Hotel Bali Beach entrance, has good food at affordable prices. Fast-food addicts can get a fix at the *Kentucky Ayam Goreng* (KFC) or *Swensen's Ice Cream*, both next to the supermarket, on the Bypass road opposite the golf course.

Entertainment

Nightlife is not great in Sanur, but there are a few places to go. The fanciest nightspot is the *Matahari disco* at the Hyatt, but drinks are expensive and it's not usually a very energetic scene. The *No 1 Club* has been pretty popular, while *Rumours Nightclub* (☎ 288054 ext 71) is a new place that promises more action, and you can arrange for them to pick you up from your hotel. The slick *Subec disco* is supposed to be popular with locals but tourists also come here, along with some of the local beachboys and non-local bar girls.

Things to Buy

Sanur has many shops selling everything from fluoro-print beachwear to the whole range of handcrafts from Bali and other Indonesian islands. The Sanur Beach market, just south of the Hotel Bali Beach, has a variety of stalls so you can shop around. There are plenty of other shops down the main street, as well as two small market areas, each with a cluster of shops. Several art and antique shops have very interesting stock – browse on the Bypass road as well as the main tourist road. Sanur is also close to many of the villages which produce stone and wood carvings, jewellery, weavings, basketry and so on.

There's a supermarket on the Bypass road, and another at the southern end of town near the Bali Hyatt. The night market, between the Bypass road and Jalan Danau Toba near the northern end of the main street, is open most of the day. It caters a bit for tourists, but still sells fresh vegetables, dried fish, pungent spices, plastic buckets and other household goods that the local people need for themselves.

Getting There & Away

Air Most airlines serving Bali have offices in the Hotel Bali Beach; they generally open Monday to Friday from 8.30 am to 4.30 pm (usually closing for an hour at lunch time), and also on Saturday morning. Telephone numbers for these airlines are:

Airline	Telephone
Air France	☎ 287734
Ansett Australia	☎ 289635
Cathay Pacific	☎ 288576
China Air	☎ 287840
Continental	☎ 287774
Garuda	☎ 288243, 287920
KLM	☎ 287576/7
Korean Air	☎ 289402
Lufthansa	☎ 287069
Malaysian Airlines	☎ 288716

Qantas	☎ 288331
Singapore Airlines	☎ 288124, 287940
Thai International	☎ 288063, 288141

Sempati (☎ 281117, 288824), the efficient domestic airline, is open 24 hours a day, every day.

Bemo There is a bemo stop at the southern end of town near where the main street rejoins the Bypass road, and another stop at the northern end of town outside the entrance to the Hotel Bali Beach. There are two different bemos operating between Sanur and Denpasar. Coming from Sanur the blue ones go past Kereneng station, across town to Tegal station (the Kuta station) and then back to Kereneng. The green bemos *sometimes* take this route around town but usually just go straight to the Kereneng station. The fare is about 600 rp.

To get from Kuta to Sanur you have to go into Denpasar and then out again. You get one bemo from Kuta into the Tegal bemo station, then get a blue bemo to Sanur via Kereneng. If you get a green bemo at Tegal, it will stop at Kereneng and you'll have to get a third one out to Sanur.

Charter Vehicles Charter cars or minibuses congregate at certain points on the main street, and offer their services to any tourist who's on foot. They should take 4000 rp for a trip to Denpasar, 8000 rp to Kuta and 15,000 rp to Ubud, but you'll have to haggle to get them down to these prices.

Boat Boats to Nusa Lembongan leave from the northern end of the beach, in front of the Ananda Hotel & Restaurant. There's a ticket office there, and the fixed price is 15,000 rp (including your surfboard) to get to the island.

Getting Around

To/From the Airport The taxi fare from Sanur to the airport is between 8000 and 10,000 rp.

Bemo Small bemos shuttle up and down the

beach road in Sanur at a cost of 200 rp. Make it clear that you want to take a public bemo, not charter it. Know where you want to go and accept that the driver may take a circuitous route to put down or pick up other passengers.

Car & Motorbike Rental There are numerous places around Sanur renting cars, motorbikes and bicycles, from about 50,000 rp, 12,000 rp and 4000 rp a day respectively. Vehicle hire is more expensive in Sanur than elsewhere, and some heavy bargaining may be called for.

PULAU SERANGAN

Very close to the shore, south of Sanur and close to the mouth of Benoa Harbour, is Pulau Serangan (Turtle Island). Turtles are captured and fattened here in pens before being sold for village feasts. Eggs are also obtained and hatched, but it's not really a breeding programme – most of the animals (or their eggs) have been taken from the wild, so it's not making any contribution to the maintenance of natural turtle populations, and may even be depleting them further. The island has an important temple, Pura Sakenan, noted for its unusual shrines *(candi)*. Twice a year major temple festivals are held here, attracting great crowds of devotees.

Day trips to Serangan have become popular with the travel agencies at Kuta and Sanur, but Serangan has a very strong tourist-trap air and is not terribly popular with visitors. You can get to Serangan on an organised tour or charter a boat from Suwang – you should be able to negotiate the price down to around 12,000 rp per person. Allow about 20 minutes each way for the trip, and an hour to look around the island.

JIMBARAN BAY

Just south of the airport, Jimbaran Bay is a superb crescent of white sand and blue sea. Jimbaran is a fishing village which has acquired some luxury hotels over the last few years, and no budget hotels, shops or eating places will be allowed to sully the 1st-class

ambience. It's accessible from Kuta, only a short distance away.

Places to Stay

The only place resembling budget accommodation, *Puri Indra Prasta*, is away from the beach, on the other side of Jalan Ulu Watu at number 28A. Unfortunately, it's not a well run place – the rooms are grimy and unattractive, the service is reluctant and the swimming pool is murky. They charge 25,000 rp for singles or doubles, and breakfast is extra.

Puri Bambu Bungalows (☎ 753377; fax 753440) is on the western side of Jalan Ulu, a short walk from the beach. It's a new place, with air-con rooms in three-storey blocks round the pool. Prices range from US$55/65 to US$75/90 which is cheap for Jimbaran, but because it's a new place they may give a good discount.

The first of the 1st-class hotels here, the *Pansea Puri Bali* (☎ 752605; fax 752220),

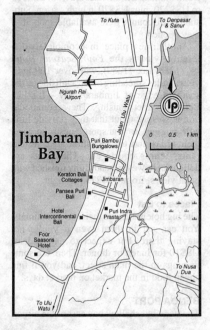

has a full range of facilities and services, including a big swimming pool, two bars, two restaurants and about 40 air-con bungalows and rooms. They cost US$115/130/160 for singles/doubles/triples (US$30 more in the high season), and dinner, breakfast and water sports facilities are included. You can come just for lunch at the beachfront restaurant.

A bit to the north, the *Keraton Bali Cottages* (☎ 753991; fax 753881), opened in 1991, are a really fine example of Balinese hotel architecture, with spacious rooms in two-storey cottages surrounded by tastefully landscaped gardens which extend to the beach. They cost from US$100/110 to US$120/140 (US$10 extra in the high season).

Further south you'll find the massive *Hotel Intercontinental Bali* (☎ 755055; fax 755056), opened in 1993. The architecture has some Balinese elements, but the scale is so huge that it resembles a fortress from the front. Published room rates are from US$165 to US$220, plus US$20 in high season. Substantial discounts were available soon after they opened.

Another new place, in a completely different style, is the *Four Seasons Hotel* (☎ 71288; fax 71280), with over 100 individual villas spreading down a hillside on the southern edge of Jimbaran Bay – it's like Bali-style tract housing. The accommodation is so spread out that they provide little golf buggies to transport guests between their villas and the reception area, restaurants, tennis courts etc. The villas are delightful however, beautifully finished with great views, from US$275 per night.

Places to Eat

The big hotels all have their own restaurants. You can eat in them even if you're not staying there, but expect to pay at least US$10 for lunch or dinner. There are some warungs in the main street, and you'll find cheap food in the market on market days.

BENOA PORT

The wide but shallow bay east of the airport runway, Labuhan Benoa (Benoa Harbour), is one of Bali's main ports. It's the main harbour for visiting yachts and there's nearly always a few overseas vessels moored here. Pelni ships stop here on their circuits through the islands; see the introductory Getting Around chapter for details of their routes. It's also a base for luxury cruises like the *Bali Hai*, and for fishing, diving and surfing trips. The *Mabua Express* luxury catamaran provides a fast boat service from here to Lombok.

Benoa is actually in two parts. Benoa Port is on the northern side, with a two-km long causeway connecting it to the main Kuta to Sanur road. It consists of little more than a wharf and a variety of port offices. Benoa village is on Tanjung Benoa, the point on the southern side of the bay.

A public bemo from Denpasar will cost around 600 rp from Suci bemo station, or 1000 rp from Tegal station. A chartered bemo to/from Kuta or Sanur should cost around 5000 rp.

TANJUNG BENOA

On the southern side of Benoa harbour, Tanjung Benoa peninsula extends north from the resort of Nusa Dua, and at its northern tip is the village of Benoa. Benoa is one of Bali's multidenominational corners, with an interesting Chinese temple, a mosque and a Hindu temple within a hundred metres of each other.

The peninsula has become a water sports centre for Nusa Dua, with places for windsurfing, parasailing, scuba diving etc. Typical prices are US$10 for an hour of windsurfing, half an hour of snorkelling for two people or one round of parasailing. Water skiing is US$15 for 15 minutes and a jet ski is US$18 for 15 minutes.

Places to Stay

Benoa has mostly upper mid-range places, but not nearly as opulent or expensive as the top-end ones in the enclave of Nusa Dua.

The *Sorga Nusa Dua* (☎ 71604; fax 71394) is the northernmost hotel, an attractive place with pool, gardens and tennis

BALI

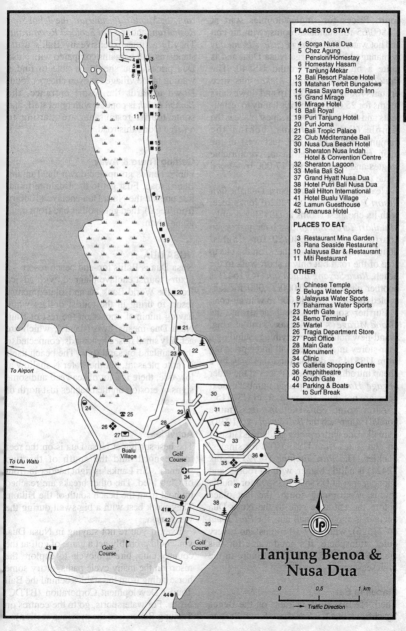

PLACES TO STAY

4 Sorga Nusa Dua
5 Chez Agung
   Pension/Homestay
6 Homestay Hasam
7 Tanjung Mekar
12 Bali Resort Palace Hotel
13 Matahari Terbit Bungalows
14 Rasa Sayang Beach Inn
15 Grand Mirage
16 Mirage Hotel
18 Bali Royal
19 Puri Tanjung Hotel
20 Puri Joma
21 Bali Tropic Palace
22 Club Méditerranée Bali
30 Nusa Dua Beach Hotel
31 Sheraton Nusa Indah
   Hotel & Convention Centre
32 Sheraton Lagoon
33 Melia Bali Sol
37 Grand Hyatt Nusa Dua
38 Hotel Putri Bali Nusa Dua
39 Bali Hilton International
41 Hotel Bualu Village
42 Lamun Guesthouse
43 Amanusa Hotel

PLACES TO EAT

3 Restaurant Mina Garden
8 Rana Seaside Restaurant
10 Jalayusa Bar & Restaurant
11 Miti Restaurant

OTHER

1 Chinese Temple
2 Beluga Water Sports
9 Jalayusa Water Sports
17 Baharmas Water Sports
23 North Gate
24 Bemo Terminal
25 Wartel
26 Tragia Department Store
27 Post Office
28 Main Gate
29 Monument
34 Clinic
35 Galleria Shopping Centre
36 Amphitheatre
40 South Gate
44 Parking & Boats
   to Surf Break

To Airport

To Ulu Watu

Bualu
Village

Golf
Course

Golf
Course

Golf
Course

Tanjung Benoa &
Nusa Dua

0   0.5   1 km

→ Traffic Direction

court. Prices for singles/doubles start at US$60/65 for standard rooms, with air-con and hot water. *Chez Agung Pension/Homestay* is managed by the Sorga Nusa Dua, and is quite a bit cheaper, around US$40. The *Pondok Wisata Tanjung Mekar* has nice upstairs rooms for 35,000 rp and downstairs rooms for 25,000 rp, and it's handy to restaurants and the beach. The cheapest place is the simple *Homestay Hasam*, behind the Tanjung Mekar on a lane just west of the main road, which has clean, comfortable singles and doubles from 17,000 rp – good value for the area.

Heading south towards Nusa Dua, the *Bali Resort Palace Hotel* (☎ 72026) looks nice, with its cheapest rooms at US$80 a double. *Matahari Terbit Bungalows* have just seven apartments for US$40/50 for singles/doubles. Just down from there, on the cheap side of the road but only a short walk to the beach, *Rasa Sayang Beach Inn* (☎ 71643) is another cheapie, at 20,000/25,000 for fan-cooled rooms, 32,000/40,000 rp with air-con.

Further south, on the beachfront, the *Grand Mirage* (☎ 72147; fax 72148) is a big, brand-new hotel with everything including a four-storey interior waterfall and a price tag from US$145 a double (and that may be a cheap introductory offer). Prices at the older *Mirage Hotel* (same phone number), next door, are not quite so grand, from US$115.

After some construction sites (more hotels!) you reach the *Bali Royal* (☎ 71039), a small place with a pretty garden and just 14 air-con suites from US$95/140 for singles/doubles. The *Puri Tanjung* (☎ 72121; fax 72424) is a little bigger, with 64 rooms, and a lot cheaper at US$60 to US$90 for double rooms. Continuing south, the last place before the entrance gate to the Nusa Dua enclave is another small one, the *Puri Joma* (☎ 71526), with only 10 rooms and a very quiet atmosphere. It's good value for this area at US$45/55, and US$10 more in the high season.

Places to Eat

There are several restaurants on the Benoa beachfront, like the *Barakuda Bar & Restau-*rant, the *Mentari Restaurant*, the *Jebal Suta Restaurant* and the *Rai Seafood Restaurant*. They're a little expensive by Bali's usual standards, but bargains compared with Nusa Dua prices. You should be able to find a warung in the village for even cheaper food. Down towards the resort entrance, the *Bambu Indah* is popular with hotel staff, and some tourist restaurants are starting to emerge along this road.

Getting There & Away

Public bemos go up and down the Tanjung Benoa road. First get to the Bualu terminal just outside the Nusa Dua enclave (1000 rp from Tegal), then get another one from there going north.

NUSA DUA

Nusa Dua is Bali's top-end beach resort – a luxury tourist enclave planned, with advice from the World Bank, as an isolated luxury resort to bring in the tourist dollars while having minimal impact on the rest of Bali. Nusa Dua means 'two islands', which are actually small raised headlands, connected to the mainland by sand spits. The beach itself is quite pleasant, but the water is shallow at low tide, there is a lot of seaweed and some signs of erosion on the beaches just north of the resort.

Activities

The best surfing at Nusa Dua is on the reef to the north and the south of the two 'islands'. 'Sri Lanka' is right hander in front of Club Med. The other breaks are reached by boat from the beach south of the Hilton. They work best with a big swell during the wet season.

Even if you're not staying in Nusa Dua, you could probably get a game of golf at the country club, hire a bicycle to explore the resort on the many cycle paths, or try some horse riding from the stables behind the Bali Tourist Development Corporation (BTDC) office. For watersports, go to the centres on Tanjung Benoa (see the previous section).

Places to Stay

The Nusa Dua hotels all have swimming pools, a variety of restaurants and bars, entertainment and sports facilities and various other international hotel mod cons. All these places will add 17.5% tax and service, and many will charge an extra US$25 or so as a high-season supplement.

Starting at the northern end of the resort enclave, *Club Méditerranée Bali* is strictly a package-tour operation, at around US$90 per person per night in the low season, all inclusive.

A Westin Resort is under construction next to Club Med, and south of that is the five-star *Nusa Dua Beach Hotel* (☎ 71210; fax 71229), which is huge (400 rooms), with all the luxuries you could expect and prices from around US$140 to US$150 for standard rooms, plus service and tax.

The *Sheraton Nusa Indah Hotel* (☎ 71906; fax 71908) hasn't as many Balinese decorative touches, but it has all the luxuries, and it pitches for the conference market with the adjacent Bali International Convention Centre, which has a large auditorium and exhibition facilities.

The *Sheraton Lagoon* (☎ 71327; fax 72326) has a huge swimming pool (they call it a swimmable lagoon) which features sandy beaches, landscaped islands and cascading waterfalls. Rooms start at US$165, but for US$205 you can get one with a balcony from which you can flop straight into the pool.

The 500-room *Hotel Melia Bali Sol* (☎ 71510) is run by a Spanish hotel group, with rooms from US$150. It's just north of Nusa Dua's 'amenity core', which has the large Galleria shopping centre, restaurants, bank, phones, an amphitheatre and an emergency clinic.

South of amenity core is the new, 750-room *Grand Hyatt Nusa Dua* (☎ 71234; fax 71084), which is pressing for the title of one of the best hotels in Bali, and charges US$150/170 for its cheapest rooms. South again is the *Hotel Putri Bali Nusa Dua* (☎ 71020; fax 71139), which has 384 rooms, plus suites, cottages and so on, from US$110/125 to US$165. The *Bali Hilton* (☎ 71102;

fax 71199) is the most southerly hotel on the Nusa Dua beach; a massive place with a full range of convention and leisure facilities, and rooms from US$110.

Just inland from the Hilton is the smaller *Hotel Bualu Village* (☎ 71310; fax 71313). Formerly Hotel Club Bualu, it was the first hotel at Nusa Dua, and was used as a training facility by the Hotel & Tourism Training Institute (BPLP). It's away from the beach, and not as elegant as its newer neighbours, but it's smaller with just 50 rooms, and it has a more friendly, informal atmosphere. Rooms cost US$69/79 for single/doubles, and US$112 for a suite.

Adjacent to the Club Bualu is the closest you will come to budget accommodation in Nusa Dua. The *Lamun Guesthouse* (☎ 71983; fax 71985) is the current training ground of the BPLP, and has air-con rooms for US$22/25, including tax. The rooms are very ordinary, the location is nowhere and the service could be anything from overattentive to nonexistent.

On a hill overlooking the golf course to the south of the resort area, the *Amanusa* (☎ 72333; fax 72335) is one of Bali's three new Aman resorts. Small, understated, with sublime architecture, superb decorations and brilliant views, they are setting new standards for taste and elegance, with rooms from US$300 to US$700.

Places to Eat

The Nusa Dua hotels offer a large number of 1st-class restaurants, usually several in each hotel. There are also a few eating possibilities in the Galleria shopping centre, but they're almost as expensive. If you walk a km or so to Bualu village, just west of the resort enclave, you can find the places where the hotel staff eat, which offer better value for money.

Things to Buy

The large Galleria complex in the middle of the resort enclave has an excellent range of clothing, footwear and leather goods, from local manufacturers and major international brand names. There are also handcrafts from

Bali and all over Indonesia – not the cheapest, but some of the most interesting examples. It's fully air-con, they take credit cards and the service is attentive but not pushy. Prices are competitive by international standards, and they have occasional sales with some real bargains. Unexpected delights, like a Rangda undulating through the complex, add a touch of fun and remind you that it's not really a mall in California, even if it looks like one. Just outside the Nusa Dua enclave are a number of tourist shops, and the Tragia supermarket and department store. They're probably a bit cheaper than the Galleria, but not as flashy. There's actually a bit of Kuta bustle out here, and it's a refreshing change from the orderly, uncrowded enclave inside the gates. If you want to shop for quality goods, you'll probably enjoy a day trip to Nusa Dua.

Getting There & Away

A bemo from Denpasar costs around 700 rp from Suci bemo terminal to Bualu village, just outside the Nusa Dua compound. There's usually one every hour, and more when the hotel staff are finishing their shifts – many people commute from Denpasar to Nusa Dua. If you want to shop, call the Galleria (☎ 71662, 71663) or Tragia (☎ 72170, 72172) and they may provide transport.

BUKIT PENINSULA

The southern peninsula is known as Bukit (*bukit* means 'hill' in Indonesian), but was known to the Dutch as Tafelhoek (Table Point). The road south from Kuta goes around the end of the airport runway, and the main route goes south then east to Nusa Dua. A couple of turn-offs to the west will take you to Jimbaran village and the road continues right down to the end of the peninsula at Ulu Watu. There are fine views back over the airport, Kuta and southern Bali.

Pura Ulu Watu

The temple of Ulu Watu perches at the southwestern tip of the peninsula, where sheer cliffs drop precipitously into the clear blue sea – the temple hangs right over the edge!

Ulu Watu is one of several important temples to the spirits of the sea to be found along the southern coast of Bali. Others include Tanah Lot and Rambut Siwi. Most of them are associated with Nirartha, the Javanese priest credited with introducing many of the elements of the Hindu religion to Bali. Nirartha retreated to Ulu Watu for his final days.

Surfing

Ulu Watu is Bali's surfing Mecca, made famous through several classic surfing films. Just before the Ulu Watu car park, a sign indicates the way to the Suluban Surf Beach (Pantai Suluban). There will be a crowd of guys on motorbikes here, waiting to taxi you down towards the beach. It's two or three km down a narrow footpath, which is OK for motorbikes but nothing more. From a motorbike park at the end of the track you continue on foot another 250 metres, down to the small gorge which gives access to the surf. There are half a dozen warungs on the northern side of the gorge, perched on a cliff with great views of the various surf breaks. You can get wax, ding repair stuff, food, beer and a massage, depending on what you need most.

There are other great surf breaks around the south-west tip of the Bukit Peninsula, notably Padang Padang, Bingin and Balangan. Most of them are accessible by somewhat rough roads, and a short walk. Typically, there is a car park at the end of the road (parking costs a few hundred rupiah), and a warung or two with snacks and beer. These are some of the prettiest beaches on Bali, and practically deserted when the surf isn't working. For the latest information, ask in the Kuta surf shops or at Tubes Bar.

Places to Stay

The surf spots have warungs around the cliff tops which offer basic Indonesian food (nasi and mie), Western fare (jaffles and pancakes) and expensive beer. These warungs are not really places to stay, but surfers are sometimes able to crash in them to get an early start on the morning waves.

At the very south end of the peninsula, the *Bali Cliffs Resort* is a luxury hotel perched on the cliff top, with the rooms offering great ocean views. A scenic elevator goes down the cliff to the restaurant and the beach. It costs from around US$110, but you might be able to negotiate a good rate in the off season until it's well established on the package tour market – they won't get any passing trade here.

Places to Eat

There are a few places to eat along the road into Ulu Watu. The *Pub Batu Karung* has food and beer at near Kuta prices, and is planning to provide some bungalows. The *Restaurant Puncak Pesona* is expensive, probably a stop for tour groups. *Ugly Boys* is mainly for beer, while the *Warung Indra*, opposite, looks more like a restaurant and has good, cheap food and a shop selling a few basics like sunblock and film. Further on is the *Corner Pub* and a place to buy petrol.

Denpasar to Ubud

The road from Denpasar via Batubulan, Celuk, Sukawati, Batuan and Mas is lined with places making and selling handcrafts. Many tourists stop and shop along this route, but there are also alternative, quieter routes between the two towns, where much of the craft work is done, in small workshops and family compounds. There are regular bemos along this route, but if you want to stop at craft workshops and buy things, it's more convenient to have your own transport.

BATUBULAN

Soon after leaving Denpasar the road is lined with outlets for stone sculpture, the main craft of Batubulan, which means 'moon stone'. The sculpting is often done by quite young boys and you're welcome to watch them chipping away at big blocks of stone. Not surprisingly, the temples around Batubulan are noted for their fine stone sculptures. Pura Puseh, just a couple of hundred metres to the east of the busy main road, is worth a visit.

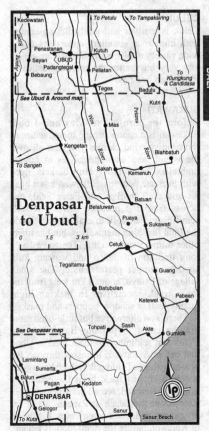

Batubulan is also a centre for antiques and a variety of crafts, textiles and woodwork, and has some well regarded dance troupes. A Barong & Kris dance, popular with tourists, is held in Batubulan every day at 9.30 am. It's touristy and there's a stampede of souvenir sellers afterwards, but if you don't get a chance to see a performance elsewhere then it's worth catching.

Batubulan also has the main bemo terminal for eastern Bali – see under Getting There & Away in the Denpasar section earlier in this chapter for details.

CELUK

Celuk is a silver and goldsmithing centre, with numerous jewellery specialists and a wide variety of pieces on sale. All are generally very busy after the morning dance in Batubulan finishes.

SUKAWATI

Before the turn-off to Mas and Ubud, Sukawati is a centre for the manufacture of those noisy wind chimes you hear all over the island, and also specialises in temple umbrellas and *lontar* (palm) baskets, dyed with intricate patterns. Sukawati has a busy art and craft market, the Pasar Seni, just across from the produce market. It sells semifinished artwork to craft shops who do the final finishing themselves, but has many other things worth seeing. The town has a long tradition of dance and wayang kulit shadow puppet performance. The small village of **Puaya**, about a km west from the main road, specialises in making high-quality leather shadow puppets and masks.

There's an alternative but little-used route via the coast, bypassing Batubulan and Celuk and rejoining the main road to Ubud just before Sukawati. It passes through the coastal village of Gumicik (which has a good beach) and, just back from the coast, the village of Ketewel. A road branches off from Ketewel to the beach at Pabean, a site for religious purification ceremonies. Just north of Ketewel, before the main road, is Guang, another small woodcarving centre.

BATUAN

Batuan is a noted painting centre with a number of galleries. It came under the influence of Bonnet, Spies and the Pita Maha artists' co-operative at an early stage. Batuan painters produced dynamic black-ink drawings, good examples of which can be seen in Ubud's Puri Lukisan Museum. Today the distinct Batuan style of painting is noted for its inclusion of some very modern elements, like the odd windsurfer or a tourist with a video camera in an otherwise traditional Balinese scene. Batuan is also noted for its traditional dance classes and is a centre for carved wooden relief panels and screens.

MAS

Mas means 'gold' but it's woodcarving, particularly mask carving, which is the craft here. The great Majapahit priest Nirartha once lived here and Pura Taman Pule is said to be built on the site of his home. During the three-day Kuningan festival, a *Wayang Wong* performance (an older version of the Ramayana ballet) is put on in the temple's courtyard.

The road through Mas is almost solidly lined with craft shops which do most business by the tour-bus load, but there are plenty of smaller carving operations in the small lanes off the busy main road. The bigger and more successful outlets are often lavishly decorated with fine woodcarvings. The renowned artist Ida Bagus Tilem, whose father was also a noted woodcarver, has a particularly fine gallery.

If you want to stay in Mas, *Taman Harum Cottages* has elegant individual bungalows, some of them two-storeyed with balconies overlooking the rice fields, and there's a swimming pool – prices are from about US$40.

BLAHBATUH

Blahbatuh is a detour from the more direct road to Ubud. Its Pura Gaduh has a metre-high stone head said to be a portrait of Kebo Iwa, the legendary strongman and minister to the last king of the Bedulu kingdom (see under Bedulu and Gunung Kawi in the Around Ubud section later in this chapter). Gajah Mada, the Majapahit prime minister, realised that he could not conquer Bedulu, Bali's strongest kingdom, while Kebo Iwa was there so he lured him away to Java (with promises of women and song) and had him killed. The stone head is thought to be very old, but the temple is a reconstruction of an earlier temple destroyed in the great earthquake of 1917.

KUTRI

Just north of Blahbatuh, near the village of

Kutri, on the western side of the road is Pura Kedarman (also known as Pura Bukit Dharma). If you climb Bukit Dharma nearby (*bukit* means hill), you'll find a panoramic view, and a hill-top shrine with a stone statue of the eight-armed goddess Durga. The statue, in the act of killing a demon-possessed water buffalo, is thought to date from the 11th century and shows strong Indian influences.

Another theory is that the image is of Airlangga's mother Mahendradatta, who married King Udayana, Bali's 10th-century ruler. When her son succeeded to the throne she hatched a bitter plot against him and unleashed evil spirits (*leyaks*) upon his kingdom. She was eventually defeated but this incident eventually led to the legend of the rangda, a widow-witch and ruler of evil spirits. The temple at the base of the hill has images of Durga and the body of a barong can be seen in the *bale barong* (literally 'barong building'); the sacred head is kept elsewhere.

Ubud

Perched on the gentle slopes leading up towards the central mountains, Ubud is the cultural centre of Bali and has attracted visitors interested in Bali's arts & crafts ever since Walter Spies established it as the centre for the cultured visitors of the 1930s. Apart from the many places of interest in Ubud itself, there are also numerous temples, ancient sites and interesting craft centres around the town.

Ubud has undergone tremendous development in the past few years, and now has problems of traffic congestion in the centre and urban sprawl on the edges. On the whole though, Ubud has managed to stay relaxed and beautiful, a place where the evenings are quiet and you can really tell you're in Bali. There's an amazing amount to do in and around Ubud so don't plan to do it in a day. You need at least a few days to appreciate it properly and Ubud is one of those places where days can quickly become weeks and weeks become months.

Orientation

The once small village of Ubud has expanded to encompass its neighbours – Campuan, Penestanan, Padangtegal, Peliatan and Pengosekan are all part of what we see as Ubud today. The crossroads, where the bemos stop, marks the centre of town. On the north (*kaja*) side is the Ubud Palace, on the south (*kelod*) side is the market. Running south beside the market is Monkey Forest Rd, while the main east-west road is Jalan Raya Ubud.

There's a one-way traffic system in the centre of town, with a clockwise-only circuit east of Monkey Forest Rd and south of the main road. It means a substantial detour if you want to drive through town on the main road from east to west.

West of Ubud, the main road drops steeply down to the ravine at Campuan, then bends north past many craft shops and galleries. Penestanan, famous for its painters, is just west of Campuan. Further west again is Sayan, where musician Colin McPhee lived in the 1930s. Peliatan, famous for its dance troupe, is south-east of the centre.

Information

Ubud is just high enough to be noticeably cooler than the coast. It's also noticeably wetter. For getting around Ubud, and especially the surrounding villages, the best map is *Bali Pathfinder*, obtainable in the main street just west of the tourist office – look for its logo, a figure with a pointing hand instead of a head.

Tourist Office Ubud has a very friendly and helpful tourist office (*bina wisata*) on the main street. The Ubud tourist office is a local venture, set up in an effort to defend the village from the tourist onslaught – not by opposing tourism but by generating a respect amongst visitors for Balinese culture and customs.

The sheer number of tourists, and the insensitivity of a few, can still be intrusive, but to some extent these problems have been alleviated by increasing commercialisation of the tourist industry. Most visitors who

BALI

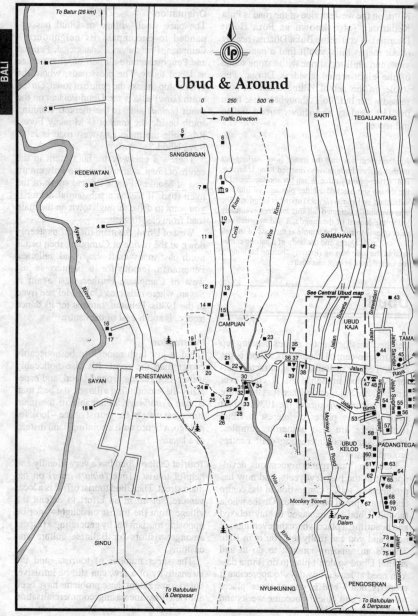

To Batur (26 km)

Ubud & Around

0   250   500 m

→ Traffic Direction

1
2
KEDEWATAN
3
4
SANGGINGAN
5
6
7
8
9
10
11
Cerik River
Wos River
SAKTI
TEGALLANTANG
12   13
14
15
CAMPUAN
16
17
19
SAYAN
PENESTANAN
20   21
22
23
24
25
27
28
26
30
31 32
33   34
35
36 37
38
39
40
18
41
Wos River
SINDU
To Batubulan
& Denpasar
NYUHKUNING
SAMBAHAN
42
43
See Central Ubud map
UBUD
KAJA
Sriwedari
Suweta
Jalan
Jalan
Jalan
TAMA
44
45
Jalan Sandat
Jalan Raya
47 48
Jalan Sugriwa
54
55
56
Jalan Hanoman
Jalan Bima
53
Jalan
57
58
59
60
61
62
PADANGTEGA
63
64
65
66
68
69
70
67
71
72
UBUD
KELOD
Monkey Forest Road
Monkey Forest
Pura
Dalem
73
74
75
76
Hanoman
PENGOSEKAN
To Batubulan
& Denpasar

BALI

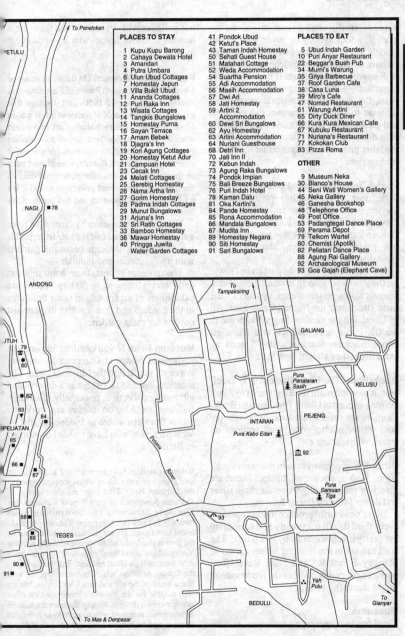

PLACES TO STAY

1 Kupu Kupu Barong
2 Cahaya Dewata Hotel
3 Amandari
4 Putra Umbara
6 Ulun Ubud Cottages
7 Homestay Jepun
8 Villa Bukit Ubud
11 Ananda Cottages
12 Puri Raka Inn
13 Wisata Cottages
14 Tangkis Bungalows
15 Homestay Purna
16 Sayan Terrace
17 Amam Bebek
18 Djagra's Inn
19 Kori Agung Cottages
20 Homestay Ketut Adur
21 Campuan Hotel
22 Cecak Inn
24 Melati Cottages
25 Gerebig Homestay
26 Nama Artha Inn
27 Gorim Homestay
28 Padma Indah Cottages
29 Munut Bungalows
31 Arjuna's Inn
32 Sri Ratih Cottages
33 Bamboo Homestay
36 Mawar Homestay
40 Pringga Juwita
   Water Garden Cottages

41 Pondok Ubud
42 Ketut's Place
43 Taman Indah Homestay
50 Sehati Guest House
51 Matahari Cottage
52 Weda Accommodation
54 Suartha Pension
55 Adi Accommodation
56 Masih Accommodation
57 Dwi Ari
58 Jati Homestay
59 Artini 2
   Accommodation
60 Dewi Sri Bungalows
62 Ayu Homestay
63 Artini Accommodation
64 Nuriani Guesthouse
68 Detri Inn
70 Jati Inn II
72 Kebun Indah
73 Agung Raka Bungalows
74 Pondok Impian
75 Bali Breeze Bungalows
76 Puri Indah Hotel
78 Kaman Dalu
81 Oka Kartini's
84 Pande Homestay
85 Rona Accommodation
86 Mandala Bungalows
87 Mudita Inn
89 Homestay Negara
90 Siti Homestay
91 Sari Bungalows

PLACES TO EAT

5 Ubud Indah Garden
10 Puri Anyar Restaurant
22 Beggar's Bush Pub
34 Murni's Warung
35 Griya Barbecue
38 Roof Garden Cafe
38 Casa Luna
46 Miro's Cafe
47 Nomad Restaurant
65 Warung Artini
65 Dirty Duck Diner
66 Kura Kura Mexican Cafe
67 Kubuku Restaurant
71 Nuriana's Restaurant
77 Kokokan Club
83 Pizza Roma

OTHER

9 Museum Neka
30 Blanco's House
44 Seni Wati Women's Gallery
45 Neka Gallery
46 Ganesha Bookshop
48 Telephone Office
49 Post Office
53 Padangtegal Dance Place
69 Perama Depot
79 Telkom Wartel
80 Chemist (Apotik)
82 Peliatan Dance Place
88 Agung Rai Gallery
92 Archaeological Museum
93 Goa Gajah (Elephant Cave)

witness traditional ceremonies, do so through a tour agency or guide. Part of the guide's job is to ensure that his/her charges go only where they are welcome and behave with appropriate decorum. If they don't, the community will hold the guides responsible. Also, the Balinese have made some decisions as to which ceremonies can be open and public, and which must be conducted with discretion, and visitors will not learn of the latter ones through the normal sources of information.

Post & Telecommunications The pleasant little post office, with a poste-restante service, is towards the east end of Jalan Raya. Have mail addressed to Kantor Pos, Ubud, Bali, Indonesia. You can also get stamps at a few places around town, identified by a 'postal services' sign.

A Telkom wartel is at the east end of town, on the road going north towards Penelokan. There's also a private wartel, upstairs on the main street near the Nomad Restaurant. All of Ubud and the surrounding villages are in the 0361 telephone district. Old five-digit phone numbers starting with 95 need an extra digit; they should now start with 975.

Bookshops The Ubud Bookshop is excellent; it's on the main road right next to Ary's Warung in central Ubud. The Ganesha Bookshop, on the main street almost opposite the post office, is also good, with sections on travel, women, arts etc.

Other The supermarket is in the main street, along with a couple of banks. There are plenty of moneychangers on the main street and down Monkey Forest Rd.

Ubud's colourful produce market operates every third day. It starts early in the morning but pretty much winds up by lunch time. The craft market in the building on the corner of Monkey Forest Rd and Jalan Raya Ubud operates every day, as does the *pasar malam* (night market).

Museums
Ubud has two interesting museums, numerous galleries with art for sale and there are a number of artists' homes which you can visit to view their work.

Puri Lukisan Museum On the main street of Ubud, the Puri Lukisan (Palace of Fine Arts) was established in the mid-1950s and displays fine examples of all schools of Balinese art. It was in Ubud that the modern Balinese art movement started, where artists first began to abandon purely religious and court scenes for scenes of everyday life. Rudolf Bonnet, who played such an important role in this change, helped establish the museum's permanent collection in 1973. It's a relatively small museum and has some excellent art.

You enter the museum by crossing a river gully beside the road and wander from building to building through beautiful gardens with pools, statues and fountains.

The museum is open from 8 am to 4 pm daily and admission is 500 rp. There are exhibitions of art for sale in other buildings in the gardens and in a separate display just outside the main garden.

Museum Neka If you continue beyond the suspension bridge at Campuan for another km or so, you'll find the Museum Neka. The museum, opened in 1982, has a diverse and interesting collection, principally of modern Balinese art. Also on display are works by artists from elsewhere in Indonesia, and by Western artists who have resided or worked in Bali.

Balinese paintings have been defined as falling into four groups or styles, all of which are represented in the Museum Neka. First there are the classical or Kamasan paintings from the village of Kamasan near Klungkung. Then there are the Ubud paintings which basically fall into two subgroups. The older or traditional Ubud paintings are still heavily influenced by the prewar Pita Maha artists' circle, while the postwar Young Artists' styles were influenced by Dutch artist Arie Smit, still an Ubud resident. The third group is the Batuan paintings which, in some respects, look like a blend of the old and new Ubud styles, but are also notable for the modern elements which often sneak into their designs. Finally, there are the modern or 'academic' paintings, which can be loosely defined as anything which doesn't fall into the main Balinese categories. They show influences of everything from the Post-Impressionists to Rothko, and look like the work of 'modern' artists who are abreast of international trends, which is what they are.

The Balinese collection includes numerous works by I Gusti Nyoman Lempad, the Balinese artist who played a key role in the establishment of the Pita Maha group. Some of these works were from the collection of Walter Spies. Other works read like a role call of the best Balinese artists, including Gusti Made Deblog, Gusti Ketut Kobot, Ida Bagus Made, Anak Agung Gede Sobrat, Made Sukada and many others. Works by artists from other parts of Indonesia include those of Abdul Aziz, Dullah, Affandi and Srihadi Sudarsono.

Western artists represented include current residents like Arie Smit, Han Snel and Antonio Blanco, as well as earlier works by Theo Meier, Willem Hofker, Le Mayeur de Merpres, Walter Spies and Rudolf Bonnet. Miguel Covarrubias, who painted and wrote on Bali in the 1930s, is represented, as is Australian artist Donald Friend who worked here until 1977.

Galleries There are countless galleries and shops exhibiting artwork for sale, but there are two 'must see' Ubud art galleries. One is the Neka Gallery, run by Suteja Neka (who also operates the Museum Neka). It has a huge variety of work displayed, generally of a very high quality, including fine pieces from all the schools of Balinese art as well as work by European residents like Han Snel and Arie Smit. Most of them are for sale, often at pretty high prices. It's across the road from the post office at the eastern end of the main road.

Ubud's other important commercial gallery is the Agung Rai Gallery at Peliatan, south east of central Ubud. Again the collection extends for room after room and covers the full range of Balinese styles plus works by Western and Javanese artists like Antonio Blanco, Arie Smit, Han Snel, Theo Meier and Affandi. The gallery also has some important works which are not for sale,

including paintings by I Gusti Nyoman Lempad and Walter Spies.

Artists' Homes The home of I Gusti Nyoman Lempad is on the main street of Ubud, just across from the market, and is open to the public, although there are no works by the artist on display. He is well represented at the Puri Lukisan Museum and the Museum Neka.

Walter Spies and Rudolf Bonnet, the two Western artists who played a key role in changing the course of Balinese art from a purely decorative skill, both lived for some time at Campuan, near the suspension bridge. Spies' home is now one of the rooms at the Campuan Hotel and can be inspected if it is not in use; you can even stay there if you book well ahead.

Just beside the Campuan suspension bridge, across the river from Murni's Warung, the driveway leads up to Filipino-born artist Antonio Blanco's superbly theatrical house. Entry to the beautiful house and gallery is 500 rp. Blanco's speciality is erotic art and illustrated poetry, though for Blanco, playing the part of the artist is probably just as important as painting.

Arie Smit and Han Snel are other well-known Western artists currently residing in Ubud. In the 1960s, Smit sparked the Young Artists' school of painting in Penestanan, just west of Campuan. Han Snel's work is exhibited in a private collection at his restaurant and hotel, just off the main road through Ubud.

Walks Around Ubud
The growth of Ubud has engulfed a number of nearby villages, though these have still managed to retain their distinct identities. It's interesting to walk to the surrounding villages, where you frequently see artists at work in open rooms and verandahs on the quieter streets.

Monkey Forest Monkey Forest Rd is lined with hotels, restaurants and shops for its whole length, but at the far end, at the bottom of the hill, you'll arrive in a small but dense forest. It's inhabited by a handsome band of monkeys ever ready for passing tourists who just might have peanuts available for a hand-out. Peanut vendors are usually waiting to provide monkey sustenance but be warned, the monkeys have become far too used to visitors and can put on ferocious displays of temperament if you don't come through with the goods, and quick. If you're not planning on feeding them don't give any hint that you might have something interesting in a pocket or a bag. You buy a ticket (500 rp) before entering the forest.

Ubud's interesting old **Pura Dalem** (Temple of the Dead) is in the forest – look for the rangda figures devouring children at the entrance to the inner temple. The road swings east at the Monkey Forest, and you can follow it round to Padangtegal or Pengosekan.

Nyuhkuning is a small village south of the monkey forest, noted for its woodcarving, there is a small woodcarving museum.

Campuan   At the confluence of the Wos and Cerik rivers (Campuan actually means 'where two rivers meet'), and far below the bridges, is the Pura Gunung Labuh, a temple thought to date back as far as 1000 years. From beside the temple a walking track leads away to the north along the ridge between the rivers.

Penestanan   The road bends sharply as it crosses the river at Campuan and then runs north, parallel to the river. If you take the steep uphill road which bends away to the left of the main road you reach Penestanan. There are galleries, many of them specialising in paintings of the Young Artists' style, and some losmen and houses to rent.

Sayan & Kedewatan   West of Penestanan is Sayan, the site for Colin McPhee's home in the 1930s, so amusingly described in *A House in Bali*. North of Sayan is Kedewatan, another small village where a road turns east and swings back towards Ubud via Campuan. Just west of the villages and the main road is the Ayung River (Yeh Ayung). The deep gorge of the swift-flowing river offers magnificent

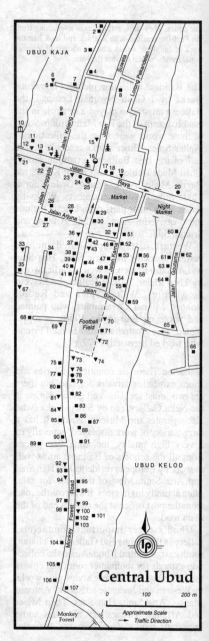

Central Ubud

0   100   200 m

Approximate Scale
→ *Traffic Direction*

PLACES TO STAY

1	Kajeng Home Stay
2	Gusti's Garden Bungalow
3	Lecuk Inn
4	Arjana Accommodation
5	Siti Bungalows
7	Shanti's Homestay
8	Suci Inn
9	Roja's Homestay
11	Mumbul Inn
13	Puri Saraswati Cottages
18	Sudharsana Bungalows
26	Anom Bungalows
27	Suarsena House
29	Happy Inn
30	Canderi's Losmen & Warung
31	Yuni's House
34	Oka Wati's Sunset Bungalows
35	Igna 2 Accommodation
37	Alit's House
38	Puri Muwa Bungalows
40	Dewa House
41	Igna Accommodation
42	Pandawa Homestay
44	Badra Accommodation
46	Gandra House
47	Sudartha House
48	Seroni Bungalows
49	Mertha House
50	Surawan House
51	Widiana's House Bungalows
52	Sania's House
53	Wija House
54	Ning's House
55	Devi House
56	Sayong's House
57	Dewi Putra House
58	Raka House
59	Esty's House
60	Wayan Karya Homestay
61	Wena Homestay
62	Shana Homestay
63	Nirvana Pension
64	Agung's Cottages
65	Sidya Homestay
66	Ramasita Pension
68	Bendi's Accommodation
71	Wahyu Bungalows
75	Accommodation Kerta
77	Karyawan Accommodation
79	Frog Pond Inn
80	Ubud Village Hotel
82	Mandia Bungalows
83	Puri Garden Bungalow
85	Pertiwi Bungalows
86	Adi Cottages
87	Rice Paddy Bungalows
88	Sri Bungalows
89	Jati 3 Bungalows & Putih Accommodation
90	Villa Rasa Sayang
91	Nani House (Karsi Homestay)
93	Jaya Accommodation
95	Ibunda Inn
96	Ubud Bungalows
97	Dewi Ayu Accommodation
98	Ubud Tenau Bungalows
101	Sagitarius Inn
102	Fibra Inn
103	Ubud Inn
104	Lempung Accommodation
105	Pande Permai Bungalows
106	Monkey Forest Hideaway
107	Hotel Champlung Sari

PLACES TO EAT

6	Han Snel's Garden Restaurant
12	Mumbul's Cafe
14	Lotus Cafe
15	Coconut's Cafe
19	Restaurant Puri Pusaka
21	Menara Restaurant
23	Ary's Warung
28	Satri's Warung
32	Seroni's Warung
33	Oka Wati's Warung
36	Ayu's Kitchen
43	Gayatri Restaurant
67	Beji's Cafe
69	Bendi's Restaurant
70	Legian Cafe & Video
72	Ubud Dancer Restaurant
73	Ibu Rai Restaurant
74	Cafe Bali
76	Dian Restaurant
81	Coco Restaurant
84	Cafe Wayan
92	Jaya Cafe
94	Yudit Restaurant & Bakery
99	Warsa's Cafe
100	Ubud Restaurant

OTHER

10	Puri Lukisan Museum
16	Bemo Stop
17	Palace & Hotel Puri Saren Agung
20	I Gusti Nyoman Lempad's home
22	Supermarket
24	Ubud Bookshop
25	Tourist Office (Bina Wisata)
39	Bookshop
45	Ibu Rai Gallery
78	Batik Workshop & Crackpot Cafe

panoramas, and several expensive hotels, and the homes of a number of modern-day McPhees, are perched on the edge. White-water rafting trips offer another perspective on the river.

Petulu In the late afternoons you can enjoy the spectacular sight of thousands of herons arriving home in Petulu. They nest in the trees along the road through the village and make a spectacular sight as they fly in and commence squabbling over the prime perching places.

The road north of Ubud's bemo terminal continues through the village of **Junjungan**, which is heavily into the carving of garudas. Half a dozen shops by the roadside offer them in all sizes from a few cm high to giant two-metre garudas, which probably weigh a ton. A little further on there's a well marked right turn to Petulu.

Other Activities

Bird enthusiasts should inquire about the three-hour guided walks departing from the

Beggar's Bush pub (☎ 975009) at 9.15 am on Sunday, Tuesday and Friday. They cost US$28, including lunch and a guide book.

There are quite a few courses on offer – for more information, start by asking at the tourist office. Possibilities include Balinese music, dance, painting, woodcarving, mask making, batik, Balinese and Indonesian cooking, meditation, Balinese language and Bahasa Indonesia.

Places to Stay

Ubud and the surrounding villages have many small homestays, where a simple, clean room in a pretty garden will cost around 10,000 to 12,000 rp for a single/double, with private bathroom and a light breakfast. For a little more, up to 25,000 or 35,000 rp, you can get a very nice room or bungalow, often well decorated with local arts & crafts, perhaps with a view of rice fields, jungle or garden. Upper mid-range tourist hotels, with swimming pools, hot water and prices from US$25 to US$50, are mostly on Monkey Forest Rd and near Jalan Raya. The really expensive hotels are perched on the edges of the deep, steep valleys of nearby rivers, with superb views and decorative art & craft works that rival many galleries.

Many small losmen are run by people involved with the arts, who are interesting to talk to and often have useful information about what's happening. At most cheaper and mid-price places, breakfast is included in the price. Some of the accommodation is geared to longer stayers (several weeks at least) and usually offers cooking facilities rather than meals.

Just about everyone who stays in Ubud says they had a wonderful place run by lovely, helpful people, and they will recommend it highly.

Places to Stay – bottom end

Many cheap places are very small, just two, three or four rooms. What follows is just a sample; there are many other excellent places apart from those mentioned.

Ubud In central Ubud, the *Mumbul Inn* (☎ 975364) is near the Puri Lukisan Museum on Jalan Raya, and has simple, spartan rooms from 12,000/20,000 rp. *Rojas II* (☎ 975107) bungalows are right by the Museum Puri Lukisan, with a jungle setting close to the middle of town.

Close to the top of Monkey Forest Rd, near the market, is *Canderi's* (also Candri's or Tjanderi's depending on which sign or spelling style you choose), one of Ubud's really long runners. It's a typical, straightforward losmen-style place with singles from 8000 to 10,000 rp and doubles at 15,000 rp. In the small street off the other side of Monkey Forest Rd, *Anom Bungalows* and *Suarsena House* cost about the same.

Going down Monkey Forest Rd, other cheap places include *Pandawa Homestay* at 10,000/15,000 rp, *Igna Accommodation* at 6000/8000 rp, *Karyawan Accommodation* with nice, traditional-style rooms from 12,000/15,000 rp and the very clean and well-kept *Frog Pond Inn*, with a welcoming atmosphere and breakfast for 10,000/15,000 rp a single/double. Nearby *Mandia Bungalows* are well-kept and friendly at 20,000/25,000 rp for singles/doubles. Further down is *Ibunda Inn*, a pleasant place with rooms from 12,000/15,000 rp, or 25,000 rp with hot water. At the south end of Monkey Forest Rd is the secluded *Monkey Forest Hideaway* (☎ 975354), with rooms at 15,000/20,000 rp, some romantically overlooking the forest and others far too close to the road.

The small streets to the east of Monkey Forest Rd, including Jalan Karna and Jalan Goutama, have heaps of small homestays – just look for the small signs near the gates. They are mostly family compounds with three or four bungalows at around 10,000/15,000 including breakfast and tax, though prices depend somewhat on demand. There's nothing to choose between these numerous losmen, just wander down the narrow lanes, have a look in a few, compare the prices and facilities and make your choice.

North of the Centre A few roads run north of Jalan Raya, to the rice fields on the fringe of town. Jalan Kajeng has a number of more expensive places with great views over the river gorge to the west, and a few budget places like *Roja's Homestay*, with rooms at 8000/10,000 rp and 12,000/15,000 rp. Jalan Suweta has the *Suci Inn*, across from the banyan tree, which is a very straightforward losmen-style place with simple rooms with bath from 9000 rp in front rooms and 12,000 rp at the back. The rooms look out on to the central garden, and it's a friendly, relaxed place, quiet yet very central.

Continue up this road for about 10 minutes to Sambahan, where there's a small group of places, best known of which is *Ketut's Place* (☎ 975304), with rooms in a family compound from 10,000/15,000 rp for singles/doubles in the front rooms to 25,000 rp for cottages at the back, or 35,000 rp with hot water. *Sambahan Village Guest House* has also been recommended. A really secluded place is *Taman Indah Homestay*, a walk into the rice fields at the north end of Jalan Sandat, with three rooms at 8000/10,000 rp.

South-East of Ubud More accommodation can be found in **Padangtegal**, in the streets east of central Ubud which run south of Jalan Raya; Jalan Hanoman, Jalan Sugriwa and Jalan Jembawan. *Puri Asri*, on Jalan Hanoman, has six rooms at 20,000/25,000 rp, while *Nuriani Guesthouse* (☎ 975346), just off to the east side on the rice fields, costs 25,000 to 30,000 rp a double. Hanoman continues south to **Pengosekan**, past the pleasant *Jati Inn*, which has two-storey rooms for only 8000/10,000 rp, and the *Bali Breeze* with bungalows at 30,000 rp.

Further east is **Peliatan**, where Jalan Tebesaya has some possibilities, including the popular *Rona Accommodation* (☎ 976229), a very nice place with rooms at 10,000/12,000 rp and 17,000/20,000 rp, and a book exchange with a good selection. They have lots of useful information and can organise tours, car and bike rental, and even baby-sitting.

On the main road south, *Mudita Inn* has two rooms in its shady garden for 8000/12,000 rp for singles/doubles, and there are

other places nearby. At the junction where the road bends sharp left to Denpasar, you'll see a sign for the *Sari Bungalows*, just 100 metres or so off the road. It's a pleasantly quiet location and good value with singles from 5000 to 6000 rp and doubles from 8000 rp, all including a 'big breakfast'. Nearby is the pleasant *Siti Homestay*, with a garden and rooms at 8000/12,000 rp, and also *Nyoman Astana Bungalows* and *Mandra Cottages*.

West of Ubud Heading west on Jalan Raya brings you to **Campuan**, where the rivers meet. Cross the suspension bridge by Murni's, and take the steep road uphill by Blanco's house to **Penestanan**, a quiet but arty area. Along this road you'll find a little group of pretty homestays, including the attractive *Arjuna's Inn*, run by the artist's daughter, with rooms at 15,000 to 20,000 rp. Also along here are *Sri Ratih Cottages* and *Bamboo Homestay*.

There are more places further back into the rice fields, but you have to walk to get to them. The ones near this road include *Gerebig*, *Gorim*, *Reka* and *Made Jagi*. Others are in the rice fields further north, more easily reached by climbing the stairs west of the Campuan road, and following the sign boards. Places to look for include *Siddharta*, *Danau* and *Pugur*. Asking price is from around 15,000/20,000 rp for singles/doubles, up to around 40,000 rp per night for a larger bungalow, but many people stay much longer and negotiate a much lower rate. Further west is **Sayan**, where there are a few small places with great views over the Ayung River; one of cheapest is *Putra Umbara* at 20,000/25,000 rp.

Places to Stay – middle
Many good mid-range places cost from 25,000 to 35,000 rp, with hot running water being the most touted feature (in coastal areas it's air-con). There are a growing number of new or renovated hotels with prices up to US$50, almost always equipped with a swimming pool. For lower mid-range hotels, service, tax and breakfast are usually

included, but the more expensive ones, with US-dollar prices, often add 10 to 15%.

Ubud Near the top of the Monkey Forest Rd and off to the right you'll find *Oka Wati's Sunset Bungalows* (☎ 975063), still with a rice field in view but being built out. It's pretty quiet, and very handy to the centre of town. The rooms range from US$25/30 to US$45/55. There's a swimming pool and a restaurant presided over by Oka Wati herself, a familiar face to visitors to Ubud since the early 1970s.

A little further down, the *Ubud Village Hotel* (☎ 975069) is one of the few new places built with some imagination and taste. The pleasantly decorated rooms, each with a separate garden entrance, cost from US$35. There's a swimming pool with swim-up bar and other luxuries.

Also on Monkey Forest Rd and almost at the forest, the *Ubud Inn* (☎ 975188) is a well-established place with a variety of bungalows and rooms dotted around a spacious garden area with a swimming pool. Rooms cost US$25/35 with fan, US$30/40 with aircon, and two-storey family rooms are US$45. The brick rooms have carved wood and thatched roofs and they're quite cool, each with a private bathroom. The upstairs verandah on the two-storeyed rooms is ideal for gazing out over the fast-disappearing rice fields. Next door, the *Fibra Inn* (☎ 975451) has a pool, and bungalows from US$30.

The newer Monkey Forest Rd hotels are not always so interesting. *Pertiwi Bungalows* (☎ 975236) has comfortable rooms, plenty of outdoor space for kids and a swimming pool, but there's nothing very special about it. They charge from US$32/38 to US$65/75 but service, tax and breakfast are all extra.

There are a number of places along the main road through Ubud but one of the nicest has to be artist Han Snel's *Siti Bungalows* (☎ 975699), hidden away behind the Lotus Cafe. Some of the very pleasant individual cottages are perched right on the edge of the river gorge, looking across to the Puri Lukisan Museum on the other side. There are

seven rooms, the nightly cost is US$40/50 for singles/doubles and it's pleasantly quiet, back off the main road, yet close to the town centre. Further west, another good place is *Abangan Bungalows* (☎ 975082), up a steep driveway off the main road; you'll see the sign on the south side. It has a pool, and 12 rooms from US$20/30 to US$35.

Several places to stay along the main road are associated with the old palaces of Ubud. The pleasant and well-kept *Puri Saraswati Cottages* (☎ 975164), near the Saraswati palace, has rooms for US$17/22 and US$32/37. The *Hotel Puri Saren Agung* (☎ 975957), near the bemo stop in the centre of Ubud, is part of the home of the late head of Ubud's royal family. It's not signposted as a hotel, but walk into the courtyard and inquire – it costs US$30/40. Balinese dances are held regularly in the outer courtyard, and the bungalows have displays of Balinese antiques.

Some small streets climb the slope south of the main road, with a few places to stay – *Pringga Juwita Water Garden Cottages* (☎ 975734) is family-run, with pretty gardens, ponds and a swimming pool from US$37/45. *Pringga Juwita Inn*, not unrelated, is also a very nice and friendly place; a bit cheaper at US$23.

East & South of Ubud In Padangtegal, *Dewi Sri Bungalows* are an attractive midrange option, with a pool and a good restaurant, and nicely decorated rooms from US$25 to US$50. Further east in Peliatan, on the main road, is *Oka Kartini's* (☎ 975135), another long-term survivor now with a swimming pool and other mod cons, but retaining a family atmosphere; rooms cost from US$25/30 to US$35/45. On the main road south, *Mandala Bungalows* (☎ 975191) are another long-standing Ubud establishment, with rooms from about 35,000 rp.

West of Ubud Close to the river junction in **Campuan**, the *Cecak Inn* (☎ 975238) is good value, with attractive, well located bungalows from around 25,000/32,000 rp and up. *Murni's House*, run from Murni's

Warung, has apartments with verandahs for US$40 and also complete six-roomed houses for US$80. Right across the river from the warung, squeezed between the river and Blanco's house behind the Bridge Café, is the *Pondok Tjampuhan Guest House* (☎ 975085), with doubles at US$25. Further out on the main road, opposite and a little before the Museum Neka, the relaxed and pretty *Ananda Cottages* (☎ 975376) has rooms at US$35/45 or two-storey family rooms for US$95; prices include breakfast.

In the rice fields of Penestanan, up the stairs west of the road through Campuan, some of the cottages have mid-range facilities and prices, including the charming *Kori Agung* at 35,000/40,000 rp for singles/doubles, and *Penestanan Bungalows* (☎ 975604), with a pool and tranquillity, which will cost a bit more. For even more rice-field luxury, *Melati Cottages* (☎ 975088) also has a pool, restaurant and quiet location, for US$25/35. Remember that to get here, you have to walk.

Further west in Sayan, overlooking the Ayung River, *Sayan Terrace* (☎ 975384) has a brilliant view and attractive rooms for US$20, bungalows for US$25 and family-size accommodation for US$60. Also overlooking the river, *Djagra's Inn* is a bit hard to get to and impossible to phone, but delightfully secluded, with good-sized rooms from US$30.

Places to Stay – top end

Top-end hotels in Ubud feature some combination of artistic connections, traditional decor, lush landscaping, rice-field views and modern luxuries. They all charge about 17.5% for tax and service, on top of the advertised prices.

Just up beyond the suspension bridge, the long-established *Hotel Tjampuhan* (they prefer the old spelling of Campuan) (☎ 975368; fax 975137; is beautifully situated overlooking the river confluence and Pura Gunung Labuh. The hotel is built on the site of artist Walter Spies' 1930s' home and his small house is now one of the rooms. The rooms are individual bungalows in a wonderful garden and cost from US$45/52 to US$65/80. Up the steep road opposite the Tjampuhan, the *Padma Indah Cottages* (☎ 975719; fax 975091) were established by a collector of Balinese art, and his collection is displayed in all the cottages and in a gallery in the main building. Rooms with a garden view cost US$90; US$10 more for a rice-field view.

Going north from Campuan, about a km past the Neka Gallery, you'll find *Ulun Ubud Cottages* (☎ 975024; fax 975524). The bungalows are beautifully draped down the hillside overlooking the Cerik River, and there are some wonderful carvings, paintings and antiques. Double rooms cost US$55, US$65 or US$90, and there are also larger, two-bedroom family units at US$110. Rates include breakfast, taxes and service, and there's a restaurant, bar and swimming pool.

Beyond Ulun Ubud Cottages, near the Kedewatan junction, is Ubud's most beautifully designed hotel, the *Amandari* (☎ 975333; fax 975335). Accommodation is in private pavilions, simply priced at US$300, US$400, US$500, US$600 and US$700 (plus 17.5% service and tax). It's spacious, exquisitely decorated and with superb views over the rice fields or of the Ayung River. The most expensive rooms have their own private swimming pool. The hotel's main swimming pool seems to drop over the edge right down to the river.

If you head north from the Kedewatan junction you soon come to *Cahaya Dewata* (☎ 975495; fax 975495), which overlooks the same magnificent river gorge. The rooms are US$55/60 for singles/doubles or US$80 for suites, plus 15.5% service and tax. It has great views and some really interesting artworks and decorations. A little further north is *Kupu Kupu Barong* (☎ 975478/9; fax 975079). Clinging precariously to the steep sides of the Ayung River Gorge, each of the beautiful two-storey bungalows has a bedroom and living room and costs from US$305 to US$635 a night, plus 17.5% tax and service. Six of the 17 bungalows have two bedrooms, and some of them have open-air spa baths. The views from the rooms, the pool and the restaurant are unbelievable. Children under 12 years of age are not allowed (they might fall out of the restaurant).

Other expensive hotels are found around the edges of Ubud – nowhere is a view of wet-rice cultivation more bankable than here. The *Hotel Champlung Sari* (☎ 975418; fax 975473) at the bottom end of Monkey Forest Rd has nice views but very ordinary rooms for US$50/60 to US$70/90 for singles/doubles. The new *Puri Kamandalu* (☎ 975825; fax 975851), four km north-east of Ubud, seems to be aiming more for the convention market, but it has a wonderful outlook, and attractive, well decorated, thatched bungalows from US$175 to US$300. Down in Pengosekan, *Puri Indah* (☎ 975742; fax 975332) is owned by Agung Rai, proprietor of the well respected gallery, and has nice views, interesting architecture and fine decor. There's a range of rooms from US$65 to US$120, or US$200 for a complete house.

Places to Eat

Ubud's numerous restaurants probably offer the best and most interesting food on the island. You can get excellent Western food, all the Indonesian standards, and Balinese

dishes will often be on the menu as well. The very best places might cost 20,000 rp to 30,000 rp per hungry person, but they are well worth it for the quality, service and atmosphere, and many good places will cost less than half that price range. A bottle of wine will cost from 50,000 to 100,000 rp, or 4500 rp by the glass.

Jalan Raya The main east-west road offers plenty of interesting dining possibilities. The pasar malam (night market) sets up at dusk right beside the main market area, and probably feeds more foreigners than any other market in Bali. It's the only one where visitors seem to outnumber locals. There are the usual range of market warung dishes, and you can really fill yourself up going from one stall to another trying them all out. It looks healthier at night than in the light of day, but most people survive and come back for more. Dishes start at about 500 rp.

Just east of the pasar malam is the *Nomad Restaurant*, which does serve meals but is mainly a spot for a sociable drink, as it stays open later than most places in Ubud.

West of the tourist office along Jalan Raya are some of Ubud's trendiest restaurants – it's a really excellent area to go out for dinner. *Ary's Warung* is very central and does good

---

A Balinese Feast

Finding real Balinese food in Bali is often far from easy but Ketut Suartana, who can be contacted at the Suci Inn (near the bemo station, off the main road opposite the market) or at Ketut's Place (further up the same road), puts on regular Balinese feasts at 12,500 rp per person. They're held in a pavilion in his parent's family compound where Ketut's Place is also located.

This is an opportunity to sample real Balinese food at its best. Typical meals include duck or Balinese satay, which is a minced and spiced meat wrapped around a wide stick and quite different from the usual Indonesian satay. A variety of vegetables will include several that we normally think of as fruits – like papaya, nangkur (jackfruit) and blimbing. *Paku* is a form of fern and *ketela potton* is tapioca leaves, both prepared as tasty vegetables. Red onions known as *anyang* and cucumber known as *ketimun* will also feature. Then there might be gado gado and mee goreng, both prepared in Balinese style, and a special Balinese dish of duck livers cooked in banana leaves and coconut. Of course there will be krupuk (prawn crackers) and rice. To drink there will be *brem* (Bali rice wine) and you'll finish up with Balinese coffee, peanuts and bananas or Balinese desserts like *sumping*, a leaf-wrapped sticky rice concoction with coconut and palm sugar or banana and jackfruit.

The dining area is hung with palm-leaf decorations, again as for a Balinese feast, and a gamelan player tinkles away in the background. It's fun, delicious and a rare chance to sample real Balinese food but it's also a great opportunity to learn more about Bali and its customs as Ketut talks about his house, his family and answers all sorts of questions about life in Bali. ■

Indonesian and Western food from an extensive menu. Further along, on the other side, the *Lotus Cafe* was for a long time *the* place to eat, and it is still very fashionable; the lotus pond outlook is delightful, and the food is good but pricey – main courses are 6000 to 8000 rp. Try it at least for a light lunch or a snack, just for the atmosphere (closed on Monday). A little further on is *Mumbul's Cafe* – small, friendly with good service and excellent food, and even a children's menu. The *Menara Restaurant*, opposite the Lotus, does good Balinese banquet dishes and has laser disk video entertainment, but don't attempt to enjoy both at the same time.

Further down is *Casa Luna*, with a superb international menu including tiropitakia, Vietnamese salad, tandoori chicken, Balinese paella and Tex-Mex pizza. It also serves bread and pastry from its own bakery, great desserts and small (half) serves for kids. The service is efficient and the atmosphere is pleasant and friendly; they even run courses in Balinese cooking. It's not too expensive, with main courses at around 7500 rp, but the food is worth blowing your budget on.

The *Roof Garden Cafe*, a little further west, is well established with excellent dessert. Up the slope south of the road is *Miro's Cafe*, another top place to eat, with a varied menu and a cool garden setting. The prices are upper mid-range but worth it, with well-prepared Indonesian dishes at 3500 rp, and other main courses at around 8000 rp. On the other side of Jalan Raya, the *Griya Barbeque* serves very good pork, chicken, steak and fish in outdoor and indoor settings.

Continuing to Campuan, *Murni's Warung*, right beside the suspension bridge, offers excellent Indonesian and Western-style food in a beautiful setting. It's been amazingly consistent for years and is still a place to see and be seen – like Ubud's answer to Poppies in Kuta. The sate, hamburgers, lasagne, nasi campur and desserts are all first class, and the staff are charming. Again, it's not cheap, but good value (closed on Wednesday). Above the bridge and across the river from Murni's, *Beggar's Bush* is a British-style pub but with better food.

North of Jalan Raya One of Ubud's real dining pleasures is *Han Snel's Garden Restaurant*, north of the main road and more or less directly behind the Lotus Cafe. The setting is beautiful, with frogs croaking in the background. It's a bit expensive, but the food is OK with generous serves – their rijsttafel is famous – but it's mainly the atmosphere and the hospitable owners which make this place attractive (closed on Sunday). For a Balinese feast, book into *Ketut's Place*, up beyond the palace on the north side of the town centre, and for 12,500 rp per person you get a great Balinese meal, and an excellent introduction to Balinese life and customs.

Monkey Forest Rd Near the northern end, *Satri's Warung*, is an inexpensive place with good food. *Canderi's Warung* is an old Ubud institution, with standard Indonesian and Western dishes. *Gayatri Restaurant* is recommended for families, with inexpensive meals and a play area for kids. Just off the Monkey Forest Rd, *Oka Wati's* is another Ubud institution, and still a pleasant, friendly and economical place to eat. *Ibu Rai Restaurant*, near the football field, also has some good dishes.

Further south, *Cafe Wayan* is more expensive but has some of the best food in town, with a small room in the front and delightful tables in the open air at the back. The nasi campur at 5500 rp is terrific, and the curry ayam (curried chicken) at 7500 rp is superb. Western dishes like spaghetti at 6500 rp also feature, and desserts include the famed coconut pie and 'death by chocolate', a great way to go.

Continue on to *Yudit Restaurant & Bakery*, which makes pretty good pizzas for around 6500 rp, as well as good bread, rolls and other baked goods. The long-running *Ubud Restaurant* is towards the bottom end of the road, but worth the walk.

Around Ubud Anywhere with tourist accommodation will usually have a selection of places to eat. On Jalan Karna, east of Monkey Forest Rd, you'll find top food at the budget-priced *Seroni's Warung*. Further east in Peliatan, on Jalan Tebesaya, these are a couple of good, inexpensive places, including *Pizza Roma*, where the Italian food will not disappoint you.

South of Ubud, Padangtegal has some really interesting places. The *Dirty Duck Diner* does delectable deep-fried duck dishes, and has a menu full of good food and bad puns. Going south you pass the *Kura Kura Mexican Cafe* and, near Perama, *Ubud Raya* with a selection of well prepared Japanese and international dishes.

Around the corner in Pengosekan is a great splurge possibility, the *Kokokan Club* (☎ 975742), a restaurant of the Puri Indah Villas. It serves delicious Thai, seafood and other dishes in opulent surroundings, and the prices are not excessive – soups at 4000 rp, main courses around 7000 rp and desserts at 4000 rp. It's in a beautiful, open-sided bale building, with marble floors, potted palms, linen table-cloths, and a general air of understated elegance. If you phone them they may help with transport.

There are fewer restaurants west of Ubud, but you can eat at the expensive hotels overlooking the Ayung River. Try the *Amandari* for excellent food in a sophisticated atmosphere, or *Kupu Kupu Barong* for a brilliant view.

Entertainment
Music & Dance The main entertainment in Ubud is Balinese dancing. If you're in the right place at the right time you can still catch dances performed for temple ceremonies and an essentially local audience, but even the tourist dances are conducted with a high degree of skill and commitment, and usually have appreciative locals in the audience. The competition between the various Ubud dance troupes is intense, and local connoisseurs speculate endlessly about whether the Peliatan troupe is still the best, or if standards have slipped at Bona.

The tourist office has information on current performances, and sells tickets, which are also widely available in town. The usual entry price for the dances is 5000 rp –

sometimes with transport to performances away from central Ubud. They start at about 7 to 7.30 pm; for out-of-town performances, transport leaves at 6 pm. The programme has several performances every day, including Kecak, Sanghyang, Legong, Mahabharata, Barong and Rangda dances, a women's gamelan and dance, wayang kulit, Ramayana and so on.

Other A number of restaurants run laser-disk video movies, which are becoming popular. Casa Luna sometimes has a kids session at 4.00 pm. Some restaurants also have Balinese dances, but it's much better to attend one of the performances listed above.

Things to Buy
Ubud has a wide variety of shops and galleries, or you can use Ubud as a base to explore and plunder craft and antique shops all the way down to Batubulan (see under Batubulan in the previous Denpasar to Ubud section). The art & craft market at Sukawati is a great place to look, but you should get there early – between 6 and 8 am.

You'll find paintings for sale everywhere. The main galleries have excellent selections, but prices are often well over the US$100 mark. You should be able to get better prices direct from the artist or an artist's workshop. If your budget is limited, look for a smaller picture of high quality, rather than something that resembles wallpaper in size and originality. Small shops by the market and along the Monkey Forest Rd often have good woodcarvings, particularly masks. There are some other good woodcarving places along the road from Peliatan to Goa Gajah and south to Mas, and also north from Tegal Lalang to Pujung.

Getting There & Away
In Ubud, bemos leave from the stop in Jalan Suweta, in the middle of town. You can get bemos from here to nearby villages like Kedewaten, Pejeng, Bedelu, Mas, Sakah and Blahbatuh (from around 350 rp). To get to Denpasar or the southern tourist centres, you first take a bemo to the Batubulan terminal

for about 1000 rp. There are direct bemos between Batubulan and Sanur, but for Kuta you have to take a bemo from Batubulan to the Tegal terminal on the Kuta side of Denpasar for 700 rp and another bemo from there. For bemos to eastern or northern Bali, go via Gianyar.

A typical charter fare to Sanur or Denpasar is about 15,000 rp; Kuta or the airport is about 23,000 rp, while the official taxi fare from the airport to Ubud is 34,000 rp.

Tourist shuttle buses go directly to other tourist areas. Fares to Sanur, Kuta, the airport, Padangbai, Candidasa or Kintamani cost 7500 rp; and to Singaraja or Lovina it's 12,500 rp.) The Perama depot (☎ 975513) is way down towards Pengosekan. Some companies pick up closer to town – try the place at the Nomad Restaurant. There are lots of signs around Ubud announcing departure times and ticket sales with other companies.

Getting Around

There are numerous places in Ubud which rent mountain bikes for 5000 rp a day or 4000 rp a day for long-term rental. Places hiring out cars and motorbikes are equally plentiful, but it pays to shop around and to haggle. It's hard to get them for Kuta prices, and the range of vehicles is not as good.

Numerous tours (day trips or longer) are also operated from Ubud. Tours offered by the tourist office are good value – between 15,000 rp and 30,000 rp for a full day tour, with full itineraries which don't include shopping (except those to craft centres).

Around Ubud

The Pejeng region around Ubud encompasses many of the most ancient monuments and relics in Bali. Many of them pre-date the Majapahit era, and raise as yet unanswered questions about Bali's history. At some sites, newer structures have been built on and around the ancient remains.

The majority of sites are found along the route round Goa Gajah (south-east of Ubud)

and Bedulu, and near the road from there to Tampaksiring. This route follows the Pakerisan river, descending from the holy spring at Tirta Empul near Tampaksiring. Some of the temples and ancient sites in this area are heavily overrun by tourist groups, others are just far enough off the beaten track to leave the crowds behind; some lesser sites are overgrown and so difficult to access that you'd probably need a guide.

You can reach most of the places around Ubud by bemo and on foot. If you're planning to see a lot of them it's a good idea to start at Tirta Empul (about 15 km from Ubud), then any walking you have to do is back downhill.

GOA GAJAH

Only a short distance beyond Peliatan, on the road to Pejeng and Gianyar, a car park on the northern side of the road marks the site of Goa Gajah (Elephant Cave). The cave is carved into a rock face, reached by a flight of steps down from the other side of the road. There were never any elephants in Bali; the cave probably takes its name from the nearby Petanu River which at one time was known as Elephant River.

You enter the cave through the cavernous mouth of a demon. The gigantic fingertips pressed beside the face of the demon push back a riotous jungle of surrounding stone carvings. Inside the T-shaped cave you can see fragmentary remains of *lingams*, the phallic symbols of the Hindu god Shiva, and their female counterpart the *yoni*, plus a statue of the elephant-headed god Ganesh.

Goa Gajah was certainly in existence at the time of the Majapahit takeover of Bali. One tale relates that it was another example of the handiwork of the legendary Kebo Iwa, but it probably dates back to the 11th century and shows elements of both Hindu and Buddhist use.

The cave was discovered in 1923 but it was not until 1954 that the fountains and pool were unearthed. You can clamber down through the rice fields to the Petanu River where there are crumbling rock carvings of stupas (domes for housing Buddhist relics) on a cliff face and a small cave.

Admission to Goa Gajah is 550 rp, and you'll have to pay if you use the car park, and run the gauntlet of souvenir shops. There are places to buy food near the cave.

YEH PULU

Though the path to Yeh Pulu is well marked and easy, you do have to walk to it – just follow the signs off the road beyond Goa Gajah. Eventually, a small gateway leads to the ancient rock carvings at Yeh Pulu (there is a compulsory 'donation' of 550 rp).

Only excavated in 1925 these are some of the oldest relics in Bali. The carved cliff face is about 25 metres long and is believed to be a hermitage dating from the late-14th century. Apart from the figure of elephant-headed Ganesh, the son of Shiva, there are no religious scenes here. The energetic frieze includes various scenes of everyday life – two men carrying an animal slung from a pole, a man slaying a beast with a dagger (and a frog imitating him by disposing of a snake in like manner – clearly the Balinese sense of humour is not new!), and a man on horseback, either pulling a captive woman along behind him or with the woman holding the horse's tail.

On the way through the rice fields to Yeh Pulu you pass a bathing place with female fountain figures remarkably similar to those at Goa Gajah. The Ganesh figures of Yeh Pulu and Goa Gajah are also quite similar, indicating a close relationship between the two sites. *Yeh* is the Balinese word for water and, as at Goa Gajah, water and fountains play an important part at Yeh Pulu.

BEDULU

Just beyond Goa Gajah, Bedulu is the road junction where you can turn south to Gianyar or north to Pejeng and Tampaksiring. It's hard to imagine this small village as the former capital of a great kingdom, but the legendary Dalem Bedaulu ruled the Pejeng dynasty from here and was the last Balinese king to withstand the onslaught of the powerful Majapahits from Java. He was eventually defeated by Gajah Mada in 1343. The capital shifted several times after this, ending up at Gelgel and then later at Klungkung.

A legend relates how Bedaulu possessed magical powers which allowed him to have his head chopped off and then replaced. Performing this unique party trick one day the servant entrusted with lopping off his head and then replacing it unfortunately dropped it in a river and, to his horror, watched it float away. Looking around in panic for a replacement he grabbed a pig, cut off its head and popped it upon the king's shoulders. Thereafter the king was forced to sit on a high throne and forbade his subjects to look up at him; Bedaulu means 'he who changed heads'.

The Pura Samuan Tiga (Temple of the Meeting of the Three, probably a reference to the Hindu trinity) is about 100 metres east of the Bedulu junction. This important 11th-century temple is packed with Balinese during the Odalan Festival.

Bedulu Arkeologi Gedong Arca (the Bedulu Archaeological Museum) is about two km north of Bedulu and includes a collection of pre-Hindu artefacts, including stone sarcophagi from the time before cremations were practised in Bali. It's not particularly interesting, unless you're into archaeology.

PEJENG

Continuing up the road to Tampaksiring you soon come to Pejeng and its famous temples. Like Bedulu this was once an important seat of power, the capital of the Pejeng kingdom which fell to the Majapahit invaders in 1343.

Pura Kebo Edan

The Crazy Buffalo Temple (Pura Kebo Edan) with its nearly four-metre-high statue of Bima, also known as the **giant of Pejeng**, is on the western side of the road as you come in to Pejeng (entry is 500 rp).

There's considerable conjecture over what this fearsome image is all about. The dead body which the image tramples upon appears to relate to the Hindu Shiva cult but it may also have Tantric Buddhist overtones. Other figures flank the main one and male and female buffaloes lie before it. There is also conjecture about the giant's genitalia – it has either six small penises or one large one, and if that large thing is a penis, what are the interesting lumps and the big hole in the side?

Pura Pusering Jagat

The large Navel of the World Temple (Pura Pusering Jagat) is said to be the centre of the old Pejeng kingdom. Dating from 1329, this temple is visited by young couples who pray at the stone *lingam* and *yoni*.

Pura Penataran Sasih

In the centre of Pejeng, Pura Penataran Sasih was once the state temple of the Pejeng kingdom. In the inner courtyard, high up in a pavilion where you really cannot see it very well, is the huge bronze drum known as the **Moon of Pejeng**.

The hourglass-shaped drum is more than three metres long, the largest single piece cast drum in the world. Estimates of its age vary from 1000 to 2000 years, and it is not certain whether it was made locally or imported. The intricate geometrical designs are said to resemble patterns from as far apart as Irian Jaya and Vietnam.

A Balinese legend relates how the drum came to earth as a fallen moon, landing in a tree and shining so brightly that it prevented a band of thieves from going about their unlawful purpose. One of the thieves decided to put the light out by urinating on it but the moon exploded, killed the foolhardy thief and fell to earth as a drum – with a crack across its base as a result of the fall.

TAMPAKSIRING

Tampaksiring is a small town with a large and important temple, and the most impressive ancient monument in Bali.

Gunung Kawi

On the southern outskirts of Tampaksiring, a sign points off the road to the right to Gunung Kawi. From the end of the access road a steep stone stairway leads down to the river, at one point making a cutting through an embankment of solid rock. In the bottom of this lush green valley is one of Bali's oldest, and certainly largest, ancient monuments.

Gunung Kawi consists of 10 rock-cut *candi* – memorials cut into the rock face in a similar fashion to the great rock-cut temples of Ajanta and Ellora in India. Each candi is believed to be a memorial to a member of the 11th-century Balinese royalty but little is known for certain. They stand in seven-metre-high sheltered niches cut into the

sheer cliff face. There are four on the west side of the river which you come to first, and five on the east side. Each of the sets of memorials has a group of monks' cells associated with it. A solitary candi stands further down the valley to the south.

Legends relate that the whole group of memorials was carved out of the rock face in one hard working night by the mighty finger-nails of Kebo Iwa. It's uncertain who the real builders were but they may date from the Udayana dynasty of the 10th and 11th centuries. It's said that the five monuments on the eastern bank are to King Udayana, Queen Mahendradatta, their son Airlangga and his brothers Anak Wungsu and Marakata. While Airlangga ruled eastern Java, Anak Wungsu ruled Bali. The four monuments on the western side are, by this theory, to Anak Wungsu's chief concubines. Another theory is that the whole complex is dedicated to Anak Wungsu, his wives, concubines and, in the case of the remote tenth candi, to a royal minister. Entry to Gunung Kawi is 550 rp.

Tirta Empul

North of Tampaksiring, the road branches. The left fork runs up to the grand palace once used by Soekarno, which overlooks the temple and its bathing pools. The right fork dips down past the temple at Tirta Empul and continues up to Penelokan. You can look back along the valley and see Gunung Kawi from this road, just before you turn into Tirta Empul. The holy springs at Tirta Empul are believed to have magical powers so the temple here is an important one. The springs are a source of the Pakerisan River, which rushes by Gunung Kawi only a km or so away.

The springs, used since 962 AD, bubble up into a large, crystal-clear tank within the temple, and gush out through waterspouts into a bathing pool. According to legend, the springs were created by the god Indra who pierced the earth to tap the 'elixir of immortality' or *amerta*. The temple was totally restored in the late 1960s.

There is an admission charge (550 rp) and parking fee, and you have to wear a temple scarf. Come early in the morning or late in the afternoon to avoid the tour-bus hordes.

Other Sites

Between Tirta Empul and Gunung Kawi is the temple of Pura Mengening where you can see a freestanding candi similar in design to those of Gunung Kawi. There is a spring at this temple which also feeds into the Pakerisan River.

Places to Stay & Eat

Apart from the usual selection of warungs there's also the expensive *Tampaksiring Restaurant* for tourist groups; it's some distance below the village. It's not easy to find a place to stay here, but it's an easy day trip from Ubud or Bangli, or a stopover between Ubud and Kintamani.

UBUD TO BATUR

The usual road from Ubud to Batur is through Tampaksiring but there are other lesser roads up the gentle mountain slope. If you head east out of Ubud and turn away from Peliatan, towards Petulu at the junction, this road will bring you out on the crater rim just beyond Penelokan towards Batur. It's a sealed road all the way. Along this road you'll see a number of woodcarvers producing beautiful painted birds, frogs, garudas and tropical fruit. Tegalalang and the nearby village of Jati, just off the road, are noted woodcarving centres. Further up, other specialists carve stools and there are a couple of places where whole tree trunks are carved into whimsical figures.

East Bali

The eastern end of Bali is dominated by mighty Gunung Agung, the 'navel of the world' and Bali's 'mother mountain'. Towering at 3142 metres, Agung has not always been a kind mother – witness the disastrous 1963 eruption. Today Agung is quiet but the 'mother temple' Pura Besakih, perched high on the slopes of the volcano, attracts a steady stream of devotees...and tourists.

The route east goes through Klungkung, the former capital of one of Bali's great kingdoms, then runs close to the coast passing Kusamba, the bat-infested temple of Goa Lawah and the beautiful port of Padangbai. There are lots of beachside places to stay from there to the resort of Candidasa. When you reach Amlapura, another former capital, you can continue past Tirtagangga to the east coast, or return via a route higher up the slopes of Gunung Agung. Bemos from Batubulan go to the towns on this route, and do shorter connections in beween them.

GIANYAR

Gianyar is the administrative centre of the Gianyar district which also includes Ubud, but is of minimal interest in its own right. There a number of small textile factories on the Denpasar side. You can drop in, see materials being woven and buy some of the work. Busloads of free-spending visitors can push prices up to higher levels than in Denpasar.

The Gianyar royal family saved their palace by capitulating to the Dutch. The original palace dates from 1771, but was destroyed in a conflict with the neighbouring kingdom of Klungkung in the mid-1880s, it was rebuilt, and then severely damaged again in the 1917 earthquake. It's a fine example of traditional palace architecture, but the royal family of Gianyar still live there so you can't go inside the walls.

Gianyar's warungs are noted for their fine roast piglet, *babi guling*. Eat early though, as the warungs are usually cleaned out by late morning.

BONA

The village of Bona, on the back road between Gianyar and Blahbatuh, is credited with being the modern home of the Kecak dance. Kecak and other dances are held here every week and are easy to get to from Ubud. Tickets (including transport) from Ubud cost around 5000 rp.

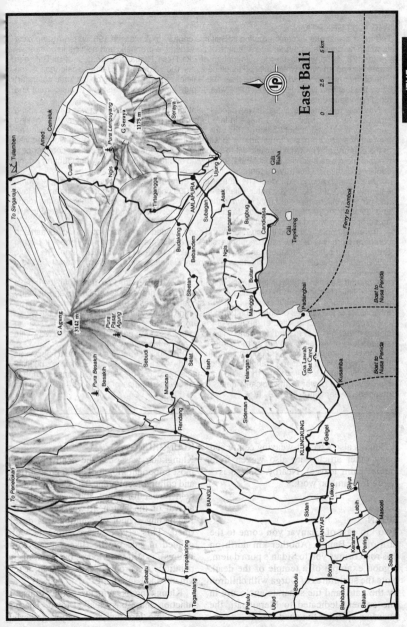

THE 1963 ERUPTION

The most disastrous volcanic eruption in Bali this century took place in 1963 when Agung blew its top in no uncertain manner and at a time of considerable prophetic and political importance.

March 8, 1963 was to be the culmination of Eka Desa Rudra, the greatest of all Balinese sacrifices and an event which only takes place every 100 years on the Balinese calendar. At the time of the eruption, it had been more than 100 Balinese years (115 years on the lunar calendar) since the last Eka Desa Rudra, but there was dispute amongst the priests as to the correct and most propitious date.

Naturally the temple at Besakih was a focal point for the festival but Agung was already acting strangely as preparations were made in late February. The date of the ceremony was looking decidedly unpropitious, but Soekarno, then the president of Indonesia, had already scheduled an international conference of travel agents to witness the great occasion as a highlight of their visit to the country, and he would not allow it to be postponed. By the time the sacrifices commenced, the mountain was belching smoke and ash, glowing and rumbling ominously but Gunung Agung contained itself until the travel agents had flown home.

On 17 March Agung exploded. The catastrophic eruption killed more than 1000 people (some estimate 2000) and destroyed entire villages – 100,000 people lost their homes. Streams of lava and hot volcanic mud poured right down to the sea at several places, completely covering roads and isolating the eastern end of the island for some time. The entire island was covered in ash and crops were wiped out everywhere.

Torrential rainfall followed the eruptions, and compounded the damage as boiling hot ash and boulders were swept down the mountain side, wreaking havoc on many villages, including Subagan, just outside Amlapura and Selat, further along the road towards Rendang. The whole of Bali suffered a drastic food shortage and many Balinese were resettled in west Bali and Sulawesi.

Although Besakih is high on the slopes of Agung, only about six km from the crater, the temple suffered little damage from the eruption. Volcanic dust and gravel flattened timber and bamboo buildings around the temple complex but the stone structures came through unscathed. The inhabitants of the villages of Sorga and Lebih, also high up on Agung's slopes, were all but wiped out. Most of the people killed at the time of the eruption were burnt and suffocated by searing clouds of hot gas that rushed down the volcano's slopes. Agung erupted again on 16 May, with serious loss of life, although not on the same scale as the March eruption.

The Balinese take signs and portents seriously – that such a terrible event should happen as they were making a most important sacrifice to the gods was not taken lightly. Soekarno's political demise two years later, following the failed communist coup, could be seen as a consequence of his defying the power of the volcanic deity. The interrupted series of sacrifices finally recommenced 16 years later, in 1979. ■

Bona is also a basket-weaving centre and many other articles are also woven from *lontar* (palm leaves). Nearby, Belega is a centre for bamboo work.

SIDAN

Two km east of Gianyar you come to the turn-off to Bangli. Another km north on this road brings you to Sidan's pura dalem, a good example of a temple of the dead. Note the sculptures of Durga with children by the gate, and the separate enclosure in one corner, dedicated to Merajapati, the guardian spirit of the dead.

KLUNGKUNG

Klungkung was once the centre of Bali's most important kingdom and a great artistic and cultural focal point. The Gelgel dynasty held power for about 300 years, until the arrival of the Dutch. It was here that the Klungkung school of painting was developed. This style, where subjects were painted in side profile (like wayang kulit figures), is still used today, but most of the paintings are produced in Kamasan, a few km outside Klungkung.

Klungkung is a major public transport junction and a busy market town. The bus and bemo terminal is a major gathering point, particularly at night when a busy night market operates there.

Royal Palace

When the ruling Dewa Agung dynasty moved here from Gelgel in 1710, they established a new palace, laid out as a large square with courtyards, gardens, pavilions and moats, and built by the best artisans available. Most of the palace and grounds were destroyed during Dutch attacks in 1908, and the two pavilions you see now have been extensively restored and rebuilt. The complex, called Taman Gili, is surrounded by a stone wall on the south side of the road from Denpasar. Entry costs 500 rp.

Kertha Gosa The Kertha Gosa (Hall of Justice) stands in the north east corner of the Taman Gili, a marked contrast to the busy intersection and modern town. The pavilion is a superb example of Klungkung architecture, with the ceiling completely covered with paintings in the Klungkung style. The paintings, done on asbestos sheeting, were installed in the 1940s, replacing the cloth paintings which had deteriorated. Further repainting and restoration took place in the 1960s and 1980s, but the style of the paintings appears to have been fairly consistent. Virtually the only record of the earlier paintings was a photograph of the ceiling taken by Walter Spies in the 1930s. In Bali's humid climate there is rapid deterioration and already the current paintings are looking very second-hand.

The Kertha Gosa was effectively the 'supreme court' of the Klungkung kingdom, resolving disputes and cases which could not be settled at the village level. The defendant, standing before the three priests who acted as judges (kerthas), could gaze up at the ceiling and see wrongdoers being tortured by demons and the innocent enjoying the pleasures of Balinese heaven. In the colonial period, the court was used to deal with questions of traditional law (adat) while colonial law was handled by Dutch courts.

Bale Kambang Also in the Taman Gili, is

the beautiful Bale Kambang (Floating Pavilion), which has been extensively rebuilt this century. Its ceiling, decorated with Klungkung-style paintings, was redone in 1945. Around the Kertha Gosa and the Bale Kambang, note the statues of top-hatted European figures, an amusing departure from the normal statues of entrance guardians.

Museum

Across the courtyard to the west of the Bale Kambang is a new museum. It exhibits paintings and handcrafts of Klungkung, and might give you a good introduction to the wayang and Kamasan styles. All exhibits are labelled in English. The museum is open from 7 am to 4pm, and admission is 500 rp.

Places to Stay & Eat

Few travellers stay in Klungkung, but there are a couple of possibilities, the nicest of which is the *Ramayana Palace Hotel* (☎ 0366 21044) on the Candidasa side of town. The good rooms are quite big and cost 20,000 rp with bathroom. Small and fairly spartan rooms with shared mandi cost 10,000 rp. There's a pleasant restaurant in a pavilion out the back. Less attractive alternatives include the *Losmen Wisnu*, near the bus terminal in the centre of town (the upstairs rooms are much brighter), and the very basic *Bell Inn*, almost opposite the Ramayana Palace.

Apart from the Ramayana Palace's restaurant, you can eat at the *Restaurant Bali Indah* and *Restaurant Sumber Rasa*, across from the market.

Things to Buy

There are a number of good shops along Jalan Diponegoro in Klungkung selling Klungkung-style paintings and some interesting antiques. Klungkung is also a good place for buying temple umbrellas – several shops sell them.

Getting There & Away

Bemos bound for Candidasa and Amlapura all pass through Klungkung. Bemos also shuttle up and down the mountain road from Klungkung to Besakih. The fare to Batubulan is about 1200 rp.

KUSAMBA
Turning south off the main road brings you to the coast, and the fishing village of Kusamba, where you'll see lines of colourful fishing *perahus* (outriggers) lined up on the beach. They take supplies from here to the islands of Nusa Penida and Nusa Lembongan. If you want to take one of these cargo perahus, get there early, but it would be safer and more convenient to go from Sanur or Padangbai.

Just beyond Kusamba you can see the thatched roofs of salt-panning huts along the beach. Salt-water-saturated sand from the beach is dried out around these huts and then further processed inside the huts. Although salt processed by machine is cheaper, connoisseurs still demand real sea salt.

GOA LAWAH
Beyond Kusamba the road continues close to the coast and after a few km you come to the Goa Lawah (Bat Cave). The cave in the cliff face here is packed, crammed, jammed full of bats.

The cave, part of a temple, is said to lead all the way to Besakih. The bats provide sustenance for the legendary giant snake Naga Basuki, which is said to live in the cave. A distinctly batty stench exudes from the cave, and the roofs of the temple shrines in front of the cave are liberally coated with bat droppings.

Entry to the bat cave temple is 500 rp (children 100 rp), including hire of a temple scarf. The souvenir sellers are very pushy. It's hard to think of a good reason to stop here.

PADANGBAI
Padangbai is the port for the ferry service between Bali and Lombok. It's a couple of km off the main Klungkung to Amlapura road, 54 km from Denpasar. There's a perfect little bay, and it's one of the two main shipping ports in southern Bali. There are other pretty and secluded beaches to the north and south. Out on the northern corner of the bay is the temple of Pura Silayukti, where Empu Kuturan, who introduced the caste system to Bali in the 11th century, is said to have lived. Cruise ships visiting Bali use Padangbai, and the town is temporarily transformed into a cacophonous souvenir market with sellers flocking in from all over the island.

Information
There are moneychangers in the main street, a post office and a wartel from where you can make international calls at higher than normal prices. The tourist information office is in the car park near the dock. It's not a great place for shopping, but one interesting speciality is the beautiful model jukungs, made by Made Sawela on Jalan Silayukti.

There's some pretty good diving on the coral reefs around Padangbai, but there doesn't seem to be a local operator. Ask at the beachfront restaurants which cater to dive groups.

Places to Stay
Most visitors to Padangbai stay at one of the pleasant beachfront places – the gentle arc of beach with colourful fishing boats drawn up on the sand is postcard perfect. Closest to the village is the *Rai Beach Inn* which has a collection of two-storey cottages for 20,000 rp and single-storey rooms with bathroom at 15,000 rp.

Next along the beach is the *Kerti Beach Inn*, with simple rooms at 8000 rp and also double-storey thatched cottages at 12,000 rp. The third place in the central beachfront cluster is the *Padangbai Beach Inn* where rooms are 7000/9000 rp for singles/doubles. The rooms are a standard losmen design and they all face the sea.

If you continue along the beach right to the end of the bay, you'll find the *Topi Inn & Restaurant*. It has small rooms upstairs at 8000/10,000 rp for singles/doubles, and dorm beds at 2000 rp.

Pantai Ayu Homestay is back from the beach behind the cemetery, but still a good place to stay, with a variety of rooms from

BALI

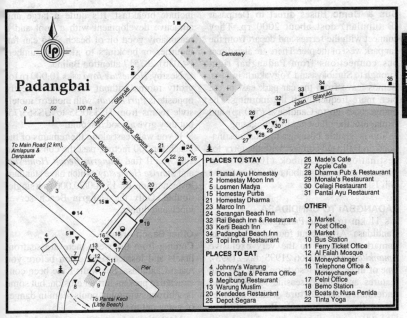

Padangbai

0   50   100 m

To Main Road (2 km),
Amlapura &
Denpasar

Cemetery

Pier

To Pantai Kecil
(Little Beach)

PLACES TO STAY
1 Pantai Ayu Homestay
2 Homestay Moon Inn
5 Losmen Madya
15 Homestay Purba
21 Homestay Dharma
23 Marco Inn
24 Serangan Beach Inn
32 Rai Beach Inn & Restaurant
33 Kerti Beach Inn
34 Padangbai Beach Inn
35 Topi Inn & Restaurant

PLACES TO EAT
4 Johnny's Warung
6 Dona Cafe & Perama Office
8 Megibung Restaurant
13 Warung Muslim
20 Kendedes Restaurant
25 Depot Segara

26 Made's Cafe
27 Apple Cafe
28 Dharma Pub & Restaurant
29 Monala's Restaurant
30 Celagi Restaurant
31 Pantai Ayu Restaurant

OTHER
3 Market
7 Post Office
9 Market
10 Bus Station
11 Ferry Ticket Office
12 Al Falah Mosque
14 Moneychanger
16 Telephone Office &
    Moneychanger
17 Pelni Office
18 Bemo Station
19 Boats to Nusa Penida
22 Tinta Yoga

8000/10,000 rp up to 20,000 rp. In the village, *Homestay Dharma* is a plain family compound with very neat and tidy rooms at 9000 rp for a double. Other places in town include *Homestay Purba*, with rooms from 6000/8000 rp to 8000/10,000 rp, *Marco Inn* and *Serangan Beach Inn*.

Places to Eat

Right across from the Rai Beach Inn there's a line-up of simple beachfront warungs where Ibu Komang, the 'mama' of the *Pantai Ayu Restaurant* wins the popularity contest hands down. Other places along the beach are the long-running *Celagi Restaurant*, *Monala's Restaurant*, the *Dharma Pub & Restaurant* (popular with visiting dive groups), *Apple Cafe* and *Made's Cafe*. At the eastern end of the beach, the *Topi Restaurant* has a sand-floored dining area and a colourful menu featuring fish dishes plus the Indonesian regulars.

In the town but near the beach there's

Depot Segara and *Kendedes Restaurant*, while along the main street there are a host of small Indonesian places, including the *Warung Muslim*, in front of the mosque, and *Dona Cafe*. Round past the post office, *Megibung Restaurant* may also be worth a try. None of these places will be expensive.

Getting There & Away

To/From Lombok Ferries are scheduled to depart for Lombok every two hours from about 4 am to 10 pm, but sometimes they are late, and sometimes early. The fare is 4800 rp, or 8700 rp in 1st class. The ticket office is down by the pier. If the fast boat service to Bangsal and Senggigi is operating again, get information and a ticket from the office in the main road (☎ 234428).

To/From Nusa Penida On the beach just east of the pier car park you'll find the twin-engined fibreglass boats that run across the strait to Nusa Penida (4000 rp).

Bus & Bemo Buses direct to Denpasar (Batubulan) cost about 2000 rp. They connect with the ferries and depart from the car park west of the pier. There are also direct bus connections from Padangbai right through to Surabaya and Yogyakarta in Java. Bemos leave from the car park east of the pier, more frequently in the morning. The orange ones go to Candidasa (500 rp) and Amlapura; the blue ones to Klungkung.

Tourist shuttle buses go to most destinations on Bali, and connect with the ferry for destinations on Lombok (10,000 rp to Mataram or Senggigi, about 20,000 rp for the Gili Islands).

PADANGBAI TO CANDIDASA

It's 11 km from the Padangbai turn-off to Candidasa. After about four km, there's an unmarked turn-off to the very exclusive *Amankila* hotel (☎ 0366 21993; fax 21995). One of three Aman resorts on Bali, this one features an isolated seaside location, and understated architecture which complements the environment. Prices start at US$300.

Balina Beach (Buitan)

Balina Beach is the name bestowed on the tourist development in the village of Buitan, about five or six km from the Padangbai turn-off, just after a substantial girder bridge.. It's a quiet, pretty place, in the process of acquiring its first luxury hotel, and losing its beach to erosion.

Diving

Diving trips from the Nelayan Village Cottages, including transport and two full tanks, range from US$40 to US$50 on the trips closer to Balina, US$70 for Nusa Penida and US$85 to Pulau Menjangan on the north coast.

Places to Stay

Nelayan Village Cottages has rooms at a host of prices from as low as US$16/20 for singles/doubles and up to US$40/45 for fancier rooms, or US$65 for a large family unit, plus 15% tax and service. All prices

include breakfast. It's quite a large and attractive development with a pool and a reasonably good bit of beach. You can fax inquiries or bookings to a Sanur number: (☎ 0361 287517 attention Balina.

Nearby, *Homestay Java* asks 10,000 rp for grotty rooms without breakfast. Directly opposite is *Puri Buitan*, with modern, motel-style rooms from US$30/35 to US$65/75, but they give a good discount.

If you walk east along the remains of the beach for 200 metres, past the construction site, you'll find *Cangrin Beach Homestay* and *Sunrise Homestay*, which have standard losmen rooms for 15,000/20,000 rp a single/double. Only the Cangrin Beach serves lunch and dinner.

Other Beach Areas

Coming from the west, there are seafront hotels and losmen several km before you reach Candidasa. Sea walls have been constructed to prevent further erosion, but some beachfront swimming pools seem in danger of going out to sea.

Most places to stay are secluded, mid-range to top-end package-tour hotels like the *Candi Beach Cottage* (☎ 0361 751-711/2/3 /4), with all mod cons and rooms from US$60/70 to US$70/80. To get there, turn right at the volleyball court about two km or so west of Candidasa. Take a Candidasa-bound bemo from Batubulan and ask to get off at Sengkidu. The fare is about 2000 rp.

The same side street leads to the *Amarta Beach Inn Bungalows*, which has a great location, friendly atmosphere and is good value at 15,000 rp a double, including breakfast. Opposite, *Anom Beach Inn Bungalows* (☎ 0361 233998) are a bit fancier with standard bungalows at US$22/28, and superior air-con bungalows up to US$40/50. In the same area, *Nusa Indah Beach Bungalows* are around 15,000 rp, but they are isolated with no restaurant, so you really need your own transport to get into town for meals.

About one km from Candidasa, *Nirwana Cottages* (☎ 0361 236136) have only ten rooms in a quiet location from US$35/40 to US$50. Another mid-range place is the

Rama Ocean View Bungalows (☎ 0361 751864/5), with pool, tennis court, satellite TV etc for US$33/35 to US$70.

As you approach Candidasa there are a few more cheapies on the beach side of the road. *Sari Jaya Seaside Cottage* is OK and quiet, and costs 10,000 rp for singles or doubles, including breakfast. A group of three cheap places, *Pelangi, Tarura* and *Flamboyant* is just before the bridge, but not too far to walk into town.

TENGANAN

At the turn-off to Tenganan, just west of Candidasa, a little posse of motorbike riders waits by the junction, ready to ferry you up to Tenganan for about 1000 rp. Make a donation as you enter the village. There's also a walking path to Tenganan from Candidasa but the trail is sometimes hard to follow.

Tenganan is a Bali Aga village, a centre of the original Balinese who predate the Majapahit arrival. Tenganan is a walled village with two neat rows of identical houses stretching up the gentle slope of the hill. The houses face each other across a grassy central area where the village's public buildings are located. The Bali Aga are reputed to be exceptionally conservative and resistant to change but even here the modern age has not been totally held at bay – crafts are sold to tourists and TV aerials sprout from the traditional houses.

Tenganan is full of strange customs, festivals and practices. Double ikat cloth known as *gringsing* is still woven here – the pattern to be produced is dyed on the individual threads, both warp (lengthwise) and weft (crosswise), *before* the cloth is woven. It's only produced in small quantities and at great expense, so don't expect to buy some for a bargain price. The magical *kamben gringsing* is also woven here – a person wearing it is said to be protected against black magic! The peculiar, old-fashioned 'gamelan selunding' is still played here, and girls perform the ancient Rejang dance.

At the annual Usaba Sambah festival, held around June or July, men fight with their fists wrapped in sharp-edged pandanus leaves – similar events occur on the island of Sumba, far to the east in Nusa Tenggara. At this same festival, small, hand-powered Ferris wheels are brought out and the village girls are ceremonially twirled round.

In recent years, festivals have often been cancelled in Tenganan because the village's population has been in steep decline. If a villager marries outside the Tenganan circle he or she loses their Bali Aga status. With such a small population pool and declining fertility, this village and its unique culture may eventually disappear.

CANDIDASA

The road reaches the sea just beyond the turn-off to Tenganan, and runs close to the coast through Candidasa. Not long ago it was a quiet little fishing village; now it's shoulder to shoulder tourist development. Nevertheless, many visitors enjoy Candidasa – it's quieter than Kuta, cheaper than Sanur, and a good base from which to explore eastern Bali. It's particularly popular with scuba divers.

The main drawback is the lack of a beach, which eroded away as fast as the new hotels were erected. The erosion started when the offshore coral was dug up to make lime for cement, much of it used to build the new hotels. Without the protection of the reef the sea soon washed the beach away. Mining the coral reef stopped completely in 1991, but the erosion continues, even a dozen km along the coast. A series of large and intrusive T-shaped piers have been built (ironically constructed out of concrete blocks), where sand has started to rebuild, providing some nice, sheltered bathing places if the tide is right. It's quite good for kids, but nothing like a wide, white palm-fringed beach.

Information

Candidasa has the full complement of shops, moneychangers, travel agencies, bicycle, motorbike and car-rental outlets, film developers and other facilities. There are a couple of bookshops and book exchanges, and a number of postal agencies. All the services are easily found along the main street.

You can make international phone calls from the private phone office at the Kubu Bali restaurant. Candidasa is in the 0361 phone district; many numbers have changed, and the new ones should have six digits.

Things to See & Do

Candidasa's temple is on the hillside across from the lagoon at the eastern end of the village strip. The fishing village, just beyond the lagoon, has colourful fishing perahus drawn up on the beach. The owners regularly canvas visitors for snorkelling trips to the reef and the nearby islets.

The main road east of Candidasa spirals up to the Pura Gamang Pass (gamang means 'to get dizzy'), from where there are fine views down to the coast. On a clear day, Agung rises majestically behind the range of coastal hills.

Diving Two reliable dive operators are: Baruna Water Sports, Bali's biggest and most established operator, with a branch at the Puri Bagus Beach Hotel; and Barrakuda, based at Candidasa Beach Bungalows II, which can offer a full, open-water course with PADI and CAMS certification.

Places to Stay

Candidasa has plenty of low-cost places to choose from, particularly in the original fishing village, hidden in the palm trees east of the lagoon. Basic doubles can be found from less than 10,000 rp. If the first price

PLACES TO STAY		
	17 The Watergarden	39 Homestay Natia
	(Taman Air)	40 Cantiloka Beach Inn
1 Sari Jaya Seaside	18 Puri Bali	44 Homestay Ida
Cottage	22 Wiratha's Bungalows	45 Homestay Kelapa Mas
2 Flamboyant	23 Puri Pandan Losmen &	46 Dewi Bungalows
3 Pelangi & Tarura	Restaurant	52 Rama Bungalows
6 Bali Samudra Arirang	27 Homestay Sasra Bahu	53 Sindhu Brata Homestay
Hotel	28 Candidasa Beach	54 Pandawa Homestay
7 Homestay Catra	Bungalows II	55 Srikandi Bungalows
12 Candidasa Sunrise	29 Homestay Lilaberata	56 Satria
Beach Bungalows	32 Agung Bungalows	57 Barong Beach Inn
13 Homestay Geringsing	36 Pondok Bamboo	58 Ramayana Beach Inn
14 Homestay Segara	Seaside Cottages	59 Dutha Homestay
Wangi	37 Dewa Bharata	60 Nani Beach Inn
15 Homestay Ayodya	Bungalows	61 Genggong Cottages

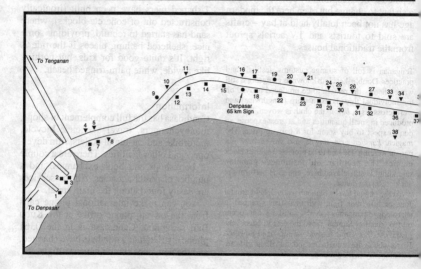

seems excessive, ask for a discount. A number of newer hotels offer air-con, swimming pools and other luxuries – some are standard package-tour places but a couple are unusual and interesting. The more expensive places add about 15% for tax and service.

Places to Stay – bottom end

Look into a few places before making a decision about where to stay. Starting at the Denpasar side, *Sari Jaya Seaside Cottage*, *Pelangi*, *Tarura* and *Flamboyant* are cheap places just before town. On the right, about

200 metres from the Tenganan turn-off as you enter town, *Homestay Geringsing* has cottages from 8500/12,500 rp for singles/doubles, and beachfront cottages for 15,000 rp a double; they're all crammed into a small garden, but it's very good for the price. Continuing east, the *Puri Bali* (☎ 229063) has simple, clean and well-kept rooms for 10,000/12,000 rp, including breakfast, and the cheap rooms at *Wiratha's Bungalows* (☎ 233973) are also good value at around 10,000 rp.

Further along, also on the beach side, there's *Puri Pandan* (☎ 235541), at 15,000/

62	Puri Tinarella Hotel	11	Candidasa Restaurant	41	Legend Rock Cafe
63	Puri Oka	16	TJ's Restaurant	42	Warung Srijati
64	Ida Beach Village	21	Ciao Restaurant	43	Warung Rasmini
65	Puri Pudak Bungalows	24	Chez Lilly Restaurant	47	Kusuma Restaurant
66	Asoka Beach Bungalows	25	Restaurant Candra	48	Raja's Restaurant
67	Sekar Orchid Bungalows	26	Hawaii Restaurant	49	Pizzeria Candi Agung
68	Puri Bagus Beach Hotel	30	Restaurant Sumber	50	Ngandi Restaurant
69	Bunga Putri Homestay		Rasa	51	Mandara Giri Pizzaria
		31	Tirtanadi (The TN)		
PLACES TO EAT			Restaurant	**OTHER**	
		33	Sanjaya Beer Garden		
4	Restaurant Flamboyant	34	Kubu Bali Restaurant	9	Perama
5	Molly's Garden Cafe	35	Murni's Cafe	19	Bookshop
8	Baliku Restaurant	38	Pondok Bamboo	20	Pandun Harum
10	Arie's Restaurant		Restaurant		

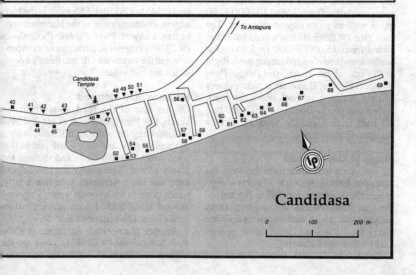
Candidasa

20,000 rp for a room with breakfast, and the popular but rock bottom *Homestay Lilaberata*, at 8000/10,000 rp, with a good location, squat toilets and chickens. The *Pondok Bamboo Seaside Cottages* (☎ 235534) is fancier, with rooms at 27,000/32,000 rp and a beachfront restaurant.

Homestay Ida, close to the lagoon, is spacious, with pleasantly airy, bamboo cottages dotted around a grassy coconut plantation. Smaller rooms are 20,000 rp, and larger rooms with a mezzanine level are 40,000 rp, including breakfast and tax. The *Homestay Kelapa Mas* (☎ 233947), next door, is also well-kept and spacious, from 10,000 rp for the smallest rooms to 15,000, 17,000 and 25,000 rp for larger ones – the seafront rooms are particularly well situated.

Beyond the Kelapa Mas is the lagoon, and there are plenty of small losmen further along the beach, as well as some newer, more expensive places. Three fairly standard losmen east of the lagoon are *Dewi Bungalows*, *Rama Bungalows* and the *Sindhu Brata Homestay*, all with rooms from 15,000/20,000 rp upwards, and the cheaper *Pandawa Homestay*. Further along the beach, *Barong Beach Inn*, *Ramayana Beach Inn* and *Nani Beach Inn* all have basic accommodation from around 10,000/15,000 rp, as well as more expensive rooms. The *Puri Oka* (☎ 224798) has somewhat better rooms from 15,000/20,000 rp for singles/ doubles, and there's a swimming pool. Right at the end of the beach, the *Bunga Putri* (Princess Flower) *Homestay* is picturesquely situated with a view back down the coast, with cheap rooms from 10,000/15,000 rp – it's hard to find and the touts are more a deterrent than an attraction.

Places to Stay – middle

As you come into town from the west, the *Samudra Arirang Hotel* (☎ 234795) is right beside the Tenganan turn-off at the start of the Candidasa village. It's a pretty tacky package-tour place with rooms in concrete boxes for US$45 to US$65, minus at least US$10 discount for asking.

Candidasa Sunrise Beach Bungalows

(☎ 235539) are well located with a pool and pleasant rooms, somewhat crowded together, for US$24 to US$27 a double, including tax. Right in the centre of Candidasa, the *Candidasa Beach Bungalows II* (☎ 235536) takes considerable liberty with the word 'bungalow': it's a three-storeyed hotel which gives the distinct impression that the maximum number of rooms has been crammed into the minimum amount of space. Air-con singles are US$30 and doubles or twins US$35 to US$52; there are some fan-cooled rooms for US$25. Breakfast is included but service and tax are an extra 15%. *Dewa Bharata Bungalows* have a pool, bar and restaurant, and are good value at US$13/15, or US$25/30 with air-con.

Past the lagoon are a number of newer mid-range places, like the *Tinarella Puri Hotel* (☎ 221373, 233971), in a pleasant location with a pool and very elaborate decor for US$16/20 for singles/doubles. *Ida Beach Village* (☎ 229041) is meant to resemble a traditional Balinese village, and it's attractive if not authentic (there are not many villages where half the people live in rice barns). Nevertheless, the cottages are very comfortable, well finished and decorated, and the garden is pretty. Low-season prices are US$45 to US$50; US$5 more in the high season. Prices may rise as the place becomes better known. *Puri Pudak Bungalows* (☎ 233978) are not as attractive or as expensive, but the rooms are OK and there's a pool, so it's not bad value.

Places to Stay – top end

On the side of the road away from the beach, *The Watergarden* (☎ & fax 235540) is something delightfully different, with a swimming pool and fish-filled ponds that wind around the buildings and through the lovely garden. The rooms are tasteful and each one has a verandah area like a jetty, which projects out over the water. They cost around US$60/65. Room service offers meals from TJ's restaurant next door.

Another place with a difference is *Kubu Bali Bungalows* (☎ 235531), also on the north side of the road, behind the restaurant of the same name. Beautifully finished individual bungalows, streams, ponds and a swimming pool are landscaped into the steep hillside and offer views over palm trees, the coast and the sea. You'll have to climb a bit to get to your room, but it's worth it. Prices are from about US$55.

Finally, the *Puri Bagus Beach Hotel* (☎ & fax 235666) is right at the end of the beach, hidden away in the palm trees which surround the original fishing village, beyond the lagoon. It's a handsome beachfront place in the Kuta-Sanur style but without the neighbours. The nicely designed rooms cost US$60/65; suites from US$125.

Places to Eat

Quite good food is available in Candidasa, particularly fresh seafood. Restaurants are dotted along the main road, mostly on the inland side, with the price usually corresponding to the size of the place and the quality of the decor. The better hotels also have restaurants; the one at the *Puri Bagus Beach Hotel* is probably the best and the most expensive.

Working along the road from the Denpasar end, some of the more interesting places include *Molly's Garden Cafe* and *TJ's Restaurant*, which is related to the popular TJ's in Kuta, but the food is not as Mexican and not quite as good. *Ciao Restaurant* serves good Italian food, while *Chez Lilly* is a newer place which already has a reputation for excellent food. *Restaurant Candra* is good for Indian dishes, while *Sumber Rasa* and the *Hawaii Restaurant* are both long-term survivors. *Tirtanadi Restaurant* (The TN) is one of the few eating places on the beach side of the road, with a cheerful atmosphere and a long cocktail list. The beachside restaurant at the *Pandan Losmen* serves Balinese feasts and good Chinese dishes.

Back on the north side of the road, the *Kubu Bali Restaurant* is a big place built around a pond with a bright and busy open kitchen area out the front, where Indonesian and Chinese dishes are turned out with great energy and panache. It's in the middle price range, but usually worth it. For cheaper eating, try *Warung Srijati* and *Warung Rasmini*, on the same side of the road but closer to the lagoon; the latter is recommended for Indian food. Just beyond the lagoon, the *Pizzeria Candi Agung* and the *Mandara Giri Pizzaria* display different approaches to spelling, although pizza is definitely on the menu at both places!

Entertainment

Barong, topeng or legong dance performances take place at 9 pm on Tuesday and Friday at the Pandan Harum dance stage in the centre of the Candidasa strip. Entry is 4000 rp. Some of the restaurants have video movies, and there's even music and dancing on some nights, but probably not in the low season when Candidasa is very quiet.

Getting There & Away

Candidasa is on the main route between Amlapura and Denpasar. A bus from the Batubulan terminal should cost about 2500 rp. Tourist shuttle buses also operate to Candidasa; to the airport, Denpasar or Kuta it costs 10,000 rp, to Ubud 7,500 rp, or to Singaraja and Lovina beaches, 20,000 rp. Buy tickets from the agents in the main street. There are cars, motorbikes and bicycles for rent.

AMLAPURA

Amlapura is the main town in the eastern end of Bali and the capital of the Karangasem District. The Karangasem kingdom broke away from the Gelgel kingdom in the late 17th century and 100 years later had become the most powerful kingdom in Bali, also ruling much of Lombok. After the 1963 eruption of Agung, lava flows cut the roads and isolated the town, which was then called Karangasem. The name was changed to get rid of any influences which might provoke another similar eruption!

Information

Amlapura is the smallest of the district capitals, and a very quiet place. There are banks (but it's probably easier to change money in Candidasa), a wartel and a couple of post offices.

The Palaces

Amlapura's three palaces are decaying reminders of Karangasem's period as a kingdom. They date from the late 19th and early 20th centuries, but only one of the palaces is open for general inspection. Admission to Puri Agung (also known as Puri Kanginan) costs 550 rp, and you can buy an explanation sheet at the entry desk for 200 rp – it's more informative than many 'guides'. There's an impressive three-tiered entry gate and beautiful sculptured panels on the outside of the main building.

The main building is known as Maskerdam (ie Amsterdam), because it was the Karangasem kingdom's acquiescence to Dutch rule which allowed it to hang on long after the demise of the other Balinese kingdoms. This may be your best opportunity to view a Balinese palace but it's certainly not impressive. A number of old photographs and paintings of the royal family are displayed on the verandah. Inside you can see into several rooms, including the royal bedroom and a living room with furniture which was a gift from the Dutch royal family.

On the other side of this main courtyard is the Balai Kambang, surrounded by a pond like the Bale Kambang in the palace grounds at Klungkung. The ornately decorated Balai Pemandesan, in between Maskerdam and the pool, was used for royal tooth-filing and cremation ceremonies. Opposite this, the Balai Lunjuk was used for other religious ceremonies.

There are other courtyards around the main one. It's said that about 150 members of the old family and their servants still live in this slowly deteriorating relic of a now-forgotten era of Balinese history.

Ujung Water Palace

A few km beyond Amlapura, on the road down to the sea, are the remains of the Ujung Water Palace, an extensive and crumbling ruin of a once-grand palace complex. It has been deteriorating for some time but most damage was done by an earthquake in 1979. The last king of Karangasem, Anak Agung Anglurah, was obsessed with moats, pools, canals and fountains, and he completed this grand palace in 1921. You can wander around the remnants of the main pool or admire the view from the pavilion higher up the hill above the rice fields.

Places to Stay & Eat

Not many travellers pause here – Candidasa is not far away and it's only another six km to Tirtagangga. On the right after you enter the town, a short distance in towards the centre, is the Homestay Sidha Karya which is pretty basic, but OK, with rooms at about 10,000 rp.

There's the usual collection of warungs around the bus terminal, plus the Rumah Makan Sedap on Jalan Gajah Mada. Amlapura tends to shut down early so don't leave your evening meal until too late.

Getting There & Away

There are buses from here to Singaraja and the north coast (about 2500 rp), as well as to Denpasar and points in between. Plenty of bemos go to villages in the area, for which Amlapura is a service town.

TIRTAGANGGA

Anak Agung Anglurah, Amlapura's water-loving raja, having constructed his masterpiece at Ujung, later had another go at Tirtagangga. This water palace, built around 1947, was damaged in the 1963 eruption of Agung and during the political events that wracked Indonesia two years later. It's not grand, but it's still a place of beauty and a reminder of the power the Balinese rajas once had. The palace has a swimming pool as well as the ornamental ponds. Entrance to the water palace is 550 rp (children 300 rp) and another 2000 rp to use the big swimming pool (children 1000 rp), or 1000 rp for the smaller, lower pool (500 rp for children). These prices have increased a lot lately, but there are some signs that the pools and grounds are being improved.

The beautiful rice terraces sweep out from Tirtagangga almost like a sea surrounding an island. A few km beyond here, on the road to the east coast, there are more dramatically beautiful terraces, often seen in photographs of Bali.

This is one of the most traditional areas on Bali. Quite a few of the villages have special or unique attractions. There are Buddhist communities near Budakling, and traditional goldsmiths, painters, carvers and so on. Some of the dances and ceremonies are found nowhere else on Bali, and have links with Lombok which was ruled from Karangasem for many years. Ask at your losmen for suggested walks in the surrounding countryside.

Places to Stay & Eat

Actually within the palace compound the *Tirta Ayu Homestay* has pleasant individual bungalows for 20,000/25,000 rp, and two large bungalows with great views for 100,000 rp. Prices include admission to the water palace swimming pools. The restaurant has a superb outlook over the palace pools.

Right by the water palace is the peaceful *Losmen Dhangin Taman Inn*, with rooms for 10,000/12,000 to 15,000/20,000 rp, including breakfast. The most expensive rooms are large and have an enclosed sitting area. You can sit in the courtyard, gazing across the rice fields and the water palace while doves coo in the background. The losmen owner here is a character, and the food is not bad.

Across the road from the palace, the *Rijasa Homestay* is a small and simple place with extremely neat and clean rooms for 10,000/12,000 rp, including breakfast and tea. A few steps back towards Amlapura, the *Taman Sari Inn* has rooms at 8000 rp and 10,000 rp but it looks rather derelict.

Alternatively, you can continue 300 metres beyond the water palace and climb the steep steps to the *Kusuma Jaya Inn*. The 'Homestay on the Hill' with a fine view over the rice fields. Its prices have increased a lot – it now costs from 25,000 to 45,000 rp, and staff are not as helpful as they used to be. A km or so further on is a new 'homestay on the hill', with good rooms and outstanding views for 12,000/16,000 rp, including breakfast.

There are several good warung on the access track to the palace; the one nearest Tirta Ayu serves excellent food. Next to the car park, the *Good Karma* has good food and plays good music.

Getting There & Away

Tirtagangga is about five or six km from the Amlapura turn-off on the main road that runs around the eastern end of Bali. Bemos from Amlapura cost 300 rp. Buses on the main road continue to Singaraja, but you can usually flag them down for transport to Culik or Tulamben – ask at your losmen about the best time.

BEYOND TIRTAGANGGA

Soon after leaving Tirtagangga, the road starts to climb. Look for the sign to Pura Lempuyang, one of Bali's nine 'directional temples', perched on a hilltop at 768 metres.

Further on, the main road climbs over a small range of hills and descends past some of the most spectacular rice terraces in Bali. The road gets back down towards sea level at Culik where there's a turn-off to Amed and the road round Bali's south-east corner. The main road goes north to Tulamben and continues round the east coast to Singaraja.

Amed

This corner of Bali is not much visited by tourists, but there is some accommodation now, and there are enough signs on the main road pointing to the 'Hidden Paradise' cottages to ensure that they won't stay hidden for long. Follow these signs from Culik to Amed, and on to where you can stay. The coast has extensive rows of troughs for evaporating sea water to extract salt – one of the main industries here. The coastline is superb and unspoilt, with views across to Lombok and back to Gunung Agung.

Apart from the places listed in the following Places to Stay & Eat section, tourist facilities are nonexistent – bring enough cash. The diving in this area is excellent but there are no local operators; the closest one is in Tulamben. Snorkelling is easy as the coral reef is just offshore.

Places to Stay The first place to stay is *Kusumajaya Beach Inn* (☎ 0363 21250 for inquiries), a couple of km past Amed itself. It has a restaurant and a few elaborately decorated Bali-style bungalows on a barren slope between the sea and the road – the proprietors are trying to establish a garden. They charge 30,000/40,000 rp for singles/ doubles.

Next are the *Hidden Paradise Cottages* themselves (☎ 0361 231273 for inquiries), which are lovely, isolated and comfortable, with restaurant, pool and a great little private beach. It's a surprise to find such a quality place way out here, but with rooms from US$30 to US$65 it's not a low-budget option.

Continuing south along the coast you arrive at *Vienna Beach Bungalows*, a cosy complex with bamboo cottages near the water for 24,000 rp, and others closer to the road for 17,000 rp. They can arrange diving, fishing and sailing trips. Crossing one or two more little hills brings you to *Good Karma*, with basic, bamboo beachside bungalows on stilts for 15,000 rp and 20,000 rp, including breakfast. The main attraction advertised is 'talking and laughing with Baba', the friendly proprietor.

Getting There & Away It's easy to find these places if you have your own transport. Public transport is easy to Culik, but from there to Amed might be difficult – try to be there early in the day as there are always more bemos then.

The South-East Peninsula

The road around the south-east peninsula is narrow, winding and hilly, but it's mostly sealed and definitely passable. You might almost be safer with a motorbike than a car, because you'll have more chance to get out of the way of an oncoming vehicle – be extremely careful. A bemo would be uncomfortable, and you wouldn't see the views. Mostly the road follows the slopes of Gunung Seraya, way above the sea, and there's spectacular coastal scenery. It's a pretty dry area and there are no rice fields, but some places have extensive vineyards so it can look almost Mediterranean. From Amed round to Amlapura is probably only about 30 km, but allow at least two hours to enjoy the trip.

Tulamben

The small village of Tulamben has the only places to stay around the east coast. The beach here is composed of pebbles rather than sand but the water is clear and the snorkelling good. It's an interesting place to pause on a trip around the barren east coast.

The Wreck of the Liberty Tulamben's prime attraction is the huge WW II wreck of a US cargo ship, the most popular dive site on Bali. Snorkellers can appreciate a good deal of it, but the most interesting parts are between 15 and 30 metres down.

Diving To find the wreck simply walk about

USAT Liberty

On 11 January 1942 the armed US cargo ship USAT *Liberty* was torpedoed by a Japanese submarine about 15 km south-west of Lombok. It was taken in tow by the destroyers HMNS *Van Ghent* and USS *Paul Jones* with the intention of beaching it on the coast of Bali and retrieving its cargo of raw rubber and railway parts. When its condition looked perilous the crew were evacuated and, although it was successfully beached, the rapid spread of the war through Indonesia prevented the cargo from being saved.

Built in 1915, the *Liberty* sat on the beach at Tulamben, a prominent east coast landmark, until 1963 when the violent eruption of Gunung Agung toppled it beneath the surface. Or at least that's one version of the story. Another relates that it sank some distance offshore and the lava flow from the eruption extended the shoreline almost out to the sunken vessel. Whatever the course of events it lies just 40 or 50 metres offshore, almost parallel to the beach with its bow only a couple of metres below the surface. ■

BALI

100 metres north of the Gandu Mayu Bungalows, the northernmost beach losmen, to the small white toilet-block building by the beach. Swim straight out from the white building and you'll suddenly see this huge wreck rearing up from the depths. It's within easy reach of snorkellers, who can easily swim around the bow which is heavily encrusted with coral and a haven for colourful fish. For qualified scuba divers, it costs about US$50 for two dives on the wreck, all inclusive – there is a dive guide, compressor and equipment to rent at the Paradise Palm Beach Bungalows. It's best to stay locally and dive early or late in the day.

Places to Stay *Paradise Palm Beach Bungalows*, the village's first accommodation, is a cheerful little losmen with a restaurant right on the beach. Singles/ doubles cost 20,000/ 25,000 rp with breakfast; cheaper rooms are available away from the beach and closer to the compressor. The bungalows are neat, clean and well kept with bamboo chairs and a table on the verandahs which overlook a pleasant garden.

The *Bali Timur Bungalows*, just on the Amlapura side, are OK at 15,000/20,000 rp, and the *Gandu Maya Bungalows*, closest to the wreck, charge 25,000 rp. About 1½ km to the south-east, there's a new, up-market place called the *Saya Resort*, which seems to cater only to divers on package tours.

Tulamben to Yeh Saneh

Beyond Tulamben the road continues to skirt the slopes of Agung, with frequent evidence of lava flows from the 1963 eruption. Beyond Agung, Gunung Abang and then the outer crater of Gunung Batur also slope down to the sea. Shortly before Yeh Sanih (see the North Bali chapter) there's a famous (but not very interesting) horse bath at **Tejakula**. The scenery is stark but an interesting contrast to the rest of Bali, there are frequent vistas of the sea and the rainfall is so low you can count on sunny weather. None of the towns or villages along this route are set up for tourists.

AMLAPURA TO RENDANG

A back road to Rendang road branches off from the Amlapura to Denpasar road, just a km or two out of Amlapura. The road gradually climbs up into the foothills of Gunung Agung, running through some pretty countryside. It's a less-travelled route, which makes it difficult on public bemos. If you have your own wheels (a bicycle is fine), you'll find it very scenic, with some interesting places to stop. At Rendang you can turn north to Besakih, south to Klungkung, or take the very pretty minor road across to Bangli. If you have the time, the energy, and a smattering of Bahasa Indonesia, this would be a wonderful area for trekking. There are very traditional villages between Bebandem and the coast (you could walk down to Tenganan), and lovely views everywhere. You can also climb Agung by heading north from Selat.

The road runs through Abian Soan, Bebandem (which has a busy market every three days), Sibetan, Selat and Muncan before reaching Rendang. Sibetan and Rendang are both well known for the *salaks* grown there. This delicious fruit has a curious 'snakeskin' covering. It's worth diverting a km or so at Putung to enjoy the fantastic view down to the coast.

Shortly before Selat you can take a road that runs south-west through Iseh and Sideman and meets the Amlapura to Klungkung road. The German artist Walter Spies lived in Iseh for some time from 1932. Later, the Swiss painter Theo Meier, nearly as famous as Spies for his influence on Balinese art, lived in the same house. Sideman was a base for Swiss ethnologist Urs Ramseyer, and is also a centre for traditional culture and arts, particularly weaving of songket, with threads of silver and gold.

Places to Stay

Three km along the Rendang from the junction as you leave Amlapura, *Homestay Lila* is a very pretty little place in the rice fields at Abian Soan.

Further along towards Rendang, 11 km beyond Bebandem, you can turn off the road a km or so to the superbly situated *Putung Central Country Club*, a set of government-run bungalows with a restaurant, tennis court and brilliant view. It's somewhat run down, and charges 25,000/30,000 rp for two-storey bungalows, with a bathroom and small sitting area downstairs; they also have some rooms which might be cheaper.

There's a delightful place to stay at Sideman, but it's a bit expensive at around 45,000 rp per person, though that includes all meals. It's called *Homestay Sideman*, and it's pleasantly old fashioned with four-poster beds, interesting decorations and lots of books to read.

BANGLI

Halfway up the slope to Penelokan the town of Bangli, once the capital of a kingdom, is said to have the best climate in Bali. It also has a very fine temple and quite a pleasant place to stay. Bangli is a convenient place from which to visit Besakih, and makes a good base for exploring the area. Bangli is home to a psychiatric institution and a prison, and is therefore the subject of unkind jokes in other parts of Bali.

Three km from Bangli, along the Tampaksiring road, is Bukit Demulih, a hill just off the south side of the road. At the top there's a small temple and good views back over Bangli; walk along the ridge line to a viewpoint where all of southern Bali spreads out below.

Information & Orientation

Bangli has a post office, telephone office (automatic exchange, so it's quite efficient) and a couple of banks.

Pura Kehen

At the top end of the town, Pura Kehen, the state temple of the Bangli kingdom, is terraced up the hillside. A great flight of steps leads up to the temple entrance and the first courtyard, with its huge banyan tree, has colourful Chinese porcelain plates set into the walls as decoration. Unfortunately, most of them are now damaged. The inner courtyard has an 11-roofed meru and thrones for

the three figures of the Hindu trinity – Brahma, Shiva and Vishnu. This is one of the finest temples in Bali.

Pura Dalem Penunggekan

Beside the road to Gianyar, there's an interesting temple of the dead, the Pura Dalem Penunggekan. The reliefs on the front illustrate particularly vivid scenes of wrongdoers getting their just desserts in the afterlife.

Places to Stay & Eat

The *Artha Sastra Inn* is a former palace residence and is still run by the grandson of the last king of Bangli. Rooms, some with private bathrooms, cost from 10,000 to 20,000 rp. It doesn't look much from the outside, but it's a pleasant, friendly place, and quite popular.

The *Losmen Dharmaputra*, a short distance up the road towards Kintamani, is a YHA affiliate. It's cheap, but pretty basic and not very attractive. Rather drab singles/doubles cost 5000/7000 rp; you can also get food there. *Adnyana Homestay* (☎ 0366 91244), near the sports ground, is newer and brighter, and costs about 10,000 rp for a room.

Bangli has a good pasar malam (night market) in the square opposite the Artha Sastra and there are some great warungs but they all close early.

BESAKIH

Perched nearly 1000 metres up the side of Gunung Agung is Bali's most important temple, Pura Besakih. In all, it comprises about 30 separate temples in seven terraces up the hill, all within one enormous complex.

The temple was probably first constructed more than 1000 years ago; 500 years later, it became the state temple of the powerful Gelgel and Klungkung kingdoms. Today, it's the 'mother temple' of all Bali – every district in Bali has its own shrine or temple at Besakih and just about every Balinese god you care to name is also honoured there. There are also temples for local families, with shrines and memorials going back several generations.

As well as being the Balinese mother temple, Besakih is also the mother of Balinese financial efforts. You pay to park (300 rp per car; 100 rp for a motorbike), pay to enter (550 rp per person), pay to rent a scarf (1000 rp!) and then brave the usual large collection of souvenir sellers. You don't need a guide to see Besakih, but if someone latches on to you and begins to tell you about the temple, let them know quickly whether you want their services.

Places to Stay & Eat

About five km below Besakih the *Arca Valley Inn* has a restaurant and rooms for about 12,000/15,000 rp. It's prettily situated in a valley by a bend in the road. This is a good place to stay if you want to climb Gunung Agung from Besakih and want an early start.

Getting There & Away

The usual route to Besakih is by bemo from Klungkung, for about 1000 rp. If there are no direct bemos about to depart, get one to Rendang or Menanga, then another to Besakih. After about 2 pm you may have trouble getting a bemo back, so leave early or be prepared to charter or hitch.

GUNUNG AGUNG

Gunung Agung is Bali's highest and most revered mountain, an imposing peak from most of southern and eastern Bali, though it's often obscured by cloud and mist. Although most books and maps give its height as 3142 metres, some say it lost its top in the 1963 eruption and is now only 3014 metres. The summit is an oval crater, about 500 metres across, with its highest point on the western edge above Besakih.

Climbing Agung

It's possible to climb Agung from various directions, but the two shortest and most popular routes are from the temple at Besakih, and up the southern flank from Selat, via Sebudi. The latter route goes to the lower edge of the crater rim, and you can't make your way from there round to the very

highest point. If that's important to you, climb from Besakih. To have the best chance of seeing the view before the clouds form, try to get to the top before 8 am. This means starting well before dawn, so plan your climb when there will be some moonlight, and take a torch. Also take plenty of water and food, waterproof clothing, a warm woollen sweater and extra batteries – just in case.

You should take a guide for either route. Before you start, or early in the climb, the guide will stop at a shrine and make an offering and some prayers. This is a holy mountain and you should show respect. Besides, you will want to have everything going for you on the climb.

Climb from Selat This route involves the least walking because there is a serviceable road from Selat to the temple Pura Pasar Agung, high on the southern slopes of the mountain. From there you can climb to the top in as little as two hours, but allow at least three or four. You should report to the police station at Selat before you start, and again when you return. If you haven't already arranged transport and a guide, the police will be able to help. One recommended guide is Ketut Uriada, a primary school teacher at Muncan, a few km west of Selat – he'll charge from around 20,000 rp plus whatever it costs for food, transport etc. You can stay the night in Selat and drive up early in the morning, or drive up the day before and stay overnight at the temple. Start climbing from the temple at around 3 or 4 am.

Climb from Besakih If you want to climb Gunung Agung from Besakih you must leave no later than 6.30 am if you want to get down before nightfall; much earlier if you want a clear view from the top. Allow five to six hours for the climb, and four to five for the descent. It's easy to get lost on the lower trails so hire a guide at Besakih – the cost could be anything from 20,000 to 30,000 rp depending on the size of your party, plus a few thousand rp as a tip. Arrange the details the day before, and stay in a losmen near Besakih so you can start early.

South-West Bali

Many of the places regularly visited in south-western Bali, like Sangeh or Tanah Lot, are easy day trips from Denpasar, Kuta or Ubud. Tabanan district has some fine rice-field scenery and, further west, spectacular roads head across the mountains to the north. The south coast has long stretches of wide black-sand beach, with fishing villages that rarely see a tourist.

SEMPIDI, LUKLUK & KAPAL

Kapal is the garden gnome and temple curlicue centre of Bali. Numerous shops line the road displaying the many standard architectural motifs for temples, along with garden ornaments like comic-book deers and brightly painted Buddhas.

Kapal's **Pura Sadat** is the most important temple in the area. Although it was restored after WW II (it was damaged in an earthquake earlier this century), the Sadat is a very ancient temple, possibly dating back to the 12th century.

TANAH LOT

The spectacularly placed Tanah Lot is possibly the best known and most photographed temple in Bali. The tourist crowds here are phenomenal, especially at sunset, and the commercial hype is terrible. The temple, perched on a little rocky islet, looks superb whether delicately lit by the dawn light or starkly outlined at sunset. But can it ever live up to the hype?

It's a well organised tourist trap – you pay the parking attendants (350 rp) and they show you where to park. Dozens of souvenir shops are in a sort of sideshow alley, which you can easily bypass. There's a ticket office to collect the entry fee (550 rp), then you follow the crowd down the steps to the sea. You can walk over to the temple itself at low tide, or climb up to the left and sit at one of the many tables along the cliff top. Order a drink (5000 rp for a beer!) or dinner, get your camera ready and wait for 'The Sunset'.

For the Balinese, Tanah Lot is one of the important and venerated sea temples. Like Pura Luhur Ulu Watu, at the southern end of the island, Tanah Lot is closely associated with the 16th-century Majapahit priest Nirartha. It's said that Nirartha passed by

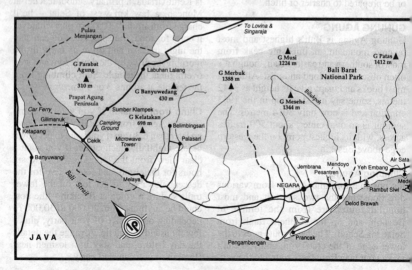

here and, impressed with the tiny island's superb setting, suggested to local villagers that this would be a good place to construct a temple.

Places to Stay & Eat

The *Dewi Sinta Cottages* (☎ 0361 23545) are in souvenir shop alley, not far from the ticket office. It's new, clean and unexciting, with standard rooms for US$12/16, and air-con rooms with 'hot and cold raining shower' for US$23/25.

Getting There & Away

By bemo, you go from Ubung terminal to Kediri (1000 rp) then catch another bemo to the coast (about 350 rp). There is no regular service out of Tanah Lot, so if you stay for the sunset, you may have to charter a bemo back. Tours to Tanah Lot usually take in a few other sites like Bedugul, Mengwi or Sangeh; a basic half-day excursion will cost from 20,000 rp, and an up-market tour with dinner for US$28.

MENGWI

The huge state temple of Pura Taman Ayun, surrounded by a wide moat, was the main temple of the kingdom which ruled from Mengwi until 1891. The temple was originally built in 1634 and extensively renovated in 1937. It's a huge, spacious temple and the elegant moat gives it a very fine appearance. The first courtyard is a large, open grassy expanse and the inner courtyard has a multitude of *merus* (multi-tiered shrines).

Across the moat from the temple is a rather lost-looking arts centre and a small museum with models and dioramas of Balinese festivals, both are unspectacular and not very informative. The *Water Palace Restaurant* overlooking the moat is not a bad place for lunch, but it's not quick.

BLAYU

In Blayu (or Belayu), a small village between Mengwi and Marga, traditional songket sarongs are woven with intricate gold threads. These are for ceremonial use only, not for everyday wear.

MARGA

Near Marga, west of the road three km north of Mengwi, is a memorial to Lt Colonel I Gusti Ngurah Rai, a local hero. In 1946 Rai led his men in a futile defence against a larger

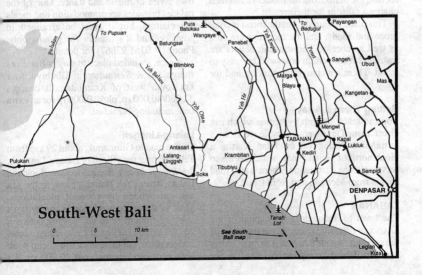

BALI

and better armed Dutch force trying to recover Bali after the departure of the Japanese. The Dutch called in air support but the Balinese refused to surrender, and all 94 of Ngurah Rai's men were killed.

SANGEH

About 20 km north of Denpasar, near the village of Sangeh, stands the monkey forest of Bukit Sari. It is featured, so the Balinese say, in the *Ramayana*.

To kill the evil Rawana, king of Lanka, Hanuman had to crush him between two halves of Mahameru, the holy mountain. On his way to performing this task, Hanuman dropped a piece of the mountain near Sangeh, complete with a band of monkeys. Of course, this sort of legend isn't unique – Hanuman dropped chunks of landscape all over the place!

There's a unique grove of nutmeg trees in the monkey forest and a temple, Pura Bukit Sari, with an interesting old garuda statue. And of course there are lots of greedy monkeys. They'll pick your pockets in search of peanuts, and have been known to steal hats, sunglasses and even thongs from fleeing tourists! A new variation on this mischief has been created by some local people, who reclaim the items from the monkeys and then charge a ransom for their return.

This place is touristy, but the forest is cool, green and shady, and the monkeys are cute as well as cheeky. The souvenir sellers are restricted from certain areas and are easy to avoid. There's a charge for parking and for entry.

Getting There & Away

You can reach Sangeh by bemos which run direct from Denpasar – they leave from a terminal at Wangaya, on Jalan Kartini a block north of Gajah Mada, which seems to serve only one destination. There is also road access from Mengwi and from Ubud.

TABANAN

The town of Tabanan is the capital of the district of the same name. It's at the heart of the rice belt of southern Bali, the most fertile and prosperous rice-growing area on the island. It's also a great centre for dancing and gamelan playing.

It's quite a large town, with shops, banks, hospital, market etc. You could probably find a place to stay here, but no-one does. The only attraction is the **Subak Museum**, with exhibits on the irrigation and cultivation of rice, and the intricate social systems which govern it. The museum is on the left, just before you come into town from Denpasar, and is easy to miss. It's open from 8 am to 2 pm Monday to Thursday, closing 11 am Friday and 12.30 pm Saturday.

AROUND TABANAN

There's not a lot of tourist activity in the southern part of Tabanan district, but it's very accessible, and a good area to see some more of Bali's most important industry, which is still agriculture rather than tourism. At nearby **Kediri**, the Pasar Hewan is one of Bali's busiest markets for cattle and other animals.

A little west of Tabanan a road turns down to the coast through **Krambitan** (or Kerambitan), a village noted for its old buildings (including two 17th-century palaces); its tradition of wayang-style painting and its own styles of music and dance. One of the palaces provides accommodation and meals for visitors, but it must be arranged in advance, and it's usually for groups only. Phone (☎ 0361 92667) for details.

A nice, secluded place to stay is *Bee Bees Bungalows & Restaurant* at Tibubiyu, four km south west of Krambitan. It charges 32,000/40,000 rp, plus 10,000 rp for an extra bed, including breakfast.

Lalang-Linggah

On the road to Gilimanuk, about 29 km from Tabanan near the village of Lalang-Linggah, the *Balian Beach Bungalows* overlook the Balian River (Yeh Balian), close to the sea and surrounded by coconut plantations. Most of the accommodation is in pavilions sleeping from three to six, costing between 35,000 and 50,000 rp. It's not really a low-budget place, but there are a few cheap bunk beds and some rooms from 20,000 rp. It's very peaceful, well run and friendly. Families are welcome. To get there from Denpasar, take any Negara or Gilimanuk bus and ask the driver to stop at Lalang-Linggah, near the 49 km post near Balian River.

JEMBRANA COAST

Jembrana is Bali's most sparsely populated district. The main road parallels the coast most of the way to Negara, the district capital. There's some beautiful scenery but little tourist development along the way.

Medewi

About 30 km from Soka, and 25 km before Negara, a large but faded sign announces the side road south to 'Medewi Surfing Point'. The beach is nothing spectacular, but Medewi is noted for its *long* left-hand wave. It works best at mid to high tide on a two-metre swell – get there early before the wind picks up.

The *Hotel Nirwana*, on the right, and the fancier *Medewi Beach Cottages* on the left, are now under the same management. The cottages have a swimming pool, restaurant, and air-con rooms with hot water and TV for 47,000 to 100,000 rp. Rooms in the two-storey block opposite are more basic, and expensive for what they offer at 23,000/30,000/42,000 rp for singles/doubles/triples. A couple of very basic bamboo huts nearby cost 10,000/15,000 rp. A little further west are the *Tinjaya Bungalows*, with quite pleasant rooms in two-storey grass-and-bamboo cottages, but still no bargain at 20,000 to 25,000 rp.

Rambut Siwi

The coastal temple of Pura Luhur at Rambut Siwi is picturesquely situated on a cliff top overlooking a long, wide stretch of beach. A superb temple with numerous shady frangipani trees, this is one of the important coastal temples of southern Bali. It is another of the temples established in the 1500s by the priest Danghyang Nirartha who had such a good eye for ocean scenery (see also Tanah Lot earlier in this section and Ulu Watu in the

Denpasar to Ubud section earlier in this chapter).

NEGARA

Negara, the capital of the Jembrana District, comes alive each year when the **bull races** take place around September and October (ask at the tourist office in Denpasar for the exact dates). The racing animals are actually water buffaloes, normally docile creatures, which charge down a two-km stretch of road pulling tiny chariots. Riders stand on top of the chariots forcing the bullocks on, sometimes by twisting their tails. Style also plays a part and points are awarded for the most elegant runner! Gambling is not legal on Bali but...

Places to Stay & Eat

Accommodation may be fully booked during the bull-racing season, and will cost more than the figures given here. *Hotel Ana*, on Jalan Ngurah Rai, the main street through town, is a standard, cheap losmen with rooms for less than 10,000 rp. Nearby is the *Hotel & Restourant Wira Pada* (☎ 0365 41161) at Jalan Ngurah Rai 107, which costs 10,000/12,500 rp including breakfast, 15,000/18,000 rp for a room with a shower or 25,000/30,000 rp with air-con. The Wira Pada serves good food, as does the *Rumah Makan Puas*, a little further east on the same street.

The Denpasar to Gilimanuk road, which bypasses the town centre, has several cheap accommodation possibilities, including *Hotel Ijo Gading*, west of the town, which is clean and friendly, and the *Losmen & Rumah Makan Taman Sari* (☎ 0365 41154), on the other side of the road.

Getting There & Away

Public transport from Denpasar's Ubung terminal costs around 3500 rp – try to get a direct bus rather than a bemo that will stop at every village en route. For the bull races, agents in the southern tourist areas offer day tours at various prices.

AROUND NEGARA

There's a bulge in the coastline south of Negara which has quite a few beaches, though none are particularly attractive, some are dangerous. There are no tourist hotels here.

Jembrana

The town of Jembrana, once capital of the region, is the centre of the *gamelan jegog*, a gamelan using huge bamboo instruments that produce a very low-pitched, resonant sound. Performances often feature a number of gamelan groups engaging in musical contest.

Belimbingsari & Palasari

Christian missionaries were discouraged by the Dutch, but sporadic activity resulted in a number of converts, many of whom were rejected by their own villages. In 1939, they were encouraged to resettle in Christian communities in the wilds of West Bali – Protestants in Belimbingsari and Catholics in Palasari. Both communities have survived, and each has a large and impressive church with distinctly Balinese architectural touches. They're easily accessible from the main road with your own transport, but public bemos are infrequent.

CEKIK

About a km before Gilimanuk, Cekik is the point at which the road to the north coast branches off to the right. Near the junction is a curious pagoda-like structure which commemorates sea battles in 1946, between republican forces and the Dutch.

Archaeological excavations at Cekik during the 1960s yielded the oldest evidence of human life on Bali. Finds include burial mounds with funery offerings, bronze jewellery, axes, adzes and earthenware vessels from around 1000 BC, give or take a few centuries.

BALI BARAT NATIONAL PARK

On the south side of the road in Cekik, the headquarters of the West Bali National Park (Taman Nasional Bali Barat) is open from 7.30 am to 2 pm Monday to Saturday. The visitors' centre does not have much information, but is the place to make arrangements for trekking in the southern part of the park. Be there by 7 am, or arrange it the day before. All trekking groups must be accompanied by an authorised guide, and you may need to organise transport to the starting point of the trek. Two, four and seven-hour treks are usually offered, but overnight trips are possible. There's a park entry fee of 2000 rp per person. For information about the northern part of the park, and diving trips to Menjangan Island, go to the other park office at Labuhan Lalang (see the North Bali section later in this chapter).

GILIMANUK

At the far western end of the island, Gilimanuk is the terminus for ferries across the strait to Java. There's a bus station and a market on the main street, as well as shops, cheap restaurants, and a couple of places to change money. Most travellers buy combined bus and ferry tickets and don't need to stop in Gilimanuk. There's little of interest here, but it's the closest accommodation to the national park, if you want to trek or dive there early in the morning.

Places to Stay

There are several places to stay along the main road. *Homestay Surya*, *Lestari Homestay* and *Nirwana* are all cheap, basic losmen which will have rooms for less than 10,000 rp. *Nusantara II* is 100 metres east of the main drag, through a split gate to the south of the ferry port. It's also basic, and no cheaper, but it's away from the busy road.

Getting There & Away

The bus and bemo terminal is about a km south of the ferry port, on the east side of the road. There are direct buses to Denpasar (about 4000 rp) and Singaraja (2500 rp), and more frequent bemos to places along the way.

To/From Java The ferries to Ketapang (near Banyuwangi) on Java leave every 30 minutes or so, 24 hours a day. One-way fares are 650 rp for an adult, 450 rp for a child, 950 rp for a bicycle, 1800 rp for a motorbike and 7400 rp for a car. Rental contracts usually prohibit the vehicle being taken out of Bali.

Central Mountains

Bali's mountains are mostly volcanoes, some dormant, some definitely active. Apart from the mighty Gunung Agung (see the earlier East Bali section), the most interesting mountain areas are Gunung Batur, with its spectacular caldera containing a lake and numerous smaller craters, and the pretty area around Bedugul, another complex of volcanic craters and lakes with much lusher vegetation. A popular round trip goes to the north coast via Batur, and returns south via Bedugul, but you can do it just as easily in the other direction. The central mountain range extends west of Bedugul, with some less-travelled routes between the south and north coasts.

GUNUNG BATUR AREA
Penelokan
Penelokan appropriately means 'place to look', and has superb views across to Gunung Batur and down to Lake Batur at the bottom of the crater. You can stay here, but those intending to tour the lake or climb Batur mountain might find it more convenient to stay at the bottom of the crater, in either Kedisan or Toyah Bunkah,

Penelokan has a well-deserved reputation as a money-grubbing place where you're constantly badgered to buy things and where you need to keep an eye on your gear. It can get surprisingly chilly up here so come prepared. Clouds often roll in over the crater, obscuring the view and making the crater rim towns cold and miserable places to be.

Information There's a fee of 500 rp per person to enter the crater rim area, plus 400 rp for a car and another 50 rp for insurance. Keep the tickets if you plan to go back and

forth around the crater rim or you may have to pay again. You can change money at the Lakeview restaurant.

Places to Stay If you arrive from the south, the first place to stay in Penelokan is the *Lakeview Restaurant & Homestay* (☎ 32023), with economy rooms for US$8 and more comfortable bungalow-style rooms with bathroom for US$15. It's not very clean and the economy rooms are impossibly small, but the view, the view...!

Continuing past the side street down into the crater, you come to *Losmen & Restaurant Gunawan* which may be slightly better value. Again, the view is terrific and the economy rooms for 20,000 rp are small; there is a bigger bungalow for 25,000 rp.

Places to Eat Along the road from Penelokan towards Kintamani you'll find a crowd of restaurants which are geared to bus loads of tour groups. All the restaurants have fine views and all prepare buffet-style lunches at international tourist prices. The restaurants, from Penelokan to Kintamani, include the *Caldera Batur, Lakeview, Batur Garden, Gunawan, Puri Selera, Puri Aninditha* and the *Kintamani Restaurant*. Lunch costs from around 10,000 rp if you order from the menu. The *Restaurant Mutiara* is better value, and there are also cheap warungs along the main road like the *Warung Makan Ani Asih* or the *Warung Makan Sederhaña*.

Getting There & Away To get to Penelokan from Denpasar, you can either get a Kintamani-bound bemo from Batubulan station (1800 rp) which will pass through Penelokan, or you can take one of the more frequent bemos to Gianyar (1000 rp) or Bangli (1200 rp) first and then another from there up the mountain. From Ubud, go first to Gianyar. Bemos shuttle back and forth fairly regularly between Penelokan and Kintamani (300 rp) and less frequently down to the lakeside at Kedisan (500 rp or more) and Toyah Bunkuh.

With your own transport you can take the roads from Gianyar or Tampaksiring, which

BALI

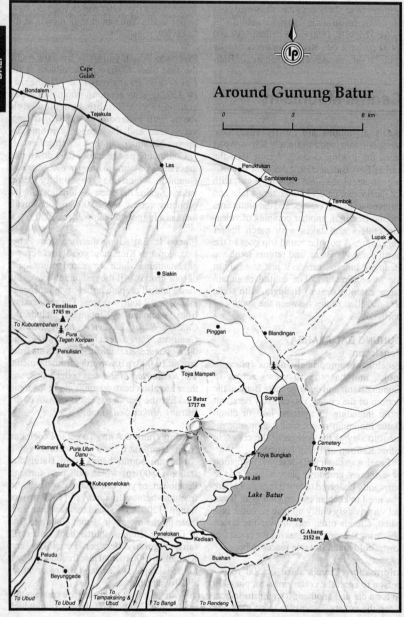

Around Gunung Batur

0   3   6 km

Cape
Gulah

Bondalem

Tejakula

Les

Penuktukan

Sambirenteng

Tembok

Lupak

Siakin

G Penulisan
1745 m

To Kubutambahan

Pura
Tegeh Koripan

Penulisan

Pinggan

Blandingan

Toya Mampeh

G Batur
1717 m

Songan

Kintamani

Pura Ulun
Danu

Batur

Kubupenelokan

Toya Bungkah

Cemetery

Pura Jati

Trunyan

Lake Batur

Penelokan

Kedisan

Abang

Buahan

G Abang
2152 m

Peludu

Beyunggede

To Ubud

To Ubud

To
Tampaksiring &
Ubud

To Bangli

To Rendang

meet just before Penelokan. The roads from the Ubud area are OK but have very little public transport. The road down to Rendang is rougher, but has great views.

Getting Around From Penelokan you can hike around the crater rim to Gunung Abang (2152 metres), the high point of the outer rim, though trees hide the view almost to the top. You can't continue hiking in this anti-clockwise direction as the trail stops.

Batur & Kintamani

The village of Batur used to be down in the crater. A violent eruption of the volcano in 1917 killed thousands of people and destroyed more than 60,000 homes and 2000 temples. Although the village was wiped out, the lava flow stopped at the entrance to the villagers' temple.

Taking this as a good omen, they rebuilt their village, only to have Batur erupt again in 1926. This time the lava flow covered all but the loftiest temple shrine. Fortunately, the Dutch administration anticipated the eruption and evacuated the village, partly by force, so very few lives were lost. The village was relocated up on the crater rim, and the surviving shrine was also moved up and placed in the new temple, Pura Ulun Danu, which was commenced in 1927. It's one of the Bali's nine directional temples.

The villages of Batur and Kintamani run together – it's basically one main street around the western rim of the crater. Although often cold and grey, it is famed for its large and colourful morning market, held every three days. The high rainfall and cool climate up here make this a very productive fruit and vegetable growing area, though the orange crops have recently been depleted by disease.

Places to Stay Nearest the Penelokan end of town (about 4.5 km away) is *Losmen Superman's*, on the west side of the road, which asks between 10,000 and 20,000 rp for pretty squalid rooms. They may take less.

About two km further north on the same side of the road, the *Hotel Miranda* has rooms from 6000 to 10,000 rp for singles/

doubles, including breakfast; the most expensive rooms have bathrooms. It has good food and an open fire at night. Made Senter, who runs it, is very friendly and informative and also acts as a guide for treks into the crater and around Gunung Batur.

Continuing along the road for a few hundred metres you come to *Losmen Sasaka* on the right. The plumbing is suspect but the rooms are large, the place is clean, the views are great and the price (15,000/20,000 rp for singles/doubles) includes breakfast.

Further along again, a sign points off the road to the *Puri Astini Inn* – it says 400 metres, but the distance is more like 800 metres, down quite a rough track. The rooms have a minimal bathroom, no view and cost 12,000 to 20,000 rp, including breakfast. It's a convenient spot from which to start a trek into the crater, but has nothing else to recommend it.

Getting There & Away From Denpasar (Batubulan station) a bemo to Kintamani is about 2000 rp, though there will be more frequent bemos from Gianyar or Bangli. Buses run between Kintamani and Singaraja on the north coast for 2000 rp.

Penulisan

The road continues along the crater rim beyond Kintamani, gradually climbing higher and higher. If it's clear, there are more fine views down over the crater. At Penulisan, a steep flight of steps leads to Bali's highest temple, Pura Tegeh Koripan, at 1745 metres. Inside the highest courtyard are rows of old statues and fragments of sculptures, some dating back as far as the 11th century. Towering over the temple is a shrine to a new and powerful god – Bali's television repeater mast!

Around Lake Batur

A hairpin-bend road winds its way down from Penelokan to Kedisan on the shore of the lake. To get to the hot springs at Toya Bunkah, take the quaint little road which winds around the lakeside from Kedisan, over many turns and switchbacks, through the lava field. The road continues to Songan, under the north-eastern rim of the crater, and a side road goes around to the north side of Gunung Batur until it is stopped near Toya Mampeh by a huge 'flow' of solidified black lava from 1974. You can climb to the summit of Gunung Batur in just a few hours from either Kedisan or Toya Bunkah, or make longer treks over and around the central volcano and up the crater rim.

Expect to be hassled by touts from top to bottom, and around the lake shore. They will offer to take you to a place to stay, but their real objective is to act as your guide for a trek in the area. Finding a room yourself is not difficult.

Kedisan Coming into Kedisan from Penelokan you reach a T-intersection. Turning left towards Toya Bunkah you come first to the *Segara Bungalows*, where basic singles/doubles cost from 8000/10,000 rp and more comfortable rooms for 15,000/25,000 rp, including breakfast. A bit further on is the *Surya Homestay & Restaurant*, with rooms from 10,000 to 25,000 rp. The cheapest rooms are not fancy, but definitely OK. They ask up to 40,000 rp for rooms with hot water. Turning right as you come into town will bring you to the *Segara Homestay* which has very cheap and basic rooms from 6000 rp.

Buahan A little further around the lake is Buahan, a small place with market gardens right down to the lake shore. *Baruna Cottages* is a more peaceful place to stay, but not without its hustlers. It has a restaurant and singles/doubles with mandi from 8000/10,000 rp to 10,000/15,000 rp.

Trunyan & Kuban The village of Trunyan is squeezed tightly between Lake Batur and the outer crater rim. This is a Bali Aga village, inhabited by remnants of the original Balinese, the people who predate the Majapahit arrival. It's not an interesting or friendly place. It's famous for its four-metre high statue of the village's guardian spirit, Ratu Gede Pancering Jagat, but you're not allowed to see it. There are only a couple of

the traditional Bali Aga style dwellings, some old structures in the temple, and a huge banyan tree, said to be over 1100 years old.

A little beyond Trunyan, and accessible only by the lake (there's no path) is the village cemetery at Kuban. The people of Trunyan do not cremate or bury their dead – they lie them out in bamboo cages to decompose. A collection of skulls and bones lies on a stone platform. This is a tourist trap for those with morbid tastes.

Getting Around the Lake Boats to Trunyan leave from a jetty near the middle of Kedisan, where there is a ticket office and a secure car park (and a few persistent hawkers of second-rate souvenirs). The listed price for a boat for a round-trip stopping at Trunyan, the cemetery at Kuban, the hot springs at Toya Bunkah and returning to Kedisan is around 38,000 rp depending on the number of passengers (maximum is eight). With four people it works out at 9,500 rp each, including entry fees, insurance and a not-very-informative guide. It's cheaper with more passengers, but still not worth it. The first boat leaves at 8 am and the last at 4 pm; the complete trip is about two hours.

Don't try hiring a canoe and paddling yourself – the lake is bigger than it looks from the shore and it can get very choppy. A better alternative is to follow the track around the lakeside from Buahan to Trunyan, an easy hour or two's walk. The walk will be the best part of the trip. From Trunyan you may be able to negotiate a cheaper boat to the cemetery and hot springs, but don't count on it.

Toya Bungkah (Tirta)
Directly across the lake from Trunyan is the small settlement of Toya Bunkah, also known as Tirta, with its hot springs – *tirta* and *toya* both mean 'water'. The hot springs (*air panas*) bubble out in a couple of spots and are used to feed an unattractive bathing pool before flowing out into the lake. It costs 1000 rp to bathe in the pool. The water is soothingly hot, ideal for aching muscles after a volcano climb, but you are stared at by

locals, hassled by hawkers and surrounded by litter.

It's a grubby little village, but many travellers stay here to climb Gunung Batur in the early morning – and most get out as quickly as possible afterwards. There's a ticket office as you enter, which charges 550 rp for entry into the hot springs area, plus 400 rp for a car and 50 rp for insurance.

Places to Stay There are quite a few places to stay in Toya Bunkah, most of them pretty basic. More are being built, including a big place to cater for package tourists.

On the left as you enter, *Arlina Bungalows* is a new place, clean and well-run, and soon to have a restaurant. Good-size rooms with fanciful fairy grotto bathrooms cost 10,000/15,000 rp for singles/doubles, 10,000 rp more with hot water. Next on the left, *Under the Volcano Homestay* (one of two by that name) has basic singles/doubles from around 12,000 rp. *Nyoman Pangus Homestay & Restaurant*, on the right as you come in from Kedisan, is one of the originals here, clean and friendly with rooms from 10,000 to 15,000 rp.

The *Balai Seni Toyabungkah* (Toya Bungkah Arts Centre), up the hill on the western side of the village, is a 'centre for international understanding and co-operation based on the arts'; but mostly it's just a slightly better place to stay, with rooms from 15,000 rp and bungalows from 25,000 rp, sometimes with hot water. *Awangga Bungalows*, at the other end of the village near the lake, advertises itself as the 'cheapest', with simple rooms from 10,000 rp, including breakfast. The nearby *Wisma Tirta Yastra*, right by the lake costs only 8000/10,000 rp with breakfast, looks quite OK and is situated in a very good position. Around 10,000 rp is the going rate for simple rooms with a basic breakfast, give or take 2000 rp. Places in this category include the *Black Lava Homestay*, *Siki Inn* and *Puri Bening Hayato Hotel*.

Places to Eat Fresh fish from the lake is the local speciality, usually barbecued with onion and garlic. The fish are tiny but tasty, and sometimes you get three or four for a meal as there is not much meat on them. There are a number of warungs and restaurants, mostly with similar menus and prices.

Songan

The road continues from Toya Bunkah around the lake to Songan, quite a large village, with some old buildings and market gardens which extend to the edge of the lake. Not many tourists come this far but there is one place to stay, the *Restiti Inn Homestay & Restaurant*, on the left side of the road past the main part of the village, which looks quite OK and costs 10,000/15000 rp for a room with a mandi.

At the end of the road there's a temple at the crater edge – from there you can climb to the top of the outer crater rim in just 15 minutes, and see the east coast, only about five km away. It's an easy downhill stroll to the coast road at Lupak but, unless you want to walk back, remember to take your stuff with you as there's no direct public transport back to Toya Bunkah.

Trekking

Soaring up in the centre of the huge outer crater is the cone of Gunung Batur (1717 metres). It has erupted a number of times this century, and the crater has a number of volcanic features, including lava flows, lava tubes, parasitic cones and craters-within-craters. The usual trek is to climb to the top for sunrise – it's a magnificent sight, though it can get crowded up there. At the summit it's possible to walk right around the rim of the volcanic cone, or descend into the cone from the southern edge. Wisps of steam issuing from cracks in the rock, and the surprising warmth of the ground, indicate that things are still happening down below.

There are several refreshment stops along the way, and people with ice buckets full of cold drinks. It'll cost you more than 2500 rp for a small coke, but it's been carried a long way. The warung at the top has tea and coffee (1500 rp), sometimes jaffles (2500 rp) and a brilliant view (free).

If you have a reasonable sense of direction, and it's not totally dark when you start climbing, you won't need a guide for the usual routes, but if you're not confident about it, take a guide. There are plans to provide a relatively easy, well marked trail to the summit, with a moderate trail fee which will benefit the whole community and support environmental and safety improvements. In the rainy season it may be cloudy in the morning and clear somewhat during the day.

Information If you want to find out about trekking, look for the sign of Jero Wijaya, who has excellent information about the area, and can arrange a guide at a reasonable rate if you think you need one. He has some useful maps showing the whole crater area, with a variety of treks on Gunung Batur, up to the outer rim and beyond to the east coast. His knowledge of the history and geology of the area is way ahead of some of the local amateurs, who can do little more than show you the path.

Guides In and around Toya Bunkah you will be hassled by people offering to guide you up the mountain, sometimes asking outrageous prices, starting at 24,000 rp. About 6000 rp would be a fair price for guiding you up and back on one of the standard routes.

Eggs Would-be guides will offer to provide breakfast on the summit, and this often includes the novelty of cooking eggs (more recently, bananas) in the steaming holes at the top of the volcano. Some of these holes are extremely hot, and it is indeed possible to cook eggs in them. Unfortunately, the practice has resulted in an accumulation of litter – egg shells, banana peels, plastic bags etc – around the summit. By all means take some food to the top, but make sure it does not result in any more rubbish, and discourage your guide from using the volcano as a stove.

North-East Route The easiest route is from the north east, where a new track enables you to take a car to within about 45 minutes' walk from the top. From Toya Bunkah take the road north-east towards Songan, and take the left fork after about 3.5 km. Follow this small road for another 1.7 km to a well-signed track on the left, which climbs another km or so to a parking area. From here the walking track is easily followed to the top. One of the guides should be able to arrange transport, for a price. You may decry the new vehicle access track, but this is hardly a wilderness area. If you want a more challenging climb, take another route.

From Toya Bunkah There is also a pretty straightforward route from Toya Bunkah. Walk out of town on the road to Kedisan and turn right just after the office where you buy the entry ticket. There are quite a few paths at first but they all rejoin sooner or later – just keep going uphill, tending south-west and then west. After half an hour or so you'll be on a ridge with quite a well-defined track; keep going up. It gets pretty steep towards the top, and it can be hard walking over the loose volcanic sand – climbing up three steps and sliding back two. It takes about two hours to get to the top.

Other Routes Other popular routes are from Kedisan or from Pura Jati, the ruined village on the Kedisan to Toya Bunkah road. Another possible route is from Kintamani, first descending the outer crater rim and then climbing the inner cone. For an interesting round trip, you can climb Gunung Batur from Toya Bunkah, follow the rim around to the other side, then descend on the route back to Kedisan. Climbing up, spending a reasonable time on the top and then strolling back down can all be done in four or five hours.

LAKE BRATAN AREA

Approaching Bedugul from the south, you gradually leave the rice terraces behind and ascend into the cool, damp mountain country. There are several places to stay on the southern slopes and near the lake, and Bedugul can be an excellent base for walking trips around the other lakes and surrounding hills. There is also an interesting temple, botanical gardens, colourful market, an excellent golf course and a variety of activities on Lake Bratan itself.

Taman Rekreasi Bedugul

The Bedugul Leisure Park (Taman Rekreasi Bedugul) is at the southern end of the lake. It's along the first road to the right as you come in from the south, and it costs 500 rp to get into the lakeside area. Along the waterfront are an expensive restaurant, souvenir shops, a hotel and facilities for a number of water activities. You can hire a canoe and paddle across to the temple – at the ticket office they charge 20,000 rp for a canoe for half an hour, but independent touts come down to 15,000 rp for 'a long time' (it's cheaper if you go round the lake past the Ashram hotel). Various motorised water sports are available, the noise of which detracts greatly from the pleasantness of the area.

Botanical Gardens

North of Bedugul the road climbs a hill and descends again to an intersection, conspicuously marked with a large, phallic sculpture of a sweet corn cob. The smaller road leads west up to the entrance of the Kebun Raya Bali, the botanical gardens. The gardens were established in 1959 as a branch of the national botanical gardens at Bogor, near Jakarta. They cover more than 120 hectares on the lower slopes of Gunung Pohon, and have an extensive collection of trees and some 500 species of orchid. It's a lovely place, cool, shady and scenic. Usually there are very few visitors, but groups of Balinese like to come for picnics, especially on Sunday when the atmosphere is more festive. Some plants are labelled with their botanical names, but apart from that there is almost nothing in the way of visitor information. Some visitors have been annoyed here by stray dogs – carry a stick to deter them. The gardens open every day from 7 or 8 am to 4.30 pm. Entry is 500 rp and parking is 500 rp for a car, 150 rp for a motorbike. You can drive a car right into the gardens for an extra 2500 rp.

Candikuning

Continuing north on the main road past the botanical gardens turn-off, the turn-off to the flower and produce market is on the left. It's very colourful and well recommended; at its best early in the morning when truck loads of flowers, fruit and vegetables are dispatched to the hotels and restaurants in south Bali.

The road swings back to the lakeside past the Ashram Guesthouse, and there's a small landing where you can hire canoes more cheaply than in Bedugul – 7500 rp for half an hour, 10,000 rp for 'a long time', which should enable you to paddle yourself round most of the lake.

It's possible to paddle across Lake Bratan to some caves which the Japanese used during WW II. You can also walk there in about an hour. From there a very well-marked path ascends to the top of Gunung Catur. It takes about two hours for the climb up and an hour back down. The final bit is steep and you should take some water but it is well worth the effort. There is an old temple on the summit with lots of monkeys.
Anne Whybourne & Peter Clarke, Australia

An interesting two to three-hour circuit walk is from the Bedugul Hotel up to the market, through to the Botanical Gardens then back down the road to the lakeside and through the grounds of the Hotel Ashram to skirt the lakeside back to the Bedugul Hotel. This walk takes in great views of the countryside and Balinese lifestyle. A visit to the market is an absolute must.
Justin Dabner & Angela Johnson, Australia

Pura Ulu Danau Also at Candikuning, a few km north of Bedugul, and actually projecting into the lake, is the Hindu/Buddhist temple of Pura Ulu Danau. It's very picturesque, with a large banyan tree at the entrance, attractive gardens and one courtyard isolated on a tiny island in the lake. The temple, founded in the 17th century, is dedicated to Dewi Danau, the goddess of the waters. Ulu Danau has classical Hindu thatched-roof merus and an adjoining Buddhist stupa. There are the usual admission and parking charges.

Around the Lakes

North of Candikuning, the road descends

BALI

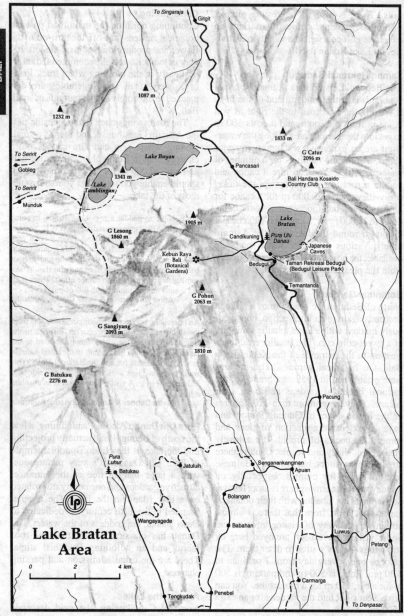

To Singaraja
Gitgit

1087 m

1232 m

1833 m

G Catur
2096 m

To Seririt
Gobleg

Lake Buyan

Pancasari

Bali Handara Kosaido
Country Club

1341 m

Lake
Tamblingan

To Seririt
Munduk

1905 m

Lake
Bratan

Candikuning

Pura Ulu
Danau

Japanese
Caves

G Lesong
1860 m

Kebun Raya
Bali
(Botanical
Gardens)

Bedugul

Taman Rekreasi Bedugul
(Bedugul Leisure Park)

G Pohon
2063 m

Temantanda

G Sangiyang
2093 m

1810 m

G Batukau
2276 m

Pacung

Pura
Luhur
Batukau

Jatuluih

Senganankanginan

Apuan

Bolangan

Luwus

Wangayagede

Babahan

Petang

**Lake Bratan
Area**

0   2   4 km

Tengkudak

Penebel

Carmarga

To Denpasar

past the Bali Handara Kosaido Country Club, with its beautifully situated, world-class **golf course**. Green fees are US$57.75 for 18 holes, and you can hire a half-set of clubs for US$10.

If you continue to Lake Buyan, there's a fine walk around the southern side of Buyan, then over the saddle to the adjoining, smaller **Lake Tamblingan**. From there you can walk uphill, then west to the village of **Munduk** (about two to three hours) and then take the road around the northern side of the lakes back to Bedugul. Alternatively, you can follow the road west from Munduk, and then north, descending through picturesque villages to Seririt on the north coast.

Places to Stay

There are some new places along the road up to Bedugul from the south, starting at Pacung on the southern slopes with a wonderful panorama of southern Bali. The *Pacung Mountain Hotel* (☎ 0361 262460/1/2) is a top-end place perched on a steep hillside looking west to Gunung Batukau. It has a pool, restaurant and comfortable rooms from US$65/70 to US$80. The *Green Valley Hotel* (☎ 0368 21020, 21207) is on the other side of the road, with great views east to Gunung Agung, and rooms from 25,000/30,000 rp.

Opposite the turn-off to the Taman Rekreasi, the *Hadi Raharjo* (☎ 0362 23467), is an OK losmen with a restaurant and rooms at 15,000/20,000 rp (it threatens to become a mid-range place and change its name to 'Strawberry'). Inside the Taman Rekreasi area, the *Bedugul Hotel* (☎ 226593) has motel-style rooms next to the lake for 45,000 rp and older rooms on the slope behind from 35,000 rp. The ones next to the lake have less character and more noise, especially at weekends.

Continuing north, the road climbs higher up the hillside to the turn-off for the pricey *Bukit Permai Hotel* (☎ 0362 23662). Rooms cost from US$22.50 to US$35, including tax, breakfast, TV, hot water, a fireplace and a great view. It's OK, but doesn't look like a fun place to stay.

Back on the lakeside street you come to the well-located *Lila Graha* (☎ 0362 23848), up a steep drive on the left, with singles/doubles from 25,000/30,000 rp, or 60,000 for a suite. It is clean and comfortable, and it incorporates an old Dutch resthouse. On the other side of the road, right by the lake, is the popular *Hotel Ashram* (☎ 0362 22439), with ordinary rooms from 15,000 rp up to 60,000 rp for bigger rooms with hot water. People enjoy staying here.

Top-end accommodation is at the *Bali Handara Country Club* (☎ 0361 288944, 0362 22646; fax 0361 287358) north of Candikuning, with rooms from US$65 to US$350. The view from the bar might be worth the price of a drink. As well as the golf course, there are tennis courts, a gym and a Japanese bath.

Places to Eat

The lakeside restaurant at the Taman Rekreasi is a bit expensive – 3750 rp for a mie goreng! The restaurant at the Bedugul Hotel does buffet lunches for tour groups. In Candikuning, you'll find the *Restaurant Pelangi, Rumah Makan Mini Bali* and others in the same area. Further north, the lakeside *Taliwang Restaurant* has food which is not so tourist-oriented, and is one of the best options. There are a few places near the Ulu Danau temple which should provide a reasonable meal at a reasonable price. The restaurants at the Bali Handara and the Pacung Mountain hotels probably have the best food, at a price.

Getting There & Away

Bedugul is on the main north-south road so is easy to get to from either Denpasar or Singaraja. It costs 1800 rp from Denpasar's Ubung bus terminal, a bit less from the western bus station in Singaraja. The road is sealed all the way and signposted, so it's easy to follow if you have your own transport.

GITGIT

Heading north from the Lake Bratan area, a very scenic road goes to Singaraja, about 30 km away (see the North Bali section later in this chapter). On the way there's the beautiful **Gitgit waterfall**, west of the road just past Gitgit village. There are plenty of signs and a car park. You buy a ticket (450 rp) at the office near the west side of the road, and follow the concrete path between the rows of souvenir stalls for about 500 metres. The new *Gitgit Hotel* has clean but uninteresting rooms for 25,000/35,000 rp, or 10,000 rp more with hot water. There's a good view from here, but this hotel doesn't take advantage of it.

GUNUNG BATUKAU

West of the Mengwi-Bedugul-Singaraja road rises 2276-metre Gunung Batukau, the 'coconut-shell mountain'. This is the third of Bali's three major mountains and the holy peak of the western end of the island.

Pura Luhur

Pura Luhur, on the slopes of Batukau, was the state temple when Tabanan was an independent kingdom. The temple has a seven-roofed meru to Maha Dewa, the mountain's guardian spirit, as well as shrines for the three mountain lakes: Bratan, Tamblingan and Buyan. There are several routes to Pura Luhur but none of them are particularly high-class roads – it's a remote temple. You can reach it by following the road up to Penebel from Tabanan. Or turn off the Mengwi to Bedugul road at Baturiti, near the 'Denpasar 40 km' sign and follow the convoluted route to Penebel.

Jatuluih

Also perched on the slopes of Gunung Batukau, but closer to Bedugul and the Mengwi to Bedugul road, is the small village of Jatuluih, whose name means 'truly marvellous'. The view truly is – it takes in a huge chunk of southern Bali.

ROUTES THROUGH PUPUAN

Less travelled routes over the mountains branch north from the Denpasar to Gilimanuk road, one from Pulukan and the other from Antosari. They meet at Pupuan before dropping down to Seririt, on the north coast to the west of Singaraja.

The Pulukan to Pupuan road climbs steeply up from the coast providing fine views back down to the sea. The route runs through spice-growing country and you'll often see spices laid out on mats by the road to dry – the smell of cloves rises up to meet

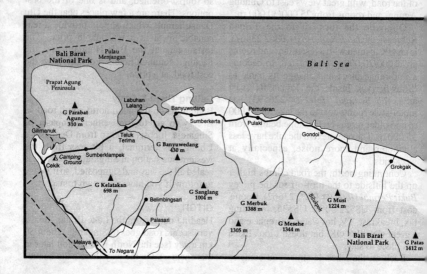

you. At one point, the narrow and winding road actually runs right through an enormous banyan tree which bridges the road. Further on, the road spirals down to Pupuan through some of Bali's most beautiful rice terraces.

The road from Antosari starts through rice fields, climbs into the spice-growing country, then descends through the coffee growing areas to Pupuan.

If you continue another 12 km or so towards the north coast you reach Mayong, where you can turn east to Munduk and on to Lake Tamblingan and Lake Buyan. The road is rough but passable, and offers fine views of the mountains, lakes and out to the northern coast. Munduk is a traditional village, and there are some interesting walks in the area.

North Bali

Northern Bali, the district of Buleleng, makes an interesting contrast with the south of the island. Lovina, a string of beaches west of Singaraja, is popular with budget travellers. Many arriving from Java go straight from Gilimanuk to the north coast, rather than taking the south-coast road.

The north coast has been subject to European influence for longer than the south. Although the Dutch had established full control of northern Bali by 1849, it was not until the beginning of this century that their power extended to the south. In 1845 the rajas of Buleleng and Karangasem formed an alliance, possibly to conquer other Balinese states or, equally possibly, to resist the Dutch. In any case, the Dutch were worried, and attacked Buleleng and Karangasem in 1846, 1848 and 1849, seizing control of the north in the third attempt. The western district of Jembrana came under Dutch control in 1853, but it was not until 1906 that the south was finally subdued.

From the time of their first northern conquests, the Dutch interfered increasingly in Balinese affairs. It was here that Balinese women first covered their breasts – on orders from the Dutch to 'protect the morals of Dutch soldiers'.

Buleleng has a unique artistic and cultural tradition. Its dance troupes are highly regarded and a number of dance styles have originated here, including Joged and Janger.

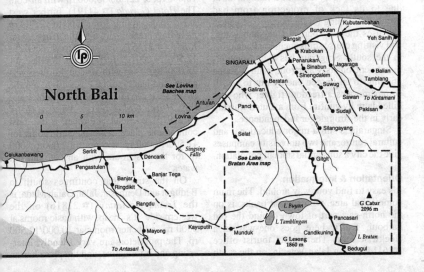

Gold and silverwork, weaving, pottery, musical-instrument making and temple design all show distinctive local styles. The Sapi Gerumbungan bull race is a Buleleng tradition and quite different from the races of Negara, in south-west Bali. Events are held at Kaliasem, near Lovina, on Independence Day (August 17), Singaraja Day (March 31) and other occasions.

SINGARAJA

Singaraja was the centre of Dutch power in Bali and remained the administrative centre for the islands of Nusa Tenggara (Bali through to Timor) until 1953. It is one of the few places in Bali where there are visible reminders of the Dutch period, but there are also Chinese and Muslim influences. With a population of around 85,000 Singaraja is a busy town, but orderly, even quiet compared with Denpasar. Dokars are still used on the pleasant tree-lined streets, and there are some interesting Dutch colonial houses. The 'suburb' of Beratan, south of Singaraja, is the silverwork centre of northern Bali.

For years the port of Singaraja was the usual arrival point for visitors to Bali – it's where all the prewar travel books started. Singaraja is hardly used as a harbour now, due to its lack of protection from bad weather. Shipping for the north coast generally uses the new port at Celukanbawang, and visiting cruise ships anchor at Padangbai in the south. Singaraja has a conspicuous monument on its waterfront, with a statue pointing to an unseen enemy out to sea. It commemorates a freedom fighter who was killed here by gunfire from a Dutch warship early in the struggle for independence.

Singaraja is still a major educational and cultural centre, and two university campuses give the city a substantial student population.

Orientation & Information

It's easy to find your way around. The main commercial area, with several banks, is on the north-east part of town behind the old harbour. Traffic here goes one-way in a clockwise loop. The helpful tourist office (☎ 61141) is on Jalan Veteran, on the south side of town, open from 8 am to 2 pm, closing noon on Friday and 1pm Saturday.

The post office and telephone office are near each other on Jalan Imam Bonjol. The telephone code for Singaraja, and all of Buleleng district, is 0362.

Gedung Kirtya Historical Library

This small institution has a collection of around 3000 old Balinese manuscripts inscribed on lontar (palm). These lontar books include literary, mythological, historical and religious works. Some older written works, in the form of inscribed metal plates, are kept here, but most valuable works have been transferred to Denpasar. There are also some old publications in Dutch. You're welcome to visit, but it's more a place for scholars than tourists. It opens from 7 am to 1 pm Monday to Friday – donation requested.

Places to Stay & Eat

Most of the hotels are used by local business travellers. You'll find a few of them along Jalan Jen Achmad Yani, starting in the east with the *Hotel Sentral* (☎ 21896), a good choice with basic singles/doubles at 7000/10,000 rp, or 22,500/30,000 rp with air-con. The *Hotel Garuda* (☎ 41191), further west at No 76, has rooms from 7500 to 12,500 rp including breakfast, while the *Hotel Duta Karya* (☎ 21467), across the road, is OK at 12,500/14,000 rp for singles/ doubles, or 25,000/30,000 rp with air-con. Further west again, and handy to the bus station, are the *Hotel Saku Bindu* (15,000 rp a double) and the *Hotel Gelar Sari*. *Wijaya Hotel* (☎ 21915), on Jalan Sudirman, is the most comfortable place, with standard rooms for 11,500/14,000 rp, and up to 62,000/69,000 rp for the best room with air-con and hot water.

On the street that continues south to Bedugul and Denpasar, Jalan Gajah Mada, is the *Tresna Homestay* (☎ 21816) on the western side. It's cheap, with basic rooms at 5000 rp and better rooms at 10,000/12,500 rp. The proprietors are very friendly, interesting and informative, and the place has an

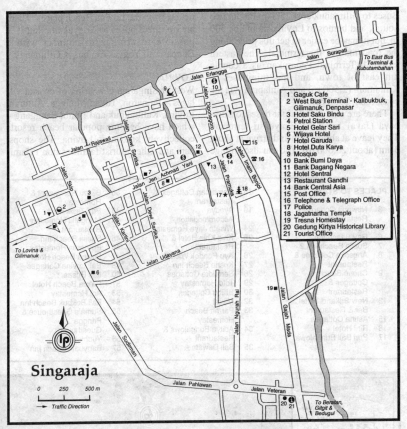

1 Gaguk Cafe
2 West Bus Terminal - Kalibukbuk,
   Gilimanuk, Denpasar
3 Hotel Saku Bindu
4 Petrol Station
5 Hotel Gelar Sari
6 Wijaya Hotel
7 Hotel Garuda
8 Hotel Duta Karya
9 Mosque
10 Bank Bumi Daya
11 Bank Dagang Negara
12 Hotel Sentral
13 Restaurant Gandhi
14 Bank Central Asia
15 Post Office
16 Telephone & Telegraph Office
17 Police
18 Jagatnartha Temple
19 Tresna Homestay
20 Gedung Kirtya Historical Library
21 Tourist Office

Singaraja

0   250   500 m

→ Traffic Direction

amazing collection of antiques and old junk, some of it for sale.

Places to Eat

There are plenty of places to eat in Singaraja, including a batch of places in the small Mumbul market on Jalan Jen Achmad Yani. You'll find the popular *Restaurant Gandhi* here, with a good Chinese menu and glossy, clean surroundings. Across the road is the *Restaurant Segar II*, where a good Chinese meal will run to about 6000 rp. There are also a few restaurants along Jalan Imam Bonjol, and some warungs near the two bus stations.

Gaguk Cafe, an open-fronted place just west of the western bus terminal, is very friendly and popular with local students, and great for a snack or a meal. It's also a good place for information about things to see and how to get around.

Getting There & Away

Singaraja is the north coast's main transportation centre with two bus terminals. From the Banyuasri terminal, on the western side of town, buses to Denpasar (Ubung station) via Bedugul leave about every half hour from 6 am to 4 pm and cost around 2000 rp.

Buses to Gilimanuk cost 2500 rp (about two hours), and bemos to Lovina should be 500 rp, but it may be easier to get this price along the road than at the terminal. The eastern terminal, Terminal Penarukan, is a couple km east of town, and has minibuses to Kintamani (2,500 rp) and Amlapura (via the coast road; 2500 rp).

There are also direct night buses to Surabaya (Java) from the Banyuasri terminal. They leave at about 5 pm and arrive at about 3 am (about 20,000 rp). You can also arrange tickets from the Lovina Beach places. There are no direct buses to Yogyakarta, but it is possible to arrange to connect with a Denpasar to Yogyakarta bus in Gilimanuk.

LOVINA

West of Singaraja is a string of coastal villages – Pemaron, Tukad Mungga, Anturan, Lovina, Kalibukbuk and Bunut Panggang – which have become popular beach resorts collectively known as Lovina. The shops, bars and other tourist facilities don't domi-

PLACES TO STAY		
3 Nirwana Cottages & Restaurant	18 Rambutan Cottages & Restaurant	36 Billibu Restaurant & Homestay
5 Palestis Hotel	19 Ayodya Accommodation	43 Puri Tasik Madu
6 Ray Beach Inn	24 Wisata Jaya Homestay	44 Mangalla Homestay & Restaurant
7 Susila Beach Inn 2	25 Khie Khie Hotel & Restaurant	45 Susila Beach Inn
8 Angsoka Cottages & Restaurant	26 Ayu Pondok Wisita	46 Purnama Homestay
9 Chono Beach Cottages & Restaurant	27 Krisna Beach Inn	47 Lovina Beach Hotel
	28 Samudra Cottages	48 Bali Lovina Cottages
12 New Srikandi Hotel, Bar & Restaurant	29 Toto Homestay	50 Las Brisas
	30 Billibu Cottages	51 Palma Beach Hotel
15 Astina Cottages	32 Miami	53 Adi Homestay
16 Rini Hotel	33 Parma Beach Homestay	54 Kali Bukbuk Beach Inn
17 Puri Bali Bungalows	34 Aditya Bungalows & Restaurant	55 Suma's Guesthouse & Pringga Guesthouse
	35 Bali Dewata	56 Yudhistra Inn
		57 Banyualit Beach Inn

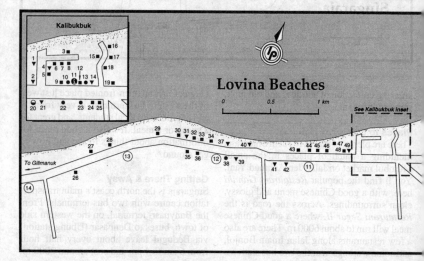

nate the place as they do at Sanur or Kuta. Visitors are hassled with people trying to sell dolphin trips, snorkelling, sarongs and so on, but they don't seem to sell as hard as at Kuta, and the intensity of the harassment seems to wax and wane. It's a good place to meet other travellers, and there's a bit of night life.

The beaches here are black volcanic sand, not the white stuff you find in the south. It doesn't look as appealing but it's perfectly clean and fine to walk along. Nor is there any surf – a reef keeps it almost flat calm most of the time. The sunsets here are every bit as spectacular as those at Kuta, and as the sky reddens, the lights of the fishing boats appear as bright dots across the horizon. Earlier in the afternoon, at fishing villages like Anturan, you can see the perahus being prepared for the night's fishing.

Orientation & Information

Going along the main road, note the km posts which show distances from Singaraja (they are marked on the map). The tourist area

58	Janur's Dive Inn	71	Permai Beach	41	Superman Restaurant
59	Awangga Inn		Bungalows	42	Singa Pizza
60	Lila Cita	72	Baruna Beach		Restaurant
61	Celuk Agung Cottages		Cottages	49	Wina's Bar &
62	Hotel Perama & Postal				Restaurant
	Agency	**PLACES TO EAT**		63	Harmoni Restaurant
64	Mandhara				
	Cottages	1	Bali Bintang	**OTHER**	
65	Gede Homestay		Restaurant		
66	Simon's Seaside Cot-	2	Puri Taman Restaurant	10	Perama Office
	tages	4	Kakatua Bar &	11	Tourist Office & Police
67	Homestay Agung &		Restaurant		Station
	Restaurant	14	Surya Restaurant	13	Malibu Club
68	Bali Taman Beach	21	Arya's Cafe	20	Bus Stop
	Hotel	31	Karina Restaurant	22	Moneychanger
69	Happy Beach Inn	37	Johni's Restaurant	23	Air-Brush T-Shirt Shop
70	Jati Reef Bungalows	39	Restaurant Adi Rama	38	Spice Dive
		40	Marta's Warung	52	Radio Mast

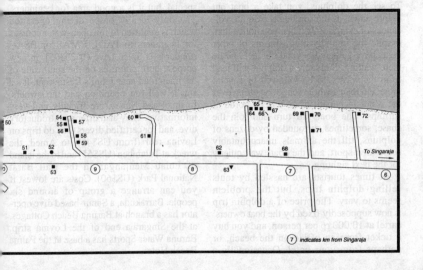

To Singaraja

⑦ indicates km from Singaraja

stretches out over seven or eight km, but the main focus is at Kalibukbuk, about 10½ km from Singaraja. This is where you'll find the tourist office and the police station, which share the same premises. The tourist office is open Monday to Thursday and Saturday from 7 am to 5.30 pm, Friday until 1 pm. If you need information outside these hours the police may be able to help. There's a moneychanger nearby, and some of the hotels also change money.

The postal agent is on the main road near Khie Khie restaurant, and you can also buy stamps and post letters at the Hotel Perama. Local and long-distance telephone calls can be made from the postal agent and also at Aditya Bungalows, but international calls are much cheaper at the Telkom telephone office in Singaraja.

East of Arya's you'll find Beny Tantra's Air-Brush T-shirt shop. It's not cheap, but it's worth a look because his designs are so good, brilliant in fact. He'll also make T-shirts to order, and some of his cartoons are available as postcards. Other shops around here sell souvenirs, sarongs, second-hand books and so on.

Dolphins

To see the dolphins, you take a boat out before dawn, as the sun bursts over the volcanoes of central Bali. Then you notice that, despite the ungodly hour, dozens of other boats have gathered beyond the reef and lie there waiting. Suddenly a dolphin will leap from the waves, to be followed by several more and then a whole school, vaulting over the water in pursuit of an unseen horde of shrimps. The boats all turn and join the chase, sometimes surrounded by dozens of dolphins, till the animals unaccountably cease their sport, and the boats wait quietly for the next sighting.

At times tourists are hassled by touts selling dolphin trips, but the problem seems to vary. The price of a dolphin trip is now supposedly fixed by the boat owners' cartel at 10,000 rp per person, and you buy a ticket from an office on the beach, or perhaps from your hotel. Occasionally a tout will sell a dolphin trip for more than this rate (maybe 15,000 rp) and pocket the difference, prompting a new round of direct marketing, which can be a major annoyance.

There are reports that the number of dolphins in the morning show has declined, perhaps because of too much attention. It's not clear whether this is a temporary, seasonal or long-term decline.

Snorkelling & Diving

Generally, the water is very clear and the reef is terrific for snorkelling. It's not the best coral you'll find but it's certainly not bad and getting out to it is very easy. In many places you can simply swim out from the beach, or get a boat to take you out; the skipper should know where the best coral is. The price of snorkelling trips is also fixed by the boat owners, at 5000 rp per person for an hour, including the use of mask, snorkel and fins. There is some technicality about whether or not you can see dolphins and snorkel on the one trip for a special rate, or whether you have to return to shore and do a separate trip to snorkel.

Scuba diving on the reef is nothing special, but it is a good area for beginners. The only locally based diving operation which is qualified to run open-water courses for beginners to PADI, CMAS or BSAC standards is Spice Dive (☎ 23305), in new purpose-built premises on the south side of the main road near Johni's Restaurant. It's a small, well run operation and the owners, Imanuel and Nancy, are friendly and very informative. They also offer an introductory dive, and for certified divers they do trips on Lovina reef (from US$45), to Amed, the wreck at Tulamben (US$55) and to the island of Pulau Menjangan in the Bali Barat National Park (US$60). Costs are lowest if you can arrange a group of around six people. Barrakuda, a Sanur-based dive operator has a branch at Baruna Beach Cottages, at the Singaraja end of the Lovina strip. Baruna Water Sports has a base at the Palma Beach Hotel.

Places to Stay

There are so many places to stay along the Lovina beach strip that it's impossible to list them all, or to keep the list up to date. The first hotel is north of the main road just after the six km marker, the last is nearly 14 km from Singaraja. Places are usually clustered in groups on one of the side roads to the beach, then there might be nothing for a half km or so.

During peak times (mid-July to the end of August and mid-December to mid-January) accommodation can be tight and prices are somewhat higher. Generally the cheapest places are away from the beach, some on the south side of the main road. Upstairs rooms are cooler and a bit more expensive, especially if they have a view. There's a 5% tax on hotel accommodation, but not on the cheaper homestays, and the fancier places have a 10% service charge as well. Mostly it's budget accommodation, but there are a few mid-range places – generally they're the ones with phone numbers. They are all in the 0362 zone.

Singaraja to Anturan Starting from the Singaraja end, the first place is the *Aldian Palace Hotel* (☎ 23549), a mid-range place but not well-located, with double rooms from US$16 to US$35. Then there's the nice looking *Baruna Beach Cottages* (☎ 22252), with individual cottages and rooms in a larger two-storey block. All have bathrooms, and prices range from US$17 for losmen-style rooms, US$24 for cottage-style rooms and up to US$52 for beachfront rooms with air-con, plus 15.5% tax and service. There's a swimming pool, a bar/restaurant on the beach, and you can also rent water-sports equipment and arrange diving trips.

On the next side road, *Jati Reef Bunga-lows*, in the rice fields close to the beach, doesn't look very pretty but have comfortable double rooms with private, open-air bathrooms and cost around 12,000 to 15,000 rp. The nearby *Happy Beach Inn* is in fact a cheerful place, with good food and rooms from 7000 to 10,000 rp. In between those two, *Puri Bedahulu* is right on the beach and

has some Balinese-style rooms for 20,000 rp, or 35,000 rp with air-con. Further inland are the *Permai Beach Bungalows,* where basic rooms cost from 10,000/15,000 rp and rooms with hot water and air-con cost from 30,000 rp. The reef off the beach here is reputed to be the best along the Singaraja to Lovina coastal strip.

Fronting onto the main road, but extending all the way down to the beach, is the up-market *Bali Taman Beach Hotel* (☎ 22126). Standard singles/doubles cost US$22.50/27.50 and air-con rooms cost US$45/55.

Anturan From the main road, another turn-off goes to the scruffy little fishing village of Anturan, where there are a few places to stay. The *Mandhara Cottages* have basic singles/doubles with bathroom for 8000/10,000 rp, 2000 rp more for bigger rooms, including breakfast. The friendly *Gede Homestay*, just behind, costs 7000/10,000 rp for smaller rooms and 12,000/20,000 rp for the best rooms. Gede is a musician, and also provides entertainment, information and good Balinese food.

Walk a short distance east along the beach to the refurbished *Simon's Seaside Cottages* (☎ 41183), with comfortable rooms for US$20. There's actually a little track leading from the main road directly to Simon's, but it's hard to spot. The beach here is a bit nicer than at Mandhara, at the end of the Anturan road. Next door to Simon's is *Homestay Agung*, at around 10,000 rp, which gets mixed reports from travellers.

Anturan to Kalibukbuk Continuing west from Anturan you pass the *Hotel Perama* (☎ 21161) on the main road, with basic rooms from 6000/8000 rp, including breakfast. This is also the office for the Perama bus company, and a good source of information for tours. The next turn-off goes down to the *Lila Cita*, right on the beach front. It's simple and reasonably clean, with singles/doubles for 8000/10,000 rp, or 15,000/20,000 rp with private mandi, and the sea is just outside your window. On the way there you'll pass the

Celuk Agung Cottages (☎ 23039), with rooms from US$20/25, up to US$50/55 for a suite room with air-con, fridge and 'luke-warm water'. Other facilities include satellite TV, tennis courts and a pool.

The next side road down to the beach has quite a few places to stay. The pleasant *Kali Bukbuk Beach Inn* (☎ 21701) has rooms from 15,000/20,000 rp to 30,000/35,000 rp with air-con. On the other side, back a bit from the beach, is *Banyualit Beach Inn* (☎ 25889) with fan-cooled doubles for 22,000 rp, up to 40,000 rp with air-con – it's pretty good value for the location and the facilities it offers. Other budget places here include *Yudhistra, Indra Pura, Awangga Inn* and *Janur's Dive Inn*.

Back on the main road, on the side away from the beach, is the *Adi Homestay*, with ordinary rooms from 9000 rp up to 20,000 rp, which seems steep for a plain losmen in this location. On the beach side of the main road is the new *Palma Beach Hotel* (☎ 23775; fax 23659), with a big pool and air-con rooms with fridge, hot water and TV from US$60/67.50 to US$78/85; you can use the pool for just 5000 rp.

Kalibukbuk A little beyond the 10-km marker is the 'centre' of Lovina – the village of Kalibukbuk. Here you'll find *Ayodya Accommodation*, a traditional place in a big old Balinese house. Rooms cost from 7000 to 8000 rp and are bare and functional, but you sit outside and take your meals there. It's very pleasant in the evening, although the traffic noise can be annoying.

Follow the track beside Ayodya down towards the beach and you'll come to the delightful *Rambutan Cottages* (☎ 23388). The beautifully finished rooms cost from 30,000 to 45,000 rp, or 55,000 rp with hot water; 5000 rp more in peak seasons. They have a new swimming pool set in a pretty garden, and a spacious restaurant with ace food. Next along are the *Puri Bali Bunga-lows* where singles/doubles cost 8000/10,000 rp, good value for this location. Closest to the beach is the super-clean and well-run *Rini Hotel* (☎ 23386), with a

variety of comfortable rooms from 25,000 rp. There's a good restaurant, and families and children are welcome. Opposite Rini are the *Astina Cottages*, in a pretty garden setting, with a variety of rooms and bunga-lows from 9000 to 15,000 rp; prices are a bit higher in the peak season.

On the south side of the main road, west of Ayodya, you'll find the *Khie Khie Hotel & Restaurant*, with a not-very-attractive pool, and rooms at 20,000 rp. A bit further along is the small *Wisata Jaya Homestay*, one of the cheapest around, with basic but satisfactory rooms for 8000 rp. On the beach side of the road is the *New Srikandi Hotel Bar & Restaurant*, which is also cheap, and *Chono Beach Cottages* which are more expensive.

The next turn-off, just beyond the 11-km marker, takes you down to *Nirwana Cottages* (☎ 22288). This is the biggest development at Lovina, with a large slab of beachfront property and double rooms from 20,000 to 45,000 rp; some people think it's overpriced, and have found that the cleaning and the management are not as good as the location.

Right behind Nirwana is *Angsoka* (☎ 22841), which has a pool and advertises 'luxury on a shoestring' but only has a couple of cheap rooms – most are over 35,000 rp, up to 65,000 rp with air-con and hot water. *Susila Beach Inn 2*, beside the Angsoka, is a small, straightforward losmen with cheap rooms for 7000/8000 rp. The *Ray Beach Inn*, next door, has rooms at 8000/10,000 rp in cell-block style. *Palestis Hotel*, on the road to the beach, is new and very colourful, with quite good rooms for 20,000 rp, including breakfast.

Back on the main road there's a string of cheaper places with prices from about 8000 rp. They include the *Purnama Homestay*, *Mangalla Homestay* and *Susila Beach Inn* which are all grouped together on the north side of the road, some extending through to the beach. *Lovina Beach Hotel* (☎ 23473) has a variety of rooms extending to the beach – pretty basic ones are US$5; better ones are up to US$25 with air-con and hot water. *Puri*

Top: Wooden sculpture, Sanur, Bali (PM)
Bottom: Detail of sarcophagus at a funeral procession, Bali (PM)

Top left: Gamelan orchestra at Yoga kraton, Yogyakarta, Java (PM)
Top right: A funeral gathering, Ubud, Bali (VT)
Bottom: Mancong dancers, East Kalimantan (BD)

Tasik Madu costs 12,000 rp for downstairs rooms, 15,000 rp upstairs, and is close to the beach.

Beyond Kalibukbuk Continuing further along there's *Aditya Bungalows & Restaurant* (☎ 22059), a big mid-range place with beach frontage, pool, shops and a variety of rooms with TV, phone, fridge etc. Some of the rooms are right on the beach and costs range from US$20 to US$60. Next, there's the friendly *Parma Beach Hotel*, with cottages from 10,000/12,000 rp to 20,000/25,000 rp, set in a garden extending down to the beach. *Bali Dewata* is on the south side of the road, a basic but clean and friendly place for 10,000/15,000 rp. The *Toto Homestay* is another bottom-end beachfront place with spartan rooms for 7500 rp a double. *Samudra Cottages*, with a secluded location further along the road, are from 10,000/15,000 rp, and have a new hotel building growing beside them. *Krisna Beach Inn* is the next one, at 10,000/15,000 rp for singles/doubles, and there are now even more places extending west of here. The *Adirama Beach Hotel* (☎ 23759) offers a pool, beachfront location and not much in the way of style, with rooms from US$22, US$30 with air-con, or US$45 with TV.

Places to Eat
Most of the places to stay along the beach strip also have restaurants. Many of the restaurants are also bars, depending on the time of night, and you can stop at any of them just for a drink. With all these places, plus a handful of warungs, there are dozens of places to eat. Some of them are listed here, but you'll do well just looking around and eating anywhere that takes your fancy.

Starting from the Singaraja end, the *Harmoni Restaurant*, on the main road, has great fresh fish and other seafood dishes, but service can be slow in between meal times. The restaurant at *Happy Beach Inn* is good, with friendly service – order Balinese roast duck a day in advance. In Kalibukbuk village, the *Surya Restaurant* is very well regarded, and will also serve good Balinese

dishes. The *BU Warung*, next to the tourist office, is good value, or you could try *Chono's*, a little bit to the west. Across the road, *Arya's Cafe* is a favourite with locals – everyone recommends it; try its cakes and desserts.

On the road down to Nirwana there's the *Kakatua Bar & Restaurant*, which offers a good meal in a very convivial atmosphere. The restaurant at *Nirwana* is pricey, and it's been redesigned so it doesn't overlook the beach as nicely as it used to.

Further along are *Singa Pizza Restaurant*, the *Superman Restaurant*, *Marta's Warung* and then *Johni's Restaurant*. All these places are popular, and their menus and prices are similar. *Wina's Bar & Restaurant* is more of a night-time hangout, as is the *Malibu*, but they both serve meals.

Entertainment
Some of the hotel restaurants have special nights with an Indonesian buffet meal and Balinese dancing. At about 6000 rp for entertainment and all you can eat, this can be very good value. *Rambutan* does a good one, usually on Wednesday and Sunday. *Aditya*, the *New Srikandi* and *Angsoka* also have buffet nights which are well advertised by leaflets that circulate around the beach and the bars. There's often live music at the *Malibu*, and they also have video movies.

Quite a few Balinese guys hang round the bars in Lovina. Most of them are pretty harmless, and some of then are a lot of fun. The shameless con artists of a few years ago have mostly moved on, but you should still be sceptical if local guys offer elaborate pretexts for wanting large amounts of money.

Getting There & Away
To get to Lovina from the south of Bali by public transport, you first have to get to Singaraja, then take a bemo from there. The regular bemo fare from Singaraja to the middle of Lovina's beach strip is 500 rp.

There are direct public buses between Surabaya (Java) and Singaraja, but if you're coming in from the west you can get off along the Lovina beach strip, rather than have to backtrack from Singaraja. Public buses to Surabaya (20,000 rp) leave Singaraja at 5 pm; call the ticket office on ☎ 25141 to arrange a pick up, or get the staff at your losmen to help. Alternatively, there are frequent buses to Gilimanuk, where you can take the ferry to Java, and arrange onward transport. If you're just going a short way west, to Sing Sing, Banjar or Seririt, you can flag down a bemo on the main drag.

The Perama office (☎ 21161) and bus stop is at the Perama Hotel in Anturan, about eight km from Singaraja. Fares are 12,500 rp to Kuta or Ubud, 20,000 rp to Candidasa or Padangbai, 30,000 rp to Lombok.

Getting Around
The Lovina strip is very spread out, but you can get back and forth on bemos, which should cost 300 rp for a short trip (two or three km), or 500 rp all the way to Singaraja – they will try to charge you more if they can. You can also rent bicycles (3000 rp per day), motorbikes (around 10,000 rp per day) and cars (about 40,000 rp per day without insurance; less for longer). Inquire at the places in Kalibukbuk, or ask at your losmen. For a charter bemo, try at the Banyuasri terminal in Singaraja where there might be a few to compete for your business.

WEST OF SINGARAJA
The road west of Singaraja follows the coast through Lovina then cuts through the Bali Barat National Park to join the south coast road near Gilimanuk, the port for ferries to Java. There are several places along this road, or near to it, which are worth a visit.

Waterfalls
At the village of Labuhan Haji, five km from the middle of the Lovina beach strip, there's a sign to Singsing Air Terjun (Daybreak Waterfall). About one km from the main road there's a warung on the left and a car park on the right. It's a 200-metre walk along a path to the lower falls, which drop about 12 metres into a deep pool. The pool is good for a swim, though the water isn't crystal clear, but it's much cooler than the sea and very

refreshing. Clamber further up the hillside to the second waterfall (Singsing Dua), which is slightly bigger and has a mud bath which is supposedly good for the skin.

There are some other falls in the area which you have to walk to – ask at your losmen for details. They are more spectacular in the wet season, and may be turned off in the dry season.

Banjar
Buddhist Monastery Bali's only Buddhist monastery *(wihara)* is about half a km beyond the village of Banjar Tega, which is about three km up a steep track from the main coast road – get a lift on the back of a motorbike for about 500 rp. It is vaguely Buddhist-looking, with colourful decoration, a bright orange roof and statues of Buddha, but overall it's still very Balinese. There are good views down the valley and across the paddy fields to the sea. The road continues past the monastery, winding further up into the hills.

Hot Springs The hot springs (air panas) are only a short distance west of the monastery if you cut across from Banjar Tega, rather than return to the main road. Turn west in the centre of the village and take the small road for a km or so to the village of Banjar. From there it's only a short distance uphill before you see the 'air panas 1 km' sign on the left. Buy your ticket from the little office (400 rp, children 200 rp) and cross the bridge to the baths. There are changing rooms under the restaurant, on the right side.

Eight carved stone *nagas* (mythological serpents) spew water from a natural hot spring into the first bath, which then overflows (via the mouths of five more nagas), into a second, larger pool. In a third pool, water pours from three-metre-high spouts to give you a pummelling massage. The water is slightly sulphurous and pleasantly hot, so you might enjoy it more in the morning or the evening than in the heat of the day. You must wear a swimsuit and you shouldn't use soap in the pools.

The whole area is beautifully landscaped

with lush tropical plants. The restaurant, a striking Balinese-style building, is not too expensive and has good Indonesian food.

Getting There & Away The monastery and hot springs are both signposted from the main road. If you don't have your own transport, it's probably easiest to go to the hot springs first. At the Banjar turn-off (around the 18-km marker) there are guys on motorbikes who will take you up to the air panas for 500 rp one way. From there you can walk across to the monastery and back down to the main road.

Seririt

Seririt is a junction town for the roads that run south over the mountains to Pulukan or Bajera, on the way to Denpasar. The road running west along the coast towards Gilimanuk is quite good, with some pretty coastal scenery and few tourists.

Seririt has a petrol station and a reasonable selection of shops. If you need to stay there, the *Hotel Singarasari* (☎ 92435), near the bus and bemo stop, has rooms for 8000 rp, or 20,000 rp with air-con and TV. There are places to eat in the market area, just north of the bemo stop.

Celukanbawang

Celukanbawang, the main port for northern Bali, has a large wharf. Bugis schooners, the magnificent sailing ships which take their name from the seafaring Bugis people of Sulawesi, sometimes anchor here. The *Hotel Drupadi Indah*, a combination losmen, cinema, bar and restaurant, is the only place to stay; it costs 15,000 rp for a very ordinary room.

Pulaki

Pulaki is famous for its Pura Pulaki, a coastal temple which was completely rebuilt in the early 1980s. The temple has a large troop of monkeys. Pulaki itself seems to be entirely devoted to grape growing and the whole village is almost roofed over with grapevines. A local wine is made which tastes a little like sweet sherry – mixed with lemon-

ade it's drinkable, sort of. The grapes are also exported as dried fruit.

Pemuteran

One km past Pulaki is the Pemuteran temple, with some hot springs just outside, but it's not particularly interesting. North of the road near here is the *Pondok Sari Accommodation & Restaurant*, all by itself with its own little beach. It's used as a base for diving trips to Menjangan island, about 16 km away, but it would also be a nice place to get away from it all. Very comfortable, attractive rooms cost 35,000 rp without breakfast, plus 10% tax and service. There's a Sanur number for bookings (☎ 289031).

BALI BARAT NATIONAL PARK

The Bali Barat (West Bali) National Park covers nearly 20,000 hectares of the western tip of Bali. In addition, 50,000 hectares are protected in the national park extension, as well as nearly 7000 hectares of coral reef and coastal waters. On an island as small and densely populated as Bali, this represents a major commitment to nature conservation.

The park headquarters is at Cekik, near Gilimanuk, and some treks can be done from there (see the South-West Bali section earlier in this chapter for details). Coming from the north coast, there is a visitors centre at Labuhan Lalang (open from 7 am to 4 pm every day), with some information and a good relief model of the national park. There are a couple of trekking possibilities here, but the main attraction is diving and snorkelling on Menjangan Island. The standard of facilities and information for visitors is quite limited.

The main north coast road connects with Gilimanuk through the national park, and you don't have to pay any entrance fees just to drive through. If you want to visit any places of interest (they're called 'visitor objects'), then you have to buy an entry ticket – 2000 rp for the day. In addition you pay for parking at some of the visitor objects.

Flora & Fauna

Most of the natural vegetation in the park is

not tropical rainforest, which requires rain all year, but a coastal savannah, with deciduous trees which become bare in the dry season. The southern slopes have more regular rainfall, and hence more tropical vegetation, while the coastal lowlands have extensive mangroves. Over 200 species of plant inhabit the various environments.

Animals include black monkey, leaf monkey and macaque; barking deer, sambar deer, mouse deer, Java deer and muncak; squirrel, wild pig, buffalo, iguana, python and green snake. The bird life is prolific, with many of Bali's 300 species represented.

Bali Starling Bali's most famous bird is the Bali starling (*Leucopsar rothschildi*), also known as the Bali mynah, Rothschild's mynah, or locally as *jalak putih*; it's Bali's only endemic. This striking white bird, with black tips on wings and tail and a distinctive bright blue mask, is greatly valued as a caged bird. Its natural population fell as low as 40 pairs, but efforts are being made to rebuild the population by reintroducing captive birds to the wild. Initially this is taking place on Menjangan Island and the Prapat peninsula, so trekking in both these areas is currently restricted.

Banyuwedang Hot Springs
Coming from the north coast, this is the first 'visitor object' you will encounter. There's a temple, and water from the springs is supposedly therapeutic, but the place is smelly and unattractive.

Labuhan Lalang & Pulau Menjangan
At Labuhan Lalang you must buy a 2000 rp ticket to enter the park, even if you just want to look at the foreshore area, and parking a car costs 2000 rp for a day, or for half an hour. There's a jetty for the boats to Menjangan, a warung with the usual sort of menu and a pleasant white-sand beach 200 metres to the east. There are coral formations close to the shore which are good for snorkelling.

Excursions from Labuhan Lalang to Pulau Menjangan start at 42,000 rp per person, for the half-hour boat trip, three hours on or

around the island and the return trip. If you want to stay longer, each additional hour costs about 5000 rp. Both snorkelling and scuba diving are excellent around the island, with great visibility, superb unspoiled coral, caves, lots of tropical fish and a spectacular drop-off. Boats should use fixed moorings, which have been installed to prevent the coral being damaged by anchors. Diving is usually best in the early morning. Diving trips to the island can be arranged by various dive operators in Bali, but it's a long way to come for a day trip from the south. The closest dive operation is at Lovina Beach. Trekking on the island is currently restricted.

Trekking
Three-hour guided treks around the Labuhan Lalang area can be arranged at the visitors centre. You must take a guide, who will cost about 15,000 rp with from one to four people. Arrange things the day before, or just be at the visitors centre at 7.30 am.

A seven-hour trek across to Belimbingsari is also possible. Prapat Agung, the peninsula north of the Terima to Gilimanuk road, has some good places to see wildlife, but access is currently restricted. More treks can be arranged from the park headquarters in Cekik. (See under Cekik in the South-West Bali section earlier in this chapter for details.)

Jayaprana's Grave
A 10-minute walk up some stone stairs from the south side of the road will bring you to this site. The foster son of a 17th-century king, Jayaprana, planned to marry Leyonsari, a beautiful girl of humble origins. The king, however, also fell in love with Leyonsari and had Jayaprana killed. In a dream, Leyonsari learned the truth of Jayaprana's death, and killed herself rather than marry the king. This Romeo and Juliet story is a common theme in Balinese folklore, and the grave is regarded as sacred even though the ill-fated couple were not deities. From the site, there's a fine view to the north and, according to a national park pamphlet,

'...you will feel another pleasure which you can't get in another place'.

Places to Stay
There are no lodgings at all in the national park area. The closest places are in Gilimanuk, or at Pemuteran on the north coast. For overnight treks there are some rough shelters, and you need to bring your own food, cooking and sleeping gear. There is a campground near Cekik.

Getting There & Away
The road east follows the coast to Lovina and Singaraja. The road west goes to Cekik, three km from Gilimanuk. There are regular public buses and bemos between Gilimanuk and the towns on the north noast road.

EAST OF SINGARAJA
Interesting sites east of Singaraja include some of Bali's best known temples. The north-coast sandstone is very soft and easily carved, so temples are heavily decorated, often with delightfully whimsical scenes. Although temple architecture is similar to that in the south, there are some important differences. In northern temples, there is a single pedestal with 'houses' for the deities to use on their earthly visits, structures for storing important religious relics, and probably a padmasana or 'throne' for the sun god. In southern temples these are all in separate structures.

At Kubutambahan you can turn south to Penulisan and Kintamani, or you can continue east to the lovely spring-fed pools at Yeh Sanih. From there the road continues right around the east coast to Tulamben and Amlapura – see the East Bali section earlier in this chapter.

Sangsit
At Sangsit, only a few km beyond Singaraja, you'll find an excellent example of the colourful architectural style of northern Bali. Sangsit's Pura Beji is a subak temple, dedicated to the spirits that look after irrigated rice fields. It's about half a km off the main road towards the coast. The sculptured

panels along the front wall set the tone with their Disneyland demons and amazing nagas. The inside also has a variety of sculptures covering every available space, and the inner courtyard is shaded by a frangipani tree. The pura dalem at Sangsit shows scenes of punishment in the afterlife, and other pictures which are humorous and/or erotic.

If you continue beyond Sangsit to Bungkulan, you'll find another fine temple with an interesting kulkul (warning drum).

The Sara & Dewa Guesthouse in Bungkulan is a cheap and interesting place to stay.

Jagaraga
The village of Jagaraga, a few km off the main road, has an interesting pura dalem. The small temple has delightful sculptured panels along its front wall, both inside and out. On the outer wall look for a vintage car being hijacked, a steamer at sea and even an aerial dogfight between early aircraft. Jagaraga is also famous for its legong troupe, said to be the best in northern Bali.

It was the capture of the local raja's stronghold at Jagaraga that marked the arrival of Dutch power in Bali in 1849. A few km past Jagaraga, along the right-hand side as you head inland, look for another small temple with ornate carvings of a whole variety of fish and fishermen.

Sawan
Several km further inland, Sawan is a centre for the manufacture of gamelan gongs and complete gamelan instruments. You can see the gongs being cast and the intricately carved gamelan frames being made.

Kubutambahan
Only a km or so beyond the Kintamani turn-off at Kubutambahan is the Pura Maduwe Karang. Like Pura Beji at Sangsit, the temple is dedicated to agricultural spirits, but this one looks after unirrigated land.

This is one of the best temples in northern Bali and is particularly noted for its sculptured panels, including the famous bicycle panel depicting a gentleman riding a bicycle with flower petals for wheels. The cyclist

Temple guardian, Kubutambahan

may be Nieuwenkamp, one of the first Dutch people to explore Bali, who did actually get around by bicycle. It's on the base of the main plinth in the inner enclosure – other panels are also worth inspecting.

Yeh Sanih

About 15 km east of Singaraja, Yeh Sanih (also called Air Sanih) is a popular local spot where freshwater springs are channelled into some very pleasant swimming pools before flowing into the sea. Yeh Sanih is right by the sea and the area with the pools is attractively laid out with pleasant gardens, a restaurant and a couple of places to stay. It's well worth a visit and admission to the springs and pool is 400 rp (children 200 rp). On the hill overlooking the springs is the Pura Taman Manik Mas temple.

Places to Stay & Eat The *Bungalow Puri Sanih* is in the springs complex, with a restaurant overlooking the gardens. It has doubles for 15,000 to 20,000 rp – the more expensive rooms are upstairs in little two-storeyed bungalows. Also in the springs area, on the east side, *Yeh Sanih Seaside Cottages* has rooms at 30,000 rp and cottages near the

sea at 40,000 rp. Up the steep stairs opposite, *Puri Rena* has double rooms at 15,000 rp and 20,000 rp, and a restaurant with great views.

There are warungs across the road from the springs. *Tara Beach Bungalows* are one km east of Air Sanih, with basic bungalows at 7000/10,000 rp and better ones at 10,000/20,000 rp.

Nusa Penida

Nusa Penida, an administrative region within the Klungkung district, comprises three islands – Nusa Penida itself, the smaller Nusa Lembongan to the north-west and tiny Nusa Ceningan between them. Nusa Lembongan attracts visitors for its surf, seclusion and snorkelling. The island of Nusa Penida is right off the tourist track and has few facilities for visitors, while Nusa Ceningan is virtually uninhabited. There are some challenging scuba diving possibilities, but you'll have to organise it all from the mainland.

Nusa Penida has been a poor region for many years and there has been some transmigration from here to other parts of Indonesia. Thin soils and a lack of water do not permit the cultivation of rice, but other crops are grown – maize, cassava and beans are staples here. Tobacco is grown for export to mainland Bali. Fishing is another source of food, and some sardines and lobster are also sold to Bali. The cultivation of seaweed is now well established, and the underwater fences on which it is grown can be seen off many of the beaches. After harvesting, the seaweed is spread out on the beach to dry, then exported to Hong Kong, Japan and Europe where it is used as a thickening agent in processed foods and cosmetics.

NUSA LEMBONGAN

Most visitors to Nusa Lembongan come for the quiet beach or the surf, and they stay around the beach north of Jungutbatu. The surf breaks on the reef, which shelters a nice beach with white sand, clear blue water and

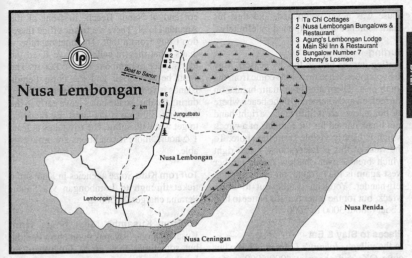

Map legend:
1 Ta Chi Cottages
2 Nusa Lembongan Bungalows & Restaurant
3 Agung's Lembongan Lodge
4 Main Ski Inn & Restaurant
5 Bungalow Number 7
6 Johnny's Losmen

Nusa Lembongan

0   1   2 km

Boat to Sanur

Jungutbatu

Nusa Lembongan

Lembongan

Nusa Penida

Nusa Ceningan

superb views across the water to Gunung Agung on mainland Bali. There's also good snorkelling on the reef, with some spots accessible from the beach. To reach other snorkelling spots you need to charter a boat, which costs about 5000 rp per hour.

There's no jetty – the boats usually beach at the village of Jungutbatu and you have to jump off into the shallows. Your boat captain might be able to leave you at the northern end of the beach where most of the bungalows are, but otherwise you'll have to walk a km to reach them.

Apart from the few basic bungalows and restaurants there are virtually no tourist facilities, though some of the cruise boat operators are planning improvements at the beaches they visit. There's no post office and the bank doesn't change travellers' cheques. The notice board at the Main Ski restaurant advertises excursions and day trips to various locations around the three islands, bicycle and motorbike hire, and a local doctor who specialises in coral cuts and surfing injuries.

Lembongan Village

It's about three km south-west along the sealed road from Jungutbatu to Lembongan village, the island's other town. You get the feeling that tourists are a rarity here – the people aren't hostile, but neither do they display the welcoming smiles that greet you elsewhere in Bali. It's possible to continue right around the island, following the rough track which eventually comes back to Jungutbatu.

The Underground House

As you enter Lembongan you'll pass a warung on the right with a couple of pool tables. For 1000 rp the kids here will offer to take you through the labyrinthine underground 'house', 100 metres back off the road. It's a crawl and scramble through the many small passages, rooms and chambers, supposedly dug by one man. Bring your own torch (flashlight) and be very careful as there are big holes in unexpected places.

The story goes that the man lost a dispute with an evil spirit and was condemned to death, but pleaded to be allowed to finish his house first. The spirit relented, and the man started excavating his cave with a small spoon. He always started a new room before he finished the last one, so of course the house was never completed, and thus his death sentence was postponed indefinitely.

Surfing

Surfing here is best in the dry season, May to September, when the winds come from the south east. There are three main breaks on the reef, all aptly named. Off the beach where the bungalows are is Shipwreck, a right-hand reef break named for the remains of a wreck which is clearly visible from the shore. To the west of this is Lacerations, a fast right which breaks over shallow coral. Further west again is Playground, an undemanding left-hander. You can paddle out to Shipwreck, but for the other two it's better to hire a boat (about 3000 to 5000 rp).

Places to Stay & Eat

In the village, *Johnny's Losmen* is basic but quite OK, and cheap at 4000/5000 rp for singles/doubles, although not many people stay here. There are some other small places near the village – *Bungalow Number 7* is OK, and cheap.

Most of the accommodation is further along the beach to the north. Don't deal with the touts here – go to the desk of the losmen yourself, and don't pay money to anyone else. The conspicuous *Main Ski Inn & Restaurant* has upstairs rooms at 12,000/15,000 rp for singles/doubles, downstairs rooms at 10,000/12,000 rp. Its two-storey restaurant, right on the beach, is a little more expensive than some of the others, but serves good food and has a great view.

Agung's Lembongan Lodge has cheap double rooms from 6000 rp, and better ones at 15,000 rp. Their restaurant has cheap but tasty food. Next to that is the more expensive *Nusa Lembongan Restaurant & Bungalows*. Finally there's *Ta Chi* (or Tarci) with rooms from 12,000 to 15,000 rp and reputedly the best cook on the island.

Getting There & Away

The following boat trips are available to/from Nusa Penida.

To/From Sanur Boats leave from the north-ern end of Sanur Beach, in front of the Ananda Hotel. There's a ticket office there; don't buy from a tout. The boat captains – that's what they're called – have fixed the tourist price to Lembongan at 15,000 rp. The strait between Bali and the Nusa Penida islands is very deep and huge swells develop during the day, so the boats leave early in the morning, 8.30 am at the latest. Be prepared to get wet with spray. The trip takes at least 1½ hours, more if conditions are unfavour-able.

To/From Kuta Some agencies in Kuta sell a ticket through to Lembongan via Sanur. Perama charges 22,500 rp.

To/From Kusamba Most boats from Kusamba go to Toyapakeh on Nusa Penida, but sometimes they go to Jungutbatu on Lembongan. Boats from Sanur are safer and quicker.

To/From Nusa Penida There are boats which take the local people between Jungutbatu and Toyapakeh on Nusa Penida, particularly on market days. You'll have to ask around to find when they leave, and discuss the price. The public boats will be chock full of people, produce and livestock. A charter boat will cost about 30,000 rp, which would be OK between six or eight people.

Getting Around

The island is fairly small and you can easily walk around it in a few hours. You can also hire a motorbike or get a lift on the back of one.

NUSA PENIDA

Clearly visible from Bali's south-east coast, the hilly island of Nusa Penida has a popula-tion of around 40,000 and was once used as a place of banishment for criminals and other undesirables from the kingdom of Klung-kung.

Nusa Penida is the legendary home of Jero Gede Macaling, the demon who inspired the Barong Landung dance. Many Balinese

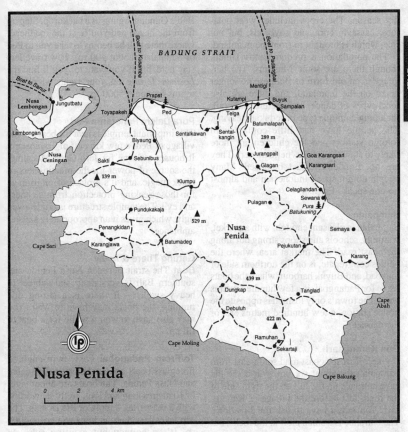

Nusa Penida

BADUNG STRAIT

Boat to Kusamba

Boat to Padangbai

Boat to Sanur

Nusa Lembongan

Jungutbatu

Lembongan

Nusa Ceningan

Toyapakeh

Prapat

Ped

Biyaung

Sakti

Sebunibus

▲ 139 m

Pundukakaja

Penangkidan

Karangjawa

Batumadeg

Klumpu

Sentalkawan

Mentigi

Kutampi

Telga

Sentalkangin

Batumalapan

▲ 289 m

Jurangpait

Giagan

Buyuk

Sampalan

Goa Karangsari

Karangsari

Celagilandan

Pulagan

Sewana

Pura Batukuning

Nusa Penida

▲ 529 m

Semaya

Pejukutan

Karang

▲ 439 m

Dungkap

Tanglad

Cape Abah

Debuluh

▲ 422 m

Ramuhan

Sekartaji

Cape Bakung

Cape Sari

Cape Moling

0   2   4 km

believe the island to be a place of enchantment and evil power *(angker)* – thousands come every year for religious observances aimed at placating the evil spirits. The island has a number of interesting temples dedicated to Jero Gede Macaling, including Pura Ped near Toyapakeh and Pura Batukuning near Sewana.

There is also a huge limestone cave, Goa Karangsari, on the coast about four km from Sampalan. The mountain village of Tanglad in the south-east, with its throne for the sun god, Surya, is also interesting.

The north coast has white-sand beaches and views over the water to the volcanoes on Bali. This coastal strip, with the two main towns of Toyapakeh and Sampalan, is moist and fertile, almost lush. The south coast has limestone cliffs dropping straight down to the sea – a spectacular sight if you're coming that way by boat. Rickety bamboo steps enable fresh water to be collected from springs near the base of the cliffs. The interior is a hilly, rugged landscape, not barren but with sparse-looking crops and vegetation and unsalubrious villages. Rainfall is low, and there are large square concrete tanks called *cabang* in which water is stored for the dry season. The crops include sweet potatoes, cassava, corn and soybeans, but not rice, which is brought in from the mainland.

The population is predominantly Hindu, though there are some Muslims. The language is an old form of Balinese no longer heard on the mainland, and there are also local types of dance, architecture and craft, including a unique type of red ikat weaving. The people have had little contact with foreign visitors and the children are more likely to stare than shout 'hello mister'. They are not unfriendly, just bemused. Many people do not speak Indonesian and almost no-one speaks English.

Sampalan

Sampalan is pleasant enough, with a market, warungs, schools and shops strung out along the coast road. The market area, where the bemos congregate, is on the northern side of the road, and Buyuk harbour, where the boats leave for Padangbai, is a few hundred metres west. The town's only losmen is opposite the police station, a few hundred metres east of the market.

Goa Karangsari

If you follow the coast road south-east from Sampalan for about six km, you'll see the cave entrance up the hill on the right side of the road, just before the village of Karangsari. You might have to ask for directions. The entrance is a small cleft in the rocks, but the cave is quite large, extending for over 200 metres into the hillside. Many small bats live in the cave – they're noisy but harmless. During the Galungan Festival there is a torch-lit procession into the cave, followed by ceremonies at a temple by the lake in one of the large chambers. If you want to do more than put your head in the entrance, bring a good torch.

Toyapakeh

If you come by boat from Nusa Lembongan you'll probably be dropped at the beach at Toyapakeh. It's a pretty town with lots of shady trees. The beach has clean white sand, clear blue water, a neat line of perahus and

Bali's Gunung Agung as a backdrop. Step up from the beach and you're at the roadhead, where there will be bemos to take you to Ped or Sampalan (about 400 rp). Few travellers stay here, but if you want to, you'll find the *Losmen Terang* on your right, which has rooms for about 5000 rp.

Pura Dalem Penetaran Ped

This important temple is near the beach at the village of Ped, a few km east of Toyapakeh. It houses a shrine for Jero Gede Macaling, the source of power for the practitioners of black magic, and it's a place of pilgrimage for those seeking protection from sickness and evil. The temple structure is crude, even ugly, which gives it an appropriately sinister ambience.

Getting There & Away

Boat The strait between Nusa Penida and southern Bali is very deep and subject to heavy swells – if there is a strong tide running, the boats may have to wait. You may also have to wait a while for a boat to fill up.

To/From Padangbai Fast, twin-engined fibreglass boats operate between Padangbai and Nusa Penida. The boats are about eight or 10 metres long and look pretty seaworthy, with a reassuring supply of life jackets. The trip takes less than an hour and costs 4000 rp. It's a bouncy but exciting ride. At Padangbai, the boats land on the beach just east of the car park for the Bali to Lombok ferry. On Nusa Penida, the boats land at the beach at Buyuk Harbour, just west of Sampalan, or on the beach at Toyapakeh.

To/From Kusamba Perahus carry produce and supplies between Nusa Penida and Kusamba, which is the closest port to Klungkung, the district capital. The boats leave when they're full, weather and waves permitting, and cost about 2500 rp one way. They are slower than the boats from Padangbai, and may be heavily loaded (overloaded?) with provisions.

To/From Nusa Lembongan The boats which carry local people between the islands usually land at Toyapakeh. Ask around the beachfront area to find when the the next boat is leaving, and discuss the price. Get there early. You may have to wait quite a while, or charter a boat.

Getting Around

There are regular bemos on the sealed road between Toyapakeh and Sampalan, on to Sewana and up to Klumpu, but beyond these areas the roads are rough or nonexistent and transport is uncertain. If you want to charter a bemo, try to find Wayan Patra, from Banjar Sentral Kanjin in Ped. He knows Nusa Penida well, and speaks English. You may be able to get someone to take you on the back of a motorbike, although this can be a high-risk form of transport. If you really want to explore the island, bring a mountain bike from the mainland, or plan to do some walking.

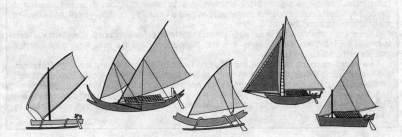

Sumatra

Sumatra is an island with an extraordinary wealth of natural resources, abundant wildlife, astonishing architecture and massive rivers. It is also home to people of diverse cultures: the former head-hunters and cannibals of the Batak regions, the matrilineal Muslim Minangkabau and the indigenous groups of the Mentawai Islands who, until early this century, had little contact with the outside world.

Sumatra is almost four times the size of neighbouring Java, but supports less than a quarter of the population. During Dutch rule it provided the world with large quantities of oil, rubber, pepper and coffee. And its seemingly inexhaustible resources continue to prop up the Indonesian economy today.

HISTORY

Geography goes a long way towards explaining the remarkable diversity of cultures on Sumatra and its outlying islands. Sumatra's northern tip faces the west, while much of the island's eastern shore borders the Selat Melaka (Straits of Malacca) – a natural gateway to the South China Sea for ships trading between India, Java and China.

This trade, controlled initially by Hindu merchants, led to the development of coastal Hindu city-states. The kingdom of

---

Highlights

The majority of Sumatra's attractions are in the north. Most spend about a month taking in the main highlights along the well-trodden trail between the major cities of Medan and Padang.

Top of the itineraries are a visit to the orang-utans at Bukit Lawang and time-out at spectacular Lake Toba. Toba remains a fine place to unwind despite large-scale tourism and it has some of the county's best accommodation bargains. Nias gets a lot of visitors, drawn by both the ancient megalithic culture and the surf.

The cool mountain town of Bukittinggi is the cultural heart of Minangkabau, West Sumatra, and is one of the main travellers' centres. It is also the place to organise treks among the isolated villages of the Mentawai islands.

Few travellers spend much time in the southern part of Sumatra, where the main attractions are Krakatau and the elephant training centre at Way Kambas. Aceh province in the north is also off the main route, but is becoming increasingly popular and Pulau We is the main attraction.

If your time in Sumatra is limited, a week is enough to visit Bukit Lawang and continue to Lake Toba via the Karo-Batak highland town of Berastagi. The three are conveniently linked by tourist bus. ■

Sriwijaya, which arose in the second half of the 7th century with its capital on or near the site of modern Palembang, grew to become a major power in South-East Asia. Unlike the more insular Javanese kingdoms of the time, Sriwijaya remained an outward-looking trading nation. With foreign trade came other developments, including Buddhism and court-centred Brahmanism.

Sriwijaya's control of Selat Melaka continued for seven centuries before it was ended by the Javanese Majapahits in 1377. Allegedly, a Sriwijayan prince, Parameswara, fled to the Malay Peninsula and arrived in the tiny port-settlement of Melaka, which he developed into a thriving international port. The centre of power in the region thus shifted from Sumatra to the Malay Peninsula.

About the same time, Islam became an important religion in Sumatra. Islamic communities are known to have existed in northern Sumatra since the 13th century (Marco Polo mentions finding Muslims here when he visited Sumatra in 1292 on his way home from China.) By the early 16th century, most kings of the Sumatran coastal states – stretching from Aceh in the far north to Palembang in the south – were Muslim. The peoples south of Palembang and in the southwest continued to follow old beliefs and customs, as did the peoples of the interior.

When the Dutch colonial forces arrived in the early 19th century, they found the cultural stew harder to digest than first expected. Their inability to tame the populace subsequently lead to some of the most protracted fighting of the colonial era. The Dutch wanted Sumatra for its strategic position as much as for its spices (mainly pepper) and resources such as tin.

This proved the subject of intense colonial rivalry with the British. The United East India Company (Vereenigde Oost-Indische Compagnie or VOC) had been active in Sumatra since the early days of Dutch involvement in Indonesia. But the company's demise, combined with a short period of British rule in Indonesia during the Napoleonic Wars, meant that the Dutch had to rebuild their influence in Sumatra from scratch.

Palembang was first attacked by the Dutch in 1818, but wasn't subdued until 1849. Jambi was claimed in 1833, but resistance in the interior continued until 1907.

In West Sumatra, Dutch designs on the Minangkabau districts clashed with the first major Islamic revival movement of Indonesia – known as the Padri movement because its leaders had made their pilgrimage to Mecca via the Acehnese port of Pedir. Civil war erupted between the Islamic reformists and the supporters of traditional law *(adat)*. The Dutch entered the Padri War in support of the latter in 1821, but it was not until 1838 that all the Minangkabau territories were subdued.

The Dutch needed three military expeditions – in 1847, 1855 and 1863 – to establish their authority over the island of Nias, while diplomacy persuaded the British to vacate Bengkulu which was traded for guarantees not to challenge British rule on the Malay Peninsula and Singapore. Treaties and alliances brought other areas of Sumatra under Dutch rule; war with the Bataks in 1872 ended in Dutch victory, although Batak resistance was not curbed until 1895.

The war with the Acehnese, however, proved both bloody and lasting. The only remaining Acehnese sultan, Tuanku Muhamat Dawot, surrendered to the Dutch in 1903 after battles raged for more than 30 years. Unrest subsequently continued, and the Dutch were forced to keep a military government in the area until 1918. The Dutch did not try to return to Aceh after WW II. From 1945 until Indonesian independence in 1949, Aceh was ruled chiefly by Daud Beureueh, the leader of an Islamic modernist movement. The region was in the throes of rebellion from 1953 until 1961, when it became a province of Indonesia. Even today it retains a semi-autonomous status within the republic.

GEOGRAPHY

Stretching nearly 2000 km and covering an area of 473,607 sq km, Sumatra is the sixth-largest island in the world.

The main feature is the Bukit Barisan

Sumatra

0   100   200 km

mountains which run most of the length of the west coast, merging with the highlands around Lake Toba and central Aceh in the north. Many of the peaks are over 3000 metres (the highest is Gunung Kerinci, at 3805 metres). Spread along the range are almost 100 volcanoes, 15 of them active. The mountains form the island's backbone, dropping steeply to the sea on the west coast but sloping gently to the east. The eastern third of the island is low-lying, giving way to vast areas of swampland and estuarine mangrove forest bordering the shallow Selat Melaka. It's traversed by numerous wide, muddy, meandering rivers, the biggest being the Batang Hari, Siak and Musi rivers.

The string of islands off the west coast, including Nias and the Mentawai Islands, are geologically older than the rest of Sumatra.

FLORA & FAUNA

Large areas of Sumatra's original rainforest have been cleared for agriculture, but some impressive tracts of forest remain – particularly around Gunung Leuser National Park in the north and in the south-western reaches of the Bukit Barisan mountains.

The extraordinary *Rafflesia arnoldi*, the world's large flower, is found in pockets throughout the Bukit Barisan – most notably near Bukittinggi – between August and November.

You'll be lucky to set eyes on such rare and endangered species as the Sumatran tiger and the two-horned Sumatran rhino, but elephants and orang-utans are easier to see. Elephants are the main attraction at Way Kambas National Park, two hours east of Bandarlampung in southern Sumatra, and Bukit Lawang in North Sumatra is one place where an orang-utan sighting is a certainty.

ECONOMY

Sumatra is enormously rich in natural resources and generates the lion's share of Indonesia's export income. The important income earners are oil and natural gas. The fields around the towns of Jambi, Palembang and Pekanbaru produce three-quarters of Indonesia's oil. The town of Llokseumawe, on the east coast of Aceh Province, is the centre of the natural gas industry.

The Dutch first found oil in Sumatra in the 1860s and were exploiting it in commercial quantities by the 1880s.

Rubber and palm oil are the next biggest income earners. The first rubber plantations were established in West Java and eastern Sumatra and by 1930, Indonesia was producing nearly half the world's rubber. There has also been a big increase in palm oil plantations in recent years.

Timber is another heavily exploited resource. Other crops are tea, coffee and tobacco. Sumatra was noted as a source of prized black pepper by the Chinese more than a thousand years ago, and it remains a major crop in southern Sumatra.

PEOPLE

Sumatra is the second most populous island in the archipelago with 36 million people. Population density is, however, but a fraction of Bali or Java.

Continuing transmigration from these two islands has added to the remarkably diverse ethnic and cultural mix. (See under Bataks in the Lake Toba section; the Acehnese in the Aceh section; the Minangkabau in West Sumatra, the Mentawaians in the Mentawai Islands section, and the Kubu under Jambi later in this chapter.)

GETTING THERE & AWAY

The international airports at Medan, Padang and Pekanbaru are visa-free, as are the seaports of Belawan (Medan), Sekupang and Batu Ampar (Pulau Batam) and Tanjung Pinang (Pulau Bintan).

Most travellers arrive and depart through Medan, either by air on the daily connections to Kuala Lumpur, Penang and Singapore or by sea on the high-speed catamarans that run between Penang and Belawan. Most of northern Sumatra's main attractions are within easy reach of Medan.

A more unusual approach is to travel by boat from Singapore to Batam in the Riau Islands (where you clear customs) and then take a boat to the mainland city of Pekanbaru.

There are also regular flights from Batam to Medan, Padang and a host of smaller destinations.

Coming from Jakarta, the main route is by bus and ferry from Merak to the southern Sumatran ferry terminal of Bakauheni, and then north by bus on the Trans-Sumatran Highway. A popular alternative which eliminates the long haul by bus is to catch the fortnightly Pelni boat from Jakarta to Padang.

If you're heading to Sumatra from the Americas, Europe or Oceania, a good way to travel is to reach Kuala Lumpur, Penang or Singapore first. They are much closer to Medan than Jakarta, and open up more options for onward travel.

To/From Malaysia

Air Malaysian Airlines System (MAS) and Sempati both operate flights on the 40-minute journey between Penang and Medan for US$60. Sempati sometimes offers special deals. It is a popular flight to satisfy the ticket-out requirement.

Sempati flies between Medan and Kuala Lumpur three times a week, while Garuda and MAS have daily flights for US$77. Sempati also flies to Kuala Lumpur twice a week from Padang, while Pelangi Air has four flights a week from Padang via Pekanbaru for US$107.

Boat Penang-Medan is the most convenient of the many ferry routes operating between Malaysia and Sumatra. The Singapore-Batam-Pekanbaru route is also becoming popular.

To/From Penang The high-speed ferries *Ekspres Selasa* and *Ekspres Bahagia* journey across the Selat Melaka in about four hours. There are departures from Penang every day except Sunday for RM90. They leave Medan's port of Belawan every day except Monday for 78,500 rp, including free bus to the boat. Children pay half fare.

The *Ekspres Bahagia* leaves Penang on Monday, Wednesday and Friday at 10 am, and Medan on Tuesday, Thursday and Satur-

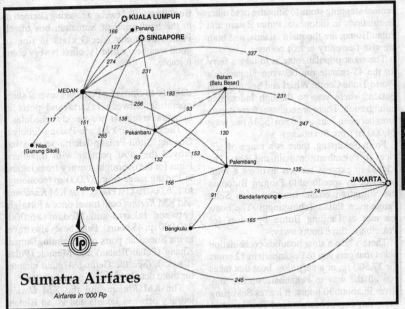

Sumatra Airfares

Airfares in '000 Rp

(Airfare map showing connections and fares between cities)

KUALA LUMPUR
Penang — 166
SINGAPORE
127
274
231
337
MEDAN — 193 — Batam (Batu Besar)
256 — 231
117 — 93
151 — 138 — 247
265 — Pekanbaru
Nias (Gunung Sitoli) — 130
63 — 132 — 153
Padang — Palembang — 135 — JAKARTA
156 — 91 — 74
Bandarlampung
165
Bengkulu
245

SUMATRA

---

day at 11 am. The Medan office (☎ 720954) is at Jalan Sisingamangaraja 92A, but tickets can also be bought at Pacto (☎ 510081), Jalan Katamso 35G. Its Penang office (☎ (04) 631943) is on Jalan Pasara King Edward.

The *Ekspres Selesa* leaves Penang on Tuesday, Thursday and Saturday at 9 am, and Belawan at 1 pm on Wednesday and Sunday and 11 am on Friday. Trophy Tours (☎ 514888), at Jalan Katamso 33D, is the Medan agency, while in Penang the place to go is the Kuala Perlis-Langkawi Ferry Service (☎ (04) 625630) in the PPC building on Jalan Pasara King Edward.

To/From Lumut The *Selesa Ekspres* also runs from Medan to Lumut, 200 km south of Penang on the Malaysian mainland, at 2 pm on Tuesday and Saturday, returning at 9 am on Wednesday and Sunday. The fares are the same as for the Medan-Penang trip. The Lumut office (☎ (05) 934258) is by the jetty.

To/From Port Kelang There are ferries from Belawan to Port Kelang, Kuala Lumpur's port, on Monday and Wednesday at 10 am. The six-hour trip costs 87,000 rp. They return on Tuesday and Thursday. The Medan agency is Trophy Tours.

To/From Melaka The ferries between Melaka and Dumai are of little interest for travellers. Dumai is an overgrown oil-pumping station and it's not a visa-free port. Still, there are ferries from Dumai at 8 am on Thursday and Sunday for 87,500 rp, returning on Monday and Friday for RM100.

To/From Singapore

Air Garuda and Silk Air both run daily flights between Singapore and Medan for US$127, while Garuda/Merpati flies from Singapore to Padang three times a week for US$110.

Boat The Riau Islands immediately south of Singapore can make an interesting and convenient stepping stone to Sumatra or to other destinations in Indonesia. Pulau Batam and Pulau Bintan are the main islands, and both are visa-free entry or exit points.

The most popular route is to take a ferry for the 45-minute run between Singapore's World Trade Centre Wharf and Sekupang on Batam, where you go through Indonesian immigration. There are constant ferry departures between 7 am and 6 pm (S$16 one way; 24,000 rp from Sekupang).

From Sekupang, there is a range of services to Pekanbaru on mainland Riau. The 35,000-rp express service involves a four-hour ride by speedboat to Tanjung Buton on the Sumatran coast, travelling via Selat Panjang on Pulau Tebingtinggi. The boats are met at Tanjung Buton by buses for Pekanbaru, three hours away.

There's also a slow boat/bus combination ticket that gets you to Pekanbaru in 12 hours for 27,500 rp, or a very slow boat that takes you all the way to Pekanbaru up the Siak River in about 30 hours. It leaves Sekupang every day except Monday and Tuesday at 11 am and costs 25,000 rp.

There are four direct services a day between Singapore and Pulau Bintan, which is the best place to find boats to the outer Riau Islands. From Bintan you can also get ships to Jakarta. (See under Tanjung Pinang for details.)

To/From Java

Air Merpati has direct flights from Jakarta to Bandarlampung (74,200 rp), Batam (231,500 rp), Bengkulu (165,500 rp), Medan (337,100 rp), Padang (245,800 rp) and Palembang (135,800 rp). It also has daily direct flights from Bandung to Palembang, continuing to Batam.

Sempati has direct flights from Jakarta to Batam, Medan, Padang and Pekanbaru. Mandala and Bouraq also have daily direct flights to Jakarta, and are slightly cheaper than the others. Other Mandala destinations from Jakarta are Padang and Palembang, while Bouraq also flies to Batam.

Boat Boat travel can be a relaxing alternative to the hard grind of Sumatran bus travel. Pelni's economy (deck) class is fine in good weather, while 1st class is very comfortable.

Jakarta to Sumatra Pelni has several ships operating between Jakarta and ports in Sumatra on regular two-weekly schedules.

The KM *Lawit's* Jakarta-Padang-Sibolga-Gunung Sitoli-Padang-Jakarta service has proved the most popular with travellers. Fares for the overnight journey from Jakarta to Padang range from 37,000 rp (economy) to 126,000 rp (1st class). The KM *Kambuna* and KM *Kerinci* both travel once a fortnight between Jakarta and Medan (56,000/ 219,000 rp; 45 hours). Pelni boats also travel to the Sumatran ports of Bengkulu, Dumai, Kijang (Pulau Bintan) and Mentok (Pulau Bangka). (See the Getting Around chapter for more details of the ships and routes.)

The KM *Rinjani* and the KM *Umsini* journey between Jakarta and Pulau Bintan, where daily ferries go to Singapore. The *Bintan Permata* also sails twice a week between Bintan and Jakarta.

Merak to Bakauheni Ferries shuttle 24 hours a day between Merak in Java and the southern Sumatran port of Bakauheni. There are departures every 36 minutes, with a brief lull between 4.30 and 6 am, so there's never long to wait. The trip takes 1½ hours and costs 1300 rp (economy), 1900 rp (2nd class) and 2400 rp (1st class). The only noticeable difference is the level of crowding.

The Bahauheni terminal is modern and efficient, and there are buses waiting to take you north to Bandarlampung's Rajabasa bus station (1700 rp; two hours). There are also share taxis that will take you to the city destination of your choice for 5000 rp.

There are regular buses to Merak from Jakarta's Kalideres bus station. The journey takes 3½ hours. Trains also run from Tanah Abang railway station.

If you travel by bus between Jakarta and destinations in Sumatra, the price of the ferry is included in your ticket. Bus fares from Jakarta to Bandarlampung start at 12,000 rp.

Long-distance share taxis, running between Jakarta and Bandarlampung, cost 30,000 rp.

To/From Elsewhere in Indonesia

Air There are occasional direct flights between Denpasar and Medan for 454,000 rp; otherwise getting to Sumatra by air means changing planes in Jakarta.

Boat Pelni boats provide links to some of the outlying islands of eastern Indonesia. Sample fares from Medan include Ambon, capital of the Maluku Islands for 134,000/522,000 rp in economy/1st class, and Ujung Padang on Sulawesi (100,000/367,000 rp).

GETTING AROUND

Getting around Sumatra presents fewer problems than it did previously, thanks to the efforts of road builders and the introduction of better boats, buses and services on the main routes.

Most travellers follow a well-trodden trail across Sumatra, starting from Medan and stopping at Bukit Lawang, Berastagi, Parapat, Lake Toba, Pulau Nias, Bukittinggi, Padang and then on to Java. It can be done in about a month if you're in a hurry, but if you want to go trekking in Mentawai or exploring the jungle, it's easy to spend a two-month visa and more.

Air

Sumatra has a comprehensive network of domestic flights. Garuda and Merpati are the main carriers, but Sempati competes on many routes. Mandala and Bouraq operate only on major routes such as Medan-Jakarta, but can be a lot cheaper. SMAC and Deraya Air fly to some remote destinations that the big airlines don't bother with.

Bus

Bus is the most popular method of travelling around Sumatra. The completion of the Trans-Sumatra Highway has made a huge difference to the speed and comfort of bus travel. The old travellers' tales of hours of bone-shaking, teeth-rattling horror on Sumatra's buses are gently fading, at least on the main highway.

On the back roads, travelling around Sumatra by bus can still be grindingly slow, diabolically uncomfortable and thoroughly exhausting, particularly during the wet season when bridges are washed away and the roads develop huge potholes.

If your only travel is on the Trans-Sumatra Highway, then the big air-con buses and tourist coaches can make travel a breeze, as long as you take it in manageable stages – two days on a bus is no fun anywhere.

You can take an air-con bus from Medan to Jakarta for as little as 65,000 rp, and from Padang to Jakarta for around 45,000 rp, which includes the ferry crossing from Java to Sumatra. Despite claims of 30 hours or less for the trip, count on 32 hours or more.

The best express air-con buses have reclining seats, toilets, video and even karaoke. The only problem is that many of them run at night, so you miss out on the scenery. Buses without air-con that travel along the Trans-Sumatra Highway are in many cases simply older versions of the air-con buses: they rattle more, the air-con no longer works and they can get very crowded, but they are fine for short sections. As on the Sumatran buses of yesteryear, the seats are usually hard and far too small for average-sized Westerners. Avoid seats at the rear of the bus where the bouncing is multiplied.

Many bus companies cover the popular routes from the major towns and prices vary according to the quality and comfort of the bus. Ticket agencies may charge 10% or more than the bus companies, but they are more convenient and in some cases the only place to buy tickets. In some places, especially in the main tourist areas, agents' charges can be excessive. It pays to shop around.

Tourist Buses Many take the convenient tourist coaches that make the Bukit Lawang-

SUMATRA

Berastagi-Parapat-Bukittinggi run. They pick up and drop off at hotels, travel during the day so you can see the scenery, and stop at points of interest on the way. While you may feel like you're on a tour group at times, they certainly are comfortable and take some spectacular routes, such as the Berastagi-Parapat trip, that normal buses don't cover. The cost and journey times are about the same as for air-con buses.

Train

Sumatra's passenger rail network is restricted to the southern line linking Bandarlampung with Palembang and Lubuklinggau, and the northern line running from Medan, north-west to nearby Binjai and south to Tanjungbalai and Rantauparapat. There are no passenger services on the line from Padang to Padangpanjang in West Sumatra.

Boat

Sumatra's rivers are also major transport routes which teem with a motley but colourful collection of multipurpose vessels: rowing boats, speedboats, outriggers, ferries, junks and large cargo vessels. Boats are usually available for charter and will take you almost anywhere.

Taking a boat is both a welcome respite from bus travel and another way of seeing Sumatra. There are also some places in Sumatra which you can't get to any other way – islands which don't have an airstrip, or river villages not connected by road.

Jambi, Palembang and Pekanbaru are important towns for river transport. There are also regular links to surrounding islands, such as Banda Aceh to Pulau We, Padang to Pulau Siberut, Palembang to Pulau Bangka, Pekanbaru to Pulau Batam and Sibolga to Pulau Nias.

Pelni ships provide links between some coastal towns, such as Bengkulu and Padang, but operate on fortnightly schedules which can be hard to catch.

Local Transport

The usual Indonesian forms of transport – bemos, opelets, becaks and dokars (horse-drawn carts) – are available for getting around towns and cities in Sumatra. The base rate for a bemo is 200 rp and the minimum fare by becak is 500 rp. Dokars also charge a minimum 500 rp.

Hang back and watch what the locals pay if you are not certain of the fare, or check the price with other travellers.

Trans-Sumatran Highway

The sealing of the central southern sections of the Trans-Sumatran Highway means that there is now a reasonable sealed road all the way from Bakauheni in the south to Banda Aceh in the north.

The worst section of the highway is now the 10-hour stretch between Bandarlampung and Lubuklinggau in the south, where the surface is badly potholed in places. The sector from Lubuklinggau north to Padang is one of the best stretches of road in Sumatra as well as being one of the most scenic. It takes about 12 hours.

Most people make one or more stops on the sector between Padang and Parapat, usually Bukittinggi and/or Sibolga (for Nias). The road as far as Bukittinggi is excellent and takes about two hours, but the stretch from Bukittinggi to Parapat is the original long and winding road. The air-con buses can do it in 12 to 13 hours, most running at night, while public buses take 16 hours or more. The special tourist minibuses also do the trip in 12 to 13 hours during the day.

The section from Parapat to Medan is plain sailing, taking about four hours. Traffic congestion near Medan is the only problem.

The coast road north from Medan to Banda Aceh is easy going apart from a winding, mountain section between Sigli and Banda Aceh. The air-con buses can do the journey in nine hours at night, while the day buses can stretch it to 12 hours.

Other important roads to have been sealed in recent years are those linking Palembang to the highway at Lubuklinggau, and between Jambi and Muarabunga. ∎

North Sumatra

The province of North Sumatra is home to many of Sumatra's most popular attractions, including the jewel in the crown, Lake Toba. Other attractions are the Orang-Utan Rehabilitation Centre at Bukit Lawang, the Karo Batak Highlands around Berastagi and the fascinating island of Nias off the west coast.

The province's 70,787 sq km straddle Sumatra from the Indian Ocean in the west to the Selat Melaka in the east, bordered by Aceh in the north to West Sumatra and Riau in the south. It has a population of more than 11 million, with Medan and Pematangsiantar the main cities.

There are five main ethnic groups in North Sumatra: the coastal Malays who live along the Selat Melaka; the five Batak groups from the highlands around Lake Toba and Pulau Samosir; the Pesisirs (central Tapanuli) along the Indian Ocean coastline; the Mandailings and Angkolas (south Tapanuli) in the south; and the people from Pulau Nias. These ethnic groups all have their own dialects, religious beliefs and traditional customs, arts and cultures, which in turn are overlaid by the dominant influences of Islam and the national language, Bahasa Indonesia.

North Sumatra produces more than 30% of Indonesia's exports and handles about 60% of them. Fine tobacco is grown around Medan and oil, palm oil, tea and rubber are also produced in large quantities and exported from the port of Belawan, about 26 km from Medan.

MEDAN

Medan is the capital of North Sumatra and the third-largest city in Indonesia with a population approaching two million.

History

Medan is an Indonesian word meaning 'field', 'battlefield' or 'arena'. It was on the fertile swamp, at the junction of the Deli and Babura rivers (near the present Jalan Putri Hijau) that the original village of Medan Putri was founded by Raja Guru Patimpus in 1590.

From the end of the 16th century through to the early 17th century, Medan was a battlefield in the power struggle between the two kingdoms of Aceh and Deli. It remained a small village until well into the 19th century. In 1823, a British government official, John Anderson, found a population of only 200.

The town began to grow after the arrival of the Dutch. An enterprising planter named Nienhuys introduced tobacco to the area in 1865 and Medan became the centre of a rich plantation district. In 1886, the Dutch made it the capital of North Sumatra. By the end of Dutch rule, the population had grown to about 80,000 – still a far cry from today's huge, sprawling city.

The solid Dutch buildings of the affluent older suburbs inspire images of bloated bureaucrats and fat European burghers from the colonial era, while jerry-built lean-tos house the bulk of today's population.

Despite some fine architecture – traditional, colonial and Islamic – and an interesting museum, there is not a lot to hold the traveller's attention.

Most people's abiding memory of Medan is of battered old motorcycle becaks belching fumes into the already heavily polluted air. That and the humidity. Most treat the city strictly as an entry and exit point.

Orientation & Information

The main street of Medan runs north-south through the city centre with a string of name changes along the way. It starts as Jalan Katamso to the south, becomes Jalan Pemuda at the junction with Jalan Suprapto and Jalan Pandu, Jalan Ahmad Yani at the junction with Jalan Palang Merah, and then Jalan Soekarno-Hatta (or Jalan Balai Kota) at the park. It then continues north to the port of Belawan as Jalan Putri Hijau.

Travellers arriving in Medan from Parapat and points south will find themselves deposited at the giant Amplas bus station, three km from town on Jalan Sisingamangaraja (often written as S M Raja). The northernmost

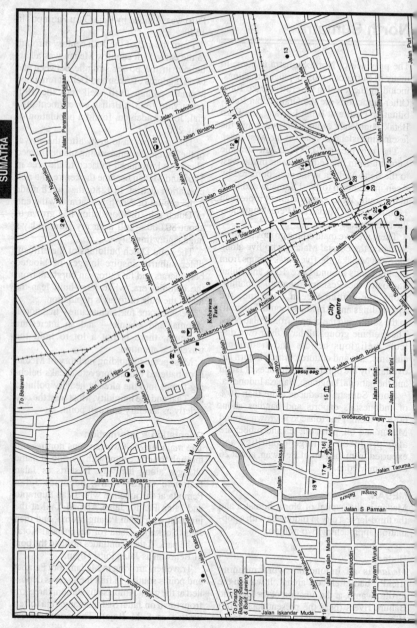

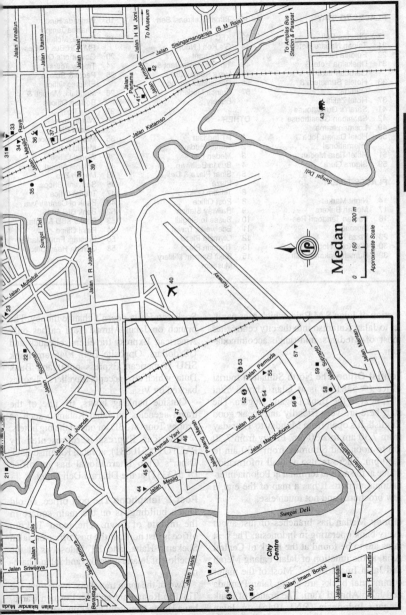

SUMATRA

Medan

0   150   300 m

Approximate Scale

SUMATRA

PLACES TO STAY		34	Taman Rekreasi Seri Deli	16	Parisada Hindu Dharma Temple
7	Dharma Deli	39	KFC	19	Kurnia, Melati &
21	Taipan Nabaru Hotel	44	G's Koh I Noor		PMTOH Bus Offices
22	Polonia Hotel		Restaurant	20	Governor's Office
31	Dhaksina Hotel &	46	Tip Top Restaurant &	24	Trophy Tours
	Garuda Plaza		Lyn's Restaurant	25	Pacto & Selesa
33	Hotels Sumatera &	55	Restaurant Agung		Ekspres Office
	Garuda	57	France Modern	26	Mandala, Merpati &
37	Hotel Zakia		Bakery		Bouraq Offices
41	Sarah's Guesthouse			27	Inda Taxi
42	Shahibah Guesthouse	**OTHER**		28	Water Tower
49	Losmen Irama			29	Gelora Plaza
50	Hotel Danau Toba	1	PT Indosat	35	Maimoun Palace
	International	2	Taman Budaya	36	Mesjid Raya
51	Hotel Tiara Medan	3	Medan Fair	38	Wartel Office
59	Sigura Gura	4	Bus to Belawan	40	Polonia Airport
		5	Sinar Plaza & Deli Plaza	43	Medan Zoo
PLACES TO EAT		6	Telkom Office	45	Souvenir Shops
		8	Post Office	47	Tourist Office
14	Night Market	9	Railway Station	48	Bank of Central Asia
17	Medan Bakers	10	Buses to Singkil	52	Bank BNI 1946
18	Farhan Tandoori Res-	11	Edelweiss Travel	53	Banks SBU & Duta
	taurant	12	Olympia Plaza	54	Pelni Office
23	Pizza Hut	13	Thamrin Plaza	56	Brastagi Fruits Market
30	G's Koh I Noor II	15	Bukit Barisan Military Museum	58	Garuda Head Office
32	Rumah Makan Famili				

section of Jalan S M Raja, which runs parallel to Jalan Katamso into the city centre, has most of Medan's mid-range accommodation.

Tourist Office The North Sumatran tourist office (☎ 538101) is at Jalan Ahmad Yani 107, next to the Bank Dagang Negara. The staff here are very friendly and speak good English. It's open from Monday to Thursday from 7.30 am to 2.30 pm, Friday from 7.30 am to noon and Saturday from 7.30 am to 1.30 pm. There is also a small information office at the arrival terminal at Polonia international airport. It has a map of the city, a few brochures and not much else.

Money Medan has branches of just about every bank operating in Indonesia. The best rates are to be found at the Bank of Central Asia, at the junction of Jalan Palang Merah and Jalan Imam Bonjol. Most of the major commercial banks are along Jalan Pemuda and Jalan Ahmad Yani. The branch of Bank Negara Indonesia (BNI 1946) on Jalan

Soekarno-Hatta doesn't change money. The branch on Jalan Ahmad Yani cashes only American Express travellers' cheques and US dollars. Opposite BNI 1946 are Bank SBU (American Express only) and Bank Duta, which also accepts travellers' cheques backed by Visa.

Outside banking hours, try one of the travel agencies on Jalan Katamso such as Trophy Tours at 33D, or one of the big hotels.

American Express is represented by PACTO (☎ 510081), at Jalan Katamso 35G. Diner's Club International has an office (☎ 513331) at the Dharma Deli Hotel.

Post & Telephone The post office, an old Dutch building, is on the main square in the middle of town. The main Telkom office is just north of the post office on Jalan Soekarno-Hatta, and PT Indosat is at the junction of Jalan Ngalenko and Jalan Thamrin.

Two of the main travellers' hang-outs, the Tip Top Restaurant and the Losmen Irama, have Home Country Direct phones.

If you're staying on the south side of the city, international calls can be made from the wartel office opposite KFC on Jalan Juanda.

Foreign Embassies & Consulates The following countries have consulates in Medan:

Belgium
Jalan Patimura 459 (☎ 620599)
Denmark
Jalan Hang Jebat 2 (☎ 323020)
Germany
Jalan S Parman 217 (☎ 520900)
India
Jalan Uskup Agung Sugiopranoto 19 (☎ 510418)
Japan
Jalan Suryo 12 (☎ 510033)
Malaysia
Jalan Pangeran Diponegoro 11 (☎ 518053)
Netherlands
Jalan A Rivai 22 (☎ 519025)
Norway
Jalan Zainal Arifin 55 (☎ 510158)
Singapore
Jalan Teuku Daud 3 (☎ 513134)
Sweden
Jalan Hang Jebat 2 (☎ 511017)
UK
Jalan Ahmad Yani 2 (☎ 518699)
USA
Jalan Imam Bonjol 13 (☎ 322200)

Travel Agencies Jalan Katamso is packed with travel agencies and is the place to buy ferry tickets. Trophy Tours (☎ 514888), at No 33D, is one of the biggest operators.

Edelweiss Travel (☎ 517297), at Jalan Irianbarat 47-49, is well organised and the manager speaks fluent English. It has the best choice of organised tours.

Bookshops Finding anything to read in English is a hassle. The Toko Buku Deli, at Jalan Ahmad Yani 48, has a few books in English, among them a couple of novels. It also sells *Time* and *Newsweek*.

The bookshops at the Tiara Medan and Garuda Plaza hotels both sell a range of books about Indonesia, as well as a few expensive 'airport' novels. The Tiara Medan also has foreign newspapers, such as the *London Daily Telegraph, International Herald Tribune* and the *Bangkok Post*.

Mesjid Raya & Istana Maimoon

The city's two finest buildings are located within 200 metres of each other. The crumbling Istana Maimoon (Maimoun Palace), on Jalan Katamso, was built by the Sultan of Deli in 1888, and the family still occupies one wing.

The magnificent black-domed Mesjid Raya is nearby at the junction of Jalan Mesjid Raya and Jalan Sisingamangaraja. It was commissioned by the sultan in 1906. Both buildings are open to the public, and both ask for donations rather than charging an entrance fee. (Ever noticed how the person before you always donates 10 times more than you have in mind!)

Museums

The **Museum of North Sumatra** (☎ 716792), at Jalan H M Joni 51, is open Tuesday to Sunday from 8 am to 5 pm and costs 400 rp. It has good coverage of North Sumatran history and culture. Most exhibits are well marked, and there are well-informed English-speaking guides who will happily answer any questions.

The **Bukit Barisan Military Museum**, near the Hotel Danau Toba International on Jalan H Zainal Arifin, has a small collection of weapons, photos and memorabilia from WW II, the War of Independence and the Sumatra Rebellion of 1958. Donations are welcomed.

The Hash House Harriers

Medan's two branches of the Hash House Harriers continue an eccentric approach to exercise that dates back to the mad dogs and Englishmen days of the British in South-East Asia.

The Medan Hash House Harriers organise runs every Monday at 4 pm and the Sumatra Hash House Harriers run on Sundays and Tuesdays (alternate weeks).

The run takes the form of a game of hare and hounds, a pursuit that has its origins in the hunting traditions of the British aristocracy. A 'hare' is selected to lay a trail for the 'hounds' to follow – dotted with false leads and other tricks.

SUMATRA

The Harriers were formed in Malaysia in the 1930s, supposedly at an eating house in Kuala Lumpur known as the 'Hash House'. The English would run after work on Monday afternoons – partly for amusement, partly for sport and partly to baffle the locals.

Another objective is to work up a thirst. Both sets of Harriers meet at Lyn's Bar at Jalan Ahmad Yani 98 (next to the Tip Top Restaurant) where you'll find details of coming runs. There's a fee of about 4000 rp for men and 3000 rp for women All are welcome.

Other Things to See & Do

There are some fine European buildings scattered along Jalan Soekarno-Hatta opposite the park, including the **Bank Indonesia**, the **High Court** and the **post office**. Look out for the splendidly ornate **Chinese mansion** near the Tip Top Restaurant on Jalan Ahmad Yani.

Breaking up the Medan skyline are modern edifices like the **Deli Dharma** shopping complex, three floors of glittering neon-lit shopping arcades straight out of Singapore and a nightly hang-out for Medan's gays. The top floor has a small **amusement park** with a couple of good rides for small children, as well as dodgem cars for the big kids.

The **Parisada Hindu Dharma** temple is on the corner of Jalan Teuku Umar and Jalan H Zainal Arifin. Cultural performances can be seen at **Taman Budaya**, on Jalan Perintis Kemerdekaan, near PT Indosat. The tourist office has a list of what's on. The amusement park *(taman ria)*, on Jalan Gatot Subroto, is also the site for the **Medan Fair** in August.

A bemo ride further along Jalan Sisingamangaraja is Medan's depressing zoo, the **Taman Margasawata**. The **crocodile farm** at Asam Kumbang, five km from the city centre, is something else to steer clear of.

Places to Stay – bottom end

The most popular of the budget hotels is the *Losmen Irama* (☎ 324614), close to the city centre in a little alley off Jalan Palang Merah. It's well set up for travellers – they even have a Home Country Direct phone for international calls. Dorm beds cost 3500 rp and doubles are 7000 to 10,000 rp, all with common bath.

Another good place is the *Tapian Nabaru Hotel* (☎ 512155), by the banks of the Sungai Babura, at Jalan Hang Tuah 6. It charges the same rates as the Irama. It's quiet and somewhat off the beaten track.

G's Koh I Noor (☎ 513953), an Indian restaurant at 21 Jalan Mesjid, also has a few dorm beds available for 5000 rp. The manager, Dalip, speaks excellent English and this family-run homestay is right in the heart of town.

The cheapest place in town is the *Sigura Gura* (☎ 323991), above the travel agency at Jalan Suprapto 2K. Dorm beds cost 3000 rp and doubles are 6000 rp, but the rooms are hot and dingy.

Wisma Sibayak, at Jalan Patimura 627, several km from the city centre on the road towards Berastagi, is associated with the popular Wisma Sibayak in Berastagi. It has dorm beds at 3500 rp and rooms at 5000 rp.

Places to Stay – middle

If you arrive by ferry from Penang, you'll soon meet the touts from the *Shahibah Guesthouse* (☎ 718528), a fair hike from the city centre at Jalan Armada 3, off Jalan Sisingamangaraja. The place is well run and has rooms priced up to 20,000 rp with bath and fan as well as dorm beds for 5000 rp.

Sarah's Guesthouse (☎ 719460), at Jalan Pertama 10, is a nearby alternative. It's similarly priced and the owner offers free transport to the airport.

Much more convenient is the friendly *Hotel Zakia* (☎ 722413), next to the Mesjid Raya on Jalan Sipiso-Piso. It has clean doubles with fan for 15,000 rp, which also pays for breakfast (roti and coffee).

Further north on Jalan Sisingamangaraja is a cluster of very uninspiring, one-star places such as the *Hotel Sumatera* (☎ 718807), at No 21, and the *Dhaksina Hotel* (☎ 720000), at No 20. They offer rooms with breakfast, mandi and fan for 20,000 rp and 35,000 rp with air-con. The formidable-looking *Hotel Garuda* (☎ 717733), next to the Sumatera at No 18, has rooms from 35,000 to 60,000 rp, all with air-con.

Places to Stay – top end

Top of the range is the massive *Hotel Tiara Medan* (☎ 516000), on Jalan Cut Mutiah, which has everything from a convention centre to a swimming pool and gymnasium. The cheapest double room costs 190,000 rp, while suites start at 400,000 rp.

More modestly priced are places like the *Dharma Deli* (☎ 327011), opposite the post office. It was once the Hotel de Boer, but the old part of the hotel has been completely renovated and a high-rise accommodation wing added. Singles/doubles start at 78,000/101,000 rp with breakfast.

Other good up-market places include: *Garuda Plaza* (☎ 711411) on Jalan Sisingamangaraja; the *Polonia Hotel* (☎ 325300) at Jalan Sudirman 14; and the *Hotel Dirga Surya* (☎ 321555) at Jalan Imam Bonjol.

The giant *Hotel Danau Toba International* (☎ 327000), at Jalan Imam Bonjol 17, was closed for renovations at the time of writing.

Places to Eat

Jalan Semarang is just a dirty side street between Jalan Pandu and Jalan Bandung during the day, but come nightfall, it's jam-packed with food stalls offering great Chinese food.

The *Taman Rekreasi Seri Deli*, across the road from the Mesjid Raya, is a slightly up-market approach to stall eating. You just sit down and waitresses bring round a menu that allows you to choose from the offerings of about 20 stalls.

The *Tip Top Restaurant*, at Jalan Ahmad Yani 92, is not the cheapest place in town, but it's an old favourite with foreign visitors. It's a pleasant spot, in spite of the continuous traffic jam outside. It serves European and Chinese food as well as Padang food. It also has a Home Country Direct phone.

A few doors down, at No 98, is *Lyn's Restaurant*, a gathering place for Medan businesspeople and expatriates, with a predominantly Western menu.

There are much better places to eat Padang food than the Tip Top. Try the *Restaurant Agung* at Jalan Pemuda 40, or the *Rumah Makan Famili* at Jalan Sisingamangaraja 21B.

Vegetarians looking for something other than gado-gado should check out one of the Indian restaurants. *G's Koh I Noor* has provided good, cheap curries for years at Jalan Mesjid 21. The family has now opened a second restaurant at Jalan Sisingamangaraja 23, underneath a huge advertising billboard at the junction with Jalan Rahmadayah.

The *Farhan Tandoori Restaurant*, Jalan Taruma 94, has a menu very similar to that at G's Koh I Noor – curries for 3000 rp, *nan* (bread) for 1500 rp and yoghurt drinks for 1000 rp.

There are some excellent bakeries awaiting the sweet-toothed traveller. Two to check out are the *France Modern Bakery*, at Jalan Pemuda 24C, and *Medan Bakers*, just beyond the Hindu temple at Jalan H Zainal Arifin 150.

If you're hanging out for some junk food, there is a *KFC* on the corner of Jalan Juandu and Jalan Katamso and also one at Deli Plaza. *Pizza Hut* (☎ 519956), on the corner of Jalan Multatuli and Jalan Suprapto, offers free delivery to your home or hotel, starting at 10,700 rp for a regular 'vegetarian'.

Fruit is surprisingly hard to find. The main fruit market is the Pasar Ramai, next to Thamrin Plaza on Jalan Thamrin. *Brastagi Fruits Market*, an up-market, air-con shop rather than a market, is more conveniently located on Jalan Sugiono. It has a great selection of both local and imported tropical fruit as well as apples and oranges.

Things to Buy

Medan has a number of interesting arts & crafts shops, particularly along Jalan Ahmad Yani. Try Toko Asli at No 62, Toko Rufino at No 56 or Toko Bali Arts at No 68. They all have a good selection of antique weaving, Dutch pottery, carvings and other pieces.

One of the best places to buy Sumatran handicrafts is Gelora Plaza, south of the railway line on Jalan Sisingamangaraja. The display is tucked away in a small alcove at the back of the 1st floor. Most prices are so reasonable that you don't feel driven to haggle.

Getting There & Away

Medan is Sumatra's main international arrival and departure point.

Air There are daily international flights from Medan to Singapore, Kuala Lumpur and Penang, as well as a weekly direct service to Bangkok on Saturdays. Airport tax for international departures is 15,000 rp.

Malaysian Airlines System (MAS) has daily connections with Penang for US$60. Sempati occasionally has special deals on its flights on Monday, Wednesday, Thursday and Sunday, and these are sometimes cheaper than the ferry.

Sempati also has three flights a week to Kuala Lumpur, while Garuda and MAS have daily flights for US$77. Both Garuda and Singapore-based Silk Air have daily flights to Singapore for US$127.

MAS (☎ 519333) is in the Hotel Danau Toba International at Jalan Imam Bonjol 17. Garuda has three offices: the head office (☎ 516066) at Jalan Suprapto 2; a branch at the Hotel Tiara Medan (☎ 538527); and a branch at the Hotel Dharma Deli (☎ 516400). Singapore Airlines (☎ 325300) is in the Polonia Hotel on Jalan Sudirman. Thai International (☎ 510541) is at the Dharma Deli Hotel. Merpati (☎ 514102) is at Jalan Katamso 41J; Sempati has offices at the Hotel Tiara Medan (☎ 537800) and at the Dharma Deli Hotel (☎ 327011); Mandala (☎ 538183) is at Jalan Katamso 37E; Bouraq (☎ 552333) is also on Jalan Katamso; and the SMAC office (☎ 537760) is at Jalan Imam Bonjol 59, close to the airport.

Merpati and Garuda have the most domestic flights from Medan as well as five flights a day to Jakarta (337,000 rp) and occasional direct flights to Bali (454,800 rp). Sumatran services include daily direct flights to Banda Aceh, Batu Besar (Pulau Batam), Padang and Pekanbaru. There are five flights a day to Jakarta (337,000 rp). Sempati has four flights a day to Jakarta for the same price, while Bouraq and Mandala also fly the route daily for fractionally less. SMAC has daily flights from Medan to Gunung Sitoli on Pulau Nias for 117,000 rp one way and 231,000 rp return.

The domestic terminal has a restaurant, snack bar and magazine stand.

Bus Medan is the major crossroads for bus travel in North Sumatra. Every destination used to have its own bus station, but these days most destinations are served by two major terminals.

The huge Amplas bus station, five km south of the city centre, handles departures to points south, including the most popular destination, Parapat. Buses leave every hour for the four-hour trip and cost 3500 rp. Any yellow opelet heading south should get you to Amplas for 250 rp.

The best company for long-distance travel south is ALS, whose office is at Jalan Amaliun 2, 150 metres from Jalan Sisingamangaraja. ALS will get you from Medan to Bukittinggi for 15,000/20,000 rp (without/with air-con), Padang (18,000/23,000 rp), Palembang (40,000 rp) and Bandar Lampung (45,000/70,000 rp). Real masochists can keep going to Jakarta (50,000/75,000 rp) or all the way to Denpasar (75,000/120,000 rp).

Buses to Banda Aceh, Berastagi, Bukit Lawang and other northern destinations leave from the Pinang Baris bus station. Pinang Baris is 10 km west of the city centre, towards Binjai on Jalan Gatot Subroto. Direct buses to Bukit Lawang (1300 rp; three hours) leave every half hour between 5.30 am and 6 pm. Buses to Berastagi (1200 rp; two hours) are just as frequent.

The journey to Banda Aceh takes as little as nine hours on the new buses. You can spend between 20,000 and 30,000 rp, depending on the level of comfort. There are lots of overnight services. The main companies doing the Banda Aceh-Medan run – PMTOH, Kurnia and Melati – have offices at the junction of Jalan Iskandar Muda and Jalan Gajah Mada where seats can be booked.

Opelets to Pinang Baris run along Jalan Gatot Subroto for 250 rp. A taxi to the city centre costs about 5000 rp.

North Sumatra – Bukit Lawang 509

There are also tourist buses every morning to Sibolga via Parapat, leaving from SMJ Travel – a small office opposite the junction of Jalan Sisingamangaraja and Jalan Sipiso-Piso. A seat costs 15,000 rp, regardless of how far you go. The price includes hotel pick-up.

Train There are passenger services twice a day to Pematangsiantar for 4000/2000 rp (business/economy class), Tanjungbalai (5500/2500 rp) and Rantauprapat (6500 rp business class).

Taxi There are several long-distance taxi operators in Medan. Inda Taxi (☎ 516615) is at Jalan Katamso 60. It has share taxis to Parapat (12,000 rp), Sibolga (15,000 rp), and Pekanbaru (28,600 rp).

Boat See Sumatra's introductory Getting There & Away section for information on the ferry service between Penang and Medan's port of Belawan.

The introductory Getting Around chapter has details of services operated by the national line, Pelni, connecting Medan with other east Sumatran ports and with the rest of Indonesia.

The Pelni office (☎ 518899) in Medan is at Jalan Sugiono 5, one block from Jalan Pemuda.

Getting Around
To/From the Airport The airport taxis (which are not metered) charge a minimum 5000 rp from the airport to the hotels on Jalan Sisingamangaraja, and 7000 rp to the city centre hotels. The fare in a metered cab is about half that – if you can find one.

Becaks are not allowed into the airport area, so you have to walk from the junction of Jalan Imam Bonjol and Jalan Juanda. The fare into town is between 1500 and 2000 rp.

Local Transport You're unlikely to spend enough time in Medan to work out the opelet routes. The minimum fare is, however, around 250 rp. Medan also has plenty of becaks, both pedal-powered and motorised.

It is essential to agree on the price before you set off. The going rate for tourists is 1000 rp for a short ride and up to 1500 rp for most destinations around town. A few of the drivers speak English well and can be very helpful.

Fares also start at about 1000 rp for motorised becaks, which tend to be Medan's most visible source of pollution.

BUKIT LAWANG
Bukit Lawang, 80 km north-west of Medan, is on the eastern edge of the giant Gunung Leuser National Park. The country is wild and enchanting with dense jungle and clear, fast-flowing rivers.

It is also the site of the famous Bohorok Orang-utan Rehabilitation Centre, which has made this once-remote village into one of the most popular spots in Sumatra. Many tourists opt to spend four or five days here.

It is a very popular weekend destination for Medan people, which means accommodation can be hard to find on a Saturday. The foreign tourists have the place pretty much to themselves during the week.

Orientation
The settlement exists almost solely to service the tourist industry. The bus stops where the road ends: a small square surrounded by shops and a few offices. There are a couple of restaurants by the river where you can sit and take stock. The closest accommodation is on the opposite side of the river, but the prime locations are 15 minutes' walk upstream.

Information
Tourist Office There is a small tourist office in the white building at the back of the bus lot. There is not much information to be gained, but the staff are helpful and speak English.

Money Change money before you arrive. There are no banks in Bukit Lawang and the rates at the local moneychangers are appalling. If you have to change, Sri Said, next to the bus parking lot, has the best rates. You

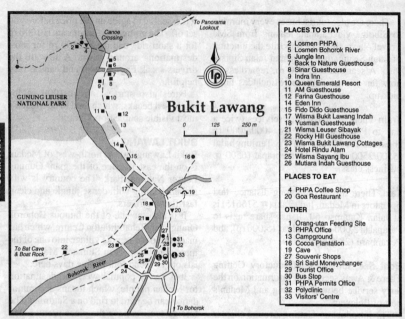

Bukit Lawang

PLACES TO STAY
2 Losmen PHPA
5 Losmen Bohorok River
6 Jungle Inn
7 Back to Nature Guesthouse
8 Sinar Guesthouse
9 Indra Inn
10 Queen Emerald Resort
11 AM Guesthouse
12 Farina Guesthouse
14 Eden Inn
15 Fido Dido Guesthouse
17 Wisma Bukit Lawang Indah
18 Yusman Guesthouse
21 Wisma Leuser Sibayak
22 Rocky Hill Guesthouse
23 Wisma Bukit Lawang Cottages
24 Hotel Rindu Alam
25 Wisma Sayang Ibu
26 Mutiara Indah Guesthouse

PLACES TO EAT
4 PHPA Coffee Shop
20 Goa Restaurant

OTHER
1 Orang-utan Feeding Site
3 PHPA Office
13 Campground
16 Cocoa Plantation
19 Cave
27 Souvenir Shops
28 Sri Said Moneychanger
29 Tourist Office
30 Bus Stop
31 PHPA Permits Office
32 Polyclinic
33 Visitors' Centre

GUNUNG LEUSER NATIONAL PARK

To Panorama Lookout

Canoe Crossing

To Bat Cave & Boat Rock

Bohorok River

To Bohorok

can also change money at the Bukit Lawang Visitor Centre and a couple of the hotels.

Post & Telephone There are no telephones and no post office. Outgoing mail can be left at the tourist office, where it is collected on Wednesday and Friday at 10 am. Stamps can be bought at the shops. The nearest post office is seven km away at Bohorok, and the nearest phone is 45 km away at Kuala.

Medical Services Minor medical problems can be dealt with by the nurse at the small clinic next to the PHPA office.

Orang-Utan Rehabilitation Centre
Bukit Lawang's famous Orang-utan Rehabilitation Centre was set up in 1973 to help the primates readjust to the wild after captivity.

The orang-utans can be seen every day at a jungle feeding platform in the adjacent national park. Before you set off, get a permit from the national parks office in Bukit Lawang which is open from 7 am every day. The permit is valid for one visit, costs 4000 rp and must be used within three days of issue. In theory, only 40 permits are issued each day, but the numbers swell at the weekend when the Medan crowds arrive.

The feeding site is 30 minutes' walk from the office in town, including a free crossing of the Bohorok River in a dugout canoe. The path into the national park from the river crossing can get very muddy.

Feeding times are from 8 to 9 am and from 3 to 4 pm. These are the only times visitors are allowed to enter the national park other than with a guide or an organised trek.

Most days about half a dozen orang-utans turn up to be fed milk and bananas, intended as supplementary feed until they learn to fend fully for themselves. It's best to get there early so that you can see the orang-utans arrive, swinging through the trees. It is forbidden to touch or feed the animals.

The cages by the Losmen PHPA are used to keep new arrivals in quarantine and sick animals under observation.

Occasionally, orang-utans can be seen by the river opposite the Jungle Inn and Losmen Bohorok River, where they come down to check out the tourists.

Bukit Lawang Visitor Centre

This fine establishment is run by the World Wide Fund for Nature (WWF). It has good displays of flora & fauna in Gunung Leuser National Park and a section to explain the orang-utan rehabilitation programme. It's backed up by some stunning photographs. The centre sells a small, but very informative, booklet about the national park by New Zealand writer and photographer Mike Griffiths. It's a good investment at 12,000 rp if you're planning on spending time in the park.

Rafting

The Back to Nature Guesthouse organises rafting trips down the Bohorok and Wampu rivers for 75,000 rp per day.

Trekking

A lot of people use Bukit Lawang as a base for trekking. Almost every losmen advertises trekking, and half the losmen workers seem to be guides – without whom you are not allowed into the park. They offer a range of treks around Bukit Lawang as well as three and five-day walks to Berastagi.

Around Bukit Lawang, expect to pay 20,000 rp for a day trek, and 25,000 per day for treks that involve camping out. Prices include meals, guide fees and the cost of the permit to enter the park.

There are a number of short walks that require no guides or permits. There is a bat cave 20 minutes' walk to the south-west of town, signposted behind the Wisma Bukit Lawang Cottages. The two-km walk passes through rubber plantations and patches of forest.

A lot of the forest trees are durians, so take care in late June and July when the spiked fruits crash to the ground (there are signs warning people not to linger). You'll also need a torch to explore the caves.

There are more bat caves a further four km downstream at a site called Boat Rock, but entry is not allowed without a guide.

The Panorama Lookout walk starts just north of the Jungle Inn. The path through the rainforest is very steep and slippery, but you can take a more leisurely route through rubber and cocoa plantations. Luntir Cave, about 20 minutes' walk from the lookout, is another bat hang-out.

Places to Stay & Eat

Bukit Lawang has a choice of 19 places, with plenty of budget options and a couple of entries at the more comfortable end of the market. Almost all the losmen have restaurants.

Accommodation is concentrated in two main areas: along the river bank opposite the town and upstream along the path to the orang-utan feeding site.

The best budget accommodation is upstream near the canoe crossing; about 15 minutes' walk from town. This is also the best spot to go swimming. The most popular place is the *Jungle Inn*, which has become a bit of a legend among travellers for its creative carpentry and incredibly relaxed style. It charges for its reputation, and its cheapest rooms are 5000 rp. The 10,000 rp rooms with balconies over the river are a bit claustrophobic for all their charm.

Some of the Jungle Inn's neighbours offer better value. The *Losmen Bohorok River* has rooms on the river bank for 3000 rp, while the nearby *Sinar Guesthouse* and *Back to Nature Guesthouse* charge 3000 and 3500 rp respectively.

There's not much of note between this group and the town. The *Fido Dido* has uninviting little huts for 3000 rp, and the *Eden Guesthouse* has the cheapest double in town at 2000 rp.

The downstream accommodation is dominated by the *Wisma Bukit Lawang Cottages* and the *Wisma Leuser Sibayak*, two large bungalow complexes that have almost half the total number of beds in town. Both have basic doubles for 7500 rp. The layout of the Wisma Bukit Lawang Cottages is far more imaginative, with bamboo bungalows set in well-tended gardens for 10,000 to 12,000 rp and modern bungalows for 20,000 rp. The Leuser Sibayak has a hotel wing with rooms overlooking the river for 15,000 rp.

Downstream budget options include the *Yusman Guesthouse*, upstream from the Leuser Sibayak. It has doubles for 3000 and 4000 rp.

Guests look to be something of a rarity at the *Rocky Hill Guesthouse*, a small group of simple bungalows set away from the crowd on the edge of a rubber plantation.

The most expensive hotel in town is the new *Rindu Alam*, where 50,000 rp gets a double with TV and breakfast but not hot water.

The food in the guesthouses is the usual travellers' fare. The best restaurant in town is at *Wisma Bukit Lawang Cottages*. It does a couple of unusual items such as banana stem curry.

No doubt the eyes of many will light up on spotting 'extremely herbal jungle tea, extra herb' on the menu at the Jungle Inn. It turns out to be very much as described – a drink made from a mixture of jungle herbs, berries, bits of bark etc.

Durian trees can be found everywhere in and around Bukit Lawang, and the town is overflowing with the fruit in late June and July. They are as fresh and as cheap as you'll find anywhere, and priced from 500 rp for a small one.

Getting There & Away

The road from Medan to Bukit Lawang has some of the biggest potholes in Sumatra – great, gaping monsters that could swallow a bus whole.

There are direct buses to Medan's Pinang Baris bus station every half hour between 5.30 am and 6 pm. The 80-km journey takes three hours and costs 1300 rp. A chartered taxi to Medan costs 65,000 rp.

A tourist bus leaves every morning at 7.30 am to Medan (7000 rp), Berastagi (12,000 rp), Lake Toba (20,000 rp) and Bukittinggi

(45,000 rp). Getting to Bukittinggi involves an overnight stay at Lake Toba.

BERASTAGI (BRASTAGI)

Berastagi is a picturesque hill town in the Karo Highlands, only 70 km from Medan on the back road to Lake Toba. The setting is dominated by two volcanoes: Gunung Sinabung to the west and the smoking Gunung Sibayak to the north.

At 1300 metres above sea level, the climate is pleasantly cool, and the town is a favourite weekend destination for Medan day-trippers and weekenders.

Travellers come for two main reasons – to experience the culture of the Karo Batak people, and to go trekking. Berastagi is crawling with guides for treks into the Gunung Leuser National Park or to surrounding volcanoes and attractions.

Orientation & Information

Berastagi is essentially a one-street town spread along Jalan Veteran. The hill to the north-west of town is Bukit Gundaling, a popular picnic spot and mid-range accommodation area.

Tourist Office The staff at the tourist office in the centre of town, near the fruit market, are friendly and helpful, but the best source of travellers' information is the noticeboards at the Wisma Sibayak.

Money It's best to change money before arriving here. The closest bank is BNI 1946 at nearby Kabanjahe, but the rates are poor and it will change only American Express US dollar travellers' cheques and US dollars.

The Wisma Sibayak will change US dollar travellers' cheques and various foreign currencies but the rates are terrible. The Hotel International Sibayak, on the northern edge of town, has marginally better rates.

Post & Telephone The post office and Telkom office are side-by-side near the memorial at the northern end of Jalan Veteran.

Orang-utans, Tanjung Puting National Park, Central Kalimantan (BD) &
bamboo, Flores, Nusa Tenggara (GE)

Top left: Horse cart and bamboo walkways, Parangtretes, Central Java (PT)
Top right: Tay Kak Sie Temple, Semarang, Central Java (PT)
Bottom: Becak, Pangandaran, West Java (PT)

SUMATRA

PLACES TO STAY

2	Rose Garden Hotel
3	Rudang Hotel
4	Hotel Bukit Kubu
6	Wisma Ikut
8	Crispo Inn
12	Ginsata Hotel
13	Ginsata Guesthouse
17	Torong Inn
19	Losmen Timur
20	Hotel Anda
21	Losmen TS Lingga
22	Losmen Trimurty
23	Merpati Inn
25	Losmen Sibayak Guesthouse
32	Wisma Sibayak

PLACES TO EAT

9	Rendezvous Restaurant
18	Asia Restaurant
26	Rumah Makan Terang
27	Europah Restaurant
29	Restaurant Ora et Labora

OTHER

1	Peceren Traditional Longhouse
5	Power Station
7	Petrol Station
10	Fruit Market
11	Memorial
14	Tourist Office
15	Telkom Office
16	Post Office
24	Public Health Centre
28	Ria Cinema
30	Bus & Opelet Station
31	Market

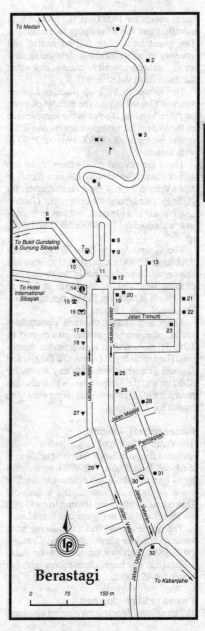

Fruit Markets

Berastagi is famous for its fruit and vegetable markets. The volcanic soils of the surrounding countryside supply much of the produce for North Sumatra. Passionfruit are a local speciality. You'll find both the *marquisa*, a large, sweet, yellow-skinned fruit, and the *marquisa asam manis*, a purple-skinned fruit that makes delicious drinks.

Places to Stay – bottom end

The *Wisma Sibayak*, at Jalan Udara 1, the Kabanjahe end of the main street, is one of the best-run travellers' places in the country. It has dorm beds at 2500 rp and small singles/doubles for 4000/6000 rp as well as larger rooms for 10,000 rp. It's packed with travellers and has a very popular restaurant. The guest books are full of useful and amusing information about sightseeing, festivals, transport, walks, climbs and other things to do in the area.

The Sibayak's back-up place is *Losmen Sibayak Guesthouse* in the middle of town on Jalan Veteran. It's not in the same league as the Wisma Sibayak, but dorms cost 2500 rp and rooms are 3000/5000 rp – or 7500 rp with mandi.

There are several good places at the top end of town. The friendly *Ginsata Hotel*, at Jalan Veteran 79, has good, clean doubles for 7000 rp. Just around the corner, the *Ginsata Guesthouse* is a pleasant, old timber bungalow with doubles for 4000, 5000 and 6000 rp.

The *Crispo Inn*, at Jalan Veteran 3, has doubles for 5000 rp, or 10,000 rp with hot shower and breakfast, while the *Torong Inn*, at Jalan Veteran 128, has dorms at 3000 rp and rooms at 5000 rp. Better rooms, including mandi, cost 7500 rp.

There is a cluster of small guesthouses around the junction at the eastern end of Jalan Trimurti, a short walk from the memorial. They include the *Losmen TS Lingga* and *Losmen Trimurty*, both with tiny rooms for 3000 rp, and the *Merpati Inn*, which also has rooms for 3000 rp as well as larger ones with mandi for 7500 rp.

Places to Stay – middle

There are a few mid-range hotels on the northern fringe of town. The best of them is the *Hotel Bukit Kubu* (☎ 20832), surrounded by its own nine-hole golf course just north of town on Jalan Sempurna. It's a fine old Dutch hotel with rooms starting from 35,000 rp. Prices include hot water and breakfast.

The hotels around Bukit Gundaling offer some of the best views. *Berastagi Cottages* (☎ 20888), halfway up the hill on Jalan Gundaling, has large, clean rooms with hot water for 45,000 rp.

Places to Stay – top end

'International' hotels are springing up every-

where, aimed largely at the Malaysian and Singaporean markets. They come complete with swimming pools, tennis courts and fitness centres. The cheapest doubles are listed at about 120,000 rp, but this is very negotiable. The biggest of them is the *Hotel International Sibayak* (☎ 20928), at Jalan Merdeka, on the road to Bukit Gundaling. It's also the only one that's been around long enough to have finished the landscaping.

Places to Eat

Most of the budget hotels also operate restaurants. The restaurant at the *Wisma Sibayak* is fast and efficient and serves good food, while the Torong Inn's *Jane & Tarzan Coffee Shop* has more typical travellers' fare.

There's Padang food at the *Ginsata* and at the *Rumah Makan Muslimin*, downstairs from the Torong Inn, where the manager speaks English and is happy to explain his dishes to Western novices.

The *Rumah Makan Terang*, at Jalan Veteran 369, and the *Eropah Restaurant*, at No 48G, do Chinese food. The *Asia Restaurant*, at No 9-10, is bigger, better and more expensive.

If you want to dine colonial style, the restaurant at the *Hotel Bukit Kubu* is the place to go. Expect to pay 15,000 rp, plus drinks, for a choice of Indonesian and European food.

At night, try the delicious cakes made from rice flour, palm sugar and coconut steamed in bamboo cylinders. You can buy them at the stall outside the Ria Cinema.

Things to Buy

There are a number of interesting antique and souvenir shops along Jalan Veteran. Crispo Antiques has particularly interesting items.

Getting There & Away

Berastagi's bus station is on Jalan Veteran. There are frequent buses from Berastagi to Medan (1200 rp; two hours).

Getting to/from Parapat, along the scenic back road through the Karo Highlands by public transport, involves a couple of bus changes and can take all day. From Parapat, the first step is to catch a Medan-bound bus as far as Pematangsiantar (600 rp; one hour). The second step is a rough bus ride from Pematangsiantar to Kabanjahe (1750 rp), that takes over three hours. Finally, you catch a minibus (250 rp) for the last 12 km to Berastagi.

The easy option is to catch one of the tourist buses making the Bukit Lawang-Parapat run. Berastagi is the midpoint and buses stop for lunch in both directions, leaving at about 1 pm. It costs 12,000 rp to both Bukit Lawang and Parapat.

The Parapat leg includes sightseeing stops at the Sipiso-Piso Waterfall at the northern tip of Lake Toba and the Batak king's huge house near Pematangpurba. Buses follow the winding road along the eastern shore of Lake Toba to Parapat.

The Bukit Lawang leg goes via Medan (5000 rp; 1½ hours) and includes stops at palm oil and rubber plantations.

Berastagi is the jumping-off point for visiting Kutacane and the Gunung Leuser National Park. For details, see Kutacane in the Aceh Province section.

Getting Around

Local transport comes in the form of dokars. Rides around town cost 750 to 1000 rp.

Opelets leave from the bus station on Jalan Veteran. They run every few minutes between Berastagi and Kabanjahe (250 rp), the major population and transport centre of the highlands. You need to go to Kabanjahe to get to many of the villages in the following section.

AROUND BERASTAGI
Gunung Sibayak

From Berastagi you can climb Gunung Sibayak (2094 metres), probably the most accessible of Indonesia's volcanoes, and have a soak in the hot springs (500 rp) on the way back. It's best to avoid going on a Sunday, when day-trippers are out in force.

You need good walking boots because the path is steep in places and is slippery all year round. It can be cold at the top, so bring

Around Berastagi

0   5   10 km

Danau Tawar

Gunung Sinabung
(2450 m) ▲

Naman

KARO BATAK

Laukawar

Gunung
Sibayak
(2094 m) ▲

Simpang Empat

BERASTAGI

Lingga

HIGHLANDS

Kandibata

Kabanjahe

Barusjahe

Sikanalu

Tigapanah

Sipiso-Piso
Falls

Merek

Situnggaling

Tongging

Seribudolok

Sibaulangit

Lake Toba

SUMATRA

something warm to wear as well as food, drink and a torch (in case you get caught out after dark).

There are three ways of tackling the climb, depending on your energy levels. The easiest way is to catch a local bus (300 rp) to Semangat Gunung, at the base of the volcano, from where it's a two-hour climb to the top. Alternatively, you can start from Berastagi, taking the track leading from the road to Bukit Gundaling. This walk takes between 3½ and four hours. The longest option is to start from the waterfall on the Medan road, about five km north of town. Allow at least five hours for this walk.

Whichever route you choose, on the way down it's worth stopping for a soak in the hot springs, a short ride from Semangat Gunung on the road back to Berastagi.

The guest books at Wisma Sibayak have more information about this climb and various other walks in the area.

Gunung Sinabung

Gunung Sinabung (2450 metres) is considerably higher than Sibayak and the views from the top are spectacular.

The climb takes six hours up and four hours down, starting from the village of Mardingding. Mardingding is 30 minutes by opelet from Kabanjahe (12 km and 250 rp by minibus from Berastagi), so you will need to start early or join an organised walk with a guide. Again, you'll need good shoes, warm clothing, food, drink and a torch.

Sipiso-Piso Waterfall

The impressive Sipiso-Piso Waterfall is at the northern end of Lake Toba, 36 km from Berastagi (24 km from Kabanjahe) and about 300 metres from the main road. The tourist bus from Bukit Lawang stops at the falls.

Kampung Peceren

This cluster of traditional houses is on the northern outskirts of Berastagi and has almost been absorbed by the town. The village has half a dozen traditional houses, most of them occupied.

Lingga

The best-known of the traditional Karo Batak villages is Lingga, 16 km south of Berastagi. The place is interesting, if rather rundown, with many traditional houses with the characteristic horned-shaped roofs. Some are in a very poor state of repair.

The houses are about 100 years old, rather than 250 as claimed by some guides. Not a single nail was used in their construction. There's a 200 rp entry fee into the village. The people, especially the women, do not like being photographed.

Opelets to Lingga (250 rp) leave from the junction of Jalan Bangsi Sembiring, Jalan Pala Bangun and Jalan Veteran in Kabanjahe.

Cingkes

Cingkes is a Simalungun Batak village about 22 km from Berastagi that will appeal to architecture buffs. There are about two dozen traditional houses, most in good condition, as well as a spirit house (tambak law burawan).

Cingkes takes a bit of getting to. By opelet from Berastagi, you have to change at Kabanjahe, Situnggaling and Seribudolok.

Barusjahe

Barusjahe has a number of traditional houses and rice barns, but their dilapidated condition suggests that they won't be around much longer.

Barusjahe is half an hour by opelet from Kabanjahe (600 rp).

PARAPAT

Almost sliding into the crater of Lake Toba is Parapat, a pleasure spot of the Medan wealthy set. Untempted by tourist literature that describes it as the 'most beautiful mountain and lake resort in Indonesia', most travellers linger only long enough to catch their ferry to Samosir – unless they arrive too late or have to catch an early bus.

Orientation & Information

Parapat is divided into two parts. The line of restaurants and shops along the Trans-

SUMATRA

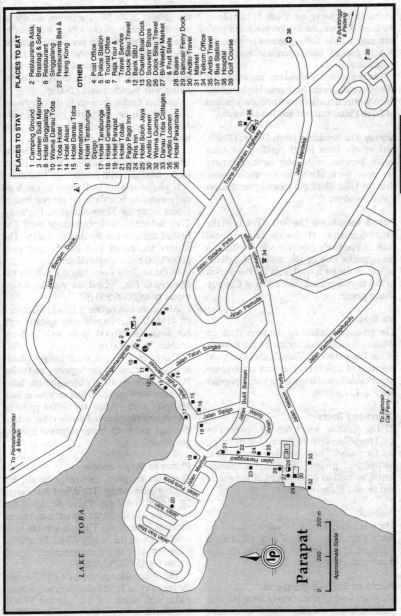

PLACES TO STAY

1 Camping Ground
3 Losmen Sud Mampir
8 Hotel Singgalang
10 Wisma Danau Toba
11 Toba Hotel
14 Hotel Atsari
15 Hotel Danau Toba International
16 Hotel Tarabunga
   Sipigo
17 Hotel Tarabunga
18 Hotel Cendrawasih
19 Hotel Parapat
21 Hotel Toball
23 Pago Pago Inn
24 Riris Inn
25 Hotel Soloh Jaya
30 Andilo Losmen
32 Wisma Gurning
33 Danau Toba Cottages
35 Andilo Losmen
36 Hotel Pakanbaru

PLACES TO EAT

2 Restaurants Asia,
   Brastagi & Sehat
8 Restaurant
   Singgalang
22 Restaurants Bali &
   Hong Kong

OTHER

4 Post Office
5 Police Station
6 Tourist Office
7 Raja Tour &
   Travel Service
9 Dolok Silau Travel
12 Bank SBU
13 Charter Boat Dock
20 Souvenir Shops
26 Dolok Silau Travel
27 Bi-Weekly Market
   & Fruit Stalls
28 Buses
29 Samosir Ferry Dock
31 Market
34 Telkom Office
35 Andilo Travel
37 Bus Station
38 Hospital
39 Golf Course

Parapat

LAKE TOBA

To Bukittinggi & Padang

To Pematangsiantar & Medan

To Samosir Car Ferry

Trans-Sumatran Highway

Jalan Merdeka

Jalan Sisoha Pintu

Jalan Joseph Sinaga

Jalan Kernel Naptupulu

Jalan Pemuda

Jalan Talun Sungkit

Jalan Pulau Pandan

Jalan Sanusar

Jalan Bangun Dolok

Jalan Sitongemangaraja

Jalan Sipigo

Jalan Bukit Bansan

Jalan Nelson Purba

Jalan Simkid

Jalan Marihat

Jalan Tarangaaol

Jalan Pora-Pora

Jalan Ikan Mas

Jalan Ikan

0   250   500 m

Approximate Scale

Sumatran Highway are about 1½ km from the heart of town, the market place and ferry terminal on Lake Toba. The area between the two is packed with countless hotels and guesthouses.

The bus station is about one km south-east of town on the Trans-Sumatran Highway and there's a small tourist office near the junction of Jalan Pulau Samosir and the highway.

Money The Sejahtera Bank Umum (SBU), part of the Toba Hotel building on Jalan Pulau Samosir, is the only bank. The rates are poor, particularly for currencies other than the US dollars, but much better than on Pulau Samosir.

Post & Telephone The post office is on the Trans-Sumatran Highway. International calls can be made from the wartel office on the opposite side of the road. The Telkom office, on the back road from the bus station to the ferry terminal, has a Home Country Direct phone.

Markets
The produce markets by the ferry dock on Wednesday and Saturday are the main events of the Parapat week. There's always a good selection of fruit here. The busy markets are remarkably free of tourists for such a popular place as Lake Toba.

Organised Tours
PT Dolok Silau, which has offices both on the Trans-Sumatran Highway and down by the ferry dock, runs weekly tours to local coffee, tea, ginger, clove and cinnamon farms, as well as other places of interest in and around Parapat.

Festival
The week-long Danau Toba Festival is held every year in mid-June. Canoe races are a highlight of the festival, but there are also Batak cultural performances.

Places to Stay – bottom end
There are several places along Jalan Harang-gaol, including the *Pago Pago Inn* close to the harbour at No 50. The rooms are not as stylish as the bamboo lobby, but they're clean and cost 5000 rp per person. On the other side of the road, at No 47, is the *Hotel Soloh Jaya*. It has some windowless little boxes (doubles) for 7500 rp as well as better rooms with mandi from 17,500 rp.

You can't get any closer to the ferry dock – or any noisier – than the losmen *Andilo Nancy* above the travel agency of the same name. A double here costs 7500 rp.

More relaxed than any of these is the *Wisma Gurning*. It's a simple, friendly place, by the lakeside, with doubles for 10,000 rp.

If you're staying in Parapat to catch an early-morning bus, there are several budget places along the Trans-Sumatran Highway. They include two at the bus station itself. The best of them is run by *Andilo Nancy*. The rooms are clean and bright and cost 5000/7500 rp for singles/doubles.

In the unlikely event that it's full, try the *Simarmata Inn*, behind the Andilo, where rooms cost 6000/7500 rp.

Also at the bus station is *Hotel Pakanbaru* (☎ 41466). It has large rooms upstairs with hot water for 50,000 rp as well as basic doubles for 15,000 rp.

There are a couple more budget places near the junction of the highway and Jalan Pulau Samosir. Directly opposite the lakeside turn-off is the small and very basic *Sudi Mampir*, with rooms for 3000 rp. The *Singgalang Hotel*, uphill on the other side of the road, has much better rooms at 5000 rp per person.

Places to Stay – middle
There are countless mid-range hotels, but nothing outstanding. The *Hotel Tarabunga* (☎ 41666), on Jalan Pulau Samosir, has rooms for 45,000/50,000 rp and a restaurant overlooking the lake. This place is not to be confused with the nearby *Hotel Tarabunga Sibigo* (☎ 41665), a giant concrete box with rooms for 45,000/54,000 rp.

The *Wisma Danau Toba* (☎ 41302), near the highway on Jalan Pulau Samosir, is better value with rooms by the lake for 32,000/45,000 rp.

The *Riris Inn* (☎ 41392), near the ferries at Jalan Haranggaol 39, has good, clean singles/doubles for 15,000/20,000 rp.

Places to Stay – top end
The *Hotel Parapat* (☎ 41012), at Jalan Marihat 1, is the best hotel in town. It's also the oldest, and occupies a prime site with fine views over the lake and a private beach. Prices start at 130,000 rp for a double.

The *Hotel Danau Toba International* (☎ 41583) is starting to look a bit too tatty to be charging 85,000/99,000 rp.

Places to Eat
Parapat is dotted with restaurants as well as hotels. The highway strip is well equipped to feed the passing traveller. The four Chinese restaurants include the unpretentious *Restaurant Singgalang*, underneath the hotel of the same name. It's the one the locals choose in preference to the flashier *Asia, Sehat* and *Brastagi*. There are also several nasi padang restaurants.

Towards the lake along Jalan Haranggaol, the side-by-side *Restaurant Hong Kong* at Nos 9 and 11 and the *Restaurant Bali* at No 13, have similar Chinese menus with main courses for about 6000 rp. Chicken with lychees at the Bali is delicious.

Getting There & Away
Bus Andilo Nancy (☎ 41548) and Dolok Silau (☎ 41467) are the main agencies for bus tickets and provide a good service, despite some annoying hard-sell practices.

Parapat agencies tend to charge a higher than average commission and have been known to bungle bus and flight reservations from Medan. Parapat is not a major travel hub, so do most of your business in Medan if possible.

Public buses leave from the bus station, but some express buses stop at the agencies on Jalan Sisingamangaraja.

Public buses to/from Medan (3500 rp; four to five hours) leave throughout the day, but most departures are in the morning. Other public bus services generally depart up until noon and include Sibolga (7000 rp; four

hours), Bukittinggi (17,000 rp; 15 hours), Padang (19,000 rp; 18 hours) and Pekanbaru (17,000 rp).

Most express buses run from Medan (via Parapat) to Bukittinggi or Padang. The best air-con luxury buses to Bukittinggi run at night, leaving Parapat at 4.30 pm, and cost 25,000 rp. They bypass Sibolga, take 12 or 13 hours and are much less arduous than the public buses. ALS and ANS buses are both recommended.

For Berastagi, you have to change buses at Pematangsiantar and Kabanjahe, and the journey takes up to six hours.

Andilo Nancy and Dolok Silau have tourist minibuses every day to Bukittinggi (25,000 rp; 13 hours). They leave early in the morning so you get to see the scenery, and they stop at points of interest, such as the equator, on the way.

The same companies also operate daily tourist buses to Bukit Lawang (20,000 rp; eight hours) via Berastagi (12,000 rp; 3½ hours) and Medan. The buses take a spectacular route between Parapat and Berastagi that winds around Lake Toba for much of the way.

Tourist buses to/from Medan to Sibolga stop at Raja Tour & Travel Service on Jalan Sisingamangaraja.

Boat See the Lake Toba section for details of ferries to Pulau Samosir.

Getting Around
Opelets charge 200 rp for the run between the highway and the ferries to Pualau Samosir.

AROUND PARAPAT
Labuhan Garaga
The village of Labuhan Garaga, 25 km from Parapat, is a centre for the weaving of the cotton Batak blankets *(kain kulos)* that are widely on sale in Parapat and on Pulau Samosir. The colour and patterns vary from group to group, but most have vertical stripes on a background of ink blue with rust-red and white the predominant colours. They're not cheap, but they are attractive and practical buys. The price range is from 30,000 to 70,000 rp; more for good-quality cloth.

SUMATRA

The Bataks

British traveller William Marsden astonished the 'civilised' world in 1783 when he returned to London with an account of a cannibalistic kingdom in the interior of Sumatra, which nevertheless had a highly developed culture and a system of writing. The Bataks have remained a subject of fascination ever since.

According to Batak legend, all Bataks are descended from Si Radja Batak, who was born of supernatural parentage on Bukit Pusuk, a mountain on the western edge of Danau Toba.

According to anthropologists, the Bataks are a Proto-Malay people descended from Neolithic mountain tribes in northern Thailand and Burma, who were driven out by migrating Mongolian and Siamese tribes.

When they arrived in Sumatra they did not linger long at the coast but trekked inland, making their first settlements around Lake Toba – where the surrounding mountains provided a natural protective barrier. They lived in virtual isolation for centuries.

The Bataks were among the most warlike peoples in Sumatra – the natives of Nias were the other – and their villages were constantly feuding. They were so mistrustful of each other (not to mention outsiders) that they did not build or maintain natural paths between villages, or construct bridges.

They practised ritual cannibalism in which the flesh of a slain enemy or a person found guilty of a serious breach of *adat* (traditional law) was eaten.

Today, there are more than six million Bataks and their lands extend 200 km north and 300 km of Danau Toba. They are divided into six main groupings – the Pakpak Batak to the north-west of Danau Toba, the Karo Batak around Berastagi and Kabanjahe, the Simalungun Batak around Pematangsiantar, the Toba Batak around Danau Toba, and the Angkola Batak and Mandailing Batak further south.

The name 'Batak' was certainly in use in the 17th century but its origins are not clear. It could come from a derogatory Malay term for robber or blackmailer, while another suggestion is that it was an abusive nickname coined by Muslims meaning 'pig-eater'.

The Bataks are primarily an agricultural people. The rich farmlands of the Karo highlands supply vegetables for much of North Sumatra as well as for export.

In contrast to the matrilineal Minangkabau, the Bataks have the most rigid patrilineal structure in Indonesia. Women not only do all the work around the house but also much of the work in the fields.

Although there is an indigenous Batak script, it was never used to record events. It seems to have been used only by priests and *dukuns* in divination and to record magic spells.

Religion & Mythology The Batak have long been squeezed between the Islamic strongholds of Aceh and West Sumatra. The Karo Batak, in particular, were constantly at odds with the Islamic Acehnese to the north, who several times tried to conquer them and convert them to Islam.

Interestingly enough, after long years of resistance to the Acehnese, the Karo were easily subdued by the Dutch, who brought with them Christianity.

The majority of today's Bataks are Protestant Christians, especially in the north around Lake Toba and the Karo Highlands. Islam is the predominant religion in the south.

Most Bataks, however, still incorporate elements of traditional animist belief and ritual. Traditional beliefs combine cosmology, ancestor and spirit worship and *tondi*. Tondi is the concept of the soul, the spirit – the essence of a person's individuality.

It is believed to develop before the child is born. It exists near the body and from time to time takes its leave, which causes illness. It is essential for Bataks to make sacrifices to their tondi to keep it in good humour.

The Bataks regard the banyan as the tree of life and relate a creation legend of their omnipotent god Ompung:

One day Ompung leant casually against a huge banyan tree and dislodged a decayed bough that plummeted into the sea. From this branch came the fish and all the living creatures of the oceans. Not long afterwards, another bough dropped to the ground and from this issued crickets, caterpillars, centipedes, scorpions and insects. A third branch broke into large chunks which were transformed into tigers, deer, boars, monkeys, birds and all the animals of the jungle. The fourth branch which scattered over the plains became horses, buffalo, goats, pigs and all the domestic animals. Human beings appeared from the eggs produced by a pair of newly created birds, born at the height of a violent earthquake.

Architecture Traditional Batak houses are built on stilts a metre to two metres from the ground. Finishing touches vary from region to region, but all follow the same basic pattern.

They are made of wood (slotted and bound together without nails) and roofed with sugar palm fibre or, more often these days, rusting corrugated iron.

The roof has a concave, saddleback bend, and each end rises in a sharp point which, from certain angles, look like the buffalo horns they are invariably decorated with. The gables are usually extravagantly embellished with mosaics and carvings of serpents, spirals, lizards and monster heads complete with bulbous eyes.

The space under the main structure is used for rearing domestic animals like cows, pigs and goats. The living quarters, or middle section, is large and open with no fixed internal walls and is often inhabited by up to a dozen families. This area is usually sectioned off by rattan mats which are let down at night to provide partial privacy. It is dark and gloomy, the only opening being a door approached by a wooden ladder.

A traditional village is made up of a number of such houses, similar to the villages of the Toraja people of central Sulawesi.

There are many interesting traditional villages around Berastagi. The houses have very high roofs, and are much larger that those of the Toba Batak. A traditional Toba village or *huta* was always surrounded by a moat and bamboo trees to protect the villagers from attack. The villages had only one gateway because of this. The houses in the village are lined up to the left and right of the king's house. In front of the houses is a line of rice barns, used for storing the harvest. Even today, walking around Samosir, you can still see how the villages were designed with defence in mind.

Culture There's evidence of a strong Indian influence on the Bataks – the cultivation of wet field rice, the type of houses, chess, cotton and even the type of spinning wheel.

A purely Batak tradition is the *sigalegale* puppet dance, once performed at funeral ceremonies but now more often a part of wedding ceremonies. The puppet, carved from the wood of a banyan tree, is a life-size likeness of a Batak youth. It is dressed in the traditional costume of red turban, loose shirt and blue sarong. A red *ulos* (a piece of rectangular cloth traditionally used to wrap round babies or around the bride and groom to bless them with fertility, unity and harmony) is draped from the shoulders.

One story of the origin of the sigalegale puppet concerns a loving but childless couple who lived on Pulau Samosir. Bereft and lonely after the death of her husband, the wife made a wooden image of him. Whenever she felt intensely lonely she hired a dalang to make the puppet dance and a dukun to communicate with the soul of her husband through the puppet.

The other story goes that there was once a king who had only one child, a son. When his son passed away the king was grieved because he now had no successor. In memory of his dead son the king ordered a wooden statue to be made in his likeness, and when he went to see it for the first time invited his people to take part in a dance feast.

The sigalegale stand up on long, wooden boxes, through which ropes are threaded and operated like pulleys to manipulate the jointed limbs of the puppet. This enables the operator to make the sigalegale dance to gamelan music accompanied by flute and drums. In some super-skilled performances the sigalegale weeps or smokes a cigarette. Its tongue can be made to poke out, and its eyelids to blink. The sigalegale is remarkably similar in appearance to the *tau tau* statues of Tanatoraja in central Sulawesi, although the tau tau do not move.

Whatever, the sigalegale soon became part of Batak culture and was used at funeral ceremonies to revive the souls of the dead and to communicate with them. Personal possessions of the deceased were used to decorate the puppet and the dukun would invite the deceased's soul to enter the wooden puppet as it danced on top of the grave. At the end of the dance, the villagers would hurl spears and arrows at the puppet while the dukun performed a ceremony to drive away evil spirits. A few days later the dukun would return to perform another ceremony, sometimes lasting 24 hours, to chase away evil spirits again.

SUMATRA

Arts & Crafts Traditionally the Bataks are skilled metalworkers and woodcarvers; other materials they use are shells, bark, bone and horns. They decorate their work with fertility symbols, magic signs and animals.

One particularly idiosyncratic form of art developed by the Toba Bataks is the magic augury book called *pustaha*. These books comprise the most significant part of their written history. Usually carved out of bark or bamboo, they are important religious records which explain the established verbal rituals and responses of priests and mourners. Other books, inscribed on bone or bamboo and ornately decorated at each end, document Batak myths.

Music is as important to the Bataks as it is to most societies, but traditionally it was played at religious ceremonies, rather than for everyday pleasure. Today they are famous for their powerful and emotive hymn singing. Most of their musical instruments are similar to those found elsewhere in Indonesia – cloth-covered copper gongs in varying sizes struck with wooden hammers, a small two-stringed violin which makes a pure but harsh sound, and a kind of reedy clarinet.

Porhalaan are divining calendars – of 12 months of 30 days each – engraved on a cylinder of bamboo. They are used to determine auspicious days on which to embark on certain activities such as marriage or the planting of the fields. ■

LAKE TOBA & PULAU SAMOSIR

Lake Toba, a remarkable volcanic crater set in the middle of North Sumatra, 176 km south of Medan, is one of Sumatra's most spectacular sights. The lake is huge – the largest in South-East Asia – occupying the caldera of a giant volcano that collapsed on itself after a massive eruption about 100,000 years ago. Measurements of ash deposits indicate that the blast made Krakatau's 1883 effort look like a hiccup. It is surrounded by steep mountains, ridges and sandy, pine-sheltered beaches.

Lake Toba is the home of the outgoing Toba Batak people. *Horas* is the traditional Batak greeting and it's delivered with great gusto.

Samosir, the impressively large, wedge-shaped island in the middle of Lake Toba, is thought to have been created by a subsequent upheaval between 30,000 and 75,000 years ago. The island has long been North Sumatra's premier attraction for foreign travellers, although it acquired a bad reputation for hustling in the late 1980s and early 1990s. Things have quietened down a bit these days. It's still a good place to rest up after the rigours of Trans-Sumatran Highway travel, and you couldn't ask for a more spectacular setting.

Most foreigners stay in Tuk Tuk where there is nothing much to do but relax. Those with a serious interest in Toba Batak culture will gain more satisfaction from scrambling over the mountain ridge to the villages on the other side of the island.

Orientation & Information

Most of the accommodation is concentrated around the Tuk Tuk Peninsula and nearby Ambarita. Tomok, the main village a couple of km south of Tuk Tuk, also has a couple of places to stay and there is a police station near Carolina's bungalows.

Money Change money before you get to Samosir. Exchange rates at the island's hotels and moneychangers make the bank in Parapat look like a top deal. The Bank Rakyat Indonesia in Ambarita doesn't change money, but the post office does.

Post & Telephone There is a post office in Ambarita. Several shops in Tuk Tuk sell stamps and have post boxes and lists of rates for overseas mail. International phone calls are marginally cheaper from the Anju Restaurant than from the resort hotels.

Bookshops There are several places selling or leasing second-hand books. The best collection is at the Gokhon Library.

Medical Services The small health centre close to the turn-off to Carolina's is equipped to cope with cuts and bruises and other minor problems.

Dangers & Annoyances Beware of theft and keep your door locked. There have been a number of reports of thieves sneaking into rooms at night and stealing cash or cameras – almost always the result of carelessness.

Things to See & Do

Tomok Although Tomok is the main village on the east coast of Samosir, it is a place to visit rather than a place to stay. Prices are

very competitive at the dozens of souvenir stalls.

There are many examples of traditional Batak houses in Tomok and also fine old graves and tombs – sarcophagi decorated with carvings of *singa*, creatures with grotesque three-horned heads and bulging eyes. Their faces also decorate the facades of Toba Batak houses.

The grave of King Sidabatu, one of the last Batak animist kings, is one hundred metres up a path that leads from the lake front through the souvenir stalls. His image is carved on his tombstone along with that of

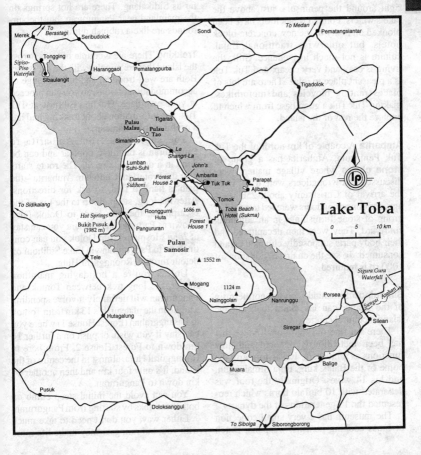

Lake Toba

0   5   10 km

his Muslim military commander and body-guard, Tengku Mohammed Syed, and that of the woman he is said to have loved for many years without fulfilment, Anteng Melila Senega. The surrounding souvenir stalls have the best range and. prices (after hard bargaining) on the island.

Nearby, a traditional house has been turned into a small museum. There are a few interesting items among the Christian religious photos and paintings.

Tuk Tuk This once small village is now a string of hotels and restaurants stretching right around the peninsula, just above the lake's waters. Pointed Batak roofs have been plonked on many of the new concrete-block hotels, but otherwise traditional Batak culture is not much in evidence. Still, the living is easy and very cheap, and Tuk Tuk is a pleasant place to relax. There are lots of places renting bicycles and motorbikes, making Tuk Tuk a good base from which to explore the rest of the island.

Ambarita A couple of km north of the Tuk Tuk Peninsula, Ambarita has a group of **stone chairs** where village matters were discussed and wrongdoers were tried. Until the arrival of Christianity about 250 years ago, serious wrongdoers were led to a further group of stone furnishings in an adjoining courtyard. They were then decapitated and their body parts supposedly chopped up and consumed. To see the chairs, a 'donation' of 1000 rp is required.

Simanindo Simanindo, on the northern tip of the island, can lay claim to being the island's cultural centre.

There's a fine old traditional house that has been meticulously restored and now functions as a museum. It was formerly the home of the Batak king, Raja Simalungun, and his 14 wives. Originally the roof was decorated with 10 buffalo horns which represented the 10 generations of the dynasty.

The museum has a very small collection of brass cooking utensils, weapons, Dutch and Chinese crockery, sculptures and other Batak carvings.

There are very polished displays of Batak dancing daily at 10.30 and 11.15 am in an adjoining traditional village compound. Entry is 3000 rp, or 500 rp to visit just the museum.

Pangururan Samosir's major population centre has virtually nothing of interest to tourists. The town is next to the narrow isthmus connecting Samosir to the mainland, so has transport links to Berastagi. It's not a popular route, and the road is very poor as far as Sidikalang. There are hot springs on the mainland near Pangururan, but the surrounds are like a rubbish dump.

Trekking There are a couple of treks across the island that are popular with the energetic. Both are well-trodden, and have a range of accommodation options, so you can proceed at your own pace. Gokhon Library, at Tuk Tuk, has information about trekking and has a useful map of Samosir.

The short trek from Ambarita to Pangururan is the more popular and can be done in a day if you're fit. The route starts near the Protestant Church in Ambarita – the path is hard to find, so ask for directions. After the long, steep climb to the top of the escarpment, the path leads to Dolok (also known as Partungkoan), where you can stay at *John's* losmen. From Dolok you can continue on to Pangururan via Lake Sidihoni on detour through Roonggurni Huta.

Unless you're a holidaying marathon runner, the long trek between Tomok and Pangururan will definitely involve spending a night on the plateau. It's 13 km from Tomok to Pasanggrahan (Forest House 1) where you can stay if you wish, or push on a further 16 km down to Forest House 2. From here to Roonggurni Huta, almost in the centre of the island, it's only four km and then another 17 km down to Pangururan.

You can avoid the initial steep climb on both these treks by starting from Pangururan.

Either way, you don't need to take much with you, but rain gear may make life more comfortable. The Samosir Bataks are hospitable people and although there are no warungs you can buy cups of coffee at villages along the way. It may also be possible to arrange accommodation in the villages.

Neither walk takes you through jungle or rainforest. In fact, most of Samosir is either pine forest or plantation – cinnamon, cloves and coffee.

Places to Stay & Eat

Samosir has some of the best value accommodation in Indonesia. You can still find some spartan places at 2000/4000 rp a single/double; some still in wooden Batak-style buildings. Most places tend to be of the concrete-box variety, but you'll get a good-sized, clean box, usually with attached mandi, from around 3000/5000 rp. A room with balcony overlooking the lake costs 4000 to 7500 rp. There is such a choice of places that the best advice is to wander around until you find something that suits.

Every losmen or hotel comes with a restaurant, but there are few surprises around – and very little difference in prices. The restaurants are good earners, and some places get pretty cranky if you don't eat where you stay. Most places still run a book for each guest, with each banana pancake or fruit salad added to a list which can stretch to a surprising length over a week or two.

Tuk Tuk This is where the vast majority of people opt to stay, and there are more than 50 places to choose from. They're strung out on the lakeside around Tuk Tuk and along the road to Ambarita. Prices range from 2000 rp for the cheapest single to 100,000 rp for a family unit at Carolina's.

Starting in the south, the first stop for the ferries is near the *Bagus Bay* on the southern neck of the peninsula. Its cheaper doubles cost 7000 rp, but the 10,000 rp rooms in the new part-stone, Batak-style houses are much better. The Bagus Bay also has a good restaurant, but uses nightly videos to lure customers – and repel others. The first stop is also the place to get off for *Linda's*, a

popular place run by the energetic Linda, with doubles for 6000 rp.

There are few places serving only food, especially on the southern side of Tuk Tuk. One is the tiny *Juwita's*, run by the sister of Pepy – responsible for the popular restaurant of the same name until she married and went to France. She passed on some of her expertise before she left, and Juwita excels at curries. It's best to order in advance.

Carolina's, easily the most stylish place on the island, is the second stop for ferries. Some of its older bungalows are excellent examples of local architecture. It's worth calling by just to look at the living, fern-covered Karo Batak roof of Room 5 – originally the best room in the place. It's worth 35,000 rp per night, a bargain compared to what you get for that money elsewhere. Its older bungalows with mandi are priced at 12,500 and 15,000 rp; for 25,000 rp you get hot water as well. Carolina's also has a range of modern rooms with hot water for 40,000 rp and family units for 100,000 rp. The restaurant is popular and the service fast and efficient, but the food is unexciting.

Next door to Carolina's is the first of Samosir's new breed of package hotels, the *Silintong 1*. It looks like a prison camp with its barbed wire fencing and guards on the gate. Its doubles for 40,000 rp are much better value than the 60,000 rp versions. The best feature of the place is the amazing collection of orchids.

A hundred metres north, the restaurant at *Bernard's* turns out consistently good food. The pizzas are good value for 3000 rp, as is chicken curry for 3500 rp and the vegetable curry for 3000 rp.

Continuing north, *Romlan* offers some of the best budget rooms. It's a very private place set on its own small headland and has a private jetty. It has rooms for 3000/4000 rp and better doubles for 7500 rp. The only drawback is the rubbish dump outside the kitchen that you have to walk through from the road.

Beyond Romlan is a cluster of big, package-type hotels offering clean, modern

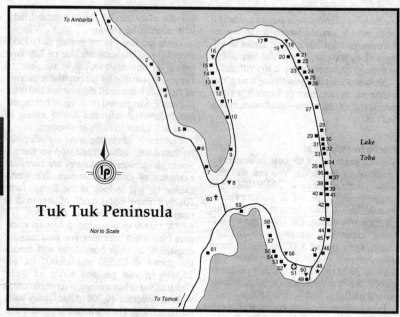

Tuk Tuk Peninsula

Not to Scale

Lake
Toba

To Ambarita

To Tomok

rooms with hot water. Doubles start at 35,000 rp, including breakfast and tax. The best of them is the expanding *Ambaroba*, which has nice rooms by the lake.

Also in this group is the *Toledo 2*, a relatively discreet little sibling of the giant *Toledo Inn* that dominates the northern end of the peninsula. Both have standard singles/doubles for 35,000/40,000 rp as well as 'luxury rooms' for 55,000/60,000 rp.

Between the two Toledos are a couple of good mid-range places: *Samosir Cottages* and *Anju* (☎ 41348). Both have rooms for 5000/8000 rp, as well as larger new rooms with hot water for 15,000 rp and 20,000 rp respectively. International phone calls can be made from the Anju.

Almost opposite the Anju is *Leo's Bar & Restaurant*, home of the cheapest cold beer on the island at 3250 rp for a large bottle. Their chicken schnitzel (3000 rp) comes with chips, fresh vegetables and a very tasty sauce.

The north-west coast of the peninsula is occupied by a string of budget places, built on the steep hillside between the road and the lake. *Abadi's*, with its good restaurant and fine views, is probably the pick of these. Rooms cost 3000/5000 rp or 5000/7000 rp for larger rooms. *Tony's* is a big place that has consumed most of its neighbours in the local monopoly game, while *Antonius* is a basic traditional Batak-style place.

There's half a dozen more places dotted along the road to Ambarita. The *Ho-l'e* looks promising, but isn't. Further along, *Tuktuk Timbul* is popular with people who want to get away from it all. It's easier to get to by boat than on foot. Singles/doubles are 4000/7000 rp.

Ambarita There are several guesthouses on the lakeside north of Ambarita, appealing to those who find Tuk Tuk too crowded. *Gordon's* has been a popular spot for years, with rooms from 3000 to 7500 rp.

PLACES TO STAY					PLACES TO EAT	
		30	Pos			
		32	Brando's Blues		8	Romlan's Beer
1	Tuktuk Timbal	33	Rodeo			Garden
2	Mas	34	Hotel Silintong 2		16	Reggae Restaurant
3	Nina's	35	Rudy's		18	Anju Restaurant
4	Sony	36	Hotel Sumber Polo		19	Leo's Bar & Restau-
5	Yogi		Mas			rant
6	Christina's	37	Romlan		24	Gokhi Bar &
7	Ho-I'e	38	Marroan			Restaurant
9	Antonius	39	Hisar's		31	France Restaurant
10	Murni	40	Lenny's		45	Franky's Restaurant
11	Laster Jony	41	Bernard's		47	Many Toba Restaurant
12	Sibayak	42	Matahari's		50	Pepy's Restaurant
13	Tony's	43	Rosita's		52	Juwita's Restaurant
14	Abadi's	44	Epy, Lacoccinelle &		56	Roy's Pub
15	Caribien		Nova			
17	Toledo Inn	46	Hotel Silintong 1		OTHER	
20	Dewi's	49	Carolina's			
21	Samosir Cottages	53	Mafir		25	Gokhon Library
22	Anju	54	Vandu		48	Police Station
23	Popy's	55	Elsina		51	Health Centre
26	Endy's	57	Dumasari		60	Church
27	Lekjon	58	Linda's			
28	Toledo 2	59	Bagus Bay			
29	Ambaroba Resort	61	Smiley's			
	Hotel					

SUMATRA

If you really are serious about getting away from it all, *Le Shangri-La* is the place, six km past Ambarita (300 rp on a Simanindo-bound bus). Clean Batak-style bungalows front a sandy beach and cost 4000/6000 rp, and there's dorm accommodation for 2000 rp. The owner, Pami, is a very jovial character and a mine of information. Boats operated by the Nasional co-operative will get you from Parapat to Le Shangri-La for 2000 rp.

Tomok Few people stay in Tomok, although there are plenty of restaurants and warungs here for day-trippers who come across on the ferry from Parapat. *Roy's Restaurant*, on the main street, near the track to the royal tombs, has accommodation on the edge of town in large Batak houses for 3000 rp per person. Tomok also has another two losmen.

Pangururan There are a couple of places at Pangururan, on the other side of the island. *Mr Barat Accommodation*, close to the wharf at Jalan Sisingamangaraja 2/4, is the budget option with rooms for 5000 rp. Much better is the *Hotel Wisata Samosir* (☎ 41150), by

the lake at Jalan Kejaksaan 42. It has rooms from 16,000 rp, and dorm beds for 6000 rp per person.

Entertainment
Tuk Tuk has a few bars and restaurants such as *Franky*, which pumps out taped music and *Roy's Pub*, which sometimes has bands.

Things to Buy
The souvenir shops of Samosir carry a huge range of cheap cotton goods, starting with dozens of brightly coloured T-shirts that let folks back home know where you've been for your holidays. Most of it is the standard tourist fare found in tourist shops throughout Indonesia.

Something a bit out of the ordinary is the embroidery work produced by peoples, such as the Gayo, living north and east of Lake Toba. The work decorates a range of bags, cushion covers and place mats.

Toba Batak musical instruments for sale include the *grantung*, consisting of several slats of wood strung out on a harness, and hit with sticks – like a xylophone.

Porhalaans, the bamboo divining calendars, are commonly sold around Tomok, Tuk Tuk and Ambarita.

Getting There & Away
Bus There is a daily bus service from Pangururan to Berastagi, via Sidikalang, but the road is very poor. From Sidikalang, it's also possible to get buses to Kutacane and Tapaktuan. (See the Parapat section for information on bus travel to/from Lake Toba.)

Every Monday at 7 am, a ferry goes from Ambarita to Haranggaol, a market town at the northern tip of the lake, and meets a bus on to Berastagi. The total cost is around 2500 rp and the trip takes about 2½ hours from Ambarita. On Thursday, a similar ferry leaves from Simanindo at 9 am and also meets a bus from Haranggaol on to Berastagi.

Boat There is a constant flow of ferries between Parapat and various destinations on Samosir.

Ferries between Parapat and Tuk Tuk Samosir operate roughly every hour, more frequently on Saturday market days. The last ferry to Samosir leaves at around 5.30 pm, and the last one to Parapat at around 4.30 pm. The fare is 800 rp one way. Some ferries serve only a certain part of Tuk Tuk, so check at Parapat and you will be pointed to the appropriate boat to get to your accommodation.

Some ferries continue on to Ambarita, but four or five boats per day go directly to Ambarita. Tell them where you want to get off on Samosir when you pay your fare, or sing out when your hotel comes around – you'll be dropped off at the doorstep or nearby. When leaving for Parapat, just stand out on your hotel jetty and wave a ferry down.

The other main destination is Tomok, with hourly ferries from Parapat for 500 rp. There is also a car ferry between Tomok and Ajibata, near Parapat. It leaves Tomok at 7 am and shuttles back and forth all day, with the last departure from Ajibata at 8.30 pm. Cars cost 10,000 rp and places can be booked

in advance through the Ajibata office (☎ 41194). The passenger fare is 500 rp.

Getting Around
It is possible to get right around the island – with the exception of Tuk Tuk – by public transport.

There are regular minibuses between Tomok and Ambarita (400 rp); some services continue to Simanindo (800 rp) and Pangururan (1500 rp). There are also occasional buses from Tomok to Nainggolan (1500 rp). From Nainggolan to Pangururan costs another 1000 rp.

Most services run in the morning and it is difficult to find anything after 3 pm.

You can rent motorbikes in Tuk Tuk for between 15,000 and 20,000 rp a day. They come with a free tank of petrol, but no insurance – so take care. There are lots of stories about travellers who have been handed outrageous repair bills.

Bicycles range in price from 3500 rp for a rattler and up to 8000 rp for a flash mountain bike.

SIBOLGA
It's hard to find a tourist with a good word to say about Sibolga, a drab little port on the west coast, 380 km north of Bukittinggi. Most people use Sibolga as a stepping-off point to Nias Island.

There's not much reason for tourists to hang around, although there are some good beaches nearby. There are also great views on the descent into Sibolga from Parapat, particularly at sunset.

Orientation & Information
The main streets in the centre of town are Jalan Suprapto, Jalan Diponegoro and Jalan Sisingamangaraja. There are two harbours. One is at the end of Jalan Horas. The other is at Jalan Pelabuhan. The centre of town is about midway between these two harbours, both only a short becak ride away.

There's a small tourist office at Jalan Horas 80. The post office and telephone office are on Jalan Sutomo.

If you're heading to Nias, the BNI 1946,

on Jalan Diponegoro, is your last chance to change money at a decent rate.

Dangers & Annoyances Tales of woe about rip-offs at the hands of the becak drivers, who operate between the buses and the port, are a dime a dozen. You need to agree on the fare and destination before you start.

Beaches

Pantai Pandan is a popular white-sand beach at the village of the same name, 11 km north of Sibolga. After a swim, 5000 rp will buy you a meal of excellent grilled fish at one of the seafood restaurants. A few hundred metres further from Sibolga is Pantai Kalangan, where there is a 250 rp entry fee. Both beaches get very crowded at weekends, but are a good way to pass the time while you're waiting for a boat from Sibolga. Opelets run to/from Sibolga to both beaches all day for 250 and 300 rp respectively.

Places to Stay

If you need to stay the night, you'll be doing yourself a favour by avoiding the budget hotels in the town centre. They are generally dirty and/or unfriendly. They include the *Hotel Sudi Mampir*, at Jalan Mesjid 100, and the *Losmen Subur*, at Jalan Diponegoro 19, with rooms from around 5000 rp.

The better cheapies are along Jalan Horas near the port. Both the *Hotel Karya Samudra*, at No 134, and *Losmen Bando Kanduang* have rooms for 5000 rp.

Many travellers speak highly of the *Pasar Baru Inn* at Jalan Suprapto 41, a very clean place run by a Chinese family. It has good doubles with fan for 8000 rp and doubles with TV and air-con for 30,000 rp.

The *Hotel Indah Sari*, at Jalan Ahmad Yani 29, is a another reasonable place with rooms for 7000 rp, and rooms with air-con and bath from 15,000 rp. The *Maturi*, opposite the Indah, is also cheap.

The flashest place in town is the *Hotel Tapian Nauli* (☎ 21116), at the northern end of town on Jalan S Parman 5. Large rooms with balcony, bathroom and breakfast cost 55,000 rp.

Places to Eat

To compensate for Sibolga's other drawbacks, there are some good restaurants and an ice-cream place on the corner across from the cinema. The *Telok Indah*, at Jalan Ahmad Yani 63-65, does good, but expensive, Chinese food.

Getting There & Away

Bus The main bus station is on Jalan Sisingamangaraja and is a busy stop on the Bukittinggi-Parapat-Medan route with a steady flow of departures north and south. A number of bus companies have their own offices and terminals around town.

Makmur and Bintang Udara bus companies, on Jalan Sutoyo, have buses to Parapat and Medan, departing in the morning or the evening only. ALS, on Jalan Sutoyo 30 also has buses to Bukittinggi and Jakarta. PO Terang, at Jalan Diponegoro 50, has buses to Padang and Bukittinggi.

Typical fares and journey times from Sibolga are: Bukittinggi (10,000 rp; 12 hours); Medan (9000 rp; eight hours); and Parapat (7000 rp; four hours).

The daily tourist bus between Medan and Sibolga is a very easy way to travel. It will take you from hotel door to hotel door for 15,000 rp, leaving at 8 am in each direction.

Taxi Shared cabs are a good alternative to the buses. Inda Taxi (☎ 22123), at Jalan Ahmad Yani 105, has seats in cabs to Medan (15,000 rp) and Parapat (12,000 rp) among other destinations.

Boat Ferries to Nias leave from the harbour at the end of Jalan Horas. There are boats to Gunung Sitoli every night except Sunday and to Teluk Dalam on Monday, Wednesday and Friday. The official departure time is 8 pm for both services. Tickets for both can be bought at PT Simeulue at Jalan Pelabuhan 2. The office closes at 8 pm, but it's often possible to buy a ticket on the boat.

It's also possible to get from Sibolga to Gunung Sitoli on the Pelni liner *Lawit* during its fortnightly circuit that provides links to Padang, Tanjung Priok, Surabaya and beyond. Pelni (☎ 21193) is at Jalan Pela-buhan 46.

Getting Around

Becaks theoretically cost 500 rp for most distances in town. But try telling this to the riders at the bus station.

Nias

Nias is an island almost the size of Bali, 125 km off the west coast of Sumatra. Magnificent beaches and one of the world's best surfing breaks combined with an ancient megalithic culture and unique customs, make it one of Sumatra's most exotic destinations.

The Indonesian government is now hoping to raise the profile of Nias as a tourist spot by pushing for the inclusion of the famous Lagundri Bay surfing break on the world professional surfing circuit. An inaugural pro tournament was held in July 1994 in a bid to persuade organisers that Nias can stage such an event.

There's talk of more resorts to follow in the footsteps of the plush new Sorake Beach Resort at Lagundri, and of a new airport to ferry in the jet set. All that may be a while off, but the changes already are being felt.

History

Local legend has it that all Niassans are the descendants of six gods who came to earth and located in the central highlands.

Academics have come up with a host of theories to explain such customs as the use of stone to produce monumental works of art. Niassans have been linked to the Bataks of Sumatra, the Naga of Assam in India, the aborigines of Taiwan, and various Dayak groups in Kalimantan.

Head-hunting and human sacrifice once played a part in Niassan culture, as it did in the culture of the Bataks.

The Niassans developed a way of life based mainly on agriculture and pig raising. Hunting and fishing, despite the thick jungle and the proximity of many villages to the coast, was of secondary importance. The Niassans relied on the cultivation of yams, rice, maize and taro. Pigs were both a source of food and of wealth and prestige; the more pigs you had, the greater your status in the village. Gold and copper work, as well as woodcarving, were important village industries.

The indigenous religion was thought to have been a combination of animism and ancestor worship, with some Hindu influences. Today, most people are either Christian or Muslim, but their beliefs are overlaid with traditional beliefs. Christianity was introduced by the missionaries who followed the arrival of the Dutch military in the 1860s. Islam is found in some villages and in larger towns like Gunung Sitoli.

Traditionally, Niassan villages were presided over by a village chief, heading a council of elders. Beneath the aristocratic upper caste were the common people, and below them the slaves (often used as trade merchandise).

Sometimes villages would band together in federations, which were often perpetually at war with other federations. Prior to the Dutch conquest, inter-village warfare was fast and furious, usually spurred on by the desire for revenge, slaves, or human heads. Heads were needed when a new village was built and for the burial of a chief. In central Nias, heads were reportedly a prerequisite for marriage. Today you can still see samples of the weapons used in these feuds: vests of buffalo hide or crocodile skin; helmets of metal, leather or plaited rattan; spears, swords and shields.

Until the first years of the 19th century, when people like the Englishman Sir Stamford Raffles began to send back reports about the island, the name of Nias rarely featured. When it did, it was as a source of slaves.

The island did not come under full Dutch control until 1914.

Today's population of just under 600,000 is spread through more than 650 villages, most inaccessible by road.

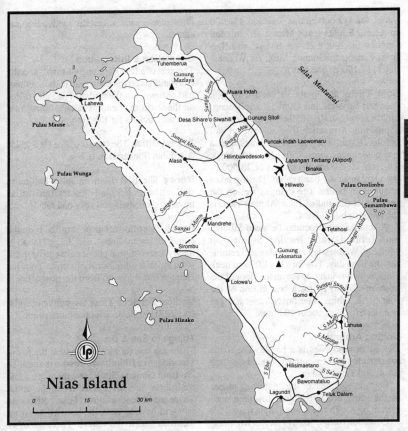

Nias Island

0   15   30 km

Orientation & Information

Most of the interesting places are in the south and that's where most travellers head. Teluk Dalam is the port and main town of the south. Gunung Sitoli, in the north, is the island's biggest town. The only airport is nearby.

Money Change money before you arrive. Exchange rates at the bank in Gunung Sitoli aren't much better than the miserable rates at the moneychangers in Teluk Dalam and Lagundri.

Health Chloroquine-resistant malaria has

been reported on Nias so take appropriate precautions.

Organised Tours

Companies like Nias Holidays (☎ 21010), at Jalan Lagundri 46 in Gunung Sitoli, offer a range of guided tours to all parts of the island. Guides can be hired through the tourist office for 25,000 rp per day if you want to set your own programme.

Getting There & Away

Air SMAC has daily flights from Medan to Binaka airport, 10 km south of Gunung

Sitoli, for 117,000 rp one way and 231,000 rp return. Flights leave Medan at 7 am and Gunung Sitoli at 8.25 am. SMAC also flies from Padang to Gunung Sitoli on Wednesday (117,100 rp one way).

Boat There are boats in each direction between Sibolga and Gunung Sitoli every night except Sunday. In theory, they leave at 8 pm, but in practice they seldom set sail before 10 pm. They are cargo boats with a few passenger cabins – often hot and airless. The fare is 9500 rp deck class or 13,500 rp for a bed in a four-berth cabin. The trip takes about eight hours. The Pelni office, on the seafront at the end of Jalan Ahmad Yani, is the place to buy tickets.

A smaller boat operates between Sibolga and Teluk Dalam, leaving Sibolga on Monday, Wednesday and Friday and returning the next day. The fare is 11,000 rp deck class, which is just a space on the floor of the boat, or 16,000 rp for a bed in one of the four-berth cabins. The boats leave at 8 pm and the trip takes about 10 hours.

Getting Around
Getting around Nias is a hassle. The roads are terrible apart from those around Gunung Sitoli and Teluk Dalam.

Fortunately, most of the interesting places in the south are fairly close together, connected by rough roads and jungle tracks.

Conditions on the 'Trans-Niassan Highway' between Gunung Sitoli and Teluk Dalam are very reminiscent of the Trans-Sumatran Highway 15 years ago. Nature continues to give the road builders a good fight in the mountains and the 120-km journey takes about five hours – if all goes well.

Motorised transport is infrequent and uncomfortable and many villages are only accessible by foot. You can also catch rides on trucks or negotiate pillion rides on motorbikes.

GUNUNG SITOLI
Situated on the north-eastern coast of Nias, this is the island's main town with a population of about 27,000. It's a fairly innocuous

little place with a certain seedy, tropical charm.

Orientation & Information
The port is a few km north of town, and the bus station is on the main road in the southern part of town past the bridge. The Pelni office on the seafront at end of Jalan Ahmad Yani also sells tickets for the Sibolga ferries.

Tourist Office The tourist office (☎ 21545) is at Jalan Soekarno 6.

Money The BNI 1946 on Jalan Pattimura will change US and Australian dollar travellers' cheques at a very bad rate.

Post & Telephone The post office is on the corner of Jalan Gomo and Jalan Hatta. In theory, international phone calls can be made from the telecommunications office on Jalan Hatta, a few doors up from the post office.

Medical Services There is a public hospital (☎ 21271) on Jalan Ciptmangunkusumo.

Things to See & Do
There are several nice **walks** near the town. The village of **Hilimbawodesolo** is about 14 km from Gunung Sitoli, and there are some traditional houses uphill from the road. There are occasional direct buses, otherwise you will have to walk the last two km from the main road to the village. There are other traditional houses on the road between the airport and Gunung Sitoli.

Places to Stay & Eat
Accommodation is generally expensive, dirty and depressing. The best place to stay is the *Wisma Soliga*, although it's four km from the town centre on the main road. It's clean, spacious and has good Chinese food. Rooms start from 10,000 rp for a double, and there are rooms with air-con for 25,000 rp. The manager can organise tickets and transport.

The *Hotel Gomo* (☎ 21926), in the centre of town at Jalan Gomo 148, has cheap rooms upstairs for 8000 rp. They are bright and airy

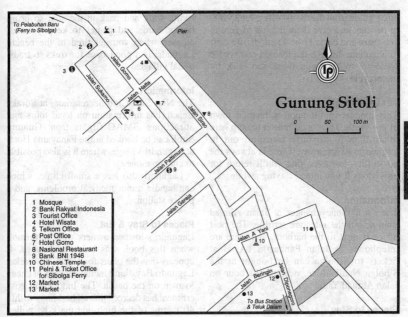

Gunung Sitoli

0   50   100 m

To Pelabuhan Baru
(Ferry to Sibolga)

Pier

1 Mosque
2 Bank Rakyat Indonesia
3 Tourist Office
4 Hotel Wisata
5 Telkom Office
6 Post Office
7 Hotel Gomo
8 Nasional Restaurant
9 Bank BNI 1946
10 Chinese Temple
11 Pelni & Ticket Office
     for Sibolga Ferry
12 Market
13 Market

To Bus Station
& Teluk Dalam

compared to the dark and more expensive air-con rooms downstairs. The *Hotel Wisata* (☎ 21858), at Jalan Sirao 2, has doubles for 9500 rp or 12,500 rp with bath, but there are no air-con rooms.

The *Hawaii Hotel*, at Jalan Ahmad Yani, has doubles with mandi for 12,500 rp and air-con for 20,000 rp.

The cell-like *Hotel Beringin*, on Jalan Beringin, has rooms for 5000 rp. Cheaper and even sadder is the *Penginapan Banuada* on Jalan Kopri.

Getting There & Around

To/From Teluk Dalam There are daily buses between Gunung Sitoli and Teluk Dalam. Normally two or three buses depart anytime between 8 and 10 am. The fare is 7000 rp and the journey takes at least five hours. Buses from Gunung Sitoli leave from the terminal on Jalan Diponegoro, and also meet the boats at the port.

There are also irregular boats connecting

the two towns, but they are not an attractive alternative, taking between seven and 10 hours and costing 9000 rp.

To/From the Airport SMAC operates a minibus between Binaka airport and Gunung Sitoli for 3000 rp.

GOMO

The most famous reminders of the island's megalithic past are the menhirs (single standing stones) and stone carvings around Gomo in the central highlands of southern Nias. The most spectacular examples are at **Tundrumbaho**, near the village of Lahusa, five km from Gomo. Some are believed to have been fashioned between 3000 and 5000 BC.

Gomo is not an easy place to get to. There's no public transport, and there's no road for the final eight of the 44 km from Teluk Dalam.

A good option from Gunung Sitoli is to

hire a guide from the tourist office for 25,000 rp per day and give them the job of getting you there and back. From Lagundri, it's best to negotiate through the losmen owners for someone to take you there and back by motorcycle.

TELUK DALAM

This nondescript little port is the main town of the south. There's no reason to stop here other than to organise transport out to Lagundri, 12 km away. There is always the possibility, however, that you'll return for provisions if you intend staying awhile.

Information

There's a moneychanger at Jalan Ahmad Yani 4, but the rates are terrible. The post office is next to the harbour, and there are telephones at Jalan Pancasila 1A. Boat tickets to Sibolga can be bought at the Sibolga Nauli office, near the harbour on Jalan Ahmad Yani.

Places to Stay

If you get stuck, *Wisma Jamburae* is on the waterfront with clean rooms for 8000 rp. The more expensive *Hotel Ampera*, on Jalan Pasar, has clean rooms with mandi from 15,000 rp.

Getting There & Away

The principal destination, Lagundri, is about 12 km from Teluk Dalam. It's 1000 rp by truck or bemo or 2500 rp by motorbike.

There are also buses to the villages of Bawomataluo and Hilisimaetano (1200 rp).

LAGUNDRI

For years, travellers have been calling this place 'Lagundi' (minus the 'r'), but every available Indonesian map and brochure insists that Lagundri is the correct name.

Whatever the spelling, its perfect horseshoe bay is the reason most people come to Nias. The surfing break is at the mouth of the bay off Sorake Beach, and there is good swimming at the back of the bay on Lagundri Beach.

There's not much to do here except surf, swim, walk and bask in the sun, so bring books, cards and games to keep yourself amused when you get tired of the beach. Lagundri is a good base for treks to traditional villages.

Information

The Nias Surf Club Secretariate, at Sorake Beach, has information on local tours and attractions. SMAC flights from Gunung Sitoli can be booked at the Fanayama Hotel at Lagundri Village, where it is also possible to change money.

Lagundri also has a small clinic, which can handle minor medical problems, and a police station.

Places to Stay & Eat

Lagundri's losmen owners were in turmoil when this book was being researched. It appears that the plans for a new, up-market Lagundri Bay didn't include dozens of cheap losmen on the beach. The Indonesian government has decreed that all buildings within 40 metres of the high-tide mark be pulled down and relocated further back.

Until this happens, the bay is ringed by dozens of ridiculously cheap losmen, all very similar in price and style, costing from around 1000 to 2000 rp for a single room, or double that for a bungalow. In spite of the dire predictions, the cheapies are likely to be around for a while longer.

All the losmen provide food and the menus are mostly the same. The cheap accommodation is subsidised by the food, so losmen owners can get justifiably peeved if their lodgers eat somewhere else.

It's possible to buy fresh fish and lobster very cheaply on the beach from local fishermen and get your losmen to cook it for you.

The most popular places to stay are those closest to the surf break, such as *Olamaya* and *Sun Beach*. The *Damai*, tucked around the corner to the west of the headland, offers comparative seclusion. There are more losmen, including the *Risky, Magdalena* and the *Yanti*, near the centre of the horseshoe bay. All three are good and cheap and the owners are friendly. If you're into swimming rather than surfing, its beach is the place to be.

The next step up the price scale is occupied by places like the bizarre *Fanayama Motel*, a crumbling concrete dump behind the Yanti, with overpriced doubles for 15,000 rp. The *Lantana Inn*, an uninspiring modern place on the road to Teluk Dalam, has doubles with breakfast for 20,000 rp.

The new *Sorake Beach Resort* is a sign of things to come, with doubles expected to cost about 80,000 rp when it opens.

Getting There & Away
Lagundri is about 12 km from Teluk Dalam: 1000 rp by truck or bemo or 2500 rp by motorbike.

Buses from Gunung Sitoli usually stop at the crossroads between Teluk Dalam and Lagundri Beach, where there are boys on motorbikes waiting to take travellers the last six km to Lagundri for 2000 rp. If you're going to Gunung Sitoli, it's better to go to Teluk Dalam first as buses are usually full by the time they reach the crossroads.

THE SOUTHERN VILLAGES
The architecture of southern Nias is completely different to that of the north. Whereas the houses of the north are free-standing oblong structures on stilts with thatch roofs, the more sophisticated houses of the south are built shoulder to shoulder on either side of a long, paved courtyard. Both the northern and southern houses emphasise the roof as the primary feature. Houses are constructed using pylons and cross-beams slotted together without the use of bindings or nails.

Southern villages were built on high ground with defence in mind. Often stone walls were built around the village. Stone was used to pave the area between the two rows of houses, the bathing pools and staircases. Benches, chairs and memorials were also made out of carved stone.

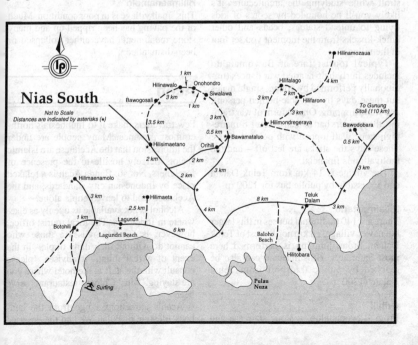

Nias South

Not to Scale
Distances are indicated by asterisks (*)

SUMATRA

Bawomataluo

This is the most famous, and the most accessible, of the southern villages. It is also the setting for *lompat batu* (stone jumping), featured on Indonesia's 1000 rp note.

As the name suggests (Bawomatuluo translates as 'sun hill'), the village is perched on a hill about 400 metres above sea level. The final approach is up 88 steep stone steps.

Houses are arranged along two main stone-paved avenues which meet opposite the impressive chief's house, thought to be the oldest and largest on Nias. Outside are stone tables where dead bodies were once left to decay, and nearby is the 1.8-metre stone structure for jumping (see below). The houses themselves look like rows of washed-up Spanish galleons.

Although it's still worth exploring, Bawomataluo is on every tourist itinerary and villagers have learned to view foreigners as money jars waiting to be emptied.

Don't arrive expecting to take a casual stroll while studying the architecture: it's likely you'll be hounded by scores of kids trying to unload statues, beads and other knick-knacks from the moment you set foot in the village.

Typical tourist fare at Bawomataluo includes fairly half-hearted war dances (traditionally performed by young, single males but these days by any able-bodied person), and stone jumping. Once a form of war training, the jumpers had to leap over a 1.8-metre-high stone wall topped with pointed sticks. These days the sticks are left off – and the motivation is financial.

The village is 14 km from Teluk Dalam and accessible by public bus for 1200 rp.

Hilisimaetano

There are 140 traditional houses in this larger but newer village, 16 km north-west of Teluk Dalam. Stone jumping is performed here most Saturdays. Hilisimaetano can also be reached by public transport from Teluk Dalam (1200 rp).

Orihili

From Bawomataluo, a stone staircase and trail leads downhill to the village of Orihili. From Bawomataluo you can see the rooftops of Orihili in a clearing in the trees.

Botohili

This is a smaller village on the hillside above the peninsula of Lagundri Beach. It has two rows of traditional houses, with a number of new houses breaking up the skyline. The remains of the original entrance way, stone chairs and paving can still be seen.

Hilimaeta

This village is similar to Botohili and also within easy walking distance of Lagundri. The stone-jumping pylon can still be seen and there are a number of stone monuments, including benches and a four-legged stone table. In the middle of the paved area stands a two-metre-high stone penis. A long pathway of stone steps leads uphill to the village.

Hilimaenamolo

This small village is in poor condition. Much of the paving has been ripped up and many stone monuments have either collapsed or been dismantled.

Aceh

Few travellers make it to Indonesia's northernmost province. Many people are under the impression that the Acehnese are Islamic zealots fiercely hostile to the presence of foreigners. Not so. Banda Aceh is a relaxed place by Indonesian city standards, and the Acehnese tend to leave people alone.

Alcohol is not available as openly as elsewhere in Indonesia. The local tourist office, however, is keen to reassure those who cannot do without their daily tipple. 'In the event of a real thirst,' it advises, 'please consult with the staff at the hotel where you are staying.' Most Chinese restaurants serve beer.

Aceh's attractions range from the laid-back lifestyle of Pulau We and the deserted

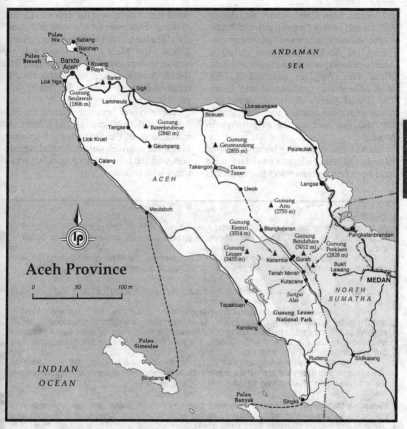

Aceh Province

0   50   100 m

beaches of the rugged west coast to the jungle wilderness of Gunung Leuser National Park that straddles the central mountains.

History

I am the mighty ruler of the Regions below the wind, who holds sway over the land of Aceh and over the land of Sumatra and over all the lands tributary to Aceh, which stretch from the sunrise to the sunset.

This extract, from a letter sent by the Sultan of Aceh to Queen Elizabeth I of England in 1585, marked the beginning of a trade agreement between Aceh and England that lasted until the 19th century. It also shows the extent of Aceh's sphere of influence as a trading nation, as well as providing a colourful assessment of Aceh's importance.

Years before Melaka fell to the Portuguese, Aceh was Melaka's chief competitor for trade. Rivalry between them was intensified by religious hostility as Aceh was one of the earliest centres of Islam in the archipelago.

Religious differences and the harsh Portuguese rule spurred many traders of different nationalities – Islamic scholars, Egyptians and Arabians, craftspeople from India and goldsmiths from China – into abandoning Melaka and setting themselves up in Aceh.

The influx of traders and immigrants contributed to Aceh's wealth and influence. Aceh's main exports were pepper and gold; others were ivory, tin, tortoiseshell, camphor, aloe-wood, sandalwood and spices. The city of Aceh was also important as a centre of Islamic learning and as a gateway for Muslims making the pilgrimage to Mecca.

Aceh is also interesting because, despite its early and strong allegiance to Islam, there have been four women rulers (although it is possible that real power lay with a council of 12 men). However, such a state of 'grace' could not last and in 1699 a legal recommendation from Mecca condemned rule by women as contrary to Islamic practice. The fourth woman ruler was deposed and replaced by a government headed by religious leaders.

Aceh's power began to decline towards the end of the 17th century, but it remained independent of the Dutch for a long time. Singapore and Aceh were active trading partners with the help of a long-standing secret treaty with Britain.

The Acehnese

As a result of their history of extensive and mixed immigration, Aceh's population is a blend of Indonesian, Arab, Tamil, Chinese and indigenous groups. Curiously, some of the tallest people in Indonesia live here.

Ethnic groups include the Gayo and Alas in the mountains, the Minangkabau along the west coast, the Kluetin in the south, and Javanese and Chinese throughout.

Religion Aceh is the most staunchly Muslim part of Sumatra and Christians and Buddhists comprise only a small percentage of the population.

Nevertheless, animism is also part of the everyday fabric of Acehnese life. There is a prevailing popular belief in the existence of spirits who dwell in old trees, wells, rocks and stones. Ghosts and evil spirits are said to be particularly malicious around dusk when they can wreak havoc on all those they come in contact with. *Dukuns* are still called in to help solve grievances, cure illnesses and cast spells on enemies.

Offerings and rituals are still observed at significant times of the agricultural year, such as harvest time, and dreams and omens are interpreted. In some parts of Sumatra, pilgrimages are made to the tombs of Acehnese scholars and religious leaders.

Weapons Metallurgy was learned early from Arab and Persian traders and, because of Aceh's continued involvement in wars, weapon-making became a highly developed skill. Acehnese daggers and swords comprise three parts: blade, handle and sheath. The blade can have both edges sharpened or just one, and can be straight, concave or convex. The handles of weapons are usually made of buffalo horn, wood or bone, and carved in the form of a crocodile's mouth, a horse's hoof or a duck's tail and embellished with gold or silver. The sheaths are made of rattan, silver or wood and fastened with bands of a mixture of gold, brass and copper called *sousa*.

The best example of this art form is the *rencong*, a dagger which has a convex iron and damascene blade with one sharpened edge. Less well-known Acehnese weapons are the *siwah* (knife) and *pedang* (a pointed sword).

Jewellery While there is a long tradition – stemming from the early days of the sultanate – of fine craftsmanship in gold and silver jewellery, there is almost no antique jewellery to be found in Aceh today. Much of it was sold to raise money for the war against the Dutch.

Excellent gold and silver jewellery is still produced but there is not much variation in design.

Weaving & Embroidery Despite its long history and high reputation, Acehnese weaving is rapidly disappearing. On the other hand, embroidery is a very vital art form. Areas around Sigli, Meulaboh and Banda Aceh are renowned for embroidery using gold-coloured metallic thread *(soedjoe)* on tapestry, cushions, fans and wall hangings. The main motifs are flowers, foliage and geometric

That came to an end in 1871 when the Dutch negotiated a treaty in which the British withdrew any objections to the possibility of a Dutch occupation of Aceh. The Acehnese tried to counteract this blow by negotiating with both the Italian and US consuls in Singapore. The draft of a US-Acehnese treaty of friendship was sent to Washington. The Dutch, however, forestalled further attempts by declaring war on Aceh in 1873.

The first Dutch expeditionary force of 7000 retreated when its commander, General Kohler, was killed. A new army contingent, twice as large, succeeded in taking the capital, the central mosque and the sultan's palace, but the war went on for 35 years before the last of the sultans, Tuanku Muhamat Dawot, surrendered. Even then, no Dutch area was safe from sabotage or guerrilla attack from the Acehnese until the Dutch surrendered to Japan in 1942.

The Japanese were welcomed at first but resistance soon sprang up when local institutions were not respected. This period saw the Islamic Party, which had been formed in 1939 under the leadership of Daud Beureuh, emerge as a political force.

SUMATRA

designs and the finished work is also decorated with mirrors, golden pailletes, sequins and beads in an effect known as *blet blot*.

Mendjot beboengo is a kind of embroidery from the Gayo and Alas regions south of Takengon, traditionally done only by men. Stylised motifs of geometric flowers in red, white, yellow and green thread are embroidered on a black background.

Other Crafts Various domestic items are made from coconut husks, tree bark, water buffalo horns, palm leaves and clay. These include spoons, baskets, mats, earthenware pots and dishes.

Music & Dance Every region in Aceh has its local dances, but there are three that are popular throughout the province – the *seudati*, *meusakat* and *ranub lam puan*.

Typical Acehnese instruments include: a three-stringed zither (called an *arbab)* made of wood from the jackfruit tree with strings of bamboo, rattan or horsetail hair; bamboo flutes *(buloh merindu, bangsi, tritit* and *soeling)*; and gongs and tambourines *(rapai)*. The tambourines are made of goatskin, while the gongs are usually brass (sometimes dried goatskin) and are struck with padded wooden hammers. They come in three sizes: *gong, canang* and *mong-mong*.

Seudati This is a quick-tempoed dance which involves a complicated pattern of forward, sideways and backward leaps. The songs are led by a dancer (called the *syech)* and two narrators *(aneuk syahi)*, and no instruments are used. The rhythm is accentuated by the variation in the movements of the dancers, who also heighten the tension by snapping their fingers and beating their chests. The pace is hotted up even more when contests are held between performing groups.

The traditional Seudati has five parts: the *salaam* (greeting), *likok* (special movements), *kisah* (story), *dhiek* (poetry) and *syahi* (songs). This dance has also been used to disseminate information on government policy and to urge people to become better Muslims.

Meusakat Known as the dance of the thousand hands, Meusakat originated in the region of Meulaboh and is performed by a group of 13 young women. It consists of a series of precise hand, head, shoulder and torso movements. Traditionally, the dance was performed to glorify Allah or to offer prayers.

Like the seudati, no instruments are used. The songs are led by a girl positioned in the middle of a row of kneeling performers.

Ranub Lam Puan This is a modern adaptation of various traditional dances from throughout Aceh. It is performed to welcome guests and to convey hospitality, which is symbolised in the offering of betel nut or snacks by the dancers.

The *seurene kalee*, a single-reed woodwind, provides the haunting musical accompaniment. ■

In 1951, the central government dissolved the province of Aceh and incorporated its territory into the province of North Sumatra under a governor in Medan. Dissatisfaction was so widespread that Daud Beureuh proclaimed Aceh an Islamic Republic in September 1953. This state lasted until 1961 when military and religious leaders had a falling out.

The central government resolved the conflict by giving Aceh provincial status again. The military yielded to this decision because it felt its objective had been achieved and the religious leaders, without the support of the military, were forced to surrender. Jakarta later granted special status to the province in the areas of religion, culture and education and in 1967, Aceh was given the title of Special Territory.

BANDA ACEH

Banda Aceh, the capital of Aceh, is a sprawling city at the northern tip of Sumatra. It's an odd mix of faded grandeur and modern architecture. Money is being poured into the region and prestige building projects – mosques in particular – are everywhere.

Orientation & Information

The city centre is dominated by the magnificent, imposing, black-domed great mosque, the Mesjid Raya Baiturrahman. Clustered around it are markets, bus stations and some hotels. The city is split in two by the waters of the Krueng Aceh River.

Tourist Office The tourist office (☎ 23692) is at Jalan Chik Kuta Karang 3.

Money The best rates are to be found at the Bank of Central Asia at Jalan Panglima Polem 38-40. The BNI 1946 is at Jalan Kh Dahlan with reasonable rates for American Express US dollar travellers' cheques and dollars. The Bank Rakyat Indonesia, on Jalan Cut Meutia, will change only US dollar travellers' cheques.

Post & Telephone The main post office is on Jalan Teukuh Angkasah, one block from Simpang Tiga. International phone calls can be made from the Telkom office at Jalan Nyak Arief 92.

Pasar Aceh

The central meat and fish market on Jalan Sisingamangaraja is one of the most striking and lively in Sumatra. At the rear, by the river, you can see the boats unloading their cargoes of shark, tuna and prawns. Nearby, running off Jalan S M Yamin, is 'Banana Street', an alley full of banana stalls. It's a great place for people-watching.

Cultural Centre

For those with a more cultural bent, there is a new complex behind the governor's official residence, Pendopo. The complex, built in 1981 for the National Koran Reading Competition, comprises two modern buildings surrounding an open-air performance centre where dances and theatre are staged on special occasions.

Mesjid Raya Baiturrahman

With its stark white walls and liquorice-black domes, this imposing building is the city's best-known landmark. The first section of the mosque was kindly built by the Dutch in 1879 as a conciliatory gesture towards the Acehnese after the original one had been burnt down. Two more domes – one on either side of the first – were added by the Dutch in 1936 and another two in 1957 by the Indonesian government. Two new minarets were under construction in 1994. Non-Muslims are not allowed to enter any part of the mosque.

Gunongan

For a contrast in architectural styles, go and see the Gunongan on Jalan Teuku Umar, near the clocktower. This 'stately pleasure dome' was built by Sultan Iskandar Muda (who reigned from 1607-36) as a gift for his wife, a Malayan princess, and was intended as a private playground and bathing place. Its three storeys are each meant to resemble an open leaf or flower. The building itself is a series of frosty peaks with narrow stairways and a walkway leading to hummocks, which were supposed to represent the hills of her native land.

Directly across from the Gunongan is a low, vaulted gate in the traditional Pintu Aceh style which gave access to the sultan's palace – supposedly for the use of royalty only.

These architectural curiosities, plus a few white-washed tombs, are about all that remains to remind today's visitor of the past glories of the Acehnese sultanates.

Dutch Cemetery (Kherkhof)

Close to the Gunongan is the last resting place for more than 2000 Dutch and Indonesian soldiers who died fighting the Acehnese. The entrance is about 250 metres from the clocktower on the road to Uleh-leh. Tablets implanted in the walls by the entrance gate are inscribed with the names of the dead soldiers.

Museum Negeri Aceh

The museum at Jalan Aloudin Mahmudsyah 12 has a good display of Acehnese weaponry, household furnishings, ceremonial costumes, everyday clothing, gold jewellery and calligraphy.

In the same compound is the **Rumah Aceh** – a fine example of traditional Acehnese architecture, built without nails and held together with cord or pegs. It contains more Acehnese artefacts and war memorabilia. In front of the Rumah Aceh is a huge cast-iron bell, the Cakra Donya, said to have been given to the Acehnese by a Chinese Emperor centuries ago.

They are both open Tuesday to Sunday from 9 am to 1 pm and 3 to 6 pm, and cost 200 rp.

Places to Stay – bottom end

There are no great budget hotel bargains to be found in Banda Aceh.

The *Losmen International*, conveniently located on Jalan Ahmad Yani opposite the night markets, has been out of action since it was gutted by fire in October 1993. There's no indication of any attempt to repair the damage.

The *Losmen Pacific* (☎ 31364), at Jalan Ahmad Yani 22 opposite the shell of the International, is an odd place that seems strangely suspicious of foreigners wanting a room. It has doubles for 12,000 rp.

Much more welcoming is the *Losmen Palembang*, nearby at Jalan Khairil Anwar 51, with doubles starting at 10,000 rp. It charges 24,000 rp for a double with air-con and bathroom. Further along the road, at No 16, is the *Losmen Aceh Barat* (☎ 23250) with similar prices.

Away from the city centre, the sprawling *Wisma Lading* (☎ 21359), at Jalan Cut Meutia 9, has doubles with mandi for 10,000 rp and with air-con for 20,000 rp.

The *Hotel Sri Budaya* (☎ 21751), on Jalan Prof A Majid Ibrahim III 5E, has basic rooms for 10,000 rp, rooms with mandi for 12,000 rp and air-con rooms for 20,000 rp.

One place to stay well clear of is the *Losmen Aceh* (☎ 21354), opposite the mosque on Jalan Mohammed Jam. After 40 years without a cent being spent on maintenance, 'dilapidated charm' has become dangerously decrepit. It has doubles for 5000 rp, if you dare. It has some better rooms out the back for 20,000 rp with air-con.

Places to Stay – middle

The *Hotel Medan* (☎ 22636), at Jalan Ahmad Yani 15, has clean but characterless rooms starting from 20,000 rp. Rooms with air-con, TV and hot water cost 50,000 rp.

Next door at No 17, the popular *Wisma Prapat* (☎ 22159) has doubles with mandi and fan for 18,000 rp. It also has rooms with air-con and TV for 27,500 rp.

The *Hotel Raya* (☎ 21427), at Jalan Mesjid Raya 30, is a small, friendly place with some air-con rooms for 20,000 rp.

The *Hotel Rasa Sayung Aya* (☎ 22846), diagonally opposite the Seutia bus station on Jalan Teuku Umar, is a long way out of town. It is, however, very well kept and the rooms have big double beds, carpet and TV for 40,000 rp.

SUMATRA

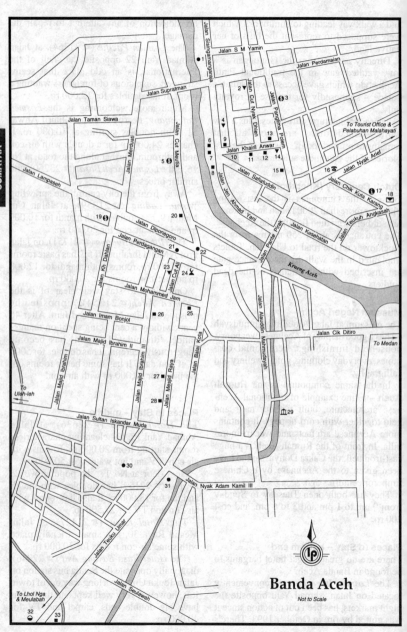

Jalan S M Yamin

Jalan Siangmangaraja

Jalan Perdamaian

Jalan Supratman

Jalan Cut Nyak Dhien

Jalan Panglima Polem

To Tourist Office &
Pelabuhan Malahayati

Jalan Taman Siswa

Jalan Merduati

Jalan Cut Meutia

Jalan Khairil Anwar

Jalan Nyak Arief

Jalan Chik Kuta Karang

Jalan Lampaseh

Jalan Safiatuddin

Jalan Jen Ahmad Yani

Jalan Teukuh Angkasah

Jalan Diponegoro

Jalan Perdagangan

Jalan Pante Pirak

Jalan Kesehatan

Jalan Kh Dahlan

Jalan Cut Ali

Jalan Mohammed Jam

Krueng Aceh

Jalan Imam Bonjol

Jalan Alauddin Mahmudsyah

Jalan Majid Ibrahim II

Jalan Cik Ditiro

Jalan Majid Ibrahim 1

Jalan Majid Ibrahim III

Jalan Mesjid Raya

Jalan Balai Kota

To Medan

To
Uleh-leh

Jalan Sultan Iskandar Muda

Jalan Teuku Umar

Jalan Nyak Adam Kamil III

Jalan Seulawah

To Lhok Nga
& Meulaboh

Banda Aceh

Not to Scale

PLACES TO STAY	PLACES TO EAT	18	Post Office

PLACES TO STAY

- 6 Losmen International
- 7 Wisma Prapat
- 8 Hotel Medan
- 9 Losmen Pacific
- 11 Losmen Palembang
- 12 Hotel Cakra Donya
- 13 Losmen Aceh Barat
- 15 Sultan Hotel
- 20 Wisma Lading
- 25 Losmen Aceh
- 26 Hotel Sri Budaya
- 27 Hotel Kuala Tripa
- 28 Hotel Raya
- 33 Hotel Rasa Sayung Aya

PLACES TO EAT

- 2 Restoran Aroma
- 4 Restoran Tropicana
- 14 Satyva Modern Bakery
- 23 Rumah Makan Aceh Spesifik

OTHER

- 1 Pasar Aceh
- 3 Bank of Central Asia
- 5 Bank Rakyat Indonesia
- 10 Night Market
- 16 Telkom Office
- 17 Tourist Office
- 18 Post Office
- 19 Bank BNI 1946
- 21 Central Market
- 22 Opelet Station
- 24 Mesjid Raya Baiturrahman
- 29 Museum Negeri Aceh & Cakra Donya
- 30 Dutch Cemetery (Kherkof)
- 31 Gunongan
- 32 Bus Station

SUMATRA

Places to Stay – top end

The best hotel in town is the three-star *Kuala Tripa* (☎ 21879), at Jalan Mesjid Raya 24. The cheapest double costs 108,000 rp. You can pay 2500 rp to use the pool if you're not staying here.

The *Sultan Hotel* (☎ 23581), also blessed with three stars, is a lot more comfortable than its concrete box exterior would indicate. It's in the heart of town in an alley leading off Jalan Panglima Polem and has pokey little rooms for 40,000 rp; otherwise singles/doubles start at 60,000/80,000 rp.

The modern *Hotel Cakra Donya* (☎ 23735), at Jalan Khairil Anwar 10, is very similar in price and style to the Sultan.

Places to Eat

The table-filled square at the corner of Jalan Ahmad Yani and Jalan Khairil Anwar, in the centre of town, is the setting for Banda Aceh's lively night food market, known as the Rek. The square is ringed by more than 30 stalls serving everything from Padang food to seafood.

If there's nothing here that takes your fancy, Jalan Jalan Ahmad Yani is a good place to start looking for food. The *Restoran Tropicana*, at Nos 90-92, does Chinese and European meals, as does the *Aroma* on nearby Jalan Cut Nyak Dhien.

The difference between Acehnese food and Padang food is hard for the amateur to detect, but you can try your luck at places such as the *Aceh Spesifik*, behind the Mesjid Raya on Jalan Cut Ali.

The Acehnese like their cakes and pastries as much as anyone in Indonesia. The *Satyva Modern Bakery*, at Jalan Khairil Anwar 3, is a good place to try.

Things to Buy

There are several markets in Banda Aceh with a colourful jumble of stalls laden with different foodstuffs. In the large area beside the mosque, a vast central market sells fresh fruit and vegetables as well as household goods or utilitarian handicrafts (on the Jalan Diponegoro side).

Most of the jewellery shops are in a row along Jalan Perdagangan. Goldsmiths can produce any design you like provided they have something to copy from. If you are interested in antiques, there are several shops worth browsing around. Toko Daud, on Jalan Perdagangan, has a good selection of Acehnese weapons, including traditional knives and swords.

H Keucik Leumik, at Jalan Perdagangan 115, specialises in Acehnese antiques, but also has a good selection of old Dutch and Chinese porcelain.

Nya'na Souvenirs, at Jalan Singgahmata 9, has a good collection of embroidered bags etc and its prices are very reasonable. Close to the police station, on Jalan Cut Meutia, the

Pusat Promosi Industri Kecil also has a limited selection of handicrafts on display.

The Fona Agency, opposite the mosque, sells *Time, Newsweek* and the *Jakarta Post*.

Getting There & Away
Air Garuda has two direct flights a day between Banda Aceh and Medan (125,900 rp) continuing to Jakarta (439,000 rp).

The Garuda office is at the Hotel Sultan (☎ 22469).

Bus The main bus station is the Terminal Bus Seuti on Jalan Teuku Umar at the southern end of town. There are lots of departures to Medan, many of them leaving at night. The road is sealed all the way and the journey can take as little as nine hours. Fares start at 20,000 rp, and the best air-con services cost 30,000 rp.

It's best to book in advance and many companies have offices on Jalan Mohammed Jam. PMTOH is at No 58, Kurnia is at No 68 and Pelangi/Melati is at No 90.

Heading down the west coast, PMTOH and Aceh Barat run buses from Banda Aceh to Meulaboh (6000 rp; five hours). From Meulaboh, it's possible to continue to Tapaktuan and Sidikalang, and then complete a loop of northern Sumatra to Medan via Berastagi.

Bemos from Banda Aceh to Uleh-leh (300 rp) and Lhok Nga (500 rp) leave from Jalan Diponegoro, near the Mesjid Raya.

Getting Around
To/From the Airport The airport operates a voucher system for taxis. The 16-km ride into town costs 12,000 rp. Other destinations covered by the system are Lhok Nga (22,000 rp) and Krueng Raya (27,000 rp). Opelets (No 1) are a much cheaper way of getting between Banda Aceh and the airport at 500 rp, but you could face a long wait – and then find that there is no room.

Local Transport Opelets (known locally at *labi-labi)* are the main form of transport around town and cost 250 rp. There are also motorised becaks, which require the usual hard bargaining before you set off.

AROUND BANDA ACEH
Uleh-leh
Five km west of Banda Aceh is the old port of Uleh-leh where you can while away a few interesting hours watching the traders come in from outlying islands. There are some attractive villages around Uleh-leh and an unattractive, exposed black-sand beach. In colonial times, the Dutch fenced off part of the beach with metal netting and came here for a dip.

Pulau Beras
It's possible to hire a boat for a day from Uleh-leh and go out to Pulau Beras or one of the other islands off the coast of Banda Aceh. You may have to get permission from the harbour master before you set off.

Pulau Beras is lightly populated but most of the other islands are uninhabited. If you like snorkelling there are some good spots around these islands, so take equipment with you. You will also need food, drink, insect repellent and, if possible, life jackets.

Ujung Bate
Ujung Bate is another popular spot for Banda Aceh day-trippers, about 15 km from town on the road to Krueng Raya. It is a black-sand beach overlooking the Selat Melaka to Pulau We. There's not much to do other than stroll, hunt for shells and eat at the seafood restaurant.

Lhok Nga
Lhok Nga, 17 km west of Banda Aceh, is a popular weekend picnic spot. The beach is dominated by the loading operations of the Semen Andalas Indonesia cement company.

There's a beautiful white-sand Indian Ocean beach at nearby **Lampu'uk**. Women should dress modestly – most local women swim fully clothed.

Both the *Pondok Wisata Darlian* and *Pondok Wisata Mitabu*, at Lhok Nga, have doubles for 7000 rp.

The place to go if you want to relax in

comfort is the *Taman Tepi Laut Cottages* (☎ 32029). It has rooms and cottages priced from 30,000 to 50,000 rp. The more expensive rooms are some of the best appointed anywhere in Sumatra. Facilities at the park include an ocean swimming pool built into the rocky shoreline and fed by the incoming tide.

Opelets to Lhok Nga from Jalan Diponegoro, in Banda Aceh, are 700 rp.

PULAU WE

This spectacular island, at the north-western tip of the Indonesian archipelago, is a couple of hours by ferry from Banda Aceh. It has some magnificent palm-fringed beaches with coral reefs and rocky coves. The rugged, jungle-covered interior has some great hillside lookouts.

There are only 24,000 people on the island, most of them in the main town and port of Sabang. During Dutch rule, Sabang was a major coal and water depot for steam ships, but it went into decline with the arrival of diesel power after WW II.

During the 1970s it was a duty-free port, but when this status was eliminated in 1986, Sabang once again became a sleepy fishing town. The only industry – other than fishing – is making rattan furniture.

For most people, Sabang is no more than an overnight stop on the way to the beaches at Gapang and Ibioh. It's pleasant enough, with some huge tamarind trees dominating the middle of town.

Picking the best time to visit the island is a bit of a lottery. Rain is never far away – different winds seem to bring rain from different directions. You can, however, be fairly sure that it will rain constantly from November until early January. July is supposedly the driest month.

Malaria has been reported on the island.

Information

The Stingray Dive Centre, in the centre of Sabang on the corner of Jalan Teuku Umar and Jalan Perdagangan, doubles as a tourist office. The manager, Mr Dodent, is a good source of information about the whys and wherefores of life on the island. There is also a small collection of second-hand books in English and German for sale or exchange.

The post office is at Jalan Perdagangan 66. The telephone office is next door, and is open 24 hours. It has a Home Country Direct phone.

Things to See & Do

The most popular beach is at **Ibioh**, the destination for most of the tourists coming to the island. Opposite Ibioh, 100 metres offshore (10,000 rp return by boat) is **Pulau Rubiah**, a densely forested island surrounded by spectacular coral reefs known as the **Sea Garden**. It is a favourite snorkelling and diving spot. The Stingray Dive Centre (☎ (0652) 21265) in Sabang hires out diving gear and snorkelling equipment as well as organising trips to a range of diving locations. It also has an 'office' at Ibioh.

Adjacent to the Sea Garden is the **Ibioh Forest**, a nature reserve with plenty of native animals in the jungle. The reserve also has **coastal caves** that can be explored by boat.

Gapang Beach, around the headland from Ibioh, is another good spot. The coral here is dead, but the beach is great for swimming and there are fewer tourists.

Other beaches of note include **Pantai Paradiso**, a white-sand beach shaded by coconut palms just outside Sabang. Not much further away is **Pantai Kasih** and about 30 minutes from town is **Pantai Sumur Tiga**, a popular picnic place.

Less than two km from town is a serene freshwater lake called **Danau Anak Laut**, the source of the island's water supply. From the nearby hills it is possible to see the port and Sabang Bay.

Gunung Merapi is 17 km from town. This semi-active volcano holds boiling water in its caldera, and occasionally emits smoke.

Places to Stay

There are several cheap places to stay in Sabang. Both the *Losmen Irma* (☎ (0652) 21128), at Jalan Teuku Umar 3, and *Losmen Pulau Jaya* (☎ (0652) 21344), further up the street at No 17-25, are well set up for travellers.

The Pulau Jaya is marginally the better of the two. Prices start at 3500 rp for singles, ranging up to 12,500 rp for doubles with fan and mandi and 15,000 rp with air-con. The front rooms are noisy but the rear ones are quiet. The shared mandis have peepholes in the doors.

Prices are almost identical at the Losmen Irma. The only difference is that there are no air-con rooms. Their front rooms also get some street noise.

Tucked away in a quiet lane down Jalan Perdagangan is *Holiday Losmen* (☎ (0652) 21131), with rooms at 6000/10,000 rp and air-con rooms for 25,000 rp.

Accommodation at Ibioh is in the form of numerous bungalows for which you'll pay from 4000 to 7000 rp. Gapang has similar, but slightly more expensive bungalows.

Places to Eat

Sabang has a remarkable number of restaurants for a town of its size. The majority are along Jalan Perdagangan and serve cheap Padang food. The *Dynasty Restaurant*, at Jalan Perdagangan 26 (they seem to be disputing the address with the Padang restaurant next door), offers something a bit different with up-market Chinese food. It does a steak for 4000 rp – and you can wash it down with a cold beer for 3000 rp.

The *Restaurant Sabang*, opposite the Dynasty at No 27, serves a huge portion of sweet & sour fish for 4000 rp.

Yulie Coffie, downstairs from the Losmen Irma, has a range of pancakes and breakfast goodies aimed at the tourist trade.

The *Café Bar* at the Losmen Pulau Jaya is another place offering a tourist menu. It includes whole 'Kentucky' fried chicken for 7500 rp. It also sells cold beer.

The beach resorts at Ibioh and Gapang both have small restaurants offering basic meals, such as rice, fish and vegetables for 2000 rp.

Getting There & Away

Bemo There are regular bemos (No 1) to

Krueng Raya from Jalan Diponegoro in Banda Aceh. The bus trip costs 1500 rp and takes 45 minutes.

Boat Boats to Pulau We leave every afternoon at 3 pm (returning at 9 am the next morning) from the port of Krueng Raya, 35 km from Banda Aceh. The voyage takes two hours and costs 3900 rp in deck class or 5500 rp in 1st class. The difference between deck class and 1st class is minimal. There are two boats each way on Sundays, leaving Krueng Raya at 11 am and 6 pm and Pulau We at 9 am and 3 pm.

Getting Around

The ferries to Pulau We arrive at the port of Balohan – the brand new ferry terminus is virtually all that exists there. From Balohan, there are bemos for the 15-minute ride to Sabang, 12 km and 1500 rp away.

There are pick-up trucks from Sabang to Gapang and Ibioh at 10.30 am and 6 pm, returning at 7 am and 4 pm. They cost 2000 rp. In Sabang, they leave from outside the Stingray Dive Centre.

The island has a good road network and motorcycles are the ideal way to get around if you want to see a bit of the island. They can be rented from Yulie Coffie, with prices starting at about 15,000 rp per day for a Honda 90.

BANDA ACEH TO SIDIKALANG

Very few travellers make it to the remote west coast of Aceh, with its seemingly endless deserted Indian Ocean beaches backed by densely forested hills.

The journey from Banda Aceh to Sidikalang used to be another Sumatran endurance test – almost 700 twisting km of potholes and mud or dust, depending on the season. These days, it's plain sailing as far south as Tapaktuan, and even the final stretch from Tapaktuan to Sidikalang isn't too bad. From Sidikalang there is a good road to Medan.

It's best to take the journey in stages, stopping off to enjoy the surroundings en route.

Calang

Calang is a fairly nondescript small town 140 km south of Banda Aceh, but the beaches along this part of the coast are superb.

About 15 km north of Calang is the small village of **Lhok Geulumpang**, home to a small collection of tree-houses known officially as *Camp Europa*, but better known as 'Dieter's Farm', after its eccentric expatriate German owner.

The place is pitched at people who want to do nothing more active than meditate. Accommodation is in tree-houses, built in littoral rainforest just 100 metres from a deserted Indian Ocean beach. Doubles are priced from 15,000 to 40,000 rp, which includes all meals and tea/coffee through the day. The food is very basic.

The place is not set up for crowds. There are only seven tree-houses and accommodation for 14 people in all. There are no phones at Camp Europa, but it is possible to book in advance by fax (0651) 32139.

While the setting is indisputably magnificent, there have been a few complaints from travellers who object to the keeping of an orang-utan and a honey bear, both of which Dieter claims to be rehabilitating.

If Camp Europa is full, the nearest accommodation is in Calang, where the *Losmen Sri Jaya* has very simple doubles for 5000 rp.

Getting There & Away PMTOH and Aceh Barat operate regular buses to Calang from Banda Aceh (3500 rp; three hours) and Meulaboh (2000 rp; two hours). Drivers know the Camp Europa stop. Some locals know Dieter as 'Daud German'.

Meulaboh

Almost 250 km from Banda Aceh on the south-western coast is the small, sleepy town of Meulaboh.

There's good surf around Meulaboh, although the beaches close to town are dangerous for swimming because of strong currents. **Lhok Bubon**, 16 km back towards Banda Aceh, is a safe swimming beach

Meulaboh has an unusual monument to Acehnese resistance hero Teuku Umar – it's shaped like a traditional Acehnese hat (*kupiah meukeutop*).

There are half a dozen losmen in Meulaboh. The *Mutiara* (☎ 21531), at Jalan Teuku Umar 157, has rooms for 5000 rp as well as rooms with TV and air-con for 50,000 rp. The tiny *Mustika* (☎ 21033), at Jalan Nasional 78, has a similar choice.

The *Losmen Pelita Jaya* and *Losmen Erna*, on Jalan Singgahmata, both have doubles for 6000 rp.

Getting There & Away Meulaboh is a five-hour trip by road from Banda Aceh (5000 rp). SMAC flies between Medan and Meulaboh on Tuesday and Thurday (84,100 rp), and from Meulaboh to Sinabang, on Pulau Simeulue (58,800 rp).

Pulau Simeulue

The isolated island of Simeulue is known for its clove and coconut plantations and not much else. The island is said to be restful and the people friendly. There are few shops and no luxuries, but there is plenty of fruit, coffee, rice, noodles and fish.

Getting There & Away There are occasional boats from Meulaboh to Sinabang in deck class/1st class for 4900/9200 rp as well as weekly flights from Meulaboh.

Tapaktuan

This quiet place is about halfway between Meulaboh and Sidikalang. Tapaktuan can be used as a base to explore the lowland Kluet region of Gunung Leuser National Park. The unspoilt swamp forests are recommended for bird-watching, and support the densest population of primates in South-East Asia. It may be possible to hire guides through the national park office in Kandang, 38 km south of Tapaktuan.

The *Losmen Bukit Barisan*, at Jalan Merdeka 37, and the *Losmen Jambu*, at Jalan Ahmad Yani, have doubles priced from 6000 to 15,000 rp with mandi and fan. Both come recommended by travellers.

The *Hotel Panorama* (☎ 21004), at Jalan

SUMATRA

Merdeka 33, is the best hotel in town. It has air-con doubles for 25,000 rp.

Getting There & Away The road between Meulaboh and Tapaktuan is good. It takes five hours and costs 4000 rp.

A lot of work has been done on the road between Tapaktuan and Sidikalang in recent years, but it is still the roughest section. The 230 km can take five to six hours (6000 rp).

Singkil

Singkil is a remote port at the mouth of the Alas River, noteworthy mainly as the departure point for the nearby Banyak Islands. The town was accessible only by boat until the recent construction of a road between Singkil and Rundeng. The people of Singkil are famous for their fishing and boating abilities.

Singkil's three losmen – *Harmonis, Purnama* and *Favourit* – have doubles for 5000 rp.

Getting There & Away There are daily minibuses between Medan and Singkil, leaving Medan at 11 am outside the Losmen Singkil Raya, on Jalan Bintang (behind Olympia Plaza). The trip takes seven hours and costs 15,000 rp. If you're travelling from Berastagi, Lake Toba or Padang, catch a bus to Sidikalang and change for Singkil.

Pulau Banyak

The Banyaks ('many' islands) are a cluster of 99 islands, 95 of them uninhabited, about 30 km off the Sumatran coast.

They are well off the beaten track, but not to hard to get to, thanks to a convenient transport link to Medan. There's guesthouse accommodation on the main island of Pulau Baleh and on nearby Pulau Rangit.

The main activities are snorkelling and beach combing.

Most travellers head for *Coco's Restaurant & Bungalows* on the beach on Pulau Rangit. A thatched bungalow for two costs 5000 rp. *Mamma's Homestay* is the place to stay on Pulau Baleh, just 50 metres from the port. It charges 5000 rp for doubles, 10,000 rp with food.

Getting There & Away Boats from Singkil leave at 7 am every day except Wednesday and Sunday for Pulau Baleh. The trip takes 2½ hours and costs 5000 rp. There are frequent small boats shuttling between Pulau Baleh and Pulau Rangit, 30 minutes and 3000 rp away. Mamma's can organise a boat for you.

BANDA ACEH TO MEDAN

There are several interesting villages on this road if you want to take it easy and stop along the way.

Saree

Saree is a small hill town about 1½ hours south of Banda Aceh. The climate is refreshingly cool after the heat of the coast.

It's advisable to take a guide if you want to climb nearby Gunung Seulawah (1806 metres). You can ask at the local police station. It takes about six hours to climb, and another three hours to descend. Take a sweater or jacket as it's cold at the top.

One of Sumatra's last elephant herds lives around Seulawah for part of the year. You may also come across monkeys, deer and tropical birds. Corn, sweet potatoes and a local variety of almond grow in abundance in this region and are usually available at the market.

The nearest accommodation is at Sigli, about 40 km further down the Trans-Sumatran Highway (800 rp by opelet).

Sigli

About three hours south of Banda Aceh, Sigli is the source of many traditional regional handicrafts. Embroidered cloth and other articles are produced at Kampung Garot, eight km from Sigli, and pottery and ceramics are produced at Kampung Klibeit.

Sigli's contribution to modern Indonesia is a factory which produces pre-stressed concrete units for bridges.

You can stay at *Losmen Paris* (☎ 21521), near the bus station, on Jalan Melati 2. There are a variety of rooms from 6000 to 19,000 rp. There is also the *Hotel Riza* (☎ 21527), on Jalan Blok Sawah, with air-con doubles for 30,000 rp.

Sigli is known for its curries. Try them at one of the many small local restaurants.

The bus from Banda Aceh to Sigli (3000 rp) takes 2½ hours.

TAKENGON TO BLANGKEJERAN

Takengon and Blangkejeran are the main towns of the Gayo Highlands in the central mountains of Aceh Province. The Gayo, who number about 250,000, lived an isolated existence until the advent of modern roads and transport. Farming is the main occupation. Pressure for land to grow coffee and tobacco led to some serious overclearing in the past. The Gayo also grow rice and vegetables.

Like the neighbouring Acehnese, the Gayo were renowned for their fierce resistance to Dutch rule; like the Acehnese, they are also strict Muslims.

It's said that one way of telling you are in Gayo country is from the number of water buffalo, replacing the hump-necked *bentang* cattle preferred by the Acehnese.

Takengon

The Dutch made Takengon, on the shores of Danau Tawar, their base when they arrived at the beginning of this century. Much of the town centre dates from that time. It is the largest town of the highlands, but not wildly exciting. The climate is pleasantly cool at an altitude of 1100 metres.

The lake is 26 km long, five km wide and 50 metres deep, surrounded by steep hills rising to volcanic peaks of more than 2500 metres. Gunung Geureundong, to the north, rises 2855 metres.

Orientation & Information The Grand Mosque is in the centre of the town on Jalan Lebe Kadar, which is where you'll find the post office and police station as well as shops and restaurants. The main bus station and the market are closer to the lake.

Things to See & Do The intricately carved home of the area's last traditional ruler is

open for inspection at the village of **Kebaya-kan**, on the lakeside just north of Takengon.

There are a couple of good walks. It's best to engage a guide before tackling **Gunung Telong**, a walk of four to six hours through moss forest with numerous exotic orchids.

There are also good views from **Gunung Tetek**, a much less energetic climb taking under an hour.

There are stalagmites at **Loyang Koro** (Buffalo Caves), six km from town. Take a torch.

Places to Stay & Eat The best of the many cheap losmen is the *Penginapan Batang Ruang* (☎ 21524), at Jalan Mahkamah 7, next to the cinema. It has clean doubles for 7500 rp.

Around the corner from the bus station, on Jalan Pasar Inpres, is the overpriced, mid-range *Triarga Inn* (☎ 21073), where doubles cost 12,500 rp and doubles with hot water and air-con are 45,000 rp.

The *Hotel Danau Laut Tawar*, opposite the Grand Mosque on Jalan Lebe Kadar, has rooms for 15,000 rp.

The flash hotel on the lakeside, 2½ km out of town, is the *Hotel Renggali* (☎ (0643) 21144). Doubles start at 60,000 rp and suites are 120,000 rp.

There are the usual Padang and Chinese-style warungs to eat at. For good sates, try *Warung Soto Surabaya*.

Things to Buy This is the place to buy the traditional Gayo/Alas tapestry which is made into embroidered clothes, belts, purses, cushion holders and tapestry. Brightly woven mats can be bought at Isak or at one of the other small villages on the road to Isak.

It's sometimes possible to buy highly decorative, engraved pottery called *keunire*, which is used in wedding ceremonies, at the market in Takengon.

Getting There & Away There are regular buses to Takengon from Bireuen, on the Trans-Sumatran Highway, 218 km south-east of Banda Aceh. The 100-km journey from Bireuen (3000 rp; 2½ hours) passes through spectacular country.

There are daily direct connections between Takengon and Medan as well as Banda Aceh. Heading south, there are now regular opelets on the much-improved road to Blangkejeran and on to Kutacane, although you wouldn't want to hold your breath waiting for a bus in the wet season.

Blangkejeran

Blangkejeran is the main town of the remote southern highlands. The area is known as the Gayo heartland and it is possible to hire guides to take you out to some of the smaller villages.

There are a couple of small guesthouses: *Penginapan Juli* at Jalan Kong Buri 12 and *Penginapan Mardhatillah* on Jalan Ahmad Yani.

There are daily opelets for the 125-km journey to Takengon.

KUTACANE & GUNUNG LEUSER NATIONAL PARK

Kutacane, in the heart of the Alas Valley, is the base camp for activities in the surrounding expanses of Gunung Leuser National Park.

Gunung Leuser National Park is one of the great flora & fauna sanctuaries of South-East Asia. Within the park's boundaries can be found four of the world's rarest animals – rhinos, elephants, tigers and orang-utans. There are perhaps 300 elephants, 500 tigers and 100 rhinos living in the park, mostly deep within its environs; however, your chances of seeing them are extremely remote. You can, however, be sure of encountering plenty of primates. The most common is the white-breasted Thomas Leaf monkey which sports a splendid, crested 'punk' hair-do.

Habitats range from the swamp forests of the west coast to the dense lowland rainforests of the interior. Above 1500 metres, the permanent mists have created moss forests rich in epiphytes and orchids.

Rare flora includes two members of the rafflesia family: *Rafflesia acehensis* and *Raf-flesia zippelni* which are found along the Alas River.

More than 300 bird species have been recorded in the park, among them the bizarre rhinoceros hornbill and the helmeted hornbill, which has a call sounding like maniacal laughter.

Crocodiles used to be common in the lower reaches of the Alas/Bengkung River, but have been virtually wiped out by poachers.

Gunung Leuser National Park was one of the first national parks in Indonesia when it was proclaimed in 1980. There are two main access points to the park. They are at Bukit Lawang – home of the famous Orang-utan Rehabilitation Centre – and at Kutacane, a small town on the Alas River in the area known as Aceh Tenggara, central Aceh.

Kutacane itself has nothing much to offer – much of the land around the town has been cleared for farming – but it is surrounded by the densely forested hills of the national park.

There is a research station in the national park north-west of Kutacane at Ketambe, but it is off limits to tourists.

Information

Permits You need to get a permit from the PHPA (national parks) office in Tanah Merah, about 15 minutes by bemo from Kutacane. The permit costs 1000 rp, and you need to provide three photocopies of your passport.

Trekking

There is a wide range of treks, from short walks to week-long hikes through the jungle to the tops of the park's mountains.

There are some good walks around Gurah. The most popular walk involves a two-hour hike from Lawe Gurah to hot springs on the Alas River.

It's compulsory to take a guide for the longer walks. Guides can be hired in Kutacane or from the PHPA office at Tanah Merah for about 15,000 rp per day. The guides will construct shelters at night, cook food, carry baggage, cut through the trails (or what's left of them) and, if possible, show you the wildlife.

Orang-Utan

Gunung Leuser National Park is one of world's largest remaining strongholds of the orang-utan, with more than 5000 animals thought to be living in the wild.

The orang-utan is found today only in Sumatra and Borneo, although fossilised remains show that its range once extended to China and Java.

It is the world's largest arboreal mammal, large males weighing up to 90 kg. Despite their size, they move through the jungle canopy with great agility and assurance, swinging on vines and branches or using their weight to sway saplings back and forth to reach the next.

The name *orang hutan* is Malay for 'person of the forest' and there are numerous myths and legends surrounding the creature. Stories were told of how the orang-utan would carry off pretty girls. Others told of how the orang-utan could speak, but refused to do so because it did not want to be made to work.

The orang-utan has a long life-span but tends to breed slowly. Females reach sexual maturity at about the age of 10 years. They have few young and they stay around their mothers until they are about seven to 10 years old. The females remain fertile until about the age of 30, and on average have only one baby every six years. The orang-utan tends to be quite a solitary creature.

They are primarily vegetarians. Their normal diet comprises fruit, shoots and leaves as well as nuts and tree bark that they grind up with their powerful jaws and teeth. They occasionally eat insects, eggs and small mammals.

Despite their remarkably human expressions, the orang-utan is considered to be the most distantly related to humans of all the great apes.

Apart from Gunung Leuser National Park, orang-utans can also be found in Tanjung Puting and Kutai national parks and the Gunung Palung and Bukit Raja reserves in Kalimantan, and in neighbouring Sarawak and Sabah. ∎

One possibility is to trek to the Lawe Mamas, one of the major tributaries of the Alas River that forms the central valley of southern Aceh Province. The Mamas is a wild, raging river which enters the Alas River about 15 km north of Kutacane, near the village of Tanjung Muda.

The trek to Gunung Kemiri takes five to six days and leads through some of the park's richest primate habitat with orang-utan, macaques, siamangs and gibbons.

It's also possible to walk to Gunung Leuser, a round trip of 10 to 14 days that starts from the village of Angusan, near Blangkejeran, to the north-west of Kutacane.

The trek to Gunung Bendahara is another

10 to 14-day outing, starting from the village of Aunan.

The trek to Gunung Kapi is a one-week round trip starting from the village of Marpunga. The area around Marpunga is supposed to offer the best chance of seeing wild elephants.

The trek to Gunung Simpali is a one-week round trip starting from the village of Engkran and following the valley of the Lawe Mamas. Rhinos live in this area.

Rafting

Rafting on the Alas River hardly qualifies as a whitewater experience. It's more like a float trip, and the companies operating on the river use makeshift rafts lashed together from truck inner tubes and bamboo rather than rubber inflatables. Trips can be organised in Kutacane and prices start at US$75 for three days/two nights. Most rafting trips start at Gurah and end at Serakut.

Places to Stay

Most of the uninspiring places in Kutacane are near the bus station on Jalan Besar. *Wisma Renggali* has rooms from 3000 to 10,000 rp, while the nearby *Wisma Rindu Alam* has dorms for 2500 rp and rooms with fan for 10,000 rp.

The *Hotel Bru Dihe*, near the mosque on Jalan Cut Nyak Dhien, has rooms with mandi and fan for 15,000 rp and with air-con for 25,000 rp.

Gurah has budget accommodation at the *Losmen Pak Ali* for 2500 rp as well as the comfortably appointed *Gurah Lodge*, with air-con doubles for 25,000 rp.

Places to Eat

There are lots of places to eat near the bus station along Jalan Besar. *Sapo Bawan*, opposite the bus station, has good nasi or mie goreng. If you're after Padang food, *Anita*, opposite Wisma Renggali, is worth a try, or you can stroll down Jalan Ahmad Yani where there's a choice of the *Roda Baru*, the *Damai Baru* or the *Nasional*.

Getting There & Away

Bus The Pinem company has occasional direct buses from Medan's Pinang Baris bus station to Kutacane via Kabanjahe, and there are more frequent services between Kutacane and Kabanjahe (4000 rp; five hours). Many travellers head to Kutacane from Berastagi, which means catching an opelet to Kabanjahe first.

The road winds its way over the mountains with fine views of Gunung Sinabung, valleys occupied by the Karo Batak people, and the Alas River valley. The winding road allows drivers plenty of opportunity to use their favourite toy – the air horn. Every bend, shack and village is an excuse for a triple or quadruple blast.

There also are buses heading north-west from Kutacane to Blangkejeran and beyond. This road is a lot better than it used to be, but it is still prone to washout in the wet season.

Minibuses run from Kutacane to Tanah Merah (250 rp) and Gurah (400 rp).

West Sumatra

The province of West Sumatra is like a vast and magnificent nature reserve, dominated by volcanoes, with jungles, waterfalls, canyons and lakes. This is the homeland of the Minangkabau, one of Indonesia's most interesting and influential ethnic groups. They make up 95% of the province's population of 3½ million.

Padang is the provincial capital. The other major cities are Payakumbuh, Bukittinggi, Padangpanjang, Solok and Sawahlunto. There are four large lakes in West Sumatra: Singkarak near Solok; Maninjau near Bukittinggi; and Diatas and Dibawah east of Padang.

The fascinating Mentawai Islands are also part of West Sumatra. Only recently emerged from their stone-age isolation, the inhabitants of these islands are quite different from the people of mainland Sumatra.

The economy of West Sumatra, although predominantly based on agriculture (coffee, rice, coconuts and cattle), is strengthened by industries like coal mining.

History

Legend has it that the Minangkabau are descended from none other than that wandering Macedonian tyrant, Alexander the Great.

According to legend, the ancestors of the Minangkabau arrived in Sumatra under the leadership of King Maharjo Dirajo, the youngest son of Alexander, more commonly known in Indonesia as Iskandar Zulkarnair. They first settled in the Padangpanjang region, and gradually spread out over western Sumatra.

History suggests that, in fact, the Minangkabau arrived in Indonesia some time

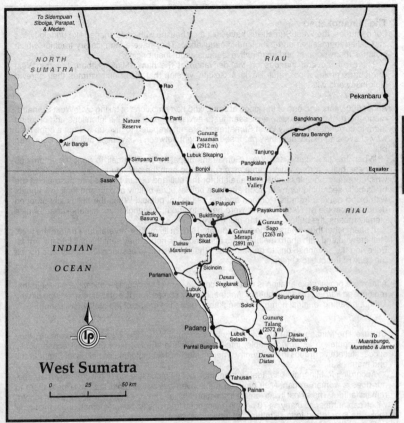

West Sumatra

between 1000 and 2000 BC. The early Malayu kingdom, which later extended to include what is now West Sumatra, was established by Hindu colonists in the 7th century and emerged as a power in the 12th century following the demise of the Sriwijaya empire. It is thought to have been founded by a prince of the Javanese Majapahit empire, and was listed as a dependent of Java in the year 1365. At its zenith, between the 14th and 15th centuries, it stretched right across central Sumatra and included Padang, Jambi, Bengkulu and other cities.

In the 14th century, Islam began to penetrate the region, which split into small Muslim states ruled by sultans. They gradually pushed the Minangkabau kingdom further inland and it had all but disintegrated by the early 17th century when the Europeans arrived.

At that time it consisted of little more than a few small-time rajas ruling over minuscule village-states.

It continued to survive in this form until the early 19th century when the Padri rebellion erupted, instigated by a group of Muslim fanatics known as the 'men of Pedir'.

The Minangkabau

For centuries, the West Sumatrans have built their houses with roofs shaped like buffalo horns and called themselves and their land Minangkabau. They have a long literary tradition which includes many popular and imaginative legends about their origins.

There are several theories on the derivation of the name Minangkabau, but the West Sumatrans prefer a colourful 'David & Goliath' version that also demonstrates their shrewd diplomacy and wit:

About 600 years ago one of the kings of Java, who had ambitions of taking over West Sumatra, made the mistake of sending a messenger to advise the people of his intentions and ordering them to surrender. The wily West Sumatrans were not prepared to give up without a fight. As a way of avoiding bloodshed, they proposed a bullfight between a Javanese bull and a Sumatran bull.

When the time came, the West Sumatrans dispatched a tiny calf to fight the enormous Javanese bull – a ruse which came as a surprise to both the bull and the onlookers. The calf, which appeared helpless, charged straight for the bull and began to press its nose along the bull's belly searching for milk. Soon after, the bull let out a bellow of pain and took to its heels with blood pouring from its stomach and the calf in hot pursuit. When the bull finally dropped dead, the people of West Sumatra were heard to shout, 'minangkabau, minangkabau!' which literally means 'the buffalo wins, the buffalo wins!'

It seems that the owners of the calf separated it from its mother several days before the fight. Half-starved and with sharp metal spears attached to its horns, they sent the calf into the arena. Believing the Javanese bull to be its mother, the calf rushed to assuage its hunger and ripped the belly of the bull to shreds.

A far more prosaic explanation is that it is a combination of two words – *minanga*, a river in that region, and *kerbau*, meaning buffalo. Another is that it comes from the archaic expression *pinang kabhu*, meaning 'original home' – Minangkabau being the cradle of the Malay civilisation.

Culture The Minangkabau are known by their compatriots as the 'gypsies of Indonesia'; they have a reputation as an adaptable, intelligent people and are one of the most economically successful ethnic groups in the country. Though Muslim, Minangkabau society is still matriarchal and matrilineal.

According to Minangkabau adat, a man does not gain possession of a woman by marriage, nor does a woman a man. Men have no rights over their wives other than to expect them to remain faithful. The eldest living female is the matriarch and has the most power in the household, which can number as many as 70 people descended from one ancestral mother, under the same roof. She is deferred to in all matters of family politics.

Every Minangkabau belongs to his or her mother's clan. At the lowest level of the clan is the *sapariouk* which consists of those matri-related kin who eat together. These include the mother, grandchildren and son-in-law. The name comes from the word *periouk* which means rice pot. A number of genealogically related *sapariouk* make up a lineage or *sapayung*. The word *payung* means umbrella.

Children born of a female member of the lineage will, by right of birth, be members of that lineage. Ancestral property, although worked collectively, is passed down this female line, rather than down the male line.

All progeny from a marriage are regarded as part of the mother's family group and the father has no say in family affairs. The most important male member of the household is the mother's eldest brother, who replaces the father in being responsible for the children's education and offers them economic advice as they grow older. He also discusses and advises them on their prospective marriages.

Arts & Crafts West Sumatra has a reputation for exquisite, hand-loomed songket cloth and fine embroidery. Songket weaving uses gold and silver threads (imitation these days) to create patterns on a base of silk or cotton, depending on the budget. The designs are usually elaborate floral motifs and geometric patterns. One of the most popular designs, used in both weaving and embroidery, incorporates stylised flowers and mountains in an ornate pattern known as *gunung batuah* or 'magic mountain'.

The material is traditionally used as a sarong, shawl or wrap. Expect to pay more than 200,000 rp for a sarong of good quality. It's also widely available in the form of such items as cushion covers, bedspreads, handbags, wallets etc.

Songket weaving is widespread in West Sumatra. Kubang, 13 km from Payakumbuh near the border with Riau Province, is the centre for commercial weaving.

The village of Silungkang, on the Agam Plateau near the coal town of Sawahlunto, specialises in vividly coloured silk songket sarongs and scarves. Other weaving villages in this area include Balai Cacang, Koto Nan Ampek and Muara.

Pandai Sikat, near Padangpanjang on the main road between Padang and Bukittinggi, is known for the finery of its cloth. The village is also known for its decorative woodcarving.

The Minangkabau are also known for their fine embroidery. Villages which specialise in this are Koto Gadang, Ampek Angkek, Naras, Lubuk Begalung, Kota Nan Ampek and Sunguyang.

Traditional weavers also used an unusually painstaking technique called 'needle weaving'. The process involves removing certain threads from a piece of cloth and stitching the remaining ones together to form patterns. These patterns include identifiable motifs such as people, crabs, insects, dogs or horses. Traditionally, such cloth is used to cover the *carano* – a brass sireh stand with receptacles for betel nut, tobacco, lime – which is used for ceremonial occasions. You're unlikely to find any examples for sale.

Another highly developed art found in West Sumatra is silverwork. Filigree jewellery, as fine as spider webs, is a speciality. Koto Gadang, near Bukittinggi, is the place to go if you're interested.

Dance & Music Dance is an important part of Minangkabau culture. Dances include: the colourful Tari Payung (Umbrella Dance), a welcome dance about a young man's love for his girlfriend; the dazzling Tari Lilin (Candle Dance), a miracle of physical coordination where the female dancers are required to rhythmically juggle and balance china saucers with burning candles attached to them while simultaneously clicking castanets; and the dramatic Tari Piring (Plate Dance), which involves the dancers leaping barefoot on piles of broken china.

The most popular of the Minangkabau dances is the Randai, a unique dance-drama performed at weddings, harvest festivals and other celebrations. The steps and movements for the Randai developed from the Pencak Silat, a self-defence routine that comes in various styles. The dance is learnt by every Minang boy when he reaches the age at which he is considered too old to remain in his mother's house but too young to move into another woman's.

It is the custom for Minang youths to spend some time in a *surau* (prayer house) where they are taught, among other things, how to look after themselves. This includes learning the Pencak Silat. The style of Pencak Silat most often performed is the Mudo, a mock battle which leads the two protagonists to the brink of violence before it is concluded. It is a dramatic dance involving skilled technique, fancy footwork and deliberate pauses which follow each movement and serve to heighten the tension.

Harimau Silat, the most aggressive and dangerous style of Pencak Silat, originated in the Painan district of West Sumatra. The steps for the Harimau Silat imitate a tiger stalking and killing its prey. With their bodies as close to the ground as possible, the two fighters circle around menacingly, springing at each other from time to time.

The Randai combines the movements of Pencak Silat with literature, sport, song and drama. Every village in West Sumatra has at least one Randai group of 20 performers. Both the female and male roles are played by men wearing traditional *gelambuk* trousers and black dress. The traditional version tells the story of a woman so wilful and wicked that she is driven out of her village before she brings complete disaster on the community. The drama is backed by gamelan music.

The percussion instruments used to accompany most of the dances are similar to those of the Javanese gamelan and are collectively called the *telempong* in West Sumatra. Two other instruments frequently played are the *puput* and *salung*, both primitive kinds of flute which are usually made out of bamboo, reed or rice stalks. ■

It was called the Padri rebellion because the Muslim hajis who started it returned to Sumatra via Pedir after their pilgrimage to Mecca. Determined to force the Minang people to follow Mohammedan law, the Padri resorted to killing and enslaving anyone who resisted them.

The Minangkabau leaders were not prepared to relinquish all power without a fight and defended their rights to follow the traditional system of matriarchy, indulge in gambling and drinking, and practise other pre-Islamic customs.

The bitter struggle lasted from 1820 to 1837 but, backed by the Dutch army and non-Muslim Bataks, the adat leaders finally overcame the Padri strongholds. Today, a curious mix of traditional beliefs and Islam is practised in West Sumatra.

Flora & Fauna

Tigers, rhinoceroses, sun bears, elephants, and various species of monkey and deer are all native to West Sumatra. Of particular interest in the Mentawai Islands is a rare species of black-and-yellow monkey (*siamang kerdil*), but usually called *simpai mentawai* by the locals. Their numbers are small and they are strictly protected. There is also diverse bird life.

The *Rafflesia arnoldi* can be seen around the small village of Palupuh, 16 km north of Bukittinggi, between August and November. Strictly speaking, the Rafflesia is not a flower. It's a parasitic fungus specific to a species of rainforest vine. Whatever its status, it's huge. Some specimens measure as much as a metre across and weigh over seven kg. Rafflesia blooms are a gaudy red-and-white and give off a putrid smell which attracts pollinating flies and insects.

West Sumatra is also famous for its many species of orchids.

Cultural Events

In addition to the dances performed by the Minangkabau, there are other important sporting and cultural events in West Sumatra.

Bullfighting Known locally as *adu kerbau*, bullfighting is a popular entertainment in West Sumatra. It bears no resemblance to the Spanish kind – there is no bloodshed (unless by accident) and the bulls, which are water buffaloes or *kerbau*, don't get hurt.

Two animals (both cows and bulls are used) of roughly the same size and weight are encouraged by their handlers to lock horns for a trial of strength. Once horns are locked, the fight continues until the losing animal tires and runs off pursued by the winner. It often ends up with both beasts charging around a muddy paddock, scattering onlookers in all directions.

The original intention was to help develop buffalo breeding in the region. As a spectator sport, the local men love to get together for a bet on the buffaloes. It's an interesting insight into local culture, and well worth seeing.

The centres for bullfighting are the villages of Kota Baru and Batagak, between Padang and Bukittinggi. The host village in each district is changed every six months or so. The first bullfight in a new location is an important day for the host village, which kicks off proceedings with a meeting of village elders, followed by a demonstration of pencak silat dancing.

They're held every Tuesday afternoon at around 5 pm around Kota Baru, and every Saturday from 4 pm around Batagak. There are bemos to the bullfights from Bukittinggi's Aur Kuning bus station for 500 rp each way. Entry is another 500 rp.

Alternatively, travel agencies in Bukittinggi charge 5000 rp for the round trip plus admission.

Horse Racing Horse racing in Sumatra is a vivid, noisy spectacle and nothing like the horse racing of Western countries. The horses are ridden bareback and the jockeys are dressed in the traditional costume of the region or village they come from. The aim is to gain prestige for the district where the horse is bred and raised. Padang, Padang-panjang, Bukittinggi, Payakumbuh and Batu Sangkar each stages one meeting a year, normally over two days.

Tabut Festival The highlight of the West Sumatran cultural calendar is the colourful Islamic festival of Tabut, staged at the seaside town of Pariaman, 36 km north of Padang.

It's held at the beginning of the month of Muharam to honour the martyrdom of Mohammed's grandchildren, Hassan and Hussein, at the battle of Kerbala. Because the date is fixed by the Islamic lunar calendar, it moves forward 10 days each year.

Central to the festival is the *bouraq*, a winged horse-like creature with the head of a woman, which is believed to have descended to earth to collect the souls of the dead heroes and take them to heaven.

Nearby villages construct effigies of bouraqs which they paint in vibrant reds, blues, greens and yellows and adorn with gold necklaces and other paraphernalia. The effigies are carried through the streets with much merriment, dancing and music and are finally tossed into the sea. Spectators and participants then dive into the water themselves and grab whatever remains of the bouraqs, the most valued memento being the gold necklace. When two bouraqs cross paths during the procession a mock fight ensues. Each group praises its own bouraq, belittling and insulting the other at the same time.

So popular has this festival become, people from all over Indonesia arrive to witness or take part in it. Admission to the area is by donation.

Other West Sumatran towns also celebrate Tabut, but usually on public holidays, such as Independence Day or Hero Day.

PADANG
Padang is a flat, sprawling city (the name means 'field') on the coastal plains between the Indian Ocean and the Bukit Barisan mountains. It is the capital of West Sumatra and its population of almost 700,000 makes it Sumatra's third-largest city.

Many travellers use Padang as an entry or exit point for Sumatra, using the Pelni boats between here and Jakarta to bypass southern Sumatra. Tabing airport is one of Indonesia's visa-free entry points with direct connections to Kuala Lumpur and Singapore.

Although not particularly inspiring itself, Padang has some fine palm-fringed beaches nearby, the mountains a few hours away and the unique Mentawai Islands for the adventurous to explore. The road between Padang and Solok takes you through some of the most picturesque scenery in Sumatra: exquisite high-peaked Minangkabau houses and lush, terraced rice paddies. The final descent into Padang from Solok offers sweeping views along the coastline.

Orientation & Information
Padang is easy to find your way around and the central area is quite compact. Jalan M Yamin, from the bus station corner at Jalan Pemuda to Jalan Azizcham, is the main street. The main bus station and opelet station are both centrally located across from the market.

Tourist Office The tourist office (☎ 55711) is at Jalan Khatib Sulaiman 22 (the northern extension of Jalan Sudirman) and is open from 7.30 am to 2 pm Monday to Thursday, 7.30 to 11 am on Friday and 7.30 am to 12.30 pm on Saturday. It's a fair way out of the city centre. Take an orange *biskota* (city bus) 14A and tell the driver where you're going. The staff are very helpful and several speak fairly good English. If you're going to Mentawai independently, you'll need to come here to get a permit, issued free in half an hour.

Money The best rates are to be found at the Bank of Central Asia at Jalan Angus Salim 10A. BNI 1946, at Jalan Dobi 1, changes foreign cash and travellers' cheques. Moneychangers include CV Eka Jasa Utama at Jalan Niaga 241. American Express is represented by PACTO Tours & Travel (☎ (0751) 37678) at Jalan Tan Malaka 25.

Post & Telephone The post office is at Jalan Azizchan 7, near the junction with Jalan M Yamin. The huge new Minangkabau-style Telkom office is on the corner of Jalan Ahmad Dahlan and Jalan Khatib Sulaiman.

SUMATRA

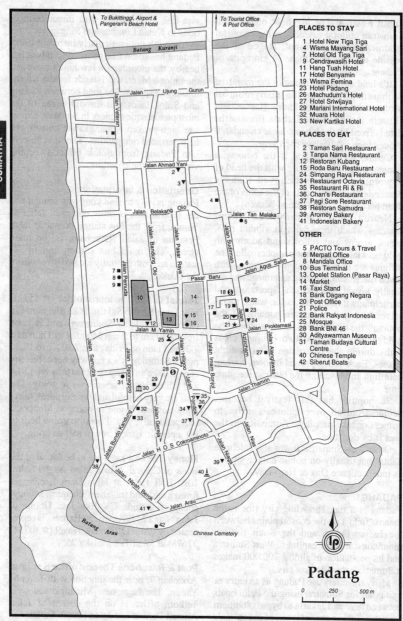

To Bukittinggi, Airport &
Pangeran's Beach Hotel

To Tourist Office
& Post Office

Batang Kuranji

Jalan Ujung Gurun

Jalan Veteran

Jalan Ahmad Yani

Jalan Belakang Olo

Jalan Tan Malaka

Jalan Bandung Olo

Jalan Pasar Raya

Jalan Sudirman

Jalan Pemuda

Pasar Baru

Jalan Agus Salim

Jalan Samudra

Jalan M Yamin

Jalan Proklamasi

Jalan Diponegoro

Jalan Hiligoo

Jalan Imam Bonjol

Jalan Azizchan

Jalan Alanglawas

Jalan Bundo Kandung

Jalan Gereja

Jalan Pondok

Jalan Thamrin

Jalan Nias

Jalan H O S Cokroaminoto

Jalan Nipah Berok

Jalan Niaga

Jalan Arau

Batang Arau

Chinese Cemetery

PLACES TO STAY
1 Hotel New Tiga Tiga
4 Wisma Mayang Sari
7 Hotel Old Tiga Tiga
9 Cendrawasih Hotel
11 Hang Tuah Hotel
17 Hotel Benyamin
19 Wisma Femina
23 Hotel Padang
26 Machudum's Hotel
27 Hotel Sriwijaya
29 Mariani International Hotel
32 Muara Hotel
33 New Kartika Hotel

PLACES TO EAT
2 Taman Sari Restaurant
3 Tanpa Nama Restaurant
12 Restoran Kubang
15 Roda Baru Restaurant
24 Simpang Raya Restaurant
34 Restaurant Octavia
35 Restaurant Ri & Ri
36 Chan's Restaurant
37 Pagi Sore Restaurant
38 Restoran Samudra
39 Aromey Bakery
41 Indonesian Bakery

OTHER
5 PACTO Tours & Travel
6 Merpati Office
8 Mandala Office
10 Bus Terminal
13 Opelet Station (Pasar Raya)
14 Market
16 Taxi Stand
18 Bank Dagang Negara
20 Post Office
21 Police
22 Bank Rakyat Indonesia
25 Mosque
28 Bank BNI 46
30 Adityawarman Museum
31 Taman Budaya Cultural Centre
40 Chinese Temple
42 Siberut Boats

Padang

0   250   500 m

Medical Services If you need a good hospital, you can try the privately owned Ruman Sakit Yos Sudarso on Jalan Situjuh.

Things to See & Do
In the centre of town, down the road from the bus station, is the **Adityawarman Museum** on Jalan Diponegoro, built in the Minangkabau tradition with two rice barns out the front. It has a small but excellent collection of antiques and other objects of historical and cultural interest from all over West Sumatra, and a particularly good textile room. The museum is open daily except Monday, from 9 am to 6 pm. Admission is 200 rp.

Next to the museum is the **Taman Budaya** (Cultural Centre) where local, regional, national, traditional and modern music and dances are performed regularly. They also hold poetry readings and stage plays and exhibitions of paintings and carvings.

Festivals
Padang's colourful annual boat race to commemorate Independence Day is on August 17.

Places to Stay – bottom end
Padang has some decent budget hotels. The best of them is the *Hotel Sriwijaya* (☎ 23577), at Jalan Alanglawas, which has clean singles/doubles from 6000/8000 rp. The rooms are small and simple, but each has a little porch area. It's a quiet, small street, although not far from the centre.

Another good place is the spotless *Hotel Benyamin* (☎ 22324), 100 metres down the lane next to Hotel Femina, at Jalan Azizchan 15. The airy rooms on the top floors are better than the rather dingy rooms on the ground floor. They cost 10,000 rp per person and all rooms have fans – a good investment in steamy Padang.

There are no fans in the budget rooms at the *Hotel Old Tiga Tiga* (☎ 22633), opposite the bus station at Jalan Pemuda 31. The budget singles/doubles cost 7500/12,500 rp, but you'll need to fork out 17,500/22,500 rp to qualify for a fan or 22,500/27,500 rp for air-con.

Almost next door, at No 27, is the *Cendrawasih Hotel* (☎ 22894) with rooms from 8000/13,000 rp, or 12,000/18,000 rp with mandi and fan. A double with air-con costs 36,000 rp.

Places to Stay – middle
The *Hang Tuah Hotel* (☎ 26556) is a modern hotel at Jalan Pemuda 1, near the Jalan M Yamin intersection. It has singles/doubles with mandi and fan for 18,000/23,000 rp. The best rooms cost 45,000/50,000 rp and come with air-con, satellite TV and hot water.

There's a second *Tiga Tiga* (☎ 22173) further out at Jalan Veteran 33; prices in this newer version are the same as at the Old Tiga Tiga, except that there are no budget rooms.

The *Hotel Padang* (☎ 31383), at Jalan Azizcham 28, has a large garden area and a variety of rooms starting from simple singles with fan for 22,000 rp. Better rooms with a bathroom and a pleasant little porch out the front start at 36,000 rp for a double, rising to 84,000 rp for air-con and the works.

Further north, at Jalan Sudirman 19, is the excellent guesthouse-style *Wisma Mayang Sari* (☎ 22647). It's an old Dutch villa with clean, well-appointed rooms with air-con, hot water and TV for 30,000/35,000 rp. The upstairs rooms, with their own verandahs for 35,000/40,000 rp, are particularly good.

Places to Stay – top end
The *Muara Hotel* (☎ 25600), at Jalan Gereja 34, is Padang's number-one establishment, complete with swimming pool; rooms start at 85,000 rp.

Pangeran's Beach Hotel (☎ 31333), at Jalan Ir Juanda 79, is on the outskirts of Padang and on the road towards the airport. It's on the beach (unsafe for swimming, but there is a swimming pool), and rooms cost from 86,850 rp.

Places to Eat
What else would you eat here but Padang food, the spicy Minangkabau cooking that is found throughout Indonesia?

The most famous Padang dish is *rendang*,

chunks of beef or buffalo simmered very slowly in coconut milk until the sauce is reduced to a rich paste and the meat becomes dark and dried. Fabulous.

Other dishes include eggs dusted in red chillies *(telor balado)*, fish *(ikan balado)* and a mutton stew *(gulai kambing)*.

Padang food would have to qualify as the world's fastest food. There are no menus in a Padang restaurant. You simply sit down and almost immediately the waiter will set down at least half a dozen bowls of various curries and a bowl of plain rice. You pay only for what you eat, and you can test the sauces for free.

The food is normally displayed in the front window so you can take a look at what you're going to eat before entering, and go somewhere else if you don't like what you see. Don't be overly concerned about the odd fly cruising around the food on display – you'll starve if you try to find a restaurant without flies. Fresh fruit, usually pineapple and bananas, is offered for dessert.

Some of the well-known Padang food specialists include *Roda Baru* upstairs at Jalan Pasar Raya 6, in the market buildings, and *Simpang Raya* at Jalan Azizcham 24, opposite the post office. *Pagi Sore* is towards the end of Jalan Pondok at No 143.

There are also some Chinese-Indonesian restaurants, particularly along Jalan Pondok and Jalan Niaga. *Restaurant Octavia*, at Jalan Pondok 137, is a simple little place with the standard nasi goreng, mie goreng menu. Across the road are *Chan's*, at No 94, and the *Ri & Ri* at No 86A.

The *Restoran Kubang*, at Jalan M Yamin 138 near the bus station, really turns out the martabaks at night. It's a busy scene with tables set up across the pavement and lots of obviously satisfied customers.

There are also several big restaurants like the *Taman Sari* and *Tanpa Nama* along Jalan Ahmad Yani north of the centre. The *Restaurant Sari*, at Jalan Thamrin 71B, does excellent seafood. Expect to pay at least 10,000 rp per person for such luxuries as a crooner on piano.

No Sumatran city would be without its bakeries, and Padang has its share. The *Aromey Bakery* at the southern end of Jalan Niaga has a good selection.

Getting There & Away

Air Merpati, Pelangi Air and Sempati operate international flights to and from Padang. Merpati flies three time a week to Singapore (US$110), Sempati flies to Kuala Lumpur on Monday and Tuesday (US$123) and Pelangi Air flies to Kuala Lumpur via Pekanbaru four times a week (US$107). The Pelangi Air office (☎ 54516) is at Jalan Diponegoro 13.

Merpati (☎ 31850) is at Jalan Sudirman 2. It has three direct flights daily to Jakarta as well as direct connections to Batam, Medan and Palembang.

Sempati (☎ 51612) is based at Pangeran's Beach Hotel, Jalan Ir Juanda. It has one direct flight a day to Jakarta and direct flights to Pekanbaru. Mandala (☎ 32773), at Jalan Pemuda 29A, has two flights a day to Jakarta and easily the best fare at 184,500 rp one way.

SMAC (☎ 55367), also at Jalan Sudirman 2, flies to Gunung Sitoli on Nias on Wednesday for 117,100 rp.

Bus Padang's bus station is conveniently central. Every north-south bus comes through here, so there are a number of options.

There are heaps of buses to Bukittinggi, the prime destination for travellers. The trip costs 1500 rp and takes about two hours, passing through some fine scenery. If you arrive in Padang by air, there's no need to go into town – the main road to Bukittinggi is only 100 metres from the airport terminal.

There are also buses to Jambi (10,000 rp; 10 hours); Palembang (18,000 rp or 25,000 rp with air-con; 22 hours); Pekanbaru (6500 rp or 10,000 rp with air-con; eight hours); and Parapat (15,000 rp; 18 hours). You can get all the way to Jakarta in 30 hours for 35,000 rp, or 60,000 rp air-con.

Train The railway line from Padang to Bukittinggi used to be quite an attraction for railway enthusiasts, but now it's only used as far as Padangpanjang and only for freight trains. You can see some old steam engines permanently parked at Padangpanjang. The line beyond here is spectacular, crossing and recrossing the road, but derelict and overgrown.

Boat The Pelni ship *Lawit* calls at Padang's port of Teluk Bayur every two weeks en route to Sibolga (20,000/58,000 rp in economy/1st class) and Gunung Sitoli (22,000/74,000 rp). It stops again on the way south to Jakarta (42,000/131,000 rp), Semarang and Pontianak. The Pelni office (☎ 33624) is at Jalan Tanjung Priok 32, Teluk Bayur.

The Pelni boat *Baruna Dwipa* operates between Padang and Bengkulu (13,700/60,200 rp) every two weeks on a route that includes Pulau Enggano and Krui on the way to Jakarta. There's a regular shipping service from Padang to Pulau Siberut, with fares starting at 14,000 rp.

Getting Around
To/From the Airport Padang's Tabing airport is nine km north of the centre on the Bukittinggi road. The 'fixed' taxi fare into town is 8000 rp, while a metered taxi the other way costs under 4000 rp. The budget alternative is to walk from the airport terminal to the main road and catch any opelet into town for 250 rp. Heading out to the airport, city bus (biskota) 14A is the best one to get.

Local Transport There are numerous opelets and mikrolets around town. Their station is Pasar Raya at Jalan M Yamin. The standard fare is 250 rp. Dokars are also numerous and cost 1000 rp. There's a taxi stand beside the market building on the corner of Jalan M Yamin.

AROUND PADANG
Air Manis
Four km south of Padang is the fishing village of Air Manis, which literally means 'sweet water'. To get there, take a bemo to Muaro, then hire a *perahu* across the river and walk to the Chinese cemetery which overlooks the town. A one-km walk will take you to the village of Air Manis. There, at low tide, you can wade out to a small island or take a sampan to a larger one. According to local mythology, the rock at the end of the beach is the remains of Malin Kundang (a man who was transformed into stone when he rejected his mother after making a fortune) and his boat.

In the village you can stay at cheerful *Papa Chili-Chili's*, and yes, his food is hot! It costs 3000 rp per person, or 6000 rp plus food.

Climb the hill beyond Air Manis for a good view of the port of Teluk Bayur. You can walk to Teluk Bayur, take a look around the harbour and from there get an opelet for 400 rp back into the city centre.

Pasir Jambak
This beach, 15 km north of town, is the best of several beaches north of Padang. You can stay at *Uncle Jack's Homestay* for 10,000 rp with meals. Jovial Jack can organise snorkelling trips to nearby Pulau Sawo for 30,000 rp. Opelet 423 will get you to Pasir Jambak for 400 rp.

Islands
There are four islands – Pisang Besar, Sikoai, Pagang and Bintangur – within easy reach of Padang and not too expensive to get to. And all four offer good diving and snorkelling opportunities, with lots of fish and coconut palms. Although it's not difficult to catch your own dinner, take food with you. There are camping grounds on each island and fresh water is available.

The closest island is **Pulau Pisang Besar** (Big Banana Island), which is only 15 minutes from Muara River Harbour. Hire a sampan with an outboard motor from there. The others are between one and two hours from Teluk Bayur.

Sikoai has a resort hotel and regular boats for 2500 rp per person. Visiting the other islands involves arranging your own transport. You can arrange to be dropped off and picked up at a stipulated time a few days later. Ask the harbour master who to approach to take you to whichever island you choose. It's best to organise a few people to go on this trip. A sampan which can hold up to eight passengers will cost about 40,000 rp to charter.

Contact the tourist office in Padang for more information if you are interested in staying on one of these islands.

PADANG TO BUKITTINGGI

The 90-km drive north from Padang to Bukittinggi is beautiful with its rice paddies, Minangkabau houses, glimpses of the sea and views of the towering Singgalang and Merapi volcanoes – each almost 3000 metres high.

Along this route is the Lembah Anai Nature Reserve, renowned for its waterfalls, wild orchids and the giant rafflesia flowers. Danau Singkarak, bigger than Danau Maninjau but undiscovered by the tourist trail, is nearby.

Padangpanjang

Padangpanjang is the main town on the Padang-Bukittinggi road. It's interesting for its conservatorium (ASKI) of Minangkabau culture, dance and music. This is the best place to get accurate information on live dance and theatre performances. It has a fine collection of musical instruments which includes Minangkabau and Javanese gamelan outfits. There are also excellent costume displays, which are particularly interesting for bridal jewellery and ornaments like the headdress, necklace and the deceptively light bracelet called *galang-gadang*.

Places to Stay The *Hotel Ma Kmur*, at Jalan Dahlan 34, charges 4000/7500 rp for grotty singles/doubles. The other option is the modern *Wisma Singgalang Indah* (☎ 82213), which has clean doubles with breakfast starting from 31,000 rp.

Getting There & Away Padangpanjang is a comfortable afternoon or morning trip from either Padang or Bukittinggi. There are regular buses between Bukittinggi, Padang and Padangpanjang.

BUKITTINGGI

This cool, easy-going mountain town has long been one of Sumatra's most popular tourist destinations. Many travellers heading north from Java make Bukittinggi their first stop. The town is sometimes referred to as Kota Jam Gadang('Big Clock Town'), after its best-known landmark – the Minangkabau-style clocktower that overlooks the large market square.

Bukittinggi is also known as Tri Arga, after the three majestic mountains that encircle it – Merapi, Singgalang and Sago. The name actually translates as 'high mountain'.

A Dutch stronghold during the Padri rebellion (1821-37), Bukittinggi is today a centre for Minangkabau culture and has a small university.

Orientation & Information

The town centre is conveniently compact. Most of the cheap hotels, restaurants and travel agencies are at the northern end of the main street, Jalan Ahmad Yani. The famous clocktower is at the junction of Jalan Ahmad Yani and Jalan Sudirman, which leads south to the post office and bus station. Jalan M Yamin, below the market, is also known as Jalan Perentis Kemerdekaan.

Tourist Office The tourist office is beside the market car park, overlooked by the clocktower. The staff are friendly and helpful, although they don't have much other than the standard leaflets and brochures. It's open Monday to Thursday from 8 am to 2 pm, Friday from 8 to 11 am, and Saturday from 8 am to 12.30 pm.

Money There's a BNI 1946 in the Pasar Atas (market) building. You can also change money at the Toko Eka, on Jalan Minangkabau, in the central market.

Post & Telephone The main post office, with its well-organised poste restante section, is on Jalan Sudirman. The Telkom office is 150 metres along the road opposite the post office. It has a Home Country Direct phone. International calls can also be made from the 24-hour telephone office on Jalan Ahmad Yani, next to the Grand Hotel.

Travel Agencies There are lots of travel agencies in town. One of the best is Mitra Wisata (☎ 21133), at Jalan Ahmad Yani 99. The manager, Yan, speaks excellent English and is very helpful. Standard offerings at the various agencies include trips to the bullfights, full-day excursions to surrounding places of interest and trips to Pulau Siberut.

Market

Bukittinggi's large and colourful market is crammed with stalls of fruit and vegetables, clothing and crafts. The central market is open every day, but the serious action is on Wednesday and Saturday when the markets overflow down the hill. There are some good antiques and arts & crafts to be found around the market.

Fort de Kock, Museum & Zoo

Apart from the defensive moat and a few rusting cannons, not much remains of Bukittinggi's old Fort de Kock, built during the Padri Wars (1821-37) by the Dutch. It does, however, provide fine views over the town and surrounding countryside from its hilltop position.

A footbridge leads from the fort over Jalan Ahmad Yani to Taman Bundokanduag, site of the museum and zoo. The museum, which was built in 1934 by the Dutch 'controleur' of the district, is a superb example of Minangkabau architecture with its two rice barns (added in 1956) out the front. It is the oldest museum in the province and has a good collection of Minangkabau historical and cultural exhibits. The zoo is reportedly a disgrace. There's a 1000 rp entry fee to see the fort and zoo, plus an extra 300 rp for the museum.

Panorama Park & Japanese Caves

Panorama Park, on the southern edge of the town, overlooks the deep Sianok Canyon to the west of town. From the park you can enter the extensive grid of caves built by the Japanese using slave labour during WW II.

Many of the tunnels open onto the cliff face of the canyon. Entry to the park is 300 rp and entry to the Japanese Caves (Lobang Jepang) costs a further 500 rp. At the entrance there's a bas-relief showing the Japanese herding helpless locals inside.

Military Museum

Next to the Minang Hotel and overlooking Panorama Park is the Military Museum, the final resting place of a collection of faded photographs from the war of independence against the Dutch. There are also photos of the bodies of five Indonesian generals murdered at the time of the supposed Communist-led attempted coup of 1965, plus war souvenirs and photos from Indonesia's war against the Fretilin guerrillas in East Timor.

Organised Tours

Almost every hotel, coffee shop and travel agency offers tours of the district. They range from trips to the bullfighting for 5000 rp to full-day tours of the area's attractions to activity tours like mountain climbing and pig hunting.

Places to Stay – bottom end

Bukittinggi's budget hotels are a pretty charmless lot, but they're certainly cheap. Most are close together at the bottom of Jalan Ahmad Yani.

The two most popular are *Murni's* at No 115 and the *Nirwana*, next door at No 113. Both have clean singles/doubles for 4000/6000 rp. Murni's also has a nice upstairs sitting area.

Across the road, there's the *Hotel Rajawali* with rooms for 5000/7000 rp, and you can have an outside sitting area if you take the rooms on the roof. The *Singgalang Hotel* (☎ 21576), 50 metres up the hill, is a light and airy place with rooms for 6000 rp.

The *Hotel Yany* (☎ 22740), at No 101, has overpriced rooms for 10,000 rp, while the *Wisma Tiga Balai* (☎ 21824), at Jalan Ahmad Yani 100, is about as cheap as they come with rooms at 3500/5000 rp. The *Gangga Hotel* (☎ 22967), at No 70, is a sprawling place with many styles of room.

SUMATRA

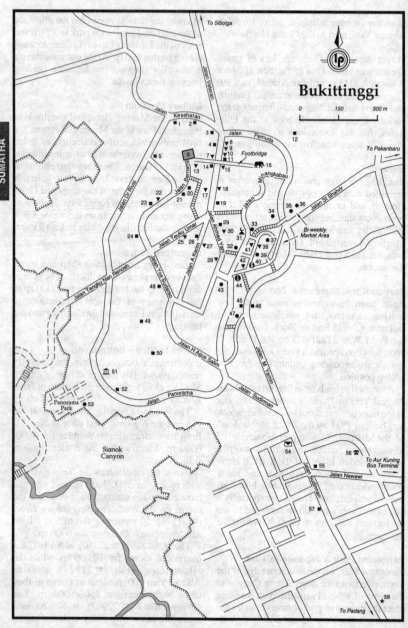

SUMATRA

Bukittinggi

0   150   300 m

To Sibolga

To Pekanbaru

To Padang

To Aur Kuning
Bus Terminal

Panorama
Park

Sianok
Canyon

Footbridge

*Bi-weekly
Market Area*

Jalan Veteran

Jalan Kesehatan

Jalan Pemuda

Jalan Benteng

Jalan Dr Rivai

Jalan Teuku Umar

Jalan Minangkabau

Jalan St Shahrir

Jalan Tengku Nan Renceh

Jalan Yos Sudarso

Jalan A Karim

Jalan Ahmad Yani

Jalan H Agus Salim

Jalan M Yamin

Jalan Panorama

Jalan Sudirman

Jalan Sudirman

Jalan Nawawi

PLACES TO STAY	PLACES TO EAT	OTHER
1 Hotel Denai	7 The Coffee Shop	6 Fort de Kock
2 Lima's Hotel	8 Rendezvous Coffee	16 Zoo & Museum
3 Sri Kandi Hotel	Shop	31 Mosque
4 Hotels Murni & Nirwana	9 Three Tables Coffee	32 Toko Eka
5 Merdeka Homestay	House	33 Gloria Cinema
11 Singgalang Hotel	10 Mexican Coffee Shop	34 Roda Barn
12 Tropic Hotel	13 Family Restaurant	35 Pasar Bawah (Market)
14 Hotel Yany	15 Bukittinggi Coffee Shop	36 Bemo & Opelet Station
19 Wisma Tiga Balai	17 Jazz & Blues Coffee	37 Pasar Wisata
20 Benteng Hotel	Shop	39 Pasar Atas
21 Suwarni Guesthouse	18 Bouganville Coffee	40 Bank BNI 46
23 Mountain View	Shop	43 Clocktower
Guesthouse	22 Restaurant Sari	44 Tourist Office & Small
24 Wisma Bukittinggi	25 Canyon Coffee Shop	Post Office
26 Surya Hotel	27 ASEAN Restaurant	47 Medan Nan
29 Gangga Hotel	28 Selecta Restaurant	Balituduang
45 Hotel Jogja	30 Mona Lisa Restaurant	(Saliguri Dance
46 Hotel Antokan	38 Roda Group Restaurant	Group)
48 Hotel Sari	41 Simpang Raya	51 Military Museum
49 Gallery Hotel	Restaurant	53 Japanese Cave Entry
50 Sumatera Hotel	42 Simpang Raya	54 Post Office
52 Minang Hotel	Restaurant	56 Telkom Office
55 Dymen's Hotel		58 Police
57 Hotel Bagindo		

SUMATRA

Simple rooms cost 3500/6000 rp, better rooms with mandi are 5000/8000 rp and the best rooms with hot water are 20,000/25,000 rp.

A good alternative to Jalan Ahmad Yani are the places on the way to Fort de Kock. The quiet *Suwarni Guesthouse* is in an old Dutch house with a lot more character than the cheap hotels. It has dorm beds for 3500 rp, and rooms cost from 7000 to 10,000 rp. It also does food and has information on the attractions around Bukittinggi.

Another good old-style guesthouse is the *Wisma Bukittinggi*, with small rooms for 4000 rp and larger rooms for 7500 rp or 10,000 rp with attached bathroom.

The *Merdeka Homestay* (☎ 21253), at the corner of Jalan Dr Rivai and Jalan Yos Sudarso, is a solid old Dutch house with dorms for 5000 rp and rooms for 10,000 rp.

Places to Stay – middle
There's a string of mid-range places on the roads leading up to the fort. The *Mountain View Guesthouse* (☎ 21621), at Jalan Yos Sudarso 3, is a modern place with well-kept rooms from 14,000 rp with mandi.

The very comfortable *Benteng Hotel* (☎ 21115) is a bit more expensive, but it's the pick of the mid-range places with great views over the town towards Merapi. Prices start at 24,000/32,500 rp, and all rooms have baths, hot water and TV. The price includes a breakfast of fried rice and coffee.

The *Hotel Jogja* (☎ 21142), below the market on Jalan M Yamin, looks like the owners spent their money on satellite TV rather than paint. Nevertheless, it's a friendly places with basic singles/doubles for 10,000/15,000 rp, and rooms with satellite TV for 20,000/27,500. It also has a travel agency in the foyer.

Past the post office, at Jalan Sudirman 45, the *Hotel Bagindo* (☎ 23100) is a curious mix of the functional and the traditional – a concrete box with a Minangkabau-style awning stuck on the front. It's more comfortable than it looks with doubles priced from 28,000 rp. All rooms have hot water.

Places to Stay – top end
Close by the Bagindo, at Jalan Nawawi 3, is *Dymen's Hotel* (☎ 21015) at Jalan Nawawi 3. It has rooms from 70,000 rp.

The pick of the up-market places is the *Hotel Denai* (☎ 32920), at Jalan Dr Rivai 26, with rooms starting at 70,000 rp. It also has Minangkabau-style cottages for 120,000 rp and suites for 200,000 rp.

Three km south of town is the new, enormous and empty *Hotel Pusako* (☎ 321110). Singles/doubles here start at 150,000/170,000 rp.

Places to Eat

The restaurants among the cheap hotels on Jalan Ahmad Yani feature all the favourite travellers' fare. There's half a dozen different ways to have your breakfast egg as well as various pancakes, muesli, fruit salad and buffalo yoghurt.

The most popular places to hang out are the *Three Tables Coffee House* and the *Rendezvous Coffee Shop* at the bottom end of the street. Both are also good places to pick up information, although you'll have to deal with all the guides who stop by to offer their services.

The menu is a bit more sophisticated at the *Harau Cliff Coffee Shop*, next to the Rendezvous, where you can sink your teeth into a chunk of imported American sirloin steak for 13,000 rp.

Off by itself, on Jalan Teuku Umar, is the delightful *Canyon Coffee Shop* with good food and atmosphere.

Naturally enough, Padang food is plentiful. The best places are around the market. The *Roda Group* and *Simpang Raya* are big names in the nasi padang business with branches all over Sumatra. Each has two branches in the market. The Simpang Raya also has menus, unusual in Padang restaurants. Located on the Fort de Kock hill, at the top of the road, the *Family Restaurant* also does good Padang food.

Chinese food also is well represented. The tiny *Mona Lisa*, at Jalan Ahmad Yani 58, has long been a popular spot with travellers. The food is much better at the *Selecta*, further up Jalan Ahmad Yani near the markets. The *ASEAN Restaurant*, at Jalan A Karim 12A, also has good Chinese food.

Near Fort de Kock, the *Restaurant Sari*

has excellent food and juices on its mostly Chinese menu and is moderately priced for the quality on offer. You can dine outside in the thatched area with commanding views of the surrounding valley and hills. A number of places in Bukittinggi, including the Western-oriented coffee houses, do the local speciality *dadiah campur*, a tasty mixture of oats, coconut, fruit, molasses and buffalo yoghurt.

Entertainment

The town's very professional Saliguri Dance Group puts on performances of Minangkabau dance/theatre every Tuesday and Friday night in a hall on the road linking Jalan Sudirman and Jalan M Yamin. The show starts at 8.30 pm and costs 5000 rp.

Things to Buy

Bukittinggi is a good place to go shopping. There's the usual cotton goods with clocktower and bullfight T-shirts, and there's also some excellent local handicrafts.

There are a number of antique, souvenir and curio shops around. Try Kerajinan, at Jalan Ahmad Yani 44, and Aladdin at No 14. There are more around the market area.

Box collectors can look out for a couple of Minangkabau versions. *Salapah panjang*, or long boxes, are brass boxes used for storing lime and tobacco, and *salapah padusi* are silver boxes used for storing betel nut and lime.

Getting There & Away

Padang is only two hours south of Bukittinggi, a pleasant trip costing 1500 rp.

The road north to Sibolga and Parapat is twisting and narrow for much of the way. Regular buses can make the trip to Parapat in 15 hours, while the air-con buses do it in 13 hours.

The Aur Kuning bus station is about two km from the town centre but easily reached on the local opelets. Typical fares from Bukittinggi include: Medan (20,000 rp, or 25,000 rp with air-con); Parapat (17,500 rp, 22,500 rp air-con); Sibolga (12,000 rp); and Pekanbaru (7000 rp). You can also get buses through to Bengkulu, Jambi or Palembang. You can buy tickets at the bus station, and the tourist office has a list of bus companies and ticket prices. Ticket prices vary quite a lot between travel agencies, so shop around.

The tourist coaches leave for Parapat every morning at 7.30 am and cost 20,000 rp. Tickets can be booked at a number of places in town. The bus picks up from some hotels and travel agencies that sell tickets. The buses stop just outside Bonjol at the equator, site of a tacky monument and several stalls selling 'I Crossed The Equator' T-shirts and a few other souvenirs.

If you're arriving in Bukittinggi from the north (Parapat) or east (Pekanbaru), get off the bus near the town centre and save the hassle of a 200 rp opelet ride back from the main bus terminal which is south of the centre.

Getting Around
Opelets around Bukittinggi cost 150 rp for three-wheelers or 200 rp for the four-wheel variety. The four-wheelers run to the bus station. *Bendis* (horsecarts) cost from 500 to 1000 rp depending on the distance.

AROUND BUKITTINGGI
Koto Gadang
This village, known for its silverwork, is a comfortable walk, eight km south-east of Bukittinggi through the Sianok Canyon.

Pandai Sikat
The name means 'clever craftsmen' and the village is famous for its songket weaving and ornate woodcarving – too ornate for many Western tastes. The village is only 13 km from Bukittinggi and easily accessible by bemo for 200 rp from Aur Kuning bus station.

Ngalau Kamanga
The 1500-metre-long cave at Ngalau Kamanga, 15 km north-east of Bukittinggi, was used as a base for guerrilla attacks against the Dutch in the late 19th and early 20th centuries. The cave is dripping with stalactites and stalagmites and has a small, clear lake.

Batu Sangkar
Batu Sangkar is a traditional village in the Minangkabau heartlands, 41 km south-east of Bukittinggi. There are the remains of some stone tablets with Sanskrit inscriptions and lots of *rumah adat* (traditional houses) with horned roofs. There are more at **Pagaruyang**, five km to the north, as well as a massive reconstruction of a king's house. **Belimbing** is another traditional village 10 km south of Batu Sangkar.

Rafflesia Sanctuary
There is a rafflesia sanctuary about 16 km north of Bukittinggi near the village of Palupuh. A sign in the village indicates the path to the sanctuary. The Rafflesia blooms between August and November. The tourist office in Bukittinggi can tell you if there are blooms around.

Gunung Merapi
Gunung Merapi (2890 metres) can be climbed, but it is an active volcano and therefore occasionally deemed too dangerous. The last major eruption was in 1979. The tourist office in Bukittinggi can tell you when the mountain is off limits. It probably

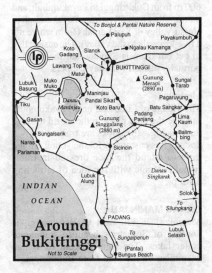

Around Bukittinggi
Not to Scale

won't stop the staff offering their services as guides.

The climb begins at the village of Kota Baru (of bullfighting fame on Tuesdays). From Kota Baru, it's a one-hour climb to the forestry station (which is no more than a shelter) and then another four hours to the top. Most people climb at night, with the objective of being on the summit at dawn. You'll need good walking boots, warm clothing, a torch and food and drink.

Travel agencies in Bukittinggi offer guided trips to Merapi with transport to Kota Baru and a snack at the top for 15,000 rp.

Harau Valley

The Harau Valley, 15 km north-east of Payakumbuh, is a popular local beauty spot that is included on many tour itineraries. The valley is enclosed by spectacular, sheer 100-metre cliffs. The cliffs are popular with rock-climbers – anyone interested should ask Dodi at the Harau Cliff Coffee Shop in Bukittinggi. Otherwise, there's walks and waterfalls. Harau village is three km up the valley.

The Harau Valley is not an easy place to get to. The first step is to catch a bemo for 600 rp from Bukittinggi to Payakumbuh, and then another for 250 rp from Payakumbuh to Harau Valley or Sari Lamak (from where it's a five-km walk to the valley). The easiest day to get out there is Sunday, but the place is normally packed with day-trippers.

Limbuku

The village of Limbuku, near Payakumbuh, must be the only place in the world to stage duck racing – the ducks are trained to fly a course! It is customary for the young village girls to attend the race dressed in traditional costume with the idea of attracting a suitor.

DANAU MANINJAU

Maninjau, 38 km west of Bukittinggi, is another of Sumatra's beautiful mountain crater lakes. The final descent to Danau Maninjau, on the road from Bukittinggi, is

unforgettable. The road twists and turns through 44 (most of them numbered) hairpin bends in quick succession, and offers stunning views over the shimmering blue lake and surrounding hills.

It is well set up for young travellers, but remains relatively unspoiled. At 500 metres above sea level, the air is pleasantly cool – cool enough, in fact, to warrant a blanket at night.

The lake is 17 km long, eight km wide and 480 metres deep in places.

Orientation & Information

Most people arrive from Bukittinggi. The bus stop is at the crossroads where the Bukittinggi road meets the main street of Maninjau.

To the south is Jalan H Udin Rahmani. It has most of the town of Maninjau's shops (which isn't many), several restaurants and three or four guesthouses.

To the right is Jalan SMP which leads off around the lake to the north. It has the majority of Maninjau's 20-odd losmen and numerous coffee shops, as well as the only bank.

Money The Bank Rakyat Indonesia will change US dollars only – either cash or travellers' cheques.

Post & Telephone International calls can be made from the telephone office next to the bus stop. The post office is opposite the police station on the road running down to the lake.

Things to See & Do

The waters of Maninjau are considerably warmer – and cleaner – than at Lake Toba, so it's a good place for swimming. Some of the guesthouses hire/lend dugout canoes or inflated truck inner tubes.

There are some good walks, and **hot springs** are signposted up the hill near the Km 1 marker, north of Maninjau. A far more strenuous hike leads to **Sakura Hill** and **Lawang Top**, which have excellent views

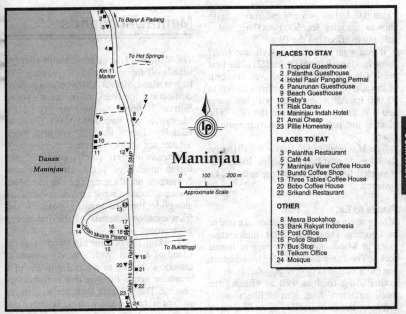

PLACES TO STAY

1 Tropical Guesthouse
2 Palantha Guesthouse
4 Hotel Pasir Pangang Permai
6 Panurunan Guesthouse
9 Beach Guesthouse
10 Feby's
11 Riak Danau
14 Maninjau Indah Hotel
21 Amai Cheap
23 Pillie Homestay

PLACES TO EAT

3 Palantha Restaurant
5 Café 44
7 Maninjau View Coffee House
12 Bundo Coffee Shop
19 Three Tables Coffee House
20 Bobo Coffee House
22 Srikandi Restaurant

OTHER

8 Mesra Bookshop
13 Bank Rakyat Indonesia
15 Post Office
16 Police Station
17 Bus Stop
18 Telkom Office
24 Mosque

Maninjau

of the lake and the surrounding area. It's much easier to do this hike in reverse, catching a Bukittinggi-bound bus as far as Matur and climbing Lawang from there before descending to the lake on foot. A fit person can do it in a couple of hours, but allow longer.

Places to Stay

Maninjau has more than 20 guesthouses to choose from as well as a couple of larger, up-market hotels. There are a few hotels in the village itself, but the majority are dotted along the lakeside for a km or so to the north.

While there are lots of places to choose from, there is not much between them. The main difference is between those on the shore of the lake and those set back from the water. Those on the water's edge are understandably more popular.

The best place in Maninjau village is the spotless *Pillie Homestay*, 150 metres from the bus stop on Jalan H Udin Rahmani. It has singles for 3000 rp and doubles for 6000 rp.

The nearby *Amai Cheap* (☎ 61054) is a striking old colonial Dutch house with a huge balcony and rooms priced from 5000 to 7000 rp.

Heading north from Maninjau on Jalan SMP, there's little to choose between the *Riak Danau*, *Feby's* and the *Beach Guesthouse*, next to each other on the lake's edge 500 metres from town. All have singles/doubles for 4000/7500 rp and virtually identical menus.

Further north still, about 1½ km from town, are two more good places: *Palantha Inn* and the *Tropical Guesthouse*. The Palantha Inn is an intriguing old timber rabbit warren that looks like it was built by a dozen carpenters working off different plans. It charges 4000/7000 rp for singles/doubles. If there's nobody home, ask at the Palantha Restaurant. The Tropical Guesthouse is a more modern place, 100 metres north of

Palantha. It has some good rooms with shower upstairs for 5000/8000 rp and a balcony overlooking the lake.

If you want to rest up in style, the *Hotel Pasir Panjang Permai* (☎ 61022) is the best bet. It's an efficiently run place, one km north of town, with doubles priced from 50,000 to 75,000 rp. All rooms come with hot water and TV, and most overlook the lake. The place is just past the Km 1 marker north of town.

The *Maninjau Indah Hotel* (☎ 61018), on the lakeside past the post office, looks like it started falling down before it could be finished.

Places to Eat

Most guesthouses provide meals like mie or nasi goreng. There are several small restaurants in Maninjau offering typical tourist tucker. The *Three Tables Coffee House* (there are more upstairs) is very popular. It serves both Padang food as well as offering the usual travellers' fare. Animal liberationists can enjoy the unavailability of the 'Kentucky Freed Chicken'.

Down the road, the *Srikandi* does a very tasty sweet & sour fish for 8000 rp, which is heaps for two people. Sweet & sour spaghetti for 1300 rp was one of several unusual items on the menu.

The *Maninjau View Coffee House*, set on a small rise back from the lake 500 metres north of town, is a good place to relax and study the view.

Café 44 is a popular restaurant and party spot on the lakeside, reached down a path next to the Panururan Homestay.

Getting There & Away

There are buses between Maninjau and Bukittinggi every hour for 800 rp. The journey takes almost an hour. There are two direct buses a day to Padang (2500 rp; 2½ hours) which go via the coast road rather than the Bukittinggi road.

Getting Around

There are a number of places renting mountain bikes for about 4000 rp per day.

Mentawai Islands

The Mentawai Islands are a remote chain of islands off the west coast of Sumatra. The largest island, Siberut, has become a popular destination for trekkers in recent years. Siberut is home to the majority of the Mentawais' population of 30,000. The other islands, Sipora, Pagai Utara and Pagai Selatau, are seldom visited.

After being left quietly on their own for thousands of years, change is now coming at an alarming rate for the Mentawaians. Tourism is but a minor development alongside the pro-logging policies and transmigration schemes of the Indonesian government.

Trekking has become big business on the island of Siberut, with a steady stream of travellers coming to catch a glimpse of a primitive jungle lifestyle that is fast disappearing. The villagers, their bodies covered with ritual tattoos and wearing little but loin clothes and decorative bands and rings, are a photogenic lot who have found tour groups to be good sources of extra income.

History

Very little is known about the origins of the Mentawaians but it is assumed that they emigrated from Sumatra to Nias and made their way to Siberut from there.

They remained isolated and undisturbed by other cultures until late in the 19th century when the Dutch permitted Protestant missionaries to attempt to convert them to Christianity.

There are several references to the islands before the 19th century. In 1621, it appears that Siberut was the only island inhabited. The Mentawaians are also mentioned in a scientific paper presented in 1799 by the Englishman John Crisp. Sir Stamford Raffles appears to have been particularly impressed by the Mentawaians and their culture. In one of the many reports he wrote urging the British government to compete with the Dutch in colonising Indonesia he states:

Formerly, I intended to write a book to prove that the Niassans were the most contented people on earth. Now I have to acknowledge the fact that the people of the Mentawai Islands are even more admirable and probably much less spoiled than we.

In 1864, the Mentawai Archipelago was nominally made a Dutch colony, but it was not until 1901, at the time of the Russo-Japanese War, that the Dutch placed a garrison on the islands to prevent another foreign power using them as a naval base.

Apart from taking a few minor precautions to protect the Mentawai Islands from being taken over by other imperialist nations, the Dutch showed very little interest in them. It was the missionaries who had the most influence on the people, creating fundamental changes in their culture.

The first permanent mission was set up in 1901, in Pagai Utara, by a German missionary, August Lett. Eight years later, Lett was murdered by the local people but the mission survived and by 1916 there had been 11 baptisms recorded. There are now more than 80 Protestant churches throughout the islands. Over half the population claims to be Protestant, 16% Catholic, 13% Muslim, while the rest have no official religion.

It was over 50 years after the advent of the Protestant missionaries that the Catholics moved into the islands to vie for converts. They opened a mission in south Siberut which combined a church, a school and a clinic. Free medicines and clothes were given to any islander who became a Catholic and by 1969 there were almost 3000 converts.

The Islamic influence began to make inroads once government officials were regularly appointed from Padang during the Dutch era. To complicate religious matters further, the eclectic Baha'i faith was introduced in 1955.

Economy

Taros and bananas are the staple crops of both the Pagai Islands and Sipora, while on Siberut, sago is also cultivated. Traditionally, the women own the taro fields and are

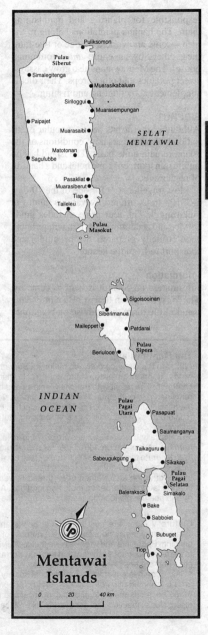

Mentawai
Islands

0   20   40 km

responsible for planting and maintaining them. The banana plantations belong to the men – some are worked by one or two families, others by an entire *uma* (communal house). The Mentawaians also grow cassava, sweet potatoes and other crops. Their diet is supplemented by hunting and fishing.

SIBERUT

Although Siberut has been a popular destination for some years now, conditions on the island remain quite basic. The island has no public transport, only one hotel and a handful of restaurants.

Most travellers opt for one of the 10-day, US$125 treks offered by various guides in Bukittinggi. The tour price includes guide service and accommodation (in village huts), food (usually prepared by the guide) and transport to/from the island.

Banana Palm

Information

Information on Siberut is hard to come by. The West Sumatran tourist office in Padang can do little more than advise on boat times and show you a booklet called *Saving Siberut* that was put out by the WWF in the early 1980s. It can, however, issue permits (free, but requiring two passport photos) and

---

The Mentawaians

Although the distance between mainland Sumatra and the Mentawai Islands is not great, strong winds, unpredictable seas and coral reefs made navigation to the islands difficult in earlier centuries. The result was that the Mentawaians had very little contact with the outside world and remained one of the purest indigenous Indonesian societies until early in the 20th century when the missionaries arrived. The Mentawaians had their own language, their own adat and their own religion. They were skilled in boat building, but had not developed any kind of handicraft nor cultivated rice.

Physically, the Mentawaians are slim and agile. Traditional clothing consists of a loin cloth made from the bark of the breadfruit tree for men and a bark skirt for women. They sharpen their teeth and decorate themselves with tattoos which cover part of their faces and most of their bodies and wear bands of red-coloured rattan, beads and imported brass rings on their arms, fingers and toes. Both men and women often thread flowers through their long hair. The government has banned tattoos, sharpened teeth and long hair. Although the ban has not been enforced, it's now rare to see people looking like this, except in the more remote villages.

Culture Villages are built along river banks and consist of one or more uma surrounded by single-storey family houses *(lalep)*. A number of families (between five and 10) live in the same building. Bachelors and widows have their own living quarters, known as *rusuk*, which are identical to the family longhouse except that they have no altar. Traditionally all the houses stand on wooden piles and are designed without windows.

Although it is essentially a patriarchal society, it is organised on egalitarian principles. There are no inherited titles or positions, and no subordinate roles. It is the uma, not the village itself, which becomes the pivot of social, political and religious life in Mentawai society. It is here that discussions affecting the community take place. Everyone – men, women and children – are

tell you about any special requirements for independent visits to the islands.

Money There are no banks and no money-changers so you will need to bring your cash requirements with you. Although some villagers prefer gifts to payment in cash, most places on what is now a well-trodden trail prefer cash. You'll certainly need cash in Muarasiberut.

When to Go May is generally the driest month, but it can rain on Siberut at any time of year. The seas between Siberut can get very rough in June and July, which means tours may be cancelled if boats aren't running. October and November tend to be the wettest months on Siberut.

What to Bring If you're heading off independently, you will need your own food supplies – rice, noodles, dried food as well as tea and sugar. Essential items for jungle living are a mosquito net, insect repellent, torch and plastic bags for keeping things dry.

You can buy most supplies in Muarasiberut and Muarasikabaluan, but they are much cheaper if bought in Padang.

The smaller your backpack the better. It will be easier to carry in the jungle and transport in the sampans.

You will also need to bring things for barter and gifts. Pens, pencils and paper are much sounder choices than cigarettes, which unfortunately are the accepted gift currency.

Medicines should on no account be given away as gifts.

The demand for gifts has become a constant hassle. Most islanders already seem to think that White people are rich fools who will willingly part with anything asked of them. It's wise to give things only to people who have helped.

Health Chloroquine-resistant malaria is a common problem and each year many locals die from it. There are plenty of snakes around, but they are not likely to be a problem. The rivers are used for washing and as running toilets, and thus are a source of

present at meetings, but the prominent men make most of the major decisions, including choosing a *rimata* (the person who leads religious affairs and is the community's spokesperson to the outside world), building an uma, clearing forests, or laying out a banana plantation.

On such occasions the people of the uma carry out a religious festival known as *punen*. This usually involves ritual sacrifices of both pigs and chickens and, depending on the importance of the occasion, can last for months on end and sometimes years. All kinds of everyday jobs and activities become taboo; work in the fields is stopped and strangers are denied access to the uma – its isolation being marked by a cordon of palm leaves and flowers.

Religion The native Sibulungan religion was a form of animism, involving the worship of nature spirits and a belief in the existence of ghosts as well as the soul. The chief nature spirits are those in the sky, sea, jungle and earth. There are also two river spirits: Ina Oinan (mother of rivers) is beneficent while Kameinan (father's sister) is regarded as being evil. Apart from these nature spirits all inanimate objects have spirits (*kina*) which give them life. There is no hierarchy among the spirits, although the sky spirits are considered the most influential, nor do they have any particular gender, but like human beings there's a mixture of men, women and children.

As with all religions in Indonesia, the worship of the soul is of the utmost importance, being vital to good health and longevity. The soul is believed to depart the body at various times during life before its ultimate escape at death. Sickness, for example, is the result of the temporary absence of the soul from the body, while dreams also signify that the soul is on 'vacation'. When the soul leaves the body at death it is transformed into a ghost *(sanitu)*. Mentawaians try to avoid these ghosts, whom they suspect of malevolently attempting to rob the living of their souls. To protect themselves from such an awful fate, they place fetish sticks at every entrance to the village. This tactic is considered foolproof, provided no-one has committed a ritual sin or broken a taboo. ∎

disease. Never drink water unless it has been boiled or purified.

Dangers & Annoyances Theft can be a problem but normally only of small items left lying around. Also remember that elderly people dislike cameras and are afraid of flashes. You will not be well received in a village if you arrive with camera at the ready.

Things to See & Do
Despite recent changes, about two-thirds of the island is still covered with tropical rainforest. It's also surrounded by magnificent coral reefs teeming with fish. The two main towns on Siberut are **Muarasikaba-luan** in the north and **Muarasiberut** at the southern tip of the east coast. There is no public transport on the island so you either have to walk between villages, catch public boats or charter private boats.

Sakelot is the most interesting of the four villages. It's a traditional village accessible on foot (one km) from Muarasiberut. The others are new – a legacy of the government's policy of moving the people out of the jungle and setting them up in villages along the coastal strip.

One of the easiest villages to get to from Muarasiberut is **Tiap**, which is two hours by boat along a narrow branch of jungle river. A more adventurous, but still comparatively easy trip is to **Rokdok**, where people live in small, traditional houses. It takes between five and six hours to get there and back by boat.

Two more remote villages are **Sakudai** and **Madobak**. The journey to Sakudai takes two days – one day by boat and the other trekking through the jungle. The trip to Madobak takes six hours by boat.

Organised Tours
Most people take the easy option of joining a guided tour. It is also the cheap option, in view of the costs involved in getting around Siberut alone – getting around by charter boat is an expensive way to travel.

Bukittinggi is the place to go to check out the tour offerings. Almost everywhere in town seems to advertise treks. The best approach is to spend some time in the coffee shops seeking out the experiences of those who have just returned. Prices are all much the same – US$125 for 10 days/nine nights is the going rate. Some places offer shorter five-days treks for US$100. Rates include fares, accommodation, guides and most meals. Some travel agencies arrange deluxe outings, such as 10 days for US$285; it's worth asking about the size and composition of a group before signing up.

Some critics claim the tours are no good because they are run by Sumatrans, who are not liked by the Mentawaians. The tour agencies counter that they employ Mentawaian guides.

The comment books run by the agencies can sometimes by helpful, although a glance at the spine of the books shows what happens to pages with negative comments.

The treks usually include plenty of mud-slogging, river crossings and battles with indigenous insects, so don't set off expecting a gentle jaunt through the jungle.

The return on your suffering is the chance to experience unspoiled rainforest and the local culture of Siberut. Most people come away very happy with their trekking package.

Places to Stay & Eat
The only losmen on Siberut is *Syahruuddin's Home Stay*, at Muarasiberut, where a bed costs 6000 rp. In more remote areas, it's often possible to stay at missionary buildings, schools or with private families, but don't expect any comforts. Accommodation is usually on the floor. Payment is normally made in the form of a gift rather than money.

The situation is much the same for food. There are a few basic restaurants in Muarasiberut and Muarasikabaluan, elsewhere you will be expected either to pay or make a donation for meals.

Getting There & Away
Air The islands' only airport is on Pulau Sipora, but there are no scheduled flights.

Boat There are boats from Padang to Siberut

three times a week. The boats leave from the Muara River Harbour in Padang. The offices of PT Rusco Lines (☎ 21941) at Jalan Batang Arau 31 and Nusa Mentawai Indah (☎ 28200), Jalan Batan Arau 88, are the places to ask about services. The better boats cost from 15,000 rp economy to 20,000 rp cabin class, and the journey takes 10 to 12 hours. Sometimes people get groups together to charter a boat across and back, giving them transport around the coast as well.

Other options include chartering private boats from Padang or Nias. Small boats are available for charter but are not advised as the sea and winds are rough and unpredictable in this region – the journey is not only likely to be uncomfortable, but could also be dangerous. If you only intend chartering the boat one way, you will have to pay the return passage if it goes back empty.

Getting Around

Boats are the main form of local transport. They are used both around the coast and for river transport. You need to bargain hard.

If you're planning on organising your own way around Siberut, the biggest expense will be the cost of getting around. Getting to villages that are off the beaten track will mean chartering boats as well as hiring your own guide. Most of the interesting villages will cost about 100,000 rp to get to, while a guide will cost about 15,000 rp per day. If you want a porter as well, set aside another 10,000 rp per day.

Riau

The province of Riau is split into two distinct areas, mainland Riau and the Riau Islands.

Mainland Riau covers a huge expanse of eastern Sumatra's sparsely populated east coast and has the modern oil town of Pekanbaru as its capital. It has Indonesia's richest oil fields as well as huge deposits of tin and bauxite. Much of the land is dense forest or mangrove swamp – too low-lying and poorly drained for agriculture. Several animistic and nomadic peoples (including the Sakai, Kubu and Jambisal) still live in the jungle, mostly around the port of Dumai.

Offshore Riau is made up of more than 3000 islands spread over more than 1000 km of ocean. The islands' capital is the town of Tanjung Pinang, on Pulau Bintan south-west of Singapore, although attention is fast turning to the boom island of Pulau Batam next door.

The islands are home to a third of Riau Province's population of 2.7 million.

Mosquitoes are rife throughout Riau and chloroquine-resistant malaria has been reported.

History

Before the advent of air travel, Riau occupied a strategic position at the southern entrance to the Selat Melaka, the gateway for trade between India and China.

From the 16th century, the Riau Islands were ruled by a variety of Malay kingdoms, who had to fight off constant attacks from pirates and the opportunistic Portuguese, Dutch and English. The Dutch eventually won their struggle with the Portuguese for control over Selat Melaka, and mainland Riau (then known as Siak) became a Dutch colony in 1745 when the Sultan of Johore surrendered his claim to the Dutch East India Company.

The Dutch were more interested in ridding the seas of pirates so their fleet could trade without losses and danger than in governing or developing the region, so they left Riau alone.

PEKANBARU

The capital of mainland Riau is made up of a sleazy port on the banks of the Sungai Siak, and a modern administrative centre stretching away from the river to the south. The further away from the port you go, the better Pekanbaru gets.

There's little to see or do in Pekanbaru. For most travellers it's no more than a transit stop between the Riau Islands and Bukittinggi.

SUMATRA

Oil was discovered around Pekanbaru by US engineers before WW II, but it was the Japanese who drilled the first well at Rumbai, 10 km north of Pekanbaru. Rumbai is now the base for Caltex Pacific Indonesia. The wilderness of dense rainforest and mangrove swamps around Pekanbaru is crisscrossed by pipelines connecting the oil wells to refineries at Dumai because ocean-going tankers cannot enter the heavily silted Sungai Siak.

The jungle is also home to such rare creatures as the Sumatran rhinoceros and tiger as well as bears, tapirs and elephants.

Orientation & Information

The main street of Pekanbaru is Jalan Sudirman. Almost everything of importance to travellers – banks, hotels and offices – can be found on Jalan Sudirman or close by.

The main port area and ferry wharf is at the end of Jalan Saleh Abbas, while speedboats leave from the wharf at the end of Jalan Sudirman. The bus station is at the other end of town on Jalan Nangka, and the airport is out of town on the road to Bukittinggi.

Tourist Office The new regional tourist office (☎ 31562) is at Jalan Diponegoro 24A, while the provincial office (☎ 31452) is at Jalan Merbabu 16.

Money Pekanbaru has branches of all the major banks. The Bank of Central Asia, at Jalan Sudirman 8, is the best place to go. The BNI 1946 is at Jalan Sudirman 63. It's possible to change money at the airport, but the rates are poor, as they are from the moneychanger at Toko Firmas, Jalan Sudirman 27.

Post & Telephone The main post office and the Telkom office are on Jalan Sudirman, between Jalan Hangtuah and Jalan Kartini. There is a small post office nearer the port at the corner of Jalan Sudirman and Jalan Juanda.

Travel Agencies Kota Piring Kencana Travel (☎ 21382), conveniently located at

Jalan Sisingamangaraja 3, can handle flight and bus bookings as well as tours.

Things to See & Do

Few people hang around Pekanbaru for long enough to do anything other than buy a ticket out. Not a bad idea, really, but if you've got time to burn there's always the **Museum Negeri Riau** and neighbouring **Riau Cultural Park** towards the airport on Jalan Sudirman. They are open from 8 am until 2 pm Monday to Thursday and Saturday, 8 am until 12 pm on Friday.

The **Balai Adat Daerah Riau**, on Jalan Diponegoro, has displays of traditional Malay culture and is open the same hours as the museum. The **Great Mosque** (*Mesjid Raya*), near the junction of Jalan Riau and Jalan Ahmad Yani, dates back to the 18th century when Pekanbaru was the capital of the Siak sultans. The courtyard holds the graves of the fourth and fifth sultans.

Places to Stay – bottom end

If you have to stay overnight, there are a few decent places around the bus station. *Tommy's Place*, half a km from the bus station on Gang Nantongga at Jalan Nangka 41D, has rooms for 5000 rp and can arrange tickets for the Batam boats. From the bus station, turn right and Gang Nantongga is the second gang on your right side. Walk down and ask for Tommy's.

Poppie's Homestay (☎ 33863), a few minutes' walk from the bus station on Jalan Cempedak II, is another traveller-friendly place. It has doubles for 10,000 rp and dorm beds for 3500 rp, and can also arrange boat tickets. You will be picked up from the port if you phone. *Penginapan Linda*, on Jalan Nangka, has clean rooms from 7500 rp.

If you're departing by boat, there are a couple of rundown and depressing hotels with little going for them other than their proximity to the port. The *Nirmala*, at Jalan Yatim 11, is typical with rooms from 7000 rp.

There are a few cheapies on Jalan Sisingamangaraja in the town centre. They include the *Hotel Tutenja Atas* (☎ 22985), at

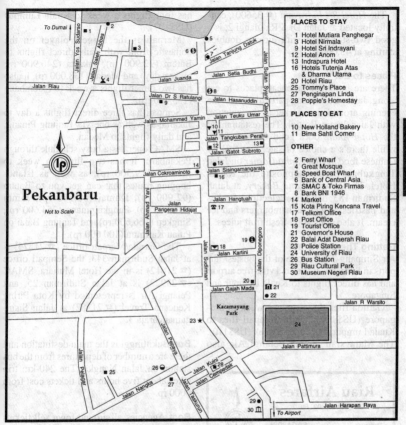

Pekanbaru

Not to Scale

PLACES TO STAY
1 Hotel Mutiara Panghegar
3 Hotel Nirmala
9 Hotel Sri Indrayani
12 Hotel Anom
13 Indrapura Hotel
16 Hotels Tutenja Atas
   & Dharma Utama
20 Hotel Riau
25 Tommy's Place
27 Penginapan Linda
28 Poppie's Homestay

PLACES TO EAT
10 New Holland Bakery
11 Bima Sahti Corner

OTHER
2 Ferry Wharf
4 Great Mosque
5 Speed Boat Wharf
6 Bank of Central Asia
7 SMAC & Toko Firmas
8 Bank BNI 1946
14 Market
15 Kota Piring Kencana Travel
17 Telkom Office
18 Post Office
19 Tourist Office
21 Governor's House
22 Balai Adat Daerah Riau
23 Police Station
24 University of Riau
26 Bus Station
29 Riau Cultural Park
30 Museum Negeri Riau

SUMATRA

No 4, and the extremely basic *Hotel Dharma Utama* (☎ 22171) at No 10. Both have doubles for 10,000 rp.

Places to Stay – middle

There are a some good mid-range places around the town centre. The *Hotel Anom* (☎ 22636), at the corner of Jalan Sudirman and Jalan Gatot Subroto, has reasonable rooms set around a courtyard. Doubles with mandi cost 18,000 rp, rising to 30,000 rp with air-con.

The *Riau* (☎ 22986) is a good, quiet hotel at Jalan Diponegoro 34. Clean rooms with

mandi and fan cost 20,000 rp, while air-con rooms are 50,000 rp.

Places to Stay – top end

The flashest hotel in town is the *Mutiara Panghegar* (☎ 23637), at Jalan Yos Sudarso 12, before the bridge across the Siak. It had oil executives rather than travellers in mind when pricing its cheapest doubles at 120,000 rp. Non-guests can pay 3500 rp to use the swimming pool.

There's also a pool at the Mutiara's slightly cheaper three-star rival, the *Indrapura Hotel* (☎ 36233), at Jalan Dr Sutomo 86.

The *Hotel Sri Indrayani* (☎ 35600), centrally located at Jalan Dr S Ratulangi 2, is a good two-star place with air-con doubles starting at 45,000 rp.

Places to Eat
There are innumerable cheap places to eat along Jalan Sudirman, particularly in the evening around the market at the junction with Jalan Imam Bonjol. The restaurant at the *Hotel Anom* does good Chinese food, while there's a choice of sate, martabak or Chinese food at *Bima Sahti Corner* on Jalan Tangkuban Perahu, opposite the Rauda Hotel. The *New Holland Bakery*, at Jalan Sudirman 153, has a fine selection of cakes and pastries as well as hamburgers and ice cream. It also does good fresh fruit juices.

Getting There & Away
Air Simpang Tiga is one of the busiest airports in Sumatra. It is also a visa-free airport and has direct flights to Kuala Lumpur and Singapore.

Garuda flies three times a week to Singapore (US$102), while Sempati flies to Kuala Lumpur four times a week (US$110). The Malaysian airline Pelangi Air also

has four flights a week to Kuala Lumpur (US$107).

Merpati is the biggest player on the domestic front with daily direct flights to Batam (92,900 rp), Jakarta (246,900 rp; twice a day) and Medan (138,000 rp). It also has two direct flights a week to Palembang (153,400 rp).

Sempati has three direct flights a day to Jakarta, as well as one via Tanjung Pinang, and daily flights to Medan.

SMAC operates a busy schedule through Pekanbaru. It has two flights a week to Medan (119,300 rp), as well as island-hopping routes that can get you to Batam (92,900 rp), Dumai (68,700 rp), Jambi (116,000 rp), Pangkalpinang (254,600 rp), Singkep (166,600 rp) and Tanjung Balai on Pulau Karimun (100,600 rp).

The Garuda/Merpati office (☎ 21575) is at Jalan Sudirman 343, the Sempati office (☎ 21612) is in the Hotel Mutiara, SMAC (☎ 23922) is at Jalan Sudirman 25, and Pelangi Air is represented by Kota Piring Kencana Travel (☎ 21382) at Jalan Sisingamangaraja 3.

Bus Bukittinggi is the main destination and there are a number of departures from the bus station on Jalan Nangka. The 240-km trip takes about five hours and tickets cost from 6000 rp.

Boat Agencies all around town sell tickets for the boats to Batam. Tickets include the bus fare to Tanjung Buton and the speedboat from there to Batam, usually via Selat Panjang. There is not a lot of difference between the speedboat services, though the prices vary from around 28,000 to 35,000 rp. Garuda Express goes by speedboat down the river to Perawang, then by bus to Tanjung Buton and then another speedboat to Batam. It is an interesting trip, though no quicker despite the claims. It is slightly cheaper to do the trip in stages yourself, but you may miss connections.

The other alternative is the slow boat on Monday, Wednesday and Friday at 5 pm, travelling down the Siak River and then on

Riau Airfares
Airfares in '000 Rp

SINGAPORE

Medan
221
Batu Besar
Tanjung Balai — 63 — 46 — Tanjung Pinang
204   92   115
145
Pekanbaru
131   92
Jambi
220
164   84
65
JAKARTA
Palembang   Dabo

to Selat Panjang (9500 rp; 12 hours). It then continues to Batam (25,000 rp; 24 hours) and Bintan. Buy tickets at the wharf – an extra 3000 rp will get you a 'cabin', which is just a bare, wooden sleeping platform, but a luxury compared to deck class.

It's a good idea to take food and drink with you since two meals of boiled rice garnished with a bit of dry, salted fish and a dollop of chilli is all your ticket includes. All is not lost if you forget – or don't have the time – to stock up. The boat stops at various river villages along the way and flotillas of sales people circle around hawking soft drinks, peanuts and fruit.

Getting Around
To/From the Airport Airport cabs charge 10,000 rp for the 12-km trip into town. Metered cabs charge about 6000 rp the other way. It's a one-km walk from the airport to the main road if you want to catch a bemo into town.

SIAK SRI INDERAPURA
Some 120 km down river from Pekanbaru is Siak Sri Inderapura, site of the beautiful Asserayah el Hasyimiah Palace built by the 11th sultan of Siak, Sultan Adbul Jalil Syafuddin, in 1889. The palace was restored five years ago as a museum. The site also includes a dazzling white mosque with a silver dome.

Siak can be reached by a variety of river transport from Pekanbaru, starting with speedboats that will do the trip in two hours. There's reportedly a cheap losmen near the dock in Siak, with doubles for 5000 rp.

DUMAI
Dumai, 158 km from Pekanbaru, is the port through which the bulk of Riau's oil is exported. Apart from the port and a Pertamina refinery, there is not much to Dumai. There is certainly little to interest travellers apart from boat connections. Given that Dumai is not a visa-free port, even these are largely academic.

If you get stuck, try the *City Hotel* (☎ 21550) on Jalan Sudirman. Expect to pay

about 10,000 rp for a double with fan and 25,000 rp for air-con.

There are ferries from Dumai to Melaka in Malaysia at 8 am on Thursday and Sunday (87,500 rp) and from Melaka on Monday and Friday (RM100). The Pelni boats *Rinjani* and *Umsini* also call at Dumai in the course of their fortnightly circuits out of Jakarta, stopping at Pulau Bintan.

RIAU ARCHIPELAGO
The islands of the Riau Archipelago are scattered across the South China Sea like confetti. There are as many islands, locals say, as there are grains in a cup of pepper (3214 islands in all, more than 700 of them uninhabited and many of them unnamed).

The term Riau originally applied only to the group of islands immediately south-west of Singapore, including Batam, Bintan, Rempang and Galang islands. The modern administrative region also takes in the nearby Karimun Islands and the Lingga Islands further south, as well as stretching 1000 km to the north-east to take in the remote South China Sea island groups of Anambas, North and South Natuna and Tambelan.

Tanjung Pinang, on Pulau Bintan, is the traditional capital of the islands, but much attention is focused these days on Pulau Batam, which is rapidly being developed as an industrial extension of Singapore.

History
The early history of the Riau Archipelago suggests a wave of migration from southern India. Around 1000 AD, Pulau Bintan emerged as a separate kingdom which was enlarged by a propitious marriage to the son of a king of Palembang. A capital was built in Temasik (now Singapore) and the principality was renamed Bintan Temasik Singapura.

By 1500, the kingdom of Melaka held sway through the islands of Kundur, Jemaja, Bunguran, Tambelan, Lingga and Bintan. The Portuguese ruled Riau for a brief period following their conquest of Melaka, but from 1530 to the end of the 18th century, the

SUMATRA

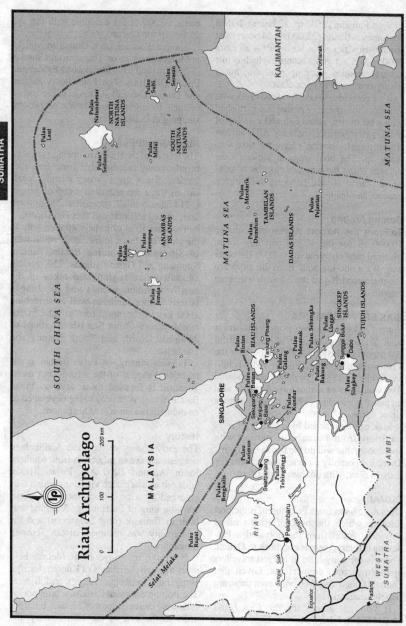

archipelago was a stronghold of Malay civilisation with its main centres at Penyenget and Lingga.

In 1685, Sultan Mahmud Syah II was coerced into signing an agreement with the Dutch which greatly diminished his authority. The Dutch gradually reduced the authority of the rajas, and finally assumed control of the archipelago on the death of the raja in 1784.

Opposition to the Dutch did not really re-emerge until the early 1900s when the Rusydiah Club was formed by the last sultan of Riau-Lingga. This was ostensibly a cultural and literary organisation, but later assisted in the struggle for Indonesian independence.

People
Most of the inhabitants of the islands are of pure Malay origins, but there are several indigenous groups like the *orang laut* (sea gypsies) of the Natuna Islands, the Mantang peoples of Penuba and Kelumu islands and the Baruk people of Sunggai Buluh, Singkep.

Bintan is the largest and most populous of the Riau Islands. The majority of people are of Malay origin, but the ethnic melting pot includes Sumatran peoples such as the Batak and Minangkabau, as well as a comparatively large Chinese community. The population is about 90% Muslim.

Architecture
The traditional architecture of the Riau Islands is called *rumah lipat kijang*, meaning 'hairpin' and refers to the shape of the roof. The style is undergoing a revival at present and is used for most new public buildings.

Houses are usually adorned with carvings of flowers, birds and bees. Often there are wings on each corner, said to symbolise the capacity to adapt. Four pillars have much the same meaning: the capacity to live in the four corners of the universe. The flowers are supposed to convey a message of prosperity and happiness from owner to visitor, the birds symbolise the one true god and the bees symbolise the desire for mutual understanding.

Festivals
The islanders of remote Pulau Serasan in the South Natuna Islands hold an annual Festival of the Sea. They hang packets of sticky rice on trees near the beach, then cut logs from the forest which they cart down to the beach, load into canoes and drop into deep water to appease the gods of the ocean and protect them from drowning. The islanders also uphold the principal festivals of the Islamic calendar.

PULAU BATAM
Nowhere in Indonesia is the pace of development more rapid than on Pulau Batam. Until the island was declared a free-trade zone in 1989, it was a backwater comprising little more than the shanties of Nagoya and a few coastal villages.

Several years of frantic construction later, it is fast emerging as an industrial overflow of Singapore. Batam is also set to supply water to the thirsty city-state following the building of the huge Duriankang Reservoir in the centre of the island.

Although much of the island is set for industrial development, there are a number of resort hotels on the north coast around Nongsa. For the most part, however, there's a distinct frontier town atmosphere to the place, with high prices, ugly construction sites and no reason to pause other than to catch one of the daily boats to Pekanbaru on the Sumatran mainland.

The seaports of Sekupang and Batu Ampar and Hang Nadim airport are all visa-free entry and exit points.

Orientation & Information
Most travellers arrive on Batam by boat from Singapore to Sekupang. After immigration, there are counters for money exchange, taxis and hotels. Boats to Pulau Bintan leave from Kabil on the opposite side of the island.

The main town, Nagoya, is the original boom town, complete with bars and preening prostitutes. The old shanties can still be seen peeping out between the flash new hotels, offices and shopping centres. Nagoya's port area of Batu Ampar is just north of town.

SUMATRA

SUMATRA

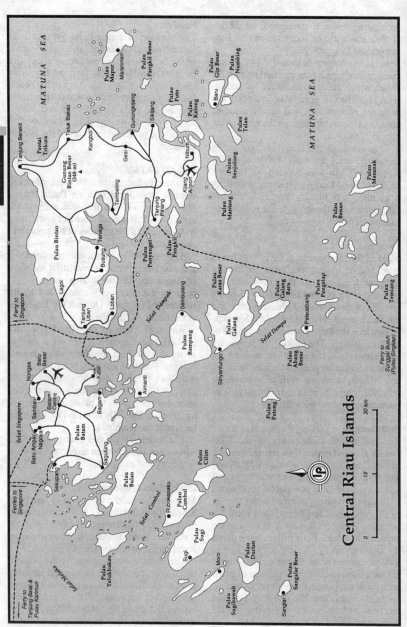

Central Riau Islands

MATUNA SEA

MATUNA SEA

Selat Melaka

Selat Singapore

Ferry to
Singapore

Ferries to
Singapore

Ferry to
Tanjung Balai &
Pulau Karimun

Ferry to
Sungai Buluh
(Pulau Singkep)

Tanjung Berakit
Pantai
Trikora
Teluk Bakau
Kangboi
Gunungkilang
Sekijang
Pulau Mapor
Marannen
Pulau Pangkil Besar
Pulau Poto
Pulau Kelong
Baru
Pulau Gin Besar
Pulau Numbing
Pulau Telan
Gunung Bintan Besar (348 m)
Gesi
Nibum
Kijang Airport
Pulau Senjdong
Pulau Bintan
Tembeling
Tanjung Pinang
Pulau Mantang
Pulau Mesanak
Tenaga
Busung
Pulau Penyenget
Pulau Pangkil
Lagoi
Loban
Tanjung Uban
Pulau Benan
Pulau Pengelap
Pulau Temiang
Selat Danpak
Sembulang
Pulau Karas Besar
Pulau Galang Baru
Palauabang
Nongsa
Batu Besar
Pulau Rempang
Pulau Galang
Selat Dempo
Sambau
Batam Centre
Kabil
Bagam
Airmanti
Sinyantungo
Pulau Abang Besar
Batu Ampar
Nagoya
Pulau Batam
Sekupang
Saguilung
Pulau Bulan
Pulau Petong
Pulau Cilim
Selat Combol
Rubokepaku
Pulau Combol
Pulau Sugi
Sigi
Moro
Pulau Durian
Sanglar
Pulau Sanglar Besar
Pulau Sugibrawah
Pulau Teliukbakaru

30 km
15
0

Batam Centre is a new administrative centre that is being built from the stumps up in the north between Nagoya and Hang Nadim airport at Batu Besar.

Tourist Office The Batam Tourist Promotion Board (☎ 322852) has a small office outside the international terminal at Sekupang. It can help with hotel bookings, and puts out a small brochure that gets a bit carried away in describing Batam as a tropical paradise.

Money Singapore dollars are easier to spend than Indonesian rupiah on Batam. There's a money exchange counter at the Sekupang ferry building, but the rates are better in Nagoya where all the major banks are based. They include the Bank of Central Asia, opposite the Nagoya Plaza Hotel on Jalan Imam Bonjol.

Post & Telephone International phone calls can be made from the Telkom office at the junction of Jalan Teuku Umar and Jalan Sriwijaya (near the cheap hotel strip), and from the wartel office opposite the Batamjaya Hotel on Jalan Imam Bonjol. The main post office is one of the few completed buildings in the new town of Batam Centre, but there is a small post office opposite the Bank of Central Asia on Jalan Imam Bonjol.

Places to Stay – bottom end

Budget accommodation on Batam is some of the worst in Indonesia, and another argument for not sticking around. There is a line-up of utterly rock-bottom places about a km out of town at Blok C, Jalan Teuku Umar. The *Minang Jaya* (☎ 457964) is the best of a bad bunch with bare, partitioned singles for 15,000 rp – absurdly expensive compared to anywhere else in Indonesia.

Cheaper, but certainly not better, is the *Penginapan Asia* (☎ 457903), nearby at Jalan Sriwijaya 1. It has tiny singles for 10,000 rp and doubles for 16,000 rp.

A better choice is the *Wisma Star International* (☎ 457372), close to the town centre

at Jalan Complek Sriwijaya Abadi 9/10A, with rooms from 20,000 rp.

Places to Stay – middle

Mid-range accommodation is similarly uninspiring and overpriced. Prices are quoted in Singapore dollars, and staff will reach for the calculator if you want to pay in rupiah.

It's hard work to find a place asking under S$50 per night. The *Bukit Nagoya Hotel* (☎ 458271), occupying a small hill near the junction of Jalan Abdul Rahman and Jalan Imam Bonjol, has doubles with fan for S$30 and with air-con for S$40, but the place smells like it hasn't seen fresh air in months. The *Batamjaya Hotel* has clean air-con doubles with hot water for S$50, and facilities include a swimming pool.

Places to Stay – top end

Three-star hotels are everywhere in Nagoya. There are some smart-looking places on Jalan Imam Bonjol, like the *Nagoya Plaza* (☎ 459888) and the *New Holiday Hotel* (☎ 459308), both charging from S$110 for the cheapest doubles.

The beach resorts around Nongsa were built with wealthy, golf-loving Singaporeans in mind. Places like *Palm Spring Golf & Country Club* (☎ 459899) and the *Turi Beach Resort* (☎ 310075) won't give you much change from S$200 for a double.

Places to Eat

Restaurants on Batam are expensive, much like everything else, but there are a lot of good seafood places. The best eating in Nagoya is found at the night food stalls along Jalan Raja Ali Haji or at the big and raucous *Pujasera Nagoya* food centre. There are some good Padang food places like *Mak Ateh* on Jalan Raja Ali Haji.

There are a number of waterfront seafood places dotted around the coast, particularly around the resorts at Nongsa. The southeastern village of Telaga Punggur has a string of *kelong* seafood restaurants built over the water. Places like the *Penggat Seafood Restaurant* keep their catch in underwater cages under the restaurant.

SUMATRA

SUMATRA

Getting There & Away

Air The ramshackle Hang Nadim airport at Batu Besar is set to be replaced by a flash new international airport in early 1995. At the moment, it's international in name only.

Merpati and Sempati both operate busy domestic schedules through Batam with at least six direct flights a day to Jakarta (231,500 rp) as well as direct flights to Medan (193,000 rp).

Merpati also has daily direct flights to Padang (132,500 rp), Palembang (130,300 rp), Pangkalpinang (129,200 rp), Pekanbaru (92,900 rp) and Pontianak (221,000 rp).

Bouraq also stops at Batam en route between Medan and Denpasar, Jakarta, Yogyakarta and Surabaya.

Island-hoppers should check out SMAC. Destinations include: Pulau Karimun (48,900 rp); Tanjung Pinang (47,800 rp); Pulau Singkep (84,100 rp); and Ranai in the North Natuna Islands (209,500 rp).

Bouraq (☎ 458344) is at Jalan Raden Patah 6; Merpati (☎ 457288) at Jodoh Square Blok A 1; Sempati (☎ 451612) at Gedung Astek on Jalan Imam Bonjol; and SMAC (☎ 458710) is behind the Bank of Central Asia at Complex Sakura Anpan 10.

Boat There are numerous services to Singapore as well as daily links to the Sumatran mainland.

To/From Singapore Several companies operate ferries between Singapore's World Trade Centre and Sekupang. The first ferries leave Singapore at 8 am and Sekupang at 7.45 am, while the last ferries leave at 7 pm in both directions. The fare from Singapore is S$16 (24,000 rp from Sekupang for those who insist on using rupiah). The trip takes about 40 minutes.

There are also four ferries a day in each direction from the World Trade Centre to Nagoya's port of Batu Ampar for S$12. The last ferry leaves Batu Ampar at 8.40 pm. There also are ferries from Batu Ampar to Johore Bahru in Malaysia.

To/From Pulau Bintan There is a steady stream of boats from the tiny east coast port of Kabil to Tanjung Pinang on neighbouring Pulau Bintan. The fastest boats do the trip in 40 minutes for 12,500 rp, other boats do the trip in an hour for 10,000 rp and slow boats take at least three hours and cost 6000 rp. The first boat leaves Kabil at 8 am and the last at 5.15 pm.

Slow boats also operate on the shorter route between Kabil and Tanjung Uban, on Bintan's north-west coast, charging 3000 rp for the 45-minute trip. From Tanjung Uban, there's a bus to Tanjung Pinang, taking two hours and costing 2500 rp.

To/From Elsewhere in Indonesia The main reason most travellers come to Batam is to catch a boat to Pekanbaru from Sekupang. Boats leave from the domestic wharf, 100 metres north of the international terminal. The *Dumai Express* is one of the best boats, departing at 9.30 am. Most departures to Pekanbaru or Selat Panjang (on Pulau Tebingtinggi) are before noon.

You can do the trip from Batam in stages, but you run the risk of missing connections. Selat Panjang is a grotty, bustling, oversized water village with a strong Chinese influence – interesting for an hour or so and it has hotels but there is no reason to stay. Tanjung Buton is just a bus/ferry terminal with no facilities.

Other destinations from Sekupang include: Pulau Karimun (13,000 rp); Pulau Kundur (15,000 rp); Dumai (35,000 rp); Tembilahan (40,000 rp); and Kuala Tungkal, on the Jambi coast (50,000 rp).

Getting Around

To/From the Airport There are cabs queued up at the airport waiting to take people to Nagoya for 7000 rp and to Sekupang for 10,000 rp. Bargaining is hard work because there are plenty who are ready to pay the asking price after a flight arrives.

Local Transport There is a token bus service between Nagoya and Sekupang for 800 rp, but most people use the share taxis that cruise the island: just stand by the roadside and call out your destination to passing cabs. Sample fares from Nagoya include 1000 rp to Sekupang and Batam Centre, and 2500 rp to Kabil. There is a taxi counter in the Sekupang ferry terminal. The large hotels provide free cabs for guests.

PULAU BINTAN

Bintan is twice as large as Batam and many times more interesting. Singapore development is, at present, very low key on Bintan, although a mega-resort is planned for the north coast.

For visitors, the island has three areas of interest: the town of Tanjung Pinang (a visa-free entry/exit point and a hub of inter-island shipping), nearby Penyenget Island and the relatively untouched beaches of the east coast.

After development-mad Batam, **Tanjung Pinang** comes as a very pleasant surprise. It may be the largest town in the Riau Archipelago – being the modern administrative centre – but it retains much of its old-time charm, particularly the picturesque, stilted section of the town that juts over the sea around Jalan Plantar II.

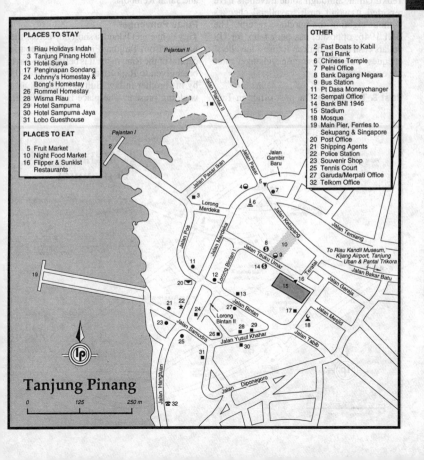

PLACES TO STAY
1 Riau Holidays Indah
3 Tanjung Pinang Hotel
13 Hotel Surya
17 Penginapan Sondang
24 Johnny's Homestay & Bong's Homestay
26 Rommel Homestay
28 Wisma Riau
29 Hotel Sampurna
30 Hotel Sampurna Jaya
31 Lobo Guesthouse

PLACES TO EAT
5 Fruit Market
10 Night Food Market
16 Flipper & Sunkist Restaurants

OTHER
2 Fast Boats to Kabil
4 Taxi Rank
6 Chinese Temple
7 Pelni Office
8 Bank Dagang Negara
9 Bus Station
11 Pt Dasa Moneychanger
12 Sempati Office
14 Bank BNI 1946
15 Stadium
18 Mosque
19 Main Pier, Ferries to Sekupang & Singapore
20 Post Office
21 Shipping Agents
22 Police Station
23 Souvenir Shop
25 Tennis Court
27 Garuda/Merpati Office
32 Telkom Office

Tanjung Pinang
0   125   250 m

SUMATRA

The harbour sees a constant stream of shipping of every shape and size, varying from tiny sampans to large freighters.

Information

There is no tourist office, but PT Info Travel, one of the shipping agencies at the main wharf in Tanjung Pinang , is used to dealing with visitors and has all the shipping information. It also rents motorbikes.

Money The banks and moneychangers are all in Tanjung Pinang. The best rates can be found at the Bank Dagang Negara on Jalan Teuku Umar, although some travellers have reported it won't cash travellers' cheques without sighting the purchase receipt. The BNI 1946, opposite, has poor rates for US dollars cash and American Express travellers' cheques. The PT Dasa moneychanger rates are even worse.

Post & Telephone The post office in Tan-jung Pinang is near the harbour on Jalan Merdeka, while international phone calls can be made from the wartel office on Jalan Hangtuah.

Riau Kandil Museum

This museum contains a treasure trove of artefacts from the days of the sultanates and the Dutch, including old guns, ceramics, charts, antique brassware and other memorabilia. It is a short bemo ride from the centre of Tanjung Pinang along Jalan Ketapang, on the right-hand side past the junction of Jalan Bakar Batu (an extension of Jalan Ketapang) and Jalan Kemboja.

Pulau Penyenget

Tiny Penyenget Island, a short hop across the harbour from Tanjung Pinang, was once the capital of the Riau rajas. It is believed to have been given to Raja Riau-Lingga VI in 1805 by his brother-in-law, Sultan Mahmud, as a wedding present. The place is littered with

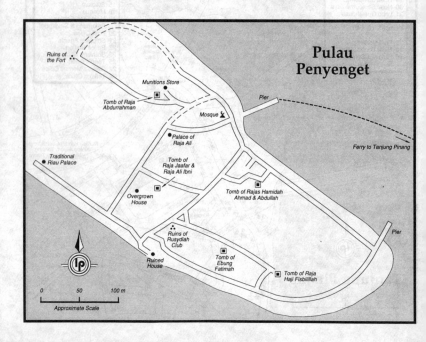

Pulau Penyenget

Ruins of the Fort

Munitions Store

Tomb of Raja Abdurrahman

Mosque

Pier

Palace of Raja Ali

Traditional Riau Palace

Tomb of Raja Jaafar & Raja Ali Ibni

Ferry to Tanjung Pinang

Overgrown House

Tomb of Rajas Hamidah Ahmad & Abdullah

Ruins of Rusydiah Club

Pier

Ruined House

Tomb of Ebung Fatimah

Tomb of Raja Haji Fisbilillah

0   50   100 m

Approximate Scale

reminders of its past and there are ruins and graveyards wherever you walk.

Penyenget is said to take its name from a certain type of bee which had the habit of stinging pirates whenever they landed on the island.

There's not much danger of getting stung on Penyenget these days. The island is a charming place, with a very different feel to Tanjung Pinang. The coastline is dotted with stilted traditional Malay houses. The ruins of the **old palace** of Raja Ali and the **tombs** and graveyards of Raja Jaafar and Raja Ali are clearly signposted inland.

The most impressive site is the sulphur-coloured **mosque** with its many domes and minarets. The mosque houses a historic library which is also worth seeing. You won't be allowed into the mosque if you're wearing shorts or a short skirt.

There are frequent boats to the island from Bintan's main pier for 500 rp per person. There's a 500 rp entry charge on weekends.

Beaches

Bintan's beaches are relatively untouched apart from the inevitable overlay of bottles and other drift plastic.

Pantai Dwi Kora is a long strip of white, palm-fringed beach on the west coast, about 20 minutes' drive from Tanjung Uban. It's a fine place for a swim, but gets very crowded on weekends.

The best beaches are along the east coast, where there is also good snorkelling outside the November to March monsoon period. Getting there can be a battle, but there is a choice of accommodation at the main beach, Pantai Trikora. There are share taxis to Trikora for 4000 rp per person from the bus and taxi station, on Jalan Teuku Umar, in Tanjung Pinang.

Senggarang

Senggarang is a fascinating village across the harbour from Tanjung Pinang. The star attraction is an old Chinese temple held together by the roots of a huge banyan tree that has grown up through it.

The temple is to the left at the end of the pier, coming by boat from Tanjung Pinang. Half a km along the waterfront is a big square with three Chinese temples side-by-side.

Boats to Senggarang leave from Pejantan II.

Snake River

You can charter a sampan from Tanjung Pinang to take you up the Sungai Ular (Snake River) through the mangroves to see the Chinese Temple with its gory murals of the trials and tortures of hell. Nearby you can see the ruins of old Sea Dayak villages.

Other Attractions

Bintan is fairly flat except for the peaks Gunung Bintan Besar and Gunung Kijang. You can climb the 348-metre **Gunung Bintan Besar**, although getting there and getting permission is not easy. Other nearby islands include **Pulau Mapor** and the tiny **Pulau Terkulai**, where the lighthouse keeper lives in solitary splendour. The trip out takes 20 minutes.

Organised Tours

There are a couple of tour operators in Tanjung Pinang. Try PT Riau Holidays (☎ 22573) in the Hotel Riau Holidays Indah, or Pinang Jaya Tours & Travel (☎ 21267) at Jalan Bintan 44.

Places to Stay – bottom end

Tanjung Pinang has some good budget accommodation. Lorong Bintan II, a small alley between Jalan Bintan and Jalan Yusuf Khahar in the centre of town, is the place to look. The popular *Bong's Homestay*, at No 20, has dorm beds for 4000 rp and doubles for 10,000 rp, including breakfast. Next door, at No 22, *Johnny's Homestay* is also good. *Rommel Homestay* (☎ 21081), on the corner of Lorong Bintan II and Jalan Yusuf Khahar, also has dorm beds for 4000 rp.

The friendly *Lobo Guesthouse*, nearby at Jalan Diponegoro 8, has dorm beds for 5000 rp and rooms are 7000/12,000 rp. Its hillside location means that it catches what little breeze there is.

Penginapan Sondang is a basic place on

Jalan Yusuf Khahar with doubles for 15,000 rp.

At Pantai Trikora (Km 46 marker) is *Yasin's Guesthouse*. It has simple wooden huts with a bed, mosquito nets, verandah and not much else. It's on the beach and charges 15,000 rp per day, including three meals.

Places to Stay – middle

The *Hotel Surya* (☎ 21811), on Jalan Bintan in Tanjung Pinang, has clean, simple singles/doubles with fan for 14,000/18,000 rp or 20,000 rp with bath.

The *Tanjung Pinang Hotel* (☎ 21236), on Jalan Pos, charges 32,500 rp for spartan rooms with fan, while the 70,000 rp air-con suites have some of the dirtiest carpet ever seen on a hotel floor.

Much better value are the *Wisma Riau* (☎ 21023) and the *Sampurna Inn* (☎ 21555), side-by-side on Jalan Yusuf Khahar. Both have clean, comfortable air-con rooms with TV for 40,000 rp.

On the beach at Pantai Trikora (Km 38 marker) is the *Trikora Country Club*, with singles from S$50 to S$70 and doubles from S$60 to S$80.

Places to Stay – top end

The *Hotel Sampurna Jaya* (☎ 21555), at Jalan Yusuf Khahar 15 in Tanjung Pinang, is probably the best of the up-market hotels. Standard doubles cost 57,500 rp, while suites are 125,000 rp.

The *Riau Holidays Indah* (☎ 22644), off Jalan Plantar II, is an unusual place built on pylons over the water in the midst of the old stilted part of town. It has very comfortable air-con rooms with bath and TV from 84,700 to 127,600 rp.

Places to Eat

Tanjung Pinang has a superb night market which sets up in the bus station on Jalan Teuku Umar. The grilled seafood is particularly good. A plate of grilled squid for 2500 rp, washed down with a cold beer, is a fine way to dine.

During the day, there are several pleasant cafes with outdoor eating areas in front of the stadium on Jalan Teuku Umar. Try *Flipper* or *Sunkist*. There are some good Padang food places along Jalan Plantar II where you can get a tasty fish curry for 1500 rp, or jackfruit curry *(kare nangka)* for 800 rp.

The fruit market on Jalan Merdeka is well stocked with imported as well as local produce.

Getting There & Away

Air Bintan's airport, at Kijang, has taken something of a back seat following the upgrading of Batam.

Garuda/Merpati (☎ 21267) no longer flies out of Bintan, but has a representative at Jalan Bintan 44. Sempati has daily direct flights to Jakarta (220,500 rp) and also flies direct to Pekanbaru (113,800 rp). The Sempati office (☎ 21612) is at Jalan Bintan 9.

The best bet for island-hoppers is SMAC (☎ 22798). Its office is five km from the city centre at Jalan Ahmad Yani (Batu 5). It also has a regular shuttle which can fly you to Batam (46,700 rp), Dabo on Pulau Singkep (92,900 rp), Pangkalpinang on Pulau Bangka (128,100 rp) and Tanjung Balai on Pulau Karimun (65,400 rp) as well as out to Ranai in the remote North Natuna Islands (208,400 rp). It also flies to Jambi (144,600 rp) and Pekanbaru (113,800 rp).

Boat Although most of the boats to mainland Riau now operate from Batam, Bintan (Tanjung Pinang) retains its traditional role as the hub of Riau's inter-island shipping as well as having international links to Singapore and Malaysia. There are shipping agencies all over town, but the main concentrations are around the entrance to the main pier – where PT Info is recommended – and at the junction of Jalan Pos and Jalan Ikan Pasar.

To/From Singapore There are four boats a day direct to Singapore's World Trade Centre wharf for 55,000 rp.

To/From Malaysia There's a daily boat to Johore Bahru in Malaysia for 40,000 rp.

To/From Pulau Batam There are regular speedboats leaving Tanjung Pinang's Pejantan 1 wharf for Kabil, on Pulau Batam, from 7.15 am to 5 pm. The fastest boats cost 12,500 rp and take 40 minutes. There is also a boat every midday from the main pier to Sekupang for 8000 rp. It takes about 1½ hours. There are slow boats from Tanjung Uban to Kabil for 3000 rp.

To/From Pulau Karimun There are two fast boats a day to Tanjung Balai (21,000 rp; 2½ hours) and one slow boat (16,000 rp; 3½ hours).

To/From Lingga & Singkep Islands Three ferries a day go to Dabo on Singkep Island. Fares range from (16,000 rp; 10 hours) to (25,000 rp; four hours). There also are ferries to Daik on Lingga Island (12,500 rp).

To/From Sumatra There are two boats a week to Pekanbaru (25,000 rp; 40 hours), and a boat to Jambi on Tuesdays (25,000 rp). Occasional boats go to Tembilahan (20,000 rp).

To/From Jakarta Pelni's KM *Rinjani* and KM *Umsini* call in every two weeks on their way between Jakarta and Dumai in Sumatra. Sailings are from Kijang, the port at the south-eastern corner of the island. The fares to Jakarta are 38,000 rp in economy and up to 143,000 rp in 1st class. The Pelni office (☎ 21513) is at Jalan Ketapang 8 in Tanjung Pinang. There are shared taxis to Kijang, from Jalan Merdeka for 1500 rp.

A new service to Jakarta on the MV *Bintan Permata* leaves Tanjung Pinang every Tuesday and Friday at 8 am, arriving at 6 am the following day. It costs 91,500 rp in economy and 111,500 rp in 1st class. The ship leaves Jakarta on Wednesday and Saturday. Bookings can be made through Primkopal, 18 Jalan Samudra, Tanjung Pinang.

Getting Around
To/From the Airport Kijang airport is about 17 km from Tanjung Pinang on the south-eastern tip of Pulau Bintan (5000 rp by share taxi).

Local Transport Buses to other parts of Bintan leave from the bus and taxi station on Jalan Teuku Umar. There are frequent departures to Tanjung Uban (2500 rp; two hours). Share taxis cost 7000 rp to Tanjung Uban and 4000 rp to Pantai Trikora.

PT Info Travel rents motorcycles for 15,000 rp per day.

PULAU SINGKEP
Few travellers make the trip south to Pulau Singkep, the third-largest island in the archipelago. The place has become even more of a backwater since the closure of the huge tin mines that provided most of the island's jobs. Much of the former population has now gone elsewhere in search of work.

The main town, **Dabo**, is shaded by lush trees and gardens and is clustered around a central park. A large **mosque** dominates the skyline. **Batu Bedua**, not far out of town, is a white-sand beach fringed with palms. It's a good place to spend a few hours and there

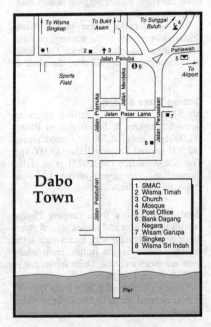

are a couple of others nearby called **Sergang** and **Jago**. There are fine views from the top of the hill just past the residential district of Bukit Asem.

The fish and vegetable **markets**, near the harbour, are interesting and Jalan Pasar Lamar is a good browsing and shopping area.

Information
In Dabo, the Bank Dagang Negara changes money at quite good rates. The post office is on Jalan Pahlawan and there is also an overseas telephone office about three km out of town on the road to Sunggai Buluh.

Places to Stay & Eat
Wisma Sri Indah, on Jalan Perusahaan, has rooms from 15,000 rp. It's spotlessly clean and has a comfortable sitting room. Similar places are the *Wisma Gapura Singkep*, on the opposite side of the street and a bit north, and *Wisma Sederhana*. Some travellers have reported very good deals at the best place in town, the *Hotel Wisma Singkep*, which overlooks the town.

You can eat at the markets behind Wisma Sri Indah or try any of the warungs on Jalan Pasar Lama and Jalan Merdeka. Food stalls and warungs pop up all over the place at night.

Getting There & Away
Air SMAC is the only airline operating through Singkep. It has flights to Batam (81,900 rp), Jambi (68,700 rp), Pangkalpinang (92,900 rp) and Tanjung Balai (89,600 rp). The SMAC office (☎ 21073) is on Jalan Pemandian. The airport is five km from Dabo, on Jalan Pahlawan.

Boat The boat trip from Tanjung Pinang crosses the equator and passes several shimmering islands on the way. Boats dock at the northern port Sunggai Buluh, from where there are buses to Dabo. Daily ferries run to Daik on Pulau Lingga.

There's also a weekly boat from Dabo to Jambi. Several shops in Dabo act as ticket agencies.

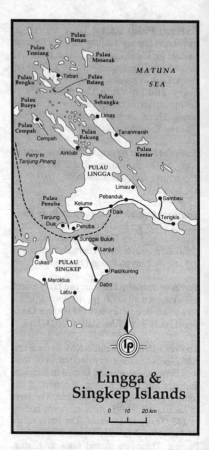

Lingga & Singkep Islands

0   10   20 km

PULAU PENUBA
Penuba is a small island wedged between Pulau Lingga and Pulau Singkep. It's an idyllic place to do nothing but swim, walk and read. The main settlement on this island is the village of the same name, which is tucked into a small bay on the south-east coast.

The **Attaqwa Mosque** stands in the centre of the village. Several good beaches are within 10 minutes' walk, and there are more fine beaches near the north coast village of **Tanjung Dua**.

A house next to the Attaqwa Mosque is

now used as a *guesthouse* for foreign visitors. Expect to pay about 5000 rp for a room. Ask around for the caretaker. There are several warungs along Jalan Merdeka, the main street.

To get to Pulau Penuba you'll need to charter a boat from Sunggai Buluh (on Pulau Singkep) for the half-hour trip.

PULAU LINGGA
Not much remains of the glory that was once Lingga except a few neglected ruins. The arrival point is Daik, which is hidden one km up a muddy river. It has that all-enveloping atmosphere of tropical seediness and oppressive humidity that pervades many of Somerset Maugham's stories.

Daik is pretty much a single street, some cargo wharves and about a dozen Chinese shops, with dirt roads and tracks branching out to the Malay villages around the island. You must report to the police as soon as you arrive.

Things to See & Do
The main site of historical interest is the ruin of the **old palace** of Raja Suleiman, the last raja of Lingga-Riau. Next to the palace are the foundation stones of a building which is said to have housed the raja's extensive harem. Otherwise there's not much left of the palace. The surrounding jungle hides overgrown bathing pools and squat toilets. The ruins are a two-hour walk from Daik, and you'll need someone to guide you through the maze of overgrown forest paths. Along the same trail is the **tomb** of Raja Muhammed Jusuf, who reigned from 1859-99.

A half-hour walk from Daik is the **Makam Bukit Cenckeh** (Cenckeh Hill Cemetery). Situated here are the crumbling graves of Raja Abdul Rakhman (who ruled from 1812-31) and Raja Muhammed (who ruled from 1832-41).

On the outskirts of Daik is the **Mesjid Sultan Lingga**, in the grounds of which is the tomb of Raja Mahmud I, who ruled in the early 19th century.

Inland is **Gunung Daik**, its three peaks looking like a crown. It's possible to scale the two outer peaks but the central one is said never to have never been climbed because it's too steep and too dangerous.

Places to Stay & Eat
There is one hotel in Daik, near the ferry dock on the main street. Expect to pay about 8000 rp for a double. There are a few small warungs on the main street.

Getting There & Around
There are daily boats for the two-hour trip from Daik to Dabo on Pulau Singkep (2000 rp) and occasional boats between Tanjung Pinang and Daik.

There's no public transport on Lingga, or transport of any sort for that matter.

PULAU KARIMUN
Karimun is a small island to the south-east of Singapore with a few resort hotels that cater to visitors from the city state. The main centre is the port of Tanjung Balai.

Tanjung Balai has a few small losmen with doubles from 10,000 rp as well as the *Hotel Holiday Karimun* (☎ 21065), at Jalan Trikora Laut 1, with air-con doubles for 50,000 rp.

There are several boats a day from Pulau Karimun to Tanjung Balai. The faster boats charge 21,000 rp and take 2½ hours, while the slow boats charge 16,000 rp and take 3½ hours. Tanjung Balai airport is also a regular stop on SMAC's island hop around the Riau Islands. There are direct flights to Batam (45,600 rp) and Singkep (88,500 rp), as well as flights from Pekanbaru via Dumai (100,600 rp).

PULAU GALANG
You need an official permit (yellow ticket) to go to this island, which is a temporary home to 13,000 Vietnamese refugees. Indonesia reportedly hopes to include Galang in the Batam free-trade zone.

THE EASTERN ISLANDS
These islands are right off the beaten track and difficult to get to, although oil has been found on the largest of the islands, Pulau Natuna Besar in the North Natunas. A road

now links Bangurun Timor on the east coast to Bunguran Barat on the west coast.

The population of the island is fairly small, although there's an extensive transmigration programme on the Sungai Ulu with settlers from Java growing cash crops like peanuts and green peas.

The islands are noted for fine basket-weave cloth and various kinds of traditional dance. One particularly idiosyncratic local dance is a kind of *Thousand & One Arabian Nights* saga, incorporating episodes from Riau-Lingga history.

There are two flights a week between Tanjung Pinang and Bunguran Timor for 208,400 rp.

Jambi

The province of Jambi occupies a 53,435-sq-km slice of central Sumatra, stretching from the highest peaks of the Bukit Barisan mountains in the west to the coastal swamps facing the Selat Melaka in the east.

Jambi's main attractions are natural. Sumatra's highest mountain, Gunung Kerinci (3805 metres), is on the border of Jambi and West Sumatra, while the Batang Hari River is Sumatra's longest at about 800 km.

Sumatran tigers – Jambi's fauna mascot – and Sumatran rhinos live in the remains of the forests that once covered the lowlands.

Today, much of the forest has been replaced by the rubber and palm oil plantations that, together with timber products, generate most of Jambi's revenue.

The province is sparsely populated with around two million people, many of them migrants from Java and Bali.

Few travellers visit Jambi. Roads are no longer the problem they once were, but Jambi remains a long way from anywhere else of interest.

The Trans-Sumatran Highway town of Bangko, in the west of the province, is the base for visits to the forest habitat of the nomadic Kubu people who once lived throughout the forests of southern Sumatra.

History

The modern city of Jambi is close to the site of the ancient capital of the Malayu kingdom, which was recorded as sending a delegation to the Chinese court in 644 AD. Shortly afterwards, Malayu was conquered by the Sriwijayan empire that ruled southern Sumatra from Palembang.

When Sriwijayan power began to wane in the 11th century, Malayu re-emerged as an independent kingdom. It stayed that way until it became a dependency of Java's Majapahit empire, which ruled from 1294 until 1520. It then came under the sway of the Minangkabau people of West Sumatra.

In 1616, the Dutch East India Company opened an office in Jambi and the Dutch quickly formed a successful alliance with Sultan Muhammed Nakhruddin to protect their ships and cargoes from pirates. They also negotiated a trade monopoly with Nakhruddin and his successors. The predominant export was pepper, which was grown in great abundance. In 1901, the Dutch moved their headquarters to Palembang and effectively gave up their grip on Jambi.

JAMBI

The modern city of Jambi, capital of the province of the same name, is a busy river port about 155 km from the mouth of the Batang Hari River.

Orientation & Information

Jambi sprawls over a wide area, a combination of the old city spreading out around the port and the new administrative centre of Telanaipura to the west. Most of the banks, hotels and restaurants are in the old city centre around the port.

Tourist Office The regional tourist office (☎ 25330) is a fair way from the city centre at Jalan Basuki Rahmat 11, in the district of Kota Baru.

Post & Telephone The main post office is at Jalan Sultan Thaha 9. International phone

> ## The Kubu
> The Kubu are the indigenous people of southern Sumatra, nomadic hunter-gatherers who once lived throughout the region's lowland forests. They are descended from the first wave of Malays to migrate to Sumatra.
>
> Today, their domain is restricted to a reserve called Bukit 12 – 287 sq km of forest to the east of the Trans-Sumatran Highway town of Bangko.
>
> The traditional Kubu way of life came to end when large-scale transmigration from Java and Bali began. The migrants cut down the forests for plantation farming, and brought with them diseases like measles and tuberculosis.
>
> The Kubu steadfastly resisted attempts to persuade them to settle in government-built villages. In 1985, they were granted the forest preserve around Bukit 12. It is home to about 1000 people, divided into five groups. Each group is led by a *temenggung* (chief).
>
> A road leads off towards the reserve from the town of Limbur, on the main highway about 25 km east of Bangko. There are buses to Limbur from Bangko, where you can stay at the *Bangko Indah Hotel* in Jalan Lintas. ■

SUMATRA

calls can be made from the Telkom office on Jalan M Taher.

Travel Agencies Jambora Kencana (☎ 23926), close to the port on Jalan Gatot Subroto, and Mayang Tour & Travel (☎ 25450) can handle ticketing as well as organise trips around the province.

Museum Negeri Jambi
The museum is on the corner of Jalan Urip Sumoharjo and Jalan Prof Dr Sri Sudewi. It has a small collection of costumes, handicrafts and household accessories from the province. It's open daily from 9 am to 4 pm. Admission is 200 rp.

Muara Jambi Temples
The temples at Muara Jambi, 26 km downstream from Jambi, date from between the 11th and 13th centuries, the golden age of the Malayu kingdom. The site was rediscovered in 1920 by a British army expedition sent to explore the Jambi area.

Nine temples have so far been identified at Muara Jambi. They are known as *candis*, the places of worship of Indonesia's Hindu age.

The temples are an easy day trip from Jambi. On Sundays, there are boats doing the trip for 6000 rp return; otherwise it costs about 45,000 rp to charter a boat.

Organised Tours
Travel agencies in Jambi and Bukittinggi offer tours to Kubu country. Expect to pay about US$100 to join a group of 10 for four nights/five days, including nights sleeping out in the forest.

Places to Stay
Most of the cheaper places are drab and unpleasant. The place to go looking is Jalan Dr Sutomo, which runs south from the port off Jalan Raden Pamuk. The *Losmen Penang* (☎ 22324), at No 9, has doubles for 12,500 rp, while the *Losmen Garuda*, at No 32, has rooms from 20,000 to 45,000 rp with air-con.

The best hotel in town is the two-star *Hotel Abadi* (☎ 24054) at Jalan Gatot Subroto 119. Doubles start at 45,000 rp and go up to 120,000 rp for rooms with satellite TV etc. Prices are very similar at the *Hotel Harisman* (☎ 24677), at Jalan Prof Dr M Yamin.

Places to Eat
Padang food is very popular. The *Simpany Raya I*, on Jalan Thamrin, is part of a chain of fine Padang restaurants – there is another at Jalan Wahidin. There are some promising places on Jalan Veteran, including the *Begadang* at No 9.

Jalan M Assa'at is the place to go for Chinese food with the *Restaurant Terkenal*, at No 124, and the *Internasional* at No 34.

Ayam Goreng Yogya, at Jalan Abdul Muis 58, serves precisely that – Yogya-style fried chicken.

Getting There & Away

Air Merpati operates two direct flights a day to Jakarta (173,800 rp) and two direct flights a week to Batam (127,600 rp). The Merpati office (☎ 22184) is at Jalan Damar 55.

SMAC has three flights a week between Jambi and Batam (128,100 rp) as well as flights to Pekanbaru (99,000 rp), Singkep (69,800 rp) and Tanjung Pinang (145,700 rp). The SMAC office (☎ 22804) is at Jalan Orang Kayo Hitam 26.

Bus Intercity services use the Simpang Kawat bus station on Jalan Prof Dr M Yamin, on the edge of town. There are lots of buses to Palembang with fares from 6000 to 13,500 rp, depending on the level of comfort. Buses to Jakarta cost 27,000 rp without air-con and take about 30 hours; 40,000 rp with air-con. Regular buses to Padang cost 10,000 rp and take 10 hours.

Boat There is a weekly boat between Jambi and the port of Tanjung Pinang on Pulau Bintan. It leaves Tanjung Pinang on Tuesdays at 9 am, returning on Friday at 9 am. The journey costs 25,000 rp and takes about 48 hours.

Getting Around

Rawasari opelet station, in the centre of town at Jalan Kenuming, is where all opelets start and finish their journeys. The standard fare is 200 rp.

SUNGAIPENUH

Sungaipenuh is the main town of the beautiful Kerinci Valley on Jambi's border with West Sumatra. It's at the heart of Kerinci Seblat National Park, which is the town's main attraction.

At the northern end of the Kerinci Valley is Gunung Kerinci (3805 metres), the highest mountain in Indonesia outside Irian Jaya. At the southern end is Danau Kerinci, yet another of Sumatra's scenic mountain lakes.

While administratively the valley may be in Jambi Province, culturally, Sungaipenuh

and the 200 surrounding villages are unmistakably Minangkabau West Sumatran, with the same matrilineal social structure.

Gunung Kerinci

Kerinci is an active volcano which last erupted in 1934. It's a tough two-day climb to the summit, where you'll find a crater measuring about 120 metres by 400 metres filled with a greenish lake.

Before you start, you'll need to get a permit (surat ijin) from the PHPA office at the Visitor Information Centre, Jalan Arga Selebar Daun 11, in Sungaipenuh. They will try to persuade you to engage a guide, which is not really necessary as there is only one well-marked trail. It starts from the village of Kersik Tua, 43 km from Sungaipenuh, among the tea plantations of the 60-sq-km Kayo Aro estate. The 16 km from the village to the top is normally tackled in two stages. It takes about five hours to climb to a campsite at about 3000 metres where most climbers spend the night before setting off for the final 90-minute scramble to the summit at dawn.

You'll need to bring food, a water bottle (water is scarce on the mountain), and a tent and sleeping bag, as it is cold (down to 2°C at night).

On the way back, you can stop at the hot springs near the Kayo Aro plantation. It's too hot to swim in the main pool, but you can get a private room with a hot-water mandi.

Other Attractions

The large, pagoda-style **Mesjid Agung**, in Sungaipenuh, is said to be over 400 years old. It has large carved beams and old Dutch tiles, but you need permission to go inside.

The village of **Sungai Tutung** is nationally renowned for its basket weaving. It's easy to find a guide for day trips there from Sungaipenuh.

There are lots of stone carvings around the Kerinci Valley, the best known being at **Batu Gong**. Locals tell stories of a great kingdom that existed in Kerinci long ago.

The village of Pelompek, 51 km from Sungaipenuh, is the starting point for visiting **Danau Tujuh**, a remote and spectacular crater lake near the summit of 2751-metre Gunung Tujuh, due east of Kerinci. The **Telun Berasap** waterfall, north of Pelompek, is a popular weekend picnic spot.

Places to Stay & Eat
The *Losmen Mata Hari*, on Jalan Basuki Rahmat, is cheap and a good source of information. Rooms cost from 5000 to 15,000 rp. More up-market places are the *Hotel Yani*, on Jalan Muradi, with rooms priced from 10,000 to 25,000 rp, and the *Hotel Busana*, on Jalan Martadinata. The *Minang Soto* restaurant has good, cheap Padang food. There are a few places to eat in the bus station/market area. Try the speciality of the region, *dending batokok*, which is strips of beef smoked and grilled over a fire.

There are half a dozen small guesthouses in Kersik Tua at the foot of Gunung Kerinci; they make a good base for climbing the mountain.

Getting There & Away
The closest major city to Sungaipenuh is the West Sumatran capital of Padang, a journey of 246 km via the coast road (4000 rp; six hours). There is also a scenic back route to Padang that takes the mountain road past Gunung Kerinci and follows the valleys north.

Sungaipenuh is 121 km (5000 rp; four hours) from the Trans-Sumatran Highway town of Bangko in Jambi Province. There are also buses south along the coast to Bengkulu for 10,000 rp.

Getting Around
The bus station is in the market area at Jalan Prof M Yamin. There are minibuses from Sungaipenuh to most of the valley villages, including Kersik Tua for 1500 rp.

Dokars cost about 500 rp per ride around Sungaipenuh.

Bengkulu

The six-hour journey through the Bukit Barisan mountains from Lubuklinggau to the town of Bengkulu, capital of the province of the same name, is like taking a journey back in time.

Nothing much seems to have changed in years – except, unfortunately, prices. Bengkulu remains Sumatra's most isolated province, cut off from its neighbours by the Bukit Barisan – particularly during the rainy season from December to March when land transport can break down completely.

Few tourists come to Bengkulu. There is not a lot to do apart from adjust to the slower pace of life.

History
Little is known of Bengkulu life before it came under the influence of the Majapahits from Java at the end of the 13th century.

It appears to have lived in something approaching total isolation until then, the territory of a number of small kingdoms such as Sungai Lebong in the Curup area. It even developed its own cuneiform script, known as *ka-ga-nga*.

The British moved into Bengkulu, or Bencoolen as they called it, in 1685, searching for pepper after being kicked out of Banten, in Java, three years previously.

From the onset things did not go well. Isolation, boredom and constant rain sapped the British will, while malaria ravaged their numbers.

When Sir Thomas Stamford Raffles arrived as Lieutenant-General of Fort Marlborough (as the British called the ruler of Bencoolen) in 1818, the colony still was not a going concern. In the short time he was there, Raffles made the pepper market profitable and planted coffee, nutmeg and sugar cane as cash crops. In 1824, Bengkulu was traded for a Dutch guarantee to leave the British alone in Malaysia and Singapore.

Bengkulu was a home in domestic exile

for Indonesia's first president, Soekarno, from 1938-41.

Flora & Fauna

Bengkulu's rainforests are home to both the *Rafflesia arnoldi* and the world's tallest flower *Amorphophalus titanum*.

While the bizarre rafflesia is found in a number of sites throughout the Bukit Barisan mountains, most notably around Bukittinggi in West Sumatra, it was in Bengkulu that Raffles first set eyes on the flower, in 1818, in company with a British government botanist named Arnold. The rafflesia is found at a number of sites dotted around Bengkulu's mountains, the most accessible being close to the main road halfway between Bengkulu and Curup.

The lily-like *Amorphophalus titanum* flowers only once every three years, when it throws up a spectacular flower spike than can stand over two metres. The flower is a rich red, with a huge yellow stamen protruding from its core. The plant is a member of the same family as the taro, the starchy tuber that is a staple food in parts of Asia and the Pacific islands. The tubers can weigh up to 100 kg. Known locally as *kibut* or *bunga bangkai*, it is Bengkulu's floral emblem, and is found mainly in the Rejang Lebong district north of Curup.

BENGKULU

Capital of the province of the same name, Bengkulu is a relaxed town of about 60,000.

Orientation & Information

Although Bengkulu is by the sea, most of the town is set back from the coast, touching only near Fort Marlborough. The coast is surprisingly quiet and rural just a km or so from the town centre.

Jalan Suprapto and the nearby Pasar Minggu Besar are the modern town centre, separated from the old town area around the fort by the long, straight Jalan Ahmad Yani.

Tourist Office The Bengkulu tourist office (☎ 21272) is inconveniently situated to the south of town at Jalan Pembangunan 14.

There's not much material in English other than a couple of glossy brochures, but the staff are friendly.

Money The best place to change money is the Bank of Central Asia, near the Gandhi Bakery at Jalan Suprapto 150. You can also change money at the Bank Dumi Daya at Jalan R Hadi 1, and American Express US dollar travellers' cheques and US dollars cash at the BNI 1946, on Jalan S Parman.

Post & Telephone The main post office (and poste restante) is south of the town centre on Jalan S Parman, but there is another post office on Jalan Ahmad Yani. The Telkom office is just around the corner on Jalan R Hadi. It has a Home Country Direct phone.

Travel Agencies Assik Tour & Travel is conveniently located next to the Hotel Asia at Jalan Ahmad Yani 922.

Fort Marlborough

Fort Marlborough (*Benteng Marlborough*) became the seat of British power in Bengkulu after it was completed in 1719 to replace nearby Fort York, of which nothing but the foundations remain.

After a long period of use by the Indonesian army, Fort Marlborough was restored in 1983 and reopened to the public in 1984. There are a few small and uninteresting exhibits about the restoration, together with a pile of cannon balls and a couple of old British gravestones. Admission is 250 rp.

Bengkulu has a few other British reminders, including the **Thomas Parr monument** in front of the Pasar Barukota and a couple of 'Monumen Inggris'. The monument near the beach is to Captain Robert Hamilton who died in 1793, 'in command of the troops'.

Soekarno's House

Soekarno was exiled to Bengkulu by the Dutch from 1938 until the Japanese arrived in 1941. The small villa in which he lived on Jalan Soekarno-Hatta is maintained as a small museum. Exhibits include a few faded

PLACES TO STAY
7 Losmen Samudera
11 Wisma Balai Bantar
12 Garden Hotel
13 Asia Hotel
14 Wisma Rafflesia
17 Hotel Samudera Dwinka
22 Penginapan Damia
25 Wisma Bumi Endah
27 Horizon Hotel
28 Nala Seaside Cottages

PLACES TO EAT
15 Rumah Makan Srikandi
16 Rumah Makan Si Kabayan
21 Gandhi Bakery
29 Kafeteria Nala

OTHER
1 Mosque
2 Pasar Barukota
3 Fort Marlborough
4 Telkom Office
5 Post Office
6 Thomas Parr Monument
8 Daerah Monument
9 Governor's House
10 Pelni Office
17 Assik Tour & Travel
17 Merpati Office
18 Mesjid Jamik
(Bung Karno Mosque)
19 Robert Hamilton Monument
20 Bank of Central Asia
23 Pasar Minggu Besar
(Market)
24 Soekarno's House
26 Bank BNI 1946

photos, a wardrobe and even Soekarno's trusty bicycle. The house is closed on Mondays and open other days from 8 am to 2 pm, except on Fridays when it closes at 11 am and on Saturday when it closes at noon. Admission is 250 rp.

Other Attractions

Soekarno, who was an architect, designed the **Mesjid Jamik** mosque at the junction of Jalan Sudirman and Jalan Suprapto during his stay. It is commonly known as the Bung Karno mosque.

The **Bengkulu Museum Negeri** is near the tourist office on Jalan Pembangunan. It's open the same hours as Soekarno's house.

Dendam Taksudah is an aquatic reserve area eight km south of the town. It's of little interest to travellers in spite of being described as 'exciting' by the tourist brochure. There's not much there other than water snakes and the beginnings of a resort hotel.

The graves in the **European cemetery**, behind the small church on Jalan Ditra, are a reminder of the ravages wrought by malaria among the colonialists. Many of the graves are of young men in their early 20s.

Bengkulu's main beach, **Pantai Panjang**,

is long, featureless and deserted. Strong currents make it dangerous for swimming. There is a seafood restaurant at the end of Jalan Samudera.

Organised Tours
Iwan Idrus is an English-speaking guide who can be contacted through the tourist office. He specialises in jungle trekking around Curup, but can organise trips all over the province.

Places to Stay – bottom end
The most interesting part of town is around Fort Marlborough. The *Losmen Samudera*, opposite the fort entrance on Jalan Benteng, is an old place with lots of character. Singles/doubles are 3500/7000 rp, but unfortunately the rooms are extremely basic and lack fans.

Wisma Rafflesia (☎ 21650), at Jalan Ahmad Yani 924, has slightly better doubles for 10,000 rp.

Wisma Bumi Endah (☎ 21665), at Jalan Fatmawati 29, is a much better place. Clean singles/doubles cost 10,000/15,000 rp or 25,000 rp with air-con.

Places to Stay – middle
The *Wisma Balai Buntar* (☎ 21254), near the fort at Jalan Khadijah 122, is the best value in town. It's a fine old Dutch villa with extraordinarily high ceilings. Huge singles/doubles with mandi and fan cost 20,500/27,500 rp, or 25,000/32,000 rp with air-con. All prices include breakfast. The place is run by a very friendly former Indonesia army colonel who speaks excellent English. A lot of travellers stay here and the colonel is a great source of information about Bengkulu.

The *Asia Hotel* (☎ 21901), at Jalan Ahmad Yani 922, is a clean place with a range of rooms with air-con starting from 25,000 rp. Close to the centre, at Jalan Sudirman 246, the *Hotel Samudera Dwinka* (☎ 21604) is well kept and modern. The 22,000 rp economy doubles have black & white TV; the 40,000 rp 'VIP' rooms have colour TV and air-con.

By the beach, on Jalan Pantai Nala, *Nala Seaside Cottages* (☎ 21855) has a dozen

pleasant air-con bungalows with small verandahs. Prices start at 30,000 rp, including breakfast.

Places to Stay – top end
The flashest hotel in town is the *Horizon* (☎ 21722) at Jalan Pantai Nala 142. Facilities include swimming pool and snooker room. Rooms overlooking the sea cost 95,000 rp and come with satellite TV etc.

There's also a swimming pool at the brand new *Garden Hotel* (☎ 21952), at Jalan Veteran 63, which has air-con doubles from 52,000.

Places to Eat
The *Rumah Makan Srikandi*, opposite the Asia Hotel on Jalan Ahmad Yani, does excellent southern Sumatran food very cheaply. Ask for *sayur asam*, a sour vegetable soup that is a Bengkulu speciality – you can eat everything in the bowl. A serving costs 700 rp.

The *Rumah Makan Si Kabayan* (☎ 21919), at Jalan Sudirman 51, is rated by locals as the best restaurant in town. It serves Sundanese food, but the menu includes sayur asam and other local favourites. It does delicious grilled chicken with soy sauce for 2150 rp.

The *Gandhi Bakery*, on Jalan Suprapto, has a fine collection of ice creams as well as cakes.

The *Kafeteria Nala*, overlooking the beach near the Nala Seaside Cottages, is a good place for a cold beer. You can look out to sea and wonder what brought you to Bengkulu in the first place!

Other Bengkulu delicacies to look out for are *emping melinjo*, a kind of krupuk made from the seeds of the melinjo fruit and *Lampuk*, a sweet made by boiling durian and molasses.

Getting There & Away
Air Merpati has two direct flights a day to Jakarta (165,500 rp) and three a week to Palembang (91,800 rp). The Merpati office (☎ 42337) is in the Hotel Samudera Dwinka at Jalan Sudirman 246.

Bus Terminal Panorama, the long-distance bus station, is several km east of town on the road to Curup, but most services continue to the various bus companies' city depots.

Several companies have offices on Jalan MR Haryono. Putra Rafflesia (☎ 22640), at No 57, has buses to Padang for 17,500 rp (22,500 rp air-con), Palembang for 15,000 rp and Jakarta for 30,500 rp – or 55,000 rp for the best seats. Bengkulu Indah (☎ 21811), at No 14, also has a wide range of destinations.

Sriwijaya Express, at Jalan Bali 36, runs buses up the coast to Mukomuko (6000 rp) and inland to the Kerinci Valley town of Sungai Penuh, in Jambi Province, for 10,000 rp.

Habeco, at the northern edge of town at Jalan Bali 67, has daily buses to Padang (15,000 rp; 16 hours) along the coast road via Lias (1500 rp), Ipuh (4500 rp) as well as Mukomuko.

Boat The Pelni boat *Baruna Dwipa* calls at Bengkulu in both directions on its fortnightly circuit from Jakarta to Padang. The economy/1st class fare to Jakarta is 23,700/106,700 rp. The fares to Padang are 13,700/60,200 rp. The boat also calls at Krui and Pulau Enggano (4000 rp). The boats leave from the harbour at Pulau Baai, about 15 km south of town. The Pelni office (☎ 21013) is at Jalan Khadijah 10.

Getting Around

To/From the Airport The city's Padang Kemiling airport is 14 km south of town and airport cabs charge a standard 10,000 rp to town. Metered cabs charge half that the other way. The airport is 200 metres from the main road south and there are regular bemos and buses to Bengkulu.

Local Transport There are countless minibuses shuttling around town for a standard fare of 250 rp.

NORTHERN BENGKULU

The coast road (Jalan Manusurai Pantai) north from Bengkulu to Padang, has a number of possibilities for travellers.

The road is now sealed all the way and takes about 16 hours, making it a reasonable alternative land route to the usual trip inland via Lubuklinggau and the Trans-Sumatran Highway.

The journey can be done as a number of short hops. The first town north of Bengkulu is **Lias**. It has a beach and accommodation at *Elly's Guesthouse*, on Jalan Utama, with rooms for 5000 rp.

There are reported to be elephants further north near **Ipuh**, around the mouth of the Sungai Ipuh. You can stay at the *Losmen Rindu Alam*, at Jalan Protokol 1.

Mukomuko, 200 km north of Bengkulu, was the northern outpost of the British colony of Bencoolen. Fort Anna survives as a reminder.

CURUP

Curup is a small town halfway between Bengkulu and Lubuklinggau and is the launching pad for the attractions of the surrounding Bukit Barisan. The town itself is set in a valley watered by the upper reaches of the Sungai Musi that eventually flows through Palembang.

There's nowhere to change money in Curup, although it is possible to draw money on Visa or Mastercard from the Bank of Central Asia on Jalan Merdeka.

Things to See & Do

There are many fine examples of **rumah adat**, traditional stilted wooden houses, in the villages around Curup.

Volcanic **Gunung Kaba**, 19 km east of Curup, is dotted with small craters as well as two large sulphurous craters.

The **hot springs** and **waterfall** at Suban are popular with weekend picnickers.

Places to Stay & Eat

There are a number of cheap losmen, such as the *Losmen Nusantara* at Jalan Merdeka 794, with doubles for 6000 rp.

Much better is the *Hotel Aman Jaya* (☎ 21365), at Jalan Dr A K Gani 10. It has standard doubles with shower and fan for 25,000 rp and huge rooms upstairs with hot water and air-con for 35,000 rp. It's a friendly place with lots of information on surrounding attractions and how to get to them.

The *Restaurant Sari Buana*, on Jalan Merdeka 120, is a busy Padang food place, while the *Warkop Ramanda*, around the corner at Jalan Cut Nyak Dhien 1, does Palembang food.

Getting There & Away
There are frequent connections to Bengkulu and Lubuklinggau. Both cost 2500 rp and take three hours. Buses leave from the busy central market.

PULAU ENGGANO
Pulau Enggano is a remote island with an area of 680 sq km, 100 km off the coast of South Bengkulu. Its isolation is such that, until as recently as 100 years ago, some Sumatrans believed it was inhabited entirely by women. Apparently, these women managed to procreate miraculously through the auspices of the wind or by eating certain fruit.

The island is featured on a map of Asia drawn in 1593. The name, Enggano, is Portuguese for deceit or disappointment, which suggests that the Portuguese were the first Europeans to discover it. It wasn't until three years later that Dutch navigators first recorded it.

The original inhabitants are believed to be native Sumatrans who fled from the mainland when the Malays migrated there. The present day inhabitants live by cultivating rice, coffee, pepper, cloves and copra. Wild pigs, cattle and buffalo are abundant.

There are five villages on the island: Banjar Sari on the north coast; Meok on the west; Kaana and Kahayupu in the east; and Malakoni, the harbour. The island is relatively flat (the highest point is Bua Bua which rises to 250 metres) and the coastline is swampy. It's worth visiting only if you are a keen anthropologist and/or a real adventurer with plenty of time.

Places to Stay
The only place to stay is the *Losmen Apaho*, at Malakoni, which has rooms for 5000 rp.

Getting There & Away
The only way to get to Enggano is by boat from Bengkulu. The Pelni boat *Baruna Dwipa* stops at the island's port of Malakoni three times a fortnight on its route between Jakarta and Padang. The fare is 4000 rp.

Getting Around
The villages on the island are connected by tracks originally made by the Japanese and not very well-maintained since. Once you're there, the only way of getting around is to walk.

South Sumatra

The province of South Sumatra stretches from Lubuklinggau in the Barisan foothills in the west, to the islands of Bangka and Belitung in the east. All roads, rivers and the railway lead to Palembang, the provincial capital.

PALEMBANG
Palembang is a huge, heavily polluted industrial city of almost 1.5 million people – the second largest in Sumatra. The main industries are oil refining, fertiliser production and cement manufacture. The Pertamina refineries at Plaju and Sungai Gerong can handle a combined capacity of 180,000 barrels of oil per day, while the giant Pusri fertiliser plant is the largest producer of urea in South-East Asia.

People glancing at a map could be forgiven for not realising that Palembang was also a major port, 80 km from the mouth of the Musi River.

When Sumatra's oil fields were discovered and opened early in the century, Palembang quickly became the main export outlet for South Sumatra.

The port also handles exports from the

province's seemingly endless plantations of rubber, coffee, pepper and pineapples.

Palembang has little to offer travellers apart from transport connections.

History

A thousand years ago, Palembang was the centre of the highly developed civilisation of Sriwijaya. When the Chinese scholar I Tsing was in Palembang in 672, he recorded that a thousand monks, scholars and pilgrims were studying and translating Sanskrit there.

Few relics from this period remain – no sculpture, monuments or architecture of note – nor is there much of interest from the early 18th century when Palembang was an Islamic kingdom. Most of the buildings of the latter era were destroyed in battles with the Dutch, the last of which occurred in 1811.

Palembang translates as 'gold from the ground', which probably stems from the city's name in Sriwijayan times, *Swarna Dwipa*, which translates as 'Golden Island'.

Orientation & Information

Palembang sits astride the Musi River, once the city's pride but now suffering badly from the ravages of industrial waste. The city's skyline is dominated by the giant Ampera Bridge, built in the 1960s, that links the two halves of the city.

A hodgepodge of wooden houses on stilts crowd both banks of the Musi River. The south side, known as Seberang Ulu, is where the majority of people live. Some of the streams feeding into the Musi River look positively corrosive, not merely polluted.

Seberang Ilir, on the north bank, is the city's better half where you'll find most of the government offices, shops, hotels and the wealthy residential districts.

The main street is Jalan Sudirman, which runs north-south to the bridge. The bus and railway stations are both on the southern side.

Be careful, especially at night, as many locals will warn you about pickpockets and muggings.

Tourist Office The tourist office (☎ 28450)

is at the Museum Sultan Machmud Badaruddin II. You can also get information and maps from the South Sumatra regional tourist office (☎ 357348) at Jalan POM IX.

Money The best rates are available from the Bank of Central Asia at Jalan Kapitan Rivai 22, next to the Telkom administration building. It won't change cash or travellers' cheques after 1 pm. The Bank Rakyat Indonesia, nearby at No 15, has reasonable rates for American Express US and Singapore dollars and is open until 3 pm. Bank Duta, at Jalan Sudirman 72, handles travellers' cheques backed by Visa. BNI 1946 offers its standard below-par rates for American Express US dollars at its Jalan Sudirman branch, just south of Jalan Iskandar.

Outside banking hours, the bigger hotels are a better bet than moneychangers such as Dhrama Perdana, at Jalan Kol Atmo 446, opposite the Hotel Lembang, which will change only cash US dollars and Singaporean dollars at very poor rates.

Post & Telephone The post office is close to the river, next to the Garuda monument on Jalan Merdeka. International phone calls can be made next door at the Telkom office. It has a Home Country Direct phone.

Museums

There are two museums in Palembang. The **Museum Budaya Sultan Machmud Badaruddin II** is in the city centre, near the Musi River and Ampera Bridge. There are three rooms where you can see traditional Palembang decor, and a number of ancient Hindu statues.

The other museum, the **Museum of South Sumatra**, is 5½ km to the north of the city centre at Jalan Sriwijaya 1. The place is built in traditional Palembang-style and is strong on cultural material – costumes, weaving, furniture and miniature replicas of traditional houses. It also has some of the best megalithic remains from the Pasemah Highlands, including the *batu gajah* (elephant stone). The museum is open from 9 am

SUMATRA

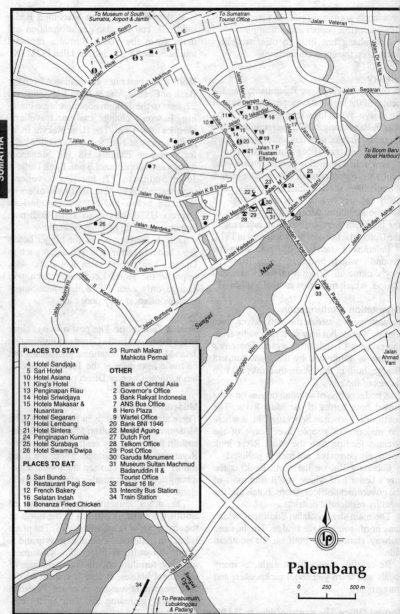

PLACES TO STAY

4 Hotel Sandjaja
5 Sari Hotel
10 Hotel Asiana
11 King's Hotel
12 Penginapan Riau
14 Hotel Sriwidjaya
15 Hotels Makasar & Nusantara
17 Hotel Segaran
19 Hotel Lembang
21 Hotel Sintera
24 Penginapan Kurnia
25 Hotel Surabaya
26 Hotel Swarna Dwipa

PLACES TO EAT

5 Sari Bundo
6 Restaurant Pagi Sore
12 French Bakery
16 Selatan Indah
18 Bonanza Fried Chicken

23 Rumah Makan Mahkota Permai

OTHER

1 Bank of Central Asia
2 Governor's Office
3 Bank Rakyat Indonesia
7 ANS Bus Office
8 Hero Plaza
9 Wartel Office
20 Bank BNI 1946
22 Mesjid Agung
27 Dutch Fort
28 Telkom Office
29 Post Office
30 Garuda Monument
31 Museum Sultan Machmud Badaruddin II & Tourist Office
32 Pasar 16 Ilir
33 Intercity Bus Station
34 Train Station

Palembang

0   250   500 m

to 2 pm Tuesday to Saturday, 8 am to 2 pm on Sunday, and is closed on Monday.

Close by the museum is the impressive **Limas House**, a fully furnished traditional Palembang house.

Opelets heading north from Jalan Sudirman go within 100 metres of the museum for 200 rp, or you can spend 2500 rp on a taxi.

Markets
Next to the Ampera Bridge, on the other side of the museum, is the Pasar 16 Ilir, Palembang's frenetic and fascinating market. The main part is housed in an old building built by the Dutch. The colourful market is full of food, household goods and clothing.

Other Attractions
The remains of the late 18th-century **Dutch fort**, occupied today by the Indonesian army, can be seen to the north of Jalan Merdeka. Sections of the outside walls still stand.

There's also the **Mesjid Agung** mosque, at the junction of Jalan Sudirman and Jalan Merdeka, which was built by Sultan Machmud Badaruddin in the 18th century. You can also while away an hour or two observing Musi River life drift by from the middle of the Ampera Bridge.

Palembang's annual tourist event is the *bidar* (canoe) race held on the Musi River in the middle of town every August 17 (Proclamation Day). A bidar is about 25 metres long, a metre wide, and powered by up to 60 rowers.

Places to Stay – bottom end
Cheap hotels in Palembang aren't anything to look forward to – and they're not particularly cheap either. The *Hotel Asiana*, at Jalan Sudirman 45 E, north of the intersection with Jalan Iskandar, doesn't look too good until you've checked out the opposition. The Asiana's rooms are bare but reasonably clean and the rooms away from the main street are surprisingly quiet. Singles/doubles are 9000/12,500 rp.

Two other similarly styled and priced hotels are *Penginapan Riau*, at Jalan Dempo 409C, and *Hotel Segaran*, at Jalan Segaran

207C. The numbers of Jalan Segaran follow no discernible pattern.

A step up from these is the *Hotel Makasar*, a popular place next to the Hotel Nusantara, off Jalan Iskandar. It has clean doubles with mandi and fan for 15,000 rp, which represents good value.

If price is your sole concern, the cheapest place in town is the gloomy *Penginapan Kurnia*, on Jalan Mesjid Lama, with doubles for 8000 rp and 10,000 rp.

Places to Stay – middle
There's much more to choose from if you're prepared to spend a few thousand rupiah more. The area to look is around the junction of Jalan Iskandar and Jalan Sudirman.

The *Hotel Sriwidjaja* (☎ 355555) is as good a place as any to start. Its address of Jalan Iskandar 31 is actually a small cul de sac, close to the junction with Jalan Sudirman. It has doubles with fan for 18,000 rp and rooms with air-con, hot water and TV for 47,000 rp. All prices include breakfast.

Occupying a very similar cul de sac 50 metres further along Jalan Iskandar, at No 17, is the *Hotel Nusantara* (☎ 353306). It has clean doubles with fan starting at 17,500 rp.

The cheapest rooms at the *Hotel Sintera* (☎ 354618), right in the thick of things at Jalan Sudirman 38, aren't up to much, but there are large doubles with mandi and fan for 29,000 rp.

The *Sari Hotel* (☎ 313320), on the corner of Jalan Sudirman and Jalan Kapitan Rivai, is a rather rundown modern hotel with rooms from 29,500/49,000 rp, including breakfast. *Hotel Surabaya*, at Jalan Sayangan 669, has clean doubles for 20,000/30,000 rp with fan/air-con.

Places to Stay – top end
King's Hotel (☎ 310033), at Jalan Kol Atmo 623, is a fine three-star hotel in the heart of town. All rooms have air-con and the usual amenities and prices start from 90,000 rp.

The *Hotel Swarna Dwipa* (☎ 313322) is tucked away at Jalan Tasik 2, some distance west of the centre. Singles/doubles start from

90,000/110,000 rp and facilities include a gymnasium and swimming pool.

Places to Eat

While Palembang is hardly a name to make the taste buds tingle in anticipation, the city gives its name to the distinctive cuisine of southern Sumatra (including Lampung and Bengkulu) in the same way as Padang gives its name to the cooking of West Sumatra.

The favourite item on the Palembang food menu is *ikan belida*, an eel-like river fish that used to be caught in great numbers in the Musi River in pre-industrial days. These days, the fish come from other coastal South Sumatran rivers. The fish is served with a range of fiery sauces that a novice could easily confuse with Padang food.

The difference is in the accompaniments. The main one is *tempoyak*, a combination of fresh/salted durian, *terasi* (shrimp paste), lime juice and chilli that is mixed up with the fingers and added to the rice. *Sambal buah* (fruit sambals), made with pineapple or sliced green mangoes, are also popular.

Pindang baung is a spicy fish soup very similar in style to Thailand's famous *tom yum*.

A good place to try Palembang food is the *Rumah Makan Mahkota Permai*, at Jalan Mesjid Lama 33, near the junction with Jalan Sudirman. It has ikan belida prepared a couple of ways for 3000 rp, plus a range of other dishes.

The *Selatan Indah*, at Jalan Iskandar 434, reportedly does the best Palembang food in town.

Another Palembang speciality is *pempek*, also known as *empek-empek*, a mixture of sago, fish and seasonings which is formed into balls and deep-fried or grilled. They are served with a spicy sauce and are widely available from street stalls and warungs for 100 rp each.

At night, Jalan Sayangan, to the east of Jalan Sudirman, is packed with some excellent Chinese food stands and sate places. Around the corner on Jalan Rustam Effendy, there are fruit stalls and stands selling *pisang goreng* (fried bananas) and other snacks.

The *Sari Bundo*, part of the Hotel Sari set-up, and the *Pagi Sore*, diagonally opposite at Jalan Sudirman 96, are a couple of Padang food places that come recommended.

There are a number of bakeries along Jalan Sudirman which also do noodle dishes and other simple meals, or try the *French Bakery* at Jalan Kol Atmo 481B, opposite King's Hotel.

Fast food has arrived in the form of places like *Bonanza Fried Chicken* at Jalan Kol Atmo 425. *Rooster Fried Chicken*, next to Hero Plaza on Jalan Diponegoro, also does burgers.

Getting There & Away

Air Merpati operates a busy schedule out of Palembang. There are seven direct flights a day to Jakarta (135,800 rp), as well as direct connections to Bandarlampung, Bandung, Batam, Bengkulu, Padang, Pekanbaru and Rengat (halfway to Pekanbaru). It also flies daily to Pangkalpinang on Pulau Bangka for 59,900 rp and twice a week to Tanjungpandan on the neighbouring island of Belitung for 113,800 rp. The Merpati office (☎ 310675) is in the Hotel Sandjaja building on Jalan Kapt Rivai.

Mandala also has two direct flights a day to Jakarta. Its office (☎ 350634) is also in the Hotel Sandjaja.

Deraya Air has daily flights between Palembang and Tanjungpandan for 85,000 rp. Deraya Air's Palembang office (☎ 353700) is at Jalan Sudirman 2954.

Bus The main bus station is south of the Musi River at the junction of Jalan Pangeran Ratu and Jalan Kironggo Wiro Sentiko. ANS is a reliable company with daily air-con buses north to Bukittinggi (25,000 rp; 24 hours), Medan (50,000 rp) and through to Banda Aceh (74,000 rp). It also has daily buses to Jakarta (33,000 rp; 20 hours) and points east. ANS has an office in town at Jalan Diponegoro 100 (☎ 350029). There are numerous services to Jambi, and a five-hour trip costs from 6000 to 13,000 rp with air-con. Bengkulu Indah has daily buses to Bengkulu (15,000 rp; 12 hours).

Train The Kertapati railway station is on the south side of the river, eight km from the town centre. There are two trains a day to Bandarlampung, at 9 am and 9 pm. The morning train is economy class only (4500 rp) and takes 10 hours, while the night train has only business class (18,000 rp) and 1st class (28,000 rp).

There are also trains to Lubuklinggau at 8 am and 8 pm, returning at 9 am and 9 pm. The day trains cost 4500 rp and the night trains cost 10,000 rp.

Boat There are two daily jetfoil services between Palembang and Mentok (25,000 rp). They leave Palembang's Boom Baru jetty at 7.30 and 9.30 am, and Mentok at 11.30 am and 1 pm. The journey takes between three and 3½ hours, depending on conditions. For your money you get a snack and a numbered seat in an air-con saloon that has more in common with an airliner than a boat. If you want to enjoy the scenery on the banks of the Musi River, you can go out through the engine room and sit on the bench at the back of the boat.

There's also a daily slow boat from Palembang to Mentok (13,000 rp; six hours).

Getting Around
To/From the Airport Sultan Badaruddin II airport is 12 km north of town and a taxi costs a standard 10,000 rp. It's a two-km hike from the airport to the main road if you want to catch an opelet into town for 350 rp.

Local Transport Opelets around town cost a standard 200 rp. There is no longer a city centre opelet station. They leave from around the huge roundabout at the junction of Jalan Sudirman and Jalan Merdeka. Opelets to Kertapati railway station cost 200 rp.

AROUND PALEMBANG
Kayuagung
Kayuagung is a village on the banks of the Komering River that's known for its unusual

pottery. The pots, mostly cooking and household utensils like jugs and rice dishes, are fired under a kiln of brushwood in the open air.

Gold and red inlaid Palembang cabinets are still made in this village, which is also known for its sago cakes and krupuks.

Kayuagung is 66 km south of Palembang. There are regular buses from the main bus terminal in Palembang. They cost 1500 rp and take 90 minutes.

DANAU RANAU
Remote Ranau, nestled in the middle of the Bukit Barisan mountains in the south-western corner of South Sumatra, is one of the least accessible – and least spoiled – of Sumatra's mountain lakes. It is about 300 km, and at least seven hours by bus, from Palembang.

Temperatures at Ranau seldom get above 25°C. It is a good place to relax or go hiking in the surrounding mountains. It's possible to climb Gunung Seminung (1881 metres), the extinct volcano that dominates the region.

Change money before you get there.

Organised Tours
The Palembang travel agency Varita Tours & Travel (☎ 355669), at Jalan Iskandar 16A, specialises in tours to Danau Ranau.

Places to Stay & Eat
Bandingagung, on the north side of the lake, is the area's main town and has half a dozen losmen with rooms for around 8000 rp. The lakeside places south of Simpangsender, on the lake's western shore, are a better place to be. The best of them is the *Wisma Pusri*, a smarter than average guesthouse with great views over the lake. It costs a bit more than average, but is worth it. Doubles with mandi and fan are 17,500 rp; 30,000 rp with air-con.

Getting There & Away
Most routes to Danau Ranau go through the Trans-Sumatran Highway town of Baturaja. All north/south buses go through Baturaja, and from Palembang there are buses every

hour from the main bus terminus (5000 rp; 4½ hours). Baturaja is also a stop on the Palembang-Bandarlampung railway, about 3½ hours south of Palembang.

There are regular buses for the remaining 120 km from Baturaja to Ranau for 1700 rp. The road is not too good and the journey takes at least three hours.

It's a good idea to time your travelling so you arrive in Baturaja as early in the day as possible to give yourself plenty of time to get a bus out again. If you do get stuck, there are dozens of uninspiring budget losmen to choose from.

PASEMAH HIGHLANDS
The Pasemah Plateau, tucked away in the foothills of the Bukit Barisan west of Lahat, is famous for the dozens of mysterious megalithic monuments that dot the landscape. The origins of the stones remain unknown, but they have been dated back almost 2000 years.

Orientation & Information
It's 80 km and two hours by bus from Lahat to Pagaralam, the main town of the highlands. Lahat has a tourist office at Jalan Amir Hamzeh 150 (☎ 22496). The Losmen Mirasa is a good source of information in Pagaralam. There's nowhere to change money, so bring enough rupiah to see you through.

Megalithic Sites
Megalithic remains are everywhere in Pagaralam, and in the surrounding villages of Pajarbulam, Tanjung Aro and Belumai.

The museums of Palembang and Jakarta now house the pick of the stones. The best of those remaining are found around the village of **Tegurwangi**, about five km from Pagaralam.

There are two distinct styles of sculpture. The older style features figures squatting with hands on knees or arms folded over chests; the second is more sophisticated and has single statues as well as groups.

The sculptures in this group are dynamic, powerful and passionate studies of men, women, children and animals. They include several of men riding buffaloes or elephants, groups of people standing next to elephants and buffaloes, two men battling with a snake, a man struggling with an elephant lying on its back, and a couple of tigers – one guards a representation of a human head between its paws.

These carvings have expressive facial features and are thought to date from the Bronze Age. Their makers used the natural curve of the rocks to create a three-dimensional effect, though all the sculptures are in bas-relief.

A couple of stone graves at the village of **Tanjungraya** contain fragments of paintings in broad bands of black, yellow, red, white and grey on the inner walls, in the same style as the sculptures. Two are scenes of a warrior and a buffalo; the third is of a man with an elephant.

Other Attractions
The dormant volcano **Gunung Dempo** (3159 metres) is the highest of the peaks surrounding the Pasemah Highlands. It's a tea-growing area, and there are opelets from Pagaralam to the tea factory.

Elephant safaris are among the activities offered by the elephant training centre near Bukit Serelo, a striking landmark about 20 km from Lahat that is shaped like a fist giving a thumbs up. The hill is known locally as Bukit Tunjuk (Finger Mountain).

Places to Stay
Few travellers stay in Pagaralam, even though it's much cooler than Lahat and there are half a dozen places to stay. The tiny *Wisma Mess*, on Jalan Purwasari, charges 6000 rp for simple doubles. The best place is the *Losmen Mirasa* on the main street, Jalan Mailan, where rooms are priced from 10,000 to 25,000 rp.

Lahat's super cheapies are grouped together close to the railway station on Jalan Stasiun. The places on Jalan Mayor Ruslam III are much better, starting with the *Losmen Simpang* (☎ 21940) and the *Simpang Baru*, where doubles start at 7500 rp. The best rooms in town are at the *Nusantara Hotel*

(☎ 21336), where you can pay up to 60,000 rp for air-con doubles with hot water.

Getting There & Away

Lahat's location on the Trans-Sumatran Highway makes it easy to get to by bus. It's nine hours from Bandarlampung, 12 hours from Padang and 4½ hours from Palembang. Lahat is also a stop on the railway line between Palembang and Lubuklinggau.

Getting Around

There are regular buses between Lahat and Pagaralam (1500 rp; two hours). If you are staying in Lahat, note that the last bus from Pagaralam leaves at 4 pm. There are opelets to the villages around Pagaralam for 200 rp.

PULAU BANGKA

Bangka is a large, relatively unpopulated island 25 km off the east coast of Sumatra, surrounded by some of the finest palm-fringed, deserted beaches in Indonesia. They appear destined to stay that way for some time since they are hard to get to and there are no cheap places to stay. All the beach hotels are priced with wealthy visitors from Singapore and Malaysia in mind, but they too appear to be staying away in droves.

The island's name is derived from the word 'wangka', meaning tin, which was discovered in 1710 near Mentok. The island is covered with old mine workings. Tin is still mined on the island, although operations have been greatly scaled down in recent years.

There are only small pockets of natural forest left on Bangka. Rubber, palm oil and pepper are major crops.

Orientation & Information

The island's tourist office (☎ 92496) is just south of Sungailiat on the main road from Pangkalpinang.

Pangkalpinang, the island's main town, is a fairly small town with most banks, travel agencies and the post office along Jalan Sudirman (the main street). The post office is the only place not centrally located (it is at the edge of town) on the road to Sungailiat.

The BNI 1946 is at Jalan Sudirman 119, while Visa and Mastercard holders can draw money from the Bank of Central Asia on Jalan Masjid Jamik. You can't miss it: its sign is the highest structure in town.

Merpati, Sempati and SMAC all have offices around the central junction of Jalan Sudirman and Jalan Masjid Jamik, while local travel specialist Duta Bangka Sarana (DBS) (☎ 21698) is at Jalan Sudirman 10E. The bus station and markets are nearby on Jalan N Pegadaian.

Things to See & Do

Pangkalpinang Pangkalpinang is a bustling business and transport centre with a population of about 50,000. There is a colourful **market** in the centre of town. **Pantai Pasir Padi** is a beach 2½ km south of town that is easily reached by opelet for 300 rp. The swimming is poor and the main attraction is the seafood restaurant.

Travelling golfers can have a round at the **golf course** built on the southern edge of town by the island's tin company. It costs 3000 rp for nine holes, plus 500 rp club hire.

The huge **cemetery** on the northern edge of town, divided into sections for Muslim, Buddhist and Christians, has some extravagant looking graves. There are supposedly 100,000 people buried here.

Mentok Mentok, on the north-western tip of the island, is the port for boats to/from Palembang. Few people bother to stay here longer than it takes to catch a bus to Pangkalpinang.

There's a **memorial** close to Mentok's lighthouse to 22 Australian nurses who were shot dead by the Japanese during WW II. The nurses had survived the sinking of the SS *Vyner Brooke* during the evacuation of Singapore.

The hilltop guesthouse, at nearby **Gunung Menumbing** (445 metres), served as a home in domestic exile for future President Soekarno and Vice-President Hatta during negotiations on independence from February until July 1949.

SUMATRA

Other Attractions The islands' star attractions are its beaches. The best are **Pantai Parai Tenggiri**, four km from Sungailiat and monopolised by the Parai Beach Hotel, and the deserted **Pantai Matras**, five km further up the coast.

The hot springs and children's playground at **Pemali**, about seven km from Sungailiat, were developed for the families of workers at the nearby tin mine. The springs feed two large swimming pools. The entry fee is 600 rp. There is no public transport to the hot springs.

Places to Stay

Pangkalpinang There are quite a few cheap losmen around the centre of town. A good choice is the friendly *Penginapan Srikandi* (☎ 21884), at Jalan Masjid Jami 42. It has singles/doubles for 9000/15,000 rp, and newer rooms for 12,500/22,000 rp. Both categories come with mandi and fan.

Immediately opposite, at No 43, is the *Bukit Shofa Hotel* (☎ 21062). It's a clean, modern place with singles/doubles from 11,000/20,000 rp with mandi and fan, or doubles with air-con for 50,000 rp.

If you want to go further down-market, try the *Losmen Maras* at Jalan Sudirman. It has singles/doubles for 7500/10,000 rp or 12,500 rp with mandi. The grotty *Penginapan Sederhana*, next to the Bank of Central Asia on Jalan Suraiman Arief, has rooms for 4000/8000 rp.

Mid-range hotels are plentiful. The best value is the *Sabrina Hotel* (☎ 22424), on Jalan Diponegoro, a quiet side street off Jalan Sudirman. It has very comfortable doubles with air-con, TV, hot water and breakfast for 45,000 rp. Don't bother with the economy 'Japan-style' rooms (mattress on the floor).

The *Menumbing Hotel* (☎ 22991), at Jalan Gereja 5, has doubles starting from 20,000 rp. Rooms with bath, air-con and TV cost 75,000 rp. The hotel has a restaurant and a nice pool, which non-guests can use for 2500 rp.

Mentok The *Losmen Mentok*, near the harbour at Jalan Ahmad Yani 42, has rooms

for 5000 rp. The splendid-sounding *Tin Palace Hotel*, which overlooks the market place from Jalan Major Syafrie Rahman 1, has rooms with shower and fan for 20,000 rp and with air-con for 30,000 rp.

Beaches The beaches around Sungailiat are tourist resort territory, although there's not much evidence of tourists. The *Parai Beach Hotel* (☎ 92335) is the best of this lot, with accommodation in air-con bungalows by the beach. Few guests would be paying the advertised prices, which start from 110,000 rp and peak at 300,000 rp for suites.

The glossy brochure put out by *Tanjung Pesona Beach Cottages*, just south of Sungailiat, promises an 'unforgettable experience'. It's unforgettable all right – the aquaria in the foyer were full of floating dead fish, and by the beach there were miserable, moulting sea eagles held in a cage so small they could hardly spread their wings. Great beach, though.

The best of the resort accommodation is at *Remodong Cottages*, on the north coast beyond the port town of Belinyu. Cottages for two cost 60,000 rp and family cottages go for 100,000 rp. The setting here is great, but the beach is not much good for swimming – the water disappears at low tide. There are no phones, but cottages can be booked through an office in Pangkalpinang (☎ 21573).

Places to Eat

The island is well known for its small but fiery chillies. In Pangkalpinang there are plenty of places to eat Indonesian and Chinese food along Jalan Sudirman and in the market area.

For Padang-style food, try *Sari Bundo* at Jalan Sudirman 77. Nearby, opposite Video Queen, is a small restaurant serving the Palembang speciality, pempek (fish balls). The flashiest restaurant in town is the *Tirta Garden*, an up-market Chinese and seafood restaurant about three km from the city centre at Jalan Sudirman 3.

If it's seafood that you're after, the place to go is the *Restaurant Asui Seafood*, behind

Ship mast, Karimunjawa, Central Java (PT)

Top: Karimunjawa, Central Java (PT)
Middle: Children playing in the water, Togian Islands, Sulawesi (BD)
Bottom: Pulau Antuk Barat, West Java (PT)

the Bank of Central Asia on Jalan Kampung Bintang. It's the original no-frills restaurant, but the food is great and the place does a roaring trade. It's run by a fisherman who decided that there was more money to be made from cooking fish than catching them. Try *gebung*, known locally as 'chicken fish' because of the firmness of the flesh. Delicious!

Getting There & Away

Air Merpati has two flights a day between Pangkalpinang and Jakarta (136,000 rp; 50 minutes) and at least one flight a day between Pangkalpinang and Palembang (59,900 rp; 30 minutes). Pelita (135,000 rp) and Bouraq (122,000 rp) also have daily connections to Jakarta.

Merpati and SMAC also fly to Batam (129,000 rp). Between them, there are flights on Monday, Thursday, Friday and Sunday.

Deraya Air flies to the neighbouring island of Pulau Belitung daily (52,275 rp).

Boat There are two daily jetfoil services between Palembang and Mentok (25,000 rp). They leave Palembang at 7.30 and 9.30 am, and Mentok at 11.30 am and 1 pm. The journey takes between three and 3½ hours, depending on conditions.

There's also a daily slow boat from Palembang (13,000 rp; six hours).

The Pelni liner *Rinjani* stops at Mentok on Fridays in each direction during fortnightly journeys between Medan and Jakarta. The economy fare between Jakarta and Mentok is 25,000 rp, and 36,000 rp between Mentok and Medan. The Pelni office (☎ 22743) in Mentok is outside the port gates.

Getting Around

To/From the Airport Airport taxis charge 5000 rp for the seven-km run into Pangkalpinang, or you can walk to the main road and catch an opelet for 300 rp.

Local Transport There is regular public transport between Bangka's main towns, but most opelets stop running in mid-afternoon. After that, taxis are the only option.

There are public buses between Mentok and Pangkalpinang (3500 rp; four hours), but the best way to travel between the two towns is by the private DBS Travel buses that connect with the jetfoil services. They do the journey in 2½ hours for 5000 rp, including hotel pick-up/drop-off. The bus can be booked in Palembang through Carmeta Travel (☎ 314970), at Jalan Dempo Luar 29. The buses leave Pangkalpinang at 7.30 and 8.30 am for Mentok.

Lampung

Sumatra's southernmost province was not given provincial status by Jakarta until 1964. The Lampungese, however, have a long history as a distinct cultural entity.

There's evidence that Lampung was part of the Palembang-based Sriwijayan empire until the 11th century, when the Jambi-based Malayu kingdom became the dominant regional power.

Megalithic remains at Pugungraharjo, on the plains to the east of Bandarlampung, are thought to date back more than 1000 years and point to a combination of Hindu and Buddhist influences. The site is believed to have been occupied until the 16th century.

From the earliest times, Lampung has been famous for its pepper, and it was the prized pepper crop that was the target for the West Javanese sultanate of Banten (today no more than a fishing village) when it moved in at the beginning of the 16th century. It was Banten that introduced the Islamic faith to Lampung.

Lampung pepper also interested the Dutch, and the Dutch East India Company built a factory at Menggala in the late 17th century in a failed attempt to usurp the pepper trade.

When the Dutch finally took control of Lampung in 1856, they began to move large numbers of people from West Java to farm

SUMATRA

the fertile plains of eastern Lampung in the first of the transmigration schemes that have sought to ease the chronic overcrowding on Java. The Javanese brought with them the music of the gamelan and wayang shadow puppetry.

Transmigration has made east Lampung something of a cultural melting pot. Other newcomers came from Hindu Bali, and trips to 'Balinese villages' are on some organised tour agendas.

The majority of the province's eight million people live in the main city of Bandarlampung and in the transmigration areas to the east. Very few people live on Lampung's rugged western seaboard, most of which is taken up by Bukit Barisan Selatan National Park.

Today, coffee is Lampung's most important income earner, closely followed by timber. Pepper remains a major crop, while there are also large areas of rubber and palm oil plantation.

The main tourist attractions are trips to the volcano at Krakatau and the elephants of Way Kambas National Park.

BAKAUHENI

Bakauheni is the major ferry terminal on Sumatra's southern tip, and the main transit point between Java and Sumatra. There is no point in staying here.

There are 40 ferries a day between Bakauheni and Merak in Java, leaving – according to the timetable – every 36 minutes. The trip across the Selat Sunda to Merak takes two hours and the cost for economy/1st class is 1300/2400 rp.

The Bakauheni Terminal is large, well-organised and designed to shift people as quickly and smoothly as possible. Buses (1700 rp) and share taxis (5000 rp) are waiting to take passengers to Bandarlampung, two hours' drive away. The taxis are the better bet for those planning to stay in Bandarlampung as they will take you directly to the hotel of your choice, thus avoiding the hassles of the chaotic Rajabasa bus station.

KRAKATAU VOLCANO

While the movie moguls decided that Krakatau was West of Java, they might just have easily opted for South of Sumatra.

The Indonesian government considers Krakatau to be Sumatran anyway, and Lampung promotes the famous volcano as its attraction. It's certainly cheaper and reportedly safer to get to Krakatau from Lampung than from Java.

For the story of Krakatau and details on the area, see the Krakatau section in the Java chapter.

Getting There & Away
From Bandarlampung The Lampung provincial tourist office can arrange speedboat charter for 400,000 rp, which covers up to six passengers. The trip takes 1½ hours each way. Tour operators charge US$75 per person (minimum four) to take you by bus to Canti and then by boat to Krakatau.

From Kalianda/Canti The Beringin Hotel in Kalianda is a good place to meet up with other travellers wanting to see Krakatau. The hotel can organise a boat for up to eight people for 80,000 rp. Alternatively, you can head to the nearby small port of Canti and charter a larger boat for about 200,000 rp. The trip takes about three hours each way.

KALIANDA
Kalianda is a quiet little town, 30 km north of the ferry terminal at Bakauheni. It has a great setting overlooking Lampung Bay with Gunung Rajabasa as a backdrop. There are boats to Krakatau and other islands in Lampung Bay from Canti.

Things to See & Do
The main reason for stopping here is to visit Krakatau (see Krakatau Volcano earlier), but there are a couple of other things you can do while you organise that.

Volcano climbers can add **Rajabasa** (1281 metres) to their list, while there are hot springs on the tide line at **Wartawan Beach**, just beyond Canti; 300 rp by opelet.

There are scheduled boats from Canti to

the nearby islands of Sebuku (1500 rp) and Sebesi (2000 rp). The boats leave at 9 am and 3 pm. It is reportedly possible to camp on both islands and there are self-contained bungalows on Sebesi with room for six people for 75,000 rp.

Organised Tours
The manager of the Beringin Hotel organises a range of tours for small groups, including trips to Krakatau.

Places to Stay & Eat
The *Hotel Beringin* (☎ 2008) is a fine old Dutch villa with high ceilings and fans slowly stirring the air. It's close to the centre of town at Jalan Kesuma Bangsa 75, and has huge rooms with mandi for 9300 rp and smaller rooms without mandi for 6000 rp. The manager is very friendly and has lots of information about local attractions.

The street stalls that emerge in the town centre at night are the best place to eat. There's Padang food at the *Rumah Makan Palapa* on Jalan Raya.

Merak Belantung Beach Cottages (☎ 43747), 10 km north of Kalianda, are tucked away among the palm trees just metres from a perfect horseshoe beach outside the town of Merak Belantung. A night in one of the half dozen bungalows will set you back 40,000 rp.

Getting There & Away
There are regular buses between Kalianda and Bandarlampung's Rajabasa bus station (1500 rp; 1½ hours). There are less regular bemos from the Bakauheni ferry terminal to Kalianda for 1200 rp. It's also possible to get a north-bound bus from Bakauheni to Merak Belantung, and then catch an opelet back to Kalianda for 500 rp.

Getting Around
There are regular opelets from Kalianda to Canti (300 rp) and along the road that rings Gunung Rajabasa via Gayam and Pasuruan. Motorcycles can be rented from the Beringin Hotel for 15,000 rp per day.

BANDARLAMPUNG
The major city and administrative centre of Lampung Province is Bandarlampung, at the northern end of Lampung Bay.

Bandarlampung is the new name that marks the official merger of the old towns of Telukbetung (coastal) and Tanjungkarang (inland), which have grown together over the years. The merger has produced the fourth largest city in Sumatra, with a population around 600,000.

When Krakatau erupted in 1883, almost half the 36,000 victims died in the 30-metre high tidal wave that funnelled up Lampung Bay and devastated Telukbetung. A huge steel maritime buoy, now located on a hillside overlooking the city, was erected as a memorial – in the position it came to rest after the wave had receded. (See Things to See & Do later.)

These days, Bandarlampung has acquired a reputation as something of a bogey town for travellers. It must be the only place in Sumatra where you can venture off the beaten track simply by leaving the bus station.

Still, some people take distrust to sorry extremes.

One example concerns a traveller who was shown to the railway station by a policeman. He was given a cup of coffee in the policeman's office and assumed, on the strength of what he'd heard about Bandarlampung, that the policeman was protecting him because it wasn't safe on the streets. It never occurred to him that the policemen might have been a friendly local keen to talk to a rare Western visitor!

Orientation & Information
Most of the places of relevance to travellers are in Tanjungkarang, including the bulk of the hotels and the railway station. The Rajabasa bus station is on the northern edge of town, and the airport is 15 minutes' drive further north.

Tourist Office The tourist office (☎ 51900) is at Jalan Kotaraja 12, 150 metres from the railway station. Several of the staff speak good English and are very helpful. Yaman Aziz, of the Lampung Provincial Tourist

Association (☎ 428565), at Jalan WR Suprat-man 39, also speaks good English.

Post & Telephone The main post office is inconveniently located halfway between Tanjungkarang and Telukbetung on Jalan Kh Dahlan 21, off Jalan Sudirman. There is a small branch post office on Jalan Kotaraja, near the railway station. International telephone calls can be made from the 24-hour Telkom office on Jalan Kartini, which has a Home Country Direct phone.

Money Many banks have branches in both Tanjungkarang and Telukbetung, including the Bank of Central Asia. Its Tanjungkarang branch is at Jalan Raden Intan 98, and the Telukbetung branch is at Jalan Yos Sudarso 100. BNI 1946 has a branch on the round-about in the heart of Tanjungkarang.

Tour Agencies If you want to join an organised tour it's best to check out the tour companies working at the big hotels; there's more chance of them getting the numbers required for a trip. The Indrah Palace and the Sheraton are the places to ask. Elendra Tour & Travel (☎ 53942), at Jalan Agus Salim 112, also offers a range of tours.

Things to See & Do

Not even the enthusiastic crew at the tourist office can come up with much to do in Bandarlampung. The **Krakatau monument**, a huge steel maritime buoy washed out of Lampung Bay by the post-eruption tidal waves, is worth a look to satisfy curiosity about the scale of what happened in 1887. The buoy has been mounted in concrete and sits in a small park opposite Kupang Kota police station, off Jalan Veteran.

The **Lampung Provincial Museum**, five km north of central Tanjungkarang on Jalan Teuku Umar, houses a diverse collection of bits and pieces – everything from neolithic relics to stuffed animals. A museum brochure gives visitors a good idea of what to expect when it announces matter-of-factly that the collection 'would benefit from improved conservation, labelling and display'!

Places to Stay – bottom end

As is so often the case in big cities, things are a bit grim at the budget end of the scale. There are a couple of rock-bottom places on Jalan Kotaraja, less than 100 metres from the railway station. The *Hotel Gunungsari*, at No 21, has dingy doubles for 7500 rp. Avoid the *Hotel Berkah* next door. Another couple of cheapies are *Penginapan Tambak Baya* and the *Hotel Cilimaya*, 50 metres apart on Jalan Imam Bonjol. Both have singles/doubles for 5000/8000 rp with shared mandi. The Cilimaya also has rooms with mandi for 6500/10,000 rp. No fans, though.

Places to Stay – middle

Things start to improve rapidly if you are prepared to spend a bit more. A good place to look is around the junction of Jalan Raden Intan and Jalan S Parman.

The *Kurnia City Hotel* (☎ 62030), on the junction at Jalan Raden Intan 114, has very clean singles/doubles with air-con starting from 24,000/26,500 rp. Across the road, the *Kurnia Dua* (☎ 61985) also has economy rooms starting at 15,000/17,500 rp.

In the centre of town, off Jalan Kartini on Jalan Dwi Warna, is the *Hotel Garden* (☎ 55512), with doubles ranging from 13,500 rp for a simple room to 29,500 rp with shower and air-con. The *Hotel Ria* (☎ 53974), around the corner from the Garden on Jalan Kartini, has doubles with air-con starting at 25,000 rp.

Places to Stay – top end

Bandarlampung has a growing band of up-market hotels. The latest addition is the *Hotel Arinas* (☎ 66778), in the heart of town at Jalan Raden Intan 35A, set back from the main road on a small cul-de-sac. It has very comfortable modern rooms, all with air-con, TV and hot water, at prices ranging from 45,000 to 80,000 rp. A bit out of town is the *Marco Polo Hotel* (☎ 62511), at Jalan Dr Susilo 4, where 45,000 rp will get you a double with a view of Lampung Bay and use of the Olympic-size pool.

Other top-end offerings are the classy *Hotel Indrah Palace* (☎ 62766) and the

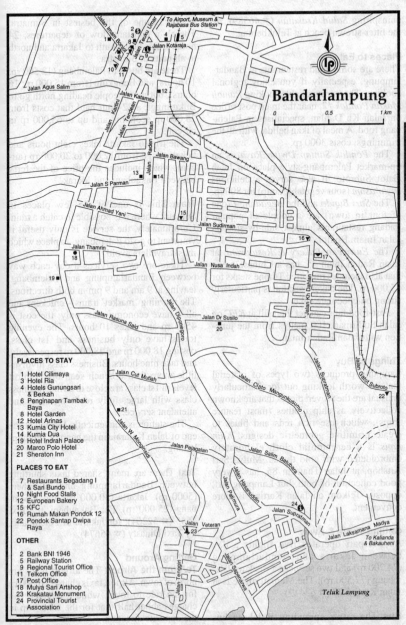

Bandarlampung

0   0.5   1 km

SUMATRA

PLACES TO STAY
1 Hotel Cilimaya
3 Hotel Ria
4 Hotels Gunungsari & Berkah
6 Penginapan Tambak Baya
8 Hotel Garden
12 Hotel Arinas
13 Kurnia City Hotel
14 Kurnia Dua
19 Hotel Indrah Palace
20 Marco Polo Hotel
21 Sheraton Inn

PLACES TO EAT
7 Restaurants Begadang I & Sari Bundo
10 Night Food Stalls
12 European Bakery
15 KFC
17 Rumah Makan Pondok 12
22 Pondok Santap Dwipa Raya

OTHER
2 Bank BNI 1946
5 Railway Station
9 Regional Tourist Office
11 Telkom Office
16 Post Office
18 Mulya Sari Artshop
23 Krakatau Monument
24 Provincial Tourist Association

To Airport, Museum & Rajabasa Bus Station

Jalan Imam Bonjol
Jalan Teuku Umar
Jalan Kotaraja
Jalan Agus Salim
Jalan Kartini
Jalan Katamso
Jalan Teladan
Jalan Raden Intan
Jalan Bawang
Jalan S Parman
Jalan Ahmad Yani
Jalan Sudirman
Jalan Thamrin
Jalan Nusa Indah
Jalan KH Dahlan
Jalan Rasuna Said
Jalan Diponegoro
Jalan Dr Susilo
Jalan Cut Mutiah
Jalan Cipto Mangunkusumo
Jalan Supratman
Jalan Gatot Subroto
Jalan W Monginsidi
Jalan Pejagalan
Jalan Salim Batubara
Jalan Hasanuddin
Jalan Patimura
Jalan Supratman
Jalan Veteran
Jalan Tenggiri
Jalan Sarena
Jalan Laksamana Madya

Teluk Lampung

To Kalianda & Bakauheni

uninspiring *Sahid Krakatau* (☎ 46589), by the litter-strewn beach at Telukbetung.

Places to Eat

There are some good restaurants in Bandarlampung, especially if you enjoy regional cooking. The unremarkable-looking *Rumah Makan Pondok 12*, near the main post office on Jalan Kh Dahlan, specialises in Palembang food. A meal of ikan belida, with all the trimmings, costs 3000 rp.

The *Pondok Santap Dwipa Raya*, is an up-market Palembang-style place on Jalan Gatot Subroto. It also serves a delicious *sayur asam* (sour vegetable soup) for 800 rp.

The *Sari Bundo* and the *Begadang I* (one of four in town) are a couple of popular Padang restaurants almost side-by-side on Jalan Imam Bonjol.

The *European Bakery & Restaurant*, at Jalan Raden Intan 35, has a Chinese menu that also includes imported T-bone steaks for 15,000 rp. The bakery section is particularly strong on chocolate cake.

Fast-food fans can get their fill at *KFC* on Jalan Sudirman, 100 metres from the junction with Jalan Raden Intan.

Things to Buy

Lampung produces two types of material that are worth looking out for. Particularly unusual are the woven pieces that are known collectively as ship clothes (most feature ships), which use rich reds and blues to create primitive geometric designs. *Kain tapis* is a ceremonial cloth elaborately embroidered with gold thread. Mulya Sari Artshop, at Jalan Thamrin 85, has a very good collection of both, but Lampung Art, opposite Telkom on Jalan Kartini, is more convenient.

Getting There & Away

Air Merpati operates five flights a day between Jakarta and Bandarlampung (74,200 rp) and two services a week to Palembang (77,500 rp). The Merpati office is at Jalan Kartini 90 (☎ 63419).

Bus The city's sprawling Rajabasa bus station is one of the busiest in Sumatra. There's a constant flow of departures, 24 hours a day, both south to Jakarta and north to all parts of Sumatra.

There are buses to Palembang (12,500 rp; 10 hours) and Bengkulu (from 15,000 rp; 16 hours), but most people heading north go to Bukittinggi; a 22-hour haul that costs from 25,000 rp economy and up to 65,000 rp in air-con.

The trip to Jakarta takes eight hours and tickets range from 12,000 to 20,000 rp (aircon), which includes the price of the ferry between Bakauheni and Merak.

Train This is one of the few places in Sumatra where it is possible to catch a train. Unfortunately, the service is only useful if you want to go to Palembang – a place which most travellers avoid.

There are two services a day each way between Bandarlampung and Palembang, leaving at 9 am and 9 pm in both directions. The morning 'market' trains – chickens and all – have economy class only; the cost is 4500 rp and takes 10 hours. The evening trains have only business and 1st class, costing 18,000 rp and 28,000 rp respectively, and take nine hours. Business class involves little more than a bench seat, but comfort levels in 1st class are close to airline business class with large, fully reclining seats and attendant service.

The station is conveniently located at the end of Jalan Kotaraja in the heart of Tanjungkarang.

Taxi There are many shared taxis shuttling between Bandarlampung and Bakauheni (5000 rp), Jakarta (30,000 rp) and Palembang (25,000 rp). For Bakauheni, try Taxi 4545 (☎ 52264); for Jakarta or Palembang, try Taxi Dinasty (☎ 45674).

Getting Around

To/From the Airport The airport is 22 km north of town. Airport taxis charge 16,000 rp for the ride to town, while a metered cab charges about half that for the same trip in the opposite direction.

Local Transport There are frequent opelets between the Tanjungkarang railway station and Rajabasa bus station. They cost 300 rp.

WAY KAMBAS NATIONAL PARK
The national park occupies 1300 sq km of coastal lowland forest around the Way Kambas River on the east coast of Lampung, 110 km from Bandarlampung.

The park is home to five pairs of rhinos, the occasional Sumatran tiger and – the main attraction – elephants.

Elephants
The elephants in question are Sumatran elephants *(Elephas maximus sumatrensis)*, a subspecies of the Asian elephant found only in Sumatra and Kalimantan.

Way Kambas is home to about 350 elephants, about 250 of them still living wild – but don't head out there expecting to see any of them. What you'll find is something much closer to a circus show than a brush with nature: the Way Kambas elephant training centre.

The centre was set up to do something about the 'problem' of wild elephants that has been created by the clearing of elephant habitat for farming.

The elephants are rounded up and taught to be productive employees of the tourism industry. Some of them learn such useful tricks as how to kick a football and get to star in the circus-type shows that are put on for tour groups.

The most popular activities are two-hour elephant safari rides, which can be arranged on request for 20,000 rp per person. Mornings are the best time. Short rides cost 2500 rp.

One time when there's a good chance of seeing wild elephants around the training centre is during the mating season in June and July. Late afternoon is the time to be there.

Way Kanan
The Way Kanan 'resort', as the tourist blurb rather optimistically calls it, is little more than a small guesthouse and a few ramshackle huts in a jungle clearing on the banks of the Way Kanan River, about 13 km from the entrance to the national park.

An official guide is based at the camp during daylight hours. Guided activities include three-hour jungle treks for 15,000 rp, and two-hour canoe trips on the Way Kanan River and surrounding waterways for 75,000 rp.

Judging by the piles of evidence on the road, elephants visit Way Kanan from time to time. There's certainly more chance of seeing an elephant than a Sumatran tiger, sightings of which are extremely rare.

What you will see – and hear – is lots of primates and birds.

There is very little virgin forest in the national park. The only parts the loggers left alone were the parts they couldn't get to. They did, however, leave a few big trees. They include some massive scaly-barked meranti trees with trunks rising 30 metres as straight as an arrow before the first branch.

Organised Tours
Prices for day trips to Way Kambas and Way Kanan start at about $US60 per person for a minimum of two, falling to US$30 per person for larger groups. Some tours also include a stop at the Pugungraharjo archaeological site.

Places to Stay
There is no cheap accommodation in the park. The *Way Kambas Visitors' Centre*, at the elephant training centre, has reasonable double rooms for 25,000 rp. There is nowhere to eat after the stalls that cater for the day-trippers close, so bring food. Conditions are very basic at the *Way Kanan Guesthouse*, and the price is way over the top at 25,000 rp for a double. That's what you'll have to pay, though, for the privilege of waking up in the jungle. You'll need to bring your own food, but cooking facilities and utensils are provided.

Otherwise, the nearest accommodation is the *Losmen Lindung* at Jepara, 10 km south of the turn-off to Way Kambas, where singles/doubles are 10,000/15,000 rp

If you turn up at the park entrance late, the

staff will normally let travellers bunk down somewhere.

Getting There & Away

There are occasional buses from Bandarlampung's Rajabasa bus station direct to Jepara (3500 rp; 2½ hours). These buses go past the entrance to Way Kambas, an arched gateway in the village of Tridatu, 10 km

north of Jepara. Otherwise, catch a bus to Metro (1500 rp; one hour) and then another to Tridatu (2500 rp; 1½ hours).

From the park entrance, it is easy to find someone to take you into the park by motorbike. The going rates are 6000 rp to Way Kambas and 7500 rp to Way Kanan. You will also need to negotiate a time to be picked up again.

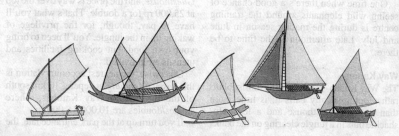

Nusa Tenggara

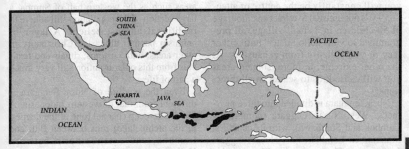

Nusa Tenggara (the name means 'South-East Islands') is quite different from the rest of Indonesia. As you travel east, the climate becomes drier, so people raise corn and sago rather than rice; the flora & fauna are more evocative of parts of Australia than of tropical Bali; the people are poorer than those elsewhere in Indonesia; and there is a great variety of cultures and religions.

Each island has its own peculiar sights, some of which rival anything seen on Java or Bali. The great stone-slab tombs and traditional villages of Sumba, the intricate ikat weaving of Sumba and Flores, the brilliantly coloured lakes of Keli Mutu in Flores and the dragons of Komodo must rate as some of the finest attractions in South-East Asia. Though there are few beaches where you can peel off and lie back undisturbed by a crowd of curious locals, there's fine coral off some of the islands.

Although a steady stream of travellers passes through, until recently the lack of transport confined most of them to a limited route. There are now more opportunities

---

Highlights

The string of islands east of Bali attracts a growing stream of travellers looking for a taste of different cultures, with some unique sights and good beaches thrown in.

Lombok gets a lot of the Bali overflow, attracted by fine beaches, towering Gunung Rinjani, interesting crafts and a more relaxed approach to tourism.

Sumba has a wonderful mix of the most intact traditional culture in Nusa Tenggara and long white, but as yet undeveloped, beaches. Sumba is best known for its spectacular *ikat* weaving in the east and south-east.

Komodo is home to those fabulous dragons, and seeing a dragon in the wild is awesome. Rinca, Komodo's smaller neighbour, also has dragons and abundant wildlife.

Flores is a high volcanic island, and the most visited. In the mountains, Keli Mutu is home to spectacular coloured lakes. The Bajawa area has interesting traditional villages, while Labuhanbajo and its nearby beaches are the place to kick back for a few days.

The interior of west Timor still has some interesting traditional areas that are starting to open up or there are other oddities such as the whaling village of Lamalera on Lembata.

The islands of Nusa Tenggara can be stepping stones to or from Darwin in Australia's north, or can be approached from Bali. A good way to see Nusa Tenggara is to fly from Bali to Timor or Flores and then island hop back via the regular ferry services. You need at least a month to look around the whole chain. ∎

for off-the-beaten-track explorations, and the lack of tourists in these places will mean that your reception will be more natural. It does create one problem, though: you will constantly be the centre of attention – it's not unusual to attract an entourage of 50 children in a small village, all programmed to yell 'hello mister' until either they or you collapse from exhaustion. At the other extreme, in more isolated areas you will cause kids to scatter in all directions!

Nusa Tenggara is divided into three provinces: West Nusa Tenggara (comprising Lombok and Sumbawa), with its capital at Mataram in Lombok; East Nusa Tenggara (comprising Flores, Sumba, Timor and a number of small islands), with the capital at Kupang in Timor; and East Timor, with its capital at Dili.

Only about 2% of the Indonesian population live in Nusa Tenggara, but there are so many different languages and cultures that it's impossible to think of these people as one group. There are several languages on the tiny island of Alor alone, though you won't have any trouble getting by with Bahasa Indonesia anywhere in Nusa Tenggara.

Many of its people are now at least nominally Christian; Christians predominate on Flores, Roti and Timor. Muslims form a majority on Lombok and Sumbawa, while in isolated areas such as the western half of Sumba, a large section of the population still adhere to traditional animist beliefs. A layer of animism persists alongside Christianity in other areas, with customs, rituals and festivals from this older tradition still very much a part of life.

Even the wildlife of Nusa Tenggara is different from that of western Indonesia. A 300-metre-deep channel (one of the deepest in the archipelago) runs between Bali and Lombok, and extends north between Kalimantan and Sulawesi. The channel marks the 'Wallace Line', named after 19th-century naturalist Alfred Russel Wallace, who observed that from Lombok eastwards, the islands are characterised by more arid country, thorny plants, cockatoos, parrots, lizards and marsupials, while from Bali westwards, the vegetation is more tropical. It's actually not as clear cut as Wallace thought, but Nusa Tenggara is definitely a transition zone between Asian and Australian flora & fauna.

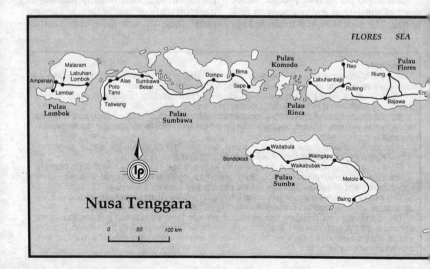

HISTORY

Despite Portuguese interest in the region in the late 16th century, and Dutch interest from the 17th century onwards, Nusa Tenggara was never in the mainstream of colonial activity in Indonesia. Because the area offered few economic temptations, the Dutch largely concentrated on Java, Sumatra and the Spice Islands of Maluku. In Nusa Tenggara they set up trading posts, but didn't find it necessary to exercise much authority. Local rulers and their conflicts, and traditional ways of life, including animist religions, were largely left to run their own course until around 1840, when the Dutch were spurred into action for a variety of reasons: to protect their ships from pirates; because of disputes (such as those with the Balinese) over the salvaging of shipwrecks; and to protect their possessions from other powers. As the Europeans scrambled for the last available morsels of territory in Asia and Africa in the last quarter of the 19th century, the Dutch grabbed anything that was left in the archipelago.

Piracy and disputes over shipwrecks motivated the first Dutch assault on Bali, in 1846. When the indigenous Sasaks of Lombok rebelled against their Balinese overlords in 1891 and appealed to the Dutch for help, the Dutch took the opportunity to send in a military expedition to finish off the Balinese and take control of Lombok themselves. Flores, further east, was another target. A desire to control the slave trade, and disputes over the rights to shipwrecks, led to two Dutch expeditions against the island, in 1838 and 1846, and a local rebellion in 1907 prompted a complete takeover. The Dutch waited until the early 1900s to subdue the tribespeople of the interior of the Nusa Tenggara islands, and the eastern half of Timor never fell into Dutch hands (it was a Portuguese colony until 1975, when Indonesia invaded and took it over).

After Indonesia achieved independence, in the 1940s, Nusa Tenggara remained a remote and lonely outpost, administered by a handful of Javanese officials and soldiers, who considered themselves virtual exiles. The difficulty of the mountainous terrain, poor communications and, in particular, the islands' location on the path to nowhere all helped to deter visitors and maintain this isolation, at least until the late 1980s, when regular air connections between Darwin and Timor began.

NUSA TENGGARA

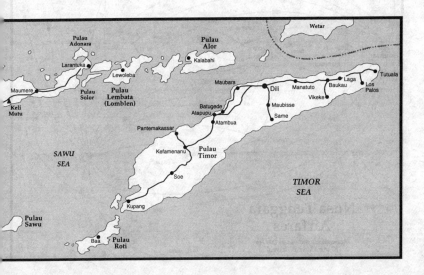

MONEY

As you travel eastwards, banks are few and far between, and the exchange rate often falls below that in Bali or Java. As well, some banks change only cash, and will refuse to change notes if they are damaged in the slightest way. 'Damaged' can mean worn, faded, torn or marked. Any cash you bring should be as new as possible. Without a doubt, the safest currency to bring is US dollars; travellers' cheques should be from the larger companies (such as American Express, Thomas Cook or Bank of America).

GETTING THERE & AROUND

The good news is that transport in Nusa Tenggara has improved immensely in the last decade. There are now more surfaced roads, more regular ferries and buses, and more flights. Previously, a lot of travel in Nusa Tenggara was just plain awful – you'd spend days in dreary ports waiting for boats, or hour upon hour shaking your bones loose

in trucks, attempting to travel on roads which resemble minefields. Some of it is still like that, but on the whole, if you stick to the main routes, you shouldn't have much trouble. Sections of the roads on Flores were swallowed by the earthquake of December 1992, but they've all been reopened, and in some areas upgraded. The only time problems are likely to occur is during the rainy season – roughly November to March, but it's shorter and less intense in the eastern and southern parts of the chain. Rainy season still takes its toll on Flores, though, and roads are sometimes cut by floods or landslides during this time.

Air

You can fly direct between Darwin (Australia) and Kupang (Timor) with Merpati, and Kupang is an international gateway (no visa is required for most Western nationalities). Merpati has a good network of flights in Nusa Tenggara. Many flights start or

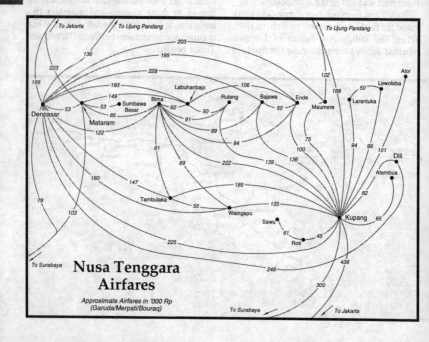

Nusa Tenggara Airfares

Approximate Airfares in '000 Rp
(Garuda/Merpati/Bouraq)

finish in Kupang or Bima (Sumbawa), with Ende and Maumere (on Flores), Dili (Timor), Waingapu (Sumba) and Mataram (Lombok) the other busiest airports. Some flights come straight through from Bali or Java, and from Kupang or Maumere you can fly to Ujung Pandang (Sulawesi) and Kalimantan without changing planes. Bouraq has a number of flights between Bali and Maumere, Waingapu and Kupang.

While it is possible to get a seat even on the morning of departure, it's wise to book, and reservations are essential in the peak August tourist season. The most popular routes are Mataram-Bima-Labuhanbajo and Maumere-Denpasar. If flights from Labuhanbajo or Maumere are full, try Ende or Ruteng. Overbooking sometimes occurs, so make sure your booking has been made when you buy your ticket, and always reconfirm. On the other hand, if you've been told a flight is full, it can sometimes be worth going to the airport before the flight leaves, if the airport is easy to get to. Merpati offices don't have computers, so no-show seats are not reoffered.

Boat

The Pelni passenger liner *Kelimutu* loops around from Surabaya and back every two weeks, stopping at Benoa (Bali), Bima (Sumbawa), Waingapu (Sumba), Ende (Flores), Dili (East Timor), Kupang (West Timor), Kalabahi (Alor), Maumere (Flores), Lembar (Lombok) and Banjarmasin (Kalimantan).

The Pelni ships *Tatamailau* and *Dobonsolo* also service ports in Nusa Tenggara.

Most of the islands are connected by ferries, which are regular, if rarely comfortable. There are several trips daily between Bali and Lombok and between Lombok and Sumbawa, three trips a week in each direction between Sumbawa and Flores (stopping at Komodo Island along the way), one ferry a day between Timor and Roti, three a week between Timor and Flores and two a week between Timor and Alor and between Timor and Sawu. The ferry boat *Ile Mandiri* connects Kupang with Ende (Flores), Waingapu

(Sumba) and Sawu once a week. Small boats chug every day from Flores to the islands of Adonara, Solor and Lembata. A small ferry links Lembata and Alor three times a week, and another links Alor and Timor twice a week. Details are provided in the relevant sections.

If you want to do something different, try finding one of Pelni's other, more basic ships, or a freighter working its way through the islands – you can often make quite an interesting trip on the same ship, since they usually sail at night and unload during the day, giving you at least a full day in each port. Ask around the harbour, at the office of the harbour master *(syahbandar)* or at the shipping offices. Once you find something, it's a matter of bargaining your fare with the captain and making friends with the cook!

For shorter hops, you can often charter sailing boats or small motorboats. A popular way of travelling between Flores and Lombok is on a five-day boat run out of Labuhanbajo, stopping at Komodo and other islands along the way. Some Bugis schooners find their way right down into Nusa Tenggara, for those who want a really different way of getting to Sulawesi.

Motorbike

If you like living dangerously, motorcycling is an interesting way to see Nusa Tenggara, and you can transport your bike on ferries between most of the islands. It's best to bring your own machine – it's possible to find short-term hires in a few large Nusa Tenggara towns, but it's difficult to convince anyone to let you take their bikes to other islands.

Bicycle

Bicycles are for rent around the main centres of Lombok, but they are not a popular form of transport anywhere in Nusa Tenggara. Long-distance cycling is a possibility on Sumba, where there's a lot of flat terrain, but cycling on hilly Flores or Timor requires legs of iron and a state-of-the-art mountain bike.

Lombok

Lombok has both the lushness of Bali and the starkness of outback Australia. Parts of the island drip with water, while pockets are chronically dry, and droughts can last for months, causing crop failure and famine. Recent improvements in agriculture and water management have made life on Lombok less precarious.

The indigenous Sasak people make up about 80% of the population. They follow the Islamic religion, but have a culture and language unique to Lombok. There is also significant evidence here of Balinese culture, language and religion – a legacy of the time when Bali controlled Lombok. Balinese-style processions and ceremonies are conducted, and there are a number of substantial Balinese temples.

History

Islam may have been brought to the island from Java, but there's no firm evidence that Java controlled the island. Not much is known about Lombok before the 17th century, at which time it was split into numerous, frequently squabbling petty states, each presided over by a Sasak 'prince' – a disunity which the neighbouring Balinese exploited.

Balinese Rule In the early 1600s, the Balinese from the eastern state of Karangasem established colonies and took control of western Lombok. At the same time, the roving Makassarese crossed the straits from their colonies in western Sumbawa and established settlements in eastern Lombok. The war of 1677-78 saw the Makassarese booted off the island, and eastern Lombok temporarily reverted to the rule of the Sasak princes. Balinese control soon extended east, and by 1740 or 1750 the whole island was in their hands. Squabbles over royal succession soon had the Balinese fighting amongst themselves, and Lombok split into four separate kingdoms. By 1838 the Mataram kingdom had subdued the other three and reconquered eastern Lombok (where Balinese rule had weakened during the years of disunity). Mataram forces then crossed the Lombok Straits to Bali and overran Karangasem, reuniting the 18th-century state of Karangasem-Lombok.

In western Lombok, where Balinese rule dated from the early 17th century, relations between the Balinese and the Sasaks were relatively harmonious. The Sasak peasants, who adhered to the mystical Wektu Telu religion, easily assimilated Balinese Hinduism. They participated in Balinese religious festivities and worshipped at the same shrines. Intermarriage between Balinese and Sasaks was common, and they were organised in the same irrigation associations (*subak*) that the Balinese used for wet-rice agriculture. The traditional Sasak village government had been done away with, and the peasants were ruled directly by the raja or by a landowning Balinese aristocrat.

Things were very different in eastern Lombok, where the recently defeated Sasak aristocracy hung in limbo. Here the Balinese maintained control from garrisoned forts. Although the traditional Sasak village government remained intact, the village chief became little more than a tax collector for the local Balinese *punggawa* (district head). The Balinese ruled like feudal kings, taking control of the land from the Sasak peasants, reducing them to the level of serfs. With their power and land holdings slashed, the Sasak aristocracy of eastern Lombok was hostile to the Balinese, and retained the loyalty of the peasants. This enabled the aristocracy to lead rebellions against the Balinese in 1855, 1871 and 1891.

Dutch Involvement The Balinese succeeded in suppressing the first two revolts. The uprising of 1891 was almost put down when the Sasak chiefs sent envoys to the Dutch resident in Buleleng, asking for help and inviting the Dutch to rule Lombok. The Dutch were initially reluctant to take military action, partly because they were still fighting a war in Sumatra and partly because of the

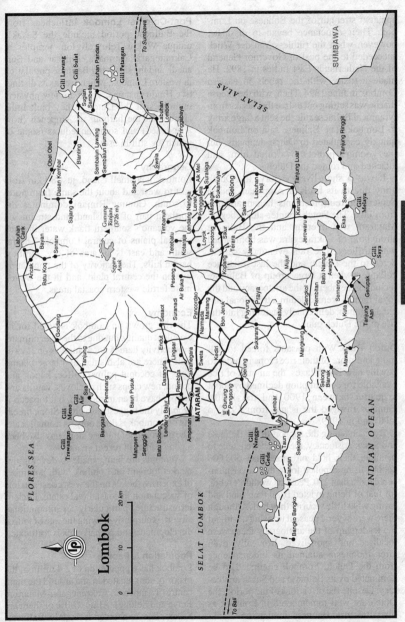

FLORES SEA

Lombok

0   10   20 km

Gili Trawangan
Gili Meno
Gili Air Sira
Bangsal
Pemenang
Mangset
Senggigi
Batu Bolong
Lendang Bajur
Ampenan
Baun Pusuk

MATARAM

Gunung Pengsong

Sekotong
Taun
Pelangan
Bangko Bangko
Gili Nanggu
Gili Gede

SELAT LOMBOK

To Bali

Gili Lawang
Gili Sulat
Gili Petangan
Labuhan Pandan
Sugian
Sembelia
Blanting
Obel Obel
Dasan Kembar
Sembalun Lawang
Sembalun Bumbung
Sapit
Labuhan Lombok
Pringgabaya
Sweta
Sajang
Senaru
Batu Koq
Bayan
Anyar
Labuhan Carik
Gunung Rinjani (3726 m)
Segara Anak
Timbanun
Tetebatu
Kotaraja
Lendang Nangka
Loyok
Pomotong
Masbagik
Pringgasela
Suralaga
Ak Mel
Lanek
Selong
Labuhan Haji
Sakra
Terara
Sikur
Kopang
Janapria
Mujur
Peseng
Air Buka
Suranadi
Endut
Sesaot
Lingsar
Dasangria
Cakranegara
Rembiga
Narmada
Mantang
Bon Jeruk
Kediri
Sweta
Pancordao
Gerung
Sukarara
Puyung
Praya
Batujai
Sengkol
Mangkung
Selong Blanak
Lembar
Mawan
Kuta
Tanjung Aan
Semeng
Gerupak
Awang
Batu Nampar
Rembitan
Keruak
Jerowaru
Ekas
Serewei
Tanjung Luar
Tanjung Ringgit
Gili Melaya
Gili Saya

SELAT ALAS

SUMBAWA

To Sumbawa

INDIAN OCEAN

apparent strength of the Balinese on Lombok. Their reluctance began to dissipate, however, when the ruthless Van der Wijck succeeded to the post of Governor-General of the Netherlands East Indies in 1892. He made a treaty with the rebels in eastern Lombok in June 1894. Then, with the excuse that he was setting out to free the Sasaks from tyrannical Balinese rule, he sent a large army to Lombok. The Balinese raja on Lombok quickly capitulated to Dutch demands, but the younger princes overruled him, and attacked and routed the Dutch.

It was a short-lived victory; the Dutch army dug in its heels at Ampenan, and in September reinforcements began arriving from Java. The Dutch counter-attack began: Mataram was overrun and the Balinese stronghold of Cakranegara was bombarded with artillery. The raja eventually surrendered to the Dutch, and the last resistance collapsed when a large group of Balinese, including members of the aristocracy and the royal family, were killed in a traditional suicidal puputan, deliberately marching into the fire of the Dutch guns.

Dutch Rule With peasants forced to sell more and more of their rice crops in order to pay the new Dutch taxes, the amount of rice available for consumption declined by about a quarter between 1900 and the 1930s. Famines ravaged the island from 1938 to 1940 and in 1949.

By maintaining the support of the Balinese and Sasak aristocracy, the Dutch were able to maintain their hold on more than 500,000 people, using a police force that never numbered more than 250. Peasants wouldn't rebel, for fear of being evicted from their land and losing what little security they had. Although there were several peasant uprisings, without the leadership of the aristocracy these were localised and short-lived. Ironically, even after Indonesia attained its independence from the Dutch, Lombok continued to be dominated by its Balinese and Sasak aristocracy. Despite the privations of the period, the Dutch are well remembered in Lombok as liberators from Balinese domination.

Post-Colonial Lombok Influences from the Balinese period include the Sasak's unique Wektu Telu religion, temples at Cakranegara, Narmada, Lingsar and Suranadi, and the surviving Balinese population in western Lombok, which retains its distinctive Hindu customs. There are few physical reminders of the Dutch – they built little, apart from the harbour at Ampenen (now abandoned) and some aqueducts (some of which are still in use).

Geography

Lombok is a small island, just 80 km from east to west and about the same from north to south. Gunung Rinjani dominates the northern part of the island, and streams on the volcano's southern flank water the rich alluvial plains of central Lombok. The far south and east is an area of dry, scrubby, barren hills. The majority of the population live on the central plain, and in the wetter, more fertile western coastal areas.

Economy

The rice grown on Lombok is noted for its excellent quality, but due to the drier climate, productivity here is not as high as on Java or Bali. There are also small and large plantations of coconut palms, coffee, kapok and cotton; new crops such as cloves, vanilla and pepper have been introduced, but tobacco is probably the biggest cash crop. Stock breeding on Lombok is done only on a small scale. The quarrying of pumice stone has also been a good earner in recent years.

Attempts are being made to develop upmarket tourism on Lombok, with a number of expensive hotels on the west coast and lots of speculation in coastal real estate. Lack of infrastructure, particularly an international airport, is currently slowing the rate of tourist development, and perhaps this is fortunate.

Population & People

Lombok has a population of 2.4 million, the majority congregated in and around the main centres (Ampenan, Cakranegara, Mataram, Praya and Selong). Almost 80% of them are Sasak. The remainder is mainly Balinese,

Clove

with minority populations of Chinese, Javanese and Arabs. Some Sumbawanese live in the east of the island, and Buginese along the coast. There may still be some isolated villages of the Bodha (or Boda), said to be the aboriginal people of Lombok.

Sasaks Physically and culturally, the Sasaks have much in common with the Javanese, the Balinese and the Sumbawanese; they're Malay people, agriculturalists and animists who practised ancestor and spirit worship. Basically hill people, the Sasaks are now spread over central and eastern Lombok, and are generally much poorer than the Balinese minority. Officially, most Sasaks are Muslims, but in practice they retain many of their ancient animist beliefs.

There are a number of more-or-less traditional Sasak villages scattered over the island; the most accessible are Sukaraja, Bayan and Senaru. Typical Sasak huts are square or rectangular, constructed on wooden frames, daubed with lime and covered with grass, with a high thatched roof. Some sit squat on the ground, but generally they rest on stilts. The village is usually surrounded and protected by a high paling fence and the houses are built in long, straight lines.

Chinese Most of the Chinese living in Lombok are based in Ampenan or Cakranegara. The Chinese first came to Lombok with the Dutch, as a cheap labour force, but were later fostered as economic intermediaries between the Dutch and the Indonesian population. The Chinese soon became a privileged minority and were allowed to set up and develop their own businesses. When the Dutch were ousted in 1949, the Chinese stayed, and continued to expand their business interests. Many of those in eastern Lombok, however, were killed in the aftermath of the attempted 1965 coup.

Culture
Lombok has a number of traditional dances and contests of physical prowess, but they are not well developed as tourist attractions.

Religious Festivals Most of the Wektu Telu religious festivals of Lombok take place at the beginning of the rainy season (from October to December) or at harvest time (April to May), with celebrations in villages all over the island. Many of these ceremonies and rituals are annual events but do not fall on specific days – getting to see one is a matter of luck and word of mouth. Lombok's Muslims celebrate the various events in the Islamic calendar (see the introductory Facts for the Visitor chapter), especially the end of Ramadan.

Dances The popular Cupak Gerantang tells the story of Panji, a romantic hero. The dance, which is usually performed at celebrations and festivals, probably originated in Java in the 15th century. The Kayak Sando, another version of a Panji story, in which the dancers wear masks, is found only in central and eastern Lombok.

The Gandrung is about love and courtship – *gandrung* means being in love, or longing. It's a social dance, usually performed by the young men and women of the village.

Everyone stands around in a circle and then, accompanied by a full gamelan orchestra, a young girl dances by herself for a time before choosing a male partner from the audience to join her. It's performed in Narmada, Suangi, Lenek and Praya.

The Oncer is a war dance performed vigorously by men and young boys in central and eastern Lombok. Participants play a variety of musical instruments in time to their movements, and wear severe black costumes with crimson and gold waistbands, shoulder sashes, socks and caps.

The Rudat, with a combination of Islamic and Sasak influences, is performed by pairs of men dressed in black caps and jackets and black-and-white checked sarongs. They're backed by singers, tambourines and cylindrical drums called *jidur*.

Music The Tandak Gerok is an eastern Lombok performance which combines dance, theatre and singing to music played on bamboo flutes and on the bowed lute called a *rebab*. The unique feature of the Tandak Gerok is that the vocalists imitate the sound of the gamelan instruments. It's usually performed after harvesting or other hard physical labour, but is also put on at traditional ceremonies.

The Genggong involves seven musicians using a simple set of instruments, including a bamboo flute, a rebab and knockers; they accompany their music with dance movements and stylised hand gestures.

The Barong Tengkok is the name given to the procession of musicians who play at weddings or circumcision ceremonies.

Contests The Sasaks show a fascination with physical prowess, heroic trials of strength and one-on-one contests.

The Peresehan is held all over Lombok, usually outside, in the late afternoon. A huge crowd (all men, apart from the occasional female traveller) gathers to watch two men fight with long rattan staves and small rectangular shields.

The Lanca, originally from Sumbawa, is another trial of strength, this time between two well-matched men who use their knees to strike each other. It is performed on numerous occasions, particularly when the first rice seedlings are planted.

Religion

Islam and Balinese Hinduism are the two main religions on Lombok – see the introductory Facts about the Country chapter and the Bali chapter for details. Wektu Telu is an indigenous religion, unique to Lombok and thought to have originated in the northern village of Bayan. The number of adherents is officially quite small (less than 30,000), though this may be understated, as Wektu Telu is not one of Indonesia's officially recognised religions. There are also small numbers of Christians and Buddhists.

Wektu Telu In the Sasak language, *wektu* means 'result' and *telu* means 'three'. The name probably denotes the complex mixture of Hindu, Islamic and animist influences that make up this religion, and the concept of a trinity is embodied in many Wektu Telu beliefs, eg the sun, moon and stars (representing heaven, earth and water) and the head, body and limbs (representing creativity, sensitivity and control). Wektu Telu stresses *adat* (traditional law and beliefs), while Wektu Lima is a more orthodox form of Islam – *lima* means 'five', referring to the five pillars of Islam (which are considered obligatory for the believer to follow).

The Wektu Telu observe only three days of fasting during Ramadan, they do not pray the five times a day laid down by Islamic law, they do not build mosques and they have no objection to eating pork. Their dead are buried with their heads facing Mecca, but Wektu Telu do not make pilgrimages there. In fact the only fundamental tenet of Islam to which the Wektu Telu seem to hold firmly is the belief in Allah and that Mohammed is his prophet. They regard themselves as Muslims, but are not accepted as such by orthodox Muslims, and relations between the two groups have not always been good. The number of Wektu Telu has been declining as more young people turn to orthodox Islam.

Books

There are few books devoted solely to Lombok. One is Alfons van der Kraan's *Lombok: Conquest, Colonization and Underdevelopment, 1870-1940* (Heinemann, 1980), which describes the economic destitution of the island during the Dutch administration.

Getting There & Away

There is no international airport on Lombok, but the island is quite accessible by air and sea from the neighbouring islands. The vast majority of travellers arrive from Bali, less than 100 km away, while those island-hopping from the east reach Lombok from Sumbawa.

Air Lombok is served by Garuda-Merpati and Sempati, both with offices in Mataram. Agents in Mataram and Senggigi can also sell tickets and reconfirm flights (it's important to reconfirm). Merpati has eight flights per day to/from Denpasar (47,500 rp; 25 minutes) and Sempati has two flights a day, at the same price. There are flights at least once daily with Merpati and/or Sempati to/from Sumbawa Besar (54,500 rp), Bima (90,500 rp), Surabaya (118,000 rp), Yogyakarta (135,500 rp), Semarang, Jakarta (228,000 rp) and Ujung Pandang (158,000 rp).

Boat There are numerous options for those who wish to travel to or from Lombok by boat.

Ferry To/From Bali Ferries run every two hours between Padangbai (Bali) and Lembar (Lombok). Scheduled departure times from both ports are 6, 8 and 10 am, noon, and 2, 4, 6, 8 and 10 pm, but actual times may be later or earlier. Economy costs around 4800 rp (2500 rp for children), 1st class 8700 rp (4700 rp for children). You can take a bicycle (800 rp), motorbike (5300 rp) or car (price depends on size – over 50,000 rp for a Suzuki

Jimny). The trip takes at least four hours, sometimes up to seven.

Fast Boats To/From Bali The *Mabua Express* is a luxury jet-powered catamaran which travels between Lembar and Benoa. It leaves Benoa at 8.30 am and 2.30 pm, and Lembar at 11.30 am and 5 pm, and takes about two hours (US$17.50 for 'Emerald Class' and US$25 for 'Diamond Class'). For details call their office in Bali (☎ (0361) 72370, 72521) or Lombok (☎ 25895, 37224).

A small, fast catamaran service was running between Padangbai (Bali), Bangsal (for the Gili Islands), Senggigi and Lembar (20,000 rp; two hours plus), but it wasn't very reliable. The service was suspended for a time but may resume. Inquire in Padangbai (☎ (0361) 234428), Senggigi (☎ 93045, ext 339) or Mataram (☎ 27295).

Tourist Shuttles To/From Bali Perama has services running between the main tourist centres on Bali and Lombok, with prices which include the ferry ticket and minibus connections at each end. Other companies have similar services at similar prices, but a less comprehensive network. Tourist shuttle services are more expensive than public transport, but quicker and more convenient. For example, a Perama ticket from Ubud through to Gili Meno (off Lombok) costs 27,500 rp. On public transport, you could probably do this trip for about 10,000 rp (if you weren't overcharged), but it would involve five bemo trips, a pony cart, the ferry and a boat. It would take longer, and if you missed a connection, you might have to spend a night somewhere in between.

Ferry To/From Sumbawa Passenger ferries leave Labuhan Lombok (in eastern Lombok) for Poto Tano (Sumbawa) just about every hour from 7 am to 6 pm, but the exact times vary. In the other direction, ferries are scheduled to depart at half past the hour. The trip takes about 1½ hours and costs 3100/2000 rp in ekonomi A/ekonomi B (1600/1300 rp for a child), 2500 rp for a bicycle, 3200 rp for a motorbike and 32,000 rp for a small car.

Direct buses run from Sweta terminal (on Lombok) to destinations on Sumbawa, including Sumbawa Besar (five buses per day, 9000 rp, 10,000 rp with air-con), Dompu (at 6 am and 4 pm, 15000 rp, 21,000 rp with air-con) and Bimà (8 am and 2 pm, 18,000 rp, 22,000 rp with air-con). Fares include the ferry.

To/From Other Islands The Pelni ship *Kelimutu* typically calls at Lembar once a fortnight, usually on a Wednesday or a Thursday. The usual stops before and after Lembar are Bima (Sumbawa) and Surabaya (Java). For exact dates and routes, inquire at the Pelni office (☎ 21604) at Jalan Industri 1 in Ampenan.

Getting Around

There is a good main road across the middle of the island, between Mataram and Labuhan Lombok, and quite good roads to the south of this route. You can get around the whole island and to many of the more remote locations if you have your own transport. Public buses and bemos are generally restricted to main routes; away from these, you have to hire a pony cart *(cidomo)*, get a lift on a motorbike or walk. In remote regions, food, drinking water and petrol are often scarce, and there are few lodgings.

During the wet season, many roads are flooded or washed away, and others are impassable because of fallen rocks and rubble, making it impossible to get to many out-of-the-way places. The damage may not be repaired until well into the dry season.

Most public transport stops at 10.30 or 11 pm, often earlier in more isolated areas.

Bemo & Bus There are several bus and bemo terminals on Lombok. The main one is at Sweta, at the eastern end of the main urban area. Other terminals are at Praya and Kopang, and you may have to go via one or more of these transport hubs to get from one part of Lombok to another. For main routes, fares are fixed by the provincial government, and a list is displayed at the terminals. The bus and bemo drivers may still try to over-

charge, so check the fare list before setting off, and watch what the locals are paying. You may have to pay more if you have a big bag.

With a few people together, chartering a bemo by the day can be convenient and quite cheap – perhaps 45,000 to 60,000 rp, depending on distance. Many vehicles are licensed to operate only in certain areas.

Car & Motorbike Hotels in Ampenan, Mataram or Senggigi can often arrange car or motorbike hire, as can some of the tourist-type shops. There are some 'official' car rental companies in Mataram which have a wider range of vehicles, but these tend to be more expensive. (See the Ampenan, Mataram, Cakranegara & Sweta section.) It costs about 35,000 to 50,000 rp per day for a small vehicle such as a Suzuki Jimny, depending on the insurance cover, where you get the vehicle and how you bargain; if you rent for a few days or a week, you should get a discount. Large Toyota 4WD vehicles are actually cheaper (around 35,000 rp), though you will pay more for petrol. Between four people, it can be a cheap way to get around.

You can rent motorbikes in the main town, and at Senggigi, from around 10,000 rp per day. Elsewhere, you might find one if you ask around. There are petrol stations around the larger towns, while in rural areas you can only get fuel from small wayside shops – look out for signs that read *premium*, or *press ban* (literally 'tyre repair'). It may be wise to take some with you, if you can carry it safely.

Bicycle Although bicycles are available for hire in the main centres of Lombok, they are not generally a popular form of transport around the island – among the locals or with travellers. If you want to explore Lombok by bicycle, you'll probably have to bring your own or be prepared to do a lot of maintenance work on one of the rusty specimens you will find there.

Tours Costs start at US$10 for a half-day tour and US$15 for a full day. Specialised tours, such as a 'nature tour' or a 'handcraft tour', can give a quick introduction to a specific aspect of the island. Many hotels have an arrangement with a tour operator, or you can ask at the tourist office for suggestions.

AMPENAN, MATARAM, CAKRANEGARA & SWETA

Although officially four separate towns, Ampenan, Mataram, Cakranegara and Sweta actually merge, so it's virtually impossible to tell where one stops and the next starts. Collectively, they're the main 'city' on Lombok, with banks, travel agencies, some interesting shops and markets, and a few things to see, but it's not a major attraction.

Ampenan

Once the main port of Lombok, Ampenan is now not much more than a small fishing harbour. It's a bit run-down and dirty, but has character. The main road does not actually reach the coast at Ampenan, but simply fades out just before it gets to the port's grubby beach. Apart from Sasaks and Balinese, Ampenan's population includes some Chinese, and a small Arab quarter known as Kampung Arab. The Arabs living here are devout Muslims, usually well educated and friendly towards foreigners.

Mataram

Mataram is the administrative capital of the province of Nusa Tenggara Barat (West Nusa Tenggara). Some of the public buildings, such as the Bank of Indonesia, the new post office and the governor's office and residence, are substantial. The large houses around the outskirts of town are the homes of Lombok's elite.

Cakranegara

Now the main commercial centre of Lombok, bustling Cakranegara is usually referred to as Cakra. Formerly the capital of Lombok under the Balinese rajas, Cakra today has a thriving Chinese community, as well as many Balinese residents. Most of the shops and restaurants in Cakranegara are run or owned by Chinese, and there are many friendly, Balinese-run losmen.

Sweta

Seven km east of Ampenan and only about 2½ km beyond Cakra is Sweta, the central transport terminal of Lombok. This is where you catch bemos and buses to other parts of the island and on to Sumbawa. Stretching along the eastern side of the terminal is a vast, covered market, the largest on Lombok. If you wander through its dim alleys, you'll see stalls spilling over with coffee beans, eggs, rice, fish, fabrics, crafts, fruit and hardware. There's also a bird market.

Orientation

The 'city' is effectively divided into four functional areas: Ampenan (the port), Mataram (the administrative centre), Cakranegara (the trading centre) and Sweta (the transport centre). The towns are spread along one main road, a one-way street running west to east, which starts as Jalan Pabean in Ampenan, quickly becomes Jalan Yos Sudarso, changes to Jalan Langko and then to Jalan Pejanggik, and finishes up in Sweta as Jalan Selaparang, though it's difficult to tell where the road changes names. Indeed, it seems that they overlap, since some places appear to have more than one address.

A second one-way street, Jalan Sriwijaya/Jalan Majapahit, brings traffic back in the other direction. Bemos shuttle between the bemo stop in Ampenan and the big terminal in Sweta, about seven km away, so getting back and forth is dead easy. You can stay in Ampenan, Mataram or Cakra, since there are hotels and restaurants in all three places.

Mataram has a small commercial 'centre' (near the river) and a larger shopping area (past the Jalan Selaparang/Jalan Hasanuddin intersection). You'll find the Cakra market just east of here, south of the main road. The Mataram government buildings are chiefly found along Jalan Pejanggik. The main square, Lampangan Mataram, is on the south side of Jalan Pejanggik. Art exhibitions, theatre, dance and wayang kulit performances are held in the square, but you'll only find out about these shows by word of mouth. Alternatively, look for the swarms of

NUSA TENGGARA

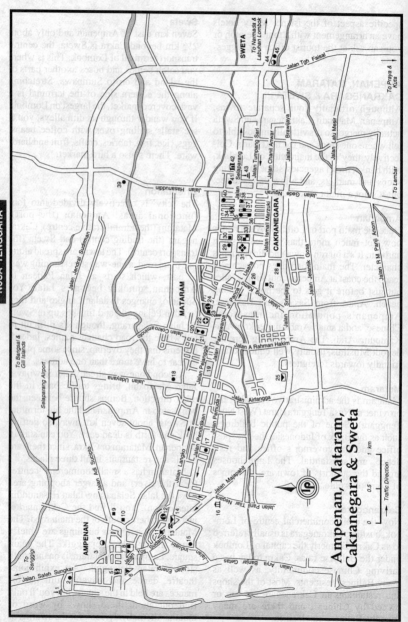

Ampenan, Mataram,
Cakranegara & Sweta

PLACES TO STAY			7	Kiki Restaurant		19	Main Square
			20	Garden House			(Lampangan
8	Hotel Zahir			Restaurant			Mataram)
9	Losmen Wisma Triguna		38	Sekawan Depot Es		21	Governor's Office
10	Losmen Horas					22	Hospital
11	Nitour Hotel &		**OTHER**			24	Perama Office
	Restaurant					25	GPO (Poste Restante)
23	Hotel Kertajoga		1	Pura Segara Temple		29	Rinjani Hand Woven
26	Hotel Granada		2	Sudirman Antiques		31	Cilinaya Shopping
27	Graha Ayu		3	Ampenan Market			Centre
28	Puri Indah Hotel		4	Ampenan Bemo		34	Bank Ekspor-Impor
30	Selaparang Hotel			Terminal		35	Merpati Office
32	Hotel & Restaurant		5	Moneychangers		39	Lombok Handicraft
	Shanti Puri		12	Tourist Office			Centre
33	Oka Homestay		13	Telephone Office		40	Motorbike Rental
36	Losmen Ayu		14	Post Office		41	Selamat Riady
37	Adiguna Homestay		15	Pelni Office		42	Mayura Water Palace
			16	Museum		43	Pura Meru Temple
PLACES TO EAT			17	Mataram University		44	Sweta Bus/Bemo
			18	Immigration Office			Terminal
6	Pabean & Cirebon					45	Sweta Market
	Restaurants						

police and military personnel that are the most obvious sign of such an occasion.

Information

Tourist Offices The main Lombok government tourist office, the Kantor Dinas Pariwisata Daerah, or DIPARDA (☎ 21866, 31730), is at the Ampenan end of Mataram, at Jalan Langko 70, on the north side, almost diagonally opposite the telephone office. The people at the tourist office are friendly, helpful and well informed. They keep standard government office hours – 7 am to 2 pm most days, closing at 11 am on Friday and at 12.30 pm on Saturday.

The Perama office (☎ 22764; fax 23368) is at Jalan Pejanggik 66. The very helpful staff provide good information, organise shuttle-bus connections, change money (unless they're out of cash), arrange day tours around Lombok and try to sell Land-Sea Adventure tours to Komodo and Flores.

Money A number of banks along the main drag will change travellers' cheques, although it can take some time. The Bank Ekspor-Impor seems to have longer opening hours than other banks: weekdays from 7.30 am to noon and 1 to 2 pm. There are also moneychangers in Ampenan, and in Mata-

ram's Cilinaya shopping centre (on the south side of Jalan Pejanggik). They're efficient, and open for longer hours. You can also change travellers' cheques at the airport and at the Perama office.

Post & Telecommunications Mataram's main post office, on Jalan Sriwijaya, has the only poste restante service. It's open from 8 am to 2 pm Monday to Saturday (until 11 am on Friday).

The Telkom telephone office, at the Ampenan end of Mataram on Jalan Langko, has telegram and fax services; it's open 24 hours every day. The international telephone service from here is very efficient, and you can usually get an overseas call through in minutes. There's another wartel in Cilinaya Centre in Cakra.

Immigration Lombok's kantor imigrasi (immigration office) is on Jalan Udayana, the road out to the airport.

Bookshops There are a number of bookshops along the main road through the towns. Toko Buku Titian (in Ampenan) has some English-language magazines and maps. The bookshop in Cilinaya, the Mataram shopping centre on the south side of Jalan

Pejanggik, also has some English titles. The daily *Jakarta Post* usually arrives at 2 pm the day after publication.

Weaving Factories

There are a few weaving factories in Mataram, where you can see the dyeing and weaving processes – the hand-and-foot-powered looms are amazing contraptions. You can buy ikat cloth and handwoven sarongs – in fixed-price shops they charge around 15,000 rp per metre (1200 mm width) for ikat woven in mercerised cotton. One place to look is Selamat Riady, off Jalan Hasanuddin. A bemo will drop you within a few metres of the factory (open from 7.30 am), and you're welcome to wander around. Rinjani Hand Woven, at Jalan Pejanggik 44-46, beside the Selaparang Hotel, also has an interesting collection of woven materials. Another place to try is Sari Kusuma, Jalan Selaparang 45, Cakranegara; open from 8 am to 4 pm.

Ikat motif

Pura Segara

This Balinese sea temple is on the beach a few km north of Ampenan. Nearby are the remnants of a Muslim cemetery and an old Chinese cemetery – worth a wander through if you're visiting the temple.

Museum Negeri

The Museum Negeri Nusa Tenggara Barat is on Jalan Panji Tilar Negara in Ampenan. With exhibits on the geology, history and culture of Lombok and Sumbawa, it's well worth browsing around if you have a couple of free hours. If you intend buying any antiques or handcrafts, have a look at the krises, songket, basketware and masks to give you a starting point for comparison. The museum is open from 8 am to 2 pm Tuesday to Sunday. Admission is 200 rp (100 rp for children).

Mayura Water Palace

On the main road through Cakra, this 'palace' was built in 1744 and was once part of the royal court of the Balinese kingdom in Lombok. The centrepiece is a large artificial lake with an open-sided pavilion in the middle, connected to the shoreline by a raised footpath. This *bale kambang* (floating pavilion) was used both as a court of justice and as a meeting place for the Hindu lords. There are other shrines and fountains dotted around the surrounding park. The entrance to the walled enclosure of the palace is on the western side (entry 500 rp). Today the palace grounds are used as a place to unleash fighting cocks and make offerings to the gods. It's a pleasant retreat from Cakra, although less than a century ago it was the site of bloody battles with the Dutch.

Pura Meru

Directly opposite the water palace on the main road is the Pura Meru, the largest temple on Lombok. It's open every day, and a donation is expected (about 500 rp is fine). It was built in 1720 under the patronage of the Balinese prince Anak Agung Made Karang of the Singosari kingdom, as an attempt to unite all the small kingdoms on Lombok. Intended as a symbol of the universe, the temple is dedicated to the Hindu trinity of Brahma, Vishnu and Shiva, though it's nothing great to look at.

The outer courtyard has a hall housing the wooden drums that are beaten to call believers to festivals and special ceremonies. In the middle courtyard are two buildings with large raised platforms for offerings. The inner court has one large and 33 small

Mayura Water Palace

In 1894 the Dutch sent an army to back the Sasaks of East-Lombok in a rebellion against the Balinese rajah. The rajah quickly capitulated but the crown prince decided to fight on while the Dutch-backed forces were split between various camps.

The Dutch camp at the Mayura Water Palace was attacked late at night by a combined force of Balinese and western Sasaks. The camp was surrounded by high walls, and the Balinese and Sasaks took cover behind them as they fired on the exposed army, forcing the Dutch to take shelter in a nearby temple compound. The Balinese also attacked the Dutch camp at Mataram, and soon after the entire Dutch army on Lombok was routed and withdrew to Ampenan where, according to one eyewitness, the soldiers 'were so nervous that they fired madly if so much as a leaf fell off a tree'. The first battles resulted in enormous losses of men and arms for the Dutch.

Although the Balinese had won the battle they had just begun to lose the war. They then had to fight the Dutch as well as the eastern Sasaks, and the Dutch were soon supplied with reinforcements from Java. The Dutch attacked Mataram a month after their initial defeat, fighting street to street not only against Balinese and west Sasak soldiers but also the local population. The Balinese crown prince was killed in the battle for the palace and the Balinese retreated to Cakranegara, where they were well armed and where the complex of walls provided good defence against infantry. Cakra was attacked by a combined force of Dutch and eastern Sasaks and, as happened in Mataram, Balinese men, women and children staged repeated suicidal lance attacks, to be cut down by rifle and artillery fire. The rajah and a small group of punggawas (commanders) fled to the village of Sasari near Lingsar. A day or two later the rajah surrendered to the Dutch, but even his capture did not lead the Balinese to surrender.

In late November the Dutch attacked Sasari and a large number of Balinese chose the suicidal puputan. With the downfall of the dynasty the local Balinese population abandoned its struggle against the Dutch. The conquest of Lombok had taken the Dutch barely three months. The old rajah died in exile in Batavia in 1895. ■

shrines, as well as three *meru* (multiroofed shrines). The three meru are in a line: the central one, with 11 tiers, is Shiva's house; the one in the north, with nine tiers, is Vishnu's; and the seven-tiered one, in the south, is Brahma's. The meru are also said to represent the three great mountains Rinjani, Agung and Bromo. A festival is held here each June.

Places to Stay – bottom end

The most popular cheap places to stay are in Ampenan and Cakranegara. Jalan Koperasi branches off Jalan Yos Sudarso in the centre of Ampenan. Only a short stroll from the centre is the *Hotel Zahir* (☎ 22403) at Jalan Koperasi 12. It's a basic, straightforward place with singles/doubles for 6000/7500 rp (8000/10,000 rp with bathroom). Prices include breakfast, and tea or coffee throughout the day. This is a popular, convenient and friendly losmen, with rooms facing a central courtyard. The owners can arrange motorbike rental (about 10,000 rp per day).

Continue along the road to *Losmen Horas*

(☎ 21695) at Jalan Koperasi 65. It's pretty basic, but has singles/doubles with Indonesian-style bathrooms for only 5000/7500 rp. Continuing further east you come to *Losmen Wisma Triguna* (☎ 31705), which is operated by the same people as the Horas. It's a little over a km from central Ampenan, and a quiet, relaxed place. Spacious rooms opening on to a bright verandah or the garden start at 10,000 rp, including breakfast. The people at Horas and Wisma Triguna have good information on climbing Gunung Rinjani. The nearby *Losmen Angi Mammire* is cheaper. It's not as roomy, but quite OK.

Back in the centre of Ampenan is *Losmen Pabean* (☎ 21758) at Jalan Pabean 146 (also known as Jalan Yos Sudarso). It's basic, but a bit better inside than it looks from the outside. You'll pay 4500/7000 rp for singles/doubles with shared mandi.

In Mataram, the pleasant *Hotel Kambodja* (☎ 22211) on the corner of Jalan Supratman and Jalan Arif Rahmat has rooms for about 8500 rp.

In Cakranegara, south of the main drag

and just north of Jalan Panca Usaha, are a number of Balinese-style losmen which are quite good places to stay. The *Oka Homestay* on Jalan Repatmaja has a quiet garden. Singles/doubles cost 8000/10,000 rp, including breakfast. The *Astiti Guest House* (☎ 27988) on Jalan Subak has rooms from 6000/8000 rp with shared bathroom, 8000/10,000 rp with private bath and 35,000 rp with air-con, including breakfast, and tea any time. It's popular with surfers, and staff can help with transport information, rental cars etc. The *Adiguna Homestay*, Jalan Nursiwan, is another good budget place, with rooms from 8000/11,000 rp. The very friendly *Losmen Ayu* (☎ 21761) on the same street has cheap rooms (about 10,000 rp a double). The bemos from Lembar come close to this area; get off on Jalan Gede Ngurah and walk west on Jalan Panca Usaha.

In the same area, at Jalan Maktal 15, the *Hotel & Restaurant Shanti Puri* (☎ 32649) is almost mid-range quality, but has cheap singles/doubles for 5000/7000 rp. Very comfortable rooms cost up to 12,000/15,000 rp. It's run by friendly, helpful people, who can also arrange motorbike and car hire.

Places to Stay – middle
There are quite a few good value, mid-range places in the Mataram-Cakra area. The *Selaparang Hotel* (☎ 32670) at Jalan Pejanggik 40-42 in Mataram, has air-con singles/doubles at 42,500/47,500 rp and fan-cooled rooms for about half the price. Across the road at No 105 is the *Mataram Hotel* (☎ 23411). Double rooms are 25,000 rp, and rooms with air-con, TV, hot water and other mod cons cost up to 50,000 rp. Both these mid-range hotels have pleasant little restaurants. At Jalan Pejanggik 64, just west of the Perama office, is the *Hotel Kertajoga* (☎ 21775). It's good value, with fan-cooled rooms at 15,000/18,500 rp (20,500/25,500 rp with air-con).

The *Hotel Pusaka* (☎ 33119) at Jalan Hasanuddin 23, is mainly for Indonesian travellers, but has a variety of quite good rooms priced from 12,500/15,000 rp (up to 45,000/60,000 rp with air-con), including

tax and breakfast. The cheap rooms are pretty basic, but OK, and the mid-range rooms are quite good. The Pusaka is close to the mosque.

Places to Stay – top end
At Jalan Yos Sudarso 4 in Ampenan, the *Nitour Hotel & Restaurant* (☎ 23780; fax 36579) is quiet and comfortable, with carpets, air-con, telephone etc. 'Superior' rooms are US$30, 'deluxe' rooms US$35. This place used to be called the Wisma Melati.

The heavily advertised *Hotel Granada* (☎ 22275) is on Jalan Bung Karno, south of the shopping centre in Mataram. There's a swimming pool, and all rooms are air-conditioned. It has vaguely Iberian architecture and a caged menagerie. The prices include breakfast, and start at 59,000 rp a double, plus 10% tax; ask for a low-season discount whenever you get there. If you want this kind of comfort, the *Puri Indah* (☎ 37633) on Jalan Sriwijaya also has a restaurant and a pool, but is much better value at 15,000/20,000 rp (25,000/30,000 rp with air-con). The nearby *Graha Ayu* has rooms from 50,000 rp, with all mod cons, but doesn't look appealing.

Places to Eat
Ampenan has several Indonesian and Chinese restaurants, including the very popular *Cirebon* at Jalan Pabean 113, with a standard Indonesian/Chinese menu and most dishes from around 2000 rp. Next door at No 111 is the *Pabean*, with similar food. *Poppy*, in the same area, is also recommended. On the other side of the intersection, upstairs from the art shop, *Kiki Restaurant* has a pleasant atmosphere and very good food for reasonable prices. The tables on the balcony overlooking the town centre are fun. *Rumah Makan Arafat*, Jalan Saleh Sungkar 23, has good, cheap Indonesian food. Other alternatives are the *Setia* at Jalan Pabean 129 and the *Depot Mina* at Jalan Yos Sudarso 102. *Timur Tengah* at Jalan Koperasi 22, right across from the Hotel Zahir, is also popular (it's closed on Sunday and during Ramadan).

There are a couple of interesting restaurants at the Mataram shopping centre off Jalan Pejanggik, a few hundred metres up the road from the governor's residence on the same side. The *Garden House Restaurant* is a pleasant open-air place with inexpensive nasi campur, nasi goreng and other standard meals. *Denny Bersaudra*, a bit further east, is well known for Sasak-style food. The nearby *Taliwang* also offers local dishes. *Flamboyan Restaurant*, on the south side of Pejanggik, is a good place for Indonesian dishes and seafood. *Flamboyan Restaurant II*, on the road to Senggigi, also has good food.

In Cakra, the *Sekawan Depot Es* has cold drinks downstairs and a seafood and Chinese restaurant upstairs. Around the corner, on Jalan Hasanuddin, the *Rumah Makan Madya* serves very good, cheap food in authentic Sasak style. There are a number of other restaurants in this area, a handful of bakeries and, of course, plenty of places to buy food at the market.

Things to Buy

Surdiman Antiques, on Jalan Saleh Sungkar (the road north to Senggigi), is one of the biggest and best known antique and handcraft shops. There are a few others nearby, so this is a good area to look around. Rora Antiques, in Ampenan at Jalan Yos Sudarso 16A, sells some excellent woodcarvings, baskets and traditional Lombok weavings (songket and so on). Renza Antiques, Jalan Yos Sudarso 92, is also a good place to browse. Musdah, at Dayan Penen, Jalan Sape 16, has an interesting collection of masks, baskets, krises and carvings for sale.

The Lombok Handicraft Centre is at Sayang Sayang, north of Cakra. It has a number of shops with a good selection of crafts from Lombok and elsewhere. An excellent place to look for local products is the Sweta market, next to the Sweta bemo station. For sarongs and fabrics, see the weaving factories mentioned earlier.

Getting There & Away

Air There's a Garuda/Merpati office (☎ 23762)

which can book and reconfirm flights at Jalan Yos Sudarso 6 in Ampenan. It's open from 8 am to 5 pm Monday to Saturday. The main Merpati office (☎ 32226, 36745) is on Jalan Selaparang in Cakra. A third office (☎ 22670, 23235) is at the Selaparang Hotel, Jalan Pejanggik 40-42 in Mataram. The Sempati office (☎ 21226, 24844/5) is in the Cilinaya shopping centre in Mataram.

Bus Sweta has the main bus terminal for the entire island. It's also the eastern terminus for the local bemos to/from Ampenan. There's an office in the middle of the place, with a noticeboard on which you can check the fare before you're hustled on board one of the vehicles. Some distances and approximate fares from Sweta to other parts of Lombok include:

Destination	Fare
East (Jurusan Timor)	
Narmada (six km)	200 rp
Mantang (17 km)	600 rp
Kopang (25 km)	700 rp
Terara (29 km)	800 rp
Sikur (33 km)	900 rp
Pomotong (34 km)	950 rp
Masbagik (36 km)	1000 rp
Selong (47 km)	1400 rp
Labuhan Haji (57 km)	1800 rp
Labuhan Lombok (69 km)	2000 rp
South & Central	
(Jurusan Selatan & Tenggara)	
Kediri (five km)	500 rp
Lembar (22 km)	700 rp
Praya (27 km)	700 rp
Mujur (36 km)	1100 rp
Kuta (56 km)	1500 rp
North (Jurusan Utara)	
Senggigi (12 km)	500 rp
Pemenang (31 km)	700 rp
Tanjung (45 km)	900 rp
Bayan (79 km)	1800 rp

Boat The ferry docks at Lembar, 22 km south of Ampenan (see the Lembar Getting There & Away section for details). The Bali ferry office is at Jalan Pejanggik 49 in Mataram. The *Mabua Express* office (☎ 25895, 37224) is in Lembar. The office of the national shipping line, Pelni (☎ 21604), is at Jalan Industri 1 in Ampenan.

Getting Around

To/From the Airport Lombok's Selaparang Airport is only a couple of km from Ampenan. Taxis from there cost about 5000 rp to Ampenan, Mataram or Cakra, 6000 rp to Sweta, 8000 rp to Senggigi and 15,000 rp to Bangsal. Alternatively, you can walk out of the airport car park to the main road, and take one of the frequent No 7 bemos which run straight to the Ampenan bemo stop (250 rp).

Bemo & Cidomo Ampenan-Mataram-Cakra-Sweta is very spread out, so don't plan to walk from place to place. Bemos shuttle back and forth along the main route between the Ampenan terminal at one end and the Sweta terminal at the other. The fare is a standard 250 rp, regardless of the distance. There are plenty of cidomos for shorter trips around town, although they are not permitted on the main streets. The bemo terminal in Ampenan is a good place to charter a bemo.

Car & Motorbike Hotels in town can often arrange car rental. Metro Photo (☎ 32146), Jalan Yos Sudarso 79 in Ampenan, can arrange pretty cheap rental cars.

There are some 'official' car rental companies, but these tend to be more expensive. Rinjani Rent Car (☎ 21400), opposite the Hotel Granada on Jalan Bung Karno in Mataram, has Suzuki Jimnys for 50,000 rp per day (without insurance). Yoga Rent Car (☎ 21127), in the Cilinaya shopping centre in Mataram, has similar cars for 45,000 rp per day.

Your hotel might be able to get you a rental motorbike. If not, go to Jalan Gelantik, off Jalan Selaparang near the junction with Jalan Hasanuddin, at the Cakranegara end of Mataram. The motorbike owners who hang around there have bikes to rent for 10,000 to 12,500 rp a day. As usual, the more you pay the better you get, and it's wise to check a bike over carefully before saying yes.

Bicycle You can rent good bicycles from the Cirebon Restaurant for about 5000 rp per day.

GUNUNG PENGSONG

This Balinese temple is built, as the name suggests, on top of a hill. It's nine km south of Mataram and has great views of rice fields, the volcanoes and the sea. Try to get there early in the morning, before the clouds envelop Gunung Rinjani. Once a year, generally in March or April, a buffalo is taken up the steep, 100-metre slope and sacrificed to celebrate a good harvest. The Bersih Desa festival also occurs here at harvest time – houses and gardens are cleaned, fences whitewashed, roads and paths repaired. Once part of a ritual to rid the village of evil spirits, it is now held in honour of the rice goddess, Dewi Sri. There's no set admission charge, but you will have to pay the caretaker 200 rp or so, especially if you use the car park.

LEMBAR

Lembar, 22 km south of Ampenan, is the main port on Lombok. The ferries to and from Bali dock here, as does the *Mabua Express*. There's a canteen at the harbour, where you can buy snacks and drinks while waiting to catch the ferry. The only place to stay, the *Serumbung Indah* (☎ 37153), has a restaurant, and rooms from around 15,000 rp. It's not very convenient, though, being about two km north of the harbour on the main road.

Getting There & Away

You can buy your tickets to Bali at the wharf on the day of departure, or from the offices in Mataram. Ferries leave every two hours from 6 am. The *Mabua Express* leaves at 11.30 am and 5 pm.

In theory you should be able to get a bemo from Lembar to Sweta for about 700 rp; in practice they will try to get you on a special charter bemo, or otherwise manage to charge you more – maybe 1000 rp. If you come on the *Mabua Express* and want a public bemo to town, you have to leave the dock area and walk 200 metres to the left, then turn right to find the bemos waiting at the roadside. There are set fares for 'taxis'; the price per person depends on the number of passengers. To Mataram, it's 7000 rp each with two people, or 12,000 rp by yourself. Minibuses from the hotels in town sometimes meet the ferry.

Regular buses and bemos to Lembar from Sweta cost 700 rp.

SOUTH-WESTERN PENINSULA

If you approach Lembar by ferry, you'll see a hilly and little-developed peninsula on your right. A road from Lembar runs on to this peninsula in Lombok's south-west, but it's pretty rough after Sekotong. Bangko Bangko is at the end of the track, and from there it's two or three km to Desert Point, which has great surf but no places to stay or eat. There are a number of picturesque islands off the north coast of the peninsula, and one of them, Gili Nanggu, has some tourist bungalows. *Istana Cempaka* charges US$11 per person, including all meals. Enquiries and bookings can be made by phoning a Cakra number (☎ 22898).

SENGGIGI

On a series of sweeping bays between three and 12 km north of Ampenan, Senggigi has become the most developed tourist area on Lombok. All the tourist facilities are here, plus a range of top-end and mid-range accommodation, and some budget places too. One day Senggigi might be a pleasant, mid-range beach resort in the Sanur mould, but at its present stage of development it's more like a construction site, with lots of new buildings not yet been softened by landscaping, and without the unspoiled beauty of a few years ago. The nicest places are the isolated groups of bungalows north of the central area.

Senggigi has fine beaches, although they slope very steeply into the water. There's some snorkelling off the point and in the sheltered bay around the headland. The beautiful sunsets over Lombok Strait can be enjoyed from the beach or from one of the beach-front restaurants. As it gets dark, the fishing fleet lines up offshore, each boat with its bright lanterns. Senggigi has the only nightlife on Lombok, and it can be good fun.

Orientation

The area known as Senggigi is spread out along nearly 10 km of coastal road. Most of the shops, travel agencies and other facilities, and a fair concentration of the accommodation, are on the stretch of road near the Senggigi Beach Hotel, about six km north of Ampenan.

Information

Kotasi is the tourist office of the local cooperative, and is good for transport information. Nearby is a private telephone office and a postal agency. You can change money or travellers' cheques at the Graha Beach Hotel, in the middle of the Senggigi strip, and also at most of the big hotels, if they have the cash.

The staff at the Graha Beach can make bookings and reconfirm flights for Garuda and Merpati, as can a number of travel agencies, such as Nazareth Tours (☎ 93033). The Perama office (☎ 93007/8/9), further north, runs tours and tourist transport and will also provide information and change money. There are some tourist shuttle-bus agencies, including Lombok Independent. The town also has a supermarket, a Telkom telephone office and some photo-processing places.

Batu Bolong Temple

This temple is on a rocky point which juts into the sea about a km south of Senggigi Beach, five km north of Ampenan. The rock on which it sits has a natural hole, giving the temple its name (which literally means 'rock with hole'). Being a Balinese temple, it's oriented towards Gunung Agung, Bali's holiest mountain, across the Lombok Strait. There's a fantastic view, and it's a good place to watch the sunsets. Legend has it that beautiful virgins were once thrown into the sea from the top of the rock. Locals like to claim that this is why there are so many sharks in the water here.

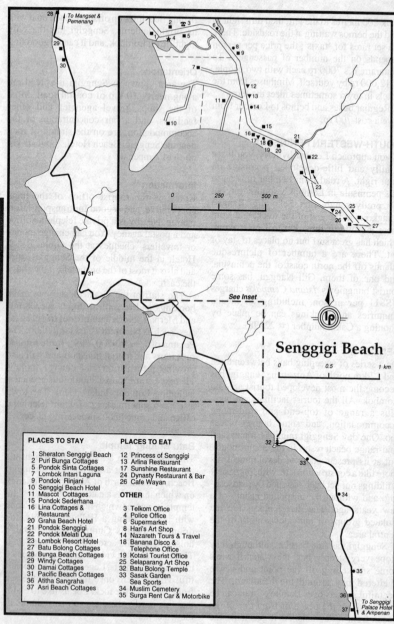

Senggigi Beach

PLACES TO STAY

1 Sheraton Senggigi Beach
2 Puri Bunga Cottages
5 Pondok Sinta Cottages
9 Lombok Intan Laguna
9 Pondok Rinjani
10 Senggigi Beach Hotel
11 Mascot Cottages
15 Pondok Sederhana
16 Lina Cottages & Restaurant
20 Graha Beach Hotel
21 Pondok Senggigi
22 Pondok Melati Dua
23 Lombok Resort Hotel
27 Batu Bolong Cottages
28 Bunga Beach Cottages
29 Windy Cottages
30 Damai Cottages
31 Pacific Beach Cottages
36 Atitha Sangraha
37 Asri Beach Cottages

PLACES TO EAT

12 Princess of Senggigi
13 Arlina Restaurant
17 Sunshine Restaurant
24 Dynasty Restaurant & Bar
26 Cafe Wayan

OTHER

3 Telkom Office
4 Police Office
6 Supermarket
8 Hari's Art Shop
14 Nazareth Tours & Travel
18 Banana Disco & Telephone Office
19 Kotasi Tourist Office
25 Selaparang Art Shop
32 Batu Bolong Temple
33 Sasak Garden Sea Sports
34 Muslim Cemetery
35 Surga Rent Car & Motorbike

To Mangset & Pemenang

See Inset

To Senggigi Palace Hotel & Ampenan

Places to Stay – bottom end

Senggigi is moving up-market. Although there's plenty of mid-range accommodation and an increasing number of expensive places, there's not that much for shoestring travellers. The most popular travellers' centre at Senggigi is the *Pondok Senggigi* (☎ 93273). It's expanded quite a bit, but still has some cheaper rooms (10,000/13,0000 rp for singles/doubles with shared bathroom). Rooms with Western-style bathrooms start at 15,000/20,000 rp, and deluxe air-con rooms are 70,000/80,000 rp. There's also a 15% tax and service charge. The rooms run off a long verandah with a pleasant garden area at the front. There's a good restaurant, which is very popular, and sometimes live music, so it's not the most serene place to stay.

About the cheapest place to stay is *Pondok Sederhana*, north-west of Pondok Senggigi. The rooms are a bit dirty, but very cheap (from about 7000 rp with shared mandi and toilet), and the position is good. There are some small places off the main road away from the beach, such as the *Astiti Guesthouse*, with singles doubles at 8000/10,000 rp and 10,000/14,000 rp. They're not far from the centre of things, but still quiet and pretty good value.

The *Pondok Sinta Cottages* are further north and closer to the beach, and they're cheap: 6000/7500 rp (10,000/12,000 rp with private bathroom), including breakfast and tax. *Damai Cottages*, way north in Mangset, are moderately cheap at 13,000/16,000 rp.

Places to Stay – middle

About the first place you'll strike coming in from Ampenan is *Asri Beach Cottages*, with standard rooms at 12,500 rp and bungalows at 17,500 rp, including tax and breakfast. They're basic but clean, and near the beach. Just north of Asri is *Atitha Sangraha*, a nice new place with spotlessly clean cottages near the beach from around 20,000 rp.

Batu Bolong Cottages (☎ 24598) have bungalows on both sides of the road. On the beach side they cost from 35,000 rp, and on the other side from 30,000 rp, including tax.

The small *Pondok Melati Dua* (☎ 93288), on the right as you enter Senggigi central, has standard rooms at 20,000/22,000 rp and cottages at 30,000/32,500 rp, including tax and breakfast. It's a short walk to the beach, and generally a nice place.

Lina Cottages (☎ 93237), with rooms at 25,000/35,000 rp, is central, friendly and good value, and its restaurant has a good reputation. A little further north, *Pondok Rinjani* has cottages with private bathrooms at 22,000/28,000 rp plus tax.

Windy Cottages are out by themselves, north of Senggigi in an area known as Mangset. It's a great location if you want to get away from it all, and the restaurant has good food. There are only eight rooms, at 20,000 rp for standard rooms and 35,000 rp for bungalows.

Places to Stay – top end

The first place you see coming north from Ampenan is the new *Senggigi Palace Hotel* (☎ 93045/6/7/8/9; fax 93043), and you'll certainly see it – the central lobby building is massive. The rooms are plain and clean (sterile?), with fridge, phone, TV and video, and cost US$60/70 (US$75/85 with an ocean view). It has a vast swimming pool, and may look prettier when the garden is established.

Senggigi's first big 'international-standard' hotel is right on the headland. Operated by Garuda, the *Senggigi Beach Hotel* (☎ 93210; fax 93200) charges from US$60/ 75 for an air-con room and up to US$160 for a deluxe bungalow. The hotel has a beautiful setting, a swimming pool and other mod cons, though it's almost old enough to need a facelift. At least as classy is the *Lombok Intan Laguna* (☎ 93090; fax 93185), a large and handsome luxury hotel with a big pool. Rooms start at US$80/95 and suites at US$200, plus 21% tax and service.

Mascot Berugaq Elen Cottages (☎ 93365; fax 22314), near the Senggigi Beach Hotel, are pleasant individual cottages costing US$29 to US$33, plus 21% service and tax. (Formerly they were just 'Mascot Cottages'.) The *Graha Beach Hotel* (☎ 93101; fax 93400) has air-con singles/ doubles with TV from US$40/45 (US$5 extra for an ocean view), and a beach-front restaurant.

Puri Bunga Cottages, formerly Ida Beach Cottages (☎ 93013; fax 93286), are stepped up the hillside on the east side of the road, with great views, but it's a bit of a trek to the higher rooms and to the beach. The place has air-con, telephones, TV, hot water, a swimming pool, a restaurant and indifferent staff. The published rate is US$60/65, but they offer big discounts.

Further north, the new *Sheraton Senggigi Beach* (☎ 93333; fax 93140), is the best hotel in Senggigi, and also the most expensive, with rooms from US$105 to US$125 and suites from US$275 to US$800, plus 21% tax and service. The rooms are comfortable, stylish and tastefully decorated with local handcrafts. The pool and gardens are lovely, and the staff are friendly and efficient. There's a children's pool and playground, and special family packages. The Sheraton is making an effort to train local staff and to promote local crafts and culture, and is one of the first places to recycle some of their waste water for the gardens.

At the northern end of Senggigi, *Pacific Beach Cottages* (☎ 93006; fax 93027) have all the standard luxuries – air-con, TV, hot water, swimming pool – but the rooms are ordinary and the place has no character at all. Standard singles/doubles cost US$25/30 (add US$5 for deluxe rooms or US$20 for 'executive deluxe' bungalows), plus 21% tax and service. Even further north in Mangset you'll find the well-run *Bunga Beach Cottages*, with a splendid beach-front position, a pool, and 28 comfortable, air-con bungalows in a pretty garden (US$42/45 to US$52/55).

Other top-end places under construction include the *Lombok Resort Hotel* and a *Holiday Inn*.

Places to Eat

Most of the places to stay have their own restaurants, and you can eat at any one you like. The restaurant at *Pondok Senggigi* is popular from breakfast time until late at night. It's not the cheapest (nasi goreng is

2500 rp, a main course of fish is around 5000 rp), but the food and the atmosphere are good. The restaurant at *Lina Cottages* has some very tasty dishes and is also popular.

There's not much at the bottom end of the scale; local warungs seem to have been priced out of the real estate market. *Cafe Wayan*, south of the centre, is related to the excellent Cafe Wayan in Ubud, which should be recommendation enough. The centrally located *Princess of Senggigi* is also a good eatery. The *Sunshine Restaurant* has a typical tourist menu and good Chinese food. Further north, the *Arlina Restaurant* is also good value. At the other end of the Senggigi strip, the restaurant at *Windy Cottages* serves very good food at reasonable prices in a delightful seaside setting.

Entertainment

Pondok Senggigi, the *Graha Beach Hotel* and *Dynasty Restaurant & Bar* have live music on occasions, with both tourists and young locals crowding the dance floor. The local bands do good rock and reggae music with an Indonesian flavour, as well as covers of popular Western numbers.

Getting There & Away

A public bemo from Ampenan to Senggigi costs about 500 rp. To get to Senggigi from the airport, get a bemo to the Ampenan terminal (250 rp), then take another to Senggigi. Officially, a taxi from the airport to Senggigi is 10,000 rp, but you can walk out of the airport and charter a bemo for about 7000 rp.

The fast catamaran from Padangbai used to call at Senggigi, and may resume service. Other boats run directly to the Gili Islands – not a cheap option, but very scenic.

NARMADA

Laid out as a miniature replica of the summit of Gunung Rinjani and its crater lake, Narmada is a hill about 10 km east of Cakra, on the main east-west road crossing Lombok. It takes its name from a sacred river in India. The temple, **Pura Kalasa**, is still used, and the Balinese Pujawali celebration

Top: Market scene, Lombok (JL)
Middle left : Kuta beach, Lombok (JL)
Middle right: Lotus plants in a rice field, Lombok (JL)
Bottom: Lombok landscape at sunrise (JL)

Top left: The caldera, Mt Bromo, East Java (PT)
Top right: Kawah Ijen, East Java (PT)
Middle: Keli Mutu (green & turquoise lake), Flores, Nusa Tenggara (GE & TW)
Bottom: Outer crater, Mt Bromo, East Java (PT)

is held here every year in honour of the god Batara, who dwells on Gunung Rinjani.

Narmada was constructed in 1805 by the king of Mataram, when he was no longer able to climb Rinjani to make his offerings to the gods. Having set his conscience at rest by placing offerings in the temple, he spent at least some of his time in his pavilion on the hill, lusting after the young girls bathing in the artificial lake. Along one side of the pool are the remains of an aqueduct built by the Dutch and still in use.

It's a beautiful place to spend a few hours, although the gardens are neglected. Don't go there on weekends, when it tends to become very crowded. Apart from the lake, there are two other pools in the grounds. Admission is 500 rp, and there's an additional charge to swim in the pool.

Places to Eat

Right at the Narmada bemo station is the local market, which sells mainly food and clothing; it's well worth a look. There are a number of warungs scattered around, offering soto ayam (chicken soup) and other dishes.

Getting There & Away

There are frequent bemos from Sweta to Narmada (200 rp). When you get off at the bemo station at Narmada, you'll see the gardens directly opposite. If you cross the road and walk 100 metres or so south along the side road, you'll come to the entrance. There are parking fees for bicycles, motorbikes and cars.

LINGSAR

This large temple complex just a few km north of Narmada is said to have been built in 1714. The temple combines the Bali Hindu and Wektu Telu religions in one complex. Designed in two separate sections and built on two different levels, the Hindu pura (in the northern section) is higher than the Wektu Telu temple (in the southern section).

The Hindu temple has four shrines. On one side is Hyang Tunggal, which looks towards Gunung Agung, the seat of the gods in Bali. The shrine faces north-west, rather than north-east as it would in Bali. On the other side is a shrine devoted to Gunung Rinjani, the seat of the gods in Lombok. Between these two shrines is a double shrine symbolising the union between the two islands. One side of this double shrine is named in honour of the might of Lombok; the other side is dedicated to a king's daughter, Ayu Nyoman Winton, who according to legend gave birth to a god.

The Wektu Telu temple is noted for its small, enclosed pond devoted to Lord Vishnu. It has a number of holy eels, which look like huge swimming slugs and can be enticed from their hiding places by the use of hard-boiled eggs as bait. The stalls outside the temple complex sell boiled eggs – expect to pay around 200 rp or so. Get there early to see the eels, because they've had their fill of eggs after the first few tour groups. Next to the eel pond is another enclosure, with a large altar or offering place bedecked in white and yellow cloth and mirrors. The mirrors are offerings from Chinese businesspeople asking for good luck and success. Many local farmers also come here with offerings.

At the annual rain festival, held at the start of the wet season (somewhere between October and December), the Hindus and the Wektu Telus make offerings and pray in their own temples, then come out into the communal compound and pelt each other with ketupat – rice wrapped in banana leaves. The ceremony is to bring the rain, or to give thanks for the rain. Be prepared to get attacked with ketupat from both sides if you visit Lingsar at this time!

Getting There & Away

Lingsar is off the main road. Take a bemo from Sweta to Narmada (200 rp), then catch another to Lingsar village (also 200 rp), and walk the short distance from there to the temple complex. It's easy to miss the temple, which is set back off the road behind the school.

SURANADI

A few km east of Lingsar, Suranadi has one of the holiest temples on Lombok. This small temple set in pleasant gardens is noted for its bubbling, icy-cold spring water and for the restored baths with their ornate Balinese carvings. The eels here are also sacred and seldom underfed – how many hard-boiled eggs can an eel eat? You can bathe here (it's polite to ask first), or use the swimming pool at the hotel (1000 rp, kids 500 rp).

Not far from Suranadi, on the road towards Sesaot, there's a small jungle sanctuary, the **Hutan Wisata Suranadi** (*hutan* means 'forest' or 'jungle'), but it's sadly neglected.

Places to Stay & Eat

The *Suranadi Hotel* (☎ 33686) has rooms and cottages which are grossly overpriced at US$12 to US$50 plus 21% tax and service. The hotel is an old Dutch building, originally an administrative centre, although it's no great example of colonial architecture. There are two swimming pools, tennis courts, a restaurant and a bar. There's a cheaper *homestay* nearby (10,000/12,000 rp, including breakfast) – ask at the warungs in the main street.

SESAOT

About five km north of Suranadi, and also worth a visit, Sesaot is a small, quiet market town on the edge of a forest where wood-felling is the main industry. There's regular transport from Suranadi to Sesaot, and you can eat simple but tasty food at the warung on the main street.

Go up the main street and turn left over the bridge. There are some nice picnic spots, popular with locals on holidays, and you can swim in the river. The water is very cool, and is considered holy, as it comes straight from Gunung Rinjani. You can continue up the road about three km to **Air Nyet**, a small village with more places for swimming and picnics.

CENTRAL LOMBOK

Central Lombok, or Lombok Tengah, is the name of one of the three administrative districts (kabupaten) on Lombok, but for this section the term is used more generally, to cover the inland towns and villages in the rich agricultural area south of Gunung Rinjani. The area is well watered and lush, and offers opportunities for scenic walks through the rice fields and the jungle.

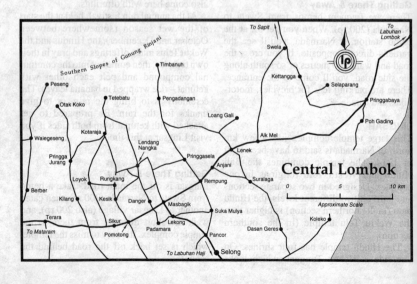

Towards the south coast, the country is drier, and dams have been built to provide irrigation during the dry season. Most of the places in central Lombok are more or less traditional Sasak settlements, and several of them are known for particular types of local handcrafts. Villages tend to specialise in a particular type of craft.

Tetebatu

A mountain retreat at the foot of Gunung Rinjani, Tetebatu is 50 km from Mataram and about 10 km north of the main east-west road. It's quite a bit cooler here, and it can be misty and rainy, particularly between November and April.

There are magnificent views over southern Lombok, east to the sea and north to Gunung Rinjani. You can climb part way up Rinjani from here, but the formerly magnificent stands of mahogany trees have virtually disappeared. Other destinations for walks include **Jukut Waterfall**, six km to the east, and the **hutan** (forest) four km north-west, where lots of jet-black monkeys will shriek at you.

Places to Stay & Eat The original place to stay is *Wisma Soedjono*, an old colonial house that was once a country retreat for a Dr Soedjono. A number of rooms and bungalows have been added, as well as a restaurant and a good-sized swimming pool. Prices start at 15,000 rp for a simple double, peaking at 35,000 rp for 'VIP' accommodation. The better rooms have Western-style toilets, and showers with hot water, and all prices include continental breakfast. The staff provide good information about walks in the area. Food here is excellent, but costs extra – you can even get a packed lunch if you want to spend the day walking. There are also two or three warungs in the town.

Some cheap accommodations are sprouting in the lovely rice fields. One such place is *Diwi Enjeni*, on the south side of town and with a nice outlook. Bungalows cost 7500 rp, including breakfast, and there's a small restaurant. *Pondok Tetebatu* is nearby, at a similar price. Turn right in Tetebatu to the

Green Ory bungalow, which costs 25,000 rp but could sleep several people. Continue on the road to the waterfall to find *Wisma Paradiso*, another nice cheapie.

Getting There & Away Getting to Tetebatu involves a number of changes if you haven't got your own wheels. There is a direct bus from Sweta to Pomotong (950 rp), but as you may have to wait around for a while, it may actually be quicker to take a bemo to Narmada then another to Pomotong. From Pomotong, take a bemo or cidomo to Kotaraja (400 rp), and from there another bemo or cidomo to Tetebatu. Or go straight to Tetebatu on the back of a motorbike (1000 rp or so). If you're not in a hurry and you're not carrying too much, you can walk from Pomotong to Tetebatu. It's an easy 2½ to three hours, through attractive country.

Kotaraja

Kotaraja means 'city of kings', although no kings ruled from here and it's hardly a city. Apparently, when the Sasak kingdom of Langko (located at Kopang in central Lombok) fell to the Balinese invaders, the rulers of Langko fled to Loyok, the village south of Kotaraja. After the royal compound in that village was also destroyed, two sons of the ruler of Langko went to live in Kotaraja. The aristocracy of Kotaraja trace their ancestry back to these brothers.

The area around Kotaraja is noted for blacksmithing and basketware. Traditional blacksmiths still use an open hearth and human-powered bellows, but old car springs are the favoured 'raw material' for knives, farm implements and other tools.

Getting There & Away There are no losmen in Kotaraja, so visit from Tetebatu or Lendang Nangka. With your own transport you can make a day trip from the capital – it's only 32 km from Sweta.

Loyok

Loyok, a tiny village just a few km from Kotaraja, is noted for its fine handcrafts, particularly basketware and natural-fibre weaving. Most of the craftspeople work from their homes, but there's a place in the main street where you can buy some of the excellent basketware. There's also a Handcraft Centre, with some work on display. You can stay at the *Wisma Loyok* for 12,500 rp, including dinner and breakfast.

Getting There & Away To get to Loyok, catch a bemo from Pomotong to Rungkang (the turn-off to the village), and then either walk the last km or get a cidomo (250 rp per person). If you're setting out from Kotaraja for Loyok, you have the same options – either take a cidomo or walk. It's a very pretty drive, with traditional thatched Sasak huts and lush rice terraces along the way.

Rungkang

This small village less than a km east of Loyok is known for its pottery, which is made from a local black clay. The pots are often finished with attractive cane work, which is woven all over the outside for decoration and for greater strength. Similar pottery is made in a number of other villages in the area south of the main road.

Masbagik

Quite a large town on the main road at the turn-off to Selong, Masbagik has a market on Monday morning and is well known for production of pottery and ceramics. There's a post office and a Telkom wartel here. Just east of the wartel, follow the track to the left for 500 metres to Repo village, where you can stay at *Sasak House* for 12,000/15,000 rp (with three meals). It's not very well located, but Gep, the guy who runs it, was looking for a better place, so it may be worth asking for.

A bemo from Sweta to Masbagik (42 km) costs 1000 rp, and you can hire a motorbike to get around.

Lendang Nangka

This village has similar surroundings to those of Tetebatu, seven km away. In and around the village you can see blacksmiths making knives, hoes and other tools using indigenous techniques. Silversmiths are also starting work here. **Jojang**, the biggest freshwater spring in Lombok, is a few km away. Or you can walk to a waterfall with beautiful views, and look for black monkeys in a nearby forest. In August you should be able to see the traditional Sasak stick-fighting at Lendang Nangka. Local dances are a possibility at Batu Empas, one km away.

Hadji Radiah is a local primary school teacher who has been encouraging people to stay in Lendang Nangka. His family homestay has become quite popular among travellers who want an experience of typical Lombok village life. He speaks English very well, and is a mine of information on the surrounding countryside and customs. He has a map for local walks and enjoys acting as a guide.

Places to Stay Staying at Radiah's *homestay* will cost you about 10,000/15,000 rp for a basic single/double, including three excellent meals per day of local Sasak food, and tea or coffee. You will get customary Sasak cake and fruit for breakfast. It's not luxury, but good value and highly recommended. His house is fairly easy to find (see the map, but everyone knows him), and has 12 bedrooms for guests. There's a new place to stay on the west side of Lendang Nangka, *Wisma Ewira*, which is quite nice. It, too, costs 10,000/15,000 rp with three meals.

Getting There & Away First take a bemo from Sweta to Masbagik (42 km; 1000 rp). Then take a cidomo to Lendang Nangka

Lendang Nangka

Radiah's House ■

School

Mosque

Monument

Market

To Loyok & Kotaraja

To Masbagik

(about four km) – this should cost 350 rp per person, but the driver will want at least three passengers, or 1000 rp for the whole cart.

Pringgasela
This village is a centre for traditional weaving (sarongs, blankets etc). You can see the weavers in action, and buy some of their beautiful work at a bargain price – that is, you'll have to bargain.

Lenek
Lenek has a traditional music and dance troupe which does performances for tourists on a more-or-less regular basis. Ask at the tourist office in Mataram for the times. A little north and east of Lenek is the village of **Loang Gali**, where the *Loang Gali Cottage* charges 12,500 rp per person for a room and three meals.

Sapit
At Aikmel, near Lenek, a side road heads north up the shoulder of Gunung Rinjani, past Swela to Sapit. This place offers cool air, stunning views and the attractive forest area of Lemor. You can walk from Sapit to Sembalun Bumbung, and from there do a climb up Rinjani from the east side. The road north of Sapit is not driveable.

The *Hati Suci Homestay* in Sapit has bungalows at 10,000 to 12,000 rp and bunk beds at 4000 rp, all including breakfast. There's a restaurant, and staff can help with information about climbing Rinjani. Get there by bemo from Masbagik (1000 rp).

Sukarara
Twenty-five km south of Mataram, not far off the Kediri to Praya road, is the small village of Sukarara. Nearly every house here has an old wooden handloom. Along the main street are lots of places with looms set up outside, and displays of sarongs hanging in bright bands. Typically, there are young women working out the front, in the traditional black costume with brightly coloured edgings. More women work inside, often wearing jeans and watching TV as they

work, but most of the material is actually made in homes in surrounding villages.

Before you go to Sukarara, it may be a good idea to check prices in the Selamat Riady weaving factory in Cakranegara to get some idea of how much to pay and where to start bargaining. There's a range of quality and size that it's impossible to give a guide to prices, but the best pieces are magnificent and well worth paying for. If you're accompanied to Sukarara, your guide or driver will inevitably get a commission, which will add a little to the price you'll pay. The village is a regular stop for tour groups, but don't let that deter you.

Getting There & Away Get a bemo from Sweta towards Praya and get off at Puyung (about 600 rp). From Puyung you can hire a cidomo for about 250 rp to take you the two km to Sukarara.

Penujak
This small village six km south of Praya is well known for its traditional *gerabah* pottery, made from a local red clay. You'll see the pottery places from the road, and you can watch the pots being made by hand and fired in traditional kilns. There's a lot worth buying, but the bigger pieces would be hard to carry. Pots range in size up to a metre high, and there are kitchen vessels of various types, and decorative figurines, usually in the shape of animals.

Rembitan & Sade
The area from Sengkol down to Kuta Beach is a centre of traditional Sasak culture, and there are many relatively unchanged Sasak villages where the people still live in customary houses and engage in indigenous craftwork.

The village of Rembitan is a few km south of Sengkol and has a population of about 750. It's a slightly sanitised Sasak village where tourists are welcome to look around, with one of the local kids as a guide. Masjid Kuno, an old thatched-roof mosque, tops the hill around which the village houses cluster. A little further south is Sade, a traditional village which was apparently constructed just for tourists. Hawkers here give the hard sell.

SOUTHERN LOMBOK
Kuta Beach

The best known place on the south coast is Lombok's Kuta Beach, a magnificent stretch of white sand and blue sea with rugged hills rising around it, but not much else. It is a very small development with far fewer tourists than the famous (infamous?) Kuta Beach in Bali, but there are perennial plans to develop not only Kuta but a whole stretch of the superb south coast with luxury hotels.

People flock to Kuta for the nyale fishing celebration, usually falling in February or March each year, with thousands sleeping on the beach, and visiting celebrities and TV crews. For the rest of the year it's very quiet. There are surf breaks on the reefs round here, but they're still 'secret' – the locals will take you out on boats, the charter rate is about 40,000 to 50,000 rp per day.

Information You can change money at Anda Cottages, but the rates are not very good. Wisma Segara Anak is a postal agency, and has a booking desk for Perama. There are phones in Kuta, but no wartel. There's a market twice a week, on Sunday and Wednesday.

Nyale Fishing Festival On the 19th day of the 10th month in the Sasak calendar – generally February or March – hundreds of Sasaks gather on the beach. When night falls, fires are built and the young people sit around competing with each other in rhyming couplets called *pantun*. At dawn the next morning, the first nyale are caught, after which it is time for the Sasak teenagers to have fun. In a colourful procession, boys and girls put out to sea – in different boats – and chase one another with lots of noise and laughter. The worm-like nyale fish are eaten raw or grilled, and are believed to have aphrodisiac properties. A good catch is a sign that the rice harvest will also be good.

Places to Stay & Eat Most of Kuta's accommodation is along the beach-front road to the east of the village – all of a similar price and quality. The following are low-season prices; expect to pay up to 5000 rp more if there are other tourists around. *Kuta Beach Bungalows* are on the edge of the village, at the west end of the beach, and charge 6000/8000 rp, including breakfast. After the police station you pass *Rambutan*, with rooms at 6000 and 8000 rp, including tea and breakfast. The *Wisma Segara Anak* next door has a restaurant. Rooms cost 4000/6000 rp and bungalows are 12,000/15,000 rp, including breakfast. Next along, *Pondok Sekar Kuning* (Yellow Flower Cottage) has double rooms downstairs for 5000 rp, and upstairs, with a nice view, for 10,000 rp (10,000 and 15,000 rp in the high season). *Anda Cottages* (☎ 54836), next door, is the original place at Kuta. It has some trees and shrubs, which make it more pleasant, a good restaurant, with Indonesian, Chinese and Western dishes, and rooms from 8000 to 10,000 rp, including breakfast.

A bit further along is *Florida Bungalows*, with good food, and singles/doubles at 5000/8000 rp, and the *Rinjani Agung Beach Bungalows*, with standard rooms from 12,0000/15,000 rp. *Mascot* is only a place for a beer and music, it's almost a pub. Continue to the *Cockatoo Cottages & Restaurant*, the last place along the beach, which has a nice restaurant area, and rooms for 6,000/10,000 rp, including breakfast.

There are a few cheap, basic *homestays* in the village, and also the *Losmen Mata Hari*, near the market on the road to Mawan. It has a restaurant, and nine small, clean rooms with private shower at 8000/10,000 rp, including breakfast.

Getting There & Away There is some direct public transport from Sweta to Kuta (1500 rp), or get a bemo to Praya (700 rp) then another from there to Sengkol (500 rp) and a third down to Kuta (300 rp). Travel early, or you may get stuck and have to charter. Market day in Sengkol is Thursday, so there may be more transport then. Perama has connections to Kuta from Mataram and Senggigi (10,000 rp) and other tourist areas. Lombok Independent shuttle buses from Senggigi cost the same. If you have your own transport, it's easy as the road is sealed all the way. The final five km to Kuta is a steep and winding descent which suddenly leaves the hills to arrive at the coast.

East of Kuta

Quite a good road goes east along the coast, passing a series of beautiful bays punctuated by headlands. There's some public transport, but you will see more with your own transport – a bicycle would be good. All the beach-front land has been bought by speculators for planned tourist resorts. **Segar Beach** is about two km east around the first headland, and you can easily walk there. An enormous rock about four km east of the village offers superb views across the countryside if you climb it early in the morning. Five km east is **Tanjung Aan (Cape Aan)**, where there are two classic beaches with very fine, powdery white sand. This is an area slated for up-market resort hotels.

The road continues another three km to the fishing village of **Gerupak**, where there's a Tuesday market. From there you can get a boat across the bay to Bumgang. Alternatively, turn north just before Tanjung Aan and go to Sereneng. Beyond here the road deteriorates, but you can get to Awang with a motorbike or on foot, then get a boat across to Ekas, a not-so-secret surf spot (see under South of Labuhan Lombok in the following East Lombok section).

West of Kuta

The road west of Kuta has recently been sealed as far as Selong Blanak, a lovely sandy bay. It doesn't follow the coast closely, but there are regular and spectacular ocean vistas. In between are such fine beaches as Mawan, Tampa, Rowok and Mawi, but you have to detour to find them. They are all known to have surfing possibilities in the right conditions.

Selong Blanak Cottages are by themselves, 1½ km north of Selong Blanak

beach, but they provide transport to the beach and back for nothing, and to more isolated spots for a small price. It's a very nice place to stay, with a restaurant, and a variety of rooms from 15,000/20,000 rp (5000 rp more in the high season). The road between Selong Blanak and Penujak is mostly sealed and quite passable.

The coast road continues west to Pengantap, but beyond there it gets very rough. In the dry season, with a motorbike or 4WD, you might make it through to Blongas and north to Sekotong and Lembar. Don't try it in the wet season.

EAST LOMBOK

For most travellers, the east coast is just Labuhan Lombok, the port for ferries to Sumbawa, but improvements to the road around the north coast make a round-the-island trip quite feasible. Similarly, the once-remote south-eastern peninsula is becoming more accessible, particularly to those with their own transport.

Labuhan Lombok

There are fantastic views of mighty Gunung Rinjani from the east coast port of Labuhan Lombok. From the hill on the south side of the harbour, you look across the Alas Strait to Sumbawa. The town is a sleepy little place with concrete houses, thatched shacks and stilt bungalows in the Sulawesi style. Ferries to Sumbawa leave from the jetty on the east side of the bay.

If you're just passing through Labuhan Lombok on your way to Sumbawa, there's no need to stay overnight. A bus from Sweta only takes a couple of hours, and there are regular ferries.

Places to Stay & Eat In the village itself is the very basic *Losmen Dian Dutaku*, with singles/doubles at 2600/3600 rp. On Jalan Khayangan, the road that runs round to the ferry port, the *Losmen Munawar* is a much better place, with rooms at 3000/5500 rp; it's pretty basic, but quite OK. There are a few warungs near the bemo terminal.

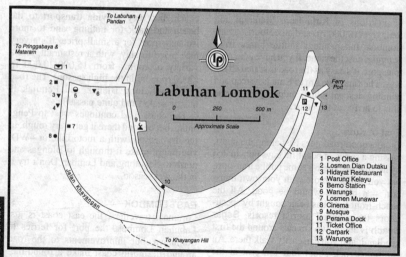

Labuhan Lombok

To Labuhan
Pandan

To Pringgabaya &
Mataram

Ferry
Port

0   250   500 m

Approximate Scale

Gate

Jalan Khayangan

To Khayangan Hill

1 Post Office
2 Losmen Dian Dutaku
3 Hidayat Restaurant
4 Warung Kelayu
5 Bemo Station
6 Warungs
7 Losmen Munawar
8 Cinema
9 Mosque
10 Perama Dock
11 Ticket Office
12 Carpark
13 Warungs

Getting There & Away Regular buses and bemos run between Labuhan Lombok and Sweta (about 2000 rp; 69 km; two hours). If you're zipping straight across Lombok bound for Bali, you can take a bus via Sweta to Lembar. Other road connections go to Masbagik (1000 rp) and Kopang (1500 rp).

Regular passenger ferries leave Labuhan Lombok for Poto Tano (Sumbawa). According to one schedule, they leave at 7, 8.30, 11 and 11.30 am and 2.30, 4 and 5 pm, but at the harbour, they said it was every hour on the hour from 7 am to 6 pm. If you get a through bus from Sweta, you won't have to worry about it; if you're travelling independently, try to get to the port before 11 am, to make the 1½-hour crossing and the two-hour bus trip to Sumbawa Besar before dark. The ferry costs 3100 rp in ekonomi A (children 1600 rp), 2000 rp in ekonomi B, 2500 rp for a bicycle, 3200 rp for a motorbike and 32,000 rp for a small car. There's a 300 rp harbour tax as well. Ekonomi A has air-con, which may be worth it – it can be a bloody hot trip! If you go in ekonomi B, take a water bottle and a hat, and arrive at the dock early to get a seat. The ferries can get very

crowded, especially at times when local people are travelling, such as Ramadan.

The boats depart from a new port on the east side of the harbour. It's about two or three km from the port to the town of Labuhan Lombok, on the road which skirts the south side of the bay. It will be too hot to walk, so take a bemo for 250 rp. The ticket office is beside the car park. There are a couple of food stalls and warungs at the port, and food vendors come on board the boat.

North of Labuhan Lombok

Foreigners are still a curiosity along this coast. Look for the giant trees about five km north of Labuhan Lombok, and **Pulu Lampur**, 14 km north, with a black-sand beach which is popular with locals on Sunday and holidays.

Another few km to the north you can stay at the pleasant and secluded *Siola Cottages*, by themselves in a coconut grove on the seashore, just before the village of **Labuhan Pandan**. It's 12,000/20,000 rp for singles/doubles, with three meals, or you can just stop for a meal or a snack. From here you can charter a boat to the uninhabited islands of Gili Sulat and the **Gili Petangan** group, with lovely white beaches and good coral for snorkelling. There are virtually no facilities, but a boat costs about 30,000 rp for up to five passengers for a day trip out and back, with a few hours on the island. Take drinking water and a picnic lunch.

Perama has a camp on one of the islands, which is a stopover on its expensive Land-Sea Adventure tours. A short trip to the so-called **Perama Island** from Labuhan Lombok costs about 25,000 rp, including transport, snorkelling gear and three meals. It's best to arrange it with Perama in Mataram.

The road continues through Sambelia and Sugian to the north coast (see the following Around the North Coast section). It's in the process of being sealed, and new bridges are under construction, but it's quite passable on a motorbike or Suzuki jeep, at least during the dry season. By public transport, you can get a bemo to Anyar (near Bayan) from Labuhan Lombok.

South of Labuhan Lombok

The capital of the East Lombok administrative district is **Selong**, which has some old Dutch buildings but is certainly not a tourist town. It has grown a lot in recent years, and there is an almost-continuous urban strip from Pancor to Tanjung. Pancor is a bus and bemo terminal for the region, and you can change money at the BPD Bank. The *Wisma Erina*, on the east side of the main road, is not a bad place to stay.

On the coast is **Labuhan Haji**, accessible from Selong and Tanjung by bemo. Formerly a port for those departing on a *haji*, or pilgrimage to Mecca, the port buildings are abandoned and in ruins. The black-sand beach here is a bit grubby, but OK for swimming. There's accommodation at *Melewi's Beach Cottages*, on the beach just north of where the road from Selong comes in. They ask 20,000 rp a double, including breakfast, and can arrange other meals. It doesn't look a very well-run place, but it's isolated and has great views across to Sumbawa. It would be a good place to feed mosquitoes, so take precautions.

Further south you come to **Tanjung Luar**, one of Lombok's main fishing ports, with a strong smell of fish and lots of Sulawesi-style houses on stilts. From there the road swings west to Keruak, and continues to **Sukaraja**, a very traditional Sasak-style village which tourists are welcome to visit.

Just west of Keruak there's a road south to Jerowaru (3.6 km), and to the south-eastern peninsula, which was inaccessible until recently. This peninsula is sparsely populated, with a harsh climate and scrubby vegetation, but the coastline has some interesting features. Turn right at Jerowaru and follow the road about 16 km to **Kaliantan**, on the south coast, which has nowhere to stay but does have a wonderful white beach and brilliant ocean views. A sealed road branches west 6.4 km past Jerowaru – it gets pretty rough, but eventually reaches **Ekas**. There's no accommodation there, but you can get a small boat to take you a few km south to *Laut Surga Cottages*. In the dry season you can reach the cottages by road, turning left after 5.2 km on the Ekas road and following the small blue signs. Laut Surga is mainly a place where surfers stay, but it has a lovely little beach. 'Laut Surga' means 'heaven sea', but it's hell to get to. You might make it to Ekas by bemo from Keruak, and you can also get there by boat from Awang (see under East of Kuta in the previous Southern Lombok section).

On the east coast of the peninsula, **Tanjung Ringgit** has some large caves which, according to local legend, are home to a demonic giant. Tanjung Ringgit is a day's walk from the nearest road, or you might be able to charter a boat from Tanjung Luar. There's a cultivated-pearl operation at Teluk Sunut, on the north coast of the peninsula.

AROUND THE NORTH COAST

It's possible to go by road around the north coast, though it's pretty rough between Bayan and Sambelia. It's very scenic, with a variety of landscapes and seascapes, but few tourists and even fewer facilities. You'll need a reliable motorbike, or a vehicle with good ground clearance as you're unlikely to make

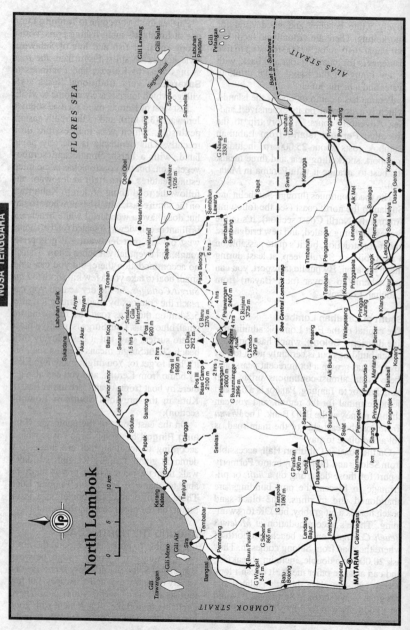

NUSA TENGGARA

North Lombok

0   5   10 km

FLORES SEA

LOMBOK STRAIT

Gili Trawangan
Gili Meno
Gili Air
Sira
Bangsal
Pemenang
Tembabar
Tanjung
Karang Kates

Baun Pusuk
G Saberis 865 m
G Wengsit 541 m
Batu Bolong
G Tampole 1080 m
G Punikan 490 m

Lendang Bajur
Rembiga
Cakranegara
Ampenan
MATARAM
Narmada
Sesaot
Suranadi
Selat
Sung
Pemepek
Pringgarata
Pengantjek
Mantang
Barabali
Kopang

Endut
Dasangra
Peseng
Waleganang
Berber
Pancoordao

Aik Buka

Sikur
Kilang
Pringga Jurang
Kotaraja
Terebatu
Masbagik
Anjani
Pringgasela

Timbanuh
Sembalun Bumbung
Sembalun Lawang
Sapit
Swela
Ketanga
Suralaga
Lenek
Aik Mei
Rempung
Suka Mulya
Lekong
Dasan Geres
Korleko

Labuhan Lombok
Pringabaya
Poh Gading

Boat to Sumbawa

ALAS STRAIT

Gili Lawang
Gili Sulat
Gili Pelangan
Labuhan Pandan

Sugian Strait

Sugian
Sambelia
Blantung
Lepeang

Obel Obel
Dasan Kembar
waterfall

Salang
G Ankabare 1926 m
G Nangi 2330 m

Pade Belong
G Baru 2376 m
Pelawangan II 2400 m
G Rinjani 3726 m
G Kondo 2947 m
G Daja 2912 m
Lake Segara Anak
Pelawangan I 2600 m
Base Camp 2100 m
Pos III 1850 m
Pos II
Pos I 920 m
G Buamangge 2896 m

Sendang Gila Waterfall

Torean
Senaru
Bayan
Anyar
Batu Koq
Akar Akar
Labuhan Cenk
Sukadana

Amor Amor
Lokorangan
Siduten
Santong
Papak
Ganga
Seelas
Gondang

See Central Lombok map

km

2

it in a normal car. You can do it on public transport, but east of Bayan that might mean standing in the back of a truck rather than sitting on a bus or a bemo. The road is being improved, but the improvements are an obstacle in themselves, with long sections piled with stones or covered in loose gravel, and rough detours over creeks where the new bridge is under construction.

From Ampenan, a road goes north to Senggigi, Mangset and Pemenang. It's a winding and wonderfully scenic coastal route, but does not yet have a regular bemo service. The inland route north from Mataram is a good road, through Lendang Bajur and the Pusuk Pass (Baun Pusuk) to Pemenang. It's also scenic, and it's worth stopping on the pass for the view and the monkeys. A bemo for the 31-km trip costs about 700 rp. Pemenang is where you turn off for Bangsal and the Gili Islands (see under Gili Islands later in this section), but you can keep going to Sira and the north coast.

Sira

Just a few km north of Pemenang, on the coast facing Gili Air, Sira has a white-sand beach, and there's good snorkelling on the nearby coral reef. There is a proposal to develop a big three-star hotel here, but at the moment there's no accommodation.

Tanjung

This town is quite large and attractive, and has a big cattle market on Sunday. Further on is **Karang Kates** (Krakas for short), where fresh water bubbles from the sea bed 400 metres offshore – the people here collect their drinking water from the sea. From nearby Gondang, you can walk about four km to the **Tiu Pupas waterfall**. There are a number of traditional villages south and west of here, where Wektu Telu is the prevailing religion. Tanjung is 45 km from Sweta (about 900 rp by bemo).

Bayan

Bayan is the birthplace of the Wektu Telu religion, and also a home for traditional Muslims. The mosque here is 300 years old,

and said to be the oldest on Lombok. Bayan is at the turn-off to Batu Koq and Senaru, the usual route for climbing Rinjani (see the next section for details). There are a couple of warungs here, and accommodation a few km away, in Batu Koq.

There are several buses daily from Sweta to Bayan (about 1800 rp, 79 km), the first leaving at around 9 am. It's a three-hour trip, and you should try to get on an early bus. There may be more frequent bemos to intermediate places like Pemenang or Tanjung.

East of Bayan

The north coast road continues about nine km to a junction. The road south goes to Sembalun Bumbung and Sembalun Lawang, traditional villages which can also be used as approaches to Rinjani.

Continue 35 km east on a winding road, through landscapes alternately lush and arid, to reach Sambelia and Labuhan Pandan, on the east coast. There's one place to stay there (see under North of Labuhan Lombok in the previous East Lombok section), or you can continue to Labuhan Lombok.

GUNUNG RINJANI

Rinjani is the highest mountain in Lombok and, outside Irian Jaya, about the highest in Indonesia. At 3726 metres, it soars above the island and dominates the landscape, but by mid-morning on most days, the summit is shrouded in cloud. The mountain is actually an active volcano – its last eruption was in 1901. A huge crater contains a large, green, crescent-shaped lake, Segara Anak, which is about six km across at its widest point. A series of natural hot springs on the north-eastern side of the caldera testify to the fact that Rinjani is still geologically active. These springs, known as Kokok Putih, are said to have remarkable healing powers, particularly for skin diseases. The lake is 600 vertical metres below the caldera rim, and in the middle of its curve is a new cone, Gunung Baru (or Barujari), only a couple of hundred years old.

Both the Balinese and the Sasaks revere Rinjani. To the Balinese it is equal to Gunung

Agung, a seat of the gods, and many Balinese make a pilgrimage here each year. In a ceremony called *pekelan*, people throw jewellery into the lake and make offerings to the spirit of the mountain. Some Sasaks make several pilgrimages a year – full moon is the favourite time for paying their respects to the mountain, and curing their ailments by bathing in its hot springs.

The main approaches to Rinjani are from Batu Koq and Senaru, on a northern ridge, or from Sembalun Lawang, to the east.

Batu Koq

Batu Koq is the usual starting point for a climb up Gunung Rinjani. There are several *homestays* in the village, some of which have superb views over the valley to the east, and up to the rim of Rinjani. Most of them have places to eat, and there are a few which sell biscuits, canned fish, eggs, chocolate and other food you can take trekking. There are also places to rent trekking equipment.

Sendang Gila Waterfall Make sure you go to this magnificent waterfall. It's a very pleasant half-hour walk, partly through forest, and partly alongside an irrigation canal which follows the contour of the hill, occasionally disappearing into tunnels where the cliffs are too steep. Watch for the sleek black monkeys swinging through the trees. Splash around near the waterfall – the water cascades down the mountain slope so fast that it's strong enough to knock the wind out of you. A much longer walk takes you through more forest to the upper part of the falls.

Getting There & Away There are bemos from Bayan to Batu Koq for about 700 rp. There are even Perama buses going direct to Batu Koq from Mataram.

Senaru

Perched high in the foothills of Rinjani, about seven km from Bayan, the small, traditional village of Senaru has an air of untainted antiquity. Until the 1960s, these villagers lived largely in isolation from the

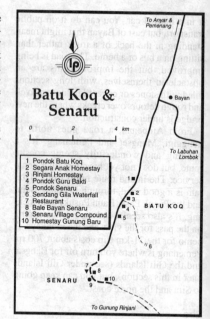

Batu Koq & Senaru

0   2   4 km

1 Pondok Batu Koq
2 Segara Anak Homestay
3 Rinjani Homestay
4 Pondok Guru Bakti
5 Pondok Senaru
6 Sendang Gila Waterfall
7 Restaurant
8 Bale Bayan Senaru
9 Senaru Village Compound
10 Homestay Gunung Baru

To Anyar & Pemenang

Bayan

To Labuhan Lombok

BATU KOQ

SENARU

To Gunung Rinjani

rest of the world. Even though trekkers pass by all the time, and are welcome to visit, Senaru retains a sense of isolation, as if modern civilisation is a world away. The village, surrounded by a wooden fence, comprises about 20 thatched wooden huts, some on stilts, others low to the ground. As you enter, there is a visitors' book, a donation tin, and a notice indicating how proceeds are used to benefit the village. For all its quaintness, this is obviously a poor village, and you should give something, though no-one hassles you at all.

This is as close as you'll get to Rinjani in a vehicle, and there are a couple of places to stay outside the traditional village. The *Bale Bayan Senaru* has quite adequate rooms (5000/10,000 rp, including breakfast), and there's a warung opposite. The basic *Homestay Gunung Baru* asks the same amount, and as it's a bit higher up the ridge, you can see the sunset as well as the sunrise, and be 500 metres closer to the summit when you start walking. It's only a km or so from Batu Koq to Senaru, an easy walk.

Sembalun Bumbung & Sembalun Lawang

High up on the eastern slopes of Gunung Rinjani is the cold but beautiful Sembalun Valley. The inhabitants of the valley claim descent from the Hindu Javanese, and a relative of one of the Majapahit rulers is said to be buried here. In the valley are the traditional Sasak villages of Sembalun Bumbung and Sembalun Lawang. It's only a 45-minute walk from one village to the other, and there are many pleasant walks in the surrounding area. From Sembalun Bumbung, there is a steep 1½-hour climb to a saddle with a beautiful panoramic view.

In Sembalun Lawang you may be able to stay with the kepala desa for about 5000 rp per person. Accommodation with the kepala desa in Sembalun Bumbung is more basic. Bring your trekking food and equipment, as none is available here.

Getting There & Away From the north coast road nine km east of Bayan, a rough but usable road climbs to Sembalun Lawang and continues to Sembalun Bumbung. There may be public transport up this road, but there won't be much and you'll have to start early.

From the south you can reach Sembalun Bumbung in a beautiful five-hour walk from Sapit, through coffee, paw paw, rice and vegetable fields, then through forest. Sapit has bemo connections to Pringgabaya on the main east-west road.

Climbing Rinjani

Many people climb up to Rinjani's crater lake every year. They are mostly local people making a pilgrimage or seeking the curative powers of the hot springs. Many foreign visitors make the climb, too, though very few people go the extra 1700 or so metres to the very summit of Rinjani. Even the climb to the crater lake is not to be taken lightly. Don't try it during the wet season, as the tracks will be slippery and very dangerous; in any case, be

you would be lucky to see any more than mist and cloud. During the full moon, it's very crowded.

There are a few possibilities, from a quick dash to the rim and back to a four or five-day trek around the summit. Most visitors stay in Batu Koq or Senaru, climb from there to the crater lake, and return the same way. The other main route is from Sembalun Lawang, on the eastern side. The northern route is more easily accessible, and has facilities for trekkers.

The people at the losmen Wisma Triguna in Ampenan can give good information about the climb. For a price (over US$100) they will organise the complete trip for you – food, tent, sleeping bag and a guide. But if you don't come at that, they can tell you how to go about it on your own. A number of agencies in Mataram or Senggigi organise guided all-inclusive treks (from US$100). A sleeping bag and tent are essential; you can rent them in Batu Koq.

Guides You can do the trek from Batu Koq without a guide, but in some places there's a confusion of trails branching off, so you could get lost. Guides can also be informative, good company, and act as porters, cooks and water collectors. When you're doing this walk with a guide, make sure you set your own pace – some guides climb Rinjani as often as 20 or 30 times a year and positively gallop up the slopes! A guide will cost about 15,000 rp per day, porters about 10,000 rp per day. From Sembalun Lawang you'll definitely need a guide (again, about 15,000 rp per day).

Equipment There are some very crude shelters on the way, but don't rely on them. In Batu Koq you can rent a two or three-person tent (12,500 rp for up to five days), a stove and cooking gear (2500 rp) and a sleeping bag (10,000 rp). You could probably get the whole lot for about 20,000 rp for three days. Check the equipment before you take it. It gets cold, so bring thick woollen socks, a sweater and a ground sheet as well.

Food & Supplies You need to take enough food to last three days, including food for your guide. Consider taking rice, instant noodles, sugar, coffee, eggs, tea, biscuits or bread, some tins of fish or meat, onions, fruit, and anything else that keeps you going. Don't forget matches, a torch (flashlight) and plenty of water; the bottles you buy it in are adequate containers. Even if you don't smoke, the guides really appreciate being given cigarettes. It's better to buy most of it in Mataram or at the supermarket in Senggigi, as there's more choice available, but you can get a fair range in Batu Koq.

Environmental Care A lot of rubbish is dropped along the route. The only reason it doesn't look worse is that student groups from the university come and clean it up every few months. Carry all rubbish out. Don't try to burn it or bury it. The other problem is firewood – there's none left up by the lake, so people have burned the floors of the shelters and are now destroying live trees. Bring a stove and fuel for cooking, and enough clothing to keep warm.

The Northern Route This is the most popular route for visitors, ascending via Batu Koq and Senaru and returning the same way. It takes about three days (the walking times given are pretty slow).

Day 1 Depart from Batu Koq at about 8 am for Senaru (altitude 600 metres). From there it's about 1½ hours to the first post, Pos I (920 metres), then another two hours to Pos II (1850 metres), where there is a hut and a water supply (sterilise the water). A further two hours brings you to the base camp at Pos III (2100 metres), where there is also water. The climb is relatively easy going through dappled forest, the quiet broken only by the occasional bird, animal, bell or woodchopper. At base camp, pitch the tent, collect wood and water and, if you have enough energy left, climb up to the clearing and watch the sunset. The ground is rock hard at base camp, and it's very cold.

Day 2 Set off very early, to arrive at the crater rim for sunrise. It takes about two hours to reach Pelawangan I, on the rim of the volcano, at an altitude of 2600 metres. Rinjani is covered in dense forest up to 2000 metres, but at around this height the vegetation changes from thick stands of mahogany and teak trees

to the odd stand of pine. As you get closer to the rim, the pines become sparser and the soil becomes rubbly and barren. Monkeys, wild pigs, deer and the occasional snake inhabit the forest. Once you get above the forest and up to the clearing, the going is hot, as there's not much shade – the land here is harsh and inhospitable – but you have superb views across to Bali and Sumbawa.

From the rim of the crater, it takes up to six hours to get down to Segara Anak and around to the hot springs, though some people will say it takes as little as two. The descent from the rim into the crater is quite dangerous – for most of the way the path down to the lake clings to the side of the cliffs and is narrow and meandering. Watch out for rubble as in certain spots it's very hard to keep your footing. Close to the lake, a thick forest sweeps down to the shore. There are several places to camp along this part of the lake, but if you head for the hot springs, there are many more alternatives. The track along the lake is also narrow and very slippery – be careful, and take it slowly. There are several species of small water birds on the lake, and the lake has been stocked with fish over the last few years.

After setting up camp at the lake, it's time to soak your weary body in the springs and recuperate. It's not as cold here as it is at base camp, but it's damp and misty from the steaming springs.

Day 3 Start early to do the hard climb back to the crater rim before it gets too hot. Then it's all downhill to Senaru. It's a full day's walk, between eight and 10 hours, arriving back in Batu Koq in the afternoon. The last bemo down the mountain from Senaru leaves at 4 pm.

The Eastern Route You can climb to the crater of Rinjani directly from Sembalun Lawang, but come prepared with sleeping bag, tent, food and other supplies. You can hire a guide in Sembalun Lawang – and you'll need one to get through the maze of trails as you climb west from the village. It will take about six hours to get to the village of Pade Belong, and another four hours to get to Pelawangan II, on the crater rim, at 2400 metres. Near here there's a crude shelter and a trail junction, with one track climbing southwards to the summit of Rinjani and the other heading west, to much more comfortable camp sites near the hot springs or the lake, about four hours away.

Going the other way, you can get from the crater rim down to Sembalun Lawang in about seven hours. It's quite possible to

Either route will involve at least one night's camping in the jungle, and you may not see any views at all until you get above the tree line. Again, a guide is essential.

Gunung Baru, the 'new' cone in the middle of Segara Anak, may look tempting, but it's a very dangerous climb. The track around the lake to the base of the Baroe is narrow, and people have drowned after slipping off the track. The climb itself is over a very loose surface – if you start sliding or falling, there is nothing to stop you and nothing to hang on to.

To the Very Top The path to the summit branches off the Sembalun Lawang track near Pelawangan II. From the shelter there, allow four hours to reach the summit. Start early in the morning, because you have to get to the top within an hour or so of sunrise if you want to see more than mist and cloud.

The first two days were pretty much as described, but on the third day we warmed up in the springs before making a three-hour climb to a shelter by the path just before the junction with the summit route. This shelter is just a hollow scooped out of the ground and lined with dry grass. A few old sheets of iron serve as a roof. It fits three people, or maybe an intimate four.

The next morning we watched the sun rise over Sumbawa from the junction of the paths, before starting the final ascent. The view from the rim is great, but it's nothing compared with the view from the very top! From the top, you look down into the crater, which fills up with 'cotton wool' cloud streaming through the gap in the crater wall at the hot springs. In the distance, you look over Bali in one direction and Sumbawa in the other.

It's a difficult three-hour climb from the shelter; the air gets thinner and the terrain is horrible to walk on. It's powdery to start with, then you find loose stones on a steep slope (offering little support for your weight). It's a case of climbing one step up, then sliding two-thirds of a step back down, and the peak always looks closer than it is! Climbing without strong-toed shoes or boots would be masochistic.

Richard Tucker, England

about seven hours. It's quite possible to ascend by the northern route and descend by the eastern route, or vice versa, but you'll have to work out how to get yourself and, particularly, your guide back to your starting point.

A Night Climb If you travel light and climb fast, you can reach the crater rim from Senaru in about six hours or even less – it's an 800-metre altitude gain in 10 km, approximately. With a torch and some moonlight, and/or a guide, set off at midnight and you'll be there for sunrise. Coming back takes about four hours, so you'll be down in time for lunch. Take lots of snack food and a litre of water.

Other Routes on Rinjani You can climb up to the crater from Torean, a small village just south-east of Bayan. The trail follows Sungai Kokok Putih, the stream that flows from Lake Segara and the hot springs, but it's hard to find; you'll need a guide.

You can also climb the south side of Rinjani, from either Sesaot or Tetebatu.

THE GILI ISLANDS

Off the north-west coast of Lombok are three small, coral-fringed islands: Gili Air, Gili Meno and Gili Trawangan. Each has superb, white sandy beaches, clear water, coral reefs, brilliantly coloured fish and excellent

NUSA TENGGARA

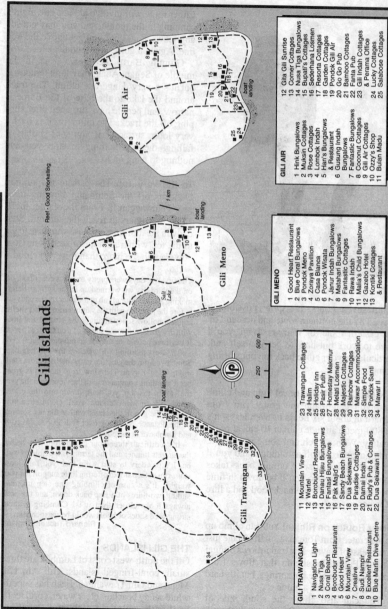

Gili Islands

Reef – Good Snorkelling

Salt Lake

Gili Meno

Gili Air

Gili Trawangan

boat landing

boat landing

boat landing

0   250   500 m

1 km

GILI TRAWANGAN
1 Navigation Light
2 Nusa Tiga
3 Coral Beach
4 Borobudur Restaurant
5 Good Heart
6 Mountain View
7 Sudi Nampir
8 Creative
9 Excellent Restaurant
10 Blue Marlin Dive Centre
11 Mountain View
12 Wartel
13 Borobudur Restaurant
14 Danau Hijau Bungalows
15 Fantasi Bungalows
16 Pak Majid's
17 Sandy Beach Bungalows
18 Dua Sekawan I
19 Paradise Cottages
20 Dal Indah
21 Rudy's Pub & Cottages
22 Dua Sekawan II
23 Trawangan Cottages
24 Halim
25 Holiday Inn
26 Pasir Putih
27 Homestay Makmur
28 Melati Losmen
29 Majestic Cottages
30 Rainbow Cottages
31 Mawar Accommodation
32 Simple Food
33 Pondok Santi
34 Mawar II

GILI MENO
1 Good Heart Restaurant
2 Blue Coral Bungalows
3 Pondok Meno
4 Zoraya Pavillion
5 Casa Blanca
6 Pondok Wisata
7 Janur Indah Bungalows
8 Matahari Bungalows
9 Fantastic Cottages
10 Rawa Indah
11 Maia's Child Bungalows
12 Gazebo Hotel
13 Kontiki Cottages
   & Restaurant

GILI AIR
1 Hink Bungalows
2 Muksin Cottages
3 Rose Cottages
4 Lombok Indah
5 Han's Bungalows
   & Restaurant
6 Ijusung Indah
   Bungalows
7 Fantastic Bungalows
8 Coconut Cottages
9 Gili Air Cottages
10 Ozzy's Shop
11 Bulan Madu
12 Gita Gili Sunrise
13 Corner Cottages
14 Nusa Tiga Bungalows
15 Bupati's Cottages
16 Sederhana Losmen
17 Resorta Cottages
18 Garden Cottages
19 Pondok Gili Air
20 Go Go Pub
21 Bamboo Cottages
22 Fanta Pub
23 Gili Indah Cottages
   & Perama Office
24 Lucky Cottages
25 Salaloose Cottages

snorkelling. Although known to travellers as the 'Gili Islands', *gili* actually means 'island', so this is not a local name. There are lots of other gilis around the coast of Lombok!

A few years ago, people were granted leases to establish coconut plantations on the islands, and they diversified into fishing, raising livestock, and growing corn, tapioca and peanuts. As tourists started to visit Lombok, many people on the Gilis found that the most profitable activity was 'picking white coconuts' – a local expression for providing services to tourists. The islands have become enormously popular with visitors, especially young Europeans, who come for the very simple pleasures of sun, snorkelling and socialising. It's cheap, and the absence of cars, motorbikes and hawkers adds greatly to the pleasure of staying here.

The very popularity of the Gilis may be a problem, as numbers sometimes exceed the available rooms and put pressure on the island environments, especially the supply of fresh water and the capacity of septic systems to cope with waste. The locals, aware of environmental issues, are trying to retain the unspoilt quality of the islands while improving the facilities, but there is always the temptation to put up just one more bungalow.

Other problems in this paradise include occasional outbreaks of illness: bouts of food poisoning, typhoid and cholera have been reported, and the islands are definitely in a malaria risk area. In 1993, 15 or 20 bungalows were destroyed in a fire, apparently caused by a candle left burning in a bungalow – be careful with candles and mosquito coils.

Avoiding Offence

The islanders are Muslims, and visitors should respect their sensibilities. In particular, topless (for women) or nude sunbathing is offensive to them, although they won't say so directly. Away from the beach, it is polite for both men and women to cover their shoulders and knees.

Information

You can change money and make international phone calls at any of the islands. Most places have electricity, sometimes from their own generators, but supply is sometimes erratic, and usually stops at about 10 pm. There are small shops, with a bare minimum of supplies, second-hand books and some handcrafts, clothing and souvenirs.

Activities

A few places rent paddle boards (called canoes), some of which even have a window so you can see the coral. Windsurfers are available on Trawangan and Meno, and you can rent a boat to go fishing.

Diving The coral round the islands is good for snorkelling, but much has been damaged by fish bombing. Ask locally to find the best spots, most of which you can reach from the shore. For scuba divers, the visibility is fair to good (best in the dry season), and there is some very good coral reef accessible by boat. Marine life includes turtles, rays, sharks (harmless) and a giant clam. There are a number of scuba-diving operations, some more reliable than others. Albatross is the longest-established outfit, and can take out certified divers. Blue Marlin, the only one with an instructor qualified to PADI standards, can offer a full range of diving courses, from beginners to advanced level. A complete PADI open-water course costs about US$290.

Accommodation & Food

Most places to stay come out of a standard mould – you get a plain little bungalow on stilts, with a small verandah out the front and a concrete bathroom block out the back. (It's very easy to see which bungalows have their own bathroom.) Inside, there will be one or two beds, with mosquito nets.

Accommodation prices are pretty well fixed, though there is some cost cutting in the low season. Some places charge more because they're a bit better. Low-season

Gili Islands Development

Big business interests are trying to cash in on the popularity of the Gili Islands. There is a proposal to build a luxury resort on the mainland at Sira, and golf courses on Gili Air and Gili Trawangan. This would effectively destroy the simple charm that makes the islands so attractive to current visitors, and would have substantial environmental implications, such as a pipeline from the mainland, over the coral reefs, to supply fresh water for the fairways. The proposal is not supported by many of the local people who lease the land on which they've built tourist bungalows and restaurants.

In 1992 a number of bungalows on Trawangan were closed down and/or relocated by the government authorities; it's not clear whether this was to make way for a grandiose development project, or because the bungalows contravened the lease conditions, or because they did not meet environmental and health standards. The owners were told to vacate the leased land, and were offered new sites and compensation (the adequacy of the compensation is another question). Some of the owners did not move, and after repeated requests, the authorities closed down their bungalows by the simple but effective means of cutting the legs off with chainsaws.

Most of the businesses have now been re-established at the south end of Gili Trawangan, and others are to be set up at the north end, but not right on the beach – the plan seems to be to build the golf course in a 'U' shape around them. The changes to date have left the northern end of the beach looking bare and desolate, and the southern end crowded with shoulder-to-shoulder bungalows and restaurants. A few bungalows on the south-west side of Gili Air are also to be removed to make way for the golf course. ■

prices are about 9000/15,000 rp for singles/doubles with bed and breakfast (B&B) only, 15,000/22,000 rp with three meals. Add 2000/5000 rp in the high season. Most places provide only B&B these days; you can order dinner as an extra, or eat somewhere else. Rooms with shared bathroom are cheaper, but becoming rare.

Getting There & Away

From Ampenan or the airport, you can get to one of the islands and be horizontal on the beach within a couple of hours. Start with a short bemo ride north to Rembiga (about 200 rp), then a scenic bus trip to Pemenang (600 rp). Alternatively, get a bemo from Sweta direct to Pemenang (about 700 rp). From there, it's a km or so off the main road to the harbour at Bangsal (200 rp by cidomo).

There's a small office at Bangsal Harbour which charges the official fares out to the islands – 900 rp to Gili Air, 1000 rp to Gili Meno and 1200 rp to Gili Trawangan. It's a matter of sitting and waiting until there's a full boat load (about 20 people). If you have almost that number waiting, the boat will leave if you can pay the extra fares between you. As soon as you do this, you'll be amazed at how many local people appear from nowhere to fill the boat. Try to get to Bangsal by 10 am. It's not an unpleasant place to hang around while you're waiting for a boat, and the shaded warungs, such as the Para-hiangan Coffee House, have good food and coffee. You can charter a whole boat to any of the islands, or any combination, but it's expensive – 60,000 rp to visit all three islands.

Perama shuttle buses go from Mataram or Senggigi to Bangsal (5000 rp) and the Gili Islands (about 10,000 rp, including the boat). Lombok Independent has a slightly cheaper service at around 6500 rp from Senggigi.

Getting Around

There is now a shuttle service between the islands, so you can stay on one and have a look, or a snorkel, around the others. The boat fares for 'island hopping' are 4000 rp between Gili Air and Gili Trawangan, 3000 rp between Gili Meno and either of the other two islands. There are two runs a day, one between 9 and 10 am and the other between 3 and 4 pm.

On the islands themselves, cidomos trot around the tracks (500 rp is the usual charge). If you're in a hurry (almost inconceivable on the Gilis), you can rent a bicycle, but the main transport is walking.

Gili Air

Gili Air is the closest island to the mainland. It's also the smallest, but has the largest population (about 600). There are beaches around most of the island, and a small village at the southern end. Homes and small farms are dotted amongst the palm trees, along with a few losmen and a couple of 'pubs'. Because the buildings are so scattered, the island has a pleasant, rural character and is delightful to wander around. There are plenty of other people to meet, but if you stay in one of the more isolated places, socialising is optional. Gili Indah Cottages is where you'll find the Perama office, telephone office and moneychanger. You can also change money at Gita Gili Sunrise, which may give a better rate.

Places to Stay & Eat Most of the accommodation is scattered round the southern end of the island, at the harbour, though there are losmen near the east, north and west coasts. Most of the places, about 15 of them, charge the standard rates (9000/15,000 rp with breakfast), and are so similar that it wouldn't be fair to mention any in particular. Pick one that appeals to you in a location you like, or one that's been recommended by other travellers.

Coconut Cottages is very nice, with great food, and is only slightly more expensive than average. *Gili Indah* (☎ 36341) is the biggest place on Gili Air. Rates start at US$7 /10, up to US$20/30 for very nice, spacious, pavilion-style rooms. Up north, at the other end of the island, *Han's Bungalows* are above average in price (15,000/20,000 rp), though they do have a beautiful outlook and a forthcoming swimming pool. (These bungalows are popular with German visitors, though the owner, Han, is actually a local.) *Bulan Madu* has a few very attractive, comfortable rooms, but they're also much pricier, at 50,000/60,000 rp.

Gili Meno

Gili Meno, the middle island, has the smallest population (about 300). It is also the quietest of the islands, with the fewest tourists. There's a salt lake in the middle of the island which produces salt in the dry season and mosquitoes in the wet season. The mozzies are probably no worse than in other places at that time of year, but the usual precautions are called for – mosquito net, insect repellent, long sleeves and long pants around dusk. You can change money here, and make phone calls at the Gazebo Hotel.

Places to Stay & Eat The accommodation here is mostly on the east beach, with a few places which are pretty up-market by Gili standards. The *Zoraya Pavillion* (☎ 33801) has a variety of rooms, from 15,500 to 40,000 rp a double, with various water sports and a tennis court. The *Gazebo Hotel* (☎ 35795) has tastefully decorated Bali-style bungalows with private bathrooms, air-con and electricity (if it's working). It costs about US$45 a double for B&B. Anyone can eat in the fancy balcony restaurant. *Casa Blanca* seems overpriced at US$25/30, even with its tiny swimming pool. *Kontiki* (☎ 32824) has both standard-price and more expensive rooms – look at them first to make sure they're worth the extra rupiah. The other half-dozen places have pretty much standard Gili Islands bungalows (perhaps a little more spacious than on the other two islands) and charge standard prices.

Gili Trawangan

The largest island, with a local population of about 400, Trawangan also has the most visitors, the most facilities and a reputation as the 'party island' of the group. The accommodation and restaurant/bars are all along the south and south-east coast beaches, where some of them were forced to shift. It's a compact layout, perhaps a little too compact, though there are a couple of places away from the others. Some places may be rebuilt on the north-east of the island, but not right on the beach. There's a wartel in the middle of the beach strip.

Lots of places on Gili Trawangan will change money, but you'll get a better rate on the mainland. The Blue Marlin Dive Centre will give a cash advance on your credit card. You can rent windsurfers from them, too.

A hill at the south of the island has traces of two Japanese WW II gun emplacements. At sunset, it's a good place to enjoy the view across the straits to Bali's Gunung Agung. The sunrise over Gunung Rinjani is also impressive; one islander described Trawangan's three main attractions as 'sunrise, sunset and sunburn'!

Places to Stay & Eat The accommodation and prices here are even more standardised than on the other islands. Typical basic bungalows cost 10,000/15,000/20,000 rp for singles/doubles/triples, with breakfast and private mandi. *Pondok Santi* is a bit more expensive, but probably worth the extra. Pick a place you like the look of (some have prettier gardens), or one recommended by a recent visitor. Otherwise, go with one of the friendly people who meet the boats.

Most of the places to stay also serve food, but there are a few convivial restaurants which are more like bars in the evening. There's usually music and dancing in at least one of them. *Pasih Putih* and *Halim* are reputed to have the best food.

Sumbawa Island

Between Lombok and Flores and separated from them by narrow straits is the rugged land mass of Sumbawa. Larger than Bali and Lombok combined, Sumbawa is a sprawling island of twisted and jutting peninsulas, with a coast fringed by precipitous hills and angular bights, and a mountain line of weathered volcanic stumps stretching along its length.

Sumbawa is the most predominantly Muslim island anywhere east of Java or south of Sulawesi – Islam seems to have overshadowed Sumbawa's indigenous traditions, and Christian missionaries never even bothered to try here. The people, particularly in the western half, are curious about foreigners, and friendly – they're more reserved in the east, and you should always dress respectfully if you're visiting mosques or government offices.

Sumbawa is a scenic island, with plenty of scope for exploring off the beaten track. The mountain and coastal regions in the south – not converted to Islam until around the turn of the century – and the Tambora peninsula, in the north, are rarely visited by travellers. If you're in the right place at the right time (on holidays and festivals), you might see traditional Sumbawan fighting, a sort of bare-fisted boxing called *berempah*. Horse and water-buffalo races are held before the rice is planted.

Towards the east end of the island, the narrow Teluk Bima (Bima Bay) cuts deep into the north coast, forming one of Indonesia's best natural harbours. It's surrounded by fertile lowlands which reach west into the rich interior Dompu plains.

History

For centuries Sumbawa has been divided between two linguistically – and to some extent ethnically – distinct peoples; the Sumbawanese speakers, who probably reached the west of the island from Lombok, and the Bimanese speakers, who independently occupied the east and Tambora peninsula. The squatter, darker-skinned Bimanese are more closely related to the people of Flores, while the western Sumbawans are closer to the Sasaks of Lombok. Both their languages have considerable variation in dialect, but the spread of Bahasa Indonesia has made communication easier in the last couple of decades.

Sumbawa, with its rich timber resources in the west, was probably an early trading call for Javanese merchants on the way to or from the Spice Islands in Maluku. Bima and

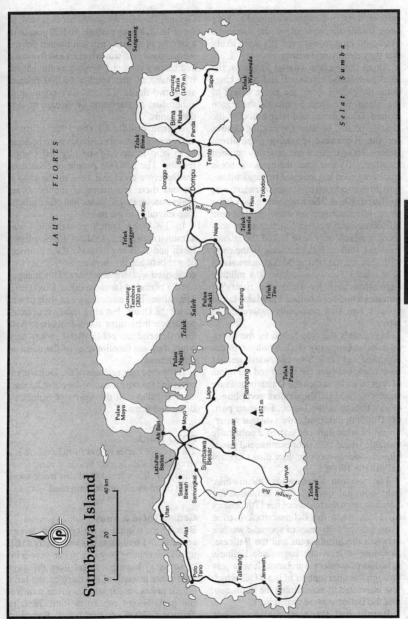

Sumbawa Island

0   20   40 km

LAUT FLORES

Selat Sumba

Pulau Sangeang

Gunung Daria (1479 m)

Sape

Teluk Wanorada

Bima
Raba

Panda

Teluk Bima

Tente

Sila

Dompu

Donggo

Kilo

Teluk Sangger

Tolodoro

Huu

Teluk Sumla

Napa

Sungai Nae

Gunung Tambora (2820 m)

Teluk Saleh

Pulau Rakit

Empang

Teluk Tiro

Pulau Ngali

Plampang

1452 m

Teluk Panas

Pulau Moyo

Lape

Lenangguar

Alk Ban

Moyo

Labuhan Badas

Sesat Bawah

Semongkat

Sumbawa Besar

Lunyuk

Teluk Lampui

Sungai Bak

Utan

Alas

Poto Tano

Taliwang

Jereweh

Maluk

NUSA TENGGARA

parts of western Sumbawa are said to have been under the control of the Javanese Majapahit empire, although it's more likely that they simply sent tribute.

Along the western coastal lowlands, the local population expanded, and petty kingdoms developed along the entire length of the island. In eastern Sumbawa, the region around Teluk Bima, and later probably the Dompu plains, became the leading centres for the Bimanese-speaking population. Before 1600 these were probably animist kingdoms. By that time, the domestic horse was being used and irrigated rice agriculture, possibly introduced by Javanese traders, was well established. There appears to have been some intermarriage between the Balinese aristocracy and western Sumbawanese aristocracy which may have linked the islands from the 15th or 16th centuries. In the early 17th century, the Islamic Makassarese states of southern Sulawesi undertook a military expansion, and by 1625, the rulers of Sumbawa had been reduced to Makassarese vassals and had nominally converted to Islam.

Makassar's rise was halted by the Dutch East India Company (VOC), whose forces occupied it in 1669. Soon afterwards treaties were made between the Dutch and the rulers of Sumbawa by which the Dutch hegemony was recognised and these rulers were obliged to pay tribute to the Dutch. For their part, the Dutch maintained only a distant supervision of what they considered a politically unstable island with poor commercial possibilities, taking more or less direct control only in the 1900s.

The western Sumbawans, meanwhile, held nominal control over neighbouring Lombok from the middle of the 17th century till 1750, when the Balinese took it over. Then followed 30 years of sporadic warfare between the Sumbawans and the Balinese, including at least one large-scale Balinese invasion of western Sumbawa. It was only through the intervention of the VOC, which was interested in maintaining the status quo, that the Balinese were turned back.

Barely had the wars finished when Gunung Tambora on Sumbawa exploded, in April 1815, killing perhaps 10,000 people in a shower of choking ash and molten debris. Agricultural land was wrecked and livestock and crops wiped out throughout the island. It's estimated that another 66,000 people, about two-thirds of Sumbawa's population, either died of starvation or disease or fled their lands.

By the middle of the 19th century, immigrants from other islands were brought in to help repopulate the blighted coastal regions. The 850,000 people of Sumbawa are therefore a diverse lot – in the coastal regions there are traces of the Javanese, Makassarese, Bugis, Sasak and other groups who migrated to the island.

In 1908 the Dutch government sent administrators and soldiers to Sumbawa Besar and Taliwang to head off the prospect of war between the three separate states that comprised western Sumbawa. This inaugurated a period of far more direct Dutch rule. The sultans kept a fair degree of their power under the Dutch, but after Indonesian independence their titles were abolished; now their descendants hold official power only when they are functionaries of the national government.

Little evidence remains of the Dutch presence, and the only traces of the old sultanates are the palaces in the towns of Sumbawa Besar and Bima.

POTO TANO

The port for ferries to and from Lombok is a straggle of stilt houses beside a mangrove-lined bay. It's a few km of dirt track away from Sumbawa's single main road.

Getting There & Away

Bus There's quite a melee when ferries arrive from Lombok as bus jockeys try to fill up all the waiting buses. You can save a bit of stress by buying a ticket from the guys who come around selling them on the ferry – their prices are the same as in the scrum at the port. Buses run from Poto Tano to Taliwang (1000 rp; one hour), Sumbawa

Besar (2000 rp; two hours) and Bima (8500 rp; nine hours).

Boat Ferries run hourly from Poto Tano to Lombok between 5.30 am and 5.30 pm. The crossing takes about 1½ hours and costs 2000 rp. You can buy tickets at Poto Tano, or get a combined bus and ferry ticket from Bima or Sumbawa Besar all the way to Lombok, Bali or even Java. From Lombok, the fare is the same, with departures almost hourly between 7 am and 6 pm.

TALIWANG
During the 19th century, Taliwang was one of the 'vassal states' of the kingdom of Sumbawa based in Sumbawa Besar. Today, it's a sleepy, oversized village, with friendly people and bemo drivers who haven't yet discovered 'tourist price'. It lies close to the west coast of Sumbawa, 30 km south of Poto Tano along a narrow road winding through the hills. **Danau (lake) Taliwang**, close to the Poto Tano road near Taliwang, is quite a picture when covered in water lilies.

Poto Batu, six km from Taliwang, is a local sea resort with caves and a decent beach. Trucks and bemos from Taliwang cost 250 rp. **Labuhanbalat**, a Bugis stilt fishing community of just eight houses, is seven km from Taliwang – take a truck or bemo there.

Places to Stay & Eat
Taliwang's market is next to the bus station. Behind the market and directly opposite the mosque, the friendly but spartan *Losmen Azhar* has rooms for 5000 rp per person. *Losmen Taliwang* on Jalan Jenderal Surdiman is the newest place in town, with a 1st-floor porch overlooking the hills, and a friendly manager who speaks good English. Double rooms are 10,000 rp with shared mandi, 15,000 rp with shower. The same family run the *Rumah Makan Taliwang Indah* next door, with a long menu of excellent, cheap food. On the same street, opposite the cinema, *Losmen Tubalong* has rooms (with attached mandi) for 7500/10,000 rp. There's a small restaurant in the front of the losmen. *Rumah Makan Anda* in the bus

station has only three dishes on the menu, but it does have cold drinks.

Getting There & Away
Direct buses from the ferry at Poto Tano to Taliwang cost 1000 rp. There are some direct buses from Taliwang to Sumbawa Besar (2500 rp; three hours). You can buy a combined bus and ferry ticket from Taliwang to Mataram, Lombok (6000 rp; five hours). Several buses leave Taliwang for Poto Tano and Lombok between 6 and 9 am.

South of Taliwang
From Taliwang, bemos and trucks run south over a good, paved road to **Jereweh** (500 rp). Further south along a rough road are deserted surf beaches at **Maluk** and **Sekongkang**. Maluk has bungalow accommodation (5000 rp per person); at Sekongkang, see the kepala desa. A truck leaves Taliwang for Maluk (2000 rp; 1½ hours) at 8 am every day.

ALAS
'Alas' (Javanese for 'forest') may have received its name from Javanese timber traders. Most buses between Sumbawa Besar and Poto Tano stop here. *Losmen Anda* on Jalan Pahlawan has rooms with small patios around a garden (4000 rp per person). A couple of rumah makan around the market/bus station serve decent food.

Labuhan Alas
This little port just off the Sumbawa Besar road, about three km east of Alas, was until recent years the terminal for ferries from Lombok. Set in a pretty bay, it's now not much more than a dock and a few houses. A Sulawesi fishing village clusters offshore on stilts, television antennae jutting up from its roofs. Dokars (250 rp) run between Labuhan Alas and Alas.

Getting There & Away
Buses go to Sumbawa Besar (1500 rp; 1½ hours), to Poto Tano (1500 rp; one hour) for the ferries and to Taliwang (2000 rp; two hours).

SUMBAWA BESAR

At one time the name 'Sumbawa' only applied to the western half of the island – the region over which the sultan of the state of Sumbawa held sway; the eastern half of the island was known as Bima. Almost all that remains of the old western sultanate is the wooden palace in Sumbawa Besar – the showpiece of the town.

Sumbawa Besar is the chief town of the western half of the island – a laid-back, friendly place where dokars still outnumber bemos and Muslims flood out of the mosques after midday prayer. There are some lovely tree-lined boulevards around the new palace, but the town has no remarkable attractions except for the old palace. A trip out to **Pulau Moyo** (Moyo Island) or to nearby villages might be rewarding.

If you arrive at the central bus station, you'll probably meet Abdul Muis, who speaks very good English and is helpful with information. However, he also works as a guide, so if shows you around, establish whether or not you're paying for his time.

Information

Tourist Office The PHPA (national parks) people (☎ 21358) are in the Direktorat Jenderal Kehutanan office at Jalan Garuda 12. They can give you information about Pulau Moyo, but will probably refer you to one of the tour companies for arrangements. Still, this is a good place to start if you want to go there. The office is open until 2 pm Monday to Thursday, until 11 am on Friday and until noon on Saturday.

Money The Bank Negara Indonesia is at Jalan Kartini 10. It's open Monday to Friday from 7.30 am to 2.30 pm, and until noon on Saturday.

Post & Telecommunications For poste restante, go to the GPO, which is about 1½ km from the Hotel Tambora on Jalan Kebayan. For stamps, there's a sub-post office near the town centre, on Jalan Yos Sudarso. Both are open Monday to Thursday from 8 am to 2 pm, on Friday until 11 am and on Saturday until 12.30 pm. The new, state-of-the-art Telkom office is on Jalan Setiabudi, and is open 24 hours.

Dalam Loka (Sultan's Palace)

Back in the early 1960s, Helen and Frank Schreider passed through Sumbawa Besar in their amphibious jeep, and later described the remnants of this palace in their book *The Drums of Tonkin*:

Sumbawa Besar...had a sultan. A small man with tortoise-shell glasses and a quiet, friendly dignity...his old palace, now deserted except for a few distant relatives, was a long barn-like structure of unpainted wood that seemed on the point of collapsing. Beneath the ramshackle entrance, a rusted cannon from the days of the Dutch East India Company lay half-buried in the ground...Mothers and fathers and naked little children made the palace shake as they followed us up the ramp into a great empty room that was once the audience chamber...Only when the few remaining court costumes, the faded silver brocade kains, the gold-handled krises and the long gold fingernails that were a sign of royalty's exemption from labour were modelled for us did we have any idea of the extravagance of this past era. By government decree, the sultan's are no longer in power.

The palace was restored in the early 1980s, but only a few of the original pillars and carved beams remain. Boys will show you around and tell you (in Indonesian) that each room was used for, though there's little in them except a couple of old palanquins. Then they'll ask you for a donation towards the cost of turning the place into a museum – but don't count on this happening in the near future.

New Palace

The imposing building with the bell tower at its gate on Jalan Merdeka is the headquarters of the *bupati* (head government official) of West Sumbawa. It's built in imitation of the style of the old sultan's palace – a reminder that the national government now holds the power that was once the sultan's.

Pura Agung Girinatha

This Balinese Hindu temple is on Jalan Yos Sudarso, near the corner of Jalan Setiabudi.

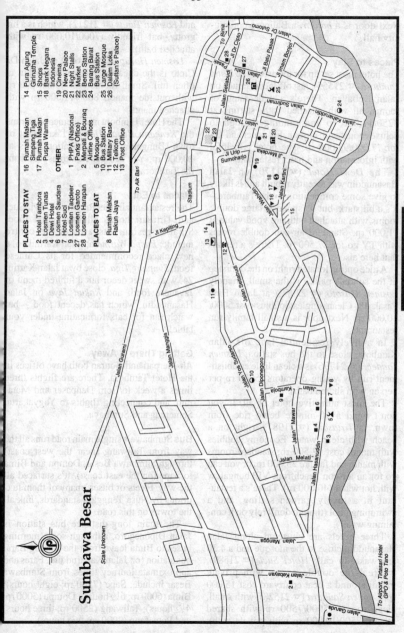

PLACES TO STAY
2 Hotel Tambora
3 Losmen Tunas
4 Dewi Hotel
6 Losmen Saudara
7 Hotel Suci
9 Losmen Taqdeer
27 Losmen Garoto
28 Losmen Harapan

PLACES TO EAT
8 Rumah Makan
  Rakun Jaya

16 Rumah Makan
   Simpang Tiga
17 Rumah Makan
   Puspa Warma

OTHER
1 PHPA (National
  Parks Office)
3 Merpati & Bouraq
  Airline Offices
5 Mosque
10 Bus Station
11 Military Base
12 Telkom
13 Post Office

14 Pura Agung
   Girinatha Temple
15 Shops
18 Bank Negara
   Indonesia
19 Cinema
20 New Palace
21 Night Stalls
22 Market
23 Bemo Station
24 Baera Barat
   Bus Station
25 Large Mosque
26 Dalam Loka
   (Sultan's Palace)

Sumbawa Besar

Scale Unknown

To Bima

To Aik Bari

To Airport, Tirtasari Hotel
GPO & Poto Tano

NUSA TENGGARA

Next door is a *banjar*, a Balinese community hall.

Places to Stay

The hotel most set up for tourists is the *Hotel Tambora* (☎ 21555), just off Jalan Garuda on Jalan Kebayan. There's a wide range of rooms, all with attached bath, starting at 8250/11,000 rp and running through to deluxe rooms with air-con, hot water and TV for 77,000/93,000 rp. The hotel is helpful with information and has a restaurant.

The *Dewi Hotel* (☎ 21170) on Jalan Hasanuddin was recently rebuilt and is likely to give some competition to the Tambora – it's a bit stark, but its spotless, large double rooms with attached bath are good value at 11,000 rp. Standard air-con double rooms with TV go for 27,500 rp. There's a restaurant here also.

A nice option located right on the doorstep of the sultan's palace is the small, friendly *Losmen Garoto* (☎ 22062) at Jalan Batu Pasak 48. Clean singles/doubles cost 5000/10,000 rp. Next door is a small family-run restaurant.

In a lively residential lane off Jalan Kamboja, close to the bus station, *Losmen Taqdeer* (☎ 21796) is a clean little establishment run by young operators (5000 rp per person with shared bath).

The most attractive hotel of all, if you don't mind a 10-minute bemo ride from town, is *Tirtasari* (☎ 21987), right on a beach with clean water. Economy doubles with mandi cost 12,500 rp; standard rooms with mandi and fan are 25,000 rp; or you can go for an air-con beachfront VIP bungalow with hot water (40,000 rp). There's a restaurant in a lovely garden setting, and a swimming pool (though don't rely on it containing water).

Three hotels are clustered along Jalan Hasanuddin close to the mosque and a 4.30 am wake-up call: *Hotel Suci* (☎ 21589), where large double rooms with private mandi around a neat courtyard cost 15,000 rp; *Losmen Saudara* (☎ 21528), with small, clean rooms (5000/7500 rp with shared mandi, 7500/10,000 rp with private bath);

and *Losmen Tunas* (☎ 21212), which is a bit grotty, but friendly (7000/10,000 rp with attached bath).

Losmen Harapan (☎ 21629) on Jalan Dr Cipto is the cheapest place in town but is often full. Small rooms cost 4500/6000 rp with outside mandi, 8000/11,000 rp with attached mandi.

The Hotel Tambora management also runs the *Kencana Beach Hotel*, 11 km west of town. Bungalow accommodation starts at 20,000 rp. You can get free transport from the Tambora.

Places to Eat

The restaurants in the Tambora, Dewi, Suci and Tirtasari hotels all have good food. Smaller restaurants around the centre include: *Puspa Warma* at Jalan Kartini 16, a new place recommended for its Chinese food; *Simpang Tiga*, close by at Jalan Kartini 24, with sweet decor but a limited menu of Javanese food; and *Rakun Jaya* on Jalan Hasanuddin, which has decent food – but watch out for cats fornicating under your table!

Getting There & Away

Air Merpati and Bouraq both have offices in the Hotel Tambora. There are flights three times a week to/from Denpasar and Mataram, and connecting flights to Yogyakarta, Semerang and Surabaya.

Bus Sumbawa's single main road runs all the way from Taliwang (near the west coast) through Sumbawa Besar, Dompu and Bima to Sape (on the east coast). It's surfaced all the way. Fleets of buses, many of them luxurious by Nusa Tenggara standards, link all the towns on this road.

The main long-distance bus station is Jalan Diponegoro, although some morning buses to Bima leave from the Barang Barat bus station (on Jalan Kaharuddin). Fares and approximate journey times from Sumbawa Besar include: Sape (7500 rp; eight hours); Bima (6000 rp; 6½ hours); Dompu (5000 rp; 4½ hours); Taliwang (2500 rp; three hours) and Poto Tano (2000 rp; two hours).

Buses for Poto Tano leave every hour until late afternoon; ferry departures from there to Lombok are hourly from 5.30 am until 5.30 pm. Morning buses leave for Bima between 7 and 10 am, but after that you have to hope for a seat on a bus coming through from the ferries at Poto Tano.

You can buy combined bus and ferry tickets from Sumbawa Besar through to Lombok (10,000 rp) or Bali. Get tickets from Toko Titian Mas at Jalan Kartini 89; most hotels can also tell you of similar services.

Boat Labuhan Sumbawa, about three km west of town on the Poto Tano road, is just a small fishing harbour. Labuhan Balas, seven km further along the road, is the port of Sumbawa Besar – you *might* be able to pick up a coastal or interisland craft there. A public bemo from town costs 300 rp, but this is not a very well-trodden route.

Getting Around
Sumbawa Besar is small; you can easily walk around most of it, except maybe to the main post office.

To/From the Airport It's about 300 metres from the airport to the Hotel Tambora, and you can easily walk – turn to your right as you exit the airport terminal and cross the bridge. Alternatively, take a bemo (250 rp).

Bemo The streets here, apart from the bemo speedway along Jalan Hasanuddin, are relatively stress free. Bemos and dokars cost 250 rp for trips anywhere around town.

The local bemo station is on Jalan Setiabudi, in front of the market; dokars congregate along Jalan Urip Sumohardjo near where it meets Jalan Setiabudi. For trips to villages around Sumbawa Besar, there should be public bemos. Get to the station early in the morning, as sometimes there's only one bemo daily; after that you'll have to charter (prices are negotiable).

AROUND SUMBAWA BESAR
Pulau Moyo
Two-thirds of Pulau Moyo, an island off the coast just north of Sumbawa Besar, is a nature reserve. There are good coral reefs with lots of fish at the southern rim of the island (watch out for currents and sharks), and a number of villages in the north. Moyo rises to 648 metres, its centre composed mainly of savannah with stands of forest. The reserve is inhabited by wild domestic cattle, deer, wild pigs and several varieties of birds.

For travel to the island, start at the PHPA office in Sumbawa Besar, which has a good map of Moyo. They may be able to help you find a ride to Aik Bari on the coast, half an hour north of Sumbawa Besar. They may just refer you to tour operators who run one or two-day snorkelling and diving trips.

It's possible to get to Aik Bari by public bemo, but they run infrequently – there should be one at around 7 am, costing 2000 rp. Ask around the bemo station and the turn-off to Aik Bari, behind the market on the north side. Otherwise, you'll have to charter a bemo (around 7500 rp, if you bargain hard).

From Aik Bari, you can hire a fishing boat for the three-km crossing to the south coast of the island. Again, you must bargain – 10,000 rp each way should do it, petrol included.

There are four PHPA guard posts on Moyo; one at the south end, the others in villages, where you can stay overnight (5000 rp per person). Take your own food and water. It's about an eight-hour walk from the south to the centre of the island, and about six hours across the middle from east to west.

If getting there independently sounds like too much trouble, several tour operators run trips from Sumbawa Besar; the Tirtasari and Suci hotels can also arrange trips. A day trip, including transport, lunch and snorkel gear, costs around 50,000 rp.

For those travelling on someone else's money, a new ultra-exclusive resort has been set up on the island, costing a cool $US500 per day.

Other Attractions
Look out for 'horse racing' – in reality, boys

on ponies, but still a big local event – around Sumbawa from August to October. Some of the best songket sarongs are made in the village of **Poto**, 12 km east of Sumbawa Besar (600 rp by bus or bemo) and two km from the small town of Moyo. At **Semongkat**, about 15 km up the road which leads south-west from Sumbawa Besar into the hills, there's an old Dutch swimming pool fed by a mountain river. A stretch of the coast near **Lunyuk**, about 60 km from Sumbawa Besar, is said to be a nesting ground for turtles. **Liang Petang** and **Liang Bukal** are caves near Batu Tering village, and locals say they're worth a visit. Take a torch. Batu Tering is about 30 km by bemo from Sumbawa Besar.

CENTRAL SUMBAWA

It's a beautiful ride from Sumbawa Besar to Bima. After Empang you start moving up into the hills through rolling green country, thickly forested, with occasional sprays of palm trees along the shoreline.

Gunung Tambora

Dominating the peninsula which juts north in central Sumbawa is the 2820-metre volcano, Gunung Tambora. It can be climbed from the western side; the huge crater contains a two-coloured lake, and there are views as far as Gunung Rinjani (on Lombok). The base for ascents is the small logging town of Cilacai, which is eight hours by truck from Dompu or an hour by speedboat from Sumbawa Besar. Not many people bother though, since the climb takes three days.

Tambora's peak was obliterated in the explosion of April 1815 (see Sumbawa History), but since then all has been quiet. The eruption wiped out the entire population of Tambora and Pekat (two small states at the base of the mountain), as well as devastating much of the rest of Sumbawa.

AROUND EASTERN SUMBAWA

This part of Sumbawa is little explored by travellers; there aren't many traditional areas left around eastern Sumba, but the coastline

to the south is quite beautiful, and developers are eyeing several sites along it.

Dompu

The seat of one of Sumbawa's former independent states, Dompu is now the third biggest town on the island. If you're travelling between Sumbawa Besar and Bima, you don't get to see it: buses detour via the lonely Ginte bus station (on a hill two km out of Dompu). From there, bemos run into town (250 rp). The town has a big, colourful market snaking around narrow back streets, but otherwise it's probably a stopover on the way to the south coast.

There are three hotels in town; the cheapest is *Wisma Kuta Baru*, at around 3500 rp per person. *Hotel Manuru Kupang* has singles/doubles for 5000/10,000 rp, while the more up-market *Hotel Samada* costs 10,000/15,000 rp. Around the market there are a couple of small rumah makan.

Buses run from Ginte bus station to Huu (1500 rp; one hour), Bima (1400 rp; two hours), Sape (2500 rp; 3½ hours) and Sumbawa Besar (5000 rp; 4½ hours). You can get a combined air-con bus/ferry ticket through to Mataram (15,000 rp; 21,000 rp with air-con).

Huu

Huu is best known as a stronghold of one of the most traditional cultures in the world – surf culture. Several surf camps have been set up along the beach, but lately an attempt has been made to woo the average garden-variety tourist to Huu's long stretch of palm-tree-lined, white-sand beach. However, if you're a male and not surfing, be prepared to have your masculinity questioned! The best waves are between June and August.

Places to Stay & Eat *Mona Lisa Bungalows* is one of the longest-established places, and its restaurant is draped with surfing paraphernalia and surfboard art. Well-appointed bungalows facing the beach cost 15,000/20,000 rp with private mandi, or there are comfortable economy rooms with outside mandi for 7500/12,500 rp.

Intan Lestari is the other original place; it has a rustic little restaurant, and rooms for 10,000/15,000 rp with mandi.

Prima Dona, a swanky new place with a huge restaurant, is flash, but lacks character and is expensive. Bungalows with TV and bathroom cost 17,500/30,000 rp.

There are several small homestays along the beach, all with basic rooms for around 7500 rp per person. *Periscopes* is around 1½ km from the main beach towards the village, near the surf break of the same name. *Lakey* is next door to Mona Lisa, and has a restaurant with good food.

Getting There & Away From Bima, a direct bus goes to Huu (2000 rp; three hours) at least once a day, at 8 am. Otherwise, take a bus to Dompu and change there for Huu. Buses to Dompu from Huu leave around 6 and 10 am and noon. From Sumbawa Besar, get off at Dompu and take a local bus (1500 rp; one hour) to Huu.

Donggo

Buses from Sila run to the village of Donggo on the Dompu to Bima road (800 rp). You should be able to stay with the kepala desa in Donggo, on the flank of the mountainous west side of Bima bay. The Dou Donggo ('mountain people') living in these highlands speak an archaic form of the Bima language, and may be descended from the original inhabitants of Sumbawa. Numbering about 20,000, they've adopted Islam and Christianity over their traditional animism in the last few decades, with varying degrees of enthusiasm; they're being absorbed into Bimanese culture and will probably disappear as a distinct group. The most traditional village is Mbawa where, at least until a few years ago, people still wore distinctive black clothes, and a few *uma leme* (traditional houses whose design was intimately connected with the traditional region) were still standing.

BIMA & RABA

Bima and Raba combined form the major town in the eastern half of Sumbawa. Bima,

Sumbawa's chief port, is the main centre; Raba, a few km east, is the departure point for buses east to Sape, where you get the ferry to Komodo or Flores.

Bima is one of the more orthodox Muslim areas in Indonesia: you'll see girls playing volleyball in brightly coloured headscarves and full body coverings, but you'll also see local girls in *short* denim shorts. The locals seem to have become used to the behaviour of tourists – you can show respect by wearing long pants, but generally you shouldn't attract more attention here than elsewhere in Nusa Tenggara.

The Bima region has been known since the 14th century for its sturdy horses, which even then were exported to Java. Local tradition claims that before the 17th century, when Bima fell to the Makassarese and its ruler was converted to Islam, this region had some sort of political control over Timor, Sumba and parts of western Flores.

Today, the former sultan's palace apart, Bima is a rather practical place – it certainly has a good range of services and shops, and the Jalan Flores night market is worth a wander. Western heavy metal bands dominate the posters on sale there.

Information

Money The Bank Rakyat Indonesia on Jalan Sumbawa changes foreign currency and travellers' cheques. The bank is open Monday to Friday from 7.30 am to noon, and until 11 am on Saturday. The Bank Negara Indonesia 1946 on Jalan Sultan Hasanuddin also changes money, and is open until 1.30 pm on weekdays and until noon on Saturday. If you're heading east, this is the last place to change money before Labuhanbajo (in Flores).

Post & Telecommunications The main post office is on Jalan Sultan Hasanuddin, about 500 metres east of the Hotel Sangyang. Opening hours are from 8 am to 2 pm Monday to Saturday (until 11 am on Friday). The Telkom office is on Jalan Soekarno Hatta about 1½ km from the town centre, and is open 24 hours. It's also possible to

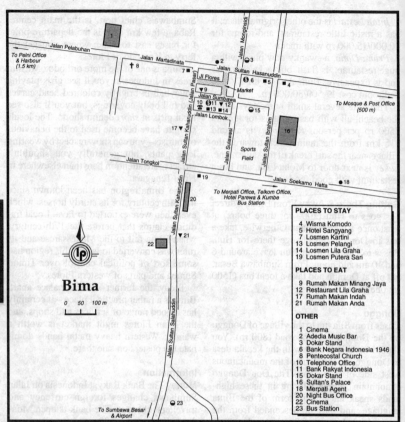

Bima

0   50   100 m

PLACES TO STAY

4 Wisma Komodo
5 Hotel Sangyang
7 Losmen Kartini
13 Losmen Pelangi
14 Losmen Lila Graha
19 Losmen Putera Sari

PLACES TO EAT

9 Rumah Makan Minang Jaya
12 Restaurant Lila Graha
17 Rumah Makan Indah
21 Rumah Makan Anda

OTHER

1 Cinema
2 Adedia Music Bar
3 Dokar Stand
6 Bank Negara Indonesia 1946
8 Pentecostal Church
10 Telephone Office
11 Bank Rakyat Indonesia
15 Dokar Stand
16 Sultan's Palace
18 Merpati Agent
20 Night Bus Office
22 Cinema
23 Bus Station

make international calls from the Telkom Warpostel Remaja on Jalan Lombok, in the centre of town.

Sultan's Palace

The former home of Bima's rulers – until they were put out of a job after Indonesia's independence – is now partly a museum. The building itself is less impressive than its counterpart in Sumbawa Besar, but the exhibits inside (chainmail shirts, sedan chairs, battle flags, weapons, a chart comparing the alphabets of Indonesian languages with the Latin alphabet) hold some interest. The palace had fallen into complete disrepair by the late 1950s, but has been restored. If you look interested, someone will show you around, explaining things in Indonesian. You can see the royal bedchamber (with its four-poster bed, and Koran on the dressing table), and photos of the tombs of some early Bima rulers which still stand somewhere in the hills outside town.

Places to Stay

Bima is compact, and most hotels are in the middle of town. You might have to bargain a bit to get the right room price.

A good place to start looking is the *Losmen Lila Graha* (☎ 2740) at Jalan Lombok 20. Small singles/doubles with shared mandi are not cheap at 7500/11,000 rp; better value are the larger, brighter rooms with private mandi (11,000/13,000 rp). Air-con double rooms with hot showers go for 42,000 rp.

Just next door is the dingy but cheap *Losmen Pelangi* (☎ 2878). Boxy double rooms are 6000 rp per person with shared mandi, or 7500 rp with private mandi.

The friendly *Wisma Komodo* on Jalan Sultan Ibrahim has long been popular with travellers. Good-value doubles with shared mandi are 7500 rp (15,000 rp with mandi and fan). Triples with private mandi are 12,500 rp, but are often full.

The basic *Losmen Kartini* (☎ 2072) at Jalan Pasar 11 is cheap (4000 rp per person), but they seem keen to send you to the other hotels. *Losmen Putera Sari* (☎ 2870) at Jalan Soekarno Hatta 7 is also less than salubrious, and their prices are seriously out of synch with the surroundings. Singles/doubles are 5000/10,000 rp with shared bath, 6000/12,000 rp with attached bath.

Hotel Sangyang (☎ 2017) on Jalan Sultan Hasanuddin is popular with tour groups, but they'll give discounts if they aren't busy. Large, carpeted rooms with air-con and hot water go for 25,000/30,000 rp.

Bima's most up-market hostelry is the *Hotel Parewa* (2652), one km from the town centre at Jalan Soekarno Hatta 40. It's comfortable and roomy, but pricey. All rooms are doubles and have private bath. Economy rooms with fan are 20,000 rp; the standard rooms with air-con, hot water and TV go for 35,000 rp.

Places to Eat

Restaurant Lila Graha, attached to the hotel of the same name, has a long menu of excellent, fresh Chinese, Indonesian and seafood cuisine, with a few Western dishes thrown in. The *Hotel Parewa* restaurant also has good Chinese food, while the cheapest cold beer in town is at *Rumah Makan Anda*, opposite the cinema. There's a good, clean Padang restaurant, the *Rumah Makan Minang Jaya*

on Jalan Sumbawa, and a couple more basic restaurants along Jalan Kaharuddin. The night market has stalls selling sate, curry, gado gado, rice creations and interesting snacks.

Getting There & Away

Air Merpati (☎ 2697) has its office at Jalan Soekarno Hatta 60, and there's a Merpati agent a little closer to town at No 30. There are flights between Bima and the following places: Bajawa, Denpasar, Ende, Kupang, Labuhanbajo, Mataram, Ruteng, Surabaya, Tambulaka (Waikabubak) and Waingapu. There are also connecting flights to Yogyakarta, Semerang, Ujung Pandang and Jakarta.

Bus Bima bus station, for most buses to and from the west, is a 10-minute walk from the centre of town. In addition to the daytime buses, there are night buses to Lombok, Bali or Java with ferry fares included. Several bus ticket offices are around the corner of Jalan Sultan Kaharuddin and Jalan Soekarno Hatta. For night buses it's advisable to get a ticket in advance – some of them leave from the town instead of from the bus station.

Destinations on Sumbawa from Bima include Dompu (1500 rp; two hours) and Sumbawa Besar (6000 rp; seven hours). At least one bus daily goes through to Huu (2000 rp; three hours) via Dompu, leaving at around 8 am.

Buses east to Sape go from Kumbe bus station in Raba, a 20-minute (300 rp) bemo ride east of Bima. You should be able to pick up a bemo easily on Jalan Sultan Kaharuddin or Jalan Soekarno Hatta. Buses leave Kumbe for Sape (1100 rp; 1½ hours) from about 7.30 am till late afternoon. Don't rely on these local buses to get you to Sape in time for the morning ferry to Komodo or Flores. Hotels in Bima usually sell tickets for a special bus to Sape that picks you up early in the morning. The fare is 1600 rp.

If you are on a long-distance bus from Lombok or Bali and plan to arrive in Sape the night before the ferry leaves, be careful – some of the long-distance buses don't go through to Sape, and there may not be a late connecting bus. Try to time your arrival in Bima before late afternoon to keep your options open.

Boat The Pelni office is in the port of Bima at Jalan Pelabuhan 103. The *Kelimutu* calls at Bima twice a fortnight, one week sailing on to Waingapu, Ende and Kupang and the next week sailing to Lembar.

Getting Around
To/From the Airport The 16-km trip from the town centre to the airport takes about 20 minutes over an excellent road. If you're at the bus station, announce to the crowd of bemo drivers that you want to go to the airport, then let them fight it out among themselves! You should be able to get a bemo for 6500 rp.

If you're heading straight to Sumbawa Besar from the airport, you can walk out to the main road about 100 metres in front of the terminal and catch a bus there. It is possible to catch a bus coming from Sumbawa Besar into Bima, but these are less frequent, so a taxi may be your best bet.

Local Transport Bemos around town cost 250 rp per person; dokars are 200 rp.

SAPE
Sape is a pleasant little town with amiable people, and an immense number of dokars, which the locals call 'Ben Hurs'. These jingling little buggies with their skinny, pompommed horses don't look much like Roman chariots, but the drivers obviously think they're Charlton Hestons as they race each other along the main street after dark. The overloading of the buggies and the treatment of the horses can be distressing – if this is likely to worry you, walk.

There are two colourful daily markets in town, one right in the centre and the other behind the bus station. If you have to wait for the ferry to Komodo or Flores, then it's as well to wait here as in Bima. The ferry leaves from Pelabuhan Sape, about four km down the road from Sape. There's lots of boat building going on along the street running down to the port.

Information
The PHPA office is about 2½ km from the town centre along the road to Pelabuhan Sape. The office has some interesting brochures and maps, and is open every day until 2 pm.

Places to Stay
The most convenient place to stay if you arrive the night before the ferry leaves is *Losmen Mutiara*, nestled just outside the entrance to the port. The best rooms are upstairs, with access to a back balcony overlooking the harbour. All rooms have shared mandi and cost 6000/8000 rp. There are a couple of small warungs and shops opposite the hotel, but if you're in Sape for more than a day or so, the four-km dokar ride into town could get tiresome.

In town, *Losmen Friendship* lives up to its name. Clean doubles with shared mandi cost

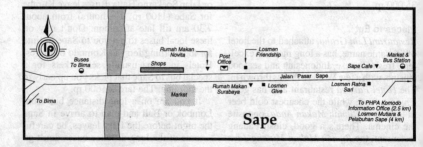

7000 rp (10,000 rp with private mandi). Also OK is *Losmen Ratna Sari*, where rooms with outside mandi cost 4000 rp per person (5000 rp with private mandi). *Losmen Give* apparently gives you the bedbugs free! Dingy singles/doubles with shared bath are 4000/8000 rp (5000/10,000 rp with private bath).

Places to Eat
Sape Cafe is the new place in town. The staff are friendly and speak some English, and they serve up a mixture of Western dishes and seafood. The beer's cold, and the music's OK as well. Next door, the *Rumah Makan Slamet Timur* is also a friendly place, but has a limited menu. *Rumah Makan Novita* is a casual little place near the post office, with decent food. Otherwise, there are two cheap warungs on either side of Losmen Give, one specialising in nasi everything and the other offering Padang food. The area around the central market has a few warungs and push-carts in the evening.

Getting There & Away
Bus Buses always meet ferries arriving at Pelabuhan Sape – they are usually express services direct to Bima, Lombok or Bali. You can purchase tickets on the boat – in fact, if you don't want tickets you'll have to fight off the offers. Some sample fares for express air-con buses are: Mataram (25,000 rp), Denpasar (38,000 rp), Surabaya (45,000 rp) and Jakarta (77,500 rp). Buses without air-con are slightly cheaper.

For most destinations on Sumbawa, you need to go to Bima for an onward bus. Buses leave from Sape bus station for Bima about every half-hour during the day and cost 1100 rp, but a few night buses charge 2000 rp. Beware of taxi drivers who may approach you at the bus station to tell you that no more buses are running and you must charter a taxi to Bima – walk away and ask someone else if buses are still running. Also, some long-distance buses from Lombok finish in the late afternoon at Bima, and buses through to Sape may have finished – if you're making a late run for the ferry the next morning, it's better to arrive in Sape (or Bima) earlier in the day.

Boat The ferry to Labuhanbajo (on Flores), stopping in at Komodo Island on the way, leaves three times a week from Pelabuhan Sape. This ferry was running every day until one of two ferries was 'broken' – it's not known when, or if, it'll be back in action.

The ferry departs at 8 am every Monday, Wednesday and Saturday. Tickets can be purchased at the pier about one hour before departure – get on the boat early if you want a position out of the sun. The boat returns from Labuhanbajo every Tuesday, Thursday and Sunday. In both directions, it stops in at Komodo Island. Sape to Labuhanbajo or Sape to Komodo each costs 9000 rp. You can take a bicycle from Sape to Labuhanbajo for 1600 rp, a motorbike for 7900 rp or a car for 78,000 rp. The duration of the crossing varies with the tides and weather, but allow seven hours to Komodo, nine or 10 hours to Labuhanbajo.

If you miss the ferry and are in a hurry to get to Labuhanbajo or Komodo, ask around the pier – you may find a boatload of rich tourists who'll take you along as a mascot. Otherwise, if you have enough people, you can charter your own boat, but it'll be expensive – and make sure you check the boat out first.

Getting Around
A dokar between Sape and the ferry pier costs 250 rp (more at night or if you have luggage). Shorter hauls within the city cost 200 rp.

Komodo & Rinca

A hilly, desolate island sandwiched between Flores and Sumbawa, Komodo's big attraction is lizards – three-metre, 100-kg monsters, known as *ora* to the locals and tagged 'Komodo dragons' by Westerners. The island is surrounded by some of the most tempestuous waters in Indonesia, fraught with rip tides and whirlpools. From the sea it looks a far more fitting habitat for a

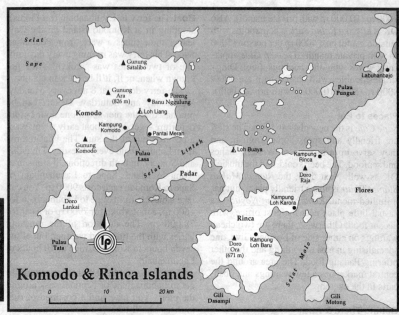

Komodo & Rinca Islands

0   10   20 km

monstrous lizard than for the few hundred people who live in the island's lone village.

Komodo gets a constant stream of visitors these days, but to understand how far off the beaten track it used to be, read *Zoo Quest for a Dragon*, by naturalist-adventurer David Attenborough, who filmed the dragons in 1956. Dragons also inhabit the nearby islands of Rinca and Padar, and coastal western Flores. Some people now prefer to visit Rinca than Komodo, since it's closer to Flores, has fewer visitors and dragon-spotting is less organised.

Komodo Dragons

There were rumours of these awesome creatures long before their existence was confirmed in the West. Fishers and pearl divers working in the area had brought back tales of ferocious lizards with enormous claws, fearsome teeth and fiery yellow tongues. One theory holds that the Chinese dragon is based on the Komodo lizard. The

first Dutch expedition to the island was in 1910; two of the dragons were shot and their skins taken to Java, resulting in the first published description.

The Komodo dragon is actually a monitor lizard. Monitors range from tiny 20-gram things just 20 cm long, to the granddaddy of them all, the Komodo dragon (*Varanus komodoensis* in science-speak). All monitors have some things in common – the head is tapered, the ear openings are visible, the neck is long and slender, the eyes have eyelids and round pupils, and the jaws are powerful. But the dragons also have massive bodies, four powerful legs (each with five clawed toes) and long, thick tails (which function as rudders, and can also be used for grasping or as a potent weapon). The body is covered in small, nonoverlapping scales – some may be spiny, others raised and bony.

The monitors' powerful legs allow them to sprint short distances, lifting their tails when they run. Many species stay in or near the water and can swim quite well, with an undulating movement of the trunk and tail. When threatened they'll take refuge in their normal resting places – holes, trees (for the smaller monitors) or water. They *are* dangerous if driven into a corner, and will then attack a much larger opponent. They threaten by opening the mouth, inflating the neck and hissing. The ribs may spread or the body expand slightly, making the monitor look larger. It often rises up on its hind legs just before attacking, and the tail can deliver well-aimed blows that will knock down a weaker adversary. Their best weapons are their sharp teeth and dagger-sharp claws which can inflict severe wounds.

All monitors feed on other animals – small ones on insects, larger ones on frogs and birds, and the ora on deer, wild pig and even water buffalo which inhabit the islands. The ora also eat their own dead. They can expand their mouth cavity considerably, enabling them to swallow large prey – the ora can push practically a whole goat into its throat.

Being such a large reptile, the ora rarely moves until warmed by the sun. They seem to be stone deaf, but have a very keen sense of smell. Of all the monitors, the ora lays the largest eggs – up to 12 cm long and weighing around 200 grams. The female lays 20 or 30 eggs at a time and usually buries them in the wall of a dry river, where they hatch by themselves nine months later.

Monitors are *not* relics of the dinosaur age – they're a remarkably versatile, hardy modern lizard – if not exactly sensitive and new age. Why they exist only on and around Komodo Island is a mystery – as is why males outnumber females by a ratio of 3.4 to one. Today there are around 2500 ora on Komodo, 800 on Rinca and fewer in the other locations.

The villagers never hunted the monitors, which weren't as good to eat as the numerous wild pigs on the island – and for other reasons not too hard to imagine! Today the ora is a protected species.

Orientation & Information

Komodo The only village is Kampung Komodo, a fishing village in a bay on the east coast. On the same bay and a half-hour walk north of the village is Loh Liang, the tourist accommodation camp run by the PHPA (the Indonesian government body responsible for managing nature reserves and national parks). You pay a 2000 rp park entrance fee when you arrive at Loh Liang. If you are going on to Rinca Island, keep your park entrance ticket, as Rinca is part of the same national park.

The PHPA warns you not to walk outside the camp without one of their guides – hire one for 3000 rp for up to five people for three hours. Longer treks around the island can be organised, and the PHPA office has a list of guides' fees for them. A lot of emphasis is put on 'danger' – this includes encounters with Komodo dragons that can snap your leg as fast as they'll cut a goat's throat, or having a cobra spit poison at you, as happened to one trekker recently. The PHPA staff will probably get the blame if you have to be shipped home in a box – or if you ship home some rare dragon's eggs in a box for that matter. Several years ago an elderly European did wander off alone and was never found. Locals are attacked periodically, most commonly while sleeping out in the open. In any case, many trails around the island are overgrown and you could get lost. The best reasons for having the guides are simply the information they provide, and their trained eyes can spot wildlife better than the average tourist can.

Rinca The PHPA tourist camp is at Loh Buaya, and it's possible to camp in some of the villages. The park entrance fee here is also 2000 rp; PHPA guides cost 5000 rp. Again, keep your entrance ticket if you're going on to Komodo.

Dragon Spotting

Komodo You're likely to see dragons all year at Banu Nggulung, a dry river bed about a half-hour walk from Loh Liang. Banu Nggulung is where the dragons are fed every

Saturday by the PHPA, using goats provided by tourists. The dragons used to be fed at least two days a week, until the PHPA decided they were getting too fat and lazy! These dragons still don't stray too far in search of food, but this may change, as some of them have started to look decidedly hungry. Poreng Valley, 5½ km from Loh Liang, is also a favourite dragon haunt, and has a more out-in-the-wild feeling than Banu Nggulung. Komodo is very hot most of the year; take water if you're going further afield than Banu Nggulung.

Unlike the 'good old days' when you had to trek out into the interior, string out the bait, hide behind a bush and hope something would happen, these days lizard hunting at Banu Nggulung is a bit like going to the theatre. A little 'grandstand' overlooks the river bed where the dragons are fed. The PHPA feeds the dragons on Saturday – usually twice (one session in the morning and one in the afternoon). They don't string the goats up these days – although it was a spectacular sight for tourists, the dragons were suffering back problems and breaking teeth off trying to rip the goats apart!

It's not uncommon to see several dragons, ranging from relatively lively youngsters to lumbering three-metre monsters, clambering over each other to get to the last legs of a goat. The guides may let you go down to the river bed for a closer look if there aren't too many of you. A telephoto lens is handy but not essential – either way, don't think you can walk up to the dragons and have them say 'cheese'.

Rinca There are no established dragon feeding places on Rinca, so spotting monitors is more a matter of luck and your guide's knowledge. But other wildlife is much more abundant than on Komodo – there are several monkey colonies, wild water buffalo, deer, horses, pigs, bush turkeys and eagles.

Around Komodo Island
Kampung Komodo is a half-hour walk from the tourist camp. It's a friendly Muslim Bugis village of stilt houses infested with goats, chickens and children. The inhabitants are all descendants of convicts who were exiled to the island last century by one of the sultans on Sumbawa. The old sultan mustn't have realised the island's potential for attracting the tourist dollar – although the village still doesn't get too many visitors.

If you trek around the island, or climb Gunung Ara (about a six-hour round trip), or go to Poreng Valley or anywhere else, be warned that this place can get bloody hot! The PHPA guides perform like mountain goats, marching up and down the hilly terrain in the fierce heat. Sights around the island include wild deer and huge, poisonous (but not deadly) spiders.

There's good coral just off **Pantai Merah** (east of Loh Liang), and around the small island of **Pulau Lasa** (near Kampung Komodo) – the PHPA guys say there's little danger from sea snakes or sharks. The PHPA no longer charter boats – ask around at Kampung Komodo, or perhaps hitch a ride with one of the tour boats moored off the pier.

Wild deer are often seen close to the camp or on the beach in front of it in the morning. Komodo dragons occasionally wander into the camp looking for food. Dolphins are common in the seas between Komodo and Flores, and the area is also on a whale migration route from the Indian Ocean to the South China Sea.

Places to Stay & Eat
The PHPA camp at Loh Liang (on Komodo Island) is a collection of large, spacious wooden cabins on stilts. Each cabin has four or five rooms, a sitting area and two mandis. You pay 8500 rp per person in a room with two beds, 12,500 rp per couple in a room with a double bed. Electricity, produced by a noisy generator, operates from 6 to 10 pm. Some travellers have complained of beady-eyed, long-tailed nocturnal visitors, but we can't substantiate these reports.

There's also a restaurant at the camp, but the menu is limited to very average nasi goreng or mie goreng, plus some drinks (including beer and drinking water). Bring other food yourself, or pick up basic supplies at Kampung Komodo. You should be able to buy fish or eggs there as well, or perhaps get them to kill and cook a chicken.

Accommodation at the PHPA camp at Loh Buaya (on Rinca Island) is similar to that on Komodo, at the same prices, but there's no restaurant here so bring your own food. The PHPA guides are very friendly – they don't get many people staying at the camp and are glad of the company!

Getting There & Away

Air You can fly to Labuhanbajo with Merpati from Denpasar, Mataram, Kupang, Ende or Ruteng. There are a few Komodo tours run from Bali – look around the travel agencies there.

Boat With one of the two vessels running the route between Sape, Komodo and Labuhanbajo out of action indefinitely, the ferries are running on a reduced timetable. From Sape, the ferry departs at 8 am every Monday, Wednesday and Saturday. Going the other way, the Labuhanbajo-Komodo-Sape ferry departs from Labuhanbajo at 8 am every Tuesday, Thursday and Sunday.

The ferry to Komodo costs 9000 rp from Sape, or 2800 rp from Labuhanbajo, plus 1500 rp per person for a small boat to transfer you between the ferry and the Komodo shore. Tickets can be purchased from the harbours in Sape and Labuhanbajo an hour before departure. With the reduced timetable in operation, these ferries get seriously crowded, so it's worth boarding early to stake out a good position. If you arrive at Komodo by ferry but don't really want to stay overnight, ask around the charter boats moored off the pier – you might be able to get a ride through to Labuhanbajo or Sape.

If you don't want to wait for the ferry to get you to Komodo, you can charter a boat for a one-way or return journey. (It's easier to do this from Labuhanbajo than from Sape.) You can fix this through the hotels in Labuhanbajo or by asking around the waterfront. A reliable boat costs about 60,000 rp for a day trip for up to six people, or 90,000 to 100,000 rp for a two-day trip with an overnight stay on the boat. Other options include a two-day trip from Labuhanbajo through to Sape, stopping at Bidadari, Rinca and Komodo Islands (about 40,000 rp per person), or the five-day trips through to Lombok (around 100,000 rp per person). See under Labuhanbajo in the following Flores section for more details.

If you get enough people together, you can charter a boat and create your own itinerary. Make the agreement with the boat operator very clear – you may want to get something in writing. If you're recruiting other passengers, let the operator know well before you leave, as they may need to buy extra food and water. Labuhanbajo to Komodo takes three to four hours in an ordinary boat, which gives you maybe four hours on the island if you're making a day trip – enough time to see the dragons and to have lunch and a swim.

To Rinca, there are no regular passenger ships or ferries, so the only option is to charter a boat. It's only about two hours by motorboat from Labuhanbajo to Rinca; a charter boat costs around 50,000 rp for up to six people. Ask at the hotels or around the harbour. Komodo*

Flores

Flores is one of the biggest, most rugged and most beautiful islands in Nusa Tenggara. You'll find some interesting cultures here, with a layer of animism beneath the prevalent Christianity.

Geographically, the island's turbulent volcanic past has left a complicated relief of V-shaped valleys, knife-edged ridges and a collection of active and extinct volcanoes. One of the finest volcanoes is the caldera of Keli Mutu in central Flores, with its three coloured lakes. There are 14 active volcanoes on Flores – only Java and Sumatra have more. The central mountains slope gently to the north coast, but along the south coast the spurs of the volcanoes plunge steeply into the sea.

The island is part of one of the world's

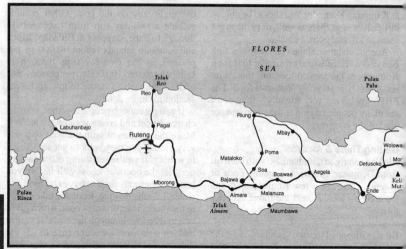

FLORES SEA

most geologically unstable zones, and earthquakes and tremors hit every year – in December 1992, an earthquake measuring 6.8 on the Richter scale, and the massive tidal wave that followed it, killed around 3000 people in eastern Flores and almost flattened the large town of Maumere.

The rugged terrain makes road construction difficult; although Flores is only about 375 km long, its end-to-end road winds, twists, ascends and descends for nearly 700 km, and heavy wet-season rains as well as the frequent earthquakes and tremors mean that it has to be repaired year-round.

Difficulties of communication have also contributed to the diversity of Flores' cultures. In some remoter areas, you'll find older people don't speak a word of Bahasa Indonesian and whose parents grew up in purely animist societies.

Physically, the people at the western end of the island are more 'Malay', while the other inhabitants of Flores are more Melanesian. The island's 1½ million people are divided into five main language and cultural groups: from west to east, the Manggarai (main town Ruteng), the Ngada (Bajawa), the closely related Ende and Lio peoples

(Ende), the Sikkanese (Maumere) and the Lamaholot (Larantuka).

Around 85% of the people are Catholic (Muslims tend to congregate in the coastal towns), but in rural areas particularly, Christianity is welded onto traditional beliefs. Animist rituals are still important here for a variety of occasions, ranging from birth, marriage and death to the building of new houses or to mark important points in the agricultural cycle. Even educated, English-speaking Florinese still admit to the odd chicken, pig or buffalo sacrifice to keep their ancestors happy when rice is planted or a new field opened up. In former times, it took more than animal blood to keep the gods and spirits friendly: there are persistent tales of children or virgin girls being sacrificed.

Flores has a thriving ikat-weaving tradition, a developing beach spot at Labuhanbajo and some fine snorkelling off some parts of the coast. The island has attracted a steady flow of visitors in recent years, but has nothing like the tourist scene of Bali or even Lombok.

The rainy season (November to March) is more intense in western Flores, which receives the brunt of the north-west monsoon and has the highest mountains. Ruteng, near Flores'

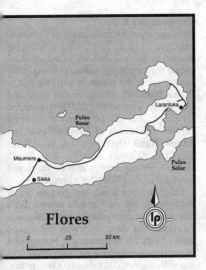

Flores

0   25   50 km

highest peak (the 2400-metre Ranaka), gets an average 3350 mm of rain every year, but Ende has only 1140 mm and Larantuka just 770 mm.

History

Flores owes its name to the Portuguese, who called its easternmost cape Cabo das Flores, meaning 'Cape of Flowers'. The island's diverse cultures have enough similarities to suggest that they developed from a common type, differentiated by geographical isolation and the varying influence of outsiders. Long before Europeans arrived in the 16th century, much of coastal Flores was firmly in the hands of the Makassarese and Bugis from southern Sulawesi. The Bugis even established their own ports as part of a trading network throughout the archipelago. They brought gold, coarse porcelain, elephant tusks (used for money), a sort of machete known as *parang*, linen and copperware, and left with rubber, sea cucumber (much of it fished from the bay of Maumere), shark fins, sandalwood, wild cinnamon, coconut oil, cotton and fabric from Ende. Bugis and Makassarese slave raids on the coasts of Flores were a common problem, forcing people to retreat inland.

Fourteenth-century Javanese chronicles place Flores (rather imaginatively) within the Majapahit realm. In the 15th and 16th centuries, most of western and central Flores is thought to have become a colony of the Makassarese kingdom of Gowa in south Sulawesi, while eastern Flores came under the sway of Ternate in Maluku.

As early as 1512, Flores was sighted by the Portuguese navigator Antonio de Abreu, and Europeans had probably landed by 1550. The Portuguese, involved in the lucrative sandalwood trade with Timor, built fortresses on Solor (off eastern Flores) and at Ende (on Flores), and in 1561 Dominican priests established a mission on Solor. From here the Portuguese Dominicans extended their work to eastern Flores, founding over 20 missions by 1575. Despite attacks by pirates, local Islamic rulers and raiders from Gowa, the missionaries converted – it is claimed – tens of thousands of Florinese. The fortress at Ende was overrun in 1637 by Muslims, and the mission abandoned, as eventually were all the other missions on southern Flores. The growth of Christianity continued, however, and today the church is the centrepiece of almost every village.

In the 17th century, the Dutch East India Company (VOC) kicked the Portuguese out of Flores and the surrounding area, and concentrated on monopolising the trade in sappan wood (used to make a red dye) and wild cinnamon. The slave trade was also strong; a treaty with Ende outlawed it in 1839, but it was reported to exist into the first years of the 20th century.

Though Ternate and Gowa ceded all their rights on Solor, Flores and eastern Sumbawa to the Dutch in the 17th century, Flores was too complex and isolated for the Dutch to gain real control. Around 1850 the Dutch bought out Portugal's remaining enclaves in the area, including Larantuka, Sikka and Paga on Flores. Dutch Jesuits then took over missionary work on Flores and founded their new bases in Maumere and Sikka – still their centres on Flores today.

Even into the first decade of this century, the Dutch were constantly confronted with rebellions and intertribal wars, until a major military campaign in 1907 brought most of the tribes of central and western Flores firmly under control. Missionaries moved into the isolated western hills in the 1920s.

LABUHANBAJO

A small Muslim/Christian fishing town at the extreme western end of Flores, this is a jumping-off point for Komodo and Rinca, and also the most popular swimming and sunning spot on Flores. If you've got a few days to while away, Labuhanbajo is a good place to do it. There aren't any readily accessible walk-on-and-flop beaches, but many of the small islands nearby have white-sand beaches, and good snorkelling offshore. The harbour is littered with outrigger fishing boats and is sheltered by the islands, giving the impression that you're standing on the shores of a large lake.

Information

Tourist Office The PHPA administers Komodo National Park, which takes in Komodo and Rinca islands and other parts of western Flores, including the Riung area. The PHPA information booth, a two-minute walk from the Bajo Beach and Mutiara Beach hotels, provides some practical information for Komodo and Rinca islands. The new PHPA office is a little out of town – they don't really encourage tourists to visit, but can be helpful if your Indonesian is OK.

Money The Bank Rakyat Indonesia is open Monday to Friday from 7 am to 1 pm, and on Saturday until 11.30 am. For currencies other than US dollars, expect a very poor exchange rate, and the banks are fussy about some brands of travellers' cheques. If you're heading west, this is the last place to change money before Bima in Sumbawa.

Post & Telecommunications The post office is open Monday to Saturday from 8 am to 2 pm (closing at 11 am on Friday). The Telkom office is a bit of a hike from town, near the PHPA office.

Things to See & Do

Walking down the main street of Labuhanbajo, you're likely to be offered boats for charter to the uninhabited island of your choice for swimming and snorkelling. Otherwise, ask at the hotels. A half-day trip to **Pulau Bidadari**, where there's coral and clear water, costs around 20,000 rp for up to six people. For divers, there's good coral between the islands of **Sabolo Besar** and **Sabolo Kecil**. Operators such as Varanus and Dive Komodo, near the Bajo Beach Hotel, offer day trips with two tanks and lunch for around $US60 per person.

Other beaches worth lounging on are at **Batugosok** and on **Kanawa Island**. Both places have accommodation, and transport is free if you stay there. Otherwise, ask around where boats for **Weicucu** and **Batugosok** leave, at the north end of the main street. The trip to Batugosok costs about 4000 rp return. **Pantai Weicucu** itself is just a beach, but there's a white-sand beach on a small island opposite – you should be able to get there for 2000 rp return.

Batu Cermin (Mirror Rock) is about four km from town and has a good cave – take a torch. Walk there, or charter a bemo.

Places to Stay

You can stay in Labuhanbajo itself or at one of the beach hotels. Several new mid-range hotels have sprung up recently, and competition between them is keeping prices reasonable for the moment.

Central The well-appointed *Bajo Beach Hotel* (☎ 41009) has a range of clean rooms set around a central eating area. Economy rooms with outside mandi go for 4000/7000 rp, while large rooms with private bath cost 10,000/15,000 rp.

Across the road, the *Mutiara Beach Hotel* (☎ 41039) has a waterfront restaurant with a fine harbour view, but several travellers have given the food and service the thumbs down. Small, windowless singles/doubles with mandi cost 3500/7000 rp.

A popular new place is the *Gardena Hotel*,

with an attached restaurant serving good seafood. The bungalow-style rooms overlook the harbour and cost 8000/10,000 rp with private mandi. It is set above the road.

Another good new hotel is the up-market but reasonably priced *Hotel Wisata* (☎ 41020). Spotless rooms with shower and fan cost 5000/10,000 rp; large double rooms facing the courtyard cost 15,000 rp. The restaurant here is recommended by travellers.

The *Golo Hilltop Resort*, set 600 metres above the town, offers spectacular views. Standard rooms with shower and fan cost 15,000/20,000 rp, while deluxe rooms with

hot water and air-con cost 50,000/60,000 rp. The restaurant has some reasonably priced dishes, and is worth a visit around sunset for hopeless romantics.

Labuhanbajo also has a number of small homestays. The best of these is *Chez Felix*, run by a friendly family that speaks good English. Rooms are clean, with large windows, and there's a pleasant porch area for eating. Singles/doubles are 4000/6000 rp with shared bath, 6000/8000 rp with fan and attached bath.

Nearby is the quiet *Sony Homestay*, with a nice hilltop view. Basic but clean singles/doubles with private bath are 3500/7000 rp.

Three other basic places scattered around town are the *Bahagia Homestay*, in a nice position along the waterfront (5000/10,000 rp), the cheap *Homestay Gembira* (3000 rp), next to the mosque, and the dingy *Losmen Sinjai* (5000 rp).

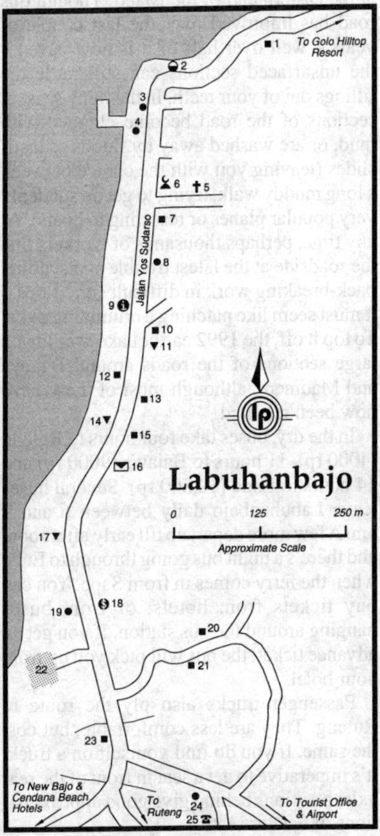

NUSA TENGGARA

PLACES TO STAY

1 Bahagia Homestay
7 Homestay Gembira
10 Gardena Hotel
12 Mutiara Beach Hotel
13 Bajo Beach Hotel
15 Losmen Sinjai
20 Chez Felix Homestay
21 Sony Homestay
23 Hotel Wisata

PLACES TO EAT

11 Dewata Restaurant
14 Restaurant New Tenda Nikmat
17 Sunset Restaurant

OTHER

2 Boats to Weicucu & Batugosok
3 Bus Station
4 Harbour Master's Office & Ferry Office
5 Church
6 Mosque
8 Pelni Agent
9 PHPA Information Booth
16 Post Office
18 Bank Rakyat Indonesia
19 Art Shop
22 Market
24 PHPA Office
25 Telkom

Beach Hotels You'll need to take a boat ride to get to most of these hotels from Labuhanbajo – for guests, the hotels will provide free transport.

Batugosok Beach Hotel is set on a fine white-sand beach on the mainland, a half-hour boat ride from town. Bungalow accommodation costs 12,500 rp, including three meals.

Kanawa Island Bungalows is on Kanawa Island, one hour by boat from Labuhanbajo. The hotel's information centre is in a house opposite the Wisata Hotel. The beach and snorkelling here are both very good, and accommodation costs 7500/15,00 rp (with three meals a day).

The *Weicucu Beach Hotel* requires a 20-minute boat ride from Labuhanbajo. The beach here is not very appealing, but the small island opposite offers a white-sand beach and good snorkelling. Basic bungalow accommodation costs 7500 rp per person with three meals, 10,000 rp per person with attached toilet.

The *Cendana Beach Hotel*, four km south of town, can be reached by road. Rooms with nice views cost 10,000 rp per person, including breakfast.

The *New Bajo Beach Hotel* is 2½ km south of town and is more up-market, but the beach is ordinary. Air-con double rooms cost 60,000 rp.

Places to Eat

Labuhanbajo now has a few good restaurants specialising in seafood at reasonable prices. One of the best is the *New Tenda Nikmat*, a colourful, relaxed place with excellent seafood and sate. Next door, the *Rumah Makan Indah* offers a wide range of juices and good, fresh Padang food. The *Dewata Restaurant*, set above the road with lovely views, also does good seafood, and cheaper Indonesian dishes.

The *Sunset Restaurant* is in a prime position on the harbour side of the road, overlooking the water, but the menu is limited. Otherwise, the restaurants in the Gardena, Bajo and Wisata hotels all have long menus and reasonable prices.

Getting There & Away

Air Merpati has direct flights between Labuhanbajo and Bima, Ende and Ruteng, and connecting flights to Denpasar, Kupang and Mataram. The airfield is 2½ km from town. You can get there by bemo for 1000 rp, or the hotels can arrange a taxi (5000 rp). The Merpati office is between Labuhanbajo and the airport, about two km from town.

Bus & Truck What one Indonesian tourist leaflet charitably calls the 'Trans-Flores Highway' loops and tumbles nearly 700 scenic km from Labuhanbajo to Larantuka, at the eastern end of the island. Though this road has improved over the last couple of years – well over half of it is now paved – the unsurfaced sections can still rattle the fillings out of your teeth. In the rainy season, sections of the road become clogged with mud, or are washed away by floods or land-slides (leaving you with the choice between a long muddy walk, trying to get on suddenly very popular planes or resorting to boats). At any time, perhaps thousands of workers line the roadside at the latest trouble spots, doing back-breaking work in difficult conditions – it must seem like patching a crumbling dyke. To top it off, the 1992 earthquake swallowed large sections of the roads around Bajawa and Maumere, although most of these have now been repaired.

In the dry, buses take four hours to Ruteng (4000 rp), 11 hours to Bajawa (9000 rp) and 14 hours to Ende (12,500 rp). Several buses leave Labuhanbajo daily between 6 and 7 am. A few more depart up till early afternoon, and there's a night bus going through to Ende when the ferry comes in from Sape. You can buy tickets from hotels, or from buses hanging around the bus station. If you get an advance ticket, the bus will pick you up from your hotel.

Passenger trucks also ply the route to Ruteng. They are less comfortable, but cost the same. If you do find yourself on a truck, it's imperative to get a seat in front of the rear axle; positions behind give good approximations of ejector seats.

Boat At the time of research, one of the two ferries chugging the route to/from Labuhanbajo was in dry dock, and no-one was sure when, or if, it would be back in action. Consequently, the schedule between Labuhanbajo and Sape (Sumbawa) via Komodo was reduced to three runs a week in each direction – it may be wise to work around this schedule until you hear reliable information to the contrary. As it is, the ferry leaves Labuhanbajo for Sape at 8 am every Tuesday, Thursday and Sunday, costing 11,800 rp. Going the other way, departures from Sape are at 8 am every Monday, Wednesday and Saturday. In both directions, it stops in at Komodo. You can get tickets from the harbour master's office (in front of the pier) one hour before departure. The ferries get very crowded, so it's definitely worth boarding as early as possible.

A very popular way to travel between Labuhanbajo and Lombok is on the boat tours run from several of the hotels in Labuhanbajo. The trip is cheaper from Labuhanbajo than from Lombok. A typical itinerary takes in Komodo Island to see the dragons, makes several snorkelling stops off islands, including Pulau Moyo (Moyo Island), off Sumbawa, and finally docks at Bangsal (on Lombok). Usual departure days are Tuesday and Friday, depending on demand, and the trip costs 100,000 rp, including all meals and water, snorkel gear and mattress. It seems that several hotels recruit passengers for the same trip; get details through the New Bajo Beach or Mutiara hotels, or at Chez Felix Homestay.

If the ferry schedule to Komodo is not convenient, charter boats to the island are available at reasonable prices. You should be able to charter a boat for a day trip for around 60,000 rp for up to six people, which will give you about three or four hours wandering around the island. Other options are two-day trips through to Sape or back to Labuhanbajo, with a stop at Pulau Rinca (Rinca Island) and snorkelling stops, for around 40,000 rp per person. Ask around at the hotels – the Bajo Beach is a good place to start. If you get a few people together, it's

viable to charter a boat and create your own itinerary. Boat owners are usually open to ideas. Make sure the agreement is well understood (and perhaps in writing).

The Pelni passenger ship *Tatamailau* stops in at Labuhanbajo about once a week.

REO
Set on an estuary a little distance from the sea, Reo's focal point is the large Catholic compound in the middle of town. Reo has a couple of cheap losmen and a few small rumah makan.

From the port of Kedidi, regular boats leave for Labuhanbajo, but if you want to do a boat trip between the two towns, it's probably better to do it from Labuhanbajo – then, if you have to wait a few days for a boat, you do it in a more interesting place.

A good surfaced road links Reo to Ruteng. The 60-km trip by bemo or bus takes around two hours and costs 2000 rp.

RUTENG
A market town and meeting point for the hill people of western Flores, Ruteng is the heart of the Manggarai country, the region extending to the west coast from a line drawn north from Aimere. The town is surrounded by rice fields on gentle slopes beneath a line of volcanic hills. The crisp air and dung smells give Ruteng the feeling of a hill town, even though it's quite a sizable place.

The Manggarai hill people are shy but friendly – you'll see them in their distinctive black sarongs, trailing droopy-stomached black-haired pigs into market or herding beautiful miniature horses. The Manggarai language is unintelligible to the other people of Flores.

Makassarese from Sulawesi have mixed with the coastal Manggarai for well over 100 years, and the Bimanese dominated the area for at least 300 years until early this century, when the Dutch took over all of Flores. Christianity now predominates among the upland Manggarai, and Ruteng has several large Christian schools and churches. Traditional animist practices still linger, but are dwindling – traditionally, the Manggarai

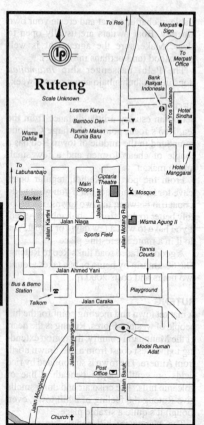

Ruteng

Scale Unknown

To Reo

To Merpati Office

Merpati Sign

Bank Rakyat Indonesia

Losmen Karyo

Bamboo Den

Rumah Makan Dunia Baru

Wisma Dahlia

Hotel Sindha

Jalan Yos Sudarso

To Labuhanbajo

Ciptaria Theatre

Main Shops

Jalan Pasar

Mosque

Hotel Manggarai

Market

Jalan Kartini

Jalan Niaga

Jalan Motang Rua

Wisma Agung II

Sports Field

Tennis Courts

Jalan Ahmed Yani

Bus & Bemo Station

Telkom

Jalan Caraka

Playground

Jalan Bhayangkara

Model Rumah Adat

Jalan Monginsidi

Post Office

Jalan Baruk

Church

would carry out a cycle of ceremonies, some involving buffalo or pig sacrifices, to ask favour from ancestor and nature spirits and the supreme being, Mori. In some villages you can still find the *compang*, a ring of flat stones on which offerings were placed, or you may be shown ritual paraphernalia used during sacrificial ceremonies.

Trials of strength and courage known as *caci* still take place in Ruteng during the national Independence Day celebrations (on 17 August). The two combatants wear wooden masks like uptilted welder's helmets. One carries a rawhide oval shield and a metre-long whip, the other a short, springy stick and a thick cloth wrapped around his forearm.

The Manggarai traditionally practised slash-and-burn agriculture. They were introduced to rice cultivation around 1920 by the Dutch, but only in the last few decades has the area been devoted to permanent rice terraces. Maize (sweet corn) is the other main crop, though other crops (such as coffee and onions) are grown for export. The Manggarai also raise fine horses and large water buffalo, the latter primarily for export.

Information

The Bank Rakyat Indonesia is on Jalan Yos Sudarso, and is open Monday to Friday from 7.30 am to 1 pm, and on Saturday until 11 am. The post office, at Jalan Baruk 6, is open Monday to Saturday from 8 am to 2 pm (closing at 11 am on Friday). The Telkom office is on Jalan Kartini, and is open 24 hours.

Things to See & Do

Ruteng's lively, sprawling market is a meeting place for people from the surrounding hills. **Golo Curu**, a hill to the north of Ruteng, offers spectacular early morning views of the hills, valleys, rice paddies, terraced slopes and distant mountain valleys. Go down the Reo road, and 20 minutes past the Losmen Karya turn right at the small bridge across a stream. There's a derelict shrine on the hilltop, with a statue of the Virgin Mary on a pedestal.

Manggarai sarongs are black with pretty embroidered patterns. You can find them in Ruteng market, or visit the weaving village of **Cibal**. Women at Cibal work their looms mainly from May to October. To reach Cibal, there are occasional direct bemos from Ruteng; otherwise, take one to Pagal (600 rp), 21 km north of Ruteng on the main road to Reo, then walk about three km east over the hill to Cibal. Make sure you head for Cibal Timur – there are other Cibals in the area.

The 2400-metre volcano **Gunung Rana-ka** is Flores' highest peak, and can be climbed from Ruteng. Take a bemo to Robo village, from where you begin the the tough eight-km ascent. **Danau (lake) Ranamese**, known as 'little Keli Mutu' to locals, is 21 km from Ruteng, close to the main Bajawa road.

Places to Stay

The central *Hotel Sindha* (☎ 21197) on Jalan Yos Sudarso seems to be moving up-market – bargaining may still help with the prices. Small rooms with outside mandi go for 6000/12,000 rp, rooms with Western bathroom and TV cost 12,000/15,000 rp, and new, spacious rooms with Western bath, TV and balcony are 15,000/18,000 rp. The attached restaurant serves good Chinese food, and has satellite TV if you're desperate for news.

Hotel Manggarai (☎ 21008) on Jalan Adi Sucipto is also convenient, and very quiet, except for a wall clock that strikes the hour with heavy metal guitar solos of classical tunes! The few rooms with outside mandi go for 5000/10,000 rp, but better value are the large, clean rooms with mandi for 7000/12,000 rp.

Wisma Dahlia (☎ 21377) on Jalan Kartini is close to the market and has a nice green courtyard. Economy rooms with outside mandi cost 7500/10,000 rp and singles/doubles with Western bathroom are 15,000/20,000 rp. There's a small restaurant off the back courtyard.

Wisma Agung 11 (☎ 21835), behind Toko Agung on Jalan Motang Rua, is right in the town centre, but a bit dingy. Economy rooms with outside mandi cost 6600/8250 rp.

Losmen Karya, on Jalan Motang Rua, is the cheapest place in town at 4000 rp per person, but it's very dark and often 'full'.

Places to Eat

For meals out, there's a cluster of restaurants along Jalan Motang Rua near Losmen Karya – *Rumah Makan Dunia Baru*, with good Chinese food, *Rumah Makan Masakan Padang*, serving big fresh prawns, and the cosy and friendly *Bamboo Den*. A couple of warungs around the market serve Padang

food, buffalo soup and sate. Otherwise, the *Hotel Sindha* serves tasty (but pricey) Chinese food.

Getting There & Away

Air There are direct flights most days to/from Bima, Kupang, Denpasar and Mataram, and a couple a week to Labuhanbajo. The Merpati office (☎ 21147) is out in the rice paddies, about a 10-minute walk from the centre of town.

Bus Most buses will drop you at hotels on your arrival in Ruteng. Buses to Labuhanbajo (4000 rp; four hours), Bajawa (4000 rp; five hours) and Ende (8500 rp; 10 hours) leave in the early morning at around 7 am. There are noon buses to Bajawa and Labuhanbajo. You can buy tickets for the morning buses at the bus station or from one of the ticket agencies along Jalan Niaga. Most hotels will also get them for you, and arrange for the bus to pick you up – probably first, so you get a free tour of Ruteng's backstreets as you cruise for other passengers.

Buses, trucks and bemos run frequently until midday to Reo (1500 rp; 2½ hours). You can pick them up at the bus and bemo station or as they circle the streets.

Getting Around

The airport is about two km from the town centre, about a half-hour walk. The Sindha Hotel offers guests free transport to the airport. Otherwise, you can charter a bemo.

BAJAWA

The small hill town of Bajawa (population around 12,000) is the centre of the Ngada people, one of the most traditional groups on Flores. The town is at an altitude of 1100 metres and is surrounded by volcanic hills, with the 2245-metre Gunung Inerie (to the south) predominant. Bajawa is cool, low-key and clean – it even has street cleaners. It also has a good range of restaurants and accommodation, making it a popular place to spend a few days exploring the countryside and making trips to the Ngada villages.

Orientation & Information

Bajawa is three km north of the Ruteng-Ende road. The town is centred around the market, and everything is within walking distance, except the long-distance bus terminal, Watujaji, which is near the main Ruteng-Ende road.

The Bank Rakyat Indonesia on Jalan Soekarno Hatta is open Monday to Friday from 8 am to noon, and until 11 am on Saturday. The post office is close by, and is open Monday to Saturday from 8 am to 2 pm (until 11 am on Friday).

Places to Stay

Homestay Sunflower (☎ 21230), on a small path off Jalan Ahmad Yani, is a friendly place that's popular for its balcony overlooking the valley. It's a good place for information, and runs trips to villages, with knowledgeable local guides. Small singles/doubles with attached mandi are 6000/8000 rp.

The *Hotel Nusa Tera* (☎ 21357) on Jalan El Tari is run by a switched-on young host.

Large, bright rooms with mandi cost 7000/10,000/12,500 rp, while smaller rooms with outside mandi go for 4000 rp per person.

In the same street is the *Hotel Kambera* (☎ 21166), where coffin-sized rooms with outside bath cost 3000 rp per person. Rooms for swinging very small cats are 5000/10,000 rp with attached mandi. The hotel is partly redeemed by its bright, clean 1st-floor restaurant.

Close by, the *Hotel Anggrek* (☎ 21172) is good value – clean singles/doubles with attached mandi are 6000/10,000 rp. The restaurant here serves excellent food.

The *Hotel Virgo* (☎ 21061) on Jalan Mayjen Dipanjaitan is one of the better budget places in town, with singles/doubles for 5000/8000 rp with attached bath.

The staff at the *Hotel Kencana*, Jalan Palapa 7, seemed surprised to see a visitor at the hotel – so surprised they couldn't remember their address or phone number! Rooms with mandi cost 5000/10,000 rp.

The *Hotel Dam* (☎ 21145) is a quiet and delightful little place near the church, run by

---

NGADA

The 60,000 Ngada people inhabit both the upland Bajawa plateau and the slopes around Gunung Inerie stretching down the south coast. They were subdued by the Dutch in 1907 and Christian missionaries arrived about 1920. Older animistic beliefs remain strong and the religion of many Ngada, to a greater extent than in most of Flores, is a fusion of animism and Christianity.

The most evident symbols of continuing Ngada tradition are the pairs of *ngadhu* and *bhaga*. The ngadhu is a parasol-like structure about three metres high consisting of a carved wooden pole and thatched 'roof', and the bhaga is like a miniature thatch-roof house. You'll see groups of them standing in most Ngada villages, though in the less-traditional ones some of the bhaga have disappeared.

The functions and meanings of ngadhu are multiple, but basically they symbolise the continuing presence of ancestors. The ngadhu is 'male' and the bhaga 'female' and each pair is associated with a particular family group within a village. Though the carved trunks of ngadhu often feel like solid stone, their tops are usually dilapidated – some are said to have been built to commemorate people killed in long-past battles over land disputes, and may be over 100 years old. Periodically, on instruction from ancestors in dreams, a pair of ngadhu and bhaga is remade according to a fixed pattern, accompanied by ceremonies which may involve buffalo sacrifices.

The main post of a ngadhu, known as *sebu*, should come from a tree which is dug up complete with its main root, then 'planted' in the appropriate place in the village. Each part of the post has specific designs carved on it on different days: an axe and a cassava on the top part, a dragonhead in the form of a flower in the middle, and a geometric design around the base. The three parts are also said to represent the three classes of traditional Ngada society: from top to bottom, the *gae*, *gae kisa* and *hoo*. A crossbeam with two hands holding an arrow and a sword links the top of the pole to the roof. The walls of the bhaga must be cut from seven pieces of wood. Near the ngadhu there's usually a small stone post which is the 'gate keeper', and the bases of both ngadhu and bhaga are often surrounded by circles of stones, said to symbolise meeting places.

a friendly family. Singles with outside bath go for 4000 rp (7500 rp with attached bath).

On Jalan Ahmad Yani, in front of Homestay Sunflower, the *Hotel Melati Dagalos* is also pleasantly located, with a nice front porch. Rooms cost 3500 rp per person with outside mandi, 5000/8000 rp with *kamar mandi di dalam* (attached bath).

The *Hotel Korina* (☎ 21162) at Jalan Ahmad Yani 81 is one of the better places, with friendly and efficient staff. Single/doubles/triples with mandi go for 6000/10,000/12,000 rp.

Hotel Johny (☎ 21079) has basic rooms with shared bath for 3500 rp per person and small singles/doubles for 7000/14,000 rp.

The up-market *Hotel Kembang* (☎ 21072) on Jalan Marta Dinata has well-appointed double rooms with private bath for 15,000 rp.

Places to Eat

For a small town, Bajawa has a good range of restaurants – one of the rare places of this size in Nusa Tenggara where it's worth stepping out for a meal.

The travellers' favourite is the small and friendly *Restaurant Carmellya* (probably something to do with the free spring rolls and fruit they hand out late at night). The restaurant also has good maps of the area and lots of other information. Oh, and the food isn't bad either – even stretching to a few Indonesian-style Italian and Swiss dishes.

Rumah Makan Wisata, near the market, is good value. There's plenty of information here too, and excellent gado gado and Chinese food. Two other smaller restaurants right in the market, *Rumah Makan Pondok Salero* and *Rumah Makan Roda Baru*, are cheap, and popular with locals.

A little further along Jalan Gajah Mada, *Rumah Makan Kasih Bahagia* has cold beer and decent food at reasonable prices. You'll go a long way for tastier gaucamole. The *Hotel Anggrek* and the *Hotel Kambera* both have attached restaurants with long menus – the Hotel Anggrek, in particular, does excellent home-style cooking.

The traditional Ngada village layout – of which there are still a few examples left – is two rows of high-roofed houses on low stilts. These face each other across an open space which contains ngadhu and bhaga and groups of man-high stone slivers surrounding horizontal slabs. The latter, which appear to be graves of important ancestors, have led to some exotic theories about the Ngada's origins.

Traditionally, the Ngada believe themselves to have come from Java and they may have settled here three centuries ago. But stone structures which are in varying degrees similar to these 'graves' crop up in other remote parts of Indonesia – among them Nias Island, Sumatra's Batak highlands, parts of Sulawesi, Sumba and Tanimbar – as well as in Malaysia and Laos. The common thread is thought to be the Dongson culture, which arose in southern China and north Vietnam about 2700 years ago then migrated into Indonesia, bringing, among other things, the practice of erecting large monumental stones (megaliths). This practice, it's thought, survived only in isolated areas which were not in contact with later cultural changes.

Some writers also claim to have recognised Hindu, Semetic, even Caucasian elements in Ngada culture – and one theory seeking to explain apparent similarities between Indonesian and Balkan culture, suggests that the Dongson culture originated in south-east Europe!

What makes the Ngada unusual today is their preservation of animistic beliefs and practices. 'Straight' Christianity has made fewer inroads in the villages than in Bajawa itself. Apart from ngadhu and bhaga and the ancestor worship which goes with them, agricultural fertility rites continue (sometimes involving gory buffalo sacrifices) as well as ceremonies marking birth, marriage, death or house building. The major annual festival is the six-day *Reba* ceremony at Bena, 21 km from Bajawa, held around late December/early January, which includes dancing, singing, buffalo sacrifices and the wearing of special black ikat costumes. The highest god in traditional Ngada belief is Gae Dewa who unites Dewa Zeta (the heavens) and Nitu Sale (the earth). ■

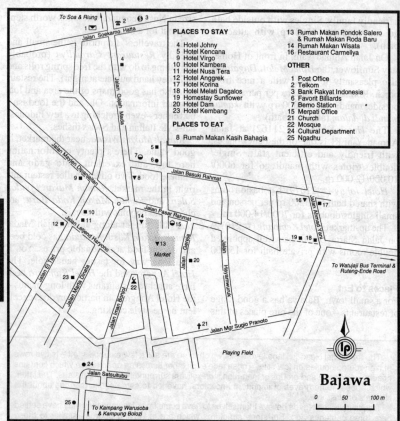

PLACES TO STAY
4   Hotel Johny
5   Hotel Kencana
9   Hotel Virgo
10 Hotel Kambera
11 Hotel Nusa Tera
12 Hotel Anggrek
17 Hotel Korina
18 Hotel Melati Dagalos
19 Homestay Sunflower
20 Hotel Dam
23 Hotel Kembang

PLACES TO EAT
8   Rumah Makan Kasih Bahagia

13 Rumah Makan Pondok Salero
    & Rumah Makan Roda Baru
14 Rumah Makan Wisata
16 Restaurant Carmellya

OTHER
1   Post Office
2   Telkom
3   Bank Rakyat Indonesia
6   Favorit Billiards
7   Bemo Station
15 Merpati Office
21 Church
22 Mosque
24 Cultural Department
25 Ngadhu

Bajawa

Things to Buy

Bajawa market is busy and colourful, with lots of women from the Ngada area and from further afield wearing ikat cloth, some of which is for sale. The better local stuff is black with white motifs, often of horses. The fruit here is plentiful and of good quality. It's also a good place to pick up betel nut or pens to take out to villages.

Getting There & Away

Air Merpati has two flights a week to and from Mataram, Bima and Denpasar, and three each week to/from Ende and Kupang.

The Merpati office is near the market, behind the Toko Suma Damai.

Bus Long-distance buses leave from Watujaji Terminal, about three km east of town near the Ende-Ruteng road. Several buses to Ende and Ruteng leave around 7 am and a few leave around noon. The buses usually do a pick-up from Homestay Sunflower, so you can go either there or to the terminal. Most hotels can arrange ticket purchase. Buses to either place cost 4000 rp and take around 5½ hours.

There are also several buses doing the

entire Bajawa-Labuhanbajo trip in one day, leaving at around 6 am. This takes about 11 hours and costs 9000 rp. There's a daily bus to Riung doing the long route via Aegela and Mbay. At least once a week, usually on Wednesday morning, a truck runs the direct route to Riung via Soa.

Bemo & Truck The town bemo station is on Jalan Basuki Rahmat. Regular bemos go from here to Soa, Mangulewa, Mataloko, Langa and Boawae. A bemo to Bena runs perhaps once or twice a day, depending on passengers, but not to any schedule. Otherwise, at least one truck a day runs to Jerebuu, passing through Bena. The bemos roam around town a lot, so you can also pick them up on the street.

Getting Around
To/From the Airport The airport is 25 km from Bajawa and about six km outside Soa. Regular bemos go to Soa (1000 rp) from the town bemo terminal on Jalan Basuki Rahmat. You should be able to pick up another from Soa to the airport for 500 rp. There are less regular bemos doing the whole run from Bajawa to the airport, and Merpati runs a bus (5000 rp).

Bemo There are no regular bemo routes around town, so you'll have to charter.

AROUND BAJAWA
Kampung Bolozi
Only a 30 to 45-minute walk from Bajawa, Kampung Bolozi has some ngadhu, a few traditional houses and an old tomb. See the town map for directions – if in doubt, ask for Kampung Warusoba, which is on the way to Kampung Bolozi.

Langa
There are 10 ngadhu and bhaga and several steep-roofed houses in Langa, seven km from Bajawa. From Bajawa's bemo terminal, there should be bemos going all the way. Otherwise, take one to Watujaji bus terminal. You'll probably be asked to pay 1000 rp to take photos, and you might be offered cere-

monial sarongs for sale. Three km from Langa is another traditional village, **Borado**.

Bena
Right underneath the Inerie volcano, 19 km from Bajawa, Bena is one of the most traditional Ngada villages, and its stone monuments are a protected site. High thatched houses line up in two rows on a ridge, the space between them filled with ngadhu, bhaga and strange megalithic tomb-like structures. Some of these 'tombs' are said to contain hoards of treasure. The house of the leading family in each part of the village has a little model house on top of its roof. A small Christian shrine sits on a mound at the top of the village, and behind it a recently built shelter offers a spectacular view of Gunung Inerie and the south coast. From Bena you can climb **Gunung Inerie** in about four hours.

You will be asked to sign in and pay 500 rp (1000 rp if you have a camera). During the

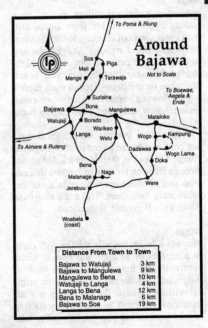

Around Bajawa

Not to Scale

To Poma & Riung

To Boawae, Aegela & Ende

To Aimere & Ruteng

Distance From Town to Town	
Bajawa to Watujaji	3 km
Bajawa to Mangulewa	9 km
Mangulewa to Bena	10 km
Watujaji to Langa	4 km
Langa to Bena	12 km
Bena to Malanage	6 km
Bajawa to Soa	19 km

day, most of the men and some of the women are out in the fields – only a few mothers and elderly women remain in the village, pounding rice or doing other chores. Try to at least chat to the villagers before wandering around and taking photos. You will probably be shown weavings here as well, some now decidedly commercial. If you want to stay with the kepala desa, you could offer to pay about 3000 rp for accommodation rather than paying the 'visitor's fee'.

Bena is 12 km from Langa. Occasionally, bemos go from Langa to Bena, but more often they finish in Langa and want you to charter the rest of the way. Otherwise, you have to walk. An easier walk is from Mangulewa, which can be reached by regular bemo from Bajawa. The 10-km walk from Mangulewa to Bena is downhill all the way. There's a daily truck from Bajawa to Jerebuu which passes through Bena – usually early in the morning or around noon.

Nage

Nage is a traditional village located on a plateau about seven km from Bena, also with great views of Gunung Inerie. Several well-maintained ngadhu and bhaga and some tombs lie between two rows of high-roofed houses. Just before you reach Malanage on the Bena-Jerebuu road, there's a fast-flowing, emerald-green hot river. Unfortunately, the water is too hot to bathe in!

To get there, you can walk from Bena – just continue on the paved road through the village. Otherwise, there's a truck that passes through Bena on the way to Jerebuu that can drop you at Malanage – Nage is a one-km uphill walk from there. This truck returns to Bajawa via Bena and Mangulewa.

Wogo

Wogo is a large, friendly village with eight or nine sets of ngadhu and bhaga. Some nontraditional houses have been built at Wogo, but they are not allowed in the original village, where the buildings are all traditional. You will be asked to pay 1000 rp to take photos, but you might want to take

some betel nut and pens for the kids as well. About one km further on from Wogo, at Dadawea, a track runs off to the left to Wogo Lama, the site of several megalith tombs.

Wogo is about a 10-minute walk from Mataloko, which is about 18 km from Bajawa on the Ende road. Regular bemos run from Bajawa to Mataloko.

Boawae

Forty-one km from Bajawa on the road to Ende, Boawae is the centre of the Nage-Keo people (related to, but distinct from the Ngada). Boawae is the source of most of the best Bajawa-area ikat. Gory buffalo-sacrifice rituals take place here, and an equally messy form of boxing called *etu* is part of the May to August harvest festivities. The boxers wear garments made of tree bark and painted with animal blood, and their gloves may be studded with broken glass!

Soa

About 19 km north of Bajawa, Soa's main attraction is the weekly market (on Thursday), which brings in villagers from a wide area. Villagers tramp into Soa with sacks of rice or lone melons perched on their heads. There are hot springs (air panas) in a river about a 1½-km walk from a village six km beyond Soa. Bungalows are being constructed nearby, but Soa is easily reached by bemo from Bajawa for a day trip.

RIUNG

This small Muslim/Christian fishing village of 2000 people is one of the few places on Flores with access to white-sand beaches and excellent snorkelling over intact reefs. The main village itself is fairly nondescript, although there's a Muslim Bugis stilt village built around the harbour. Like Labuhanbajo, most of the action is on offshore islands, and getting to them requires a charter boat. About seven of the 17 uninhabited islands off Riung have white-sand beaches. Most of the homestays can arrange day trips to several of the islands (about 20,000 rp for up to six people, with lunch included).

Another attraction are the giant iguanas

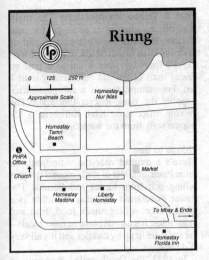

Riung

0   125   250 m
Approximate Scale

Homestay Nur Iklas

Homestay Tamri Beach

PHPA Office

Church

Market

Homestay Madona

Liberty Homestay

To Mbay & Ende

Homestay Florida Inn

Places to Stay & Eat

There are five homestays in Riung, all offering bed-and-meals deals. The best choice for information and originality is *Homestay Nur Iklas*, right next to the harbour, in the Bugis stilt village. The building, originally a traditional stilt house, features precarious step ladders and a large 1st-floor balcony. The manager speaks excellent English and has a good boat available for hire. Rooms with mosquito nets are 7000 rp per person.

Liberty Homestay has a nice balcony area and large rooms (8000 rp per person, with discounts for groups). Next door, *Homestay Madona* is run by a friendly couple and costs 7000 rp per person.

Homestay Tamri Beach is popular with travellers and has good maps and information. Rooms cost 7000 rp per person. *Homestay Florida Inn*, on the road into town, is a bit far from the harbour. Large rooms go for 7500 rp.

Getting There & Away

Bus Until the long-awaited direct road from Bajawa is completed, the trip to Riung usually requires a long ride via Aegela and Mbay. From Ende, one bus leaves every morning between 6 and 7 am from Ndao terminal. This bus sometimes finishes at Mbay, so you either have to take a truck (ask everything that comes into the market) or wait for a bus from Bajawa to come through. Altogether, travelling time is four hours over a good road and the fare is 4000 rp.

From Bajawa, there's usually a bus every day, leaving at around 6 am – this takes the Ende road to Aegela and goes on to Riung via Mbay, taking six hours and costing 4000 rp. There is also at least one truck a week from Bajawa, on Wednesday morning, that takes the direct route to Riung via Soa. This road is brand new and about the best on the island for the first 50 km or so, but the unmade last 25 km is one of the worst stretches on the island, so the trip is good value for variety. When this road is finally finished, bemos will make the trip from Bajawa in about 2½ hours. Buses return from Riung to Ende and Bajawa every day.

that can be seen further north along the mainland coast at **Torong Padang**. The beasts are more brightly coloured than Komodo dragons, with yellow markings, and some readers reported seeing one three metres long. Patience is needed, however – when we were there, one traveller had been crouching behind a bush all day watching his strung-up dead dog and was still waiting for a bite! Getting there involves a boat trip along the coast – you can do a combined snorkelling/dragon stake-out day trip for around 30,000 rp.

Watujapi Hill, about three km from Riung, offers a magnificent view of the 17 islands lying offshore. If you count them, there are actually more than 21 islands, but the government authorities decided on the number as a neat tie-in with Independence Day!

Information

The PHPA office is near the Homestay Tamri Beach and is helpful with information about the Riung area. You don't normally have to use one of their guides, but you must sign in and pay 500 rp before going to the islands. The office also rents snorkel equipment (5000 rp per day).

Boat There's a market boat leaving Riung for Reo at around 7 am on Tuesday morning (5000 rp; about six hours). From Reo, there are regular boats on to Labuhanbajo. You can also charter a boat to or from Labuhanbajo for up to 10 people for around 250,000 rp.

ENDE

Like their neighbours, the people gathered in south-central Flores in and around the port of Ende have a mix of Malay and Melanesian features. The aristocratic families of Ende link their ancestors, through mythical exploits and magical events, with the Hindu Majapahit kingdom of Java. Today most of the 60,000 people living in Ende are Christian, but there are also many Muslims.

Ende is a pleasant enough town, surrounded by fine mountain scenery. The perfect cone of Gunung Meja rises almost beside the airport, with the larger Gunung Iya occupying a promontory south of Gunung Meja. Most travellers will use Ende as a stopover to eastern Flores, or as a launching pad to Sumba. Trips to nearby villages are worthwhile, and there's interesting weaving from around Flores and Sumba to look at.

The December 1992 earthquake caused extensive damage in Ende; a lot of building is going on around the north-eastern suburbs, but things are pretty much back to normal.

Orientation

Ende is at the neck of a peninsula jutting south into the sea. The port of Ende and most of the shops are on the western side of the neck; another port, Pelabuhan Ipi, is on the eastern side. There are two bus terminals: Wolowana, about five km east of town (for buses going east), and Ndao, along the waterfront one km north of town (for buses going west, and north to Riung).

Information

Money The Bank Rakyat Indonesia is in the same building as the Dwi Putri Hotel, on Jalan K H Dewantara. It's open from 7.30 am to noon Monday to Friday, and until 11 am on Saturday.

Post & Telecommunications The main post office, where you must go for post restante, is out in the north-eastern part of town on Jalan Gajah Mada. It's open Monday to Thursday from 8 am to 2 pm, on Friday until 11 am and on Saturday until 1 pm. For stamps, there's a sub-post office opposite the Bank Rakyat Indonesia. The Telkom office is on Jalan Kelimutu, a 15-minute walk from the waterfront.

Things to See

There's a **market** near the waterfront, on Jalan Pasar, and lots of stalls around the port selling ikat from Flores and Sumba. The **Pasar Potulando** on Jalan Kelimutu is a night market selling snack food, fruit and vegetables. It's a good place to meet locals – the stalls are lit up by candles and it's all very laid back.

In 1933, the Dutch exiled Soekarno to Ende – his house on Jalan Perwira is now a **museum**. There's not a lot to see, apart from some photographs, but the caretaker, a friend of Soekarno's brother, can tell you a few stories if your Indonesian is good enough. It's open Monday to Saturday from 7 am to noon.

The Ende area has its own style of ikat weaving, mostly using abstract motifs. Some of the best local stuff comes from the village of **Ndona**, eight km east of Ende. There are irregular bemos to Ndona (300 rp) from Ende, but it might be quicker to go to Wolowana (five km out) and take another bemo from there to Ndona.

Wolotopo, about eight km east of Ende, has traditional houses built on several levels, and some reasonable ikat weaving. Bemos run from Ende (300 rp) about twice a day. Otherwise, it's a 45-minute walk from Wolowana along the black-sand beach of Nanga Nesa to Wolotopo.

Places to Stay

Accommodation is fairly spread out, but frequent bemos make it easy to get around. Several hotels damaged in the 1992 earthquake are being rebuilt, and prices are likely to alter as the work is completed.

NUSA TENGGARA

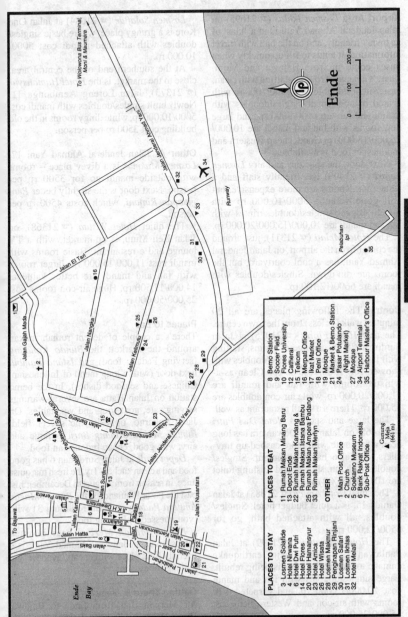

Ende

0   100   200 m

To Wolowona Bus Terminal,
Moni & Maumere

Runway

Pelabuhan
Ipi

Ende Bay

To Bajawa

Jalan Gajah Mada

Jalan El Tari

Jalan Nangka

Jalan Kelimutu

Jalan Sudirman

Jalan Pasar

Jalan Pabean/Garuda

Jalan Jenderal Jenderal

Jalan Banteng

Jalan Jenderal Ahmad Yani

Jalan Pahlawan (Suprapto)

Jalan J K H Dewantara

Jalan Soekarno

Jalan Pawira

Jalan Kartini

Jalan Hatta

Jalan Baki

Jalan Pelabuhan

Jalan Kemanunan

Jalan Nusantara

Gunung
Meja
▲ (661 m)

PLACES TO STAY

3   Losmen Solafide
4   Losmen Nirwana
6   Hotel Dwi Putri
14 Hotel Flores
20 Hotel Hamansyur
23 Hotel Amica
26 Hotel Wisata
28 Losmen Makmur
29 Penginapan Rinjani
30 Losmen Safari
31 Losmen Ikhlas
32 Hotel Melati

PLACES TO EAT

11 Rumah Makan Minang Baru
13 Depot Ende
22 Rumah Makan Kandang &
25 Rumah Makan Istana Bambu
    Merpati Office
16 Rumah Makan Ampera Padang
33 Rumah Makan Merlyn

OTHER

1   Main Post Office
2   Church
5   Soekarno Museum
6   Bank Rakyat Indonesia
7   Sub-Post Office
8   Bemo Station
9   Soccer Field
10 Flores University
12 Catheral
15 Telkom
16 Merpati Office
17 Ikat Market
18 Peini Office
19 Mosque
21 Market & Bemo Station
24 Pasar Potulando
    (Night Market)
27 Mosque
34 Airport Terminal
35 Harbour Master's Office

Airport Area *Losmen Ikhlas* (☎ 21695) on Jalan Jenderal Ahmad Yani is in a 'klas' of its own – friendly, and on the ball with travel information. It tends to fill up quickly when buses come in from Bajawa and Moni. There's a range of rooms, starting with clean, basic singles/doubles for 3500/7000 rp with shared mandi. Small singles/doubles with mandi and fan are 6000/9000 rp, and large new rooms with fan and mandi are 10,000/15,000/18,000 rp. Good, cheap Western and Indonesian food is available.

Next door, the spacious and airy *Losmen Safari* (☎ 21499) has friendly staff and a restaurant. Rooms are more expensive, but still good value – 5000/10,000 rp with mandi. Bigger singles/doubles/triples with fan and mandi are 10,000/15,000/20,000 rp.

The *Hotel Melati* (☎ 21311), just around the corner from the airport, on Jalan Jenderal Ahmad Yani, has a cool courtyard, but the rooms are run-down. Singles/doubles with mandi are 6600/12,100 rp.

Central The following places are all 20 minutes' walk (or less) from the town centre. The new *Hotel Flores* (☎ 21075) at Jalan Surdiman 28 has a range of rooms, starting with 1st-floor economy singles/doubles with shower for 7500/15,000 rp. Clean-as-a-whistle rooms with fan and mandi are 11,000/20,000 rp, while air-con doubles are 35,000 rp. There's a small restaurant as well.

The large and spotless *Hotel Dwi Putri* (☎ 21465) on Jalan K H Dewantara has long been a favourite with more cashed-up travellers, and also has a restaurant. Singles/doubles with fan, shower and flushing toilet are 10,000/15,000 rp.

The small *Hotel Amica* (☎ 21683) at Jalan Garuda 15, is a quiet budget hotel. Singles/doubles, all with attached bath, go for 6500/12,000 rp.

The *Hotel Nirwana* (☎ 21199) at Jalan Pahlawan 29 suffered major earthquake damage to its 2nd floor but is being rebuilt. Large singles/doubles with fan and mandi cost 10,000/15,000 rp, and carpeted VIP rooms with air-con and Western bath cost 15,000/25,000 rp.

Losmen Solafide (☎ 21084) at Jalan One Kore is a grungy place, where basic singles/doubles with attached mandi cost 5000/10,000 rp.

At the southern end of the central area, close to the market, is the *Hotel Hamansyur* (☎ 21373), Jalan Loreng Aembonga 11. Newly built singles/doubles with mandi cost 5000/10,000 rp, while dingy rooms in the old building cost 3500 rp per person.

Other At Jalan Jenderal Ahmad Yani 17, *Losmen Makmur* is a divey place – rooms with outside mandi go for 3500 rp per person. Next door is the slightly better *Penginapan Rinjani*, which costs 4500 rp per person.

The quiet *Hotel Wisata* (☎ 21368), on Jalan Keli Mutu, is up-market, with a TV lounge and a restaurant. Basic rooms with mandi cost 11,000/15,000 rp; larger rooms with fan and mandi are better value at 14,000/17,500 rp. Huge air-con rooms cost 25,000/50,000 rp.

Places to Eat
There's a couple of decent rumah makan around the market: the *Bundo Kandang* (serving Padang food) and *Istana Bambu*, next door (with a long menu of Indonesian, Chinese and seafood dishes). In the bemo station on Jalan Hatta are several warungs serving sate, goat soup and vegetables. On Jalan Sukarno, opposite the soccer field, *Rumah Makan Minang Baru* is large and airy, with good, cheap Indonesian food.

Depot Ende at Jalan Surdiman 6 has good food and a clean kitchen. Try the fresh marquisa juice, in season from August to December. Just past the Pasar Potulando is the *Rumah Makan Ampera Padang* at Jalan Kelimutu 31 with (you guessed it) Padang food.

Rumah Makan Merlyn, near Losmen Ikhlas on Jalan Jenderal Ahmad Yani, is a friendly little place with cheap Javanese and Padang food.

Getting There & Away
Air Merpati flies from Ende to Bajawa, Bima, Denpasar, Kupang, Labuhanbajo and

Mataram almost daily. The Merpati office (☎ 21355) is on Jalan Nangka, a short bemo ride from the airport.

Some readers have reported getting seats on flights after being told the flight is full, as no-shows are not reoffered. If you're desperate, it might be worth going to the airport before departure to check.

Bus Terminal Wolowana, for buses going east, is easily reached by bemo. Buses to Moni (2000 rp; 2½ hours) leave throughout the day between 6 am and 2 pm. To Maumere (5000 rp; six hours), buses leave at 8 am and 5 pm. If you take this late bus to Moni, you'll have to pay the full fare to Maumere. There's supposed to be a daily bus to Nggela (3000 rp; 3½ hours), leaving at 7 am, but it may go only as far as Wolojita.

Terminal Ndao is one km north of town, reachable by bemo. Buses to Bajawa (4000 rp; five hours) leave at 7 and 11 am. One bus a day leaves for Riung (5000 rp; six hours), at 6 am, and there's one to Ruteng (8500 rp; 10 hours) at 7 am. If you have a well-developed sense of humour, it's possible to do the long haul to Labuhanbajo (12,500 rp; 14 hours) in one hit; the bus leaves at 7 am.

Most hotels can arrange tickets for the Bajawa bus and have it pick you up, but for most other destinations you'll have to go to one of the terminals.

Boat The ferry boat *Ile Mandiri* loops once a week around Kupang, Ende, Waingapu, Savu and back. It leaves Kupang for Ende (15,400 rp; 12 hours) on Monday afternoon, continuing on from Ende to Waingapu (10,400 rp; 10 hours) at 7 pm on Tuesday. It returns from Ende to Kupang on Saturday at 1 pm. The ferry docks at Pelabuhan Ipi.

The *Kelimutu* calls in at Ende twice a fortnight, sailing on to Waingapu and Bima one week and to Kupang the next. It departs for Waingapu on Wednesday at 6 pm, and the following week for Kupang on Thursday at 6 am. It now docks at Pelabuhan Ipi. The Pelni office is on the corner of Jalan Pabean and Jalan Sukarno, a five-minute walk from the pier.

Other boats sail irregularly to these and other destinations – ask at the harbour masters' offices at Ende and Pelabuhan Ipi.

Small boats also chug regularly along the south coast of Flores. A boat to Nggela (2000 rp; about three hours) should leave at 7 am every day, except Friday, from Pelabuhan Ipi. The boat puts in at the village of Ngaluroga, and from there it's a good two-km walk uphill to Nggela. If you can, leave your backpack in Ende.

Getting Around

To/From the Airport You could walk to town, or just walk 100 metres to the roundabout on Jalan Jenderal Ahmad Yani and catch a bemo (300 rp).

Bemo Bemos run frequently just about everywhere in town for a flat fare of 300 rp, even out to Pelabuhan Ipi. You can easily flag one down in the street; if not, pick one up at the bemo stop, or on Jalan Hatta (near the pier).

Car You can charter a car to Keli Mutu for up to six people for 75,000 rp. Ask at your hotel.

DETUSOKO & CAMAT

Between the villages of Detusoko and Camat, 35 km from Ende, *Wisma Santo Fransiskus* is quiet and peaceful. It's presided over by Sister Maria Graciana, who has the distinction of producing a book with over 100 recipes for tapioca roots! The nightly price (7000 rp) includes good meals. It's a popular retreat from Ende, and there are some lovely walks around the area – it should even be possible to walk along foot trails all the way to Keli Mutu.

KELI MUTU

Of all the sights in Nusa Tenggara, the coloured lakes of Keli Mutu are the most singularly spectacular. The three lakes, set in deep craters at an altitude of 1600 metres, near the summit of the Keli Mutu volcano (in this region 'keli' means mountain), have a habit of changing colour from time to time.

Most recently, the largest was a light turquoise, the one next to it olive green, and the third one black. A few years ago the colours were blue, maroon and black, while back in the 1960s the lakes were blue, red-brown and cafe-au-lait.

No-one has managed to explain the cause of the colours, or why they change (apart from what those '60s travel writers were on), except to suppose that different minerals are dissolved in each lake. The moonscape effect of the craters gives the whole summit area an ethereal atmosphere. There's a story among the locals that the souls of the dead go to these lakes: young people's souls go to the warmth of the green lake, old people's to the cold of the milky turquoise one, and those of thieves and murderers to the black lake. No-one explains how a soul knows which lake to hop into when the colours keep changing!

Keli Mutu has attracted sightseers since Dutch times, and today there's a paved road up to the lakes from Moni, 13½ km away at the base of the mountain. You even get an occasional busload of tourists, and a small helipad has been constructed for VIP guests. There's a staircase up to the highest lookout point, from where you can see all three lakes.

Fortunately, there's a wonderfully spacious feeling up here and you can scramble round the perimeters of two of the lake-craters for a bit of solitude. Hope for a sunny day – sunrise is stunning at the top, and the turquoise lake only reaches its full brilliance in the sunlight. If the weather is bad, come back the next day, because it really is worth seeing!

You could camp up here, but it gets very cold and there's no water available. The nearest losmen are in Moni.

Getting There & Away

The easiest and best way of seeing Keli Mutu is to base yourself in Moni, 52 km east of Ende on the Maumere road. Staying in Moni

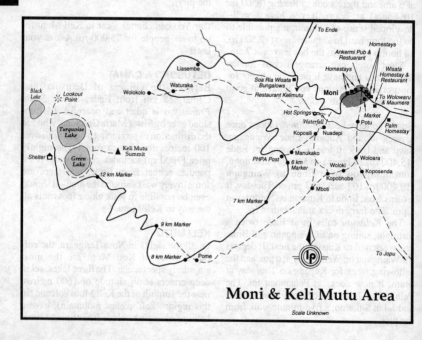

Moni & Keli Mutu Area

Scale Unknown

allows you to get to the lakes for sunrise, and also to assess the weather before going up. Be warned, though, that even if it looks clear in Moni, there can be cloud cover at Keli Mutu. The most convenient way of getting up there is to take the truck at 4 am (3000 rp one-way). The truck returns to Moni at about 7 am, which can be a little hurried, so you may want to linger until the sun brings out the full brilliance of the lakes, then walk down. The sun rises earlier at the top than in the valley below. Later in the day, clouds roll in and block out the view.

The walk down takes about 2½ hours and isn't too taxing. A few masochists walk or ride mountain bikes both ways. It's 13½ km of winding (but not steep) road up to the lakes. After about six km there's a PHPA post, where you have to pay 400 rp per person (more if you've hired a vehicle) to continue up to the protected summit area. Beware of false 'PHPA posts', which have been known to set up lower down the road and extract 1000 rp from unsuspecting visitors. A short cut (jalan potong) leaves the Moni-Ende road about 750 metres from the centre of Moni (see the Moni & Keli Mutu Area map), and comes out on the Keli Muti road beside the PHPA post. This cuts about six km off the journey, but is easier to follow in daylight, so most people only use it on the way down unless they've checked it out the day before.

Another path branches off the short cut at Koposili and goes via the villages of Mboti and Pome, reaching the Keli Mutu road about 5½ km from the summit. It's no shorter, but it passes through villages where you can have a drink and fruit and see weaving. This one is almost impossible to find in the dark, but on the way down may be marked by a small sign ('Suka Pome tu Moni'!) and an arrow made of sticks, erected by an enterprising family in Pome. On the way down, at Nuadepi, we were accosted by a pint-sized 11-year-old genius with curlers in her hair. After engaging us in quick-fire repartee we were whisked into her house, Rumah Makan Agnes, for breakfast.

MONI

It's no hardship if you have to wait a few days in Moni to see Keli Mutu. This is quite a pretty village, and is developing as a tourist destination – witness the number of homestays that have sprung up in the last few years. There are several good walks, a lovely waterfall and hot springs nearby, traditional dances and a pub for a spot of nightlife, and about the best food you'll find in Flores.

The village is strung alongside the Ende-Maumere road and is the heart of the Lio region, which extends from just east of Ende to beyond Wolowaru. Lio people, who speak a dialect of the Ende language, are renowned for their ikat weaving, and a colourful market spreads over the playing field in front of Moni's earthquake-damaged church every Monday morning. The local ikat is quite attractive, with bands of blue and rusty-red. You'll also see cloth from the Nggela and Maumere regions in stalls set along the street in Moni. Prices are not much higher than in the villages.

In the kampung opposite the market, there's a genuine high-thatched rumah adat, still inhabited, with some carved woodwork. You may be asked 500 rp to enter. Dance performances are held in the kampung at night.

Apart from the trek to or from Keli Mutu, there are several other walks from Moni. About 750 metres along the Ende road from the centre of Moni, paths lead down to a 10-metre waterfall, with a pool big enough for swimming, and a couple of hot springs (air panas). Locals use these springs to wash in, and don't mind if you join them – men to the left pool, women to the right. Another short walk is out past the church to Potu and Woloara (about 2½ km from Moni). From Woloara you could continue on through several villages to Jopu (about five km). If you're energetic and well prepared, walk on to Wolojita and Nggela, or you can loop back to Wolowaru and catch a bus or truck back to Moni.

Places to Stay & Eat
Several new places have sprung up in Moni,

and competition between them can be keen. Apart from one or two more expensive options, the standard is fairly similar. The bulk of places are within five minutes' walk of each other, so it's worth checking a few out.

Along the main road opposite the market are several cheap places where beds are rented mostly on a per person basis: *Homestay Amina Moe* (3000 rp), *Homestay Friendly* and *Homestay Maria* (both 4000 rp with mandi), *Homestay Daniel* (4000 rp) and *Homestay John* (3500 rp). All do decent meals for around 2000 rp – the buffet meals at Homestay Amina Moe and Homestay Maria continue to get rave reviews.

More homestays are clustered about five minutes' walk along the road to Ende, with *Nusa Bunga* (3000 rp), *Regal Jaya* (3500 rp), *Lovely Rose* (3000 rp) and *Sylvester* (3000 rp) the most popular. Another option is the *Wisata Homestay & Restaurant* (4000 rp), a large place with a popular restaurant; it's about 500 metres back along the road to Maumere. The quiet *Palm Homestay* (4000 rp) is on a side road to Woloara, a few hundred metres past Wisata Homestay.

On the Ende road 1½ km from Moni is the more expensive *Sao Ria Wisata*, with bungalows for 7500 rp per person.

A popular place for its views and music is the *Ankermi Pub & Restaurant*, situated above the main road, between the two clusters of homestays. The food is basic, but the music and cold beer make up for it. Another good cheap place is the *Restaurant Moni Indah*, next to Homestay Daniel. *Restaurant Kelimutu* is a decent tourist-oriented restaurant 200 metres down the road from Sao Ria Wisata.

Getting There & Away
Moni is 52 km from Ende and 96 km from Maumere. The first bus for Moni (2000 rp; 2½ hours) leaves Ende at 7 am. From Moni to Ende, there's an early morning truck at 8 am. Otherwise, a few buses pass through Moni on the way to Ende at about 11 am, and a late bus comes through at around 9 pm. Buses originating in Wolowaru come

through Moni between 7 or 8 am. On Monday (market day) trucks go to Ende and Wolowaru throughout the day.

From Maumere to Moni, you probably need to take an Ende bus. The morning buses leave between 7 and 8 am, and a late bus leaves around 5 or 6 pm. Maumere to Moni costs 4000 rp and takes about four hours (including a lunch break in Wolowaru, just 13 km before Moni). In the opposite direction, the first buses to Maumere start coming through Moni between 8 and 9 am. Buses through Moni from Ende or Maumere are often crowded; sometimes you'll be sitting in the aisle on a sack of rice, or a pig – if you're lucky!

AROUND MONI
Wolowaru
The village of Wolowaru, straggling along the Maumere road 13 km east of Moni, is a convenient base for trips to the ikat-weaving villages of Jopu, Wolojita and Nggela. The road to these villages branches south from the main road in Wolowaru. The daily market winds down around 9 am, except on Saturday, the main market day. As you come into Wolowaru from Moni, you'll see a group of five traditional houses with high sloping roofs.

Places to Stay & Eat There are two losmen in the village: *Losmen Kelimutu* has basic singles/doubles with shared bath for 6000/7500 rp, and *Losmen Setia*, down near the market on Jalan Pasar Wolowaru, has rooms with shared bath for 5000 rp per person.

Rumah Makan Jawa Timur, where the buses stop, has a reasonably long menu. There are three other small restaurants in the village.

Getting There & Away Buses come through from Maumere for Moni/Ende between 9 and 11 am, and between 8 or 9 am from Ende to Maumere. Buses originating in Wolowaru go both ways in the morning as well – ask at the Rumah Makan Jawa Timur. Fares and journey times from Wolowaru are: Ende (2500 rp; 2½ hours), Maumere (4000; four hours) and Moni (500 rp; half an hour).

Nggela, Wolojita & Jopu

Beautiful ikat sarongs and shawls can be found here, and in other villages between Wolowaru and the south coast. Impromptu stalls will spring up before your eyes as you approach the villages.

Nggela is worth a visit for its hilltop position above the coast, but the chief attraction is its weaving, usually done by hand and still using many natural dyes. The weaving is among the finest in Flores, and you'll be able to watch women weaving and see at least part of the process that makes up the final product. In former times the size, colour and pattern of the ikat shawls of this region indicated the status of the wearer. Nggela ikat typically has black or rich, dark-brown backgrounds, with patterns in earthy reds, browns or orange.

Bargain hard – and watch out for synthetic dyes, which are becoming more common (you should pay less if the dyes aren't natural). There are a couple of homestays in the village (around 7500 rp, including a couple of meals).

Wolojita, about seven km inland from Nggela, has similar-quality weavings, but not Nggela's fine location. At Jopu, six km further inland (and the same distance from Wolowaru), weaving has taken a plunge in the last few years. Old weaving may still be worth looking at.

Getting There & Away A road branches off the Ende-Maumere road at Wolowaru to Jopu (six km), Wolojita (12 km) and Nggela (19 km). There's usually a bus or truck every day from Moni at about 8 am (1500 rp), at least as far as Wolojita. This should also pass through Wolowaru. Otherwise, it's a good half-day's walk to Nggela from Wolowaru. It's only two or three km further from Moni, so you could just as easily start from there. The volcano-studded scenery is beautiful, particularly on the downhill stretch to Nggela. From Wolojita to Nggela, you can either follow the road or take a short cut past the hot springs (ask for the *jalan potong ke Nggela*). You'd be pushing it to do the return

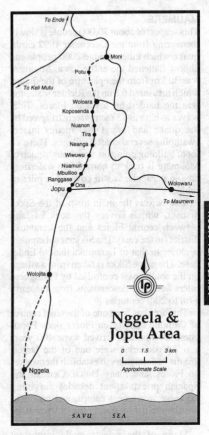

NUSA TENGGARA

Nggela & Jopu Area

0   1.5   3 km

Approximate Scale

walk the same day, but you might find a truck going back to Wolowaru.

An alternative is the small boat that chugs along the coast from Pelabuhan Ipi (at Ende) to Nggela and back. It's supposed to go every day (except Friday) at around 7 am, but it's not always a definite starter. The trip takes about three hours and costs 2000 rp. The boat actually puts in at the village of Ngaluraga; Nggela is a two-km uphill walk from there. Ask at the harbour master's office at Pelabuhan Ipi (in Ende) about availability. From Nggela to Ende, the boat leaves at around 11 am.

MAUMERE

This seaport of about 70,000 people is slowly recovering from the December 1992 earthquake which killed around 2000 people and almost flattened the entire town. Maumere was 30 km from the epicentre of the quake, which measured 6.8 on the Richter scale, and was the hardest-hit town on Flores. Tidal waves as high as 23 metres were triggered by the quake and swept 300 metres inland, swamping several coastal villages. There's a lot of building going on, and though much of Maumere is back to normal, the waterfront area in particular is still covered in piles of rubble.

Maumere is the main town of the Sikka district, which covers the neck of land between central Flores and the Larantuka district (in the east). The Sikkanese language is closer to that of Larantuka than to Endenese. The name Sikka is taken from a village on the south coast controlled by Portuguese rulers and their descendants from the early 17th to 20th centuries.

This area has been one of the chief centres of Catholic activity on Flores since Portuguese Dominicans arrived some 400 years ago. Missionaries were one of the largest groups of foreigners to establish themselves on Flores, and many Dutch, German and Spanish priests spent decades surviving Japanese internment camps, and an often-hostile population during the independence wars.

Many of the priests made important studies of the island and its people. They also encouraged local arts and crafts and helped the Florinese with improved tools and seed for agriculture – as recently as two decades ago, many Florinese were still tilling the soil with sharpened sticks, and moving slash-and-burn farming is still common. Today the European priests are being replaced by Florinese.

To prove that God isn't always White, the interior of Maumere's cathedral is adorned with a series of paintings of a very Indonesian-looking Jesus. This cathedral was shaken to its foundations by the earthquake, and huge cracks run along the walls from floor to ceiling. You can still enter, but tread lightly ye of little faith!

There's a strong ikat-weaving tradition in the Maumere region, and some interesting trips can be made out of town. Toko Harapan Jaya, beside the market on Jalan Pasar Baru Timur, has the most comprehensive collection of ikat (from Flores and other islands) that you'll find anywhere in Nusa Tenggara except Sumba. They also sell carvings and other artefacts.

Orientation & Information

Central Maumere is fairly compact, and most of what you're likely to need is within walking distance of the central market – apart from the east and west bus terminals, the airport and a couple of hotels.

The Kantor Dinas Pariwisata (☎ 21652) is on Jalan Wairklau. The Bank Rakyat Indonesia on Jalan Soekarno Hatta is open from 8 am to noon Monday to Friday, and until 11 am on Saturday. The post office is on Jalan Pos, opposite the soccer field. Opening hours are from 8 am to 2 pm Monday to Saturday (closing at 11 am on Friday). The Telkom office, opposite the Bank Rakyat Indonesia on Jalan Soekarno Hatta, is open 24 hours.

Places to Stay

Quite a few losmen were 'broken' in the earthquake; new ones have since sprung up and old ones are being rebuilt or are in the process of renovation. Some of the losmen now operating in half-demolished buildings will put their prices up when building is finished.

A little far from the town centre but close to the west bus terminal, *Losmen Wini Rai* (☎ 21388) on Jalan Gajah Mada has plenty of rooms and serves meals. Single/double economy rooms with shared mandi are not cheap (7500/12,500 rp), while rooms with private mandi and fan jumped in price recently to 20,000/25,000 rp.

If you fly to Maumere, you'll probably be steered to the *Gardena Hotel* (☎ 21489) on Jalan Pattirangga, which is central but in a quiet street. Clean singles/doubles/triples with mandi and fan are 10,000/15,000/20,000 rp.

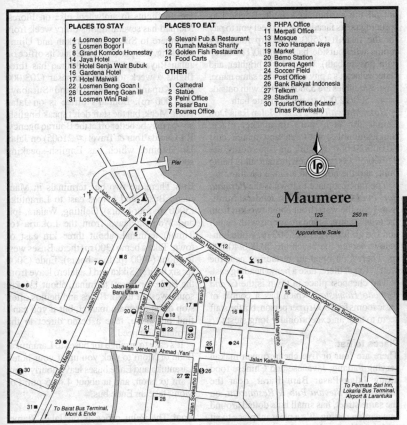

PLACES TO STAY	PLACES TO EAT	
4 Losmen Bogor II	9 Stevani Pub & Restaurant	8 PHPA Office
5 Losmen Bogor I	10 Rumah Makan Shanty	11 Merpati Office
8 Grand Komodo Homestay	12 Golden Fish Restaurant	13 Mosque
14 Jaya Hotel	21 Food Carts	18 Toko Harapan Jaya
15 Hotel Senja Wair Bubuk		19 Market
16 Gardena Hotel	**OTHER**	20 Bemo Station
17 Hotel Maiwali		23 Bouraq Agent
22 Losmen Beng Goan I	1 Cathedral	24 Soccer Field
28 Losmen Beng Goan III	2 Statue	25 Post Office
31 Losmen Wini Rai	3 Pelni Office	26 Bank Rakyat Indonesia
	6 Pasar Baru	27 Telkom
	7 Bouraq Office	29 Stadium
		30 Tourist Office (Kantor Dinas Pariwisata)

Maumere

0   125   250 m

Approximate Scale

NUSA TENGGARA

A new place that's well set up is the *Hotel Senja Wair Bubak* (☎ 21498) on Jalan Komodor Yos Sudarso, near the waterfront. There's a wide range of rooms, from singles/doubles with fan and shared bath (6600/11,000 rp) through to air-con rooms with private bath (25,000/30,000 rp). Meals are available, and the hotel can arrange motorbike hire.

On Jalan Hasanuddin near the centre of town, the *Jaya Hotel* has friendly staff, and rooms with fan and mandi go for 10,000/15,000 rp.

One of the cheapest places in town is the

Losmen Beng Goan III (☎ 21284), in an old stable-like building next to where the original hotel stands (just). It's a bit dark and dingy. Rooms with mandi and fan cost 5500/10,000 rp. *Losmen Beng Goan I* (☎ 21041), beside the market on Jalan Moa Toda, fared better than its stablemate and has already been partially rebuilt. It offers a range of rooms: basic singles/doubles/triples are 5000/8000/12,000 rp, while rooms with private bath start at 10,000/16,000 rp.

Losmen Bogor 1 and *Losmen Bogor 11* (☎ 21137), opposite each other on Jalan Slamet Riyadi, are both a bit tragic, but it's not all the earthquake's fault. Bogor 1 is sprucing up its facade; they expect you to pay for the facelift (7500/10,000 rp for dingy rooms with outside bath, 10,000/11,500 rp with private bath). Bogor 11 is brighter, and better value; it's a pity it carries the same name. Singles/doubles are 5500/9000 rp with outside bath, 7500/12,000 rp with private bath.

Hotel Maiwali (☎ 21220), Jalan Raja Don Tomas 40, is a more up-market place. Singles/doubles with fan and mandi cost 10,000/20,000 rp and air-con rooms are 31,000/55,000 rp. A new restaurant is being built, and the hotel can arrange car hire.

The fanciest place in town is the *Permata Sari Inn* (☎ 21171) at Jalan Jenderal Surdiman 1, on the waterfront about two km from the town centre. Standard rooms with mandi and fan go for 17,500/22,500 rp, while bungalows facing the beach are 30,000/40,000 rp. There's an open-air restaurant near the water. To get there, take a bemo heading east.

The cheapest place in town is the *Grand Komodo Homestay*, which has a couple of basic rooms for 3500 rp per person, but the staff seem to take an exceptionally long siesta.

Places to Eat

There are four or five cheap rumah makan serving Padang, Javanese and Chinese food along Jalan Pasar Baru Barat, near the market. The *Stevani Pub & Restaurant*, on the same street, has small huts dotted around in a garden setting. It's a pleasant place to sit with a drink, and the food is OK as well. You can get Western food such as hamburgers and chips; if you've come overland from the east, it's a bit like being in heaven. *Rumah Makan Shanty* is spacious and has a long menu of Chinese food and seafood. The *Golden Fish* restaurant, on the waterfront, has good seafood and air-con. The *Bamboo Den* near the Losmen Wini Rai has cheap Indonesian and Western food. Night food stalls set up behind the market, near Jalan Jenderal Ahmad Yani.

Getting There & Away

Air Maumere is probably the easiest place on Flores to fly into from other islands, but there are no flights to anywhere else on Flores. Merpati has several flights every week from Maumere to Surabaya, Tarakan and Ujung Pandang. Merpati (☎ 21342) has its office on Jalan Raya Don Tomas. Bouraq has three flights a week to/from Denpasar (203,000 rp), Kupang (75,000 rp) and Surabaya (258,000 rp). Bouraq's office is on Jalan Nong Meak, but the staff don't speak English, so you may be better off at the Bouraq agency, P T Garuda Tour & Travel (☎ 21605) on Jalan Dr Sutomo, which has English-speaking staff.

Bus There are two bus terminals in Maumere. Buses and bemos east to Larantuka (5000 rp; four hours), Geliting, Waiara, Ipir and Wodong leave from the Lokaria (or Timur) terminal, about three km east of town. Take a bemo (300 rp) there. Buses west to Moni (4000 rp; four hours), Ende (5000 rp; six hours), Sikka and Ladalero leave from the Ende (or Barat) terminal, about 1½ km south-west of town. Buses and bemos often stop off at the main market, but if you can't find one there, take a bemo direct to the terminal you need.

It's easy to arrange for buses to Larantuka, Ende or Moni to pick you up at your hotel. Larantuka and Ende buses leave hourly from 8 am to noon, and at about 4 or 5 pm. For Moni, take an Ende bus.

Boat The Pelni office is on Jalan Slamet Riyadi, across the road from Losmen Bogor I. The *Kelimutu* stops in Maumere on its way to Ujung Pandang. You may be able to find something else if you ask around the harbour.

Getting Around

To/From the Airport Maumere's Wai Oti airport is three km from town, 800 metres off the Maumere/Larantuka road. A taxi to/from town is 5000 rp. Otherwise, it's about a one-km walk out of the airport to the Maumere-Larantuka road to pick up a bemo (500 rp) into town.

Bemo Bemos run around town regularly, and cost 300 rp anywhere within the city.

Motorbike A few places around town hire motorbikes for around 15,000 rp per day – ask at your hotel or the travel agencies.

AROUND MAUMERE
Ladalero & Nita
Many Florinese priests studied at the Roman Catholic seminary in Ladalero, 19 km from Maumere on the Ende road. The chief attraction here is the museum run by Father Piet Petu, a Florinese. It houses a collection of historic stone implements and Florinese ikat – you'll see designs and natural dyes that are either rare or extinct, including softly textured, pastel-coloured old Jopu sarongs. It's a good place to try to piece together the jigsaw of Florinese culture. Admission is free, but you might leave a donation. Nita, two km beyond Ladalero on the main road, has a Thursday market. There are bemos to Ladalero and Nita from Maumere's Ende terminal (500 rp).

Sikka
On the south coast, 27 km from Maumere, Sikka was one of the first Portuguese settlements on Flores, dating from the early 17th century. Its rulers dominated the Maumere region until this century. Today it's interesting mainly as the home of the distinctive Sikkanese ikat. A lot of Sikka weaving is predominantly in maroons, blues and browns, and design has been heavily influenced by the Dutch – you'll see the Dutch coat of arms and pairs of baby cherubim!

If you're in Sikka overnight, you may be able to stay with the Dutch priest. The road to Sikka leaves the Ende road 20 km from Maumere. Take a bemo from Maumere to Sikka (1000 rp).

About four km before Sikka is **Lela**, another Catholic and weaving centre. It has a few colonial buildings, and a long, rocky black-sand beach.

Geliting
Geliting, about 10 km east of Maumere on the Larantuka road, has a huge, colourful market on Friday. There's lots of beautiful ikat around – more being worn than for sale

– and thousands of people come from surrounding villages. Get there by bemo from Maumere's east terminal (500 rp).

Watublapi
Watublapi, in the hills 20 km south-east of Maumere, is a large Catholic mission. From here, you can walk to **Ohe**, where you can see both coasts of Flores. **Bola** is a large village six km from Watublapi, and two km further on is the traditional coastal weaving village of **Ipir**. Market day in Ipir is Friday, and bemos and trucks go there from Maumere (1500 rp; 1½ hours). On other days, trucks usually finish at Bola. You should be able to stay with villagers or the kepala desa in Bola or Ipir.

Pantai Waiara
Thirteen km east of Maumere, just off the Larantuka road, Waiara is the jumping-off point for the Maumere 'sea gardens'. Unfortunately, some of the reefs were damaged in the 1992 earthquake, although others are still intact.

There are two resorts here – the cheaper one, *Sea World Club* (☎ 21570), is the friendlier and cleaner. Cabin accommodation starts at 22,000/35,000 rp with fan and shower, with air-con rooms costing 55,000/65,000 rp. A snorkelling day trip will cost 30,000 rp, while a room and dive package is around 150,000 rp per day, including meals.

The newer *Flores Sao Resort* (☎ 21555) is group-tour territory, with prices to match, but is looking tired. Accommodation starts at 70,000/80,000 rp, plus 15% tax, for singles/doubles with fan and bath. A day's diving will cost another 110,000 rp.

To get there, catch a Talibura bus from Maumere to Waiara (500 rp), or take a bemo to Geliting and walk 1½ km along the Larantuka road. You'll see the signs for the turn-off to Sea World Club first, and Flores Sao Resort is about 500 metres further along the road.

Wodong
Wodong village is 28 km east of Maumere, a short walk off the Maumere-Larantuka

road. A French couple have built lovely bamboo beachside huts (*Flores Froggies*) near the village, where you can stay for 4000 rp in 'dorm huts', 7500/15,000 rp in bungalows with private mandi and balcony. They serve French and Indonesian food, have canoes you can take out to snorkel and offer boat trips to nearby islands.

To get there, take a Talibura, Nangahale or Larantuka bemo or bus and get off at Wair Terang (1000 rp; 40 minutes).

LARANTUKA

A busy little port at the eastern end of Flores, Larantuka (population 30,000) nestles round the base of the Ili Mandiri volcano, separated by a narrow strait from the islands of Solor and Adonara. Larantuka is the departure point for boats to the Solor Archipelago (east of Flores) and for a twice-weekly ferry to Kupang.

The Larantuka area has long had closer links with the islands of the Solor Archipelago – Adonara, Solor and Lembata – than with the rest of Flores. It shares a language, Lamaholot, with the islands. The whole area, particularly outside the towns, fascinates anthropologists because of its complex social and ritual structure, which in some parts survives pretty well intact.

There's a web of myths about the origins of the Lamaholot people: one version has them descended from the offspring of Watowele (the extremely hairy female god of Ili Mandiri) and a character called Patigolo, who was washed ashore, got Watowele drunk, cut her hair (thus removing her magic powers and discovering that she was female) and made her pregnant. Alternatively, locals believe their forbears came from Sina Jawa (China Java), Seram or India – take your pick.

At some stage, probably before the 16th century, the Lamaholot area became divided between two groups known as the Demon and the Paji. The Demon, associated with the 'Raja' of Larantuka, were mainly grouped in eastern Flores and the western parts of Adonara, Solor and Lembata; the Paji, with their allegiance to the 'Raja' of Adonara, were centred in the eastern parts of the three islands. Anthropologists tend to believe that the conflict between the two groups was mainly a ritual affair – as one writer puts it, 'two groups representing the two halves of the universe engaged in regular combat to

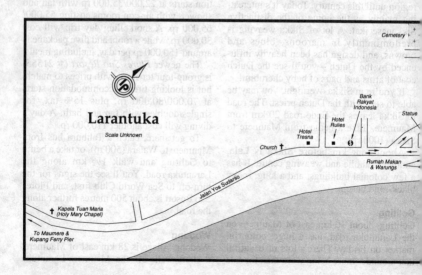

Larantuka

Scale Unknown

Cemetery

Bank Rakyat Indonesia

Statue

Hotel Rulies

Hotel Tresna

Church

Rumah Makan & Warungs

Jalan Yos Sudarso

Kapela Tuan Maria (Holy Mary Chapel)

To Maumere & Kupang Ferry Pier

produce human sacrifices for the securing of fertility and health'. Such a pattern was not uncommon in eastern Indonesia. Today, people still know who is Paji and who is Demon, but ritual warfare has subsided. Other animist rites survive, including those for birth, name-giving, marriage, the building of a new house, the opening of new fields in *ladang* (slash-and-burn) agriculture, and the planting and harvesting of crops.

This corner of Indonesia, though always isolated, was one of the first to attract European interest. Lying on sea routes used by the Portuguese seeking sandalwood from Timor, the Larantuka-Solor area saw Portuguese forts and over 20 Dominican missions being built by 1575. Portugal even maintained a few enclaves until the mid-19th century – among them Larantuka, which was the centre of a community of Topasses (from *tupassi*, a south Indian word for 'interpreter'), the descendants of Portuguese men and local women. The Topasses are still a significant group in Larantuka today.

Orientation & Information
Most hotels, the ferry pier, shipping offices and the main bus stop are in the compact southern part of the town (shown on the Larantuka map). Further north-east are the homes, mosques and fishing boats of the Muslim population, and the post office, Telkom office and airport. To the south is the pier for boats to Kupang.

The only place in town to change money, the Bank Rakyat Indonesia on Jalan Yos Sudarso, will change US and Australian dollar travellers' cheques.

Things to See
Portuguese-style Catholicism flourishes in Larantuka. There's a large **cathedral**, and the smaller **Holy Mary Chapel** (Kapela Tuan Maria) contains Portuguese bronze and silver known as *ornamento*. On Saturday in this chapel, the women say the rosary in Portuguese, and on Good Friday an image of the Virgin Mary from the chapel is carried in procession around the town to the accompaniment of songs in Latin.

The **market** at Larantuka has some weaving – look for ikat from Lembata, Adonara and Solor.

Six km north of Larantuka is a white-sand beach at **Weri**; get there by bemo (300 rp)

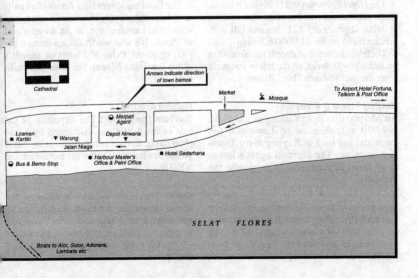

from the central bemo stop in Larantuka. **Waibalun** is a weaving village about four km north of Larantuka. The villages of **Lewoloba**, **Lewohala** and **Badug** are traditional weaving villages, accessible by bemo (300 rp). Some bemos are direct to the villages; others finish in **Oka**, and you can walk from there. In Oka, ask the kepala desa for someone to show you the short walk to the villages.

Places to Stay & Eat

The friendly, family-run *Hotel Rulies* (☎ 21198) at Jalan Yos Sudarso 44 is recommended; clean singles/doubles/triples with shared bath are 8000/13,000/18,000 rp. The manager speaks good English and meals are available.

Next door, the *Hotel Tresna* (☎ 21072) caters mainly for business travellers. Rooms with private mandi are 11,000 rp per person (6000 rp with shared mandi). Meals are served here, too.

Right in the middle of town, opposite the bus stop, the drab *Losmen Kartiki* (☎ 21083) has the cheapest rooms in town (4000 rp per person). The *Hotel Sederhana* has a similar deal, but may be 'full'.

The *Hotel Fortuna* (☎ 21140) is a relaxed, clean place about two km north-east of town at Jalan Diponegoro 171. Rooms (all with private bath) go for 11,000/16,500 rp.

There are a couple of decent rumah makan on Jalan Yos Sudarso, on the left as you walk from the pier towards Hotel Rulies.

Getting There & Away

Air Merpati flies from Kupang to Larantuka (94,000 rp), then on to Lewoleba (on Lembata) and back to Kupang every Thursday morning. The Merpati agent's house is at Jalan Diponegoro 64, opposite the cathedral.

Bus Buses to/from Maumere cost 5000 rp and take about four hours. If you're coming in from the Solor Archipelago, there'll be enthusiastic bus jockeys ready to arm-wrestle you into waiting buses and whisk you away to Maumere. Buses leave Larantuka hourly throughout the morning, and you can arrange for the bus to pick you up at your hotel.

Boat The Kupang-Larantuka ferry leaves Kupang on Thursday and Sunday afternoons. Going the other way, ferries leave Larantuka on Tuesday and Friday at 2 pm. You can buy tickets at the office at the pier entrance on the day of departure. The price for the 12-hour voyage is 12,500 rp. There are some seats on board, but they get pretty crowded – the earlier you board the better, since the undercover deck space fills up quickly. Take some food and water, as there's none on board. Departures from Larantuka are from a pier five km southwest, which is reached by taking a yellow-bulb bemo (300 rp).

Smaller boats go to Adonara, Solor and Lembata daily from the pier in the centre of town. Boats run twice a day to Lewoleba (4000 rp; four hours) at around 8 am and 1 pm. All these boats stop in at Waiwerang (on Adonara). A boat goes once a week to Lamalera (5000 rp; seven hours) on Friday at 9 am.

The Pelni passenger ship *Tatamailau* calls in at Larantuka every two weeks or so, and sails on to Labuhanbajo, at the western end of Flores. It's also worth asking around the pier, or at the Pelni and harbour master's office (on Jalan Niaga), for other possibilities.

Getting Around

To/From the Airport The airport is 12 km east of town. It's possible to go by bemo (500 rp) from the central bemo stop, but if you're in a hurry it's better to charter (around 5000 rp).

Bemo The bemo system is efficient but doesn't dominate the town. Bemos run up and down Jalan Niaga and Jalan Pasar, and to outlying villages. Bemos in town cost 250 rp, but many are trying out a new price – 300 rp.

Solor & Alor Archipelagos

A chain of small islands stretches out from the eastern end of Flores: volcanic, mountainous specks separated by swift, narrow straits. Andonara is directly opposite Larantuka; south of Adonara is Solor, where the Portuguese first established themselves in the 16th century; further east is Lembata, with the whaling village of Lamalera, where whales are still hunted with small boats and harpoons; and beyond Lembata are the islands of Pantar and Alor, whose people were still head-hunting in the 1950s. The Solor Archipelago – Solor, Adonara and Lembata – has close cultural links with the Larantuka area on Flores, and together these people are known as the Lamaholot. Pantar and Alor are the main islands of the Alor Archipelago.

The scenery is spectacular, all the islands (notably Lembata) produce distinctive ikat weaving, and there are some traditional, almost purely animist villages, despite the spread of Christianity and (less so) Islam.

In remote villages, people are poor and not used to Westerners: children will follow you in excited bunches. They won't follow you into the toilet, but will wait enthusiastically outside the door for your return. Food is generally poor. If you can't deal with all this, limit your stay to the urban centres of Kalabahi and Lewoleba and make a few day trips into the surrounding countryside.

One thing you should bring is plenty of money. You can change money in Kalabahi, but that's it for the entire group of islands! Even Lewoleba has no place to change money. Take 1000 and 5000 rp notes into the countryside, as you'll find it hard to change anything bigger.

Alor has some bemos and ancient buses, but most of the islands have only one decent road, and transport to more isolated areas is limited to a few trucks per week. Asking around the ports may prove more fruitful; on Alor and Lembata, the most reliable transport to their south coasts is by boat.

History

European contact was made as early as 1522, when the only remaining ship of Magellan's fleet sailed through the Lembata-Pantar strait. By the middle of the century, the Dominican Portuguese friar Antonio Taveira had landed on Solor and set about spreading Catholicism. The Solor mission became the base for extending Christianity to mainland Flores, and a fort was built to protect the converts from Muslim raids. The Portuguese were eventually kicked out of Solor by the Dutch, but until the mid-19th century, Portugal held on to Wurek (on Adonara) and Pamakajo (on Solor).

SOLOR

Rita-Ebang is the main town on the island. Lohajong (towards the eastern end of the north coast) has the ruins of the Portuguese fort. Lamakera (on the north tip) is a whaling

NUSA TENGGARA

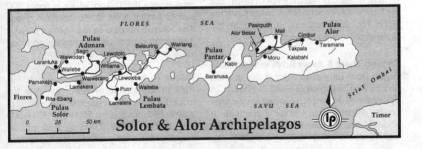

Solor & Alor Archipelagos

village, but is losing the battle against commercialism of its tradition.

Getting There & Away

From Larantuka there are boats to Pamakajo and Lohajong every morning at about 8 am. From Waiwerang (on Adonara), boats cross several times a day to Lohajong and Lamakera.

ADONARA

Adonara was known as the 'Island of Murderers' because of a feud between two clans. The feud apparently ran for hundreds of years, with people in the hills being killed and houses burned year in, year out – very likely a case of ritual conflict between the Demon and Paji groups (see under Larantuka in the previous Flores section). Though extremes of animism have died out, there are villages in the hinterland where Christianity has only the loosest of footholds. One traveller reported placing her hands on a sacred rock above one village and being unable to remove them! The chief settlements are Wailebe (on the west coast) and Waiwerang (on the south). A few bemos link the main villages.

Waiwerang

There's an uninspiring market every Monday and Thursday – follow the streets about 400 metres in the Lembata direction from the pier. There are three places to stay in Waiwerang: *Losmen Taufiq*, close to the pier, is run by a friendly Muslim woman and costs 5000/10,000 rp; the more up-market *Ile Boleng Homestay* is a little out of town; and the cheapest accommodation in town is at the *Hotel Tresna*. A few rumah makan dot the main street around the pier.

Getting There & Away

Boats to Waiwerang depart from Larantuka twice a day at 8 am and 1 pm. The trip takes about 2½ hours. To Wailebe and Waiwodan (further up the west coast), boats usually leave Larantuka at about 11 am. You can pick up boats to Solor and Lembata every day, to Lamalera (on

Lembata) on Friday, and to Alor and Pantar perhaps twice a week.

LEMBATA

Lembata is well known for the whaling village of Lamalera, and for the smoking volcano, Ili Api, which towers over the main town of Lewoleba. As in the rest of the Lamaholot region, many Lembata villagers still use the slash-and-burn method of clearing land. Corn, bananas, papayas and coconuts are grown; most rice is imported.

Lewoleba

Despite the ominous smoking of Ili Api volcano in the background, the chief settlement on Lembata is a relaxed little place.

Boats unload you at a pier about a 10-minute walk west of the town – take a becak, or the town's one dokar (which hangs around the pier). Below town, on the water, is a Bugis stilt village built out over the sea – some of its people are pearl divers, and you can arrange to go out with them on diving trips. Have a good look at the pearls you're offered in town as many are just shells. Locals will take you out to a sandbank off Lewoleba – it's the closest place to town for a swim in beautifully clear water.

Orientation & Information The centre of Lewoleba is the market place, which comes alive every Monday evening with buyers and sellers from around Lembata and other islands – watch out for the character with the python and megaphone flogging some kind of miracle elixir.

The post office is near the south side of the market, and the Telkom office is about 500 metres further west along the main street. The Merpati agent is in the Losmen Rejeki. The banks do not change money, so bring sufficient funds with you.

Places to Stay & Eat *Losmen Rejeki 1* is right in the middle of town, opposite the market. Clean, bright singles/doubles/triples with outside mandi cost 5500/11,000/16,500 rp (10,000/15,000/20,000 rp with private mandi). Meals are generous and cheap, and there's always fresh seafood on the menu. Check your bill here, as they seem to have problems adding up. *Losmen Rejeki 11* is about a 10-minute walk south of the market. It's cheaper (4500 rp per person), but a bit out of the way.

The basic *Losmen Rahmat*, near the waterfront on Jalan Aulolon (turn left at the far end of the market as you come from the pier), has rooms for 4000 rp per person.

There are a few restaurants around the market. *Rumah Makan Bandung*, right next to the market on Jalan Aulolon, serves basic Indonesian dishes for about 1500 rp and is popular with locals. *Rumah Makan Sinar Masakan*, on the main street opposite the market, has Padang food – check out the window displays.

Getting There & Away Merpati flies Kupang-Larantuka-Lewoleba once a week on Thursday (98,400 rp).

Boats ply daily both ways between Lewoleba and Larantuka. They normally leave at 8 am from Lewoleba and at 7 am from Larantuka, take about four hours and cost 4000 rp. Most of these boats stop at Waiwerang (on Adonara).

Boats leave Kalabahi (Alor) for Belauring (Lembata) on Tuesday, Thursday and Sunday. The trip takes nine hours and costs 9000 rp. There should be boats through to Lewoleba (4000 rp; four hours) from there – certainly on Monday morning for the Lewoleba market. You'll probably have to stay overnight in Belauring, where there's now one decent losmen. Going the other way, boats leave Lewoleba for Belauring on Tuesday, Wednesday and Friday. Boats from Belauring return to Kalabahi at 7 am on Wednesday, Friday and Monday – the Tuesday boat from Lewoleba is the best for connections to Kalabahi.

Getting Around Around town there are a few becaks and one dokar. Passenger trucks go to other parts of the island, most regularly on Monday (market day) and Tuesday. Losmen Rejeki 1 can rent you a motorbike for around 40,000 rp per day.

Around Lewoleba
Some of Lembata's finest ikat – recognisable by its burgundy-coloured base and highly detailed patterning – comes from the villages on the slopes of Ili Api, 15 or 20 km from Lewoleba. **Atawatun** and **Mawa**, on the north coast, are two of the best places to see fine ikat. Trucks go there three times a week. **Jontona** is on the east side of the deep inlet in Lembata's north coast. Trucks make the one-hour trip every day. It's possible to stay there with the kepala desa. An hour's walk from Jontona towards Ili Api is the **Kampung Lama** (Old Village), with at least 50 traditional houses. These contain many sacred and prized objects, including a huge number of elephant tusks, but are occupied by villagers only for ceremonies such as the *kacang* (bean) festival in late September/early October. It is possible to climb Ili Api – it takes about four hours.

Belauring
A laid-back little town on the peninsula jutting off the eastern end of Lembata, Belauring is the major port of call for ferries linking Alor and Lembata. If you're doing

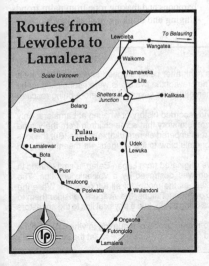

Routes from Lewoleba to Lamalera

Scale Unknown

To Belauring
Lewoleba
Wangatea
Waikomo
Namaweka
Lite
Kalikasa
Shelters at Junction
Belang
Bata
Pulau Lembata
Lamalewar
Bota
Udek
Lewuka
Puor
Imuloong
Posiwatu
Wulandoni
Ongaona
Futongtolo
Lamalera

this trip, you'll probably have to spend a night here. There are wonderful views of Ili Api as you come into Belauring. The town has one good place to stay, *Losmen Telaga Sari*, run by a friendly Chinese family, though it's in a swampy area and mosquitoes are a problem. Walk straight down the road leading off the end of the pier, and the losmen is the second last building in the street. It costs 7000 rp per person, with three good meals a day. Otherwise, you may be able to sleep on the boat. Trucks occasionally run the 53 km from Belauring over a shocking road to Lewoleba.

Lamalera

Like characters out of *Moby Dick*, the people who live in this village on the south coast of Lembata still use small boats to hunt whales. The whaling season is limited from May to October, when the seas aren't too rough. Even then, the whales are infrequent, with only about 25 caught each year. The villagers probably qualify as subsistence whalers and are therefore exempt from international bans on whaling.

The meat is shared according to traditional dictates. The heads go to two families of original landowners – a custom observed, it is said, since the 15th century. The blubber is melted to make fuel for lamps, and some is traded for fruit and vegetables in a barter-only market in the hills.

Most whales caught are sperm whales, though smaller pilot whales are occasionally taken. When whales are scarce, the villagers harpoon sharks, manta rays and dolphins, which are available all year round. Using nets is alien to these people, and fishing rods are used only for sharks.

The whaling boats are made entirely of wood, with wooden dowel instead of nails. Each vessel carries a mast, and a sail made of palm leaves, but these are lowered during the hunt, when the men (usually a crew of 12) row furiously to overtake the whale. As the gap between the boat and the whale narrows, the harpooner takes the three-metre-long harpoon and leaps onto the back of the whale. An injured whale will try to dive, dragging the boat with it, but cannot escape, since it has to resurface.

Your chances of actually seeing a whale hunt, or the bloody business of butchering a whale, are quite small. The village is difficult to reach, but a worthwhile trip for the cultural experience, even if you don't see any whaling. It's a friendly, relaxed village, and it's interesting poking around the boat sheds and small shrines on the beach, and watching men forge harpoons and making rope from palm fronds, singing and drinking tuak as they work.

Lamalera

In March 1994, two small boats from Lamalera sank after being dragged almost to Timor by a wounded whale, a distance of around 80 km. The crew of the two boats were later picked up by a third boat from the village, and the 36 men then drifted for several days before being rescued by the P & O Spice Islands cruise ship.

Throughout several hundred years of oral and recorded history of whaling at Lamalera, only one or two similar incidents have occurred (there is a story that some children from the village were named Kupang after one), and these are remembered as remarkable events. But the loss of boats from the village was more than an economic blow to the villagers – it meant losing an important part of their heritage.

The villagers of Lamalera are thought to have originated from Lapan Batan, a small island in the straits between Lembata and Pantar which was destroyed by a volcanic eruption. The ancestors arrived in boats that each clan has kept as the model for all future boats. While the original boats have been repaired and added to over generations, the villagers consider them to be the same boats. To the villagers, each boat is a living being, and a physical link to the ancestors and the ancestral home.

The loss of the boats sent the village into a two-month period of mourning in which no whaling was allowed. When the mourning period finished, a ceremony took place to 'let the boats go'. ∎

On Saturday, there's an interesting barter-only market at **Wulandoni**, about a 1½-hour walk along the coast from Lamalera. Another nice walk along the coast is to **Tapabali**, where you can see local weaving. In Lamalera, common ikat motifs are whales, mantarays and boats.

Places to Stay & Eat There are four small homestays in the village. *Homestay Ben Guru* is above the village, perched on a hill overlooking the shoreline. The cost is 7000 rp per person, with three meals a day. The most salubrious accommodation in the village is *Bapa Yosef's*, also known as the 'White House', which is right on the point at the end of the beach. The house sleeps four, and you can have it to yourself for 7500 rp per person – someone will come in three times a day to cook meals. *Mama Maria's Homestay* is right in the heart of the village, behind the shady town square. The cost is 7000 rp per person, including three meals and a good breakfast. *Abel Losmen* is on the main path through the village, past the town square, and costs 6500 rp, food included.

Getting There & Away The easiest way to get to Lamalera is by boat from either Lewoleba or Larantuka. The boat from Lewoleba leaves after the Monday night market (any time between 1 and 5 am, depending on tides) and takes about six hours (3500 rp). From Larantuka, a boat leaves on Friday at 8 am (5000 rp; seven hours). Going the other way, a boat leaves Lamalera for Lewoleba on Monday at 8 am, for the market. To Larantuka, a boat leaves on Wednesday at 8 am, stopping in Waiwerang on the way. It's possible to connect back to Lewoleba from Waiwerang.

The alternative is to take a truck to Puor or Bota and walk from there. Trucks go to Puor from Lewoleba at least twice a week, and from there it's a three-hour walk, mostly downhill. Trucks go more frequently to Bota, closer to Lewoleba on the same road, from where it's at least a four-hour walk, with the first half uphill. Bring plenty of water. It may be possible to charter or hire a motorbike in

Lewoleba. If you want to walk the entire way from Lewoleba, it's quicker via Nanaweke and Udek, but still takes about 10 hours – it might be worth finding a guide through Losmen Rejeki.

ALOR & PANTAR

East of the Solor group are the islands of Alor and Pantar. Alor, in particular, is quite scenic, and has a wide mix of cultures in a small area. Diving around the island is reportedly some of the best in South-East Asia. The island is so rugged and travel there so difficult that the roughly 140,000 inhabitants of Alor are divided into some 50 tribes, with about as many different languages. To this day there is still some isolated occasional warfare between the tribes.

Although the Dutch installed local rajas along the coastal regions after 1908, they had little influence over the interior, whose people were still taking heads in the 1950s. The mountain villages were hilltop fortresses above valleys so steep that horses were useless, and during the rainy season the trails became impassable. The different tribes had little contact with each other except during raids.

When the 20th century came, the warriors put Western imports to good use by twisting wire from telegraph lines into multibarbed arrowheads, over the tip of which they pressed a sharpened, dried and hollowed chicken bone. When the arrow hit, the bone would splinter deep inside the wound.

The coastal populations are predominantly Muslim. Christianity has made inroads into the interior, but indigenous animist cultures still survive, mainly because travel remains very difficult. Roads are few, with boats a more common form of transport.

Alor's chief fame lies in its mysterious *mokos* – bronze drums about half a metre high and a third of a metre in diameter, tapered in the middle like an hourglass, and with four ear-shaped handles around the circumference. They're closed at the end with a sheet of bronze that sounds like a bongo when thumped with the hand. There are thousands of them on the island – the Alorese apparently found them buried in the ground and believed them to be gifts from the gods.

Most mokos have decorations similar to those on bronze utensils made in Java in the 13th and 14th-century Majapahit era, but others resemble earlier South-East Asian designs and may be connected with the Dongson culture which developed in Vietnam and China around 700 BC and then pushed its influence into Indonesia. Later mokos even have English or Dutch-influenced decorations.

Theories about the mokos' origins usually suggest they were brought to Alor from further west by Indian, Chinese or Makassarese traders, but this doesn't explain why they were buried in the ground. Maybe the Alorese buried them in some long-forgotten times, as an offering to spirits at a time of plague or to hide them during attacks.

Today mokos have acquired enormous value among the Alorese, and families devote great time and energy to amassing

collections of them, along with pigs and land. Such wealth is the only avenue to obtaining a bride in traditional Alorese society. In former times, whole villages would sometimes go to war in an attempt to win possession of a prized moko.

Kalabahi & Around

Kalabahi is the chief town on Alor, at the end of a long, narrow and spectacular palm-fringed bay on the west coast. It's a cliché tropical port – lazy and slow-moving, with wooden boats scattered around the harbour. Kalabahi is relatively prosperous, but outside the town, living conditions are poor. There are a few interesting villages and nice beaches nearby. Some of the beaches have spectacular snorkelling and diving, but also dangerous currents.

Money It's best to bring enough cash with you, as there are restrictions on currencies and exchange rates are not good.

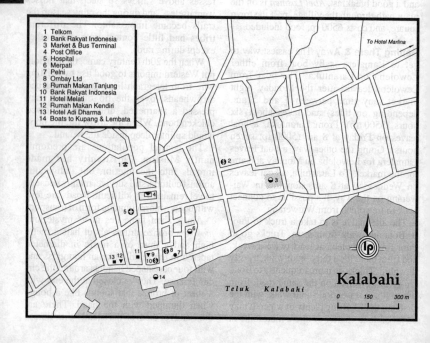

1 Telkom
2 Bank Rakyat Indonesia
3 Market & Bus Terminal
4 Post Office
5 Hospital
6 Merpati
7 Pelni
8 Ombay Ltd
9 Rumah Makan Tanjung
10 Bank Rakyat Indonesia
11 Hotel Melati
12 Rumah Makan Kendiri
13 Hotel Adi Dharma
14 Boats to Kupang & Lembata

To Hotel Marlina

Teluk   Kalabahi

Kalabahi

0   150   300 m

The Bank Rakyat Indonesia has two branches that will change money. One is on the street running along the harbour opposite the pier, but it only changes US dollars (cash). The other main branch will change US and Australian dollar travellers' cheques, though you'll get a better rate for Australian dollars at Ombay Ltd, one block back from the port.

Things to See It's worth strolling around the Pasar Inpres market in Kalabahi. It has a huge variety of fruit, and you'll see women making bamboo mats.

Takpala is a traditional village about 13 km east of Kalabahi. To get there, take a bus from the Kalabahi market (500 rp). From where the bus drops you, walk about one km uphill on a sealed road. There are several traditional high-roofed houses, and the view over the Flores Sea from the village is stunning. The people welcome visitors, and occasionally put on dance performances for tour groups. From Takpala it's possible to continue on to **Atimelang**, another traditional village rarely visited. You can take a bus to Mabu, but from there it's about a four-hour walk; a guide is recommended. It's possible to stay with the kepala desa in Atimelang.

The villages of **Alor Kecil** and **Alor Besar** have good beaches nearby, with excellent snorkelling. The water is wonderfully cool but the currents are very strong. Alor Kecil has some weavings and offers great views across to other islands. This area is being promoted as a potential diving resort, and may soon have bungalows. Buses to Alor Kecil and Alor Besar leave from the Kalabahi market but also wait around outside the Hotel Melati.

Near the airport at the northernmost tip of the island is **Mali**, a lovely white-sand beach with good snorkelling. It's possible to rent a boat for a tour of the area, and at high tide you can walk to Suki Island, off the beach at Mali – there's an old grave there, said to be that of a sultan from Sulawesi.

Places to Stay & Eat Most travellers head

for the *Hotel Adi Dharma* (☎ 21049) at Jalan Marta Dinata 12, on the waterfront about 100 metres from the main pier. Singles/doubles/triples with outside bath are 6000/10,000/12,000 rp, while large, clean rooms with fan and bath are 12,500/ 20,000/24,000 rp. Meals are served (around 4000 rp for lunch or dinner, 2500 rp for a breakfast of eggs). The staff speak English, and the charming owner, Mr Enga, is a wealth of information.

The nearby *Hotel Melati* (☎ 21033) has a shady garden and a faded charm about it. Singles/doubles with bath go for 7000/16,000 rp.

The *Hotel Marlina* (☎ 21141) gets few travellers, because of its location (three km out of town on Jalan El Tari), but you can get there by bemo. Room rates are 5000 rp per person in three-bed rooms with shared bath, 15,000 rp with private bath.

There are a few restaurants dotted around the harbour. Close to the pier, the *Rumah Makan Kendiri* on Jalan Marta Dinata serves tasty Javanese food, such as soto ayam and mie goreng. The *Rumah Makan Tanjung*, just off the main drag on Jalan Dr Sutomo, has good Chinese food, cold beer and friendly owners. There are also two Padang restaurants, opposite the market.

Getting There & Away Merpati flies from Kupang to Kalabahi (100,600 rp) and back four times a week.

The Perum ASDP ferry leaves Kupang's Bolok Harbour on Thursday and Saturday at 2 pm (15,000 rp; about 16 hours). Ferries run from Kalabahi to Kupang on Tuesday and Friday.

There are three boats per week from Kalabahi to Belauring (Lembata) on Sunday, Tuesday and Thursday, departing at 7 am and returning to Kalabahi the following morning, probably stopping in Baranusa (Pantar) on the way. The trip takes nine hours and costs 9000 rp. Take food and water, as there's none on the boat. There should be boats on to Lewoleba (4000 rp; four hours) from Belauring, at least on Monday morning for the Lewoleba market.

Going the other way, a boat leaves

Lewoleba on Tuesday and stays overnight in
Belauring before sailing on to Kalabahi on
Wednesday morning. Other boats leave
Belauring for Kalabahi on Friday and
Monday.

The Pelni ship *Kelimutu* calls in at
Kalabahi twice every fortnight, sailing on to
Dili (East Timor) one week and to Maumere
the next.

From Dili, there's usually one boat a week
on Monday. The fare is 4600 rp and the trip
somehow takes 14 hours. Another option is
to/from the port of Atapupu (in Timor). A
boat leaves Kalabahi for Atapupu every
Sunday at 10 pm (9000 rp; eight hours). It
returns to Kalabahi from Atapupu on Monday at 10 am.

Getting Around Kalabahi airport is 28 km
from town. Merpati or the Hotel Adi Dharma
will run a minibus (2500 rp) to meet flights.
There are also bemos (300 rp). As yet
Kalabahi has no taxis or becaks, so local
transport is by bus and bemo, which finish
by 7 pm. It's also possible to rent a motorbike
through the Hotel Adi Dharma (about 15,000
rp per day).

Timor

If you arrive in Timor from Darwin, it will
hit you with all the shock of Asia. Kupang,
the main city, is very Indonesian, with its
buzzing streets and honking horns and its
Third World sights and smells. Away from
Kupang, Timor is not very touristy, although
it's a scenic island, with some traditional
areas in the south-west that are off the track
and worth exploring. New interest was
added in 1989, when East Timor, a former
Portuguese colony, was opened up to foreign
tourists for the first time since Indonesia
invaded and took it over in 1975.

Timor's landscape is unique, with its
spiky lontar palms, rocky soils and central
mountains dotted with villages of beehive-
shaped huts. The island has some fantastic
coastline. There are no tourist-type beach

spots yet, though you can take trips from
Kupang to nearby islands for swimming and
snorkelling. East Timor's beaches, which
attracted travellers before 1975, are again
accessible.

Timor is 60% mountainous; the highest
peak, Tata Mai, stands at about 3000 metres.
Along the north coast, the mountains slope
right into the sea. Aggravated by dry winds
from northern Australia, the dry season is
distinct and results in hunger and water
shortages. To remedy the water problem,
there is an intensive programme of small
earth-dam building. Maize is the staple crop,
but coffee and dry rice are important, and
some irrigated rice is grown in the river
valleys.

Thanks to Merpati's twice-weekly flights
between Kupang and Darwin, more travellers to or from Australia are passing through
Timor, and there are interesting options for
onward travel from East Timor to the Solor
and Alor archipelagos, or from Kupang on to
Roti, Sawu and Sumba.

Apart from Kupang (one of the most prosperous towns in Nusa Tenggara) and Dili
(something of a showcase town for the
Indonesian government), Timor is poor,
especially the eastern half. West Timor has a
population of 1.3 million and East Timor
about 700,000. Christianity, both Catholic
and Protestant, is widespread, though still
fairly superficial in some rural areas: the old
animistic cultures have not been completely
eradicated. In the hills of the centre and the
east, villagers still defer to their traditional
chiefs, though major damage seems to have
been done to traditional East Timorese
society by decades of war and oppression.

About 14 languages are spoken on the
island, both Malay and Papuan types, though
Tetum (the language of the people thought to
have first settled in Timor in the 14th
century) is understood in most parts.

History
The Tetum of central Timor are one of largest
ethnic groups on the island. Before the Portuguese and Dutch colonisation, they were
fragmented into dozens of small states.

Skirmishes between them were frequent, with head-hunting a popular activity, although when peace was restored, the captured heads were kindly returned to the kingdom from which they came.

Another major group, the Atoni, are thought to be the earliest inhabitants of Timor. One theory is that they were pushed westward by the Tetum. The Atoni form the predominant population of West Timor and, like the Tetum, were divided into numerous small kingdoms before the arrival of Europeans. It's thought that their traditional political and religious customs were strongly influenced by Hinduism, possibly as a result of visits by Javanese traders, but they held to a strong belief in spirits, including ancestor spirits.

The first Europeans in Timor were the Portuguese, perhaps as early as 1512, the year after they captured Melaka. Like Chinese and western Indonesian traders before them, the Portuguese found the island a plentiful source of sandalwood (prized in Europe for its aroma and for the medicinal santalol made from the oil). In the mid-17th century the Dutch occupied Kupang, Timor's best harbour, beginning a long con-

flict for control of the sandalwood trade. In the mid-18th century the Portuguese withdrew to the eastern half of Timor. The division of the island between the two colonial powers, worked out in agreements between 1859 and 1913, gave Portugal the eastern half plus the enclave of Oekussi (on the north coast of the western half), while Holland got the rest of the west. Today's Indonesian province of East Timor has the same boundaries as the former Portuguese Timor.

Neither European power penetrated far into the interior until the second decade of this century, and the island's political structure was left largely intact, both colonisers ruling through the native kings. Right through until the end of Portuguese rule in East Timor, many ostensibly Christian villages continued to subscribe to animist beliefs. When Indonesia won independence, in 1949, the Dutch left West Timor, but the Portuguese still held East Timor, setting the stage for the tragedy that continues today.

East Timor (Timor Timur) Until the end of the 19th century, Portuguese authority over their half of the island was never very strong.

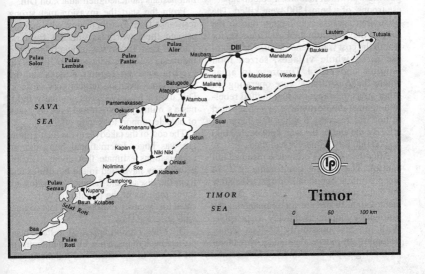

Their control was often effectively opposed by the *liurai*, the native Timorese rulers, and by the *mestico*, the influential descendants of Portuguese men and local women. The Dominican missionaries were also involved in revolts or opposition to the government. Eventually a series of rebellions between 1894 and 1912 led to bloody and conclusive 'pacification'.

The colony had been on the decline much earlier, as the sandalwood trade fizzled out, and when Portugal fell into a depression after WW I, East Timor drifted into an economic torpor. Neglected by Portugal, it was notable only for its modest production of high-quality coffee and as a distant place of exile for opponents of the Portuguese regime. The ordinary Timorese were subsistence farmers using the destructive ladang (slash-and-burn) system, with maize (sweet corn) the main crop.

In WW II, although Portugal and her overseas territories were neutral, the Allies assumed that the Japanese would use Timor as a base from which to attack Australia. Several hundred Australian troops were landed in East Timor, and until their evacuation (in January 1943), they carried out a guerilla war which tied down 20,000 Japanese troops, of whom 1500 were killed. The Australian success was largely due to the support they got from the East Timorese, for whom the cost was phenomenal. The Japanese razed whole villages, seized food supplies and killed Timorese in areas where the Australians were operating. In other areas the Japanese had incited rebellion against the Portuguese, which resulted in horrific repression when the Japanese left. By the end of the war, between 40,000 and 60,000 East Timorese had died.

After the war the Portuguese resumed full control. The turning point came in 1974 when a military coup in Portugal overthrew the Salazar dictatorship. The new government sought to discard the remnants of the Portuguese empire as quickly as possible. With the real possibility of East Timor becoming an independent state, two major political groups, the Timorese Democratic

Union (UDT) and the Timorese Social Democrats (later known as Fretilin), quickly formed in the colony. A third group, known as Apodeti, was a minor player, but its stated preference for integration with Indonesia eventually turned it into little more than a front for Indonesia's goals.

Although both major political groups advocated independence for East Timor, Fretilin gained the edge over the UDT, partly because of its more radical social policies. Indonesian leaders had had their eyes on East Timor since the 1940s, and as Fretilin was regarded by them as communist, they were itching for a reason to step into East Timor.

It came on 11 August 1975, when the UDT staged a coup in Dili which led to a brief civil war between it and Fretilin. Military superiority lay from the outset with Fretilin; by the end of August, the bulk of the fighting was over and the UDT withdrew to Indonesian Timor.

Fretilin proved surprisingly effective in getting things back to normal, but by the end of September Indonesia had decided on a takeover. East Timor and Fretilin now faced Indonesia alone; the Portuguese were certainly not coming back. On 7 December the Indonesians launched their attack on Dili.

From the start the invasion met strong resistance from Fretilin troops, who quickly proved their worth as guerilla fighters. Though East Timor was officially declared Indonesia's 27th province on 16 July 1976, Fretilin kept up regular attacks on the Indonesians, even on targets very close to Dili, until at least 1977. But gradually, Indonesia's military strength and Fretilin's lack of outside support took their effect.

The cost of the takeover to the East Timorese was huge. International humanitarian organisations estimate that about 100,000 people may have died in the hostilities and from the disease and famine that followed. Large sections of the population were relocated for 'security reasons', and lost contact with ancestral sites.

By 1989, Fretilin appeared to have been pushed back to just a few hidden hideouts in the far east of the island and Indonesia was confident to open up East Timor to foreign tourists. But on 12 November 1991, about 1000 Timorese staged a rally at a cemetery where they had gathered to commemorate the death of an independence activist two weeks earlier. Indonesian troops opened fire on the crowd. The number killed was variously reported from 19 to 200. Other unconfirmed reports claim scores of injured people were killed in the days following the incident.

In the wake of the 1991 massacre, Indonesia once again restricted travel to and around East Timor. This situation has since eased, and currently there are no official restrictions on travel to East Timor, with travellers getting right through to Tutuala, East Timor's most easterly point.

Books Probably the best account of events surrounding the Indonesian invasion of East Timor is John Dunn's *Timor – A People Betrayed* (Jacaranda Press, Brisbane, Australia, 1984). Dunn was Australian consul in East Timor from 1962 to 1964; he was also part of an Australian government fact-finding mission to East Timor from June to July 1974, and returned in 1975, just after the Fretilin-UDT war. To balance Dunn's book, read *Timor, The Stillborn Nation*, by Bill Nicol (Widescope International, Melbourne, Australia, 1978), which tends to criticise Fretilin's leaders and places much more blame on the Portuguese. For the inside story from the Fretilin point of view, read *Funu: The Unfinished Saga of East Timor*, by Jose Ramos Horta (Red Sea Press, New Jersey, USA, 1987). Horta is Fretilin's United Nations representative. A book detailing recent travellers' experiences in East Timor may also be worth reading: *Opening Up: Travellers' Impressions of East Timor*, edited by Kirsty Sword & Pat Walsh (Australia East Timor Association, Fitzroy, Australia, 1991).

KUPANG

Kupang is virtually a booming metropolis compared with the overgrown villages that pass for towns in other parts of Nusa Tenggara. It's the capital of East Nusa Tenggara

(Nusa Tenggara Timur, or NTT) province, which covers West Timor, Roti, Sawu, the Solor and Alor archipelagos, Sumba, Flores and Komodo. As such it comes equipped with footpaths (watch your step, though, or you could find yourself knee-deep in green slime), brightly coloured bemos with sophisticated sound systems and a nightlife of sorts.

The centre is busy, noisy and untidy; the wealthier residential areas are in the suburbs. There's a lot of building going on, particularly on the eastern edge of town.

Merpati's twice-weekly Darwin to Kupang flights are attracting many short-term tourists from Australia, and have put Kupang well and truly on the South-East Asia travellers' route. It's not a bad place to hang around for a few days – Captain Bligh did after his *Bounty* misadventures.

History

The Dutch East India Company occupied Kupang in the middle of the 17th century, mainly in an attempt to gain control of the sandalwood trade. The Portuguese had built a fort at Kupang, but abandoned it before the Dutch arrived, leaving the Portuguese-speaking Christian mixed-blood mestico population (or the 'black Portuguese', as they were known) to oppose the Dutch. It was not until 1849, after an attack by the mestico on Kupang had been decisively defeated, that the Dutch went more or less unchallenged in western Timor.

Timor was, however, very much a sideshow for the Dutch. Supplies of sandalwood had already dwindled by 1700, and by the late 18th century, Kupang was little more than a symbol of the Dutch presence in Nusa Tenggara. Not until the 20th century did they pay much attention to the interior of the island.

The original inhabitants of the Kupang area were the Helong. Squeezed by the Atoni, the Helong had, by the 17th century, been limited to a small coastal strip at the western tip of the island. Later, partly because of the Dutch-supported migration to Kupang of people from the nearby island of Roti, most of the Helong migrated to the small island of Semau (off Kupang). By the mid-20th century they were confined to just one village near Tenau (the port of Kupang) and several villages on Semau.

Orientation
Kupang is hilly, with the downtown area hugging the waterfront. The central bemo station, Kota Kupang (or simply Terminal), almost doubles as a town square, though you're not likely to stroll leisurely across it with bemos coming at you from all directions. Many of the shops and restaurants are around here. Kupang's El Tari Airport is 15 km east of town; Tenau Harbour is eight km west.

Information
Tourist Office The tourist office is way out of town, grouped with other government offices east of Kupang. The office is helpful for maps and a few brochures, but that's about it. To get there, take bemo No 10 or 7.

Get off on the corner of Jalan Raya El Tari and Jalan K B Mandiri (where the SMP5 secondary school is), and walk 200 metres east along Jalan Raya El Tari. The office is open Monday to Thursday from 7 am to 2 pm, on Friday until 11 am and on Saturday until 12.30 pm.

Money The Bank Dagang Negara at Jalan Urip Sumohardjo 16 is the best place to change money. It's open Monday to Friday from 7.30 am to noon and 1 to 2.30 pm, and on Saturday until noon. The Bank Negara Indonesia at Jalan Sumatera 33 is open Monday to Saturday from 8 am to noon and 1 to 3 pm. The Bank Danamon a few doors away also changes money. A moneychanging office opens at the airport when flights come in from Darwin, offering the same rate as the banks.

Post & Telecommunications The main post office, with poste restante, is at Jalan

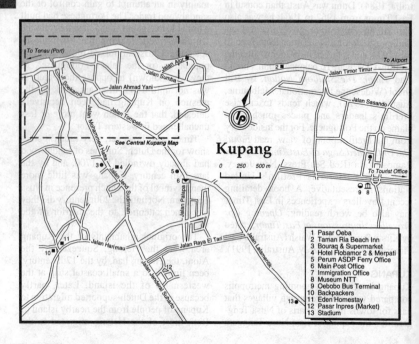

Kupang

0   250   500 m

1 Pasar Oeba
2 Taman Ria Beach Inn
3 Bourag & Supermarket
4 Hotel Flobamor 2 & Merpati
5 Perum ASDP Ferry Office
6 Main Post Office
7 Immigration Office
8 Museum NTT
9 Oebobo Bus Terminal
10 Backpackers
11 Eden Homestay
12 Pasar Inpres (Market)
13 Stadium

To Tenau (Port)
To Airport
Jalan Alor
Jalan Sumba
Jalan Timor Timur
Jalan Ahmad Yani
Jl Soekarno
Jalan Sasando
Jalan Tompelo
Jalan Mohammad Hatta
See Central Kupang Map
To Tourist Office
Jalan Jend Sudirman
Jalan Palapa
Jalan Harimau
Jalan Raya El Tari
Jalan Lalamentik
Jalan Jenderal Suharto

Palapa 1. It's open Monday to Saturday from 8 am to 2 pm (closing at 11 am on Friday). To get there, take a No 5 bemo from the city centre. There's a sub-post office near the Terminal at Jalan Soekarno 29. The Telkom office is at Jalan Urip Sumohardjo No 11, and is open 24 hours a day.

Markets

The main market is the rambling Pasar Inpres off Jalan Jenderal Suharto in the south of the city. To get there, take bemo No 1 or 2, and follow the crowd when you get off. There's a wide range of good quality fruit and vegetables, and some crafts and ikat from out of town. A lesser market is on Jalan Alor two km east of town. There's a large supermarket (the Western variety) at Jalan Surdiman 20.

Museum NTT

The East Nusa Tenggara Museum, near the tourist office, is worth a look for a taste of what you're heading into, or to round up your Nusa Tenggara experience. It houses a collection of arts, crafts and artefacts from all over the province. Aurora Arby, an anthropologist, will be happy to show you around. To get there, take a No 10 bemo from the Terminal. It's open Monday to Thursday from 8 am to 2 pm, on Friday until 11 am and on Saturday until 12.30 pm. Entry is free, but drop a donation in the box as you leave.

Pulau Semau

Semau, visible to the west of Kupang, has some good beaches where you can snorkel, and freshwater springs. You may be able to organise a boat from one of the fishing villages outside Kupang or from Tenau for around 2000 rp per person, and stay with villagers on the island. Teddy's Bar in Kupang runs trips to Semau. A day trip with a barbecue lunch on the island will cost 35,000 rp per person – there's a discount for groups. You can stay overnight in the bungalows run by Teddy's Bar, and for some reason, the total price is the same for a single – 35,000 rp per night – with three meals thrown in. Doubles are 60,000 rp. *Savanah*

Homestay has rooms for 25,000 rp per person, with breakfast included.

Monkey Island (Pulau Kera)

Monkey Island is the blob of trees and sand visible from Kupang. This small, uninhabited island has sandy beaches and clear water. Taman Ria organises day trips, or talk to the people operating the fishing boats.

Pantai Lasiana

Lasiana Beach, about 10 km east of Kupang, is a busy picnic spot on Sunday. It's a lovely setting, but the litter left along the beach is a bit depressing. Outside the wet season, the water is clear. There are also stalls selling drinks and snacks. To get there, take bemo No 17 from the Terminal – you'll see the 'Welcome to Lasiana Beach' sign when you get off.

Tablolong

The government recently opened up a new development area at Tablolong, 15 km west of Kupang. Locals reckon the white-sand beach, Air Cina, has it all over Lasiana. Take bemo No 8 from the Terminal.

Places to Stay – bottom end

Accommodation in Kupang is spread out, with the highest concentration of hotels a few blocks south of the Terminal (near the Bank Dagang Negara) and about one km east along the beach front on Jalan Sumatera. Many of the hotels have a range of prices, so the bottom, middle and top end overlap to some extent. There are also some good options a little further out if you want to escape the bustle of central Kupang.

One of the best of these is the *Taman Ria Beach Inn* (☎ 31320) at Jalan Timor Timur 69, on the beach front about three km from the Terminal. Dorm rooms go for 4000 rp, singles/doubles with shared bath are 8000/10,000 rp and singles/doubles with private bath are 11,000/15,000 rp. To get there, catch a No 10 bemo.

Two options for those on a budget are in a quiet area a bit out of town, on Jalan Kencil. *Backpackers* at No 37B and *Eden Homestay*

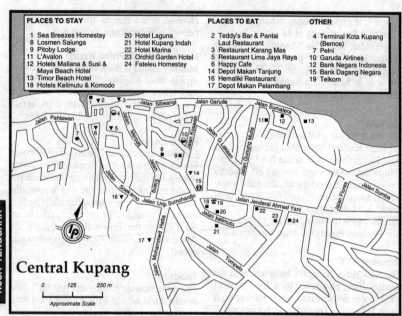

PLACES TO STAY		PLACES TO EAT	OTHER
1 Sea Breezes Homestay	20 Hotel Laguna	2 Teddy's Bar & Pantai	4 Terminal Kota Kupang
8 Losmen Salunga	21 Hotel Kupang Indah	Laut Restaurant	(Bemos)
9 Pitoby Lodge	22 Hotel Marina	3 Restaurant Karang Mas	7 Pelni
11 L'Avalon	23 Orchid Garden Hotel	5 Restaurant Lima Jaya Raya	10 Garuda Airlines
12 Hotels Maliana & Susi &	24 Fateleu Homestay	6 Happy Cafe	12 Bank Negara Indonesia
Maya Beach Hotel		14 Depot Makan Tanjung	15 Bank Dagang Negara
13 Timor Beach Hotel		16 Hemaliki Restaurant	19 Telkom
18 Hotels Kelimutu & Komodo		17 Depot Makan Pelambang	

Central Kupang

0   125   250 m

Approximate Scale

(☎ 21931) at No 6 have rooms for 3000 rp per person. Eden offers basic meals, or there's a gado gado warung where Jalan Kencil meets the main road. There's a shady freshwater pool nearby to swim in. To get there from the Terminal, catch a No 3 bemo.

A new place at Jalan Sumatera 8, *L'Avalon* (☎ 32278), is run by local character Edwin Lerrick. Beds go for 4000 rp per person, and it's a good place to make contact with guides. Willy D Kadati is one we found to be competent and knowledgeable.

The central *Pitoby Lodge* (☎ 32910) at Jalan Kosasih 13 is popular for its budget rooms with shared bath (5500 rp per person).

Fateleu Homestay (☎ 31374) at Jalan Gunung Fateleu 1 is a friendly place close to the city centre. Rates start at 7500 rp per person for rooms with fan and shared bath; doubles with private bath are 15,000 rp.

Sea Breezes Homestay is on Jalan Ikan Tongkol (Tuna Fish St), next to Teddy's Bar. Dorm rooms are 4000 rp per person and singles/doubles are 5000/8000 rp, all with shared bath.

Places to Stay – middle

Along the beach front on Jalan Sumatera, a short bemo ride from the Terminal, are four hotels, with the *Timor Beach Hotel* (☎ 31651) the standout for its restaurant with panoramic sea views. Economy singles/ doubles with fan and bath are 12,500/16,500 rp; air-con rooms go for 24,500/30,000 rp.

Heading back into town, the recently renovated *Maya Beach Hotel* (☎ 32169) is next to the BNI Bank at No 31. Singles/doubles with air-con and bath are 22,500/25,000 rp and family rooms for triples cost 50,000 rp, including hot water and TV. *Hotel Maliana* (☎ 21879) is at No 35, and offers air-con rooms with private bath for 19,000/24,000 rp, while the *Hotel Susi* (☎ 22172) at No 37 has a range of rooms, starting at 12,500/ 16,000 rp with fan and bath. Some rooms upstairs have views and are more expensive.

Clustered on Jalan Kelimutu close to the city centre are another four hotels, three of which, *Hotel Kelimutu* (☎ 31179) at No 38, *Hotel Komodo* (☎ 21913) at No 40 and *Hotel Kupang Indah* (☎ 22638) at No 21, are owned by the same group. The standard at these three is similar. Singles/doubles with bath and fan start at 15,000/25,000 rp and air-con rooms with bath at around 25,000/30,000 rp.

A cheaper option is the *Hotel Laguna* at Jalan Kelimutu 36, where singles/doubles with shared bath cost 7500/11,500 rp and doubles with air-con and private bath go for 31,000 rp.

Close by at Jalan Kakatua 20 is the dark *Losmen Salunga* (☎ 21510). Single/double rooms with air-con and bath are 17,500/22,500 rp.

Another option is the friendly *Hotel Marina* (☎ 22566) at Jalan Jenderal Ahmad Yani 72. The spacious rooms start at 12,500/15,000 rp with fan and shared bath (25,000/30,000 rp with air-con and private bath).

Places to Stay – top end

Located on the beach front one km west of town at Jalan Pahlawan 91, is the *Hotel Ausindo* (☎ 32873). There's a popular swimming spot across the road, rooms are spacious and the hotel offers full service. Singles/doubles start at 27,500/33,000 rp, but you can do better if it's quiet. More expensive rooms on the top floor feature balconies with great views.

Hotel Flobamor II (☎ 33476) is at Jalan Surdiman 21, next to the Merpati office. All rooms have air-con and hot water, with prices starting at 30,000/60,000 rp. There's a swimming pool and restaurant as well.

At the top of the comfort range is the *Orchid Garden Hotel* (☎ 33707; fax 33669) at Jalan Gunung Fateleu 2. It features a swimming pool, and rooms with hot water, TV and minibar. Singles/doubles go for 111,200/127,500 rp.

Places to Eat

Kupang has a greater variety of food than most places in Nusa Tenggara, so tuck in while you can. There are some good seafood and Chinese restaurants close to the Terminal, while a few of the best restaurants require a short walk.

Depot Makan Pelambang, opposite the hospital, at Jalan Mohammed Hatta 54, has an extensive menu of tasty Chinese and Indonesian food, including seafood and pigeon. It's popular with locals, so get there early. Close by you can get a taste of the West at the *California Fried Chicken*. Back towards the Terminal, on the corner of Jalan Soekarno and Jalan PRC Cendana, *Hemaliki* has seafood, as well as Chinese, Indonesian and, supposedly, Japanese dishes.

Around the Terminal, *Restaurant Lima Jaya Raya*, Jalan Soekarno 15, has Chinese and Indonesian food, including sea cucumber, frogs' legs and hens' feet. Upstairs is a nightclub of sorts; it's loud and sweaty, and a good place to meet locals. Across the road, at Jalan Ikan Paus 3, the *Happy Cafe* is a bright place serving cheap Chinese and Indonesian food. *Restaurant Karang Mas* at Jalan Siliwangi 88 attracts a lot of travellers, but more for its seafront balcony and cold beer than for its food.

When you can't eat another noodle or grain of rice, step into the *Gunung Intan Bakery* opposite the Happy Cafe and sniff the air. It has a delicious selection of pastries, doughnuts and buns.

Depot Makan Tanjung, on the corner of Jalan Kosasih and Jalan Sumahardjo, has good, cheap Chinese food, and takeaway snacks like biscuits and cakes. *Teddy's Bar*, on the waterfront near the Terminal, caters for the short-term tourist crowd, and does seafood, spit roasts, pies and steak sandwiches. *Pantai Laut*, next door, has good food and amiable staff. *Rumah Makan Beringin Jaya* on Jalan Garuda has an interesting selection of Padang dishes – especially if you're into offal.

The *Timor Beach Hotel* has good food and probably the most romantic location in town. Nearby, at Jalan Sumatera 44, *Rujak Cinjur* has good Javanese food, such as gado gado and nasi campur, for around 1000 rp.

You'll see night warungs around town,

NUSA TENGGARA

particularly around the Terminal. Try the bubur kacang (mung beans and black rice in coconut milk). In case you're interested, some of these warungs sell dog meat.

Things to Buy

Timorese ikat is colourful, with a huge variety of designs, and there are lots of other embroidered textiles. Purists will be disappointed that natural dyes are now rare in Timor, but interestingly, the tourist trade is starting to create a demand for it. You may also see some at Kupang's market, Pasar Inpres, where villagers sometimes bring their weavings to sell.

Several shops in Kupang sell ikat, handcrafts, old silver jewellery, ornamental *sirih* containers and more. Bizarre hats from Roti (*ti'i langga*) make a fun purchase – but try fitting one in your backpack! These shops also have ikat from other parts of East Nusa Tenggara, including Roti and Sawu. Prices are quite high, and bargaining won't bring them down dramatically, but you won't often find Timorese stuff elsewhere in Nusa Tenggara. Try Dharma Bakti at Jalan Sumba 32, out towards Jalan Tim Tim. Toko Sinar Baru, on Jalan Siliwangi opposite the Terminal, has an interesting range, but it's hard to shift them on prices.

You can watch weavers at work in Kupang at Ibu Bunga's Sentra Tenun Ikat on Jalan Tifa, about one km south-west of the Terminal.

Getting There & Away

Kupang is the transport hub of Timor, with buses and flights to and from the rest of the island, plus planes and regular passenger boats to many destinations in Nusa Tenggara and beyond.

Air Merpati flies to and from Darwin twice a week – you can get a return ticket from Kupang for around US$250 or a one-way ticket for US$150. Kupang is a gateway city, so you can enter here without a visa.

Merpati has direct flights from Kupang to Dili (81,900 rp), Sawu (85,200 rp), Alor (100,600 rp), Lewoleba (98,400 rp), Wain-

gapu (134,700 rp), Maumere (77,500 rp), Ende (99,500 rp) and Labuhanbajo (206,200 rp).

Bouraq flies from Kupang to Denpasar, Maumere, Surabaya and Waingapu, while Sempati flies to Dili and Surabaya.

Merpati (☎ 33221) is at Jalan Surdiman 21, next to the Hotel Flobamor. Bemo Nos 1 and 2 go there. The office is open Monday to Friday from 7.30 am to 5 pm, and on Saturday and Sunday from 9 am to 2 pm. Bouraq (☎ 21421) is close by, next to the supermarket at Jalan Surdiman 20. Garuda (☎ 33654) is more central at Jalan Kosasih 13. There are also numerous ticket agencies around town, including P T Ultra Tours (☎ 31064), right next to the Terminal at Jalan Soekarno 15A (open on Sunday).

Bus Kupang's main bemo terminal (Terminal Kota Kupang) is *not* where long-distance buses depart from. For out-of-town buses, you need to take a No 10 bemo to Oebobo Terminal, in the eastern part of the city, near the Museum NTT. Buses leave from here for Soe (3500 rp; two hours), Niki Niki (4300 rp; 3½ hours), Kefamenanu (6200 rp; five hours) and Atambua (8700 rp; eight hours). Express night buses go to Dili (15,000 rp; 12 hours).

Boat Regular ships to Flores, Roti, Sawu, Sumba, Alor and further afield leave from Tenau and Bolok harbours, eight and 10 km west of Kupang respectively. Generally, Pelni passenger ships leave from Tenau, and ferries leave from Bolok. From the bemo station, bemo Nos 12 and 13 both go to the harbours (750 rp).

Pelni and the ferry company Perum ASDP have ticket offices in Kupang. Pelni is at Jalan Pahlawan 3, within walking distance of the Terminal – you should buy tickets for Pelni ships two days before departure. The *Kelimutu* calls in at Kupang twice every fortnight, one week sailing on to Dili (17,000 rp in economy class), Kalabahi and Maumere, and the next week sailing to Ende (17,600 rp), with further stops at Waingapu, Bima, Lembar, Banjarmasin and Surabaya.

The *Dobonsolo* also calls in at Kupang twice a fortnight, heading on to Dili one week and to Surabaya the next, with a stop at Benoa (Bali).

Perum's ferries link Kupang with Larantuka and Ende (Flores), Kalabahi (Alor), Roti and Sawu. The Perum office at Jalan Cak Doko 20 sells tickets the day before departure, but it's easier to buy a ticket at the harbour. The *Ile Mandiri* leaves Kupang every Monday for its circuit around Ende, Waingapu, Sawu and back. A ferry goes to Roti every day of the week (4,500 rp; four hours), to Sawu on Tuesday and Friday afternoon (12,000 rp; nine hours), to Larantuka (12,000 rp; 12 hours) on Wednesday and Sunday afternoon, and to Kalabahi (14,000 rp; 12 hours) on Thursday and Saturday afternoon.

Getting Around

To/From Airport Kupang's El Tari airport is 15 km east of the city centre. A taxi from the airport is a fixed 7500 rp.

To get a bemo from the airport, walk out of the terminal and follow the road to your left a full km to the junction with the main highway. The fare to town is 500 rp. The taxi drivers will tell you it's four km to the highway and point you in four different directions, so ask someone who doesn't have an interest. From the city centre, bemo Nos 14 and 15 go to the airport.

Bemo The bemo system is efficient but loud, with music played at full blast and the bass set to maximum. The bemos are plastered with pictures of heavy-metal dinosaurs, but all you'll hear is syrupy pop music.

Kupang is too spread out to do much walking. The hub of bemo routes is the Terminal Kota Kupang, usually just called 'Terminal'. All bemos in town cost 300 rp, and they stop running by 9 pm. Bemos are numbered, with the main bemo routes as follows:

Nos 1 & 2 Kuanino-Oepura – passing the following hotels: Maya, Maliana, Timor Beach, Fateleu, Orchid Garden, Marina and Flobamor II

No 3 Aimona-Bakunase – to Eden Homestay and Backpackers
No 5 Oebobo-Airnona-Bakunase – passing the ferry office and the main post office
No 6 Oebobo-Oebufu – to the stadium but *not* to the bus terminal
No 10 Kelapa Lima-Walikota – from the Terminal to the Taman Ria Beach Hotel, tourist information office and Oebobo bus terminal
No 12 Tenau
No 13 Bolok
Nos 14 & 15 Penfui – useful for getting to the airport
No 17 Tarus – to Pantai Lasiana.

Car & Motorbike It's possible to rent a motorbike for 30,000 rp per day, or a car with driver for 100,000 rp. Ask at your hotel, P T Ultra Tours or Teddy's Bar.

OEBELO

Oebelo, 22 km from Kupang on the Soe road, is where Pak Pah and his family have set up a workshop producing the traditional 20-stringed Rotinese instrument, the *sasando* (featured on the 5000 rp note). They also make the Rotinese lontar-leaf hat, ti'i langga. If you're interested, Pak Pah will play the Rotinese version of *Waltzing Matilda* for you.

BAUN

A small, quiet village 30 km south of Kupang in the hilly Amarasi district, Baun is an ikat-weaving centre, with a few Dutch buildings. You can visit the *rumah raja*, the last raja's house, now occupied by his widow. She loves to chat to foreigners and will show you her weavings and rose garden. Market day in Baun is Saturday. From Baun to the south coast is a solid day's hike – reportedly, there's a good surf beach down there.

To get to Baun, take a bemo from Kupang's Inpres market (700 rp).

CAMPLONG

Camplong, 46 km from Kupang on the Soe road, is a cool, quiet hill town and a refreshing change from Kupang. Camplong has some caves, a small forest and a freshwater spring to swim in.

The Camplong convent, *Wisma Oemat Honis*, has rooms for 5000 rp per person with shared mandi, 15,000 rp with private mandi and two meals.

To get there, take a bus from Kupang's Oebobo terminal (2500 rp).

SOE

The road from Kupang passes through rugged countryside, reminiscent of the Australian bush, to the regional centre of Soe. At an elevation of 800 metres, it's cool at night, but hot enough for shorts and T-shirts during the day. Soe is an excellent base for side trips to traditional villages and colourful markets around the area. Soe itself is a sprawl of modern houses, but has a large market, where you'll see people in their traditional garb.

Like most of rural Timor, the Soe district is poor. Australian aid projects in the area include building dams to cope with the water shortages and health education.

Outside Soe, you'll see the beehive-shaped houses (*lopo*) which give the region a distinctive character. Lopo have been banned by authorities, who deem them unhealthy, as they're small and smoky. The locals, however, consider their new houses unhealthy, as they're cold, so they construct new lopos behind the approved houses. Another type of lopo, which acts as a meeting place, has no walls and a toadstool-like roof.

Orientation

Soe's bus and bemo terminal is on the far side of Soe if you're coming from Kupang. Accommodation is on and near Jalan Diponegoro in the town centre, a km or so back from the terminal. The market is a km in the opposite direction from the terminal. To get to the hotels, turn left out of the bus station and walk uphill past the post office, then turn right at the first junction.

Money

The Bank Rakyat Indonesia changes only cash, and only if the notes are in 'good condition'. Outside Kupang and Dili, this is the only official place in Timor to change money.

Places to Stay

The travellers' favourite is the basic but friendly *Hotel Anda* at Jalan Kartini 5. Rooms with shared mandi are 4000 rp per person. The hotel is run by an interesting

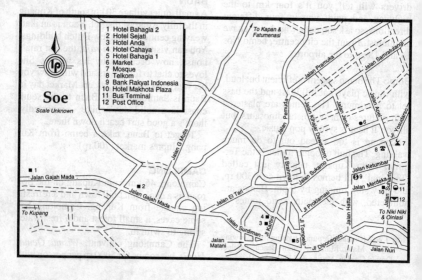

```
1  Hotel Bahagia 2
2  Hotel Sejati
3  Hotel Anda
4  Hotel Cahaya
5  Hotel Bahagia 1
6  Market
7  Mosque
8  Telkom
9  Bank Rakyat Indonesia
10 Hotel Makhota Plaza
11 Bus Terminal
12 Post Office
```

Soe
Scale Unknown

English/Dutch/German-speaking man who plays good guitar and is a wealth of knowledge on the area's history and attractions.

If this is full you could try the *Hotel Cahaya*, next door, where rooms are 6000 rp with outside mandi, 7500 rp with attached mandi.

Right across the road from the bus terminal is the up-market *Hotel Makhota Plaza* at Jalan Jenderal 11. Clean singles/doubles with mandi are 15,000/20,000 rp.

Hotel Bahagia 1 at Jalan Diponegoro 72 has singles/doubles with outside mandi for 15,000/17,500 rp (17,500/30,000 rp with private mandi). *Hotel Bahagia 2*, on the way in from Kupang, has air-con singles/doubles at a flat rate of 27,500 rp.

Hotel Sejati at Jalan Gajah Mada 18 has a range of accommodation, starting with economy rooms with shared bath for 7000/10,000 rp.

Places to Eat

There are a few good restaurants around the bus terminal, including the *Rumah Makan Padang*, the *Rumah Makan Suka Jadi* (with Javanese food), the *Rumah Makan Harapan* (with tasty, good-value Chinese food – try the ikan tauco, fish with sweet sauce) and the *Hotel Makhota Plaza*. Other recommended restaurants are near the market on Jalan Hayam Wuruk, including the *Sri Solo* and the *Sari Bundo*.

Things to Buy

The shop attached to the Hotel Bahagia I has an excellent but expensive range of weaving and carvings. Bargaining is definitely worthwhile and probably expected. If you are heading out to village markets, wait to see what's there, and if you don't find what you want, go back to the shop.

Getting There & Away

Buses from Kupang cost 3500 rp, and the 110-km journey takes three to four hours. It's best to set off early, as the chances are your bus will fill up quickly and leave sooner. If you ask, your bus can drop you off at a losmen.

Regular buses run from Soe to Kefamenanu (2500 rp; 2½ hours), Kolbano (3000 rp; six hours) and Oinlasi (1600 rp; 1½ hours), while bemos cover Niki Niki (800 rp) and Kapan (700 rp).

Getting Around

For journeys around town, bemos cost 300 rp.

AROUND SOE
Oinlasi

Regular buses from Soe make the 51-km trip along a winding mountain road to Oinlasi in around 1½ hours. Its Tuesday market, probably the biggest and best in West Timor, is a great place to meet local people from around the region wearing their traditional ikat. There are weavings, carvings, masks and elaborately carved betel-nut containers to buy. A direct bus from Kupang makes the trip in about four hours.

Boti

This small, isolated kingdom is about 10 km from Oinlasi along a rugged mountain road. The village welcomes visitors – the raja has a bizarre collection of cards and photos he will proudly show you. There are now tour companies organising trips to Boti from Kupang. You can see the process of hand-weaving ikat in the village's cooperative, and at night there are often performances of traditional dance. Boti is one of the last remaining villages in Timor where men let their hair grow long, but only after they are married.

It's possible to stay with the raja in his house, with all meals provided (around 10,000 rp per person). It's a good idea to bring gifts for the raja, such as betel nut and fruit. Try to remember that this is a royal family – gifts should be placed in the box provided for offerings.

Taking a guide is a very good idea, as few people in the village speak Indonesian.

Getting There & Away From Oinlasi, you may be lucky and find a truck going to Boti,

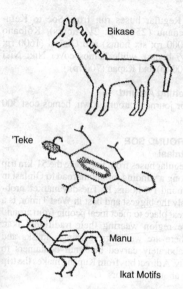

Bikase

'Teke

Manu

Ikat Motifs

or a local who will guide you (about a four-hour walk on a dry, rocky and hilly road – take plenty of water).

The other approach is to catch a bus from Soe to Oenai and walk from there. The two-hour walk follows a river most of the way. However, this route is only a series of tracks, so a guide is essential. Bring water from Soe, as there isn't any to buy in Oenai. Alternatively, you may be able to charter a bemo in Soe for about 30,000 rp.

The kingdom is surrounded by a system of gates and fences; unless you are with a local, you must wait at the first gate until someone comes along to guide you into the village.

Niki Niki

Niki Niki, 34 km east of Soe along the Soe-Kefa road, is the site of some old royal graves. It has a busy market on Wednesday. There are a couple of restaurants, but no accommodation. Regular buses run to Niki Niki from Soe (800 rp). The village is about two km off the main road – you can walk or hitch a ride.

Kapan

Twenty-one km north of Soe, Kapan has an interesting market on Thursday, when the roads are blocked with stalls. The village is situated on steep slopes, from where you can see Gunung Mutis (2470 metres). From Kapan, some trucks run to **Futamenasi**, 20 km away, which has even more spectacular alpine scenery, or you can take a bemo there from Soe.

Kolbano

The village of Kolbano, on the south coast 110 km from Soe, has white-sand beaches, and good surf between May and August. The easiest access is probably by bus from Noilmina on the Kupang-Soe road (about six hours over a decent road). There's also a bus from Soe, but it's not very regular. A joint Australian-American-Indonesian oil research project has begun in the area, so access should become easier in the near future.

KEFAMENANU

Kefamenanu, 217 km from Kupang, is cool and quiet, with some pleasant walks to the surrounding hills. The town is very Catholic and has a few impressive churches. 'Kefa', as it's known to locals, once had a reputation as a place to buy fine rugs, and though this tradition declined, it is gradually being revived. Locals bring around reasonable ikat to the losmen, and you could strike a bargain. **Oelolok**, a weaving village 26 km from Kefa by bus and a further three km by bemo, has a Tuesday market.

Orientation & Information

Kefa is fairly spread out – the old market (pasar lama), a few km north of the bus terminal, is the town centre. The post office is on Jalan Imam Bonjol, opposite the market. The Telkom office is on Jalan Surdiman.

Places to Stay & Eat

Losmen Soko Windu (☎ 21122) is a clean, friendly place on Jalan Kartini, a short bemo ride from the bus terminal but close to the centre of town. Large, clean rooms with shared bath cost 6500 rp per person. Breakfast is included.

Losmen Ariesta (☎ 21007) on Jalan Basuki Rachmat looks up-market but is good value. Clean rooms with shared mandi are 11,000 rp, single or double. There's a good restaurant here.

The cool, quiet *Hotel Cendana* (☎ 21168) on Jalan Sonbay offers rooms with mandi and fan at 12,500 rp, single or double, while air-con rooms go for 35,000 rp. The staff can help you charter bemos and rent motorbikes.

Losmen Sederhana on Jalan Patimura is a long way from the bus terminal, but there are bemos. Singles/doubles with outside mandi go for 6500/10,000 rp, while rooms with attached mandi are 8000/12,500 rp.

The *Stella Maris*, on the corner of Jalan El Tari and Jalan Surdiman, has good Chinese food. Around the centre of town, try *Warung Sami Jaya* and *Warung Padang* on Jalan Kartini. The *Hotel Ariesta* and the *Hotel Cendana* also serve meals.

Getting There & Away

The main bus and bemo terminal, Terminal Bus Kefa, is a few kilometres south of the town centre. Buses to Soe, Kupang and Atambua leave from here, but the bus to Oekussi leaves from the Pasar Lama, in the centre of town. Buses to Kefa leave Kupang early in the morning. From Kefa to Kupang, there are several buses in the morning and a few at night. The last bus leaves at 8 pm from the Rumah Makan Minang Jaya, near the Cendana Hotel. Regular buses run to and from Soe (2500 rp; two hours) and Atambua (2500 rp; two hours). Buses to Oekussi (2500 rp; three hours) leave about every two hours from 8 am until 2 pm.

Getting Around

Within Kefa there are no regular bemo routes; just tell the driver where you are going. Bemos cost 200 rp around town.

TEMKESSI

Temkessi, a traditional village around 50 km north-east of Kefa, has seen few travellers, because of its isolation. Sitting high on a

hilltop, its only entrance a small passage between two huge rocks, the village has about 18 families and 25 traditional houses. The raja's house sits on top of rocks over the village. There's lots of weaving here, but little Indonesian is spoken, so a guide may be necessary.

To get there, regular buses run from Kefa to Manufui, about eight km from Temkessi. On market day in Manufui, Saturday, trucks or buses should run through to Temkessi. Otherwise, it may be possible to charter a bemo in Manufui.

OEKUSSI

This former Portuguese coastal enclave north-west of Kefamenanu is part of East Timor province. When East Timor was reopened to tourists in 1989, travellers were only allowed to pass through Oekussi, but this restriction has now been dropped.

PANTEMAKASSAR

Pantemakassar, the capital of Oekussi province, was the first permanent Portuguese settlement on Timor in the 17th century. The locals never accepted Portuguese domination, rebelling and forcing the Portuguese to flee to Dili in 1769. It was later taken back by the Portuguese and a fort, garrison and mission were built. Today Pantemakassar is a sleepy coastal town of around 8000 people, sandwiched between hills and the coast – a pleasant place to wind down for a few days.

Information

The post office is on the corner of Jalan Alimurtopo and Jalan Jose Osorio. The Telkom office is further east, past the fountain, on Jalan Santa Rosa.

Things to See

There are some good **beaches** near Pantemakassar; the black-sand beach five km west is where locals say the Portuguese first landed. Many Portuguese buildings, including the old garrison known as **Fatusuba**, are scattered around the town. **Poto Tano**, 12 km east on the Kefa road, has a large, colourful market on Tuesday, with people coming from all over the region. The market's location is idyllic, nestled under the shade of huge fig trees next to the Tono River.

Places to Stay & Eat

The town has one losmen, the friendly and clean *Aneka Jaya* on Jalan Soekarno, which runs off the beach front. Singles/doubles with bath are 7500/11,000 rp. The hotel is also an agent for the Dili-Atambua-Oecusi bus. A small restaurant, *Rumah Makan Sri Jaya*, is just around the corner, one block east of the hotel, on Jalan Oecusi.

Getting There & Away

Buses run every two hours through the morning to and from Kefa (2500 rp; three hours), starting at 7 am. Regular buses run to/from Dili via Atambua.

ATAMBUA & BELU

Atambua is the major town at the eastern end of West Timor. It's quite a cosmopolitan place; the shops have a wide range of goods and the streets are lively at night, with lots of people strolling around. Since the bus route to Dili has changed to the coast road, it's only a three-hour journey between the two cities.

Atambua is the capital of Belu province, which borders East Timor. The district is mainly dry farming, using traditional time-consuming methods, though there are some wet paddy lands on the south coast. Belu has some beautiful scenery and traditional villages.

Betun, a prosperous town 60 km south near the coast, has a couple of losmen and restaurants. A few intrepid travellers visit the nearby villages of **Kletuk**, **Kamanasa** and **Bolan** – you can see flying foxes, and watch the sun set over the mountains at Kletuk.

Places to Stay & Eat

There are six losmen near the town centre, within walking distance of each other, all of which offer a free breakfast. You can ask the bus to drop you at a hotel.

Centrally located on Jalan Soekarno is *Losmen Nusantara* (☎ 21117), but it's a bit

dark and noisy, and rooms are not cheap (11,000/16,000 rp with mandi).

From Losmen Nusantara, walk 200 metres north-east and turn right at the roundabout, into Jalan Merdeka. Three losmen line the street: the cool and quiet *Losmen Merdeka* (☎ 21197) at No 37 has rooms with private mandi for 9000/15,000 rp; the sparkling new *Intan Hotel* at No 12 has rooms starting at 12,000/19,800 rp with outside mandi; and *Losmen Sahabat* at No 7 has slightly grungy rooms for 7500/15,000 rp with outside mandi.

Coming back out of Jalan Merdeka, walk through the roundabout and veer to the right, into Jalan Jenderal Gatot Subroto. *Losmen Kalapataru* (☎ 21351) at No 5 is a homey place, where clean doubles with shared bath cost 12,500 rp. Next door at the *Losmen Liurai*, four-bed rooms with shared bath are 5500 rp per person. Having said that Atambua is a cosmopolitan place, you shouldn't be surprised by the manager of the Liurai!

There are a couple of good restaurants along Jalan Soekarno, all close to the losmen. Try the friendly *Rumah Makan Surabaya*, on the corner of Jalan Merdeka and Jalan Soekarno, for good, cheap sate, or *Rumah Makan Meriah* at No 37 for Padang food.

Getting There & Away

Bus Buses from Kupang to Atambua cost 8700 rp and take about eight hours. Atambua to Dili is 5000 rp, and buses leave regularly until about 11 am. If you're heading straight to Dili, the 'Belu Express' is the quickest bus. You can easily arrange for the bus to pick you up at your hotel in the morning.

The three-hour trip to Dili is quite scenic, hugging the coast most of the way (sometimes closer than you'd like!). The road is surfaced, though three unbridged rivers could make things tricky in the wet season (there is an alternative route via Maliana).

Boat The passenger ferry *Kambaniru* sails from the port of Atapupu, 25 km from Atambua, to Kalabahi (Alor) on Monday morning at 10 am, and costs 9000 rp for the eight-hour crossing. You might find boats here to other islands.

BATUGEDE, MAUBARA & LICISIA
Batugede, 111 km from Dili, is the border point between West and East Timor – there's a military checkpoint, where you'll have to show your passport. Maubara, on the coast 45 km west of Dili, has a 17th-century European-built fort. This was the centre of one of the most important old kingdoms in Portuguese Timor, and it was here, in 1893, that a series of revolts took place, eventually leading to the bloody pacification of the island by the Portuguese. **Licisia** is a cool, green town with some reasonable beaches – mostly black sand – 35 km from Dili. There are regular Dili-Licisia-Maubara return buses for day trips.

MALIANA & ERMERA
Maliana is a large regional capital with one losmen, the *Purwosari Indah*, and a busy market. Ermera, 62 km south-west of Dili, was the main coffee plantation of Portuguese Timor. Both can be reached by bus from Dili.

DILI
Dili was once the capital of Portuguese Timor. When the English scientist Alfred Russel Wallace spent several months here in 1861, he noted Dili as:

...a most miserable place compared with even the poorest of Dutch towns...After three hundred years of occupation there has not been a mile of road made beyond the town, and there is not a solitary European resident anywhere in the interior. All the government officials oppress and rob the natives as much as they can, and yet there is no care taken to render the town defensible should the Timorese attempt to attack it.

Dili is now quite a pretty place centred around a harbour, with parkland edging the waterfront on either side. The town is slow-paced, though it appears fairly prosperous, with lots of new public buildings. Shops are open early in the morning, but everything closes for an afternoon siesta from noon until 4.30 pm. If you want to get amongst the people, you could go along to a soccer match at the stadium, or hang out where the night food stalls set up along the Bidau canal, about two km east of the town centre.

The dry season is *really* dry in this part of Timor, but it makes for some spectacular scenery, with rocky, brown hills dropping right into a turquoise sea lined with exotic tropical plants. To top it off, there are some beautiful sunsets over the harbour in Dili.

Information
Tourist Office The tourist office (☎ 21350), or Dinas Pariwisata, is on Jalan Kaikoli. Mr Da Silva speaks good English, and the office has a few brochures and maps.

Money The Bank Danamon on Jalan Avenida Bispo de Madeiros is the best place to change money, but accepts only US or Australian dollar travellers' cheques. They'll change cash in other currencies. The Bank Dagang Negara, next to the New Resende Inn, also changes money, with the same restrictions.

Markets
Neither of the town's two markets is very inspiring, selling mostly manufactured goods. Comoro market is about two km west of the town centre, and has mostly permanent stalls; Becora, about two km east of the centre, is more relaxed, with people from out of town crouched in front of their produce.

Pantai Pasir Putih
About four km east of town, the beach here is nice by any standards, with white sand, clear water, and sweeping views of the harbour and the hills to the south. Even on weekends, it's a nice escape from Dili – it has the feel of an abandoned resort, with small thatched shelters, and rusting paddle boats lying around. A taxi from the town centre costs around 2000 rp.

Places to Stay
The bottom end seems to have dropped out of the accommodation market in Dili – there's nothing in the budget category,

NUSA TENGGARA

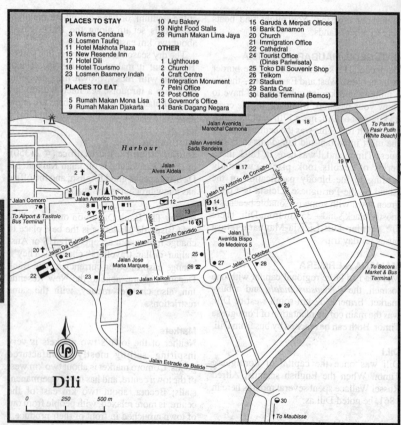

PLACES TO STAY
3 Wisma Cendana
8 Losmen Taufiq
11 Hotel Makhota Plaza
15 New Resende Inn
17 Hotel Dili
18 Hotel Tourismo
23 Losmen Basmery Indah

PLACES TO EAT
5 Rumah Makan Mona Lisa
9 Rumah Makan Djakarta

10 Aru Bakery
19 Night Food Stalls
28 Rumah Makan Lima Jaya

OTHER
1 Lighthouse
2 Church
4 Craft Centre
6 Integration Monument
7 Pelni Office
12 Post Office
13 Governor's Office
14 Bank Dagang Negara

15 Garuda & Merpati Offices
16 Bank Danamon
20 Church
21 Immigration Office
22 Cathedral
24 Tourist Office
   (Dinas Pariwisata)
25 Toko Dili Souvenir Shop
26 Telkom
27 Stadium
29 Santa Cruz
30 Balide Terminal (Bemos)

Dili

0   250   500 m

though some of the mid-range hotels are reasonable value.

Losmen Taufiq (☎ 21934) on Jalan Americo Thomas has the cheapest accommodation, and is centrally located – but it's often full. With shared bath, singles/doubles are 10,000/16,500 rp. Rooms with attached mandi cost 15,000/22,000 rp.

Losmen Basmery Indah (☎ 22151) is on Jalan Estrade de Balide, opposite the University of Timor Timur. It's also central, and relatively cheap (13,500/16,500 rp for singles/doubles with private bath).

The standout in the mid-range is the *Hotel*

Tourismo (☎ 22029) on the waterfront, on Jalan Avenida Marechal Carmona. It features a large restaurant (serving Western, Chinese and Indonesian food), cable TV and a garden eating area. Singles/doubles with fan and shower go for 20,000/24,000 rp; air-con bumps the price up to 36,000/41,000 rp.

Hotel Dili (☎ 21871) is also on the waterfront at Jalan Avenida Sada Bandeira 25. It has a faded charm about it, but is deserted most of the time. Large rooms with fan and bath start at 18,000 rp (single or double), while air-con rooms with large balconies are 33,000 rp.

Wisma Cendana (☎ 21141) on Jalan Americo Thomas is a large, government-run hotel with an impressive foyer and red-carpeted rooms. Double rooms with air-con and bath go for 25,000 rp; VIP rooms with TV and fridge are 35,000 rp.

The *Hotel Makhota Plaza* (☎ 21662), right in the town centre on Jalan Alves Aldeia, is a big hotel, and a bit soulless, though they do have karaoke in the restaurant downstairs. Singles/doubles/triples with fan and bath are 20,000/25,000/30,000 rp. Air-con rooms with shower, TV, phone and minibar go for 50,000/55,000 rp.

Top of the range is the *New Resende Inn* (☎ 22094), centrally located on Jalan Avenida Bispo Madeiros. The rooms aren't as new as the name suggests. Standard singles/doubles with air-con and bath cost 40,000/45,000 rp, while deluxe rooms are 50,000/55,000 rp.

Places to Eat

For some reason, East Timor can import directly from overseas without goods going through Jakarta, so you can buy Singapore Tiger beer and even Portuguese wines.

The best bet for the budget-minded is the *Rumah Makan Mona Lisa*, in the town centre, on Jalan Alberqueque. The friendly staff serve up tasty, fresh Javanese food – try the delicious kering tempe. Just across the road is the cosy *Rumah Makan Padang Pariaman*, serving Padang food.

The top-rated restaurant in town is the *Rumah Makan Djakarta*, also on Jalan Alberqueque. The food and decor are nice, but it's quite expensive. Slightly lower prices and less fancy decor are found at *Rumah Makan Seroja* on Jalan Avenida Aldeia, next to the cinema.

In a beautiful location on Jalan Metiaut about three km east of town is the *Rumah Makan Angin Mamiri*. Right on the waterfront, this is a great place to sit with a cold drink.

The *Tourismo Hotel* serves Western, Chinese and Indonesian food in a lovely garden setting.

To get a taste of Dili by night, check out the scores of warung set up along the Bidau canal. The food is pretty basic and beer is not cheap, but it's a good place to get some local flavour.

For cakes and pastries, try the *Aru Bakery* on Jalan Alberqueque.

Getting There & Away

Air Merpati flies daily from Kupang to Dili (81,900 rp). Sempati also has flights from Kupang to Dili. From Dili you can fly nonstop to Denpasar, or to Yogyakarta and Surabaya with a couple of stops.

Merpati (☎ 21088) and Garuda (☎ 21880) share an office in the New Resende Inn on Jalan Avenida Bispo Madeiros. Multi Perona Tour & Travel (☎ 21477) at Jalan Jose Maria Marques 23 is an agent for Sempati.

Bus From Kupang, you can take an express bus to Dili (15,000 rp; 12 hours). Buses from Atambua cost 5000 rp and leave hourly until about noon. The ride takes about 3½ hours along the winding coast road. Going the other way, buy your tickets the night before at the Belu Express agency on Jalan Avenida Bispo de Madeiros, or just turn up to the Tasitolo Terminal in the morning.

There are three terminals in Dili for out-of-town buses. Buses heading south and west to Maubara, Ermera, Maliana, Oekussi, Atambua and Kupang leave from the Tasitolo Terminal. Buses east to Baukau (4000 rp; three hours), Los Palos (7000 rp; seven hours) and Vikeke (7000 rp; seven hours) leave from Becora Terminal, and buses and bemos to Maubisse (three hours; 3000 rp) and Suai (8000 rp; 10 hours) leave from the Balide Terminal. It's best to start early, as Timorese don't seem to like travelling late in the day – most buses leave before 8 am.

Boat That nightclub-on-water, the Pelni ship *Kelimutu*, stops in Dili twice a fortnight – one week sailing on to Kupang, Ende, Waingapu, Bima, Lembar, Surabaya and Banjarmasin, and the next week sailing to Kalabahi, Maumere and Ujung Pandang. The *Dobonsolo* also calls in at Dili twice a fortnight, going on to Kupang, Surabaya and Jakarta one week and to Ambon the next. The *Tatamailau* sails from Dili every week to Larantuka, Labuhanbajo, Ujung Pandang and other ports. A Pelni ferry sails about once a week from Dili to Kalabahi, on Alor Island (4600 rp).

When buying tickets for the *Kelimutu* and other passenger liners, you must go to the Pelni office two days before departure with a photocopy of your passport. Ferry tickets can be bought at the port on the morning of departure.

Getting Around
To/From the Airport Dili's Comoro Airport is five km west of the town centre. A taxi to your accommodation costs around 5000 rp – but you'll have to bargain for it. You can also get there for 200 rp on bus A or B – the bus will drop you about a 300-metre walk from the terminal.

Car & Motorbike It's possible to rent a car from Multi Perona Tours & Travel for 120,000 rp per day. Primkopad, next to the Mona Lisa restaurant, might rent you a motorbike for 20,000 rp per day.

Local Transport Bemos and buses cost 200 rp anywhere within the city limits. Taxis are plentiful, and cost a flat 1000 rp within the town.

MAUBISSE
About 70 km south of Dili, the small town of Maubisse sits high in rugged mountains, surrounded by spectacular scenery. There's an interesting mix of traditional houses and Portuguese buildings, and the grandest building in town, the fortified former governor's residence, is also the town's only hotel. The building is run-down inside, but there are wonderful views all around from the balconies.

A bed in the hotel costs 9000 rp. It gets cold at night, but there's an open fire in the huge sitting room (if you can find some wood). There are two small warung in town, serving basic meals.

A couple of direct buses leave Balide Terminal in Dili for Maubisse (3000 rp; three hours) between 6 and 8 am. Later buses may finish in Aileu – you should be able to find a truck going through to Maubisse from there.

SAME
Same is another 45 km on from Maubisse along a scenic route. This was a centre of late-19th and early 20th-century revolts led by Boaventura, the liurai of Same. There's one losmen in town. **Betano**, a coastal village about 20 km from Same, reportedly gets good waves between April and July.

BAUKAU
The second largest centre of what was Portuguese Timor, the charmingly raffish colonial town of Baukau has many Portuguese buildings, and Japanese caves left over from WW II. Baukau once had an international airport, eight km west of the town centre, but it's now used by the Indonesian military. The altitude makes Baukau pleasantly cool, and the beaches, five km sharply downhill from the town, are breathtakingly beautiful. To get to them, you might need to charter a bemo.

Places to Stay & Eat
The Portuguese-built *Hotel Flamboyant* is the only place to stay, and costs 10,000 rp per person. It may have been special once, but now nothing seems to work (although the beds are OK).

There are a couple of restaurants in town and several warung around the market.

Getting There & Away
Dili to Baukau is a three-hour bus trip (4000 rp) along the coast. The bus stops briefly at Manatuto on the way. It might be an idea to check in at the police station when you arrive – otherwise, they may come looking for you to give them an English lesson.

BAUKAU TO TUTUALA
There's an old Portuguese fort at **Laga**, on the coast about 20 km beyond Baukau. **Lautem**, 35 km further on, is the next town

with lots of traditional houses. From Lautem the road improves dramatically for 15 km, until it reaches the regional capital of **Los Palos**, which has one losmen and a couple of warung. Los Palos to **Tutuala**, on the eastern tip of Timor, is about 30 km; you should be able to get a bemo there if it's not too late in the day. Tutuala has interesting stilt houses and spectacular sea views – the sunsets here are stunning. Tutuala has one losmen, which can organise meals.

VIKEKE

A road heads south over the mountains from Baukau to Vikeke, which is close to the south coast. There are buses from Dili (7000 rp; seven hours), and the town has one losmen.

Roti & Sawu

The small islands of Roti and Sawu (also spelled Sabu), between Timor and Sumba, are little visited but, with their successful economies based on the lontar palm, have played a significant role in Nusa Tengarra's history and development and now preserve some interesting cultures. Roti, in particular, has a few beautiful coastal villages and some of the best surf in Nusa Tenggara.

ROTI (ROTE) ISLAND

Off the west end of Timor, Roti is the southernmost island in Indonesia. The lightly built Rotinese speak a language similar to the Tetum of Timor, though nowadays almost everyone speaks Bahasa Indonesian. Traditionally, Roti was divided into 18 domains. In 1681 a bloody Dutch campaign placed their local allies in control of the island, and Roti became the source of slaves and supplies for the Dutch base at Kupang. In the 18th century, the Rotinese began taking advantage of the Dutch presence, gradually adopted Christianity and, with Dutch support, established a school system which eventually turned them into the region's elite.

The Rotinese openness to change is the main reason their old culture is no longer as strong as Sawu's – though there are still pockets of animist cultures, and a layer of old beliefs linger behind Protestantism in the villages. At some festivals, families cut chunks from a live buffalo and take them away to eat.

Ikat weaving on Roti today uses mainly red, black and yellow chemical dyes, but the designs can still be complex: typical are floral and patola motifs. One tradition that hasn't disappeared is the wearing of the wide-brimmed lontar hat, ti'i langga, which has a curious spike sticking up near the front like a unicorn's horn (perhaps representing a lontar palm, or a Portuguese helmet or mast). Rotinese also love music and dancing – the traditional Rotinese 20-stringed instrument, the sasando, features on the 5000 rp note.

NUSA TENGGARA

The Lontar Economy

For centuries, the traditional Rotinese and Sawunese economies have centred on the lontar palm. The wood from this multipurpose tree can be used to make houses, furniture, musical instruments, mats, baskets and even cigarette papers. Its juice can be tapped and drunk fresh, or boiled in a syrup and diluted with water – this syrup formed the staple traditional diet. The juice can be further boiled into palm sugar and the froth fed to pigs and goats. Meanwhile, vegetables were grown in dry fields, fertilised by animal manure and lontar leaves. Basically, it's your average useful tree, and with coconuts in abundance as well, there was no annual period of hunger on Roti or Sawu, as there was on other islands in Nusa Tenggara.

Because the lontar palm required only two or three months of work each year, the women had time for weaving and other handcrafts and the men became the entrepreneurs of Nusa Tenggara. In fact, many Rotinese and Sawunese migrated to Sumba and Timor with Dutch encouragement (it must have been persuasive to leave that setup!), and by the 20th century, Rotinese dominated both the civil service and the local anticolonial movements on those islands. ∎

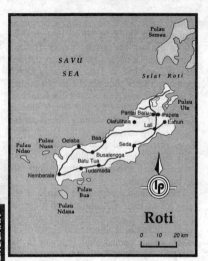

SAVU SEA

Selat Roti

Roti

0   10   20 km

Baa

Roti's main town is Baa, on the north coast. The main street, Jalan Pabean, is close to the ocean, and there are coral beaches nearby. Some houses have boat-shaped thatched roofs with carvings (connected with traditional ancestor cults) at the ends. Baa's market day is Saturday, when stalls line the area around the central town square. The Bank Rakyat Indonesia in Baa does not change money.

Places to Stay & Eat The best place to stay is *Losmen Pondok Wisata Karya* at Jalan Kartini 1, just off Jalan Pabean. Clean rooms with outside bath are 5000 rp per person. The manager speaks good English, and will change money at a reduced rate if you're desperate. Other options are *Hotel Ricki* (on Jalan Gereja) and *Hotel Kesia* (on Jalan Pabean). Both have rooms with attached mandi from 7500/10,000 rp.

Rumah Makan Karya and *Warung Makan Lumayah*, both on Jalan Pabean near the town centre, serve basic meals such as gado gado and nasi ayam for around 1000 rp. The *Hotel Kesia* also serves meals; it has a slightly more extensive menu.

Getting There & Away Merpati flies from Kupang to Roti on Saturday at 7 am (44,500 rp). The flight goes on to Sawu, then returns to Roti at 10 am and loops back to Kupang. From Kupang it connects to Denpasar and Surabaya. There's a Merpati agent on Jalan Pabean in Baa.

Direct buses go to Nemberala (5000 rp; five hours) on Wednesday and Saturday, and possibly on other days if there are enough passengers. The last 20 km of road into Nemberala is a shocker; trucks run the route during the wet season. Buses also run from Pantai Baru to Papela (1000 rp; one hour).

Ferries from Kupang run every day, leaving from Bolok at 9 am – the trip takes four hours and costs 4500 rp. Reach Bolok Harbour from Kupang by taking bemo No 12 or 13 from the Terminal (750 rp).

Getting Around The airport is eight km from Baa, and a Merpati minibus will meet the flight and drop you in Baa (2500 rp).

The ferry drops you at Pantai Baru, about 1½ hours (1500 rp) from Baa – a pack of buses and bemos will meet the ferry.

Nemberala

A surfers' secret for a few years, Nemberala is a relaxed little coastal village with white-sand beaches, and good surf between April and July. A long coral reef runs right along the main beach, with snorkelling possible inside it.

Boa, about eight km from Nemberala, has a spectacular white-sand beach and good surf. You should be able to charter a motorbike in Nemberala. The tiny island of Ndao is another ikat-weaving and lontar-tapping island. In the dry season, men take off for other islands to sell ikat and to work as gold and silversmiths. You can see weavings and jewellery in Ndao's one large village – it's possible to charter a boat in Nemberala, or you might get a lift on a fishing boat.

Ndana is another island reachable by boat from Nemberala. Local legend has it that the island is uninhabited because the entire population was murdered in a revenge act in the 17th century, and the small lake on the island turned red with the victim's blood. The island is now populated by wild deer, a wide variety of birds and (reportedly) turtles, which come to lay their eggs on the beaches.

Boni, about 15 km from Nemberala, is one of the last villages on Roti where traditional religion is still followed. Market day is Thursday. To get there, you can charter or perhaps rent a motorbike in Nemberala.

Places to Stay & Eat The best place to stay is *Losmen Ti Rosa*, right on the beach in Nemberala. It's run by the kepala desa and his family, who speak good English. The losmen has a generator. Accommodation costs 7500 rp per person, all meals included.

Losmen Anugurah seems to be the surfers' favourite – it's close to the main surf break (the cold beer could come into it, also). It costs 7500 rp, with three meals per day. *Homestay Thomas*, another small, family-run place, offers a similar deal.

A resortish place was in construction on the beach front a little way outside the village, reportedly costing around 20,000 rp per person per day.

Getting There & Away A direct bus to Nemberala meets the ferry at least on Wednesday and Saturday (5000 rp; five hours). Otherwise, you'll have to organise transport in Baa – you should be able to charter a motorbike to Nemberala for 15,000 rp per person.

Papela

This Muslim Bugis fishing village in the far west of Roti is set on a beautiful harbour. Every Saturday, it hosts the biggest market on the island. There is one losmen in Papela, the basic *Losmen Karya*, which costs 5000 rp per person. Buses go to Papela from Baa (2500 rp) and Pantai Baru (1000 rp) over the best road on the island.

SAWU (SABU)

Midway between Roti and Sumba, but with closer linguistic links to Sumba, the low, bare island of Sawu (also spelled Sabu) is still a stronghold of animistic beliefs collectively known as *jingitui*. These persist, even though Portuguese missionaries first arrived before 1600 and their work was continued by the Dutch.

Sawu's population (about 45,000) is divided into five traditional domains; the main settlement, Seba (on the north-west coast), was the centre of the leading domain in Dutch times. Sawunese society is divided into clans, named after their male founders, but also into two 'noble' and 'common' halves, determined by a person's mother's lineage: the halves are called *hubi ae* (greater flower stalk) and *hubi iki* (lesser flower stalk). Sawunese women have a thriving ikat-weaving tradition – their cloth typically has stripes of black or dark blue interspersed by stripes with floral motifs, clan or hubi emblems.

There are three places to stay on Sawu: *Ongka Da'i Homestay*, *Makarim Homestay* and *Petykuswan Homestay*, each costing around 12,000 rp, meals included. Seba has a market, and a handful of trucks provides the island's transport, although you can hire a motorbike for 15,000 rp per day. A group of stones near Namata is a ritual site: animal sacrifices, with a whole community sharing the meat, take place around August to October. Another festival in the second quarter of the year sees a boat pushed out to sea as an offering.

Getting There & Away

Air Merpati flies from Kupang to Sawu every Saturday (85,200 rp). From Sawu, the flight returns to Kupang via Roti Island.

Boat Ferries leave Kupang's Bolok Harbour for Sawu on Tuesday and Friday afternoon (12,000 rp; nine hours), returning to Kupang the following day. The Perum ship *Ile Mandiri* does a loop once a week around Kupang, Ende (Flores), Waingapu (Sumba), Sawu and back.

NUSA TENGGARA

Sumba

A great ladder once connected heaven and earth. By it, the first people came down to earth; they found their way to Sumba, and settled at Cape Sasar, on the northern tip of the island – or so the myth goes. Another Sumbanese tale recounts how Umbu Walu Sasar, one of their two ancestors, was driven away from Java by the wars. Transported to Sumba by the powers of heaven, he came to live at Cape Sasar. The other ancestor, Umbu Walu Mandoko, arrived by boat, travelled to the east and lived at the mouth of the Sungai (river) Kambaniru.

Such myths may come as near to the truth as any version of the origins of a people who are physically of Malay stock with a tinge of Melanesian; whose language falls into the same bag that holds the Bimanese of eastern Sumbawa, the Manggarai and Ngada of western Flores and the Sawunese of Sawu; whose death and burial ceremonies are strongly reminiscent of Torajaland in Sulawesi; and whose brilliant ikat textiles, fine carved stone tombs and high, thatched clan houses suggest common origins with similar traditions scattered from Sumatra to Maluku.

Wherever they came from, the island on which the Sumbanese have ended up lies far from Indonesia's main cultural currents, south of Flores and midway between Sumbawa and Timor. Sumba's isolation has helped preserve one of Indonesia's most bizarre cultures, particularly in its wetter, more fertile and more remote western half, which is home to about two-thirds of the island's 400,000 people.

Right up until this century, Sumbanese life was punctuated by periodic warfare between a huge number of rival princedoms. Though Christianity and (less so) Islam have now made inroads, around half the people in the west and a significant minority of people in the east still adhere to the animist *marapu* religion, and old conflicts are recalled every year at western Sumba's often-violent Pasola festivals – mock battles between teams of mounted horse riders.

The 'mock' battles sometimes become real, as in August 1992, when two villages went to war – several people were killed and over 80 homes were burned down.

Many Sumbanese men still carry long-

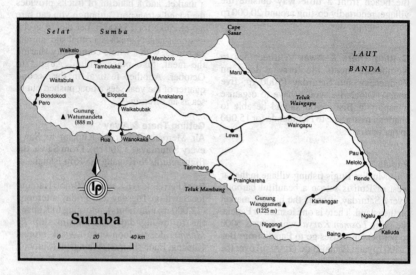

Sumba

bladed knives in wooden sheaths tucked into their waistbands; they wear scarves as turbans and wrap their brightly coloured sarongs to expose the lower two-thirds of their legs, with a long piece of cloth hanging down in front. A woman may have her legs tattooed after the birth of her first child as a recognition of status; often it will be the same motifs that are on her sarong. Another custom, teeth filing, has died out, but you'll see older people with short, brown teeth from the time when white teeth were considered ugly.

The last 20 years have seen an increasing flow of visitors to Sumba, many attracted by the ikat cloth of eastern Sumba. Other Sumbanese traditions are much stronger in the west, where you'll see exotic houses, ceremonies and tombs. The tombs are a constant reminder that, for a Sumbanese, death is the most important event in life. Against this background, the most recent attraction of Sumba – surfing – hardly seems to fit.

Despite their warlike past, the Sumbanese are friendly, and more reserved than many other peoples in Nusa Tenggara, but foreigners should consider hiring a guide when going to villages, at least until they learn some visitor behaviour. Bahasa Indonesia apart, East and West Sumbanese speak different dialects of one language. The eastern one is called Kambera.

History

Fourteenth-century Javanese chronicles place Sumba under the control of the Majapahits. After that empire declined, the island is supposed to have come under the rule of Bima in Sumbawa, then of Gowa in southern Sulawesi. But Sumbanese history is mostly a saga of internal wars, mainly over land and trading rights, between a great number of petty kingdoms. The most powerful clans claimed direct descent from the legendary original settlers, Sasar and Mandoko.

Despite their mutual hostility, princedoms often depended on each other economically. The inland regions produced horses, lumber, betel nuts, rice, fruit and dyewoods, while

the much-valued ikat cloth was made on the coast, where the drier climate was suitable for cotton growing. The coastal people also controlled trade with other islands.

The Dutch initially paid little attention to Sumba because it lacked commercial possibilities. The sandalwood trade conducted in the 18th century was constantly interrupted by wars among the Sumbanese. Only in the mid-19th century did the Dutch arrange a treaty permitting one of their representatives to live in Waingapu, buy horses and collect taxes. Towards the end of the century, Sumba's trade with other islands through Waingapu led to extensive internal wars as various princes tried to dominate it – and in the early 20th century, the Dutch decided to secure their own interests by invading the island and placing it under direct military rule.

Military rule lasted until 1913, when a civilian administration was set up, although the Sumbanese nobility continued to reign, and the Dutch ruled through them. When the Indonesian republic ceased to recognise the native rulers' authority, many of them became government officials, so their families continued to exert influence.

Sumba's extensive grasslands made it one of Indonesia's leading horse-breeding islands. Horses are still used as transport in more rugged regions; they are a symbol of wealth and status, and have traditionally been used as part of the bride-price. Brahmin bulls, first brought to Sumba in the 1920s, are also bred.

Culture

Old beliefs fade, customs die and rituals change: the Sumbanese still make textiles, but no longer hunt heads; 25 years ago the bride-price may have been coloured beads and buffaloes, while today it might include a bicycle. Churches are now a fairly common sight, and in some areas the following traditions are dying – but elsewhere, particularly in the west, they thrive.

Religion

The basis of traditional Sumbanese religion

NUSA TENGGARA

is *marapu* – a collective term for all the spiritual forces, including gods, spirits and ancestors. The most important event in a person's life is death, when they join the invisible world of the marapu, from where they can influence the world of the living. *Marapu mameti* is the collective name for all dead people. The living can appeal to them for help, especially to their own relatives, though the dead can be harmful if irritated. The *marapu maluri* are the original people placed on earth by god – their power is concentrated in certain places or objects, much like the Javanese idea of *semangat*.

Death Ceremonies On the day of burial, horses or buffalo are killed to provide the deceased with food for their journey to the land of marapu. Ornaments and a sirih (betel nut) bag are also buried with the body. The living must bury their dead as richly as possible to avoid being reprimanded by the marapu mameti. Without a complete and honourable ceremony, the dead cannot enter the invisible world, and roam about menacing the living. It was said the dead travel to Cape Sasar to climb the ladder to the invisible world above.

One Sumbanese custom – which parallels the Torajan customs of central Sulawesi – is the deliberate destruction of wealth to gain prestige, often by sponsoring festivals where many buffaloes would be slaughtered. Funerals may be delayed for several years, until enough wealth has been accumulated for a second burial accompanied by the erection of a massive stone slab tomb. In some cases the dragging of the tombstone from outside the village is an important part of the procedure. Sometimes, hundreds are needed to move the block of stone – and the family of the deceased feed them all. A *ratu* (priest) sings for the pullers, which is answered in chorus by the group. The song functions as an invocation to the stone.

When the Indonesian republic was founded, the government introduced a slaughter tax in an attempt to stop the destruction of livestock. This reduced the number of animals killed but didn't alter

basic attitudes. The Sumbanese believe you *can* take it with you!

Villages A traditional village usually consists of two more or less parallel rows of houses facing each other, with a square between. In the middle of the square is a stone with another flat stone on top of it, on which are made offerings to the village's protective marapu. These structures, spirit stones or *kateda*, can also be found in the fields around the village, and are used for offerings to the agricultural marapu when planting or harvesting.

The village square also contains the stone-slab tombs of important ancestors, usually finely carved, but nowadays often made of cement. In former times the heads of slain enemies would be hung on a dead tree in the village square while ceremonies and feasts took place. These skull-trees, called *andung* can still be seen in some villages today, and are a popular motif on Sumbanese ikat.

A traditional Sumbanese dwelling is a large rectangular structure raised on piles; it houses an extended family. The thatched – nowadays often corrugated-iron – roof slopes gently upwards from all four sides, and in the loft are placed marapu maluri objects.

Rituals accompanying the building of a house include an offering, at the time of planting the first pillar, to find out if the marapu agree with the location; one method is to cut open a chicken and examine its liver. Many houses are decked with buffalo horns or pigs' jaws from past sacrifices.

Visiting Villages An awkward situation can arise when visiting traditional villages, especially in western Sumba. If the villagers ask you to pay to take photos, or even just to visit, should you?

Some Sumbanese villages are unaccustomed to tourists, and even those that get a steady stream sometimes have difficulty understanding the strange custom of Westerners who simply want to observe 'exotic' cultures. If you're interested in their weavings or other artefacts, the villagers can put

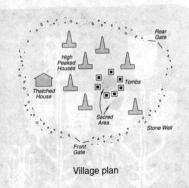

Village plan

places, appointed representatives keep a visitors' book, which they'll produce for you to sign – you should give 1000 rp or a pack of cigarettes to take photos, and in return you may be offered a drink. In off-the-beaten-track kampungs, offering 1000 rp or cigarettes is also OK, especially if you make it clear that you're offering it because you don't have any sirih. This way you still conform to the give-and-take principle. Taking pens for kids is a good idea – it's certainly more productive than handing out sweets.

Whatever the circumstances, taking a guide, at least to isolated villages, is a big help. A guide smoothes over any language difficulties, and through them you should learn enough about the behaviour expected of guests to feel confident visiting villages alone. No matter where you go, taking the time to chat with the villagers helps them to treat you more as a guest than a customer or alien. Remember that when you enter a village, you're in effect walking into a home.

you down as a potential trader. If all you want to do is chat and look around, they may be puzzled about why you've come, and if you simply turn up with a camera and start putting it in their faces, they're likely to be offended.

On Sumba, giving betel nut (sirih pinang) is the traditional way of greeting guests or hosts, and it's a great idea to take some with you – it's cheap and you can get it at most markets in Sumba. Offer it to the kepala desa or to the other most 'senior'-looking person around.

Some villages have grown used to foreigners arriving without sirih. In these

Ikat The ikat woven by the women of eastern coastal regions of Sumba is the most dramatic in Indonesia. The colours are predominantly bright (indigo blue and earthy *kombu* orange-red), and the Sumba motifs are a pictorial history, reminders of

---

Betel Nut – The Peacekeeper

One traditional custom that still thrives in parts of Nusa Tenggara, particularly Sumba and Timor, is the chewing of betel nut, or *siri pinang*. Apart from the obvious reason for chewing it – it gives you a little pep up to help you through the day – there are more complex social and cultural reasons.

Chewing betel is a statement of adulthood, and the three parts that make up the 'mix' that are chewed together have symbolic meaning. The green stalk of the siri represents the male, the nut or pinang the female ovaries and the lime *(kapor)* is symbolic of sperm. The lime causes the characteristic flood of red saliva in the mouth, and when the saliva is spat out, it is believed to be returning the blood of child birth back to the earth.

Betel nut traditionally played an important role in negotiation and discussion between different clans. Betel nut would always be offered to visitors to a village as a gesture of welcome. If a male entering a village did not accept the betel offered, it was tantamount to a declaration of war.

Even today, if you're offered betel nut never refuse it! Some foreigners have really caused offence by saying, 'No, I don't want to buy it.' If you don't want to chew it, just put it in your pocket or bag. Most foreigners find betel nut pretty disgusting – it tastes a bit like bark. It gives you a mild buzz and a bright red mouth. It also creates an amazing amount of saliva, so if you're going to be embarrassed about spitting constantly, better not have any. Whatever you do, don't swallow it – or you're likely to really embarrass yourself! ∎

tribal wars and an age which ended with the coming of the Dutch – the skulls of vanquished enemies dangle off trees and mounted riders wield spears. A huge variety of animals and mythical creatures is also depicted on Sumba ikat, including *nagas* (a crowned snake-dragon with large teeth, wings and legs), deer, dogs, turtles, crocodiles, apes and eagles.

Traditionally, ikat cloth was used only on special occasions: at rituals accompanying harvests, as offerings to the sponsors of a festival, or as clothing for leaders, their relatives and their attendants. Less than 90 years ago, only members of Sumba's highest clans, and their personal attendants, could make or wear it. The most impressive use of the cloth was at important funerals, where dancers and the guards of the corpse were dressed in richly decorated costumes and glittering headdresses. The corpse itself was dressed in the finest textiles, then bound with so many that it resembled a huge mound. The first missionary on Sumba, D K Wielenga, described a funeral in 1925:

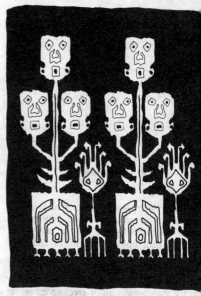

Skull tree – Ikat motif

> The brilliant examples of decorated cloths were carefully kept till the day of the burial. The prominent chief took 40 or 50 to the grave with him and the raja was put to rest with no less than 100 or 200. When they appeared in the hereafter among their ancestors, then they must appear in full splendour. And so the most attractive cloths went into the earth.

The Dutch conquest broke the Sumbanese nobility's monopoly on the production of ikat and opened up a large external market, which in turn increased production. Collected by Dutch ethnographers and museums since the late 19th century (the Rotterdam and Basel museums have fine collections), the large cloths became popular in Java and Holland. By the 1920s, visitors were already noting the introduction of nontraditional designs, such as rampant lions from the Dutch coat of arms.

A Sumbanese woman's ikat sarong is known as a *lau*; a *hinggi* is a large rectangular cloth used by men as a sarong or shawl.

WAINGAPU

Now the largest town on Sumba, Waingapu (population 25,000) became the administrative centre after the Dutch took over the island in 1906. It had long been the centre of the trade controlled by the coastal princedoms, with textiles and metal goods brought in by traders from Makassar, Bima and Ende, and the much-prized Sumba horses, dyewoods and lumber being exported.

Waingapu is the main entry point to Sumba, but the island's attractions lie elsewhere, in the west and south-east. The town does have a large group of ikat traders who run stores or hang around outside hotels (see the Things to Buy section).

Prailiu, three km out of Waingapu, is an ikat-weaving centre that's worth a look – you should be able to see at least some aspects of production going on there. Bemos to Prailiu run from Waingapu's main bus and bemo station (300 rp).

Kawangu, 10 km from Waingapu and

about 300 metres off the road south to Melolo, has some stone-slab tombs. Traditional houses may be seen at **Maru**, on the coast north-west of Waingapu. Buses go there every day, and there's a big market (pasar belakang) on Monday. **Prailiang**, another traditional village on the road between Waingapu and Maru, sees few visitors.

Orientation & Information

Waingapu has two centres: the northern one focuses on the harbour; the southern one is around the main market and bus station, about one km inland.

The Bank Rakyat Indonesia on Jalan Ahmad Yani changes major travellers' cheques (it's the only bank on the island that will). It's open from 8 am to noon Monday to Thursday and on Saturday, and from 7 to 11 am on Friday. The post office on Jalan Hasanuddin is open from 8 am to 2 pm Monday to Saturday (closing at 11 am on Friday). The Telkom office on Jalan Tjut Nya Dien is open 24 hours.

Places to Stay

Losmen Permata Sari is in a good position close to the harbour, with nice views – from

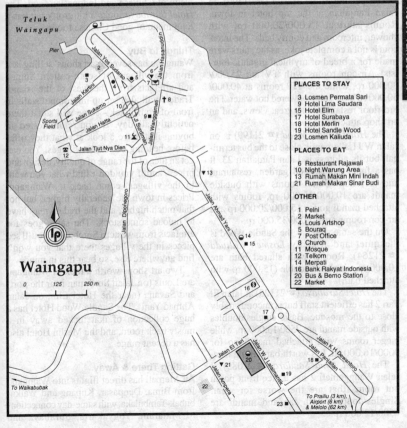

PLACES TO STAY
3 Losmen Permata Sari
9 Hotel Lima Saudara
15 Hotel Elim
17 Hotel Surabaya
18 Hotel Merlin
19 Hotel Sandle Wood
23 Losmen Kaliuda

PLACES TO EAT
6 Restaurant Rajawali
11 Night Warung Area
13 Rumah Makan Mini Indah
21 Rumah Makan Sinar Budi

OTHER
1 Pelni
2 Market
4 Louis Artshop
5 Bouraq
7 Post Office
8 Church
10 Mosque
12 Telkom
14 Merpati
16 Bank Rakyat Indonesia
20 Bus & Bemo Station
22 Market

the bathrooms! Large rooms with attached mandi are 4000 rp per person; new rooms with fan and mandi start at 10,000/15,000 rp. Basic meals are available, and Ali, the owner, is a good source of information. A Hindu temple 50 metres away provides nice background music in the evenings.

The *Hotel Elim* (☎ 21443) at Jalan Ahmad Yani 55 wins the prize for variety of rooms. Dorm rooms cost 5000/9000/12,000/15,000 rp with shared mandi, basic rooms with mandi are 7500/12,500/15,000 rp and up-market rooms with fan and mandi are 15,000/20,000/25,000 rp. The hotel has a restaurant as well.

The palatial *Hotel Merlin* (☎ 21300) on Jalan Panjaitan is the top hotel in town. Rooms start at 15,000/20,000 rp, with shower, intercom and comfy beds. The intercom is not a complete joke, as the stairs were made for a breed of mythical gigantic tourists! Air-con rooms with TV are 25,000/30,000 rp, while the VIP rooms at 40,000/50,000 rp have solar-powered hot water. The 3rd-floor restaurant has great views, and an art shop attached.

The *Hotel Sandle Wood* (☎ 21199) is on Jalan W J Lalaimantik close to the bus terminal, but its address is Jalan Panjaitan 23. It · has a fancy landscaped garden, restaurant and art shop. Small rooms with outside mandi are 10,000/15,000 rp, rooms with attached mandi go for 15,000/20,000 rp and air-con rooms are 25,000/35,000 rp.

On the same street as the Sandle Wood is the quiet and friendly *Losmen Kaliuda* (☎ 21264). Rooms with shared bath are 10,000 rp, single or double (15,000 rp with attached bath).

The *Hotel Surabaya* (☎ 21125) at Jalan El Tari 2 has efficient staff but is uncomfortably close to the mosque. Basic singles/doubles with outside mandi are 7500/13,000 rp, while bigger rooms with attached mandi go for 9000/16,000 rp. It's worth bargaining here.

The *Hotel Lima Saudara* (☎ 21083) at Jalan Wanggameti 2 has a nice front porch but rooms that are the worse for wear. Singles/doubles with fan and mandi are 6500/12,000 rp.

Places to Eat

Waingapu is not overendowed with eateries; there are a few small restaurants, but the best food is probably at the hotels.

Recommended by locals is the cheap and quick *Rumah Makan Mini Indah* at Jalan Ahmad Yani 27. *Restaurant Rajawali* on Jalan Sutomo is also popular. There are night warungs around the corner of Jalan Hatta and Jalan Surdiman. *Rumah Makan Sinar Budi*, behind the market, serves Padang food.

Otherwise, eat at the hotels. The *Hotel Merlin* has a large 3rd-floor restaurant with Indonesian and Western food, and great views. The *Hotel Sandle Wood* has a varied menu of Chinese and Indonesian food. The *Hotel Surabaya* looks a bit grotty but has a long menu of good Chinese food.

Things to Buy

Waingapu has several 'art shops' selling ikat from the villages of south-eastern Sumba and artefacts from the west of the island. Traders will also set up impromptu stalls in front of your hotel – some will squat there patiently all day. If you're interested in buying ikat, have a look at what they offer before heading out to the villages. You can get an idea of the range of quality, design and price – and if you don't find what you want in the villages, come back to Waingapu. Prices in town are generally higher, but not that much higher, and the traders may have to unload some stock. The same goes for artefacts from western Sumba, but you'll see pieces in the villages there that you won't find anywhere else, so bear this in mind.

Two art shops worth a look in Waingapu are Louis (on Jalan Surdiman near the port) and Savana (near the Hotel Elim on Jalan Ahmad Yani). The Sandle Wood Hotel has a huge collection of ikat tucked away in a musty back room, and the Merlin Hotel also has a decent range.

Getting There & Away

Air Merpati has direct flights into Waingapu from Bima, Denpasar, Kupang and Waika-bubak-Tambulaka, with same-day connections to Mataram, Yogyakarta, Surabaya and

Ujung Pandang. Bouraq has four direct flights a week from both Kupang (117,000 rp) and Denpasar (160,000 rp).

The Merpati office (☎ 21323) is on Jalan Ahmad Yani, next to the Hotel Elim. Bouraq (☎ 21363) is at Jalan Yos Sudarso 57, near the harbour.

Bus The bus station is in the southern part of town, close to the market. To Waikabubak (4000 rp; four hours), there are buses leaving at 7 am, noon and 3 pm. Your hotel can arrange for the bus to pick you up, and it's worthwhile booking a seat if you have a preference. The road to Waikabubak goes through Lewa (long the centre of horse breeding) and Anakalang. It's an excellent road, paved all the way.

Buses also head south-east to Melolo, Rende and Baing. Several travel through the morning and afternoon to Melolo (2000 rp; 1½ hours), with a few continuing on to Rende, Ngalu and Baing. Most return to Waingapu the same day.

Car Losmen Permata Sari and the Sandle Wood and Merlin hotels rent cars with driver for out-of-town trips. Some asking prices were 60,000 rp to Rende, 65,000 rp to Kaliuda and 80,000 rp to Waikabubak.

Boat The Perum ferry *Ile Mandiri* leaves Pelabuhan Ipi (in Ende) for Waingapu every Tuesday at 7 pm (10,400 rp; 10 hours). From Waingapu it sails on to Sabu, then loops back to Waingapu. It departs from Waingapu for Ende on Friday at 7 pm.

The *Kelimutu* calls at Waingapu twice a fortnight, sailing on to Ende one week and to Bima the next. It docks at a special port on the far side of Waingapu's main harbour – a bemo there from town costs 300 rp. The Pelni office is close to the harbour at Jalan Pelabuhan 2.

For other, less regular boats, ask around the harbour or at the Losmen Permata Sari, which has a view over the harbour and can tell you where boats are heading.

Getting Around
To/From the Airport The airport is six km south of town on the Melolo road. Minivans from the Elim, Sandle Wood and Merlin hotels and from Losmen Permata Sari will usually meet incoming flights and offer a free ride to intending guests. Taxi drivers may tell you that these vans don't exist – walk out into the car park and see for yourself. If you have to use a taxi, expect to pay around 3000 rp.

Bemo A bemo to any destination around town will cost 300 rp.

SOUTH-EASTERN SUMBA
Some of the villages of south-eastern Sumba have impressive stone tombs (as well as less exciting concrete ones), and produce much of the island's best ikat, but the traditional way of life is not as strong as in the west of the island. You can buy weavings in the villages, but you'll need plenty of patience if you want better prices than those offered by the competitive Waingapu merchants.

Melolo
If you don't want to visit the south-east on a day trip from Waingapu, the small town of Melolo, 62 km from Waingapu and close to some interesting villages, has one losmen, the friendly and security-conscious *Losmen Hermindo*. Clean singles/doubles with fan and mandi cost 5000/10,000 rp. The losmen can arrange car hire for a day trip around the area for around 40,000 rp. Basic meals are available on request; otherwise there's one small warung in town, if you like goat soup. Ten minutes' walk through mangroves from Losmen Hermindo, there's a long, sandy beach, although the water's a bit murky.

The market is about three km out of town, in the middle of nowhere on a dusty hill. The main market day is Friday, when you might see some good ikat, and also *hikung* cloth (distinguished from ikat by its woven, not dyed, patterns). Bemos run regularly from town to the market (250 rp).

Getting There & Away Buses to Melolo from Waingapu (2000 rp; 1½ hours) run hourly until around 4 pm. It's an excellent, paved road, and crosses mainly flat grasslands. From Melolo the road continues on to Baing. Another road from Melolo crosses the mountains to Nggongi – trucks run along this road, at least in the dry season.

Rende

Seven km towards Baing from Melolo, Rende has an imposing line-up of big stone-slab tombs and makes some fine-quality ikat. You may be asked to pay 1000 rp, as an admission and photo fee. If you sit and chat with the villagers, they might not ask you for anything, but make a small gift anyway – at least some cigarettes. You'll certainly be shown some magnificent ikat, but prices are high. Though Rende still has a raja, other traditions have declined, due to the cost of ceremonies and the breakdown of the marapu religion here.

The largest tomb at Rende is that of a former chief. It consists of four stone pillars two metres high, supporting a rectangular slab of stone about five metres long, 2½ metres wide and a metre thick. Two stone tablets stand atop the main slab, carved with human, buffalo, deer, lobster, fish, crocodile and turtle figures. A massive newly built traditional Sumbanese house with concrete pillars faces the tombs, along with a number of older *rumah adat*, although many of these now have tin roofs.

It's possible to stay with the raja, but remember that these are members of a royal family, not hotel staff. Act accordingly!

Getting There & Away Four or five buses a day go from Waingapu to Rende (2000 rp; two hours), starting at about 7 am. From Melolo, bemos and trucks run throughout the day.

Umabara & Pau

Like Rende, these two villages about four km from Melolo have traditional Sumbanese houses, stone tombs and weavings. At Umabara, the largest tombs are for relatives of the present raja, who speaks some English and is quite friendly. Apart from serving you

coffee, he may also offer you some betel nut. Again, expect to pay 1000 rp if you're looking for hospitality and/or want to take photos.

From Melolo, bemos can drop you at the turn-off to the villages on the main Waingapu-Melolo road. About a 20-minute walk up here is a horse statue, where you fork right for Umabara or left for Pau, both just a few minutes further. A trail also links the two villages. From Waingapu, ask the bus driver to drop you at the turn-off.

Mangili

This village, 38 km from Melolo, and a 20-minute walk off the road to Baing, is another high-quality weaving centre, though its people don't seem very interested in bargaining with travellers. About six buses a day from Waingapu and Melolo pass the Mangili turn-off, the first leaving Waingapu at about 7 am and passing through Melolo at about 8.30 am. From Melolo, the trip takes about 1½ hours and costs 1000 rp.

Kaliuda

This town is reputed to produce the best ikat in all of Indonesia. However, you might have trouble finding what you want here – much of the best stuff gets bought up in large quantities and shipped off to Bali! Still, the villagers are happy to chat, and you may see some of the work being produced, even if their prices make you weep. There are also some stone-slab tombs here. To get there, take a bus heading to Baing from Waingapu or Melolo and get off at Ngalu – Kaliuda is about a three-km walk from there.

Baing

There's good surf between May and August at Kalala, about two km from Baing off the main road from Melolo. An Australian has set up bungalow accommodation along the wide, white-sand beach for surfing and fishing fanatics, costing 30,000 rp per person per day. To get there, the same buses you take for Mangili continue to Baing, about one hour further on over a rough road. If you get a blank look when you ask the bus driver for

Baing, ask for Waijelu, where the buses finish further south of Baing. Baing is about two hours from Melolo and the fare is 2500 rp.

SOUTH-CENTRAL SUMBA

This part of the island is little explored and difficult to access – although there are regular trucks from Waingapu to Praing-kareha, getting around may require a jeep and, often, some hiking.

Praingkareha

The big attraction here is the 100-metre-high waterfall. There's a beautiful pool at the base of the falls. By tradition, women are forbidden to look into it, but an exception is made for foreigners!

You can drive to within eight km of the falls, then you have to walk. A guide is advisable, and can be hired for about 5000 rp per day, but you can ask directions to the falls (air terjun). It's possible to stay at the kepala desa's house.

Lumbung

As at Praingkareha, the main attraction here is the spectacular 25-metre waterfall. Although the falls are not extremely high, the volume of water is huge, and it's crystal clear. At present, you can drive to within eight km of the falls, and then you must walk. Road building is continuing, though, and eventually this trip won't require much exercise.

Tarimbang

If you're one of the crazies trudging around the outer islands carrying several surfboards looking for uncrowded waves, you might want to check this place out. Tarimbang has a beautiful surf beach, and it's possible to stay with villagers nearby. Trucks from Waingapu can drop you at the Tarimbang turn-off.

WAIKABUBAK

The neat little town of Waikabubak is located at the greener, western end of Sumba, where the tropical trees and rice paddies contrast with the dry grasslands around Waingapu.

More a collection of kampungs clustered around a main shopping street and market, Waikabubak has traditional clan houses, and small graveyards of old stone-slab tombs carved with buffalo-horn motifs. About 600 metres high, and cooler than the east, it's a good base for exploring the traditional villages of western Sumba. Although the locals are friendly towards foreigners, it seems there may be some sort of curfew after 10 pm.

Information

The Bank Rakyat Indonesia on Jalan Gajah Mada will change US and Australian dollars cash – but not travellers' cheques. However, if the notes are even slightly damaged or marked, the bank may refuse to change them. It's open from 8 am to noon Monday to Friday, and until 10.30 am on Saturday.

The post office is open from 8 am to 2 pm Monday to Saturday (closing at 11 am on Friday). The Telkom office is open 24 hours.

Tombs & Traditional Kampungs

Large stone-slab tombs are dotted around Waikabubak, and several kampungs occupy ridge or hilltop positions around the town. Some of these kampungs are more traditional and visiting them less formalised than many located further out – the only explanation is that getting to some of the hilltop kampungs around Waikabubak requires a short uphill walk on narrow paths, while some kampungs further out of town are accessible by vehicle. Still, at most of the kampungs around Waikabubak, locals are accustomed to the eccentric behaviour of tourists, so you can see some traditional culture without offending somebody. The most interesting kampungs are around Praiij-ing, Tarung and Bondomarotto.

Kampung Praiijing is especially scenic, perched on a hilltop about four km from the centre of town. There are five neat rows of traditional houses and large stone tombs. You may be offered betel nut, and you should offer 1000 rp in return to take photos – chewing a little betel nut could make the experience that little bit more vivid! Kampung Prairami and Kampung Primkateti are also beautifully located on adjacent hilltops. You can take a bemo to the turn-off to Praiijing (300 rp).

Kampung Tarung, reached by a path off Jalan Maadaelu marked by a large number of tombs at the junction, is the scene of an important month-long ritual sequence, the Wula Podhu, each November. This is an austere period when even weeping for the dead is prohibited. Rites consist mainly of offerings to the spirits – the day before it ends, hundreds of chickens are sacrificed, and on the final day people sing and dance day long. Tarung's monuments are under official protection.

Another major kampung worth visiting is Tambera, 10 km north on the road to Mamboro. At most of these kampungs, you are usually asked to give 1000 rp.

Places to Stay

The *Hotel Aloha* (☎ 21024) has friendly staff, good food and excellent information about the culture of western Sumba. Clean singles/doubles with shared bath cost 6600/8800 rp (11,000/13,750 rp with private bath).

Just around the corner at Jalan Pemuda 4 is the *Hotel Manandang* (☎ 21197). This place is up-market, but good value: large, spotless singles/doubles with wash basin and comfy beds cost 8000/13,500 rp. Rooms with private bath and fan go for 15,000/20,000 rp. The restaurant has a long menu, and satellite TV with American, Australian and French channels if you're feeling a bit isolated.

The *Hotel Rakuta* on Jalan Veteran, run by a friendly family, has rooms, beds and mandis that are vast by Nusa Tenggara standards. Singles/doubles/triples with mandi are 15,000/20,000/25,000 rp, including three meals per day.

The cheapest accommodation in town is at the *Hotel Pelita* (☎ 21104) on Jalan Ahmad Yani. Basic rooms are 4000 rp per person with shared mandi; dingy singles/

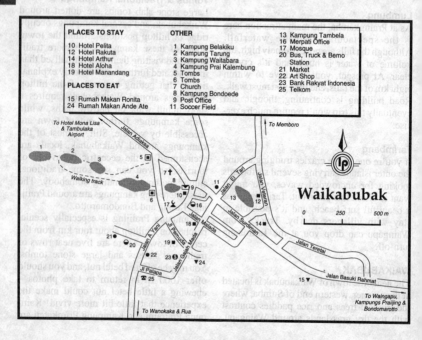

PLACES TO STAY
10 Hotel Pelita
12 Hotel Rakuta
14 Hotel Arthur
18 Hotel Aloha
19 Hotel Manandang

PLACES TO EAT
15 Rumah Makan Ronita
24 Rumah Makan Ande Ate

OTHER
1 Kampung Belakiku
2 Kampung Tarung
3 Kampung Waitabara
4 Kampung Prai Kalembung
5 Tombs
6 Tombs
7 Church
8 Kampung Bondoede
9 Post Office
11 Soccer Field

13 Kampung Tambela
16 Merpati Office
17 Mosque
20 Bus, Truck & Bemo Station
21 Market
22 Art Shop
23 Bank Rakyat Indonesia
25 Telkom

To Hotel Mona Lisa & Tambulaka Airport

Jalan Adiatsa

Walking track

To Memboro

Waikabubak

0   250   500 m

Jalan El Tari

Jalan Veteran

Jalan Sudirman

Jalan A Yani

Jalan Pemuda

Jalan Gajah Mada

Jalan Malada

Jl Palapa

Jalan Teretai

Jalan Basuki Rahmat

To Wanokaka & Rua

To Waingapu, Kampungs Praijing & Bondomarotto

doubles with private mandi are 7500/12,000 rp. Swanky new rooms out the back look like they've never been slept in. Officially, they cost 15,000/25,000 rp.

The *Hotel Arthur* (☎ 21112) on Jalan Veteran is a quiet new place with a lovely courtyard and a small restaurant. There's a range of rooms, starting at 17,000 rp, single or double, with private mandi. VIP rooms with fan, shower and fridge go for 45,000 rp.

The resortish *Hotel Mona Lisa* (☎ 21364), on Jalan Adhyaksa 2½ km from town, has bungalow-style accommodation. During the off season, prices are reasonable – large rooms with Western bathroom cost 15,000/20,000 rp, but expect to pay at least three times this during the Pasola festival and between June and August. The restaurant houses a wonderful collection of photos from around western Sumba.

Places to Eat

The restaurant situation in Waingapu has improved a bit recently; there's a few decent alternatives to the hotel restaurants. The *Rumah Makan Ronita* on Jalan Basuki Rahmat has a long menu of Indonesian and Western food, and even a karaoke section! *Rumah Makan Ande Ate* near the Hotel Aloha is cheap, and popular with locals. Otherwise, the *Hotel Manandang* and the *Hotel Aloha* have good meals.

Things to Buy

You'll get traders coming to your hotel with ikat cloth, but it's nearly all from eastern Sumba, and you're better off buying it over there. What is worth buying in western Sumba are the elaborate bone, wood, horn and stone carvings, and metal symbols and jewellery. There are bone or wooden betel-nut and *kapor* (lime) containers with stoppers carved into animal and human heads; knives with Pasola horsemen or fertility symbols carved into their wooden handles; tobacco and money containers made of wood and coconut shell; stone figures representing marapu ancestors; and metal omega-shaped symbols called *mamuli*, which are worn as earring and pendants.

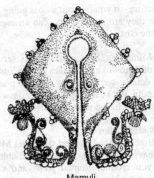

Mamuli

There's one art shop in Waikabubak – it's worth checking the range and prices there before you go out to villages.

Getting There & Away

Air The Merpati agency is on Jalan Ahmad Yani. If you're checking the Merpati timetable, look under Tambulaka; Waikabubak is not listed. There are three flights a week to and from Bima, Denpasar, Kupang, Mataram and Waingapu.

Bus Around four or five buses leave Waikabubak for Waingapu between 7 and 8 am, at least two leave around noon and there is one at 3 pm. The fare is 4000 rp and the trip takes around four hours, including a break for snacks. You can easily arrange for the bus to pick you up from your hotel. It's best to book your ticket the day before leaving – your hotel may be able to help, or visit the bus ticket agencies along Jalan Ahmad Yani.

Getting Around

To/From the Airport The airport is at Tambulaka, 42 km north of Waikabubak. The Bumi Indah bus can take you there for 2000 rp – it's supposed to go every flight day at 7 am, but it's not very reliable. If it hasn't picked you up at your hotel by 7.30 am, you'd better get a taxi or charter a bemo, which will cost a nasty 45,000 rp. It's not a bad idea to check the flight list at Merpati the day before – if you find out who is going and where they are staying, you can arrange to split the cost.

Bus Minibuses, bemos and trucks service most other towns and villages in west Sumba – for details, see under the separate places. Generally, it's best to get them early when they tend to fill up more quickly.

Car & Motorbike
The Hotel Manandang and the Hotel Mona Lisa have vehicles and drivers available to take you around. Rented jeeps and vans include petrol, and a driver who can also act as your guide. Some quoted prices were: Anakalang (45,000 rp), Bondokodi (80,000 rp), Tambulaka (45,000 rp), Waingapu (100,000 rp) and Wanokaka (70,000 rp).

The Hotel Aloha can arrange motorbike hire for 20,000 rp a day. It's not a bad idea to take a guide – you can probably get someone to go with you for around 10,000 rp per day. Kering is one we found to be honest and lots of fun – though his English is bizarre!

AROUND WESTERN SUMBA
The traditional village culture of western Sumba is one of the most intact in Indonesia. Kampungs of high-roofed houses still cluster on their hilltops (a place of defence in times past), surrounding the large stone tombs of their important ancestors. Away from the towns, old women with filed teeth still go bare breasted and men in the traditional 'turban' and short sarong can be seen on horseback. The agricultural cycle turns up rituals, often involving animal sacrifices, almost year-round, and ceremonies for events like house building and marriage can take place at any time. Some kampungs are unaccustomed to foreigners – taking betel nut and cigarettes is a good way to get a friendly reception.

You should give yourself at least a few days around western Sumba – once you have learned some basic manners as a guest arriving in a village, hopefully armed with some Indonesian, it's possible to do without a guide.

Pasola Festival
The most famous of Nusa Tenggara's festivals sees large teams of colourfully clad horse riders engaging in mock battles. Its pattern is similar to that of other ritual warfare that used to take place in Indonesia – the cause not so much a quarrel between opposing forces as a need for human blood to be spilled to keep the spirits happy and bring a good harvest. Despite the blunt spears that the combatants now use and the efforts of Indonesian authorities to supervise the events, few holds are barred; injuries and sometimes deaths still occur.

The Pasola is part of a series of rituals connected with the beginning of the planting season. It takes place in four different areas in February or March each year, its exact timing determined by the arrival on nearby coasts of a certain type of seaworm called *nyale*. Priests examine the nyale at dawn and from their behaviour predict how good the year's harvest will be. Then the Pasola can begin: it's usually fought first on the beach, then later the same day, further inland. The opposing 'armies' are drawn from coastal and inland dwellers.

The nyale are usually found on the eighth or ninth day after a full moon. In February Pasola is celebrated in the Kodi area (centred on Kampung Tosi) and the Lamboya area (Kampung Sodan); in March it's the turn of the Wanokaka area (Kampung Waigalli) and the remote Gaura area west of Lamboya (Kampung Ubu Olehka).

Anakalang & Around
Kampung Pasunga, beside the Waingapu road at Anakalang, 22 km east of Waikabubak, boasts one of Sumba's most impressive tomb line-ups. The grave of particular interest consists of a horizontal stone slab with a vertical slab in front of it. The vertical slab took six months to carve with the figures of a man and a woman. The tomb was constructed in 1926; five people are buried here and 150 buffalo were sacrificed during its construction. There's no fee to enter the kampung, and you can see the tombs from

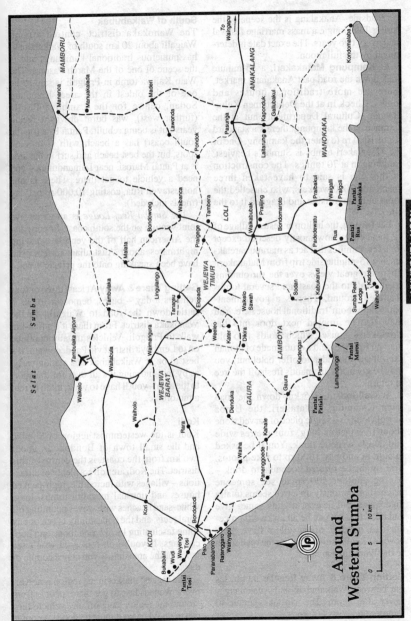

Around Western Sumba

0   5   10 km

Selat Sumba

MAMBORU

Mananca
Manuakalada
Maderi
Lawonda
Pondok
Bondoweog
Waibanca
Tambera
Malata
Praigage
WEJEWA TIMUR
Lingulango
Tanageu
Elopada
Weeleo
Kater
Waikelo Sawah
Dikira
Waingura
Wainmangura
Tambulaka
Tambulaka Airport
Waitabula
Wakelo
Walholo
Rara
WEJEWA BARAT
Denduka
GAURA
Waha
Panengpoede
Kahale
Gaura
Bondokodi
KODI
Kori
Wayengo
Tosi
Wudi
Bukabani
Pantai Tosi
Peto
Paranatakororo
Ratengaro
Wanyapou

ANAKALANG
To Wangapu
Kapondok
Gallubakul
Pasunga
Laitarung
WANOKAKA
Praijing
Praibakul
Waigalli
Praigoli
Pantai Wanokaka
Waikabubak
LOLI
Bondomaroto
Padedewatu
Rua
Pantai Rua
Sodan
Kabukaruti
Sumba Reef Lodge
Kadolu
Wahoil
LAMBOYA
Kadengar
Patiala
Lamandunga
Pantai Marosi
Pantai Patiala

Kondomalaba

the roadside. Anakalang is the scene of the Puring Takadonga, a mass marriage festival held every two years. The exact date is determined by the full moon.

At **Kampung Matakakeri**, a 15-minute walk down the road past Anakalang market, there are more traditional houses and tombs. Check in at the Departemen Kebudayaan (Cultural Department) hut at the entrance to the kampung: there's a standard fee of 1000 rp to enter the kampung. One of the Matakakeri tombs is Sumba's heaviest, weighing in at 70 tonnes. The construction of this one is said to have taken three years, and 2000 workers, who chiselled the tomb out of a hillside and dragged it to the site.

Lai Tarung, the hilltop ancestral village of 12 local clans, now mostly deserted except for a few families that act as marapu caretakers, is a 15-minute side trip from Matakakeri. There are great views over the surrounding countryside to the coast, and several tombs scattered around. There's a government-built 'showroom' traditional house here. You may also be invited next door into the caretaker's house, which holds two old marapu figurines and a drum made of human skin. It's a good idea to offer betel nut; you may be given a jeruk mantis fresh off the tree in return.

At **Gallubakul**, 2½ km down the road from Kampung Matatakeri, the Umba Sawola tomb is a single piece of carved stone about five metres long, four metres wide and nearly a metre thick. You'll be asked to sign in and pay 1000 rp to take photos. You might be offered coconuts to drink – paying another 500 rp to see someone perched precariously up a tree seems totally inadequate, but at least it adds some 'give and take' to what can be an awkward procedure. A handful of travellers have gone beyond Gallubakul, following the road south to the Wanokaka area.

Getting There & Away Regular minibuses run between Waikabubak and Anakalang – fewer after 1 pm. The trip takes about 40 minutes and costs 600 rp.

South of Waikabubak

The Wanokaka district, centred around Waigalli about 20 km south of Waikabubak, has numerous traditional kampungs and is the scene of one of the March Pasolas. The Watu Kajiwa tomb in Praigoli is said to be one of the oldest in the area. Kampung Sodan, centre for the Lamboya Pasola (further west), was burnt down in recent years but is being rebuilt. Pantai Rua (on the south coast) has a beach with swimming spots, but the best beach and surf in the area is at Pantai Marosi, near Lamandunga – you need a vehicle to get there. There is one homestay in Rua, costing 10,000 rp per day (meals included).

The *Sumba Reef Lodge* is an expensive joint venture on the south coast. Reportedly, the American half of the venture is having nightmares about Australian surfers who have been sneaking onto the private beach.

Getting There & Away At least three or four vehicles a day – buses, bemos or trucks – rattle down the road to Waigalli, in the Wanokaka district. From there it's a five-km walk to Praigoli. Vehicles usually continue on to Lemboya district via Pandedewatu. It's best to be at Waikabubak bus station early, as by mid-morning it's all over for transport to the area – you'll have to walk, hitch or rent a motorbike.

Kodi

Kodi is the westernmost region of Sumba, and the small town of Bondokodi, about two km from the coast, is the centre of this district. The Kodi area offers plenty of attractions – villages with incredible, high-peaked houses and unusual megalith tombs, long, white-sand beaches with waves pounding on coral reefs, and the opportunity to see or buy some fascinating local wood, bone and horn carvings. If you're on foot, you won't see much of the area unless you stay a couple of days.

The biggest market in the region is at Kori every Wednesday; to get there, people from around the region hang off any vehicle they can get hold of, so it must be good! A couple of buses run from Bondokodi in the morning, before 8 am.

Pero

Pero is a friendly coastal village set on spectacular coastline just a few km from Bondokodi.

To visit traditional kampungs, go either north or south along the coast. To get to **Ratenggaro**, first cross the freshwater pool that runs to the coast below Pero. At low tide you could wade across; otherwise, small boys will get you across in canoes. From the other side, follow the dirt track for about three km along Pantai Radukapal, a long stretch of white-sand beach, until you come to the fenced kampung of Ratenggaro. The kepala desa is friendly and will show you his carvings and serve you tea. You may be asked to sign in and pay 1000 rp. It's possible to stay with the kepala desa (about 8000 rp with meals included), or to pitch a tent and just pay for meals. The view from Ratenggaro along the coastline is breathtaking – coconut palms fringe the shoreline and the high roofs of Wainyapu peep out above the trees across the river. On the near side of the river mouth, some unusual stone tombs occupy a small headland. To get to **Wainyapu**, you'll probably have to wade across the river at low tide.

On the way to Ratenggaro, you may notice the roofs of **Kampung Paranobararo** through the trees about one km inland. Here are houses with even higher roofs, stone statues and an elaborate house with pig jaws and numerous buffalo horns hanging from its verandah. During the day, only women and children are in the village – you may see women weaving outside their houses, and they are happy to chat. Again, you may be asked to sign in and pay 1000 rp. Another way to reach Paranobararo is to head south from Bondokodi market for about a km, and take a dirt road to the right just past the school – if you make it past the school (we had the whole school rushing out of the schoolyard to greet us!). Keep forking right towards the coast; you'll reach Paranobararo after about two km.

To reach **Tosi**, about six km north and the scene of the Kodi Pasola in February, head north from Bondokodi market along the paved road – if you are coming from Pero, it's simply left at the T-intersection. About a km along the road you see a track on your left. Follow it for five km, past a series of tombs. You'll soon see Tosi's roofs on your right. From Tosi it's a 10-minute walk to the beach, and a track runs all the way back to Pero.

Place to Stay

The only accommodation is the *Homestay Story*. It's clean and cosy, but the beds have long since given up the ghost. The cost is 10,000 rp per person, including meals. At night, an impromptu art shop may set up on the front porch. The traders won't bother you if you aren't interested – but it's worth taking a look at the bone, horn, wood and stone carvings, because you won't see some of them anywhere else.

Getting There & Away From Waikabubak there are two direct buses a day, departing at around 6 am. The trip takes about three hours and costs 2500 rp. One bus is run by the Hotel Mona Lisa, but you can book it in town. These buses return to Waikabubak at about 9 am. On market day in Kori, return buses may finish in Waitabula – you have to change to another bus to continue on to Waikabubak.

Wejewa Timur

This region less than 20 km west of Waikabubak sees relatively few tourists because of the lack of transport – you probably need a jeep to explore the area. The people here have maintained their traditional culture and are very friendly. The villages of **Weeleo** and **Kater**, both near Elopada, make interesting day trips.

Waikelo

Occasional boats go to Sumbawa, Flores or even further afield from this small port north of Waitabula.

Kalimantan

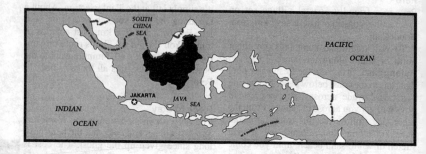

Kalimantan is the southern two-thirds of the island of Borneo. Of the 12 million people on Borneo, about nine million live in Kalimantan, most in settlements along its rivers. Mountains stretch across Borneo's interior, while heavy rainfall and poor drainage have produced a broad rim of dense, inhospitable wetlands along much of the island's coast and river basins.

Timber and mining interests have penetrated deep into Kalimantan, bulldozing and chainsawing at an alarming rate. Growing pressure for tighter controls over natural resource exploitation seems to have spurred millers and miners to accelerate the pace, to make the most of lax environmental law enforcement and to meet the demand for jobs and development. Indigenous Dayak claims to preserve traditional lands have attracted some government sympathy, yet vast tracts

of rainforest continue to fall, rivers are being fouled and indigenous cultures are reeling from the social and economic intrusions of the 20th century.

If you are expecting to see half-naked, heavily tattooed Dayaks striding down the streets of Balikpapan, Samarinda or Pontianak, you'll be disappointed. Your first impressions are likely to be of oil refineries and timber mills. Travellers in search of deepest, darkest Borneo must go further and further afield to find unlogged jungle and traditional Dayak hospitality. There are pockets of accessible culture, wildlife and jungle close to major waterways – the highway system of Kalimantan – but these are increasingly rare.

The visions of Eden that colour popular imagery of Borneo probably stem from the accounts of early European explorers.

Highlights

Kalimantan is one of the least visited parts of Indonesia, mostly because its unique cultures, spectacular flora and unusual wildlife are expensive and time-consuming to reach. Wetlands and mountains provide a buffer to the ravages of development, and it is here that you will find truly wonderful remnants of pre-colonial Kalimantan.

The Orang-Utan Rehabilitation centres and diverse forest reserves at Tanjung Puting National Park are world-class attractions. So too is the river life along the Sungai Mahakam, and the remote Kayan and Kenyah settlements in the Apokayan and around Long Bawang. Balikpapan and its river life is perhaps the main tourist attraction in Kalimantan and a good place to start exploration of this vast island. ■

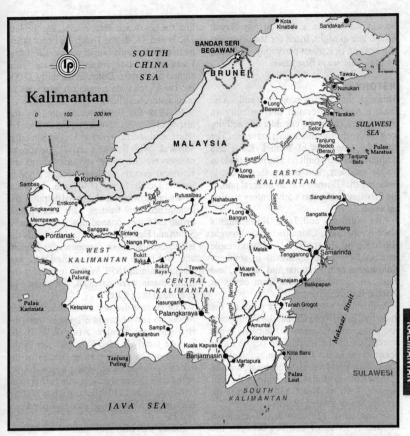

Kalimantan

SOUTH CHINA SEA

0   100   200 km

BANDAR SERI BEGAWAN

BRUNEI

MALAYSIA

Kota Kinabalu

Sandakan

Tawau

Nunukan

Long Bawang

Tarakan

Tanjung Selor

SULAWESI SEA

Pulau Maratua

Tanjung Redeb (Berau)

Tanjung Batu

Sambas

Kuching

Putussibau

Nahabuan

Long Nawan

Sungai Kapuas

EAST KALIMANTAN

Sangkulirang

Entikong

Singkawang

Mempawah

Sanggau

Sintang

Nanga Pinoh

Long Bangun

Sungai Mahakam

Sungai Belayan

Sangatta

Bontang

Pontianak

WEST KALIMANTAN

Bukit Baka

Bukit Raya

Teweh

Melak

Tenggarong

Samarinda

Gunung Palung

Muara Teweh

Panajam

Balikpapan

Pulau Karimata

Ketapang

CENTRAL KALIMANTAN

Sungai Barito

Sungai Kahayan

Tanah Grogot

Makassar Strait

Kasungan

Palangkaraya

Amuntai

Sampit

Kandangan

Pangkalanbun

Kuala Kapuas

Banjarmasin

Martapura

Kota Baru

Tanjung Puting

SOUTH KALIMANTAN

Pulau Laut

SULAWESI

JAVA SEA

KALIMANTAN

Anxious to justify their expensive exploits, they filed reports to their sponsors with exaggerated claims of the fertility and great commercial potential of the jungles of the East. It seemed one could simply clear the jungle and, with minimal effort, grow anything. Later works by naturalist Alfred Wallace and novelists such as Joseph Conrad added considerably to the mystique.

Kalimantan's unique cultures, spectacular flora and unusual wildlife remain the primary attractions for the trickle of tourists with the time, money and energy required to explore this part of the world. Wetlands and

mountains provide a buffer to the ravages of development, and it is here that you will find truly wonderful remnants of pre-colonial Kalimantan.

The orang-utan rehabilitation centres and diverse forest reserves at Tanjung Puting National Park are a world-class attraction. So too is the river life along the Sungai Mahakam, and the remote Kayan and Kenyah settlements in the Apokayan and around Long Bawang. Even in tourist precincts such as Tanjung Isuy in East Kalimantan where visitors pay by the hour to see 'primitive' culture, there are still many who believe in the old ways. Take a walk in any Dayak village late at night, listen for the drumbeat of a healing or harvest ceremony, and learn about the old ways first hand.

HISTORY

Although the pace of economic and social change has accelerated dramatically in recent years, there was considerable activity long before the multinationals moved in. The powerful kingdoms of Brunei, Kutai and Banjarmasin were built on a thriving trade in jungle products, and before then there is evidence that Borneo was an integral part of the Sriwijaya kingdom's 5th-century trading network.

Like Sumatra and Java, Kalimantan's place on the India-China trade axis brought Hinduism by about 400 AD. Hindu temple remains have been unearthed in southern Kalimantan near Amuntai and Negara, and there are Sanskrit tablets from caves at Wahau, East Kalimantan.

Kalimantan was a stopover point on the trade routes between China, the Philippines and Java and Chinese settlements were established on the island long before Europeans came to the Indonesian archipelago. The coastal ports were Islamic by around the 15th or 16th centuries and some of the sultanates, such as Kutai and Banjarmasin, became major trading centres.

In the early 17th century, Kalimantan became a scene of conflict between the British and the Dutch. The British turned their attention to Banjarmasin, reputedly a great source of pepper. Trade flourished until the British stationed a guard ship at the mouth of the Barito River and recruited Bugis mercenaries to guard their warehouses. Banjarmasin rebelled in 1701, and the British were eventually evicted six years later.

British and Dutch interests in Borneo changed markedly in the 19th century. The British wanted to protect its sailing routes between China and India, while the Dutch wanted to consolidate control over the East Indies. Borneo was a hideout for 'pirates' and the Dutch had some interest in controlling the south and west coasts. By the late 1820s and 1830s the Dutch had concluded treaties with various small west-coast states. Parts of the Banjarmasi sultanate were signed over to the Dutch in the early 1800s but the Dutch didn't establish garrisons or administrative offices.

In 1839 the Dutch were jolted by the arrival of English adventurer, James Brooke, who established a private colony at Kuching, Sarawak. With Brooke's arrival, the spectre of intervention by other private colonists and European powers suddenly became a reality for the Dutch. In the 1840s and 1850s the Dutch put down several internal disputes and established new treaties with local rulers. From 1846 they opened new coal mines in South and East Kalimantan and gradually the island became more commercially important. War broke out between the Dutch and Banjarmasin in 1859. Within four years the Banjarmasis were defeated, but resistance continued until 1905.

The current division of Borneo between Indonesia and Malaysia originates from the British-Dutch rivalry. After WW II the Brooke family handed Sarawak over to the British government, putting Britain in the curious position of acquiring a new colony at the time it was shedding others. Sarawak remained under British control when Malaya (Peninsular Malaysia) gained independence in 1957.

Sabah was also once part of the Brunei sultanate. It came under the influence of the British North Borneo Company as Brunei declined. In 1888, North Borneo's coast became a British protectorate, although fighting did not end until the death of the Sabah rebel leader, Mat Salleh, in 1900. After WW II, the administration of Sabah was handed over to the British government. In 1963, Sarawak and Sabah joined with the Malay Peninsula – and, temporarily, Singapore – to form the nation of Malaysia.

Indonesia's President Soekarno, suspicious of Britain's continuing influence in Malaysia, challenged the newly independent state with military confrontations. Long after 'Konfrontasi' was abandoned, anti-Malaysian Chinese guerrillas of the Sarawak People's Guerrilla Troops, originally trained and armed by Indonesia, remained in Kalimantan. The so-called emergency also provided a convenient, officially sanctioned excuse for Dayak people to resume head-hunting.

Towards the end of the 19th century the outer islands, rather than Java, became the focus of Dutch commercial exploitation of the archipelago. Rubber and oil became increasingly important and pepper, copra, tin and coffee plantations were developed. By the end of the century, oil was being drilled in East Kalimantan. To finance the drilling, a British company was set up in London, the Shell Transport & Trading Company. In 1907 Shell merged with the Royal Dutch Company for the Exploitation of Petroleum Sources in the Netherlands Indies (the first company to start drilling in Sumatra) to form Royal Dutch Shell, giving the Dutch the greater share. Shell expanded rapidly and soon oil was produced everywhere from California to Russia. The Russian properties were confiscated in 1917 but by 1930 Shell was producing 85% of Indonesia's oil.

Economic value aside, East Kalimantan is one of Indonesia's prime transmigration

targets. The transmigrants tend to settle on marginal lands, replacing diverse tracts of jungle with extensive monocultures of rubber and pulp-wood trees. The newcomers also provide the mining and logging industries with a ready supply of willing young labourers. Transmigrants occasionally clash with Dayak groups, whose indigenous land-use regimes and land rights are rarely recognised.

Not everyone goes to Kalimantan on government-sponsored schemes. A major group in East Kalimantan are the Bugis of southern Sulawesi, continuing a transmigration tradition 400 years old. The Kahar-Muzakar rebellion in 1951 spurred Bugis movement from Sulawesi. After the rebellion was suppressed another wave of Bugis transmigrants joined their relatives in Kalimantan, tempted by the prospect of a better life.

FLORA & FAUNA
The strangest inhabitants of Kalimantan are the orang-utan, whose almost human appearance and disposition puzzled both Dayaks and early European visitors. The English Captain Daniel Beeckman visited Borneo early in the 18th century and wrote: 'The natives do really believe that these were

Borneo's Private Colonists
Kalimantan has had its share of opportunists including the Bugis pirate Arung Singkang, a descendant of the royal family of Wajo in South Sulawesi. In 1726 he conquered Pasir then Kutai, and in 1733 his forces made an unsuccessful attempt on Banjarmasin. Singkang returned to Sulawesi a couple of years later, taking the Wajo throne in 1737, and remaining a political force there until his death 1765.

Less successful was the Briton, Erskine Murray, who tried his luck at Tenggarong (the capital of Kutai) in the early 1800s. The incumbent sultan was less than enthused about Murray's plans to rule Kutai and a short battle on the Mahakam River ended in Murray's death and the demise of his private mission.

The waning influence of Banjarmasin, Kutai and Brunei enabled another Briton, Alexander Hare, to be posted as Resident to the Sultanate of Banjarmasin in 1812. Hare quickly set about creating his own private colony, importing Javanese coolies to work the coal mines and fostering trade in jungle produce. Post-Napoleonic treaties and the return of the Dutch forced Hare to abandon his colony in 1814.

The most famous of the 'white rajahs' was the English adventurer, James Brooke, who in 1839 intervened in a dispute at Kuching, then part of Brunei. His timely intervention won him the governorship of Sarawak. The new ruler put down the inland tribes, eliminated piracy and founded a personal dynasty. He and his successors forced further territorial concessions from Brunei, extending Sarawak to its present expanse. Their rule ended with the Japanese invasion of WW II. ■

formerly men, but metamorphosed into beasts for their blasphemy. They told me many strange stories of them...' Today, one of the last orang-utan refuges is the Tanjung Puting National Park in Central Kalimantan.

The deep waters of the Mahakam River in East Kalimantan are home to freshwater dolphins, and there are gibbons in the jungles, proboscis monkeys and crab-eating macaques in the mangrove swamps, plus crocodiles, clouded leopards, giant butterflies and hornbills, including the legendary black hornbill.

The Dayaks traditionally believe that the black hornbill carries the human soul, but because of its feathers and huge beak it was almost hunted into extinction. Beaks and bony humped skulls are still immersed in water overnight, to give whoever drinks the water special spiritual powers. Some Dayaks keep juvenile hornbills as pets, releasing them when they become old enough to mate.

PEOPLE & CULTURE

The three biggest ethnic groups in Kalimantan today are the recently arrived Malay-Indonesians who tend to follow Islam and live in settlements along the coasts and along the main rivers; the Chinese, who have controlled trade in Kalimantan for centuries; and the Dayaks, the collective name for the indigenous inhabitants of the island.

The Dayaks

The tribes do not use the term Dayak. It's a slightly pejorative term often used by Indonesians, or indigenous peoples converted to Islam (such as the Banjars and the Kutais) to differentiate non-Muslim from Muslim inhabitants. Enlightened Indonesians call them *orang pedalaman* ('inland people') or *orang gunung* ('mountain people'). The tribes prefer to use their separate tribal names, such as Kenyah, Kayan, Iban and Punan.

Most were probably coastal dwellers until the arrival of Malay settlers drove them inland to the highlands and river banks. Some also live in neighbouring Sabah and Sarawak. The Dayaks are generally light-skinned, somewhat Chinese in appearance and may be descendants of immigrants from southern China or South-East Asia. Tribal dialects show linguistic similarities.

Swidden or so-called 'slash and burn' agriculture is the mainstay of Borneo's agricultural economy. Dry fields are cleared then burnt to provide ash to enrich the poor soils, crops are grown for one or two seasons, then the blocks are left to fallow for a number of years. There are also reserves set aside for hunting, traditional medicines and extraction of jungle products such as honey and rattan. Many tribes maintain small reserves of untouched rainforest, to provide emergency food supplies during periods of extreme drought.

When population growth puts too much pressure on the land, whole villages can move to find new land. One such mass migration was the recent exodus of large groups of Kayan and Kenyah from the Apokayan, to valleys in the Mahakam basin or across the border to Sarawak. The Apokayan's population dropped from 30,000 in the 1950s, to about 5000 today. The introduction of government-subsidised transport and basic services has stabilised the situation, but arable land is still scarce and goods remain prohibitively expensive.

Another, as yet unexplained migration started in the mid-16th century when Iban groups began to abandon their agricultural settlements in the Kapuas basin in West Kalimantan and move north, most to the Batang Lupar region in Sarawak. The pattern changed again after James Brooke suppressed their 'piracy', and recruited Iban forces to pacify inland tribes elsewhere in his expanding colony. Violent Iban incursions drove other tribes, notably the Kenyah and Kayan, further upstream.

The most striking feature of many older Dayak women is their pierced ear lobes, stretched with the weight of heavy gold or brass rings. This custom is increasingly rare among the young. Older Dayaks, influenced by missionaries, often trim their ear lobes as a sign of conversion.

It was once the custom for all women to tattoo their forearms and calves with bird and spirit designs. Tattooing of young women has almost disappeared, except in tribes deep in the interior. It is still seen among men, although men in many Dayak cultures are expected to earn their tattoos by taking heads.

Dayak traditions are being modified by pressure from the Indonesian government and Protestant Christian missionaries. Neither the Muslims nor the Christians seem content to leave the indigenous belief systems, the backbone of these tribal cultures, alone. Plus there is the added pressure of new industries. A miner or sex worker (often mines refuse to employ Dayaks) can bring home much more money than their parents ever could, disrupting traditional roles.

Not all Dayaks live in villages. The Punan are nomadic hunter-gatherers who still move through the jungles, although some stay in longhouses at the height of the rainy season and many have settled in permanent riverside villages. To other Dayaks, the Punan are the ultimate jungle dwellers. As logging and ethno-religious evangelism push them deeper into the interior, they can be difficult to find.

BOOKS

Borneo, Change and Development (Oxford University Press, Singapore, 1992) by Mark Cleary and Peter Eaton is a rich compilation of contemporary research on Borneo and on humanity's accelerating impact on the island. It provides excellent historical and environmental data for researchers or eco-tourists.

A Field Guide to the Mammals of Borneo (the Sabah Society in association with WWF, 1985), Junaidi Payne et al, is another must for eco-tourists.

Stranger in the Forest (Houghton Mifflin Co, Boston; Century Hutchinson, London, 1988), is an inspiring account of Eric Hansen's six-month trek across Borneo in 1982.

Into the Heart of Borneo (Vintage Departures, New York, 1987) by Redmond O'Hanlon is an entertaining read, recounting the almost slapstick adventures of a natural-

ist and an English poet as they made their way to Gunung Batu in Kalimantan, via Sarawak. It gives a good account of interior travel.

GETTING THERE & AWAY

Visa-free entry is now possible for visitors entering Indonesia by road at Entikong or by air at Pontianak and Balikpapan. Tourists enter and leave from Balikpapan so rarely that you can expect delays as the officials ferret around the bottom drawer for that rarely-used stamp, but there are no real hassles. To enter or exit Indonesia by air, sea or land elsewhere in Kalimantan you'll need to get a visa in advance. Tarakan accepts new arrivals as long as they have advance visas.

To/From Singapore

Merpati has three flights a week between Singapore and Pontianak, and two flights linking Singapore with Balikpapan. The cheapest fare is the direct Singapore-Pontianak flight for about S$264 (237,000 rp). Sempati has daily flights (via Jakarta) linking Singapore to Banjarmasin and Balikpapan. There are also daily connections from Tarakan and Palangkaraya to Singapore.

To/From Malaysia

The border post at Entikong became an official international entry point in January 1994. This means the same rules now apply at Entikong as would apply at major airports and seaports. To get a 60-day tourist pass (see the earlier Facts for the Visitor section), it's advisable to have an onward ticket. Sarawak has scrapped its 14,000 rp visa fee, but Indonesians can still expect to pay a 50,000 rp *fiskal* to leave the country. Immigration rules can change and Entikong is a long way from anywhere, so double-check with Indonesian and Malaysian authorities before setting out from Kuching or Pontianak.

Sabah to East Kalimantan is a different story. There are flights and boats between Tawau and Tarakan, but you will not be allowed into Indonesia unless you obtain a one-month visa in advance. These can be obtained at Indonesian embassies in Sabah

KALIMANTAN

at Tawau or Kota Kinabalu. If you entered Indonesia on a 60-day tourist pass and want to leave this way, you *must* do your paperwork in Jakarta before immigration will let you through at Nunukan. A few travellers on the boat to Tawau get through but most get turned back.

Air MAS flies twice weekly between Pontianak and Kuching in Sarawak for 159,000 rp, and twice weekly between Tarakan and Tawau (and on to Kota Kinabalu) for $M175.

Bus Air-con buses from Pontianak to Kuching cost 30,000 rp. Book at SJS Travel in Pontianak.

Boat To leave Indonesia by sea via Nunukan in East Kalimantan (to Tawau, Sabah), you'll need an exit permit from the immigration office in Jakarta if you entered Indonesia at a visa-free port. The exit permit isn't necessary if you entered Indonesia on a one-month

advance (paid) visa. If your paperwork is not in order, you will be turned back. There are longboats from Tarakan to Nunukan (15,000 rp), and speedboats for 25,000 rp. From Nunukan to Tawau there are speedboats (26,000 rp). Buy tickets from CV Tam Bersaudara on Jalan Pasar Lingkas in Tarakan. The boats depart most days between 7 and 8 am, although they may not run on Sunday.

To/From the Philippines
Bouraq flies twice a week between Balikpapan and Davao, via Manado, for US$200.

To/From other parts of Indonesia
Travel across some parts of Kalimantan is only possible by air or foot. It is usually much easier to go from Kalimantan to Sulawesi or Java, than from one part of Kalimantan to another. For instance, Pelni boats from Tarakan to Balikpapan will take you via Toli-Toli and Palu.

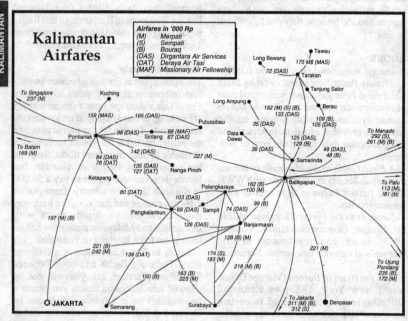

Kalimantan Airfares

Airfares in '000 Rp
(M)   Merpati
(S)   Sempati
(B)   Bouraq
(DAS) Dirgantara Air Services
(DAT) Deraya Air Taxi
(MAF) Missionary Air Fellowship

Air Merpati and Sempati have the best connections with the rest of Indonesia, while Dirgantara Air Services (DAS), Deraya Air Taxi and Mission Aviation Fellowship (MAF) are often your only options on many routes within Kalimantan. Banjarmasin and Balikpapan are the busiest and best-connected airports but, curiously, Bouraq is the only airline connecting the two. Bouraq is prone to cancellations, but it has useful flights between Kalimantan and Sulawesi, including a Banjarmasin-Balikpapan-Palu-Gorontalo-Manado hop.

Boat There are shipping connections with Java and Sulawesi, both with Pelni and other shipping companies. There are also regular passenger-carrying cargo ships between the ports on the east coast of Kalimantan to Pare Pare and Palu in Sulawesi. Apart from Pelni, Mahakam Shipping at Jalan Kali Besar Timur 111 in Jakarta may be worth trying for more information on other ships to Kalimantan.

GETTING AROUND

Kalimantan's dense jungle and flat, wet terrain make communications and travel difficult. Life in Kalimantan centres on the rivers, which are the most important transport routes on the island. All of the provinces have rivers deep into the interior, each served by an array of public transport. Where there are no navigable rivers, your only other options are usually air or foot.

The area around Pontianak has the best roads, stretching north along the coast, inland to Sintang, and across the border to Kuching. Apart from these, and the highway from Samarinda to Banjarmasin, there are few sealed roads.

There are plenty of flights to inland and coastal destinations and some shipping along the east coast. Going upriver into some of the Dayak regions is now relatively easy from Pontianak, Samarinda and Banjarmasin, but the further you go off the beaten canal the more time you'll need. For serious forays into the interior, even along the main rivers, you must allow at least two weeks per province.

Air

There are flights around the coastal cities and into the interior of Kalimantan with the regular airline companies. DAS now carries the bulk of the traffic, but Merpati, Sempati, Bouraq and Deraya Air Taxi also have useful routes. Other possibilities include planes run by the missionaries (MAF), which serve the most isolated communities.

DAS's small propeller aircraft fly to all sorts of places, with daily flights from Pontianak to inland West Kalimantan towns like Sintang or south-east to the coastal town of Ketapang. DAS also has flights between Palangkaraya and Banjarmasin. Deraya flies in and out of Pangkalanbun in Central Kalimantan to Pontianak, Palangkaraya and Banjarmasin. In East Kalimantan, DAS and MAF have the best interior routes.

DAS and Deraya have tiny planes and heavily booked services. If you are travelling solo, you might be able to buy a ticket for a fully booked service, front up to the airport, and score the spare seat next to the pilot. Be polite but firm and you can get away with it.

Boat

There are a number of variations on the river ferry theme. The *feri sungai* (river ferry/cargo boat, also known as a *kapal biasa*) carries both cargo and passengers; the *taxi sungai* (river taxi) carries cargo on the lower level and has rows of wooden bunks (sometimes with mattresses and pillows) on the upper level; and the *bis air* (water bus) has rows of seats.

Along Sungai Kapuas in Pontianak are the *bandung*, large cargo-cum-houseboats that take up to a month to move upriver to Putussibau. A bis air does the same distance in about four days. A *long bot*, as the name indicates, is a longboat – a narrow vessel with two large outboard motors at the rear and bench seats in a covered passenger cabin. Speedboats commonly ply the Barito, Kapuas, Kahayan and Kayan rivers and seem to be appearing elsewhere. Don't get too hung up on the terminology, as what may be called a bis air in one province may be a taxi sungai in another.

KALIMANTAN

Recent innovations are the coastal jet boat services which fling passengers from Pontianak to Ketapang, and from Banjarmasin to Sampit. These big, modern cruisers look more like water-bound planes than boats, and are a great way to get around.

West Kalimantan

West Kalimantan is dissected by Indonesia's longest waterway, the Sungai Kapuas (1143 km), which is the main transport artery for rafts of logs and other heavy cargo to and from the interior. Roads and buses are rapidly superseding the river as the main mode of moving people.

The province has about 3.5 million inhabitants, including the highest concentration of ethnic Chinese people in Indonesia. The proportion of Chinese residents in Pontianak is estimated at 35%, and 70% in Singkawang. Everything has a Chinese flavour, and even the major Muslim festivals are celebrated with Chinese firecrackers.

Beyond the activity on the coast and along the Kapuas, the province's interior is rela-

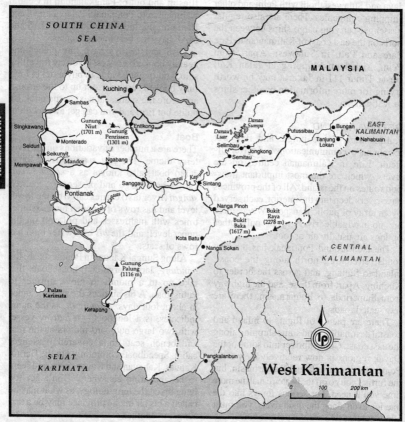

tively unexplored. There are many Iban settlements north of the Kapuas, and Punan and Kenyah-Kayan Dayak villages in the mountainous eastern part of the province. Contact with neighbouring Sarawak is increasing now that border restrictions have been relaxed.

PONTIANAK

Situated right on the equator, Pontianak lies astride the confluence of the Landak and Kapuas Kecil rivers. The city was founded in 1770 by Arab trader Abdul Rahman Al Gadri who used a barrage of cannon fire to frighten off the resident *pontianak* (spirits), clearing the way for human settlement. The discovery of sizeable gold deposits north of Pontianak a few decades later, gave the young settlement a great economic and demographic boost.

Pontianak is a sprawling city with a giant indoor sports stadium, a sizeable university and two big girder bridges upstream from the city centre. Like Banjarmasin it really needs to be seen from the canals and riverside boardwalks. Charter a sampan (rowboat) or walk over the Kapuas Bridge from Jalan Gajah Mada for a sweeping view of the river and brilliant orange sunsets.

From Pontianak you can drive north along the coast to Pasir Panjang, a lovely beach just back from the Pontianak-Singkawang road. (See the Pasir Panjang section later in this chapter.) The Mandor Nature Reserve is to the north-east. This is also the starting point for boat trips up the Kapuas, which terminate in Putussibau in the north-eastern corner of the province. From Putussibau, at the edge of Kalimantan's shrinking frontier country, you can walk to the headwaters of Sungai Mahakam in East Kalimantan.

Orientation & Information

The commercial hub is on the southern side of the junction of the Kapuas Kecil and Landak rivers. Here you'll find several markets, the main *bemo* station (Kapuas Indah), hotels, airline and Pelni offices, banks and markets.

Tourist Offices The Kalimantan Barat tourist office is way out at Jalan Ahmad Sood 25 (☎ 36172). It has fine intentions but lousy maps and little English. Staff at the big hotels and private travel agencies often offer better advice. (See Travel Agencies.)

The conservation office (Balai Konservasi Sumber Daya Alam) at Jalan Rahman Saleh 33 (☎ 34613) has Indonesian-language brochures on nature reserves, and information on getting to each, but their enthusiasm can be misleading. None of their parks cater for visitors.

Money US and Malaysian cash is easy to change, everything else is not. The banks around the Merpati office in Jalan Rahadi Usman handle foreign currency and travellers' cheques, and there are moneychangers along Jalan Tanjungpura (at Nos 12, 14 and 236B), at Pasar Nusa Indah I Blok AA 4, and in the Kapuas Indah building. As a last resort try the bigger hotels though their rates are lousy.

Post & Telephone You can collect poste-restante mail from the regional post office at Jalan Sultan Abdurrakhman 49. It's open Monday to Friday from 8 am to 7 pm (closed Friday 11 am to 2 pm), Saturday from 8 am to 1 pm and Sunday from 9 am to 2 pm. There's an older post office at Jalan Rahadi Usman near the Kartika Hotel, and an agency on Jalan Diponegoro.

There are private telephone agencies next to the Warung Somay Bandung in Jalan Sisingamangara and next to the Hotel Wijaya Kusuma, but to call collect (reverse-charges) you must go to the Telkom office on Jalan Teuku.

Foreign Embassies The Malaysian Consulate is at Jalan Jen Ahmad Yani 42, but neighbouring Sarawak no longer insists on a visa, nor do visa-free tourists need an exit permit from Indonesian immigration. (It seems improving relations between Malaysia and Indonesia are finally delivering dividends for tourists.) Consulate hours are from 7 am to 3 pm Monday to Saturday (closed Friday from 11 am to 1.30 pm).

Immigration The Pontianak immigration office (☎ 34516) at Jalan Sutoyo, near the national museum, is a bustling, friendly place. For visa extensions, it's easier to take a bus to Kuching and get a new two-month pass when you return via the border post at Entikong.

Travel Agencies PT Asia Jaya Nusantara (☎ 37432) at Jalan Tajungpura 236B, and Amir at PT Citra Tour & Travel (☎ 36436), Jalan Pak Kasih 6, can provide general information on touring and trekking. The DAS agent, PT Gajahmada Nusantara, at Jalan Gajah Mada 67 (☎ 34383) is good for airline schedules.

River Life
Pontianak's wealth stems from its river trade, and the best vantage point of the river activity is from the river itself. Hire a sampan for an hour or two from next to the ferry terminals or behind the Kapuas Indah building for 5000 rp or so. The price depends on your itinerary and your bargaining prowess, but the views are worth every last rupiah.

For an interesting experience of riverfront life, take a walk from the Mesjid Abdurrakhman along the wobbly wooden boardwalks past the stilt houses at washing time, either early or late in the day. You will find the people of the kampung extremely friendly and curious. Take your camera. There are plenty of willing models, especially the kids.

If there is the slightest breeze in the evening, young men crowd the boardwalks along the south bank to fly huge paper kites, many decorated with swastika. They seem much more interested in the swastika's pattern than its politics.

If you follow Jalan Sultan Muhammad south along the Kapuas Kecil you eventually come to the pisini (schooner) harbour, where you can see Bugis-style sailing schooners. Also docked in this area are the large houseboats, or bandung, peculiar to West

Kalimantan. Bandungs function as floating general stores that ply Sungai Kapuas, trading at villages along the way. Their family owners live on board and a typical run up the Kapuas might last as long as a month.

Mesjid Abdurrakhman
Also known as the Mesjid Jami, this was the royal mosque of Syarif Abdul Rahman (in Indonesian, Abdurrakhman), who reigned as Sultan of Pontianak from 1771 until his death in 1808. The Sumatran-style mosque has a square-tiered roof, and is made entirely of wood. Beautiful inside and out, it's worth the short canoe trip across the river from the pisini harbour. Charter a boat for 500 to 700 rp or wait for a shared canoe taxi for only 150 rp per person. The beautiful wooden **Mesjid Jihad** near the main post office is also a pleasant stop.

Istana Kadriyah
About 100 metres behind the sultan's mosque is his former palace, a double-storey ironwood building which is now an interesting museum. It displays the personal effects of the sultan's family. Eight sultans reigned after the death of the first in 1808. The last died in 1978. Visiting hours are from 8.30 am to 6 pm daily. There is no admission fee, but a donation is encouraged.

Museum Negeri Pontianak
Located near Tanjungpura University, south of the city centre on Jalan Ahmad Yani, this recently built national museum has a collection of *tempayan*, South-East Asian ceramics (mostly water jugs) from Thailand, China and Borneo. The jugs displayed vary in size from tiny to tank-like and date from the 16th century.

Tribal exhibits include dioramic displays of the clothing, musical instruments, tools and crafts of the Dayak cultures of West Kalimantan. All the labels are in Indonesian. The museum is open Tuesday to Sunday from 9 am until 1 pm. Around the corner in Jalan Sutoyo is a replica of a Dayak longhouse.

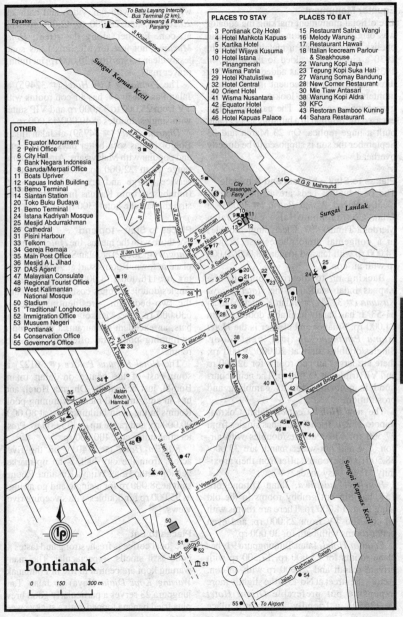

PLACES TO STAY

3 Pontianak City Hotel
4 Hotel Mahkota Kapuas
5 Kartika Hotel
9 Hotel Wijaya Kusuma
10 Hotel Istana Pinangmerah
19 Wisma Patria
29 Hotel Khatulistiwa
32 Hotel Central
40 Orient Hotel
41 Wisma Nusantara
42 Equator Hotel
45 Dharma Hotel
46 Hotel Kapuas Palace

PLACES TO EAT

15 Restaurant Satria Wangi
16 Melody Warung
17 Restaurant Hawaii
18 Italian Icecream Parlour & Steakhouse
22 Warung Kopi Jaya
23 Tepung Kopi Suka Hati
27 Warung Somay Bandung
28 New Corner Restaurant
30 Mie Tiaw Antasari
38 Warung Kopi Aldra
39 KFC
43 Restoran Bamboo Kuning
44 Sahara Restaurant

OTHER

1 Equator Monument
2 Pelni Office
6 City Hall
7 Bank Negara Indonesia
8 Garuda/Merpati Office
11 Boats Upriver
12 Kapuas Indah Building
13 Bemo Terminal
14 Siantan Station
20 Toko Buku Budaya
21 Bemo Terminal
24 Istana Kadriyah Mosque
25 Mesjid Abdurrakhman
26 Cathedral
33 Pisini Harbour
33 Telkom
34 Gereja Remaja
35 Main Post Office
36 Mesjid A L Jihad
37 DAS Agent
47 Malaysian Consulate
48 Regional Tourist Office
49 West Kalimantan National Mosque
50 Stadium
51 'Traditional' Longhouse
52 Immigration Office
53 Musuem Negeri Pontianak
54 Conservation Office
55 Governor's Office

Pontianak

0   150   300 m

KALIMANTAN

Equator Monument

The official monument marking the equator was originally erected in 1928 as a simple obelisk mounted with a metallic arrow. In 1930 a circle was welded to the arrow, in 1938 another circle was added in the other direction and its subsequent incarnation is unintentionally funny, looking like a giant gyroscope on a pillar. The caretakers then encased the original in a building in 1991 and built a huge replica. On 23 March and 23 September the sun is supposed to be directly overhead.

Places to Stay – bottom end & middle

The best budget beds are at the inconveniently placed *Wisma Patria* (☎ 36063) at Jalan Cokroaminoto (also called Jalan Merdeka Timur) 497. Clean single/doubles in a congenial atmosphere cost 12,000/14,000 rp with fan and mandi, 18,000/20,000 rp with air-con.

Backing on to the river opposite the Kapuas Indah station is the *Hotel Wijaya Kusuma* (☎ 32547) at Jalan Kapten Marsan 51-53. It has barely habitable doubles from 14,000 rp. Smaller and cleaner is the *Hotel Istana Pinangmerah* just next door. Singles/doubles start at 20,000/29,000 rp; there are larger air-con rooms for 32,500 rp and VIP triples at 35,000 rp. The neighbourhood is notorious for its gambling and prostitution.

The new *Hotel Central*, Jalan Cokroaminoto 232, is friendly and has singles from 27,500 rp. Clean singles/doubles with air-con, TV and hot-water mandi are 33,000/38,500 rp. The rooms suffer from their proximity to two busy roads.

Hotel Khatulistiwa, Jalan Diponegoro 151, has big but grubby rooms in the old wing from 14,000 rp. There are rooms with air-con and TV from 25,000 rp, and even better rooms with bath for 30,000 rp.

Equator Hotel, Jalan Tanjungpura 91, has clean rooms for 15,000 rp, 17,500 rp with private mandi and 25,000 rp with air-con. Across the street at No 45 is the slightly more expensive but preferable *Orient Hotel* (☎ 32650), a friendly, family-run place

where rooms with fan, video and bath are 25,200 rp, and 28,000 to 42,000 rp with air-con. Further along the street, *Hotel Muslim* ('not just for Muslims') has spotlessly clean rooms from 20,000 rp, including prayer mats.

The *Pontianak City Hotel* (☎ 32495) at Jalan Pak Kasih 44, has air-con rooms with TV from 25,000 to 35,000 rp and VIP suites with singles/doubles at 40,000/45,000 rp.

Dharma Hotel (☎ 34759) at Jalan Imam Bonjol 10 has seen better days but is clean and popular with Malaysians. Air-con rooms range from 22,000 to 40,000 rp, plus a service charge and tax. Yellow *mikrolets* (minibuses) from Kapuas Indah station run straight past the hotel (300 rp).

Places to Stay – top end

For those with the means, the *Hotel Mahkota Kapuas* (☎ 36022) at Jalan Sidas 8 is the best place in town. Rooms start at 94,000 rp plus tax or 116,000/138,000 rp for standard singles/doubles. Suites cost 266,000 rp and the two-bedroom 'presidential suite' is 630,000 rp. The Mahkota has a couple of bars, an excellent restaurant, a disco and a swimming pool, and often discounts its rooms.

The *Hotel Kapuas Palace* (☎ 36122) is south-east of the centre on Jalan Imam Bonjol, just behind the Dharma Hotel, and has an amazing 100-metre swimming pool. Rooms in the main building start at 80,000/90,000 rp, and range up to 175,000 rp. Presidential suites cost 400,000 rp.

Kartika Hotel (☎ 34401), on the river across from the city hall, is an up-market version of the Hotel Wijaya Kusuma. Rooms start at 58,000 rp for a single and go as high as 95,000 rp for doubles with sweeping river views.

Places to Eat

The local coffee is fresh, strong and tastes as good as it smells – spectacular. The many warung kopi are central to life in Pontianak. *Warung Kopi Djaja* (Jaya) at Jalan Tanjungpura 23 serves a particularly good brew plus fried banana topped with a sticky sweet spread. Also popular is *Tepung Kopi Suka Hati* three doors down, which serves its coffee with bread buns and a sweet jam, and has a fridge stocked with cold drinks. Both sell bags of freshly ground coffee.

The clean little *Somay Bandung*, in the theatre complex on Jalan Sisingamangaraja near Jalan Pattimura, serves delicious Chinese-style bubur ayam (sweet rice porridge with chicken) and the house speciality, *somay*, a tasty concoction of potatoes, tofu, hard-boiled egg and peanut sauce for 1100 rp. It also serves good ice drinks. Around the corner in Jalan Pattimura, the *New Corner Restaurant* serves padang-style food.

The best fare (and good coffee) is at the countless warungs. Those in the Kapuas Indah station offer a great choice but this neighbourhood gets pretty smelly when it rains. Try the night warung on Jalan Sudirman and Jalan Diponegoro for goat sate and steaming plates of rice noodles, crab, prawns, fish, vegetables – all fried up in a wok for 2000 rp.

Pontianak has a big Chinese population and excellent Chinese food. The speciality of *Mie Tiaw Antasari* on Jalan Antasari 72 is its fabulous beef *mie tiaw* (fried or rapid boiled noodles). It also offers tasty *bihun* (beef noodle dish, fried or boiled), bakso (meatball soup) and yellow noodles. There are several similar-style restaurants in nearby Jalan Diponegoro, including the *Mie Tiau Sam* at No 63 with its popular bakso, beef and bean noodle soup.

The *Restoran Hawaii* on Jalan Pasar Nusa Indah is a good choice for Chinese, as is *Restaurant Satria Wangi* on Jalan Nusa Indah II. There's a Chinese flavour to everything – even the gado-gado is served on noodles rather than rice.

For a Western food fix, there's a *KFC* on Jalan Gajah Mada, the *Italian IceCream Parlour & Steakhouse* on Jalan Nusa Indah, and good but expensive Western fare at the Mahkota Hotel.

Things to Buy

Pontianak has numerous gold shops. Prices are good, but quality is variable. A better buy

would be the *kain songket* – a material from Sambas with silver or gold thread woven into it. It is available from souvenir and material shops around the old market area, often at prices better than those at Sambas. There is a selection of old (and reproduction) trading beads, cheap bags of rough-cut gems, and beautiful old Chinese and Dutch china and glassware.

Getting There & Away

Air Garuda/Merpati (☎ 34142), Jalan Rahadi Usman 8A, is open Monday to Friday from 8 am to 4 pm, Saturday from 8 am to 1 pm, Sunday and holidays from 9 am to noon. DAS (☎ 34383), Jalan Gajah Mada 67; Bouraq (☎ 32371) Jalan Tanjungpura 253, and Deraya (office at airport) also service Pontianak.

Flights between Pontianak and Jakarta cost 197,000 rp on Merpati, and 197,500 rp on Bouraq. Merpati has five flights per day and same-day connections via Jakarta with Bandarlampung, Bengkulu, Jambi, Padang, Palembang, Pekanbaru, Semarang and Tanjungpandan.

Merpati flies to Medan (362,400 rp) and Batam (168,800 rp) on Thursday, and to Singapore three days a week for 237,160 rp (or S$264 from Singapore). There are also direct Merpati flights to and from Balikpapan twice a week.

MAS flies to/from Kuching on Monday and Thursday for US$74 (179,000 rp), and has connections to Kuala Lumpur (US$185) and Singapore (US$154).

DAS has three flights a day to Ketapang (84,000 rp), and daily services between Pontianak and Sintang (98,300 rp), Putussibau (165,400 rp), Pangkalanbun (134,600 rp) and on to Sampit (67,500). DAS flies from Nanga Pinoh to Pontianak every day (142,300 rp), but only three days a week in the other direction. Deraya has a similar schedule and prices to DAS, and better planes.

MAF (☎ 30271; fax 32757), Jalan Veteran 9, goes to big centres which don't have commercial services. If you are planning on trekking, it is worth flying in to the jungle with MAF and coming out by foot or boat.

KALIMANTAN

If you are hiking to east Kalimantan, MAF has monthly flights as far as Tanjung Lokan. It regularly flies to Kelansan, Serawai, Sungai Ayak and Sandai in the south, and is considering adding villages at the northern hills of Central Kalimantan to its network.

Bus Pontianak's intercity bus terminal is now Batu Layang, north-west of town. Take a ferry to Siantan (150 rp) and a white bemo to Batu Layang (300 rp). From there you can catch buses north along the coast to Singkawang (4000 rp; 3½ hours) and Sambas (6000 rp), inland to Sanggau (7000 rp) or Sintang (10,000 to 13,000 rp), or over to Pemangkat (7000 rp), Tebas (5200 rp) or Kartiasa (6200 rp). Singkawang buses leave throughout the day. Others are less frequent, but the mornings are busiest.

For the longer hauls to Kuching (30,000 rp; six hours), Sintang and soon to Putussibau, book early at bus offices such as SJS at Jalan Sisingamangaraja or Sinar Indah at Jalan Machmut 168 (Siantan) for the best seats. Luggage is loaded at these offices, but you must be ferried by bemo to Batu Layang to actually board the bus. Buses arriving at Pontianak in the wee hours will cut laps of the city until every last passenger is delivered to their doorstep.

Other Renting a car in Pontianak is a way to see coastal West Kalimantan at your own pace. Road conditions are good and traffic is relatively light. At Citra Tour & Travel (☎ 36436), Jalan Pak Kasih 6, you can rent a minibus or jeep for 120,000 rp per day with a driver. There is also a set schedule of taxi fares to destinations such as Singkawang 85,000 rp, Sambas 150,000 rp, Entikong 200,000 rp, and Sintang 250,000 rp. Ask at the taxi office in front of the Kartika Hotel. Motorbikes are an option for experienced riders only and cost from around 20,000 to 30,000 rp a day.

Boat There are now five Pelni ships calling regularly at Pontianak: the fortnightly *Lawit, Sirimau, Binaiya* and *Bukitraya*, and the monthly *Tatamailau*. The Pelni office is on Jalan Pak Kasih on the southern bank of the river at the Pelabuhan Laut Dwikora, and ticket sales are only in the mornings.

For other ships ask at the entrance to the port adjacent to the Pelni office. At least two non-Pelni cargo ships also take passengers on the Pontianak-Jakarta run daily for around 30,000 rp but you might have to sleep on deck. Travellers have reported miserable conditions and long delays on some of these ships.

Melyani has daily jet boats to Ketapang (55,000 rp; seven hours). This is more like a plane trip than a boat. The coastal boat leaves from just downstream of the Siantan car ferry.

Riverboats up Sungai Kapuas leave from behind the Kapuas Indah station near the Hotel Wijaya Kusuma. Some, like the houseboat bandungs, leave from the pisini harbour near the end of Jalan Sultan Muhammed. Bandungs don't usually take passengers, but they may make exceptions for curious foreigners. There are a few deluxe bandungs available for rent by up-market tourists.

Getting Around
To/From the Airport A counter at the airport sells tickets for taxis into town (15,000 rp). Alternatively, walk down the road in front of the station building to the main road in Pontianak and from there you should be able to get a bemo for 500 rp. It is a half-hour drive from the airport to the Kapuas Indah station. Ticketing agencies in Pontianak can organise lifts to the airport for 5000 rp.

Local Transport The two main bemo stations are in the middle of the city, the Kapuas Indah station near the waterfront, and the other on Jalan Sisingamangaraja. There are taxis for hire next to the Merpati office and *becaks* (bicycle-rickshaws) aplenty – the drivers overcharge but they're not too difficult to bargain with. Should you wish to tour the city and environs with a taxi, the set tariff is 10,000 rp per hour with a two-hour minimum.

Outboard motorboats depart from piers next to the Kapuas Indah building on the river. They cross the river to the Pasar Lintang and Siantan ferry terminal for 300 rp per person. A car and passenger ferry 100 metres downstream will take you to the other side for 150 rp.

KAPUAS RIVER
Pontianak is the launching point for riverboat services along Indonesia's longest river. The Kapuas basin is broad and flat, making it hard to pick where the river ends and the surrounding countryside begins. The primary attraction is the river itself, and the many vessels using it. As elsewhere in Kalimantan, take a slow boat to see and photograph the river activity

Boats of all shapes and sizes journey the Kapuas, but the standard is a double-deck bandung with beds on the upper deck which take passengers from Pontianak to Putussibau for 33,000 rp. Allow five days. A boat to Sintang (about 700 km by river from Pontianak) costs 15,000 rp per person and takes two days and one night. This includes basic meals but you're well advised to supplement the meagre fish and rice diet with food from Pontianak.

Cheap, fast and reliable buses from Pontianak to Sintang (11,000 rp; seven hours) are rapidly superseding the regular passenger services along the lower Kapuas. Boats remain the dominant mode of moving people beyond Sintang. Daily speedboats ferry passengers from Sintang to the larger centres of Putussibau (43,000 rp; eight hours) and Nanga Pinoh, as well as Semitau, Merakai, Separk and Mengkirai, or there are the irregular slow boats.

On your return to Sintang from upstream, there will be touts aplenty to meet the speedboats and shove Pontianak bus tickets into your hand. Prices and departure times vary widely, so go instead to the ticket sellers at the town bus station to hunt out the best deal.

Sintang
A wave of transmigration brought 15,000 new farming families to the Sintang area in the early 1980s, but most migrants come to this area to service the boom in logging.

1 Sesean
2 Losmen Setia
3 Ranah Minang
4 Losmen Central
5 Warkop Valentine
6 Flamboyan
7 Bemo Terminal
8 Bakso 33
9 Market
10 Bus Terminal

Speedboats to Putussibau & Nanga Pinoh

Sungai Melawi

Jalan Katamso

Jalan Supratman

Jalan Sugiono

Sintang

0   50   100 m

To Intercity Bus Terminal (5 km)

Sintang, situated halfway up the Kapuas, has nicer accommodation than you might expect for such a small town.

The nearby **Gunung Kelam** monolith offers a challenging hike, jungle, a waterfall, butterflies and panoramic views of the surrounding countryside. Take a white bemo to Pasar Impres (400 rp), then a Kelam bemo to the base (2000 rp). A road circles the hill, and you can be dropped off at the gaudy park entrance. The stepped path to the top, including steel ladders over more difficult rock faces, is one of the best you will find anywhere, but it takes hours and the going is difficult.

Places to Stay
The *Sesean*, a friendly place on the waterfront, has tiny singles from 5000 rp, doubles for 7500 rp, and rooms with bath for 20,000 rp. The *Flamboyan* charges 7500 rp for a double, 10,000 rp for a double with fan, 25,000 rp with private bath, and 30,000 rp with bath and air-con. The *Losmen Setia* and *Losmen Central* are both a little cheaper.

Places to Eat
For strong coffee, reasonable food and a

KALIMANTAN

view of the riverside activity, join the rest of the gossips at *Warkop Valentine*. *Bakso 33* has conventional Indonesian fare, and *Ranah Minang* has passable padang food. Otherwise there are coffee and cake stalls around the market.

Putussibau

The Dutch were conspicuous by their absence from much of inland Kalimantan until the turn of the century. Even then, the colonial presence tended to be for security rather than economic reasons. The first district officer was stationed in Putussibau in 1895.

Today Putussibau is an important market town, pretty and quiet. A few km upstream there are more traditional attractions, the longhouse villages of **Melapi I** and **Sayut** on the Kapuas. Along the Mendalam River there is a new longhouse at **Semangkok I** and a much older one just upstream at **Semangkok II**. Get there by speedboat for 15,000 to 30,000 rp.

Places to Stay

The *MESS Pemdaer* government lodge on Jalan Merdeka is frequented by road contractors. Apart from a noisy TV lounge at the front, it is good value with clean rooms with private mandi for 10,000 or 12,000 rp.

The *Marisa Hotel*, Jalan Melati, has a sad-looking bar downstairs, and rooms upstairs for 10,000 rp, 17,500 rp with mandi and 22,500 rp with air-con. The sleazy *Losmen Harapan Kita*, Jalan Pelita, faces the river and has small rooms from 7500 rp.

One option for solo women travellers is to put up at the Catholic mission school of the *zuster Belanda*. Offer to pay.

Places to Eat

The unnamed 'Muslim' eatery at Jalan Melati 5, next door to the Hotel Melati, has excellent sate, green vegetables, rice and mixed dishes; it's great value. There is OK bakso and coffee in the small Chinese warung on the boardwalk behind the DAS agent, and strong coffee and cake from the warung on the corner of Jalan Pelita and the boardwalk.

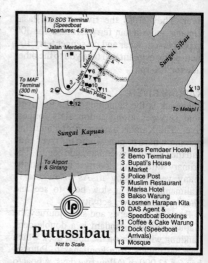

1 Mess Pemdaer Hostel
2 Bemo Terminal
3 Bupati's House
4 Market
5 Police Post
6 Muslim Restaurant
7 Marisa Hotel
8 Bakso Warung
9 Losmen Harapan Kita
10 DAS Agent & Speedboat Bookings
11 Coffee & Cake Warung
12 Dock (Speedboat Arrivals)
13 Mosque

Putussibau

Not to Scale

Getting There & Away

Air MAF, better known locally as 'air missi', flies between Putussibau and Sintang (68,000 rp), and DAS flies direct to Pontianak (168,000 rp). Occasionally MAF flies beyond Putussibau to Tanjung Lokan.

Bus Pioneering souls might like to try the buses between Sintang and Putussibau, or hitch a ride with the road contractors. Good luck. Let us know if the 'road' improves.

Boat Arriving speedboats will land you at the dock in front of the house of the *bupati* (district head), however boats heading downstream depart from Terminal SDS, 4½ km from town. Bemos to the terminal usually cost 300 rp, but if you are rushing to catch that 6 am boat, haggle for a 2000 rp charter. It is possible to connect with a bus from Sintang, and be in Pontianak, Entikong, or Singkawang that night.

Putussibau to Long Apari

The hardy, intrepid and wealthy can begin a river and jungle trek eastwards from Putussibau, across the West-East Kali-

mantan border through the Muller Range to
Long Apari at the headwaters of the Mahakam.
The going is arduous and expenses can be
considerable.

The first step is to arrange a knowledgeable guide in Putussibau – the bupati can
assist. There will be plenty of guides willing
to take your cash, but few with detailed
knowledge of the track and local languages.
If guides cannot be found in Putussibau, you
can postpone this until you reach the village
of Tanjung Lokan. Do not attempt the trip
beyond Tanjung Lokan alone, as the trails are
not well marked.

In Putussibau, stock up on provisions for
you and your guide(s) – allow about 100,000
rp for rice, sugar, coffee, eggs, canned fish
and tobacco. Then charter a motorised canoe
for 350,000 to 450,000 rp – bargain hard –
to make the one-day trip to Nangabungan.
From there you must charter a smaller canoe
for 75,000 rp for another day's travel to
Tanjung Lokan. Fuel is *very* expensive.

In Tanjung Lokan, find guides to lead you
through the jungle into East Kalimantan.
Some claim the walk takes two or three days,
but allow five or six. Guides will ask for
around 60,000 rp each, often more. Once you
reach the logging camp west of Long Apari,
the guides will turn around – you must offer
them a substantial amount of rice for their
return journey. From the logging camp it's a
four-hour walk plus a three-hour boat ride to
the village of Long Apari. You should be able
to charter a canoe for the trip for about
35,000 rp.

This is rough country so travel light. You
need food, a set of dry clothes to sleep in,
basic medicines, cooking equipment and a
sheet of strong waterproof material for
shelter. Allow plenty of time each day for
your guides to set up camp and hunt or fish
for extra protein. You will almost certainly
hanker for variation in your diet.

An added warning: many travellers report
thefts on this route. To avoid disappoint-
ments lock up anything of value, including
food, before handing your pack over to an
assistant. If you get 'ripped off', you might
just have to put it down to experience.

NANGA PINOH

An interesting side trip off Sungai Kapuas is
from Sintang along Sungai Melawai to
Nanga Pinoh. There are four losmen in
Nanga Pinoh with rooms for 5000 to 20,000
rp. From Nanga Pinoh catch boats further
south on the Sayan River to the villages of
Kota Bahru and **Nanga Sokan**. The journey
entails riding sections of thrilling rapids and
spending nights in Ngaju Dayak villages.
Boat fares from Nanga Pinoh to Nanga
Sokan should be about 12,000 rp. Allow a
week to do the trip from Sintang. You can fly
back to Pontianak from Nanga Pinoh (book
ahead), or hire guides for the difficult two or
three-day trek to Central Kalimantan. (See
the following section.)

Nanga Pinoh to Pangkalanbun

This route is an option for those travelling
light. Take a speedboat from Nanga Pinoh to
Nanga Sokan (25,000 rp; four hours), and
stay with the hospitable *camat* (subdistrict
head). (Just 2½ hours walk from Nanga
Sokan is a modern longhouse at Batu Beg-
ansar.) The walk from Nanga Sokan to
Central Kalimantan is a two-day adventure
across hills and rivers. Guides from Nanga
Pahan cost 40,000 rp for two.

A speedboat from Nanga Sokan to Nanga
Pahan is 50,000 rp. From Nanga Pahan walk
about four hours to Kediman and then
another five hours on to a logging base camp
of the Corindo group. If the guides tell you
after two hours of strenuous walking that
you've reached Kediman (two huts in the
forest), don't believe them. It will take at
least three hours. After Kediman, it takes
another two hours to reach the main logging
road, and another three to get to the base
camp. From the base camp, hitch a lift to
logging camps further south, then take a
15,000 rp taxi to Pangkalanbun. (See Pangkalanbun in the Central Kalimantan section
for more information.) The path between
Nanga Pahan and the logging road crosses
various rivers about 20 times. It is impossible
to find your way without a guide. Beware of
dehydration.

SINGKAWANG

This predominantly Hakka Chinese town boomed in the early 18th century when minefields from Sambas to Pontianak were realising about one-seventh of total world gold production. Powerful Chinese associations ran the show, especially on the rich Montrado fields, and an agricultural infrastructure soon sprang up to supply the miners. Hakka is still the lingua franca.

New, some say illegal, open-wash mining at Montrado is stimulating some activity, but otherwise Singkawang is pretty quiet. If you've travelled along the west coast of West Malaysia, the atmosphere and colonnaded shop architecture will seem familiar. If nothing else, it's probably the cleanest town in Indonesia. It's a day trip from Pontianak, and a good base for a day trip to Sambas.

Singkawang's main attraction is nearby Pasir Panjang beach, a three-km stretch of white sand and calm water with few people except on public holidays. Pasir Panjang is a

20-minute drive out of Singkawang just off the Singkawang-Pontianak road. (See the Pasir Panjang Beach section.)

On the road to Singkawang you could stop at **Pulau Kijing**, a seaside picnic spot just before the town of Sungaiduri, also called Seiduri for short. (Several towns along here shorten Sungai to Sei.)

Just 12 km east of Singkawang is **Gunung Poteng**, once a minor hill resort but its hotel is now closed. The largest flower in the world, the rafflesia, grows wild on these slopes. A *colt* (minibus) will get you to Poteng and the hike to the top takes about two hours.

In the hills east of Singkawang, at Samatantan, there is a privately run **Christian hospital**, reputedly the best in the province. MAF in Pontianak flies lots of folks there, and can direct you there.

Places to Stay

The cheaper (by no means cheap) hotel pre-

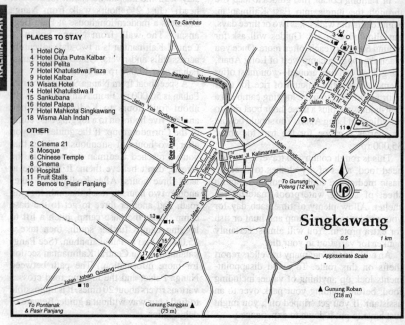

PLACES TO STAY
1 Hotel City
4 Hotel Duta Putra Kalbar
5 Hotel Pelita
7 Hotel Khatulistiwa Plaza
9 Hotel Kalbar
13 Wisata Hotel
14 Hotel Khatulistiwa II
15 Sankubana
16 Hotel Palapa
17 Hotel Mahkota Singkawang
18 Wisma Alah Indah

OTHER
2 Cinema 21
3 Mosque
6 Chinese Temple
8 Cinema
10 Hospital
11 Fruit Stalls
12 Bemos to Pasir Panjang

To Sambas

Sungai Singkawang

Jalan Yos Sudarso

See Inset

Pasar Jl Kalimantan

Jalan Sudirman

To Gunung Poteng (12 km)

Jalan Diponegoro

Jalan Stasiun

Jl Selamira

Jl Stasiun

Jl Setapuk Bulang

Jl Sejahtera

Jl Niaga

Jl Setia I

Singkawang

0   0.5   1 km

Approximate Scale

Jalan Johan Godang

To Pontianak & Pasir Panjang

Gunung Sanggau ▲ (75 m)

▲ Gunung Roban (218 m)

cinct is in the noisy commercial hub, at the northern end of Jalan Diponegoro near the main mosque and Chinese temple. The *Hotel Khatulistiwa Plaza* (☎ 31697) at Jalan Selamat Karman 17 has fairly nice rooms from 8000 rp with private mandi. Across the road, the *Hotel Pelita* has surly staff and rundown rooms for 10,000 rp.

The best hotel in this price range is the *Hotel Duta Putra Kalbar* (☎ 31430) at Jalan Diponegoro 32, diagonally opposite the Khatulistiwa Plaza. The 8000 rp rooms are small but all have fans and clean mandi. Larger rooms are 10,000 rp and for an extra 21,500 rp you get air-con.

In the Kal-Bar Theatre complex in nearby Jalan Kepol Machmud, the *Hotel Kalbar*, has reasonable rooms for 12,500 rp. There's a fridge in the lounge area stocked with cold beer – a rarity in Singkawang. Air-con rooms cost 22,000 rp.

Hotel City at Jalan Yos Sudarso 27 has quiet, air-con rooms from 20,000 rp, or 30,000 rp if you want a TV.

About one km south of town is Singkawang's best mid-range accommodation, the *Hotel Palapa* (☎ 31449) on Jalan Ismail Tahir. It's a pleasant, clean place, if a little isolated, with economy rooms with air-con and TV from 26,000 rp, ranging up to VIP rooms for 52,000 rp. Just opposite is the depressingly quiet *Sankubana*, with rooms from 15,500 rp (25,500 rp with air-con).

The 10,000 rp rooms in the *Wisata Hotel* at Jalan Diponegoro 59 are dingy and airless. Better value are the rooms around the rear garden of the *Hotel Khatulistiwa II* (☎ 31082), just opposite, for 11,000 rp or 22,000 rp with air-con and mandi.

The top accommodation in town is the *Hotel Mahkota* (☎ 31244) on Jalan Diponegoro 1. It has a swimming pool, disco and air-con rooms ranging from 70,000 to 175,000 rp.

Places to Eat

Chinese food is your best bet. The *Rumah Makan Tio Ciu Akho*, at Jalan Diponegoro 106, serves fabulous *kue tiaw goreng* (fried rice noodles), loaded with shrimp, squid, wheat gluten and freshly made fishballs.

Most of their dishes are prepared in the savoury Chiu Chao (Chao Zhou, Tae Jiu) style and the beer is ice-cold (3000 rp). Look for the giant wood stove in front.

Also on Jalan Diponegoro are the *Bakso 68* and *Bakso 40* noodle shops, serving variations on bakso (Chinese meatballs) with mie (wheat noodles), bakmi (egg noodles) and kue tiaw (rice noodles). The *Rumah Makan Indonesia* on the same street serves mostly Javanese food, a rarity in this town.

Toko Kopi Nikmat on Jalan Sejahtera is one of many coffee shops in this part of town serving excellent brews, but little else. Along Jalan Johan Godang at the Jalan Diponegoro intersection is a string of good Chinese coffee shops, all with Bentoel International signboards – the *Mexico, Malang, Asoka* and *Tahiti*. The Mexico has the best selection of pastries.

Along Jalan Niaga (Pasar Lama) you'll find three or four decent padang-style places serving Banjar and Sumatran food. In front of the cinema, on Jalan Pasar Hilir (Budi Utomo), is a Chinese night market.

Getting There & Around

Catch a ferry (150 rp) to Pontianak's Siantan terminal and take a white colt (300 rp) from there to the Batu Layang terminal a few km past the equator monument. Opelets to Singkawang (4000 rp; 3½ hours) leave throughout the day. There is no longer a main depot in Singkawang, so let your driver know where you want to get off. When leaving town, you will find buses outside Rumah Makan Asun, Rumah Makan Aheng or along Jalan Niaga.

From Singkawang to Gunung Poteng, catch a Bengkayang bus east for the 12-km trip (700 rp). Let the driver know where you're going and he'll let you off at the foot of the hill. Or offer him a little extra to take you up the hill to Wisma Gunung Poteng, the closed hotel.

Beyond Singkawang there are opelets as far as Sintang, a nine-hour ordeal for a mere 12,500 rp. You can also get colts north-east to Sanggau (5200 rp), north to Pemangkat

(700 rp) and Sambas (see later in this section) or east to Mandor (2200 rp).

CERAMIC FACTORIES

En route to Pasir Panjang there are a series of ceramic factories which make huge Chinese jars with colourful motifs. The Semanggat Baru, about 100 metres off the main road, five km from Singkawang, has a long, ancient kiln and ceramics at various stages of manufacture. If you like what you see, the factory can ship your purchase to Jakarta. Another kiln, the Sinar Terang, is just 400 metres down the road. See the following Pasir Panjang section for transport information.

PASIR PANJANG BEACH

Just 12 km south of Singkawang, this marvellous stretch of sand and flat grassy picnic areas is deserted on weekdays and in the mornings. However the locals dress up and descend en masse on weekends and public holidays. At the northern end of the beach is a recreational park, the Taman Pasir Panjang Indah, with a swimming pool, disco and warung area.

Beyond Pasir Panjang, *Hotel Palapa* runs overnight snorkelling tours to a tiny, deserted island beyond Pulau Lemukutan. Facilities are basic, so bring your own food. It is a great escape.

Places to Stay

The *Hotel Palapa* has taken over a shabby hotel with rooms/cottages for an outrageous 25,000/30,000 rp. Much better are its cottages set back from the beach in its 'motel' section for 40,000 rp, or 50,000 rp on weekends and public holidays. Camping is an attractive option, particularly among the casuarina trees that line the beach at the quieter southern end.

Getting There & Away

To get there from Singkawang take a bemo from Toko Olimpik on the corner of Jalan Suman Bajang and Jalan Sintut (700 rp; 15 to 20 minutes) and get out at the Taman Pasir Panjang gate, or at the warung 200 metres

further on. From there, you'll have a 500-metre walk to the beach.

SAMBAS

Archaeological finds of Indian materials indicate Sambas had connections with the Sriwijaya kingdom and perhaps India in the 6th century, and became an important port city in its own right from the late 13th century. The Dutch established a factory in Sambas from 1608-10, but showed little interest in colonising the area.

Palace ruins show a hint of the city's former prosperity, but Sambas is now better known for its cloth – kain songket – a material with silver or gold thread woven into it. Check the prices in Pontianak before taking on the weavers or vendors at Sambas market. It might still be cheaper down south.

Colts from Singkawang to Sambas cost 2200 rp.

Central Kalimantan

Central Kalimantan was formed in 1957, after a Dayak revolt calling for greater autonomy from centuries of domination by Banjarmasin. It remains the only province with a predominantly Dayak population, mostly Ngaju, Ot Danum and Ma'anyan peoples. It is also the least populated, with just 1.4 million people.

Bahasa Ngaju is the most widely spoken dialect, and is the lingua franca of the Kapuas, Palangkaraya and southern Barito regencies.

The main faith is nominally Islam, but *kaharingan* is still widely observed. Kaharingan, which means 'life', is an indigenous tradition passed from generation to generation through story-telling, rituals and festivals. Jakarta recognises the creed as a kind of 'Hinduism', the name used for any religion that won't fit neatly into an officially-recognised category. Every few years a major inter-tribal religious festival called a *tiwah* takes place in Central Kalimantan (see

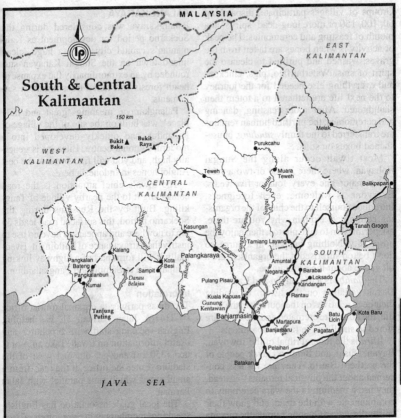

MALAYSIA

EAST
KALIMANTAN

**South & Central
Kalimantan**

0   75   150 km

WEST
KALIMANTAN

Bukit
Baka
Bukit
Raya

Purukcahu

Teweh

Muara
Teweh

Balikpapan

CENTRAL
KALIMANTAN

Sungai Lamandau

Sungai Seruyan

Sungai Sampit

Sungai Katingan

Kasungan

Sungai Kahayan

Sungai Kapuas

Sungai Barito

Tanah Grogot

Kalang

Kota
Besi

Palangkaraya

Tamiang Layang

SOUTH
KALIMANTAN

Pangkalan
Bateng

Sampit

Danau
Belaiau

Sungai Mendawai

Pulang Pisau

Amuntai

Negara

Sungai Negara

Barabai

Loksado

Pangkalanbun

Kumai

Kuala Kapuas
Gunung
Kentawan

Kandangan

Rantau

Muratus Mountains

Tanjung
Puting

Banjarmasin

Sungai Barito

Batu
Licin

Kota Baru

Martapura

Banjarbaru

Pagatan

Pelaihari

Batakan

JAVA   SEA

KALIMANTAN

next section) and features a month of feasting, drinking and ritual dancing.

The northern reaches of Central Kalimantan are mountainous, while most of the province is low, flat and poorly drained. Timber extraction has stripped most of the province. Natural attractions include the mountains north of Muara Teweh and Tanjung Puting National Park near Pangkalanbun in the south.

The major river thoroughfares run roughly parallel from the northern hills to the coast. Five canals built in the Dutch era join the Kahayan with the Kapuas and two lower

branches of the Barito, cutting miles off the route from Banjarmasin to Palangkaraya. The bigger rivers also carry phenomenally long rafts of logs, some stretching almost a km and requiring three tugs to keep them in line.

Tiwah, Ijambe & Wara
The region is famous for its tiwah, colourful interment ceremonies in which dozens of Ngaju Dayak families retrieve the remains of their dead from temporary graves and send them on their way to the next life according to the traditions of the kaharingan faith.

Groups of villages participate, dispatching 60, 100, 150 or more long-dead 'spirits' in a month of feasting and ceremonies. The peak of activity is when bones are taken from the graves, washed and purified to cleanse the spirit of sins. Waterbuffalo, pigs, chickens and everything else needed for the journey to the next life are tethered to a totem then slaughtered. After more feasting, dancing and ceremonies, the purified human remains are transferred to the family *sandung,* house-shaped boxes on stilts.

Most tiwah occur along the Sungai Kahayan, where there is one or two a year, and a major one every four or five years. Everyone is welcome, even foreigners. Introduce yourself to the chief of the organising committee, explain why you are there, ask permission to take photos, then enjoy the hospitality. Nothing happens in a hurry, so don't be too surprised if the organisers are a bit vague about the programme.

The *ijambe* is a Ma'anyan and Lawangan Dayak variation on the tiwah. In sending their dead relatives on the journey to the next life, the bones are cremated and the ashes are stored in small jars in family apartments.

Wara is the funeral ritual of the Tewoyan, Bayan, Dusun and Bentian Dayak people of the northern Barito. They are far less concerned about the physical remains – instead, they use a medium in the wara ceremony to communicate with the dead, and show their spirits the way to Gunung Lumut, the nirvana of this branch of the kaharingan faith.

Potong Pantan

Another kaharingan tradition is the *potong pantan* welcoming ceremony in which important guests are met by the head of the village, offered a machete and invited to cut through *pantan,* lengths of wood blocking the entrance to the village. As they cut, guests introduce themselves and explain the purpose of their visit to purge themselves of bad spirits. *Tapung tawar* is an extension of the potong pantan, in which guests have their faces dusted with rice flour and their heads sprinkled with water to protect them from bad spirits and illness.

PALANGKARAYA

Palangkaraya was considered during the Soekarno period for development as Kalimantan's capital city. It is a large, clean inland town on the Sungai Kahayan surrounded by an extraordinarily flat expanse of heath forests and failed transmigration settlements.

Palangkaraya, meaning 'great and holy place', was built on the site of the village of Pahandut, and quickly developed into a modern, regional centre. Literacy is generally high, and you will find some of the best Anglophones in Indonesia here.

The town's chief attraction is the road connecting it to the nearby village of Tangkiling. Built by the Russians during the Soekarno period, this surfaced road leads 35 km to nowhere and appears to have no use to justify the extravagance of building it. Eventually it will form part of a highway linking Banjarmasin to Sampit and Pangkalanbun.

Information

The dinas pariwisata regional tourist office (☎ 21416), Jalan Parman 21, has helpful, English-speaking staff with brochures and useful information on tiwah. Take an A or C taxi (350 rp) and get out just west of the stadium. Enter the office at the rear, from a small street which runs parallel with Jalan Parman.

The local guide association has English-speaking members who are often a step ahead of the dinas pariwisata. Association secretary Yusuf Kawaru (☎ 23341; fax 21254) at the Dandang Tingang Hotel, can refer you to helpful guides such as Aprianus Dulimar. These people are young, educated and articulate, with an obvious affection for their province.

Things to See

There is a lively **market** south of Dermaga Flamboyan, a traditional house and art centre near the post office, the sort of monuments and public buildings that befit a well-planned regional capital, lots of river traffic to watch, and a string of souvenir shops between the Laris and Melati Halmahera

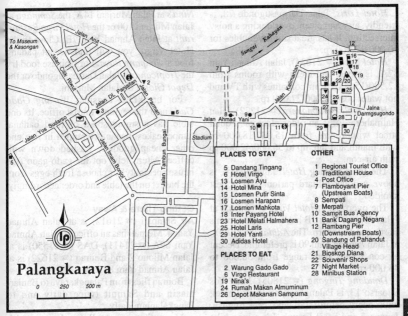

Palangkaraya

0   250   500 m

PLACES TO STAY

5 Dandang Tingang
6 Hotel Virgo
13 Losmen Ayu
14 Hotel Mina
15 Losmen Putir Sinta
16 Losmen Harapan
17 Losmen Mahkota
18 Inter Payang Hotel
23 Hotel Melati Halmahera
25 Hotel Laris
29 Hotel Yanti
30 Adidas Hotel

PLACES TO EAT

2 Warung Gado Gado
6 Virgo Restaurant
19 Nina's
24 Rumah Makan Almuminum
26 Depot Makanan Sampurna

OTHER

1 Regional Tourist Office
3 Traditional House
4 Post Office
7 Flamboyant Pier
   (Upstream Boats)
8 Sempati
9 Merpati
10 Sampit Bus Agency
11 Bank Dagang Negara
12 Rambang Pier
   (Downstream Boats)
20 Sandung of Pahandut
   Village Head
21 Bioskop Diana
22 Souvenir Shops
27 Night Market
28 Minibus Station

KALIMANTAN

hotels. Other than that, Palangkaraya is just a place to recharge your batteries before launching inland.

The **museum** on Jalan Cilik Riwut (Km 2½), is open from 8 am to noon and 4 to 6 pm (closed Monday); admission is free. Take an A taxi (350 rp) to Km 2½. Most wings were closed for renovation at the time of researching this edition, but the single working display was interesting.

Tangkiling National Park

A nature reserve 35 km north of Palangkaraya with sweeping views and a ship-shaped rock, the **Tangkuban Parahu** on the northern face of the hill. Near Tangkiling is **Danua Tahai**, a lake, recreation area and nature reserve.

Places to Stay

There's a cluster of cheap hotels by the Rambang pier where the longboats, river ferries and speedboats depart for Banjar-masin. Even the cheapest places provide 'breakfast', usually sweet tea and banana in sticky rice.

Hotel Mina (☎ 22182), Jalan Nias 17, is cool, clean and friendly. Singles/doubles with fan go for 10,000/15,000 rp, 20,000/27,000 rp with air-con; it's recommended.

Losmen Putir Sinta (☎ 21132), next door at Jalan Nias 15, is bright and busy with clean singles/doubles with fan and mandi for 7000/10,000 rp, and rooms with shared mandi for 5000/8000 rp.

Losmen Mahkota (☎ 21672) across the road at No 5 has old rooms from 5500/8800 rp with threadbare curtails and shared bath. New rooms out the back with mandi and car parking cost 24,700/35,200 rp.

Losmen Ayu at Jalan Kalimantan 147 near Rambang Pier, is small, grotty, but cheap. Singles start at 4400 rp, doubles from 6600 rp.

Losmen Harapan, Jalan Nias 18, is markedly nicer – a tiny, family place with clean rooms, fan, and shared mandi for 5000/8000 rp.

Hotel Laris, Jalan Darmasugondo 78, is friendly, airy and clean, overlooking a noisy intersection. It has great singles/doubles for 10,000/12,000 rp.

Hotel Yanti (☎ 21634), Jalan Ahmad Yani 82A, is smart and clean with rooms from 12,500/15,000 rp; air-con suites with TV and hot water cost 25,000/27,000 rp.

Hotel Melati Halmahera (☎ 21222), Jalan Halmahera 24, is an older place on a quiet street with rooms from 15,000/18,000 rp with mandi and fan, up to 36,000/42,000 rp with air-con.

The *Inter Payang Hotel*, Jalan Nias 6, is above a noisy billiard parlour and is best avoided.

The overpriced *Hotel Virgo* (☎ 21265) at Jalan Ahmad Yani 7B has fan-cooled rooms starting at 15,000 rp. The *Adidas* (☎ 21770), at Jalan Ahmad Yani 90 is preferable. Decent air-con rooms here range from 38,000 to 43,000 rp.

Dandang Tingang (☎ 21805), Jalan Yos Sudarso 13, is Palangkaraya's luxury hotel, with cheery, helpful staff who speak English, Japanese and basic French. It's a long hike from the centre but C taxi buses run straight past the front. The hotel has a restaurant, bar and disco. All air-con singles/doubles start at 35,000/55,000; it's highly recommended.

Places to Eat

Fish and freshwater cray hold pride of place in Banjarmasin cuisine. *Depot Makanan Sampurna*, Jalan Jawa 49, serves some of the best barbecued fare, including delicious river cray and patin fish. The patin is considered a delicacy upriver, selling at markets for up to 20,000 rp a kg. Nearby *Rumah Makan Almuminum* in Jalan Halmahera is reputedly the best fish place in town.

Both restaurants face stiff competition from a lively, colourful night market on Jalan Halmahera and Jalan Jawa where there are plenty of cheap noodle and rice dishes plus a colourful range of very cheap seasonal fruit. There are coffee warungs around the docks and a few stalls opposite Bioskop Diana.

For moderately priced Indonesian fare, try *Nina's* at Jalan Murjani 14A, the *Sampaga* at Jalan Murjani 100 or the *Hotel Virgo Restaurant* at Jalan Ahmad Yani 7B. Close to the Hotel Virgo, you will find decent padang food at *Simpang Raya*. For Chinese food try the *Tropicana* on Jalan Darmasugondo or the *Depot Gloria* on Jalan Murjani.

For breakfast, consider *Warung Gado Gado* near the regional tourist office. Its one table has a smorgasbord of fried banana, tempe, cakes, bananas wrapped in rice and other cheap goodies, washed down with coffee. Alternately, opt for gado-gado (the house speciality) or choose fresh eggs from the basket on the table and order accordingly.

Getting There & Away

Air Sempati (☎ 21612) is at Jalan Ahmad Yani 4. Merpati has an office at Jalan Ahmad Yani 69A (☎ 21411), DAS (☎ 21550) is at Jalan Milono 2 and Bouraq (☎ 21622) is at Jalan Ahmad Yani 84.

Bouraq flies from Palangkaraya to Banjarmasin and Sampit twice daily and to Pangkalanbun daily.

Merpati connects Palangkaraya with Balikpapan for 100,000 rp net, Banjarmasin 74,000 rp, Buntok 62,000 rp, Jakarta 232,000 rp, Sampit 62,000 rp, Muara Teweh 76,000 rp, Surabaya 183,000 rp and Tubangsamba 67,000 rp.

DAS flies daily to Pangkalanbun (103,000 rp) with connections to West Kalimantan, and to Kuala Kurun for 60,000 rp. Sempati has daily flights to Balikpapan and Surabaya, and connections onto various other destinations.

Bus & Jeep Patas Tours (☎ 23307), Jalan Yani 52, has jeeps leaving for Kuala Kapuas twice daily (four hours; 15,000 rp). Alternatively, take a regular minibus to Pulang Pisau (6000 rp), cross the river for 500 rp, then take another regular bus to Kuala Kapuas for 2750 rp. From there you can connect with regular buses to Banjarmasin (5100 rp).

Patas claims it can get you to Sampit in less than seven hours (15,000 rp), weather permitting.

Dimendra Perkasa Travel at Jalan Yani 30

charges 17,000 rp to Sampit, and 41,000 rp to Pangkalanbun. Wet-season trips require three vehicle changes and 20-plus hours. It is probably better to wait until roads are built.

Boat Boats downstream to Banjarmasin leave from the Dermaga Rambang (Rambang Pier) near the hotel cluster. Speedboats to Banjarmasin cost 20,100 rp and take about six hours, 17,100 rp to Kuala Kapuas and 14,100 rp to Pulang Pisau. Buy your ticket from the little office at the pier. The river ferries (bis air) take about 18 hours to Banjarmasin but they're much cheaper – 6500 rp. Buy your ticket from the larger office at the dock.

Boats heading upstream leave from Dermaga Flamboyan. Two daily speedboats terminate at Tewah, six hours (35,000 rp) upstream. The slow boats take two days and cost 25,000 rp.

To go beyond Tewah, you can charter a small boat. Tewah to Tubangkurik will cost about 50,000 rp, or up to 200,000 rp by *klotok* (motorised canoe). Your choices usually depend on the condition of the water: too high is dangerous, too low is too much like hard work.

Getting Around
To/From the Airport The airport is on the edge of town, but there are no direct roads. Taxis cost 7500 rp, but you can share with up to four others.

Local Transport Efficient taxi buses – marked A, B, C or D – cost just 350 rp. Choose your destination, then ask a local which taxi will get you there. You can charter a colt for 4000 rp an hour, or a motorbike for about half that. Hotels all advertise the recommended rates. Becak drivers congregate around the dock and along Jalan Halmahera at the night market.

The station for bemos to Tangkiling is way past the western boundary of Palangkaraya. It's a long way and it seems to take ages to catch a bemo. There are frequent bemos for the 25-minute trip from the station to Tangkiling.

AROUND PALANGKARAYA
The main challenge is to get beyond the logging areas, or find sections which have escaped the ravages of the chainsaw. Palangkaraya guide association members (see the earlier Palangkaraya Information section) can assist at a reasonable price, but travel to the interior is always an uncomfortable, expensive proposition.

One route is to take a speedboat from Palangkaraya to Tewah (35,000 rp, more in dry season), charter a klotok to Batu Suli Hill and on to the longhouse settlement of Tumbang Korik (200,000 rp), hike from there to Tubang Mahuroi spending a night in the jungle, then head back downstream to Tewah or on Kuala Kurun.

Another option involves motorbikes. Go from Tewah to Tubang Miri, by motorbike south to Tubang Rahuyan, by klotok to Tumbang Baringei, by motorbike to Tubang Malahoi (the site of a longhouse), then by klotok or speedboat south to Tangkiling.

Or take motorbikes from Kuala Kurun north to Seihanyu, a klotok up the upper reaches of the Kapuas to Seimandown and by river to Jakarta Masupa. Hike from there to Masupa Rai, a gold-rush field in a natural depression in the jungle, continue by motorbike to Tubang Masao then by klotok downstream. Alternately, take a boat from Tubang Masao to the Sungai Barito headwaters, past a series of rapids north of Tubang Tuan, and into territory the logging companies are yet to venture into. These last options are the most difficult and expensive, but well worth considering if you have the cash and the stamina.

MUARA TEWEH AREA
Muara Teweh is the last riverboat stop on Sungai Barito. Beyond Muara Teweh, travel is then by speedboat to **Puruk Cahu** in the foothills of the Muller Range. Hire Dayak guides for treks into the mountains in Puruk Cahu. Near Gunung Pancungapung, at the border of Central and East Kalimantan, a cement pillar marks the geographical centre of Borneo.

There is a bat cave, **Liang Pandan**, 10 km

from Muara Teweh, and the **Bukit Pararawan** forest reserve and lookout 40 km from town. The area is also known for its gold and diamond mining, particularly around Tumbang Lahung.

From Muara Teweh trek overland to Long Iram in East Kalimantan, then catch a boat down the Sungai Mahakam to Samarinda. (See Samarinda and Long Iram in the East Kalimantan section.) The trek takes up to two weeks and can be done on your own, following logging roads. Be sure to take sun protection and iodine to purify your water. You can trek along more interesting trails if you hire a guide in Banjarmasin or Muara Teweh.

Places to Stay

The *Barito* and the *Permai* have adequate rooms for 6000 rp per night. The Barito also has more expensive rooms with private mandi. The *Gunung Sintuk* may be a bit better at 9000/12,500 rp, and all rooms have private mandi. In Puruk Cahu you can stay at a longhouse.

Getting There & Away

It's 56 hours by longboat from Banjarmasin to Muara Teweh. The fare is 13,000 rp per person and most boats have beds and a warung. Speedboats from Muara Teweh to Puruk Cahu take about 2½ hours and cost 18,500 rp.

Merpati links Muara Teweh with Palangkaraya for 76,000 rp net and Banjarmasin for 115,000 rp. There are also flights from Muara Teweh to Balikpapan.

PANGKALANBUN

Pangkalanbun is a dusty stopover where you register with the police if you intend to visit Tanjung Puting National Park. It is a fairly important harbour for the cargo boats that run from here to Java. Very few ply the Kalimantan coast. Most travellers avoid Pangkalanbun.

Orientation & Information

Pangkalanbun is little more than an overgrown village with a small downtown area between Jalan P Antasari and Jalan Kasu-

mayuda. Many businesses, banks, the post office, travel agencies and mosques are along these streets. There are also several cafes, a few hotels and a large, swampy market. Bank Negara Indonesia near the passenger pier on Jalan Antasari will change US-dollar travellers' cheques.

Try PT Dimendra Travel (☎ 22954) Jalan Rangga Santrek 11 for air tickets, Bayu Angkasa Tours & Travel at the Blue Kecubung Hotel for tour and trekking advice, and Yessoe Travel for overland travel to Sampit and Palangkaraya.

Places to Stay – bottom end

The choice is not brilliant at this end of the market. Once you have restocked and made onward travel arrangements, consider staying at Kumai. (See the Tanjung Puting National Park section.)

Losmen Selecta (☎ 21526) behind the bemo station for Kumai, is central, very basic and friendly. Singles/doubles cost 6000/ 10,000 rp.

Nearby on Jalan Antasari is the *Abadi* (☎ 21021) with fan-cooled singles starting at 7000 rp, better singles/doubles for 14,000/ 18,000 rp, and air-con ones for 30,000/ 35,000 rp.

Losmen Mawar (☎ 21358) around the corner in Jalan Blimbing Manis is very friendly. Its rooms are grungy but cheap with singles for 4500 rp.

The hospitable *Losmen Bahagia* (☎ 21226) is recommended. Renovated singles/doubles cost 5500/8000 rp with shared mandi, 10,000/12,500 rp with private mandi.

Losmen Candi Agung (☎ 21183), Jalan Suradilaga, has also been renovated. Singles/ doubles in the old section next to the cafe are 4000/7000 rp with shared mandi.

Losmen Rangga Santrek (☎ 21125), Jalan Kasumayuda, is a lovely place for the price (5500 rp for economy singles), but foreigners often find that it is 'full'. *Losmen Rahayu* next door is cheaper but is also reluctant to take foreigners.

Away from the centre, towards the end of Jalan Domba, is *Losmen Anda*, with clean rooms for only 5000 rp.

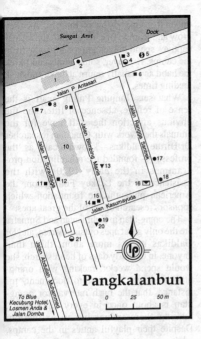

1	Market
2	Speedboat Hire
3	Losmen Selecta
4	Bemos to Kumai
5	Bank Negara Indonesia (BNI)
6	Losmen Abadi
7	Losmen Bahagia
8	Supermarket
9	Losmen Mawar
10	Market
11	Losmen Candi Agung (Under Construction)
12	Candi Agung Losmen & Restaurant
13	Warung Sate
14	Losmen Rahayu
15	Losmen Rangga Antrek
16	Post Office
17	Travey Agency
18	Travel Agency
19	Cinema
20	Rumah Makan Antomoro
21	Bus Station & Night Market

Pangkalanbun

To Blue
Kecubung Hotel,
Losmen Anda &
Jalan Domba

0   25   50 m

Places to Stay – top end

The *Blue Kecubung* (☎ 21211; fax 21513), Jalan Domba 1, has well-kept singles/doubles for 40,000/50,000 rp, and air-con rooms for 57,500/71,000 rp. It's a little overpriced but is the best in town. The owner is a good source of information about Tanjung Puting. The hotel has its own facilities – *Rimba Lodge* – in the national park.

Better value in the upper end is *Hotel Andika* (☎ 21218), Jalan Hasanuddin 51A, around the corner from Losmen Anda. It's clean, the staff are helpful and the restaurant is good. Rooms are 15,000 to 42,500 rp plus tax.

Places to Eat

On Jalan Blimbing Manis, *Warung Sate* serves tasty sate. An even better selection of sate, soups and other Indonesian fare is available from *Rumah Makan Antomoro*, in the tiny lane beside the cinema.

At night, there is a great choice of dishes from warungs at the bus station, including the local speciality, *es kolak*, a kind of pineapple-coconut smoothie.

There is barbecued chicken and friendly service at the warung adjoining *Losmen Candi Agung*, and loads of snacks in the small supermarkets on Jalan Antasari.

If you're staying in the Jalan Domba area away from the centre, you can get good *nasi kuning* (a kind of South Kalimantan-style chicken biryani) in the morning at Jalan Hasanuddin 2, near the Merpati office.

Getting There & Away

Air Bouraq flies to Pangkalanbun from Banjarmasin (126,000 rp) and Surabaya (162,800 rp). DAS flies from Pangkalanbun to Palangkaraya (103,000 rp), Sampit (68,000 rp), and Banjarmasin (126,000 rp). On Merpati, fares to Sampit are 66,000 rp, Palangkaraya 103,000 rp, Surabaya 223,000 rp and Jakarta 268,000 rp.

Deraya and DAS are the only services that fly from west Kalimantan, both with flights from Pontianak for 135,000 rp (DAS) and 127,000 (Deraya). Deraya also flies via Ketapang (80,000 rp).

The Merpati and DAS offices are on Jalan Hasanuddin in Pangkalanbun, near Hotel Andika. The Deraya Air Taxi agency is at Jalan Antasari 51 near the swampy market.

KALIMANTAN

Kijang Travel by road is really only an option for the poor or the desperate, though 'road' is probably not an accurate description for the 450-km nightmare stretch of mud from Pangkalanbun to Palangkaraya. Yessoe Travel can get you to Palangkaraya via Sampit for 41,000 rp, but be prepared to share your six-seat *kijang* (4WD) with a dozen other adults, plus children and luggage.

Boat Pelni passenger ships from Semarang and Surabaya call at Kumai every two weeks. The trip takes a full day and night and the economy fare is about 27,000 rp. There are also many cargo boats with berths or at least deck space, but most go direct to Java.

If you can find a boat to Pontianak, expect to pay about 35,000 rp including meals. The trip takes three days and two nights. For an extra 15,000 rp you can usually get a bed in a crew cabin; otherwise you sleep on the deck. If you can find a boat to Banjarmasin, you'll pay around 25,000 rp. Failing that, catch a boat to Semarang, and get a Pelni boat from Pontianak or Banjarmasin there. Pelni ships to Pangkalanbun leave every 11 days and cost 23,000 rp economy and 31,000 rp with a cabin.

Getting Around

From the airport it's 10,000 rp to your destination in town, or 30,000 rp for a two-hour charter. If you are going direct to Kumai, you could charter a taxi at the airport for 28,000 rp – this includes a stop at the Pangkalanbun market to photocopy your passport and visa, and at the Pangkalanbun police station for your registration to enter the reserve. In Pangkalanbun, the easiest way to get around is to flag down an *ojek* (motorbike taxi) for around 500 rp.

TANJUNG PUTING NATIONAL PARK

The orang-utan rehabilitation camps at Tanjung Harapan and Camp Leakey are like nowhere else in Indonesia: a sanctuary for humans and primates alike. Juvenile orang-utan orphaned or rescued from captivity are reintroduced to the jungle at these centres,

under the supervision of rangers. As they grow and learn to live in the wild, the former captives spend longer and longer away from the camps. However, some adults can't kick the habit and usually return at dawn and dusk feeding times.

What sets Tanjung Puting apart is the sense of refuge, absence of litter and the obvious affection the staff have for the animals they work with. Canadian researcher Dr Birute Galdikas – known locally as 'the professor' – founded the rehabilitation programmes in the early 1970s with the assistance of the Leakey Foundation, the American philanthropic foundation which sponsors research on all of the great apes.

The orang-utan in Kalimantan and Sumatra are the only great apes outside Africa, and Dr Galdikas knows more about them than anyone. In the early days of her research, she would spend weeks tracking wild orang-utan, and was the first to document, for instance, that the birth interval for orang-utan is about once in every eight years, making them vulnerable to extinction. Despite their playful antics in the camps, adult orang-utan are solitary in the wild.

Tanjung Puting National Park, now an Indonesian conservation showpiece, encompasses 305,000 hectares of tropical rainforest, mangrove forest and wetlands. It is home to a vast variety of flora & fauna, including crocodiles, hornbills, wild pigs, bear cats, crab-eating macaques, orang-utan, proboscis monkeys, gibbons, pythons, dolphins and mudskippers (a kind of fish that can walk and breathe on land). This is also a habitat for the dragon fish, an aquarium fish worth 700,000 rp and highly valued by Chinese collectors throughout South-East Asia. Unfortunately, both the dragon fish and the crocodiles are occasionally prey to poachers.

Most visitors go straight to the research centre at Camp Leakey, or the quieter rehabilitation centre at Tanjung Harapan, established in 1989 to cope with the excess from Camp Leakey. At Natai Lengkuas, further up the Sungai Sekonyer, there is a project to research the large populations of proboscis monkeys and gibbons. Another idea is to follow Sungai Kumai south into Kumai Bay to visit the deserted beach of Tanjung Keluang, said to be a fine vantage point to enjoy a lovely sunrise and sunset.

Supporters of the orang-utan research and rehabilitation work in Tanjung Puting could send donations to Orang-Utan Fund Australia Inc, PO Box 447, St Leonards NSW 2065 (☎ 61-2-4896341).

Orientation & Information

A trip into the park begins at the Pangkalanbun police station, where you must register and give the friendly cop a bit of English practice. Make sure you have photocopies of the photo page of your passport, and of the page with your current immigration stamp.

Then head to Kumai, on the banks of Sungai Kumai about 25 km south-east of Pangkalanbun, and register at the riverside conservation office (PHPA) north of town. It's open Monday to Friday from 7 am to 2 pm, Saturday 7 am to 1 pm, and is closed Sunday. If you're not planning to spend the night in the park it's best to register a day in advance, as the whole procedure takes at least an hour.

Registration costs 2000 rp per person per day, 2000 rp a day for a boat 'parking' fee, plus life insurance of 2500 rp (you can talk your way out of this one). You *must* provide a copy of your police letter from Pangkalanbun and a copy of your passport. The Park Office will give you three letters: one for you, one for the ranger stationed at Tanjung Harapan (or whichever other post you choose to visit inside the park), and

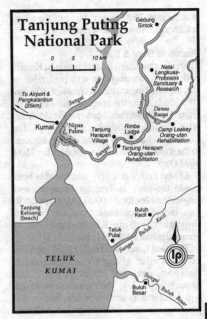

the third for the ranger at the Orang-Utan Research & Conservation Project at Camp Leakey.

Organised Tours

The PHPA may try to talk you into hiring a guide or two but they're really not necessary, as the boatmen know where to go and the rangers in the park are happy to accompany you on walks. However, some PHPA guides speak some English and will also cook on overnight trips. The official PHPA guide rate

---

The Primate Pet Trade

Sadly, the cruel and destructive trade in primates persists throughout Indonesia, although legal sanctions and a growing green consciousness are helping curb the trade.

The trade usually starts with poachers shooting mothers nursing baby primates in the wild. The baby falls from the trees with its mother and, if it survives, is sold at a local market for 50,000 to 100,000 rp. They are then resold in larger centres, often direct to private collectors.

Disease, poor nutrition and boredom usually kill these pets well before they reach maturity. Only the lucky ones get sent to rehabilitation centres like Camp Leakey. ■

is a bargain 7500 rp per day, but they may ask more. Use your discretion.

Places to Stay & Eat

There are two small budget hotels in Kumai, both clean, comfortable and preferable to staying in Pangkalanbun. *Losmen Kumara* (☎ 22062), near the river on the main road from Pangkalanbun, has singles/doubles with shared mandi for 10,000 rp. The *Losmen Cempaka* is above a bank adjacent to the market, with singles/doubles for 7500/10,000 rp.

Rimba Lodge is a very comfortable hotel inside the park at Tanjung Harapan, with singles/doubles for 77,000/117,000 rp. Bookings, including package deals, can be made through the Blue Kecubung Hotel in Pangkalanbun (☎ 21211; fax 21513).

The Baso family's *Garuda* klotok represent excellent value, giving you accommodation, transport, meals and guides for just 75,000 rp per boat per day. Their smaller two klotok will comfortably accommodate four or five passengers, while their large one will take eight to 10. Hire the klotok for at least two days, preferably more, stop at the market to stock up on food and drink, and enjoy Tanjung Puting at a leisurely pace. At night the crew moors the boat well away from settlements, allowing passengers to enjoy the sunsets and wildlife in peace. Sleep on mattresses on the lower deck, wake to the haunting cries of gibbon at dawn, and watch for the tell-tale splash of big crocodiles. Swim and wash in the river pool at Camp Leakey, but be wary of the mercury-contaminated waters of Sekonyer River. Allow time to explore the glorious jungle reserves around the rehabilitation camps, and plan your river movements for dawn or dusk, when various primates come down to the river's edge.

The Basos' boats are in high demand around school and public holidays, the only time you will need a reservation. To book, write to *Boat Garuda,* Baso (Yatno), Jalan Idris Rt 6, No 507, Kumai Hulu 74181, Pangkalanbun, Kalimantan Tengah. Agencies handling bookings (and charging commissions) are the Loksado in Banjarmasin (☎ 64833), Arjuna in Banjarmasin (☎ 58150), and Ethanim Expresindo in Jakarta (☎ 4216373).

Getting There & Away

Colt Kumai is about half an hour away from Pangkalanbun by colt. You can catch colts to Kumai (1000 rp) near the market by Sungai Arot in Pangkalanbun, or on the road to Kumai, which skirts the northern end of Pangkalanbun. This is the same road that goes to the airport. A detour to the airport will cost a little extra. Haggle hard.

Boat Pelni ships from Semarang and Surabaya call at Kumai every two weeks. Inquire at the Kumai and Pangkalanbun docks.

Getting Around

Klotok Public klotok overloaded to within an inch or two of sinking, carry passengers to the tiny village at Tanjung Harapan for 2000 rp, and to the illegal gold-mining fields upstream for 3000 rp.

Klotok hire is 75,000 rp a day, takes four to five hours to reach Camp Leakey, plus stops along the way, and is considerably more pleasant. The added bonus of this option is that the klotok doubles as comfortable, airy accommodation and as your restaurant. (See Places to Stay & Eat earlier.)

Speedboat Speedboat charter to Camp Leakey costs 100,000 rp a day, and will get you from Kumai to Tanjung Harapan in 45 minutes, to Camp Leakey in 90 minutes, or Natai Lengkuas in 90 minutes. Most day-trippers opt for this.

Dugout Canoe Dugout canoes with crew can be hired in Tanjung Harapan for 7500 to 14,000 rp per day. This is a better way around Sekonyer River and its shallow tributaries. The canoes are also much quieter so you're likely to see more wildlife. It is not unusual to see three to four-metre crocodiles in this area.

South Kalimantan

South Kalimantan (Kalimantan Selatan, or Kal-Sel) is Kalimantan's smallest and most densely populated province with an area of 37,660 sq km and a population of 2.8 million. Kal-Sel is an important centre for diamond mining, rattan processing and, of course, timber. It is also the centre of Banjarese culture and a good starting point for treks into Central and East Kalimantan.

Traditional Banjarese clothing is made from *kain sasirangan*, cloth produced by a striking tie-dyeing process. The traditional Banjar-style house is the 'tall roof' design and the best examples can be seen in the town of Marabahan, 50 km north of Banjarmasin on Sungai Barito. There are still a few around Banjarmasin and Banjarbaru, the remains of some in Negara and some impressive public buildings such as the governor's office on Jalan Bali which draw on this style.

In the mountainous north-eastern interior of South Kalimantan are groups of Dayaks said to be descendants of the original Banjar race. These original Banjars may have been families from the Barito delta area who fled to the mountains to avoid Muslim conversion in the 15th and 16th centuries. Communal houses, *balai*, house up to 30 or more families and serve as a ritual centre for these mountain villages.

The province also has one million hectares of wetlands, including 200,000 hectares of tidal marshlands, and 500,000 hectares of freshwater swamps. As elsewhere in Kalimantan, these rich reserves are heavily exploited and becoming degraded, but their sheer size still makes them a valuable refuge for wildlife.

BANJARMASIN

This Venice of the East is far and away Kalimantan's most interesting city. The residents of Banjarmasin are up to their floorboards in water, and much of the city's commerce occurs on water. Many houses are perched on stilts or ride the tides on bundles of floating logs.

The upstream city of Negara is the site of the region's first kingdom. Banjarmasin rose to prominence in 1526 when Pangeran Samudera, a descendant of one of Negara's Hindu kings, overthrew the ruler in Negara and moved the capital to Bandar Masih, the present site of Banjarmasin. The sultanate became an important commercial power, on a par with Brunei.

Competing English and Dutch interests each established factories in Banjarmasin between 1603 and 1814. Trouble erupted in 1701, after the British stationed a warship on the Barito River to guard their warehouses. The Banjars revolted, and took six years to evict the foreigners.

The Dutch felt the sting of Banjar resistance after placing an unpopular prince on the Banjarmasin throne in 1857. Incidents followed, building to full-blown rebellion and the Banjarmasin War of 1859-63. Rural Islamic leaders led a courageous resistance, heavily taxing Dutch financial and human resources. The Dutch declared the sultanate to be 'lapsed' in 1860, had regained control by 1863, but sporadic resistance continued until 1905.

Orientation

Banjarmasin is big, but just about everything you'll need is packed into the city centre around the Pasar Baru markets along Jalan Pasar Baru. There are two cheap 'homestays' just off Jalan Hasanuddin and most of the big banks are along Jalan Lambung Mangkurat. Travellers arriving by ship can catch small yellow *bis kota* (literally 'city minibus') direct to Jalan Hasanuddin (300 rp), but most others terminate at the Antasari market, a few hundred metres east of the centre. Sungai Barito lies to the west of the city centre.

Information

Tourist Office The South Kalimantan regional tourist office at Jalan Panjaitan 3, near the Grand Mosque, is open from 7.30 am to 2.30 pm Monday to Thursday, 7.30 to 11.30 am Friday and 7.30 am to 1.30 pm

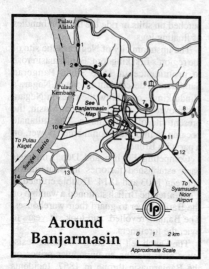

1   Hand Sawing Timber
2   Pasar Kuin
3   Graves of Banjarese Sultans
4   Banjarese
5   Rattan Mat Making
6   People's Struggle Museum & Banjarese
    Traditional House
7   Banjarese
8   Pengambangan Floating Shops
9   Lokbaintan Floating Market
10 Trisakti Sailing Boat Harbour
11 Bouraq Airline
12 Km 6 Bus Station (Inter-City)
13 Basirih Floating Shops
14 Mantuil Floating Village

Around Banjarmasin

0   1   2 km
Approximate Scale

Saturday. The helpful staff can put you in touch with the South Kalimantan Tourist Guide Association and its adventure/jungle guides. There is also a city tourist office next to the Banjarmasin city hall on Jalan Pasar Baru, and an information counter at the airport.

Money Bank Dagang Negara, next to the Telkom office on Jalan Lambung Mangkurat, has the best rates for travellers' cheques but insists on seeing your purchase agreement. Rates are less generous at the moneychanger next to Diamond Homestay, and even worse at Lippobank and the handful of other banks willing to handle travellers' cheques or foreign currency.

Post & Telephone The Telkom office for long-distance phone calls is on Jalan Lambung Mangkurat, and the main post office is further south at the Jalan Pangeran Samudera intersection. There is a Home Country Direct-Dial phone in the departure lounge of Banjarmasin's airport.

Travel Agencies Adi Angkasa Travel (☎ 53131), Jalan Hasanuddin 27, is run by the friendly and informative Pak Mariso who, along with his staff, speaks English. It also accepts credit cards. Other good agencies are Arjuna on Jalan Lambung Mangkurat (☎ 54927) and Loksado at Jalan Seberang Mesjid (☎ 64833).

Bookshops Detailed blueprint maps of South and Central Kalimantan are available at Toko Cenderawasih Mas, Jalan Hasanuddin 37, between the Merpati office and Jalan Pos. Across the street a bookshop sells week-old copies of *Newsweek* and *Asiaweek*, and there is an excellent Gramedia bookshop in Mitra Plaza for maps and magazines.

Guides The going rate for guides is about 5000 rp per hour for local tours, including transport to nearby Pulau Kaget, the floating markets or Pulau Kembang, or 40,000 to 50,000 rp per day for jungle tours (eg to Loksado). A local guide and good source of information is the smooth-talking Johan at the Borneo Homestay on Jalan Pos. At the regional tourist office, Akhmad Arifin speaks excellent English and moonlights as a guide on weekends and holidays.

Mesjid Raya Sabilal Muhtadin

On Jalan Jenderal Sudirman, this is a giant modern mosque with a copper-coloured flying saucer dome and five minarets with lids and spires. Also called the Grand Mosque, it was completed in 1981 at the monumental cost of US$4.5 million, and is the second largest in Indonesia. Despite the gaudy exterior, the interior is a work of art.

Floating Markets

The floating markets are groups of boats, large and small, to which buyers and sellers paddle in canoes. Trading begins at dawn and is usually over by 9 am. **Pasar Kuin** at the junction of the Kuin and Barito rivers is a particularly fine floating market with canoe cafes among the hundreds of boats that converge here. Pull up beside the canoe cafe and, using a bamboo pole with a nail pushed through the end, spike your choice from the generous smorgasbord.

Canal Trips

Everything happens on or around the waterways, so hire someone to take you around for 5000 rp per hour in a motorised canoe. Allow two or three hours, including a dawn visit to one of the two floating markets. Start from the mosque, go to Pasar Kuin where the Kuin River runs into the Barito, perhaps stop at Pulau Kembang (see the next section), head past the sawmills of the Alalak River, and back to town via the Sungai Andai. Johan at Borneo Homestay will provide a boat, or ask around the wharf near the junction of Jalan Lambung Mangkurat and Jalan Pasar Baru. Don't hire a speedboat – they go too fast to observe or photograph anything.

The kampung of **Muara Mantuil** is a floating village of houses and shops built on logs lashed together. It's on a tributary of the Barito close to the Trisakti pisini harbour.

Pulau Kembang

The island is 20 minutes from the town centre by boat and home to a large tribe of long-tailed macaques who congregate at an old Chinese temple near shore. On Sundays the temple becomes a virtual circus when Chinese families give the monkeys huge offerings of eggs, peanuts and bananas.

You can buy bags of peanuts to feed the macaques, but it's best to keep the bags in your pockets, withdrawing a few nuts at a time. The aggressive simians are apt to jump on the visitor and steal all their peanuts in one fell swoop. There are also long-nosed proboscis monkeys in the interior of Pulau Kembang.

Pulau Kaget

About 12 km downstream from Banjarmasin is a wetland reserve inhabited by the comical long-nosed proboscis monkeys. Indonesians call them *kera belanda* or Dutch monkeys because of their long noses, red faces and pot bellies. Borneo Homestay or the tourist office can tell you the best time to leave Banjarmasin (this depends upon the tide) so you can reach the island when the monkeys come out to feed. Because they're very shy creatures the boat pilots should cut the engines and glide beneath tree perches so the monkeys won't flee. Avoid boats with loud sound systems.

Speedboats at the pier at the end of Jalan Pos ask 45,000 to 50,000 rp for a round trip, or you can pay 20,000 to 25,000 rp for a round trip in a klotok, two hours each way. Smaller boats can take you via south Banjarmasin's narrow canals. You will also pass Banjarmasin's giant plywood mills, most of which were built after a total ban on log exports in the late 1980s.

Festivals

During Ramadan, the Muslim fasting month, Banjarmasin is the site for the festive *pasar wadai* or cake fair. Dozens of stalls sell South Kalimantan's famous Banjarese pastries near the city hall or the Grand Mosque. Muslims don't eat these delicious pastries until after sundown of course, but non-believers can gorge themselves all day.

Places to Stay – bottom end

Diamond Homestay (☎ 66100) is a relative newcomer to the budget scene and one of the cleanest and friendliest places in Kalimantan. It is run by terrific staff at a nearby moneychanger. Ring the bell above the door at the homestay on Jalan Simpang Hasanuddin or knock on the blue shutters at No 58. This pleasant place charges 10,000/15,000 rp for singles/doubles.

The recently relocated *Borneo Homestay*

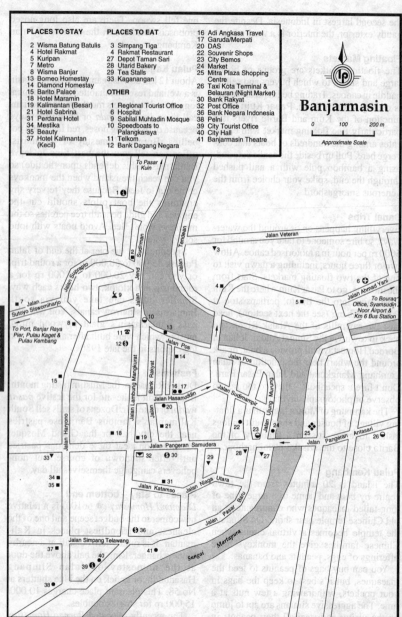

PLACES TO STAY

2 Wisma Batung Batulis
4 Hotel Rakmat
5 Kuripan
7 Metro
8 Wisma Banjar
13 Borneo Homestay
14 Diamond Homestay
15 Barito Palace
18 Hotel Maramin
19 Kalimantan (Besar)
21 Hotel Sabrina
31 Perdana Hotel
34 Mestika
35 Beauty
37 Hotel Kalimantan (Kecil)

PLACES TO EAT

3 Simpang Tiga
4 Rakmat Restaurant
27 Depot Taman Sari
28 Utarid Bakery
29 Tea Stalls
33 Kaganangan

OTHER

1 Regional Tourist Office
6 Hospital
9 Sabilal Muhtadin Mosque
10 Speedboats to Palangkaraya
11 Telkom
12 Bank Dagang Negara
16 Adi Angkasa Travel
17 Garuda/Merpati
20 DAS
22 Souvenir Shops
23 City Bemos
24 Market
25 Mitra Plaza Shopping Centre
26 Taxi Kota Terminal & Belauran (Night Market)
30 Bank Rakyat
32 Post Office
36 Bank Negara Indonesia
38 Pelni
39 City Tourist Office
40 City Hall
41 Banjarmasin Theatre

Banjarmasin

0   100   200 m

Approximate Scale

To Pasar Kuin

Jalan Veteran

Jalan Tendean

Jalan Jend Sudirman

Jalan Suprapto

To Bouraq Office, Syamsudin Noor Airport & Km 6 Bus Station

Jalan Ahmad Yani

Jalan Sutoyo Siswomiharjo

To Port, Banjar Raya Pier, Pulau Kaget & Pulau Kembang

Jalan Hanyono

Jalan Lambung Mangkurat

Bank Rakyat

Jalan Pos

Jalan Pos

Jalan Hasanuddin

Jalan Sudimampir

Jalan Ujung Murung

Jalan Pangeran Antasari

Jalan Pangeran Samudera

Jalan Niaga Utara

Jalan Katamso

Jalan Pasar Batu

Jalan Simpang Telawang

Sungai Martapura

Sungai Martapura

KALIMANTAN

(☎ 66545), on Sungai Martapura at Jalan Pos 87, is a good information centre. The owner, Johan, speaks English and knows South and Central Kalimantan well. The rooms are tiny but there is a pleasant verandah overlooking the river and the 7500/11,000 rp tariff includes breakfast. There are plans to clear the river bank, so the Borneo might have to move again. It already has an option on a place on Jalan Simpang Hasanuddin II, about 20 metres away. Be warned, both Diamond and Borneo suffer from their proximity to a very noisy mosque.

Just over the iron bridge, the *Hotel Rakmat* (☎ 54429) at Jalan Jen Ahmad Yani 9 is sizeable with a friendly manager. Singles/doubles cost 9900/13,750 rp with shared mandi and no fan, or 11,000/14,850 rp. The *Hotel Kalimantan* on Jalan Haryono near Jalan Telawang (not to be confused with the luxury hotel of the same name) has singles/doubles for 7500/13,850 rp.

There are two other cheapies which will do, although you would have to be desperate to lodge at either. The spartan *Mestika* at Jalan Haryono 172 has singles for 6600 rp. Next door is the *Beauty* – a beauty it's not, but it is preferable to the Mestika, with 10,000 rp singles.

Somewhat preferable, but more expensive is the popular *Wisma Banjar* (☎ 53561) 100 metres from the Grand Mosque on Jalan Suprapto 5. Singles/doubles cost 7000/10,000 rp with shared mandi, 8500/12,500 rp with private mandi, and 20,000/25,000 rp with air-con.

Places to Stay – middle & top end

Many places are willing to discount their rates for walk-in guests. The *Barito Palace* (☎ 67300) at Jalan Haryono 16-20 boasts excellent restaurants and a swimming pool. The listed prices for air-con singles/doubles with satellite colour TV start at 120,000/140,000 rp, and suites range from 250,000 to 600,000 rp. There are staff who speak English, German and some Japanese.

The rate card for the *Kalimantan* (☎ 66818) on Jalan Lambung Mangkurat boasts 'we never mix business with pleasure', which makes you wonder why the owners are in the hospitality industry. The place is top class, with a restaurant and pool. Singles/doubles start at 130,000/150,000 rp and rise to 1,200,000 rp – ask for discount rates.

Once Banjarmasin's number-one hotel, the *Hotel Maramin* (☎ 68944), at Jalan Lambung Mangkurat 32, now lags behind the Barito Palace and Kalimantan. Correspondingly, it's less expensive and its rooms start at 55,000 rp. The hotel has a popular disco, a bar, restaurant and convention facilities.

In the middle range, the comfortable *Hotel Sabrina* (☎ 54442), Jalan Bank Rakyat 21, has singles/doubles for 18,000/23,000 rp with fan, and 30,000/35,000 rp with air-con and TV; prices include breakfast.

The *Perdana Hotel* (☎ 68029), Jalan Katamso 3, has economy singles for 28,400 rp, doubles with fan for 33,300 rp, and air-con doubles for 45,400 rp.

The city has a pleasant government guesthouse near the Grand Mosque, the *Wisma Batung Batulis*, which has large air-con singles/doubles with hot water for 45,100/60,200 rp. Foreigners are welcome. Also near the Grand Mosque, the *Metro* (☎ 52427), Jalan Sutoyo Siswomiharjo 26, has big fan-cooled rooms at 20,000/25,000 rp and air-con rooms at 30,000/35,000 rp.

The *SAS Hotel* (☎ 53054) at Jalan Kacapiring has loads of character and pleasant staff. Singles start at 22,500, or 34,650 with air-con. Another option is the *Hotel Kuripan* on Jalan Jen Ahmad Yani with singles/doubles for 26,500 rp (☎ 53313).

Places to Eat

Banjarmasin's excellent array of kueh (cake) includes deep-fried breads, some with delicious fillings, and sticky banana rice cakes – a cheap but tasty option for breakfast at the tea stalls. Stuff yourself for 300 to 400 rp, or even less at the canoe warung at the floating markets. Other breakfast fare includes nasi kuning (a local rice and chicken dish) from the *Warung Makan Rakmat* next door to the Rakmat Hotel on Jalan Jen Ahmad Yani; it's open between 6 and 10 am. Across the street is a no-name warung that serves cheap and tasty *soto banjar*, another local speciality.

There is *ayam panggang* (chicken roasted and served in sweet soy) but fish and freshwater cray hold pride of place in Banjar cuisine. There are a string of eateries along Jalan Pangeran Samudera, but try the *Kaganangan* at No 30 for local dishes. As with most regional cuisine, you only pay for what you eat. The *Lejat Baru* on the same street has excellent Chinese food.

Behind the Hotel Rakmat (Jalan Veteran) is a string of moderately priced Chinese rumah makan – like the *Rumah Makan Sari Wangi* at No 70, the *Flamingo* across the road, and *Rumah Makan Simpang Tiga* at No 22.

The *Depot Miara*, on the corner diagonally opposite the Flamingo on Jalan Veteran, has good bubur ayam, as does the *Rumah Makan Jakarta* on Jalan Hasanuddin near the Garuda office. For pastries check out the famous *Utarid* (also called the Menseng) bakery at Jalan Pasar Baru 22-28, near the Jalan Antasari bridge. The Utarid has cakes, whole wheat bread, a range of biscuits and ice cream.

The best views are from a rooftop cafe next to the Jalan Antasari bridge, *Depot Taman Sari*, where you can bring pastries from the Utarid and have coffee or tea – the owners don't mind. The Depot Taman Sari is a good place for evening libations, with the odd breeze and views of the Martapura and surrounds.

If you're on a tight budget or want a taste of street culture, eat at the tea stalls along Jalan Niaga Utara between Jalan Katamso and Jalan Pangeran Samudera near Pasar Baru. There is a friendly *tea stall* next to the Jalan Jen Ahmad Yani bridge and another at Jalan Simpang Hasanuddin. Kalimantan's version of night markets are *belauran*. Banjarmasin's is a huge affair at the Antasari terminal, another cheap eatery.

The Arjuna Plaza complex on Lambung Mangkurat offers some superlative non-Indonesian fare for those willing to spend more. Carnivores will love the *Rama Steak House* where grilled fillets begin at 10,000 rp. Cheaper here are char-grilled hamburgers

and hot dogs. Japanese businesspeople congregate at the Arjuna's *Hakone Restaurant* for a taste of home.

The Mitra Plaza shopping complex also has a good Japanese restaurant, the *Eiyu*. The Mitra's *Hero Supermarket* is a good place to stock up on goods for trekking and the complex also has several fast-food places. Those craving Western fare will find the Kalimantan Hotel complex on Jalan Lambung Mangkurat harbouring a *KFC* and a *Swenson's Ice Cream*.

Things to Buy
The central market area sells hats of every shape, colour and material – the locals love them.

The city is famous for its kain sasirangan, a kind of colourful tie-dye batik. There are a few shops along Jalan Hasanuddin with sasirangan, and stalls in the market near the Antasari bridge. Otherwise troop out to the Citra factory at Km 12 to see the dyeing process and make your purchases there.

Polished stones are a hot item on the streets of Banjarmasin. Just as touts fling boxes of wrist watches at you in Kuta, the touts here will show you their stones. Most are polished and cut for bulky jewellery, but some offer cut crystals, agates and other interesting bits.

The Malabar souvenir shops adjacent to the bemo terminal off Jalan Pangeran Samudera offer a rag-tag selection of worm-ridden carvings, but the occasional real antique appears on their shelves too. Bargain very hard.

Getting There & Away
Air Garuda/Merpati (☎ 54203), at Jalan Hasanuddin 31, is open Monday to Thursday from 7 am to 4 pm, Friday from 7 am to noon and from 2 to 4 pm, Saturday from 7 am to 1 pm, and Sunday and holidays from 9 am to noon. Bouraq (☎ 52445) is inconveniently situated at an office four km from the centre on Jalan Jen Ahmad Yani 343. DAS (☎ 52902), Jalan Hasanuddin 6, Blok 4, is across the road from Garuda.

Bouraq has daily flights to Balikpapan

(98,600 rp). It also services Jakarta (221,000 rp), Surabaya (128,000 rp), Semarang (150,000 rp), Palu (181,000 rp) and a variety of other destinations. Occasionally there aren't enough passengers and flights are delayed a day or so.

Merpati has direct flights to Surabaya (147,000 rp net) and Jakarta (242,500 rp), and connecting flights from there. Sempati has direct flights to its Surabaya hub (146,800 rp), where it offers same-day connections across Indonesia. DAS has handy flights to Palangkaraya (74,000 rp), Muara Teweh, Pangkalanbun (125,800 rp), and on to Kalimantan Barat.

Adi Angkasa Travel at Jalan Hasanuddin 27 is a good place to buy air tickets and offers some discounts.

Bus Buses and colts depart frequently from the Km 6 terminal for Martapura and Banjarbaru (1100 rp). Night buses to Balikpapan (16,000 rp or 22,000 rp with air-con) leave daily between 4 and 4.30 pm and arrive in Panajan, across the river from Balikpapan, about 12 hours later, where you must take a speedboat across the river (1200 rp, bargain hard).

You can break the trip from Banjarmasin to Balikpapan halfway by spending the night in Tanjung. From Banjarmasin to Tanjung costs 7500 rp and takes five hours. Tanjung to Panajan/Balikpapan costs 7500 rp and takes six hours.

Regular day buses from Km 6 go via Rantau, Amuntai and Tanjung and there are buses to other destinations in the south-east corner of the island. To get to the Km 6 terminal, take a yellow minibus (300 rp) from the newspapers kiosks behind the BCA bank.

Boat All sorts of vessels leave from Banjarmasin. From here you can travel by ship to another island or head inland by river. The main terminal for longboats heading upriver is conveniently located on the Sungai Martapura, adjacent to the Grand Mosque.

Passenger Ship Ships leave for Surabaya about twice a week and the trip takes about 24 hours. The ships dock at Trisakti pisini harbour. To get there take a bemo from the taxi kota terminal on Jalan Pangeran Samudera for 300 rp. The bemo will take you past the harbour master's and ticket offices.

The harbour master's office (☎ 54775) is on Jalan Barito Hilir at Trisakti. Opposite is a line of shops with several agencies for boat tickets to Surabaya, but Pelni fares are cheapest from the Pelni counter inside. Pelni fares from Banjarmasin to Surabaya are 32,500 rp in economy class, 76,000 rp in 2nd class and 92,000 rp in 1st. Going to Semarang costs 37,500 rp (economy), 81,000 rp (2nd), 109,600 rp (1st).

Another agency for these ships is at the Km 6 bus terminal, and others can be found off Jalan Pasar Baru near the Antasari bridge. The Pasar Baru agents also sell less expensive passenger tickets for cargo boats that leave about every two days – fares are usually 25,000 to 30,000 rp to Surabaya.

Pelni also sells tickets to Pangkalanbun in Central Kalimantan. The ship leaves every 11 days and costs 23,000 rp by economy, or 31,000 rp with a cabin.

Sailboat Schooners constantly ply the route from Banjarmasin to Surabaya. First, go to the harbour master's office for information and for permission to sail. You are more likely to get permission if you have a demonstrated interest in sailing, or want to photograph or write about the trip. Then approach the individual captains for permission to board.

Ferry & Speedboat Heading inland, one of the more obvious courses to take is from Banjarmasin to Palangkaraya, a journey of 18 hours in a bis air (river ferry) or about six hours in a speedboat. You go up three rivers – the Barito, Kapuas and the Kahayan – and through the two artificial canals that link them.

Speedboats to Palangkaraya leave from a dock at the mosque end of Jalan Pos. From Banjarmasin to Palangkaraya is 20,100 rp and there are boats daily.

KALIMANTAN

River ferries (bis air) to Palangkaraya depart from the Banjar Raya pier on the Barito River, and cost 6,500 rp.

Long-distance bis air which journey up the Barito leave from the river taxi terminal near the Banjar Raya fish market. To get there take a yellow colt (300 rp) to the end of Jalan Sutoyo Siswomiharjo west of the city centre. The end of the route is the town of Muara Teweh in Central Kalimantan, 56 hours away and costing only 13,000 rp. The tariff includes the price of a bed.

Jet Boat These coastal speedboats are the fast, cheap and comfortable way to get to Sampit. The *Hoover* (40,000 rp; eight hours) and the *Soon Soon Express* (40,000 rp; six hours), leave on alternate days from Pasar Lima, opposite city hall. Get tickets from Sarikaya Supermarket, Jalan Pasar Lima II, next to the Banjarmasin Theatre, or from PT Lamun Lamun Express, Jalan Pasar Baru 137, (☎ 64232).

Getting Around

To/From the Airport Banjarmasin's Syamsudin Noor Airport is 26 km out of town on the road to Banjarbaru. To get there take a bemo from Pasar Baru to the Km 6 terminal. Then catch a Martapura-bound colt, get off at the branch road leading to the airport and walk the 500 metres to the terminal. A taxi all the way to the airport will cost you 10,000 rp. They cluster near the Garuda office and the Sabrina Hotel.

From the airport to the city, buy a taxi ticket at the counter in the terminal, or walk out of the airport, through the car park, past the MIG aircraft, turn left and walk to the Banjarmasin to Martapura highway. From here pick up one of the frequent colts to Banjarmasin.

Local Transport You can hire a boat operator to navigate the canals. Expect to pay about 5000 rp per hour, including a guide.

On dry land, the area around Pasar Baru is very small and easy to walk around. You don't need wheels since the hotels, taxi terminal, airline offices etc are all grouped

together. For longer trips there are taxis (60,000 rp a day, 12,000 rp for two hours), bemos (300 rp), becaks (500 rp minimum), ojeks (motorbike taxis, 500 rp minimum) and *bajaj* (three-wheel motorised taxi, 1000 rp minimum). A bajaj from the centre to Banjar Raya pier is around 1500 to 2000 rp; by motorcycle it costs 1000 rp.

Bemos go to various parts of town including the Km 6 terminal, which is the departure point for buses to Banjarbaru, Martapura and Balikpapan. The standard fare is 300 rp.

Banjar becak drivers aren't predatory but they are hard to bargain with. The bajaj drivers work the same way. Motorbike taxis wait at Pasar Baru and Km 6 and will take you anywhere. If you're travelling light this is a good way to get to the airport.

MARABAHAN & MARGASARI

For a glimpse of river life, take a speedboat from Banjarmasin to Marabahan, 65 km (5100 rp) up the Barito. It is a small town with old houses, including traditional Banjar-style wooden houses. The losmen on the river, such as the *Hotel Bahtera,* have rooms for 5000 rp.

From Marabahan there are charter boats to Margasari (15,000 rp), a handicraft village which produces lots of rattan and bamboo products such as fans, hats and maps. From there you can take a colt to Rantau (1000 rp), and another colt back to Banjarmasin (2500 rp), or hang around for a riverboat up to Negara.

BANJARBARU

The chief attraction of this town, on the road from Banjarmasin to Martapura, is its museum collection of Banjar and Dayak artefacts, and statues found at the site of Hindu temples in Kalimantan. Exhibits include a replica of Banjar riverboat equipment used in traditional Banjar circumcision ceremonies (including an antibiotic leaf and a cut-throat razor), cannon, swords and other artefacts from wars with the Dutch, a small cannon used by British troops in Kalimantan, Dayak and Banjar swords, knives and other pointy things.

Probably the most interesting exhibit is of items excavated from the Hindu Laras Temple and Agung Temple in East Kalimantan, including a Nandi bull and a Shiva lingam. The remains of the Laras Temple are in Margasari village, near Rantau. Agung Temple is near Amuntai, 150 km from Banjarmasin. Unless you're a hard-core archaeology freak, it's not worth going all the way to these villages to view what are mainly heaps of rubble.

The museum is on the Banjarmasin to Martapura highway. Ask the colt driver to drop you off. The museum is open from 8 am to 1 pm, closes earlier on Friday, and is closed all Monday. Dance performances are held every Sunday at 9 am.

MARTAPURA

Continuing on from Banjarbaru you come to Martapura. On a good day the large market is a photographer's paradise, with every type of food on sale and lots of colourfully dressed Banjar women.

A section of the market sells uncut gems, silver jewellery and trading beads – the choice, both strung and unstrung, is excellent. Be prepared to bargain diligently. The market is behind the Martapura bus station. A few minutes' walk diagonally across the sports field near the bus station is a diamond-polishing factory and shop. There they let visitors through to the back, where the diamond polishers work.

Backing on to the market is the *Wisma Penginapan Mutiara*, Jalan Sukaramai, which has quite decent rooms starting at 5000 rp.

Frequent colts leave from the Km 6 terminal in Banjarmasin. The fare is 1100 rp and it takes about 45 minutes along a good surfaced road.

CEMPAKA

A must-see are the Cempaka diamond fields, a short detour off the Martapura road. It is one place where you can see some of the smaller diamond and gold digs. The mines are, in fact, silt-filled, water-logged holes dug from muddy streams. The diggers spend the day up to their necks in water, diving below and coming up with baskets of silt

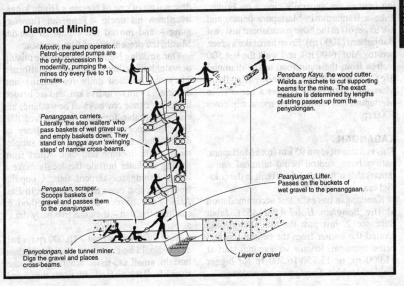

Diamond Mining

Montir, the pump operator. Petrol-operated pumps are the only concession to modernity, pumping the mines dry every five to 10 minutes.

Penanggaan, carriers. Literally 'the step waiters' who pass baskets of wet gravel up, and empty baskets down. They stand on *tangga ayun* 'swinging steps' of narrow cross-beams.

Pengautan, scraper. Scoops baskets of gravel and passes them to the *peanjungan*.

Penyolongan, side tunnel miner. Digs the gravel and places cross-beams.

Penebang Kayu, the wood cutter. Wields a machete to cut supporting beams for the mine. The exact measure is determined by lengths of string passed up from the *penyolongan*.

Peanjungan, Lifter. Passes on the buckets of wet gravel to the *penanggaan*.

Layer of gravel

which is washed away to separate the gold specks, diamonds or agates.

There are records of 20-carat diamonds from these fields as far back as 1846, a 106.7-carat monster in 1850, and the biggest of all, the 167.5-carat Tri Sakti ('Thrice Sacred') found in August 1965. Most diamonds are a fraction of the size, but the hope of another big find keeps the miners focused on the job.

Diggers usually work in teams of 10 to 15, digging one day, sluicing the next, with men and women sharing the back-breaking work. Typically, there is a 'chief' who pays the miners 2000 rp a day lunch money to work the claim. If and when there is a find, 10% of the dividend usually goes to the land owner, 10% to the chief, 15% to the pump operator and wood cutter, 10% for tax, and the remaining 55% is divided between the team. By-products such as sand and large stones are sold for building and road construction. The activity on the fields tends to follow the big finds. There are touts aplenty to show you the way, give you a lift and sell you polished stones.

Note that the diamond mines and polishing centres are generally closed on Friday. Take a Banjarmasin-Martapura bemo, and ask to get off at the huge roundabout just past Banjarbaru (1000 rp). From here take a green taxi to 'Alur' (400 rp), and walk the last 500 metres from the main road to the diamond digs. Bemos leave infrequently from Martapura; otherwise charter a bemo from Martapura bus station. The round trip costs 5000 rp.

KADANGAN

This is a transit town 95 km from Martapura, with a busy, central bemo terminal and a remarkable old marketplace built in the colonial era.

Kadangan has excellent accommodation at the *Bangkau Hotel* (☎ 21455), Jalan Suprapto 2, just past the taxi station, and around the corner from the central bus and bemo terminal. Rooms with mandi start at 11,000 rp, or 13,750/16,500 rp for bigger singles/doubles. Foreigners are welcome.

Or there are three not-so-friendly losmen opposite the central bus station. At the time of writing, *Hotel Mandapni* had singles/doubles for 4000/6000 rp but was 'full'; *Losmen Andalas* wouldn't even discuss rates; and *Hotel Sentosa* will open its doors for 5000/7500 rp.

There is excellent nasi bungkus (take away rice parcels) with chicken or liver at the barrow stalls that set up at the bemo terminal after 3 pm.

The bus from Banjarmasin's Km 6 terminal to Kandangan costs 3000 rp, and takes about three hours.

NEGARA

The north-western section of South Kalimantan is mostly wetlands, and towards the end of the wet season there is nothing but water in, under and for miles around Negara, making the city look like a very waterlogged island. The only land above water is the roads, but even they disappear occasionally.

Negara was the capital of South Kalimantan's first kingdom, the Hindu realm of Negara Dipa first ruled by Maharaja Empu Jatmika. In 1526, Pangeran Samudera, a descendant of one of Negara's Hindu kings, overthrew his uncle – Pangeran Tumenggung – and moved the capital to Bandar Masih, the present site of Banjarmasin.

One amazing Negara custom is the raising of water buffalo herds on wooden platforms. They are released daily for grazing and drinking, swim up to five km, and are herded home by 'canoe cowboys'. The wetlands are also remarkable for their prolific bird life, fish, the occasional snake and plenty of ducks. Duck eggs are an important supplement to the income and diet. Apart from trading in water buffalo the locals make a living fishing for serpent fish, a popular freshwater fish eaten throughout South-East Asia. They have a distinctive method of catching the fish – they use live baby ducks as bait.

Tour the town by boat – 10,000 rp for half a day should be enough to visit the wetland buffalo, small sawmills, wharves and other river life. Back on land, ask to see the sword-making. Local craftsmen forge beautiful swords, machete and kris in a variety of styles, complemented by remarkably decorative sheaths.

Surprisingly for such a large town, Negara has no hotel. Ask around for homestay accommodation, which should set you back 5000 to 10,000 rp a night. Negotiate a rate in advance. The cafes opposite the tiny cinema serve a delicious ayam panggang, chicken roasted and served in sweet soy. For breakfast, look out for the eateries with trays of doughnut-style kueh.

Getting There & Away
The bus from Banjarmasin to Kandangan costs 3000 rp and takes 2½ hours. From Kandangan to Negara you have the option of buses (1000 rp), shared taxi (2500 rp per person), chartered taxi (8000 rp) or ojek (6000 rp). Twice-weekly boats direct from the Banjarmasin river taxi pier cost 7000 rp and take a day and a night to reach Negara.

LOKSADO
East of Kandangan in the Muratus Mountains is a collection of villages which are the remnants of an animist Banjar society that may have moved here from the Barito delta to avoid the Javanese immigration of the 15th and 16th centuries. About 20 villages are spread over about 2500 sq km between Kandangan and Amuntai to the west and the South Kalimantan coast to the east.

Loksado is an important market village in the area and a good base from which to explore. One of the best times to be in Loksado is market day on Wednesday.

Places to Stay & Eat
There's good accommodation at the government cottages on a river island in the village (10,000/15,000 rp a single/double). The Loksado *kepala desa* (village chief) takes guests for 5000 rp a night, but charges a fortune for food. Many of the villages in this area – such as Niih, to the south-west of Loksado – will take guests for 5000 to 10,000 rp per night.

Eateries along the main lane from the suspension bridge are basic, and shut down shortly after dusk. The best breakfast is roti fresh from the wok at a warung about 20 metres from the bridge.

Getting There & Away
There is a good road to Loksado, terminating just before the suspension bridge. Bemos and pick-ups leave Loksado first thing in the morning, and return from Kandangan later in the day (2500 rp).

Coming back from Loksado, many travellers charter a bamboo raft and pole down Riam Kiwa River. The usual drop-off point is Tanuhi, just two hours downstream (20,000 rp), but it is much nicer to stay on board for eight hours and get off at Bubuhi (35,000 rp). From the nearby road, you can catch a bemo or ojek back to Kandangan.

AROUND LOKSADO
From Loksado there are hundreds of paths through mountain garden plots to other villages over the hills, many crossing mountain streams via suspension bridges. Locals bound across effortlessly, but the rest of us manage to send the tangle of wire and planks into a frenetic rhythm.

Follow the path upstream on Sungai Riam Kiwa for three hours to a series of **waterfalls** just past Balai Haratai. It is easy enough to find the first waterfall, but local knowledge is handy if you want to climb to the middle and top falls, and find the nearby cave. Ask at Haratai, or get someone from Loksado to tag along in exchange for some English practice.

Malaris
A 30-minute walk through a bamboo forest south-east of Loksado is the village of Malaris, where 32 families (about 150 people) live in a large balai (communal house). Stay the night at the invitation of the village head *(balai kepala)*, and offer to pay 5000 rp or so.

Treks
There is an excellent three-day trek through primary forest, via Haratai and Hudjung to

Pagat and Barabai. Start from either end, take guides and stay at longhouses along the way. Expect to pay 7500 rp a day per guide for assistance, plus 5000 rp for their return fares (by public transport). There are plenty of places to stay in Barabai, most looking much nicer from the outside than inside. Try the *Fusfa* where doubles start at 15,000 rp. Doubles elsewhere cost around 5000 rp per room.

There are also paths over the hills from Loksado to the coast. The trek to Kota Baru on Pulau Laut takes three or four days to reach by a combination of foot, bemo and boat. It takes you through hillside gardens, forests and over Gunung Besar, the province's highest peak at 1892 metres.

Or there are other treks downstream to Kandangan.

SUNGAI BARITO

From Banjarmasin, you can travel by river-boat up Sungai Barito all the way to Muara Teweh in Central Kalimantan and then by speedboat to the Dayak village of Puruk Cahu. From Puruk Cahu a logging road leads to Long Iram in East Kalimantan.

A boat from Banjarmasin to Muara Teweh costs 13,000 rp and takes about 56 hours. There are several budget hotels in Muara Teweh where you can stay for about 5000 rp. You can charter a speedboat to Puruk Cahu for 25,000 rp one way and stay in longhouses there. See Muara Teweh in the earlier Central Kalimantan section for more information.

SOUTH COAST

An alternative route between Banjarmasin and Balikpapan is the coastal route via Pagatan and Batulicin. Set out from Banjarmasin's Km 6 terminal before 7 am, and take a Batulicin air-con bus (7000 rp), and get out at **Pagatan**. Get a 1000 rp becak to the losmen on the beach. Nearby, there are schooners under construction, and on April 17 each year, local Bugis make offerings to the sea at the end of week-long celebrations.

From Pagatan, take a bemo to Batulicin and 75 km on to **Bangkalan**. Get out at Km 325, and look for Pak Tiang Han three km

off the main road. He will be able to direct you to nearby caves, where locals collect cave swiftlet nests. The nests are used to make birds' nest soup and medicine. Black ones sell for 300,000 rp, and white ones for 800,000 rp, or up to 1.5 million rp in Surabaya.

Local transport connections continue through to Balikpapan in East Kalimantan.

East Kalimantan

East Kalimantan is the largest (202,000 sq km) and richest province in Kalimantan, with a population of 2.1 million people. Indonesia earns a big share of its export income from East Kalimantan's lucrative oil, timber and natural gas industries plus its rapidly expanding coal and gold ventures.

While most commercial activity is along the coast and Mahakam river valley, far into the interior once-thriving Dayak cultures are confronting dramatic change in the face of logging and mining activity. With time and planning you can reach places that rarely see a foreign face, and enjoy pockets of wilderness, but loggers and the military are ever-present.

Fifth-century Sanskrit inscriptions found in the Wahau valley north of Tenggarong are all that remains of one of Indonesia's oldest Hindu kingdoms and its contact with Indian and Sriwijaya merchants. Its successor, the Sultanate of Kutai, was founded in the 13th century with the assistance of refugees from strife-torn East Java. Kutai became an important regional trading power and its capital, Tenggarong, remained East Kalimantan's largest and busiest urban centre until eclipsed by Samarinda and Balikpapan this century.

The region has had its share of opportunists, such as the pirate Arung Singkang, a descendant of the Bugis royal family of Wajo in Sulawesi Selatan. In 1726 he conquered Pasir then Kutai, and in 1733 his forces made an unsuccessful attempt on Banjarmasin. Singkang returned to Sulawesi a couple of

East
Kalimantan

0   50   100 km

years later, taking the Wajo throne in 1737, and remaining a political force there until his death in 1765.

Full-scale exploitation of the Mahakam delta's oil reserves began in 1897, shifting the focus of commerce to the oil refineries at Balikpapan. By 1913 the province was producing more than half of the East Indies' oil output and Balikpapan has been riding the booms and busts of the oil market ever since.

Government transmigration schemes accounted for 114,000 newcomers to East Kalimantan (Kalimantan Timur or Kal-Tim) between 1954 and 1985, over half settling in

the Kutai regency. Despite an acute shortage of arable land, transmigration still accounts for a significant share of population growth.

The various Dayak tribes have adapted to the scarcity of arable land through swidden techniques in which plots of secondary jungle are slashed, burnt to provide ash to enrich the poor soils, sown for one or two seasons, then left to fallow for years. Logging, population growth and competition for arable land has shortened the fallow periods in some areas, giving the land less time to recover. Unsustainable logging and farming has been blamed for degrading

The Great Fires

Farmers and loggers blamed each other for the great fires of 1982-83, in which 35,000 sq km or 17 per cent of the province's total land area was ravaged by 11 months of wildfire. There was a similar disaster in neighbouring Sabah that year. Both followed severe drought, and the damage was considerable.

Three months of fire in 1991 claimed another 500 sq km of East Kalimantan's forests and created a haze that disrupted air traffic as far away as Singapore. Kalimantan and Sumatran wildfires in 1994 created similar havoc over Singapore and Malaysia, reducing visibility over Singapore to just 300 metres and prompting a Malaysian appeal to the United Nations for assistance.

Swidden farmers undoubtedly start many of the fires through their age-old practice of slash and burn cultivation. But logged-over, degraded forest was the worst effected, indicating that the volume of combustible material left behind by loggers and the damage done by logging had made the jungle vulnerable to fire damage. ■

200,000 hectares of the province's forests to poor grassland.

Even when areas are set aside for conservation, competing demands can still exact a heavy toll. The Kutai National Park, established as a nature reserve in 1936, was cut by 100,000 hectares in 1968 when the park's whole coastal frontage was opened for logging and oil exploration. Within a few years this area, which had been severely degraded, was returned to the park as 'compensation' for a new logging concession excised from the park – 60,000 hectares of primary forest in the south. Fires in 1982-83 then claimed a big share of the remnants of the park's undisturbed forests.

BALIKPAPAN

Balikpapan's refineries have hitched the city's fortunes to roller-coaster fluctuations in the oil market and the vagaries of history. The oilfields were a strategic target for the Japanese invasion in 1941, and again for the Allied advances in 1944-45. Australians occupied Balikpapan after a bloody invasion, and suppressed anti-colonial unrest.

Balikpapan's fortunes soared with the oil price shocks of the 1970s, but then plummeted with an oil glut and falling prices in the 1980s, crippling the city's enclave economy. The current upturn in oil, coal and timber prices has restored confidence and stimulated new activity.

The city still has a frontier feel to it, with

highly insulated Pertamina, Union Oil and Total residential areas alongside grubby and decayed back streets. The suburban area bounded by Jalan Randan Utara and Jalan Pandanwanyi near the fruit market north of the oil refinery is by far the most interesting precinct. It is built on stilts over tidal mudflats, with uneven, lurching wooden walkways.

The huge oil refinery dominates the city and flying in you can see stray tankers and offshore oil rigs. This is the centre of Kalimantan's oil business and the chief city of the province. There are 12 Jakarta-Balikpapan flights a day, a five-star hotel which could easily be ranked among the best in the world, and nearly as many American and European faces as there are Japanese motorcycles.

Orientation & Information

The best landmark is the beachfront Balikpapan Centre on the corner of Jalan Sudirman and Jalan Yani. This huge shopping complex is at the axis of the commercial and hotel district. Head north along Jalan Yani to find the restaurants, east along the shore front to get to the airport, or west along Jalan Sudirman to find the immigration, government and post offices. Jalan Sudirman joins Jalan Yos Sudarso, which loops past the seaports and oil refinery areas.

Money Bank Negara Indonesia on Jalan

Pengeran Antasari changes major travellers' cheques and cash currencies. The bank is open Monday to Friday from 8 am to noon and 1.30 to 3 pm, and on Saturday from 8 to 11 am. The branch office at Seppingan Airport also changes cash and travellers' cheques.

Bank Dagang Negara on Jalan Yani offers good rates, but insists on seeing your purchase agreement. There are fewer hassles at nearby BCA.

Post There was a grand new post office under construction on Jalan Sudirman, and old flood-prone premises on Jalan Yani at the time of researching this edition. The new place is expected to open Monday to Friday from 8 am to 6 pm and on Saturday, Sunday and holidays from 8 am to 5 pm.

Places to Stay – bottom end
There are cheaper rooms, but no bargains. The old places along Jalan Yani are the best of a bad bunch, including the adequately clean *Hotel Aida* (☎ 21006) with airless singles/doubles from 9000/14,000 rp and air-con rooms at 30,000 rp.

Close by, the *Hotel Murni* has rooms for 14,000/17,500 rp and looks OK, but get a room at the back away from the main road. On the same street, the *Penginapan Mama* is passable and has rooms from 10,000/15,000 rp.

The *Penginapan Royal* near the Pasar Baru is at the start of the airport road near the Jalan Ahmad Yani corner. It's spartan, grubby but central with singles from 6500 rp.

Places to Stay – middle
Renovations have pushed the pleasant *Hotel Sederhana* (☎ 22564), Jalan Sudirman 7, into the mid-range market. Singles/doubles now start from 42,350/48,400 rp.

Better value is the very central Hotel Gajah Mada (☎ 34634), Jalan Sudirman 14, with economy rooms for 22,500/27,500 rp, and standard ones at 45,000/50,000 rp; all with private mandi. The terrace off the 2nd floor overlooks the sea.

Hotel Balikpapan (☎ 21490), Jalan Garuda 2, is a pleasant place with a bar tucked away from the main road. Rooms are overpriced; standard rooms are more expensive and not as good value as the Hotel Gajah Mada's. Doubles range from 66,500 to 78,650 rp.

Hotel Budiman (☎ 36030) on Jalan Ahmad Yani 18 has rooms with air-con and TV for 45,000 rp, plus tax. The *Mirama Hotel* (☎ 33906) at Jalan Pranoto 16 has a good location, a restaurant, chemist, and barber shop. Its air-con rooms cost 55,000 rp plus tax for economy doubles with private mandi, and range up to 115,000 rp for suites. It is the best in this price range.

The *Bahtera Hotel* (☎ 22603), at Jalan Sudirman 2, is also central, but because its disco provides guests with more options than drinks and dancing, the hotel can get a bit noisy. Air-con rooms start at 60,500 rp.

The *Blue Sky Hotel* (☎ 22268) on Jalan Suprapto is comfortable but expensive. Doubles cost from 78,000 to 126,000 rp. All rooms are air-con and there is a sauna, gym and billiard room.

Places to Stay – top end
Balikpapan's classy *Hotel Benakutai* (☎ 31896), Jalan Ahmad Yani (PO Box 299), officially costs from 242,000/275,000 rp for singles/doubles up to 682,000 rp plus 21% service and tax. Substantial discounts are available. There's an international-style bar/restaurant with pleasant surrounds and great coffee.

There's a huge up-market hotel nearing completion just east of the Balikpapan Centre which will provide an alternative to the Benakutai.

Places to Eat
Balikpapan's saving grace is its range of restaurants. *Bondy's* on Jalan Ahmad Yani offers seafood and hearty serves of Western fare in an open courtyard. Venture through the sterile street-front bakery to the courtyard and its broad balconies where you'll find good food, attentive staff, and a pleasant atmosphere.

Carnivores can order steak at Bondy's, but across the road you will find grilled fillets the

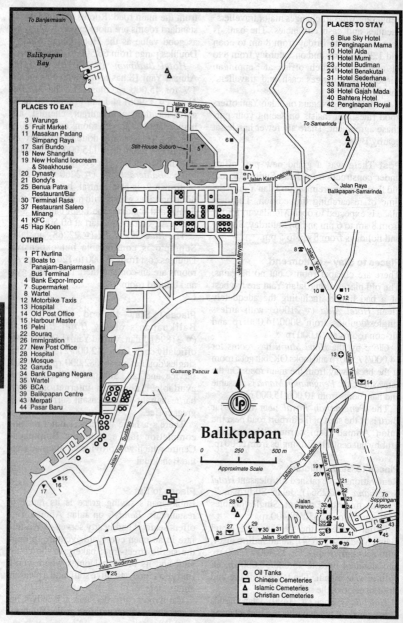

PLACES TO STAY
6 Blue Sky Hotel
9 Penginapan Mama
10 Hotel Aida
11 Hotel Murni
23 Hotel Budiman
24 Hotel Benakutai
31 Hotel Sederhana
33 Mirama Hotel
38 Hotel Gajah Mada
40 Bahtera Hotel
42 Penginapan Royal

PLACES TO EAT
3 Warungs
5 Fruit Market
11 Masakan Padang Simpang Raya
17 Sari Bundo
18 New Shangrila
19 New Holland Icecream & Steakhouse
20 Dynasty
21 Bondy's
25 Benua Patra Restaurant/Bar
30 Terminal Rasa
37 Restaurant Salero Minang
41 KFC
45 Hap Koen

OTHER
1 PT Nurlina
2 Boats to Panajam-Banjarmasin Bus Terminal
4 Bank Expor-Impor
7 Supermarket
8 Wartel
12 Motorbike Taxis
13 Hospital
14 Old Post Office
15 Harbour Master
16 Pelni
22 Bouraq
26 Immigration
27 New Post Office
28 Hospital
29 Mosque
32 Garuda
34 Bank Dagang Negara
35 BCA
39 Balikpapan Centre
43 Merpati
44 Pasar Baru

Balikpapan

O Oil Tanks
□ Chinese Cemeteries
▲ Islamic Cemeteries
□ Christian Cemeteries

speciality of the *New Holland Icecream & Steakhouse*.

For Chinese food try the *Atomic*, on a little alley near the Benakutai, the *Dynasty* on Jalan Ahmad Yani, or the *Hap Koen* on Jalan Sudirman. But the best Chinese food is at the *New Shangrila* on Jalan Ahmad Yani. Its crab in Singapore sauce is messy but unbeatable, or there is a savoury hot-plate special with pigeon eggs, vegetables and your choice of meat, chicken or seafood. The *es campur* here is pretty good too. Get there before 7 pm or you may have a considerable wait.

For padang food, try the *Restaurant Masakan Padang Simpang Raya* next to the Hotel Murni. The *Restaurant Salero Minang* at Jalan Yani 12B is similarly priced, as is the *Restaurant Sinar Minang* on Jalan Sudirman. This place serves *udang galah* (giant river prawns) and is marginally better than the Salero Minang.

If you are willing to spend an average of 30,000 rp for an excellent meal with a splendid view of the ocean, visit the *Benua Patra* on Jalan Yos Sudarso. A potpourri of cuisines, including Western, Japanese, Korean and Chinese, are skilfully prepared here and oriented to please the palate of expats.

Western breakfasts in the Benakutai Hotel's coffee shop are surprisingly reasonable. The two other restaurants in the hotel serve excellent Western and Chinese fare at moderate to expensive prices.

There's a tatty *KFC* nearby, and a *Texas Fried Chicken* in the Balikpapan Centre. The supermarket in the centre has a range to tempt homesick expats.

Entertainment

Apart from watching the twinkling lights of the oil refinery at night you could try drinking in one of Balikpapan's many bars. *Benua Patra Restaurant & Bar* on Jalan Yos Sudarso has a large bar and dance floor – some nights there's a band and other nights a disco. For a raunchier disco scene, there's the dancing emporium attached to the Bahtera Hotel on Jalan Sudirman. There's a cover charge plus a one-drink minimum unless you are staying at the hotel. Further

west, on Jalan Yos Sudarso, you'll come to a couple of smaller bar/disco affairs around the peninsula with a cover charge.

Getting There & Away

Air Garuda (☎ 22301), Jalan Ahmad Yani 14, is diagonally opposite the Hotel Benakutai. Sempati (☎ 31612) is in the Hotel Benakutai, Merpati (☎ 24477) is at Jalan Sudirman 22, and Bouraq (☎ 23117) has an office next to Hotel Budiman.

Garuda flies to Denpasar, Jakarta, Pontianak, Surabaya and Ujung Pandang.

Merpati has useful flights to Pontianak (227,100 rp), Singapore (585,000 rp), weekly flights to Batam (337,100 rp) and on to Medan (523,000 rp), Ujung Pandang (172,100 rp), Ambon (392,600 rp), Maumere (309,600 rp), and Kupang (353,600 rp). It also flies to Palu (112,700 rp) and Manado (260,600 rp), Surabaya (218,300 rp) and on to Bandung (359,600 rp), Denpasar (221,000 rp), Mataram (321,100 rp), Semarang (235,300 rp) and Yogyakarta (266,100 rp). Its only intraprovincial flight is to Tarakan (152,300 rp).

Bouraq has a smaller inter-island schedule but similar prices. It is also the only airline linking Kalimantan's two busiest airports, Balikpapan and Banjarmasin (98,600 rp). Its other useful routes include Berau (169,000 rp), Muara Teweh (201,300 rp), Kota Baru (167,200 rp), Palangkaraya (161,700 rp) and Tarakan (152,500 rp).

Bouraq (48,000 rp) and DAS (49,000 rp) both fly to nearby Samarinda.

Bus From Balikpapan you can head either north to Samarinda or south to Banjarmasin. Buses to Samarinda (2900 rp, 3500 rp aircon; two hours) depart from a bus stand in the north of the city accessible by a No 2 or 3 bemo for 700 rp (it's a long way out). Buy your ticket on the bus.

Buses to Banjarmasin (16,000 rp, 22,000 rp air-con; 12 hours) depart from the bus terminal on the opposite side of the harbour to the city. To get there, take a colt from the Rapak bus terminal to the pier on Jalan Mangunsidi. Charter a speedboat to take you to the other side (the speedboat drivers will mob you). It costs 1200 rp per person, or around 4000 rp to charter, and takes 10 minutes. Alternatively, a motorised longboat costs 800 rp and takes 25 minutes.

Boat The Pelni liners *Kambuna, Umsini,* and *Tidar* call in fortnightly, connecting Balikpapan to Tarakan, Pantoloan, Ujung Pandang, Surabaya and beyond.

In Balikpapan the Pelni office (☎ 21402) is on Jalan Yos Sudarso 76. For regular ships to Surabaya try PT Elang Raya Abadi for the MV *Hafag* services to Ujung Pandang (28,750 to 56,000 rp), or Surabaya (48,750 to 78,750 rp). Alternately try PT Ling Jaya Shipping (☎ 21577) at Jalan Yos Sudarso 40 and PT Sudi Jaya Agung (☎ 21956) at Jalan Pelabuhan 39. Fares are around 30,000 rp.

Getting Around

To/From the Airport Seppingan Airport is a 15-minute fast drive from Pasar Baru along a surfaced road. A taxi from the airport to town costs a standard 7500 rp if you buy your taxi ticket in the terminal. Walk outside and you can bargain your fare down to around 6000 rp.

In town you should be able to charter a bemo to the airport for less – from Pasar Baru for 4000 to 5000 rp, or less by ojek. Chartered bemo or taxi seems to be the only way to the airport.

Bemo Bemos cut a circular route; 300 rp gets you anywhere around town. The chief station is the Rapak bus/bemo terminal at the end of Jalan Panjaitan. From here, bemos run a circular route around Jalan Ahmad Yani, Sudirman, Yos Sudarso and Suprapto. Motorbike taxis (ojek) will take you anywhere as a pillion passenger for 1000 rp (minimum).

SAMARINDA

Balikpapan for oil, Samarinda for timber; this is another old trading port on one of Kalimantan's mighty rivers. If you want to look at a timber mill there's a giant one on the road to Tenggarong, not far from Samar-

inda. Samarinda is also the most convenient starting point for inland trips up Sungai Mahakam to the Dayak areas.

Most of the people who have settled in Samarinda are Banjars from South Kalimantan, so the main dialect is Banjarese. There are also many Kutais, who include the indigenous people of this area.

On the south side of the Mahakam, in the part of town called **Samarinda Seberang**, you can visit cottage industries where Samarinda-style sarongs are woven. The traditional East Kalimantan wraparound is woven from *doyo* leaf.

Orientation & Information

The main part of Samarinda stretches along the north bank of the river. The best orientation point is the enormous mosque on the river front. Jalan Yos Sudarso runs east from here and Jalan Gajah Mada runs west. Most of the offices and hotels are along these two streets or in the streets behind them.

Tourist Office The kantor pariwisata (☎ 21669) has excellent maps, can quote tour prices and refer travellers to decent guides. It is just off Jalan Kesuma Bangsa at Jalan Suryani 1.

Money The Bank Negara Indonesia is on the corner of Jalan Sebatik and Jalan Panglima Batur. It only changes US dollars (cash and travellers' cheques). It is open Monday to Thursday from 8 am to 12.30 pm, Friday from 1.30 to 4.30 pm, and Saturday from 8 to 11.30 am. Bank Dagang Negara on Jalan Mulawarman is the only bank in Samarinda that changes travellers' cheques in other currencies.

Post The main post office is on the corner of Jalan Gajah Mada and Jalan Awanglong, opposite the Bank Rakyat Indonesia.

Guides For good information on trekking and river journeys in East Kalimantan contact Jailani, a young Kutai guide, through the Hotel Sewarga Indah, Jalan Sudirman 11, or PT Cisma, Jalan Awang Long. The going

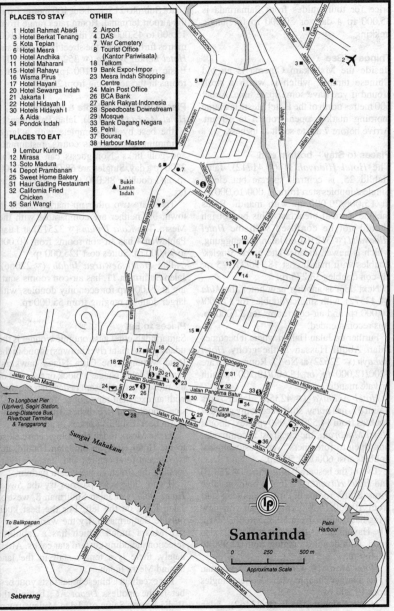

PLACES TO STAY
1 Hotel Rahmat Abadi
3 Hotel Berkat Tenang
5 Kota Tepian
6 Hotel Mesra
10 Hotel Andhika
11 Hotel Maharani
15 Hotel Rahayu
16 Wisma Pirus
17 Hotel Hayani
20 Hotel Sewarga Indah
21 Jakarta I
22 Hotel Hidayah II
30 Hotels Hidayah I
& Aida
34 Pondok Indah

PLACES TO EAT
9 Lembur Kuring
12 Mirasa
13 Soto Madura
14 Depot Prambanan
25 Sweet Home Bakery
31 Haur Gading Restaurant
32 California Fried
Chicken
35 Sari Wangi

OTHER
2 Airport
4 DAS
7 War Cemetery
8 Tourist Office
(Kantor Pariwisata)
18 Telkom
19 Bank Expor-Impor
23 Mesra Indah Shopping
Centre
24 Main Post Office
26 BCA Bank
27 Bank Rakyat Indonesia
28 Speedboats Downstream
29 Mosque
33 Bank Dagang Negara
36 Pelni
37 Bouraq
38 Harbour Master

Bukit
Lamin
Indah

To Longboat Pier
(Upriver), Segiri Station,
Long-Distance Bus,
Riverboat Terminal
& Tanggarong

To Balikpapan

Sungai Mahakam

Pelni
Harbour

Samarinda

0   250   500 m

Approximate Scale

Seberang

KALIMANTAN

price for tour guides from Samarinda is 35,000 rp a day, or 50,000 rp for jungle trekking.

Things to See

Beside the Mahakam Cinema is an old Chinese temple, which is worth a stroll around if you have some spare time. About 500 metres north of the Hotel Mesra is a large morning market, open from 5 to 10 am. Arrive before 7 am to see it at its best.

Places to Stay – bottom end

The *Hotel Hidayah II* (☎ 41712), Jalan Hahlid 25, is central, spartan but clean. Singles/doubles start from 11,000/16,000 rp, or 15,000/20,000 rp with mandi. Rates include a small breakfast. This budget inn should not be confused with the *Hotel Hidayah I* (☎ 31210), on Jalan Temenggung, which is newer, cleaner and nicer. Singles/doubles with mandi cost 18,150/21,175 rp; air-con doubles 33,275 rp.

Next door is another new hotel, the *Aida* (☎ 42572), with singles/doubles for 17,000/20,000 rp, and air-con rooms for 32,000 rp. It is recommended.

Further up Jalan Hahlid where it becomes Jalan Abdul Hassan is the grotty *Hotel Rahayu* (☎ 22622) at No 17. Rooms here are 7200/12,000 rp, or 15,600/19,200 rp with private mandi.

Hotel Andhika (☎ 42358), Jalan Agus Salim 37, has noisy, stuffy economy singles/doubles from 14,520/22,990 rp. Next door is *Hotel Maharani*, the cheapest accommodation open to foreigners. Very basic singles/doubles cost 6000/12,500 rp.

Two of the best are *Wisma Pirus* (☎ 21873) and *Hotel Hayani* (☎ 42653), both on Jalan Pirus. Stuffy rooms in Pirus's old wing start from 10,550/16,300 rp. The air-con new wing has doubles from 50,325 to 66,750 rp. The Hayani across the street at No 31 is also good, with doubles ranging from 22,990 to 31,460 rp.

Hotel Mesir (☎ 42624), Jalan Sudirman 57, is a larger cheapie with adequate singles from 10,200 rp.

Hotel Rahmat Abadi (☎ 43462), Jalan

Gatot Subroto 215, is about 100 metres from the airport terminal. Room rates range from 15,600 to 45,000 rp. A nicer option just 100 metres further down the street is the pleasant *Hotel Berkat Tenang* (☎ 35267) at No 107. Basic rooms cost 12,100 rp, or there are rooms in the new wing from 21,781 rp.

Places to Stay – middle & top end

Hotel Mesra (☎ 32772), Jalan Pahlawan 1, is the best by far, complete with a large swimming pool, tennis courts, restaurants and golf links. Non-guests can swim for 2500 rp a day. Singles are 68,000 to 187,000 rp, and doubles 88,000 to 210,000 rp, plus tax.

There are two other up-market hotels in town, but neither are comparable with the Mesra. The *Kota Tepian* (☎ 32513) at Jalan Pahlawan 4 has air-con rooms from 40,000 to 90,000 rp. Suites cost 125,000 rp.

The *Hotel Sewarga Indah* (☎ 22066), Jalan Sudirman 11, has air-con rooms starting at 29,000 rp for economy doubles, with larger doubles ranging from 55,000 rp.

Places to Eat

Samarinda's chief gastronomic wonder is the udang galah (giant river prawns) found in the local warung. The Citra Niaga hawkers' centre off Jalan Niaga, a block or two east of the mosque, is a pleasant pedestrian precinct with an excellent range of seafood, padang, sate, noodle and rice dishes, fruit juices and warm beer. Establish prices in advance.

At the Mesra Indah shopping centre close to the Hotel Hidayah on Jalan Hahlid, are two decent food centres and, upstairs overlooking the street, an ice-cream parlour.

If you like sticky pastries try the *Sweet Home Bakery* at Jalan Sudirman 8, west of Jalan Pirus on the left. For the best kueh outside Banjarmasin, try the warung opposite Mesra Indah which has a fabulous selection including custard star cakes. Alternately, there is a tempe stall in the lane behind Mesra Indah.

For excellent Chinese breakfasts your best bet is the spotless *Depot AC*, behind the Wella Beauty Salon off Jalan Mulawarman

If you prefer Indonesian soups for breakfast, there's the efficient *Warung Aida* on the south side of Jalan Panglima Batur at the Jalan Kalimantan intersection. For savoury beef soup at lunch or dinner, eat at *Soto Madura* on Jalan Agus Salim. Travellers craving a taste of home will find a *California Fried Chicken* joint on Jalan Sulawesi.

For good, albeit not cheap, Chinese fare dine at *Lezat* on Jalan Mulawarman. The *Sari Wangi* on Jalan Niaga Utara is not quite the quality of Lezat, but it's somewhat cheaper.

For a splurge, locals reckon the best hotel restaurants are at the Mesra, Sewarga Indah and the Andhika, in that order. In addition to its attractive wood-panelled restaurant serving excellent European, Indonesian and Chinese cuisine, the Mesra often has a barbecue grill for pool-side dining. The fanciest restaurant in town is the *Haur Gading Restaurant* off Jalan Sulawesi. It specialises in seafood.

Things to Buy

Rattan goods, doyo leaf cloth, carvings and other jungle products are available from a string of souvenir shops along Jalan Slamat Riadi and Jalan Martadinata. Forget the poorly stocked souvenir and antique shops along Jalan Mulawarman. Those with an environmental conscience should consider the beautiful tubular rattan baskets and wild honey which the environmental group Plasma buys direct from the isolated communities it works with. The group (☎ 35753) runs on a shoestring budget and its volunteers are busy, so only call if you are serious about buying.

Sleeping bags are essential for anyone travelling to the interior, either as a sleeping mat on the boats or for those cold nights on the verandahs of mountain longhouses. Toko Venus (☎ 33255), Jalan Citra Niaga, Blok C1, has sleeping bags for 75,000 rp, as well as masks, snorkels and other gear.

Entertainment

Several bars and discos are tucked away throughout the Kaltim Theatre complex across from the sleazy Sukarni Hotel. Most are fairly hard-core hostess bars, but the *Blue*

Pacific is a slightly up-market disco where couples are welcome. The cover charge is 5000 rp and includes a small beer.

For young Indonesians the place to dance the night away is the floating disco, *Restoran Terapung*, upstream, picturesquely situated at the foot of the Mahakam bridge. There is a cover charge.

Getting There & Away

Air DAS (☎ 35250), Jalan Gatot Subroto 92, has heavily subsidised and heavily booked flights to the interior. Fares are just 36,000 rp (plus tax) to Data Dawai, 35,000 rp to Long Ampung in the Apokayan, 125,000 rp to Tarakan and 72,000 rp from there to Long Bawang. As a general rule, the cheaper the flight, the heavier the bookings. Apart from seats set aside for VIPs and those on urgent business, you need to book weeks in advance. Telephone about a month before you want to fly: the area code is 0541.

MAF (☎ 43628), Jalan Rahuia Rahaya I, also has regular flights to Long Ampung and Data Dawai. Check for other destinations.

Merpati is at Jalan Sudirman 23, and Sempati has an agency at Jalan Imam Bonjol (☎ 38607). Bouraq (☎ 41105), Jalan Mulawarman 24, has flights to Berau (109,000 rp net), Tarakan (129,000 rp) and Balikpapan 48,000 rp.

Bus From Samarinda you can head west to Tenggarong or south to Balikpapan. The long-distance bus station is adjacent to the riverboat terminal, on the west side of the river a couple of km upstream from the bridge. Bemos run between the centre of town and the bus station for 500 rp. There are daily buses to Tenggarong (1500 rp; one hour) and to Balikpapan (2900 rp; two hours) along well-surfaced roads.

Taxi You can be driven direct to your destination in Balikpapan in less than two hours by chartering a taxi for 25,000 rp. Taxis embark from a parking lot across from the Sukarni Hotel. The drawback here is that they don't leave until they have four passengers.

Boat Many vessels leave from Samarinda including coastal ships and riverboats.

Ship Pelni (☎ 41402) is at Jalan Sudarso 40-56 or ask at the nearby Terminal Penumpang Kapal Laut Samarinda and the Direktorat Jenderal Perhubungan Laut – both on Jalan Sudarso. The *Leuser* does a fortnightly run from here to Toli-Toli and Nunukan, and south to Pare Pare, Batulicin and Surabaya. Sample fares are Nunukan 200,600 rp (1st class), 134,600 rp (2nd class), 47,600 rp (economy); Tarakan 174,600 rp (1st class), 116,600 rp (2nd class), 43,600 rp (economy); and Toli-Toli 99,600 (1st class), 66,600 (2nd class), 25,600 rp (economy).

There are many non-Pelni boats from Samarinda to other ports along the Kalimantan coast, including weekly boats to Berau (aka Tanjung Redeb), (25,000 to 40,000 rp; about 36 hours) and occasionally to Tarakan (49,000 rp; about two days and two nights). If you can't get a ship to Tarakan then take one as far as Berau. From there it's easy to get a boat to Tarakan.

For information on what leaves when, check with the harbour master at the Adpel office, on the corner of Jalan Sudarso and Jalan Nakhoda.

Riverboat Boats up the Mahakam leave from the Sungai Kunjang ferry terminal south-west of the town centre. To get there take a green city minibus A (called taxi A) west on Jalan Gajah Mada, and ask for 'feri'. The regular fare is 500 rp but if you get in an empty taxi they may try to make you charter – insist on *harga biasa* (the usual price).

A boat to Tenggarong takes four hours, one to Melak one day and a night (10,000 rp), and to Long Bagun two days and a night (conditions permitting). Most boats have a sleeping deck upstairs, which costs extra, and warungs downstairs.

Speedboats will get you to Melak and back for just one million rupiah, including a two-night stop upstream.

Getting Around
To/From the Airport The airport is quite literally *in* the suburbs. From the taxi counter in the terminal, you pay 7500 rp for a taxi into the centre of town. Alternatively, walk 100 metres down to Jalan Gatot Subroto, turn left and catch a reddish-brown colt – a taxi B – all the way to the waterfront (350 rp).

Public Taxi City colts, called taxi, run along several overlapping routes designated A, B and C. Route C goes past Hotel Mesra and the university area, route B goes past Hotel Rahmat Abadi and the airport etc. Most short runs cost 350 rp. It's a standard 500 rp to the ferry pier for boats going upriver and 350 rp to the airport.

AROUND SAMARINDA
Kutai Game Reserve
This wildlife reserve is home to orang-utan and other exotic species and can be visited either via a tour booked through agencies in Balikpapan and Samarinda, or on your own. Other than a monument to Bontang's location on the equator, some wooden houses on stilts, and an immense liquefied natural gas plant, there is little reason to spend much time in the town. Guide services cost about 12,000 rp.

Places to Stay If you stay overnight in Bontang, the best place is the comfortable *Equator Hotel* (☎ 22939). Air-con bungalows start at 30,000 rp with TV and private mandi. There are also a few cheap hotels in town and the government *Kutai Guesthouse* in the reserve where a bed costs 5000 rp. There is basic Indonesian food here, but it is recommended that you bring some of your own.

Getting There & Away Independent travellers can take a bus from Samarinda to Bontang for 3000 rp for the three-hour trip and then charter a boat from the PHPA office (50,000 rp for the round trip).

TENGGARONG
On Sungai Mahakam, 39 km from Samarinda, Tenggarong was once the capital of the sultanate of Kutai. Today it's a little riverside

PLACES TO STAY

7   Penginapan
    Zaranah I
10 Penginapan Anda
    & Warung
14 Penginapan Anda II
15 Penginapan Diana

OTHER

1   Police
2   Telkom
3   Post Office
4   Mesjid Jami
    Hasanuddin
5   Mulawarman Museum
6   Karyah Indah Art
8   Tourist Office
9   Pasar Tepian Pandan
    (Market)
11 Merpati
12 Mosque
13 Pasar Pagi (Market)
16 Bank Rakyat Indonesia
17 Cinema

KALIMANTAN

Tenggarong

Not to Scale

To Samarinda

town cut by dirty canals. Like many small towns along the Mahakam, wooden walkways lead from each house to the toilet shacks built on stilts over the waterways. Both river and canals function as a combined toilet, washroom and well.

Orientation & Information

The chief attraction of Tenggarong is its annual Erau Festival and the former sultan's palace museum, built earlier this century from the royalties from early oil exploitation. Some travellers prefer to start long river trips from here, but you can save a lot of travelling

time if you catch a bus to Kota Bangun and catch a boat from there.

A tourist office next to the sultan's palace has information on river trips and the Kutai National Park.

Mulawarman Museum

The former sultan's palace is now a museum. It was built by the Dutch in the 1930s in a futurist, monolithic, modernist style. It holds a collection of artefacts from the days of the sultan and many Dayak artefacts. Sadly, there are few of the former sultan's furnishings or personal relics remaining.

The palace is open Tuesday to Thursday from 8 am to 2 pm, Friday from 8 to 11 am, Saturday from 8 am to 1 pm and Sunday and holidays from 8 am to 2 pm; it's closed on Monday. The sultan's fine porcelain collection is only exhibited on Sundays (although if you pay the guard a tip he might show you the porcelain on other days). Admission to the museum is 500 rp. On some Sundays, there is Dayak dancing here; it can be arranged on other days for a good sum – say 100,000 rp.

Erau Festival

Once a year, Dayak people travel from various points in Kalimantan to celebrate the Erau Festival in the town of Tenggarong. Although the festival is somewhat touristy, it will give you a good opportunity to see the Dayaks in their traditional finery perform tribal dances and ritual ceremonies. Plus it is a fabulous excuse for a huge inter-tribal party. The festival is usually held the last week in September and goes for one to two weeks. Contact the tourist office in Samarinda for the exact dates.

LEMBU SUWANA

ERAU 88 - KUTAI

Places to Stay & Eat

Down on the waterfront there are two places right on the boat dock. The *Penginapan Zaranah I* has rooms for 3500/7000 rp. The

Warung & Penginapan Anda costs 4000/7500 rp. Up the road and around the corner on Jalan Sudirman are the similarly priced *Anda II* and *Penginapan Diana*. The Diana is the pick of the lot, with large rooms and a restaurant downstairs that looks decent.

Getting There & Away

Colts to Tenggarong from Samarinda take one hour and cost 1500 rp. The colt pulls into the Petugas station on the outskirts of Tenggarong. From here you have to get a taxi kota (another colt) into the centre of Tenggarong for 300 rp.

Motorcycle taxis will also take you into town for 500 rp. City taxis run between 7 am and 6 pm. It takes about 10 minutes to get from Petugas station to Pasar Tepian Pandan, where you get off for the boat dock, palace and tourist office.

There are no direct buses or colts from Tenggarong to Balikpapan, but you can get out south of Samarinda, a couple of km before the bridge, and hail a bus from the roadside.

SUNGAI MAHAKAM

Rivers are the highways of Kalimantan, and the Sungai Mahakam is the busiest of all. Daily longboats ply the Mahakam from Samarinda all the way to Long Bagun, three days and 523 km upstream. When conditions are right, four or five motorised canoes a week link Long Bagun to Long Pahangai, a one to two-day trip through gorges and rapids (40,000 rp). The return trip to Long Bagun takes just six or seven hours. *Never* tackle this stretch without local assistance. These waters can be lethal.

Beyond Long Pahangai, there are motorised canoes through to Long Apari, and from there it is possible to walk through to Tanjung Lokan on the Sungai Kapuas headwaters in Central Kalimantan.

If the Mahakam is low, you might not be able to get any further than Long Iram, 114 km short of Long Bagun. If the river's too high, the same may apply if the currents are too swift.

Many of the towns and villages along the

Mahakam are built over wooden walkways that keep them above water during the wet season. Often there will be a budget hotel or two or a longhouse where travellers can stay – the standard price everywhere is 5000 rp per person. Alcoholic beverages can be hard to come by upriver so, if you need to, bring along your own supply from Samarinda.

Kota Bangun

Kota Bangun is a dusty stop at the start of the Mahakam lake country, about three hours by bus from Samarinda along a rapidly improving road. Coal, rubber and transmigration are the major local activities. There are five buses a day to Samarinda, the first at 7 am and the last at 3 pm (3500 rp).

Penginapan & Rumah Makan Mukjizat Jalan Mesjid Raya 46, 4000/8000 rp, is directly opposite the main mosque. It has small rooms, great river views, nice people, and is just a short walk to the bus terminal and motorised canoe dock, the Liang dock. Hire a motorised canoe to Muara Muntai for 20,000 rp, or charter for two days to Muara Muntai, Tanjung Isuy, Mancong and back to Kota Bangun for 120,000 rp.

The people at Sri Bagun Lodge can run boats to the lakes at dawn and dusk to see the bird life, proboscis monkeys and other wildlife plus, if you are lucky, *pesut* – the freshwater dolphins this area is famous for.

Muara Muntai

Muara Muntai is a Kutai market town built over mud flats in the heart of the Mahakam's lake country. The streets are spotlessly clean boardwalks, but mind the mosquitoes. The town is little more than a transit stop, but its beautifully built and maintained boardwalks are an attraction. Join the hoards promenading at night, and check out the deputy bupati's fine old wooden house and huge portico, straight ahead from the dock. There is a market by the dock, as well as canoes which trade directly on the water.

Places to Stay & Eat There are two losmen. Turn left at the boardwalk parallel to the dock and you will find the first, the *Pengi-*

napan Nita Wardana, about 20 metres on. Tiny grubby rooms cost 5000 rp per head. *Penginapan Etam Sri Muntai Indah*, 50 metres down the boardwalk, is run by fun folk who don't hassle their guests. Singles/doubles cost 4000/8000 rp.

The warung between the two losmen serves *sop Muara Muntai*, a filling soup with rice, chicken, noodles, cabbage and a squeeze of lime. Warungs opposite the Nita Wardana sell fried rice, noodles etc. For breakfast, buy kueh and return to the losmen, or go to the warung on the dock for nasi kuning and a great choice of roti and kueh.

Getting There & Away Public boats leave for Tanjung Isuy via Jantur and Danau Jempang every morning. They leave at 7.15 am (be there at 7 am) and return from Tanjung Isuy at 1 pm. The price is 2500 rp, provided there are five or more passengers. If there are four, each pays 5000 rp each. If there are just two, you need to charter for 20,000 to 30,000 rp. A full day on the lakes costs about 60,000 rp.

The boat from Samarinda to Muara Muntai takes 13 hours on the 7 am express boat or 18 hours (overnight) on the 9 am boat. The fares are 5000 rp, more or less. The slower boat has mattresses on the upper deck and its own warung.

Tanjung Isuy

Tanjung Isuy is on the shores of Danau Jempang in Banuaq Dayak territory. Half the fun is getting there, via spectacular wetlands, shallow lakes and **Jantur**, a Banjar village built on a flooded mud flat. Jantur's mosque stands alone on a bend in the river, accessible only by boats and high gangplanks. Beside it is the cemetery, the highest point in town but still just 20 cm above the water table at the end of the wet season. Bodies buried here must be anchored in their watery graves to prevent them bobbing to the surface.

There is plenty of bird life on Danau Jembang, but sadly no pesut (freshwater dolphin) have been seen here since the drought and fires of 1982-83.

Tanjung Isuy is a favoured destination for

packs of aging tourists in search of an 'authentic' Dayak experience. Most arrive in speedboats from Samarinda, mob the souvenir stalls in the longhouse, watch a mix of Dayak dancing and zoom back the next day. Activity focuses on the Taman Jamrot Lamin, a longhouse vacated in the late 1970s, and rebuilt by the provincial government as a craft centre and tourist hostel. Despite the commercial nature of these pay-by-the-hour performances, they are lively, rhythmic and loads of fun for the whole town. The mix of Kenyah, Kayan and Banuaq dancing is confusing, but very entertaining.

The older, original longhouse is an inauspicious-looking building near the jetty. Unlike the other it is in bad repair and a 50-metre section has been demolished. Two families live here, but many more use it as a craft centre, meeting hall and cultural centre. You can often find healing and harvest ceremonies in progress here. The carvings here are about 20 to 30% cheaper than at the hostel.

Places to Stay & Eat There is one budget hotel in Tanjung Isuy – the *Penginapan Beringan*, which costs 5000 rp per person. The couple who run the Beringan also prepare and serve food downstairs. The *Taman Jamrot Lamin* on Jalan Indonesia Australia, 500 metres from the jetty, is also open to guests for the same rate. Unlike a real longhouse it has private guest rooms and comfortable beds. A cafe a few doors down has basic fare, or very tough chicken if you order a few hours ahead.

Getting There & Away Riverboats leave for Samarinda each Monday and Thursday, ces (motorised canoe) to Muara Muntai leave daily at 1 pm (2500 to 20,000 rp), or you could charter a ces direct to Kota Bangun (50,000 rp), catch a bus and be in Samarinda or Balikpapan that night.

Mancong

Hire a ces to get from Tanjung Isuy to nearby Mancong via Ohong River, past flocks of magnificent water birds and a gorgeous stretch of riverside jungle. Charter for 20,000 to 30,000 rp, allowing for two or three hours in each direction. It is essential to go slowly to spot the many proboscis monkeys, snakes (if you are lucky) and bird life, including hornbills. You'll pass villages with houses fronted by carved statues, folk weaving baskets and cloth, schools with steps leading into the water, and the odd ibis hanging around the house docks, hoping for a free feed.

In Mancong there is a grand wooden two-storey longhouse, built by the government as a tourist attraction in 1987. The locals will gladly show you around. You can also see Banuaq weaving cloth from doyo leaf, have the process explained to you, and buy some at very reasonable prices. Folk dances are occasionally held at the longhouse for ritual purposes or for tourist groups. You can stay for 5000 rp per person. Return to Tanjung Isuy by ces, or by motorcycle (5000 rp).

THE UPPER MAHAKAM

Melak & Eheng

Melak is the biggest town in the upper Mahakam, famous for the nearby **Kersid Luwai Orchid Reserve** where 72 different species of orchid grow, including the extremely rare green-black *Cologenia pandurata* orchids. The best time to see the orchids is supposedly January to February, but the visitors' book indicates that you never see more than a few at any time of the year. The reserve is about 16 km from Melak and may be reached via jeep or ojek charter. Pak Banen shows you around for 1000 rp per person – walk slowly, ask questions.

Inquire whether any funerals, weddings or harvest **ceremonies** are being held while you are there – they can be pretty spectacular, often including the ritual slaughter of water buffalo. Spiritual life is at its busiest in March, April and June, apparently. Look out for healing ceremonies, where the *belian* (spiritual healer) calls on her or his cosmic connections to cure all types of spiritual ills.

Barong Tongkok is a small village at the centre of the plateau. There are five warungs

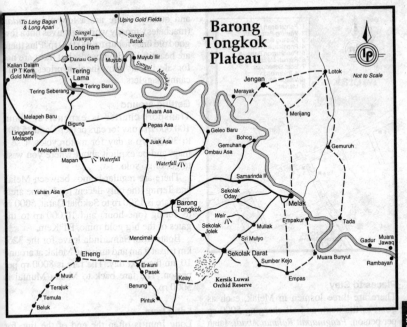

Barong Tongkok Plateau

Not to Scale

in town, most serving padang food, plus a losmen.

In nearby **Eheng** there is an unusually long Banuaq longhouse and cemetery. The longhouse was started in the 1960s, and may well be the last real Kalimantan longhouse built without government subsidy. Market day is Tuesday, the best day to visit. The final stretch of road from Mencimai to Eheng is appalling, ensuring the village's continued isolation. You can walk there, or rent a jeep or ojek from Melak. Locals sell carvings and rattan goods, and know the Melak shop prices better than most tourists.

Mencimai has an excellent museum with detailed explanations in English and Indonesian of the local systems of swidden or shifting agriculture. The Museum Mencimai Papatn Puti was set up by a Japanese student of agricultural economics, to explain the Banuaq systems of land use, the methods for collecting wild honey, traps for pigs and monkeys, bark cloth

production (revived during the Japanese occupation of WW II), and has relics including excellent old mandau and rattan ware. This tiny museum is easily one of the best in Indonesia.

PT Kem, Indonesia's biggest **gold mine**, is an Australian-run operation at Kalian which employs 800 workers. Apart from the parade of prospective employees trouping via Melak and Tering, and the occasional waste spill, you wouldn't know it was there. The shanty town at the gates is as close as you will be allowed to get without prior approval.

If you need a guide for trekking beyond Melak, travellers have recommended Agus Noto from Rojok, who can be contacted through the Penginapan Rahmat Abadi in Melak. He charges around 50,000 rp a day for local jungle treks or to Long Ampung, about five days away via Sungai Boh by boat and foot. Avoid the November-January wet season.

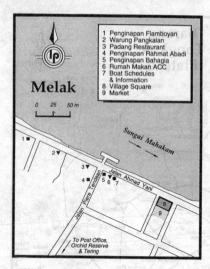

1 Penginapan Flamboyan
2 Warung Pangkalan
3 Padang Restaurant
4 Penginapan Rahmat Abadi
5 Penginapan Bahagia
6 Rumah Makan ACC
7 Boat Schedules
  & Information
8 Village Square
9 Market

and quality. There are a few old *mandau* (machetes), mostly working knives but a few good old ones for up to 300,000 rp. Plus there are beautiful trading beads, but most are not for sale. Locals know the shop prices, and are canny hagglers.

Getting around

Transport charter is expensive, about 100,000 rp a day for cars or jeeps, and 25,000 to 30,000 rp a day for motorcycles. Use a map, and be explicit about where you wish to go, or go solo.

There are regular bemos between Melak and Tering, the only decent road in the area. The fare is 1500 rp to Sekolat Darat, 5000 rp to Tering (one hour) and 10,000 rp to the gates of the big gold mine, PT Kem.

Boats from Samarinda leave for the 325-km trip at 9 am and arrive in Melak at around 10 am the next day. The fare is 8000 rp per person. The fare back to Muara Muntai is 5000 rp.

Long Iram

Long Iram is often the end of the line for many would-be explorers because of river conditions or lack of time. Get off at the floating cafe on the east bank, climb to the main road, turn right and wander down to the *Penginapan Wahtu,* Jalan Soewondo 57 (look for the tiny sign opposite the double-storey shops). Clean rooms and a good breakfast costs 7500 rp per person.

For the best food on the Mahakam, eat at *Warung Jawa Timur.* Ignore the menu. Dinner is whatever's on the stove, perhaps a curry of jackfruit and pumpkin, rice and the fattest, juiciest chicken anywhere in the tropics for 3000 rp.

Long Iram is a pleasant, quiet village with a few colonial buildings and it's an easy walk through market gardens to Tering. Go north along Jalan Soewondo, turn right at the path to the police station, and walk on over pretty bridges to **Danau Gap**, three km away. Hire or borrow a canoe to explore the lake – there are lots of monkeys. Continue to Tering Lama, and see its magnificent new church at the eastern end of town. Cross the river by

Places to Stay

There are three losmen in Melak, each as good as the next, and all charging 5000 rp per person. *Penginapan Rahmat Abadi*, Jalan Piere Tendean, is the most foreigner-friendly place, and close to the dock. *Penginapan Bahagia* is deserted, clean and overlooks the dock. *Penginapan Flamboyan* faces the river about 100 metres upstream from the dock.

In Eheng, you may be allowed to stay in the longhouse.

In the village of Barong Tongkok, there is the spartan *Wisma Orchid* costing 5000 rp per person.

Places to Eat

In Melak, the riverside *Warung Pangkalan* serves good sate. The owner does a brisk trade in beer on ice, and was setting up an extra stall on the bank opposite the warung. Warungs by the market sell coffee with hot pancakes and cakes for breakfast, and there are good rice dishes at the nameless warung opposite the Rahmat Abadi.

Things to Buy

There are great rattan bags, hats, baskets etc for 10,000 to 30,000 rp, depending on size

cat (canoe, 500 rp), or catch a riverboat back to Long Iram (1000 rp).

A few intrepid travellers have trekked overland west of Long Iram (a week to 10 days) to a tributary of the Sungai Barito in Central Kalimantan, and from there worked their way downriver to South Kalimantan and Banjarmasin. There is a logging road from nearby Tering to Tanjung Balai in Central Kalimantan. You may be able to hitch a ride to Tanjung Balai, and from there to Muara Teweh. From there regular longboats ply the Barito all the way to Banjarmasin.

Long Iram is 409 km from Samarinda, 1½ days by riverboat. The fare is usually 10,000 rp.

Datah Bilang to Muara Merak

If conditions allow you to ferry upriver beyond Long Iram, places of interest include Datah Bilang, where there are two Bahau Dayak longhouses, one of which is heavily decorated. A reader has recommended the Dayak village of **Long Hubung**, 45 minutes north of Datah Bilang by motorised canoe (7500 rp per person). Yusram, the village head, welcomes visitors.

Between Datah Bilang and Long Bagun is **Rukun Damai**, surrounded by rainforest, and home to Kenyah people who migrated here from the Apokayan in 1973. Many still hold fast to their traditions. There are five Kenyah *lamin* (longhouses) including one 250 metres long.

Less than 25 km downstream is Muara Merak, a Punan settlement. There is good trekking in this area, especially along the Merak to the north-east. With a Punan guide hired in Muara Merak, you could trek overland east for three to four days to Tabang and then travel down the Belayan River to Kota Bangun, where you can catch a boat or bus back to Samarinda.

Long Bagun to Long Apari

Long Bagun is a longhouse settlement and the end of the line for regular longboat services from Samarinda along the Mahakam. The journey costs 15,000 to 20,000 rp and

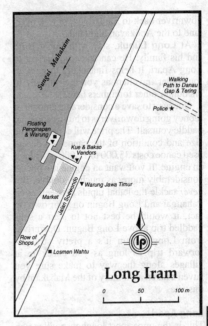

Long Iram

0   50   100 m

takes three days, conditions permitting. The boat docks in Long Iram one night each way while the crew sleeps, since night navigation can be tricky this far upriver.

From Long Bagun you must charter motorised canoes from village to village or trek through the forests. River conditions must be optimal because of river rapids between Long Bagun and the next major settlement, Long Pahangai. Under normal conditions, it's a one or two-day canoe trip from Long Bagun to Long Pahangai (40,000 rp), then another day to Long Apari. **Long Lunuk**, between Long Pahangai and Long Apari, is a good place from which to visit Kenyah villages.

Data Dawai

To start your trip from the top, fly to Data Dawai, an airstrip near Long Lunuk. DAS flies four times a week (36,000 rp each way), but you need to book weeks in advance. From there you can work your way

KALIMANTAN

downriver back to Samarinda, or trek overland to the Apokayan highlands.

At **Long Lunuk**, stay with Luhat Brith and his family. He can take you upriver to Long Apari. It helps financially to go with four other travellers as you are unlikely to encounter other foreigners here.

One way to save a considerable amount of money going downriver is to buy a canoe and paddle yourself. The price will depend on the size and condition of the canoe – a decent used canoe costs 35,000 to 75,000 rp without an engine. If you want an engine it will cost considerably more, as much as double. But *never* tackle the lethal rapids between Long Pahangai and Long Bagun on your own. In fact, it would be best not to start a self-paddled trip above Long Bagun. Downriver from Long Bagun it's a pretty straightforward trip as long as you check in at villages along the way to make sure you haven't taken a tributary of the Mahakam by mistake.

Long Apari

This is the uppermost longhouse village on the Mahakam, and it is beautiful. The longboat trip from Long Lunuk takes five to six hours. It's tiring and a stopover in Long Apari is recommended. Join the villagers for a night of dancing. Dinner is often greasy pig and bony fish – tasty supplements from the city make welcome presents. Long Apari is the stepping off point for treks to West Kalimantan.

KEDANG KEPALA RIVER

There are regular longboat services up the Kedang Kepala, which branches north off the Mahakam near Muara Kaman, from Samarinda to Muara Wahau. This trip takes three days and two nights and goes via the Kenyah and Bahau villages of Tanjung Manis, Long Noran and Long Segar. The boat fare from Samarinda to Muara Wahau is 16,500 rp. Nearby caves were the site of 5th-century Sanskrit finds, now in the museum at Tenggarong.

An alternative route from Samarinda to Berau is to take a boat north from Muara

Wahau to Miau Baru, stay with the Dutch-speaking kepala desa and his English-speaking son. Then travel by local school bus to a lumber camp four km north and hitch a ride on a jeep to the Dayak village of Marapun two hours away. From Marapun get a 12-hour boat ride down the Kelai to Tanjung Redeb/Berau.

SUNGAI BELAYAN

Another adventurous trip is up the Belayan River to Tabang. The Belayan branches north-west off the Mahakam at Kota Bangun and longboats take about three days to reach Tabang from Samarinda.

You can also reach Tabang on foot from the town of Muara Merak on the Mahakam. You can hire a Punan guide in either Tabang or Muara Merak to lead you north of Tabang into extensive rainforests that are nomadic Punan territory.

SUNGAI KAYAN

South of Tarakan is Tanjung Selor at the mouth of the mighty Kayan River. DAS flies from Samarinda to Tanjung Selor daily.

There are regular longboat services up the Kayan as far as the Kenyah villages of Mara I and Mara II, but a long section of rapids –

Kenyah godly mask of the Apo Kayan area

Kalimantan's wildest white water – further on prevents boats from reaching the headwaters of the Kayan in the Apokayan highlands.

DAS has a government-subsidised flight to Long Ampung in the Apokayan area four times a week for 36,000 rp. There is good trekking in the Apokayan headlands; you could also trek overland to the Mahakam headwaters from here in about a week with a guide from Long Ampung. The Kutai guide, Jailani (based in Samarinda) leads easy or vigorous treks to Dayak longhouses from Long Ampung.

DAYAK VILLAGES

Probably the best starting point for visits to inland Dayak villages is Samarinda. Longboats leave from here to ply the Mahakam, Kedang Kepala and Belayan rivers. DAS flies from here to Long Ampung, close to the mouth of the mighty Sungai Kayan.

There is also the relatively acculturated Kenyah Dayak village of **Pampang**, 26 km from Samarinda. You can travel there in a rented car or the yellow shared taxis departing from Samarinda's Segiri station.

Even those fluent in Indonesian will find guides a must in some areas. The drill is to introduce yourself to the camat or kepala desa, explain where you are trying to go, and ask for assistance. The money you pay for guides is one of the few opportunities many folk get to supplement their subsistence incomes, but if you arrive at harvest time or other busy periods, you might have trouble.

Your other option is to take a guide from Balikpapan or Samarinda. If you meet someone you like, then consider taking them with you. Even in easily accessible areas, it can be nice just to let someone else do the haggling, travel and other arrangements.

A good source of information about the Dayak areas in the interior is the Kutai guide Jailani, in Samarinda. He speaks English well and is very friendly and helpful. His information is free, but he can also serve as a guide at the scheduled government fee of 35,000 rp per day. Contact him through Hotel Senarga Indah, Jalan Sudirman 11, or PT Cisma, Jalan Awang Long.

Professional tour agencies in Balikpapan include Kaltim Adventure (☎ 33408) in Komplek Balikpapan Permai (ask to see Tour Manager Antoni), or PT Tomaco Tours (☎ 21747) in the Hotel Benakutai building,

KALIMANTAN

Life in a Longhouse

Many of Borneo's Dayak communities still live in communal longhouses – called *lamin* in East and West Kalimantan, *balai* in the south, and *betang* in Central Kalimantan. They are typically one room deep and up to 300 metres long with a series of self-contained apartments under one roof.

The apartments usually open on to a broad communal verandah which runs the length of the building or a central verandah between two rows of family quarters. The verandah is the place for village chores such as pounding rice and weaving, as well as the political and ceremonial centre of the village. Even in villages where individual housing is superseding longhouse life, everyone still meets in the longhouses for healing, harvest and other ceremonies.

Longhouses are built on wooden piles up to three metres high as protection against wild animals, flooding and, in the past, enemies. Stairs of notched logs leading to the house can be pulled in as needed and carved figures guard the doors from bad spirits. Domestic animals (usually pigs or chickens) are kept below the house.

During harvest and other busy periods, the longhouses are virtually empty as families migrate to their far-flung swidden plots. They tend to live in field huts until after the work is done. Occasionally longhouses are abandoned altogether as the search for arable land pushes villagers further and further afield. Religious and cultural schisms, death or disease can also divide or disperse longhouse communities.

After harvest, longhouse communities turn their attention to spiritual affairs. This is a festive period, which often includes long nights of drinking, dancing, playing cards and other nocturnal pleasures. If you visit during this period, expect to survive on minimal sleep. ■

Jalan P Antasari, Balikpapan. These agencies have good reputations for Mahakam and Kedang Kepala river trips. They have three and six-day tours going as far as Rukun Damai on the Mahakam and Tanjung Manis on the Kedang Kepala.

Rates start at about 882,000 rp per person with 10 or more on the tour, and include accommodation, river transport, meals, village performances and transport between Balikpapan and either Loa Janan or Tenggarong, the tours' starting points.

APOKAYAN

One of Jailani's most picturesque tours consists of the following itinerary: first a flight from Samarinda to Long Ampung on DAS, then a 2½-hour easy walk to stay overnight at the longhouse of Long Uro. The next day involves a 45-minute walk to the longhouse of Lidung Payau where you catch a boat back to Long Ampung for your flight back to Samarinda. Hardy travellers may include a difficult five-hour jungle walk from Lidung Payau to Long Sungai Barang. Nights are cold and longhouse verandahs can be hard, so pack a sleeping bag.

LONG BAWANG

Another inland option is the picturesque area around Long Bawang. Like the Apokayan, it is too far above the rapids to be of much interest to logging companies – yet. Like the Apokayan, there is a noticeable military presence, high prices for even the simplest commodities, and any presents from the city will be welcome – booze, toys, sweets, sugar, etc. DAS flies there from Tarakan for 72,000 rp.

Riverboat trips are a slow but very relaxing way to travel into the interior. Generally, you sleep on a covered deck with an unobstructed view of every sunset and sunrise. Every few hours, boats without cooking facilities pull in at a village dock and those who haven't brought their own food get off to eat in a warung.

Some boats have warungs on board and an upstairs sleeping area with mattresses and lockers. Either way it's a good idea to bring

snacks and plenty of bottled water. Also, take reading or writing material to help pass the time when you tire of viewing river life.

Fares vary according to conditions. When they're just right the fare is lower, and when the water level is too low or too high the fare is a bit higher. The boat dock in Samarinda is at the Sungai Kunjang pier outside town, reached by a taxi kota A for 500 rp.

BERAU (TANJUNG REDEB)

People use the names Berau and Tanjung Redeb interchangeably. Strictly speaking, Tanjung Redeb is the spit of land between Sungai Segan and Sungai Kelai, whereas Berau refers to the whole urban area. It doesn't seem to matter which you use. These days Berau is best known for its riverside coal fields downstream from the city.

Berau was once the seat of two minor kingdoms, Gunung Tabur with its palace *(kraton)* on the banks of the Segan, and Sambaliung with a palace on the Kelai. Both face each other across Tanjung Redeb. Gunung Tabur's moment in history came towards the end of WW II when the palace was mistaken for a Japanese military post and flattened by Allied bombers. The Sambaliung Palace was untouched, supposedly because of the spiritual power of cannon swaddled in the belfry.

The Gunung Tabur Palace was rebuilt, and is now the **Museum Batiwakkal**. It contains a few relics, including an old cannon found in the jungle by the very first raja. However its spiritual powers have been in doubt since the Allied bombing. Another back-room relic is the yellow birthing table in the next room, a slanted wooden bed.

In the bungalow beside the palace lives A Putri Kanik Sanipan, the daughter of the last raja of Gunung Tabur. She is a graceful woman in her 70s, speaks fluent Dutch and Indonesian, and occasionally takes tea with visitors and talks of the old days. Her collection of photographs includes many of the former palace, and of state occasions. Locals often ask her to bless their children, light incense and say prayers in the traditional

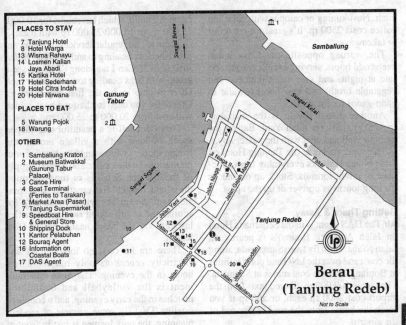

PLACES TO STAY
7 Tanjung Hotel
8 Hotel Warga
13 Wisma Rahayu
14 Losmen Kalian
   Jaya Abadi
15 Kartika Hotel
17 Hotel Sederhana
19 Hotel Citra Indah
20 Hotel Nirwana

PLACES TO EAT
5 Warung Pojok
18 Warung

OTHER
1 Sambaliung Kraton
2 Museum Batiwakkal
  (Gunung Tabur
  Palace)
3 Canoe Hire
4 Boat Terminal
  (Ferries to Tarakan)
6 Market Area (Pasar)
7 Tanjung Supermarket
9 Speedboat Hire
  & General Store
10 Shipping Dock
11 Kantor Pelabuhan
12 Bouraq Agent
16 Information on
   Coastal Boats
17 DAS Agent

Berau
(Tanjung Redeb)

Not to Scale

Gunung Tabur way. Get there by regular canoe ferry (300 rp).

The **Sambaliung Kraton** is now a private residence, occupied by the grandson of the last raja and his relatives. It is an old building with loads of character, and a belfry which once overlooked the palace grounds. There are photographs of the royal cemetery at Batu Putih, 48 km from Talisayan.

Places to Stay

Hotel Citra Indah, Jalan Soetomo, is a cavernous place built in the former Soviet style. Large clean rooms cost from 10,000/12,500 rp with shared mandi, 12,500/13,500 rp with private mandi, ranging up to 36,000/39,000 rp with air-con and TV. The staff are friendly.

Kalian Jaya Abadi, Jalan Antasari, is a tourist-friendly place with basic accommodation for 7500 rp per person, with bath.

Hotel Sederhana, Jalan Antasari, has old losmen rooms from 12,000 rp, and a much brighter hotel section with rooms from 15,000 rp plus tax, or 25,000 rp with air-con. The helpful Pak Suhartono speaks English and seems to know the boat schedules.

Hotel Nirwana (☎ 21893), Jalan Aminuddin 715, is a fair way out but the staff are eager to help. Rates are 10,500/17,500 rp.

Wisma Rahayu, Jalan Antasari, looks much nicer from the inside than out. Room rates cost from 7500 to 20,000 rp. *Tanjung Hotel & Supermarket*, Jalan Niaga II, focuses more on its grocery lines than guests. Singles/doubles are 7500/11,000 rp. *Hotel & Rumah Makan Warga* on the same street is better, with singles/doubles from 10,000/15,000 rp.

Kartika, Jalan Antasari, is unhelpful, with doubles for 10,000 rp. *Herlina* is a little way out of town, more expensive but much nicer.

Places to Eat

The warung at Jalan Yani 16, between Toko Medan Raya and Toko Logam Murni, has superb rice, curries and homemade roti and

KALIMANTAN

kueh. Nasi kuning or campur with cake and coffee costs 2500 rp. It's great for breakfast or takeaways.

The warung opposite the Citra Indah keeps odd hours, serving excellent soup and sate at night, and *soto ayam* (chicken and vegetable broth) and nasi pecel (similar to gado-gado) for breakfast.

Another dinner option is the martabak (pancake) stalls on Jalan Yani. Eat on the harbour wall and chat with the passers-by.

The supermarket at the Tanjung Hotel on Jalan Niaga II stocks everything from chocolate to infant formula. Stock up on snacks for long journeys upriver or up the coast.

Getting There & Away

Air The DAS agent is in the Sederhana Hotel on Jalan Antasari. Bouraq's is nearby on Jalan Niaga. Both fly from Samarinda, along the coast and over the LNG and port facilities at Bontang, and the coal mines at Sanggata. The fare is 109,000 rp. Shared taxis from the airport cost 2000 rp each, or 500 rp if you catch the bemo from the road at the end of the airstrip.

Boat Passenger boats to Tanjung Batu (10,500 rp; four hours) and on to Tarakan (20,000 rp) leave daily. You buy your tickets on the boat. There are also weekly boats to Samarinda. Services and departure times are advertised on the boards outside the small dock. From Tanjung Batu, hitch a lift with a local boat going to Pulau Derawan. To charter a speedboat direct from Berau to the dive resort at Pulau Derawan costs 350,000 rp. Ask at the Citra Indah wartel or at Toko Tiga Berlian.

PULAU DERAWAN

Derawan Island is part of the Sangalaki Archipelago, a marine reserve off Tanjung Batu between Berau and Tarakan. There are dive resorts on Derawan and Sangalaki islands, and their popularity is growing despite their isolation.

The daily Berau-Tarakan boat drops passengers at Tanjung Batu, a fishing village with a couple of warung and a new losmen, *Losmen Famili,* which has rooms for 10,000/15,000 rp, or 15,000/25,000 rp with meals.

There are no regular services to Derawan, just fisherfolk heading to and fro. Ask *'Boleh saya ikut?'* ('Can I tag along?') if you see a group with bags heading towards either pier. Offer to chip in for the fuel, say 5000 rp. Otherwise you need to charter a boat, which will cost from 20,000 to 25,000 rp.

Derawan itself is a beautiful tear-shaped speck of land with a village around the fringe, spotless white-sand beaches, coconut plantations in the centre and a good supply of fresh water. Schools of tuna surround the island, tongkol fish create feeding frenzies near the surface where birds dive for spoils, and at full moon rare green turtles lay eggs on the beach near the BMI Dive Resort.

There are no cars, no motorcycles and electricity generators only run for a few hours in the evening. The main entertainment is the volleyball and badminton matches in the early evening, and a couple of satellite TVs. By some miracle of modern planning, the only losmen is just in front of the only mosque, but the dawn call to prayer is a tame affair, thanks to the absence of electricity for the amplifier.

The island's main attractions, snorkelling and diving, are conducted from BMI Dive Resort. There is a Bali dive master, but his safety drills are a bit casual. The charge for two dives off Pulau Derawan, plus tanks and equipment hire, is 165,000 rp. Two dives off Pulau Sangalaki and other outer islands costs 308,000 rp.

There is also a small dive cottage with equipment on Sangalaki run by Ron Holland. Again, this isn't a budget option but the reefs in this area are reputedly spectacular. At full moon, turtles lay eggs on the beach.

Other islands in the group include **Karaban**, which has a lake in the centre, caves with swallows' nests and a population of huge coconut crabs. Another is **Maratua**, which has 2100 people in four villages, set around a lagoon. There's also a military patrol stationed here to keep 'pirates' in check.

Places to Stay & Eat

Losmen Ilham, at the western end of the island, is run by Pak Herman & Ibu Suryati who charge 15,000/20,000 rp, plus 3500 rp per person for generous serves of grilled fish. Pak Herman itemises everything, charging 800 rp for coffee, etc. He also has a karaoke machine, and adores singing at ear-splitting volumes.

BMI Dive Resort charges 55,000/110,000 rp a night for rooms in a resort still under construction, plus 22,000 rp if you use the air-con. Its new bar has an unbeatable location, set at the end of a pier, around a sea pool.

The other option is to stay with the kepala desa, a friendly man with a spare room, for around 5000 to 10,000 rp a night.

The only commercial eateries are at the losmen and dive resort. There is a tiny warung near the dive resort which serves roti and kueh in the morning. Fruit, other than coconuts, is scarce and expensive.

TARAKAN

Just a stepping stone to other places, Tarakan is an island town close to the Sabah border. It was the site of bloody fighting between Australians and Japanese at the end of WW II. Unless you're really enthusiastic about Japanese blockhouses, or want to try exiting Indonesia to Sabah, there's little of interest. It's not a bad town, just dull. Some of the houses have old Japanese cannon shells painted silver and planted in their front yards like garden gnomes.

The battle at Tarakan was one of a series of battles fought by Australian soldiers in Indonesia and New Guinea from mid-1944 onwards. There's an interesting argument put forward by Peter Charlton in *The Unnecessary War – Island Campaigns of the South-West Pacific 1944-45* (MacMillan, Australia, 1983) that these battles had no value in the defeat of the Japanese. By that time the Japanese in Indonesia were already effectively defeated, reluctant to fight, incapable of being either evacuated or reinforced, and fought only when they were forced to.

The capture of Tarakan (after six weeks of

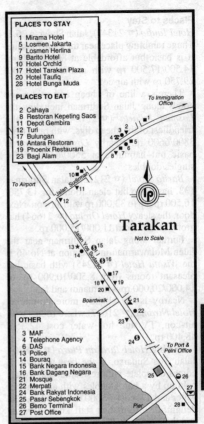

fighting and the deaths of 235 Australians) was carried out to establish an air base which was never used. After the Tarakan operation Indonesia was effectively bypassed, yet in July 1945 an assault was made on Balikpapan. This last large amphibious landing of the war managed to secure a beach, a disused oil refinery, a couple of unnecessary airfields and the deaths of 229 Australians.

Information

Money Bank Dagang Negara on Jalan Yos Sudarso will change US travellers' cheques and currency.

Places to Stay
Hotel Taufiq (☎ 21347), Jalan Sudarso 26, is a huge rambling place near the main mosque. It is basic but affordable at 8000/9000 rp, 14,500/17,500 rp with mandi, or 28,500/29,750 rp with air-con.

There's a line of cheap and mid-range hotels along Jalan Sudirman including the *Losmen Jakarta* (☎ 21704) at 112, the friendliest of the cheap digs, with rates from 3800/6600 rp. Nearby *Losmen Herlina* is basic but habitable at 5500/6400 rp for singles/doubles.

Barito Hotel (☎ 21212), Jalan Sudirman 133, has basic but clean rooms for 13,750/16,500 rp, up to 33,000 rp with air-con. Next door, the sleazy *Hotel Orchid* (☎ 21664) has grotty rooms from 11,000/15,000 rp.

Further along Jalan Sudirman near the Jalan Mulawarman intersection at No 46 is the *Wisata Hotel* (☎ 21245) with basic but pleasant rooms from 8,500/10,900 rp, or 14,000/20,000 rp with mandi and fan.

Nearby is the slightly more up-market *Hotel Nirama* (☎ 21637) where rooms with air-con, TV and hot water cost 42,350/48,400 rp.

The big *Hotel Tarakan Plaza* (☎ 21870), Jalan Yos Sudarso, is the best in town. It comes complete with restaurant and expats held up by a bar. Doubles with air-con, hot water and TV cost 77,000 to 99,000 rp. The delightful, informative staff know Tarakan and the interior well; ask for Yusuman.

Further down Jalan Yos Sudarso towards the Pelni harbour is the *Hotel Bunga Muda* (☎ 21349) at No 78, a newish concrete block with fairly clean rooms at 8500/11,000 rp.

Places to Eat
There is a good choice of cafes and mobile warungs selling fried rice and noodles at night. The lane off Jalan Sudarso near Jalan Sudirman has a wide choice after dark.

Turi on the corner of Sudirman and Sudarso is the popular choice for ikan bakar (barbecued fish), a Tarakan favourite. *Antara* and *Bagi Alam* are the other good ikan bakar places.

Rumah Makan Cahaya on Jalan Sudirman opposite the Losmen Jakarta is pretty good; the menu includes octopus, cap cai (fried vegetables), and nasi goreng. *Phoenix* in Jalan Yos Sudarso is another good choice for Chinese.

Restoran Kepeting Saos, near Losmen Herlina on Jalan Sudirman, specialises in crab dishes, and does them well.

At night the happening place is *Depot Theola* on Jalan Sudirman, where the local speciality, *nasi lalap* – battered, fried chunks of chicken served with rice and soup, is served. It also serves cold beer, ice cream, fruit juices and *jamu* (medicinal, herbal) drinks. There are only one or two tables downstairs, but there's an upstairs area with several more.

The *Nirwana* on the airport side of Jalan Sudarso has OK alfresco dining, but most patrons come here after 11 pm for the bar, disco and other diversions.

If you are craving for different food, try the *Bulungan Restoran* in the Tarakan Plaza Hotel. Its impressive array of Chinese banquet food is very tasty.

Getting There & Away
Air Sempati, Bouraq, DAS or Merpati all fly to Tarakan from Balikpapan or Samarinda. All airline flights from Tarakan to Balikpapan connect with onward flights across Indonesia and internationally.

In Tarakan, Sempati (☎ 21870) is in the Tarakan Plaza on Jalan Yos Sudarso. Merpati (☎ 21911) is at Jalan Yos Sudarso 10. Bouraq (☎ 21248) is at Jalan Yos Sudarso 9B, across from the Tarakan Theatre. DAS (☎ 51612), at Jalan Sudirman 9, has useful flights inland, as does MAF (☎ 51011), the missionary airline in the tax building at Jalan Sudirman 133. See the Kalimantan Airfares Chart in the Getting Around section at the start of this chapter for routes and fares.

Boat The Pelni office is at the main port – take a colt almost to the end of Jalan Yos Sudarso. The Pelni ship *Tidar* calls into Tarakan on its regular Pantoloan-Balikpapan-Pare Pare-Surabaya run. There's another

Pelni boat, the *Leuser*, which goes straight from Toli Toli to Nunukan and Tawau.

From Tarakan you can catch boats to other parts of East Kalimantan. There are daily boats to Berau from the pier near Pasar Sebengkok. Other longboat destinations include: Tanjung Selor (5000 rp, or 10,000 rp by speedboat); Nunukan (15,000 rp, or 25,000 to 30,000 rp by speedboat) and Pulau Bunju (7000 rp). There are also weekly boats to Toli Toli.

Getting Around

To/From the Airport Taxis (3000 rp) or chartered bemo (1000 rp) are your only option from town to the airport (five km) for those dawn flights. At all other times, bemos pass the terminal gate about 200 metres from the terminal, and can get you to and from town in 10 minutes for 300 rp.

Colt Transport around town is by colt, which cut a circular route via Jalan Sudirman and

Jalan Yos Sudarso. A 300 rp flat rate gets you anywhere.

TARAKAN TO MALAYSIA

For boats on to Tawau in the east Malaysian state of Sabah, go to Pelabuhan Tarakan. Longboats leave daily at around 9 am and arrive in Nunukan 12 hours later for 15,000 rp per person. In **Nunukan** you can catch a speedboat to Tawau for 21,000 rp – it takes about four hours. You can also spend the night at the *Losmen Nunukan* for 5000 rp and get a speedboat the next day.

There is an Indonesian immigration office in Nunukan where you must finalise your paperwork. Note that if you got a two-month tourist visa on arrival in Indonesia, you will need an exit permit from the immigration office in Jakarta. If you have a one-month tourist visa before coming to Indonesia, Nunakan can stamp your passport without an exit permit from Jakarta. Some travellers report an easy exit via this route, but most get turned back.

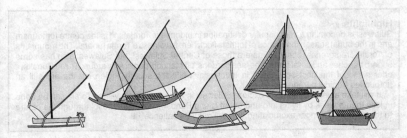

Sulawesi

The strangely contorted island of Sulawesi (formerly Celebes) sprawls across the sea between Borneo and Maluku. It was first referred to as Celebes by the Portuguese but the origins of the name are unclear. One derivation is from the Bugis *selihe* or *selire*, meaning 'sea current' or from *si-lebih*, meaning 'more islands'. Others say Celebes could be a corruption of *Klabat*, the name of the volcano which towers over Minahasa in the north. The modern name Sulawesi (and possibly Celebes too) seems to come from *sula* (island) *besi* (iron), a reference to the iron deposits around Lake Matano, the richest in South-East Asia.

Protected by mountains and walled in by thick jungle, the interior of the island has provided a refuge for some of Indonesia's earliest inhabitants, some of whom have managed to preserve elements of their idio-syncratic cultures well into the 20th century. The Makassarese and Bugis of the south-west peninsula and the Christian Minahasans of the far north are the dominant groups of Sulawesi. They have also had the most contact with the West, but it's the Christian-animist Toraja, of the Tanatoraja district of the central highlands, who attract large numbers of visitors every year.

Other minorities, particularly Bajau sea nomads, have played an integral role in the island's history. The rise of Gowa – Sula-wesi's first major power – from the mid-16th century was partly due to its trading alliance with the Bajau. The Bajau supplied much-sought after sea produce, especially trepang (sea cucumbers; a Chinese delicacy), tor-toiseshell, birds' nests and pearl, attracting international traders to Gowa's capital Makassar.

Highlights

Sulawesi is becoming a very popular destination in Indonesia. Torajaland is the centre for tourism and in the burial season thousands of tourists flock here to witness a Toraja funeral. The mountains of Toraja are serenely beautiful, as are those of Central Sulawesi, but Sulawesi also has some superb beaches and coral reefs. The 'sea gardens' off Manado, particularly around Pulau Bunaken, offer some of the best snorkelling in Indonesia, while the superb Togian islands are still an untouched tropical paradise.

It will take at least a month to explore Sulawesi in any depth, but a visit to Toraja can be done in less than a week by flying into and out of Ujung Pandang. Overland travel through the centre to the north is no longer excruciating, but still requires patience. ■

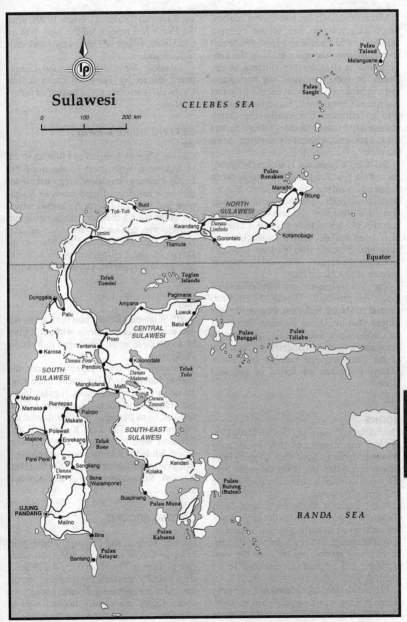

Sulawesi

0   100   200 km

CELEBES SEA

Equator

Teluk Tomini

NORTH SULAWESI

CENTRAL SULAWESI

SOUTH SULAWESI

SOUTH-EAST SULAWESI

BANDA SEA

Pulau Talaud
Melanguane

Pulau Sangir

Pulau Bunaken
Manado
Bitung
Kotamobagu

Buol
Toli-Toli
Tomini
Kwandang
Danau Limboto
Gorontalo
Tilamuta

Donggala
Palu
Ampana
Pagimana
Luwuk
Batui
Toglan Islands

Pulau Banggai
Pulau Taliabu

Poso
Tentena
Karosa
Danau Poso
Pendolo
Kolonodale
Teluk Tolo
Mangkutana
Mafili
Danau Matano
Danau Towuti

Mamuju
Mamasa
Rantepao
Palopo
Makale
Polewali
Majene
Enrekang
Teluk Bone

Pare Pare
Sengkang
Kendari
Danau Tempe
Bone (Watampone)
Kolaka

UJUNG PANDANG
Malino
Buapinang
Pulau Muna
Pulau Butung (Buton)

Bira
Benteng
Pulau Selayar
Pulau Kabaena

SULAWESI

Makassar quickly became known as a cosmopolitan, tolerant and secure entrepot which allowed traders to bypass the Dutch monopoly over the spice trade in the east. This was a considerable concern to the Dutch. In 1660 they sunk six Portuguese ships in Makassar Harbour, captured the fort and forced Gowa's ruler, Sultan Hasanuddin, into an alliance. Eventually, the Dutch managed to exclude all other foreign traders from Makassar, effectively shutting down the port.

Sulawesi's landscape is strikingly beautiful and the island, a transition zone between Asian and Australian fauna, is home to some peculiar animals. The *babirusa*, or 'pigdeer', has long legs and tusks which curve upwards like horns, the rare *anoa* is a metre-high dwarf buffalo, there's the shy but very cute bear cuscus, and various primates including the tarsier – the world's smallest primate at just 10 cm long.

The 227,000-sq-km territory is divided into four provinces: South, South-East, Central and North Sulawesi. Few visitors get further than the Ujung Pandang-Tanatoraja area in the south. Sulawesi's 12 million residents speak dozens of dialects – at least two of the nine language families in western Malayo-Polynesia are found in Sulawesi alone.

BOOKS

The Ecology of Sulawesi (Gadjah Mada University Press, Yogyakarta, 1987) by Anthony Whitten, Muslimin Mustafa & Gregory Henderson is a dated but comprehensive base reference on land and marine ecologies in and around Sulawesi.

Nigel Barley's *Not a Hazardous Sport* (Penguin, London, 1988) is the larger-than-life account of an anthropologist's 'plunge' into Tanatoraja. Barley's irreverent, self-depreciatory humour makes even the most mundane and frustrating experience sound like fun.

White Stranger – Six Moons in Celebes by Harry Wilcox was first published in 1949. This British army officer spent six months in the Rantepao district in the late 1940s, after the Dutch had reoccupied the area. Wilcox lived in the village of Labo to the south-east of Rantepao.

Sulawesi: The Celebes (Periplus, Singapore), edited by Toby Volkman & Ian Caldwell, is another good source of information.

GETTING THERE & AWAY

Air

Garuda, Merpati, Sempati and Bouraq all fly to Sulawesi, with most connections via Ujung Pandang. Singapore's regional carrier Silk now has direct flights between Singapore and Manado (North Sulawesi) which are faster but no cheaper than Sempati and Garuda who service this route via Jakarta. Bouraq flies Balikpapan-Palu-Manado to Davao in the Philippines twice a week. Manado is an approved gateway for visa-free tourists.

Sea

North Sulawesi's Bitung port is an approved gateway to enter Indonesia without a visa. However there are no ferry services from the Philippines.

Sulawesi's ferry connections are the best in Indonesia. At last count, there were 10 or so Pelni liners doing regular loops out of Java. Most call at Ujung Pandang, and five sail on to Bitung in North Sulawesi via various routes. The East Kalimantan and Sulawesi west coast ports are well serviced, while the KM *Awu* does a useful hop along eastern Sulawesi, stopping at Bau Bau, Kendari, Kolonodale, Luwuk and Kwandang.

GETTING AROUND

Air

Garuda, Sempati and Bouraq fly the busier, more profitable routes, and Merpati takes care of the rest. The Missionary Air Fellowship (MAF) services the interior, going anywhere the commercial carriers won't. Its cheap flights are usually booked well in advance.

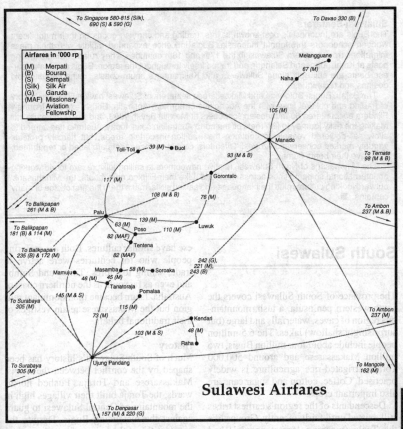

Sulawesi Airfares

Airfares in '000 rp

(M)	Merpati
(B)	Bouraq
(S)	Sempati
(Silk)	Silk Air
(G)	Garuda
(MAF)	Missionary Aviation Fellowship

Road

South Sulawesi (the south-western peninsula) has the best land transport, while nearby South-East Sulawesi has the worst and is seldom visited by tourists. The Trans-Sulawesi Highway links Ujung Pandang to Manado, but 'highway' is still too kind a word for the butt-jarring track between Palu and Gorontalo. Bitumen and bridges have greatly improved the rest of the highway, however landslides often block the mountainous stretch south of Pendolo, extending an otherwise tolerable marathon by up to 24 hours.

Boat

Pelni ships stop at all the big ports, plus there are a number of smaller boats which allow you to skirt some of the harder sections. These include regular ferries across Tomini Bay from Poso via the Togian islands to Gorontalo, and another across Bone Bay from Bajoe to Kolaka. There are boats along the western and northern coasts between Palu and Manado that call in at Toli-Toli, Paleleh and Kwandang, and others from Manado to Ternate, and to the Sangihe-Talaud group.

Sulawesi Seafarers

The Bugis are Indonesia's best-known sailors, trading and carrying goods on their magnificent wooden schooners throughout Indonesia. Bugis influence expanded rapidly with their mass migrations from southern Sulawesi in the 17th and 18th centuries. They ruled strategic trading posts at Kutai, Johor and Selangor, and traded freely throughout the region. Bugis and Makassarese boats are still built along Sulawesi's and Kalimantan's south coasts, using centuries-old designs and techniques.

The Bajau, Bugis, Butonese and Makassarese seafarers of Sulawesi have a 500-year history of trading and cultural links with the Aborigines of northern Australia. British explorer Matthew Flinders encountered 60 Indonesian schooners at Melville Bay in 1803, and many more are still making the risky journey to fish reefs off the north Australian coast today. Australia has agreed to allow sail-powered vessels to continue the tradition in certain areas, but fiercely protects vaguely-marked conservation zones. 'Offenders' caught on these reefs are jailed or repatriated, and have their boats burnt.

The Minahasans of North Sulawesi, relative newcomers to sailing folklore, are found working on international shipping lines across the world. Like their Filipino neighbours, the Minahasans' outward looking culture, plus their language and sailing skills, make them the first choice of many captains. ■

South Sulawesi

The province of South Sulawesi covers the south-western peninsula, a lush, mountainous region of caves, waterfalls and large (but surprisingly shallow) lakes. The 6.5 million people include about four million Bugis, two million Makassarese and around 500,000 Toraja. Irrigated-rice agriculture is widely practised. Coffee, cotton and sugar cane are also important crops.

Descendants of the region's earliest tribes still existed until fairly recently. Groups like the Toala (meaning 'forest people') had dwindled to a couple of villages near Maros by the 1930s and have now vanished. Other tribes have been subsumed by the dominant groups.

Torajan mythology suggests that their ancestors came by boat from the south, sailed up the Sadan River and initially dwelled in the Enrekang region, before being pushed into the mountains by the arrival of other groups.

The Bugis and the Makassarese are the main groups on the coast. The Makassarese are concentrated in the southern tip, centred on the port of Makassar (now known as Ujung Pandang). The Bugis and Makassarese have similar cultures. Both are seafaring people who for centuries were active in trade, sailing to Flores, Timor and Sumba and even as far south as the northern coast of Australia. Islam became their dominant religion but the Makassarese retain vestiges of their traditional beliefs.

History

Much of South Sulawesi's history has been shaped by the conflict between the Bugis, Makassarese and Toraja. Pushed northwards, the Toraja built their villages high in the mountains of Central Sulawesi to guard against the marauding Bugis. Despite the constant threat they never formed a united front against the common enemy. Complicating the story was the continuing rivalry between the Bugis and the Makassarese.

The southern peninsula was divided into petty kingdoms, the most powerful being the Makassarese kingdom of Gowa (centred on the port of Makassar) and the Bugis kingdom of Bone. Around 1530, before its conversion to Islam, Gowa started to expand. By the mid-16th century it had established itself at the head of a major trading bloc in eastern Indonesia. The king of Gowa adopted Islam in 1605 and between 1608 and 1611 Gowa attacked and subdued Bone, spreading Islam to the whole Bugis-Makassarese area.

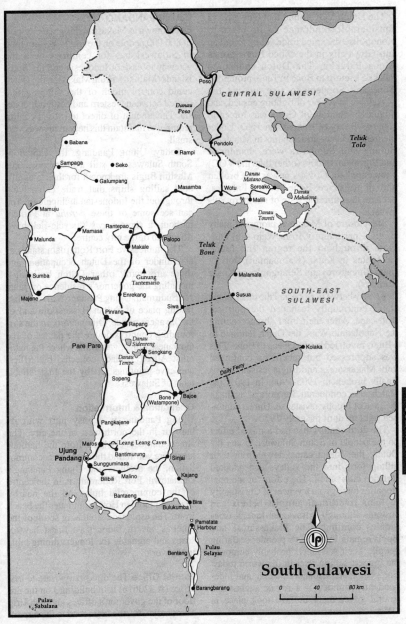

South Sulawesi

The Dutch VOC found that Gowa was a considerable hindrance to its plans to monopolise the spice trade. They found an anti-Gowa ally in the exiled Bugis prince Arung Palakka. The Dutch sponsored Palakka's return to Bone in 1666, prompting Bone and Soppeng to rise against the Makassarese. A year of fighting ensued, and Sultan Hasanuddin of Gowa was forced to sign the Treaty of Bungaya in 1667. Under the treaty, Makassarese claims to Minahasa, Butung and Sumbawa were abandoned and European traders (other than the VOC) were expelled. Gowa's power was broken and in its place Bone, under Palakka, became the supreme state of southern Sulawesi.

The closure of Makassar prompted many Bugis – particularly from Wajo – to emigrate throughout the region and found sultanates in Kutai (Kalimantan), Johore (near Singapore) and Selangor (near Kuala Lumpur).

Rivalry between Bone and the other Bugis states continually reshaped the political landscape. After their brief absence during the Napoleonic Wars, the Dutch returned to a Bugis revolt led by the Queen of Bone. This was suppressed but rebellions continued until Makassarese and Bugis resistance was finally broken in 1905-1906. In 1905, the Dutch also conquered Tanatoraja, again in the face of bloody resistance. Unrest continued right up until the early 1930s.

The 20th century has had a mixed effect on the people of South Sulawesi. Under the Dutch, the Toraja came down from their hilltop forts into the valleys and adopted wet-rice cultivation. The efforts of the missionaries have given a veneer of Christianity to their traditional animist beliefs and customs although extravagant funeral ceremonies continue. The Makassarese and Bugis remain Indonesia's premier seafaring people. Their schooners probably comprise the biggest sailing fleet in the world today. The people are staunchly Islamic and independently minded – a revolt against the central government in Java took place in 1957.

UJUNG PANDANG

Once known as Makassar, this great city-port of 800,000 people on the south-western limb of Sulawesi has for centuries been the gateway to eastern Indonesia and the Spice Islands (Maluku). From Makassar, the Dutch could control much of the shipping that passed between western and eastern Indonesia. The amount of direct territorial control required to maintain this hegemony was very small.

Today, Ujung Pandang, the capital of South Sulawesi, is still a major port. The Muslim Bugis are known for their magnificent sailing ships that trade extensively throughout the Indonesian archipelago. You can see some of these *perahu* at Paotere harbour, a short *becak* (bicycle-rickshaw) ride north of the city centre.

The impressive Fort Rotterdam stands as a reminder of the Dutch occupation, and there are many other Dutch buildings, including the governor's residence on Jalan Jen Sudirman. Ujung Pandang is also the last resting place of Sultan Hasanuddin and the Javanese prince, Diponegoro. In the surrounding countryside are the palace of the Gowanese kings, waterfalls where the naturalist Alfred Wallace collected butterflies, and cave-paintings left by the first inhabitants of Sulawesi.

Orientation & Information

Ujung Pandang is a busy port with its harbour in the north-west of the city. The streets immediately back from the harbour are where you'll find the cheapest accommodation, the brothels and Ujung Pandang's Chinatown. Fort Rotterdam is in the centre of the commercial hub, and the nearby Makassar Golden Hotel dominates the beach front. The esplanade stretching south of the hotel is one of Indonesia's finest hawker strips and arguably the longest dining table in the world.

Tourist Office The dinas pariwisata tourist office (☎ 320616) is in building J on the 3rd floor of the governor's offices on Jalan Urip Sumoharjo 269, the main road to the airport.

It is hard to find and isn't really geared to handle tourists off the street, but the staff are friendly and they have great maps of the city and region. There are also tourist office staff in Fort Rotterdam, and maps are available from the bigger hotels.

Money The Bank Rakyat Indonesia is on Jalan Jen Ahmad Yani near the Garuda office, Bank Negara Indonesia is on Jalan Nusantara, and there are moneychangers at the southern end of Jalan Martadinata. The moneychanger in the airport terminal gives the same rates as the banks and is open on Sunday.

Post & Telecommunications The post office is on the corner of Jalan Supratman and Jalan Slamet Riyadi, south-east of the fort. Wartel offices are at Jalan Balaikota 2, Jalan Veteran 28, Jalan Sulawesi and Jalan Kajaolabo. Many of the bigger hotels have card phones with international access, and the Marannu has a Home Country Direct-Dial phone for collect and credit calls.

Fort Rotterdam

One of the best preserved examples of Dutch architecture in Indonesia, Fort Rotterdam continues to guard the harbour of Ujung Pandang. A Gowanese fort dating back to 1545 once stood here, but that failed to keep out the Dutch. The original fort was rebuilt in Dutch style after the Treaty of Bungaya in 1667. Parts of the crumbling wall have been left pretty much as they were, an interesting comparison to the restored buildings. The fort now bears the rather more nationalistic title of Benteng (Fort) Ujung Pandang.

Of the two **museums** in the fort, the larger, more interesting one is on the right as you enter. It is open Tuesday to Thursday from 8 am to 1.30 pm, Friday from 8 to 10.30 am, weekends from 8 am to 12.30 pm and is closed Monday. It has an assortment of exhibits including rice bowls from Tanatoraja, kitchen tools, musical instruments and various costumes.

The museum on the left as you enter is in Speelman's House, completed in 1686 and the oldest of the fort buildings. The building itself is beautiful, but its shoddy display of stamps and coins hasn't changed for years.

Also within the walls of the fort are the National Archives, the Historical & Archaeological Institute and the Conservatory of Dance & Music.

Every Sunday, the **Benteng Conversation Club** turns the fort into a type of open university for students to practise their English. Dozens of youths meet around mid-morning, canvass a topic, then break up into small groups for sometimes heated debates – in English – on topics ranging from politics to shotgun weddings. It is a terrific way to meet people and hear what they have to say about a whole range of issues. Many are willing to show you around town.

Hasanuddin Tomb

On the outskirts of Ujung Pandang is the tomb of Sultan Hasanuddin (1629-70), ruler of the southern Sulawesi kingdom of Gowa mid-17th century. Hasanuddin is a revered figure among the Makassarese because of his struggle against the Dutch colonialists.

Outside the tomb compound is the **Tomanurung Stone**, on which the kings of Gowa were crowned. Legend has it that the Gowa kings were descended from a heavenly ancestor who first set foot on earth on this stone.

Katangka Mosque

About 15 minutes' walk from the tomb of Sultan Hasanuddin is the site of the Katangka Mosque. A mosque was first built here in 1603 – a modern building now occupies the site. More interesting is the attached cemetery with its large crypts, each containing several graves.

Diponegoro Tomb

Prince Diponegoro of Yogyakarta led the Java War of 1825-30 but his career as a rebel leader came to a sudden halt when he was tricked into going to the Dutch headquarters to negotiate peace. He was taken prisoner and exiled to Sulawesi. He spent the last 26 years of his life imprisoned in Fort Rotter-

SULAWESI

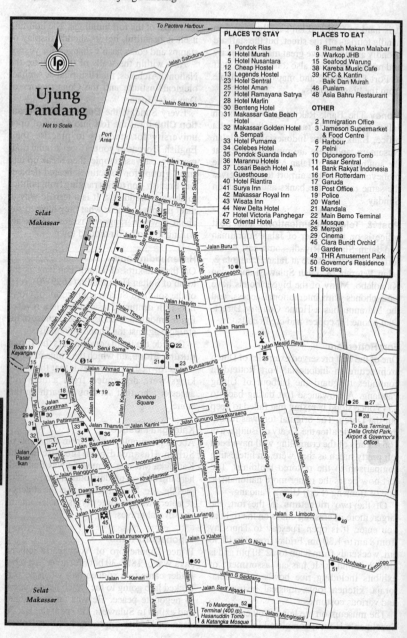

Ujung Pandang

Not to Scale

PLACES TO STAY
1 Pondok Rias
4 Hotel Murah
5 Hotel Nusantara
12 Cheap Hostel
13 Legends Hostel
23 Hotel Sentral
25 Hotel Aman
27 Hotel Ramayana Satrya
28 Hotel Marlin
30 Benteng Hotel
31 Makassar Gate Beach Hotel
32 Makassar Golden Hotel & Sempati
33 Hotel Purnama
34 Celebes Hotel
35 Pondok Suanda Indah
36 Marannu Hotels
37 Losari Beach Hotel & Guesthouse
40 Hotel Riantira
41 Surya Inn
42 Makassar Royal Inn
43 Wisata Inn
44 New Delta Hotel
47 Hotel Victoria Panghegar
52 Oriental Hotel

PLACES TO EAT
8 Rumah Makan Malabar
9 Warkop JHB
15 Seafood Warung
38 Kareba Music Cafe
39 KFC & Kantin Baik Dan Murah
46 Pualam
48 Asia Bahru Restaurant

OTHER
2 Immigration Office
3 Jameson Supermarket & Food Centre
6 Harbour
7 Pelni
10 Diponegoro Tomb
11 Pasar Sentral
14 Bank Rakyat Indonesia
16 Fort Rotterdam
17 Garuda
18 Post Office
19 Police
20 Wartel
21 Mandala
22 Main Bemo Terminal
24 Mosque
26 Merpati
29 Cinema
45 Clara Bundt Orchid Garden
49 THR Amusement Park
50 Governor's Residence
51 Bouraq

To Paotere Harbour

Port Area

Selat Makassar

Boats to Kayangan

Selat Makassar

Karebosi Square

To Bus Terminal, Delia Orchid Park, Airport & Governor's Office

To Malengera Terminal (400 rp), Hasanuddin Tomb & Katangka Mosque

SULAWESI

dam. His grave and monument can be seen in a small cemetery on Jalan Diponegoro.

Paotere Harbour
This anchorage is where the Bugis sailing ships berth, although the line-up is nowhere near as impressive as that at the Pasar Ikan in Jakarta.

Chinese Temples
You'll notice a fairly large number of ethnic Chinese Indonesians in Ujung Pandang. Both new and old Chinese temples can be seen along Jalan Sulawesi, but the most ornate is the brilliantly coloured building on the corner of Jalan Sulawesi and Jalan Serui Sama.

Clara Bundt Orchid Garden
This well-known orchid garden and shell collection is almost an institution of the city, hidden away in a compound at Jalan Mochtar Lufti 15. It's a little oasis in the middle of Ujung Pandang, founded by Clara Bundt as a hobby but subsequently developed into a business famous for its exotic hybrids. Some specimens grow up to five metres high. There's a huge collection of shells including dozens of giant clams. This is a private garden, but visitors are welcome. Admission is free.

Mr Bundt died in 1994, and there was some uncertainty about what the family would do with their inheritance, which includes a three-hectare orchid farm and hotel on the eastern edge of Ujung Pandang. Hopefully it will be preserved.

Nearby Islands
Samalona Island Samalona, a speck of land just off Ujung Pandang, is a popular spot for fishing and snorkelling. Legend Hostel and Kareba Cafe both run Sunday excursions there; the price depends on the number of people to share the costs.

Ceria Nugraha tours, Jalan Usman Jafur 9, also runs tours to Samalona, **Barranglompo** (a fishing and silversmith island), **Kudingakang Keke**, and other islands and sand bars. Or you can charter a boat from beside

the Kayangan jetty (opposite the fort) for 25,000 rp a day.

Kayangan Island This is more of a promenading circuit than a beach, and is not really a place to swim. The main interest lies in its Sunday discos and other 'entertainment'. Boats at the jetty opposite the fort ferry sightseers to and fro for 5000 rp per person.

Places to Stay – bottom end
Legend Hostel (☎ 320424), Jalan Jampea 5G, is cheap, clean and friendly with small doubles for 12,500 rp, and dorm beds for 5500 rp. There is a cafe-lounge, maps, advice, mountain bikes for hire and books of tips from other travellers.

Cheap Hostel (☎ 311922), on the same street at No 29, lets out rooms for 10,500 rp and dorm beds for 5000 rp. It is somewhat darker, quieter but just as friendly as Legend.

The *Hotel Ramayana Satrya* (☎ 442478), Jalan Gunung Bawakaraeng 121, has rooms from 14,000 rp, plus tax. It's clean, conveniently located and popular with travellers. There are also rooms from 22,000 rp with air-con and private bath. Take mosquito coils. Diagonally opposite the Ramayana is the similarly priced *Hotel Marlin*.

The *Hotel Riantira* (☎ 324133) at Jalan Ranggong 10 is looking pretty worn, but is quiet and has rooms for 15,000/18,000 rp, and the *Pondok Rias* (☎ 90112) at Jalan Bontomarannu 7 has singles/doubles for 15,000/17,500 rp, or 20,000/25,000 rp with air-con.

The other cheapies are far less impressive – many don't take foreigners. The bottom of the line is *Hotel Nusantara* (☎ 323163), Jalan Sarappo 103, east of the Pelni port, where singles go for 6000 rp. The rooms are hot, noisy little sweatboxes. Just across the road at No 60 is the slightly better appointed *Hotel Murah* (☎ 323101) with windowless rooms for 15,000 rp and 'boxes' from 7500 rp.

Rates for the dimly lit *Hotel Purnama* (☎ 323830) just south of the fort at Jalan Pattimura 3 start at 13,500/17,500 rp. *Benteng Hotel* (☎ 322172), Jalan Ujung Pandang

8, have the look and smell of old fruit on a hot day. Rooms start at 12,500 rp.

Places to Stay – middle

The choice of mid-range hotels is excellent, especially in the residential precinct south of the fort. *Pondok Suanda Indah* (☎ 312857) on Jalan Hasanuddin 12, opposite the Marannu, is highly recommended. This small, airy hotel is new, but has the feel of a classic colonial guesthouse. Singles/doubles start at 35,000/40,000 rp plus tax.

Wisata Inn (☎ 324344) just down the road at No 36 has small rooms out the back with a shared mandi for 25,000/35,000 rp, including tax. Better value are the bigger air-con rooms from 45,000/55,000 rp which over-look a courtyard garden. *New Delta Hotel* (☎ 312711), opposite the Wisata at No 43, is friendly and slightly cheaper at 42,500/55,000 rp plus tax.

The five-storey *Surya Inn* (☎ 327568), Jalan Daeng Tompo 3, offers breezy high-rise views of the city and harbour islands. Ground floor singles/doubles are 49,000/61,500 rp. Prices drop as you climb the stairs. Rooms are small, but comfortable.

The nearby *Makassar Royal Inn,* also on Jalan Daeng Tompo, has so-so economy air-con rooms for 34,500 rp, including breakfast, but you might need a map to find your way through the warren of extensions. Others range up to 74,500 rp.

On Jalan Sumoharjo 225, the road to the airport, is the *Hotel Karuwisi Indah* with basic rooms from 20,000 to 40,000 rp.

Makassar Cottages (☎ 873363), Jalan Dangko 52, are less conveniently located south of town, but offer top-value Balinese-style cottages for 24,500 to 37,500 rp. To get there take a Jalan Dangko mikrolet from the main (sentral) bemo terminal for 300 rp.

On the waterfront, there's the *Losari Beach Hotel* (☎ 326062), Jalan Penghibur 10, with singles from 69,000 to 80,000 rp, and doubles from 90,000 rp – the best views are reserved for the 210,000 rp suites. Try for a 'low season' discount, or check out the *Losari Beach Guesthouse* next door for 76,000 to 112,000 rp per room.

Delia Orchid Park (☎ 324111), at the Bundt family's three-hectare orchid farm six km east of the city, is roomy and comfort-able, with rooms from 40,000 to 87,500 rp, less discounts. It has a popular restaurant.

Hotel Afriat is a 10-minute walk from the airport terminal, facing the main road into Ujung Pandang, with rooms from 15,000 rp, or 19,000 rp with air-con.

Places to Stay – top end

Makassar Golden Hotel (☎ 314408; fax 320951) on the shore at Jalan Pasar Ikan 50 is an enormous five-star hotel with standard singles/doubles for 140,000/170,000 rp, plus tax. There are cottages for 310,000 rp and suites ranging up to 800,000 rp.

The *Makassar Gate Beach Hotel* (☎ 32-5791), a couple of doors down the road is similar value with rooms from 139,000/164,000 rp, and suites for 316,000 rp, includ-ing tax.

The recently renovated and extended *Marannu City Hotel* (☎ 315087), Jalan Sultan Hasanuddin 3, has rooms from 135,000/155,000 rp, and suites from 290,000 rp. The adjoining *Marannu Tower* starts at 155,000/175,000 rp and its suites start at 515,000 rp. The complex also has a small swimming pool open to the public for 5000 rp a day.

The classy new *Celebes Hotel* (☎ 32-0770), Jalan Hasanuddin 2, has rooms for 75,000/108,000 rp and 121,000/134,000 rp. Two young children can bunk in for the same price. Check the view from the rooftop res-taurant.

Hotel Victoria Panghegar (☎ 311556; fax 312468) Jalan Jen Sudirman 24, has standard rooms for 65,000/75,000 rp (plus tax) in its pavilion, and singles/doubles from 135,000/140,000 in the tower. Reggae bands play in a cafe overlooking the pool.

Places to Eat

Home to two of Indonesia's foremost sea-faring peoples, this place has good seafood in abundance. Barbecued fish and octopus are especially popular. Because of the size-able Chinese population, Ujung Pandang is also a good place for Chinese food. Other options include soto makassar, a soup made from buffalo innards.

The dozens of evening food trolleys along the waterfront south of the Makassar Golden Hotel make Pantai Losari the longest dining strip in Sulawesi, and also the best spot to watch Ujung Pandang's famous sunsets.

If the hustlers get too much for you, retreat to the *Minasa* or *Fajar* rooftop cafes south of the Kareba Cafe, or to the hotel at the southern end of Jalan Penghibur; the food is barely edible but the views are great.

There are good, cheap restaurants along Jalan Sulawesi. *Rumah Makan Malabar*, Jalan Sulawesi 264, specialises in Indian curries and martabak (pancakes). Try the goat head curry, cow tail soup, sate or the tastiest chicken curry east of Singapore.

The vegetable curry puffs at *Warkop JHB*, on the corner of Jalan Sulawesi and Jalan Lembah, are delicious. This sunny little cooperative also dishes up wanton noodles, nasi kuning and hot, strong filtered coffee. It's very busy on Sunday.

Asia Bahru Restaurant, near the corner of Jalan Latimojong and Jalan G Sala, specialises in seafood and when you order a big fish you get a very big fish! But the best and cheapest fish, as well as excellent fried duck, can be found at the warung opposite the fort.

Rumah Makan Ujung Pandang, Jalan Irian 42, is an air-con restaurant with a mixed Chinese and Indonesian menu, and very large servings.

Warungs around the THR amusement park serve good slabs of ikan bakar (barbe-cued fish) with cucumber, peanut sauce and rice.

The great food hunt might lead you to *KFC* or the *Kantin Baik dan Murah* (Good & Cheap Canteen) above the supermarket diagonally opposite the Marannu Tower Hotel. The supermarket downstairs panders to the tastes of homesick Westerners with Danish and Australian cheeses, imported chocolates, and other overpriced goodies. *Pizza Hut* sells expensive wedges of pizza out the front.

Things to Buy

Jalan Sombu Opu, a street to the south of the fort and one block east of the waterfront, has shops with great collections of jewellery and 'antiques'. Toko Kerajinam at No 20 is good for touristy souvenirs. CV Kanebo, on the Jalan Pattimura corner, has crafts from all over Indonesia, and the nearby Makassar Handicraft Centre is a good starting point for jewellery.

Ujung Pandang is supposed to be a good place for buying Kendari filigree silver jewellery. This is made in Ujung Pandang, not in Kendari on the south-eastern penin-sula of Sulawesi as the name might suggest. Again, Jalan Sombu Opu has a wide selec-tion and is a good starting point.

Other possible buys include Torajan hand-crafts, Chinese pottery, Makassarese brass work, silk cloth from Sengkang and Soppeng and mounted butterflies from Bantimurung.

Getting There & Away

Ujung Pandang is the gateway to southern Sulawesi and is connected to many other parts of Indonesia by air and sea. There are numerous buses to various destinations on the south-western peninsula, although for most people the next stop is the Tanatoraja district in the central highlands.

Air Shop around. There was an airfare war at the time of putting this chapter together, and agents were discounting by up to 30%. Check current prices with both carriers and agents. Garuda (☎ 322543), Jalan Slamet Riyadi 6, offers direct flights to Manado, Jakarta and Denpasar.

Merpati (☎ 24114), Jalan Gunung Bawa-karaeng 109, has the most comprehensive network within Sulawesi, particularly in the south and south-west. For destinations and indicative prices, see the Sulawesi Airfares Chart at the start of this chapter.

Bouraq (☎ 83039), Jalan Veteran Selatan 1, has useful Kalimantan-Sulawesi flights to Balikpapan, Banjarmasin, Palu, Samarinda and Ternate. Mandala, Jalan Jen Sudirman, flies to Jakarta, Surabaya and Ambon. Sem-pati (☎ 311556), in the Makassar Golden

SULAWESI

Hotel, also flies from Ujung Pandang to Denpasar and Surabaya, with connecting flights to Jakarta and other domestic destinations, plus Singapore, Perth and Taiwan.

Bus & Bemo The north-bound bus terminal is a few km out on Jalan Gowa Jaya, the airport road. You can get there by *pete-pete* (bemo) for 300 rp. South-bound buses leave from Malengera terminal. To get there, take a red pete-pete on Jalan Jen Sudirman for 400 rp.

From Ujung Pandang, most people head north to Pare Pare and inland to Rantepao, the centre of Tanatoraja. The road from Ujung Pandang to Rantepao is surfaced all the way, and Damri and Liman Express have the best buses. Most buses to Makale and Rantepao leave at around 8 am, plus there are buses in the afternoon and early evening. The 8000 rp trip takes 10 to 12 hours. Liman also has buses from Ujung Pandang to Palopo and Malili. A number of other companies run buses and minibuses to Tanatoraja and other parts of South Sulawesi.

An alternative path to Rantepao is via the south coast road to Bantaeng, Bulukumba and popular Bira. From Bulukumba, turn north to Bone (Watampone), and head further north to Palopo, or stop off at the highland silk areas of Sengkang and Soppeng.

Shared taxis to Pare Pare leave from Jalan Sarappo, in the same block as the Hotel Nusantara. There are also shared taxis to other places around Ujung Pandang.

Boat Pelni (☎ 27961), Jalan Martadinata 38 on the waterfront, has 10 modern liners which make regular stops in Ujung Pandang on their various loops around Indonesia. For full schedules, visit the Pelni office or the photocopy shop opposite Warkop JHB on Jalan Sulawesi.

Other possibilities include the cargo ships which leave Ujung Pandang for various Indonesian ports. For inter-island shipping, try PT PPSS at Jalan Martadinata 57. If they're not helpful, find out what ships are in port and where they're going, and bargain directly with the captains.

Getting Around

To/From the Airport Pete-petes to Ujung Pandang's Hasanuddin airport (22 km out of town) leave from the main terminal on Jalan Cokroaminoto. If you're staying at the Ramayana Hotel they run past the large intersection just east of the hotel.

A taxi from the airport to the city centre is 10,000 to 14,000 rp, or walk to the main road and catch a pete-pete to the city for 1000 rp.

Local Transport Ujung Pandang is too big to do much walking – you'll need becaks and pete-petes. The main pete-pete station is on Jalan Cokroaminoto and the standard fare is 300 rp.

Becak drivers kerb-crawl for potential passengers yet are hard bargainers – the shortest fare costs 500 rp. They are fearless drivers but its your life in the front line.

AROUND UJUNG PANDANG
Sungguminasa

Once the seat of the Sultan of Gowa, Sungguminasa is 11 km from Ujung Pandang. The former residence of the sultan is now the **Museum Ballalompoa** and houses a collection of artefacts similar to those in the Fort Rotterdam museums. Although the royal regalia, which includes a stone-studded gold crown, can be seen on request, it is the palace itself which is the real attraction. It is constructed of wood and raised on stilts. To get there take a pete-pete (300 rp) or Damri bus (200 rp) from the central station.

Bantimurung

About 45 km from Ujung Pandang, Bantimurung Falls are set amid lushly vegetated limestone cliffs. Bantimurung is crowded with Indonesian day-trippers on weekends and holidays; at other times it's a wonderful retreat from the congestion of Ujung Pandang. Entrance to the park costs 800 rp.

Past the 15-metre waterfall there's a **cave** at river level. Bring a flashlight to look inside. Scramble along the rocks past the waterfall and get onto the track, but you will encounter an admission gate where you must pay an additional 800 rp.

Dayak dancing, Tanjung Isuy, East Kalimantan (BD)

Top left: Diamond polishing, South Kalimantan (BD)
Top right: Wood cutter at a diamond mine, Cempaka, South Kalimantan (BD)
Bottom: Workers at a diamond mining site, Cempaka, South Kalimantan (BD)

There are many other caves in these cliffs but apart from the scenery the area is also famous for its numerous beautiful butterflies. The naturalist Alfred Wallace collected specimens here in the mid-1800s.

To get to Bantimurung, take a bemo from Ujung Pandang's central bemo terminal. The trip takes a bit over an hour. If you can't find a direct bemo then take one to Maros (1000 rp; one hour) and another from there for the rest of the way (500 rp; 30 minutes).

Leang Leang Caves

A few km before the Bantimurung turn-off is the turn-off for the Leang Leang Caves, noted for their ancient paintings. The paintings in Leang Pettae and Leang Peta Kere caves are images of human hands. The age of the paintings is unknown, but other relics from nearby Leang Burung II, Ulu Leang and Leang Burung I caves have provided glimpses of life from 30,000 to 8000 years ago.

There are 60 or so known caves in the Maros district. Most are inactive. A notable exception is the recently discovered Salukan Kalang, the largest known cave in Sulawesi at 11 km long; access is restricted.

To get to the Leang caves, take a bemo from Ujung Pandang to Maros, and another from there to the turn-off then walk the last couple of km – or charter a bemo from Maros.

Malino

Malino is a hill resort 74 km east of Ujung Pandang on the pine-covered slopes of Gunung Bawakaraeng. Its moment in history was July 1946, when a meeting of Kalimantan and East Indonesian leaders in Malino endorsed the Netherlands' ill-fated plans for a federation.

The Dutch influence is still highly visible in Malino's architecture, and there are many scenic walks. Deer-hunting on horseback in these parts was once a favoured sport of the Makassarese royalty. The spectacular **Takapala Waterfalls** are set amid rice fields four km east of town. There are two small losmen charging 5000 to 10,000 rp a night.

SOUTH COAST

South Sulawesi's south coast is remarkably barren compared to the peninsula's rich agricultural hinterland. The climate is drier, rice gives way to maize and lontar palm, and traditional boat-building and fishing are the main foci of activity. The landscape is unique, with salt pans by the sea and occasional stands of cactus.

Minibuses and 4WD run from Ujung Pandang to the ports of Bulukumba and Bira, and the wide flat road is also an increasingly popular cycling route.

Bantaeng

Bantaeng (also known as Bontain), 123 km from Ujung Pandang, is a Makassarese boat-building centre with a rich maritime history. It was noted as a dependency of the Javanese kingdom of Majapahit and its ships were mentioned in 14th-century Javanese poetry. It was ceded to the Dutch under the Treaty of Bungaya in 1667, and became an administrative centre. These days it is a town much like any other, with fairly ordinary homestay accommodation. North of town, near the village of **Bissapu**, is a 100-metre-high waterfall.

Bulukumba

The Bugis and Makassarese villages on the coastline near Bulukumba are known for their traditional boat-building. The biggest sail major trade routes through Indonesia and beyond, but the main commissions these days seem to be for smaller fishing boats. Bulukumba is also the port for the Pulau Selayar ferry when the May-July currents close Bira's jetty. For cheap accommodation try the grotty *Sinar Jaya* (☎ 81032) on Jalan Sawerigading 4 which has dorm beds for 3500 rp, or rooms from 10,000 rp.

Tanah Beru

Tanah Beru is the undisputed capital of traditional south coast boat-building. Recent commissions include two full-size boats for Australian customers. Tanah Beru is a fishing village with many of the attractions of Bira, including a beach, but none of the facilities. *Losmen Anda* on the main road has very basic singles/doubles for 5000/7000 rp, including breakfast.

BIRA

Fishing, boat-building and weaving are the primary commercial activities in Bira. Its white-sand beaches are now drawing travellers off the main Ujung Pandang to Tanatoraja tourist trail, but Bira has neither the beauty nor the comfort of Bali's beach resorts. There is swimming, snorkelling, fishing and dolphin-watching (if you can find them), but most people peg out a shady corner of the long west beach and drift off with a book.

Bira's facilities are basic, the food is functional and the beach occasionally disappears under feral tides. Those same tides occasionally dump alarming mounds of garbage on the beach, apparently from nearby shipping lanes. The locals are used to it. Indeed, beach-combing is a time-honoured pastime and in an area with little of its own timber, the currents' supply of driftwood for fires and other general use is invaluable. Note the artistically sculptured lines of driftwood fencing around houses in Tanateng village.

Fresh water is scarce. Theoretically this should cap the frenetic tourist development on Paloppalakaya Bay, but unless areas are set aside for conservation it is likely developers will keep on building. The main spin-off for locals not directly involved in the tourist trade is a new market for the region's cottage industries, especially weaving.

Places to Stay

Bira View Inn has a row of 14 Bugis-style cottages on a cliff overlooking Paloppalakaya Bay, and is the only sea-front hotel to exploit its superb location. Singles/doubles with mandi go for 22,000/40,000 rp, or less for longer stays. Bira View has a shop, snorkelling gear for rent (5000 rp a day), and a restaurant under construction; it is highly recommended.

Anda Bungalows' gritty thatched-roof cottages cost 8000/10,000 rp a night, including a doughy pancake breakfast. The

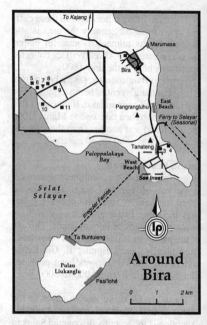

Around Bira

0   1   2 km

1   Yaya Homestay
2   Market
3   Riswan Guesthouse
4   Cliff-top Guesthouse
5   Hotel Sapolohe
6   Bira Beach Hotel
7   Warung
8   Riswan Bungalows
9   Anda Bungalows
10   Bira View Inn
11   Riswan Guesthouse II

manager has his own boat and can organise snorkelling and fishing trips; it's quiet and cheap.

Riswan Bungalows are nicer but they all face the main road. The 13,000 rp singles and 15,000 to 17,000 rp doubles include breakfast. If you need to hire a snorkel, mask (5000 rp a day) or fins (5000 rp), negotiate with the room price. You can find overpriced postcards here too.

Riswan was building a fine-looking guesthouse on the quiet rise behind Bira View Inn.

Don't confuse it with *Riswan Guesthouse* in Tanateng village near East Beach, which has rooms with three meals a day for 9500 rp per person. It is close to village life.

Yaya Homestay, actually in Bira village, has rooms and three meals for 10,000 rp per person, per day.

Bira Beach Hotel has comfortable modern doubles for 40,000 rp, including breakfast, but the price is negotiable. It has a good restaurant and friendly staff. The best views of the beach are given over to a dusty car park for picnicking day-trippers.

Hotel Sapolohe next door has a beautiful new Bugis-style house with a 75,000 rp suite and 60,000 rp doubles with ocean views, plus a neat row of clean, comfortable bungalows (40,000 rp) out the back, all with views of the rear of the hotel.

For good views and a pleasant setting, there was a guesthouse nearing completion on the cliff overlooking East Beach. Follow the street that runs past Riswan Guesthouse right to the end. This area is better known for its dawn views and for the monkeys that occasionally appear in the wee hours. Most other building activity is on west beach where the choice of accommodation is rapidly expanding. Look out for places at the prettier north-western end of Paloppalakaya Bay, which is ripe for development.

Places to Eat
Bira is no place for a gastronomic getaway. Fish, rice and chilli are the order of the day, but the choice might expand as the flow of tourists increases. The *warung* between Bira Beach Hotel and Riswan's is the cheapest and best, serving simple Indonesian fare, plus the cheapest beer.

The restaurant at *Bira Beach Hotel* has a long menu and is happy to fry any fish you catch. The cooks have garlic, oil and good intentions, but lack imagination.

The restaurant at the *Anda* is the oldest, serving reasonably priced Indonesian dishes. There are fabulous views from the restaurant nearing completion at *Bira View Inn*. Here's hoping the food will be as good.

Things to Buy
Weavers gather under raised Bugis houses to work and gossip. You can hear the click-clack of their looms as you walk along the streets. Show an interest, wait for an invitation to take a closer look and, if you like what you see, make an offer. For many women, weaving provides a useful cash supplement for school fees and other essentials.

Getting There & Away
From Ujung Pandang's Malengera terminal there are 4WD kijang that go the full 195 km direct to Bira for 4000 rp, but most terminate at Bulukumba (4000 rp). From there you can go to the market to find very crowded bemos to Tanah Beru (25 km; 1200 rp), then wait at the five-way intersection at the centre of town for a lift to Bira (18 km; 700 rp). Kijangs direct to Bulukumba and Ujung Pandang leave from outside the Bira Beach Hotel every morning.

Bemos from Bulukumba's intercity bus terminal to Bone (4000 rp) take you through some of Sulawesi's greenest, prettiest countryside, a stark contrast to the barren limestone surrounding Bira. The road is good.

Ferries from Bira to Pamatata Harbour on Pulau Selayar (4000 rp) depart from the East Beach jetty at 2 pm daily. When the seasonal currents bring waves to Bira, usually between May and July, the ferry service switches to Bulukumba and goes direct to Benteng on Pulau Selayar (5000 rp).

AROUND BIRA
Pulau Liukanglu
Weavers at **Ta'Buntuleng** on Liukanglu Island make heavy, colourful cloth on hand looms under houses in the village. On the beach west of the village there is an interesting old graveyard, and off the beach there are acres of sea grass and coral, but mind the currents and snakes. To see the best coral further out, you need fins or a boat to get back to the island.

Kajang
There are people inland from Kajang supposedly living at one with nature with no

SULAWESI

modern equipment or mechanised transport, under the leadership of a man known as Ammatoa. To visit this community, you are obliged to wear black and can hire appropriate attire at the entrance to the village. These days, however, you and Ammatoa are likely to be the only ones respecting the traditional ways.

En route to Kajang, stop over at **Ara** north of Bira to see the caves. The rubber plantations in this area are quite interesting too.

PULAU SELAYAR

This long, narrow island lies off the tip of the south-western peninsula of Sulawesi and is inhabited by Bugis and Makassarese people. Most reside along the infertile west coast, and **Benteng** is the chief settlement. Like Bira, Selayar's long coastline is a repository of flotsam from nearby shipping lanes, perhaps accounting for the presence of a 2000-year-old Vietnamese Dongson drum. This metre-wide bronze drum was excavated more than 300 years ago and is now kept in an annexe near the former Bontobangun Palace, a few km south of Benteng.

Another explanation for the drum is that Selayar once supported a significant population which traded with Dongson, situated in present-day Vietnam 2000 years ago. Interestingly, motifs on Dongson drums are similar to the designs found on *tongkonan* (traditional houses) in Tanatoraja.

Selayar's other attraction is its sandy beaches and picturesque scenery. Try renting a perahu and snorkelling near small **Pasi Island** opposite Benteng.

Few foreigners visit Selayar. When they do, most stay at the *Hotel Berlian* in Benteng, which has singles/doubles for 8000/10,000 rp. There is no set price at the older *Harmita Hotel* but expect to pay around 7000 rp a double. Benteng's newest hotel is the *Selayar Beach*.

Getting There & Away

Take a bus or kijang from Bone or Ujung Pandang to Bira (4000 rp), and a boat from Bira to Pamatata Harbour (4000 rp), the northern end of Pulau Selayar. Seasonal currents around May-July often force the ferry operators to reroute the ferry from Bulukumba to Benteng (5000 rp). If this is the case, there will be plenty of people telling you so when you get to Bulukumba.

TAKA BONE RATE

South-east of Selayar and north of Pulau Bone Rate is the 2220-sq-km Taka Bone Rate, the world's third-largest coral atoll. The largest is Kwajalein in the Marshall islands, just 20% bigger. Taka Bone Rate's extensive patch and barrier reefs are now a marine reserve, and the focus of conservation projects working with the atoll's inhabitants to document and preserve the area's rich variety of marine and bird life. One threat is cyanide, used in dilute doses to stun rare and beautiful tropical fish for aquariums. Even if the fish survive, the coral usually dies. Nine of the atoll's 21 islands are inhabited.

BONE (WATAMPONE)

Bone, also known as Watampone, became a major centre of power under the authoritarian rule of Arung Palakka in the 17th century. Bone had been a semi-autonomous state under the overlordship of Gowa, the strongest anti-Dutch power in the East Indies. Palakka and his followers returned from exile in 1666, and rallied the Bugis of Bone and Soppeng for a long overland campaign, forcing Hasanuddin to cede territory, including Bone. Palakka emerged the most powerful man in South Sulawesi, creating a system of unprecedented autocratic rule.

Information

Wisata Bone, a combined tourist information and travel agency, has set up a small office at the Bone bus terminal. It has maps and brochures, excellent advice on accommodation, can explain how to get to regional attractions. The manager, Pak Bohari, speaks English very well.

Change your cheques and cash in Tanatoraja or Ujung Pandang. It is hopeless trying to change foreign currency in Bone.

Things to See

Bone is a pretty town with the bupati's residence, museum and other public buildings centred on a well-kept square. A statue of Arung Palakka, the 15th king, dominates the square. South of the centre, in the streets behind Hotel Wisata Watampone, is the **Bola Soba**, a Bugis house built in 1881.

Bone is surrounded by rich agricultural land and is famous for its variety of primary industries. By arrangement with the tourist office, visitors can see prawn farming and processing, crab farms at **Pallime** and a sugar estate.

Museum Lapawawoi The museum (open daily from 8 am to 2 pm) is a former palace housing one of Indonesia's more interesting regional collections. Just inside the door there are war flags featuring cocks, remarkably similar to flags flown by Bone's opponent, Gowa. There is an odd array of other court memorabilia, and dozens of photographs of state occasions. VIP photos as recent as 1993 show that the special place of *pajogge* transvestites in Bugis court tradition still survives. These *waria* (transvestite) priests are responsible for special ceremonies, and are often found attending to

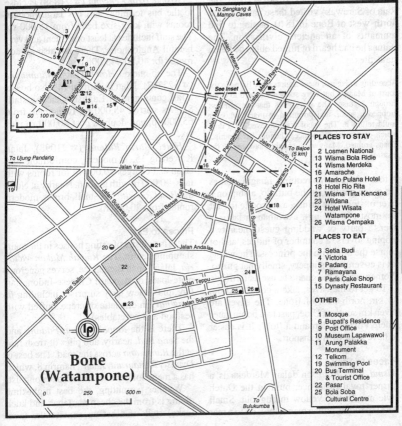

Bone (Watampone)

PLACES TO STAY
2 Losmen National
13 Wisma Bola Ridie
14 Wisma Merdeka
16 Amarache
17 Mario Pulana Hotel
18 Hotel Rio Rita
21 Wisma Tirta Kencana
23 Wildana
24 Hotel Wisata Watampone
26 Wisma Cempaka

PLACES TO EAT
3 Setia Budi
4 Victoria
5 Padang
7 Ramayana
8 Paris Cake Shop
15 Dynasty Restaurant

OTHER
1 Mosque
6 Bupati's Residence
9 Post Office
10 Museum Lapawawoi
11 Arung Palakka Monument
12 Telkom
19 Swimming Pool
20 Bus Terminal & Tourist Office
22 Pasar
25 Bola Soba Cultural Centre

SULAWESI

spiritual matters at the museum after hours. One of the inner rooms is reserved for offerings to Bone's former kings – visitors may enter, but please don't take photographs. On the wall to the right is a complex family tree. Lines of royal succession can be hard to follow. For instance Toappainge, the 24th raja, had two wives, 200 consorts and dozens of kids.

Bojoe The nearby harbour of Bajoe is a busy centre of commerce, five km (500 rp) from Bone. Charter a canoe to see the floating village and port area.

Mampu Caves James Brooke (later the Raja of Sarawak) visited these caves 40 km north-west of Bone in 1840, hoping to find remnants of an ancient civilisation. The statues he had heard of turned out to be fallen stalactites.

According to legend, these figures were living in the court of Mampu but were suddenly turned to stone through a curse. The story goes that the princess dropped a spool, and promised to marry whoever could return it. The spool was retrieved by a dog, which demanded the princess honour her promise. Chaos erupted. Many were caught unawares by the disaster.

A tour of the caves requires imagination as the guide points out the buffalo, a ship on a river of stone, the prince, a crocodile (by far the most convincing), a woman in labor, a deer, a party of wedding guests near two eloping lovers, a chamber of judges, and of course the dog with the princess. The whole lot is covered by slippery, smelly bat guano. Women scrape the guano to use as fertiliser.

To get to the caves, take a bemo to **Uloe**, 34 km north-west of Bone. The caves are seven km south of Uloe, past two boom gates where villagers demand a 'toll'. It is easier to have your own transport.

Places to Stay

Wisma Bola Ridie on Jalan Merdeka is a former royal residence, built in the Dutch style and 'royal' yellow throughout. Small 7500 rp rooms with a mandi look on to a rear courtyard, or there are huge rooms in the main building for 15,000 rp; it's excellent value.

Wisma Merdeka next door at No 4 – a former army hostel – is more modern, but again there are huge rooms in the main house for 15,000 rp, and smaller ones out the back for 7000 to 8000 rp.

Losmen National, Jalan Mesjid Raya 86, is an old-style mansion built in 1952, and recently carved into losmen rooms. High ceilings compensate for the lack of fans, and the nearby mosque will take care of your wake-up calls. Singles/doubles cost 7500/15,000 rp.

Wisma Tirta Kencana (☎ 21838) is close to the bus terminal and has large modern rooms with king-size beds from 15,000 rp. The staff includes at least one fluent and very helpful Anglophone. There are also air-con rooms for 40,000/45,000 rp.

The up-market *Hotel Wisata Watampone* (☎ 322367), Jalan Sudirman 14, also boasts a fair contingent of English-speaking staff. Singles start at 45,000 rp, twin-share from 65,000 rp, and doubles cost 80,000 rp plus tax.

Hotel Mario Pulana (☎ 21098), Jalan Kawerang 15, is modern, comfortable and clean and charges 20,000 rp for rooms with fans, 30,000 rp with air-con. Nearby at No 4, the *Hotel Rio Rita* has small, bright, modern rooms from 20,000 rp.

Places to Eat

There is a cluster of eating houses in the main shopping centre. The *Rumah Makan Victoria*, Jalan Tanah Bangkalae, serves generous plate-loads of standard Chinese-Indonesian fare, plus a few tasty surprises including *fu yung hai* (an omelette or crepe stuffed with seafood and vegetables).

There is the *Rumah Makan Padang* and the *Setia Budi* nearby, and piles of fresh fare at the *Ramayana* across the road. The best is *Dynasty Restaurant*, Jalan Thamrin 8, which has a menu longer than its karaoke song list.

Weather permitting, the best night-time dining is from the cheap martabak and kueh (cake) stalls that set up next to the town

SULAWESI

square, or try Javanese *cat* (rice-flour cakes) steamed over the humming barrows of wandering vendors.

If you are invited home you might get to try *serba*, a Bugis elixir of ginger, red sugar and coconut, or some of the many Bugis-style cakes. Otherwise you'll find a few in the mouth-watering windows of *Paris*, the corner shop next to Ramayana.

Getting There & Away

Bus & Bemo Watampone can be reached by bus from Ujung Pandang, a pretty ride through mountainous country (six hours; 5000 rp). A number of companies have buses on the route. There are bemos from Bulu-kumba for 4000 rp, and to Sengkang for 2500 rp via a very rough road. Buses direct to Rantepao cost 9000 rp.

Boat Three ferries ply the route between Bone and Kolaka in South-East Sulawesi. They leave Bajoe late afternoon and early evening for the eight-hour journey across the gulf. Fares are 10,300/8500/6800 rp in 1st/2nd/3rd class, or you can book a combined bus/boat ticket direct to Kendari for 25,000 rp. Cahaya Ujung supposedly has the best buses.

Getting Around

The minimum becak fare is from 300 to 500 rp. Bemos from behind the market to Bajoe cost 500 rp, plus another 1000 rp to enter the dock area.

SENGKANG

The lakeside resort of Sengkang between Bone and Pare Pare has only recently been discovered by tourists and is still little visited. Scenic Danau Tempe, a large shallow lake fringed by wetlands, is the main attraction, and is best admired by taking a boat trip. Geologists believe the lake was once a gulf between southern Toraja and the rest of Sulawesi Selatan. As the two merged, the gulf disappeared. It is thought the lake will eventually disappear too.

There are floating houses, magnificent

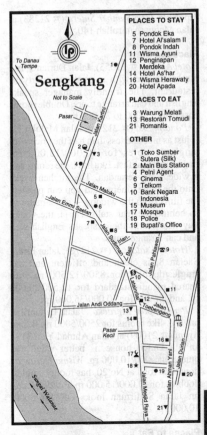

PLACES TO STAY

5 Pondok Eka
7 Hotel Al'salam II
8 Pondok Indah
11 Wisma Ayuni
12 Penginapan Merdeka
14 Hotel As'har
16 Wisma Herawaty
20 Hotel Apada

PLACES TO EAT

3 Warung Melati
13 Restoran Tomudi
21 Romantis

OTHER

1 Toko Sutera Sutera (Silk)
2 Main Bus Station
4 Pelni Agent
6 Cinema
9 Telkom
10 Bank Negara Indonesia
15 Museum
17 Mosque
18 Police
19 Bupati's Office

bird life and a range of commercial activities on the lake. Lake tours will usually take in Batu Batu on the other side, but the most interesting part is along the river around Sengkang. Boats can be chartered for 10,000 to 15,000 rp each.

The other main attraction of Sengkang is the *sutera* (silk) weaving industry. You can visit the silk villages, or go to the factories and get things made to order. Most visitors buy ready-made silk products at bargain prices in the town's silk market, but be very wary of cotton blends. To get an idea of the quality and prices available, visit the

SULAWESI

reputable *Toko Sumber Sutera* (☎ 21383) at Jalan Magga Amirullah 140.

Places to Stay

Hotel Apada (☎ 21053), Jalan Durian 9, is a pleasant place with a gorgeous courtyard restaurant. The friendly manager speaks English and can arrange tours. Double rooms cost from 25,000 to 35,000 rp.

Pondok Eka (☎ 21296), Jalan Maluku 12, is just as nice and less than half the price with singles/doubles for 10,000/15,000 rp, including breakfast. Eka has large rooms and a wide front verandah. The kitchen backs onto the town cinema and you can preview the films from the window – just a metre or so behind the rear stalls. Harja, the young guy who works there, speaks English well and can arrange tours.

Hotel Al'salam II (☎ 21278), Jalan Emmi Saelan 8, is clean and efficient and has singles/doubles for 8500/12,500 rp with shared mandi, standard for 12,500/20,000 rp, and air-con for 30,000/35,000 rp.

Penginapan Merdeka, Jalan Latainrilai, has box-like rooms for 2500/5000 rp. *Wisma Ayuni* (☎ 21009) at Jalan Ahmad Yani 31 in an old Dutch house, is better value and quieter at 5000/10,000 rp. *Wisma Herawaty* down the road at No 20, has roomy singles/doubles for 10,000/15,000 rp. *Pondok Indah* on Jalan Sudirman looks OK for 8000/10,000 rp.

Places to Eat

Warung Melati, opposite the bus station on Jalan Kartini, has fresh Indonesian fare including chunky serves of tasty nasi campur and Western-style dishes such as potato fries and scrambled eggs. The martabak from the *night stall* in front of the bus station is also good.

There's a cluster of eating houses on the corner of Jalan Latainrilai and Jalan Andi Oddang, the best of which is *Restoran Tomudi* at Jalan Andi Oddang 52.

Getting There & Away

Sengkang is readily accessible from Pare Pare by bus or bemo (two hours; 2500 rp). If you're coming from or going to Rantepao, bemos go through Palopo and take about six or seven hours. There are plenty of buses south to Bone (horrible road, 2000 rp) and the port of Bajoe, and bemos from Bone to Bulukumba and Bira for 4000 rp.

SOPPENG

Soppeng, or Watansoppeng, is the other big silk producer in this region, and the source of silk-worm eggs for Sengkang's silk industry. The breeding cycle is the same as Sengkang's, so you will see the same thing at either area. It is a pleasant detour and easy to get to by bemo from either Pangkajene or Sengkang.

There is a small choice of places to stay. *Hotel Kayangan* on Jalan Kayangan 4 has basic rooms from 12,500 rp, up to 22,500 rp with air-con. *Hotel Makmur* (☎ 21038), Jalan Makmuran 104, is nicer with rooms from 20,000 rp, and *Hotel Aman* (☎ 21206), Jalan Merdeka 92, has rooms from 15,000 rp.

PARE PARE

The second-largest city in southern Sulawesi is a smaller, greener version of Ujung Pandang. Pare Pare is a seaport through which a good deal of the produce of southern Sulawesi (rice, corn, coffee etc) is shipped out. It's a pleasant stopover between Tanatoraja or Mamasa and Ujung Pandang. There are also frequent ships to the east coast of Kalimantan and to northern Sulawesi from here.

At **Bangange**, a few km south of Pare Pare, there is a small museum housing a collection of cloth, ornaments, tools and other remnants of the royal house of Bacukiki. About 10 km further south there is a quiet, swimmable beach, much cleaner than the effluent pools around Pare Pare.

Orientation & Information

Pare Pare is stretched out along the waterfront. At night, the street by the water turns into a lively pedestrian mall with warungs and stalls. Most of what you need (hotels, restaurants etc) is on the streets running parallel with the harbour.

Bank Negara Indonesia is the only bank in town that changes money. It's right next to the large mosque (see the Pare Pare map). There's also a moneychanger at Jalan Hasanuddin 59.

Places to Stay

The *Hotel Gandaria* (☎ 21093) at Jalan Baumassepe 171 is clean, comfortable and run by friendly people. Economy singles with attached toilet and shower cost 15,000 rp. Air-con singles cost from 25,000 rp.

The *Hotel Gemini* (☎ 21754) at Jalan Baumassepe 451 has small rooms from 6500 rp, rooms with mandi for 8500 rp, and newly renovated airy rooms with TV for 16,500 rp.

Hotel Cahaya Ujung (☎ 22810), Jalan Mangga Barat 2, is above a new shopping centre on the corner of Jalan Baumassepe. New rooms with pre-aged mandi cost from 10,000 rp, up to 45,000 rp with air-con. Discounts are available.

Tanty Hotel (☎ 21378), Jalan Sultan Hasanuddin 5, has clean, basic rooms from 10,000 rp.

Nurlina Hotel (☎ 21278) at Jalan Pawero 10, off Jalan Andi Makassau, is on the north-eastern edge of the city centre. It boasts antechambers for all its rooms, even the 20,000 rp economy ones.

Places to Eat

Restaurant Asia has good Chinese food and excellent but pricey seafood dishes from 8000 to 14,000 rp per serve. There are a couple of vegetarian dishes and fresh, meaty corn and crab soup for 6000 rp.

Restaurant Sempurna, a few km to the south of town on Jalan Baumassepe, is pretty good value with both Indonesian and Chinese food. *Warung Sedap* has good ikan bakar next door to the Asia. There are many small warungs along the main street in the vicinity of the Hotel Siswa.

At night there's a string of warungs along the waterfront, each with exactly the same choice of mie, rice and bakso dishes. At the northern end there are fruit stalls selling whatever's in season.

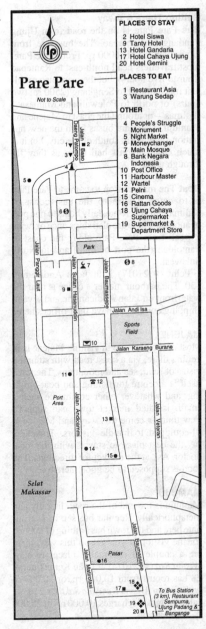

Pare Pare

Not to Scale

PLACES TO STAY
2 Hotel Siswa
9 Tanty Hotel
13 Hotel Gandaria
17 Hotel Cahaya Ujung
20 Hotel Gemini

PLACES TO EAT
1 Restaurant Asia
3 Warung Sedap

OTHER
4 People's Struggle Monument
5 Night Market
6 Moneychanger
7 Main Mosque
8 Bank Negara Indonesia
10 Post Office
11 Harbour Master
12 Wartel
14 Pelni
15 Cinema
16 Rattan Goods
18 Ujung Cahaya Supermarket
19 Supermarket & Department Store

Jalan Daeng Patompo
Jalan Baso
Park
Jalan Panggi Laut
Jalan Sultan Hasanuddin
Jalan Baumassepe
Jalan Andi Isa
Sports Field
Jalan Karaeng Burane
Port Area
Jalan Andicamm
Jalan Veteran
Selat Makassar
Jalan Matirolasi
Pasar
Jalan Baumassepe
To Bus Station (3 km), Restaurant Sempurna, Ujung Padang & Bangange

SULAWESI

Getting There & Away

Bus Pare Pare is on the road from Ujung Pandang to Rantepao. The bus fare from Ujung Pandang is 6000 rp. From Pare Pare, most travellers head north-east to Rantepao (four to five hours), but there are also excellent roads inland to Sengkang (2500 rp; two hours) or north to Polewali and Mamasa – 'Polmas'– or around the coast to Majene and Mamuju. There are buses from the new bus station several km south of the city, but it is much easier to just hail them as they fly through town.

Boat The main reason to come to Pare Pare is to catch a ship to the east coast of Kalimantan. There are daily boats to one port or another. There are also ships once or twice a week from Pare Pare along the coast to Pantoloan (the port of Palu) and to North Sulawesi.

Pelni (☎ 21017) is at Jalan Andicammi 130. The harbour master's office is near the waterfront on Jalan Andicammi, and several shipping companies have their offices here.

MAJENE

Most of the pleasure in visiting Majene is in getting there, via a coast road with stunning vistas of sand, sea and mountains. The town itself is a centre for fishing and boat-building, and whatever other commerce such a small, isolated market town can support. Few tourists come this way, and Majene is ill-equipped to handle visitors. Travellers say the best place to stay is with the local doctor. Ask at the market for directions. The food is supposed to be good there too.

MAMUJU

Mamuju is the end of the road, literally and metaphorically. Regular bus services terminate here and the town has nothing of interest for the visitor. If you get up this way, there are a couple of reasonable places to stay. *Wisma Rio* (☎ 21014) at Jalan Kemakmuran 28 has rooms from 10,000 rp, or 30,000 rp with air-con. *Wisma Kencana Sakti* (☎ 21039), Jalan Langsat 2, charges 10,000 rp, or 25,000 rp with air-con.

MAMUJU TO MASAMBA

From Mamuju there are bemos to **Tarailu**. Stay at the losmen there for 2500 rp, then get a motorised canoe to **Galumpang** on the Karama River, where archaeologists have excavated remains of Neolithic villages. Galumpang to Tambing, Bau, Seko, Emo, Seka Tenggah and Seko Padang is a three or four-day walk. You can fly from Seko Padang to Masamba by MAF. If you head this way, travel light, pay around 5000 rp a night for accommodation and leave gifts – pencils, cards, tobacco etc.

Tanatoraja

Despite long conflict with their Bugis neighbours to the south, it was only in the early years of this century that the Toraja came into serious contact with the West. The Toraja and their culture had survived the constant threat from the Bugis, but in 1905 the Dutch decided to bring central Sulawesi under their control. The Toraja held out against the Dutch for two years, until the last substantial resistance was wiped out in the mountains of Pangala, north-west of Rantepao.

The missionaries moved in on the heels of the army and by WW II many of the great Toraja ceremonies (except for their remarkable funeral ceremonies) were already disappearing. Tourism, mining and transmigration have aided the work the missionaries began.

The Toraja

Despite the isolation caused by the rugged landscape of central Sulawesi, similar cultures have existed in the territory bordered by the Bugis to the south-west, the Gorontalo district in the north, and the Loinang and Mori peoples in the east. The people in this vast area are collectively referred to as the Toraja. The name is derived from the Bugis word *toriaja*, meaning 'men of the mountains', but the connotations of the name are something like 'hillbilly' – rustic, unsophisticated, oafish highlanders.

Torajan Food

Going to the ceremonies provides a chance to try Torajan food. The best-known is *pa'piong*, the spinach-like vegetables with pork, chicken or fish cooked in bamboo tubes. The chicken pa'piong has the added flavour of coconut. If you want to try it in a warung, order several hours in advance as it takes ages to cook. The pork pa'piong tends to have a high fat content, because fat is considered as tasty as the meat. *Pamerasan*, buffalo meat in a black sauce, is delicious if the meat is tender.

Fresh fish from Palopo is rushed to Toraja by would-be WW II fighter pilots on ancient motorbikes, laden with huge pannier baskets. They fly down the two-hour stretch of twists and turns to Palopo often twice a day, returning with glittering baskets of silver fish ready for frying in warung everywhere. *Ikan mas* (gold fish) and *ikan belut* (eels) are caught in padi fields and barbecued.

Indulge your sweet tooth with *kue baje*, cakes of sticky rice and palm sugar rolled in a dry corn leaf like a Christmas cracker. They go off quickly so it's a good idea to try before you buy. *Kue deppa* are triangular rice flour cakes bought loose from street stalls, and *kacang goreng* is an over-sweet concoction of peanuts and treacle wrapped in corn leaves. A hard to find delicacy is *kolak*, a kind of sweet banana soup based on coconut milk and palm sugar, and spiced with ginger.

Toraja produces an incredible variety of bananas, the only fruit available year-round. Choose from tiny finger banana, *pisang susu* or milk banana (the speckled brown skin looks off, but it's not), the 30 cm *pisang tanduk* or *hom* banana, or the *pisang molen* – banana wrapped in pastry and deep-fried.

The cool climate makes Toraja ideal for fresh vegetables such as cabbage, beans and spinach-type leaves. See tiny women carrying huge baskets of these vegetables to market early in the morning. ■

Torajan Drinks

Rantepao and Makale markets have whole sections devoted to the sale of the alcoholic drink known locally as *balok*. Although known as 'palm wine', balok is actually sap from the sugar palm. It is probably the strongest proof yet of a benevolent creator.

Every few months the palm, with its huge, dark metallic-green fronds and untidy black-haired trunk, produces a great cluster of round, dark fruit. The stem is pierced close to the fruit and if sugary sap flows from the wound the fruit cluster is cut off and a receptacle is hung to catch the juice dripping from the amputated stump. This ferments naturally, producing one of creation's finest brews. The sap can also be boiled down to produce crystalline red sugar – *gula merah*.

Balok, known nationally as *tuak* and internationally as *toddy*, used to be available by the bamboo-tube full in the market, but these days plastic containers are considered more practical. Otherwise drink it by the glassful at night in the warung and restaurants around town. Tuak is collected in long bamboo tubes, is left to ferment all day and then consumed at night. It comes in a variety of strengths, and ranges from lemonade-coloured to the orange or red – made by adding tree bark and reputedly potent.

It also ranges from sweet to bitter, depending on its age. It doesn't keep for more than a day so be wary of buying blends of old and new. Torajans also advise against eating durian or nangka with balok. Supposedly the best balok is sold at the Alang Alang bridge between Rantepao and Makale. Stop and see.

Coffee is Toraja's other famous brew, an excellent antidote to a night of balok tasting. *Robusta* is the most widely available variety, drunk strong and black with equal portions of coffee and sugar. The tastier *arabica* is also available at much higher prices. It is largely produced for export and you can see the whole process of growing, harvesting, drying and roasting throughout Tanatoraja. In villages, coffee is sometimes roasted with ginger, coconut or even garlic for an unusually fragrant and delicious taste. For souvenirs, buy carved boxes and fill them with coffee yourself – the pre-packaged ones in the shops are usually only half full. ■

SULAWESI

The Bugis traded Indian cloth, Dutch coins and porcelain with the Toraja in return for coffee and slaves. The Bugis are even said to have introduced cockfighting to the Toraja, who incorporated the sport into the death rituals of their noble class. Islam brought a new militancy to the Bugis and under Arung Palakka they attacked the Toraja in 1673 and 1674. However, Islam never spread much further than the southern Toraja areas because, it is said, of the people's fondness for pork and palm wine.

Customarily the Toraja have been split by ethnologists into western, eastern and southern groups. To some extent these divisions represent the varying degrees of influence the old kingdoms of Luwu, Gowa and Bone have had on the Toraja. It *doesn't* reflect any political organisation among the Toraja. In the past there has been no organisation beyond the level of the local village or small groups of villages. Sometimes villages would band together in federations to resist the Bugis invaders, but there have never been any large Torajan states.

Of all the Toraja peoples the best known to the Western world are the southern Toraja, also known as the Sadan or Saqdan Toraja. These people live in the mountainous Sadan Valley. Their main concentration is in the area called Tanatoraja around the towns of Rantepao and Makale. Tanatoraja has become the chief tourist destination in Sulawesi where, like Bali, the impact of tourism is evident in the rapid emergence of hotels, losmen and restaurants around Rantepao. The area, however, is unspoilt and the tourist trade is peripheral. The vast majority of the Toraja make a living from rice farming and pig breeding.

The introduction of wet-rice cultivation after the Dutch conquest has sculpted and terraced the slopes of the steep mountainsides, with streams originating near the hilltops harnessed to flow in a succession of little waterfalls before escaping once more into the natural rivers below. Toraja villages were once built on the summits, sometimes surrounded by fortified walls with the settlement itself reached by tunnels. This was partly for protection, partly because the original clan ancestors were supposed to have arrived from heaven on hilltops.

Before the Dutch there were several groups of head-hunters in the archipelago, including the Toraja. Their head-hunting was not on any great scale and their raids were basically tests of manhood for the young men of the tribe. Head-hunting was also necessary to find heads for a chief's death-feast to provide slaves for his afterlife. If enough enemies could not be captured in raids then the chief's family would buy slaves and sacrifice them. Under Dutch rule the wars and raids came to an end and the Sadan were ordered to build their villages on the plains.

Buffaloes are a status symbol for the Toraja, and are of paramount importance in various religious ceremonies. Pigs and chickens are slaughtered at many rituals, the pigs mostly at funerals and at the consecration of new *tongkonan* (traditional houses). Dogs are eaten in some parts of Tanatoraja, occasionally as sacrificial offerings. Coffee (reputedly the best in Indonesia) is the main cash crop and fish are caught in ponds in the rice fields.

Religion

Despite the strength of traditional beliefs, most of the Toraja are nominally Christians. The Christian Church of Toraja is a very active force. One of the first questions asked is your religion, and Protestant Christians are given immediate approval as *'saudara'* (sister/brother).

Physical isolation and the lack of a written language resulted in considerable variations in beliefs, customs and mythology, although the ancestor cult has always been very strong. Prior to the arrival of Christianity the Toraja believed in many gods but worshipped one in particular as the special god of their family, clan or tribe. Puang Matua was the nearest the Toraja originally came to the concept of a supreme being, and early missionaries began prayers in their churches with his name.

The Toraja have a long and involved cre-

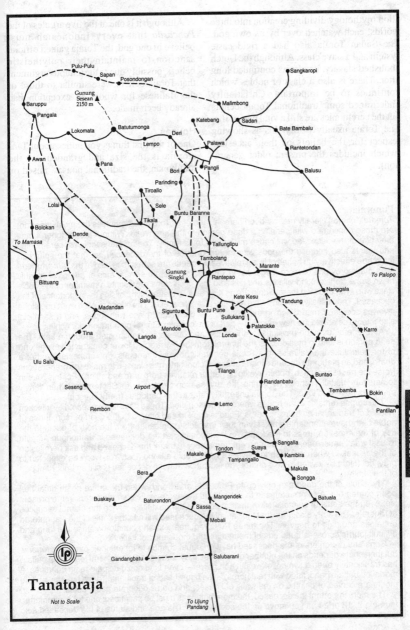

Tanatoraja

Not to Scale

To Ujung Pandang

ation mythology dividing creation into three worlds, each watched over by its own god. The Sadan Toraja also had a rigid caste system and a slave class. Although the Dutch abolished slavery, its effects continued long after. There is also a class of nobles which continues to be important. Christianity undermined some traditional Toraja beliefs but the ceremonies are still a vital part of life. The Toraja usually justify this as showing respect for the beliefs of their ancestors (which includes the present older generation).

Although it is one of the five articles of the *Pancasila* that every Indonesian must believe in one god, the Toraja gained official sanction to maintain their polytheistic beliefs, possibly due to the tenuous argument that Toraja beliefs were similar to those of the Balinese for whom an exception had already been made.

Houses

One of the first things you notice about Tanatoraja is the size and grandeur of the tongkonan, the traditional houses, raised on

Funerals

Tomate (funeral) literally means 'dead person', and of all Torajan ceremonies the most important are those concerned with sending a dead person to the afterworld. Without proper funeral rites the spirit of the deceased will cause misfortune to its family. The funeral sacrifices, ceremonies and feasts also impress the gods with the importance of the deceased, so that the spirit can intercede effectively on behalf of living relatives. Funerals are sometimes held at the *rante*, funeral sites marked by one or more megaliths. In Tanatoraja there are several arcs or groups of roughly hewn stone slabs around villages and it is said that each stone represents a member of the noble class who lived and died there. Some are as high as four metres, symbolising the importance of the deceased. They usually surround a big rock like a sacrificial altar. The efforts to raise even one stone involves scores of men dragging the stone to the designated place with ropes, and a sacrificial slaughter to celebrate the new megalith – part of the complex funeral preparations for nobles.

At a funeral, bamboo pavilions for the family and guests are constructed around a field. The dead person is said to preside over the funeral from the high-roofed tower constructed at one end of the field. Like the Balinese, the Toraja generally have two funerals, one immediately after a death, and an elaborate second funeral after sufficient time has elapsed to make the preparations (raise the necessary cash, obtain livestock, gather relatives from afar, and so on). For this reason *tomate* are usually scheduled during the dry season from July to September, when family members have free time. The Toraja cheerfully refer to this period as 'party season'.

The corpse remains in the house where the person died. These days it is preserved by injection instead of traditional embalming herbs. Food is cooked and offered to the dead person; those of noble birth have attendants who stay in their immediate presence from the hour of death to the day of their final progress to the tomb. An invitation to visit the deceased is an honour. A polite refusal won't cause offence. If you accept, remember to thank the deceased and ask permission of the deceased when you wish to leave – as you would a living host. You won't be expected to pray, but might be invited to take photos, an indication that the deceased is still an important part of the family.

The souls of the dead can only go to Puya, the afterworld, when the entire death ritual has been carried out. A spirit's status in the afterlife is the same as its owner's status in the present life; even the souls of animals follow their masters to the next life – hence the animal sacrifices at funerals. The story also goes that the soul of the deceased will ride the souls of the slaughtered buffaloes and pigs to heaven. The trip to Puya requires a strong buffalo because the long and difficult journey crosses hundreds of mountains and thousands of valleys.

Sons and daughters of the deceased have an equal chance to inherit their parents' property, but their share depends on the number of buffaloes they slaughter at the funeral feast. The buffalo has traditionally been a symbol of wealth and power – even land could be paid for in buffaloes. A modelled buffalo head, fitted with real horns, is the figurehead of traditional Toraja houses, buffalo motifs are carved or painted on the walls of houses, and horns decorate gable poles.

The more important the deceased, the more buffaloes must be sacrificed: one for a commoner, four, eight, 12 or 24 as you move up the social scale. The age and status of the deceased also

piles and topped with a massive roof. The tongkonan houses of Tanatoraja are closely bound up with Torajan traditions – one of their important functions is as a constant reminder of the authority of the original noble families whose descendants alone have the right to build such houses.

Tanatoraja is one of the few places in Indonesia where traditional houses are still being built and the skills to make them survive. The owners often live in modern houses, keeping the tongkonan for ceremonies and as a symbol of the family's status. The tourist trade has also inspired the renovation of some older houses and construction of new ones purely for the benefit of visitors. There are a number of villages in the region still composed entirely of traditional houses. Most of these houses have rice barns, surrounded by several ordinary bungalows on stilts, like the houses of the Bugis and Makassarese.

The roof, rearing up at either end, is the most striking aspect of a tongkonan house and is somewhat similar to the Batak houses of northern Sumatra. Some people think that

determines the number of animals slaughtered. Large pesta where more than 100 buffalo are slaughtered are talked of with awe for years afterwards. The type of buffalo is also significant – the most prized being the *tedong bonga* (spotted buffalo) which may cost millions of rupiah per head.

The Dutch imposed limits on the number of buffalo that could be slaughtered at a funeral, since the temptation to honour the dead and impress the living by extravagant sacrifices was so great that whole families would be bankrupted. Today the Indonesian government is also trying to limit the destruction of wealth by taxing each slaughtered animal. However, the funeral ceremonies of today seem to have lost none of their ostentation – they are still a ruinous financial burden on families. Some are now refusing to hold tomate, despite their social obligation to do so.

Those with strong stomachs can see freshly killed pigs roasted on open fires to scorch the skin before the pig is gutted and the meat mixed with piles of vegetables and stuffed into bamboo tubes. The bamboo tubes are cooked slowly over low flames to produce tasty *pa'piong*, a Torajan specialty. Cuts of buffalo meat are also distributed – the funeral season is the only time of year families are guaranteed regular supplies of meat.

Funerals can be spread out over several days and involve hundreds of guests. The wooden effigies alone can cost nearly a year's wages for many Indonesians. Bamboo pavilions are constructed specially for the occasion, with a death tower at one end.

After the guests display their presents of pigs and buffaloes, the traditional Mabadong song and dance is performed. This is a ceremonial re-enactment of the cycle of human life and the life story of the deceased. It is a slow-moving circular dance performed by men in black sarongs, who stand shoulder to shoulder and chant for hours. It also bids farewell to the soul of the deceased and relays the hope that the soul will arrive in the afterworld safely.

Cigarettes are circulated, and endless supplies of food and tuak (palm wine) are served to the guests by immaculately clad women. Each family member is responsible for a pavilion and its kitchen. Women recruited from friends and family cater for the constant flow of guests.

Ceremonies last from one to seven days, depending on the wealth and social status of the deceased. There may be buffalo fighting in which the bulls, agitated by the insertion of chilli up their behind, lock horns and strain against each other. The winner is the one which makes its opponent slide backwards. The crowd urges them on with frenzied whoops and yells, but is ready to scatter in case one breaks loose and charges in panic. You might also see *sisemba* kick-fighting, and maybe cockfights at the end of the ceremony.

As well as the Mabadong, you might see orchestras of Sunday school children playing painted bamboo wind instruments. Reward their serious performing by putting a donation on the ground in front of them – there will be donations from other spectators, in response to your effort if not the children's. The programme might also include dances like the Maranding, a war dance performed at the burial service of a patriotic nobleman to remind the people of his heroic deeds, or the Makatia, which reminds the people of the deceased's generosity and loyalty. Songs may also be sung, and these are meant to console the bereaved family or convey their grief to the other guests at the funeral. ∎

the house represents the head of a buffalo and the rising roof represents the horns. Others suggest that the roof looks more like a boat and that the raised ends represent the bow and the stern. The houses all face north – some say because the ancestors of the Toraja came from the north, carrying their boats to the safety of the hills and inverting them to use as shelter. Others maintain that the north (and the east) are regarded as the sphere of life, the realm of the gods.

The high gables are supported by poles and the wall panels are decorated with painted engravings of a geometrical design, of which the stylised buffalo head is the most striking. Other designs may include the entire buffalo, or two buffaloes fighting with horns locked. On these panels red is meant to symbolise human life, as red is the colour of blood; white is the colour of flesh and bone, and a symbol of purity; yellow represents god's blessing and power; and black symbolises death and darkness. Traditionally the colours were all natural – black is the soot from cooking pots, yellow and red are coloured earth, and white is lime. Tuak (palm wine) was used to improve the staying power of the colours. Artisans would decorate the houses and be paid in buffaloes. A realistic carving of a buffalo's head decorates the front part of the house. Numerous buffalo horns, indicating the wealth of the family, are attached to the front pole which supports the gable.

The beams and supports of Torajan houses are cut so that they all neatly slot or are pegged together; no metal nails are used. The older houses have roofs of overlapping pieces of bamboo but newer houses use corrugated metal sheets. Standing on thick solid piles, the rectangular body of the house is small in contrast to the roof, and consists of two or three dark rooms with low doors and small windows. If necessary the whole house can actually be put on runners and moved to another location. Traditionally, buffaloes were kept under the houses. Although health workers discourage this, some can still be seen tethered by the nose.

Graves & Tau Tau

The Toraja believe you can take it with you and the dead generally go well equipped to their graves. Since this led to grave plundering, the Toraja started to hide their dead in caves or hew niches out of rock faces.

These caves were hollowed out by specialist cave builders who were traditionally paid in buffaloes – and since the building of a cave would cost several buffaloes, only the rich could afford it. Although the exterior of the cave grave looks small, the interior is large enough to entomb an entire family. The coffins would go deep inside the caves, and you can see, sitting in balconies on the rock face in front of the caves, the *tau tau* – life-size, carved wooden effigies of the dead.

Tau tau are carved only for the upper classes. Their expense alone rules out their use for poor people. Traditionally, the statues only showed the sex of the person, not the likeness, but now they attempt to imitate the likeness of the person's face. The making of tau tau appears to have been a recent innovation, possibly originating in the late 19th century. The type of wood used reflects the status and wealth of the deceased, jackfruit (nangka) wood being the most expensive. After the deceased has been entombed and the tau tau placed in front of the grave, offerings are placed in the palm of the tau tau. You can see the carvers at work at Londa, across the padi opposite the caves.

Apart from cave graves there are also house graves – houses made of wood in which the coffin is placed when there is no rocky outcrop or cliff face to carve a niche in. Most of the hanging graves in which the wooden coffins were hung from high cliffs have rotted away. Sometimes the coffins may be placed at the foot of a mountain. Babies who died before teething were placed in hollowed-out sections of living trees; such graves can be seen at Suaya and Pana (see the Around Rantepao section).

Most tau tau seem to be in a permanent state of disrepair but in a ceremony after harvest time the bodies are re-wrapped in new material and the clothes of the tau tau replaced. Occasionally left lying around the more obscure grave caves is the *duba-duba*, a platform in the shape of a traditional house which is used to carry the coffin and body of a nobleman to the grave. ∎

Torajan houses always face a line-up of rice barns – wealthy owners may have a whole fleet of barns. The barns look like miniature houses and, like the living area in a house, the rice storage area is surprisingly small considering the overall size of the structure. The barn has a small door at one end and the surface of the walls and the high gables are usually decorated. The rice storage chamber is raised about two metres off the ground on four smooth columns of wood, polished to prevent rats climbing up them. About 60 cm from the ground is a wooden platform stretched between the pillars, an important meeting place to sit and wile away the hours, as well as a shelter from downpours. The boat-shaped roof shelters an area about twice the size of the rice chamber.

The Toraja have a number of ceremonies connected with the construction of a tongkonan. Construction is preceded by the sacrificial killing of a chicken, pig or buffalo; its successful completion is celebrated with a large feast in which many pigs and at least one buffalo are killed.

Sport

As on the islands of Sumbawa and Lombok, there's a unique form of man-to-man combat in Tanatoraja, an unarmed contest called *sisemba*. The aim of the game is to kick your opponent into submission. It's something like Thai boxing except that use of the hands is banned, and you can't kick your opponent when he is down (very sporting). More a feat of strength and endurance now, the original aim of the contest was to instil courage in Torajan youths – a useful attribute for a people once hemmed in by their coastal enemies and occasionally at war with each other.

The fights are held at the time of the rice harvest or just after (June to early August), which is also the most popular time for funerals and house ceremonies. Fights are held between individuals or teams of two or more and the women look on and cheer their favourites. When the men of one village challenge another, anything up to 200 a side is possible.

The Toraja had another contest known as the *sibamba*, in which the contestants used wooden clubs to hit each other, protecting themselves from the blows with a bull-hide shield (very similar to the contests found on Lombok, eastern Bali and Sumbawa). Apparently it was banned during Dutch rule.

A more docile sport is the game known as *takro*, where a rattan ball is kicked and bounced over a metre-high bamboo stick fixed parallel to the ground. It's something like volleyball but uses only two or three players, and only the head and hands can touch the ball.

Language

The weary 'Hello misters' will instantly change to radiant grins if you attempt a word or two of the Torajan dialect. Bahasa Toraja and its variations remains the predominant language, despite the lack of books written in Bahasa Toraja. Many villages and older people do not speak Bahasa Indonesia at all. The following phrases will guarantee instant laughter and appreciation. If you can't get your tongue around the characteristic glottal stop, there will be a crowd of teachers to help.

Thank you.	*kurre sumanga.*
You're welcome.	*bole paria.*
How much is this, grandmother/father?	*se pira te' indok?*
Very expensive!	*masuli' liu!*
How are you?	*apa kareba?*
I'm well.	*kareba melo.*
good/fine	*melo*
Where are you going?	*umba me sule?*
I'm just going for a walk.	*su malong-malong.*
I don't have any sweets!	*ta'e ku ampui gula-gula!* ∎

RANTEPAO

Rantepao, with a population of roughly 15,000, is the largest town and commercial centre in Tanatoraja. It is also the major travellers' centre in Sulawesi. The places to see are scattered around the lush, green countryside surrounding Rantepao. This area has pleasant, cool evenings and rain throughout the year – even in the 'dry' season.

In *Six Moons in Sulawesi,* Harry Wilcox devotes a whole chapter to the Rantepao market in the 1940s. Little has changed, except for the fleets of blaring bemos inching their way through the chaos. Tourism seems to have been absorbed into the commercial life of the town.

Information

Tourist Office The tourist office is on the south side of town and is open from 7.30 am until 2 pm Monday to Saturday. It's helpful, has a good map of the area and keeps a list of dates and locations of the funeral ceremonies.

Money The Bank Rakyat Indonesia and Bank Danamon are opposite each other on Jalan Jen Ahmad Yani. Bank Danamon gives slightly better rates, but both give lower exchange rates than banks in Ujung Pandang. The best exchange rates are available from the moneychanger at the Hotel Indra. Abadi, the moneychanger at the intersection of Jalan Jen Ahmad Yani and Jalan Diponegoro, often gives better rates than the banks.

Post & Telecommunications The post office is on Jalan Jen Ahmad Yani opposite the Bank Rakyat Indonesia. The Telkom office next to the post office provides numbers, codes and information. There are card phones in foyers of banks and hotels, and a private wartel near the Setia Kawan on Jalan Yani.

Travel Agencies Private agencies such as JET provide bicycles, motorbikes, cars and guides.

Books The locally produced *A Guide to Toraja* by A T Marampa is available in some

Rantepao shops in English, German and French. It lists dances, ceremonies and some local walks, and is quite useful.

Also locally produced is *Toraja – An Introduction to a Unique Culture* by L T Tangdilintin & M Syafei in their own unique and impenetrable style. Much more readable is *Life & Death of the Toraja People* by Stanislaus Sandarupa. These books are sold in the souvenir shops.

Things to See

The height of the tourist season in Tanatoraja is July and August – the European holiday period – when Rantepao is packed out with French, German, Italian and Japanese tour groups, and hotel prices skyrocket.

The best time to visit Tanatoraja is in the gap between the end of the rainy season and the onset of the tourist season. The rainy season usually begins in December and ends in March – although there can still be a considerable amount of rain after that. Then the rice crops are harvested (from May to August) and the ceremonies begin.

The **buffalo and pig market** *(bolu)* is held every six days. Inquire at your hotel or the tourist office to learn the exact day. The market is two km from the town centre, easily reached by minibus opposite the Fuji shop on Jalan Diponegoro.

Ceremonies To get the most out of Tanatoraja you have to be here for the ceremonies. Otherwise what you see is a lot of nicely decorated houses, caves full of coffins and *tau tau* (carved wooden effigies of the dead). It's all a bit like an open-air museum with nothing happening. Forget about going in the rainy season – apart from being poured on day in and day out, most of the roads turn into long trails of sludge. You can still get to the main spots like Londa and Kete Kesu easily enough (see Around Rantepao & Makale later in this section), but there's a lot more to be seen that's only accessible by foot or motorbike.

Some of the locals in Rantepao will take you to the ceremonies for a negotiable price – if they speak enough English or if you

SULAWESI

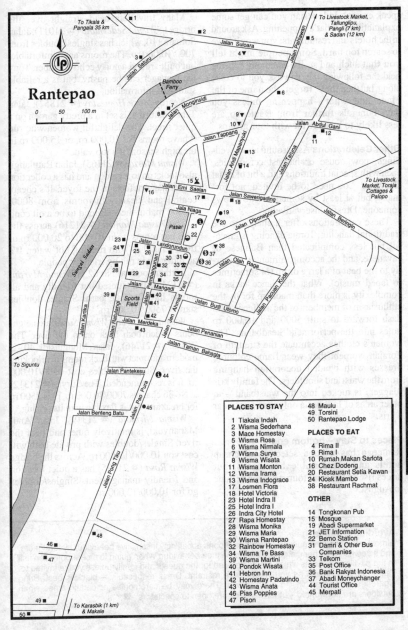

Rantepao

0   50   100 m

To Tikala & Pangala 35 km

To Livestock Market, Tallunglipu, Pangli (7 km) & Sadan (12 km)

Jalan Suloara
Jalan Setutu
Jalan Pahlawan
Bamboo Ferry
Jalan Monginsidi
Jalan Abdul Gani
Jalan Tappang
Jalan Andi Mapanyuki
Jalan Tandu
Jalan Emi Saelan
Jalan Sawerigading
Jala Niaga
Jalan Diponegoro
Jalan Beringin
Jalan Landorundun
Jalan Olah Raga
Jalan Pembangunan
Jalan Mangadi
Jalan Budi Utomo
Jalan Jen Ahmad Yani
Jalan Pacan Kuda
Jalan Merdeka
Jalan Penanian
Jalan Taman Bahagia
Jalan Pantekesu
Jalan Ratulangi
Jalan Kartika
Jalan Pao Pura
Jalan Benteng Batu
Jalan Pong Tiku
Sungai Sadang
Sports Field
Pasar

To Livestock Market, Toraja Cottages & Palopo

To Siguntu

To Karasbik (1 km) & Makale

SULAWESI

PLACES TO STAY		PLACES TO EAT
1	Tiakala Indah	48 Maulu
2	Wisma Sederhana	49 Torsini
3	Mace Homestay	50 Rantepao Lodge
4	Wisma Rosa	
6	Wisma Nirmala	PLACES TO EAT
7	Wisma Surya	4 Rima II
8	Wisma Wisata	9 Rima I
11	Wisma Monton	10 Rumah Makan Sarlota
12	Wisma Irama	16 Chez Dodeng
13	Wisma Indograce	20 Restaurant Setia Kawan
17	Losmen Flora	24 Kiosk Mambo
18	Hotel Victoria	38 Restaurant Rachmat
23	Hotel Indra II	
25	Hotel Indra I	OTHER
26	Indra City Hotel	14 Tongkonan Pub
27	Rapa Homestay	15 Mosque
28	Wisma Monika	19 Abadi Supermarket
29	Wisma Maria	21 JET Information
30	Wisma Rantepao	22 Bemo Station
32	Rainbow Homestay	31 Damri & Other Bus
34	Wisma Te Bass	Companies
39	Wisma Martini	33 Telkom
40	Pondok Wisata	35 Post Office
41	Hebron Inn	36 Bank Rakyat Indonesia
42	Homestay Padatindo	37 Abadi Moneychanger
43	Wisma Anata	44 Tourist Office
46	Pias Poppies	45 Merpati
47	Pison	

speak enough Indonesian you can get some explanation of what's happening. Ask around in the hotels and restaurants; you won't have to search too hard. Some people might tell you that such and such a ceremony is being held the following day and ask you to come along, but then they 'forget' the name of the place and what's happening unless you pay. Funerals further from Rantepao are less likely to be overrun with tour groups.

Other Celebrations Ask around about weddings, new house or harvest ceremonies, each with special traditions and a bit of ritual slaughter. You need to be invited, not formally, but at least by someone who knows someone. Dress conservatively.

These celebrations offer a chance to see traditional dancing. Toraja dancing is graceful but less complicated than Balinese or Javanese, and the accompaniment is primarily to the beat of a large drum (or sometimes to taped music). What the dance lacks in complexity is more than made up for by the enthusiasm of members of the audience who dash forward to stuff 5000 and 10,000 rp notes into the performers' headbands. The women's clothes accentuate the strength of Torajan women: they wear flame-coloured dresses with beaded decoration hanging from the waist and shoulders. The family kris (dagger) is tucked into the waistband – in other areas of Indonesia only men may wear a kris.

Places to Stay – bottom end

Rantepao has a good selection of cheap hotels and comfortable homestays, but prices rise in the peak tourist season of June to August.

Many travellers head straight over the bridge to *Wisma Sederhana* (☎ 21011), Jalan Suloara 110, which has singles/doubles from 7000/10,000 rp. The rooms are comfortable, but built around a noisy echo chamber. Tony the manager can be pushy, but is a reliable source of information.

Nearby *Mace Homestay* (☎ 21852), Jalan Tenko Saturu 4, is set in a pretty garden on a quiet street. The delightful women who run it have rooms for 10,000 rp, or 15,000 rp in the high season; it's top value.

Wisma Maria (☎ 21165), Jalan Ratulangi, also looks on to a garden and has a collection of Torajan artefacts in the foyer. It's cheap, central and clean with rooms from 8000/12,000 rp, but the staff tend to be a bit cool.

The *Wisma Monika* (☎ 21216) across the road has rooms from 10,000 to 20,000 rp or from 25,000 rp with running hot water. It's an older place run by friendly people.

Further south at No 62 is *Wisma Martini* (☎ 21240). It's tattered but friendly and all rooms have private bath. Singles/doubles start at 7500/10,000 rp.

Wisma Wisata and *Wisma Surya* are neighbours which both back on to the river. The Wisata (☎ 21746), Jalan Monginsidi 40, is modern and quiet with back rooms overlooking the river. Singles/doubles cost 8500/10,000 rp. It is recommended. The Surya (☎ 21312) at No 36 charges 7000/10,000 rp, plus 2500 rp for breakfast, but is flexible with its pricing.

Wisma Nirmala (☎ 21319), Jalan Andi Mapanyuki, is relatively quiet and near the river. Singles/doubles with private bath will cost you 10,000/17,500 rp. Across the bridge *Wisma Rosa* (☎ 21075) has a quiet location and friendly management. Singles/doubles go for 10,000/12,000 rp.

Avoiding Offence

Almost everyone who goes to Tanatoraja reports appallingly insensitive behaviour by foreigners, and it seems the larger the group, the worse their behaviour. When going to a ceremony don't sit in the pavilions or areas which are designated for the guests and family unless you're invited to. Take as many photos as you want – with restraint. Dress respectfully – black is best. Bring cigarettes and other gifts to offer around. There may be ceremonies or certain times when outsiders are not wanted – otherwise they are open to spectators. ■

SULAWESI

Wisma Rantepao (☎ 21397) is very central and good value with reasonable rooms ranging from 10,000 to 25,000 rp.

The *Rapa Homestay* (☎ 21517) on Jalan Pembangunan has two rooms. Bed and breakfast costs 10,000 rp, or 15,000 rp in the high season. *Rainbow Homestay*, almost opposite at No 11A, has modern and quiet singles/doubles for 15,000/20,000 rp. *Homestay Padatindo*, a few doors down on the corner of Jalan Merdeka, has 10,000 rp rooms.

Wisma Indograce, on busy Jalan Andi Mapanyuki, suffers from street noise but has rooms with private bath for 7500/10,000 rp.

Losmen Flora (☎ 21586) is right next to a mosque, so you can look forward to wake-up call. It's also quite basic, but one of the cheapest in town with 5000 rp singles. The nearby *Hotel Victoria* (☎ 21038) on Jalan Sawerigading is also on a busy street and a bit noisy, but all rooms have private bath. Singles/doubles are 11,000/15,000 rp.

Places to Stay – middle

The *Hotel Indra I* (☎ 21163) at Jalan Landorundun 63 is very pleasant, with a central courtyard garden and singles with private bath for 21,000 rp. (There are actually two Indras; the Indra II is in the top-end category.) There is a moneychanger here, and a very good restaurant.

Almost next door at No 55, the *Indra City Hotel* is under the same management and has good carpeted singles/doubles at 39,000/50,700. It lacks the pleasant garden that distinguishes some of the better hotels.

Pondok Wisata is a large place on Jalan Pembangunan with spotless singles/doubles for 20,000/25,000 rp, or 45,000 rp for a large room with balcony. Just a few doors to the south on the same street is *Hebron Inn* (☎ 21519), a clean and quiet place with doubles for 49,000 rp.

Around the corner is *Wisma Te Bass* (☎ 21415), an old but pleasant place run by a couple – the husband speaks English and the wife speaks Dutch. Rooms are 20,000 rp, or 25,000 rp in the high season.

Just a little further south at the end of the street is *Wisma Anata* (☎ 21356), where all rooms are triples and cost 20,000 rp for one or two persons, 25,000 rp for three.

Wisma Irama (☎ 21371) at Jalan Abdul Gani 16 is a beautiful and quiet hotel with a large garden. It's to the north-east of the town centre and has rooms with mandi for 20,000 rp. Deluxe rooms with hot showers go for 45,000 rp.

Wisma Monton (☎ 21675) at Jalan Abdul Gani 14A is in an alley behind the Irama. Its clean modern rooms start at 20,000 rp, or 25,000 rp with hot running water.

Places to Stay – top end

The *Hotel Indra II* (☎ 21442) is the new wing of the Hotel Indra complex, with singles/doubles for 68,700/86,000 rp, including breakfast and tax. The rooms are beautiful, and face a courtyard garden.

Rantepao's main tourist hotel is the *Toraja Cottages* (☎ 21089) on Jalan Diponegoro, three km to the north-east of town. Singles/doubles start at 80,000/92,000 rp.

Places to Eat

Many of the restaurants, rumah makans and warungs around Rantepao serve Torajan food. A local speciality is pa'piong, a mix of meat (usually pork or chicken) and leaf vegetables smoked over a low flame for hours. Order a couple of hours in advance and enjoy it with black rice.

Rumah Makan Rima I at the northern end of Jalan Mapanyuki is an old favourite with travellers, offering cheap and generous serves of Indonesia fare, as well as the best banana pancakes north of Bali. *Chez Dodeng*, Jalan Emi Saelan, is another Rantepao landmark. It serves basic warung fare.

Kiosk Mambo, Jalan Ratulangi, serves Indonesian and Torajan food but is also great for Western breakfasts. Nearby *Hotel Indra I* has an up-market Indonesian and Torajan restaurant – the chicken pa'piong is especially recommended. *Rumah Makan Sarlota* at the northern end of Jalan Andi Mapanyuki is also popular with travellers.

Restaurant Setia Kawan (☎ 21264), Jalan Andi Mapanyuki 32, does good Chinese

SULAWESI

food. The *Restaurant Rachmat* on Jalan Diponegoro at the traffic circle caters mainly to tourist groups. The food is quite expensive, although servings are usually large.

If you want to self-cater, Toko Remaja and Toko Abadi are the main grocery and department stores. Both are on Jalan Jen Ahmad Yani, near the Setia Kawan.

Entertainment

The *Tongkonan Pub* on Jalan Andi Mapanyuki offers the only real nightlife in town. Opening hours are from around 8 pm until midnight or 1 am. There were also whispers of plans for a pub/disco just outside of town.

Things to Buy

Woodcarving, weaving and basketry are the main crafts of Tanatoraja – some villages are noted for particular specialities, such as Mamasan boxes (used to store magic, as well as salt, betel nut etc), huge horn necklaces and wooden figurines. Woodcarvings include panels, clocks and trays, carved like the decorations on traditional houses and painted in the four traditional colours – black, white, yellow and brown. Look for those being hand etched at Kete Kesu. Bamboo containers with designs carved and burnt on them are decorative as well as functional – formerly used for storing important documents, but now ideal for keeping spaghetti.

Other artefacts sold in the souvenir shops include mini replicas of Torajan houses with incredibly exaggerated overhanging roofs. Other interesting pieces include hand spun Toraja weaving, especially from Sadan, and the longer cloths of the Mamasa Valley. Necklaces made of plant seeds and chunky silver and amber or wooden beads festoon the gift shops, but the orange beaded necklaces are the authentic Torajan wear. Black and red velvet drawstring bags are popular with tourists, much to the amusement of locals who use them for carrying betel nut ingredients to funerals.

The Barre Allo gallery above the bus terminal has an impressive range, beautifully displayed and priced (unlike the souvenir shops below). Note that the prices are not fixed, and ask about packaging and shipping. The Tengko Situru workshop, one km out on the Tikala road, sells crafts from local villages as part of a handcraft development scheme.

Getting There & Away

Air Flying gives you an idea of the dramatic contrasts in Sulawesi Selatan's geography, and thrilling descents over tongkonan kampung amid bamboo groves. There is an airport near Makale, 25 km south of Rantepao. Merpati (☎ 21485), Jalan Pao Pura, flies daily from Ujung Pandang and twice on Sunday. The fare is 87,000 rp (including tax). Be prepared for delays and always reconfirm flights – staff often double book.

Bus & Bemo There are regular buses between Ujung Pandang and Rantepao. In Rantepao the bus company offices are around Jalan Andi Mapanyuki in the centre of town. The main bus companies on the Rantepao-Ujung Pandang route are Damri, Fa Litha, Liman and Alam Indah. Departures in each direction are typically at 7, 10 and 11 am, and 1, 6 and 9 pm. The trip to Ujung Pandang (330 km) costs 8000 rp (15,000 rp for the Fa Litha executive bus with air-con, TV and leg room). Pare Pare to Rantepao takes four to five hours and costs 5000 rp.

The main bus company heading north from Rantepao through Central Sulawesi to Tentena and Palu is Damri. There are daily buses, and fares from Rantepao to Pendolo (10 hours), Tentena (12 hours) and Poso (13 hours) are all 20,000 rp. To Palu (20 hours), it's 25,000 rp. You can also make this trip by bemo – see Getting There & Away under Pendolo in the Central Sulawesi section later in this chapter for details.

Bemos run down to the coastal city of Palopo (4500 rp), taking two hours for the journey or 2½ hours in the uphill direction. There are daily buses from Rantepao to Soroako on Danau Matano, leaving at about 10 am from the Rantepao bus terminal (10 hours; 8000 rp); the road is surfaced all the way.

Getting Around

To/From the Airport A Merpati bus collects passengers from their hotels and guarantees that you will reach your flight on time, but the bus costs a steep 5000 rp.

Local Transport Central Rantepao is small and easy to walk around. Becaks hang around the bus terminals, but you probably won't have much use for them.

Bemos run from Rantepao to various destinations in the surrounding region. Kijang run almost continuously from Rantepao south to Makale (500 rp) and you can get off at the signs for Londa (400 rp), Tilanga (400 rp) or Lemo (400 rp) and walk. There are also frequent bemos east towards Palopo for the sights in that direction, eg Nanggala (500 rp). Bemos north to Sadan cost 800 rp. All stop at 6 pm, after then you need to charter. Makale-bound punters can sometimes hitch a free lift on the 9 pm Ujung Pandang bus.

Motorbikes can be rented for 3000 rp per hour, or 10,000 to 20,000 rp per day. Allow for two days of recovery after one day of riding! It can be cheaper for a group to charter a bemo or a jeep.

Apart from the roads to Makale, Palopo, Sadan, Kete Kesu and a few other places, most of the roads around Rantepao are terrible. Some are constructed out of compacted boulders – you don't get stuck but your joints get rattled loose. If trekking, bring good footwear to negotiate the mud and the rocks. Take a water bottle, something to eat, a flashlight in case you end up walking at night and an umbrella or raincoat. Even in the dry season it's more likely than not to rain.

MAKALE

Makale is the capital of Tanatoraja, but has few of the amenities of Rantepao. Makale is a small, pretty town built around an artificial lake and set amid cloud-shrouded hills. There are whitewashed churches atop each hill and a good market, and Dutch houses in the older part of town.

Market day is every six days, a blur of noise, colour and commotion. There are pigs aplenty, strapped down with bamboo strips

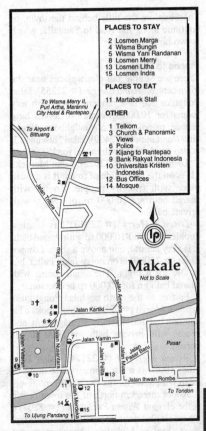

for buyers' close inspection, buckets of live eels, piles and piles of fresh and dried fish, and a corner of the market reserved for *induk* sales. The induk women are constantly mixing and blending fresher, sweeter induk with the older more alcoholic brews. Taste before you buy, either by pouring the proffered capful on to your palm and slurping from there, or by flicking the lot into your mouth. When you find the perfect brew, pay around 5000 to 10,000 rp for five litres, including the container.

Heading out of the market towards Tondon, there are a few tau tau hidden in a rock face.

SULAWESI

Then explore the hills behind the town, or continue along the road to Sangalla, which is two hours by foot.

Places to Stay
There are simple but clean places near the town centre. *Wisma Bungin* (☎ 22255), Jalan Pongtiku 35, is a modern place with airy rooms for 10,000 rp each. All rooms have private mandi. Bungin's neighbour, *Wisma Yani Randanan* (☎ 22409), Jalan Nusantara 3, is also good value, with rooms for 15,000 rp.

Losmen Indra (☎ 22022), Jalan Merdeka 11, is on the south side of town. It is a clean place with friendly people. Rooms with shared bath are 10,000 rp, or 15,000 with private mandi.

Losmen Merry (☎ 22013) has singles/doubles for 5000/10,000 rp with shared bath. It is very central, and above a shop. *Losmen Litha* (☎ 22009) is on noisy Jalan Pelita, but is OK for a night. The small rooms with shared bath go for 10,000 rp per person.

Further to the north on Jalan Pongtiku is *Losmen Marga* (☎ 22011), which looks a bit tattered but has friendly management and rooms with private bath for 5000 rp per person.

Wisma Merry II (☎ 22174), Jalan Pongtiku 100B, is a big, homey place north of town with quiet rooms for 10,000 rp.

About three km north of the town centre is the elegant *Wisma Puri Artha* (☎ 22047), where singles/doubles are 38,500/45,500 rp. Next door is Makale's expensive tourist resort, the *Marannu City Hotel* (☎ 22028), where singles/doubles go for 95,000/108,000 rp. This place comes complete with tennis courts and a swimming pool. At 1500 rp, the pool provides welcome refuge from the attentions of the local kids.

Places to Eat
Dining out is limited to basic warungs. Self-caterers can supplement market purchases with goods from Toko Sahabat or Sinar Mada. The main alternatives are the hotel restaurants are the *Puri Artha* (ordinary menu) or the *Marannu City Hotel* (expensive, tasty Western food but slow service).

Pa'piong is the local speciality, smoked in bamboo tubes in the market through the day, and sold in the warung around the market at night. Eat there or take some back to your hotel.

Throughout the day seasonal fruit and kueh (cakes), such as banana fried in a shortcrust pastry, are available from the stalls along the lanes near the market.

Getting There & Away
Makale shares its airport with Rantepao, and airline offices are in Rantepao.

There are kijang all through the day from Rantepao, the trip takes 40 minutes and costs 500 rp. However the last kijang home from Rantepao leaves around dusk, making dining out in Rantepao a tricky proposition. From Makale you can get buses to the same places (and for the same prices) as you can from Rantepao. The offices and agents for the buses are all in the middle of town, clustered near the corner of Jalan Merdeka and Jalan Ihwan Rombe.

AROUND RANTEPAO & MAKALE
The following places are all within fairly easy reach on day trips, but you can make longer trips staying overnight in villages or camping out. If you stay in villages don't exploit Torajan hospitality – pay your way. Guides are useful if you have a common language, but in some ways it's better without a guide. The Toraja are friendly and used to tourists so they rarely bother you and it's great to get out on your own into the beautiful countryside around Rantepao. If you're really short on time you could hire a bemo or motorbike and whip around the main sites in a day or two – but that's not the way to see this place.

North-West of Rantepao
At 2150 metres above sea level, **Gunung Sesean** is not the highest peak in Sulawesi, but it's certainly the most popular with hikers. The summit is accessible via a trail which begins in the town of Batutumonga, 23 km and four hours' walk to the north-west of Rantepao. You can spend the night in

Batutumonga, and from there, the return trip to the summit takes five hours. A guide might be useful, but the trail is so well established that you can probably manage on your own.

Batutumonga itself is a haven with sweeping views over Tanatoraja and is an ideal stopover for trekking trips. Take a bemo from Rantepao to **Lempo**, 11 km and two hours (plus waiting time as the bemo fills) up a hideously bumpy track and walk from there (half an hour).

Batutumonga has several losmen but no telephones. Get there by afternoon to secure a room. *Mama Siska's* is up a small track to the right as you enter the village. Stay in creaky, bamboo houses with clean mandi below. Mama Siska cooks superb meals over an open fire. Prices average around 15,000 rp per head for dinner, bed and breakfast.

Londoruden Homestay has its own generator, restaurant and amazing views over the valley. Twin rooms with private mandi and garden settings cost 20,000 rp, including breakfast. Ask Aras to explain the name. There are a few of other places and a couple of reasonable restaurants to choose from, all with views.

From Batutumonga you can walk to **Lokomata** and return on the same day. Lokomata (26 km from Rantepao) has some cave graves in one rocky outcrop, and more beautiful scenery.

After the morning cloud lifts the next day, walk the well-marked path from Batutumonga to Tikala via **Pana** with its ancient hanging graves among bamboo. Pass kampung along the way, see children pounding rice, men scrubbing their beloved buffalo and kids splashing happily in pools.

Alternatively, you could take the bemo up from Rantepao to Lokomata, walk back down the same road to the Rantepao to Sadan road, and catch a bemo back to Rantepao. This is a very pleasant downhill walk of about five hours through some of the finest scenery in Tanatoraja.

Beyond Batutumonga, the sleepy village of **Pangala** (35 km from Rantepao) is noted for its fine dancers and is the place made famous by Nigel Barley's book, *Not a Hazardous Sport*. It is a hair-raising 2½-hour bemo ride from Rantepao, starting by the river then up a pot-holed road for as far as you can bear. Eventually walking seems a better option.

The village's only losmen, *Losmen Sando,* is a surprisingly elegant place with comfortable rooms, clean mandi, carved doors, a spacious lounge-restaurant with big windows looking out to the owner's coffee plantation. Peter charges about 10,000 rp per person, and offers free advice on treks back to Rantepao or across to Batutumonga.

North of Rantepao

The traditional village of **Palawa**, two km north of Pangli, is just as attractive but less popular than Kete Kesu, with tongkonan houses and rice barns. In the dry season you can walk to **Bori**, fording a river and walking through padi fields. Bori is the site of an impressive rante and some towering megaliths. A km south is **Parinding**, which has tongkonan houses and rice barns which you pass on the two hour walk from Bori to Tikala. Rantepao-bound bemos occasionally pass this way.

Pangli, seven km north of Rantepao, has tau tau and house graves. House graves are an interesting innovation used when there are no rock faces available for carving out burial niches. Graves are dug in the earth and a small Toraja-style house is built over the top. Each grave is used for all the members of the family and the bodies are wrapped in cloth and entombed without coffins.

Further north is **Sadan**, the weaving centre of Tanatoraja, where the women have a tourist market to sell their weaving. All of it is handmade on simple, back-strap looms, but not all is produced in the village. Many of the large, earthy blankets come from the west. You can see the women making the cloth using this technique. There are bemos from Rantepao direct to Sadan 13 km along a surfaced road (500 rp). Stop for a drink at the *River Cafe* on the way back and enjoy slightly exotic dishes (at slightly exotic prices), while overlooking the second campus of the region's only university; then check out the crafts downstairs.

SULAWESI

West of Rantepao

Gunung Singki is a rather steep hill just a km west across the river from Rantepao. There's a slippery, somewhat overgrown trail to the summit with its panoramic view across the town and the surrounding countryside. Rantepao looks surprisingly large from high up. From Singki you can continue walking down the dirt road to **Siguntu**, seven km from Rantepao and an interesting walk past the rice fields. The path is not obvious so keep asking directions. From Siguntu to the main road at Alang Alang is also a pleasant walk. Stop on the way at the traditional village of **Mendoe**, six km from Rantepao. At Alang Alang, where a covered bridge crosses the river, you could head to Londa or back to Rantepao or Makale or, alternatively, remain on the west side of the river and continue walking to the villages of Langda and Madandan.

South of Rantepao

On the outskirts of Rantepao, just off the road leading to Makale, is **Karasbik** with traditional-style houses arranged in a horseshoe around a cluster of megaliths. The complex of houses may have been erected some years ago for a single funeral ceremony, but some are now inhabited. In the past, temporary houses would be built around a rante for use at a funeral and when the funeral was finished these would be demolished or burnt.

Just off the main road south of Rantepao (on the way to Kete Kesu) is **Buntu Pune** where there are two tongkonan houses and six rice barns. The story goes that one of the two houses was built by a nobleman named Pong Marambaq at the beginning of this century. During the Dutch rule he was appointed head of the local district, but planned to rebel and was subsequently exiled to Ambon where he died. His corpse was brought back to Toraja and buried at the hill to the north of this village.

A km or so further along the road is **Kete Kesu** (six km from Rantepao), reputed for its woodcarving. On the cliff face behind the village are some grave caves and some very

old hanging graves. The rotting coffins are suspended on wooden beams under an overhang. Others, full of bones and skulls, lie rotting in strategic piles. If you continue along the vague trail heading uphill you'll come to another grave cave. There are no tau tau, just coffins and bones, similarly neglected. One of the houses in the village has several tau tau on display.

The houses at Kete Kesu are decorated with enough handcrafts to fill a souvenir floor at Harrods; the village is a tourist museum, no-one seems to live here any more and there are surfaced paths to the main caves, but it's still an interesting site. To get there take a bemo from Rantepao.

From Kete Kesu you can walk to **Sullu-kang**, which has a rante marked by a number of large, rough-hewn megaliths, and on to **Palatokke** (nine km from Rantepao). In this beautiful area of lush rice paddies and traditional houses there is an enormous cliff face containing several grave caves and hanging graves. Access to the caves is difficult but the scenery alone makes it worthwhile.

The Palatokke Story

There is a story among the Toraja that Palatokke is the name of a person who was able to climb the rock face, his palms being like those of a gecko and able to cling to walls. When he died, it is said, his corpse was put into an *erong* (wooden coffin) and hung on these cliffs. In another part of Tanatoraja there is a story that Palatokke refers to a group of people who were able to climb the rock face like geckos. These people are said to have been a special class of workers whose job it was to hang the erong of noblemen on the cliff face by climbing the cliff without using ladders. ■

From Palatokke you could walk to Labo and on to Randanbatu, where there are supposed to be more graves, then continue to Balik, Sangalla, Suaya and Makale.

Six km south of Rantepao is the very extensive burial cave of **Londa** at the base of a massive cliff face. A bemo from Rantepao heading towards Makale will drop you at the Turon to Londa, from where it's a short walk (two km).

The entrance to the cave is guarded by a balcony of tau turn-off. Inside the cave is a collection of coffins, many of them rotted away, with the bones either scattered or thrown into piles. Other coffins hold the bones of several family members – it's an old Toraja custom that all people who have lived together in one family house should also be buried together in a family grave. There are other cave graves in Tanatoraja where no coffin is used at all – the body is wrapped in cloth, placed in a niche in the rock face and then the door of the niche is tightly closed. A local myth says that the people buried in the Londa caves are the descendants of Tangdilinoq, chief of the Toraja at the time when they were pushed out of the Enrekang region by new arrivals and forced to move into the highlands.

Kids hang around outside the Londa caves with oil lamps to guide you around (3000 rp). Unless you've got a strong torch you really *do* need a guide with a lamp. Inside the caves, the coffins (some of them liberally decorated with graffiti) and skulls seem to have been placed in strategic locations for the benefit of sightseers. Ask to see 'Romeo and Juliet' and (if you are thin and don't suffer from claustrophobia) squeeze through the tunnel connecting the two main caves. It is a 10-minute crawl past some interesting stalactites and stalagmites. Walk up the path by the padi opposite to where tau tau are carved. New red coffins up the nearby cliff show the old traditions are continuing.

Close to the Londa graves is **Pabaisenan** (Liang Pia), where the coffins of babies can be found hanging from a tree.

Further south, just off the Rantepao-Makale road, is **Tilanga**, a pretty, natural cool-water swimming pool. Coming from Makale, it's an interesting walk along the muddy trails and through the rice paddies from Lemo to Tilanga, but keep asking directions along the way. The natural pool at Tilanga is uphill from a derelict concrete swimming pool and decaying changing rooms.

Lemo (11 km south of Rantepao) is probably the most interesting burial area in Tanatoraja. The sheer rock face has a whole series of balconies for the tau tau. The biggest balcony has a dozen figures, with white eyes and black pupils and outstretched arms like spectators at a sports event.

There is a story that the graves are for descendants of a Toraja chief who, hundreds of years ago, reigned over the surrounding district and built his house on top of the cliff into which the graves are now cut. Because the mountain was part of his property only his descendants could use it. The chief himself was buried elsewhere, as the art of cutting grave caves had not been developed then.

It's a good idea to go early in the morning so you get the sun on the rows of figures – by 9 am their heads are in the shadows. A bemo from Rantepao will drop you off at the road to Lemo. From there it's a 15-minute walk to the tau tau.

Apart from those at Lemo, it is becoming increasingly difficult to see many tau tau in Rantepao. This is because so many of them have been stolen that the Toraja have taken to keeping the remaining ones in their own homes.

One place where you can still see substantial numbers of tau tau is at **Tampangallo**, due east of Makale and very close to Suaya. Coming from Sangalla, there's a signpost about a km before you get to Suaya. Turn off the road and walk about 500 metres through the rice paddies to a place where there are over 40 tau tau.

The local graves belong to the chiefs of Sangalla, descendants of the mythical divine being, Tamborolangiq, who is believed to have introduced the caste system, the death rituals and techniques of agriculture into Torajan society. The former royal families of Makale, Sangalla and Menkendek all claimed descent from Tamborolangiq who is said to have descended from heaven by a stone staircase.

East of Rantepao

Marante is a fine traditional village close to the road to Palopo. Near Marante there are stone and hanging graves with several tau

tau, skulls on the coffins and a cave with scattered bones. From Marante you can cross the river on the suspension bridge and walk to the village of **Ba'ta**, which is set in attractive padi fields.

In the same direction but further off the Palopo road, is the traditional village of **Nanggala** (16 km from Rantepao). It has a particularly grandiose traditional house and an impressive fleet of 14 rice barns! The rice barns have a bizarre array of motifs carved into them, including soldiers with guns, Western women and automobiles. Bemos from Rantepao take you straight there for 300 rp. Keep an eye out for a colony of huge black bats hanging from trees at the end of the village.

From Nanggala you can walk to **Paniki** and **Buntao**, a very long walk along a dirt track up and down the Toraja hills. The trail starts next to the rice barns. It's a three-hour walk from Nanggala to the Paniki district, and along the road you'll see coffee-plantation machines grinding and packing coffee into sacks. It's a long, tedious trudge and can be very hot, so take lots of water. From Paniki it's a two-hour walk to Buntao which has some house graves and tau tau. Alternatively, catch a bemo from Paniki to Rantepao. Buntao is about 15 km from Rantepao.

Two or three km beyond Buntao is **Tembamba**, which has more graves and is noted for its fine scenery.

South of Buntao and 22 km from Rantepao is **Sangalla** from where you can head south-east to the hot spring at **Makula**, west to the Rantepao-Makale road, or north to Labo and the road to Kete Kesu. There are occasional bemos from Makale and Rantepao to Sangalla.

White-Water Rafting

The canyon of the Sadan River makes for an interesting white-water rafting trip that can be completed in one day. There are over 20 rapids, none of them terribly dangerous. All equipment, transport and guides can be provided by Sobek Expeditions (☎ 0423-22143) in Makale. You can also make bookings in Ujung Pandang at Wira Karya Tours

(☎ 0411-312298; fax 314652), Jalan Gunung Lokon 25.

Toranggo Buya (☎ 0411-81791) is the other professional outfit running rafting tours down the Sadan. This US-Indonesian company offers one-day (120,000 rp per person), two-day (220,000 rp) and three-day (430,000 rp) all-inclusive expeditions. It's base is at Jalan Bulukunyi 9A, PO Box 107, Ujung Pandang 90131, Sulawesi Selatan.

PALOPO

This Muslim port town is the administrative capital of the Luwu district. Before the Dutch this was once the centre of the old and powerful Luwu Kingdom; the former palace is now the minuscule **Museum Batara Guru**. It's at Jalan Andi Jemma 1, opposite the police station, and contains relics of the royal era. On the waterfront is a Bugis village and a long pier where you can get a closer look at the fishing boats.

Places to Stay

The *Palopo Hotel*, Jalan Kelapa 11, is opposite the bus station. Grubby singles with bath are 6500 rp, while rooms with air-con go for 20,000 rp.

Buana Hotel, Jalan Dahlan, is an attractive place with a friendly manager. Prices range from 8500 to 20,000 rp.

Hotel Bumi Sawerigading is an old echo chamber, but it's not bad and all rooms have private bath. It's about a 15-minute walk from the bus station, or take a becak. Economy singles/doubles are 7500/10,000 rp. *Hotel Adifati* is newer and classier, with budget rooms for 8800 rp, and rooms with air-con for 22,000 rp.

Getting There & Away

The frequent bemos from Rantepao twist and turn their way down to the coast in 2½ hours. The fare is 4500 rp and the views are spectacular. There are buses and bemos from Palopo's main market *(pasar sentral)* to Pare Pare and Ujung Pandang, Soroako and Malili, Pendolo and Poso, and to Sengkang and Watampone.

From Rantepao you could take a bus to

Palopo and then head down the east coast back to Ujung Pandang, via Sengkang and Bone (Watampone). Palopo to Bone takes six hours. The road is good for the first half of the journey but disappears into huge potholes for the last two hours.

There are irregular boat services from Palopo to Malili, but the buses are faster and more frequent. A useful ferry connection is the service between Siwa and Susua.

MALILI & SOROAKO

Any town as distant, isolated and forgotten as Malili is hardly a candidate for a short colourful history, but thanks to the rich iron deposits around nearby Lake Matano, that's what it has. The Dutch built a thriving settlement here that was largely destroyed by the Japanese during WW II. Malili was also a rebel stronghold in the Sulawesi rebellion of the 1950s and was repeatedly razed and burnt.

Southern Sulawesi rebelled in 1950 under the leadership of Kahar Muzakar. He was a native of the Luwu region of South Sulawesi and had played a founding role in one of the Sulawesi youth organisations fighting the Dutch on Java after WW II. Sent to Sulawesi in June 1950, Muzakar teamed up with some of the Sulawesi guerrillas who had been fighting the Dutch and led them in a rebellion against the central government. His reasons seem to have been mixed: a combination of personal ambition coupled with a general opposition to Javanese and Minahasan domination of the civil and military services. By 1956, Kahar Muzakar's guerrillas controlled most of the southern Sulawesi countryside and the rebellion continued until Muzakar was killed by government troops in 1966.

Next came the mining company PT Inco which officially opened its US$850 million nickel mining and smelting project at Soroako in 1977. The project mines converts low-grade ore (a nickel content of only 1.6%) into a high-grade product with a nickel content of 75%. The company not only built a smelting plant, but also a town at Malili for its Western employees with schools, a hospital, an airport (at Soroako), administration

buildings, a road to connect Soroako and Malili with the Bone Bay, a wharf and a satellite station to link Soroako directly with its offices in Ujung Pandang and Jakarta.

Danau Matano, Mahalona & Towuti

The most striking natural feature of this area is the series of mountain-fringed lakes linked by rivers and streams. Soroako is on the shores of the 16,400-hectare Danau Matano. With depths of up to 540 metres, it is Sulawesi's deepest lake. It forms the headwaters of the Malili River system, with overflows pouring into Mahalona, then into Towuti and finally out into the rivers.

With an area of 56,100 hectares and depths of up to 203 metres, Danau Towuti is the second-largest lake in Indonesia – Sumatra's Danau Toba is bigger. Towuti is still quite elevated, so the outflow passes through a series of rapids and waterfalls before reaching the sea near Malili. The lakes support impressive bird life and other fauna.

Getting There & Away

There is a great road between Palopo and Soroako via Malili. There are bemos and buses from Rantepao to Malili and Soroako. There is also an airport at Soroako, and Merpati flies there via Tator and Masamba once a week.

Mamasa Valley

The Mamasa Valley is often referred to as West Tanatoraja, but this probably overstates the connection between Mamasa and Rantepao. A key factor distinguishing the people of Mamasa from their more famous neighbours is isolation. There is no air access, and the recently sealed road linking Mamasa to Polewali is closed by mud slides almost every time there is heavy rain. The provincial government is funding construction of an all-weather road from Mamasa to Bittuang, near Rantepao, but it is likely Mamasa will retain its Shangrila-like isolation for a few years yet.

SULAWESI

Mamasans have embraced Christianity with unfettered enthusiasm, or at least they have embraced that aspect of Christianity which encourages hymn-singing. Choir groups meet up and down the valley every dawn and dusk, flexing their vocal chords in praise of god. Interest in the old ways is waning. Tongkonan (the traditional houses) are falling into disrepair, and no new ones are being built. Torajan ceremonies survive, notably funerals, but on the whole these are far less ostentatious affairs than those around Rantepao.

Sambu weaving is a craft which still thrives in the hills around Mamasa. These long strips of heavy woven material are stitched together to make blankets, ideal insulation for the cold mountain nights. Most use factory-dyed thread, but ask around and you can find the few still using the old time-consuming natural-dye techniques.

Like Tanatoraja, the best way to see this area is by foot. Paths tend to follow the ridges, giving hikers stunning views of the clean, mountain-fringed countryside. There are few roads, and far too many paths to choose from. The only sensible way to choose between the dozens of alternatives is to constantly ask directions as you go. Open-ended questions (such as: 'Where does this path lead to?') are better than those requiring a yes or no. The other confusing factor is that village districts, such as Balla, cover a broad area and there are few villages per se. Even centres within the village area, such as Rante Balla, Balla Kalua and Buntu Balla, are very spread out. There are frequent invitations to sit, drink the local coffee and talk. Take your time, listen and enjoy.

MAMASA

Mamasa, population 2000, is the only large town in the valley. The air is cool and clean, and the folk hospitable – everyone makes time for a chat. The rhythm of life has a surreal, fairytale-like quality for those used to the hustle of Indonesia's big cities. The town wakes to choirs at dawn, prayer groups punctuate the daily routine, electricity runs from 6 pm to midnight, and dogs roam misty streets in the wee hours. The highlight of the week is the **market**, where hill people trade their produce. Look for locally made woven blankets, a must for those cold mountain nights. Trekkers will also be offered plenty of fine-looking blankets direct from weavers while walking through hill villages, so take money.

Places to Stay & Eat

Mamasa has several *penginapan* (lodging houses), all clean, comfortable and cheap. Most serve reasonably priced food. *Losmen Mini* on Jalan Yani is a rambling mountain lodge in the heart of town with sunny upstairs doubles, mandi and bibles for 15,000 rp. The 10,000 rp rooms out back are a little darker but fine; you'll wake to the lilting voices of a gospel choir which meets a few doors down each dawn.

Mantana Lodge's tiled interior is so bright that you might mistake it for an advertisement for cleaning products. Singles start at 10,000 rp, and doubles range from 15,000 to 25,000 rp. There is a good restaurant, cold beer for 3500 rp, souvenir sales and a manager who speaks English.

Guest House BPS off Jalan Demmatande is a big old-fashioned place run by the Mamasa Toraja church with 5000 to 7500 rp rooms backing on to the gurgling waters of the Mamasa River.

Losmen Marapan, Jalan Yani 39, is one of the older penginapan. Its small clean doubles with mandi cost 9000 rp, or there are economy rooms for 6000 rp. If antiques take your fancy, ask to see Papa's collection in the attic.

Mamasa Guest House on the northern edge of town near the hospital is new, with views of the surrounding mountains and the high Mambulilin Waterfall (for more details see Around Mamasa). Doubles at this pleasant place cost 15,000 rp.

Wisma Mamasa is an old Dutch house on the rise overlooking the rest of town. At 10,000 rp a double, it is less attractive than its more popular competitors, but the views are fantastic.

Mamasa Cottage is an ambitious hotel

project built over hot springs at Kole, three km north of Mamasa, with lovely rooms for around 95,000 to 113,000 rp. Hot spring water flows to every room, there is a restaurant and the staff speak fluent English.

Getting There & Away

Take a bus from Pare Pare to Polewali and then a bum-numbing bemo to Mamasa. Bittuang is connected by road to Makale, but foot is the main mode on this route. Getting to Ujung Pandang is comfortable and easy if you can score a seat on one of the express buses that leave from in front of the market early in the morning. The cost is 10,000 rp. These buses occasionally drop passengers at Pare Pare for 7000 rp, but prefer passengers bound for Ujung Pandang.

AROUND MAMASA

The countryside surrounding Mamasa is strikingly beautiful. You can hire motorbikes or hitch along the valley's couple of roads, but footpaths and slender suspended bridges link most of the villages. The following places (with distances in km from Mamasa in brackets) are within easy reach, but take warm clothes and gifts for your hosts if you

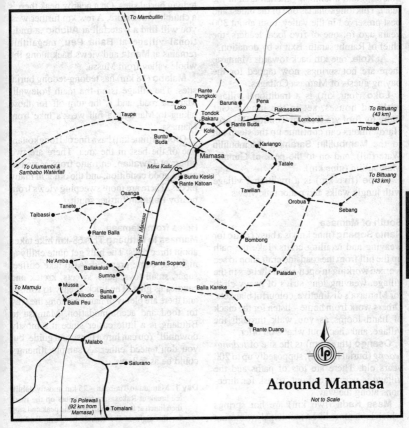

Around Mamasa

Not to Scale

plan to stay overnight in the hills. Most people grow their own coffee here. Instead, put condensed milk, chocolate, sugar, kretek (clove cigarettes) and other goods from the city on your gift list.

North of Mamasa

Rante Buda (four km) has an impressive 25-metre-long tongkonan house known as Banua Layuk (High House), an old chief's house with colourful motifs. Visitors are invited to inspect the *tado*, the reception room at the front. Beyond that there is a *ba ba* guestroom, *tambing* (the owners' private quarters) and a *lombon* (kitchen area at the rear). This tongkonan is one of the oldest and best preserved in the valley, built about 300 years ago for one of five local leaders, the chief of Rambusaratu. Exit is by donation.

At **Kole**, one km back towards Mamasa, there are hot springs, now tapped for the paying guests of Mamasa Cottages.

Loko (four km) is a traditional village with old houses, set in the jungle. Get there by foot via Kole or Tondok Bakaru. Hardy hikers can continue up the steep hill to the **Mambulilin Sarambu** (Mambulilin Waterfall), and on to the peak of Gunung Mambulilin (nine km).

Taupe (five km) is a traditional village with jungle walks and panoramic views.

South of Mamasa

Rante Sopang (nine km) is a busy centre for weaving and retailing crafts. Take the path up the hill from the roadside craft shop to see women working in open-sided shelters in the village, weaving long strips of heavy cloth for Mamasa's distinctive, colourful blankets. Others work from home – listen for the clack of hand looms as you walk through the village, and check out what's on offer.

Osango (three km) is the site of *tedong-tedong* (burial houses), supposedly up to 200 years old. There are lots of paths and the village is *very* spread out, so ask for directions along the way.

Mesa Kada (two km) are hot springs which look more like a municipal swimming

pool than fresh water from the earth, but are still nice for a swim.

Tanete (eight km) has mountain graves under a cave. Tanete and nearby **Taibassi** are also centres for traditional weaving and carving.

Rante Balla (12 km) has big beautiful tongkonan, many with dozens of buffalo horns adorning the front, honouring the former residents. The village is also a centre for traditional weaving, and there are fantastic weaved baskets from this area.

Buntu Balla (15 km) is another section of Balla with traditional houses, beautiful vistas, traditional weaving and tedong-tedong burial sites. On a nearby peak there's a church with a spire. A few km further west you will find a waterfall at **Allodio**, a traditional village at **Balla Peu**, megalithic remains at **Manta** and views back along the whole valley from Mussa.

Malabo (18 km) has tedong-tedong burial sites. The village is on the main Polewali-Mamasa road, and is the turn-off for those hiking to Mamuju, a full week's hike from Mamasa.

Orobua (nine km) has a fine old tongkonan, one of the best in the area. There are two others at **Tawalian**, en route from Mamasa, one in good condition, and the other in many pieces. There are more sweeping views from nearby **Paladan** further south.

Hikes from Mamasa

Mamasa to Bittuang This 68-km hike takes about three days. The hills get quite chilly at night, so come prepared. Also take coffee, sugar, small toys, pens, sweets, kretek and candles as gifts. The track is easy to follow, and there are plenty of hamlets along the way for food and accommodation. Mamasa to Bittuang is a little easier since it's mostly downhill. You can hire a horse and guide, but you don't need either. A sample itinerary could be as follows:

Day 1: Mamasa to Timbaan – 25 km, mostly uphill; tea break at Rakasasan, two hours up the road, then lunch at Lombonan. Cross the peak and stop for the night at Ibu Kaka's house in Timbaan

A, B, E & F: Annual Biak Islanders' festival, representing all tribal cultures from Biak Island (PG)
C: Firewalker, Adoki, Biak Island (PG)
D: Burning coal and wood for firewalking, Adoki, Biak Island (PG)

Top left: Women scaling and gutting the catch, Mahakam River, East Kalimantan (BD)
Middle left: A Banuaq woman preparing doyo leaf for dying and weaving,
Mancong, East Kalimantan (BD)
Top right: Peanut seller at the Makale market, Sulawesi (BD)
Bottom: Live pigs for sale at the Makale market, Sulawesi (BD)

(10,000 rp, including dinner and breakfast); she has beer for 5000 rp a bottle.

Day 2: Timbaan to Paku – tea and coconut (1000 rp) from a house at Bau, swim at a crossing 2½ hours down the road, stay at *Homestay Papasado* in Ponding (10,000 rp per night, including two meals; it's next to the traditional house), or continue to Paku and stay at *Mountain Homestay* for 10,000 rp. It is run by a young couple with children, and has a clear view of the perfect sunsets.

Day 3: Paku to Bittuang – three-hour walk or half an hour by car (2500 rp) over a rough track. It's better to walk. There are three losmen at Bittuang; try *Losmen Pabongian* (5000 rp a night, plus 5000 rp for meals and drinks). There are bemos from Bittuang to Makale.

Mamasa to Mamuju The hike to Mamuju takes from three days to a week, depending on your luck with transport. Salarindu, the halfway mark, can be reached by a road of sorts. The trail from there to Mamuju is somewhat rougher. You'll need a guide and some fluency in Indonesian to find your way. Try to persuade someone in Salarindu to join you.

South-East Sulawesi

South-East Sulawesi and the Buton (Butung) and Tukangbesi island groups off its southern tip, is rarely visited by travellers. It is a relatively small and sparsely populated province inhabited by diverse ethnic groups, including many who look very Torajan and who once practised customs similar to those of the Toraja. Islamic influence from the Bugis kingdom of Bone was also strong and Islam now predominates.

Perhaps the best documented area is the 96,800-hectare **Aopa Wetlands** between Kendari and Kolaka. Aopa consists of two lakes both about 25 km across, with a rich array of aquatic plant life and birds. Water temperature in these shallow lakes often exceeds air temperature.

KOLAKA

A port town on the west coast of the peninsula, Kolaka is readily accessible by boat from Bajoe, the port of Bone. Ferries from Bajoe leave nightly and the trip to Kolaka takes about eight hours. Fares are 10,300 rp for 1st class, 8500 rp for 2nd and 6800 rp for 3rd, or you can book a combined bus/boat ticket direct to Kendari for 25,000 rp. From the harbour in Kolaka there are hordes of minibuses eager to take you to Kendari (4500 rp, four hours).

Kolaka has several budget losmen, including the *Monalisa*, Jalan Konggoasa 67, for 10,000 rp; *Rachma*, Jalan Kadue 6, for 10,000 rp; and the *Mustika*, Jalan Replita 22, for 7500 rp. The Rachma is better than most, but unless you are hanging around for market day or the ferry, there is no reason to stop in Kolaka. The Lamadai Game Reserve, a 500-hectare ironwood and wildlife sanctuary, is 40 km from Kolaka.

KENDARI

This is a small provincial capital (population 150,000) and nickel mining town on the east coast of the peninsula, linked to Kolaka by an excellent road. It has one very long main street, and is surrounded by wilderness.

The tiered **Morame Waterfalls**, 100 metres of tumbling water on the Sungai Kali Osena, is 65 km south of the capital. It takes over an hour to get there by bemo, or one to two hours by boat. There is a deep pool at the base of the falls, which is excellent for swimming. Those with the energy can beat their way through the bush to mountain lakes 10 km upstream. If returning to Kendari by boat, stop off at **Lapuko Bay**, a good swimming and snorkelling spot with white-sand beaches and clear water.

Hari Island is a nature reserve just off the Kendari coast, with a white-sand beach, snorkelling and walks. To get there, get a group together and charter a boat for around 50,000 rp for the day.

There is a hill resort and beach 20 km north of Kendari, **Toli-Toli Hill** and Batu Gong beach, worth a visit if you have time to kill. There is also a bathing beach much closer to Kendari at **Maya Ria**, a half-hour walk from the end of Kendari Bay or a 300 rp bemo ride.

SULAWESI

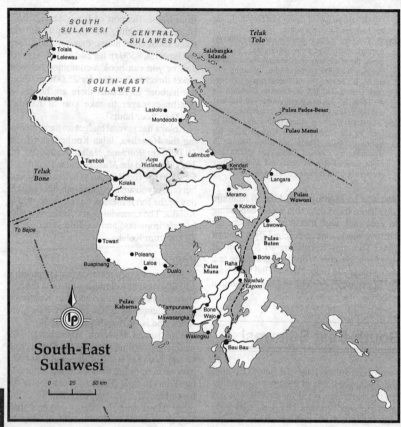

South-East Sulawesi

0   25   50 km

Information

The regional Dinas Pariwisata (☎ 21764) is at Jalan Mesjid Raya 1, Kendari.

Places to Stay & Eat

The cheapest losmen are *Wisma Cendra-wasih* (☎ 21291), Jalan Diponegoro; *Wisma Bunga Tanjung*, Jalan Bunga Tanjung 11; and *Wisma Kodrat* (☎ 21388) at Jalan Parman. By the harbour, near the cinema, are more losmen, including the *Penginapan Kendari* and the expensive *Wisma Andika*.

There are several intermediate hotels, including the *Armins* (☎ 21418) at Jalan

Diponegoro 55, but easily the best place in town is the comfortable *Kendari Beach Hotel* (☎ 21988), Jalan Hasanuddin 44, with rates ranging from 65,000 to 190,000 rp.

There is a good restaurant at the Kendari Beach Hotel, in a town otherwise not known for its cuisine. There is variety available from the night-time food stalls at the waterfront, about one km from the harbour, plus a lot of dingy places near the market.

Getting There & Away

Air Kendari is well connected by air via Ujung Pandang. Sempati (☎ 51612), Jalan

Silondae 26, has direct flights to Ujung Pandang twice a week, with connections to Surabaya, Jakarta, Singapore, Medan, Taipei etc. Merpati (☎ 21896), Jalan Sukarno 85, flies daily to Ujung Pandang for 103,000 rp.

Bus & Bemo A minibus from Kolaka to Kendari drops you at a station 10 km from Kendari. From there you have to take two different bemos to get into town.

Boat Four Pelni ferries call in at Kendari, including the KM *Awu* on its Ujung Pandang to Bitung port hop. The Pelni office (☎ 21935) is at Jalan Gereja. Another option is the Meratus shipping company which has about two ships per month on this route. The trip takes about four days and nights and the crew members on the ships will rent out their cabins.

Ferries leave Kendari every afternoon, calling at Raha and arriving at Bau Bau the following dawn. These boats stop for eight hours at Bau Bau, then return by the same route.

RAHA
Raha, the main settlement on Muna Island, is famous for its horse fighting, prehistoric cave paintings and lagoons. The **horse fighting** is a Muna tradition with a robust following – not for tender-hearted foreigners. It occurs on special occasions, especially around Raha, or can be commissioned by arrangement with guides in Raha. Allow a day or two for the owners to get organised, and the local crowd to get wind of what's on.

Horses of a different kind can be viewed at caves and rock shelters near **Bolo** village, about 10 km from Raha. Less than an hour's walk from Bolo are a dozen or more caves with **prehistoric ochre paintings** depicting hunting scenes, warriors on horses, and even boats. Guides can take you to a selection of the best caves. There used to be coffins and bones in some of the caves, until scientific papers describing the caves in 1983 and 1984 prompted a team of Jakarta archaeologists to plunder the site.

By far the prettiest spot on Muna is the clean, green **Napabale & Motonunu lagoons**, 15 km south of Raha. The swimming is excellent in both, and you can also hire canoes to paddle around. Napabale is at the foot of a hill and linked to the sea via a natural tunnel, which you can paddle through when the tide is low. Motonunu also opens to the sea. Bemos from Raha to Napabale cost 250 rp.

Raha itself is a forgettable town with a long jetty. Reasonable accommodation is available at *Andalas*, Jalan Sukawait 62; *Reodah*, Jalan Sudarso 25; *Tani*, Jalan Sutomo 27; and *Aliah* on Jalan Sudirman. Travellers have recommended the Andalas, which has singles/doubles for 15,000/30,000 rp.

BAU BAU
Bau Bau is the main settlement on Pulau Buton, and is strategically situated at the southern entrance of the Buton Strait. It was once a fort, the seat of the former sultanate of Wolio which reigned over the scattered settlements on Buton and the neighbouring islands of Muna, Kabaena, Wowini and Tukangbesi. Wolio's political history is punctuated by competing territorial ambitions of Makassar and Gowa to the west, and Ternate in the east. It enjoyed relative autonomy after the subjugation of Makassar, until coming under direct Dutch rule early this century.

The people of this island group are all closely related culturally and speak similar languages. As in South Sulawesi, most of the cultural influences seem to have come from the Bugis. The Butonese are Muslim and they were noted sailors and traders who emigrated widely, especially to Maluku. The Buton island group was also once a pirate bastion and a slave-trading centre.

The main attraction is the partly restored **Bau Bau Fort** on the hill behind the town. There is also **Pantai Nirwana**, a beach near Bau Bau.

If you are inclined to stay, try the *Deborah* at Jalan Kartini 15, the *Liliana* on the same street at No 18, or the *Elizabeth* at No 21; they are all basic budget losmen.

There are daily boats from Kendari to Bau

Bau. Four Pelni ships now call at Bau Bau. Inquire at the Bau Bau port, or at the Pelni office in Kendari.

Central Sulawesi

The inhabitants of the interior of the eastern peninsula of central Sulawesi are traditionally known to the coastal dwellers as the Loinang – the term is somewhat derogatory. The highlanders are a mixed bunch, some more akin to the inhabitants of Central Sula-

wesi, while others appear to have mixed with later immigrants from Ternate, the dominant pre-Dutch kingdom in this part of the world.

History

Evidence of Neolithic settlements found along the Karama River north of the Quarles mountain range and undated remains from a cave near Kolonodale, indicate a long history of human settlement. But by far the most spectacular prehistoric remains are the Bronze Age megaliths found throughout Central Sulawesi. The meaning and creators of these statues, cylindrical vats, urns and

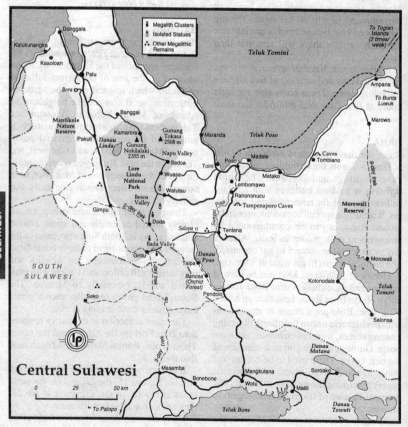

mortars are unknown. The highest concentration are along the Sungai Lariang in the Bada Valley, and near the village of Besoa, but there are others from this era throughout the region and down to Tanatoraja.

There was no single dominant power on the coast. The Portuguese built a fort at Parigi at the eastern end of Tomini Bay in 1555, and were followed by two Muslim Minangkabau traders who settled in Palu and Parigi in 1602 to trade gold and propagate their faith. Ternate, competing with Gowa for dominance of Sulawesi, had extended its influence over Palu and Toli-Toli by 1680.

The inland people in this era tended to live in fortified settlements, because of recurrent inter-tribal unrest. The earthworks surrounding their stockades are still visible in Besoa, Padang Lolo and Bala. Remains of Chinese porcelain are evidence of their trade with the outside world.

Ternate held some sway over the Banggai islands off the eastern peninsula of Sulawesi. Banggai's inhabitants are a diverse bunch, but include a large number of Bajau sea traders. At one time a royal dynasty of Javanese origin ruled here, subject to the sultanate of Ternate. After the Dutch took over in 1908 indigenous rulers were set up to run the islands.

The period of Dutch rule was brief. Their earliest settlements on Teluk Tomini were on the north coast at Gorontalo in the late 17th century and another at Parigi at the western end of the bay in 1730. Along with Makassar, these were the principle Dutch settlements of the time. The rest of the island was controlled by local tribes. In the late 1780s the Dutch attempted to take Toli-Toli (because of its fine harbour), but without success.

PENDOLO

Pendolo is a sleepy village on the southern shore of beautiful Danau Poso (Lake Poso). The reason it escaped development in the past was, simply, the horrible road connecting it to the outside world. The road was only surfaced in 1991, and foreign aid projects are paying for new bridges. Keeping this road open will be a challenge – it's a shelf carved

out of the mountains and subject to frequent landslides. As transport improves, more travellers will pass through.

Danau Poso and its lovely beaches are the main attractions – although the beaches disappear under rising waters towards the end of the wet season. You can swim, there are boat rides on the lake and the surrounding countryside has some decent walks. The lake is 600 metres above sea level so the evenings are pleasantly cool without being too cold. The area is also famous for its wild orchids, especially on the western shores near **Bancea**.

Places to Stay & Eat

The *Pondok Wisata Masamba* and the *Pondok Wisata Victory* on Jalan Pelabuhan both overlook the beach adjacent to the jetty and have small rooms with tiny mandis for 5000 rp. Both have pavilions on the beach for pleasant lakeside dining. The food is good and the prices reasonable. Masamba also offers good travel advice. The *Pamona Indah* is on the beach behind Masamba in a quieter locale.

Penginapan Danau Poso, about 100 metres back from the jetty, has singles/doubles for 5000/10,000 rp, or 3500/7000 rp upstairs. The homey *Penginapan Sederhana* across the road has beds for 3000/6000 rp with shared mandi.

The new *Mulia Hotel*, about a km out, has clean, comfortable lakeside accommodation for 15,000 rp per room, including breakfast. The Damri bus company has shares in this venture, so its buses go straight there. The staff might then announce that the losmen in town are 'full' or 'flooded'. Don't believe them. Choose the Mulia for its good rooms (the best in Pendolo) or expensive food, not for its fairytales about the competitors. Canoes ferry guests to the Pendolo jetty for 1000 rp per person.

If you tire of the home cooking and unbeatable views of the lakeside losmen, the main eatery and bus stop is *Rumah Makan Cahaya Bone* on Jalan Pelabuhan, just up from Penginapan Danau.

Getting There & Away

Damri has daily buses from Rantepao to Pendolo (10 hours), Tentena (12 hours) and Poso (13 hours) for 20,000 rp. The buses continue to Palu, an extra seven hours and 5000 rp. Litha, Acam Indah and others also run regular services.

Tentena, on the north shore of the lake, is larger and prettier than Pendolo. Most people take the ferry to enjoy the spectacular vistas, but in rough weather this trip is no fun. It costs 2000 rp, takes three hours and leaves daily at 8 am from Pendolo and at about 4 pm from Tentena.

You can also reach Tentena by bus and bemo. Right near the beach at Pendolo is a sign indicating the Jawa Indah bus company. The fare to Tentena is 2500 rp and to Poso it's 5000 rp. From Poso, there are weekly flights to elsewhere in Sulawesi. There is a track running along the western edge of the lake which is much better for hikers and bikers than drivers.

From Rantepao, there are normally no direct bemos, but you can make the trip in about 11 hours by taking three separate bemos, first to Palopo, then to Mangkutana and finally to Pendolo. Another option is to charter a bemo from Rantepao, which will cost 175,000 to 200,000 rp. Split among seven or eight people, this costs only a little more than the bus. The main advantages of this are that you can time your trip to do the Watu to Pendolo stretch in daylight hours, stopping whenever you please to photograph the rugged ranges, huge butterflies and monster spiders.

TENTENA

Tentena is surrounded by clove-covered hills at the northern end of Danau Poso. It has long had good roads connecting it to the outside world and is consequently far more developed than Pendolo. Tentena has excellent accommodation and a varied cuisine, but lacks Pendolo's fine beaches.

The nearby **Salopa Waterfalls** are a class attraction, a crystal clear series of pools, cascades and falls set amid unspoilt forest. A path to the left of the falls will lead you to the upper levels and to some pristine swimming holes, but take care not to get caught in the tumbling currents. Best of all, there's hardly any rubbish and very little graffiti, largely due to the efforts of Papa Pia, the old man living at the base of the falls. He carries loads of litter out every couple of days, and asks potential name carvers to leave their knives at his house while they visit the falls.

On the way out, stop to enjoy a glass of coffee or tuak with Papa Pia, check out the photo of the enormous python unlucky enough to tangle with his pig and, if you like, stay the night. The price for his hospitality is whatever cash and gifts you care to leave.

Mornings are the best time to catch the cascades on film. Take a bemo to the Balinese transmigration village north of Tonusu (750 rp), then walk the last three km through padi fields and winding lanes. Bemo charter will cost around 15,000 rp – perhaps prearrange a chartered bemo to meet you for the return journey, or hope to hitch a lift.

There is another waterfall at **Sulewana**, a sunken gully of steaming white water 12 km north of Tentena. Take a bemo to Watunoncu, then walk three km west to reach Sulewana.

The **Pamona Cave** is an attraction right in town, just across the big covered bridge near the missionary airstrip. It's an inactive cave about 80 metres long, nominated as a reserve but far too busy for the local bats – they moved out long ago. Another cave in town is **Latea Cave** near Panorama Hotel, off the Kolonodale road. It contains, among other things, bones and skulls from burials long ago.

Danau Poso is Indonesia's third-largest lake, covering an area of 32,300 hectares and reaching 450 metres in depth. There's a handful of beaches around Tentena, and these disappear when levels are high. Bathing spots include a sandbar near the big silver Jesus south of town, and the stretch of sand near Siuri Cottages on the western shore. The water is clear, cold and clean; hire a boat and go exploring.

The lovely old covered bridge marks where the lake ends and the outflowing Sungai Poso begins its journey to the coast. V-shaped eel traps north of the bridge snare

1   Losmen Ue'Datu
14 Penginapan Wisata Remaja
15 Horison Homestay
16 LosmenVictory
18 Wasantara Hotel
19 Pamona Indah

OTHER

2   Telkom
3   Hospital
4   Danau Poso Festival Grounds
5   Airstrip
6   MAF
7   Pamona Cave
8   Live Eels
9   Pasar
10 Police
11 Post Office
12 Church
13 Jeeps to Bada Valley
17 Mosque
20 Big Crucifix & Silver Jesus

the two-metre monsters Tentena is famous
for. Live specimens are available for inspection and sale at the warung next to the bridge.

Places to Stay

The *Losmen Victory* (☎ 21392) on Jalan Yos
Sudarso is a new place run by the friendly
and capable Bu Doris. It's doing a brisk
trade, with spotless rooms for 10,000 to
15,000 rp with breakfast.

The *Pamona Indah* (☎ 21245), adjacent to
the main jetty, has doubles for 15,000 rp with
breakfast, up to 35,000 rp with TV, hot water
and other amenities. The staff are fun.

The *Hotel Wasantara* (☎ 21345) by the
lake is large and cheery. Room rates range
from 11,000 to 19,250 rp; there are top views
from the better rooms.

Horison Homestay (☎ 21038), Jalan Setia
Budi, has small 10,000 rp rooms, and larger
rooms with mandi for 12,000 rp. It's quiet,
clean and pleasant.

Siuri Cottages, on a beach past Tonusu,
provide a little luxury for 25,000 to 50,000 rp.
The huts are lined up like army barracks, but
are good for those with spare days and dollars.

Penginapan Wisata Remaja has doubles
for 7500 to 10,000 rp. *Penginapan Pan-*
orama is on a hill set back from the lake and
affords fine views. It's a pleasant place to
stay and costs 15,000 rp for a double with
private bath. *Penginapan Tiberius* charges
10,000 rp per room.

Places to Eat

The local speciality is *sugili* or eel, one to
two-metre monsters from the river flowing
out of the lake. These 10 to 20-kg beasties
sell for up to 4500 rp a kg from the stall next
to the bridge, but it is much easier to get the
competent cooks at *Pamona Indah* to do the
shopping and cooking for you. It's worth
every last rupiah. Pamona Indah also does a
lovely ikan mas (gold fish) in arak.

For fabulous pisang molen, banana fried
in a sweet pastry, try the stalls in front of the
ikan mas boxes at the bridge.

Getting There & Away

Air MAF (☎ 21020) has a base in Tentena
and flies folk between isolated villages and
the local hospital. It takes passengers, space-
permitting, at very reasonable rates. From
Tentena, MAF flies to Bada (35,500 rp,
including insurance), Besoa (35,500 rp),
Kantewu (58,500 rp), Masamba (81,500 rp),

Palu (81,500 rp), Rampi (41,500 rp), Seko (64,500 rp) and Uentangko (92,500 rp). There are waiting lists for most flights. You can also charter to Bada for 238,000 rp (maximum of five passengers). If there's no-one at the base, contact the pilot on ☎ 21201.

Bus & Bemo Tentena is 57 km from the coastal city of Poso. Bemos and buses make the run for 2000 rp in about two hours. Be sure to set out early from the Tentena bridge, when five or more bemos depart en masse. After that, you might have a long wait. For long-distance buses there is a 'terminal' at a fork in the road, two km from the town centre, and bus agents near the bridge. There are jeeps to Gintu in Lore Lindu National Park four times a week – 73 km, eight hard hours and 20,000 rp away. Ask at the shop near the bridge. There are also buses to Kolonodale 152 km away, the stepping off point for treks into the Morowali Reserve.

Boat Boats across the lake to Pendolo (three hours; 2000 rp) leave from Tentena at 4 pm, and return at 8 am the next morning. (See under Pendolo earlier in this section for more details.)

Treks from Tentena
Tentena is the starting point for treks west to Lore Lindu National Park and through to Palu (see under Palu later in this section), east to the Morowali Reserve and along Sulawesi's eastern peninsula, or south-west through rugged countryside to Rampi or Seko in Sulawesi Selatan and back to Tanatoraja. All require energy, planning and various degrees of local assistance.

If you meet a guide in Tentena or Pendolo who you get along with, consider contracting them for an extended trek. Guides recommended by travellers include Rudy Ruus, a quiet, nature-loving Minahasan who knows Lore Lindu well; Simson Onara at the Losmen Victory in Pendolo; Marthen Gonti a fun and informative Mori man at the Pamona Indah; and Jeng, a woman who knows the Morowali area, its people and customs well– contact her at the Victory in

Tentena. Guides can save a lot of time and hassle, and cut through indigenous language barriers. Rudy Ruus also owns an old boat based at Ampana, which he uses for tours through the Togian islands.

LORE LINDU NATIONAL PARK
Covering an area of 250,000 hectares, this large and remote national park has been barely touched by tourism. It's a wonderful area for trekking – the park is rich in exotic plant and animal life, including incredible butterflies larger than your hand. It is also home to several indigenous tribes, most of whom wear colourful clothing, at least for traditional ceremonies. Other attractions include ancient megalithic relics, mostly in the Bada, Besoa and Napu valleys. It's even possible to climb remote peaks, as high as 2613 metres above sea level.

There are two main approaches to the park: from Palu to the north, or from Tentena on the east side of the park. From Palu, it's 100 km or 2½ hours by car south to Gimpu, from where the road deteriorates into a 4WD track. The other approach, from Tentena, usually takes visitors by 'road' 73 km to the isolated village of Gintu. It is also possible to fly to Bada Valley in a Cessna aircraft operated by the Missionary Aviation Fellowship (MAF) in Tentena. Roads within the park consist chiefly of mud and holes, and transport is usually by jeep, horseback and foot.

Getting to the park is a bit of an expedition, but you are likely to meet some of the friendliest people in Indonesia here. A permit and a guide are required, but not compulsory. The government tourist office can put you on to some licensed tour operators, though they tend to recommend their most expensive friends. Negotiate 50,000 to 200,000 rp per person per day, or wait until you get into the park and contract a local for around 15,000 rp a day – most guides in the park speak at least a little English. You need guidance to find the megaliths, most of which are concentrated around Gintu and Doda. Food is readily available, but it's wise to bring other necessities such as mosquito repellent and sunblock lotion. Accommodation in the Lore

Lindu area ranges from nights huddled under the roofs of covered bridges (hard and cold – wrap up well) to homestay accommodation throughout the park.

Treks

The main approaches to Lore Lindu are from Tentena via Tonusu, from Poso via Watutau or from Palu via Gimpu or Banggai. Porters are difficult to find, so consider sending non-essential gear ahead by car or bus for around 20,000 rp.

Tentena to Gintu hikers can start from Tonusu and walk for two days, sleeping under covered bridges both nights. You'll need to carry food, and water-purification tablets. You could shorten the hike by chartering a motorbike to Peatua (26 km) and walking to the Malei bridge (four hours). The next day, hike from Malei to Bomba (18 km; five hours), and get a local guide to help you find the Bomba, Bada and impressive Sepe megaliths (10,000 to 15,000 rp per day). At **Bomba**, stay at the friendly *Ningsi Homestay* for 7500 rp, including breakfast, lunch and dinner.

At **Gintu** there is *Losmen Merry* with five clean rooms at 10,000 rp, including three meals. *Losmen Sanur* is also clean and friendly, charging 7500 rp with two meals, 10,000 rp with three – two of the rooms have their own mandi.

Gintu to **Tuare** is an easy three-hour walk. (Tuare's kepala desa takes guests for 7500 rp, including breakfast and dinner.) **Moa** is several hours beyond Tuare, over two difficult rivers. Repairs to the bridges might shorten the hike. Moa's kepala desa takes guests for 10,000 rp (dinner, bed and breakfast). Moa to **Gimpu** is a strenuous eight-hour hike, again over two rivers with broken bridges. (Gimpu's kepala desa offers the same deal as Moa's.) From Gimpu to Palu there are five buses a day, starting at 7.30 am and taking three to six hours (4000 rp).

An alternative from Gintu might be to take horses through dense jungle to Gimpu. Horses and handlers are available for 30,000 to 60,000 rp a day. You need a guide for this section. There is also a path to **Doda**, another

centre for megalithic remains, where you can stay at the *Losmen Rindu Alam* (7500 rp, including three meals). Other paths from Gintu cross the peaks to Gimpu, or north to Watutau. The bird sanctuaries in the north of the park are easier to get to from Palu.

MOROWALI RESERVE

This nature reserve was established in 1980 on the east side of Teluk Tomori (Tomori Bay). Aside from the scenic beauty, the area is inhabited by the Wana people who still live mostly by hunting and gathering, and shifting agriculture.

Organised treks of the area usually take four or five days and can be organised in Tentena, Poso or Palu. In Tentena, inquire about trips at the Pomona Indah Hotel or at the Victory.

There are daily buses from Poso to Kolonodale via Tentena (10 hours; 10,000 rp, or 8500 rp by Jawa Indah bus). Most visitors spend the night in **Kolonodale** at the *Losmen Sederhana* or the more luxurious *Hotel Tomor Indah*. Other penginapan include the *Lestari* and *Rejeki Jaya*. Jabar at the Sederhana can introduce guests to local English-speaking guides.

From Kolonodale it's a two-hour boat trip across Teluk Tomori and a two-km trek to the first Wana village, then a four-hour trek to the next village. There are opportunities to see the tiny tangkasi monkey and maleo birds. Trips can also include a canoe trip on a lake, and exploration of **Gua Tapak Tangan** (Clapping Hands Cave), a sea cave with paintings of human hands on the walls. There is the **Apali stone**, a rock shaped like a statue, and relics of the Mori Kingdom.

To leave, either backtrack to Kolonodale or catch a ferry to Baturube, and ferries and buses from there through to Luwuk on the eastern peninsula. Hardy trekkers can hike (with a guide) north all the way through to Ampana.

LUWUK

Luwuk is the biggest town on the eastern peninsula, and the stepping-off point for the Banggai islands. Attractions include the 75-

metre-high **Hengahenga Waterfall** three km west of Luwuk, the **Suaka Margasetwa Reserve** eight km north, and the daily ferries to the Banggai islands. The **Bangkiriang Wildlife Reserve**, home to Central Sulawesi's largest maleo bird population, is near the coast 80 km south-west of Luwuk.

Peleng is the biggest and most populous island while **Banggai**, which is on the ferry route, has sandy beaches. There is a pearl-diving site at **Kokungan**, near Bandan, and good snorkelling at **Mukalayo** reef. **Tikus Island**, three hours from Banggai, is an uninhabited snorkelling spot making a name for itself as a secluded getaway.

Getting There and Away

Luwuk's connections with the outside world include daily buses from Poso 390 km away (20 hours; 17,500 rp). There are daily Merpati flights from Palu (139,000 rp), and weekly flights from Poso (110,000 rp). Pelni's *KM Awu* calls regularly at Kolonodale, Banggai and Luwuk en route from Ujung Pandang to Bitung.

POSO

Poso is the main town and port on the northern coast of central Sulawesi. For most travellers it's only a rest stop and transit point. However, it's quite a pleasant town. The southern side of town is the new section and looks much like a suburb in Australia or the USA, with manicured lawns and neat houses.

From Poso you can head west to Palu and continue on to northern Sulawesi, or take a ship across Teluk Tomini to Gorontalo on the northern peninsula. A rarely visited alternative is to head out to the peninsula that juts out into the Maluku Sea.

The city itself is not rich in sights. Most folks head for the beaches which, unfortunately, are not within walking distance. **Pantai Madale** is a snorkelling spot five km to the east of Poso and costs 350 rp by bemo. **Pantai Matako** is a white-sand beach 25 km to the east (1000 rp), and **Tombiano**, 40 km east, has huge wet caves occupied by bats (1500 rp by bemo).

Seven km west of Poso (500 rp) is **Pantai Toini** with a great seafood dining spot back from the beach. Further west (40 km), **Maranda** offers a small waterfall, a hot-water spring and a swimming spot (1500 rp).

The village of **Lembomawo** four km south of Poso is known for its ebony carving. To get there take a bemo from the main terminal, and you will need to cross two hanging bridges on foot. A circular route from Lembomawo to Ranononucu will bring you back to the main road, and to the roadside stalls selling the carvings.

Gua Tampenaporo is a cave off the main road to Tentena, 22 km and 1000 rp south.

Information

There is a tourist information service (☎ 21211), Jalan Kalimantan 15, run by Amir Kiat. Travellers either love him or hate him – judge for yourself.

Places to Stay

The *Hotel Kalimantan* (☎ 21420), Jalan Haji Agus Salim 14, is quite old but big, bright and airy. It's also relatively cheap at 7000/12,500 rp for rooms with bath.

Hotel Alamanda (☎ 21233), Jalan Bali 1, is better value than most at 3500 to 5000 rp per person. The new but basic *Losmen Alugoro* (☎ 21336), Jalan Sumatera 33, has rooms for 10,000 rp, or 15,000 rp with fan.

Up the road at the corner of Jalan Haji Agus Salim and Jalan Imam Bonjol is the *Penginapan Sulawesi* (☎ 21294), which has singles for 3000 rp. The rooms are tiny, but clean.

Anugrah Inn (☎ 21820), Jalan P Samosir 1, is on the southern edge of town close to the Jawa Indah bus terminal and Merpati office. It's friendly and quiet with doubles for 15,000 rp, or 25,000 rp with air-con.

Bambu Jaya Hotel (☎ 21570), Jalan Haji Agus Salim 101, was built in the charmless style once favoured by Soviet architects. The economy rooms are 16,500 rp, while a room with air-con is 25,000 rp. The breezy terrace out back has great views of the bay.

Hotel Nels (☎ 21013) is in the northern part of town on Jalan Yos Sudarso. It's old

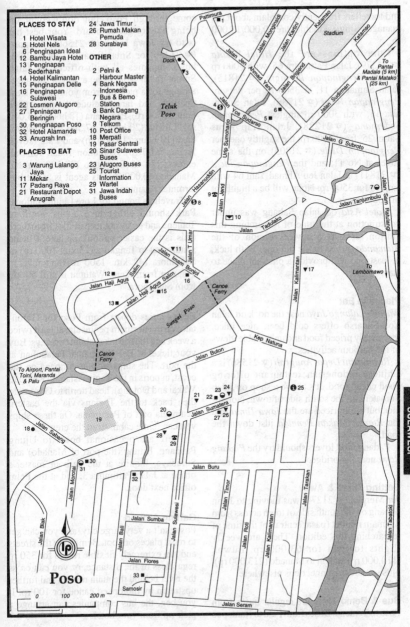

PLACES TO STAY
1 Hotel Wisata
5 Hotel Nels
6 Penginapan Ideal
12 Bambu Jaya Hotel
13 Penginapan Sederhana
14 Hotel Kalimantan
15 Penginapan Delie
16 Penginapan Sulawesi
22 Losmen Alugoro
27 Peninapan Beringin
30 Penginapan Poso
32 Hotel Alamanda
33 Anugrah Inn

PLACES TO EAT
3 Warung Lalango Jaya
11 Mekar
17 Padang Raya
21 Restaurant Depot Anugrah

24 Jawa Timur
26 Rumah Makan Pemuda
28 Surabaya

OTHER
2 Pelni & Harbour Master
4 Bank Negara Indonesia
7 Bus & Bemo Station
8 Bank Dagang Negara
9 Telkom
10 Post Office
18 Merpati
19 Pasar Sentral
20 Sinar Sulawesi Buses
23 Alugoro Buses
25 Tourist Information
29 Wartel
31 Jawa Indah Buses

SULAWESI

Poso

0   100   200 m

and travellers frequently complain about the manager. Singles/doubles are 10,000/15,000 rp.

Other options are the *Hotel Wisata* (☎ 21379), Jalan Pattimura 65, with 5000 rp rooms; *Penginapan Beringin* (☎ 21815), Jalan Sumatera 11, at 3500 rp per person; *Penginapan Poso* (☎ 21788), Jalan Sumatera 15, with 3000 rp singles; *Penginapan Sederhana* (☎ 21228), Jalan Haji Agus Salim 25, from 5000 rp; the slightly cheaper *Penginapan Delie* (☎ 21805) on the same street at No 11; and the *Penginapan Ideal* (☎ 21841) at Jalan Jen Ahmad Yani 64 with singles for 3500 rp. None will be a highlight of your travels.

Hotel Asia on Jalan Sabang was under construction at the time of researching this edition, as was a newer version of the *Alamanda* – next to the old one. With luck, at least one will provide a pleasant place to stay.

Places to Eat

Warung Lalango Jaya near the dock on Jalan Yos Sudarso offers cold beer, nice juice, reasonably priced food and unbeatable views of the harbour activities.

Restaurant Depot Anugrah (☎ 21586) is a Chinese-Indonesian restaurant offering good cheap food. It's above a shop on Jalan Sumatera on the south side of town. Not-so-nice but well priced are the *Jawa Timur* and the *Rumah Makan Pemuda* just down the road.

Padang food lovers should try the *Padang Raya* near the bridge.

Getting There & Away

Air Merpati (☎ 21274) was moving to Jalan Sabang on the south side of town across from the main market (pasar sentral) at the time of researching this edition. There are weekly flights to Palu for 63,000 rp, Luwuk (110,000 rp) and on to Manado (213,000 rp), plus same-day connections elsewhere.

Bus & Bemo There are regular buses from Poso to Tentena. Buses from Palu to Rantepao

come through Poso, but don't count on being able to get on board. Your best bet is to try Jawa Indah (☎ 21560), Alugoro (☎ 21336) or Sinar Sulawesi (☎ 21298), bus companies all with offices on Jalan Sumatera. If you have a lot of luggage, arrange for a pick-up from your hotel. Destinations and fares include Ampana (five hours; 5500 rp), Pagimana (18 hours; 15,000 rp), Luwuk (20 hours; 17,500 rp), Kolonodale (10 hours; 10,000 rp) and Palu (seven hours; 8000 rp). Tomohon Indah runs an express bus to Gorontalo (27,500 rp) and Manado (40,000 rp). Its agent is at the bus terminal Kasintuwu.

Travellers bound for Lore Lindu National Park should either take a bus south to Tentena and go by air, jeep or foot from there (this is the easier option), or take a bemo south-west to Tangkura (25 km; 1000 rp) or Sanginora (42 km; 1500 rp) and hike to Watutau from there. Watutau is still 50 km from Sanginora.

Boat Ferries depart from Poso for Gorontalo, on the northern peninsula, at least twice a week and the trip takes about two days. Buy your ticket at Pos Keamanan Pelabuhan at the port. The ships stop at Ampana on the coast, at ports in the Togian islands (Katupat, Wakai and Dolong), head north to Gorontalo then back to the Togians via the eastern peninsula port of Pagimana. On these ships you can rent a cabin from the crew.

There are occasional boats to Ujung Pandang, Bitung (the port of Manado) and Surabaya. Inquire at the harbour master's office at Jalan Pattimura 3, and at the Pelni office next door.

Getting Around

Poso isn't a very large city, and you can get to most places on foot. Bemos ply the streets and run extremely flexible routes for 350 rp regardless of the distance, or you can cross the river behind the main market and further upstream by motorised canoe for 100 rp. If you beg, the bus companies can arrange a pick-up from your hotel.

PALU

Palu is the capital of Central Sulawesi. One of the more interesting things about Palu is the climate. It's possibly the driest place in Indonesia, with only about four or five good rainstorms a year. On the outskirts of town you'll see huge prickly pear cactus, once a major pest. There is also plenty of tropical vegetation in the area, partly because of ground water from the mountains. Days are hot, nights are tolerably cool and the brilliant sunshine is amenable to sunbathing and snorkelling.

There are inland attractions too, such as the mineral springs at **Bora** 12 km south-east, and the **Mantikole Nature Reserve** 25 km south of town.

Orientation

Like Poso, Palu is spread out and the street names constantly change. The airport is on the south-eastern outskirts, and the town is split neatly in two by the Sungai Palu. The tiny commercial centre is between Jalan Wahidin and Jalan Sudirman, north of Jalan Hasanuddin.

Information

The regional tourist office, on Jalan Raja Moili, has plenty of brochures and good maps of the city. The office is open from around 7.30 am until 2 pm.

The post office is way out on Jalan Yamin, and the main Telkom office is at the southern end of Jalan Yani. There are card phones, and a wartel next to Central Hotel.

Things to See & Do

The **Central Sulawesi Museum** (☎ 22290), or Museum Negeri Propinsi Sulawesi Tengah, is at Jalan Sapiri 23. The museum houses cultural relics, natural history exhibits and a collection of books in Dutch, Indonesian and English. It's open from about 8.30 am until about noon.

Palu Beach is not especially clean or nice. Fortunately, there is an excellent beach north of nearby Donggala (see the following Donggala section).

Places to Stay – bottom end

Hotel Karsam (☎ 21776) at Jalan Suharso 15, near Pantai Palu, is a pretty good deal with singles/doubles for 8000/15,000 rp or 12,500/20,000 rp, although it's about a 15-minute walk from the shopping centre.

The *Purnama Raya Hotel* (☎ 23646), Jalan Wahidin 4, has singles/doubles for 8500/14,000 rp, all with private bath. It's clean, central (therefore a bit noisy) but recommended.

Hotel Pasifik, Jalan Gajah Mada 130, is central but supernaturally noisy. Rooms start at 6000 rp. *Hotel Garuda* (☎ 252994), with rooms for 8000/12,000 rp, is supernaturally smelly. *Taurus Hotel* (☎ 21567) across the road at Jalan Hasanuddin 36 is much better – clean, friendly and soccer mad, with singles/doubles from 8000/13,000 rp.

Places to Stay – middle

New Dely Hotel (☎ 21037), Jalan Tadulako 17, is clean, quiet and good value, with rooms from 20,000/25,000 rp plus tax, or 35,000/40,000 rp with air-con. It's about a 10-minute walk from the town centre.

Buana Hotel (☎ 21475), Jalan Kartini 8, is a respectable place and one of the better deals in this price range. Rooms with mandi start at 20,000 rp.

The *Central Hotel* (☎ 22789), next to the Buana, is a quiet, spotlessly clean place with English-speaking staff. Rooms start at 40,000 rp.

The *Hotel Pattimura* (☎ 21775), Jalan Pattimura 18, is a decent place with its own restaurant. Standard rooms are 35,000 rp, less discounts.

Places to Stay – top end

Palu Golden Hotel (☎ 21126), Jalan Raden Saleh 22, Palu's top hotel, has a lousy beach but a fabulous swimming pool. With singles/doubles starting at 93,000/120,000 rp, it's not surprising that it has plenty of vacancies. Discounts are available.

Places to Eat

Jalan Hasanuddin II is a busy market lane with many places to eat, including *Milano*

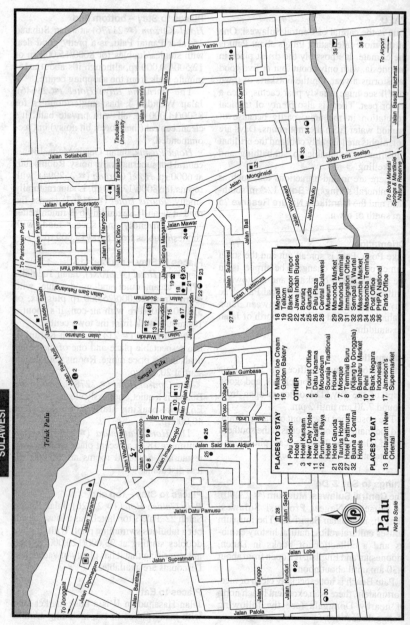

PLACES TO STAY

1 Palu Golden Hotel
3 Hotel Karsam
4 New Dely Hotel
11 Hotel Pasifik
12 Purnama Raya Hotel
21 Hotel Garuda
23 Taurus Hotel
27 Hotel Pattimura
32 Buana & Central Hotels

PLACES TO EAT

13 Restaurant New Oriental
15 Milano Ice Cream
16 Golden Bakery

OTHER

2 Tourist Office
5 Datu Karama Mousoleum
6 Souraja Traditional House
7 Mosque
8 Terminal Buru (Kijang to Dongala)
9 Bambaru Market
10 Petni
14 Bank Negara Indonesia
17 Jannata's Supermarket
18 Merpati
19 Telkom
20 Bank Expor Impor
22 Jawa Indah Buses
24 Bouraq
25 Palu Plaza
28 Central Sulawesi Museum
29 Manonda Market
30 Manonda Terminal
31 Immigration Office
32 Sempati & Wartel
33 Masomba Market
34 Masomba Terminal
35 Post Office
36 PHPA National Parks Office

Palu

Not to Scale

Ice Cream (☎ 23857), open from 8 am to 2 pm, and from 5 until 10 pm. Avoid the burgers and hot dogs, but the bubur ayam is good, and the ice cream outstanding. Most travellers stop here to chat with the owners, Peter & Maureen Meroniak, who organise trekking tours and operate a beach-side hotel in Donggala (see Donggala's Places to Stay section).

Restaurant New Oriental (☎ 23275) is also on Jalan Hasanuddin II, and serves excellent Chinese food in addition to Indonesian dishes.

Golden Bakery, just around the corner on Jalan Wahidin, is excellent for breakfast and midnight snacks. It's no place to visit if you're on a diet – too many tempting cakes, rolls and pastries.

If you want to self-cater, Jamesons is a supermarket in the busy Jalan Hasanuddin area. An even larger supermarket is Sentosa, Jalan Monginsidi 59, next to the Central Hotel.

Entertainment
The slim pickings include barbecues and other weekly activities at the *Palu Golden Hotel*. Watch out for occasional concerts at the *Stadion Gawalise Palu*.

Getting There & Away
Air Aside from the usual daytime office hours, Merpati, Garuda and Bouraq also sell tickets in the evening from about 7 pm until the staff feel like going home. Bouraq (☎ 22563), Jalan Mawar 58, offers flights west to Balikpapan and Banjarmasin, or east to Gorontalo, Manado and Davao.

Garuda (☎ 21095) is on Jalan Said Idus Aldjufrie, south of the intersection with Jalan Gajah Mada. Merpati (☎ 21295), centrally located at Jalan Hasanuddin 33, has the broadest network and oldest planes, with direct flights to Toli-Toli (117,000 rp), Luwuk (139,000 rp), Poso (63,000 rp), Gorontalo (108,000 rp), Ujung Pandang (145,000 rp) and Balikpapan (114,000 rp).

Sempati (☎ 21612), at the Central Hotel, Jalan Kartini 6, has five flights a week to Ujung Pandang and beyond.

Bus Buses to Poso, Palopo, Rantepao, Gorontalo and Manado all leave from the Inpres station. At Masomba station you can get buses to inland cities. Palu to Gorontalo takes 1½ days over a bone-jarring road. Jawa Indah buses depart from the company's Jalan Hasanuddin office to Poso (eight hours; 7000 rp), Kilo (6500 rp), Tambarana (6000 rp), Sausu (5000 rp), Tolai (4500 rp) and Parigi (4000 rp).

Boat There are three ports near Palu. Larger vessels, such as Pelni, dock at Pantoloan which is north-east of Palu, and some dock at Donggala which is north-west of Palu. Smaller ships dock at Wani, two km past Pantoloan.

In Palu, the Pelni office is on Jalan Kartini, about 100 metres past Sempati. It also has an office at Pantoloan, opposite the road to the wharf. The offices of the other shipping companies are at the various ports. Three modern Pelni boats now call at Pantoloan – see the introductory Getting Around chapter for Pelni's ferry routes. You can avoid the long and winding road through central Sulawesi by taking a ship from Palu to Ujung Pandang or Pare Pare.

Getting Around
To/From the Airport Palu's Mutiara airport is seven km from town, not far past the post office, take a bemo (10 minutes; 1000 rp) or taxi (5000 rp).

Local Transport Transport around town is by bemo – 300 rp gets you anywhere. Routes are very flexible. Just flag down one that looks like it is going your way and state your destination. Terminal Buru near Pasar Bambaru has kijang to Donggala for 1500 rp, or 4000 to 6000 rp to charter all the way to the beach at Tanjung Karang.

DONGGALA
As the administrative centre under the Dutch, Donggala was briefly the most important town and port in central Sulawesi. When the harbour silted up, the ships switched to the harbours on the other side of

the bay and Palu became the regional capital. Today Donggala is a quiet backwater.

The main attractions are sun, sand and water at **Tanjung Karang**, north of town. The reef off the Prince John Dive Resort is a delight for snorkellers and attracts a steady stream of travellers. The losmen is run by a German expat, Peter Meroniak, and his Indonesian wife, Maureen. Bring your own gear, or rent a mask and fins for 10,000 rp per day. There are also tanks and weights (40,000 rp), regulators (10,000 rp), BCDs (10,000 rp) and wetsuits (5000 rp). It all adds up. Day dives cost 65,000 rp, and night dives 75,000 rp. Beginners can dive for 95,000 rp, including tuition.

Donggala caters well for experienced divers, not so well for beginners. One traveller completed her tuition at Prince John's, and was given her PADI certification and card. The next dive centre laughed long and loud when they saw it, claiming that the card was worthless. Do your dive training *before* coming to Sulawesi.

Towale, 12 km south-west of Donggala, is another excellent swimming and snorkelling spot, especially in the lagoons around Bukit Pusentasi. This is an easy excursion from Tanjung Karang.

Places to Stay

Prince John Dive Resort offers simple, clean accommodation set in pleasant gardens. Singles/doubles are 22,500/35,000 rp, or 27,500/40,000 rp for a bungalow. Three basic meals are included, and vegetarians are catered for on request. Everyone gathers for communal dining at dusk.

Harmoni Cottages (☎ 21235) is right on the tip of the peninsula, a five-minute walk past the dive resort. Its beach cottages cost 15,000 rp, including three meals.

Getting There & Away

From Palu, you can catch a *taksi Donggala* for 1500 rp; the ride takes 40 minutes. It's another 20 minutes on foot to the beach. Alternatively, you could charter to Tanjung Karang beach for 4000 to 6000 rp.

KASOLOAN & KALUKUNANGKA

This area to the west of Palu is off the main tourist track, but makes for fascinating trekking. The people who live in the hills around Kasoloan and Kalukunangka lead traditional lives – they wear little clothing and still use blow guns. Despite the blow guns, the locals are quite used to trekkers and there is no danger.

The inland people of Central Sulawesi are also famous for their bark cloth manufacture. The inner bark of trees is treated, dyed and beaten to create a felt fabric, reputed to have spiritual power, that is used primarily for ceremonial clothing.

There is also a very large cave filled with thousands of bats. The locals eat them, and part of the thrill for travellers is a chance to sample bat stew.

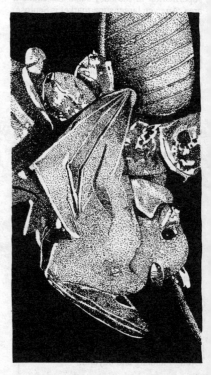

A visit to this area requires three or four days. The trek itself is fairly easy and even suitable for older children. A guide is necessary, available from the National Parks Office in Palu or through the Prince John Dive Resort at Donggala. The latter is also a good place to assemble a party to share the adventure.

AMPANA

Ampana, a port on Sulawesi's eastern peninsula, is the stepping off point for ferries and chartered boats to the Togians. There is a small market and dock, then a continual string of fishing villages around to **Tanjung Api** (Cape Fire), a nature reserve east of town. Its wildlife includes anoa (dwarf buffalo), babirusa (pig-deer), crocodiles, snakes and maleo, but most people come to see the burning coral cliff fuelled by a leak of natural gas. Try cupping the gas bubbling through the water and putting a match to it! To get there, you need to charter a boat around the rocky peninsula. Try to get there at night.

Places to Stay

There are four losmen within easy walking distance from the Ampana market. On weekends in wedding season they are flat out catering for wedding receptions and accommodating guests, a fun time for all.

Losmen Irama, Jalan Kartini 11, about 200 metres west of the market, is a modern place run by pleasant people with a better than usual appreciation of music and volume control. Rates are 5000 rp per person per night or 15,000 rp with meals. There is an air-con room for 25,000/30,000 rp.

Penginapan Rejeki (☎ 21274) at Jalan Talatako 45, about 400 metres south of the market, is the other relatively modern place, with pleasant singles for 4000 rp.

Penginapan Mekar, Jalan Kartini 5, is the cheapest, at 3500 rp for old singles or 4500 rp per person for quieter rooms out the back.

Hotel Plaza (☎ 21091), Jalan Kartini 45, is airy and pleasant, with a stock of English-language magazines. Singles cost 5000 rp, or 15,000 rp with meals.

Places to Eat

For dining out, the pokey *Warung Iraham Piasu* at the beach end of Jalan Kartini has great gado gado, or try the coffee shops in the market.

Getting There & Away

Bus Ampana is on the main road from Poso (five hours; 5500 rp) to Luwuk. The Gorontalo ferries start from Poso – take the boat from Poso on Monday, Thursday or Saturday or join it at Ampana. If there's no ferry you may be able to hitch a lift from Ampana on a smaller boat.

Boat You can catch the thrice-weekly ferries bound for Gorontalo via the Togian ports of Wakai, Katupat and Dolong, and charter boats from there, or ask around for boats available for charter in Ampana. Charter companies should provide a rough itinerary, photos and details of other trips they have done, and visitors' books with testimonials of previous travellers.

Togian Islands

This archipelago of pristine coral and volcanic isles in the middle of Teluk Tomini is a riot of blue, gold and green. Undisturbed jungle shelters a variety of wildlife, reefs around the islands support rich marine life, and the seven or so ethnic groups sharing this place are extraordinarily hospitable.

This is the only place in Indonesia where you can find all three major reef environments – atoll, barrier and fringing reefs – in one location. Two atolls and their deep lagoons lie off the north-west of **Batudaka Island**, barrier reefs surround the islands at the 200-metre depth contour (five km to 15 km offshore), and fringing reefs surround all of the coasts, merging with sea grass and mangroves.

The mix of coral and marine life is unusually diverse. The more conspicuous residents include gaily marked coral lobsters, a colony of dugong (the world's only vegetarian marine mammal), schools of dolphins numbering 100 or more, the occasional great whale, commercially important species of trepang (sea cucumbers), natural pearls, plus fish, fish and more fish.

On land, there is a cave with a colony of bats in the hills behind **Bomba** on Batudaka Island, as well as pleasant walks and prolific bird life. Even smaller islands such as **Malenge**, north-east of Katupat, support diverse fauna, including the babirusa, hornbill, very cute cuscus, salamander and even a species of primate just 'discovered' in the early 1990s.

The islands are part of an active volcanic belt. **Pulau Una Una**, which consists mostly of Mount Colo, was torn apart in 1983 when the volcano exploded to life for the first time in almost 100 years. Ash covered 90% of the island, destroying all of the houses, animals and most of the crops. Una Una's population had been safely evacuated, and access to the island remains restricted. Islanders return to tend their crops, but no-one may live there.

The Bajau

Nomadic Bajau hunter-gatherers dive for trepang, pearl and other commercially important marine produce, just as they have done for hundreds, perhaps thousands of years. Unlike the Bugis, Sulawesi's other famous seafarers, the Bajau people, spend more or less their whole lives on boats, travelling as families wherever they go. There are several permanent Bajau settlements on the Togians, and even some stilt villages on offshore reefs, but the itinerant character of Bajau culture still survives. Newly-weds are put in a canoe and pushed out to sea to make their place in the world. When they have children, the fathers dive with their three-day-old babies to introduce them to life on the sea.

Intrusions from the outside world are rare, and the consequences are sometimes tragic. When Bugis and Chinese traders introduced air compressors to enable the Bajau to dive longer and deeper for their trepang, no-one explained the lethal nature of caisson disease (the bends), which killed 40 or more in one area, and crippled many others. These days Bajau divers' only concession to modernity is goggles fashioned from wood and glass, and hand-made spearguns. Many Madurese divers working the Togian reefs still use compressors.

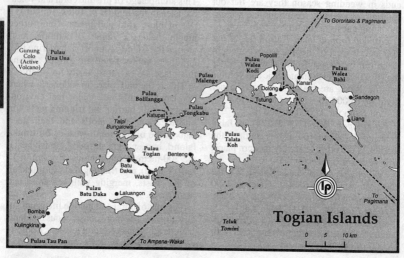

Togian Islands

Getting There & Away

The best way to see the Togians is by boat. There are a few available in Ampana, including an ancient craft owned by Rudy Ruus from Poso, a nature-loving Minahasan who knows the Togians and its people well. His friends include a Bajau community living in huts high above a reef several km offshore. Prices vary according to the number of people, the number of days and itinerary, but usually include meals and accommodation. Facilities are basic – sleep at least a few nights on the boat – and be prepared to hang out the back for the call of nature. There is no shelter, not even a platform, just a slim handhold as everything else stretches over the churning water. Rudy's postal address is Jalan Pulau Seram Nusa Indah 8, Poso.

Another option is to base yourself at Katupat or Pulau Tongkabu, and do short snorkelling and whale-watching excursions from there.

WAKAI

There is little of interest in Wakai itself, except the port, a fine hotel and some well-stocked general stores. The store owned by the hotel people also trades in a variety of local produce, including cloves, pearl shell, trepang and coconut crabs. The huge crabs are kept out the back in holding boxes, ready to sell to travelling traders.

Coconut crabs, the world's largest terrestrial arthropod, once lived on islands throughout the western Pacific and eastern Indian oceans, but unsustainable human exploitation has reduced stocks to a handful of isolated islands, including the Togians. Mature crabs weigh up to five kg and their large-clawed legs can span 90 cm. Despite popular myth, there is little evidence to support stories of crabs climbing trees to snip coconuts off, removing the husk, then carrying the nut up again to drop from a great height. In any case, the crabs will eat almost any organic matter and defend it from competitors.

Places to Stay & Eat

The *Togian Islands Hotel* is a beautiful, breezy weatherboard hotel built over the water near Wakai jetty. Prices range from 6000 rp up to 50,000 rp for the big rooms over the water. The kitchen here will cook the fish and lobsters you bring in from the reefs, as well as generous serves of rice and noodles. The hotel's speedboat is available for charters to Ampana (150,000 rp plus 100,000 rp fuel) or for excursions to the reefs. There's a small selection of diving gear available for hire – expensive.

The hotel also runs *Taipi*, a couple of beach bungalows on a tiny island off the coast of Togian Island for 15,000 rp a night. There is little else on the island, so bring supplies. The beach is OK, but the snorkelling and sunsets are fantastic. A walk west of the beach huts will eventually bring you to a series of craggy coral cliffs, home to coconut crabs the size of small footballs. Put your hand in an occupied burrow and you are likely to lose a finger.

KATUPAT

Katupat is a relaxed village on Togian Island in the heart of the Togians, and a favourite stop for travellers looking to unwind. It has simple accommodation, a small market and a couple of stores, plus some decent walking for those who need exercise. Katupat is one of the ports of call for the Pelni ferries. Katupat to Gorontalo costs 17,500 rp, or double if you hire a bed in one of the crew's cabins.

Places to Stay & Eat

Losmen Bolilanga Indah is a delightful place built over the water adjacent to Katupat's main jetty. Singles/doubles cost 12,500/20,000 rp, including meals and snacks for excursions. Boats are available for 20,000 rp a day for snorkelling excursions to nearby reefs, or more for longer trips. Fun, friendly local guides are readily available, and seem to know their reefs pretty well. They entertain with stories of 10-metre whales jumping out of the water, and tend to know where to look for smaller varieties.

Losmen Indah Tongkabu on nearby Tongkabu Island offers friendly homestay accommodation for 10,000 rp a night, and was planning to build a losmen nearby. Tongkabu Island is quieter than nearby Katupat, just on a much smaller patch of land. Guides and transport are available.

DOLONG

Dolong, on Walea Kodi Island, is the last port of call for Ampana to Gorontalo ferries, and one of the largest towns on the islands. It is set in a sheltered harbour, but has no accommodation as such. There are several restaurants that thrive on the rush of hungry ferry passengers who arrive late at night.

North Sulawesi

The people of North Sulawesi have a long history of trade and contact with the outside world, and were probably always oriented to the sea. Together with the Sangir-Talaud group, North Sulawesi forms a natural bridge to the Philippines, providing a causeway for the movement of peoples and cultures back and forth between Indonesia and to the north. Languages and physical features related to the Philippines can be found among the Minahasans at the tip of the

peninsula, and the inhabitants of the Sangir group. The Minahasans also have the Filipinos' love of music.

The three largest distinct groups of people in north Sulawesi are the Minahasans, the Gorontalese and the Sangirese, plus many more dialects and subgroups. The tribes in Bolaang Mongondow, sandwiched between Minahasa and Gorontalo, were important political players too.

The Dutch have had a more enduring influence on this isolated northern peninsula than anywhere else in the archipelago. This influence was established while the Bugis and the Makassarese were trying to repel the Dutch from the south-west peninsula. The greatest economic development in Sulawesi has also taken place in the north.

History

At the time of the first contact with Europeans the sultanate of Ternate held some sway over North Sulawesi, and the area was often visited by seafaring Bugis traders from South Sulawesi. The Spanish and the Portuguese, the first Europeans to arrive, landed in North Sulawesi in the 16th century. The main Portuguese trade route rounded South Sulawesi at the port of Makassar, but also included the Sulu islands (off the north coast

---

Coconut Economy

Northern Sulawesi's three million inhabitants are among the most prosperous in Indonesia. Cloves, nutmeg, vanilla and coffee are important cash crops, but much of northern Sulawesi is covered by a solid canopy of coconut trees. The coconut palm is one of the most important plants in the tropical economy, not only producing edible fruit but also oil, waxes, fibres and other products.

The coconut flesh is enclosed in a light-coloured inner shell, which eventually turns into the hard, dark shell of the ripe nut that you see in the West. It takes a year for the nut to reach maturity, at which point the hard-shelled nut within the fibrous husk is about 12 cm in diameter and full of sweet liquid and hard, white flesh. Copra is the dried flesh and the second-most important export product of northern Sulawesi. Coir is the fibre from the husk of the coconut.

Like bamboo, the uses of the coconut tree are manifold. You can eat the meat, drink the juice, dry the meat for export as copra, burn the dried husks as fuel, build your house with coconut timber, use the fronds to thatch the roof or make mats and baskets, use the oil to provide lighting at night or put it in your hair to keep it moist and glossy, use the leaf as a sieve to strain the sago flour that is the staple of the Maluku Islands, make rope and mats with the fibre, use the thin centre spine of the young coconut leaf to weave hats, or bag your midday meal of rice in a palm leaf.

Coconut oil, made from copra, is used instead of cooking fat, and is also used in the manufacture of soaps, perfumes, face creams, hair dressings, and even nitro-glycerine. ∎

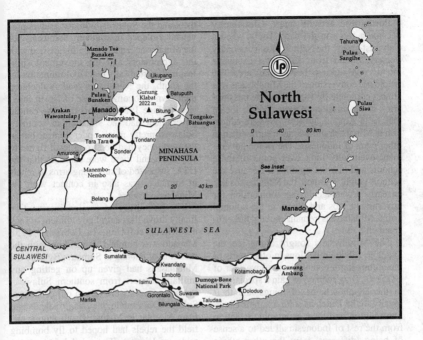

of Borneo) and the port of Manado (at the tip of North Sulawesi). The Spanish set themselves up in the Philippines. Although they had sporadic contacts with North Sulawesi, the Spanish and Portuguese influence was limited by the power of Ternate.

The Portuguese left reminders of their presence in the north in subtle ways. Portuguese surnames and various Portuguese words not found elsewhere in Indonesia, like *garrida* for an enticing woman and *buraco* for a bad man, can still be found in Minahasa. In the 1560s the Portuguese Franciscan missionaries made some converts in Minahasa, and the Jesuit priest Mascarenhas had great success in the Sangir and Talaud islands. At the same time, however, Islam was arriving from Ternate.

By the early 17th century the Dutch had toppled the Ternate sultanate, and then set about eclipsing the Spanish and Portuguese. As was the usual pattern in the 1640s and 50s, the Dutch colluded with local powers to throw out

their European competitors. In 1677 the Dutch occupied Pulau Sangir and, two years later, the Dutch governor of Maluku, Robert Padtbrugge, visited Manado at the tip of the northern peninsula. Out of this visit came a treaty (some say a forced one) with the local Minahasan chiefs, which led to domination by the Dutch for the next 300 years.

Although relations with the Dutch were often less than cordial (a war was fought around Tondano between 1807 and 1809) and the region did not actually come under direct Dutch rule until 1870, the Dutch and the Minahasans eventually became so close that the north was often referred to as 'the 12th province of the Netherlands'. A Manado-based political movement called Twaalfe Provincie even campaigned for Minahasa's integration into the Dutch state in 1947. For the most part the history of northern Sulawesi is the history of the Minahasans, who have dominated events on the peninsula for the past century.

Portuguese activity apart, Christianity became a force in the early 1820s when a Calvinist group, the Netherlands Missionary Society, turned from an almost exclusive interest in Maluku to the Minahasa area. The wholesale conversion of the Minahasans was almost complete by 1860. With the missionaries càme mission schools, which meant that, as in Ambon and Roti, Western education in Minahasa started much earlier than in other parts of Indonesia. The Dutch government eventually took over some of these schools and also set up others. Because the schools taught in Dutch, the Minahasans had an early advantage in the competition for government jobs and places in the colonial army. Minahasans remain among the educated elite today.

The Minahasans fought alongside the Dutch to subdue rebellions in other parts of the archipelago, notably in the Java War of 1825-30. They seemed to gain a special role in the Dutch scheme of things and their loyalty to the Dutch as soldiers, their Christian religion and their geographic isolation from the rest of Indonesia all led to a sense of being 'different' from the other ethnic groups of the archipelago. .

The Minahasan sense of being different quickly became a problem for the central government after independence. As in Sumatra there was a general feeling that central government was inefficient, development was stagnating, money was being plugged into Java at the expense of the outer provinces and that these circumstances favoured the spread of communism.

In March 1957 the military leaders of both southern and northern Sulawesi launched a confrontation with the central government with demands for greater regional autonomy, more local development, a fairer share of revenue, help in suppressing the Kahar Muzakar rebellion in southern Sulawesi, and that the cabinet of the central government be led jointly by Soekarno and Hatta. At least initially the 'Permesta' (Piagam Perjuangan Semesta Alam) rebellion was a reformist rather than a separatist movement.

Negotiations between the central govern-

ment and the Sulawesi military leaders prevented violence in southern Sulawesi, but the Minahasan leaders were dissatisfied with the agreements and the movement split. Inspired, perhaps, by fears of domination by the south, the Minahasan leaders declared their own autonomous state of North Sulawesi in June 1957. By this time the central government had the situation in southern Sulawesi pretty much under control but in the north they had no strong local figure to rely upon and there were rumours that the USA, suspected of supplying arms to rebels in Sumatra, was also in contact with the Minahasan leaders.

The possibility of foreign intervention finally drove the central government to seek a military solution. In February 1958 Manado was bombed, coinciding with the bombing of Padang in Sumatra. By May the Minahasans had given up on getting any military support from southern Sulawesi. Permesta forces were driven out of Central Sulawesi, Gorontalo, the Sangir islands and from Morotai in Maluku (from whose airfield the rebels had hoped to fly bombing raids on Jakarta). The rebels' few planes (supplied by the USA and flown by US, Filipino and Taiwanese pilots) were destroyed. US policy shifted, favouring Jakarta, and in June 1958 central government troops landed in Minahasa. The Permesta rebels withdrew into the mountains and the rebellion was finally put down in mid-1961.

The effect of both the Sumatran and Sulawesi rebellions was to strengthen exactly those trends the rebels had hoped to weaken: central authority was enhanced at the expense of local autonomy, radical nationalism gained over pragmatic moderation, the power of the communists and Soekarno increased while that of Hatta waned, and Soekarno was able to establish 'guided democracy' in 1959.

GORONTALO

The port of Gorontalo, population 120,000, is the second-largest centre in North Sulawesi. It has the feel of a large, friendly country town. Islam probably arrived here when the Ternate sultanate extended its influence over the tribes of the Gorontalo region before the Dutch took over in the late 17th century.

Gorontalo features some of the best preserved colonial houses in Sulawesi. The town's local hero is **Nani Wartabone**, an anti-Dutch guerilla, and there is a large statue of him dressed like a boy scout in the sports field adjacent to the Hotel Saronde.

On the outskirts of Gorontalo are some European-built fortresses. There's some confusion over whether it was the Dutch or the Portuguese who built them. On a hill at **Dembe** overlooking Danau Limboto is Otanaha Fort, which was probably built by the Portuguese; you can see the remains of three towers. To get there take a *bendi* (pony cart) to the path up the hill from Jalan Belibis, or take a *mikrolet* (bemo) from the bus station, though these are infrequent. There's a sign at the foot of the path pointing to the fort. There is another fort on the shore of the lake to the south-east.

Pantai Indah is the name of the local beach on the southern side of the city. Local musicians occasionally perform here. You can get there by bendi or mikrolet.

Air Panas Lombongo are 40 km from Gorontalo and reachable by mikrolet. There's a swimming pool filled with hot springs water and a nearby river with cold water.

Beyond Lombongo there is the **Dumoga Bone National Park** – a large reserve with the highest conservation value in North Sulawesi. Despite its importance, Dumoga Bone and its unique flora & fauna are facing a new threat from illegal gold miners working deep inside the park. If approaching the park from the east, you'll need to obtain a permit from the national parks office at Doloduo.

Orientation

Although rather spread out, most of the hotels, shops and other life-support systems are concentrated in a small central district. The intercity bus station is three km north of the city, and the port is 2½ km east. Minibuses fan out in all directions from the

terminal opposite the main market (pasar sentral) on Jalan Sam Ratulangi.

Places to Stay – bottom end
Melati Hotel (☎ 21853), Jalan Gajah Mada 33, is a lovely old place facing the Nani Wartabone square. It was built around the turn of the century for the then harbour master whose grandson, Alex Velberg, has opened the house to guests. Large airy rooms with shared bath cost 7000/14,000 rp, plus 1500 rp per person for breakfast. Pak Alex's advice in English, Dutch or Indonesian is accurate and free.

Hotel Saronde (☎ 21735), Jalan Walanda Maramis 17, just across the square, has singles/doubles with fan for 12,100/18,700 rp, and air-con for 25,850/34,100 rp. Breakfast is included.

Penginapan Teluk Kau at Jalan Parman 42 has large rooms with high ceilings, big double beds and singles/doubles for 5000/10,000 rp. It is rundown and noisy.

Hotel Wisata (☎ 21736), Jalan 23 Januari 19, is an excellent place, and is also the location of the Merpati office. Singles/doubles range from 10,000/15,000 rp to 30,000/40,000 rp. The *Hotel Indah Ria* (☎ 21296) at Jalan Yani 20 has doubles with mandi from 19,250 rp, including three meals and tax. It's a very congenial place.

Places to Stay – middle
Hotel Saronde II (☎ 21735), Jalan Walanda Maramis 17, is attached to the Hotel Saronde. Double rooms come in at least three standards for 38,000, 44,000 and 55,000 rp, including tax and breakfast. All rooms are big and bright, with refrigerator, TV and air-con.

Karawang City Hotel, Jalan Basuki Rachmad 31, is a new place with motel-style rooms for 44,000 rp, including tax and breakfast. It's cool, clean and pleasant.

Places to Eat
The local delicacy is *milu siram*, a corn soup with grated coconut, fish, salt, chilli and lime. Look for it at stalls and warung.

Brantas Bakery on Jalan Sultan Hasa-nuddin opposite the main mosque, is a depot of delights with an exquisite selection of cheap cakes and pastries. Wash them down with coffee back at your losmen or pack them for your onward journey. The warung next door has simple fare such as nasi goreng.

Gantiano across the street from the Karawang City Hotel, is a padang restaurant with an airy seating area. It's worth a visit, as is *Salero,* the padang place just south of the post office.

Viva is convenient for guests of the Melati, and *Agung* around the corner in Jalan Januari 23 is not bad either.

The *Boulavard* is known for its sweet-water fish and Chinese food. The *Dirgahayu*, on Jalan Pertiwi, serves goat sate with peanut sauce.

Getting There & Away
Air Merpati (☎ 21736) is in the Hotel Wisata at Jalan 23 Januari 19; Bouraq (☎ 21070) is at Jalan Ahmad Yani 34 next to the Bank Negara Indonesia. Merpati and Bouraq fly to Manado (93,000 rp) and Palu (108,000 rp) daily.

Bus The main bus station is three km north of town. There are direct buses to Palu and Poso in Central Sulawesi, one day away. Buses to Manado take 10 hours if the road is clear. If it rains, mud slides are common between Gorontalo and Kwandang. There are small, crowded buses (13,000 rp), big, air-con buses (17,500 rp) and top-of-the-range Tomohon Indah buses (21,000 rp).

We don't recommend Tomohon Indah, and not just because someone threw a large rock through a side window as we sped by. These buses go too fast, and have far too many heart stopping near misses.

Boat Pelni (☎ 20419), Jalan 23 Januari 31, also has an office at the port in Kwandang. Pelni's *KM Awu* calls at Gorontalo on its fortnightly run from Ujung Pandang to Bitung.

Another shipping line, Gapsu, has an office at Jalan Pertiwi 55 in central Goron-talo, and also at Gorontalo port on Jalan

Mayor Dullah. There are two ferries a week to Pagimana, the Togians, Ampana and Poso, and one which goes to Pagimana every even day and back on odd days.

The port of Kwandang, two hours by bus from Gorontalo, is a stop for the large Pelni liner *Umsini*.

Getting Around

To/From the Airport The shared Merpati and Bouraq bus will transport you from town to the airport 32 km away. It's a half-hour drive and costs 5000 rp per person. You can go to the Merpati or Bouraq office and arrange to have the bus pick you up at your hotel on the day of departure.

Local Transport Gorontalo is rather spread out and you really need the bendis; 300 rp will get you almost anywhere. For longer routes take mikrolets which cruise the streets, and can also be found at the mikrolet terminal across the road from the pasar sentral. Mikrolets to either the port of Gorontalo or the main bus station cost 250 rp and take 15 minutes. Mikrolets direct from the port to the main bus terminal cost 1500 rp per person.

KWANDANG

Kwandang is a port on the north coast of the peninsula, not far from Gorontalo. On the outskirts of Kwandang are the remains of two interesting fortresses, built by either the Portuguese or the Dutch, but no-one is certain. While the town itself is nothing special, the forts are worth checking out. Both are just off the Gorontalo to Kwandang road as you enter Kwandang.

Fort Ota Mas Udangan stands on flat ground and at first glance appears to be ill-placed to defend anything. One suggestion is that the ocean once came right up to the fort, but has since receded. All that remains of the once-sizeable fort are the ruins of a tower alongside the road, a gateway further back, and traces of the walls.

Fort Oranje lies on a hill some distance back from the sea and just a short walk from the Gorontalo-Kwandang road. It's been partly restored, though Fort Ota Mas Udangan is probably the more interesting of the two.

To get to Kwandang, take a bus from Gorontalo bus station (two hours; 2500 rp).

MANADO

When the naturalist Alfred Wallace visited in 1859 he described the town as 'one of the prettiest in the East'. Only 14 years earlier Manado had been levelled by earthquakes, enabling the Dutch to redesign the thriving settlement from scratch.

Today neat rows of wooden houses with picket fences line orderly streets. This provincial capital of 290,000 people is clean, confident and cosmopolitan, with the highest standard of living in eastern Indonesia. The locals are affable, the kids won't hound you and Westerners can mingle freely without constant assaults of 'Hello Misteerrrr'.

Manado is the centre of Minahasa, the name given to the territory around the city and sometimes to Sulawesi's whole northern peninsula. Minahasa literally means 'united, becomes one', referring to a pre-colonial defence pact which united clans against the neighbouring Bolaang Mongondow regency.

History

The original Minahasans are said to originate from Lumimuut, who rose from the sea and gave birth to Toar. After many years' separation, mother and son met again. Not recognising each other, they married and their descendants populated the region. Minahasan lands and languages were divided by the god Muntu Untu at Watu Pinabetengan (the 'dividing stone'), a carved rock on the foothills of Gunung Soputan.

Rice surpluses from Minahasa's volcanic hinterland made Manado a strategic port for European traders sailing to and from the Spice Islands of Maluku. Spain established a fort at Manado in 1627, but by 1643 the Manado rulers wanted their unruly and corrupt Spanish guests out, and appealed to the Dutch VOC in Ternate for help. The Dutch and their Minahasan allies eventually gained the upper hand in 1655, built their

SULAWESI

own fortress in 1658 and expelled the last of the Spaniards a few years later.

The Dutch helped unite the linguistically diverse Minahasan confederacy, and in 1693 the Minahasans scored a decisive military victory against the Bolaang to the south. Dutch influence flourished as the Minahasans embraced European goods and god. Missionary schools in Manado in 1881 were among the first attempts at mass education in Indonesia, giving their graduates a considerable edge in gaining civil service, military and other positions of influence.

By the mid-1800s compulsory cultivation schemes were producing huge crops of cheap coffee for a Dutch-run monopoly. Minahasans suffered from this 'progress', yet economic, religious and social ties with the colonists continued to intensify. Minahasan mercenaries put down anti-Dutch rebellions in Java and elsewhere, earning them the name 'anjing Belanda' – 'Dutch dogs'.

The Japanese occupation of 1942-45 was a period of deprivation, and the Allies bombed Manado heavily in 1945. During the war of independence that followed, there was bitter division between pro-Indonesian unitarians and those favouring Dutch-sponsored federalism. The appointment of a Manadonese Christian, Sam Ratulangi, as the first republican governor of eastern Indonesia, was decisive in winning Minahasan support for the republic.

As the young republic lurched from crisis to crisis, Jakarta's monopoly over the copra trade seriously weakened Minahasa's economy. Illegal exports flourished and in June 1956 Jakarta ordered the closure of Manado port, the busiest smuggling port in the republic. Local leaders refused and Jakarta backed down. Soon the Permesta rebels confronted the central government with demands for political, economic and regional reforms. Jakarta responded in Manado by bombing the city in February 1958 then invading in June.

Manado has prospered under Indonesia's New Order, which implemented many of the economic reforms (but few of the political reforms) sought by the Permesta rebels. The city has a tolerant, outward-looking culture with a promising future.

Orientation & Information

Mikrolets from every direction loop around Pasar 45, a block of shops, fruit stands and department stores in the heart of town. The market backs on to Jalan Sam Ratulangi, the main road running south, where you will find up-market restaurants, hotels and supermarkets. Pasar Jengki fish market, north of the centre, is the main launching place for boats to Bunaken Island.

Tourist Offices The North Sulawesi Tourism Office (☎ 64911) is on Jalan 17 Agustus, and there is an information booth at Sam Ratulangi airport. Mikrolets marked '17 Aug Wanea' leave from Pasar 45.

The Sub Balai Konservasi Sumber Daya Alam (National Parks Office) is at Jalan Babe Palar, but has little useful information on the national parks it administers.

There is a Central & South Sulawesi information office (☎ 51723, 51835) on Jalan Diponegoro 111, and a central Sulawesi tourist office (☎ 21795, 21808) on Jalan Teuku Cik Ditiro 32.

Immigration The immigration office (☎ 63491), near the tourist office on Jalan 17 Agustus, is helpful. There's another at Bitung to process sea-bound travellers. The Philippines has a consulate general (☎ 62365) at Jalan Sam Ratulangi 176.

Money Manado is overflowing with banks, most of which can change money. Bank Rakyat Indonesia is on Jalan Sarapung, and Bank Expor Impor Indonesia is on Jalan Sudirman.

Post & Telecommunications The post office is on Jalan Sam Ratulangi 21. The Telkom office is at Jalan Sam Ratulangi 4, there are card phones all over town and a wartel on Jalan Bethesda.

Things to See
There are good movies, shopping and food in Manado, but otherwise the main attractions are outside the city.

The **Provincial Museum of North Sulawesi** on Jalan Supratman is worth a look, as is the **Kienteng Ban Hian Kiong** Confucian-Buddhist temple, a colourful landmark on Jalan Panjaitan.

There are monuments on every second corner dedicated to Minahasan and Indonesian heroes. The **Sam Ratulangi** monument on the street bearing the same name, honours the first republican governor of east Indonesia, hailed as the 'father to the whole Minahasan people' after his death in June 1949. The **Toar Lumimuut** monument at the eastern end of Jalan Sudarso depicts the Adam and Eve characters of Minahasan mythology, Lumimuut and her son-husband, Toar. On the same street there is a monument to **Ibu Walanda Maramis**, a pioneer of the Indonesian women's movement, and the grave of **Imam Bonjol**, a hero of the Padri War (1821-38) – just one of many anti-Dutch rebels to die in exile in Manado during the 19th century.

Festivals
Minahasans love an excuse to party. Watch out for festivals, including the Tai Pei Kong festival at Ban Hiah Kong temple in February; the Pengucapan Syukur (Minahasan Thanksgiving Day) in June/August; the Bunaken Festival in July; the Anniversary of Manado on 14 July; traditional horse races in the second week of August; and the anniversary of North Sulawesi province on 23 September.

Places to Stay – bottom end
Two new central hotels have drastically improved the budget accommodation scene in Manado. The friendly *Rex Hotel* (☎ 51136), Jalan Sugiono 3, is modern and clean, with economy singles/doubles for 7500/12,500 rp, and air-con rooms for 25,000 rp. If you have trouble finding Jalan Sugiono, try asking for Jalan Marambak – its old name.

Manado Bersehati Hotel (☎ 55022), Jalan Sudirman 1, is a large new Minahasan-style house set about 20 metres off the main road. Singles/doubles with shared mandi go for just 7500/12,500 rp. It's highly recommended.

Manado Homestay (☎ 60298), Wanea Lingkungan III, Komplex Diklat Rike, is less conveniently located, but well worth considering with rooms from 15,000 rp per night, or 85,000 rp per month. It is a professional outfit with its own minibus, and runs tours to Minahasa (55,000 rp), Bunaken (110,000 rp) and Tangkoko National Park (90,000 rp). To get there, take a Teling mikrolet from Pasar 45 and ask to get off at Komplex Diklat.

The once-popular *Hotel Kawanua*, now the *Kawanua Kecil* (☎ 63842), Jalan Sudirman 40, is quiet, quirky but a little rundown. The name is unfortunate, because everyone you ask directs you to the similarly named Kawanua City Hotel, the most expensive place in town. Singles with shared bath are 12,500 rp, while double rooms with private bath are 16,000/19,000 rp, including breakfast.

Ahlan City Hotel (☎ 63454) is in the same neighbourhood at Jalan Sudirman 103. It's basic but clean. Singles with shared bath are 8300 rp, while singles/doubles with private bath cost 11,000/13,750 rp.

The *Hotel Jeprinda* (☎ 64049), Jalan Sam Ratulangi 33, is clean and cheery, with singles/doubles for 21,000/25,000 rp. The manager speaks English.

The *Hotel Mini Cakalele* (☎ 52942) is at Jalan Korengkeng 40, a street running off Jalan Sam Ratulangi south of the main post office. Rooms with fan are 18,700 rp, or from 26,400 rp with air-con. It's clean and comfortable.

The *Hotel Minahasa* (☎ 62059), Jalan Sam Ratulangi 199, is an elegant hotel with an old colonial feel to it. The friendly manager speaks Dutch and English. Spotlessly clean singles/doubles with fan are 20,000/25,000 rp, or 25,000/30,000 rp with private bath. Air-con rooms are 35,000/42,500 rp.

The *Angkasa Raya Indah Hotel* (☎ 52039), Jalan Sugiono 2A, has rooms with fan for 20,000 to 30,000 rp, and suites for 40,000 rp, plus tax.

SULAWESI

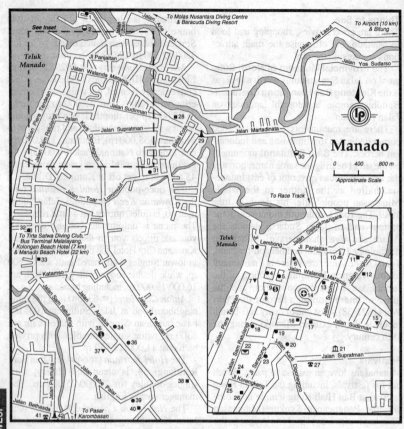

Manado

Teluk Manado

To Molas Nusantara Diving Centre & Baracuda Diving Resort

To Airport (10 km) & Bitung

Jalan Arie Lasut

Jalan Yos Sudarso

Jalan Martadinata

To Race Track

0   400   800 m

Approximate Scale

See Inset

Jl Panjaitan

Jalan Walanda Maramis

Jalan Sudirman

Jalan Supratman

Jalan Toar

Jalan Pierre Tendean

Jalan Sam Ratulangi

To Tirta Satwa Diving Club,
Bus Terminal Malalayang,
Kolongan Beach Hotel (7 km)
& Manado Beach Hotel (22 km)

Katamso

Jalan 17 Agustus

Jalan 14 Pebruari

Jalan Sam Ratulangi

Jalan Pramuka

Jalan Babe Palar

Jalan Bethesda

To Pasar
Karombasan

Teluk Manado

Jl Sindangmangara

Lembong

Jl Panjaitan

Jalan Walanda Maramis

Jalan Subroto

Jalan Sudirman

Jalan Supratman

Jalan Kenti Dotonegoro

Sarapung

Jl Korengkeng

Jalan Pierre Tendean

Jalan Sam Ratulangi

Places to Stay – middle

Hotel New Queen (☎ 65979; fax 65748), Jalan Wakeke 12-14, is clean, and even has an award to prove it. It's on a quiet street and is one of the best mid-range places in Manado, with singles/doubles from 65,250/78,300 rp, plus tax. All rooms have air-con.

Kolongan Beach Hotel (☎ 51001) is seven km south of the city and is the last stop for many of the mikrolets. This is a good place for snorkelling and diving. Rooms cost from 30,000 rp.

Manado Plaza Hotel (☎ 51124), Jalan Walanda Maramis 1, is an aging landmark in

the heart of town, with a better than average disco. Motel-style rooms start at 40,000/50,000 rp, plus tax.

The *Nusantara Diving Centre*, or *NDC* (☎ 63988) at Molas Beach, five km north of town, attracts diving groups and has a popular disco. Singles/doubles with fan start at 15,000/22,500 rp, or 75,000/90,000 rp for air-con rooms. There are discount packages for snorkellers and divers: 105,000/195,000 rp for economy rooms with fan and a day of snorkelling, and 160,000/310,000 rp for the same room and two dives.

The *Baracuda Diving Resort* (☎ 62033)

PLACES TO STAY		37	Manado Hilltop Restaurant	15	Gelael Supermarket
				18	Pelni
8	Kawanua City Hotel			19	Silk Air
11	Angkasa Raya Indah Hotel	**OTHER**		20	Garuda
				21	Museum
12	Rex Hotel	1	Pasars Bersehati &	22	Post Office
13	Manado Plaza Hotel		Jengki	23	Bouraq
16	Manado Bersehati	2	Boats to Bunaken	27	Telkom
17	Kawanua Kecil	3	Ferry Ticket Offices &	29	Toar Lumimuut
24	Hotel Mini Cakalele		Port		Monument
25	Hotel Jeprinda	4	Pasar 45	30	Paal 2 Terminal
26	Hotel New Queen	5	Town Square	31	Philippines Consulate
28	Ahlan City Hotel	6	President Complex	32	Merpati
33	Hotel Minahasa		(Shops & Cimema)	34	Governor's Office
38	Garden Hotel	7	Jumbo Supermarket	35	Tourist Office
40	Manado Homestay	8	Sempati	36	Immigration
		9	Bank Rakyat Indonesia	39	National Parks Office
PLACES TO EAT		10	Ban Hian Kiong	41	Wartel
			Temple	42	Sam Ratulangi
15	KFC	14	Hospital		Monument

just past NDC, is clean, modern and has singles/doubles from 45,000/55,000 rp. It also has dive facilities.

Places to Stay – top end

The *Kawanua City Hotel* (☎ 67777; fax 65220), Jalan Sam Ratulangi 1, is Manado's top establishment, complete with swimming pool. Singles/doubles start at 165,000/185,000 rp, plus tax.

The *Manado Beach Hotel* (☎ 67001; fax 67007) is 22 km south of the city and reachable by taxi or a long bus ride. Singles/doubles start at 190,000/215,000 rp, plus tax.

Places to Eat

Manado is a Mecca for adventurous diners. The food is clean, tasty and *very* different. Regional delights include kawaok, translated into Indonesian as tikus hutan goreng – 'fried forest rat'. The name is unfortunate because this heavily spiced dish of bones and lean meat (something akin to a possum) actually tastes sensational. There's also rintek wuuk – spicy dog meat – a tough, gamy dish similar to buffalo, lawang pangang (stewed bat), the tender and tasty freshwater ikan mas (gold fish) and tinutuan (vegetable porridge).

There are few restaurants in Manado serving regional cuisine. To eat well, stop at the row of restaurants in the Lokon foothills, just before Tomohon. The food at *Tinoor Indah* and the *Pemandangan* is as incredible as their spectacular views over Manado. Get the Tomohon bus to drop you there.

The drinks of choice are *saguer,* a very quaffable fermented sago wine, and Cap Tikus (literally 'rat brand'), the generic name for distilled saguer. Cap Tikus is sold as No 1, No 2 or No 3, referring to its strength and when it was removed from the distillation process. It is best diluted and served over ice. For durian lovers, try crushed durian in saguer.

The recently completed esplanade near Pasar 45 attracts a good selection of night warung selling cheap Indonesian food. A local English-language conversation club meets here on Monday, Wednesday and Friday. There are good, reasonably priced eating houses either side of the Penginapan Keluarga and near Pasar 45, classier Indonesian and Chinese fare along Jalan Sam Ratulangi, Indonesian fried chicken at the *Kalasan* on Jalan Sudirman 9, and its *KFC* equivalent just a few doors down. For pastries and desserts to die for, check out the restaurant opposite the Bioskop Manado on Jalan Sutomo.

Also, check out the Warong Nusa Indah and Warong Souvenir, both on Jalan

SULAWESI

Panjaitan near the temple, for candied nutmeg fruit, canary halua and bagea (happiness) cake and other Manado delicacies.

Entertainment

As in the nearby Philippines, music is a way of life for the Minahasans. They love jazz and there are always small concerts and backroom gigs, so ask around.

The central *Ocean* nightclub offers 'menu' entertainment, with a disco upstairs and a mix of fashion shows, drinking competitions, aerobic displays, dancers and other events downstairs. It opens at around 8 pm; get there by 11 pm. The cover charge is 5000 to 10,000 rp.

Pubs offer more conventional entertainment. Try *Panterai*, which often has bands; entry is free. So-called 'nightclubs' are for short-term match making.

A more entertaining option is to head for *Ebony Disco* in the Manado Plaza Complex (2500 rp entry) or the disco out at NDC, which starts at 8 pm.

The best cinema is the Benteng theatre opposite the Kawanua Hotel.

Getting There and Away

Air Garuda (☎ 51544) is at Jalan Diponegoro 15; Merpati (☎ 64027) is at Jalan Sam Ratulangi 138; Bouraq (☎ 62757) is at Jalan Serapung 27B; and Sempati (☎ 51612) is at the Kawanua City Hotel, Jalan Sam Ratulangi 1.

Useful connections include Bouraq's twice-weekly flights to Davao in the Philippines (330,000 rp) and Ambon (237,000 rp), and its daily flights to Ujung Pandang (214,000 rp), Surabaya (369,000 rp) and Jakarta (487,000 rp).

Singapore's regional airline, Silk Air, flies from Singapore to Manado direct twice a week for 580,000 to 815,000 rp, depending on its competitors' fares. Silk only offers discounts and packages through its agents – check the classified ads in Manado's daily newspaper or try the agency in the Plaza Hotel. Sempati and Garuda fly the same route for about the same price, but go via Jakarta.

Bus Bus fares to Gorontalo (10 hours) range from 13,000 to 21,000 rp. We suggest the mid-range 17,500 rp older air-con buses. The highway goes around the gulf to Poso and all the way to Ujung Pandang – so do the buses if you can tolerate the three-day haul. Allow for possible delays during wet weather. A better way would be to break your trip at Gorontalo, take a boat to Poso, then resume from there. The Gorontalo bus station is the Malalayang terminal south of town.

Boat Pelni (☎ 62844) at Jalan Sam Ratulangi 7, has five large boats calling at the deep-water port of Bitung, near Manado, plus there are many smaller ferries out of Manado itself. They tend to call at ports along the coast, go north to Tahuna (Pulau Sangihe) and Lirung (Talaud islands) or over to Ternate and Ambon. There has long been talk of a regular boat service from Manado to Davao in the Philippines, but never anything definite.

From Bitung, 1st-class/economy fares on the KM *Kerinci* or *Ciremai* are 51,200/15,200 rp to Ternate; 262,200/71,200 rp to Jayapura; 144,000/38,000 rp to Ambon; 180,000/54,000 rp to Bau Bau; 233,200/70,200 rp to Ujung Pandang; and 562,000/161,800 rp to Jakarta. The KM *Umsini* and *Kambuna* price scales are similar.

KM *Awu* fares from Bitung to Tahuna are 80,000/16,000 rp; to Luwuk 96,200/24,200 rp; to Kolonodale 132,200/32,200 rp; to Kendari 188,200/46,200; to Bau Bau 229,000/57,000 rp; and to Surabaya 528,000/128,000 rp.

Tickets for smaller boats from Manado are available from stalls outside the port compound, north of Pasar 45. Destinations include boats to Tahuna on Pulau Sangihe (12 hours; 15,000 to 17,000 rp), Pulau Siau (10 hours; 10,000 rp), Lirung (11 hours; 15,000 rp), Ternate (14 hours; 22,000 rp) and Ambon (28 hours; 54,000 rp).

Getting Around

To/From the Airport Mikrolets from Sam Ratulangi airport go to Paal-Paal (350 rp), and from there you can get another to Pasar

45 (300 rp) or elsewhere in the city. Taxis run on argo meters. One from the airport to the city (13 km) costs 6000 to 7500 rp. There are also Damri bases from Pasar 45.

Local Transport Transport around town is by mikrolet for a flat fare of 300 rp. Destinations are shown on a card in the front windscreen, not on the side of the van. There are various bus stations around town for destinations outside Manado – get to any of them from Pasar 45. Mercifully, the vehicles do not do endless pick-up rounds. Another option for touring the area is to hire a car for 8000 rp per hour. Boats leave for Pulau Bunaken from the fish market.

BUNAKEN ISLAND

The wildly varied shapes and colours of the fringing coral off Pulau Bunaken have become an international snorkelling and scuba-diving attraction. The flat coral off **Pantai Liang** takes a dramatic 90-degree turn about 100 metres offshore, plummeting from one to two-metre depths to dark oblivion. Floating over the edge is akin to floating from the top of a skyscraper.

Unfortunately, tourism and plastic have exacted a heavy toll. Tides occasionally swamp the island's shores with wads of garbage from nearby Manado, turning picturesque tropical beaches into refuse heaps overnight. Unchecked development on the beach has increased the boat traffic across the shallows, destroying acres of flat coral.

Despite the damage, Bunaken remains a world-class attraction. Its dramatic drop-offs are largely intact and easily accessible, and there is plenty of good diving on other reefs off Bunaken and neighbouring islands. It remains to be seen whether the government's conservation plan for the island group can slow the degradation.

The 800-hectare Pulau Bunaken has about 2000 residents, most living in **Bunaken village** at the southern tip, and in smaller settlements at **Tanjung Parigi** and **Alung Banua**. There is also a small settlement on neighbouring **Pulau Siladen**.

The scarcity of fresh water has limited development and villagers must import their drinking water from Manado. Washing water is drawn from small, brackish wells. Fishing, coconuts, fruit and now tourism provide much of Bunaken's income.

There are other coral reefs around the Minahasan peninsula. Manado Tua, or 'Old Manado', is a dormant volcano you can see off the coast. The Portuguese and Spanish once based themselves here to trade between northern Sulawesi and Maluku. Nowadays, like Bunaken Island, it's the coral reefs that pull in visitors. Other coral reefs lie off Mantehage Island and Bitung. The boatmen *say* there are no sharks in the waters around Bunaken, but sharks have been reported at the neighbouring islands of Manado Tua and Mantehage, and at Bitung.

Diving & Snorkelling

Get your feet wet and float over some of the world's most spectacular and accessible coral drop-offs, caves and valleys. You can buy snorkelling gear from sport shops in Manado, such as Toko Akbar Ali on the western boundary of Pasar 45, or hire wellworn masks and snorkels from warungs along the beaches on Bunaken.

Divers with current certificates can do two dives with Lorenzo at Lorenzo Cottages for 100,000 to 130,000 rp, including equipment and boat hire. Bring larger groups and your own gear to negotiate discounts.

The oldest and most established dive service, Nusantara Diving Centre or NDC (☎ 63988) on Molas Beach, Manado, caters for beginners, but not very well. Tours on glass-bottom boats cost 45,000 rp a day, snorkelling tours 65,000 rp and two-dive excursions, including two tanks and weights cost 130,000 rp. Equipment hire will set you back an extra 35,000 to 45,000 rp, and for another 15,000 to 90,000 rp you can stay the night at NDC's cottages – see Manado's Places to Stay section.

The similarly priced Murex (☎ 66280), Jalan Sudirman 28, also caters for beginners, and the swish Baracuda Diving Resort (☎ 62033) at Molas Beach is another combined resort/dive centre. This is the most

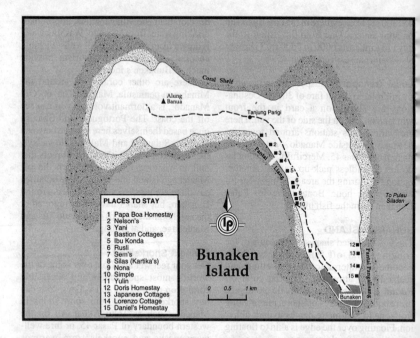

PLACES TO STAY
1 Papa Boa Homestay
2 Nelson's
3 Yani
4 Bastion Cottages
5 Ibu Konda
6 Rusli
7 Sem's
8 Silas (Kartika's)
9 Nona
10 Simple
11 Yulin
12 Doris Homestay
13 Japanese Cottages
14 Lorenzo Cottage
15 Daniel's Homestay

Bunaken
Island

0   0.5   1 km

expensive dive school, but has had good reports.

The travel agency PT Polita Express (☎ 652231), Jalan Sam Ratulangi 74, organises trips and diving tours to Pulau Bunaken, as do the major hotels.

Places to Stay & Eat

There is a range of hastily built homestays and cottages along Pantai Liang, and a few on the quieter, less developed Pantai Pangalisang near Bunaken village. Larger, more popular places such as Daniel's and Nelson's set the standard, and smaller ones adapt their rates accordingly. Most tariffs are negotiable, and all include food.

Daniel's Homestay on Pantai Pangalisang is a popular choice with budget travellers. Basic rooms cost 10,000 rp per person, including three meals, and there are cottages for 20,000/40,000 rp (singles/doubles). The staff are easy-going and informative, and the food is excellent.

Lorenzo Cottage next door is smaller, with cottages for 20,000 rp per person, and 15,000 rp (more or less) for homestay rooms. Lorenzo is a friendly young guide, Bunaken born-and-bred, who can organise scuba equipment and excursions for experienced divers.

Doris Homestay at the far end of the beach has rooms and meals for 10,000 to 15,000 rp. There's also a Japanese cottage for private tour groups on Pantai Pangalisang.

Tourism is booming along Pantai Liang, where seemingly everyone with access to land and building materials is setting up shop. *Papa Boa* is a rambling homestay at the far end, run by a lovely old bloke. It has rooms with outside mandi for 15,000 rp per person, including three meals. His neighbour is the popular *Nelson's*, a professional outfit with rooms from 15,000 rp and breezy cottages set up the hillside for 50,000 rp per night.

Yani is clean and comfortable, with simple quiet rooms from 15,000 rp per person.

Bastion Cottages are pretty flash, by Bunaken standards, with a raised airy restaurant overlooking the beach and fine rooms with private mandi for 25,000/50,000 rp a single/double. As with everywhere else, the daily price includes three meals.

Ibu Konda's prime attraction is a small canoe for guests to use plus the fact that there are no neighbours right next door. The asking price is 15,000 rp, but the sand floors in these spartan rooms make it possible to negotiate down to 10,000 rp (the sand gets into everything). Mask hire can sometimes be included in the price and the food is excellent.

Rusli has nicer rooms and mosquito nets at 10,000 rp a night, and *Sem* right next door asks 15,000 rp (more or less) a night, including mask hire and meals.

Silas or *Kartika's* (☎ 53566), *Nona* and *Simple* are three small, similarly priced homestays clustered at the southern end of the beach. They're solid and clean with rooms and meals from 10,000 to 15,000 rp per person. *Yulin* is set apart from the rest on its own little stretch of sand with simple rooms from 10,000 to 15,000 rp.

There is also *Martha Homestay* and *Lin Homestay* in the fishing village on nearby Siladen Island, both catering for budget travellers. If you get there, write to us and tell us if they are any good.

Getting There and Away

Public boats to Manado leave Bunaken at around 8 am each morning, and return to Bunaken at 3 pm. The cost is 2500 rp per person. Bunaken-bound boats depart from the quay behind the Jengki fish market. Fishing boats leave Bunaken village to take their catch to Manado around 1 pm, and are sometimes happy for passengers to tag along. Otherwise you could try chartering for 15,000 rp, including a one-hour detour to the reefs.

You need your own boat to see the reefs at their best. Try hiring or borrowing a small canoe and doing your own paddling, or there are dozens of children with small canoes willing to take passengers to and fro for a bit of pocket money. There is also a long pier at

Bunaken village. Climb down the steps at the end and you are right on the reef.

Day trippers can hire a boat in Manado and set their own pace. It's probably easiest to charter a boat from behind the fish market for about 25,000 rp, go out to the reef in the morning, paddle around for a few hours and return to Manado in the afternoon. It is worth every last rupiah!

TOMOHON

Minahasa's extraordinary cuisine is served in a string of restaurants on a cliff overlooking Manado, just a few km before Tomohon (see Manado's Places to Eat section earlier in this chapter).

Tomohon has a **vulcanology centre** which monitors and advises on the safety of active volcanoes in the area. Seek advice there and see its monitoring equipment before tackling Gunung Soputan, Lokon or Mahawu. It also has information and spectacular photographs of other volcanoes too, from Gunung Colo on the Togians, to the lethal Gunung Awu on Pulau Sangihe. Awu killed 7300 in an eruption in 1870. The work of Tomohon's vulcanology centre averts similar disasters.

About midway between Tomohon and Lahendong, there's the extensive Hutan Minahasa or **Lahendong hot springs**. Check out the booths for hot mineral baths. There are also hot springs and nice walks near **Langowan**.

Several km out of Tomohon on the road to Tara Tara are some **Japanese caves**. Take a mikrolet from Manado's Pasar Karombasan (Wanea terminal) to Tomohon and another mikrolet towards Tara Tara. There are also mikrolets between Tomohon and Tondano, and between Kawangkoan and Tomohon. Tomohon is the site of a Christian college and a centre for the study of Christian theology in Minahasa.

Tomohon has a modern, comfortable hill resort, the *Lokon Resting Place* (☎ 0436-51203) at Kakaskassen I, Tomohon 95362. It's set amid beautiful gardens with doubles from 75,000 rp, and cottages from 125,000 rp; it's recommended.

SULAWESI

SONDER

The people of Sonder are famous for their business acumen. When Minahasan incomes soared during the clove boom of 1970s, Sonder's canny business people diversified their investments and survived the subsequent drop in prices. For a while, they had the highest per capita income in Indonesia. Their wealth and industry shows today in Sonder's architecture.

The town's concession to tourism is the Komplex Walepapetaupan Toar-Lumimuut, a park, swimming pool and landscaped gardens dedicated to the Minahasans' origin myth. Guest accommodation is available for 25,000 rp, or 45,000 rp for bed and breakfast in new rooms overlooking the park. The park also has a guesthouse, *Pondok Wisata Toar Lumimuut*, 100 metres down the road, opposite the unusual white gothic Gereja Sion Protestant. Large rooms overlooking a pond cost 30,000 to 40,000 rp.

As elsewhere, the easiest way around is by chartered transport, but there are mikrolets from Manado for 1000 rp. En route to Sonder, look out for **Leilem**, a village famed for furniture making.

KAWANGKOAN

During the Japanese occupation in WW II, they dug caves into the hills surrounding Manado to act as air-raid shelters and storage space for ammunition, food, weapons and medical supplies. One such **cave** is three km from Kawangkoan on the road to Kiawa. There are mikrolets to Kawangkoan from Pasar Karombasan (the Wanea terminal) in Manado.

Close to Pinabetengan village, about 40 km from Manado and five km from Kawangkoan is **Batu Pinabetengan**, the stone said to be the place where Minahasan chiefs held meetings. According to legend, the lands of Minahasa were first divided between the different tribes at this place. The locals sometimes pronounce Batu Pinabetengan as 'Watu Pinawe-tengan' – *watu* means 'stone' and *weteng* means 'divide'.

The stone is scratched with the vague outline of human figures. These scratchings have never been deciphered, though it is thought that they may record agreements concerning the division of land amongst the tribes, and the political unification of Minahasa in the early meetings between the chiefs.

To get there, take a mikrolet to Kawangkoan from Manado's Wanea station, then a bendi from Kawangkoan to Desa Pinabetengan. The bendi will take you as far as the turn-off road that leads to Batu Pinabetengan and then you have to walk the last half hour.

TONDANO

Lake Tondano, a crater lake in an extinct volcano, is 30 km south-west of Manado. It's 600 metres above sea level, making it pleasantly cool, scenic and an excellent place to visit. In addition, some of the best **Japanese caves** are just outside Tondano on the road to Airmadidi. A bus from Airmadidi to Tondano will get you to the caves in 45 minutes. From the caves you can hitch or walk (one hour) to Tondano mikrolet station and get a mikrolet back to Pasar Karombasan in Manado. Mikrolets from Tondano to Tomohon take 30 minutes.

AIRMADIDI

Airmadidi (literally, 'boiling water') is the site of mineral springs. Legend has it that nine angels flew down from heaven on nights of the full moon to bathe and frolic here. One night a mortal succeeded in stealing a dress belonging to one of them – unable to return to heaven she was forced to remain on earth. The public baths make a refreshing stop after an overnight hike to the peak of nearby Gunung Klabat.

Airmadidi's real attraction is the odd little pre-Christian tombs known as *waruga*. Corpses were placed in these carved stone boxes in a foetal position with household articles, gold and porcelain – most have been plundered. There's a group of these tombs at **Airmadidi Bawah**, a 15-minute walk from Airmadidi bemo station.

Mikrolets go to Airmadidi from Manado's Paal-Paal terminal (400 rp). From Airmadidi you can also take a mikrolet to Tondano (45 minutes; 1000 rp) or to Bitung (40 minutes; 1000 rp). You can see more warugas at Sawangan and Likupang, and at Kema on the south coast near Bitung.

GUNUNG KLABAT

At 2022 metres, Gunung Klabat is easily the highest peak on the peninsula. The pre-dawn hike to the crater at the top is a hard five hours, but the view across the whole peninsula is spectacular. Within an hour or two of sunrise, the clouds rise and obscure the view, but the hike back to Airmadidi is a bonus because of the rainforest flora & fauna en route. This was the last hideout for the Permesta rebels. It is easy to see how they escaped detection for so long.

BITUNG

Sheltered by Pulau Lembah, Bitung is the chief port of Minahasa and lies to the east of Manado. Many ships dock at Bitung rather than at Manado. Because of the port facilities, there are also many factories here. Overall, the town is not very attractive, but there are some nice beaches along the way. The Pelni office (☎ 21167) is on Jalan Jakarta, within the harbour compound.

Places to Stay & Eat

Penginapan Sansarino near the main market has rooms for 10,000 rp and a downstairs restaurant. *Penginapan Minang* (☎ 21333) is a dark hovel above a restaurant by the same name at Jalan Sam Ratulangi 34. Rooms go for 15,000 rp with private mandi. The flashiest place in town is *Dynasty Hotel* (☎ 22111), Jalan Sudarso 10, with doubles from 50,000 to 60,000 rp.

Getting There & Away

Bitung is 50 km from Manado and is connected by a surfaced racetrack along which kamikaze mikrolet drivers break land, water and air speed records all at once. There are regular departures from Manado's Paal2 terminal (one hour; 1000 rp). The mikrolet drops you off at the Mapalus terminal just outside Bitung, where you catch another mikrolet into town (10 minutes; 300 rp).

AROUND BITUNG

Kema

Just a few km south of Bitung, Kema was formerly a Portuguese and Spanish seaport. There's supposed to be a Portuguese fortress here but if so it's been well camouflaged against assaults by tourists.

Tangkoko Batuangas Dua Saudara

This nature reserve is 30 km from the port of Bitung and is home to black apes, anoas, babirusas and maleo birds (the maleo looks like a huge hen and lays eggs five times the size of a hen's). The reserve also includes the coastline and coral gardens offshore. From Bitung hire a boat to take you to the village of **Batuputih** on the reserve's western border. There are trails into the reserve from **Kasua** village on the south-east border. The park includes a waterfall on the northern side of Gunung Tangkoko, but the real attraction is the wildlife – best seen at dawn or in the early evening.

To enter from Batuputih, you will need a 750 rp permit from the conservation office in Batuputih village. The rangers run and own three *cottages* in the park which cost 12,500 rp with two meals or 15,000 rp with three. There's another outside the park for 5000 rp.

SANGIR-TALAUD GROUP

Strewn across the straits between Indonesia and the southern Mindanao region of the Philippines are the islands of Sangir and Talaud. These small and volcanically active islands are at the end of the long chain of volcanoes that stretches from the western highlands of Sumatra, east through Java and Nusa Tenggara and then north through the Banda islands of Maluku to north-east Sulawesi. One of the more recent volcanic eruptions in northern Sulawesi was that of Gunung Api on Pulau Siau in 1974, which compelled the temporary evacuation of the entire population of the island (then 40,000 people).

The main islands in the Sangir group are Sangir Besar, Siau, Tahulandang and Biaro. The Talaud group consists of Karakelong,

SULAWESI

Salibabu, Kabaruan, Karatung, Nanusa and
Miangas. Despite their tiny size, around
300,000 people live on these islands. The
capital of the Sangir-Talaud group is Tahuna
on Sangir Besar.

History
Once upon a time these islands were subject
to strong Islamic influence from the Ternate
sultanate to the east. That was checked by the
Christian missionaries who followed in the
wake of the Dutch takeover in 1677. Most of
the population was converted to Christianity.
Prior to the arrival of the missionaries, ancestral spirits were important, and some women
(and occasionally men) became possessed
by spirits. Human sacrifice at some ceremonies was also reported.

Not only did the Dutch bring a new religion but they also encouraged the local
population to raise coconuts (for copra) and

nutmeg. The island economy came to rely
heavily on trade in these products, chiefly
carried on with Ternate and Manado. Today
the main industries are copra and cloves.

Getting There & Away
Air Merpati has three flights a week from
Manado to Naha, the airfield 20 km from
Tahuna, for 105,000 rp. Flights to Melang-
guane on Karakelong, in the Talaud group,
cost another 66,500 rp.

Boat For ships to these islands ask at the
shipping offices near the entrance to the
harbour terminal in Manado – see under
Manado earlier in this section for fare details.
There are at least three companies servicing
this route with small ferries, plus Pelni now
sends the KM *Awu* through here on its fortnightly runs. Also ask about ships to Beo and
Lirung on Karakelong.

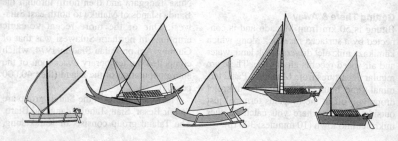

Maluku

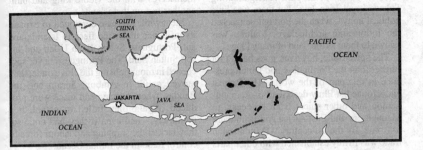

From Halmahera in the north to Wetar off the north-eastern end of Timor are the thousand islands of Maluku (previously called the Moluccas). Sprawled across a vast area of ocean but making up only a tiny proportion of Indonesia's land area, what these islands lack in size they more than make up for in historical significance. These were the fabled 'Spice Islands' to which Indian, Chinese, Arab and later European traders came in search of the cloves, nutmeg and mace which grew there and nowhere else. It was these islands which bore the brunt of the first European attempts to wrest control of the Indonesian archipelago and the lucrative spice trade.

The most popular destinations for most visitors to the region are: Ambon, the capital of Maluku province, just south of the large island of Seram; the beautiful cluster of islands south-east of Ambon known as the Bandas; and the two adjacent northern islands of Ternate and Tidore off the west coast of Halmahera. Although spices are still produced in these islands it's the fine tropical scenery, the relics of the early European invasion, some excellent snorkelling and diving, plus some enticing beaches which draw visitors today. Maluku is one of Indonesia's remotest provinces and its lesser known islands offer infinite scope for getting right off the tourist trail.

Highlights
Maluku is a vast collection of spread-out islands which will take some time (at least three weeks by plane; or five weeks by boat) to fully explore. The centre of all transport, Ambon Island, has great beaches, old forts and a modern, bustling city. Worth a diversion for several days are the nearby islands of Seram, which are undeveloped but offer great scenery and some unique cultures, and pretty Saparua, with beaches, lovely villages and old forts.

To the north, the developed and well-connected island of Ternate offers great volcanic scenery, more beaches and more forts. Close by, northern Halmahera, including Morotai island, has unspoiled beaches and diving opportunities among rusting WW II wrecks; the southern part of Halmahera is far less developed and visited.

South of Ambon is the highlight of Maluku: the Bandas, with magnificent crumbling and restored European forts, stunning volcanoes to admire and climb, and many lovely islands to explore and dive from. Further south, Aru, Tanimbar and Daya Barat islands are far less developed and have little to offer; the Kai islands are worth the effort for arguably some of the best beaches east of Bali. ■

MALUKU

HISTORY

Before the arrival of the Europeans, the sultanate of Ternate held tenuous sway over some of the islands and parts of neighbouring Sulawesi and Irian Jaya, but there was little political unity – when the Portuguese reached the Indonesian archipelago, Maluku was known to them as the 'land of many kings'.

The spice trade, however, goes back a lot further than the Portuguese and Dutch presence in this part of the world. The Roman encyclopaedist Pliny described trade in cinnamon and other spices from Indonesia to Madagascar and East Africa and from there to Rome. By the 1st century AD Indonesian trade was firmly established with other parts of Asia, including India and China, and spices also reached Europe via the caravan routes from India and the Persian Gulf.

Apart from Marco Polo and a few wandering missionaries, Portuguese sailors were the first Europeans to set foot on Indonesian soil. Their first small fleet and its 'white Bengalis' (as the local inhabitants called them) arrived in Melaka (Malaysia) in 1509; their prime objective was to reach the Spice Islands. A master plan was devised for the Portuguese to bring all the important Indian Ocean trading posts under Portuguese control. The capture of Melaka in 1511, then Goa (India), preceded the Portuguese attempt to wrest control of the Spice Islands: Ternate and Tidore, Ambon, Seram and the Bandas.

Ternate and Tidore, the rival clove-producing islands of Maluku, were the scene of the greatest Portuguese effort. They were ruled by kings who controlled the cultivation of cloves, and who policed the region with fleets of war boats with sails and more than a hundred rowers each. But they had no trading boats of their own – cloves had to be shipped out, and food and other goods imported, on Malay and Javanese ships. Early in the 16th century, Ternate granted the Portuguese a monopoly over its clove trade in return for help against Tidore. The Portuguese built their first fortress on Ternate the following year, but relations with the Muslim king were continually strained and they began fighting each other. The Portuguese were not finally thrown out until 1575 after their fort had been besieged for several years; undeterred, they ingratiated themselves with the Tidore king and built another fort on that island.

Meanwhile, Ternate continued to expand its influence under the fiercely Islamic and anti-Portuguese Sultan Baab Ullah and his son Sultan Said. The Portuguese never succeeded in monopolising the clove trade; they moved south to Ambon, Seram and the Bandas, where nutmeg and mace were produced. Again they failed to establish a monopoly – and even if they had done so, they lacked the shipping and labour force to control trade in the Indian Ocean.

By the end of the 16th century, the Dutch arrived bringing better guns, better ships, better financial backing and an even more lethal combination of courage and brutality.

The first Dutch fleet to Indonesia reached Maluku in 1599, and returned to the Netherlands with enough spices to produce a massive profit. More ships followed and the various Dutch companies eventually merged in 1602 to form the Dutch East India Company (the VOC) whose ships sailed back to Maluku with some devastating consequences for the inhabitants of the Bandas, most of whom were exterminated.

By 1630, the Dutch were established on Ambon in the heart of the Spice Islands and had their headquarters at Batavia (Jakarta) in the west. Melaka fell to them in 1641, but a monopoly of the spice trade eluded them for many years; they first had to fight the Ternateans, and the Ambonese with their Makassarese allies. It was not until around 1660 that the Dutch finally succeeded in wiping out all local opposition to their rule in Maluku and not until 1663 that the Spanish, who had also established a small presence, evacuated their remaining posts in Ternate and Tidore. Inevitably, however, the importance of the islands as an international supplier of spices faded, as European competitors managed to set up their own plantations in other countries.

Dutch rule was centred in Ambon. Intensive schooling and missionary activity

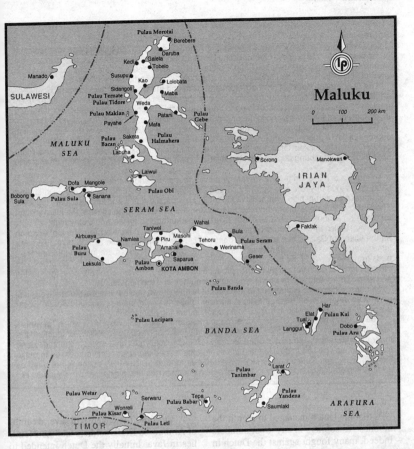

Maluku

0   100   200 km

resulted in a high standard of education among the Ambonese. A large number of them worked for the Dutch in the civil service, as missionaries or as soldiers of the Royal Netherlands Indies Army (Koninklijke Nederlandse Indisch Leger or KNIL).

Dutch rule did not go completely unopposed; the first rebellion against them was led by Thomas Matulessy – 'Pattimura' to his friends – in 1817. Pattimura is regarded as one of Indonesia's national heroes – Ambon's university is called Pattimura, and so is the army unit based on Ambon and one of the city's main streets. In the middle of the city

stands a giant statue (built in 1972) depicting Pattimura as a warrior of superhuman proportions. He came from Saparua, a small island just east of Ambon, was a professed Christian (Calvinist) and had been a sergeant-major in the British militia when the British occupied Ambon during the Napoleonic Wars. He led the revolt against the Dutch when they re-established themselves after the British left. The uprising lasted only a few months and ended with the capture and execution of Pattimura.

There were several other revolts in Maluku over the next 50 years and it was not until the

MALUKU

Spices

Spices were originally sought by Chinese and Arab traders up to 5000 years ago for medicinal purposes, and for the process of embalming the dead. Spices later became a source of incredible wealth and power, fought over by Dutch, Portuguese, English and even the Spanish, all of whom wanted spices to flavour and preserve food long before refrigeration was invented.

The Dutch took control of northern Sumatra, Java and the Celebes (now known as Sulawesi) originally to cultivate cinnamon, probably the oldest recorded spice, and pepper. Cinnamon trees grow to 15 metres high and are cut to encourage regrowth. The spice is used throughout the world as an ingredient for curries, chocolate and cakes, to name just a few uses. The island of Bangka, off the east coast of southern Sumatra, though known for its tin, is also one of the few, and best, sources of white pepper. Compared with the better known and more popular black pepper, white pepper which is picked later and then soaked to loosen its skin is less pungent and more appealing. The lampung pepper from the district in southern Sumatra of the same name, is also popular.

Indonesia is more famous, however, for cloves (cengkeh) and nutmeg (pala). The clove was used thousands of years ago by Chinese and Egyptians for freshening breath; early Dutch and Portuguese explorers also sought cloves to make an aromatic liquor, and for medicinal purposes. The Dutch colonialists destroyed most of the clove trees in the 'Spice Islands' (Maluku) except for those on Ambon and Ternate islands to create a shortage so prices would stay high.

Cloves, which thrive in tropical conditions, are still grown in Maluku – on Ternate, further south on the island of Bacan, and among the beautiful cluster of Banda islands – but have also been introduced successfully to Tanzania, Malaysia and Sri Lanka. Cloves are just dried, unopened buds from the flower of the tree, picked by hand, and then dried in the sun. Trees can grow to 15 metres high and each year are known to produce up to 30 kg of cloves, which are used for cooking and also in the manufacture of chewing gum, perfumes and toothpaste.

Nutmeg, which was indigenous to Maluku but is now grown in other tropical places like Brazil as well as Java and Sumatra, thrives in elevated positions near the sea, such as Banda Besar Island, where you can still visit functioning colonial nutmeg plantations.

The nutmeg tree stands about nine metres tall, and bears yellowish fruit, which has three sections: the outer skin is sometimes used by locals, but discarded during official production; the inner bright, orangey-red part is dried for many weeks (usually just on a sheet in the sun, along the streets, as you see in the Bandas) to become mace; and the inner nut is processed to make the nutmeg spice. Nutmeg and mace (which is regarded as spicier than nutmeg), are used as additives in cooking, particularly in fruit cakes, seafood sauces and pickles, and in liqueurs. ■

1890s that the Dutch managed to recruit the Ambonese as soldiers in any great numbers – indeed, many fought against the Dutch in the Indonesian independence wars.

The Dutch left Ambon in 1949, and a year later an independent Republic of the South Moluccas (Republik Maluku Selatan or RMS) was proclaimed in Ambon supported, it appears, by most of the 2000 or so Ambonese KNIL troops on the island. In July 1950, Indonesian government troops occupied Buru and parts of Seram and at the end of September the first landings on Ambon took place. By the middle of November most resistance on Ambon had been put down and in early December the RMS government fled to the Seram jungles (where many RMS troops had already gone).

At this time, there were still several camps of Ambonese KNIL soldiers and their families in Java. Initially the Dutch intended to demobilise them and send them back to Ambon, but it was feared that this would virtually be sending them to their deaths. Instead, the Dutch government moved them (about 12,000 people) to the Netherlands. It was hoped that once the RMS was suppressed, they could be sent back to Indonesia. They and their descendants (now numbering over 40,000) have been in the Netherlands ever since. On Pulau Seram, there continued to be pockets of RMS resistance until the mid-1960s. The impossible dream of an independent 'South Moluccas' still has its adherents among the Malukans in the Netherlands. There was a famous train hijack in the Netherlands in the mid-1970s; but there has been very little similar activity since. Nowadays many Malukans live in tight-knit communities which refuse to assimilate into ordinary Dutch society.

Today, Maluku is politically stable and 'Indonesianised' although, with its slightly Polynesian feel, it remains different from other parts of Indonesia. Despite its location in Indonesia's remote outer provinces, Ambon has as cosmopolitan an air as anywhere east of Denpasar, and its people maintain a sense of their own distinctness from other Indonesians.

Spices are still grown on many Maluku islands but they are no longer the mainstay of the economy. Large-scale fishing, logging and mining, controlled jointly by foreign companies and the Indonesian government, are growth industries. Agriculture is important: coffee, rice, sago, fruit, sugar cane, maize and copra are the major products. Tourism is slowly increasing but, despite its obvious potential, is not yet a big money earner.

FLORA & FAUNA

Maluku is a transition zone between Asia and Australia/New Guinea and there are some flora and fauna unique to the province. Vegetation is luxuriant and includes some

Sago palm

Staples

Sago The staple food of much of Maluku and other parts of eastern Indonesia is sago, from the sago palm. After 15 years the sago palm produces a flower spike; if the flower is allowed to mature, the fruit will feed off the starchy core of the trunk, leaving it a hollow shell. When the palm is cultivated, the tree is cut down when the flower spike forms and the starchy pith of the trunk is scooped out, strained and washed to remove the fibres from the starch. There's enough starch from one trunk to feed a whole family for months. Sago bread is commonly sold in Maluku in the form of thick wafers. *Papeda*, a unique local dish, is made by pulverising and straining the pulp from the sago palm and then boiling it up to make a glutinous porridge-like mass which is eaten hot.

Cassava Also known as mandioca, tapioca, manioc or yuca, cassava is another tropical staple, particularly in areas where cereals and potatoes won't grow. It's extracted from the tuberous roots of a South American plant which was brought to Indonesia by the Portuguese. These roots grow well in poor soils: they are easy to plant, harvest and store, they can be planted at different times of the year to ensure a year-round crop, the yield of starch per hectare is more than from any other crop, and it is not susceptible to many diseases. ■

Australian species, such as *kayu putih* or eucalypts, as well as the usual tropical Asiatic species. Maluku hardwoods are prized by timber companies. Ambon and Tanimbar are famous for their wild orchids, while Ternate has some of the most brilliantly coloured bougainvillea you'll ever see.

Maluku's seas teem with life, including dugongs, turtles, trepang (sea cucumber), sharks and all manner of tropical and shell fish. On land there are a few Asiatic mammals such as monkeys but there are also small marsupials such as the cuscus and the bandicoot.

Wallabies, miniature tree kangaroos, crocodiles and monitor lizards are found on the south-eastern island groups of Aru and Kai. Wild pig and deer are common, but they are introduced. Insect life abounds and butterflies are particularly brilliant.

BOOKS

The 19th-century naturalist Alfred Wallace spent six years roaming the Indonesian archipelago, spending much of that time in Maluku. His record of the journey, *The Malay Archipelago*, still makes fascinating reading. Marika Hanbury-Tenison's *A Slice of Spice* details a visit to Ambon and the wilds of Seram in the early 1970s. Lawrence & Lorne Blair's exciting *Ring of Fire* (Bantam Press, 1988) has chapters on the Bandas and Aru. For an accurate picture of the tourist scene in Banda today, read the relevant chapter of Annabel Sutton's *The Islands In Between* (Impact Books, London, 1989).

Shirley Deane's *Ambon, Island of Spices* (John Murray, London) touches on the Lease Islands, Seram, the Bandas, Kai and Aru but deals mainly with Ambon, where the author lived and worked for a couple of years in the 1970s.

GETTING THERE & AWAY

Ambon is the transport hub for all Maluku; virtually all flights around Maluku start,

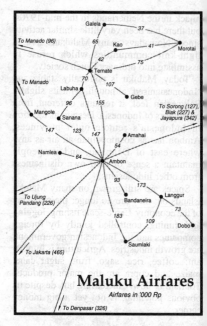

Maluku Airfares

Airfares in '000 Rp

finish or transfer at Ambon. All Indonesian internal airlines regularly connect Ambon with just about every other major transport centre in Indonesia. Large Pelni passenger liners *Kerinci*, *Tatamailau* and *Rinjani* have regular runs between Maluku and Irian Jaya, Sulawesi, Nusa Tenggara and Java.

GETTING AROUND

If you're planning to do a lot of travel in Maluku, you need either time or money – preferably both! Merpati is the major airline company linking Ambon and Ternate (the second major transport centre) with other airstrips in Maluku.

There are regular passenger ferries and speedboats to and between islands adjacent to Ambon and Ternate, but long-distance sea transport around the outer islands is more time-consuming and irregular the further away from Ambon you go. Conditions can be fairly basic on vessels other than the Pelni liners.

Pulau Ambon

Barely a dot on a map of Indonesia, the island of Ambon is the economic and transport centre of Maluku. Its landscape is dramatic and mountainous, with little flat land for cultivation or roads. There are a few good beaches, as well as coral reefs and plenty of opportunities for hiking and seeing Ambon's flora & fauna. To appreciate the island and its culture, you need to get out into the villages, where there's a definite Polynesian feel. Ambon reeks of history, especially at places like the old European fort at Hila on the north coast.

The island is just 48 km by 22 km, with a larger northern peninsula known as Leihitu and a smaller arrow-head shaped southern peninsula known as Leitimur. The peninsulas are connected only by a narrow isthmus at Passo. Kota Ambon, the capital, lies on the Leitimur peninsula, on the southern side of Teluk Ambon.

History

Ambon had the misfortune to be located almost at the dead centre of the Spice Islands. As early as the 14th century, central Maluku found the rest of the world thrust upon it because of the demand for its spices. The original trade intermediary between central Maluku and western Indonesia was the sultanate of Ternate, which brought Islam to central Maluku and also seems to have had some influence in reducing the incidence of local head-hunting. Other colonisers, like the Javanese who set up a base at Hitu on the north coast of Ambon, settled along the coasts of these islands. At this time, though Ambon grew no spices, it was an important stopover between Ternate and the nutmeg-producing Bandas.

The Ternateans were displaced on Ambon by the Portuguese; they stayed until 1605

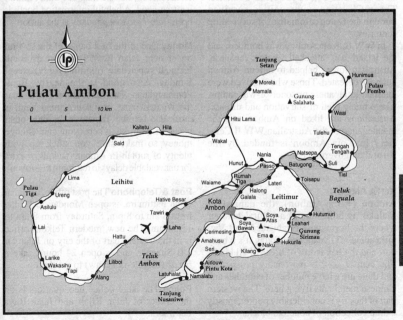

Pulau Ambon

0   5   10 km

Tanjung Setan
Liang
Hunimua
Pulau Pombo
Morela
Mamala
Gunung Salahatu ▲
Waai
Hitu Lama
Tulehu
Kaitetu   Hila
Said
Wakal
Tengah Tengah
Natsepa
Suli
Tial
Nania
Lima
Hunut
Passo
Batugong
Toisapu
Pulau Tiga
Ureng
Waiame
Rumah Tiga
Halong
Lateri
Teluk Baguala
Asilulu
Leihitu
Hative Besar
Galala
Leitimur
Rutung
Hutumuri
Tawiri
Kota Ambon
Soya Atas
Leahari
Lai
Hattu
Laha
Cerimesing
Ema
Gunung Sirimau
Naku
Hukurila
Larike
Wakasihu   Tapi
Liliboi
Amahusu
Seri
Kilang
Alang
Teluk Ambon
Airlouw   Pintu Kota
Latuhalat   Namalatu
Tanjung Nusaniwe
Soya Bawah

MALUKU

when the Ambonese teamed up instead with the newly arrived Dutch. When the Portuguese fort (in what is now Kota Ambon) was about to be attacked, the Portuguese appeared simply to have surrendered and sailed away; the Dutch occupied the fort, renamed it Victoria and made Ambon their Spice Island base.

While the Portuguese probably didn't have much effect on the political fortunes of the Maluku kingdoms, or on the overall structure of trade, there was one man among them who initiated what would be a permanent change in eastern Indonesia: the Spaniard, Francis Xavier (later canonised) who co-founded the Jesuit order. In 1546 and 1547 Xavier worked as a missionary in Ambon, Ternate and Morotai Island and laid the foundations for permanent missions there. After his departure from Maluku, others continued his work and by the 1560s there were perhaps 10,000 Catholics in the area, mostly on Ambon. By the 1590s there were said to be 50,000 to 60,000 Catholics. These Christian communities survived through the Dutch colonialism of succeeding centuries.

In WW II, Kota Ambon was bombed, and the island was attacked by the Japanese. Australian forces helped to defend Ambon but were defeated. Those who survived were interned in Japanese prisoner-of-war camps, where many died of starvation and disease. Australians are liked on Ambon and the maintenance of the Australian WW II Cemetery in Kota Ambon is funded by the Australian government.

KOTA AMBON

Ambon (Kota Ambon), the capital of Maluku, is built around a natural harbour where the Portuguese established Fort Victoria some 400 years ago. Today it's a busy port and the bay is full of boats of all kinds. The central area is reasonably prosperous and there are a large number of churches and Chinese merchants living here. The western part of the city is considerably poorer, mostly a drab collection of concrete blocks.

Orientation

On the south side of Teluk Ambon, Kota Ambon is hemmed in by the hills to the south and stretches along the waterfront for several km. The main street for shops and offices is Jalan A Y Patty and hotels are two or three blocks back (south) from here. The bemo/bus terminals and main market – the latter especially busy and colourful early in the morning – are in a relatively new complex on reclaimed coastal land about one km east. The main harbour is at the end of Jalan Yos Sudarso, a short walk from Jalan A Y Patty.

Information

Tourist Office The Maluku Government Tourist Office (☎ 52471) is on the ground floor of the Governor's Office (Kantor Gubernor) on Jalan Raya Pattimura (but enter from Jalan Sultan Hairun). It's open Monday to Thursday from 7.30 am to about 2 pm, Friday to 11 am and is closed Sunday. There are plenty of brochures and good free maps of Kota Ambon, but the map of Pulau Ambon isn't so good. A helpful information booth is open from 7 am to 4 pm daily at the airport.

Money One of the best banks of the several on or near Jalan Raya Pattimura is Bank ExIm. It's open daily (mornings only) except Sunday. Also good is the nearby Bank Pembangunan. The Bank Bumi Daya, near the Wisma Game, on Jalan Ahmad Yani, is quick and helpful. Ternate is the only other place in Maluku where you can change money so make sure you stock up with plenty of rupiah in Ambon (and allow extra for unavoidable delays in returning to Ambon).

Post & Telephone The post office, on Jalan Raya Pattimura, is open Monday to Friday from 8 am to 8 pm, Saturday from 8 am to 12.30 pm. The new, modern Telkom office is in the western part of the city on Jalan Dr J B Sitanala, and is open 24 hours; take a *becak* (bicycle-rickshaw) to get there.

Police The large police headquarters is on the corner of Jalan Rijali and Jalan Raya Pattimura.

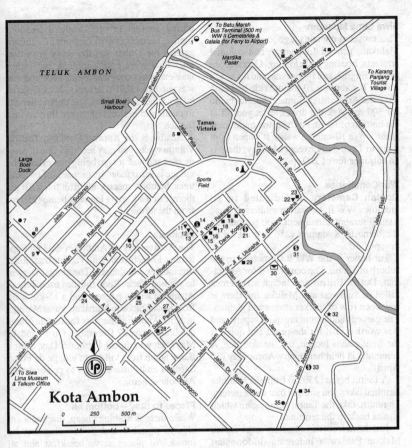

Kota Ambon

TELUK AMBON

Small Boat Harbour

Large Boat Dock

0   250   500 m

To Siwa Lima Museum & Telkom Office

Taman Victoria

Sports Field

Mardika Pasar

To Batu Merah Bus Terminal (500 m) WW II Cemeteries & Galala (for Ferry to Airport)

To Karang Panjang Tourist Village

PLACES TO STAY		PLACES TO EAT		
2	Wisata Hotel	29	Hotel Amboina	
3	Josiba Hotel	34	Wisma Game	
4	Hotel Cenderawasih			
5	Penginapan Sumber Asia	9	Ratu Gurih	
16	Baliwerti Hotel	11	Restaurant Sakura	
17	Hotel Hero	12	Tip Top Restaurant	
18	Penginapan Beta	13	Halim Restaurant	
19	Hotel Transit Rezfanny	22	Pondok Asri	
20	Hotel Mutiara	27	Restaurant Kakatoe	
23	Manise Hotel			
25	Penginapan Gamalama		OTHER	
26	Hotel Elenoor			
28	Penginapan Sahabat	1	Mardika Bus Terminal	
		6	Pattimura Monument	

OTHER

7	Pelni
8	Komplek Pelabuhan Ambon
10	Mandala
14	Tourist Office
15	Sempati
21	Bank Exim
24	Bouraq
30	Post Office
31	Bank Pembangunan
32	Police Headquarters
33	Bank Bumi Daya
35	Merpati/Garuda

MALUKU

Siwa Lima Museum

This museum contains a good collection of Malukan, general Indonesian and colonial artefacts, housing and clothing. Captions are in both English and Indonesian and it's worth a visit. It's about a 10-minute ride by bemo (take the Amahusu or Taman Makmur bemo for 300 rp). Ask the driver to let you off at the bottom of the steep road; the museum is at the top (a 10-minute walk). It's open from 8 am to 1 pm daily except Monday; there is an entrance fee of 200 rp.

War Cemeteries

Doolan Cemetery is dedicated to all unknown WW II Australian soldiers. It's just a small scrappy monument. You get there on the bemo to Kudamati (250 rp); ask to be dropped off.

Far better is the **WW II Cemetery** in the suburb of Tantui. The cemetery is for Australian, Dutch, British and Indian servicemen killed in Sulawesi and Maluku and there is row upon row of marker stones and plaques. The gardens and layout are quite superb, and it is worth a visit for the peace and quiet. If the front gate is locked, use the side gate. A ceremony is held here every Anzac Day (25 April).

A Tantui bemo (250 rp) from the Mardika terminal takes you straight past the cemetery. To return, take the Tantui bemo again which circles back to the terminal.

Just down from this cemetery is the Taman Makam Pahlawan Indonesia (**Indonesian Heroes Cemetery**) dedicated to Indonesian servicemen killed fighting the Maluku rebels during the 1950s and 1960s.

Other Attractions

The **Pattimura Monument** stands at one end of the sports field. Pattimura – really called Thomas Matulessy – is said to have been betrayed by one of the village chiefs on Pulau Saparua who took him prisoner and delivered him to the Dutch on Ambon. The monument stands on the site where he and his followers were hanged.

On a hill overlooking Kota Ambon is the **Martha Christina Tiahahu Memorial**, hon-

ouring another revered Maluku freedom fighter. Tiahahu's father supported Pattimura against the Dutch and the story goes that after they were both captured, her father was executed on Pulau Nusa Laut and she was put onto a ship to be sent to Java. Grieved by her father's execution, she starved herself to death and her remains were thrown into the sea.

Nearby is the **Karang Panjang Tourist Village** where you may see 'traditional' ceremonies and watch sago being processed. The village is surrounded by orchards of coconut trees, bamboo species and fruit trees. To get there, catch a Karang Panjang bemo (250 rp) from the terminal.

Festivals

The Anniversary of Ambon is held on September 17 each year, with various traditional ceremonies and dances. The annual Darwin to Ambon Yacht Race finishes each July at Amahusu with a pageant and a 15-km walk from Kota Ambon to Namalatu. Pasar Mardika in Kota Ambon is famous for its Christmas celebrations on 27 December. On 14 and 15 May each year during Pattimura Day, a torch flame is run from village to village on Pulau Saparua and Pulau Ambon to celebrate the Ambonese hero.

Places to Stay – bottom end

While there is nothing cheap, discounts are always possible and good value can be found. All places serve breakfast and all prices include tax. *Penginapan Gamalama* (☎ 53724), Jalan Anthony Rhebok 27, is a decent place in the quieter part of town. Singles/doubles are 12,000/16,000 rp with private mandi; ask for quieter rooms upstairs. Get there early – it is often full. Next door, the friendly and comfortable *Hotel Elenoor* (☎ 52834) has rooms with mandi for 21,600/33,600 rp or slightly more with air-con.

Penginapan Beta (☎ 53463), Jalan Wim Reawaru 114, has verandahs and a hint of tropical foliage. With mandi and fan, singles/doubles/triples start at 14,000/21,000/29,000 rp. Next door, the *Hotel Transit Rezfanny* (☎ 42300) has rooms with shared mandi for 14,000 rp; a room with private mandi costs 22,500 rp and one with air-con is 35,000 rp. *Wisma Game* (☎ 53525), Jalan Ahmad Yani 12, opposite the Merpati office has rooms from 15,000/17,500 rp with mandi and fan.

Penginapan Sahabat (☎ 52642), upstairs on Jalan Said Perintah 23, is central and quiet. Windowless rooms have hot water and start at 22,000/27,000 rp with fan. Similar prices and facilities are at the *Penginapan Sumber Asia* (☎ 56587) at Jalan Pala 34, near the small boat harbour.

Other good alternatives at about 30,000/40,000 rp are *Limas Hotel* (☎ 53269) at Jalan Kamboja 16, off Jalan Anthony Rhebok; *Hotel Carlo* (☎ 42220) at Jalan P H Latumahina 24A; and the cheaper *Avema Lestari* (☎ 43596) at Jalan W R Supratman, where the manager speaks both English and Dutch.

Places to Stay – middle

Prices in this category also include tax and breakfast. The *Hotel Hero* (☎ 42978) on Jalan Wim Reawaru 7B is a new, shiny place and is good value. All rooms including TV and air-con start at 40,000 rp with a possible discount. Next door, the modern and comfortable *Baliwerti Hotel* (☎ 55996) has singles/doubles with hot water and TV from 50,000/65,000 rp.

On Jalan Tulukabessy and near the Mardika bus terminal, are the clean and friendly *Hotel Cenderawasih* (☎ 52487) with good standard rooms for 50,000/65,000 rp, and the cheaper and seedier *Josiba Hotel* (☎ 41280). Just around the corner, *Wisata Hotel* (☎ 53293) at Jalan Mutiara 3, has similar standards starting at 42,000/46,800 rp.

A worthy alternative, to save an early morning taxi ride to the airport, or if you are just transiting Kota Ambon, is the *Hotel Maluku* (☎ 61415), five minutes by bemo or 25 minutes' walk east from the airport (ring and the people from the hotel will pick you up). Negotiable, clean rooms cost from 20,000/30,000 rp.

Places to Stay – top end

There are now several high-class places.

Recommended (with prices including tax and breakfast) are: *Hotel Mutiara* (☎ 97124), Jalan Raya Pattimura 90, with rooms from 60,000/72,000 rp; *Hotel Amboina* (☎ 41725), Jalan Kapitan Ulupaha 5, with rooms from 96,000 rp; and the *Manise Hotel* (☎ 54144), Jalan W R Supratman 1, with good-value rooms for 36,000 rp with fan, up to full luxury at 200,000 rp.

Places to Eat

Theoretically, Ambon has its own distinctive cuisine based on the staple Maluku diet of sago, along with cassava, sweet potatoes and other root dishes. *Colo colo* is a type of sweet-and-sour sauce which is used on baked fish, *kohu kohu* is fish salad and *laor* is a sea worm which is harvested at full moon at the end of March. In practice, if you want to try any of these you'd better head for the villages because the 'local' cuisine is hard to find in the city.

Three of the many places serving good Indonesian and Chinese food are next to each other on Jalan Sultan Hairun: *Tip Top Restaurant*, *Restaurant Sakura* and *Halim Restaurant* – the latter is a little more pricey but is better, and has local travel information. Most of the big hotels have restaurants. The *Hotel Mutiara's* restaurant is similarly priced to Halim. Next to the Manise Hotel, the up-market and expensive *Pondok Asri* serves Japanese food and steaks.

There are some cheap rumah makans (restaurants) around the terminals and warungs (food stalls) all over the place, particularly along the waterfront and market areas. *Ratu Gurih*, near the port on Jalan A M Sangaji 3-4, is cheap and popular with locals; great baked fish is a speciality. There are several reasonable bakeries and fast-food places on or around Jalan A Y Patty, including the 3rd floor of *Robinson's Department Store* and *Andre's* on Jalan Lola.

Destined to be a favourite place for travellers is *Restaurant Kakatoe* at Jalan Said Perintah 20 which offers good Western food, free book exchange, a message board, and local information in a lovely atmosphere.

MALUKU

Things to Buy

Model sailing ships made entirely out of cloves can be bought in Kota Ambon. Try the shops along Jalan A Y Patty. Also take a look at the 'flower arrangements' made out of mother-of-pearl. Don't buy the turtle-shell fans, ashtrays, lampshades and any other turtle-shell products. Look around for hand-woven clothes from south-eastern Maluku. Ambon is a supplier of good eucalyptus oil, and there are some interesting animist carvings from southern Maluku, available at the hotel shops and from hawkers. You'll see Ambonese women carrying loads in chocolate-brown baskets. These are finely woven and worth buying if you're into baskets. Try the villages or just make an offer when you spot one in use.

Getting There & Away

Air Kota Ambon is the gateway to Maluku, with most air travel in Maluku starting and finishing there. It is also well connected to virtually all other transport centres throughout Indonesia. Merpati flies to every major island in Maluku. For more obscure destinations check the Maluku Airfares chart at the beginning of this chapter or the other relevant sections. Regular, daily Merpati flights go to: Biak (227,100 rp), Denpasar (326,100 rp), Jakarta (464,700 rp), Jayapura (341,500 rp), Sorong (127,000 rp) and Ujung Pandang (226,000 rp).

The Merpati/Garuda office (☎ 52481, 69404 after hours) on Jalan Ahmad Yani 19 is open from 8 am to 5 pm weekdays, a little less on weekends. The office cannot (or will not) confirm any flights other than those leaving Ambon, so it pays, if possible, to confirm your return ticket before flying to an island with irregular flights. Otherwise you could easily wait a week or more (as I did) waiting to get back to Ambon.

Mandala (☎ 42551), Jalan A Y Patty 19, flies to Ujung Pandang, Surabaya and Jakarta daily at 7.30 am for exactly the same price as Merpati and Bouraq.

Bouraq (☎ 52314) flies to Ternate daily except Monday, then to Manado (236,000 rp) and to Ujung Pandang, Surabaya and

Jakarta. Its prices match those of Merpati and Mandala. The Bouraq office, at Jalan Sultan Babullah 19, is open from 8 am to 5 pm every day except Sunday.

For travel to/from other major transport centres, Sempati (☎ 51612) is worth considering. It flies to Jakarta twice a day (464,700 rp); Denpasar daily (326,100 rp); Kupang (699,400 rp) five days a week; and to Ujung Pandang daily (226,000 rp). Its office is at Jalan Wim Reawaru 9B, or bookings (☎ 61612) may be possible at the Ambon airport. International departure tax (for the very occasional international charter flight) is 13,000 rp.

Boat Every two weeks, the Pelni liner *Kerinci* goes to Bitung, Sulawesi (30,000/119,500 rp for economy/1st class) and Ternate (43,500/127,500 rp); the *Dobonsolo* goes to Dili, East Timor (35,500/121,500 rp) and Sorong (24,500/90,500 rp); and the *Rinjani* goes to Banda (12,000/41,000 rp) and Tual (25,000/100,000 rp). Every month the *Tatamailau* goes to Dili and Banda; and the *Sirimau* goes to Sorong and Kendari (Sulawesi). The Pelni office (☎ 53161) is in the main harbour area on Jalan Pelabuhan 1.

The Perintis ships *Daya Nusantara*, *Nukori* and *Nagura* go to the south-western islands of Maluku, usually through the Bandas, and then to Timor. Other Perintis ships are *Nusa Perintis*, which goes to Sanana, Mangole and Ternate; the *Katherina* and *Citra Pasific* which loop around Nusa Tenggara every month; the *Baruna Dwipa* which makes a loop to Ternate and other ports in northern Maluku; and the *Pahala* which visits Sanana, Namlea, and other places, every two weeks. Inquire at the Pelni office for Perintis boats.

Other, more basic boats going to lesser islands in Maluku usually leave from the harbour at the end of Jalan Pala. A board at the harbour entrance shows what's going where and when. The *Waisamar* leaves from the Jalan Pala harbour for Bandaneira on Monday and Wednesday at about 4 pm (19,000 rp; 13 hours).

Boats to/from Pulau Saparua and Pulau

Seram leave from Hurnala port, just north of Tulehu (take a bemo for 800 rp, but make sure you get off at Hurnala and not Tulehu town); or from Liang (1100 rp). An easier way to get to Seram, is to take the direct bus/ferry/bus – see the Pulau Seram section for more details.

Getting Around

To/From the Airport Pattimura airport is 48 km out from the city on the other side of the bay – allow an hour for all forms of transport. Official direct taxis cost 17,500 rp but in the airport car park you may be offered a fare for as little as 10,000 rp. There are occasional direct buses leaving from Mardika bus terminal in Kota Ambon which cost 1100 rp.

The quickest and most reliable way is to take a regular bemo from the airport to the port of Poka (350 rp), take the ferry across to Galala (200 rp), and then a bemo (250 rp) to Mardika terminal. The ferry operates daily from 6 am to midnight, so an early morning check-in may require a prearranged chartered taxi (or avoid this by staying at the Hotel Maluku (see Places to Stay section earlier) near the airport the night before your departure).

Local Transport Getting around town is fairly easy. There are masses of becaks (different coloured ones are only allowed to run on certain days). The correct fare around town is about 500 rp (check with your hotel for the current fare) but foreigners are usually charged 1000 rp, and it's hard to bargain.

Well-marked bemos and buses are at two terminals along the waterfront: Mardika terminal is a confusing mass of bemos which go to all places in the city and the southern peninsula but only as far as the airport in the north: eg to Galala (for the ferry), Hunut, Tantui, Natsepa, Namalatu and Amahusu (among many other destinations).

Batu Merah terminal, 10 minutes' walk further east, has bemos and buses in specific lanes going to everywhere else: eg Liang, Hila, Asilulu, and Pulau Seram. Just keep walking along the front of the terminal

until you find the lane with your bemo or bus. Public transport around Kota Ambon is cheap, but crowded, and will cost about 300 rp.

AROUND PULAU AMBON

Pulau Ambon was once two separate islands, which are now joined by a short isthmus between the northern peninsula (Leihitu) and the southern peninsula (Leitimur). There are buses throughout Leitimur; less regularly around Leihitu, especially in the sparsely inhabited western areas. Taxi drivers will charge about 100,000 rp for a full day trip all around the island, or about 20,000 rp per hour. You may be able to hire a car for as little as 50,000 rp per day – ask at Restaurant Kakatoe.

Diving

Pulau Ambon and nearby islands offer outstanding diving opportunities. The best time is from October to February. Popular dive sites include Pintu Kota, Leahari in the south, Satan's Point (Tanjung Setan), Pulau Pombo, Pulau Tiga (near Asilulu), and off

Green turtle

MALUKU

the south-western cape of Seram. New sites are constantly being discovered and explored.

For information and equipment hire in Kota Ambon, contact P T Tujuh Jaya Ekapesona (☎ 52342) at Jalan Kopra 142-3; Nanusa Tour & Travel (☎ 55334) at Jalan Rijali 53; or the Ambonia Diving Club (☎ 52342) at Jalan Sam Ratulangi 142.

The Ambon Dive Centre (☎ 55685), opposite the entrance to Namalatu beach, offers a great selection of package tours, equipment hire and other facilities. It organises the International Underwater Photography Competition as part of the annual Ambon Manise Marine Festival in October.

Far more flexible, but very expensive, are cruise ships such as the MV *Pindito* (☎ Ambon 51569) which organises diving trips all around Maluku and Nusa Tenggara.

Leihitu

Pantai Natsepa This is a lovely swimming beach 17 km (25 minutes) from Kota Ambon; avoid Sundays when it gets really crowded. On weekends there's an entrance fee of 200 rp. A bemo from Ambon costs 800 rp. Past the entrance, the *Vaneysa Losmen & Restaurant* (☎ 61451) offers individual doubles with mandi, breakfast, great views and a quiet location for 30,000 rp, and 'bungalows' sleeping four people for 50,000 rp. Nearby, on the main road, the *Miranda Beach Hotel & Restaurant* (☎ 61244) is noisier and has no views. Rooms cost 20,000 rp with fan; 30,000 rp with air-con. These places are worthy alternatives to bustling Kota Ambon.

Waai North of Natsepa, this beach has an underwater cave beneath a mountain spring, **Waiselaka Pool**, which is the home of sacred eels and carp. The villagers flick the water to draw the creatures from their cave, enticing them with eggs. If one appears it is meant to bring good luck to visitors. There are also some good murals in the nearby church. Bemos cost 900 rp.

Liang This Muslim village has a nice beach

(bemos cost 1100 rp). Not far away is **Hunimua**, where there is another pleasant beach. Ferries leave here for Waiprit on Pulau Seram.

Pulau Pombo This tiny, uninhabited island off north-eastern Pulau Ambon is pretty. Take a bemo to Tulehu (1000 rp) which will drop you at the wharf from where you can hire a speedboat to Pombo. The 20-minute speedboat ride is expensive at around 50,000 rp return; have the boat drop you off in the morning and pick you up in the afternoon, or the next day. There are some huts where you can stay on the island, but bring your own food and water.

Mamala & Morela An annual 'sweep beating ceremony' is held at these adjacent villages in March. Men from both villages stage a 'war' and 'beat' each others' bare backs with brooms. Coconut oil is then rubbed on the injuries to show its ability to heal.

Hila This village on the north coast, 42 km from Kota Ambon, is the site of Benteng (Fort) Amsterdam, an 18th-century church and a 15th-century mosque. The **fort** was built right on the coast to guard the strait between Ambon and Seram, which is at its narrowest here. There are more forts west along the coast. The **church** is just a few minutes' walk from the fort. Built in 1780, it is the oldest on Pulau Ambon, though it has virtually been rebuilt over the years. Hila has special (Christian) New Year celebrations with locals feasting and singing throughout January. There is a twin village nearby called **Kaitetu**. Bemos from Kota Ambon cost 1300 rp.

Leitimur

Amahusu Located around 10 km from Kota Ambon, Amahusu is being developed since it became the finish, and dock, for the annual Darwin to Ambon Yacht Race. The centre for this – the *Tirtha Kencana Hotel* (☎ 52979) – has bungalow-style accommodation from

60,500 rp plus 21% tax. There is no beach but ask to hire a canoe for snorkelling.

Namalatu & Latuhalat Namalatu ('king's property') is the pleasant public beach in the village of Latuhalat ('king of the west'). There's good scuba diving and snorkelling on the coral reefs offshore and nearby coves. A bemo from Kota Ambon costs 500 rp and takes about 45 minutes.

Two resorts offer good bungalow-type rooms from 55,000 to 75,000 rp with air-con and hot water: *Santai Beach Hotel* (☎ 56581) on Jalan Akihari and *Lelisa Beach Resort* (☎ 51989) at Jalan Namalatu 1. Their small artificial sandy beaches, with restaurant and bar, are available to non-guests for a small fee.

If chartering a taxi, go three km further on to the end of the south-western road, to **Tanjung Nusaniwe** for another nice beach and unusual rock formations. Also three km from Namalatu, and a 20-minute scramble up a nearby hill (ask directions), is a very tall radio mast which you can climb (if you don't mind heights!) for the best views of Pulau Ambon and nearby islands. Close by (ask directions at the houses near the mast) is a fantastic Japanese cannon *(meriam jepang)*, untouched in its original cave.

Pintu Kota This spectacular place (literally, 'city door') has a small rocky beach, and some rocks to clamber up and admire the view. It costs 500 rp to enter. You can dive around to see lobsters and moray eels. Take a bemo to the nearby village of **Airlouw** (600 rp), and then walk (about 30 minutes) from there. Airlouw is famous for its brick-making and is full of burning kilns.

Other Villages Paths connect the villages in the hills on the Leitimur peninsula to each other or to Kota Ambon. Try walking from the city to Soya on Gunung Sirimau; or catch a bemo (350 rp) to Soya Atas and then it's a one-km walk up to the summit of Gunung Sirimau – the last section is quite steep. There are great views from the top.

The Lease Group

Formerly the Uliassers, this small group of islands east of Ambon consists of Haruku, Saparua, Nusa Laut and Molana. Saparua is the largest, most populated and most developed inland. Its main claim to fame is that it was the source of the revolt against the Dutch led by Pattimura who was later betrayed, handed over to the Dutch and hanged in Ambon.

PULAU SAPARUA

Saparua island is a lovely place, so quiet and laid-back compared to Ambon which is only 70 km away. There are diving spots, a nice fort and some good beaches. Saparua, together with Pulau Seram, makes an easy and pleasant diversion of several days from Ambon.

Kota Saparua

Only one block from the main road in Kota Saparua, the large, crumbling fort **Benteng Duurstede** is set in a gorgeous location, overlooking the town and the harbour. The **museum** opposite is also well worth a look, offering dozens of dramatic dioramas of the history of Saparua and the Ambon region. All captions are in Indonesian – you could try asking the official guide there who knows his history, but his English is poor. There is the inevitable guest book to be signed and a small donation is expected.

On 14 and 15 May each year, Pattimura Day is held, jointly with Kota Ambon. A torch flame is run from village to village on

The Lease Group

both islands to celebrate the brave Ambonese hero, Pattimura, who fought the Dutch.

Places to Stay & Eat The best place in Kota Saparua is the *Penginapan Lease Indah* (☎ 21040), with views at the back of Benteng Duurstede. Good rooms with mandi and fan cost 15,000 rp; newer air-con rooms cost 25,000 rp. Great meals for 5000 rp can be ordered in advance. Look for the sign on Jalan Muka Pasar, or take a becak from the bemo terminal.

The *Mahu Village Lodge* (☎ 41136 in Ambon) is a place for divers only and is stuck among mangroves, with no beach. There is a simple restaurant, a brackish pool and diving hire. If staff at the lodge don't collect you, it's 20 minutes by bemo (400 rp); ask to be dropped off at the *Kelapa Indah* ('beautiful coconut') – the lodge's local name – in Mahu and walk down the lane beside the Protestant church – there are no signs anywhere.

Besides one or two rumah makans around the bus terminal, there is nowhere to eat on the island. Hotel food is recommended.

Getting There & Away There is a confusing and often changing variety of boats and schedules. For the latest information, ask at the port of Haria or your hotel. Boat travel around Maluku, including around these islands, can be rough in the wet season (from April to August).

To/From Seram The regular ferry to/from Seram sunk a month before I was there – there were several casualties. The only alternative at the time of writing was a speedboat to Amahai leaving every few hours from Iha-Mahu village (take a bemo for 300 rp, and ask to be dropped off at the unmarked lane). The ferry, however, is likely to be back in business soon, so check at Haria or Amahai.

To/From Ambon Boats link Haria with Hurnala port, just north of Tulehu (make sure you get off at Hurnala and not at Tulehu itself). The daily ferry (7000 rp) leaves Hurnala at 9 am and 2 pm (11 am only on

Sunday) and takes two hours. The ferry then leaves Haria at about 11.30 am and 4 pm. A speedboat leaves both ports when there are enough passengers (10,000 rp; one hour).

Getting Around
There are becaks in Kota Saparua – albeit only about six. The town is easy and pleasant to walk around.

AROUND PULAU SAPARUA
Bemos around the island leave from the terminal in Kota Saparua. They are marked: 'Hatawono' for the north-east road, including Mahu; 'Haria', the port for boats to Seram and Ambon; and 'Tenggara' for the south-east, Sirisore and Ouw. As it may take some time for a bemo to fill before it leaves, chartering is a worthy option and costs around 3000 to 5000 rp for a short ride to anywhere.

The small friendly village of **Ouw** is at the end of the south-eastern road (bemos cost 500 rp). It reportedly offers clay pottery but nothing much is evident from a walk among the streets. There is also a small, overgrown fort, which nobody knows much about. The road to Ouw is dotted with beaches such as **Pantai Waisisil**, which is great for swimming and unexplored snorkelling. Just choose a beach from the window of the bemo and get off.

In the north-east at **Nolot** there are canoe races on December 28; and more fantastic dive sites. At **Kulor**, in the north-west, there are more sandy beaches and diving spots with coral and fish life.

OTHER ISLANDS
The other two major islands in this group are Pulau Haruku and Pulau Nusa Laut. Neither has places to stay or eat, and there is irregular transport there. They are undeveloped and poor, but offer seclusion, friendliness and unspoilt scenery and beaches.

Pulau Haruku
There are ruins of another fort, **Benteng New Zeland**, and some beautiful, secluded beaches such as **Pantai Hulaliu**. In early

January, the Sasi Lompa ceremony – a mock battle at **Pelauw** where real wounds are inflicted and then healed by special oils – is held every three years, the most recent one in 1994. Normally, ferries to/from Ambon do not stop at Haruku, but the island can be reached by chartering a boat from Haria on Pulau Saparua or waiting for a fishing boat to go that way.

Pulau Nusa Laut
Though unimaginatively named 'Sea Island', it offers unspoilt beaches, an old ruined church at the village of **Ameth**, and the decrepit **Benteng Beverwyk**.

The father of famous Maluku freedom fighter Christina Tiahahu was captured on this island. The only public transport to the island is on market days – Wednesday and Saturday. Or you could charter a boat from Haria on Pulau Saparua at a high but negotiable price, or visit as part of a diving tour from Mahu Village Lodge, on Saparua.

Pulau Seram

Maluku's second-largest island (17,151 sq km), Seram is wild, mountainous and heavily forested. The Malukans call it Nusa Ina or Mother Island, as it's believed that this is where the ancestors of central Maluku came from. Much of the centre, which is difficult to visit, is home to the indigenous Alfuro peoples, some of whom have only relatively recently given up head-hunting.

One tribe, the Bati, of the southern mountains, can fly, so the story goes. They number 2000 and are supposed to have piercing eyes with the power to dominate and whisk a victim into the skies. Apparently, such is their power, the victim is quite happy to accompany them. Their flying is seasonal, but there's always one active group. Most Ambonese and Seramese believe in the powers of the Bati. The south and west coasts of Seram are populated by Malays and there are transmigrants from Java and Sulawesi. Both the Dutch and Indonesian governments resettled numbers of the indigenous people on the coast.

Seram is a bird-watcher's paradise, though other wildlife is restricted to cuscus and bandicoots plus introduced deer and pigs. Butterfly species are particularly bright in colour. The bird life includes lories, parrots, cockatoos, kingfishers, pigeons, cassowaries, hornbills, friar birds and other honeyeaters, megapodes and white eyes.

History
Before the 15th century, Seram had commercial links with the Javanese Hindu kingdoms. In 1480, Ternatean influence and Islam reached Seram and the matrilineal system of succession was replaced by a patrilineal one. Portuguese missionaries arrived in the 16th century and then, in the early 17th century, the Dutch established four coastal trading posts. The Dutch controlled Seram (they didn't bother with the wild interior) from about 1650 until it was occupied by the Japanese in 1942 and used as an air base.

Today, Seram is becoming 'Indonesianised', with oil and timber being exploited. Copra, rice, spices and a few other crops are grown for export. During the clove season (from October to January on the south coast), it seems the whole population is busy collecting, drying and shipping the spice. The indigenous peoples of the interior still do some hunting, and gather forest products such as wild sago.

MASOHI

Masohi, the main town on Seram, and the centre for all transport, except boats which dock at nearby Amahai or at Kairatu in the west, is a quiet, clean place with wide streets. Everything you will want is on the main street of Jalan Abdulla Soulissa, which connects with Amahai, and where the bus terminal is located. The very helpful tourist office (☎ 21462), Jalan Banda 2, is open from 8 am to 2 pm Monday to Saturday. Take a becak there.

Festivals

The Anniversary of Masohi is held on 3 November each year, with traditional performances and kite competitions. On 10

November – Heroes Day – a cross-country run is held.

Places to Stay & Eat

All losmen are within walking distance of the bus terminal, along Jalan Abdulla Soulissa (there are no street numbers) towards Amahai. The *Penginapan Nusantara* (☎ 21339) is being improved and has singles/doubles/triples from 14,850/23,100/ 29,700 rp. The popular *Losmen Sri Lestari* (☎ 178) has good rooms for 15,000/25,000 rp. The cheapest places are the noisy family-run *Penginapan Beilohi Indah* (☎ 251) for 12,500 rp per person, and the quiet *Wisma Nusa Ina* (☎ 221) on the corner of Jalan Cengkeh and Jalan Pala, two blocks from the market, at 11,000/18,000 rp.

On either side of the Sri Lestari, is the *Vieta Bar & Restoran* which opens late for meals and drinks, and the *Rumah Makan Sate Surabaya* which offers cheap sates in nice, simple surroundings. There are many cheap warungs and teahouses around the large busy and pleasant market.

Getting There & Away

Air Merpati flies – unreliably – to Ambon (54,400 rp) every Saturday. The Merpati agent (no telephone) is on Jalan Pemda Maluku Tengah, Amahai.

Boat Every two hours, daily from 7 am, two ferries link Waiprit port, near Kairatu, with Hunimua, near Liang, on Pulau Ambon (1700 rp, 1½ hours). This is more popular but expensive and takes longer because of the Masohi to Kairatu bus trip (9000 rp; three or four hours). A ferry leaves Amahai daily at 8 am, takes about four hours to Tulehu on Pulau Ambon (it can be rough in the wet season) and costs 7000 rp. Speedboats (10,000 rp; two hours) leave Amahai and Tulehu when there is enough passengers. A quicker alternative is the daily bus from Kota Ambon, via Hunimua and Waiprit, to Piru (6000 rp), or to Masohi (12,000 rp; six hours).

The direct ferry from Seram to Saparua was, at the time of writing, at the bottom of

Market
Jalan Cengkeh
To Wisma Nusa Ina
Bemo/Bus Terminal
Abdullah Soulissa
Jalan Pattimura
Penginapan Nusantara
Jalan Imam Bonjol
Vieta Bar & Restoran
Losmen Sri Lestari
Rumah Makan Sate Surabaya
Penginapan Beilohi Indah

Masohi

0   50   100 m
Approximate Scale

To Amahai

the sea. Ask for the latest information, as a new ferry is likely to be in operation. Chartering a speedboat will cost about 40,000 rp per hour.

Getting Around
The modern bus terminal in Masohi is quite organised; buses are well marked and wait patiently under destination signs. They regularly go to the ports of Amahai (600 rp) and Kairatu, but to other places, services are far less regular. Roads around the island are usually rough and speedboats are often the only alternative for more distant villages. Becaks are available for about 700 rp around Masohi, but it's a nice place to walk around.

AROUND PULAU SERAM
South Coast
The villages of Janeero and Bonara, about 30 km from Masohi, are 'traditional' villages of the Nuaulu people. Unfortunately, the villages are little different to others on Pulau Seram, and you will find it difficult to see any examples of Nuauluan customs and way of life. Bemos cost 1000 rp to Bonara from Masohi.

North Coast
With a population of about 1500, **Wahai** is the main town on the north coast. The road to Wahai is passable but only just. A quicker and more popular way there is to take the bus to Sawai and then catch the daily public speedboat (it leaves around 1 pm) to Wahai (total travelling time of about four hours from Masohi). But check for up-to-date information as you may be able to get a direct bus to Wahai. There are two basic losmen: *Taman Baru* and *Sinar Indah*. There is no telephone service in Wahai.

West of Wahai is the friendly Muslim village of **Sawai** with a small offshore island called Pulau Sawai. You can paddle out there or hire a motorised dugout canoe. Locals use the island for fishing and making coconut oil, and have built small houses, which you can rent cheaply. There is no fresh water on the island.

There's stunning snorkelling off the north

coast and amazing beaches – try Asele, one hour east of Wahai. There is a traditional fishing competition and cultural show here every August. *Penginapan Lisar Tour* offers the only accommodation in Sawai.

East Coast
Although it's only 100 or so km from Masohi to **Tehoru**, the road is rough and the trip can take about three hours. Buses to the east of the island leave from Amahai, so get a bemo there first. There are normally only two buses a day to Tehoru, but this could increase with more demand from passengers. There is nothing much there, but losmen *Susi Inn* and *Binaya* have basic facilities. For places further east, you will have to take infrequent public speedboats or charter one.

West Coast
Two to three hours by bus (6000 rp) from Masohi are the lovely **waterfalls** just outside the village of Rumahkai. Ask the bus driver to drop you off at the *air tejun*. Start early to allow time to get there, and to wait for a bus back.

The rough road continues to **Kairatu**, an hour further on, from where the ferry to Liang on Pulau Ambon leaves. In Kairatu, there are one or two losmen such as the *Penginapan Sudi Hampir*, about two km walk towards Masohi on the main road. There is no need to stay there, because there will always be plenty of buses connecting with the popular ferries. From Kairatu you can take buses further west to Piru and beyond, but the roads and facilities get worse.

Manusela National Park
A large part of Seram's centre is designated as Manusela National Park. It is supposedly protected, but the park management has to contend with locals who want to use the area for purposes other than conservation. The park comprises a wide lowland plain in the north; a central enclave with the small villages of Manusela, Solumena and Kanikeh in an isolated inner valley at about 700 metres; and a giant mountain range in the

south. **Gunung Manusela** (3000 metres) on the park's eastern border is Seram's highest mountain. There are some beautiful white sandy beaches and excellent coral off the north coast. The island receives very few visitors and a trek through its interior or a shorter walk along parts of the north or south coast is a real 'off-the-beaten-track' experience.

You may need a permit from the PHPA (Perlindungan Hutan dan Pelestrian Alam) office, the Indonesian national park service, at Air Besar near Wahai, or check with the tourist office in Kota Ambon or Masohi first.

Walking across Seram to or from Wahai on the north coast through the park is tough going, but could be a highlight of a trip to the island – it's far less visited than the Baliem Valley in Irian Jaya. There are limited facilities in the park so you should be self-sufficient. Check with the head of the villages, the *bapak raja*, who usually has rooms for guests – what you pay is up to you. It's recommended that you take a guide (maybe 10,000 rp per day, plus food). Good maps of the park are difficult to find but some can be obtained from the Botanical Gardens Office in Bogor, Java; or ask at the tourist office in Masohi. Or if your Indonesian is up to scratch, keep asking a lot of directions as you go. If you want to see the park, but don't want to rough it, there are travel agencies in Kota Ambon, such as Nanusa Tours & Travel (☎ 55334) at Jalan Rijali 53, which organise guided trips into the park for several days.

Routes from the South Coast To enter the park from the south coast, you must take the rough bus ride from Masohi to Tehoru and take a speedboat to Hatumetan. You can walk into the park from there or from Saunulu via Piliani; it's about 1½ hour's walk from Saunulu. This locally named 'route of sorrow' rises to 2500 metres en route to Manusela village in the inner valley, one or two days' walk away – depending on how fit you are. From Manusela it's another three or four days' walk to Wahai. The villages in the interior are almost untouched by outside

influence apart from the presence of churches and schools.

Routes from the North Coast Wahai is the starting point into the park from the north. Alternatively, look for a truck from Wahai to Pasahari, then another south to Kaloa from where it's a one-day walk to Manusela village. The PHPA park office is a half-hour walk along the road east of Wahai, past Air Besar, near the schools.

Treks There are two trekking routes of varying difficulty within the park. One is via Solea village, 15 km east from Wahai – take the path near the park office. From there you walk upriver and over **Gunung Kobipoto** (1500 metres) via Solumena in the inner valley and out via Manusela village to the south coast. Reaching Solumena takes from three days to a week.

The other route heads south-west from Wahai through Melinani, Wassa and Roho to Kanikeh in the inner valley, and out via Manusela village to the south coast – this is another hard route taking from three to six days as far as Kanikeh.

The Bandas

South-east of Ambon lies the tiny cluster of beautiful islands known as the Bandas. The group consists of seven main islands: Neira, Gunung Api, Banda Besar, Hatta, Syahrir, Ai and Run, and three smaller ones. Bandaneira on the island of Neira is the chief town. The Bandas are littered with deserted forts and deteriorating Dutch villas which are being slowly restored. There are superb deserted beaches and excellent snorkelling and diving around the numerous coral reefs. There is even a still-active volcano to climb, Gunung Api. The Bandas are well worth the effort of getting there.

History
Portuguese ships landed in the Bandas in 1512 and had the islands to themselves until

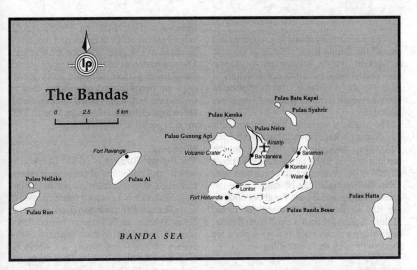

a Dutch fleet arrived in Maluku in 1599, with orders to seek out spices at their source and circumvent the Portuguese monopoly. Part of the Dutch fleet came to the Bandas, loaded a cargo of spices, alarmed the Portuguese and sailed back to the Netherlands. Soon afterwards the Dutch forced the Portuguese out of the spice trade but they still had other rivals: in 1601, the British East India Company had set up a fort on the island of Run in the Bandas, and in 1606 the Spanish got into the act by taking Ternate and Tidore.

The turning point came in 1619. Jan Pieterszoon Coen, the new VOC governor general, envisaged a Dutch commercial empire in the east, the grandeur of which would match the extent of his violent ruthlessness. He seized control of the Bandas, got rid of the unhelpful Bandanese and started producing nutmeg using imported slaves and labourers, with Dutch overseers.

In early 1621, Coen attacked Lonthor Island (Banda Besar), the most important of the group, and almost totally wiped out the indigenous Bandanese population. Coen then returned to Batavia (Jakarta) and announced that the VOC would accept applications for land grants in the Bandas if the

applicants settled permanently on the islands and produced spices exclusively for the company, at fixed prices. The company would import rice and other necessities, provide slaves to work on the plantations and defend the islands against attack.

This was not broken until the Napoleonic Wars, almost 200 years later. The Bandas, like other Dutch-held parts of the archipelago, were occupied by the English during the Napoleonic Wars and nutmeg seedlings were shipped off to Sri Lanka, Sumatra and Penang. By 1860, these areas were almost as important as the Bandas for producing nutmeg and mace. The invention of refrigeration, however, which allowed meat to be kept without the heavy use of spices, saw the end of the spice trade. The Bandas still produce nutmeg and mace for use in Indonesia, but for the most part the islands have been forgotten by the rest of the world.

Books

Willard Hanna's *Indonesian Banda*, available at the Bandaneira museum, takes you through a cannon-shot-by-cannon-shot history of the islands, from the time the first European ships sailed in until the late 1970s.

Diving

There are reportedly about 50 good dive sites around the Banda islands. Some of the best are around Syahrir, Karaka and Ai islands. The best season for all water activities is from October to March. The only place to hire equipment is the shop opposite the Hotel Maulana.

The Maulana organises half-day and full-day diving packages around the islands from 120,000 rp depending on distance and the amount of gear to be hired. Tanks will cost 44,000 rp per person per dive plus boat hire.

Snorkelling gear can be rented from the hotels Delfika and Brants for about 6000 rp per day or from the Maulana for more. Malole, a pleasant hour's stroll from Bandaneira along a shady path, is a good place for local swimming and snorkelling.

Festivals

A *kora-kora* (longboat) race is held in the Bandas every April and October, where six boats from different villages commemorate the bravery of the Malukans against the Dutch. Each kora-kora is up to 20 metres long, with a crew of about 40 people.

PULAU NEIRA

On Pulau Neira, **Bandaneira**, the only major town in the Bandas, was in its heyday, a town of spacious mansions, which are now being restored: retired foreigners are sometimes permitted to restore the mansions and live in them until their death. Neira is a great place for scrambling around old forts, walking in the hills, climbing a volcano or visiting beaches and coral reefs. Local Indonesian developers apparently plan to restrict the amount of tourists to the Bandas by charging very high resort prices, which seems a good idea but is possibly more of a money-raising venture than anything else.

Orientation & Information

There are only a handful of streets in the picturesque town of Bandaneira. Facilities are more suited to the small island it is, and not (thankfully) to the tourist trade. There is no bank, but you may be able to change money at the Hotel Maulana. There's a small, helpful tourist office at the airport, but don't be afraid to ask your hotel for information. The restoration of old colonial places is not complete or perfect, so while many attractions are beautiful and interesting, they're sometimes not well signed or explained. Often a small donation (perhaps around 1000 rp) is expected at most buildings.

Museums

The **Rumah Budaya** is an old Dutch villa with a small collection of cannons, muskets, helmets, old coins, maps, china and paintings. Next door is a restored house claimed to be the **Rumah Pengasingan** (Exile House) of Sutan Syahrir, an Indonesian independence hero. It has some Syahrir memorabilia – mainly photos – but it *was not* where he lodged during his exile to the Bandas by the Dutch in the 1930s.

Dutch Church

The pretty Dutch church (closed) on Jalan Gereja Tua dates from 1852 when it replaced an earlier stone building which was destroyed by an earthquake. A large number of people are buried beneath the floor. Note that the church's clock no longer works; its hands are stuck at 5.03, the precise moment of the Japanese invasion of 1942.

Benteng Nassau

The original stone foundations of Fort Nassau were built by the Portuguese around 1529 when they sent troops from their base in Ternate to make a show of force in the Bandas. The fort, however, wasn't completed and the foundations were abandoned. In 1608, a powerful Dutch fleet under Admiral Pieterszoon Verhoeven arrived with orders to annex the Bandas. When negotiations stalled, Verhoeven simply confronted the Bandanese with a *fait accompli* by landing soldiers on Neira and constructing a fort on the old Portuguese foundations.

Benteng Nassau was restored for use as a warehouse in the early 19th century but eventually lapsed into ruin. Today, the area around the fort is really overgrown – only

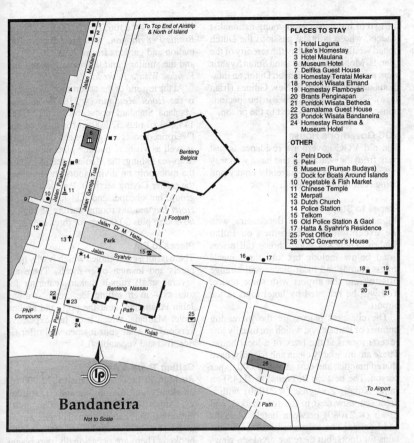

PLACES TO STAY

1 Hotel Laguna
2 Like's Homestay
3 Hotel Maulana
6 Museum Hotel
7 Delfika Guest House
8 Homestay Teratai Mekar
18 Pondok Wisata Elmand
19 Homestay Flamboyan
20 Brants Penginapan
21 Pondok Wisata Betheda
22 Gamalama Guest House
23 Pondok Wisata Bandaneira
24 Homestay Rosmina & Museum Hotel

OTHER

4 Pelni Dock
5 Pelni
6 Museum (Rumah Budaya)
9 Dock for Boats Around Islands
10 Vegetable & Fish Market
11 Chinese Temple
12 Merpati
13 Dutch Church
14 Police Station
15 Telkom
16 Old Police Station & Gaol
17 Hatta & Syahrir's Residence
25 Post Office
26 VOC Governor's House

Bandaneira

Not to Scale

three walls and a gateway remain and an old cannon lies on the ground. Still it is pleasant enough for a clamber around, and there are good views of Benteng Belgica.

Benteng Belgica

The construction of Fort Belgica began in 1611 under the direction of Pieter Both who had been appointed governor general of the region and assigned the task of creating a monopoly, and kicking out the English. With the prospect of a Banda-English alliance, his men erected the imposing Benteng Belgica on the ridge overlooking Benteng Nassau.

Belgica was maintained as a military headquarters until around 1860.

Belgica is pentagonal and its towers, in which you can climb, point out to sea. With Gunung Api looming in the distance, the fort's setting is quite beautiful. Considerable restorations make it a marvellous place to wander around. There is a small information room where you must first report (and pay a small donation).

Hatta & Syahrir's Residence

In the late 1930s, the Bandas achieved a dim sort of reflected glory as the place of exile

MALUKU

for two of Indonesia's top young nationalist leaders, whose political passions the Dutch hoped would be calmed by the serenity of the islands. Mohammed Hatta and Sutan Syahrir were moved here from Boven Digul, an infamous detention camp in New Guinea (Irian Jaya). They took up residence in the spacious house – now restored – next to the prison.

VOC Governor's House
The old VOC governor's residence is just back from the waterfront and has a walkway jutting out to sea. It's currently empty and being restored, but is worth a look.

Places to Stay
All accommodation is in Bandaneira, with the exception of one losmen on Pulau Syahrir. There's a good choice (all prices listed below include tax and three meals unless stated) and most places will arrange lifts to/from the airport with some notice. You will be accosted by hotel touts at the airport.

The cheapest places are the increasing number of homestays, which are usually just several rooms at the back of a local home. These are invariably clean and friendly, have shared mandis, and cost about 15,000 rp per person. The best are *Rosmina* (☎ 21145) on Jalan Kujali; *Zonegate* (☎ 21050) with a great sea-view next to the fish market; and *Like's* (☎ 21089) between hotels Maulana and Laguna. The rooms at Like's have curtains for doors, but there are great sea views from the garden.

Along Jalan Gereja Tua are a number of places: the clean and comfortable *Pondok Wisata Bandaneira* (☎ 21149) costs 12,500 rp per person plus 7500 rp for meals; the *Gamalama Guest House* (☎ 21053) has nice surroundings and singles/doubles from 17,500/ 30,000 rp; and the helpful *Delfika Guest House* (☎ 21027), an old Dutch house, has rooms for 20,000/35,000 rp – the new, better rooms will cost a little more. *Homestay Teratai Mekar*, on Jalan Pelabuhan, is about the same price, but not as good value.

All next to each other on Jalan Syahrir are the following restored villas: *Homestay*

Flamboyan (☎ 21067) for 20,000/35,000 rp; *Brants Penginapan*, with great local information and gardens from 17,500/30,000 rp; and the similar *Pondok Wisata Elmand* and *Pondok Wisata Betheda*.

At the top end of the accommodation scale is the *Hotel Maulana* (☎ 21022) on Jalan Maulana. Standard rooms cost from 120,000/ 144,000 rp plus 52,800 rp for three meals. Overpriced boats and guides can be arranged as well as visits to nutmeg plantations, and deep-sea fishing; the Maulana seems to have the monopoly on diving tours and hire (see the earlier Diving section). Part of the same group, but cheaper and less luxurious, the *Hotel Laguna* has rooms starting at 36,000/ 60,000 rp plus 30,000 rp for three meals.

Places to Eat
There is not a great choice which is why most hotels and losmen offer meals. There are several small rumah makans catering for tourists – even selling ice cream – along Jalan Pelabuhan, near the port, and around Hotel Maulana, which itself has expensive versions of what your losmen will offer (ie rice, fish and vegetables).

Getting There & Away
Air Merpati flies to Bandaneira (92,900 rp) on Monday and Wednesday, and on Saturday via Amahai on Pulau Seram. The pretty airport can only cater for small planes seating about 15 people so flights are often heavily booked. There are occasionally two planes for each scheduled flight, but don't count on it. The Merpati office (☎ 21041) is on Jalan Gereja Tua and is open from about 9 am to 1 pm daily. Sit on the right-hand side of the plane from Ambon for the best views of these magnificent islands.

Boat Every two weeks, the Pelni liner *Rinjani* goes to Tual (15,100/59,100 rp for economy/1st class) and Ambon (40,100/ 111,000 rp); and every four weeks the *Tatamailau* also goes to Tual and Ambon. The *Katherina*, among other passenger and cargo boats, stops in Bandaneira every week or so during the loop from Ambon to south-eastern

Maluku. The *Waisamar* connects the Bandas with Ambon – it leaves Ambon every Monday and Wednesday (19,000 rp) – and the *Daya Nusantara* goes every two weeks or so from Ambon, through Banda, and on to Tual, Saumlaki and other ports on the islands of southern Maluku. The Pelni office (no telephone) for all tickets and information is just outside the port on Jalan Pelabuhan.

Getting Around

To/From the Airport Public bemos wait for all incoming flights and cost about 1000 rp, or you can get a free lift on a bemo with a hotel tout. For passengers leaving the Bandas, there is a bemo which tours the town at about 7 am, well before the flight to Ambon (ask your hotel or the Merpati office to arrange for it to collect you).

Local Transport Pulau Neira is very small and easy to walk around. There are very occasional bemos. Bicycles are handy to get around the island and can be rented for the day at Brants for 10,000 rp and at Delfika for 7500 rp.

Boats (mainly motorised) are the major form of transport. Except for regular boats to Pulau Banda Besar, there is no public transport to the other islands. Boats holding up to 10 people can be rented by the hour or day for a very negotiable price depending on the tourist demand, distance (the most important factor being petrol costs) and length of hire. All local boats leave Bandaneira from the fish market.

Canoes with a paddler cost around 15,000 rp per day; 10,000 rp on your own. You might be able to take one out yourself but you can only reach places such as Gunung Api and Pulau Karaka on your own. Ask around at the fish market.

Organised sunset cruises are available for 25,000 rp per person – ask at the Mauluna, Brants or Delfika.

OTHER ISLANDS
Gunung Api

This volcano, jutting out of the sea directly in front of Bandaneira harbour, has been a constant threat to Banda, and some 'experts' believe it is due for a major eruption soon. In one awful hour in April 1778, a particularly destructive volcanic eruption occurred at the same time as an earthquake, a tidal wave and a hurricane – resulting in great destruction of the nutmeg trees and a massive drop in production.

Since then, Gunung Api has erupted twice in the 20th century – in 1901; and again in 1988 when two people were killed and over 300 houses on its north and south slopes and 120,000 coconut trees were destroyed. It's only a short paddle across to Gunung Api from Neira in a canoe or you can rent a motorboat all day for 25,000 rp.

You can climb the 666-metre-high volcano in about two to three hours. There are some steep sections and loose ground, so take good shoes and some gloves if you can. Start at about 5.30 am to ensure you reach the top to see the magnificent views before the early morning cloud covers it for the rest of the day. Guides are available for about 10,000 rp and are not a bad idea. Ask around at your hotel or at the fish market. A boat will cost 2000 rp to the island. Climbers who reach the summit are issued with certificates, for which a small donation is expected.

Pulau Karaka

Off the northern end of Gunung Api, Karaka has a small beach but there are some fine coral reefs in shallow water near the shore. It's close enough to paddle from Bandaneira in a dugout canoe and takes about an hour in a two-person canoe.

Pulau Banda Besar

A walk around this island makes an interesting day trip (there is no transport on the island). From the top of the obvious, steep steps in Lontor, turn left and ask directions for **Benteng Hollandia**. This fort was erected after Coen's capture of Banda Besar in 1621. Placed high on the central ridge of the island, with great views of the islands and Lontor village, it was once enormous, but an earthquake wrecked it in 1743. What little remains is derelict and overgrown, and it's a

MALUKU

real disappointment after Benteng Belgica. (Take some spare pens to really make yourself popular with the local kids.)

From the same lane way to the fort, an unmarked trail (again, you will have to ask directions) to the other side of the island past wild coconut and clove trees leads to the pretty **Namulu beach**, which is worth a swim and snorkel. Another path heads east from the speedboat dock at Lontor, along the coast, initially goes over some rocks and passes some small swimming beaches, wild cloves trees and spotless villages such as **Bioyouw**. If you keep going, you will come across some **nutmeg plantations** at Waling Besar village and beyond.

At Waer village on the north-east coast is the overgrown **Benteng Concordia**. Nearby is **Pantai Lanutu**, behind Selamon village. The only way of getting to Waer is by walking from Lontor (not really recommended without a guide or map) or by chartering a boat from Bandaneira all day for about 40,000 rp.

To get to Lontor village, the only real dock on the island, charter a longboat (about 3000 rp) one way or just take the regular public boat from the fish market for 500 rp.

Pulau Syahrir

Also known as Pulau Pisang because of its banana shape, Syahrir is about 50 minutes by motorboat from Bandaneira. It has a good sandy beach and some pretty coral (with a big drop-off) and colourful fish. You can wander uphill to the small village behind the beach. Despite a regulation stating all accommodation in the Bandas must be on Bandaneira, the friendly and secluded *Homestay Mailena* has rooms on Syahrir with three meals for 25,000 rp per person (plus 5000 rp boat fare). Otherwise, a boat there, for the day, will cost about 35,000 rp.

Pulau Ai

Ai is a couple of hours west by boat from Bandaneira and is worth visiting. It has the Benteng Revenge near a village on the north-east side. Facing Gunung Api, about one km east of the fort, there's a long sandy beach

with wonderful snorkelling. You can charter a twin-engine boat there for about 70,000 rp for the whole day.

Pulau Run

Run was once the centre of English activity in the Bandas. There is an English-built stone fort on a spit of half-exposed coral rock on **Pulau Neilakka**, which lies just off Run. A large twin-engine boat chartered all day, with a stop at Pulau Ai, will cost about 110,000 rp.

Pulau Hatta

From Bandaneira, to get to this far eastern island will take an hour and a half by twin-engine boat, which if chartered for a day, will cost about 100,000 rp.

South-East Maluku

Probably the most forgotten islands in Indonesia, the islands of South-East Maluku (Maluku Tenggara) are dispersed across the sea between Timor and Irian Jaya. The three main groups, all south-east of Banda, are Kai, Aru and Tanimbar. West of Tanimbar, two arcs of smaller islands stretch across to Timor – a southern, less fertile arc consisting of the Babar and Leti groups, Kisar and Wetar and a northern arc of volcanic, wooded islands (Serua, Nila, Teun, Damar and Romang).

South-East Maluku is inhabited mostly by people of mixed Malay and Papuan blood with the Papuan features more noticeable in people living on the islands closer to Irian Jaya. Missionaries introduced Christianity and developed the area, and Islam also became established itself in many parts. More recently, there's been logging and fishing by all and sundry. Trepang and pearls, once plentiful, are becoming scarce.

KAI ISLANDS

Also colloquially known as the 'Thousand Islands' (although there are really only 287), the Kai Islands include coral islands, atolls and beautiful beaches, which are, under-

Kai Islands

0   20   40 km

standably, being pushed by the local tourist industry. There are three main islands: Pulau Kai Kecil (known locally as Nuhu Roa), Pulau Dullah, and Pulau Kai Besar (also known as Nuhu Yut).

Orientation & Information
Langgur, on Pulau Kai Kecil, is the administrative capital of South-East Maluku, so there are lots of government buildings lining the main road. Joined by the Watdek Bridge is Tual on Pulau Dullah. It is impossible to know where Langgur ends and Tual starts. Officially, and for ease of reference below, all places in the town on Dullah Island are listed as being in Tual; all places in the town on the Kai Kecil side are in Langgur.

The very helpful tourist office (☎ 21466) – which has more staff than tourists on the islands – can provide good information. It's badly signposted; from Tual, go straight ahead rather than to the right over the bridge, walk 250 metres, it's on the left in a whitewashed building. Neither bank in Langgur changes money. The police station (☎ 21110) is on Jalan Dihir, near the port at Tual.

Things to See & Do
Pulau Kai Kecil This island has one of the most beautiful beaches in Indonesia, **Pasir Panjang** ('long sand'). Known locally as Pantai Sar Nadan, this is a completely isolated, unspoilt (so far) beach with bright blue water, powdery white sand and thousands of coconut palms. It is 17 km from Tual (500 rp by bemo) and is the best and most accessible beach in the Kai Islands, so there is really no need to go to any others.

To the north, **Ohoideertawun** offers another good beach, and the interesting **Gua Luwat** (Luwat Caves), with strange paintings. In the south, is the Pantai Danar beach at Danar village – bemos only leave five times a day (1750 rp).

Pulau Dullah The pretty, seaside village of Dullah (400 rp by bemo) claims to have the Belang Museum which is nothing more than three decaying longboats (*belang*, also called kora-kora) by the beach. (In late October races are held around Tual.) On the way to Dullah, is the developing **Taman Anggrek** (Orchard Garden) with the Ngadi Lake, and some picnic areas.

In the north of the island, there is a great beach, and marine garden, at **Pantai Sorbat Indah** (a bemo there from Tual costs 1000 rp). Nearby, at the village of **Tamadan**, is another beach with some Japanese WW II wrecks. From there, you could try to charter a motorboat for the hour trip to **Pulau Adranan**, with even more sandy beaches. Visits to the island can also be arranged through Adranan's Island Camping Club at Jalan Jenderal Sudirman 72, Tual. A bemo connects Tual with Tamadan and Sorbat every few hours.

Pulau Kai Besar Kai Besar is a long island and far less developed than its neighbours. It has rough roads and infrequent bemos. A ferry the *Tanjung Burang,* goes to Larat and Saumlaki (12,700/18,600 rp for economy/1st class; about 30 hours), both on the Tanimbar Islands, once a week; and also goes to Banda Elat on Kai Besar (2500/3500 rp) three times a week. From Banda Elat, you can charter a

MALUKU

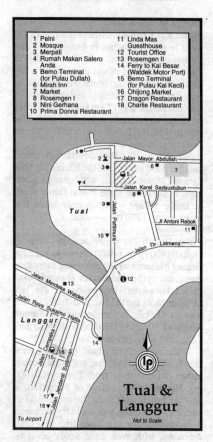

1 Pelni	11 Linda Mas
2 Mosque	Guesthouse
3 Merpati	12 Tourist Office
4 Rumah Makan Salero	13 Rosemgen II
Anda	14 Ferry to Kai Besar
5 Bemo Terminal	(Watdek Motor Port)
(for Pulau Dullah)	15 Bemo Terminal
6 Mirah Inn	(for Pulau Kai Kecil)
7 Market	16 Ohijong Market
8 Rosemgen I	17 Dragon Restaurant
9 Nini Gerhana	18 Charlie Restaurant
10 Prima Donna Restaurant	

Tual & Langgur

Not to Scale

boat to the nearby **Pulau Kelapa** (Coconut Island).

Places to Stay & Eat

Most cheap places are in older, quieter Tual. The following have basic rooms and shared mandi: the 'old' *Rosemgen I* (☎ 21045) on Jalan Karel Sadsustubun has rooms for 10,000 rp per person or 13,500 rp with simple meals, plus lots of mossies; *Nini Gerhana* (☎ 21343) on Jalan Raya Pattimura, is noisy but friendly at 15,000 rp per room; and the *Mirah Inn* (☎ 21172) on Jalan Mayor Abdullah costs 7700 rp per person. The popular,

quiet but inconveniently located *Linda Mas Guest House* (☎ 21271) on Jalan Anthony Rhebok has good rooms for a little more, plus more expensive ones with air-con and TV.

The only place in Langgur is the quiet 'new' *Rosemgen II* (☎ 21477) (not to be confused with the other Rosemgen) near the bridge, on Jalan Merdeka Watdek. Singles/doubles start at 24,000/36,000 rp with fan and mandi; ask for a room with a great water view. There are good local maps and information in the lobby.

Six km out of town, the *Coaster Cottages* (no telephone – book at the Mirah Inn) at beautiful Ohoililir Beach on Pulau Kai Kecil offers seclusion but is inconvenient (you will have to charter a bemo there which may cost about 25,000 rp – bargain). Rooms are 17,500/25,000 rp plus 2500 rp per person for meals (there is nowhere else to eat).

Neither Langgur nor Tual offers a choice of good places to eat, so hotel food is worth considering. In Tual, the *Rumah Makan Salero Anda* and *Prima Donna Restaurant* offer poor food and little variety. The *Angel Pub & Restaurant* at the 'new' Rosemgen II provides a good dinner if you order earlier in the day, and cold beer, with a great river view and live music. In Langgur, along Jalan Jenderal Sudirman are the modern Chinese *Dragon* and *Charlie* restaurants. There are plenty of warungs around the markets in both Langgur and Tual.

The only accommodation on Kai Besar is the *Adios Hotel* (no phone) at Banda Elat.

Getting There & Away

Air Merpati currently connects Langgur with Ambon four times a week (173,000 rp), with Dobo (Aru Islands) on Tuesday and Sunday (73,100 rp), and with Saumlaki (Tanimbar Islands) for 108,400 rp. But beware, these schedules often change. Unless you want to stay a while waiting for an overbooked connection, it is worth confirming your departure from Kai before you arrive. The Merpati agency (☎ 21376), on Jalan Pattimura, is open from 8 am to 4 pm, Monday to Saturday.

Boat Tual port is well connected to other islands in Maluku and to nearby Irian Jaya. Every two weeks, the Pelni liner *Rinjani* goes to Fakfak (Irian Jaya) for 15,300/99,300 rp (economy/1st class), and to Ambon (48,300/165,300 rp) through the Bandas (38,300/129,300 rp).

Every four weeks, the *Tatamailau* goes to Dobo (8300/32,300 rp), Saumlaki (16,300/70,300 rp) and Kaimana (16,300 rp). Tual is also linked to Ambon, Banda and southern Maluku by the Perintis boats *Daya Nusantara*, *Nukori* and *Nagura*; and to Irian Jaya by the *Iweri* every three weeks. The Pelni office (☎ 21181) for all bookings is on Jalan Fidnang Armau. All schedules and costs are helpfully displayed outside.

Getting Around

To/From the Airport Langgur's Dumatabun airport is five km away from Watdek Bridge. From the airport, walk to the main road for a bemo (500 rp); or take one from the terminal car park, but confirm the price as bemo drivers have no shame in charging up to 20 times the correct price!

Bemo There are reasonable roads linking the major villages throughout Pulau Kai Kecil and Dullah, but there is no regular public transport around Pulau Kai Besar.

Bemos (from 200 to 300 rp each trip) make regular runs along the main streets of Tual and Langgur, and connect both towns. For all places on Pulau Dullah, go to the terminal at the waterfront at Tual; for destinations on Kai Kecil, go to the terminal near the Ohijong market about one km from the bridge in Langgur. Chartering a bemo (worth considering to avoid the crush, and waiting for the irregular public transport to fill up) will cost at least 8000 rp per hour.

Boat A ferry, the *Tanjung Burang*, goes to Larat and Saumlaki (12,700/18,600 rp for economy/1st class; about 30 hours), both on the Tanimbar Islands once a week; and also goes to Banda Elat on Kai Besar (2500/3500 rp) three times a week. There are also daily boats to Banda Elat from Tual's Pelabuhan

Motor Watdek (Watdek Motor Port), near the bridge, at 10 am and midday; returning from Kai Besar at 2 and 4 pm (2500 rp).

TANIMBAR ISLANDS

The Tanimbar group, the most southerly of the Maluku group, consist of 66 islands, the major one being Pulau Yamdena. The islands are undeveloped, and transport service to, and on, the islands can be rough and irregular.

Orientation & Information

The main town, **Saumlaki**, on Pulau Yamdena, is little more than a 200-metre stretch of road called Jalan Bhineka. The town is busy and friendly, but less pleasant when the huge tide is at its lowest. Major currencies (cash only) can be changed at the Toko Selatan, next to the Penginapan Harapan Indah, for a slightly lower rate; the two banks won't change money.

Things to See & Do

At **Sangliat Dol**, on the east coast of Yamdena, a 30-metre-high stone staircase leads up from the beach to a large, boat-shaped, carved stone platform 18 metres long. The

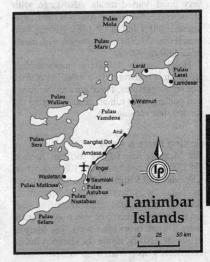

Pulau Molu
Pulau Maru
Larat
Pulau Larat
Lamdesar
Pulau Wuliaru
Watmuri
Pulau Yamdena
Arui
Pulau Sera
Sangliat Dol
Amdasa
Wasletan
Itngei
Pulau Matkusa
Saumlaki
Pulau Astubun
Pulau Nustabun
Pulau Selaru

Tanimbar Islands

0   25   50 km

stone structures are OK, and the people are friendly but it's a long, uncomfortable ride (2500 rp; 90 minutes). Two unmarked buses leave the Saumlaki terminal at 9 am and 2.30 pm (but these times are always liable to change). You can get off at Sangliat Dol, have a look around for an hour, and catch the crowded bus (which goes further north to Arui) on its way back.

Near Saumlaki is the lovely tropical **Leluan Beach**. You will need to charter a bemo there for 5000 rp return plus waiting time, or take the bemo to Olilit Lama village and get dropped off for the 20-minute walk. On the way to Sangliat Dol, the village of **Inglei** has a nice swimming beach.

Places to Stay & Eat

There are only three places to stay, all along Jalan Bhineka in Saumlaki. *Penginapan Ratulel* (☎ 14) is the cheapest at 15,000/20,000 rp for singles/doubles, plus an extra 12,500 rp for three meals. The best is the *Penginapan Harapan Indah* (☎ 21019) which has small upstairs rooms for 24,000 rp with shared mandi and clean, quiet rooms downstairs for 36,000 rp or 40,000 rp with TV, air-con and mandi. Prices include three very good, varied meals. Also large, with clean, comfortable, airy rooms is the *Penginapan Pantai Indah* (☎ 148). Rooms with mandi cost 27,500 rp per person with meals or 22,000 rp without.

Hotel food is definitely recommended, although it is invariably a variation of fish, rice and vegetables. There are a few warungs and padang-style rumah makans around the market, but nothing else.

Getting There & Away

Air Merpati has flights to/from Ambon (183,000 rp) and Langgur (108,500 rp) on Thursday and Saturday. If you want to leave by plane, it is worth ringing Merpati in Saumlaki before you arrive to confirm your departure from there, or you may be stuck there a week or so (as I was). The Merpati office (☎ 21017), inside the Harapan Indah, is officially open from 8 am to 2 pm.

Boat The Pelni liner *Tatamailau* connects Saumlaki with Tual (Kai Islands) and Dili (East Timor) every four weeks. The Perintis boats *Nukori* and *Daya Nusantara* loop around the region to/from Ambon and Banda every two weeks; as do the *Katherina* and *Citra Pasific* every four weeks. The weekly ferry *Tanjung Burang* goes to Tual and to Larat on Pulau Larat, north of Yamdena, and other places along the way. Other smaller cargo/passenger boats go to Larat, and nearby Selu, Sera and the Babar islands. Other than on the Pelni ships, conditions are usually very basic. The Pelni office, for all tickets and information, is near the port, which is just off the main street in Saumlaki.

Getting Around

To/From the Airport At the very small Olilit airport, you can charter a bemo for about 3000 rp. It is better to share a bemo with everyone else for about 300 rp, or get a lift with the friendly Merpati guys or with the Harapan Indah bemo if you want to stay there.

Local Transport There is really only one main road on Pulau Yamdena which goes north from Saumlaki up the east coast as far as Arui. Conditions are bad, and the road may be impassable in the wet season. All buses leave from the huge, incongruous Yamdena Plaza, near the port in Saumlaki. Most buses are unmarked and leave irregularly so some asking and waiting is inevitable. Chartering at about 10,000 rp per hour will offset the waiting, but you will still stop for passengers along the way.

ARU ISLANDS

The closest of the island groups to Irian Jaya, Aru is best known as home to the threatened birds of paradise, a species whose males display their full plumage during their courting season from May to December. The south-eastern part of the group is a marine reserve. The main town is Dobo on the small, northern island of Wamar. Aru is quite undeveloped for travellers and difficult to get to, so is very rarely visited.

Flights from Ambon via Langgur, on Pulau Tanimbar, leave unreliably on Tuesday and Saturday (73,100 rp). The Merpati office (☎ 21260) is at Jalan Kapitang Malitongi in Dobo. The Pelni ship *Tatamailau* connects Dobo with Timika on the southern coast of Irian Jaya, and with Tual, during its four-weekly run. The Perintis boat *Daya Nusantara* connects Wamar with Tual, Saumlaki and the Bandas. There are also smaller, local boats such as the *Ramuar* which connect Wamar with Ambon and Saumlaki.

Ternate & Tidore Islands

Pulau Ternate & Pulau Tidore

The main town and communications hub of the scattered islands of northern Maluku is Ternate on the small island of the same name, one of a chain of volcanic peaks poking out of the ocean off the west coast of the large island of Halmahera. Apart from the islands of Ternate and neighbouring Tidore, northern Maluku is rarely visited but certainly offers scope for the more adventurous traveller.

History
For centuries the sultanate of Ternate was one of the most important in Maluku, with influence as far south as Ambon, west to Sulawesi and east to Irian Jaya. Ternate's prosperity came from its abundant production of cloves, which allowed it to become a powerful regional military force. Rivalry with the neighbouring sultanate of Tidore resulted in frequent wars, and it was only in 1814 that peace was finally established.

Ternate was one of the first places where the Portuguese and Dutch established themselves in Maluku and it's dotted with the ruins of old European fortifications. Even the Spanish got into the act as the chief foreign power in Ternate and Tidore for much of the 17th century.

KOTA TERNATE
The town of Ternate is, in contrast to Kota Ambon, a relaxed place only occasionally interrupted by rumblings from the huge still-smoking volcano, Gamalama, to which all towns on the island cling.

Orientation
The town of Ternate stretches several km along the waterfront. The former sultan's palace is at the northern end of town and beyond that is the airport. The huge Benteng Oranye is near the main bemo terminal and market. The harbour Komplex Pelabuhan is at the southern end of town. If you're in a hurry you can do a loop around the island in just a few hours, taking in all the main sights.

Information
Tourist Office There's a reasonably useful tourist office inside the Kantor Bupati complex on Jalan Pahlawan Revolusi. The friendly staff speak English, but have no

MALUKU

brochures. You are strongly urged to report there before attempting to climb Gamalama volcano (see Around Pulau Ternate for more details).

Money Bank Rakyat, and the Bank ExIm, near the tourist office, both on Jalan Pahlawan Revolusi, are open from 8 am to 2 pm weekdays.

Post & Telephone The post office, near the Hotel Nirwana, is open from 8 am to midnight daily, but closed Friday lunch time for prayers. Nearby is the modern Telkom office.

Things to See
Kedaton Sultan The 13th-century sultan's palace is just back from Jalan Sultan Babullah, the road to the airport. The unkempt building now houses a museum with just a few Portuguese cannons, Dutch helmets and armour. It seems to be often closed, probably because people aren't interested in visiting it. There's a nice view of Ternate from the building. A bemo will cost 200 rp.

Benteng Oranye This Dutch fort dates from 1607 and is right in the middle of Kota Ternate, opposite the bemo station. It is pleasant to stroll around; there are cannons and crumbling walls overgrown with weeds, which still gives some idea of its past importance. It is now well used by locals for housing and sports.

Places to Stay – bottom end
Almost all of the cheap places are located near the noisy port in Kota Ternate. They are sometimes full of Indonesians waiting for boats. They often don't include breakfast, and all of them have outside mandi.

Penginapan Ujung Pandang (☎ 21836) on Jalan Ahmad Yani is very basic and noisy at 7500 rp per person. Along Jalan Pahlawan Revolusi within 200 metres of the port are the following penginapans which cost less than 10,000 rp per person: *Yamin* (☎ 21929), *Sentosa*, *Permata*, and the *Keluarga* (☎ 22250)

which offers some respite from the noisy main road.

Bastiong, the nearby *pelabuhan* (port), has one or two cheap places, such as the *Penginapan Mallioboro* and *Wisata Inn*, each for about 5000 rp per person.

Places to Stay – middle & top end
All prices in this section include tax and all rooms have a mandi. *Hotel Nirwana* (☎ 21787), Jalan Pahlawan Revolusi 58, has a disco and gym. Quiet singles/doubles with air-con, TV and good service cost 30,000/36,000 rp. Next door, *Hotel El Shinta* (☎ 21059) has noisy front rooms at 19,800/30,800 rp, and better back rooms with air-con at 33,000/44,000 rp – all prices include three meals. Across the road, the *Neraca Hotel* (☎ 21668), at Jalan Pahlawan Revolusi 30, is worth splashing out on, but is often full. Good rooms with air-con, TV and hot water cost 30,000/40,000 rp. It is also a Bouraq agency.

Hotel Indah (☎ 21334), Jalan Bosoiri 3, has air-con rooms for 27,500/38,500 rp and rooms with fan for 19,250/27,500 rp; three meals cost 10,000 rp extra.

The friendly *Chrysant Hotel* (☎ 21580) at Jalan Ahmad Yani 131 is also good value. Quiet, modern air-con rooms cost from 25,000/30,000 rp, plus 7500 rp for an extra bed. The old Dutch-built *Hotel Merdeka* (☎ 21120), at Jalan Merdeka 19, costs 20,000/30,000 rp with fan, and 30,000/40,000 rp with air-con.

Places to Eat
About a 10-minute walk west of the centre, the *Restaurant Siola* on Jalan Stadion has good Chinese food in salubrious surroundings; there's also a disco and karaoke until late. Also 10 minutes' walk north past the market, the *Bambu Kuring* on Jalan Sultan Babullah is worth the walk for its rattan decor and ponds and for its good value and selection.

Hotel restaurants include the *Neraca*, which is not expensive but its pleasant view of the ocean is now restricted by the building

PLACES TO STAY

3	Hotel Merdeka
13	Hotel El Shinta
14	Neraca Hotel
15	Hotel Nirwana
16	Hotel Indah
21	Penginapan Sentosa
22	Penginapan Permata
23	Penginapan Keluarga
24	Penginapan Yamin
26	Penginapan Ujung Pandang
28	Chrysant Hotel

PLACES TO EAT

6	Rumah Makan Gamalama
8	Restoran Garuda
10	Rumah Makan Roda Baru
17	Restaurant Siola
18	Rumah Makan Simpang Raya

OTHER

1	Market
2	Bemo Station
4	Mitra Cinema
5	Benteng Cinema
7	Bank Rakyat
9	Merpati
11	Post Office
12	Telkom
19	Tourist Office
20	Bank Exlm
25	Harbour Entrance
27	Bouraq
29	Pelni

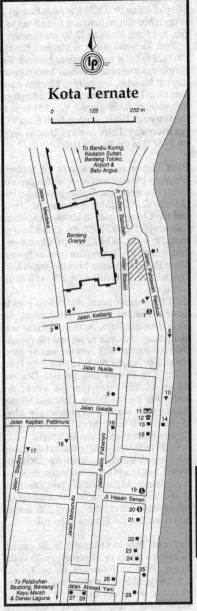

Kota Ternate

of extra rooms, and the *Nirwana* which is overpriced and has a limited choice.

Restoran Garuda is recommended for choice and cold drinks. For Padang food, the *Rumah Makan Gamalama* and *Rumah Makan Roda Baru* on Jalan Pahlawan Revolusi, are OK; as is the larger *Rumah Makan Simpang Raya* on Jalan Monunutu. There are hundreds of popular night stalls set up around the Merpati office.

Getting There & Away

Air Merpati connects Ternate with Ambon (154,500 rp) five times a week; Manado (96,200 rp) daily; Kao/Galela/Morotai (42,300/65,400/75,300 rp) on northern Halmahera irregularly; Gebe (107,100 rp); and Labuha on Pulau Bacan (69,700 rp). The

MALUKU

Merpati office (☎ 21651), at Jalan Bosoiri 2, is open Monday to Saturday from 8 am to 5 pm, and from 10 am to 12.30 pm Sunday.

With identical prices to Merpati, Bouraq (☎ 21288) is far more popular because it is simply more reliable. It flies to Ambon every day but Monday, and daily to Manado – and then on to Davao in the southern Philippines. Its office, at Jalan Ahmad Yani 131 next to the Chrysant Hotel, is open from 8 am to 5 pm every day. There is also a Bouraq agent (☎ 21327) in the Neraca Hotel.

Boat Ternate is a major port for northern Maluku – but take note of the different ports. Every two weeks the *Kerinci* goes to Ambon (24,000/82,000 rp for economy/1st class); and the *Ciremai* goes to Bitung in northern Sulawesi (15,200/51,200 rp) and to Sorong, Irian Jaya (24,200/89,200 rp). Once every four weeks, the *Tatamailau* goes to Bitung. These Pelni boats leave from the port in Kota Ternate. The Pelni office (☎ 21434) is in the port area.

Of the Perintis boats, the *Pahala* goes to Sanana, Namlea, Bacan, and Ambon; the *Nusa Perintis* links Ambon, Sanana and Mangole every week or so; and the *Baruna Dwipa* connects with Ambon, among other places. For Perintis boats, inquire at the Pelni office. The *Ternate Star* goes to Obi and Bacan islands three times a week; the *Ambera IV* goes to Tidore, Gebe and Sorong (among other places) every two weeks. Most of these boats leave from the port in Kota Ternate, where tickets can be bought.

Boats to Tidore, some to Bacan Island, and to Sidangoli leave from Bastiong (250 rp by bemo). Just to add to the confusion, there are two entrances to the Bastiong port – the first, as you come from Kota Ternate, has boats to Tidore and Bacan; the other, 300 metres further on, has the ferry to Sidangoli.

To/From Tobelo Overnight boats (which means you miss a lot of scenery) such as the *Agape Jaya* and *Garuda* go to Tobelo (15,000 rp; 15 hours) via Morotai (12,200 rp; 12 hours) every day or two; or every four weeks there's the Pelni liner *Tatamailau*.

These boats usually also go to Manado, northern Sulawesi (22,000 rp). All tickets are easily available in individual offices in or near the port in Kota Ternate.

To/From Sidangoli To Sidangoli, there are ferries from the (second) Bastiong port at 8 am and 1 pm. A combined ferry/bus ticket as far as Galela can be bought at several agencies at the (second) Bastiong port. There are speedboats, but these seem to be furtive – they do not leave from anywhere obvious, and will arrive from Sidangoli at a private jetty in Kota Ternate, such as one at the back of Toko Nelayan Jaya, opposite the Rumah Makan Gamalama.

To/From Tidore Take the bemo to the (first) Bastiong port. From there take a quick and regular speedboat (1000 rp), or a slower, less frequent wooden ferry (500 rp) to the port of Rum.

Getting Around
To/From the Airport Babullah airport is at Tarau, north of Kota Ternate. Charter a bemo for about 3000 to 5000 rp (bargain for less) or from the airport walk one km to the main road (or wait outside the nearby University) to pick up a public bemo for about 300 rp. You can also go with a hotel tout.

Bemo Ternate town is small and you can walk to all places in the central area. Bemos around town cost 200 rp. There are also horse and carts usually costing about 500 rp to any place in the central area.

AROUND PULAU TERNATE
It's easy to charter a bemo, or take individual public bemos, and visit all the sights around the island in one day starting north from Kota Ternate. The circular surfaced road (with mosques about every km) is well covered by public bemos but they are less regular in the west of the island. For instance, they go infrequently as far as Takome (550 rp) via the north, and to Togafo (750 rp) via the south, but not between the two villages because the area is mainly uninhabited. So

you can't completely circle the island by public bemo. Chartering a bemo – about 8000 rp per hour – will take at least three hours to quickly see the sights. Allow a lot longer to really explore the lakes, climb forts and take a swim.

Benteng Toloko

This small fort, built in 1512, is in better condition than the other forts on the island. A path leads off the airport road (north of the sultan's palace but south of the airport) down to Dufa-Dufa. Benteng Toloko lies on a rocky hill above the beach.

Batu Angus

Batu Angus (Burnt Rock) is a volcanic lava flow caused by an 18th-century eruption of the Gamalama volcano. There are black rocks heaped on to each other as far as you can see – great for a clamber around, and for views of Pulau Hiri. It's out past the airport and a bemo there will cost 200 rp.

Sulamadaha

Sulamadaha, near Ternate's northern tip, has the best beach (black sand) on the island. Walk to the left for 15 minutes over the rocks and headland to a tiny coral beach where the water is calm and safe for swimming and snorkelling. On Sunday it costs 300 rp to use the beach; there are a few drink and snack stalls. Public motorboats leave for the tiny villages on **Pulau Hiri** (2500 rp) from the Sulamadaha port a short walk from the beach. Just before the main beach is the friendly *Penginapan Pantai Indah* (☎ 21659) with clean rooms and mandi at 18,000 rp per person including three meals. Bemos to Sulamadaha cost 550 rp.

Danau Tolire

There are two volcanic crater lakes, Danau Tolire Kecil (Little Tolire Lake) and Danau Tolire Besar (Big Tolire Lake). The smaller one is next to a black-sand beach in a small park. The larger one is virtually opposite, and is more popular and beautiful. There is a pleasant walk around the larger lake. Bemos

to Takome (550 rp) reach this part of the island.

Afetaduma

This is a popular and clean black-sand beach, with drink and food for sale. It is especially crowded on Sunday, when you are far more likely to get a bemo there and back (750 rp).

Benteng Kastela

Built in 1522, this fort is next to the Kastela town mosque. It is fully overgrown, broken and virtually unrecognisable. Drive straight past to the next fort.

Danau Laguna

This volcanic, spring-fed lake, near Ngade, is covered with lotuses. A big whitewashed wall surrounds part of it. If the main entrance is closed, a dirt track leads down to the lake from the start of the wall as you come from Kota Ternate. Just past the main entrance to the lake is Taman Eva (entry fee 500 rp), a popular spot on Sundays with its pleasant gardens and splendid views across the bay to Tidore. You can scramble down to the rocks below and dive into the sea. Danau Laguna can be reached by bemo (250 rp).

Benteng Kayu Merah

One km from Bastiong is Red Wood Fort, also known as Benteng Kalumata. Constructed in 1540 by the Portuguese, it has a nice location but the stairs to the top are shaky. Take the Kalumata bemo for 250 rp.

Gunung Api Gamalama

This active volcano is, in fact, the entire island of Ternate. The most recent eruptions were in 1980, 1983, and in October 1994 when hot ash was sprayed 300 metres above the crater. Early detection of this eruption prevented any casualties.

Two tourists disappeared while hiking here without a guide a few years ago, so the local tourist office strongly urges climbers to report to them first. They will organise a guide for about 15,000 rp who will also help you find the impressively large 350-year-old clove tree, *cengkeh afo*, on the slopes. You

MALUKU

must report to the head of Marikurubu village for permission to climb, and to obtain the latest reports of volcanic activity. The climb will take from two to four hours, and is not difficult with some rests. The views of the volcano and the islands make it worthwhile.

PULAU TIDORE

Tidore, compared with Ternate, has had very similar influences from the outside world. Islam arrived in the middle of the 15th century and at the end of that century, the first ruler to take the title of 'sultan' assumed command. Tidore once claimed parts of Halmahera and a number of islands off the west coast of Irian Jaya. For a couple of centuries it rivalled Ternate for control of the spice trade.

Today, Tidore is a prosperous little island: hundreds of large, modern boats around the island attest to a lucrative fishing industry. The main road which links Rum to the main town of Soa Siu is virtually one long village; north from Soa Siu the island is far less populated.

Things to See & Do

A trip around the island can be completed in a couple of hours, just get off and on the bemos which regularly travel from Rum to Soa Siu (1000 rp; 40 minutes). There are less frequent bemos from Soa Siu to Maftutu in the north; and none from Maftutu back to Rum along the north – so you cannot completely circle the island without chartering.

From Rum, the port for ferries and speedboats to Ternate, there are great views of **Pulau Maitara** to which you can charter a sailboat and snorkel in the clear, blue waters. **Soa Siu** has a large, interesting market, which has some rumah makans and good baskets and weaving for sale. The decrepit ruin of Fort Tohula is not far away.

Irregular bemos leave from the Soa Siu market to the small, delightful village of **Gurabunga** perched on the side of **Gunung Api Keimatubu**. Go to the village head for current information on the volcano, and to

bargain for a guide. The climb can be tricky in parts and takes about five hours.

Festivals

On October 31 each year the Anniversary of Central Halmahera is held in Soa Siu with traditional performances and exhibitions.

Places to Stay

There is no need to stay in Tidore but if you want to there is the friendly *Losmen Jangi* (☎ 21131) on Jalan Malawat 32 in Soa Siu. Ask the bemo driver to drop you off.

Getting There & Away

From Bastiong on Ternate to Rum, there are quick and regular speedboats for 1000 rp, or the slower, less frequent ferry costs 500 rp.

Pulau Halmahera

The mainly Muslim people of Halmahera are, like the people of Ternate and Tidore, a mix of Portuguese, Gujarati (from western India), Arab, Malay and Dutch – a result of the long contact with foreign traders who came to this area in search of spices. The whole island is undeveloped, with only the northern part towards Morotai having any real infrastructure for travellers – the exception is the southern island of Bacan. An interesting, easy diversion for several days is to take a great boat ride to Morotai, then to Tobelo, from where you can catch the bus through Kao back to Ternate (or vice versa).

There was a severe earthquake, centred near Kao in the heart of northern Halmahera in early 1994 with many casualties. The road and airport near Kao were still badly damaged at the time of writing, but there is no other obvious evidence of damage, and nothing which could affect your travel there.

Getting There & Away

Air Frequent, cheaper bus/boat packages around the area have severely affected the popularity, and therefore the reliability of flights from Ternate. Officially there are

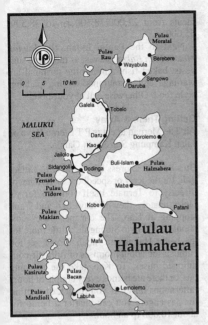

From the road you can often see huge ships and other WW II wrecks rusting in the bays.

SIDANGOLI

This is simply a place to catch your ferry, speedboat or bus between Ternate and northern Halmahera. From the ferry or speedboat, walk (10 minutes) or take a becak (to avoid the crush and get a bus seat earlier) for 250 rp to the bus terminal. Buses to Kao cost 12,500 rp and take two to three hours; and to Tobelo 15,000 rp and about five hours.

Getting off the bus from the north, you will be accosted by touts for the speedboats (they call them *spid*) and becak drivers. Take the speedboat (5000 rp; 30 minutes); it's quicker, more reliable and drops you off at an anonymous, unofficial jetty in Kota Ternate. The ferry from Sidangoli to Bastiong on Pulau Ternate leaves at 10.30 am and 3.30 pm (2500 rp), and does not necessarily connect with buses coming from the north. If the ferry has left, take the 'spid'.

KAO

Kao is not worth a stopover unless you have plenty of time or want to break up the six-hour slog between Tobelo and Ternate. It's unspoilt, friendly, with nothing to see or do, but there is a nice swimming beach nearby, which was a Japanese WW II base. Kao is literally only three dusty streets, with limited facilities and no daytime electricity, where a foreigner is a real attraction.

Places to Stay & Eat

Penginapan Dirgahayu has unexciting rooms with mandi (and plenty of mosquitoes) for 15,000 rp per person including three good meals or 12,500 rp without meals. The other losmen, *Sejahtera*, was destroyed in the earthquake but should be back in business offering similar conditions at a similar price. Your bus will drop you off at your losmen.

Next to the Dirgahayu, the *Dua Puteri* is the only place to eat. It serves basic Indonesian food, but seems to be open more for the frequent transiting bus passengers than the very few travellers staying at Kao.

Merpati flights from Ternate to Galela (65,400 rp) four times weekly; to Kao (42,300 rp) twice weekly; and to Morotai (75,300 rp) once a week – but don't count on them.

Boat About once a week, boats such as the *Garuda* connect Tobelo with Manado, Sulawesi (35,000 rp). Otherwise, all boats to northern Halmahera will start and finish in Ternate. The Pelni boat *Tatamailau* goes from Ternate to Tobelo and back once every four weeks. Bacan is well connected to nearby islands and to Ambon.

Getting Around

The recently completed road in northern Halmahera makes this the only part of Maluku with a longish bus route. (Maluku boasts 79 seaports, 25 airports and only 390 km of roads.) The road between Tobelo and Galela is the newest and best; between Tobelo and Kao it is quite bad in places; and is slightly better between Kao and Sidangoli.

Getting There & Away
Air If you want to fly from Kao to Kota Ternate or Pulau Morotai, the Merpati agent is P T Eterna Raya (no telephone). The airport was damaged during the earthquake, but should reopen.

Bus The road between Tobelo and Kao is often terrible, but serviceable. To get to Sidangoli, it's best to book a bus seat (12,500 rp) while in Tobelo. Buses like the comfortable Halmahera Indah can be booked at Toko Gelatik Utama (☎ 21034) on Jalan Kemakmuran, Tobelo. The bus will pick you up at your losmen in Kao at 6.30 am or 9.30 am – ie about 2½hours after it leaves Tobelo (at 4 and 7 am).

To head north to Tobelo, you can wait and hope for a seat on the Sidangoli-Tobelo-Galela express or take one of the irregular bemos.

TOBELO
Tobelo is a town on the move: it is the transport hub for buses and boats servicing northern Halmahera and Morotai, and there is a banana plantation nearby which ships bananas directly to Japan. The main street, with virtually everything you need, is Jalan Kemakmuran, part of the main road south to Kao and north to Galela. There are banks but they are very reluctant to change money.

Places to Stay & Eat
Penginapan Megaria on Jalan Bayankara (near the President Hotel) costs 10,000 rp per person with mandi or 7500 rp with shared mandi – no meals available. The *Hotel Karunia* (☎ 21202), on Jalan Kemakmuran, costs 15,000 rp per person with food or 9000 rp without.

The *Pantai Indah* (☎ 21068), just off the main street, on Jalan Iman Sideba, is friendly, with sea views. Singles/doubles with a fan cost 22,000/38,500 rp or 33,000/49,500 rp with air-con, including three large, varied meals. On the main street, the new but characterless *President Hotel* (☎ 21231) has a restaurant and modern, clean rooms with

meals from 22,000/38,500 rp to 38,500/ 55,000 rp.

Next to the Pantai Indah, the *Rumah Makan Ikan Bakar*, serves, as the name suggests, baked fish. Around the terminal are warungs and restaurants serving padang-style food. Otherwise, eat at your hotel.

Getting There & Away
Air The Merpati agent is P T Eterna Raya on Jalan Kampung Soa Siu in Galela.

Bus Several express buses travel to Sidangoli, for the ferry or speedboat to Ternate, or directly to Ternate itself (on the ferry). Unfortunately, they *all* leave at 4 and 7 am, stopping at Kao. The cheaper buses cost about 12,500 rp to Sidangoli, a little more for the better Halmahera Indah. Don't get too enthusiastic about promises of fully air-conditioned buses. To Kao, take the morning bus, or there are bemos every couple of hours (afternoons only). If you're sick of waiting for passengers you can charter a bemo for about 10,000 rp an hour.

Boat Tobelo is well serviced, with boats every couple of days to Ternate (15,000 rp) via Morotai (3500 rp) and often on to Manado (31,500 rp). There are weekly boats, like the *Merpati*, which connect with villages along north-eastern Halmahera.

Getting Around
Tobelo is easy to walk around, although taking one of the many becaks is useful to get from the port or the bus terminal to your hotel (500 rp). To visit the nearby beaches or islands from the port, motorboats will cost about 10,000 rp one way, or canoes about 2500 rp.

GALELA
Galela, a very sleepy Muslim village, is a worthy side trip north of Tobelo by bemo (45 minutes; 1000 rp). The road is new and lined with lovely palm trees and beaches – it's worth going just for the scenery. Along the way, there are some hot water springs (*air panas*) at the village of Mamuya; ask your

bemo driver to drop you off. Nearby are the Duma and Pive lakes created from the eruptions of the still-active Mamuju volcano.

There is nowhere to stay or eat in Galela. The Merpati agent is on Jalan Kampung Soa Siu (no telephone). A taxi from the Galela airport to Tobelo (the nearest accommodation) will cost 7500 rp, or 4000 rp just to Galela.

PULAU MOROTAI

Morotai island was an important air base during WW II for the Allies, and a headquarters for General MacArthur's forces. Now it's a sparsely populated 1600-sq-km island of unexplored tropical beaches, unused WW II airports and wrecks, and unspoilt diving sites. The major town and transport centre, Daruba, a drab, poor village where a European is a strange sight, has few facilities. For good wrecks for diving or exploring above water, ask your losmen or around the port. You will need to charter local boats to get to most places on the island, which is costly.

Penginapan Panber (no telephone) is an unsigned, light yellow building along Jalan Yasan, with passable rooms for 7500 rp per person including meals. *Penginapan Angkasa*, and *Penginapan Tonga* further out on Daruba beach, offer similar prices and

facilities. There is almost nowhere else to eat.

The Merpati agent is P T Puskopau in Auri. Every day or so, boats such as the *Garuda* and *Agape Jaya* leave Daruba for Tobelo (3500 rp), and then travel overnight to Ternate (12,500 rp). There is only one main road on the island, from Daruba to Dao, with plans for an extension as far as Berebere. Boats are still the only method of local transport.

PULAU BACAN

Bacan Island is the only part of southern Halmahera, and the adjoining islands, serviced by air and regular boat. Bacan offers some accommodation in **Labuha**: the *Pondok Indah* on Jalan Usman Shah, the *Borero Indah* on Jalan Tanah Abang, and the *Harmonis Inn* on Jalan Molon Junga. Beside Labuha, the only other major town is the port of Babang.

Babang is well connected by regular boats to Ambon and to the nearby Sula Islands (Sanana and Mangole). Several boats connect Bacan to Ternate daily – a gorgeous trip featuring spectacular mountain, volcanic and island scenery. There are flights from Labuha to Sanana (96,200 rp), Ambon (146,500 rp) and Ternate (70,100 rp). The Merpati office is at Toko Rinomar, Labuha.

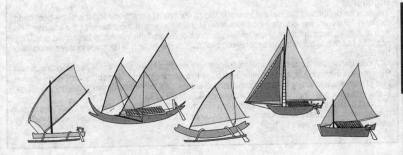

Irian Jaya

Irian Jaya presents spectacular mountains and jungle, wonderful bird life, little-known peoples who have had minimal contact with the outside world, great trekking opportunities, and some well developed coastal towns. More travellers are now going to Irian Jaya, particularly with direct Garuda flights to Biak from Los Angeles. Most visitors include a trip to the Baliem Valley, the only part of the interior which is open, accessible and developed.

HISTORY

When the Portuguese sighted the island now divided between Irian Jaya and Papua New Guinea, they called it Ilhas dos Papuas ('the island of the fuzzy hairs'), from the Malay word *papuwah*. Later Dutch explorers called it New Guinea because the black-skinned people reminded them of the people of Guinea in Africa. Towards the end of the last century the island was divided between the Dutch (western half), the Germans (north-east quarter) and the British (south-east quarter).

Irian is a word from the Biak language, and means 'hot land rising from the sea'. Under the Dutch, Irian Jaya was known as Dutch New Guinea and when sovereignty was transferred to Indonesia the Indonesians renamed it Irian Jaya (*jaya* means 'victorious'). Papuan anti-Indonesian rebel forces in the province refer to it as West Papua New Guinea; other names are West Irian and West Papua.

Highlights

There is no doubt that the Baliem Valley is the major tourist attraction (and therefore becoming touristy) for its unique culture and treks among the valleys and mountains of the interior. The Asmat region, among the swamps on the southern coast and the interior, is becoming gradually popular; but this is difficult and expensive to explore properly, and is far, far less developed than the Baliem.

Along the northern coast are several surprisingly modern cities. Only some like Manokwari and Biak are worth staying at, and for using as a base to enjoy the nearby wildlife (including the elusive bird of paradise), scenery, beaches and diving. Sentani, a better alternative to nearby Jayapura, is the place for boat trips around the magnificent Sentani Lake.

Don't underestimate the size of Irian Jaya and the amount of time and money it will take to see these places. To really experience what Irian Jaya has to offer will take at least three weeks by plane; three times longer by boat. ∎

Irian Jaya

In 1660, the Dutch recognised the Sultan of Tidore's sovereignty over New Guinea – and since the Dutch held power over Tidore, New Guinea was theoretically theirs. The British were interested too, but in 1824 Britain and the Netherlands agreed that the Dutch claim to the western half should stand. In 1828, the Dutch established a token settlement on the Bird's Head Peninsula. In the mid-19th century, missionaries started setting up shop.

After WW II, the Dutch used New Guinea as a place of exile, setting up the Boven Digul camp upriver from Merauke as a prison for Indonesian nationalists. As far back as the mid-1930s, however, the US Standard Oil Company was drilling for oil in West Irian, and the Japanese had also done some covert oil exploration. Even at the outbreak of WW II, Dutch authority was confined mainly to the coasts.

After the war the Dutch were forced to withdraw from Indonesia but clung to West Irian. In an attempt to keep the Indonesians out, the Dutch actually encouraged Irian Jayan nationalism and began building schools and colleges to train Papuans in professional skills with the aim of preparing them for self-rule by 1970.

Indonesia Takes Over

Ever since WW II many Indonesian factions – whether Communist, Soekarnoist or Soehartoist – had claimed the western side

WW II In Irian Jaya

After the bombing of Pearl Harbour, the Dutch declared war on Japan, so Irian Jaya, then part of the Dutch Indies, inevitably became an important part of the battle for the Pacific. Ironically, some Indonesians welcomed the Japanese as Asian liberators who would get rid of the hated Dutch colonialists.

In early 1944, the first of a four phase push, led by General Douglas MacArthur, commenced from New Guinea (now Papua New Guinea) to liberate Dutch New Guinea (as it was called) from Japanese occupation. The Allies were far from optimistic: this part of the world was almost completely undeveloped, inhospitable and uncharted.

Phase one was the capture of Hollandia (Jayapura). The biggest amphibious operation of the war in the South-Western Pacific, it involved 80,000 Allied troops, starting from a base at Aitape hundreds of miles east into New Guinea. The airfields at Hollandia were bombed by the Allies, the city then rebuilt and the deep Humboldt Bay (now Jayapura Bay) became a major naval base. There are now several WW II monuments around the Jayapura area, including one overlooking the magnificent Lake Sentani. Rusting wrecks can be seen along beaches near Jayapura, such as Hamadi.

The second phase – to capture Sarmi (now a transmigration town connected by road to Jayapura) via the tiny island of Wakde, where there were Japanese airfields – saw some strong fighting from the Japanese. The third phase was the taking of Biak Island – primarily to control the airfield (now the busy domestic and international airports) – and nearby Numfoor Island on the way to Sorong. Several hard battles were fought on Biak Island, not assisted by a severe underestimation by Allied intelligence of the Japanese strength. At Bosnik beach, there is a very long tunnel – unexplored since 1944 – which reaches a cave just north of Kota Biak. The cave is worth a visit; it shows obvious devastation by Allied bombing, and has rusting Japanese weapons.

By mid-1944, the Japanese knew they were losing the war and withdrew to Sansapor (now just an ordinary transmigration town) between Sorong and Manokwari – both of which have small Japanese memorials. The fourth and final phase was the continually successful push to the Japanese air bases on Morotai Island in northern Maluku, and then towards the Philippines.

The southern coast of Irian Jaya was relatively ignored by the Japanese as being virtually impossible to traverse. In early 1943, the largest Japanese base along the southern coast was near Kokenau, south of Enarotali. Merauke was continually bombed by the Japanese, but later reinforced by Allied troops who feared Merauke may be used as an air base for attacks against nearby Australia. Australian air-force radio bases were established at Yos Sudarso Island, Merauke and in Tanahmerah. The Allies won several minor battles along the coast towards Fakfak which eventually forced the Japanese out. ■

of the island as their own. Their argument was that all the former Dutch East Indies should be included in the new Indonesian republic. Throughout 1962 Indonesian forces infiltrated the area, but with little success. The Papuan population failed to welcome them as liberators, and either attacked them or handed them over to the Dutch. It was US pressure which forced the Dutch to capitulate abruptly in August 1962.

A vaguely worded 1962 agreement under United Nations (UN) auspices essentially required that Indonesia allow the Papuans of West Irian to determine, by the end of 1969, whether they wanted independence or to remain within the Indonesian republic. This 'Act of Free Choice' (or 'Act Free of Choice' as it became known) was held in 1969, 'supervised' by the UN. The Indonesian government announced that it would use the procedure of *musyawarah* under which a consensus of 'elders' is reached. In July 1969, the Indonesian government announced that the assemblies in Merauke, Jayawijaya and Paniai districts, in which the greater part of the West Irian population lives, had unanimously decided to become part of Indonesia.

Papuan Opposition

Even before the Act, the Indonesians faced violent opposition from the Papuans. In 1967, aircraft were used to bomb and strafe Arfak tribespeople threatening Manokwari town on the Bird's Head Peninsula but the fighting continued into 1969. In the same year rebellions broke out on the island of Biak and at Enarotali in the highlands. In 1977, there was serious conflict in the highlands around the Baliem Valley and Tembagapura, site of the US-run Freeport copper mine. Bombs damaged Freeport installations and cut the pipeline which takes copper concentrates to the coast. In 1981, there was heavy fighting in the Enarotali region, and in early 1984, the consequences of an attempted uprising centred on Jayapura sent thousands of Irians fleeing into PNG.

The Irians are provoked by a number of factors, among them the taking of their land

for logging, mining or other commercial purposes; transmigration, which is bringing large numbers of western Indonesians to Irian Jaya; attempts to 'Indonesianise' the locals by schooling, propaganda, and even some efforts to make them forsake their traditional attire and wear 'proper clothes'; extremely brutal Indonesian responses to conflict, protest or even uncooperativeness; and total intolerance of political dissent.

The chief anti-Indonesian guerrilla force is known as the Free Papua Movement (Organisasi Papua Merdeka or OPM). It appears to have been set up just after West Irian was handed over to the Indonesians, but there seems to be neither a single leader nor a unified command. The number of active members goes up and down: in the late '80s there were perhaps 500, mainly in the northeast of Irian Jaya. In the mid-80s, an OPM group managed to 'occupy' a 10-km-wide strip of territory on the Indonesian side of the PNG border near Mindip Tanah, south of the highlands, but activity there has since waned. Today, the group is inactive, and represents a negligible threat to the Indonesian government.

Refugees

Since the Indonesian takeover many Irians have fled to PNG as a result of Indonesian (or sometimes OPM) violence, or the fear of it. The biggest exodus occurred in 1984 when over 10,000 people fled to PNG after the abortive OPM uprising that year. Many of these were from Jayapura and included intellectuals, public servants, police, army deserters, students and their families.

Most of these refugees have ended up in camps not very far inside PNG territory – camps whose connections with the OPM provoked tension between the PNG and Indonesian governments. Indonesia complained that the camps harboured OPM activists; PNG complained about Indonesian armed incursions into its territory in pursuit of the OPM. There have been attempts by both sides to get refugees to go back to Irian Jaya – some have even been forced to do so by PNG – but most are reluctant for fear of what will happen to them. In 1987, there were an estimated 11,000 Irians in camps in PNG.

Transmigration

The Indonesian policies which provoked Papuan unrest continue. In 1988, according to official figures, about 8% of Irian Jaya's population had arrived on government transmigration schemes. Another 180,000 or so western Indonesians had come as independent settlers. So far the transmigrants are mostly grouped near main towns like Jayapura, Merauke (which has a surprisingly Javanese feel to it), Manokwari, Nabire and Sorong.

As Irian Jaya represents almost 21% of Indonesia's total territory, but has less than 1% (1.5 million) of its population, the Indonesian government continues to plan to move hundreds of thousands to Irian Jaya from overcrowded provinces in Java, Bali and Sulawesi. A number of observers, noting the poor locations and lack of planning for many existing settlements, have concluded that the main thrust of transmigration to Irian Jaya is less for the benefit of the transmigrants than to make the province truly Indonesian.

GEOGRAPHY

A central east-west mountain range is the backbone of Irian Jaya and Papua New Guinea. It reaches its maximum altitude in the west, with Puncak Jaya the highest peak (5050 metres). This and other Irian Jayan peaks such as Puncak Mandala have permanent snowfields and small glaciers. Alpine grasslands, jagged bare peaks, montane forests which include pines, foothill rainforests, ferocious rivers, gentle streams, stunning rock faces and gorges add to the varying landscape of the highlands. The most heavily populated, cultivated and developed areas of the Irian highlands are the Paniai Lake district and the Baliem Valley to the east.

South of the mountains is a coastal plain, widest in the east at the border with PNG; there are sago swamps and low-lying alluvial plains of fine-grained fertile soil, though it gets drier (with vegetation not unlike northern Australia) in the far eastern section around Merauke. The northern coastal plain is much narrower and less swampy, with larger-than-life tropical vegetation – real jungle. There are coconut-palm-fringed white sandy beaches on the north coast and the offshore islands of Biak, Numfoor and Yapen.

FLORA & FAUNA

Irian Jaya's flora is as varied as its geography. Three-quarters of the land is covered in impenetrable tropical rainforest, with the usual luxurious collection of Asiatic species and some which are endemic to the island, which is in the transition zone between Asia and Australia. The south coast's vegetation includes mangroves and sago palms (eg around the Asmat region) plus eucalypts, paperbarks and acacias in the drier eastern section. Highland vegetation ranges from alpine grasslands and heath to unique pine forests, bush and scrub.

Land animals are largely confined to marsupials, some indigenous, others also found in Australia. These include marsupial 'mice' and 'cats', bandicoots, ring-tailed possums, pygmy flying phalangers, big cuscuses, tree kangaroos and, in the south-east, wallabies. Reptiles include snakes, frill-necked and monitor lizards, and crocodiles. The spiny anteater is also found. Insects are abundant, particularly the colourful butterflies. Despite large-scale plunder, Irian Jaya's exquisite bird life is still famous. There are more than 600 species including the elusive bird of paradise, bowerbirds, cockatoos, parrots and lorikeets, kingfishers, crowned pigeons and cassowaries.

VISAS & DOCUMENTS

If you arrive at Biak's international airport (ie on a Garuda flight from the USA) you get the regular 60-day tourist pass stamped in your passport. To enter by sea or at any other airport – for example, flying in to Jayapura from PNG – you'll need an Indonesian visa before you arrive.

Saltwater crocodile

Travel Permits

Unless some political upheaval alters the picture, you can travel to, but not far from, the main northern coastal cities – eg Sorong, Manokwari, Biak and Jayapura/Sentani – without any permit, but to go elsewhere you need a *surat jalan*. You obtain this from a police station, which is particularly easy to do in Jayapura and Biak. If you're heading straight to Wamena, the most convenient place to get your surat jalan is in Sentani, the town near Jayapura's airport.

You must provide two passport-size photos and state where you want to go (and include everywhere you *may* go). They take about an hour or so to process, usually with an 'administration fee' of about 2000 rp. Don't be concerned: the police are invariably helpful and friendly, and are as bored with the paperwork as you are. Some parts of Irian Jaya are still off limits to tourists. The situation is fluid: police stations will tell you where you can and cannot go.

Take at least a dozen photocopies of your surat jalan because every village police chief will want a copy and because the back of your original will soon be full of stamps. Make sure you report to the police in each village whether you're staying or just passing through: it is only 10 minutes of paperwork, and it is not worth upsetting local authorities.

MONEY

Make sure you change plenty of money before heading into the interior. There are banks for travellers' cheques and sometimes advances on credit cards in larger Irian Jayan cities, but at places besides these getting money can be difficult. Cigarettes are a form

of currency in Wamena and other parts of Irian Jaya, such as the Asmat region. The locals love them, and they can be traded or just given away to make friends. Stock up on the cheapest brand of cigarettes and carry a cigarette lighter, even if you don't smoke.

BOOKS

Peter Matthiessen's *Under the Mountain Wall* (Collins Harvill, London, 1989), based on his long visit to the Baliem in 1961, chronicles his daily life among the Kurulu tribe. Robert Mitton's *The Lost World of Irian Jaya* (Oxford University Press, Melbourne, 1983) looks like a coffee-table book, and was compiled from his letters, diaries, maps and photographs after his sudden death in 1976. The book bitterly criticizes the reckless way in which the Irians have been shoved into the modern world.

Indonesia's Secret War: The Guerilla Struggle in Irian Jaya (Allen & Unwin, 1985), by Robin Osborne, is a documented account of events up to 1984; and *West Papua: the Obliteration of a People* (TAPOL, London, 1988), by Carmel Budiardjo & Liem Soei Liong, is also worth reading. George Monbiot's *Poisoned Arrows* (Michael Joseph, London, 1989) details a remarkable journey to the wilds of Irian Jaya with the objective of uncovering the truth about transmigration, the plight of the refugees and the true nature of the OPM resistance.

The Asmat (Museum of Primitive Art, New York, 1967) is a collection of photographs of the Asmat people (who live on the south coast) and their art, taken by Michael Rockefeller in 1961. Rockefeller disappeared on his second trip to Irian Jaya after his boat overturned at the mouth of the Betsj

River. Circumstances indicate that he may have been eaten by head-hunters.

GETTING THERE & AWAY
Air
Biak is the transport hub of Irian Jaya. Garuda flies there from the USA (and possibly from Tokyo in the future) and Garuda, Merpati, Sempati (and soon, Bouraq) connect Irian Jaya with all parts of Indonesia. Sorong and Jayapura are the other major transport centres. All flights to southern coastal cities in Irian Jaya go through Jayapura or Sorong.

To/From PNG The only way to visit PNG is by plane: there are no boats, and the border remains closed. There are two weekly return flights from Vanimo, just over the border in PNG, to Jayapura. Vanimo is connected to Port Moresby by internal PNG flights and you can book onward tickets in Jayapura. PNG visa restrictions are strict, so be prepared. (See the Jayapura section for more details.)

Boat
Transmigration to Irian Jaya has greatly increased sea links with the rest of Indonesia. Large Pelni liners, such as the *Tatamailau*, connect the rest of Indonesia with Irian Jaya's northern towns as far as Jayapura. Pelni boats, and other more basic boats, link the southern coast as far as Merauke, with the more remote islands of southern Maluku.

GETTING AROUND
The incredible impenetrable jungles and mountains of Irian Jaya (which you can only appreciate by flying over them) mean there are no roads between major towns. (There is talk of a road being built between Jayapura and Wamena.) Boats are slow, irregular, and can be uncomfortable, so flying is a popular option.

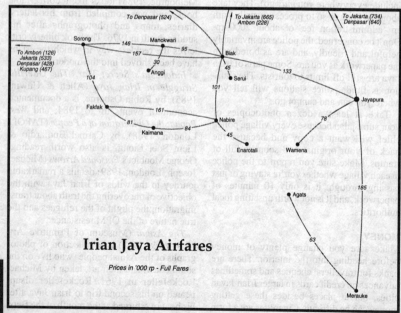

Irian Jaya Airfares

Prices in '000 rp - Full Fares

Air

Merpati still carries the bulk of traffic from major Indonesian centres to, and then within, Irian Jaya. To get to more remote parts which even Merpati doesn't reach – or occasionally as a substitute if Merpati is full or doesn't turn up – you can use flights run by the various missionary or cargo services. These cover a truly amazing network of 200-plus airstrips – nearly all grass and many on steep slopes in narrow valleys – all over Irian Jaya. They will accept passengers if they have room, but their primary concern is missionary business, and their prices are often more expensive than official airlines. Book as far ahead as possible (at least a week in advance is recommended) though you might be lucky enough to get a flight sooner. You can often also charter their planes.

The two main mission flight organisations are the Protestant-run Mission Aviation Fellowship (MAF) and the Catholic-run Associated Mission Aviation (AMA). Both have offices at Sentani airport, near Jayapura, and at other major centres where their schedules and price lists are usually posted.

Boat

Don't underestimate the size of Irian Jaya and the time it takes to travel by boat; eg from

---

Native Languages of Irian Jaya

Estimates of the number of different languages in Irian Jaya vary from 200 to over 700; nobody can really decide, and there is very little study on the linguistics in the region. There is no doubt, however, that Irian Jaya, and neighbouring Papua New Guinea, with a combined population of only a few million, speak an inordinately high percentage of the world's languages.

Since the takeover by Indonesia over 30 years ago, and because of transmigration to the region, Bahasa Indonesia has spread quickly throughout Irian Jaya through schools, media and bureaucracy. As a result there are few people in Irian Jaya, except the older, uneducated in isolated areas, who do not have at least a working knowledge of Indonesian.

The normal traveller to Irian Jaya may come across the following native languages. In the Baliem Valley, approximately 170,000 people speak either Western Dani (with at least five major dialects) which is found west of Wamena; Grand Valley Dani, found in, and to the south and north of Wamena; Yali; South Ngalik spoken towards Asmat; or North Ngalik to the east. In the Asmat region, the main language is generally referred to as Asmat (the main dialect is Kawenak) with maybe 55,000 speakers. Around Jayapura, there are several village languages like Tobati/Yotafa and Ormu, but this is a developed city run by non-Irianese.

Near Sentani, the major native language is Sentani, with about eight dialects and 6000 known speakers. Around the Bird's Head Peninsula there is Moi (particularly common around Sorong), Brat and Hattam; the latter is spoken in Manokwari, along with the Biak language. Yava is spoken on Biak and Yapen islands.

The Biak language is regarded as a lingua franca from Biak island to islands beyond Sorong. Near Merauke, the major native language is Marind.

In the unlikely event that you may need to use a native language, or want to impress an indigenous Irianese, here is a list of some common words:

	Marind	Yava	Asmat	Western Dani	Biak	Grand Valley Dani	Sentani	Moi
one	izakod	utabo	cowak	ambe	oser	opake-a	emba	mele
two	inah	jiru	yamno	bere	suru	pere	be	ali
you (s)	oh	vein	or	kat	au	kat	we	—
you (p	eoh	wea	car	kit	mko	—	me	metobou
we	nok	reia	ndar	nit	ingo	nit	meye	papetebo
I	nok	rei	ndor	an	aya	an	deye	tit
good	waninga	—	akat	op	bye	hano	foy	pobok
man	anem	ana	yipic	ap	man	ap	do	dala
name	igiz	tam	yuwus	etaxe	snon	eraxe	do	kedi
eat	havi	rais	anna	ne	kan	nan	anaiko	wak

Sorong to Jayapura will take several days, as will any boat out of Merauke to go anywhere. Pelni liners service the northern coastal towns all the way to Jayapura, and the southern coast to Merauke. To smaller towns and islands, boats are less regular, and less comfortable. Large cargo and passenger ships ply the southern coast and go as far inland as Bade and even Tanahmerah, along the Digul River.

Bird's Head Peninsula

SORONG

Sorong is the westernmost point of Irian Jaya. Since the 1930s, it has been a centre for oil exploration, and is now just a long, uninteresting port, as well as a centre for local transmigration. There is really little in the town or around the nearby countryside to interest the traveller.

Orientation

Sorong is a sprawling town, with no city centre. Most hotels and restaurants are in a small, compact area bordered by Jalan Sam Ratulangi and the esplanade of Jalan Ahmad Yani. Banks and government offices are spread out over a large area six km further away.

Information

The best two banks are Bank ExIm and BRI, both along Jalan Ahmad Yani. They are closed on Sunday. The police station (☎ 21929) is on Jalan Basuki Rahmat. No surat jalan is currently needed for Sorong or Manokwari. The post office is also way out of town on Jalan Ahmad Yani. Immigration (☎ 21393) is on Jalan Pompa Air Minum. You will need a bemo to get to all of these offices.

Beaches

About six km from Sorong, **Pantai Casuari** offers a good beach and some snorkelling, but it's not on any regular transport route, so you have to charter a bemo for about 8000

rp one way. There is a beach on **Pulau Jefman**, not too far from the airport.

Islands

Near Sorong, there are a multitude of islands, but with no regular transport linking them.

Pulau Waigeo claims to house the bird of paradise, but to get there involves at least five hours by chartered boat and then several days of trekking, carrying all your supplies. Closer islands such as **Pulau Buaya** (Crocodile Island – named for its shape, not its inhabitants) can be reached by chartering boats from Sorong for about 30,000 rp return. Tours to visit pearl farms there can be arranged with local travel agencies.

Pulau Doom, a small, friendly nearby island, can be reached by public boat for 300 rp, or by charter for 3000 rp per boat from a dock near the Hotel Indah. It takes about 40 minutes to walk around the island. (But beware, there seems to be more 'hello misters' here per second than in most other places in Indonesia!)

Tugu Arfak

This is a small unimpressive Japanese WW II memorial (also known as Tugu Jepang) in an area of Sorong with nice views. Walk a steep 500 metres along Jalan Arfak from the roundabout on the corner of Jalan Sam Ratulangi and then ask for directions; it's at the end of an unmarked goat trail.

Places to Stay

Sorong is an expensive town catering more for business people than tourists – there is no cheap accommodation. But there are several nice hotels which offer good economy singles/doubles (fan only) from about 20,000/25,000 rp including tax and breakfast, and air-con rooms for about 30,000/40,000 rp. These include the *Irian Beach Hotel* (☎ 23782), on Jalan Yos Sudarso, which has a lovely ocean setting; *Hotel Memberamo* (☎ 21564), Jalan Sam Ratulangi 35, which is friendly but has poor plumbing; the older *Hotel Batanta* (☎ 21569) on Jalan G Tamraul which has some character but dingy rooms; and the *Hotel Indah*

(☎ 21514), conveniently opposite the small boat dock, which offers cheaper, large rooms with good views.

The *Hotel Cenderawasih* (☎ 22367), Jalan Sam Ratulangi 54, offers comfortable singles/doubles with TV, fridge and breakfast at a very negotiable 50,000/55,000 rp, including tax.

The newest and flashiest place, mainly for foreign workers, is the *Grand Pacific Hotel* (☎ 22631) at Jalan Raja Ampat 105; rooms start at 85,000/105,000 rp, plus 21% tax.

Places to Eat

The *Padang Saiyo* on the roundabout at the top of Jalan Arfak does good padang-style food. The hotels all offer good Chinese and great seafood: the *Cenderawasih* has a great selection and huge prawns; the *Memberamo* is cheaper but has less choice; the *Grand Pacific* is more expensive but pleasant enough; and the *Irian Beach* offers one of the best sunset views you will ever see. Next door, the recommended *Lido Kuring* serves cheap, fresh seafood.

Getting There & Away

Air Sorong is well connected. There are daily direct flights to/from: Ambon (125,900 rp); Denpasar (428,400 rp); Jakarta (532,900 rp); and Jayapura (except Tuesday; 275,500 rp). There are less regular direct flights to Manado (204,000 rp); Fakfak (103,900 rp); Manokwari (145,700 rp); and Biak (156,600 rp). The Merpati office (☎ 23780, 21402 after hours) is in the Grand Pacific, and is open from 8 am to 6 pm daily except Sunday.

Boat Every two weeks, the Pelni ship *Dobonsolo* goes to Ambon (25,000/90,000 rp for economy/1st class) and Manokwari (16,500/66,500 rp); and the *Ciremai* goes to Manokwari and Ternate, Maluku (23,500/89,500 rp).

Every four weeks, the *Tatamailau* goes to Fakfak (15,000/60,000 rp) and Manokwari. The *Iweri*, on its semicircle from Jayapura to Merauke, also stops here every three weeks. The Pelni office (☎ 21716) and Pelni dock is on Jalan Ahmad Yani several km from the

Hotel Indah (take a bemo). Tickets are only available in the morning of the day before departure.

Getting Around

To/From the Airport Jefman airport is on Pulau Jefman, 18 km from Sorong. After arrival, walk with everyone else to the dock for the exhilarating 30-minute shared speedboat trip to Sorong. The ride should cost 5000 rp, but make absolutely sure before you leave that you will not be charged for chartering the whole boat at 10 times the normal cost. An unreliable ferry leaves Pulau Jefman at 9.30 am and 4 pm, takes one hour, but may not be there when you arrive.

Returning to the airport is potentially more difficult and/or expensive. The ferry (if it's not broken or being chartered) leaves from the Pulau Jefman ferry dock (500 rp port tax), a bemo ride away, at 6 am and 2.30 pm. If you have no luck with the ferry, try the Pulau Doom dock (opposite the Hotel Indah) for shared speedboats (which may break down anyway!) for about 5000 rp per person. Allow plenty of time to find a boat and for it to fill up; and bargain.

Twin-Otter flights to Fakfak leave from the Minland airport, five km from Sorong. Regular bemos go there for 350 rp.

Local Transport Yellow bemos (called *taksis*) will pass you every few seconds along the two or three main roads, including the various ports, for about 350 rp a trip. There is no need to take a one-person taxi anywhere as they will charge about 10,000 rp for one short trip.

MANOKWARI

Manokwari is the other main town on the Bird's Head Peninsula. As a town, and as a base for diving and trekking trips (see Teluk Cenderawasih), Manokwari has more to offer, and is more pleasant and cooler than Sorong.

Orientation

Manokwari is compact and easy to explore. Most of the town hugs the small bay, along

Jalan Yos Sudarso which heads to the airport, and Jalan Siliwangi which heads towards some pleasant beaches. The large mountains hugging the town are called *Breibe* in the local Arfak language.

Information
The best bank is Bank ExIm on Jalan Merdeka, or try the bank near the lane to the market and bemo terminal. No surat jalan is needed for Manokwari, but you may need one if you're heading into the nearby countryside; ask at the police station (☎ 21365) on Jalan Bayangkhara. Your hotel may ask for copies of your passport – have some photocopies ready (these are handy to have throughout Irian Jaya anyway). Immigration (☎ 21189) is at Jalan Merdeka 9. There is a post office near the Hotel Mulia and another just past the Pelni office.

Tugu Jepang & Taman Gunung Meja
The Japanese WW II Memorial (Tugu

Jepang) itself is of little interest, but the location (in the delightful Table Mountain (Gunung Meja) Park) does offer great views of Manokwari. To get there, head up the road behind Hotel Arfak. The memorial is about a one-km steep climb from the start of the park, at the end of an unmarked trail on the left. Continue along the main well-marked trail for the rest of the reasonably flat five-km walk through some lovely protected forest, with birds and butterflies (and, unfortunately, some mosquitoes). At the end of the trail, you reach some housing (for the University of Cenderawasih), from where you can catch a bemo back to town. You can avoid the initial steep climb by doing the walk in reverse, but the western entrance of the park is harder to find without a guide (or ask a lot of directions).

Gua Jepang
These caves are more a series of tunnels built by the Japanese in WW II. One entrance to

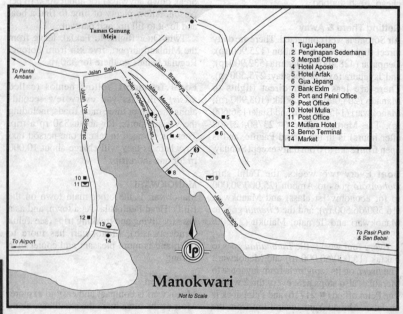

look at, but not really explore too far, is on the lane leading up from the port to Hotel Arfak.

Beaches

Pasir Sen Bebai and the adjacent Pasir Putih ('white sand') are pleasant, if not a little untidy, beaches. Take a bemo from the terminal for 400 rp. Beware of Pantai Amban to the north which reportedly has sea lice.

Places to Stay

There are very few cheap places here. All prices include tax and breakfast. At Jalan Bandung 154, *Penginapan Sederhana* (☎ 21263) – which means, aptly, 'simple inn' – has singles/doubles for 13,200/19,200 rp.

Opposite Merpati, on Jalan Kota Baru, is the friendly *Hotel Apose* (no telephone) with rooms for 8000/16,000 rp with fan and outside bathroom, and air-con rooms for 25,000/35,000 rp.

Clean, friendly and quiet (except for the nearby mosque) is the *Hotel Mulia* (☎ 21320) on Jalan Yos Sudarso with fan-cooled rooms for 19,800/27,000 rp and air-con rooms for 25,000/35,000 rp.

The old Dutch *Hotel Arfak* (☎ 21293) at Jalan Brawijaya 8 is decaying and no longer good value – economy rooms (no fan or bathroom) start from 16,500/22,000 rp and 'VIP rooms' from 27,500/41,250 rp.

In the top range the new *Mutiara Hotel* (☎ 21777) on Jalan Yos Sudarso is good value with rooms starting at 60,500/78,650 rp with air-con and TV.

Places to Eat

There is not a great choice of places to eat. The *Mutiara* serves good but overpriced Chinese and Indonesian food. For authentic Javanese food, try the *Sopo Nyono* and *Sukasari* restaurants on Jalan Trikora, not far from the airport. Several cheap Indonesian *rumah makans* (restaurants) are along Jalan Sudirman, and there are plenty of warungs (food stalls) near the terminal and market.

Getting There & Away

Air Merpati flies directly to/from Anggi on Wednesday and Friday (30,200 rp; 20

minutes); to Biak daily except Saturday (95,100 rp); and to Sorong (146,000 rp) on Wednesday and Saturday. Flights to Numfoor leave only from Biak. The Merpati office (☎ 21133), Jalan Kota Baru 37, has odd hours: it's open every morning, but not in the afternoons, and then it reopens again from 6 to 8 pm.

The Mission Aviation Fellowship (MAF) office (☎ 21155) is unsigned at the end of the airport. It flies to Anggi on Monday, Tuesday and Thursday for 42,500 rp. But don't rely on MAF flights; they are often booked out and obviously cater more for missionary work. Their postal address is c/o Kantor TEAM, Box 115, Manokwari.

Boat The Pelni boats *Ciremai* and *Dobonsolo* both go to Biak (10,000/42,000 rp for economy/1st class) and Sorong (16,500/66,500 rp) every two weeks; and the *Tatamailau* goes to Sorong, and Nabire (24,000/97,000 rp) every two weeks. The *Nuburi* does a fortnightly circle from Sorong around Cenderawasih Bay to Nabire and on to Jayapura; the *Nusa Perintis* travels between Manokwari and Jayapura every two weeks, stopping off at many smaller places on the way; and *Iweri* loops from Jayapura to Merauke through Manokwari every three weeks. For bookings for all boats go to the Pelni office (☎ 21221) at Jalan Siliwangi 24.

Getting Around

To/From the Airport Rendani airport is only five minutes' drive from most hotels. Bemo drivers may initially charge 12,500 rp, but will easily go down to 5000 rp (and even to 2000 rp!). It's better to walk straight outside to the main road and catch a bemo for 300 rp to the bemo terminal and, if necessary, take another to your hotel.

Local Transport The bemo (known locally as a taksi) terminal is next to the small and smelly *pasar sentral* (main market). Bemos leave regularly from here to the beaches, Taman Gunung Meja and the airport.

ANGGI LAKES

The twin 'male and female' lakes of Danau
Gigi and Danau Gita are spectacularly set,
and great places to walk, to swim in the
nearby rivers (but not in the lakes themselves) and to enjoy the exotic bird life,
butterflies and flora. There are regular direct
flights there. Alternatively, you could take a
bus or plane (95,000 rp) to the transmigration
centre of Ransiki, where you can hire a guide
for about 15,000 rp per day, or follow a
marked trail yourself. It will take about three
days to reach the lakes from Ransiki. There is
no accommodation on the way to, or at, the
lakes, but you can sleep in local huts for about
5000 rp per person. Take your own food or you
can buy limited vegetables along the way.

TELUK CENDERAWASIH

Increasingly popular for the more adventurous is trekking around the huge, rarely
explored Bird of Paradise Bay which offers
traditional lifestyles, bird life (even, possibly, the shy cenderawasih), butterflies and
diving.

For distant treks, the only option is to
charter a flight to/from a number of small
strips and hike, staying at local villages. For
a shorter day trip from Manokwari, take the
bus to Ransiki or halfway to Warkopi
(beware: this road is often flooded from June
to August) and walk around the nearby
jungle looking for butterflies and birds.

Guides for trekking will cost about 30,000
rp per day; porters around 10,000 rp; and
simple accommodation in local houses from
2000 to 5000 rp per night. All supplies
should be taken. A helpful, experienced and
licensed guide for this area is Joris Wanggai
who can be contacted through the Mutiara in
Manokwari. He speaks English and Dutch
well, and charges between 20,000 and
40,000 rp per day depending on the location.

Organised diving tours around Teluk Cenderawasih are expensive. Soon one or two
agencies will open in Manokwari, which can
arrange diving and hiking tours – with a
better range and cheaper prices than currently available overseas. (See Diving in the
Biak & Islands section for some details.)

Biak & Islands

KOTA BIAK

Biak is the centre of the large island of the
same name, off the north coast of the mainland of Irian Jaya. It is not a particularly
interesting town, but is a good base for
exploring some of the island's attractions,
though they can be difficult to get to. As the
transport hub for Irian Jaya, most travellers
will probably have to spend some time in
Biak anyway.

Orientation

Biak is a fairly compact town. Jalan Prof M
Yamin runs from the airport and connects
with Jalan Ahmad Yani, and then changes
names to Jalan Sudirman when it intersects
with Jalan Imam Bonjol. The majority of
hotels, restaurants and offices are around this
area which is easy to walk around.

Information

Tourist office The very helpful tourist office
(☎ 21663) is inconveniently located on Jalan
Prof M Yamin. It's open from 8 am to 2.30
pm on weekdays; take a bemo there or get
off on the way from the airport. It has free,
official brochures in English, Japanese and
Dutch, but often runs out of ones about Biak.
Little English is spoken there.

Money The large Bank ExIm on the corner
of Jalan Ahmad Yani and Jalan Imam Bonjol
is the best place to change money. It is open
Monday to Friday from 8 am to 1 pm; and
Saturday from 8 to 10 am. There are banks
at the domestic air terminal (open from 8 am
to 1 pm daily) and at the international terminal (open at times of international flights).

Post & Telephone The post office, which is
a bemo ride away on the way to the airport,
opposite the tourist office, is open from 8 am
to 6 pm every day. Telkom is also far out on
Jalan Yos Sudarso.

Police & Immigration The police headquar-

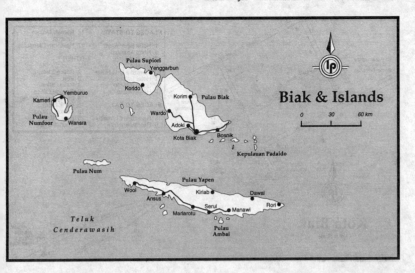

ters (☎ 21810) on Jalan Diponegoro is an excellent place to obtain a surat jalan for nearby islands and other places (a permit is not necessary for Pulau Biak). Take two photographs, there will be an 'administrative fee' of about 2000 rp, and the permit can be ready in an hour or so. The immigration office (☎ 21109) is on Jalan Sudirman.

Things to See

There is a busy **fish market** at the end of Jalan Imam Bonjol, with an extraordinary array of brightly coloured local fish during early mornings, and late afternoons.

There are two **food & clothing markets**: one on Jalan Selat Makassar, and the larger Pasar Inpres at the terminal – take a bemo there. The newish **Cenderawasih Museum** is about 15 minutes' walk from Losmen Maju. It has a mildly interesting collection, but is often closed, so check before going out there.

Activities

Diving Spectacular dive sites, and accessibility from within Indonesia and the USA, makes Kota Biak an increasingly popular base for diving tours around Pulau Biak and the general Cenderawasih Bay area. You will have to organise your own transport and gear; but Tropical Princess cruises, based at the port at Kota Biak, offers all-inclusive package tours for about US$300 per day. For bookings, contact Tropical Princess cruises c/o Jakarta Hilton Hotel, Jalan Jenderal Gatot Subroto, Senayan, Jakarta (☎ 5703500).

A new diving company called Dive Biak (☎ 21665 – no office address at time of writing) has now been established in Kota Biak. It serves dive sites around Pulau Biak, such as the Padaido Islands; the Cenderawasih Bay including Pulau Serui and the Cenderawasih Marine Park in the west of the Bay; and elsewhere along the northern coast of Irian Jaya.

Places to Stay

All places listed in the following three sections include tax and breakfast, unless stated otherwise.

Places to Stay – bottom end

Losmen Solo (☎ 21397) at Jalan Monginsidi 4 has very small singles/doubles with paperthin walls for 14,500/24,000 rp with shared bath, and no breakfast.

IRIAN JAYA

PLACES TO STAY

1 Hotel Sinar Kayu
6 Hotel Arumbai
7 Losmen Maju
8 Basana Inn
10 Titawaka Dua Hotel
11 Hotel Dahlia
16 Losmen Solo
18 Hotel Mapia

PLACES TO EAT

5 Restaurant Himalaya
9 Restaurant 99

12 Rumah Makan Jakarta
17 Restoran Cleopatra

OTHER

2 Police Station
3 Port
4 Pelni Office
13 Garuda Office
14 Immigration Office
15 Bank Exim
19 Telkom Office
20 Post Office
21 Tourist Office

Kota Biak

Not to Scale

Hotel Sinar Kayu (☎ 21933) on Jalan Sisingamangaraja has rooms for 10,000/15,000 rp.

Losmen Maju (☎ 21841), Jalan Imam Bonjol 45, is good value with fan-cooled rooms, all with bathroom, from 16,000/25,000 rp (ask for quieter rooms at the back).

Places to Stay – middle

Hotel Irian (☎ 21139) is across from the airport. It's an old place with a large seaside garden, bar and spacious restaurant (which serves ordinary food). Economy singles/doubles/triples cost 29,040/52,030/66,550 rp; or 52,030/79,860/94,380 rp with air-con. It is a great place to have a drink while waiting for a connecting flight. (Merpati will put you up there if/when your flight is cancelled.)

There are nice fan-cooled rooms at the *Hotel Dahlia* (☎ 21851), Jalan Selat Madura 6, for 22,000/27,500 rp. The new *Basana Inn* (☎ 22281) at Jalan Imam Bonjol 46, offers value and peace from 35,000/45,000 rp for economy rooms; double that for 'suites'. *Hotel Mapia* (☎ 21383) on Jalan Ahmad Yani is really run-down. Rooms start from 19,000/26,000 rp with fan and bath.

Places to Stay – top end

Hotel Arumbai (formerly Hotel Titawaka) (☎ 21835), at Jalan Selat Makassar 3, is luxurious with air-con, hot water, a swimming pool and airport transfers. Standard singles/doubles are 55,900/76,320 rp; deluxe rooms 140,000/165,165 rp. *Titawaka Dua Hotel* (☎ 22005), Jalan Selat Madura 13, has similar facilities and prices but is more open to negotiation.

Places to Eat

Restoran Cleopatra opposite the Hotel Mapia continues to be one of the best, with a varied menu. Along Jalan Imam Bonjol are the clean, modern *Restaurant 99* and *Rumah Makan Jakarta* (like many others, they have karaoke machines). For good Western food at reasonable prices, try the restaurant at the *Arumbai*.

There are some cheap places along Jalan Ahmad Yani like the *Rumah Makan Anda*, *Restaurant Megaria*, and *Cinta Rosa* (near the Hotel Mapia) which is especially recommended for good, cheap Indonesian food – and *Restaurant Himalaya* along Jalan Sudirman. There are evening food stalls around the fish market, and along Jalan Sudirman.

IRIAN JAYA

Getting There & Away

Air Biak is one of Indonesia's gateway cities, so you can enter here without a visa. Garuda has two weekly flights between Biak and Los Angeles via Hawaii. From Biak, a ticket costs US$781 one way and US$1001 return. (Payment must be made in US dollars.) There are regular flights from Biak to Denpasar and Jakarta which connect to Europe. There is a possibility of future direct flights to Biak from Tokyo. Garuda (☎ 21416) is at Jalan Sudirman 3. International departure tax is 11,000 rp.

Biak is the centre for air travel throughout Irian Jaya. Currently, only Merpati flies there. (At the time of writing, Bouraq plans to connect Biak and Jayapura with Ujung Pandang and Davao, in the southern Philippines.) The Merpati office (☎ 21386, 21752 after hours) is across the road from the airport and is open Monday to Thursday from 7.30 am to 4.30 pm, Friday from 11 am to 1 pm, and weekends from 9 am to 2 pm.

Merpati and Garuda have daily domestic flights from Biak to Ambon (228,200 rp), Denpasar (524,100 rp), Jakarta (664,900 rp), Jayapura (132,500 rp), Nabire (100,600 rp), Ujung Pandang (403,000 rp) and Serui (44,500 rp). Less regular flights go to Fakfak (179,800 rp), Manokwari (95,100 rp), Sorong (157,800 rp) and Numfoor Island (62,100 rp).

Boat The Pelni ships *Ciremai* and *Dobonsolo* go to Jayapura (26,000/108,000 rp for economy/1st class) and Manokwari (10,000/42,000 rp) every two weeks. The *Nusa Perintis*, during its two-week voyage from Jayapura, stops at Serui (Pulau Yapen), Biak, and then goes to Korido in the less accessible north of Biak Island. Every three weeks, the *Iweri* goes to Nabire. The *Teluk Cenderawasih I* connects Biak with Serui every two days. The Pelni office (☎ 21065), on Jalan Sudirman 37, handles bookings for all boats – the ticket office is open daily from 8 am to 3 pm, and Sunday from 10 am to 4 pm.

Getting Around

To/From the Airport There are regular bemos from Frans Kaisiepo airport to any place in Kota Biak for 350 rp; simply walk outside the front door of the terminal (but remember to catch one going the right way!). A taxi from the airport to the centre of town officially costs 8000 rp.

Local Transport The bemo/bus terminal is next to the Pasar Inpres market. Clearly marked boards indicate where bemos (called taksis here) are heading around the island. There are a few buses just outside the terminal which go to more distant places. Bemo charter for half a day is officially between 50,000 and 70,000 rp, but prices are very negotiable at the terminal.

AROUND PULAU BIAK

While there are some interesting places to go on Pulau Biak, the traveller is limited by the availability of transport. Public buses, along rough roads, only go as far west as Wardo, and to Korim on the east coast. North of these places an infrequent combination of trucks, boats and hiking is the only way to get around. Hiring a motorbike, from about 25,000 rp per day at the Honda dealer on Jalan Selat Makassar, could solve these transport problems. Remember, that while towns on Pulau Biak may look biggish on a map, none are really more than a handful of village huts with no accommodation or food.

Adoki

Increasingly popular for groups – but not really an option for individual travellers – is a demonstration of fire walking at the village of Adoki (bemos from Kota Biak cost 750 rp), where there is also some nice scenery and a good beach. While some women dance around the fire, the men take an hour to stoke it with coral and wood. About five men, aged between 12 and 70 years old, walk across the fire, and then back – it's all over in about three minutes. It has to be prearranged days before and will cost about 200,000 rp. Ask around the market on Jalan Selat Makassar in Kota Biak.

Gua Jepang

These Japanese caves (known locally as Binsari which means 'old woman' or 'grandmother' in the Biak language) are more like a long tunnel and are quite impressive. Ten thousand Japanese soldiers lived there during WW II, but half were eventually killed by US bombs and fire attacks. There are still many rusting remnants of the war inside. The tunnel leads from there to Bosnik beach several km away. Locals refuse to enter the dark cave, which has not been walked in since 1942. (Believe the warnings about snakes and bats!).

You can charter a bemo there for about 10,000 rp, or take a public bemo from the terminal to Komplex C (pronounced 'chay') and walk about three km along Jalan Gua Jepang. There is a small museum with Japanese WW II weapons and photos. If the museum is unattended, ask at the house next door. Across from the museum is a gate (1500 rp admission) where you enter to walk around the cave area. Ask for one of the local boys to give you an interesting commentary of the history in English. (A tip is appreciated, but not necessary.)

Bosnik

Bosnik, the former Dutch centre on the island and another landing site for the Allies, is 26 km east of Kota Biak (bemos cost 900 rp). There are some WW II relics, a lovely white, sandy beach and a small market on Wednesday and Saturday. At the end of the road from Biak to Bosnik is the monstrous Biak Beach Hotel (although currently there is no real beach within sight of it).

Pulau Padaido

From Bosnik it is possible to charter longboats for trips to some of the nearby Padaido Islands, including Undi and Owi, for swimming and snorkelling. Near the Bosnik market, Decky Rumaropen (☎ 22189) rents full snorkelling gear for 15,000 rp per day, and can arrange tours around the islands, such as Pulau Dawi, where it's possible to stay in local huts. Public boats travel from most of these islands to Bosnik on market days (Wednesday and Saturday).

Taman Burung dan Anggrek

On the way to Bosnik, your bemo can drop you off at Taman Burung dan Anggrek (Bird & Orchid Garden). The gardens are pleasant (though they were still being completed at the time of writing) with some orchids in glass houses, and several caged birds, including the bird of paradise. The entrance fee seems to vary according to who is working on the gates, but 2000 rp should be more than enough.

Pulau Supiori

Separated from Pulau Biak by only a very narrow channel, Pulau Supiori is mainly a reserve of mangrove and montane forests. To get to Korido, the main town, you can charter a boat for up to 10 people for about 300,000 rp return from Biak. Alternatively, the *Nusa Perintis* visits Korido from Kota Biak once every two weeks or so.

Korim

Korim is another small, north-eastern village which is difficult to get to, and probably not worth the effort. There is a small beach which is a bit scrappy, and it's a rough 90-minute trip. Irregular bemos cost 1900 rp, or there are buses for slightly less leaving at 8 am, 1 and 5 pm. The beach at Bosnik is far more accessible and prettier.

Wardo

In the north-west of the island, another bumpy hour or so by bemo from Kota Biak, is the very small collection of huts called Wardo ('deep water' in the Biak language) set in a beautiful bay. From here you can take a motorised longboat to visit the **waterfalls**. The falls are nice, and you can have a refreshing dip at the top (watch out for the unstable ladder), but the ride along the peaceful, overgrown jungle river is the highlight.

The two-hour return boat ride will cost about 10,000 rp per person, but bargain. An irregular bemo to Wardo costs 2200 rp, the bus a little less, or bemos can be chartered for 10,000 rp one way. You will probably be met at Wardo with offers for boat rides to the waterfalls, but also ask other local residents around the pretty bay.

PULAU YAPEN
Yapen is the elongated island south of Biak. It is undeveloped with great scenery, fishing villages and the chance of seeing the bird of paradise; but transport around the island is a problem. **Serui** is the only town of any size and the transport centre.

Orientation & Information
Serui is small, poor and fairly dirty (and you may be stuck there waiting for onward transport). The town is centred around Jalan Diponegoro, along the port, which has the only bank, the bus terminal, the market and several rumah makans. When the huge tide goes out, boys play soccer on the 'bottom of the sea' and girls look for shells.

A surat jalan, which is needed for a visit to anywhere on the island, can easily be obtained in Biak. Your hotel will arrange for your surat jalan to be stamped by local police.

Things to See & Do
In the east of the island, it is possible to see birds of paradise in the wild. Surprisingly, not many fishermen are interested in chartering and guiding, so ask at the Merpati Inn, where Eddy (who speaks Dutch) can help. He can arrange a boat (about 50,000 rp per day, plus 10,000 rp per hour for fuel) for 10 to 15 people, with a cook, but take your own food. Your guide (about 15,000 rp per day) will arrange for you to stay with villagers for up to 10,000 rp per night (no mattresses). Bargain hard and make sure everyone fully agrees with the 'contract'. Departures will vary according to the tides. Be aware that there is some sort of 'protection fee' of 50,000 rp levied on each group which wants to see a bird of paradise.

At **Pulau Ambai** there is great snorkelling (bring your own gear) among the coral and dolphins. There are plenty of cockatoos and hornbills too. Traditional dancing can be arranged for about 15,000 rp.

Places to Stay & Eat
There are only three places to stay, all in Serui. All prices include three meals, bathroom and tax. The best is the *Merpati Inn* (☎ 31154) on Jalan Yos Sudarso, which is friendly but a bit noisy, and is good for information on boat trips and Merpati flights. It has singles/doubles with fan for 27,000/45,000 rp and air-con rooms for 40,000/50,000 rp. *Hotel Bersaudara* (☎ 31376) on Jalan Sudirman, 400 metres towards the sea from the airport, has rooms for 30,000 rp with fan and 40,000 with air-con. *Losmen Marena* on Jalan Monginsidi, parallel to Jalan Yos Sudarso, costs 16,500/22,000 rp or 33,000/44,000 rp with meals.

Hotel food is recommended, although there are a couple of rumah makans serving padang food and some temporary night warungs along Jalan Diponegoro to choose from.

Getting There & Away
Air There are daily flights to/from Biak (41,500 rp) and a flight to Jayapura on Sunday (167,000 rp) but this is unreliable. (I waited three days for this flight and it didn't turn up.) The Merpati office (☎ 33) is in the Merpati Inn (next to the Toko Merpati and Merpati PhotoService!).

Boat The *Nusa Perintis* visits Serui, Ansus in the west of the island three days later, and Biak, once every two weeks; and the *Iweri* comes from Sarmi every three weeks, and returns via Biak. The *Teluk Cenderawasih I* travels overnight to Kota Biak (14 hours) every two days; and the *Teluk Cenderawasih II* travels overnight (eight hours) every two days to Nabire (16,800 rp). The Pelni liner *Tatamailau* goes direct to Jayapura (22,000/93,000 rp for economy/1st class) and to Nabire every four weeks. Pelni tickets can be bought at the Pelni office (☎ 31552) on Jalan Yos Sudarso, opposite the Merpati office; for other boats, there is a small office at the port.

Getting Around
To/From the Airport Bemo drivers will charge about 5000 rp, so take a public bemo

Birds of Paradise

Over 40 different species of the bird of paradise – known in Bahasa Indonesia as the *cenderawasih* – live in Papua New Guinea, and in small regional areas such as the north-western islands of Irian Jaya, and in southern Maluku.

The first specimens were taken back to Europe after colonial explorations around the 'East Indies'. Their feathers soon fetched remarkable prices for fashionable garments, and the birds were facing extinction. To avoid this many were transferred from Aru Island to an island near Tobago in the West Indies. Because their legs and wings had been removed to highlight the birds' beautiful plumage, and several early colonial explorers only saw them in flight and never on land, it was originally thought the birds had no feet and always flew in the air.

The male bird is usually more brightly coloured than the female. The males display their magnificent plumage during mating, often hanging upside down from branches to show off their colours; they do this alone, or in groups called leks. They mostly nest in open parts of a tree and feed on fruit and insects. They usually have remarkable thin, curled 'tail-wires' which can be up to 30 cm long with colourful tips, and often have loud calls.

The birds are scarce and very difficult to find, but with some patience, time and a good guide it is possible. The habitats are not developed, so locating the birds will involve chartering boats, organising guides and camping out on the islands of Waigeo, Misool, Batanta and Salawati, just off the coast of Sorong, or along sections of the aptly named Teluk Cenderawasih (Bird of Paradise Bay). The easiest place to travel to, and arrange a tour from, is Pulau Yapen (an island south of Biak) where several species can be found within a day's boat ride and trek from the main town of Serui. In South-East Maluku, the remote and undeveloped Aru Islands also boast the cenderawasih. For the less adventurous, you can admire several of these creatures in aviaries at the Taman Burung dan Anggrek (Orchid & Bird Park) in Bosnik, on Biak Island.

With some luck and effort, you may be able to spot the following species. The Magnificent Bird of Paradise, found on Salawati or Yapen islands, usually has gold and green sections and two long purple tail-wires and the Wilson's Bird of Paradise, found on Waigeo and Batanta islands, is smaller with blue touches on its head and partially red wings. The Red Bird of Paradise is, obviously, predominantly red, with black twisted tail-wires and is found on Batanta and Waigeo. The Lesser Bird of Paradise with its yellow tail and brownish body, found on Misool and Yapen islands has the loudest call of the species. The orange-winged Crested Bird of Paradise can be found among the mountains of Central Irian Jaya. The largest of the species, the Greater Bird of Paradise, with its bright yellow plumage, and black and maroon body, is found on Aru Island. The King Bird of Paradise is smaller, has a white belly, red head and long tail-wires with green tips, and is located around Aru, Yapen and Misool islands – as are the related, but not as spectacular with its regular black wings, Glossy-Mantled, Jobi and Crinkle-Collared Manucodes. ∎

just outside the small airport for about 300 rp. It will not take more than 20 minutes to walk to your losmen.

Local Transport There are semi-regular buses west as far as Wooi, over two hours from Serui, and to Manawi in the east, an hour away. Charters at about 10,000 rp per hour are possible. All roads in Yapen are rough, and the terrain mountainous. Motorboats can be hired to visit nearby Pulau Ambai or other villages around Yapen. Serui is very easy to walk around: no public transport is needed, and very little is offered.

PULAU NUMFOOR

Numfoor, between Biak and Manokwari, is an irresistible, unspoilt and undeveloped island, full of beautiful beaches and small villages. There is no losmen, so you must stay with a local family, and there's minimal internal transport. All planes and boats to Numfoor leave from Biak – not from Manokwari. From Biak there are irregular speedboats (known as 'Johnsons') for the eight-hour trip. This may cost up to 400,000 rp return for a boat carrying up to 15 people. The *Nusa Perintis* visits Kameri on Numfoor every 10 days from Biak. Merpati flies from Biak to Yemburuo on Tuesday and Friday for 62,100 rp.

Jayapura & Sentani

Jayapura is the name now given to the capital of Irian Jaya. In Dutch times it was known as Hollandia, (then Soekarnopura) and was deliberately placed just a few km from the border with German New Guinea, to emphasise the Dutch claim to the western half of the island. In April 1944, the Allies stormed ashore at Hamadi and captured the town after only token resistance from the Japanese. It was in Jayapura that General MacArthur assembled his fleet for the invasion of the Philippines.

Jayapura, with a population of over 250,000, is dominated by non-Irians and looks little different from any other medium-sized Indonesian city, although it has a nice enough location. There's no real reason to visit the city unless you have to deal with an airline office, bank or some other bureaucratic institution. Sentani, a small town 36 km from Jayapura, where the airport is located, is in many ways a better place to stay – it's quieter and cooler than Jayapura.

Orientation

In Jayapura, just about everything you want – most of the hotels, shops, police station and airline offices – is confined to the main streets of Jalan Ahmad Yani and, parallel to it, Jalan Percetakan. Sentani, which hugs the airport, is easy to walk around (but take a torch at night).

Information

Tourist Office The tourist bureau (☎ 23923), at Jalan Soa Siu Dok II, Jayapura, is a reasonable walk, so take a bemo. It provides helpful information and brochures about the local area, the Baliem Valley, and other places in Irian Jaya. There is a helpful information booth at the airport, open daily from 5 am to 5 pm.

Money Bank ExIm at Jalan Ahmad Yani 20, and Bank Danamon on Jalan Percetakan, both in Jayapura, are the best. They're open Monday to Friday from 8 am to 2 pm, and close a little earlier on Saturday. There are a couple of smaller banks on Jalan Kemiri Sentani Kota in Sentani, too.

It's a good idea to stock up on rupiah before heading to the Baliem Valley (although there are a couple of banks in Wamena). There is a bank at the Sentani airport (only open in the morning; closed Sunday) or you can change money at the airport shop, if you're desperate.

Post & Telephone In Jayapura, on Jalan Koti, the post office is open from 7 am to 9 pm every day. Next door, the Telkom office is open 24 hours a day. There is a small post office just back from Jalan Kemiri Sentani Kota in Sentani.

Travel Agencies A new agency, run by indigenous Irians, to promote tourism around Jayapura, Wamena and the Asmat region, is being established at Kantor YPMD, Jalan Jeruk Nipis, Kotaraja, Jayapura (☎ 81071).

Dani Sangrila (☎ 31060), Jalan Pembangunan 19, has been recommended by some readers as a good source of information on trips to the Baliem Valley (see the Baliem Valley section later).

Police & Immigration In Jayapura, the police headquarters (☎ 22161) is on Jalan Ahmad Yani; and in Sentani, near the

IRIAN JAYA

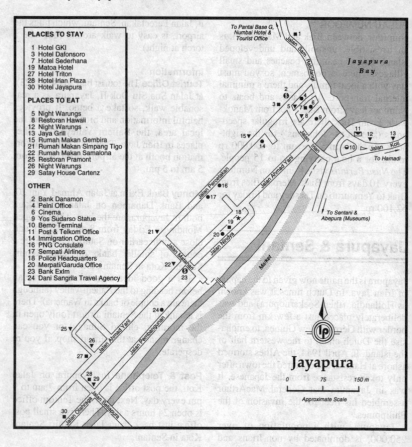

PLACES TO STAY
1 Hotel GKI
3 Hotel Dafonsoro
7 Hotel Sederhana
19 Matoa Hotel
27 Hotel Triton
28 Hotel Irian Plaza
30 Hotel Jayapura

PLACES TO EAT
5 Night Warungs
8 Restoran Hawaii
12 Night Warungs
13 Jaya Grill
15 Rumah Makan Gembira
21 Rumah Makan Simpang Tigo
22 Rumah Makan Samalona
25 Restoran Pramont
26 Night Warungs
29 Satay House Cartenz

OTHER
2 Bank Danamon
4 Pelni Office
6 Cinema
9 Yos Sudarso Statue
10 Bemo Terminal
11 Post & Telkom Office
14 Immigration Office
16 PNG Consulate
17 Sempati Airlines
18 Police Headquarters
20 Merpati/Garuda Office
23 Bank Exim
24 Dani Sangrila Travel Agency

To Pantai Base G,
Numbai Hotel &
Tourist Office

Jayapura
Bay

To Hamadi

To Sentani &
Abepura (Museums)

Jayapura

0   75   150 m

Approximate Scale

entrance to the airport (☎ 91105). The immigration office (☎ 21647) is on Jalan Percetakan 15, Jayapura.

Surat Jalan A surat jalan is not required for visiting Jayapura or Sentani, but they are the final places to get one for the Baliem Valley and most places further south or west. Get one at the police station in Jayapura or Sentani; it takes an hour or so, costs about 2000 rp and you will need two photographs. Take 10 to 20 photocopies of your surat jalan: each village police officer in the Baliem Valley will want one!

PNG Consulate The new Papua New Guinea Consulate (☎ 31250) at Jalan Percetakan 23 (PO Box 1947, Jayapura) is open weekdays from 8 am to 4 pm. At the time of writing, all foreigners needed a visa, which requires a week's notice, two photos, a 20,000 rp fee, a reason for travel, and a ticket out of PNG.

Hamadi
Hamadi is about a 15-minute bemo ride from Jayapura. Its market offers all sorts of good and not-so-good souvenirs and crafts. The swimming beach, Pantai Hamadi, another

two minutes' drive past the market, is pleasant, if a little dirty, with some nice nearby islands, and some rusting WW II wrecks. A WW II statue is nearby. Bemo No 101D goes to Hamadi from around the Jayapura streets for 350 rp. For the beach, ask the driver to drop you off outside the friendly police compound, where you will have to report and leave your surat jalan for collection when you return from the beach.

Pantai Base G

Locally known as Tanjung Ria, the pleasant Base G Beach – so-named because it was MacArthur's headquarters – is not far from Jayapura. Take bemo No 101G (200 rp), get off at the police building (called POLDA) and take bemo No 102A (300 rp) to the beach.

Museums

The **Gedung Loka Budaya Museum** is in the grounds of Cenderawasih University at Abepura, virtually a suburb of Jayapura. It exhibits a fascinating collection of Irian artefacts, including a largish collection from the Asmat area. Captions are often mostly in Indonesian and the guides are useful only if you speak Indonesian, but the displays are worthwhile, even if you don't fully understand them. A university student, wanting to practice English, would be useful as a guide. The museum is open from about 7.30 am to 2.30 pm every day except Sunday. From Sentani, take the bemo to Abepura (400 rp).

The **Museum Negeri** (State Museum) is also worth a visit for its good displays; English-speaking guides are available. Next door, is the **Taman Budaya** (Culture Park). Both are on the main road in Abepura; ask the bemo driver to drop you off outside.

Danau Sentani

The magnificent Lake Sentani covers more than 148,000 sq km with 19 islands, some of which, such as Ayapo and Nelayan, are inhabited by very small fishing villages. A boat trip is really worthwhile to enjoy the lake and visit some islands. From Yahim, the Sentani town boat harbour, a short ride from

the bemo terminal, you can rent motorboats with room for five people for about 12,000 rp per hour, but bargain hard. Canoes cost less but you can't go as far. From Yougwa Restaurant, a large motorboat for up to 15 people costs 55,000 rp per hour.

There are no public bemos around the lake, so you must hire one for about 10,000 rp per hour – ask at the terminal or your hotel. Simple, friendly villages, such as **Doyo Lama**, which offers magnificent, large woodcarvings, are worth visiting.

Tugu MacArthur

Alternatively, for the best views of Danau Sentani, visit the MacArthur monument, which itself is of little interest. Here, as the legend goes, MacArthur sat and contemplated his WW II strategies. The only way to get there is to charter a bemo, as there appears to be no public transport. The road up there, off the main road not far from Sentani, is marked 'Tugu MacArthur', and is about six km long and very steep (don't try to walk). Report to the friendly local military office (which has taken over the area) and deposit your surat jalan with them until you leave.

Sentani Waterfalls

The road behind the Hotel Minang Jaya leads to some pretty waterfalls. Despite what the hotel manager tells people, it is a long, unmarked, tiring trek of six or so km, and you will probably get lost without a guide.

Places to Stay

All places in Sentani will arrange for travel to/from the airport if you ring them when you arrive, or you could go with one of the many hotel touts. There is some choice of cheap accommodation in Sentani and Jayapura, but not much. All prices listed in each section below include tax, and breakfast.

Places to Stay – bottom end

Sentani Both the *Hotel Ratna* (☎ 91435), Jalan Kemiri Sentani Kota 7, and the *Hotel Minang Jaya* (☎ 91067) over the road, offer small rooms, friendly service and a central location. Singles/doubles with fan are about 20,000/30,000 rp, and about 30,000/36,000 rp with air-con. *Hotel Mansapur Rani* (☎ 91219), Jalan Yabaso 113, is good value – turn right just outside the airport and walk about 400 metres. Quiet rooms with fan cost 16,500/27,500 rp. *Sentani Inn* (☎ 91440) on Jalan Kemiri Sentani Kota, about two km towards Jayapura, has clean rooms for 17,000/26,000 rp with fan, or 26,000/33,000 rp with air-con. Take a bemo; it is worth the effort.

Jayapura The cheapest and most basic is the grandly named but badly signed *Hotel Jayapura* (☎ 33216) on Jalan Olahraga 4. The noisy and very ordinary singles/doubles cost 9600/14,400 rp with shared bath, or 12,000/16,800 rp with private bath.

Hotel Sederhana (☎ 31561), Jalan Halmahera 2, is good value and central. Rooms are clean, and cost 20,900/27,500 rp with air-con, a little less with a fan and no bathroom. *Hotel GKI* (☎ 33574) is a bit of a walk on the north side of town at Jalan Sam Ratulangi 12. There's a pleasant outdoor sitting area, but the dingy rooms have no bathroom. It costs 18,000/31,200 rp or 24,000/38,400 rp including three meals.

Places to Stay – middle
Sentani *Hotel Carfin* (☎ 91478) is about 500 metres east of town on Jalan Kemiri Sentani Kota. The modern rooms, which, unusually, have share baths, cost 55,450/66,550 rp a single/double. The newish, popular *Hotel Semeru* (☎ 91447) on Jalan Yabaso – five minutes' walk from the airport – has rooms with a fan for 29,200 rp, and 41,250 rp with air-con.

Jayapura One of the best in the mid-range is the busy, friendly *Hotel Dafonsoro* (☎ 31695) at Jalan Percetakan 20-24. Air-con singles/doubles are 53,240/65,340 rp; triples 79,860 rp. *Hotel Irian Plaza* (☎ 34649) at Jalan Setiapura 11, off Jalan Ahmad Yani, is clean and provides good local information. Room prices are 25,000/36,000 rp with fan, up to 60,000/75,000 rp for deluxe rooms with TV, air-con and hot water.

Hotel Triton (☎ 21218), at Jalan Ahmad Yani 52, is old and decaying – air-con rooms with hot water cost 30,000/48,000 rp. For sea views, but an inconvenient location, try *Numbai Hotel* (☎ 22185), about three km north of the centre. Rooms with fan are 25,000/28,000 rp.

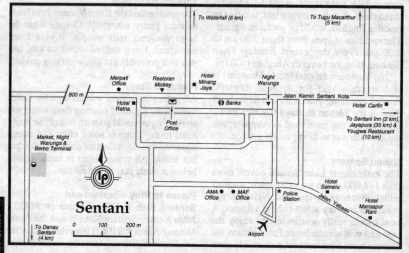

Sentani

Places to Stay – top end
In Jayapura, at Jalan Ahmad Yani 14, the
Matoa Hotel (☎ 31633) is the flashiest place.
Singles start at an exorbitant 132,000 rp and
go much, much higher.

Places to Eat
Sentani *Restoran Mickey* is the best place in
town for selection (including deer sate!) and
price. *Hotel Semeru* has a good restaurant but
with tourist prices, and no beer. There are
night warungs around the market (a fair walk
from the hotels) and more centrally along
Jalan Kemiri Sentani Kota. For good, inexpensive food, and the best views of Danau
Sentani, it is worth taking the Sentani to
Abepura bemo out to *Yougwa Restaurant*.

Jayapura Most restaurants are found on the
two main roads. Along Jalan Percetakan are
the rumah makans *Gembira* and *Simpang
Tigo*, both serving good padang food; and at
the end is the touristy *Restoran Pramont*,
which has Western food and all sorts of
liquor. Along Jalan Ahmad Yani are several
others, such as the simple, pleasant *Rumah
Makan Samalona*. For a great selection of
sates, there is the *Satay House Cartenz* on
Jalan Pembangunan. *Restoran Hawaii*,
under the IMBI theatre, serves good Chinese
food, if a little overpriced. For a splurge and
great location, try the *Jaya Grill*, at Jalan
Koti 5. There are several areas of night
warungs, and many well-stocked supermarkets.

Getting There & Away
Air Direct, daily Merpati flights go to Biak
(132,500 rp), Denpasar (639,600 rp) and
Jakarta (734,200 rp). Less regular flights go
to Merauke (185,300 rp), with direct connections to Agats (avoid the Monday flight via
Tanahmerah unless you want to be off-loaded
there – I very nearly was), Manokwari
(219,400 rp), and Nabire (157,800 rp).

There are several, heavily booked daily
Merpati flights to Wamena (77,500 rp).
Airfast cargo service (☎ 21925), Jalan Sam
Ratulangi, also takes passengers to Wamena
three times a day for 98,500 rp.

The combined Merpati and Garuda office
(☎ 33111, 33523 after hours) at Jalan Ahmad
Yani 15, Jayapura, is open Monday to Saturday from 7.30 am to 2 pm and in the
afternoons only on Sunday.

In Sentani, Merpati (☎ 91314), Jalan
Kemiri Sentani Kota, is open Monday to
Saturday from 7.30 am to 8 pm, Sunday from
5 to 9 pm. As this office can handle all
bookings and confirmations, there is no need
to go to the Merpati office in Jayapura. If
arriving by plane, sit on the right side for
truly magnificent views of Danau Sentani.

Sempati (☎ 31612) has daily flights to
Jakarta (734,700 rp) via Ujung Pandang
(529,600 rp). It has an office at Jalan Percetakan 17, Jayapura, and at Sentani airport
(☎ 91612). An interesting option is Bouraq,
which soon plans to fly to Jayapura through
Biak from Ujung Pandang and Davao, in the
southern Philippines.

The Mission Aviation Fellowship (MAF)
(☎ 91109) and Aviation Mission Association
(AMA) (☎ 91009), next door to each other
along Jalan Yabaso, Sentani, offer some
flights to more obscure places – their destinations are listed outside their offices. Take
note that their overwhelming business is,
obviously, missionary work and that they are
not interested in providing an alternative
passenger airline.

To/From PNG There are still no road or boat
connections with Papua New Guinea, so the
only alternative is to fly between Jayapura
and Vanimo, just over the border in PNG. Air
Nuigini does the return flight every Sunday,
and Sundown Air Service (SAS) every
Friday. For tickets, it is preferable to ring
these airlines in Vanimo and arrange for your
ticket to be collected at the Sentani airport.
Alternatively, try one of the several travel
agencies in Jayapura. International departure
tax from Jayapura is 13,000 rp.

Boat The huge Pelni liner *Tatamailau* goes
direct to Serui (but not Biak) every four
weeks for the economy/1st class fares of
22,000/93,000 rp; and both the *Ciremai* and
Dobonsolo go to Biak (26,000/108,000 rp)

every two weeks. The *Iweri* travels from Jayapura to Merauke via a lot of smaller ports every three weeks. The *Nusa Perintis* travels every two weeks to Manokwari and back, stopping everywhere in between. Tickets for these boats are sold at the Pelni office (☎ 33270) at Jalan Halmahera 1. Ticket sales are from Monday to Saturday – mornings only.

Getting Around

To/From the Airport A taxi from the airport to Sentani costs 5000 rp. But you can walk to your Sentani hotel in less than 10 minutes, or arrange for it to collect you. A taxi to Jayapura costs a whopping 25,000 rp. Try sharing with other equally stunned passengers; or take the bemos (see below).

Local Transport From Sentani to Jayapura take a bemo to Abepura (800 rp), get off along the main road for the bemo to chaotic Entrop terminal (400 rp), and get another to central Jayapura (300 rp). It sounds complicated but it works easily (many locals are doing it too) and takes about an hour. Bemos within the local area of Sentani and Jayapura cost around 300 rp – catch them around the streets or at the terminal. There is no public bus to Sarmi, despite the tempting road drawn on maps.

The Baliem Valley

The first White men chanced upon the Baliem Valley in 1938, a discovery which came as one of the last and greatest surprises to a world that had mapped, studied and travelled the mystery out of its remotest corners. WW II prevented further exploration and it was not until 1945 that attention was again drawn to the valley when a plane crashed there and the survivors were rescued. The first missionaries arrived in 1954, the Dutch government established a post at Wamena in 1956, and changes to the Baliem lifestyle followed. Today, the Indo-

nesians have added their own brand of colonialism, bringing schools, police, soldiers and shops, and turning Wamena into a town. But local culture has in many ways proved very resilient, helped perhaps by the absence of alcohol, which is banned in the Baliem Valley.

Geography

The Grand Valley of the Baliem River (known as the Grand Valley) starts from east and west points 120 km apart. The eastern arm rises near the summit of Gunung Trikora (4750 metres), not far west of Wamena, and flows west away from Wamena. From the confluence of the east and west arms, near Kuyawage, the river travels east then turns south into what's known as the Baliem Valley, 1554 metres above sea level, and about 60 km long and 16 km wide, with Wamena roughly at its centre. (The valley probably contained a lake at one stage and its flat expanse slows the river and allows sediment to be deposited during floods.) The river then continues south through the massive Baliem Gorge – in which it drops 1500 metres in less than 50 km, forming a spectacular series of cataracts – and on down to the Arafura Sea on the south-west coast.

The Dani

The tribes of the Baliem are usually grouped together under the name 'Dani' – a rather abusive name given by neighbouring tribes, but one that has stuck. There are a number of other highland groups, distinguished from each other by language, physical appearance, dress and social customs. The Dani are farmers, skilfully working their fertile land, digging long ditches for irrigation and drainage, and leaving the land fallow between crops. The clearing of the land and the tilling of the soil for the first crop is traditionally men's work; the planting, weeding and harvesting is women's.

Food

The sweet potato or *erom* is the staple food of the highlands. The Dani recognise 70

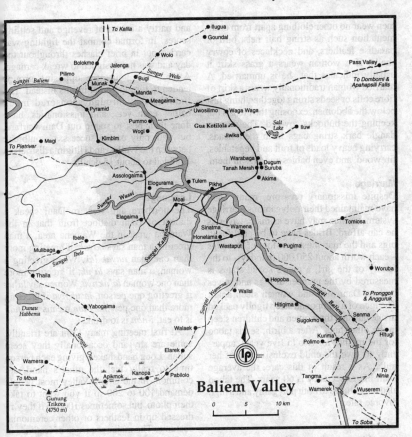

Baliem Valley

0   5   10 km

different types – some varieties can only be
eaten by a particular group such as pregnant
women or old men, and ancestor spirits get
the first potatoes from every field.

Houses

Traditional Dani kampungs are composed of
several self-contained fenced compounds,
each with its own cooking house, men's
house, women's houses, and pigsties. A
typical compound might be home to four
men and their families, perhaps 20 people. A
traditional Dani house (*honay*) is circular,
topped by a thatched dome-shaped roof.

Clothing

Dani men wear penis sheaths made of a
cultivated gourd. These penis gourds are
known locally as *horim*. The Indonesian
government's campaign in the early 1970s to
end the wearing of penis gourds was mostly
a failure. Many Dani wear pig fat in their hair
and cover their bodies in pig fat and soot for
health and warmth. The fat makes their hair
look like a cross between a Beatle's mop-top
and a Rastafarian's locks. Naked except for
their penis gourds, as the evening closes in
the men stand with their arms folded across
their chests to keep warm. Traditionally, the

men wear no other clothing apart from ornamentation such as string hair nets, bird of paradise feathers, and necklaces of cowry shells. If a woman wears a grass skirt it usually indicates that she is unmarried. A married woman traditionally wears a skirt of fibre coils or seeds strung together, hung just below the abdomen, exposing the breasts but keeping the buttocks covered. The women dangle bark string bags from their heads, carrying heavy loads of fruit and vegetables, firewood, and even babies and pigs in them.

Marriage

Despite missionary pressure, many Dani have maintained their polygamous marriage system – a man may have as many wives as he can afford. Brides have to be paid for in pigs and the man must give four or five pigs – each worth about 250,000 rp today – to the family of the girl; a man's social status is measured by the number of pigs and wives he has. Dani men and women sleep apart. The men of a compound sleep tightly packed in one hut, and the women and children sleep in the other huts. After a birth, sex is taboo for the mother for two to five years, apparently to give the child exclusive use of her milk. As a result of this care, the average Dani life expectancy is 60 years. The taboo also contributes to both polygamy and a high divorce rate.

Customs

One of the more bizarre Dani customs is for a woman to have one or two joints of her fingers amputated when a close relative dies; you'll see many of the older women with fingers missing right up to the second joint. Cremation was the traditional method of disposing of the body of the deceased, but sometimes the body would be kept and dried. At present, there are five villages in the valley which have these smoked 'mummies' which you can pay about 4000 rp to see and photograph. The five villages are Akima, Jiwika, Kimbim, Pummo and Wasalma.

Fighting between villages or districts seems to have been partly a ritual matter to appease the ancestors and attract good luck, and partly a matter of revenge and settling scores. In formal combat the fighting was carried out in brief clashes throughout the day and was not designed to wreak carnage. After a few hours the opposing groups tended to turn to verbal insults instead. The Indonesians, through sponsored mock battles each year, and missionaries, have done their best to stamp out Dani warfare, but with only partial success: an outbreak between the Wollesi and Hitigima districts in 1988 led to about 15 deaths.

Language

The northern and western Dani speak a dialect of Dani distinct from that in the Wamena area. In the Wamena area, a man greeting a man says *nayak*; if greeting more than one man *nayak lak*. When greeting a woman, a man says *la'uk*; if greeting more than one woman *la'uk nya*. Women say *la'uk* if greeting one person, *la'uk nya* if greeting more than one person. *Wam* means pig, *nan* is to eat, *i-nan* is to drink.

At first meeting many Dani are friendly, some are shy and occasionally they seem sullen. Long handshakes, giving each person time to really feel the other's hand, are common. In the Grand Valley most people demand 100 to 200 rp if you want to take their photo, but sometimes 1000 rp if they're dressed up in feathers or other ceremonial costume. The major sequence of festivals in the Grand Valley, including young men's initiation rites, mock battles and multiple marriages, takes place every five years and was last held in 1993.

WAMENA

Wamena is a spread-out, haphazard town. It has the main market in the Balien Valley, so lots of Dani come in from the surrounding villages to trade. It's also peaceful and cool, with a beautiful mountain backdrop. Accommodation and food is expensive since almost everything in Wamena has to be flown in from Jayapura, to where most things have also been shipped from western Indonesia.

Orientation

Most of the few hotels, places to eat and offices can be reached on foot. The rather dirty, crowded Pasar Nayak market serves as the centre of town. Many streets are badly signed, or not at all. Take a torch at night – there are few street lights.

Information

Money Try to change your money in Jayapura or Sentani, although the Bank ExIm (open mornings only), not far from the Pasar Nayak, on Jalan Trikora, is OK. Avoid the Bank Rakyat nearby which offers an appalling rate of exchange.

Post & Telephone The post office on Jalan Timor is open Monday to Saturday from 8 am to 2 pm, closing a little earlier on Friday. The Telkom office is at Jalan Thamrin 22.

Police The police compound (☎ 31072) is on Jalan Bhayangkara. The friendly officers are a good source of trekking information, and will tell you of any places off limits.

Travel Agencies *Chandra Nusantara* (☎ 31293) at Jalan Trikora 17 is well established and reputable for organised but flexible tours around Baliem Valley and the Asmat region. Another is *Desa Tour & Travel* (☎ 31107), PO Box 200, Wamena. There are several travel agencies in Jayapura catering for the Baliem (see the earlier Jayapura section).

Rafting trips down the Baliem River (for the brave) are being developed – ask around the Catholic Mission complex (☎ 31492).

Surat Jalan A surat jalan is absolutely essential. You can stay for a day or so in Wamena without one, but you *cannot* get one in Wamena – it's easy to get it in Biak, Jayapura or Sentani. It will be checked and stamped at Wamena airport, so have a photocopy ready to give them. You have to report to the police each time you come to a new village whether you're staying or just passing through. The back of your surat jalan will soon fill up, so keep a spare photocopy for more stamps.

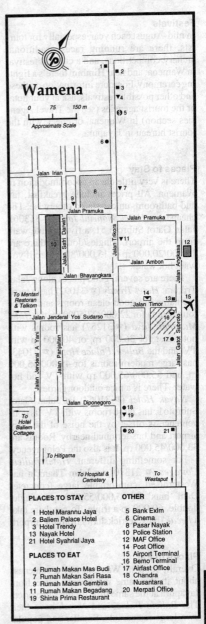

PLACES TO STAY
1 Hotel Marannu Jaya
2 Baliem Palace Hotel
3 Hotel Trendy
13 Nayak Hotel
21 Hotel Syahrial Jaya

PLACES TO EAT
4 Rumah Makan Mas Budi
7 Rumah Makan Sari Rasa
9 Rumah Makan Gembira
11 Rumah Makan Begadang
19 Shinta Prima Restaurant

OTHER
5 Bank ExIm
6 Cinema
8 Pasar Nayak
10 Police Station
12 MAF Office
14 Post Office
15 Airport Terminal
16 Bemo Terminal
17 Airfast Office
18 Chandra Nusantara
20 Merpati Office

IRIAN JAYA

Festivals

In mid-August each year, especially for tourists, there are running races, traditional archery competitions, and a cultural festival in Wamena; and near Himbim there's a fighting ceremony. For more information on these and other possible festivals, ask at your hotel or the tourist agencies (see the Travel Agencies section) in Wamena, or check with the tourist bureau in Jayapura.

Places to Stay

There is very little cheap accommodation in Wamena. All prices include breakfast, tax and bathroom, unless stated otherwise. The cheapest is *Hotel Syahrial Jaya* (☎ 31306), Jalan Gatot Subroto 51, a five-minute walk from the airport. Singles/doubles there are 10,000/20,000 rp or 15,000/30,000 rp if you want hot water.

There are several good places along Jalan Trikora: *Hotel Trendy* (☎ 31092) has a terrible name but good clean rooms and a nice lounge area for 22,000/27,5000 rp; the *Hotel Marannu Jaya* (☎ 31257) has rooms with hot water for 36,000 rp, or 40,000 rp with TV; and the *Baliem Palace Hotel* (☎ 31043) has large modern rooms for 45,000/55,000 rp, and 55,000/65,000 rp with TV and hot water. There is a nice outdoor garden.

Nayak Hotel (☎ 31067), at Jalan Gatot Subroto1, has large rooms with TV. Its convenience is offset by the noise of the busy airport and bus terminal nearby. Rooms are 33,000/45,000 rp. It is also the Pelni agency.

For something different, *Hotel Baliem Cottages* (☎ 31370) on Jalan Thamrin has Westernised, comfortable large (concrete) Dani 'huts' for 35,000/55,000 rp a single/ double, 60,000 rp a triple. To get there take a *becak* (bicycle-rickshaw) from the airport.

Places to Eat

Overall, food in Wamena has a sameness about it: the same ingredients come from Jayapura at the same time for the same price. The *Baliem Palace* and *Nayak* have their own large restaurants. Smaller and popular is *Rumah Makan Mas Budi* next to the Trendy on Jalan Trikora. Other OK places are rumah makans *Gembira*, *Sari Rosa* and *Begadang*.

Further out are the recommended *Shinta Prima*, at Jalan Trikora 17; and *Mentari Restoran*, at Jalan Yos Sudarso 47, which is worth the long walk or becak ride to get there. There are several padang places around the Pasar Nayak. Wamena is designated a 'dry' area, so no alcohol can be bought (nor should it be brought into Wamena by travellers). The local speciality is freshwater prawns *(udang)*.

Things to Buy

The Dani men are fine craftspeople (traditionally, the men are the creators), making stone axes or weaving necklaces of cowry shells or intricate bracelets. They also make the married women's fibre-coil skirts which circle the body well below the waist and defy gravity by not falling down. Palm and orchid fibres are used, the latter's texture resulting in an almost shimmering effect.

The cost of stone axe blades *(kapak)* depends on the size and amount of labour involved in making each one. Blue stone is the hardest and considered the finest material and thus more expensive, with black stone a close second. *Sekan* are thin, intricately hand-woven rattan bracelets. *Noken* are bark-string bags made from the inner bark of certain types of trees and shrubs, which are dried, shredded and then rolled into threads; the bags are coloured with vegetable dyes, resulting in a very strong smell.

And, of course, there are the penis gourds (horim). The gourd is held upright by attaching a thread to the top and looping it around the waist. Incidentally, the Indonesians refer to the penis gourd as *koteka*, from *kotek* meaning 'tail' – it's a derogatory term.

Other handicrafts include head and arm bands of cowry shells, feathers and bone; containers made of coconuts; four-pronged wooden combs; grass skirts; woven baskets and fossils (you may be approached by people with their own finds for sale). There are good souvenir shops in the market or along the road near the airport, but you can also buy items in the Dani villages.

Sometimes it's cheaper to buy direct from the Dani people, but they can strike a hard bargain so it's best to check out both shop and market prices. Expect to pay around 4000 rp for a medium-sized string bag after bargaining, at least 5000 rp for a small penis gourd, from 500 rp for a sekan, 10,000 rp for grey stone axes, and up to 200,000 rp for *asli* (genuine) stone axes. Asmat woodcarvings, shields and spears are also available in the souvenir shops, but be very wary of price and quality.

Getting There & Away

Air There are at least two Merpati flights to/from Jayapura every day (76,400 rp). As flying is the only way in and out, the flights are very popular, so confirm (and later reconfirm) your flight out as soon as you arrive in Wamena. There are no other flights from Wamena; the very convenient onward service to Agats (for the Asmat region) has been stopped. However, there may soon be direct flights to Wamena from Biak, making a stopover in Jayapura or Sentani unnecessary. The Merpati office (☎ 31488), at Jalan Trikora 41, is open daily from 7 am to 4 pm.

Airfast (☎ 31053), primarily a cargo airline, flies from Wamena to Sentani for 81,900 rp (one way) three times a day; the return from Sentani costs a lot more at 98,500 rp. Its office – opposite the Wamena airport – is open daily from 6.30 am to 3 pm.

MAF (☎ 31263) and AMA (☎ 3178) provide irregular flights to more obscure destinations, primarily for missionary work. Their schedules change weekly, and it's better to check with their larger offices near Sentani airport.

Getting Around

Almost all hotels in Wamena are within walking distance of the airport. For a rest or a longer trip around town, take a becak (about 500 rp a trip). They hang around the market.

AROUND THE BALIEM VALLEY

Getting out and wandering the valleys and hills brings you into close contact with the Dani and makes even Wamena seem a distant metropolis! This is great hiking country, but travel light because the trails are often muddy and slippery. You have to clamber over stiles, maybe cross rivers by dugout canoe or log raft, and traverse creeks or trenches on quaint footbridges or a single rough plank or slippery log. You can take all day or half-day trips out of Wamena, longer treks around the Baliem Valley staying in villages as you go, or cross the mountains to remoter areas where you may have to camp some of the time.

Mummies The mummy at Akima is a bit broken, as is the one at Musatafak. There's also a mummy at Jiwika, but the whole atmosphere there is a bit contrived. The mummy at Pummo is the best, but this involves a trek from Uwosilimo to Meagaima and then taking a canoe to Pummo, or a trek from Kimbim.

Trekking

Guides In Wamena, guides will regularly approach you at the airport, hotels and on the street. You don't have to have a guide, but taking one usually makes things easier and more interesting. They can help you decide where to go, facilitate communication with locals, find places to stay and generally keep you informed. In addition, you'll get to know a local person. They should be licensed, which usually indicates some trekking experience and an ability in English (and often Dutch).

Prices for guides have increased with the amount of tourists. For easier walks, a good, licensed guide will cost about 30,000 rp per day, a porter about 10,000 rp, and a cook 25,000 rp; but add about 25% more if it's difficult trekking – and bargain hard. An unlicensed guide will be cheaper (maybe less than 25,000 rp per day), and may or may not be as good as a licensed one. Travel agencies should have more of an idea about which guide is reliable, but the agent will take its commission too. A tip at the end of trips is expected. It's not a bad idea to test out a guide on a short walk before hiring them for a longer trip, and to ask other travellers for their recommendations.

What to Bring If you need sunblock, bring it. You can get most other things you need from Wamena's market and shops: there's no shortage of food and you can buy pots, pans, hats, mosquito coils, umbrellas and blankets. Take a torch if you want to enter any of the caves in the area. The nights are always cold and usually wet, so bring warm clothes and waterproof gear. If you need a tent, bring your own or find a guide who's adept at constructing ad hoc forest shelters (many are).

A large, hand-drawn but detailed map of the area is available at the Nayak Hotel for 7000 rp. You'll need to ask at the police station in Wamena and along the way for up-to-date information on roads, bridges and so on.

Accommodation There are losmen in a few places and in many villages you can get a wooden bed in the house of a teacher or a leading family, usually for 5000 to 10,000 rp per person, a little more for breakfast – often food is available there too. Ask at the village police station as to where you will have to report anyway. Sleeping on the floor of Dani huts is also quite possible, but make sure you've been invited before entering the compound or any particular hut. Missions can put you up in one or two places, but in general you're advised to try elsewhere.

Food Some villages have kiosks selling things like biscuits, bottled drinks, noodles and rice – heading north the last shops are at Meagaima on the east side and just beyond Pyramid on the west. Otherwise, you can usually get plenty of sweet potatoes, but don't rely on much else except some occasional eggs or fruit.

Getting Around Bemos, known locally as taksis, run to some places near Wamena during daylight hours, more often in the morning, from opposite the airport. How far and how often they go depends on the state of the roads and the number of people likely to be travelling the route.

Bemos travel as far south as Sugokmo (1500 rp), as far north as Bolokme (8000 rp), east to Uwosilimo (1500 rp) and west to Pietriver (15,000 rp). The terrain makes it hard to envisage the roads extending any further. Charters are possible for slightly longer trips, but are very expensive because petrol is flown in, and the roads are often appalling (eg, expect to be quoted 150,000 rp to get to Pass Valley in the far east!). To villages around Wamena, charters will cost about 15,000 rp per hour, which is worth considering to avoid the waiting often necessary to fill up a bemo before it goes, and the incredible number of bodies that usually fill it.

Baliem Valley – Central & South

Westaput Virtually a 'suburb' of Wamena, Westaput is across the other side of the airport – just walk across the landing strip like everyone else. At the end of the pleasant village path (a simple Dani-style losmen is being built along the way) is the traditionally built **Palimo Adat Museum**. This offers a small, interesting collection of local traditional dress, decorations and instruments. But all captions are in Indonesian, and the guide speaks little else. A donation is expected (1000 rp should be enough). At the back of the museum is the nearest hanging bridge to Wamena across the Sungai Baliem – it's about 50 metres long and unstable at times. The good path on the other side then leads to Pugima.

Sinatma This is an hour or two's stroll west of Wamena. Walk along Jalan Yos Sudarso to where it turns right at a small shop, and then go straight on past a church over the fields. Near a small hydroelectric power station you can cross the raging Sungai Wamena by a hanging bridge and walk down the far side to Wauma where you meet the main road into Wamena from the south.

Hitigima There are **salt-water wells** (*air garam*) near the village of Hitigima, an easy two to three-hour walk along the main road south from Wamena. To extract the salt, banana stems are beaten dry of fluid and put in a pool to soak up the brine. The stem is then dried and burned and the ashes are collected and used as salt.

The road to Hitigima is a flat stroll past hills with neat chequerboards of cultivated fields enclosed by stone walls. From Wamena walk down Jalan Ahmad Yani, over the bridge and straight on. Hitigima is slightly above the road on the west side. The village has a school as well as a mission, and the salt wells are a further 45 minutes or so above Hitigima.

Kurima Bemos go only as far as Sugokmo (1500 rp; 20 minutes) on a bumpy road. Over the swinging wooden bridge 30 metres above the river, there is a lovely walk for an hour to Kurima. Occasionally the terrain is hilly. The only possible obstacle is the wide Sungai Yetni – makeshift bridges often fall apart; and it's sometimes impassable in the wet season, even for the hardier locals. Like at most places, you can sleep on the floor of the local school for about 10,000 rp. Ask at (and don't forget to report to) the police station past the market, up the next hill.

Hitugi A hanging bridge leads from Kurima east to Hitugi about three hours away. From Hitugi, two trails lead north to Pugima, one nearer the river, the other more mountainous. You'll need at least two days to do a Wamena-Kurima-Hitugi-Pugima-Wamena circle.

Pugima The village of Pugima lies behind the first low line of hills as you look east across Wamena airstrip. It's a two to three-hour walk from the town. Take the rough road from the southern half of the airstrip past Westaput. At the river, turn south along the bank to the Kupelago Manunggal XIII Bridge (a half-hour walk from Wamena). The path on the other side of the bridge leads to Pugima. From Pugima to Uwosilimo is a worthwhile trek for good Dani culture.

Akima This nondescript village, about seven km north of Wamena just off the Jiwika road, is famous for its smoked mummy. It's all a bit artificial and contrived these days, but you can pay (the price is up to you) to see it. The body is hunched up in a sitting position, its head tucked down, arms wrapped around its knees, its clawed fingers draped over its feet. There are regular bemos there; look for the blue 'Mummy' sign.

Suruba & Dugum These two small villages are set beneath rocky outcrops off the Akima-Jiwika road. Suruba has nine compounds, Dugum five. Both have friendly people and a 'losmen' for visitors (ie compounds set slightly apart from the villagers' own, with Dani-style huts made of traditional materials). For about 8000 rp per person you get a floor covered in comfortable dry grass, and there's a separate hut for cooking. You wash in the creek. It's best to go with a guide who can introduce you to the villagers – they'll talk, smoke and drink with you and show you around their own compounds.

To reach Suruba, walk a few minutes east off the Jiwika road at Tanahmerah, 10 km from Wamena. For Dugum, continue one km beyond Tanahmerah then do the same. Bemos from Wamena will drop you at the turn-offs.

Jiwika There's a busy Sunday morning market at the largish village of Jiwika (pronounced 'Yiwika') 20 km from Wamena (1000 rp by bemo). Kurulu, the long-time chief here, was once such a powerful man in the valley that the Indonesians named the whole district surrounding Jiwika after him. A new Catholic church is being built in the village. About an hour's climb up the forested valley east of the village are some salt wells similar to those at Hitigima. At the foot of the path to the wells is a kiosk where you're supposed to pay an entrance fee.

Jiwika also has a mummy – the going price for seeing it is about 4000 rp.

There are two places to stay in Jiwika. The *Losmen Lauk Inn* (no telephone) has simple rooms without mandi for 11,000 rp per person with limited meals available (7000 rp); better rooms are being built. Nearby are the Dani-style *Wiyuk Huts* – you pay for tradition and not facilities – for 15,000 rp a person, which includes a Dani breakfast of sweet potato, and the possibility of some traditional dancing. Two day's walk east of Jiwika is **Wedangku** which still offers good examples of traditional Dani lifestyle.

Baliem Valley – North

You can do a loop up one side of the Baliem Valley, cross the bridge near Pyramid and walk down the other side, in three days or more, saving a day by taking a bemo between Wamena and Jiwika or Waga Waga, or lengthening the trip with deviations into side valleys of the Baliem or across the ranges into other valleys.

Waga Waga to Meagaima At Waga Waga, 21 km from Wamena and almost the furthest point on the east side for bemos, there are some caves which apparently contain the bones of victims of a past tribal war. You have to pay 1000 rp to enter and aren't likely to see the bones. The **Wikuda Caves** 500 metres past Uwosilimo are better. Locals will probably ask you for 1000 rp to enter the caves. There are plans to install some lighting, and a small losmen may be built nearby. From Uwosilimo, follow a small path west over a suspension bridge to **Danau Anegerak**, a lake apparently full of fish. Locals hire fishing equipment and can arrange basic accommodation.

From Uwosilimo, it's 1½ hours' walk through wooded country to the tiny village of Meagaima on a rise overlooking the Sungai Baliem. Before Meagaima (where there is a small losmen), another track leads down to the Sungai Baliem, which you can cross by canoe to **Pummo**, where there's another mummy.

Wolo Valley This is one of the most beautiful and spectacular side valleys of the Sungai Baliem. From Manda, just north of Meagaima, the gently rising riverside track to Wolo village is about 2½ hours' walk. Wolo, inspired by a strong strain of Evangelical Protestantism, is a nonsmoking place with lovely flower gardens. It won the 1988 'Most Progressive Village in Irian Jaya' title for a string of self-initiated projects including fish farming and a mini hydroelectric scheme which provides street lights.

From Wolo, there are walks (about two hours each) to a **waterfall** in the hills to the north, or up the **Sungai Wolo** to where it emerges from another cave. The main track up the Wolo Valley, however, leads to **Ilugua** (about 2½ hours). About two-thirds of the way to Ilugua, a side track to the right leads around a huge sinkhole and down to **Yogolok Cave** and **Goundal**, a tiny kampung on the floor of an awesome canyon. From Goundal, you can continue on to Ilugua – a full day's walk from Wolo. To see Goundal from the top of the canyon precipice, take a 10-minute side track to the right off the main Ilugua trail about 20 minutes before Ilugua. You need a guide to help you find these side tracks.

Meagaima to Kimbim It's about 3½ hours' flat walking west from Meagaima to the bridge over the Baliem just north of Pyramid, through Manda, past Jalenga, through Pilimo (a pretty place beside the Baliem) and Munak. Pyramid, a major mission and education centre near a pyramid-shaped hill about 35 km from Wamena, is about 1½ hours south of the bridge. Kimbim, with a police station and a Saturday morning market, another two hours' walk south, is a better place to stay.

Kimbim to Wamena This is a fairly dull stretch down the open west side of the main Baliem Valley – about eight hours' walk through Elagaima and Sinatma. There's a lower, usually muddier, route from Pyramid to Wamena via Miligatnem, Musatafak and Homhom.

North of the Baliem Valley

The northern end of the Baliem Valley and the regions around it are more heavily Christianised (mainly by Protestants) than the Wamena area. They were also the centre of conflict and destruction in 1977.

Directly north of the Baliem Valley, it's up-and-down walking. From Bolokme, just north of the bridge near Pyramid, it's about seven hours via Tagime to **Kelila**, which is at about 1300 metres but you climb up to over 2000 metres on the way. Kelila has a police station. From Kelila down to **Bokondini**, a missionary centre, is about 2½ hours (four or five hours coming back).

Lani Country (Western Dani)

West along the Baliem upstream from Pyramid is the country of the western Dani, who call themselves Lani.

There are tracks to Magi, the first main village, from Kimbim, Pyramid and Bolokme. Between the Sungai Pitt and Kuyawage the Baliem disappears underground for two km. Ilaga is about 60 km west of Kuyawage, beyond the western Baliem watershed. West of Sungai Pitt the going is often swampy.

Danau Habbema

From Ibele, west of the main Wamena to Pyramid track, it's two days up to this lake, at 3450 metres. Habbema is below the 4750-metre Gunung Trikora. The 1938 Archbold expedition set up a big camp beside Danau Habbema, ferrying men and supplies in by seaplane. You can charter a bemo (expensive) to where the road stops only 25 km from the lake, before walking – allow about two days – to the lake. You'll need to camp if you go there.

Pass Valley

Another popular trek is from Pass Valley, east of Uwosilimo, to Dombomi and to the **Apahapsili Waterfalls**, where birds of paradise may be seen – allow at least a week.

Yali Country

East and south of the Dani region are the Yali people, who have rectangular houses and whose men wear 'skirts' of rattan hoops, their penis gourds protruding from underneath. Missionaries are at work here, but the Indonesian presence is thinner than in the Baliem Valley. Bordering the Yali on the east are the Kim-Yal, who practised cannibalism up until the 1970s.

Reaching Yali country on foot involves plenty of ups and downs on steep trails. **Pronggoli**, the nearest centre from Wamena as the crow flies, is three days' hard walking by the most direct route, with camping needed along the way. From Pronggoli to **Angguruk** takes a day. Easier but longer is a southern loop through Kurima, Tangma (where there's a hanging bridge over the Baliem), Wet, Soba (the last Dani village, in a side valley off the Baliem Gorge), Ninia, then north to Angguruk. This takes about seven days. Along the way you can stay in teachers' or village houses. In Angguruk and Pronggoli the missions can often put you up.

Gunung Trikora

For the adventurous and physically fit, there is the possibility of climbing snow-clad Gunung Trikora. At around 4750 metres, Trikora is just 300 metres shy of Puncak Jaya, Irian Jaya's highest peak. Good equipment and a guide are essential. A special permit is also required to climb the mountain, which can only be obtained in Jakarta, or with the assistance, given plenty of notice, from travel agencies in Jayapura or Wamena which organises trips to the mountain, such as Chandra Nusantara in Wamena.

Far South

It's at least two weeks' walk from Wamena down to Dekai via Soba, Holuon and Sumo. From Dekai it could be possible to canoe downriver as far as Senggo on the fringes of the Asmat region – though you will probably need a special surat jalan to go that far.

Merauke

Although it is about the furthest you can go from Java within Indonesia, Merauke has a real Javanese feel about it, a result of the large transmigration centres in the area. There is also a northern Australian feel with the hot and dry climate (rainy season from December to May), the local flora (such as gum trees) and fauna (including kangaroos). Although pleasant and laid-back, the only real reason to visit Merauke is to change planes for Agats in the Asmat region, or to go to the Wasur National Park, which, itself, is difficult to visit.

Orientation & Information
Merauke has no town centre, and virtually everything you will need is on the long Jalan Raya Mandala. The modern Bank ExIm at the bottom of Jalan Raya Mandala is the only place that will change travellers' cheques. It's open from 8 am to 1.30 pm; closed Sunday. The police station (☎ 21706) is on Jalan Raya Mandala near the Hotel Nirmala. Immigration (☎ 21054) and the post office are on Jalan Trikora and Telkom is on Jalan Raya Mandala near the Hotel Megaria.

Surat Jalan Your surat jalan will probably be inspected at the airport. You will also need to report to the police station and give a copy of your surat jalan to your hotel; or a friendly, bored police officer may visit your hotel to look at it.

Pantai Lampu Satu
Lampu Satu ('one lamp') beach is pleasant enough, but crowded on Sunday. Take an irregular bemo from the terminal or walk for about three km from the corner where the Bank ExIm is.

Pulau Yos Sudarso
With a variety of other previous colonial names, Pulau Yos Sudarso is a huge, wild, undeveloped island near Merauke. From Merauke you can fly to the main town of

Kimam in less than 20 minutes every Wednesday or take an overnight boat. There are no losmen, so you will have to ask at the various missions or the locals, or take your own camping gear.

Festivals
The Asmat Cultural Exposition takes place in the first week of October, in both Merauke and Agats. Traditional dances, art and rowing can be seen.

Places to Stay
Transport costs have made Merauke an expensive place to stay. All prices listed include tax. The *Hotel Asmat* (☎ 21065), Jalan Trikora 3, has some character with older, comfortable singles/doubles for 15,100/20,800 rp, slightly more with a bathroom, plus 7000 rp for an extra bed. The *Losmen Merauke* (no telephone) at Jalan Raya Mandala 340, behind *Toko Sejati*, offers very, very basic rooms, with no bath or breakfast for 15,000/18,000 rp.

Along Jalan Raya Mandala, air-con, comfortable rooms with breakfast at about 35,000/50,000 rp can be found at the *Hotel Megaria* (☎ 21932) at No 166; the *Hotel Nirmala* (☎ 21849) at No 66, which also has some cheaper rooms; and at the *Flora Hotel* (☎ 21879), No 294.

Places to Eat
For some of the cheapest food, try the restaurant at the *Hotel Asmat*. Jalan Raya Mandala has the *Beautiful Nusantara Restaurant* at No 25, with karaoke (watch for overcharging); the *Nirmala* with a good selection of food; and the *Rumah Makan Sari Laut* next door, which serves great, cheap seafood but no beer. There are also plenty of places serving cheap, padang food.

A taxi ride out to the suburbs on Jalan Taman Makam Pahlawan is the *Oriental*, with good-value, up-market Chinese food (and the inevitable karaoke machine). Stalls in the Ampera market serve very cheap and delicious nasi campur.

Getting There & Away

Air Merpati goes to/from Jayapura four times a week (184,200 rp) – avoid the Monday trip via Tanahmerah; to Ewer (for Agats) three times a week (63,200 rp); and weekly to Senggo and Kepi in the Asmat region. The Merpati office (☎ 21242, 21181 after hours), Jalan Raya Mandala 163, is open from 7.30 am to 4.45 pm; closed Sunday.

Boat The Pelni ship *Tatamailau* goes to Tual in Maluku (58,000/232,000 rp for economy/1st class) every four weeks. The *Enggang*, *Teluk Sekar* and *Emprit* make fortnightly runs up the south coast, through Kimam (on Pulau Yos Sudarso), Bade, often Agats and, incredibly, as far inland as Tanahmerah. The *Iweri* links Merauke with Jayapura every three weeks. The Pelni office (☎ 21591), Jalan Sabang 318, is often closed because there are so few Pelni departures.

Getting Around

To/From the Airport Mopah airport is only four km from town. Take a chartered bemo for 7000 rp, or a bemo at the roundabout outside the airport for 500 rp. You may need to charter a bemo to the airport if your plane leaves early in the morning when public transport is less reliable.

Local Transport In Merauke, bemos have been given the Javanese name *mikrolets*. Hundreds of them go up and down the main street, as far as the airport and down to the harbour for 300 to 500 rp. They can be chartered for about 7000 rp per hour, or up to 56,000 rp for the day. The bemo terminal is next to the impressive and large Ampera market on Jalan Taman Makam Pahlawan.

WASUR NATIONAL PARK

The national park is the joint project of the World Wide Fund for Nature (WWF) and the traditional people, who contribute to, and benefit from, the park and its management. Its 412,387 hectares offers anthills, wetlands, traditional village life, bird life (74 unique species) and wildlife such as cuscus and even kangaroos. But with minimal transport and trails, these things are very, very difficult to see and enjoy, so a visit to the park is probably not worth the effort. The best (dry) season is from July to December; the wet season severely restricts travel within the park.

The WWF asks that travellers report to their Merauke office first; they arrange guides, if necessary (about 15,000 rp per day), transport and take payment for accommodation. They naturally urge users to behave and act responsibly in the park. The office (☎ 21397) is at Jalan Biak 12 (PO Box 184). To get there walk 30 metres towards the port from Flora Hotel, take the first street on the right, then walk 80 metres along an unmarked road. It's open from 7.30 am to 4.30 pm weekdays.

There is no public transport, so bemos must be hired for a day trip around the park for between 60,000 to 80,000 rp per day. Bemos to Yanggandur only will cost around 50,000 rp; prearrange a pick-up later or you will take a long time getting back to Merauke. There are good information offices at the two entrances, where you must register and pay 5000 rp.

The eastern entrance is at **Wasur**, 18 km from Merauke. The Trans-Irian Highway is good, but the road is bad to the village of **Yanggandur**, which has the only lodge in the park (there are plans to be build more soon). The accommodation is just a wooden hut, with some limited cooking facilities. Bring your own mattress, mossie net, and food. It costs 15,000 rp per person. You must get your surat jalan stamped at the police hut, from where the muddy path to the lodge starts. From Yanggandur, you can hire a horse (with guide, 10,000 rp per day) or go on foot to explore the wetlands, which, they claim, have birds of paradise. Generally, the wildlife is not abundant in areas accessible by horse or on foot.

The other, southern entrance is at **Ndalir** near some lovely beaches. You can stay at basic wooden huts at **Tomer** or at the beautiful **Onggaya Beach** (which is full of Australian pelicans around mid-year). With a 4WD in the dry season or by trekking or on horseback for several days you can go much further inland, quite close to the PNG border, and camp at several places. The information offices at the two entrances have more up-to-date details.

Asmat Region

The Asmat region is an inconceivably huge area of mangroves, pandanus and rivers with huge tides. The people are justifiably famous for their woodcarvings, and less so for their past head-hunting exploits. The area remains largely undeveloped, and one of the few truly unexplored regions left in the world. The Dutch set up an outpost along the coastline at Agats in 1953, but it was not until the highly publicised and still-controversial disappearance of US anthropologist Michael Rockefeller in 1961 near Agats that the area obtained any prominence.

To appreciate what the Asmat region has to offer will definitely take a lot of time and a lot of money. Individuals on a limited budget with no intense interest in the partic-

Central Asmat Region

ular regional culture may be very disappointed about how little they can see. Agats and the Asmat region is nowhere near as developed or accessible as Wamena and the Baliem Valley.

People

The region of Asmat has a population of over 60,000, consisting of 11 subgroups. The name Asmat either comes from the words *as akat* meaning 'right man' or from *osamat* meaning 'man from tree'. The people refer to themselves as *asmat-ow*, or the 'real people', the people of the land. The Asmat are semi-nomadic and dictated by rivers which are necessarily a source of transport and food.

Culture

Symbols The tree features heavily in Asmat symbolism, which is not surprising given the immense jungles of the region. The Asmat believe that humans are the image of a tree: their feet are its roots; the torso its trunk; the arms are the branches; and the fruit represents the head. Also an important element of their belief is that no person – except the very young and very old – dies for any other reason than through tribal fighting or by magic. So each death of a family member must be 'avenged' if the spirit of the recently dead can go to the spiritual world known as *safan*. Not so long ago, the avenging was carried out through head-hunting raids, and while it is now more ceremonial, it is still serious.

Woodcarving The Asmat have centred their belief around the figure of Fumeripitsj who first carved wooden figures, so creating the Asmat people. Through their carvings the Asmat remain in contact with their ancestors. Each village appoints a *wow ipits* or woodcarver based on their skills. Carvings are made for ceremonial purposes only, and then left to rot in the jungle. The carver uses only three colours: white, made from chalk and water; red from the earth; and black from charcoal.

There are a huge variety of carvings, and

all are important in funeral ceremonies. Decorated shields, made from mangrove roots, represent and avenge a dead relative, as do various, often huge, ancestor poles, called *bis*, and the ancestor figures *kawe*. Carved drums, made from lizard skins, are played during a feast; and wooden masks are named after a lost relative.

No longer used for head-hunting purposes, but still made for ceremonies (and tourists) are the horns which were used to herald the return of a head-hunting raid and to frighten enemies. Other ceremonial items include huge spears, paddles, and masks made from rattan and sago leaves. Figures on the carvings include birds and animals which fly such as praying mantis, hornbills, black cockatoos, cuscus and flying fox – all are head-hunting images.

Housing The centre of a village is the *yeu*, a ceremonial house used for sleeping by unmarried men. These are very smoky inside because of the permanently smouldering fireplaces called *yowse*, but also because all the men smoke tobacco! In inland areas, where the tides are very high, houses are raised up to 15 metres by poles called *yuresu*.

AGATS

Facilities in the Asmat region are very limited, and are virtually nonexistent outside Agats which itself has only two losmen, no daytime electricity (it starts at 5.30 pm every night), no telephones and limited fresh water. Due to the extraordinary tides and location, the 'streets' are simply raised, wooden and broken walkways, so, literally, watch your step.

Information

The Bank Rakyat, on Jalan Yos Sudarso, changes travellers' cheques. It's open in the mornings only, and is closed on Sunday. A surat jalan is a necessity for Agats and the Asmat region. On your arrival, report to the police station (well...hut). Give him a copy (have some ready: there are no photocopy machines for several thousand miles) and tell him which villages and areas you intend to visit.

Market

The small vegetable and fish Pasar Bhakti opposite the Asmat Inn starts at 5 am and is over in about an hour or so.

Pusat Asmat dan Pusat Pendidikan Asmat

The Asmat Centre and Asmat Education Centre are impressive buildings, of interest for their architecture if nothing else (they are usually empty). You may be able to see some carvings, and carvers at work here, if you're lucky. To get there, head north along Jalan Yos Sudarso, but watch out for the missing and loose planks.

Museum Kebudayaan dan Kemajuan

Open in 1973 to oppose a previous Indonesian government ban on local culture, the Museum of Culture & Progress is slowly improving. At present it offers some interesting, varied displays but with little or no explanations in any language. It's only open from 8 to 10 am daily except Sunday – but will definitely open for special groups (give some notice) and provide an English-speaking guide. For the enthusiast, there is a small, full library with detailed catalogues.

Festivals

The Asmat Art & Culture Festival is held in Agats every October, and includes woodcarving exhibitions, canoe races, and traditional dancing. In late September, the museum sponsors a popular woodcarving competition.

Places to Stay & Eat

There are only two losmen. To get to either, follow the signs from the dock as you come by boat from the airport, or walk towards town from the larger dock if arriving by boat. Singles/doubles at the *Asmat Inn* cost 15,000/30,000 rp, or 20,000/40,000 rp with mandi, plus tax. Rooms are clean, although noisy (honest!) from pedestrians on the creaky walkways outside. Good food (6000 rp per meal) and cold beer is available for guests, if ordered in advance.

Losmen Pada Elo has friendly service, good local information and standard rooms

To Asmat Centre

To Port

Police
Station ★

Agats

0   50   100 m

Approximate Scale
Pedestrian Streets Only

Bank Rakyat

✠ Mosque

To Dock
for Boats
to Airport

Asmat
Inn

Post
Office

Pasar Bhakti

Losmen
Pada Elo

Museum of
Culture & Progress 🏛

Warung Goyang
▼ Indah

Jalan Yos Sudarso

Jalan Kompas Agats

Pelni ●
Office

To Sjuru

from 15,000/30,000 rp, rooms with mandi from 25,000/50,000 rp (a little more for breakfast) – plus 20% tax. Guests can order food in advance for about 5000 rp a meal.

There is one – only one – rumah makan, the tiny, basic *Warung Goyang Indah* which serves nasi goreng and little else. The hotel food is definitely recommended – but remember to order all your meals in the morning.

Things to Buy

Genuine ceremonial woodcarvings, such as ancestor poles, are occasionally bought and sold despite this being sacrilege as far as Asmat beliefs are concerned – do not encourage this. Copies are available in villages, and in Agats. The copies are rarely done by the experts (wow ipits), so can be inferior to those you may see in the villages or in the museum. There is an enormous variety of masks, shields, poles, figures and drums for sale from different villages and of variable quality. The prices also vary considerably

depending on your bargaining ability, the number of tourists, the time involved in the carving and so on. As an example, expect to pay around 20,000 to 50,000 rp for a shield, and 40,000 rp for a large drum. Price and quality is not great in Agats, where there are a couple of souvenir shops.

Getting There & Away

Air The grass airstrip is at Ewer. The flight from Wamena has been stopped (due to bad weather or lack of passengers, depending on who you talk to), so this means a very long detour through Jayapura and then Merauke. (But you can get a connection from Jayapura to Ewer on the same day.) Merpati twin-otters fly to/from Merauke three times a week for 63,000 rp.

Before leaving Ewer, make absolutely sure that you quickly visit the Merpati office (well...hut) between the runway and river to confirm your flight out, because there are no telephones in the area. If this is not possible, ask the Asmat Inn to confirm with Merpati at Ewer on its short-wave radio. If you're in a real hurry or it seems you're not likely to get on a flight out of Ewer, a motorboat can be chartered to Timika, from where there are regular flights to Biak, for a mammoth 750,000 rp (nine hours) for up to six people.

Boat Boats make the trip to/from Agats and other towns in the region, but conditions are very basic. The Pelni liner *Tatamailau* stops here on its way to Merauke (25,000 rp) and returns via Timika (8000 rp) every month; the *Enggang* links Agats with Merauke every two weeks, and goes inland as far as Sawa Erma (2600 rp); and the *Iweri* goes to Timika (4000 rp) and Merauke (12,000 rp) every four weeks. The Pelni office, on Jalan Yos Sudarso, is open every day. The port for large boats is 10 minutes' walk north of the town (and is a good place for sunset-watching)

Getting Around

To/From the Airport At Ewer, follow everyone else to the river and take a shared motorised longboat for the great 20-minute trip to Agats (the official price is 5000 rp).

IRIAN JAYA

On the way from the airport to the river at Ewer, have a quick look at the well-preserved *yeu* or village long house. Returning to Ewer creates more of a problem. Make sure you ask at your hotel and find other plane passengers to share a motorboat back to Ewer to avoid chartering your own boat.

Motorboat Boats – all sorts of them – are the only form of local transport. Because of the high cost of transporting petrol (personally, I think this is not an entirely convincing argument) motorboat hire is incredibly expensive, and substantial bargaining is virtually impossible. The Asmat Inn can arrange a motorised longboat for about 250,000 rp a day, with very little room for negotiation. The boats do take between 10 and 15 passengers, but there aren't enough visitors to 'get a group together' to share hiring costs. Cheaper prices are possible – about 150,000 rp a day – if you ask around the nearby Sjuru village or at the museum, but the quality and speed of these boats will vary.

Before committing yourself to a lot of money, check the boat for the size of its motor, and therefore, its real and potential speed, and see if it has adequate cover for the harsh sun or rain. And make definite – even written – arrangements about full costs, destinations and hiring times. Boats can be hired for half a day (about 85,000 rp) at Sjuru, but this obviously limits where you can go. Boats cannot be rented by the hour.

Canoes Canoes are a far cheaper alternative but their speed severely limits where you can go. They can be hired for about 5000 rp per hour per boat plus 5000 rp per hour for each rower. These boats can carry two or three passengers, and you can see some tributaries – but little wildlife – among the mangroves near Agats. Ask at Sjuru, a small, friendly village 10-minutes' walk from Agats, or around the losmen, and bargain.

AROUND THE ASMAT REGION

While Agats is certainly the transport centre for the enormous area it services, transport to other villages is entirely by motorised longboat, and to reach anywhere of interest can take several days. Expect to pay at least 200,000 rp per day for a reputable boat, including a driver, then add 30,000 rp for a guide, 15,000 rp for a cook, and take all your own supplies. Villagers are all addicted smokers, and appreciate some tobacco, which can be bought in Agats. There are no losmen in the region outside Agats, but in the larger villages, such as **Senggo** and **Ayam**, you should be able to sleep at a mission or school house for about 10,000 rp per person, or take your own camping gear.

Within a day's motorboat ride from Agats, you can visit the simple villages of Yepem, Per, Owus, Beriten and Biwar Laut, which offer some hospitality, a chance to see some woodcarving and traditional housing. Alternatively, for bird life (and, unfortunately, mosquitoes) try **Buet-Kor** about five hours from Agats.

To experience the wildlife and jungle terrain, try walking along some shorelines – for example from Yepem to Owus in four to five hours – and be collected (you hope!) later by your motorboat.

Further out are the Kombai, Koroway and Citak Mitak people who live in tree houses raised at least 10 metres because of the tides and mosquitoes. Visits to these regions can be prearranged with travel agencies in Wamena or Jayapura. These agencies can charter planes to places like Dekai to greatly reduce what can easily be a seven-day motorboat trip, depending on tide levels, from Agats. Senggo, a larger central village can be reached from Agats in about two days, or every Wednesday by Merpati from Merauke. There are also weekly flights from Merauke to Kepi, in the southern Asmat region. But avoid travel in these regions in the wet season, from November to January, when the tides and waves make it very difficult.

Glossary

abangan – nominal Muslim, whose beliefs owe much to older, pre-Islamic mysticism

adat – traditional laws and regulations

agung – high, noble

air – water

Airlangga – 11th-century king of considerable historical and legendary importance in Bali

air panas – hot springs

air terjun – waterfall

aling aling – guard wall behind the entrance gate to a Balinese family compound; demons can only travel in straight lines so the aling aling prevents them from coming straight in through the front entrance

alun-alun – main public square of a town or village. They are usually found in front of the Bupati's (governor's) residence and were traditionally meeting areas and the place to hold public ceremonies. Nowadays they tend to be deserted, open grassed areas.

anak – child

andong – horse-drawn passenger cart

angklung – musical instrument made of differing lengths and thicknesses of bamboo suspended in a frame

angkot or **angkota** – short for *angkutan kota* (city transport), these small minibuses ply city routes

angkudes – short for *angkutan pedesaan*, these minibuses run to nearby villages from the cities, or run between villages

anjing – dog

arak – colourless distilled palm-wine firewater

Arja – particularly refined form of Balinese theatre

Arjuna – hero of the *Mahabharata* epic and a popular temple gate guardian image

ayam – chicken

Ayodya – Rama's kingdom in the *Ramayana*

Babad – early chronicle of Balinese history

babi – pork

Bahasa Indonesia – Indonesia's national language

bajaj – motorised three-wheeler taxi found in Jakarta

bakar – barbecued, roasted

bakmi – rice-flour noodles

bakso – meatball soup

balai – Dayak communal houses

bale – Balinese pavilion, house or shelter; a meeting place

Bali Aga – 'original' Balinese, who managed to resist the new ways brought in with Majapahit migration

balian – female shaman of the Tanjung Dayak people in Kalimantan

bandung – large cargo-cum-houseboats

banjar – local area of a Balinese village in which community activities are organised

banyan – see waringin

bapak – father; also a polite form of address to any older man

barat – west

baris – Balinese warrior dance

barong – mythical lion-dog creature, star of the Barong dance and a firm champion of good in the eternal struggle between good and evil

barong landung – enormous puppets known as the 'tall barong'; these can be seen at an annual festival on Serangan, Bali

barong tengkok – Lombok name for portable form of gamelan used for wedding processions and circumcision ceremonies

batik – cloth made by coating part of the cloth with wax, then dyeing it and melting the wax out. The waxed part is not coloured and repeated waxings and dyeings builds up a pattern.

becak – trishaw (bicycle-rickshaw)

belauran – night markets (Kalimantan)

belian – spiritual healer

bemo – popular local transport. Traditionally a small pickup-truck with a bench seat down each side in the back, these have mostly disappeared in favour of small minibuses. Bemo is a dated term, now rarely used in Indonesia but still widely used in Bali.

bendi – two-person dokar used in Sulawesi

bensin – petrol

berempah – traditional Sumbawan bare-fisted boxing

betang – communal house in Central Kalimantan

bhaga – miniature thatched-roof house dedicated to the ancestors of the Ngada people of Flores

bis – bus

bis air – water bus

blimbing – starfruit

bouraq – winged horse-like creature with the head of a woman; also the name of the domestic airline which mostly services the outer islands

Brahma – the creator; one of the trinity of Hindu gods

brem – fermented rice wine

bubur ayam – Indonesian porridge of rice or beans with chicken

bukit – hill

bupati – government official in charge of a regency (kabupaten)

camat – government official in charge of a district (kecamatan)

candi – shrine, or temple, of originally Javanese design, also known as a prasada

candi bentar – split gateway entrance to a Balinese temple

cap – metal stamp used to apply motifs to batik

cap cai – fried vegetables, sometimes with meat

catur yoga – ancient manuscript on religion and cosmology

cidomo – horse-drawn cart (Lombok)

cumi cumi – squid

dalang – storyteller of varied skills and considerable endurance who operates the puppets, tells the story and beats time in a wayang kulit shadow puppet performance

danau – lake

delman – horse-drawn passenger cart

desa – village

Dewi Sri – rice goddess

dokar – horse cart, still a popular form of local transport in many towns and larger villages

dukun – faith healer and herbal doctor or mystic

durian – fruit that 'smells like hell and tastes like heaven'

dwipa mulia – moneychanger

fu yung hai – sweet and sour omelette

gado-gado – traditional Indonesian dish of steamed bean sprouts, vegetables and a spicy peanut sauce

Gajah Mada – famous Majapahit prime minister

Gambuh – classical form of Balinese theatre

gamelan – traditional Javanese and Balinese orchestra, usually almost solely percussion, with large xylophones and gongs

Ganesh – Shiva's elephant-headed son

gang – alley or footpath

Garuda – mythical man-bird, the vehicle of Vishnu and the modern symbol of Indonesia; also the name of Indonesia's international airline

gereja – church

gili – islet or atoll

gringsing – rare double ikat woven cloth of Tenganan

gua – cave. The old spelling, *goa*, is also common.

gunung – mountain

haji, haja – Muslim who has made the pilgrimage to Mecca. Many Indonesians save all their lives to make the pilgrimage, and a haji (man) or haja (woman) commands great respect in the village.

halus – 'refined', high standards of behaviour and art; characters in wayang kulit performances are traditionally either halus or kasar

harga biasa – usual price

harga touris – tourist price

homestay – small family-run losmen

hutan – forest

huta – Batak village

ibu – mother; also polite form of address to any older woman

ikan – fish

ikat – cloth in which the pattern is produced

by dyeing the individual threads before weaving

Jaipongan – relatively modern, West Javanese dance incorporating elements of pencak silat and Ketuktilu

jalan – street or road

jalan jalan – to walk

jalan potong – short cut

jam karet – 'rubber time'

jamu – herbal medicine; most tonics go under this name and are supposed to cure everything from menstrual problems to baldness

jembatan – bridge

jeruk – citrus fruit

jidur – large cylindrical drums played widely throughout Lombok

jukung – prahu

kabupaten – regency

kacang – peanuts

kain – cloth

kaja – towards the mountains (Balinese)

kamar kecil – toilet, usually the traditional hole in the ground with footrests either side

kantor – office, as in kantor imigrasi (immigration office) or kantor pos (post office)

kasar – rough, coarse, crude; the opposite of halus

Kawi – classical Javanese, the language of poetry

kebaya – Chinese long-sleeved blouse with plunging front and embroidered edges

kebun – garden

kecapi – Sundanese (West Javanese) lute

kelapa – coconut

keliling – driving around (buses and bemos) to pick up passengers

kelod – towards the sea

kepala balai – Dayak village head

kepala desa – village chief

kepala stasiun – station master

kepeng – old Chinese coins with a hole in the centre, which were the everyday money during the Dutch era and can still be obtained quite readily from shops and antique dealers for just a few cents

kepiting – crab

ketoprak – popular Javanese folk theatre

Ketuktilu – traditional Sundanese dance in which professional female dancers (sometimes prostitutes) dance for male spectators

kina – quinine

klotok – canoe with water-pump motor used in Kalimantan

Konfrontasi – catchphrase of the early 1960s when Soekarno embarked on a confrontational campaign against Western imperialism, and expansionist policies in the region, aimed at Malaysia.

kopi – coffee

KORPRI – *Korp Pegawai Republik Indonesia* – the Indonesian bureaucracy.

kraton – walled city palace and traditionally the centre of Javanese culture. The two most famous and influential kratons are those of Yogyakarta and Solo.

kretek – Indonesian clove cigarette

kris – wavy-bladed traditional dagger, often held to have spiritual or magical powers

kueh – cakes

Kuningan – holy day celebrated throughout Bali 10 days after Galungan

ladang – non-irrigated field, often using slash-and-burn agriculture, for dry-land crops

lamin – communal house in East and West Kalimantan

langsam – crowded, peak-hour commuter train to the big cities

lesahan – traditional style of dining on straw mats

longbot – high-speed motorised canoe used on the rivers of Kalimantan

lontar – type of palm tree. Traditional books were written on the dried leaves of the lontar palm

lopo – beehive-shaped house found on Timor

losmen – basic accommodation, usually cheaper than hotels and often family-run

lumpia – spring rolls

Mahabharata – great Hindu holy book, telling of the battle between the Pandavas and the Korawas

Majapahit – last great Hindu dynasty in Java, pushed out of Java into Bali by the rise of Islamic power

mandi – usual Indonesian form of bath, consisting of a large water tank from which you ladle water to pour over yourself like a shower

marapu – Balinese term for all spiritual forces including gods, spirits and ancestors

martabak – pancake found at foodstalls everywhere; can be savoury but is usually very sweet

Merpati – major domestic airline

meru – multi-roofed shrines in Balinese temples; they take their name from the Hindu holy mountain, Mahameru. The same roof style can also be seen in ancient Javanese mosques.

mesjid – mosque

mie goreng – fried noodles, usually with vegetables, and sometimes meat

mikrolet – small taxi; a tiny opelet

menara – minaret, tower

moko – bronze drum from Alor (Nusa Tenggara)

muezzin – those who call the faithful to the mosque

muncak – 'barking deer' found on Java

naga – mythical snake-like creature

nanas – pineapple

nasi – cooked rice. Nasi goreng is the ubiquitous fried rice. Nasi campur is rice 'with the lot' – vegetables, meat or fish, peanuts, krupuk. Nasi gudeg is cooked jackfruit served with rice, chicken and spices. Nasi rames is rice with egg, vegetables, fish or meat. Nasi rawon is rice with a spicy hot beef soup.

ngadhu – parasol-like, thatched roof; ancestor totem of the Ngada people of Flores

nusa – island, as in Nusa Penida

Odalan – temple festival held every 210 days, the Balinese 'year'

ojek – motorcycle that takes passengers

opelet – small intra-city minibus, usually with side benches in the back

opor ayam – chicken cooked in coconut milk

Padang – city and region of Sumatra which has exported its cuisine to all corners of Indonesia. Padang food consists of spicy curries and rice, and is traditionally eaten with the right hand. In a Padang restaurant a number of dishes are laid out on the table, and only those that are eaten are paid for.

paduraksa – covered gateway to a Balinese temple

pak – shortened form of bapak

pandanus – palm plant used to make mats

pantai – beach

Pantun – ancient Malay poetical verse in rhyming couplets

parkir – a parking attendant. Anywhere a car is parked, these often self-appointed attendants will be on hand to find drivers a parking spot, look after their cars and stop traffic while they back out, all for a mere 300 rp or so tip. They may also do the job of traffic cops, blowing their whistles and directing traffic for small gratuities thrown by passing motorists.

pasanggrahan – lodge for government officials where travellers can usually stay

pasar – market

pasar malam – night market

pasar terapung – 'floating market' consisting of groups of boats to which buyers and sellers paddle to in boats

patih – prime minister

patola – ikat motif of a hexagon framing a type of four-pronged star

peci – black Muslim felt cap

pedanda – high priest

pelan pelan – slowly

Pelni – Pelayaran Nasional Indonesia, the national shipping line with major passenger ships operating throughout the archipelago

pemangku – temple priest

pencak silat – form of martial arts originally from Sumatra but now popular throughout Indonesia

pendopo – large, open-sided pavilion in front of a Javanese palace that serves as an audience hall

penginapan – simple lodging house

perbekel – government official in charge of a Balinese village (desa)

peresehan – popular form of one-to-one physical combat peculiar to Lombok, in which two men fight armed with a small hide shield for protection and a long rattan stave as a weapon

Pertamina – huge state-owned oil company

pesanggrahan – a rest house, usually a government run guest house for government officials

pinang – betel nut

pinisi – Makassar or Bugis schooner

pisang goreng – fried banana

pompa bensin – petrol station

pondok – guesthouse or lodge

prahu – traditional Indonesian outrigger boat

prasada – see candi

pulau – island

pura – temple

pura dalem – Balinese temple of the dead

puri – palace

pusaka – sacred heirlooms of a royal family

rafflesia – gigantic flower found in Sumatra, with blooms spreading up to a metre

raja – lord, prince or king

Ramadan – Muslim month of fasting, when devout Muslims refrain from eating, drinking and smoking during daylight hours

Ramayana – one of the great Hindu holy books, stories from the *Ramayana* form the keystone of many Balinese and Javanese dances and tales

rangda – witch; evil black-magic spirit of Balinese tales and dances

rattan – see *rotan*

Ratu Adil – the Just Prince who, by Javanese prophecy, will return to liberate Indonesia from oppression

rebab – two-stringed bowed lute

rijsttafel – Dutch for 'rice table'; a banquet of Dutch-style Indonesian food

rintek wuuk – spicy dog meat; a Minahasan (Sulawesi) delicacy

rotan – (rattan) – hardy, pliable vine used for handicrafts, furniture and weapons such as the staves in the spectacular trial of strength ceremony, peresehan, in Lombok

roti – bread; usually white and sweet

rudat – traditional Sasak dance overlaid with Islamic influence

rumah adat – traditional house

rumah makan – restaurant or warung (eating house)

rumah sakit – hospital

sambal – chilli sauce

Sanghyang – trance dance in which the dancers impersonate a local village god

Sanghyang Widi – Balinese supreme being, never actually worshipped as such; one of the 'three in one' or lesser gods stands in

santri – orthodox, devout Muslim

saron – xylophone-like gamelan instrument, with bronze bars struck with a wooden mallet

sarong – (or sarung) – all-purpose cloth, often sewed into a tube, and worn by women, men and children

Sasak – native of Lombok

sate (satay) – classic Indonesian dish; small pieces of charcoal-grilled meat on a skewer served with spicy peanut sauce

sawah – an individual rice field, or the wet-rice method of cultivation

sayur – vegetable

selat – strait

selatan – south

selendang – shawl

selimut – blanket

Sempati – domestic airline which flies to Kalimantan, southern Sumatra and Java

Shiva – one of the trinity of Hindu gods

sirih – betel nut, chewed as a mild narcotic

sisemba – form of kick-boxing popular with the Torajan people of Sulawesi

songket – silver or gold-threaded cloth, hand woven using floating weft technique

sop, soto – soup

sudra – lowest or common caste to which most Balinese belong

stasiun – station

suling – bamboo flute

sungai – river

syahbandar – harbour master

tahu – soybean curd (tofu)

taman – 'garden with a pond'; ornamental garden

tari topeng – type of masked dance peculiar to the Cirebon area

tarling – musical style of the Cirebon area, featuring guitar, suling and voice

tau tau – life-sized carved wooden effigies of the dead placed on balconies outside cave graves in Torajaland, Sulawesi

taxi sungai – cargo-carrying river ferry with bunks on the upper level

tedong-tedong – tiny structures over graves that look like houses found in Sulawesi

teluk – bay

telur – egg

tempe – fermented soybean cake

timur – east

tomate – Torajan funeral ceremony

tongkonan – traditional Torajan house

topeng – wooden mask used in funerary dances

tuak – alcoholic drink fermented from palm sap or rice

uang – money

udang – prawn

ular – snake

utara – north

Vishnu – one of the trinity of Hindu gods

wali songo – nine holy men who propagated Islam in Java

Wallace Line – imaginary line running between Bali and Lombok and Kalimantan and Sulawesi, which marks the end of Asian and the beginning of Australasian flora & fauna.

wantilan – open pavilion used to stage cock-fights

waringin – banyan tree; a large and shady tree with drooping branches which root and can produce new trees. It was under a banyan (bo) tree that the Buddha achieved enlightenment, and waringin are found at many temples in Bali.

wartel – private telephone office

waruga – pre-Christian Minahasan (Sulawesi) tomb

warung – food stall; a sort of Indonesian equivalent to a combination of corner shop and snack bar

wayang kulit – shadow-puppet play

wayang orang – Javanese theatre or 'people wayang'

wayang topeng – masked dance drama

wayang wong – see wayang orang

Wektu Telu – religion, peculiar to Lombok, which originated in Bayan and combines many tenets of Islam and aspects of other faiths

wisma – guesthouse or lodge

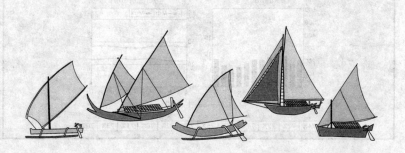

Appendix

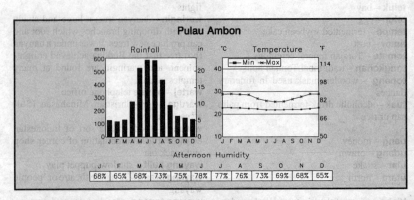

Pulau Ambon

Rainfall (mm / in)

Temperature (°C / °F) — Min —*— Max

Afternoon Humidity

J	F	M	A	M	J	J	A	S	O	N	D
68%	65%	68%	73%	75%	78%	77%	76%	73%	69%	68%	65%

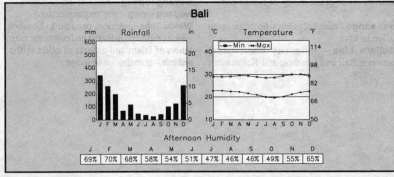

Bali

Rainfall (mm / in)

Temperature (°C / °F) — Min —*— Max

Afternoon Humidity

J	F	M	A	M	J	J	A	S	O	N	D
69%	70%	68%	58%	54%	51%	47%	46%	46%	49%	55%	65%

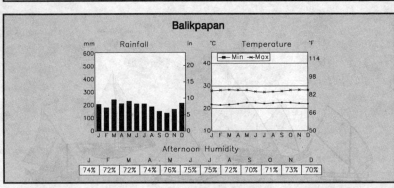

Balikpapan

Rainfall (mm / in)

Temperature (°C / °F) — Min —*— Max

Afternoon Humidity

J	F	M	A	M	J	J	A	S	O	N	D
74%	72%	72%	74%	76%	75%	75%	72%	70%	71%	73%	70%

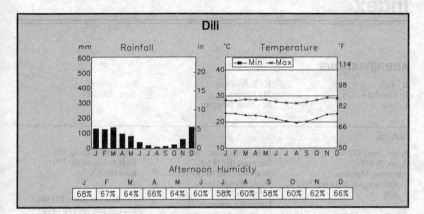

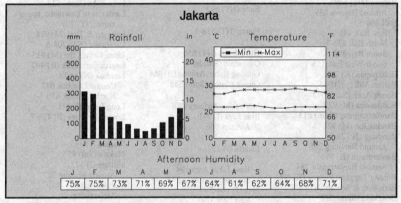

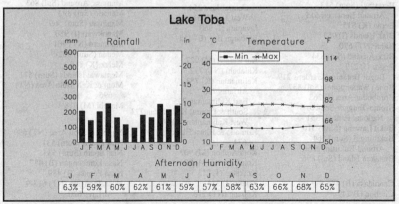

Index

988

TEXT

Map references are in **bold** type.

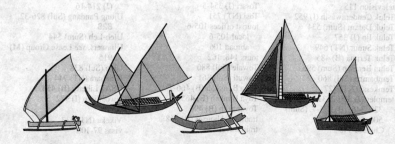

THANKS

Thanks also to those travellers who took the time and trouble to write to us about their experiences in Indonesia. Writers (apologies if we've misspelt your name) to whom thanks must go include:

Machteld Aberson (Nl), Ulrika Ahlander (S), Heather Alexander (Aus), Colin Alfandary (UK), Tim Allen (Aus), Annet & Wim van Alten (Nl), Konstanze Ammann, Michael Anacker (D), Ridwan Anaktototy, Hartley Anderson (Aus), Carolyn Magnie Applegate, Jeff & Sonja Apter (Aus), Silvia Arduini (I), Richard Aslett (UK)

Amanda Bachman (Aus), Jacqueline Baer (Aus), M W Bagnall (UK), Godely Bahher (Nl), Chris Bain (Aus), Thomas Bajor (Aus), Simon Baker (UK), Klaas Bakker (Nl), Bouwe Bakker (Nl), Goran Baltschew (S), David Banfield (UK), Anne Bang (Dk), Delia Banks (UK), John Barnett (NZ), Judy Bayens (Aus), Adrian Baron, Nicky Bean (Aus), Andre van Beeke (Nl), Greg Beel (Aus), Jerry van Beers (Nl), Driek van Beikering (Nl), Jan Bennink (Nl), Tom Benson (UK), Dr Simon Benson (Aus), Andrea & Alan Blackford (Aus), Louise Blair (Aus), Helen Bodycomb (UK), Ingrid Boelhouwer (Nl), C & C Bohlin (S), Mr M J Bos (NZ), Alexandra Botcher, Martin Bottenberg (Nl), David Boyall (Aus), Eric Bradfield (NZ), John & Barbara Brand (Nl), John Brandi (USA), Kees Brantjes (Nl), Guilio Bregliano (I), Ingrid Bremer (D), Katie Brigg (UK), M Brockotter (Nl), Adrienne Brodsky (USA), Peter & Ilonka Broekroelofs (Nl), Elizabeth Brons (Nl), Jane Brooks (USA), Joyce Brown, M Bruce (Aus), Sean, Zach & Bede Bruce-Cullen (Aus), Carina Buijs (Nl), Frank Bukkems (Nl), Kathryn Bullock (UK), Mat Burbury (UK), Peter Burton (Aus), Steve Burton (UK), Joyce & Leonard Butcher (UK), Elizabeth Butters (UK), F & T Byl (Nl)

Jane Cabutti (UK), Lisa Cadman (UK), Nigel Calvert (UK), Donald B Campbell (C), Liz Capaldi (UK), Sarah Carpenter (UK), Paola Cassone (I), Antonio Castro (I), Helena Celesnik, Dr Heather Chaffey (Aus), Jacques Chapon (F), Brigitte Carpenter (C), Yu Wa Chen, Janet Chinn (USA), Mal Clarbrough, Karen Clarke (C), David Clarke (Aus), D K Clarke (Aus), Jacqui Cleary (USA), Janet Cochrane (UK), Laurie Cohen (UK), Jan Coolhaas (Aus), Luisa Corbetta (I), Graham Cox (Aus), Peter Crayson (Aus), John Cross (USA), Suzanne Crowe (Aus), Graeme Cruickshank (UK), Rob Culham (UK), John Cusden

Hans Damen (Nl), Daphne Danen (Aus), Claire Davenport (UK), M V David-Tooze (Aus), Sue Canney Davison (UK), Tim & Melanie Dawson (USA), Liesbet De Munck (B), Anders de VosR Dean (Aus), Bronwyn Deane (Aus), Nick Debere (UK), Patrick Degreef (B), Alex Degan (USA), Janneke Delhoofen, Wendy & Alicia Denton (Aus), Andrew Dinwoodie, Glynis & Mark Dixon (Aus), Mirjam van Dongen (Nl), Michele Dowling, Martin Drake (UK), Hannie Duizings (Nl), Joanne Duret (C), Perry van Duynhoven (Nl)

Julie Easton (USA), Wilma van d Eertwegh (Nl), Ruth Eliel (USA), C M Ellery (UK), Sharon C Elliot (UK), Tony Elliott (Aus), Steve Emmerman (USA), Joachim Endress (D), Jill Ennever (Aus), Robert Esguerra (Aus), Elisabeth Euvrard (F), Mark Evans (Aus), Garry Evans (Aus), James Evard (USA), Tim Eyre (UK)

R K Faint (Aus), C Farrington Margie Figgins (USA), George Findlay, Erland Flaten (Nl), Michelle Ford (Aus), Barabara Forza (I), Stavros Fragakis, Mark Franken (Nl), John Freeman, Ariane Frey (CH), Louise Frost (UK), Mendell Fugate (USA), Dianna J Funk (C), Jane Furkert (UK)

David Galef (USA), Peter Gammzltoft (Dk), Ian Gason (Aus), Steve Geden (UK), A M Gent (UK), Grace Gevers (Nl), Hubert Gieschen (D), Sean Gilbert (USA), Tim Giles (Aus), Ty & Helen Gillespie (USA), Susan Gilmore (UK), Toni Glaser (S), Martine Glasson (CH), Tracey Gold (Aus), Bambi Goldmark (USA), Carolyn & Gary Gracie (Aus), R G Green (UK), Paul Greening, John & Lynne Griffiths (Aus), Brigitte Gronemeir (Dk), Seth Gross (USA)

Peter Haase (Nl), Christian Habliitzel (CH), Luc Hachez (B), Wolfgang Haeusl (Aus), Prof W T Hagestad (Nl), Leonard Halim, Clare Hall, David Halperin (Aus), Douglas Hamilton (USA), Ruth & Don Hanna (Aus), Leif Hansen (Dk), Mrs J Hanson (Aus), Julie Hanssens (Aus), Marcus Harley (UK), J Harper (Aus), Mr & Mrs D Harper (UK), Tracey Hartley (UK), Angelika Hautmann (D), Dirk van du Havegheu (B), Diana Headley (USA), Judith Hedley, Johannes Heermann (D), Dirk Hejndrickx (B), K v't Hek (Nl), Pete Helsby (Aus), Kimberely Henden (Aus), P Jansen Hendriks, J Higgon (Aus), Kathryn Hill (UK), Richard Hilson (UK), Finngeir Hiorth (N), Karin Hisschle (CH), M Hoenveld (Nl), Barbara Hogan (UK), Ben Hole (UK), Philip Holley (C), Christian Holm (Dk), W H Hooyer (Nl), Michael Horsburgh (Aus), Eric Hostettler (CH), Annette Hotschmann, Stephen Howell (NZ), Shirley Hoyle (UK), Una Hughes (Irl), Dr Lee Hsiao Hui (Sin), Ron & Jessica van Hunnik (Nl), J C Husband (UK), H E Huynisk (Nl)

Dr A Iyer (UK)

Oliver Jackson (UK), Patricia James (Nl), Virginia Jealous, Jane & K V Johansen (Dk), Lewis Jones (UK), Evan Jones, Richard Judge (NZ)

Anton Kalotong, Hans Kaper (USA), Jeff Kaye (Aus), Michelle Kean (Aus), Joanna Keighley (Aus), Wendy Kelton (Aus), Melodie Kemp (Aus), Alan Kettle-White (UK), Sjaak Keyers, M Kikkert (Nl), Georgiou Kitsov (G), Fred Kleinveld (Nl), Norbert Klose (NZ), Irene Koster, A Kouwenhoven (Nl), Monika Kralik, Natasha, Kraus (C), Clems Kremer (D), Jorgen Krogh (D), Marten Kuijk (Nl), Hans-Joachim Kullmann (D), Freddie Kung (CH)

Dave Laming, Christy Lanzl (USA), Jenny Latimer (Aus), Maren Lawrence (NZ), John Le Long, Rachel Lee (Aus), Elizabeth Lee (USA), Danny Leemans (B), Iene Lemmens (Nl), G Leondhard (D), Jet Levi (Nl), Beth Levy (USA), Will Lewis (UK), Claus Liebl (D), Carl Lind (Sin), Zoe Lindsay, Jasper Lloyd (UK), Jose M Lomas (S), Owen Loney (Aus), Rebecca Lord, Michel Louis (F), Janet Louise (J), Kerryn Lowe (Aus), L & C Lowson (Aus), R Lowther (UK), Linda Ludurg (Aus), Susan Luketina (Aus), Jesper Lundstedt (Dk), Ernst Lurken (D), B Luyt (J)

Liz Mackenzie (UK), Jan Maehl (D), Etienne Maes (Dk), Andrea Magri (I), Joachim Majholm (Dk), Betty Malang (M), Katie Malcom (UK), S Manicom (UK), Geoffrey Mann (UK), Chris Marjo (Aus), Chris Marriott (UK), James Martin (Aus), Jay Martin (Aus), Karen Mason (Aus), Ian Mathews (UK), Scott Mathieson (NZ), Daryl Matthews (USA), Claire Matthews (C), Johnny Mattsson (S), Boaz Mayzel (Isr), Lou & Jim McAdoo (USA), Annette McCarthy (Aus), Neil McCrindle (UK), Howard McDonald (C), Michael McGuirk (UK), Colin McKenzie (UK), Mike McLean (UK), Andrew McMeeking (UK), Ian McVittie (UK), Y Meder (J), Ben Menadue (USA), Stephen G Meredith (Aus), Hans Meyers (B), Paul van Miert (Nl), Birte Mikkelsen (Dk), C Mills (Irl), Saidie Mir (Aus), Steve Mirams (Aus), Kathleen Mitchinson, Catherine Moir-Bussy, Johan Molenaar (Nl), Christiane Moll (D), Stephen Moore (USA), Graham Morgan (Aus), Nadamo Munter (D), Allan Murphy (Aus)

Heico Neumeyer (D), Jo Anne New (UK), David Newman (UK), Kerry Nicholas (Aus), S Nielsen (Dk), Kirsten Nielsen (Dk), Ole Nielsen (Dk), K & S Nilsson (S), Jacob Noenoehitoe, Jan Noot (Nl), Bill Norman (Aus), Michelle Nuss (Aus)

Shivam O'Brien (UK), Barry O'Keeffe (Aus), Mike & Kerri Ogden (Aus), David Ogg (Aus), Mark Ogilvie (UK), Dr Robin Oldfield (UK), A & E Oldhoff (Irl), Martijn van Olst (Nl), Eugene Orwell (Aus), Sera Orzel (UK)

R Eugene Parnell (USA), Andrew Paterson (UK), Antoine Payot (CH), Jasper Pearson (UK), Michael Pearson (UK), Stephen Pelizzo (Aus), M Philippe (F), Ben Phillips (UK), Dave Pike (USA), Silvia Pisanti (I), Peter Pluymers, Rinske Potjewijd (Nl), David Powell (UK), Karsten Pries (D), E H Prillwitz (Nl)

Patricia Quintens (B)

Michael Radcliffe (Aus), Andy Rankin (Aus), Daniel Rantzen (Aus), Laura Read (UK), D R Reeves (UK), Heidi Reitmeyer (D), Tony Richards (UK), Karen Riley, Rachel Roberts (UK), Peter & Jenny Roberts (Aus), Andrew Robertson (Aus), Liz Robinson (UK), Mark Robinson (Aus), Ann Rocchi, Antonio Rodriguez (Sp), Gottfried Roelcke, Giselle Rondiltap (Nl), Bouhje Ryn (Nl)

Annika Sagnell (CH), Jack Salvador (USA), Vanessa Samson (F), Frida Sandstrom (S), Graziella Sassoe (I), Penelope Saunders (UK), Markus Schar (Aus), Astrid Scheeve (Nl), B & E Scheffer (D), Mark Scheidegger (USA), Bernhard Schindler (D), Michael Schlicht (I), Nicole Schmidt, Charlotte Schmidt Hansen (Dk), Peter Schouten (Nl), Caroline Shannon (C), Florence Shaw (Aus), Catherine Shute (UK), Malcolm Silverstone (Aus), Jo Simpson (UK), Alistair Sinclair (Aus), Eyvin Siverston (N), Pamela A Skinn (UK), Ian Skinner (Aus), Neil Sloman (UK), Meredith Small (USA), Andy Smith, Lelsey Smith (Aus), Sian Sokota (UK), Solange Souvignet (UK), Jules Spaanjaars (Nl), Lorraine Space (UK), Manfred Spliedt (Dk), J A Spykman Doornbos (Nl), Paloma Stam (Nl), Silvia Stange (D), Thijs de Ruyter van Steveninck (Nl), Dave & Phyllis Stolls (USA), Jan Stuytstraat (Nl), Pieter Swart (D), Paul Sykes (UK)

Jason Tan (Sin), Miss YC Tay (Aus), Mike Taylor, Barak Tchelet (Isr), Nicole Teuwen (Nl), Christine Thiebaut, Raphael Thiry (F), Keith & Birgid Thompson (C), Mark Thorn (UK), Jane Thurston-Hoskin (UK), Neil Tilbrook (Aus), Ryland Tippett, Rossana Tissi (I), Mark Titcombe (UK), R van Trigt (Nl), Anneke Tromp (Nl), Andrew Tyson (Aus)

Armin Uhlig (D), John E Uribe (USA)

Alice Valentine (UK), Pieter Valkenburg (Nl), R J Vastenhoud (Nl), Jurgen Veenker (Nl), Julian & Debby Veitch (UK), Mrs S A Op het Veld-Sival (Nl), Filip Verbelu (B), Monique Verbiest, Clary Verbunt (Aus), Dr E Verheij (Nl), Dorlene Verhoeven (Nl), Michel van Verk (Nl), Marina & Stella Violati (I), Christian Vogt (CH), Sabrina Volonte (I), Hans & Odette van de Vorst (Nl), Family Vos (Nl), M Vriend (Nl)

Mickey Wach (USA), Gunnar Wahlberg (S), Bryan Walter (Aus), Christine Waring, Rosalind Watson (Aus), Alan Watson (UK), David Watts (UK), Jochem Weber (D), Kees Weevers (Nl), Sven Weichert (D), Jeff Weisel (USA), Trudy Wel (Nl), Douglas Werner (UK), Gunawan & Elie Wibisono, Irsan Widarto (Nl), Jero Wijaya, Mavis Williams (Aus), Lawrence Williams (UK), Ben Williams (UK), David Williams (USA), Bev Williams, Steven Windholz (C), P M Wink (Nl), Rits Woudstra (Nl), Roger Wright (USA)

Ben Yates (UK), Jo Yoshida (C), Elizabeth Young (USA)

Martina Zegowik (D), Aase Zeuten (Dk)

Aus – Australia, B – Belgium, C – Canada, CH – Switzerland, D – Germany, Dk – Denmark, F – France, G – Greece, I – Italy, Irl – Ireland, Isr – Israel, J – Japan, N – Norway, Nl – The Netherlands, NZ – New Zealand, S – Sweden, Sin – Singapore, UK – United Kingdom, USA – United States of America

Update – March 1996

Indonesia and Australia signed a security agreement in late 1995, after 18 months of secret negotiations.

HEALTH

Make sure you get the latest information on health risks in this area. For example, Japanese encephalitis is slowly spreading (so try to avoid being bitten by mosquitos). Hot springs can spread many diseases, so don't use them if you have a cut, and don't put your head under water.

DANGERS & ANNOYANCES

Drownings of visitors are depressingly common on Kuta Beach (Bali) because of the strong currents. Make sure that you swim between the flags, and don't expect state-of-the-art rescue equipment if you do get into trouble.

We have received reports about travellers becoming lost while climbing mountains. One traveller who became separated from his guide spent four days and nights on a mountain without food or water, and when he finally made his way back he found that no-one had been looking for him.

When hiring a car in Bali, you must hold a valid international licence, otherwise you risk a very hefty fine.

GETTING THERE & AWAY
Air

Emirates Airlines has a three-weekly direct flight between Dubai/Jakarta/Melbourne.

Merpati now flies between Darwin (Australia) and Ambon, departing on Monday and Friday. The fare is about A$300 one-way, A$500 return.

Qantas now has direct flights between Perth (Australia) and Jakarta.

Boat

A traveller reports that there is a boat running between Manado (North Sulawesi) and General Santos (Mindanao, The Philippines). Contact Pelayaran Fajar Lines, at

Dear traveller

Prices go up, good places go bad, bad places go bankrupt...and every guidebook is inevitably outdated in places. Fortunately, many travellers write to us about their experiences, telling us when things have changed. If we reprint a book between editions, we try to include the best of this information in an Update section. We also make travellers' tips immediately available on our award-winning World Wide Web Internet site (http://www.lonelyplanet.com) and in a free quarterly newsletter, *Planet Talk*.

Although much of this information has not been verified by our own first-hand research, we believe it can be very useful. We cannot vouch for its accuracy, however, so bear in mind it could be wrong.

We really enjoy hearing from people out on the road, and apart from guaranteeing that others will benefit from your good and bad experiences, we're prepared to bribe you with the offer of a free book for sending us substantial useful information.

I hope you do find this book useful – and that you let us know when it isn't. Thank you to everyone who has written.

Tony Wheeler

their office in front of the Perusahaan Umum Pegadaian.

The boat company in Bitung (Harbour of Manado) is PT Fajar Line, Jalan Dr Sukarno no 77. It takes three days from Bitung to General Santos and the fare is US$50. You also need US$4 for a Philippines visa.

GETTING AROUND
Boat

Many boat timetables have changed.

The Pelni office in Ujung Pandang (Sulawesi) has moved to Jend Sudirman, just between Jalan Mochtar Lujti Sawengading and Jalan Datumusengemi.

If you're travelling by tour boat between Flores and Lombok via Komodo during the rainy season, consider taking the three-day rather than the five-day trip. Five days of rain and rough seas can be hard to take.

Motorcycle

Getting a motorbike licence on Bali is now a much more streamlined process. Travellers report that it can take as little as an hour, at a cost of 55,000 rp.

DESTINATIONS
Bali

Many telephone numbers have changed, mainly in the Lovina area. If you are having trouble getting through, try replacing the first two numbers with 41.

Irian Jaya

A group of international scientists, kidnapped by OPM (Free Papua Movement) rebels in early 1996, are about to be released unharmed. It seems that the OPM is satisfied that the kidnapping has attracted sufficient international attention to their plight. Still, having found that kidnapping works, it is possible that they will try again.

Java

Borobudur During the dry season there is a *son et lumiere* show at Borobudur. UNESCO has given permission for the controversial project, with strict limits on the numbers of people attending.

Gunung Merapi There is continuing controversy over which is the safest route. Rogier Gryus (Can) adds his opinion:

The climb from Selo is said to be easier, shorter and physically safer, but in practice it is more dangerous, as guides will take you up even if the mountain has been closed for climbing. Note the stats – on the Selo side over 30 people have been killed over the past decade, on the Kaliurang side only one.

Jakarta Not all Damri buses stop at Gambir station on the run between the airport and Blok M, despite the drivers' assurances. You'll have to read the sign on the front of the bus.

Krakatau Following increased volcanic activity, climbing Krakatau has been prohibited. This ban might be lifted if the mountain is quiet for a few months.

Kalimantan

Flights into the interior of East Kalimantan (eg, to Apokayan) are fully booked well in advance, so this option is usually out of the question.

Samarinda A group called PLASMA (☎ (0541) 35753) is concerned with helping indigenous people and the environment, both under threat from logging and development. They might be able to help you plan an upriver trip to visit the forests. The address is Jalan Pertahana Perum Yeschar no 1, Sempaja Samarinda 75119.

Nusa Tenggara

Keli Mutu Leaving the paths and wandering off on your own around the lakes might not be such a good idea any more, as earthquakes have made the ground unstable.

Komodo The park wardens have stopped feeding the dragons so they don't lose the ability to hunt. The dragons still congregate where they used to be fed and now you might see the rather more exciting sight of a dragon sprinting after one of the semi-tame deer that hang around the tourist camp.

Lombok The local Regional Authority has decreed that all tourist accommodation must have Indonesian names – for example, Fantastic Bungalows has been renamed Abdi. However, they are allowed to include the old name on the sign and will probably continue to be known by the old name for some time to come.

Maluku

A traveller reports that you can still get permits for Manusela National Park from the Paso (Pulau Ambon) office. He says that the best starting point for the park is now Mosso, from where there is a newer, shorter trail. Boats run between Amahai and Tehoru in the evenings for 7,500 rp. There are buses from Amahai to Telohu. The trip costs 5000 rp, takes about five hours and isn't too rough. From Tehoru, outriggers will take you across the bay for around 7,500 to 10,000 rp.

Sulawesi

Lore Lindu National Park A reader reports that you don't need a permit to enter Lore Lindu National Park and you can visit without first hiring a guide – you can hire one on arrival. He warns that it's nearly impossible to fly back out, as your seat will automatically be bumped for a local. The 65 km road back to Tejntena took two days by jeep.

Sumatra

Bukit Lawang Be careful if you hire tubes to float down the river. It's idyllic but the current can be very strong and there are lots of hidden trees in the water waiting to catch you. Taking a life jacket, helmet and paddle would be a good idea.

Gunung Merapi Climbing Gunung Merapi is now officially forbidden but there is an observation point you can reach to look at it. (We've had unconfirmed reports that this has been destroyed in an eruption.) Apparently some people still climb – not a good idea.

While we looked at Merapi, it rumbled and we saw a small amount of black lava move near the top. We though that the tours still being organised to climb Merapi are mad!

P Teriaca (UK)

TRAVELLERS' TIPS & COMMENTS

The Bahasa phrase *jalan jalan* (just walking) came in handy as an answer to the constant question, 'Where are you going?'

Amy Wharton & Alex Trion (USA)

The original hand-weaving workshops in the village of Sukarara (Nusa Tenggara) are gradually dying out due to three much larger, flashy, showy showrooms nearer the Puyung turning. Most visitors only go this far and don't bother to venture a further 1.5 km down the road to the old village. It's well worth it, as their 'starting prices' are much lower. They also have some unique weavings.

Nick Male

Pulau Banyak (Sumatra) are the most perfect, beautiful tropical islands I have ever visited, but they are nowhere near able to cope with the flow of travellers they receive. There is insufficient accommodation and not much food available in it. Basically, no-one has a clue out there, but if it's adventure you're after,

then go for it. Make sure you can speak some Indonesian before you head out there.

Helen Jeffs (Aus)

What can I say about Gili Trawangan, this once-beautiful Isle? At the time of writing the government goons were in full flow designing their five star golf course resort and if you want my opinion, you can let them have it.

Due to some pretty shoddy behaviour by certain fellow travellers, most of the inner road round the island is now dead and as night follows day the island's beaches are being gradually eroded.

Litter is becoming a major problem. Whilst I was there around Christmas many people got robbed in the central area and two Swiss guys were severely beaten by a group of locals.

Ray Coe

Tourist visas issued in Vanimo (PNG) are only valid for four weeks, but this may change. They can be extended in Indonesia for an additional two weeks. The consulate in Vanimo is amazingly efficient; you should be able to get the visa within an hour or so. Visas cost about K20 and you need two passport pictures.

If you are going to PNG from Irian Jaya and plan to come back again via Vanimo, you can pick up a new visa on the way through Vanimo on your way into PNG. This saves you from having to worry about it on the way out. You will be allowed to enter Indonesia for up to three months after the visa has been issued.

Banks in Irian Jaya often do not accept Thomas Cook or Visa travellers' cheques; American Express only. Apparently all branches of Bank Pembangunan Daerah in Irian Jaya with a phone will give out cash advances on Visa credit cards. Bank International Indonesia (BII; not Bank Indonesia) is a new bank which supposedly also gives cash advances on credit cards.

The Air Niugini flight from Vanimo to Jayapura has supposedly been cancelled, but there are rumours of it being taken over by Sempati.

At this time you are not allowed to cross by land and you are bound to be caught. There is an army checkpoint nine km from the border at the only bridge over a crocodile infested river, and the border area is patrolled regularly by trigger-happy soldiers. The road between Jayapura and Vanimo in PNG is nearly finished. It is supposed to open sometime next year.

There are small boats plying the waters between Vanimo and Jayapura. The owner of the Vanimo Resort Hotel has a boat and can arrange a trip to Jayapura. In Jayapura he has an agent, supposedly in the Garuda building in downtown Jayapura on Jalan Percetakan on the 3rd or 4th floor.

The luggage allowance on Twin Otters in Irian Jaya is only 10 kg. Especially on the longer flights, the overweight fee can be substantial, because it is 1% of a full-fare ticket per kg.

Be aware that in out-of-the-way places it is virtually impossible to re-route tickets issued abroad. If the flight on your ticket is cancelled and you have to get a re-routing or even a different flight number on the same route, most Merpati offices won't touch it , even if a re-routing would be the same price. Word has it that in centres like Biak they are authorised to change the tickets, but I wouldn't count on it. If they make you buy a new ticket, go into to the biggest Garuda/Merpati office you pass and ask for an XO – a rebate on the ticket you had to buy. Be sure to carry enough money to be able to buy new tickets if needed.

The system used on Merpati on the back-routes in Irian Jaya is rather simple: the Merpati office in the town of departure has a manifest with all passengers' names on it. If you are not on this 'magic' list you don't fly, simple as that. Tickets, especially international ones, don't give you any guarantee of a seat at all, no matter how many OKs the ticket sports. So make sure that your name gets written on the list.

Puncak Trikora is closed to tourists as a trekking destination. Better use Lake Habbema (near Wamena) where a lot of tourists go.

On the southwestern coast is one of Irian's hidden gems. This small district capital is nestled among steep hills. Not much has changed here since colonial days when it was a colonial administrative centre. Historically it has been an important trading town; links with other islands go back to the 17th century. This has resulted in a curious mix of Irianese and people from other nearby islands. Fak-Fak is also the only town in Irian where a significant number of indigenous people were converted to Islam. Near

Fak-Fak a lot of nutmeg and durian are grown, for which it is now well known.

Rogier Gruys (Can)

INTERNET INFO

For the latest travel information, check out the Lonely Planet web site:

http://www.lonelyplanet.com

This award-winning site contains updates, recent travellers' letters and a useful travellers' bulletin board.

Other Indonesia sites include Jendala Indonesia:

http://www.iit.edu/syafsya

This has some good links and several Indonesian magazines on-line.

ACKNOWLEDGMENTS

The information in this Stop Press was compiled from various sources and reports by the following travellers: Lou Apker (Aus); John Barraco (USA); Didier Bellet (F), Andrew Bridgman & Audrey Azad (Can); Paul & Karen Davison; Bob Else (Aus); Inge Light (Aus); Ray; Alaisdair Raynham; Mark Russell(Aus); Jenny Shaw (UK); Els Schamp (Belgium); Masato Uemor (J); Michael van Verk (Nl); Amy Wharton & Alex Trion (USA) and Monica & Christina Wojtaszewski (Denmark).